CLYMER®

MERCURY/MARINER

OUTBOARD SHOP MANUAL

75-225 HP FOUR-STROKE • 2001-2003

The world's finest publisher of mechanical how-to manuals

Business Directories & Books

P.O. Box 12901, Overland Park, KS 66282-2901

FIRST EDITION
First Printing December, 2003

Printed in U.S.A.

CLYMER and colophon are registered trademarks of PRIMEDIA Business Magazines and Media Inc.

This book was printed at Von Hoffmann an ISO certified company.

ISBN: 0-89287-876-2

Library of Congress: 2003114779

AUTHOR: Mark Rolling.

TECHNICAL PHOTOGRAPHY: Mark Rolling.

TECHNICAL ILLUSTRATIONS: Steve Amos.

WIRING DIAGRAMS: Mike Rose.

PRODUCTION: Holly Messinger.

EDITOR: Jason Beaver.

COVER: Mark Clifford Photography at www.markclifford.com. Boat courtesy of Olympic Boat Centers, San Diego, CA.

General Information 1

Troubleshooting 2

Lubrication, Maintenance and Tune-Up 3

Synchronization and Adjustments 4

Fuel System 5

Electrical and Ignition Systems 6

Power Head 7

Gearcase 8

Power Trim and Tilt 9

Midsection 10

Remote Control 11

Index 12

Wiring Diagrams 13

PRIMEDIA
Business Magazines & Media
P.O. Box 12901, Overland Park, KS 66282-2901 • 800-262-1954 • 913-967-1719

The following books and guides are published by PRIMEDIA Business Directories & Books.

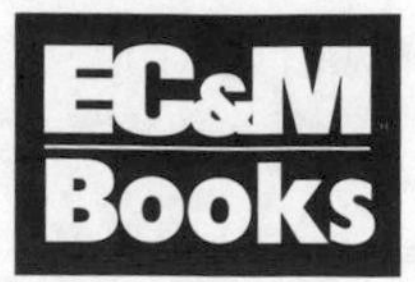

More information available at *primediabooks.com*

Contents

QUICK REFERENCE DATA IX

CHAPTER ONE
GENERAL INFORMATION 1

Manual organization 1
Warnings, cautions and notes 2
Safety 2
Service hints 3
Engine operation 5
Outboard engine identification 5
Fasteners 7
Lubricants 11
RTV gasket sealant 12
Anaerobic sealant 12
Threadlocking compound 12
Galvanic corrosion 13
Propellers 15
Basic hand tools 20
Special tools 24
Precision measuring tools 24
Electrical system fundamentals 31
Basic mechanical skills 33
Specifications 38

CHAPTER TWO
TROUBLESHOOTING 42

Electrical components 42
Preliminary inspection 42
Starting difficulty 43
Electric starting system 45
Fuel system 52
Ignition system 62
Warning system 92
Charging system 98
Power head 102
Cooling system 110
Gearcase 112
Trim/tilt system 113
Electronic fuel injection (EFI) system 119
Specifications 131

CHAPTER THREE
LUBRICATION, MAINTENANCE AND TUNE-UP 141

Before each use 141
After each use 146
Routine maintenance 147
Fuel requirements 148
Lubricants 148
Power head maintenance 149
Gearcase maintenance 158
Midsection maintenance 163
Tune up 167
Storage preparation and recommissioning 171
Submersion 172
Corrosion prevention 173
Specifications 174

CHAPTER FOUR
SYNCHRONIZATION AND ADJUSTMENTS 177

Pilot screw adjustment(75-90 hp models) 177
Linkage, throttle position sensor, carburetor synchronization and idle speed adjustments 178
Ignition timing check 187
Throttle cable adjustment 188
Shift cable adjustment 189
Valve adjustment 191
Trim tab adjustment 195
Trim position sender adjustment 195
Specifications 196

CHAPTER FIVE
FUEL SYSTEM 198

Fuel system service 198
Fuel tank 201
Fuel hose 203
Fuel filter 206
Primer bulb 209
Mechanical fuel pump 210
Silencer cover 214
Intake manifold 219
Dashpot 227
Electrothermal valve 228
Carburetor 228
Throttle body 232
Vapor separator tank 234
Secondary vapor separator tank 240
Low-pressure electric fuel pump 241
Fuel pump relay 241
Fuel pump driver 241
Fuel cooler 242
Fuel pressure regulator 244
Fuel rail and injectors 245
Idle air control motor 248
Air temperature sensor 249
Air pressure sensor 250
Throttle position sensor 250
Specifications 252

CHAPTER SIX
ELECTRICAL AND IGNITION SYSTEMS 254

Electrical components 254
Battery 254
Charging system 261
Starting system 265
Ignition system 273
Specifications 283

CHAPTER SEVEN
POWER HEAD 286

Flywheel/cover 286
Timing belt and tensioner 289
Crankshaft pulley 292
Valve cover 293
Camshaft, timing chain and camshaft pulley 295
Cylinder head removal and installation 301
Water pressure relief valve 303
Thermostat 304
Exhaust/water jacket cover 305
Cylinder head 308
Power head 314
Oil pump 317
Crankshaft pulley 318
Power head 319
Cylinder block components 333
Bearing selection 339
Engine break-in procedures 341
Specifications 342

CHAPTER EIGHT
GEARCASE 349

Gearcase operation 349
Gearcase service precautions 351
Propeller 352
Gearcase 355
Water pump 359
Water pump component 364
Gearcase 364
Specifications 405

CHAPTER NINE
POWER TRIM AND TILT 406

Trim/tilt relay 406
Trim position sender 408
Trim switch 410
Manual relief valve 410
Power trim 412
Electric trim motor 416
Trim system 423
Trim and tilt system fluid 433
Specifications 434

CHAPTER TEN
MIDSECTION 435

Lower motor mount 435
Tilt tube 444
Clamp bracket 445
Tilt lock lever 446
Oil pump 447
Upper motor mount 447
Swivel tube 448
Swivel housing 450
Power head adapter 451
Exhaust silencer 452
Exhaust tube 453
Oil pressure relief valve 453
Oil pan and oil pickup tube 454
Drive shaft housing 455
Specifications 456

CHAPTER ELEVEN
REMOTE CONTROL 458

Cable removal and installation 458
Remote control disassembly and assembly 464

INDEX 469

WIRING DIAGRAMS 472

Quick Reference Data

ENGINE DATA

MODEL:____________________YEAR:____________________

VIN NUMBER:____________________

ENGINE SERIAL NUMBER:____________________

CARBURETOR SERIAL NUMBER OR I.D. MARK:____________________

GENERAL TORQUE SPECIFICATIONS

Screw or nut size	in.-lb.	ft.-lb.	N•m
U.S. Standard			
6-32	9	–	1.0
8-32	20	–	2.3
10-24	30	–	3.4
10-32	35	–	4.0
12-24	45	–	5.1
1/4-20	70	–	7.9
1/4-28	84	–	9.5
5/16-18	160	13	18.1
5/16-24	168	14	19.0
3/8-16	–	23	31.1
3/8-24	–	25	33.8
7/16-14	–	36	48.8
7/16-20	–	40	54.2
1/ 2-13	–	50	67.8
1/ 2-20	–	60	81.3
Metric			
M5	36	–	4.1
M6	70	–	8.1
M8	156	13	17.6
M10	–	26	35.3
M12	–	35	47.5
M14	–	60	81.3

FLUID CAPACITIES

Model	Capacity
75-115 hp	
Engine oil	5.0 qt. (4.7 L)
Gearcase lubricant	24 oz. (0.71 L)
225 hp	
Engine oil	
With filter change	6.3 qt. (6.0 L)
Without oil filter change	6.1 qt. (5.8 L)
Gearcase lubricant	
Standard RH rotation gearcase	39 oz. (1.15 L)
Counter rotation LH gearcase	34 oz. (1.0 L)

SPARK PLUG RECOMMENDATIONS

Model	Recommended plug	Spark plug gap
75 and 90 hp models	NGK LFR5A-11	1.0-1.1 mm (0.039-0.043 in.)
115 hp models	NGK LFR6A-11	1.0-1.1 mm (0.039-0.043 in.)
225 hp models	NGK LFR5A-11	1.0-1.1 mm (0.039-0.043 in.)

MAXIMUM RECOMMENDED ENGINE SPEED SPECIFICATIONS

Model	Maximum recommended speed (rpm)
75 hp models	4500-5500
90 hp models	5000-6000
115 hp models	5000-6000
225 hp models	5000-6000

MAINTENANCE REQUIREMENTS AND INTERVALS

Before each use	Check the engine oil level and condition
	Inspect the fuel filter
	Inspect the fuel system for leakage
	Check for oil leakage
	Check the engine mounting bolts
	Check the steering system
	Inspect the propeller
	Check the lanyard switch operation
	Check the cooling system operation
After each use	Flush the cooling system
	Clean external engine surfaces
Initial 20 hours of operation (225 hp model only)	Change the engine oil and filter
	Change the gearcase lubricant
	Inspect the fuel filter
	Clean and inspect the spark plugs
	Check for oil leakage
	Inspect hoses and clamps
	Inspect the wiring
	Check for loose fasteners
	Adjust the throttle and shift cables
	Check the flywheel nut tightening torque
	Check or adjust the idle speed
Every 180 days or 100 hours usage (225 hp model only)	Adjust and lubricate throttle and shift linkages
	Lubricate steering cable and pivot points
	Lubricate the tilt tube and swivel tube
	Lubricate the propeller shaft
	Change the engine oil and filter
	Change the gearcase lubricant
	Clean and inspect the spark plugs
	Check for loose fasteners
	Inspect hoses and clamps
	Inspect the fuel filter
	Clean and inspect the sacrificial anodes
	Inspect the timing belt, pulleys and tensioner
	Lubricate the drive shaft splines
	Visually inspect the thermostat for damage
	Check the power trim fluid level
	Inspect the battery
	Remove carbon deposits from the power head

(continued)

MAINTENANCE REQUIREMENTS AND INTERVALS (continued)

Once a year or 100 hours of use (75-115 hp models)	Adjust and lubricate throttle and shift linkages Lubricate steering cable and pivot points Lubricate the tilt tube and swivel tube Lubricate the propeller shaft Change the engine oil and filter Change the gearcase lubricant Clean and inspect the spark plugs Check for loose fasteners Inspect hoses and clamps Inspect the fuel filter Clean and inspect the sacrificial anodes Inspect the timing belt, pulleys and tensioner Lubricate the drive shaft splines Visually inspect the thermostat for damage Check the power trim fluid level Inspect the battery Remove carbon deposits from the power head Adjust the carburetors* Check ignition timing and synchronization
Every 3 years or 300 hours of use	Replace the water pump impeller
Every 4 years or 400 hours of use (75-115 hp models)	Adjust the valves
Every 4 years or 400 hours of use (225 hp model only)	Check the oil pump pressure Inspect the timing chain tensioners* Adjust the valves
Every 5 years or 1000 hours of usage (225 hp model only	Replace the timing belt Replace the timing chains*
*This maintenance item may not apply to all models	

Chapter One

General Information

GENERAL INFORMATION

This detailed and comprehensive manual covers 75-225 hp Mercury and Mariner four-stroke outboards from 2001-2003.

This manual can be used by anyone from a first time do-it-yourself to a professional mechanic. The text provides step-by-step information on maintenance, tune-up, repair and overhaul. Hundreds of photos and drawings guide the reader through every job.

A shop manual is a reference and as in all Clymer manuals, the chapters are thumb tabbed. Important items are indexed at the end of the manual. All procedures, tables and figures are designed based on the difficulty of the task being described, but keeping in mind the reader who may be performing that task for the first time.

Frequently used specifications and capacities from individual chapters are summarized in the *Quick Reference Data* at the front of the manual. Specifications concerning a specific system are included in the tables at the end of each chapter. General torque specifications, engine codes, tap and drill sizes, conversion tables, and technical abbreviations are located in **Tables 1-5** at the end of this chapter.

MANUAL ORGANIZATION

All dimensions and capacities are expressed in U.S standard and metric units of measurements.

This chapter provides general information on shop safety, tool use, service fundamentals and shop supplies.

Chapter Two provides methods and suggestions for quick and accurate diagnosis of engine trouble. The troubleshooting procedures describe typical symptoms and provide logical troubleshooting methods.

Chapter Three explains all periodic lubrication and routine maintenance necessary to keep the outboard operating at peak efficiency. Chapter Three also includes all recommended tune-up procedures, eliminating the need to constantly refer to other chapters on the various systems.

Chapter Four describes synchronization and linkage adjustments for the fuel and shifting systems.

Subsequent chapters describe specific systems, providing disassembly, repair, assembly and adjustment procedures in simple step-by-step form.

Some of the procedures in this manual require special tools (**Figure 1**, typical). In most cases, the tool is illustrated in use. Well-equipped mechanics may be able to substitute similar tools or fabricate a suitable replacement. However, in some cases, the specialized equipment or expertise may make it impractical for the home mechanic to attempt the procedure. When necessary, such operations are identified in the text with the recommendation to have a dealership or specialist perform the task. It may be less expensive to have a professional perform these jobs, especially when considering the cost of the equipment.

WARNINGS, CAUTIONS AND NOTES

The terms WARNING, CAUTION, and NOTE have specific meanings in this manual.

A WARNING, emphasizes areas where injury or even death could result from negligence. Mechanical damage may also occur. WARNINGS *are to be taken seriously.*

A CAUTION emphasizes areas where equipment damage could occur. Disregarding a CAUTION could cause permanent mechanical damage; however, injury is unlikely.

A NOTE provides additional information to make a step or procedure easier or clearer. Disregarding a NOTE could cause inconvenience or misdiagnosis, but would not cause damage or injury.

SAFETY

Professional mechanics can work for years and never sustain a serious injury. Follow these guidelines and practice common sense to safely service the outboard.

1. Do not operate the outboard in an enclosed area. The exhaust gasses contain carbon monoxide, and odorless, colorless, tasteless and poisonous gas. Carbon monoxide levels build quickly in small, enclosed areas and can cause unconsciousness and death in a short time. Be sure to properly ventilate the work area or operate the outboard outside.
2. *Never* use gasoline or any flammable liquid when cleaning parts. Refer to *Handling Gasoline Safely* and *Cleaning Parts* in this chapter.
3. *Never* smoke or use a torch in the vicinity of flammable liquids, such as gasoline or cleaning solvent.
4. When working with the fuel system note the following:
   a. *Always* have a Coast Guard approved fire extinguisher on hand. Make sure the fire extinguisher is fully charged and read the operating instructions before beginning work.
   b. Immediately after removing the engine cover, check for the presence of fuel leakage or vapor.

   c. If a strong fuel smell is noticed, there may be a fuel leak; locate and repair the leak before proceeding.
   d. Allow the engine to air out before beginning the work.
   e. Allow the engine to fully cool. Fuel dripping on a hot engine may cause a fire.
   f. Disconnect the battery cables before working on any fuel system components. Sparks may ignite the fuel, causing a fire or explosion.
   g. Remove the fuel tank fill cap before disconnecting any fuel lines. Temperature changes can cause pressure to build within the tank.
   h. Immediately wipe up spilled fuel with suitable shop towels. Store the towels in a metal container or allow the fuel to fully evaporate before placing the towels in a safe place. *Never* leave fuel or solvent soaked towels in the boat or in an area near sparks or open flame.
   i. Inspect the fuel system after service or repair for any indication of fuel leakage. Correct the source of any fuel leakage before operating the engine.
5. Use the correct type and size of tools to avoid damaging fasteners.
6. Keep tools clean and in good condition. Replace or repair worn or damaged equipment.
7. When loosening a tight or stuck fastener, be aware of what would happen if the tool should slip. In most cases, it is safer to pull on a wrench or ratchet than to push on it.
8. When replacing a fastener, make sure to choose one with the same measurements, material and strength as the old one. Refer to *Fasteners* in this chapter for additional information.
9. Keep the work area clean and uncluttered. Keep all hand and power tools in good condition. Wipe grease or oil from tools after using them. Greasy or oily tools are difficult to hold and could cause injury or damage to equipment. Replace or repair worn or damaged tools.
10. Wear safety goggles during all operations involving drilling, grinding, using a cold chisel or *any* time the

safety of your eyes is in question. Always wear safety goggles when using solvent or compressed air.

11. Do not carry sharp tools in clothing pockets.

12. Always have an approved fire extinguisher available. Make sure it is rated for gasoline (Class B) and electric (Class C) fires. Read and fully understand the operating instructions for the fire extinguisher before beginning work.

13. Do not use compressed air to clean clothing or the work area. Debris may be blown into eyes or the skin. *Never* direct compressed air at yourself or someone else. Do not allow children to use or play with any compressed air equipment.

14. When using compressed air to dry rotating parts, hold the part so it cannot rotate. Do not allow the force of the air to spin the part. The air jet is capable of rotating the parts at extremely high speed. The part may become damaged or disintegrate, causing serious injury.

Handling Gasoline Safely

Because gasoline is used so often, many people forget that it is hazardous. Only use gasoline for fuel. Keep in mind, when working on the outboard, gasoline is always present in the fuel tank, fuel supply line and the fuel system components. To avoid an accident when working around the fuel system, observe the following precautions:

1. *Never* use gasoline to clean parts. See *Cleaning Parts* in this chapter.
2. When working on the fuel system, work outside in a well-ventilated area.
3. Do not add fuel to the tank or service the fuel system near open flames, sparks or where someone is smoking. Gasoline vapor is heavier than air. It collects in low areas and is more easily ignitable than liquid gasoline.
4. Allow the engine to cool completely before working on any fuel system component.
5. When draining the carburetors, vapor separator tank or other fuel system components, capture the fuel in a suitable plastic container and then pour it into an approved gasoline storage device.
6. Do not store gasoline in a glass container. If the glass breaks, a serious explosion or fire may occur.
7. Immediately wipe up spilled gasoline. Store cleaning rags in a metal container with a lid until they can be properly disposed of, or place them outside in a safe place until the fuel evaporates.
8. Do not pour water onto a gasoline fire. Water spreads the fire and makes it more difficult to extinguish. Use a class B, BC or ABC fire extinguisher to extinguish the fire.
9. Always turn off the engine before refueling. Do not spill fuel overboard or onto the vessel. Do not overfill the fuel tank. Leave an air space at the top of the tank to allow for expansion due to temperature fluctuations.

Cleaning Parts

Cleaning parts is one of the more tedious, time consuming and difficult service jobs performed in the home garage. There are many types of chemical cleaners and solvents available for shop use. Most are poisonous and flammable. To prevent chemical exposure, vapor buildup, fire and serious injury, observe each product warning label and note the following:

1. Read and observe the entire product label before using any chemical. Always know what type of chemical is being used and whether it is poisonous and/or flammable.
2. *Never* use more than one type of cleaning solvent at a time. If mixing chemicals is called for, measure the proper amounts according to the manufacturer.
3. Work in a well-ventilated area.
4. Wear chemical-resistant gloves.
5. Wear safety goggles.
6. Wear a vapor respirator if the instructions call for it.
7. Wash hands and arms thoroughly after cleaning parts.
8. Keep chemical products away from children and pets.
9. Thoroughly clean all oil, grease, and cleaner residue from any parts that must be heated.
10. Use a nylon brush when cleaning parts. Metal brushes may cause a spark.
11. When using a parts washer, use only the solvent recommended by the manufacturer. Make sure the parts washer is equipped with a metal lid that can be lowered in case of fire.

SERVICE HINTS

Most of the service procedures covered can be performed by anyone reasonably handy with tools. Consider personal mechanical capabilities carefully before attempting any operation that involves major disassembly.

1. *Front,* as used in this manual, refers to the side of the engine closest to the bow of the boat. Likewise, *rear* as used in this manual refers to the side of the engine furthest from the bow. *Port* as used in this manual refers to the left side of the engine relative to the corresponding side of the boat. Likewise, *starboard* as used in this manual refers to the right side of the engine. See **Figure 2**.
2. When disassembling engine, fuel, trim or gearcase components, mark the parts for location and mark all parts that mate together. Identify small parts, such as bolts, by

placing them in small plastic bags. Seal the bags and label them with masking tape and a permanent marking pen. If assembly will take place immediately, nuts and bolts may be placed in a cupcake tin or egg carton in the order of disassembly.

3. Protect finished surfaces from physical damage or corrosion. Keep gasoline and cleaning solvent off painted surfaces.

4. Apply penetrating oil to frozen or tight bolts, then strike the bolt head a few times with a hammer and punch (use a screwdriver on screws). Avoid using heat, as it can warp, melt, or alter the temper of parts. Heat also damages finishes, especially paint and plastics.

5. No parts removed or installed (other than bushings, races and bearings) in the procedures given in this manual should require unusual force during disassembly or assembly. If a part is difficult to remove or install, review the procedures and find the source of the difficulty before proceeding.

6. Cover all openings after removing parts or components to prevent debris or contaminants from falling in.

7. Read each procedure *completely* while looking at the actual parts before starting a job. Make sure you *thoroughly* understand what is to be done and then follow the procedure, step by step.

8. For the do-it-yourself mechanic, recommendations are occasionally made to refer the service to a machine shop or qualified technician. In these cases, the work will be quicker and less expensive than performing the job yourself.

9. The term *replace* means to remove and discard the affected part and replace it with a new one. *Overhaul* means to remove, disassemble, inspect, measure, repair or replace defective parts, assemble and install the assembly.

10. Some operations require the use of a hydraulic press. If a suitable press is not available, have these operations performed by a shop equipped for such work. Do not use makeshift equipment that may damage parts.

11. Repairs go faster and easier if the engine is clean before beginning work. There are many special cleaners on the market for washing engines and related parts. Follow the manufacturer's instructions on the container for the best results. Clean all oily or greasy parts with cleaning solvent upon removal.

WARNING

Never use gasoline as a cleaning agent. Work only in a well-ventilated area when using cleaning solvent. Keep a fire extinguisher rated for gasoline fires on hand at all times.

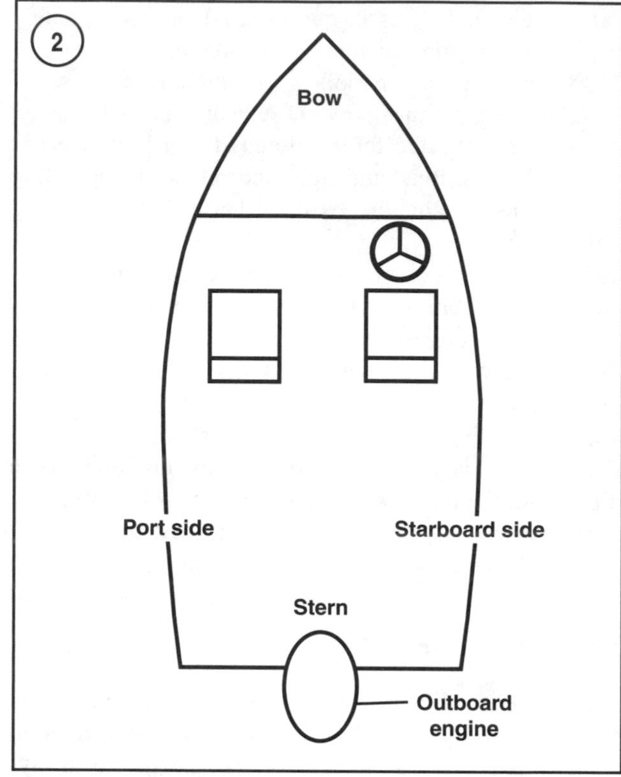

12. Much of the labor charged for repairs made by dealerships are for the time involved in the removal, disassembly, assembly and reinstallation of other parts in order to reach the defective part. It may be possible to perform the disassembly yourself and then take the defective unit to the dealership for repair. Be aware that some dealerships may not take on such jobs and many will not warranty the work unless the entire repair is performed by the dealership.

13. If special tools are required, make arrangements to get them before starting. It is frustrating and time-consuming to start a job and be unable to complete it.

14. Make diagrams or take a picture wherever similar-appearing parts are found. For instance, crankcase bolts often are not the same length. There is also the possibility of being side-tracked and not returning to work for several days or longer, in which time the carefully laid out parts may have been disturbed.

15. When assembling parts, make sure all shims and washers are replaced exactly as they came out.

16. Whenever a rotating part butts against a stationary part, look for a shim or washer. Use new gaskets, seals and O-rings upon removal.

17. When purchasing gasket material to make a replacement gasket, measure the thickness of the old gasket (at an uncompressed point) and purchase gasket material of the

same approximate thickness. Never make replacement gaskets for power head components (cylinder heads, water jackets and end covers). Many of these gaskets are of a special material and thickness; some have specially sized openings for water and oil passages. A faulty gasket can easily result in complete power head failure.

18. Use heavy grease to hold small parts in place if they tend to fall out during assembly. However, keep grease and oil away from electrical components, unless otherwise directed.

19. Never use wire to clean out jets and air passages. They are easily damaged. Use compressed air to blow out fuel, oil and cooling water passages.

20. Take the time and do the job right. Do not forget that a newly rebuilt engine must be broken in just like a new one.

ENGINE OPERATION

All models covered in this manual use a water cooled four-stroke power head. The power head is an overhead cam design with four valves per cylinder. This design provides optimum fuel economy and power output while maintaining a high level of durability.

All marine engines, whether two- or four-stroke, gasoline or diesel, operate on the Otto cycle of intake, compression, power and exhaust phases. Unlike the more conventional two-stroke outboards, four stroke models require two crankshaft revolutions to complete the Otto cycle. A brief description of typical four-stroke engine operation follows:

Intake Phase

As the piston travels downward on the intake stroke (**Figure 3**), the exhaust valves are closed and the intake valves open, allowing the fresh air-fuel mixture to be drawn into the cylinder. When the piston reaches the bottom dead center (BDC), the intake valves close and remains closed for the next one and one-half revolutions of the crankshaft.

Compression Phase

While the crankshaft continues to rotate, the piston moves upward in the cylinder (**Figure 3**). All valves are closed, and the piston compresses the fresh air-fuel mixture.

Power Phase

When the piston nears the top of its travel, the spark plug fires, igniting the compressed air-fuel mixture to start the power phase (**Figure 3**). Due to crankshaft rotation, the piston continues movement to top dead center (TDC) and is then pushed downward by expanding gasses formed by the burning fuel.

Exhaust Phase

When the piston nears the bottom of its travel on the power stroke, the exhaust valves open and remain open until the piston nears the top of its exhaust stroke (**Figure 3**). The upward travel of the piston forces the exhaust gasses out of the cylinder. The exhaust valves then close to end the exhaust phase and the cycle starts all over again.

OUTBOARD ENGINE IDENTIFICATION

Intentify the outboard correctly before performing any testing, maintenance or repairs. Test specifications and repair instructions may vary by model, production year, engine characteristics and unique serial number. Information stamped onto the serial number tag provides this information. Engine weight, maximum engine speed and power output are also listed on the serial number tag. The serial number tag is affixed to the rear side of the starboard clamp bracket (**Figure 4**) on all models covered in this manual. The unique serial number is stamped into a plug (**Figure 5**) affixed to the lower starboard side of the power head.

The serial number tag lists the model designation (3, **Figure 6**). In this example, the engine is a 75 EL with a 75 horsepower rating. Both the horsepower and kilowatt rating are listed on the serial number tag (5 and 9, **Figure 6**).

The model designation provides more than the rated horsepower output of the engine. Many engines are produced in different versions for a given horsepower. Variations include the starting system used, drive shaft length, remote or tiller control, power trim and standard or counter rotation gearcase. The letters following the horsepower rating in the model name (75 EL in this example) indicate the engine characteristics. Match the characters to the specifications in **Table 2** to identify the engine characteristics. Some models may use two or more letter codes to identify all characteristic of the engine.

The model year is listed on the serial number tag (2, **Figure 6**) directly above the model name. Specifications or test/repair instructions may change during the model year. Should this occur, the unique serial number

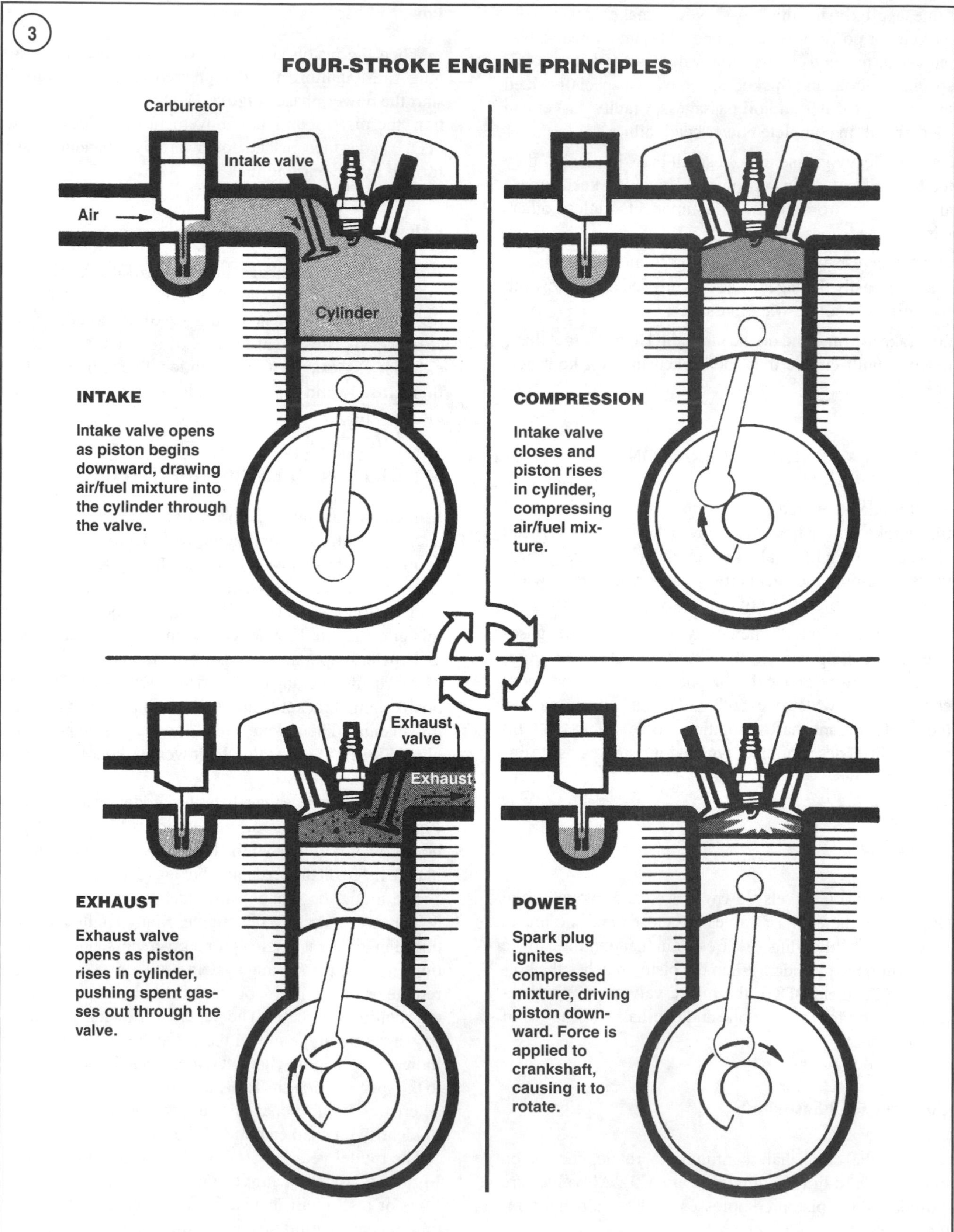
3
FOUR-STROKE ENGINE PRINCIPLES
Carburetor
Intake valve
Air
Cylinder
INTAKE
Intake valve opens as piston begins downward, drawing air/fuel mixture into the cylinder through the valve.
COMPRESSION
Intake valve closes and piston rises in cylinder, compressing air/fuel mixture.
Exhaust valve
Exhaust
EXHAUST
Exhaust valve opens as piston rises in cylinder, pushing spent gasses out through the valve.
POWER
Spark plug ignites compressed mixture, driving piston downward. Force is applied to crankshaft, causing it to rotate.

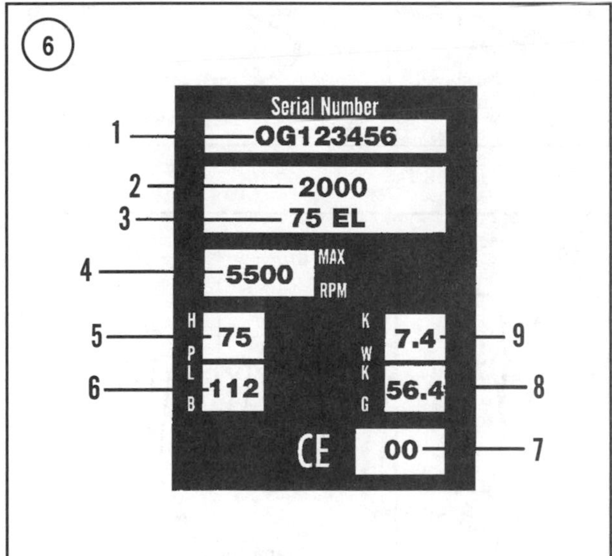

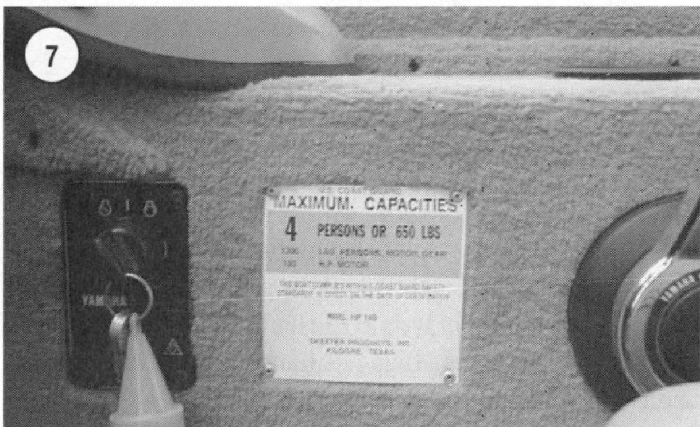

(1, **Figure 6**) is used to identify the affected engines. In many states, this number is used to register or title the outboard. Record this number and keep it in a safe place. In the event the outboard is lost or stolen this number provides accurate identification of the outboard. In the example in **Figure 6**, the first digit is 0 followed by a letter code, then six numbers. Because the serial number identifies the outboard motor, always supply it when purchasing parts.

All boats have a maximum weight carrying capacity listed on the boat rating tag (**Figure 7**). The weight of all passengers, gear, fuel, tanks, hull, and the engine must be considered prior to loading or operating the boat. Never load the boat beyond its rated capacity. When determining total weight refer to the engine weight on the serial number tag. The engine weight without fuel or tanks is listed in pounds (6, **Figure 6**) and kilograms (8).

The year of production is listed at the lower right of the tag (7, **Figure 6**). Do not assume the model year and year of production are the same.

NOTE
*The manufacturer may make changes during a model year. When ordering parts, always order by model and serial number. Record this information in the **Quick Reference Data** (QRD) section at the front of the manual. Compare new parts with old before purchasing them. If the parts are not alike, have the parts manager explain the difference and verify the part's compatibility before installing it.*

FASTENERS

Proper fastener selection and installation is important to ensure that the outboard operates as designed and can be serviced efficiently. Be sure replacement fasteners meet all the same requirements as the originals.

CAUTION
Outboards commonly use fasteners made of stainless steel or other corrosion resistant material in water exposed locations. Never install a common steel fastener in water exposed location. The fastener will corrode

and fail causing damage or loss of engine components.

Threaded Fasteners

Threaded fasteners secure most of the components on the engine. Most are tightened by turning them clockwise (meaning they have right-hand threads). If the normal rotation of a component would loosen the fastener, left-hand threads may be used. If a left-hand threaded fastener is used, it is noted in the text.

Nuts, bolts and screws are manufactured in a wide range of thread patterns. To join a nut and bolt, the diameter of the bolt and the diameter of the hole in the nut must be the same, and the threads must be properly matched.

To verify whether the threads on two fasteners are matched, start the fastener by hand. Make sure both pieces are clean; remove Loctite or other sealer residue from threads if present. If force is required, check the thread condition on each fastener. If the thread condition is good and the fasteners still jam, the threads are not compatible. A thread pitch gauge (**Figure 8**) can also be used to determine thread pitch.

CAUTION
To ensure the fastener threads are not mismatched or cross-threaded, start all fasteners by hand. If a fastener is hard to start or to turn, determine the cause before tightening with a wrench.

Two dimensions are required to match the thread size of the fastener: the number of threads in a given distance, and the outside diameter of the threads.

Two systems are currently used to specify threaded fastener dimensions: the U.S. Standard system (sometimes called American) and the metric system. Although fasteners may appear similar, close inspection shows that the thread designs differ (**Figure 9**). Pay particular attention when working with unidentified fasteners; mismatching thread types damage threads. Be aware that Mercury and Mariner outboards often use a combination of U.S Standard and metric fasteners on most models.

ISO (International Organization for Standardization) metric threads come in three standard sizes: coarse, fine and constant pitch. The ISO coarse pitch is used for most common fastener applications. The fine pitch thread is used on certain precision tools and instruments. The constant pitch thread is used mainly on machine parts and not fasteners. The constant pitch thread, however, is used on all metric thread spark plugs.

The length (**Figure 10**), diameter and threads per inch classify U.S. Standard bolts. For example, 1/4—20 × 1 indicates a bolt is 1/4 in. in diameter with 20 threads per inch, and is 1 in. long.

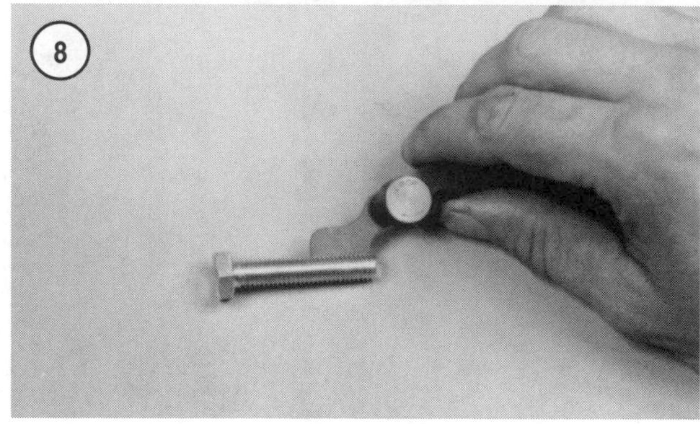

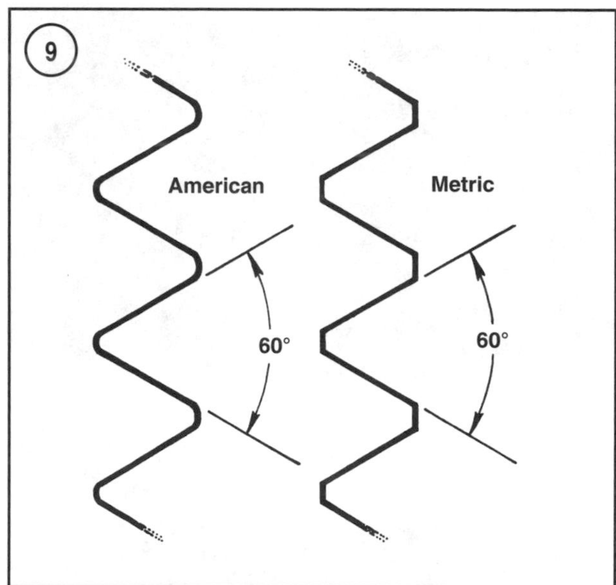

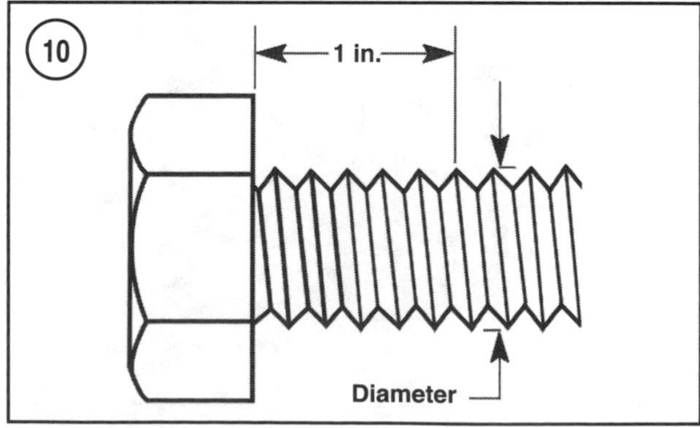

The length (L, **Figure 11**), diameter (D) and distance between thread crest (pitch) (T) classify metric screws and bolts. The numbers M8—1.25 × 130 may identify a

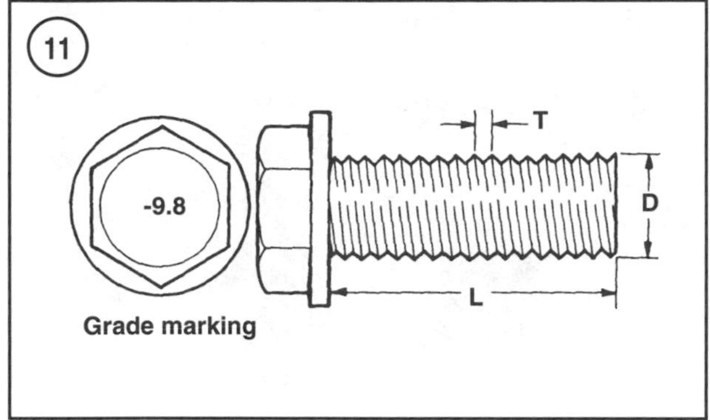

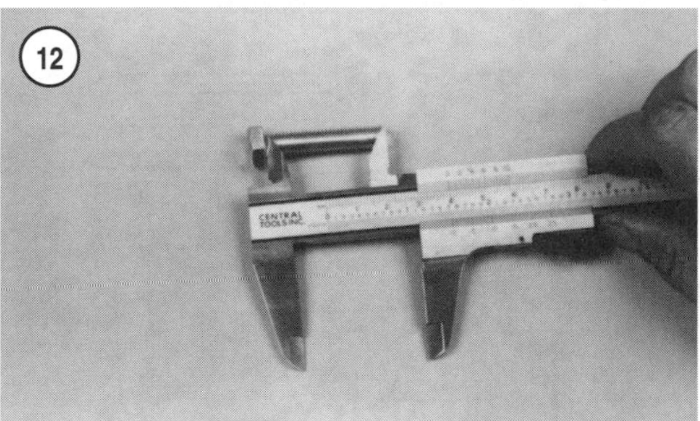

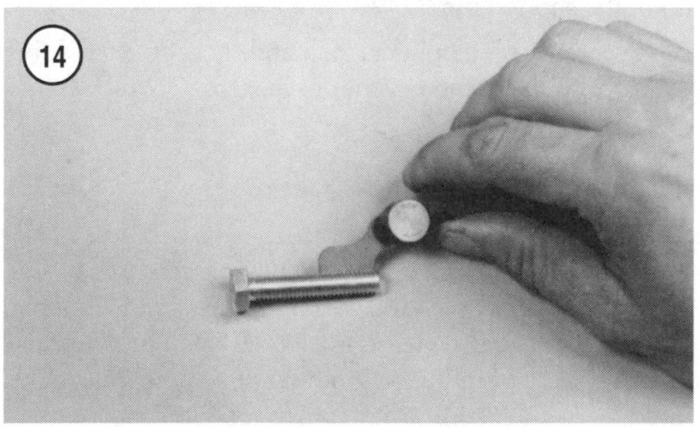

typical metric bolt. This indicates the bolt has a diameter of 8 mm. The distance between the thread crest is 1.25 mm and the length is 130 mm.

NOTE
*When purchasing a bolt from a dealership or parts store, it is important to know how to specify bolt length. The correct way to measure bolt length is to measure the length, starting from underneath the bolt head to the end of the bolt (**Figure 12**). Always measure bolt length to avoid purchasing or installing bolts that are too long.*

The numbers on the bolt head (**Figure 11**) indicate the strength of metric screws and bolts. The higher the number, the stronger the fastener. Unnumbered fasteners are the weakest.

Markings (**Figure 13**) on the bolt head indicate the strength of U.S. Standard screws and bolts. The greater the number of markings, the stronger the fastener. Similar to metric fasteners, unmarked fasteners are the weakest.

WARNING
Never install fasteners with a strength classification lower than what was originally installed by the manufacturer. Doing so may cause equipment failure and/or damage.

Use a thread pitch gauge (**Figure 14**) to identify the thread pitch of a bolt, stud or nut. Select the gauge that perfectly fits the threads. Markings on thc gauge indicate the thread pitch.

Many screws, bolts and studs are combined with nuts to secure particular components. To indicate the size of a nut, manufactures specify the internal diameter and the thread pitch. The measurement across two flats on the bolt head or nut indicates the wrench size.

Torque Specifications

The materials used to manufacture the outboard may be subjected to uneven stresses if the fasteners of the various subassemblies are not installed and tightened correctly. Fasteners that are improperly installed or work loose can cause extensive damage. It is essential to use an accurate torque wrench, described in this chapter, with the torque specifications in this manual.

Torque specifications are provided in Newton-meters (N•m), foot-pounds (ft.-lb.) and inch-pounds (in.-lb.). Torque specifications for specific components are listed in the tables at the end of the appropriate chapters. **Table 1** lists general torque specifications. Use the general torque specification for component fasteners not listed in individual chapters. To use **Table 1**, first determine the size of the fastener as described in *Fasteners* in this chapter. Torque wrenches are described in the *Basic Tools* section of this chapter.

Self-Locking Fasteners

Several types of bolts, screws and nuts incorporate a system that creates interference between the two fasteners. Interference is achieved in various ways. The most common types are the Nylon insert nut, or a dry adhesive coating on the threads of a bolt (**Figure 15**).

Self-locking fasteners offer greater holding strength than standard fasteners, which improves their resistance to vibration. Most self-locking fasteners cannot be reused. The material used to form the lock becomes distorted after the initial installation and removal. It is a good practice to discard and replace self-locking fasteners after removal. Never replace self-locking fasteners with standard fasteners.

Washers

There are two basic types of washers: flat washers and lockwashers. Flat washers are simple discs with a hole to fit a screw or bolt. Lockwashers are slightly deformed to prevent a fastener from working loose. Washers are also used as spacers and seals or help distribute fastener load and prevent the fastener from damaging the component.

When replacing washers make sure the replacement washers are of the same design and quality as the original ones.

NOTE
Avoid using washers that are made of thin or weak materials. These will deform and crush the first time they are used in a high torque application, allowing the nut or bolt to loosen.

Cotter Pins

A cotter pin is split metal pin inserted into a hole or slot that prevents a fastener from loosening. With certain applications, a cotter pin and castellated (slotted) nut are used.

To use a cotter pin, first make sure the diameter is correct for the hole in the fastener. After correctly tightening the fastener and aligning the holes, insert the cotter pin through the hole and bend the ends over the fastener (**Figure 16**). Cut excess length from the ends to prevent them from snagging on skin or clothing; remember that exposed ends of the pin will cut flesh easily. After the cotter pin is bent and the ends cut to length, it should be tight. If the cotter pin wiggles, it is improperly installed.

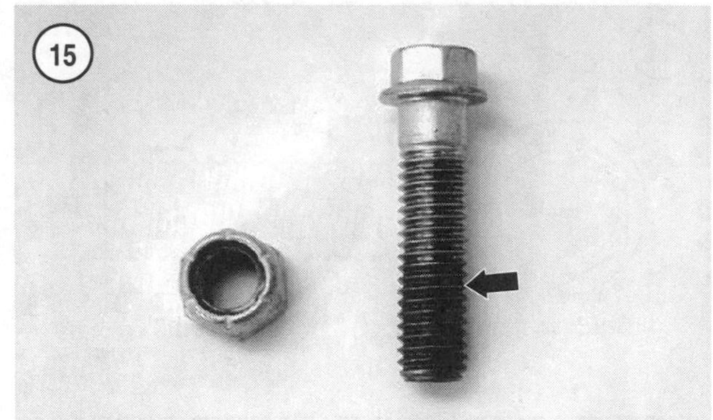

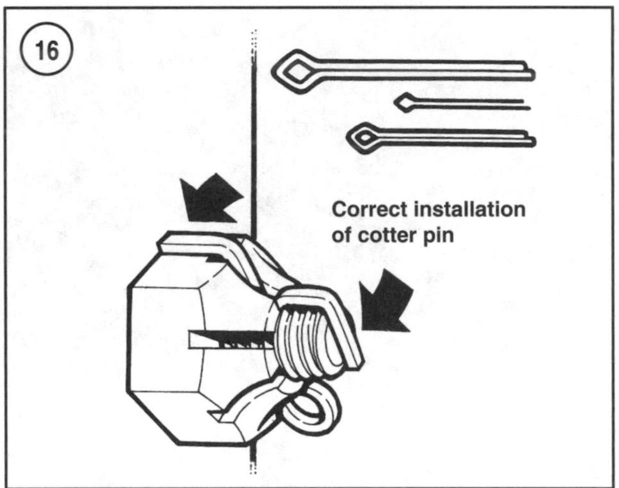

Unless instructed otherwise, never loosen a tightened fastener to align the cotter pin holes. If the holes do not align, tighten the fastener just enough to achieve alignment.

Cotter pins are available in various diameters and lengths. Measure length from the bottom of the head to the tip of the shorted pin.

Never reuse cotter pins as their ends may break, causing the pin to fail and the fastener to loosen.

Snap Rings

Snap rings are circular metal retaining clips. They help secure parts such as shafts, pins, rods, and gears. External type snap rings retain items on shafts. Internal snap rings secure parts within housing bores. In some applications, in addition to securing the component(s), snap rings of

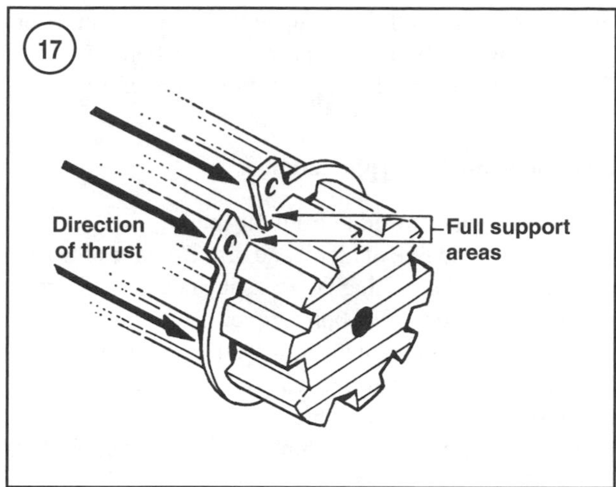

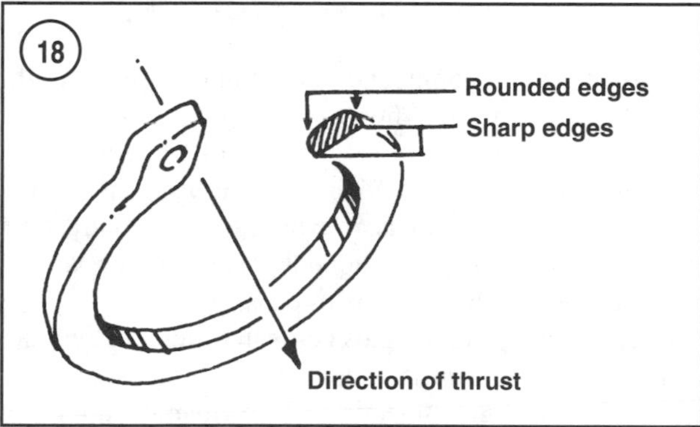

varying thickness also determine end-play. These are usually called selective snap rings.

Two basic types of snap rings are used: machined and stamped snap rings. Machined snap rings (**Figure 17**) can be installed in either direction, since both faces have sharp edges. Stamped snap rings (**Figure 18**) have a sharp edge and a round edge. When installing a stamped snap ring in a thrust application, install the sharp edge facing away from the part producing the thrust.

Observe the following when installing snap rings:

1. Remove and install snap rings with snap ring pliers. See *Snap Ring Pliers* in this chapter.
2. In some applications, it may be necessary to replace snap rings after removing, as removal weakens and deforms them.
3. Compress or expand snap rings only enough to install them. If overexpanded, they lose their retaining ability.
4. After installing a snap ring, make sure it seats completely in the groove.
5. Wear eye protection when removing and installing snap rings.

E-rings and circlips are used when it is not practical to use a snap ring. Remove E-rings with a flat blade screwdriver by prying between the shaft and the E-ring. To install an E-ring, center it over the shaft groove and push or tap it into place.

LUBRICANTS

Periodic lubrication helps ensure long life for any type of equipment. The *type* of lubricant used is just as important as the lubrication service itself, although in an emergency the wrong type of lubricant is usually better than none at all. Make sure to follow the manufacturer's recommendations of lubricant types.

Generally, all liquid lubricants are called oil. They may be mineral-based (petroleum bases), natural-based (vegetable and animal bases), synthetic-based or emulsions (mixtures). *Grease* is an oil to which a thickening agent has been added so that the end product is semi-solid. Grease is classified by the type of thickener added. Lithium soap is commonly used.

Engine Oil

Four-stroke oil

Four-cycle oil for motorcycle, marine and automotive engines is classified by the American Petroleum Institute (API) and the Society of Automotive Engineers (SAE) in several categories. Oil containers display these classifications on the top or label.

The API oil classification is indicated by letters; oils for gasoline engines are identified by an *S*.

Viscosity is the oil thickness. The SAE uses numbers to indicate viscosity. Thin oils have low numbers while thick oils have high numbers. A *W* after the number indicates that the viscosity testing was done at low temperature to simulate cold-weather operation. Four-stroke engine oils typically fall into the 5W-30 and 20W-50 range.

Multi-grade oils (for example 10W-40) are less viscous (thinner) and flow well at low temperatures. This allows the oil to perform efficiently across at wide range of engine operating conditions. The lower the number, the better the engine will start in cold climates. Higher numbers are usually recommended for engine operation in hot weather conditions. To help ensure the best performance and durability, use only the recommended oil grade and viscosity as described in Chapter Three.

Grease

Grease is lubricating oil with thickening agents added to it. The National Lubricating Grease Institute (NLGI) grades greases. Grades range from No. 000 to No. 6, with No. 6 being the thickest. Typical multipurpose grease is NLGI No. 2. For specific applications, manufacturers may recommend water-resistant grease or one with an additive such as molybdenum disulfide (MoS^2).

NOTE

A marine grade water resistant grease should be used wherever grease is required on the outboard. Chapter Three lists the greases recommended by Mercury Marine.

RTV GASKET SEALANT

Room temperature vulcanizing (RTV) sealant is used on some pre-formed gaskets and to seal some components. RTV is a silicone gel supplied in tubes and can be purchased in a number of different colors.

Moisture in the air causes RTV to cure. Always place the cap on the tube as soon as possible after using RTV. Remember that RTV has a shelf life of only one year and does not cure properly after expiration. Check the expiration date on the RTV tube before using. Keep partially used tubes tightly sealed.

RTV Sealant Application

Clean all old gasket residue from the mating surfaces. Remove all gasket material from blind threaded holes. It can cause inaccurate bolt torque. Spray the mating surface with an aerosol parts cleaner and then wipe dry with a lint-free cloth. The area must be clean for the sealant to adhere.

Apply RTV sealant in a continuous bead 0.08-0.12 in. (2-3 mm) thick. Circle all fastener holes unless specified otherwise. Do not allow sealant to enter these holes. Assemble and tighten the fasteners to the specified torque within the time frame specified by the RTV sealant manufacturer (usually 10-15 minutes).

ANAEROBIC SEALANT

Anaerobic sealant is a gel used to seal two rigid mating surfaces. It should not be used if one of the mating surfaces is flexible. Anaerobic sealant cures only in the absence of air and the presence of metal, as when squeezed tightly between two machined surfaces. For this reason it will not spoil rapidly if the cap is left off the tube. Anaerobic sealant is able to fill gaps up to 0.030 in. (0.8 mm) and generally works best on rigid, machined flanges or surfaces. Be sure to check the expiration date before use.

Anaerobic Sealant Application

Clean all gasket residue from the mating surfaces. The surfaces must be free of all oil and dirt. Remove all gasket material around attaching holes, as it can cause a hydraulic lock effect and affect bolt torque.

Apply anaerobic sealant in a 0.04 in. (1 mm) or less bead to one sealing surface. Circle all bolt holes. Do not allow sealant to enter the these holes. Assemble the unit and torque the fasteners within 15 minutes after application.

THREADLOCKING COMPOUND

Threadlocking compound is a fluid applied to the threads of fasteners. After tightening the fastener, the fluid hardens and becomes a solid filler between the threads. This makes it difficult for the fastener to work loose from vibration or heat expansion and contraction. Some threadlocking compounds also provide a seal against fluid leakage past the threads.

Threadlocking compounds come in different strengths. Follow the particular manufacturer's recommendation regarding compound selection. Two manufacturers of threadlocking compound are ThreeBond and Loctite, which offer a wide range of compounds for various strengths, temperature and repair applications.

Loctite 222 (purple), 242 (blue) and 271 (red) are recommended for many threadlocking requirements described in this manual. Loctite 222 is a low strength theadlock commonly applied to small screw head fasteners. Loctite 222 allows easy disassembly of the component. Loctite 242 is a medium strength threadlock that allows component disassembly with normal hand tools. Loctite 271 is a high strength threadlock and may require heat or special tools, such as a press or puller, for component disassembly.

NOTE

To prevent fasteners from working loose, use a threadlocking compound on all of the outboard fasteners unless specified otherwise.

Threadlock Application

Before applying threadlocking compound remove any old compound from all thread areas and clean them with

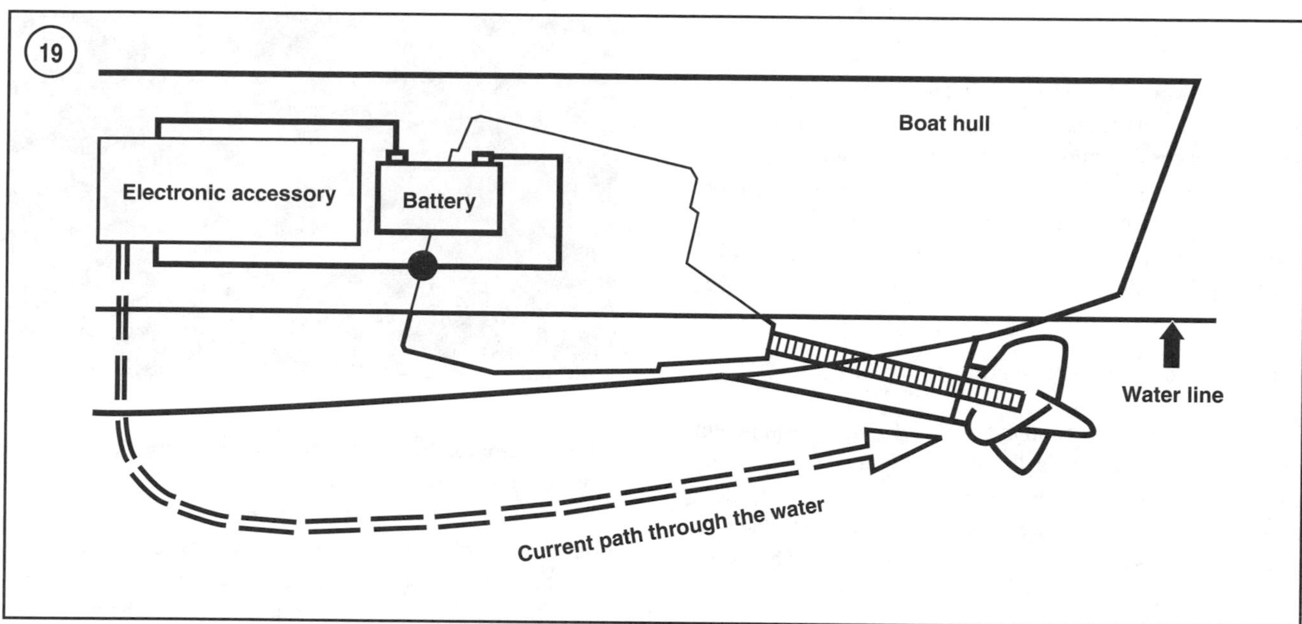

aerosol parts cleaner. Use the compound sparingly. Excess fluid can flow into adjoining parts.

Inspect the surfaces to verify that no oil or dirt is present before applying the compound. Shake the container thoroughly and apply a light coating to both surfaces, then assemble the parts and/or tighten the fasteners. Wipe cxcess compound from exposed areas to prevent it from flowing into and contaminating other components.

GALVANIC CORROSION

A chemical reaction occurs whenever two different types of metal are joined by an electrical conductor and immersed in an electrolytic solution such as water. Electrons transfer from one metal to the other through the electrolyte and return through the conductor (**Figure 19**).

The hardware on a boat is made of many different types of metal. The boat hull acts as a conductor between the metals. Even if the hull is wooden or fiberglass, the slightest film of water on the hull provides conductivity (by acting as the electrolyte). This combination creates a good environment for electron flow. Unfortunately, this electron flow results in galvanic corrosion of the metal involved, causing one of the metals to be corroded or eroded away. The amount of electron flow, and therefore the amount of corrosion, depends on several factors:

1. The types of metal involved.
2. The efficiency of the conductor.
3. The strength of the electrolyte.

Metals

The chemical composition of the metal used in marine equipment has a significant effect on the amount and speed of galvanic corrosion. Certain metals are more resistant to corrosion than others. These electrically negative metals are commonly called *noble*; they act as the cathode in any reaction. Metals that are more subject to corrosion are electrically positive; they act as the anode in a reaction. The more noble metals are titanium, 18-8 stainless steel and nickel. Less noble metals include zinc, aluminum and magnesium. Galvanic corrosion becomes more excessive as the difference in electrical potential between the two metals increases.

In some cases, galvanic corrosion can occur within a single piece of metal. For example, brass is a mixture of zinc and copper, and when immersed in an electrolyte, the zinc portion of the mixture will corrode away as a galvanic reaction occurs between the zinc and copper particles.

Conductors

The hull of the boat often acts as the conductor between different types of metals. Marine equipment, such as the engine gearcase of the outboard, can act as the conductor. Large masses of metal, firmly connected together, are more efficient conductors than water. Rubber mountings and vinyl-based paint can act as insulators between pieces of metal.

Electrolyte

The water in which a boat operates acts as the electrolyte for the corrosion process. The more efficient a conductor is, the more excessive and rapid the corrosion will be.

Cold, clean freshwater is the poorest conductor; whereas brackish or saltwater is an efficient electrolyte. Most manufacturers recommend a freshwater flush after operating in polluted, brackish or saltwater.

Galvanic Corrosion Protection

Because of the environment in which marine equipment must operate, it is practically impossible to totally prevent galvanic corrosion. However, there are several ways to slow the process. After taking these precautions, the next step is to direct the process to occur only in certain places. This is the role of sacrificial anodes and impressed current systems.

Slowing Corrosion

Some simple precautions help reduce the amount of corrosion taking place outside the hull. These precautions are not substitutes for the corrosion protection methods discussed under *Sacrificial Anodes* and *Impressed Current Systems* in this chapter, but they can help these methods reduce corrosion.

Use fasteners made of metal more noble than the parts they secure. If corrosion occurs, the parts they secure may suffer but the fasteners are protected. Major problems could arise if the fasteners corrode to the point of failure.

Keep painted surfaces in good condition. If paint is scraped off and bare metal exposed, corrosion rapidly increases. Use vinyl- or plastic-based paint, which acts as an electrical insulator.

Be careful when applying metal-based anti-fouling paint to the boat. Do not apply anti-fouling paint to metal parts of the boat or the outboard engine/gearcase. If applied to metal surfaces, this type of paint reacts with metal and results in corrosion between the metal and the layer of paint. Maintain a minimum of 1 in. (25 cm) border between the painted surface and any metal parts. Organic-based paints are available for use on metal surfaces.

Where a corrosion protection device is used, remember that it must be immersed in the electrolyte along with the boat to provide any protection. If the outboard is raised out of the water while the boat is docked, any anodes on the engine will be removed from the corrosion process rendering them ineffective. (Of course, when raised out of the water/electrolyte the engine requires less protection.) Never paint or apply any coating to anodes or other protection devices. Paint or other coatings insulate anodes from the corrosion process.

20

Any change to the boat equipment, such as the installation of a stainless steel propeller, changes the electrical potential and may cause increased corrosion. Always consider this fact when adding equipment or changing exposed materials. Install additional anodes or other protection equipment as required to ensure adequate protection. The expense to repair corrosion damage usually far exceeds that of additional corrosion protection.

If the boat is docked and connected to an on-shore power source, a galvanic isolator or other protection must be installed into the power source. Otherwise, the power line may provide an electrical connection (conductor) to on-shore pilings or other structure; resulting in greatly increased galvanic activity and corrosion. The isolator is installed in series with the power line, blocking galvanic current flow in the shore power circuit, while allowing current flow in the event of a ground fault. Always follow the manufacturer's instructions when installing a galvanic isolator.

Sacrificial Anodes

Sacrificial anodes (**Figure 20**) are designed to corrode. Properly fastening such pieces to the boat causes them to act as the anode in any galvanic reaction that occurs; any other metal in the reaction acts as the cathode and is not damaged.

Anodes are usually made of zinc. Some anodes are made of an aluminum and indium alloy. This alloy is less noble than the aluminum alloy in the drive system components, providing the desired sacrificial properties, but is more resistant to oxide coating than zinc anodes. Oxide coating occurs as the anode material reacts with oxygen in the water. An oxide coating insulates the anode, dramatically reducing the corrosion protection.

Anodes must be used properly to be effective. Simply fastening anodes to the boat in random locations does not do the job.

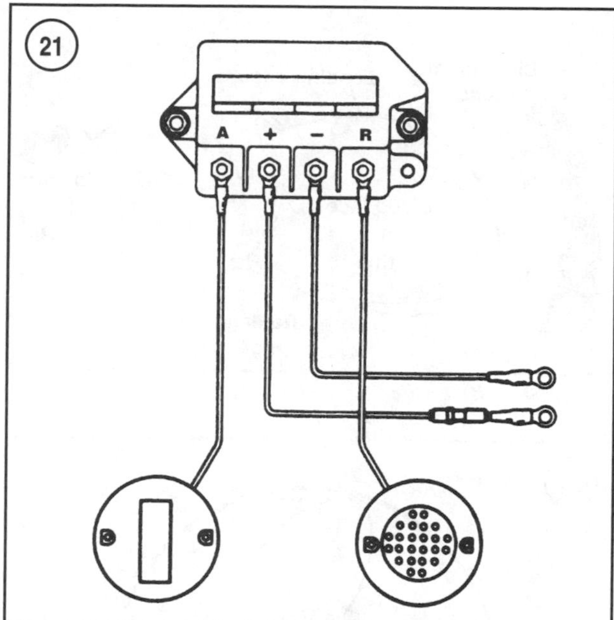

First determine how much anode surface is required to adequately protect the equipment surface area. A good starting point is provided by the Military Specification MIL-A-818001, which states that one square inch of new anode protects either:

1. 800 sq. in of freshly painted steel.
2. 250 sq. in. of bare steel or bare aluminum alloy.
3. 100 sq. in. of copper or copper alloy.

This rule is valid for the boat at rest. If underway, additional anode area is required to protect the same surface area.

The anode must be in good electrical contact with the metal that it protects. If possible, attach an anode to all metal surfaces requiring protection.

Quality anodes have inserts around the fastener holes that are made of a more noble material. Otherwise, the anode could erode away around the fastener hole, allowing the anode to loosen or possible fall off, thereby losing needed protection.

Impressed Current System

An impressed current system can be added to any boat. The system generally consists of the anode, controller and reference electrode (**Figure 21**). The anode in this system is coated with a very noble metal, such as platinum, so that it is almost corrosion-free and can last almost indefinitely. The reference electrode, under the waterline, allows the control module to monitor the potential for corrosion. If the module senses that corrosion is occurring, it applies positive battery voltage to the anode. Current then flows from

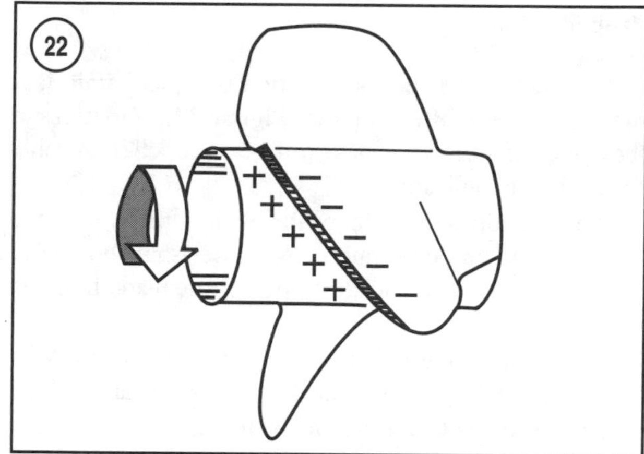

the anode to all other metal components, regardless of how noble or non-noble these components may be. Essentially, the electrically current from the battery counteracts the galvanic reaction to dramatically reduce corrosion.

Only a small amount of current is needed to counteract corrosion. Using input from the sensor, the control module provides only the amount of current need to suppress galvanic corrosion. Most systems consume a maximum of 0.2 Ah at full demand. Under normal conditions, these systems can provide protection for 8-12 weeks without recharging the battery. Remember that this system must have constant connection to the battery. Often the battery supply to the system is connected to a battery switching device, causing the operator to inadvertently shut off the system while docked.

An impressed system is more expensive to install than sacrificial anodes, but considering the low maintenance requirements and superior protection it provides, the long term cost may be lower.

PROPELLERS

The propeller is the final link between the drive system and the water. A perfectly maintained engine and hull are useless if the propeller is the wrong type, damaged, or deteriorated. Although propeller selection for a specific application is beyond the scope of this manual, the following provides the basic information needed to make an informed decision. A professional at a reputable marine dealership is the best source for a propeller recommendation.

Propeller Function

As the curved propeller blades rotate through the water, a high-pressure area forms on one side of the blade and a low-pressure area forms on the other side of the blade (**Figure 22**). The propeller moves toward the low-pressure area, carrying the boat with it.

Propeller Parts

Although a propeller is usually a one-piece unit, it is made of several different parts (**Figure 23**). Variations in the design of these parts make different propellers suitable for different applications.

The blade tip is the point of the blade furthest from the center of the propeller hub or propeller shaft bore. The blade tip separates the leading edge of the blade from the trailing edge.

The leading edge is the edge of the blade nearest the boat. During forward operation, this is the area of the blade that first cuts through the water.

The trailing edge is the surface of the blade furthest from the boat. During reverse operation, this is the area of the blade that first cuts through the water.

The blade face is the surface of the blade that faces away from the boat. During forward operation, high-pressure forms on this side of the blade.

The blade back is the surface of the blade that faces toward the boat. During forward operation, low-pressure forms on this side of the blade.

The cup is a small curve or lip on the trailing edge of the blade. Cupped propeller blades generally perform better than non-cupped propeller blades.

The hub is the center portion of the propeller. It connects the blades to the propeller shaft. On most drive systems, engine exhaust is routed through the hub; in this case, the hub is made up of an outer and inner portion, connected by ribs.

A diffuser ring is used on through-hub exhaust models to prevent exhaust gasses from entering the blade area.

Propeller Design

Changes in length, angle, thickness and material of propeller parts make different propellers suitable for different applications.

Diameter

Propeller diameter is the distance from the center of the hub to the blade tip, multiplied by two. Essentially it is the diameter of the circle formed by the blade tips during propeller rotation (**Figure 24**).

Pitch and rake

Propeller pitch and rake describe the placement of the blades in relation to the hub (**Figure 25**).

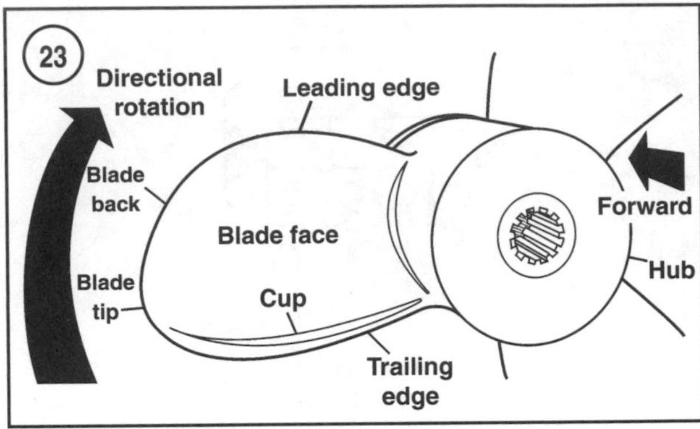

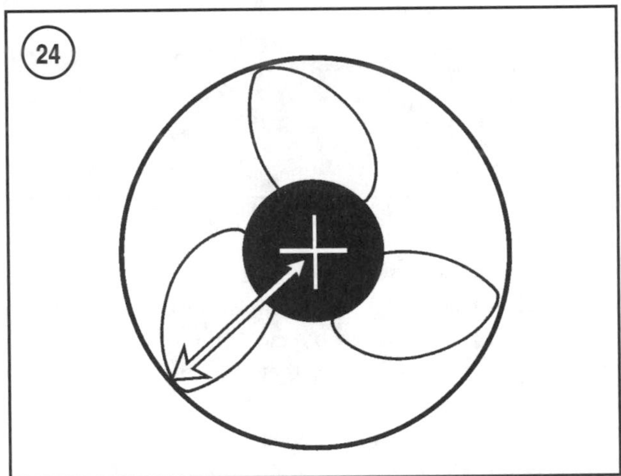

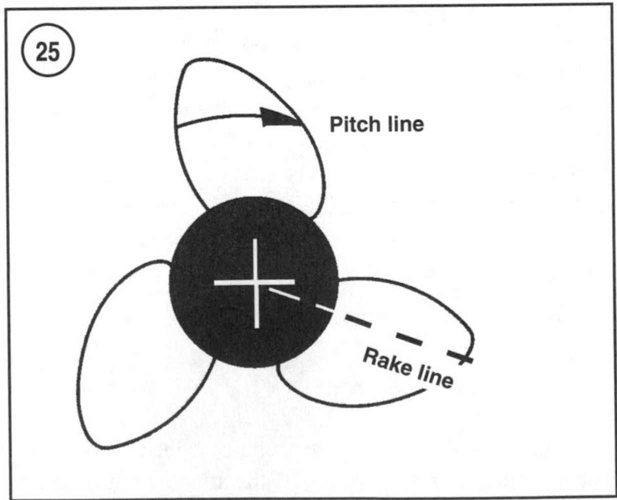

Pitch describes the theoretical distance the propeller would travel in one revolution. In A, **Figure 26**, the propeller would travel 10 in. in one revolution. In B, **Figure 26**, the propeller would travel 20 in. in one revolution. This distance is only theoretical; during typical operation,

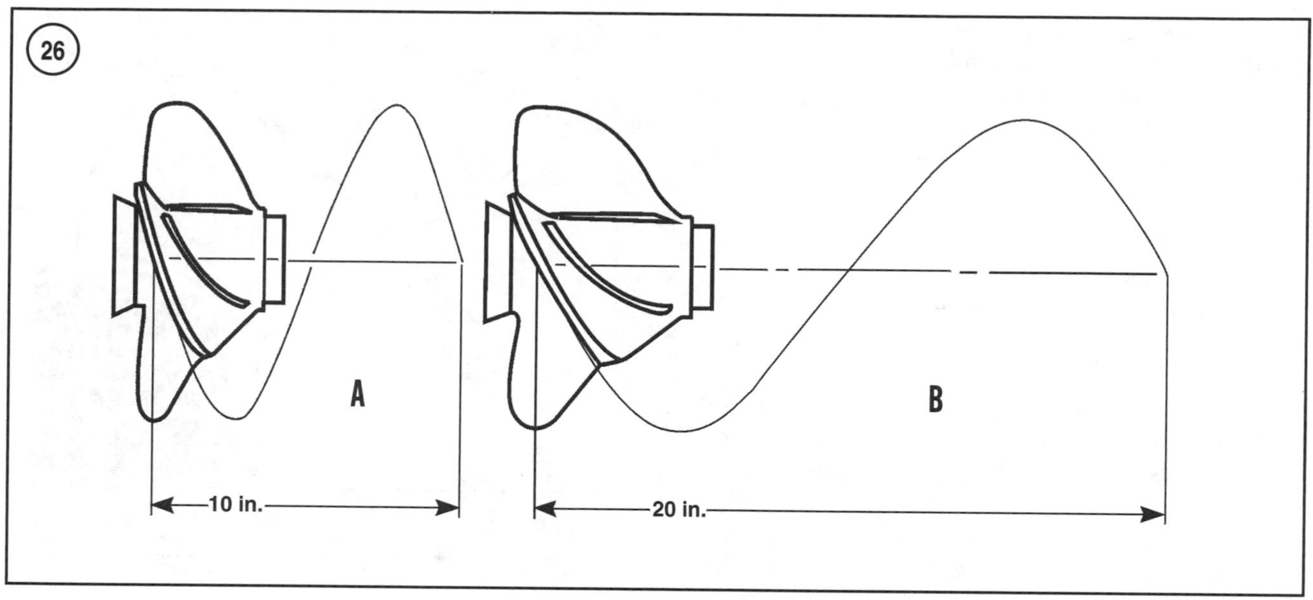

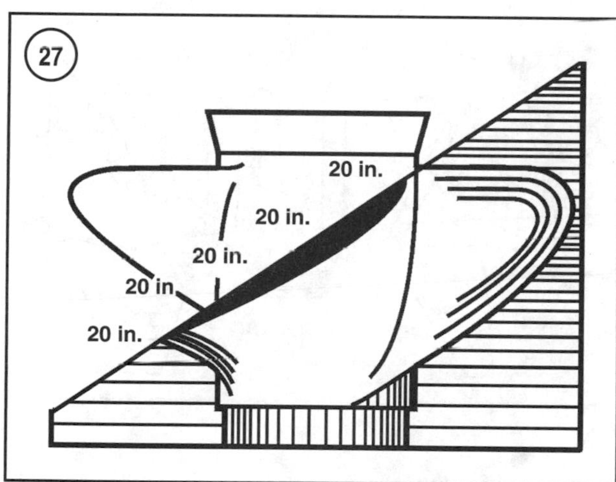

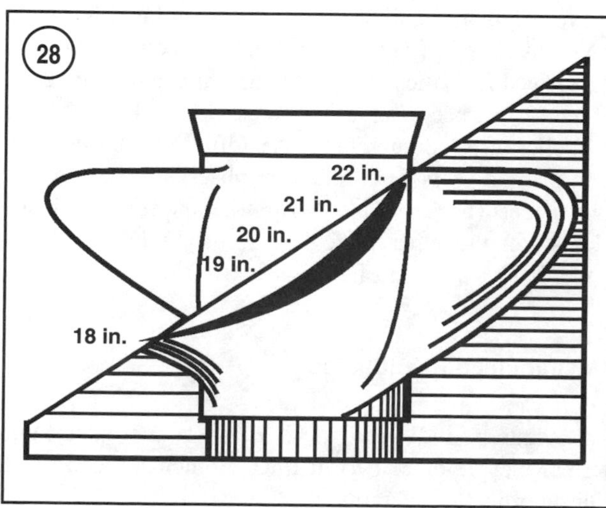

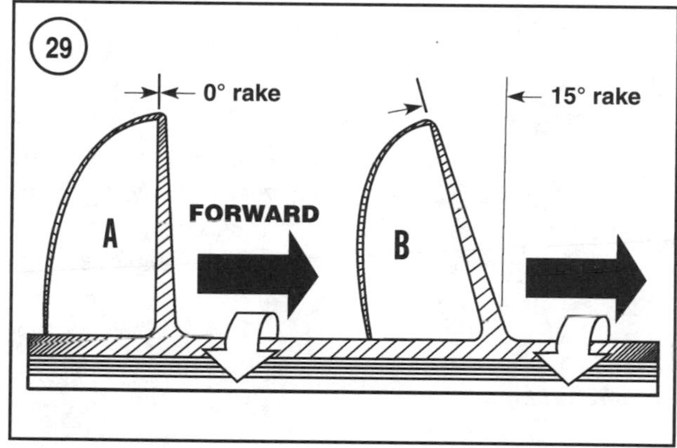

the propeller achieves only 75-85% of its pitch. Slip rate describes the difference in actual travel relative to the pitch. Lighter, faster boats typically achieve a lower slip rate than heavier, slower boats.

Propeller blades can be constructed with constant pitch (**Figure 27**) or progressive pitch (**Figure 28**). On a progressive pitch propeller, the pitch starts low at the leading edge and increases toward the trailing edge. The propeller pitch specification is the average of the pitch across the entire blade. Propellers with progressive pitch usually provide better overall performance than constant pitch propellers.

Blade rake is specified in degrees and is measured along a line from the center of the hub to the blade tip. A blade that is perpendicular to the hub (A, **Figure 29**) has 0° rake. A blade that is angled from perpendicular (B, **Figure 29**) has a rake expressed by the difference from perpendicular. Most propellers have rakes ranging from

0-20°. Lighter, faster boats generally perform better using a propeller with a greater amount of rake. Heavier, slower boats generally perform better using a propeller with less rake.

Blade thickness

Blade thickness is not uniform at all points along the blade. For efficiency, blades are as thin as possible at all points while retaining enough strength to move the boat. Blades are thicker where they meet the hub and thinner at the blade tips. This construction is necessary to support the heavier loads at the hub section of the blade. Overall blade thickness is dependent on the strength of the material used.

When cut along a line from the leading edge to the trailing edge in the central portion of the blade, the propeller blades resembles an airplane wing. The blade face , where high pressure forms during forward rotation, is almost flat. The blade back, where low pressure forms during forward rotation, is curved, with the thinnest portion at the edges and the thickest portion at the center.

Propellers that run only partially submerged, as in racing applications, may have a wedge shaped cross-section (**Figure 30**). The leading edge is very thin and the blade thickness increases toward the trailing edge, where it is thickest. If a propeller such as this is run submerged, it is very inefficient.

Number of blades

The number of blades on a propeller is a compromise between efficiency and vibration. A one-bladed propeller would be the most efficient, but it would create an unacceptable amount of vibration. As blades are added, efficiency decreases but so does vibration. Most propellers have three or four blades, representing the most practical trade-off between efficiency and vibration.

Material

Propeller materials are chosen for strength, corrosion resistance and economy. Stainless steel, aluminum, plastic and bronze are the most commonly used materials. Bronze is quite strong but rather expensive. Stainless steel is more common than bronze because of its combination of strength and corrosion resistance at a lower cost. Aluminum and plastic are the least expensive but lack the strength of stainless steel. Plastic propellers are more suited for lower horsepower applications.

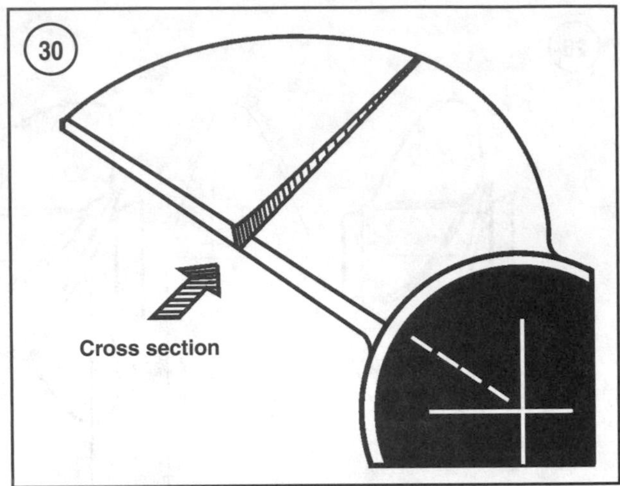

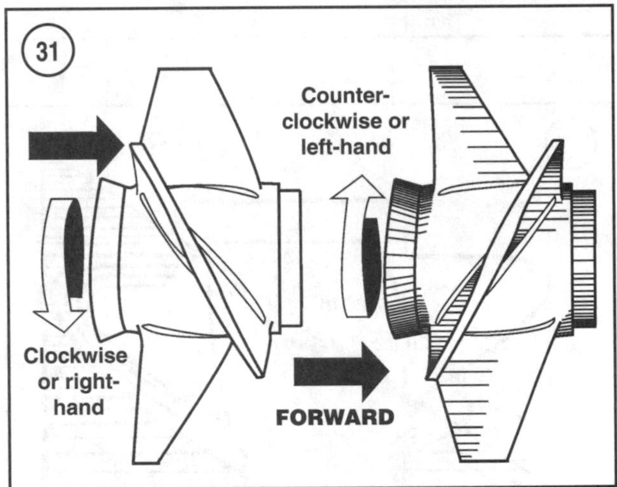

Direction of rotation

Propellers are made for both right-hand and left-hand rotations although right-hand is the most commonly used. As viewed from the rear of the boat while in forward gear, a right-hand propeller turns clockwise and a left-hand propeller turns counterclockwise. Off the boat, the direction of rotation is determined by observing the angle of the blades (**Figure 31**). A right-hand propeller blade slants from the upper left to the lower right; left-hand propeller blades are opposite.

Cavitation and Ventilation

Cavitation and ventilation are *not* interchangeable terms: they refer to two distinct problems encountered during propeller operation.

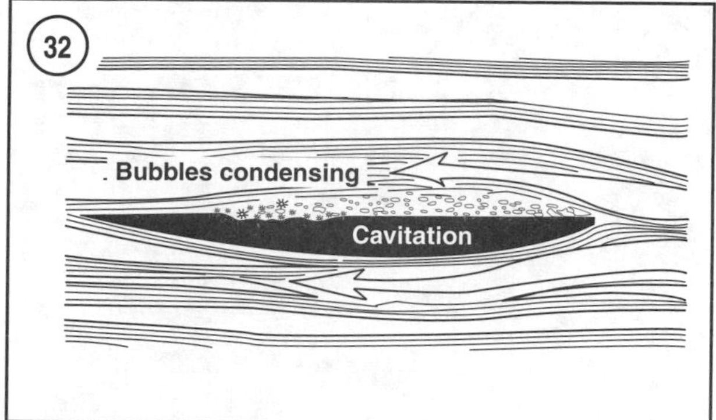

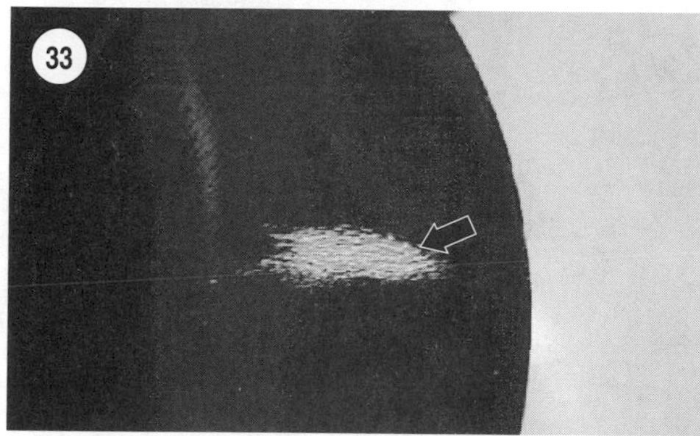

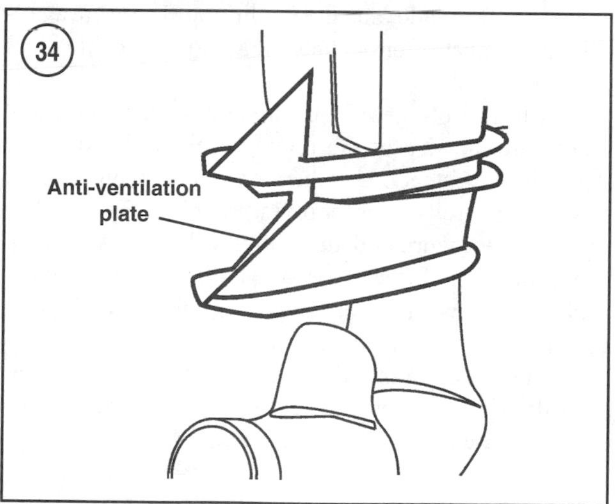

To help understand cavitation, consider the relationship between pressure and the boiling point of water. At sea level, water boils at 212° F (100° C). As pressure increases, the boiling point of water increases—it boils at a temperature higher than 212° F (100° C). The opposite is also true. As pressure decreases, water boils a temperature lower than 212° F (100° C). If the pressure drops low enough, water will boil at normal room temperature.

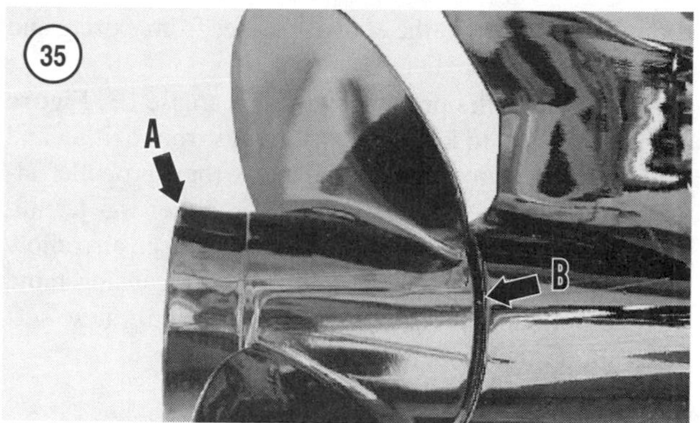

During normal propeller operation, low pressure forms on the blade back. Normally this pressure does not drop low enough for boiling to occur. However, poor propeller design, damaged blades or using the wrong type of propeller can cause unusually low pressure on the blade surface. If the pressure drops low enough, boiling occurs and bubbles form on the blade surface (**Figure 32**). As the boiling water moves to a higher pressure area of the blade, the boiling ceases and the bubbles collapse. The collapsing bubbles release energy that erodes the surface of the propeller blade.

Corroded surfaces, physical damage or even marine growth combined with high-speed operation can cause low pressure and cavitation on the outboard gearcase surfaces. In such cases, low pressure forms as water flows over a protrusion or rough surface. The boiling water forms bubbles that collapse as they move to a higher pressure area toward the rear of the surface imperfection.

This entire process of pressure drop, boiling and bubble collapse is called *cavitation*. The resulting damage is called *cavitation burn* (**Figure 33**). Cavitation is caused by a decrease in pressure, not an increase in temperature.

Ventilation is not as complex as a process as cavitation. Ventilation refers to air entering the blade area, either from above the water surface or from a through-hub exhaust system. As the blades meet the air, the propeller momentarily loses contact with the water and subsequently the engine loses thrust. The propeller and engine over-rev, causing very low pressure on the blade back and massive cavitation.

Most marine drive systems have a plate (**Figure 34**) above the propeller to prevent surface air from entering the blade area. This plate is an *anti-ventilation plate*, although it is often incorrectly called an *anti-cavitation plate*.

Most propellers have a flared section at the rear of the propeller called a diffuser ring (A, **Figure 35**). This feature forms a barrier, and extends the exhaust passage far enough aft to prevent the exhaust gasses from exiting and ventilating the propeller.

A close fit of the propeller to the gearcase (B, **Figure 35**) is necessary to keep exhaust gasses from exiting and ventilating the propeller. Using the wrong propeller attaching hardware can position the propeller too far aft, preventing a close fit. The wrong hardware can also allow the propeller to rub against the gearcase, causing rapid wear to both components. Wear or damage to these surfaces allows the propeller to ventilate.

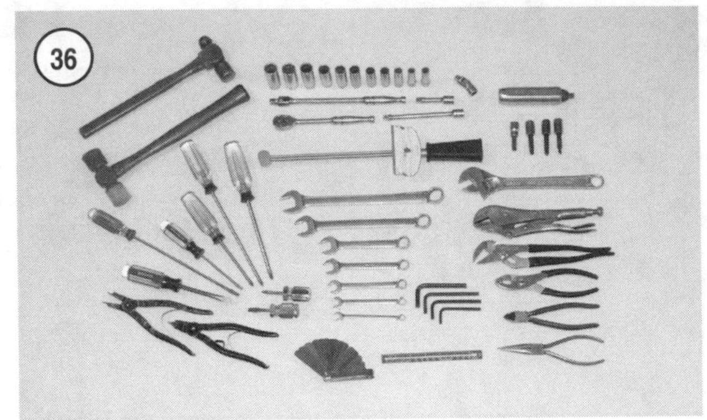

BASIC HAND TOOLS

Many of the procedures in this manual can be carried out with simple hand tools and test equipment familiar to the average home mechanic. Keep tools clean and in a toolbox. Keep them organized with related tools stored together.

After using a tool, wipe off dirt and grease with a clean cloth and return the tool to its correct place. Wiping the tools off is especially important when servicing the outboard in areas where it can come in contact with sand, salt crystals and vegetation. These contaminants can cause excessive engine wear or damage if they should enter the power head.

Quality tools are essential. The best are constructed of high-strength alloy steel. These tools are light, easy to use and resistant to wear. Their working surface is devoid of sharp edges and the tools are carefully polished. They have an easy-to-clean finish and are comfortable to use. Quality tools are a good investment.

When purchasing tools to perform the procedures covered in this manual, consider the potential frequency of use. If starting a tool kit, consider purchasing a basic tool set (**Figure 36**). These sets are available in many tool combinations and offer substantial savings when compared to individually purchased tools. As work experience grows and tasks become more complicated, specialized tools may be added.

The following basic hand tools are required to perform virtually any repair job. Each tool is described and the recommended size given for starting a tool collection. Additional tools and some duplicates may be added as you become familiar with the outboard. Both U. S. Standard and metric tools are required to work on the models covered in this manual.

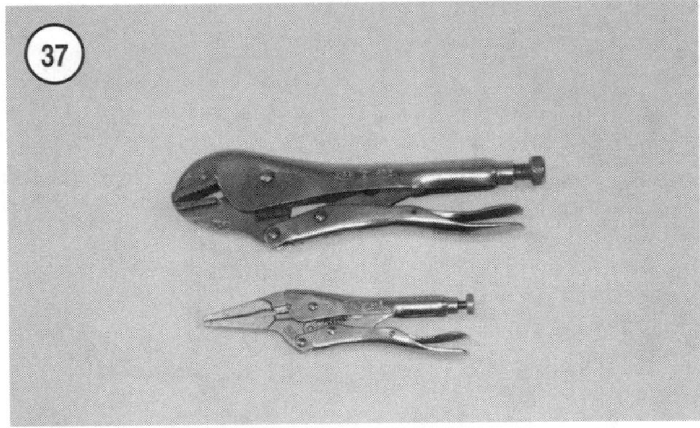

Screwdrivers

Screwdrivers of various lengths and types are mandatory for the simplest tool kit. The two basic types are the slotted tip (flat blade) and the Phillips tip. These are available in sets that often include an assortment of tip sizes and shaft lengths.

As with all tools, use a screwdriver designed for the job. Make sure the size of the tip conforms to the size and shape of the fastener. Use them only for driving screws. Never use a screwdriver for prying or chiseling metal. Repair or replace worn or damaged screwdrivers. A worn tip may damage the fastener, making it difficult to remove.

Phillips screwdrivers are sized according to their point size. They are numbered one, two, three and four. The degree of taper determines the point size. The No. 1 Phillips screwdriver is the most pointed. The points become more blunted as the number increases.

Pliers

Pliers come in a wide range of types and sizes. Though pliers are useful for holding, cutting, bending and crimping, they should never be used to turn bolts or nuts.

Each design has a specialized function. Slip joint pliers are general-purpose pliers used for gripping and bending. Diagonal cutting pliers are needed to cut wire and can be used to remove cotter pins. Needlenose pliers grip or bend small objects. Locking pliers (**Figure 37**), sometimes

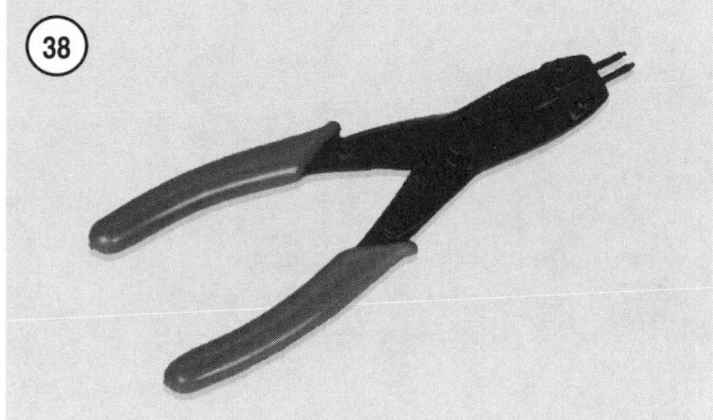
38

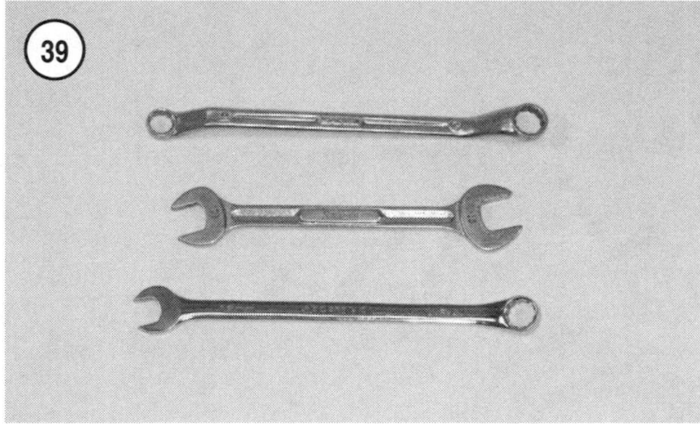
39

called locking pliers, are used to hold objects very tightly. They have many uses ranging from holding two parts together during assembly, to gripping the end of a broken stud. Use caution when using locking pliers, as the sharp jaws will damage the objects they hold.

Snap Ring Pliers

Snap ring pliers (**Figure 38**) are specialized pliers with tips that fit into the ends of snap rings to remove and install them.

Snap ring pliers are available with a fixed action (either internal for squeezing or external for spreading) or convertible (one tool works on both internal and external snap rings). They may have fixed tips or interchangeable ones of various sized and angles. For general use, select convertible type pliers with interchangeable tips.

WARNING
Snap rings can unexpectedly slip and fly off during removal and installation. Also, snap ring plier tips may break. Always wear eye protection when using snap ring pliers.

Hammers

Various types of hammers are available to fit a number of applications. A ball-peen hammer is used to strike another tool, such as a punch or chisel. Soft-faced hammers are required when a metal object must be struck without damaging it. *Never* use a metal-faced hammer on engine components. Damage will occur in most cases.

Always wear eye protection when using hammers. Make sure the hammer face is in good condition and the handle is not cracked. Select the correct hammer for the job and make sure to strike the object squarely. *Never* use the handle or side of the hammer to strike an object.

When striking a hammer against a punch, cold chisel or similar tool, the face of the hammer should be at least 1/2 in. (13 mm) larger than the head of the tool. When it is necessary to strike a steel part without damaging it, use a brass hammer. Brass will give when striking a harder object.

Wrenches

Box-end, open end, and combination wrenches (**Figure 39**) are available in sets or separately in a variety of sizes. The size number stamped near the end refers to the distance between two parallel flats on a hex head bolt or nut.

The box-end wrench is an excellent tool because it grips the fastener on all sides. This reduces the chance of the tool slipping. The box-end wrench is designed with either a 6 or 12-point opening. For stubborn or damaged fasteners, the 6-point provides superior holding ability by contacting the fastener across a wider area at all six edges. For general use, the 12-point works well. It allows the wrench to be removed and reinstalled without moving the handle over such a wide arc.

An open-end wrench is fast and works best in areas with limited access. It contacts the fastener at only two points. However, open-end wrenches can slip under heavy force, especially if the tool or fastener is worn. A box-end wrench is preferred in most instances, especially when breaking loose or applying the final tightness to a fastener.

The combination wrench has a box-end on one end, and an open-end on the other. The combination makes it a convenient tool.

Adjustable Wrenches

An adjustable wrench or Cresent wrench can fit nearly any nut or bolt head that has clear access around its entire perimeter. However, it can loosen and slip, causing damage to the nut and to the mechanic. Adjustable wrenches are best used as a backup wrench to keep a nut or bolt from turning while the other end of the fastener is being loosened or tightened with a box-end or socket wrench.

Adjustable wrenches contact the fastener at only two points, which makes them more subject to slipping off the fastener. One jaw is moveable and can unexpectedly loosen. Make certain the solid or fixed jaw is the one transmitting the force.

Socket Wrenches, Ratchets and Handles

Sockets that attach to a ratchet handle (**Figure 40**) are available with 6-point or 12-point openings and different drive sizes. The drive size (1/4, 3/8, 1/2 and 3/4 in.) indicate the size of the square hole that accepts the ratchet handle. The number stamped on the socket is the size of the work area and must match the fastener head.

As with wrenches, a 6-point socket provides superior holding ability, while a 12-point socket needs to be moved only half as far to reposition on the fastener.

Sockets are designed to be either hand or impact driven. Those designed to be impact driven are made of thicker material and offer greater strength and durability. However, the thicker sides of the impact sockets may prevent their use in areas with limited access. Use only impact sockets when using an impact driver or air-powered tools. Use hand driven sockets only with hand-driven attachments.

WARNING
Never use sockets or extensions bars designed to be hand-driven with an impact driver or air-powered tools. They may unexpectedly shatter and cause injury. Always wear eye protection when using impact or air-powered tools.

Various handles are available for sockets. The speed handle is used for fast operation. Flexible ratchet heads in varying lengths allow the socket to be turned with varying force, and at odd angles. Extensions bars allow the socket setup to reach difficult areas. The ratchet is the most versatile. It allows the user to remove or install the fastener without removing the socket.

Impact Driver

An impact driver provides extra force for removing fasteners, by converting the impact of a hammer into a turning motion. This makes it possible to remove stubborn fasteners with minimal damage to them. Impact drivers and interchangeable bits (**Figure 41**) are available from most tool suppliers. When using a socket with an impact

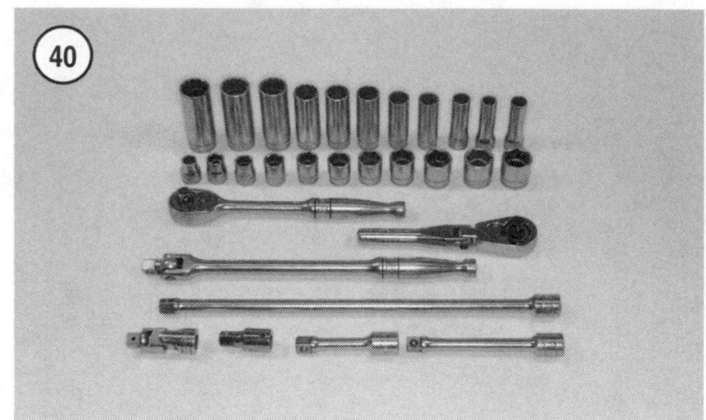

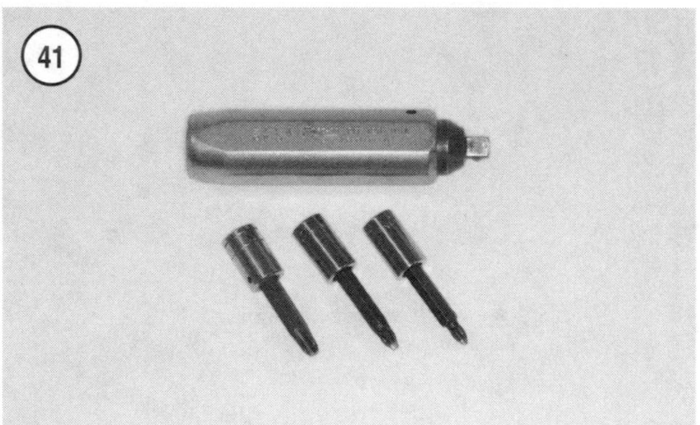

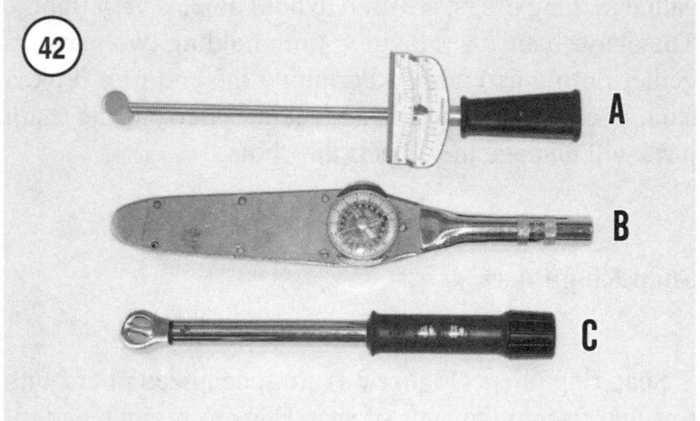

driver, make sure the socket is designed for impact use. Refer to *Sockets, Wrenches, Ratchets and Handles* in this section.

Impact drivers are great for the home mechanic as they offer many of the advantages of air tools without the need for a costly air compressor to run them.

Torque Wrenches

A torque wrench is used with a socket, torque adapter or similar extension to measure torque while tightening a

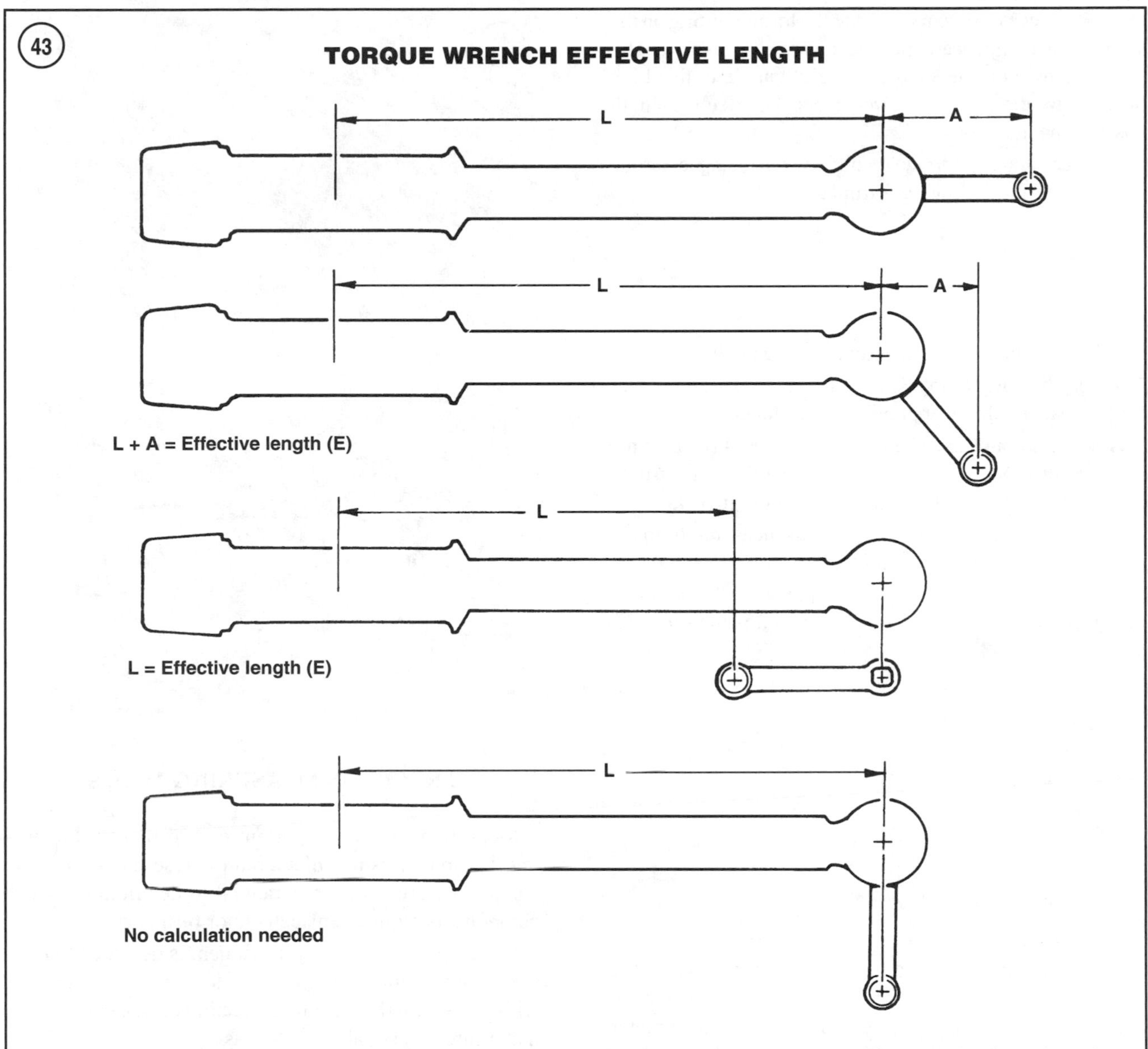

fastener. Torque wrenches come in several drive sizes (1/4, 3/8, 1/2 and 3/4 in.) and have various methods of reading the torque value. The drive size is the size of the square drive that accepts the socket, adapter or extension. Common types of torque wrenches include the deflecting beam (A, **Figure 42**), the dial indicator type (B) and the audible click type (C).

Consider the torque range, drive size and accuracy when choosing a torque wrench. The torque specifications in this manual provide an indication of the range required.

A torque wrench is a precision tool that must be properly cared for to remain accurate. Store torque wrenches in cases or separate padded drawers within a toolbox. Follow the manufacturer's instructions for their care and calibration.

Torque Adapters

Torque adapters or extensions extend or reduce the reach of a torque wrench. The torque adapter shown on the top of **Figure 43** is used to tighten a fastener that cannot be reached because of the size of the torque wrench head, drive, and socket. If a torque adapter changes the effective lever length (**Figure 43**), the torque reading on the wrench will not equal the actual torque applied to the fastener. It is necessary to recalibrate the torque setting on the wrench to compensate for the change in lever length. When using a torque adapter at a right angle to the drive head, calibration is not required, since the effective length has not changed.

To recalibrate a torque reading when using a torque adapter, use the following formula.

$$TW = \frac{TA \times L}{L + A}$$

TW is the torque setting or dial reading on the wrench.

TA is the torque specification (the actual amount of torque that should be applied to the fastener).

A is the amount that the adapter increases (or in some cases reduces) the effective lever length as measured along a centerline of the torque wrench (**Figure 43**).

L is the lever length of the wrench as measured from the center of the drive to the center of the grip.

The effective length of the torque wrench measured along the centerline of the torque wrench is the sum of **L** and **A** (**Figure 43**).

Example:

TA = 20 ft.-lb.

A = 3 in.

L = 14 in.

$$TW = \frac{20 \times 14}{14 + 6} = \frac{280}{17} = 16.5 \text{ ft.-lb.}$$

In this example, the torque wrench would be set to the recalculated torque value (TW = 16.5 ft.-lb.). When using a beam-type wrench, tighten the fastener until the pointer aligns with 16.5 ft.-lb. In this example, although the torque wrench is pre-set to 16.5 ft.-lb., the actual torque applied is 20 ft.-lb.

SPECIAL TOOLS

Some procedures in this manual require special tools. These are described in the appropriate chapter and are available from either the engine manufacturer or a tool supplier. In many cases, an acceptable substitute may be found in an existing tool kit. Another alternative is to make the tool or have a reputable machine shop make the tool. However, it is not practical or cost effective to fabricate gauging tools. Purchase or rent such tools from a reputable dealership as necessary.

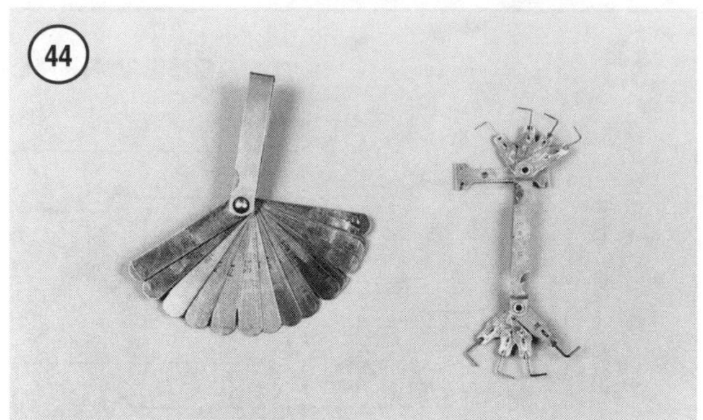

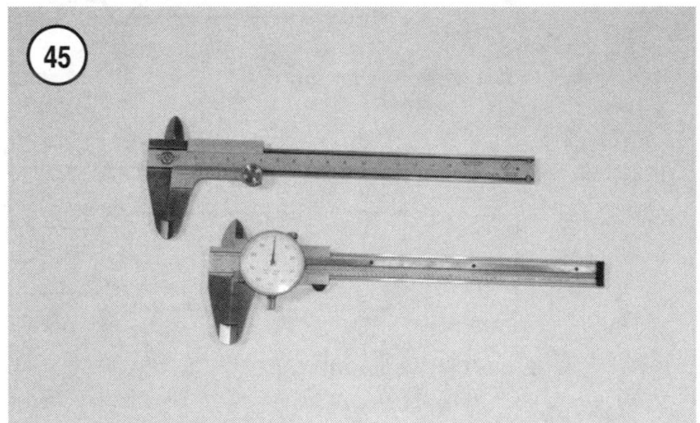

PRECISION MEASURING TOOLS

Measurement is an important part of outboard servicing. Equipment is manufactured to close tolerances. Accurate measurements are essential to determining which components require replacement or further service.

Each type of measuring instrument is designed to measure a dimension with a certain degree of accuracy and within a certain range. When selecting the measuring tool, make sure it is suitable for the task.

As with all tools, measuring tools provide the best results if cared for properly. Improper use can damage the tool and result in inaccurate results. If any measurement is questionable, verify the measurement using another tool. A standard gauge is usually provided with the measuring tool to check accuracy and calibrate the tool if necessary.

Precision measurements can vary according to the experience of the person performing the procedure. Accurate results are only possible if the mechanic possesses a feel for using the tool. Heavy-handed use of measuring tools produce less accurate results than if the tool is grasped gently by the fingertips so the point at which the tool contacts the object is easily felt. This feel for equipment produces more accurate measurements and reduces the risk of damaging tools or components.

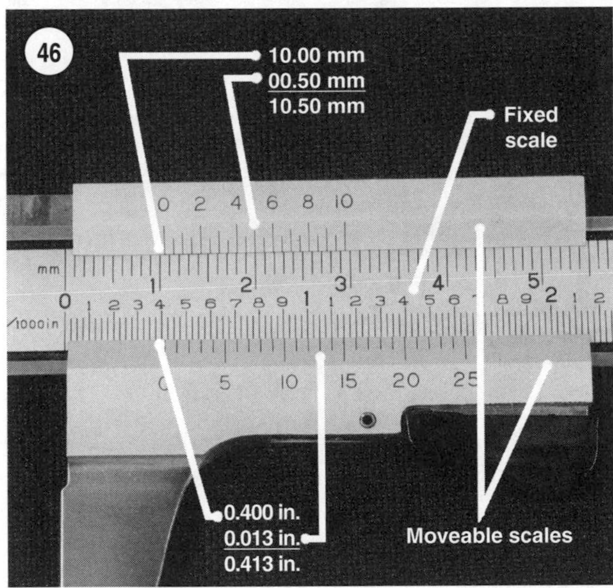

Feeler Gauges

The feeler or thickness gauge (**Figure 44**) is used for measuring the distance between two surfaces.

A feeler gauge set consists of an assortment of steel strips of graduated thicknesses. Each blade is marked with its thickness. Blades can be of various lengths and angles for use in different procedures.

A common use for a feeler gauge is to measure valve clearance. Wire (round) type gauges should be used to measure spark plug gap.

To obtain a proper measurement using a feeler gauge, make sure the blade passes through the gap with slight drag. It should not need to be forced through, but should not have any play up-and-down between the measured surfaces.

Calipers

Calipers (**Figure 45**) are excellent tools for obtaining inside, outside and depth measurements. Although not as precise as a micrometer, they allow reasonable precision, typically to within 0.001 in. (0.05 mm). Calipers are available in dial, vernier or digital versions. Dial calipers have a dial gauge readout that provides convenient reading. Vernier calipers have marked scales that are compared to determine the measurement. Most convenient of all, the digital caliper uses an LCD to show the measurement.

To ensure accurate readings, properly maintain the measuring surfaces of the caliper. There must not be any dirt or burrs between the tool and the object being measured. Never force the caliper closed around an object. Close the caliper around the highest point so it can be removed with a slight drag. Some calipers require calibration prior to use. Always refer to the manufacturer's instructions when using a new or unfamiliar caliper.

To read a basic vernier caliper refer to **Figure 46**. The fixed scale is marked in 1 mm increments. Ten individual lines on the fixed scale equal 1 cm. The moveable scale is marked in 0.05 mm increments. To obtain a reading, establish the first number by the location of the 0 line on the moveable scale in relation to the first line to the left on the fixed scale. In this example (**Figure 46**), the number is 10 mm. To determine the next number, note which of the lines on the moveable scale align with a mark on the fixed scale. Several lines will seem close, but only one will align exactly. In this example, 0.50 mm is the reading to add to the first number. The result of adding 10 mm and 0.50 mm is a measurement of 10.50 mm.

Micrometers

A micrometer is an instrument designed for linear measurement using the decimal divisions of the inch or meter. While there are many types and styles of micrometers, most of the procedures in this manual call for the common outside micrometer. The outside micrometer is used to measure the outside diameter of cylindrical forms and the thickness of material.

The usual sizes are 0-1 in. (0.25 mm), 1-2 in. (25-50 mm), 2-3 in. (50-75 mm) and 3-4 in. (75-100 mm).

Micrometers covering a wider range of measurements are available, using a larger frame with interchangeable anvils of various lengths. This type of micrometer offers a cost savings. However, its overall size may make it less convenient.

Reading a Micrometer

When reading a micrometer, numbers are taken from different scales and added together. The following sections describe how to take measurements with various types of outside micrometers.

For accurate results, properly maintain the measuring surfaces of the micrometer. There cannot be any dirt or burrs between the tool and the measured object. Never force the micrometer closed around an object. Close the micrometer around the highest point so it can be removed with a slight drag. **Figure 47** shows the markings and parts of a standard inch micrometer. Be familiar with these terms before using a micrometer in the following sections.

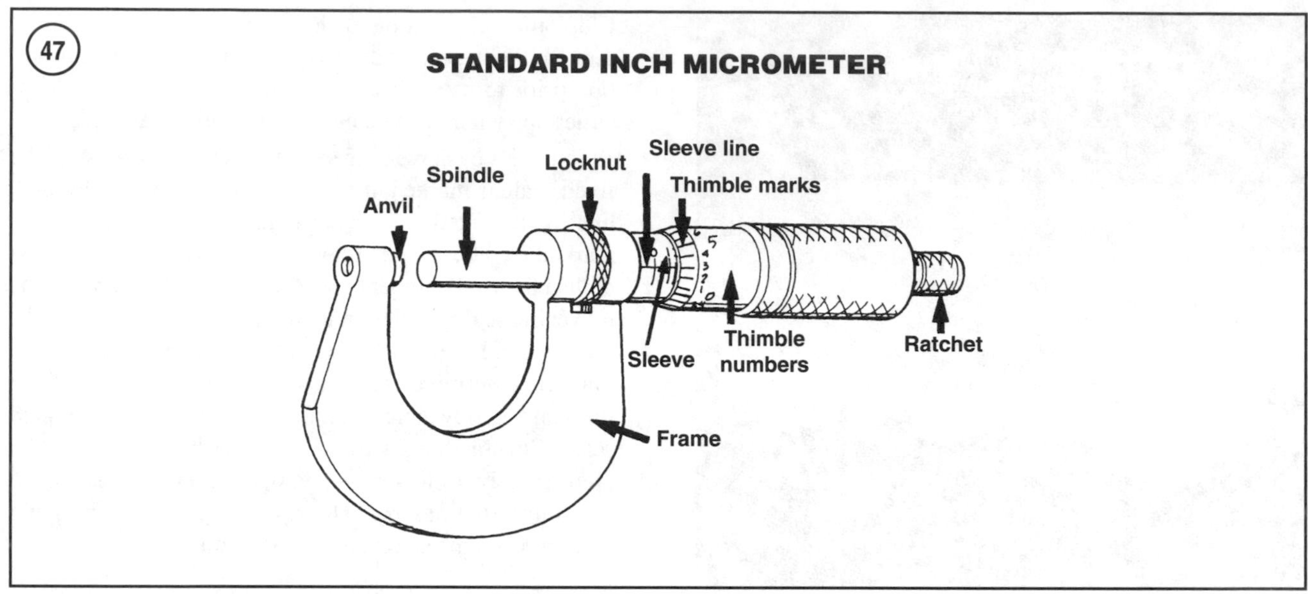

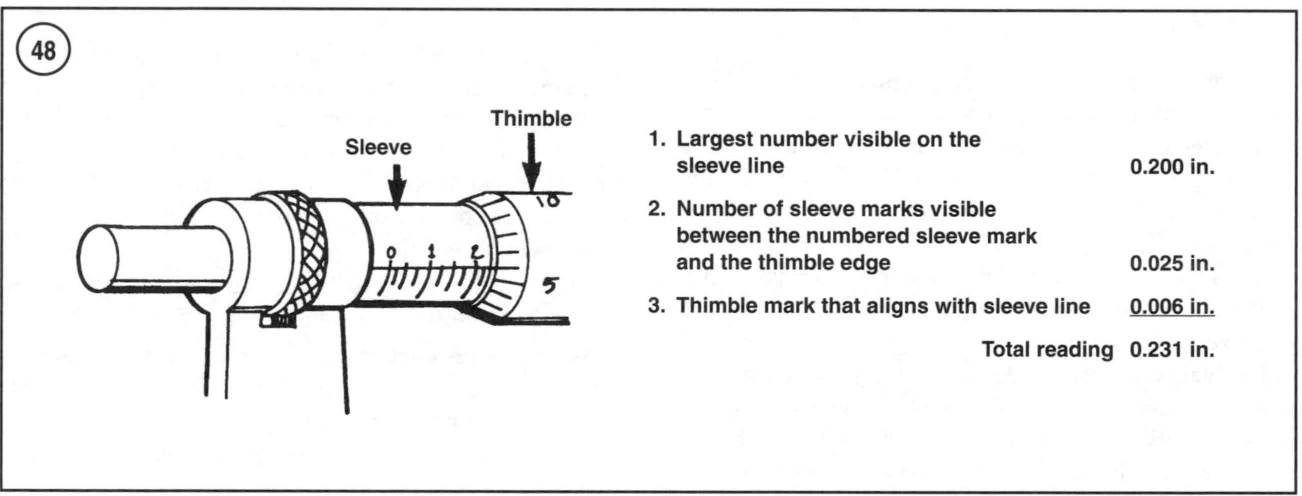

48
Thimble
Sleeve
1. Largest number visible on the sleeve line 0.200 in.
2. Number of sleeve marks visible between the numbered sleeve mark and the thimble edge 0.025 in.
3. Thimble mark that aligns with sleeve line 0.006 in.
Total reading 0.231 in.

Standard inch micrometer

The standard inch micrometer is accurate to one-thousandth of an inch or 0.001 in. The sleeve is marked in 0.025 in. increments. Every fourth sleeve marking is numbered 1, 2, 3, 4, 5, 6, 7, 8, and 9. These numbers indicate 0.100 in., 0.200 in., 0.300 in. and so on.

The tapered end of the thimble has twenty-five lines marked around it. Each marking equals 0.001 in. One complete turn of the thimble, from the closed position, will align its zero marking with the first marking on the sleeve or 0.025 in.

When reading a standard inch micrometer, perform the following steps while referring to **Figure 48**.

1. Read the sleeve and find the largest number visible. Each sleeve number equals 0.100 in.
2. Count the number of lines between the numbered sleeve markings and the edge of the thimble. Each sleeve marking equals 0.025 in.
3. Read the thimble marking that aligns with the sleeve line. Each thimble marking equals 0.001 in.

NOTE
If a thimble marking does not align exactly with the sleeve line, estimate the amount between the lines. For accurate readings in ten-thousandths of an inch (0.0001 in.), use a vernier inch micrometer.

4. Add the readings from Steps 1-3.

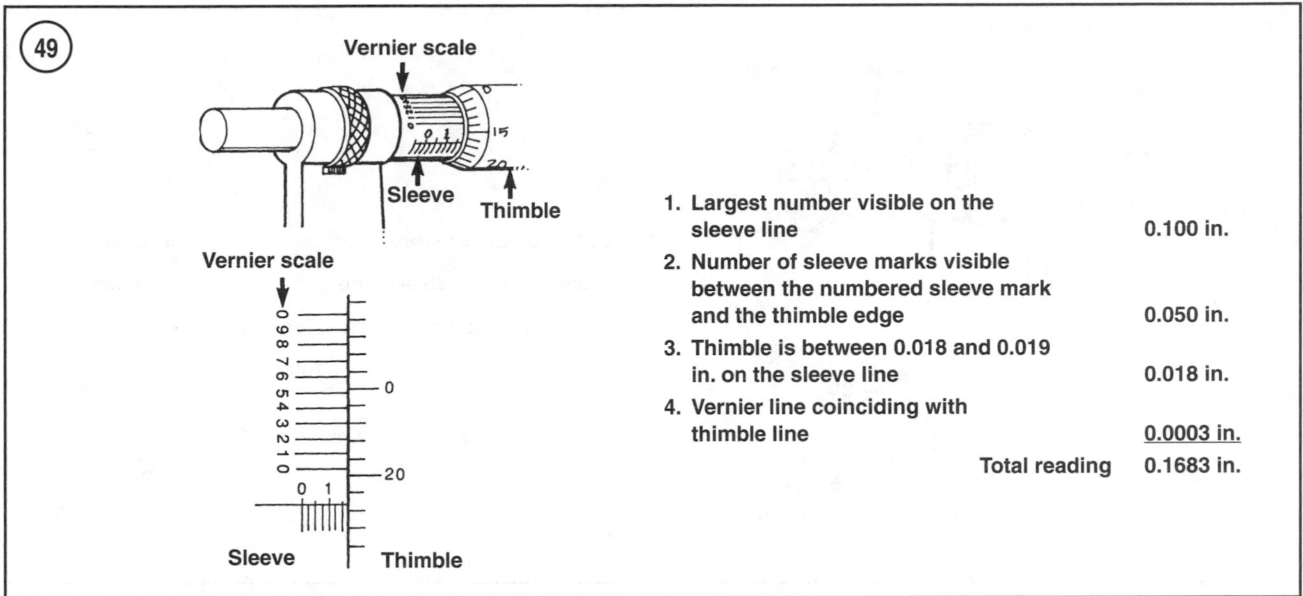

49
Vernier scale
Sleeve
Thimble
Vernier scale
Sleeve
Thimble
1. Largest number visible on the sleeve line 0.100 in.
2. Number of sleeve marks visible between the numbered sleeve mark and the thimble edge 0.050 in.
3. Thimble is between 0.018 and 0.019 in. on the sleeve line 0.018 in.
4. Vernier line coinciding with thimble line 0.0003 in.
Total reading 0.1683 in.

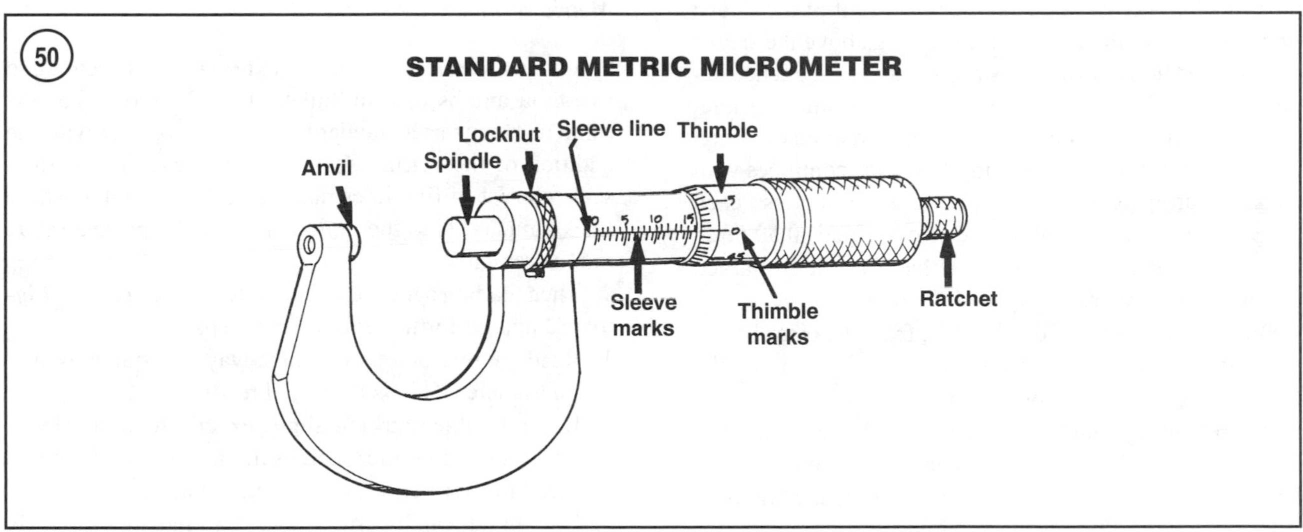

Vernier inch micrometer

A vernier inch micrometer is accurate to one ten-thousandths of an inch or 0.0001 in. It has the same markings as a standard inch micrometer with the additional vernier scale on the sleeve (**Figure 49**).

The vernier scale consist of 11 lines marked 1-9 with a 0 on each end. These lines run parallel to the thimble lines and represent 0.0001 in. increments.

When reading a vernier inch micrometer, perform the following steps while referring to **Figure 49**.

1. Read the micrometer in the same was as a standard micrometer. This is the initial reading.
2. If a thimble marking aligns exactly with the sleeve line, reading the vernier scale is not necessary. If none of them align, read the vernier scale as described in Step 3.
3. Determine which vernier scale marking aligns with one of the thimble markings. The number that aligns is the amount in ten-thousandths of an inch to add to the initial reading in Step 1.

Metric micrometer

The standard metric micrometer (**Figure 50**) is accurate to one one-hundredth of a millimeter (0.01 mm). The sleeve line is graduated in millimeter and half millimeter

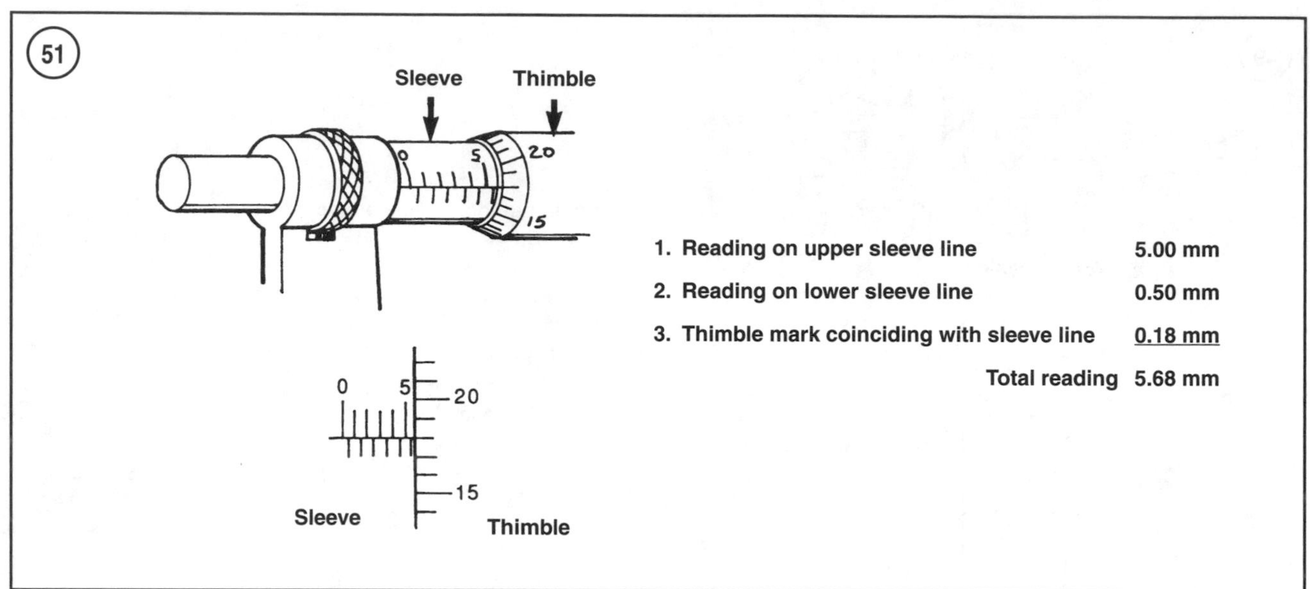

increments. The markings on the upper half of the sleeve line equal 1.00 mm. Every fifth marking above the sleeve line is identified with a number. The number sequence depends on the size of the micrometer. A 0-25 mm micrometer, for example, has sleeve markings numbered 0-25 in 5 mm increments. This numbering sequence continues with larger micrometers. On all metric micrometers, each marking on the lower half of the sleeve equals 0.50 mm.

The tapered end of the thimble has fifty lines marked around it. Each marking equals 0.01 mm.

One complete turn of the thimble, from the closed positions, will align the 0 marking with the first line on the lower half of the sleeve or 0.50 mm.

When reading a metric micrometer, add the number of millimeters and half millimeters on the sleeve line to the number of one one-hundredth millimeters on the thimble.

Perform the following steps while referring to **Figure 51**.

1. Read the upper half of the sleeve line and count the number of lines visible. Each upper line equals 1.0 mm.
2. See if the half-millimeter line is visible on the lower sleeve line. If so, add 0.50 mm to the reading in Step 1.
3. Read the thimble marking that aligns with the sleeve line. Each thimble marking equals 0.01 mm.

NOTE
If a thimble marking does not align exactly with the sleeve line, estimate the amount between the lines. For accurate readings in two-thousandths of a millimeter (0.002 mm), use a metric vernier micrometer.

4. Add the readings from Steps 1-3.

Metric vernier micrometer

A metric vernier micrometer (**Figure 52**) is accurate to two-thousandths of a millimeter (0.002 mm). It has the same markings as a standard metric micrometer with the addition of the vernier scale on the sleeve. The vernier scale consist of five lines marked 0, 2, 4, 6 and 8. These lines run parallel to the thimble lines and represent 0.002 mm increments.

When reading a metric vernier micrometer, refer to **Figure 52** and perform the following steps.

1. Read the micrometer the same way as a standard metric micrometer. This is the initial reading.
2. If the thimble marking aligns exactly with the sleeve line, reading the vernier scale is not necessary. If they do not, read the vernier scale as described in Step 3.
3. Determine which vernier scale marking aligns exactly with one thimble marking. The vernier scale number next to the marking is the amount in two-thousandths of a millimeter to add to the initial reading in Step 1.

Micrometer Calibration

Before using a micrometer, check the calibration as follows:

1. Clean the anvil and spindle faces.
2. To check a 0-1 in. or 0-25 mm micrometer:
   a. Turn the thimble until the spindle just contacts the anvil. Use very light force when turning the thimble. Excess force damages the instrument. If the micrometer has a ratchet stop, use it to ensure the proper amount of pressure is applied.

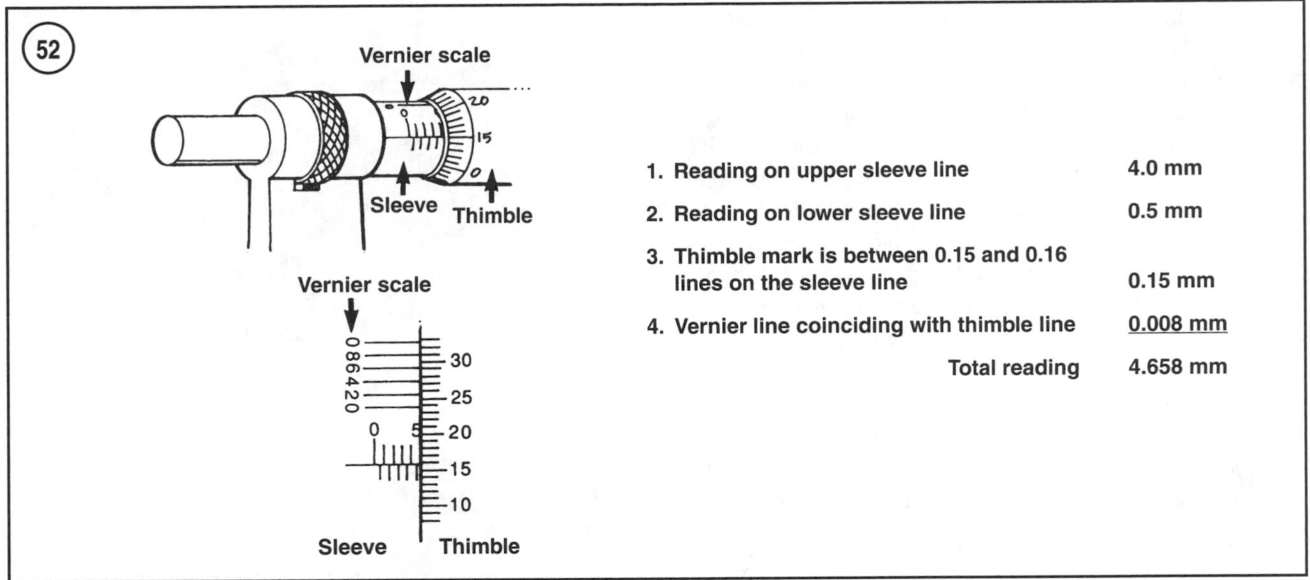

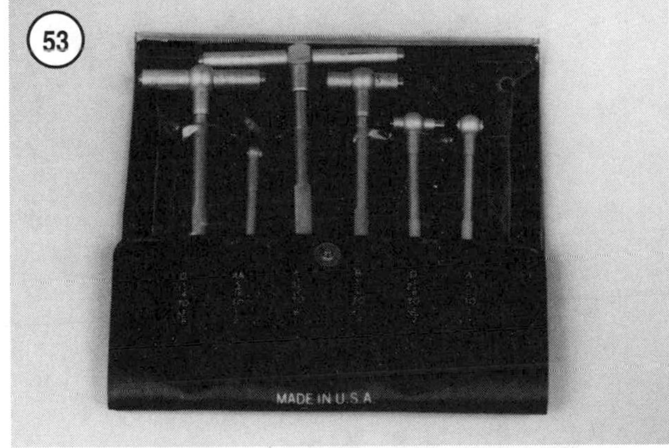

b. If the adjustment is correct, the 0 marking on the thimble will align exactly with the 0 marking on the sleeve line. If the markings do not align, the micrometer is out of adjustment.

c. Follow the manufacturer's instructions to adjust the micrometer.

3. To check a micrometer larger than 1 in. or 25 mm use the standard gauge supplied by the manufacturer. A standard gauge is a steel block or rod that is machined to an exact size.

a. Place the standard gauge between the spindle and the anvil, and measure its outside diameter or length. Use very light force when turning the thimble. Excess force damages the instrument. If the micrometer has a ratchet stop, use it to ensure the proper amount of pressure is applied.

b. If the adjustment is correct, the 0 marking on the thimble will align exactly with the 0 marking on the sleeve line. If the markings do not align, the micrometer is out of adjustment.

c. Follow the manufacturer's instructions to adjust the micrometer.

Micrometer Care

Micrometers are precision instruments. Use and maintain them with great care. Note the following:

1. Store micrometers in protective cases or separate padded drawers in a tool box.
2. When in storage, make sure the spindle and anvil faces do not contact each other or another object. If they contact, temperature changes and corrosion may damage the contact faces.
3. Never clean a micrometer with compressed air. Dirt forced into the instrument will cause rapid wear.
4. Lubricate micrometers with WD-40 or other suitable product to prevent corrosion.

Telescoping and Small Bore Gauges

Use telescoping gauges (**Figure 53**) and small bore gauges to measure bores. Neither gauge has a scale for direct reading. Use an outside micrometer to determine the reading.

To use a telescoping gauge, select the correct size gauge for the bore. Loosen the knurled knob to release the movable post. Compress the movable post, then carefully insert the gauge into the bore. Carefully move the gauge in the bore to make certain it is centered. With the gauge centered, tighten the knurled end of the gauge to lock the movable post in position. Carefully remove the gauge from the bore. Use an outside micrometer to measure the distance between the ends of the movable post. Telescoping gauges are typically used to measure cylinder bores.

To use a small-bore gauge, select the correct size gauge for the bore. Carefully insert the gauge into the bore. Tighten the knurled end of the gauge to expand the gauge fingers to the limit within the bore. Do not over-tighten the gauge, as there is no built-in release. Excessive tightening can damage the bore surface and the tool. Carefully remove the gauge from the bore. Use an outside micrometer to measure the distance between the ends of the expanded fingers. Small hole gauges are typically used to measure valve guide.

Dial Indicator

A dial indicator (**Figure 54**) is a gauge with a dial face and a needle used to measure variations in dimensions and movements such as crankshaft and drive shaft runout limits.

Dial indicators are available in various ranges and graduations and with three basic types of mounting bases: magnetic, clamp or screw-in stud. When purchasing a dial indicator for outboard repair, select a dial indicator with a continuous scale. Select a magnetic stand type to check crankshaft and camshaft runout. A screw-in stud mount is needed to check gear backlash.

Cylinder Bore Gauge

The cylinder bore gauge is a very specialized precision instrument that is only used for major engine repairs or rebuilds. The gauge set shown in **Figure 55** is comprised of a dial indicator, handle and a number of different length adapters (anvils) used to fit the gauge to various bore sizes. The bore gauge can be used to measure bore size, taper and out-of-round. When using a bore gauge, follow the manufacturer's instructions.

Compression Gauge

A compression gauge (**Figure 56**) measures the combustion chamber pressure, usually in psi or kg/cm^2, an engine is capable of mechanically generating on the compression stroke. An engine that does not have adequate compression cannot be properly tuned or expected to perform efficiently. See Chapter Three *(Engine Tune-up)*. The gauge adapter is either inserted or screwed into the spark plug hole to obtain the reading. Disable the engine so it does not start and hold the throttle in the wide-open position when performing compression testing.

54

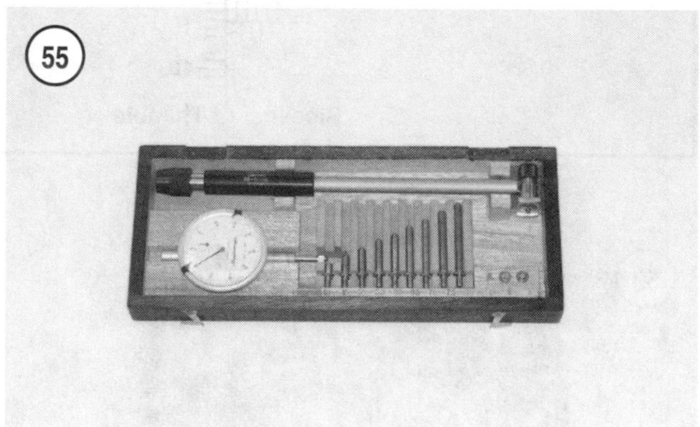
55

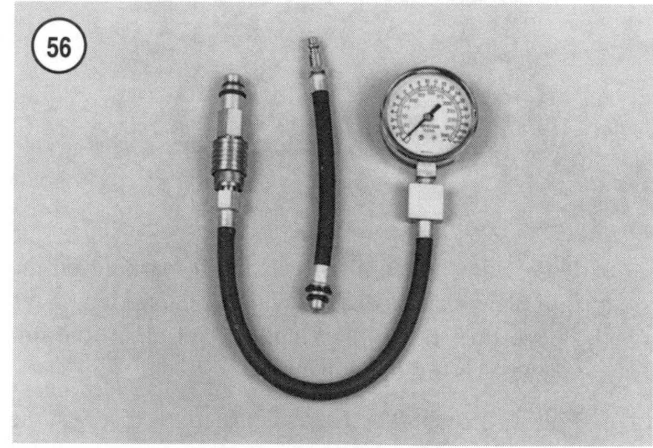
56

Multimeter

A multimeter (**Figure 57**) is an essential tool for electrical system diagnosis. The voltage function indicates the

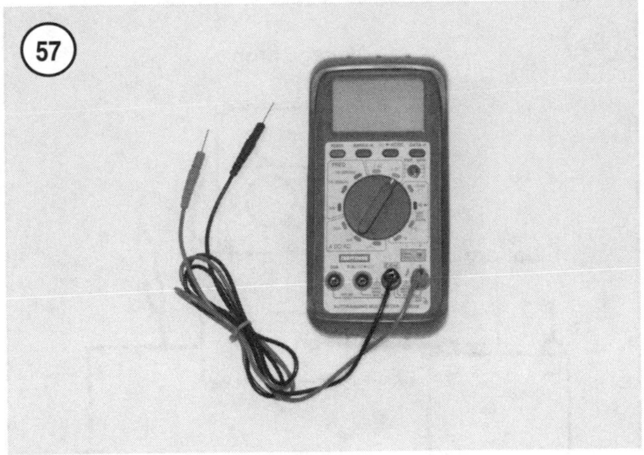

57

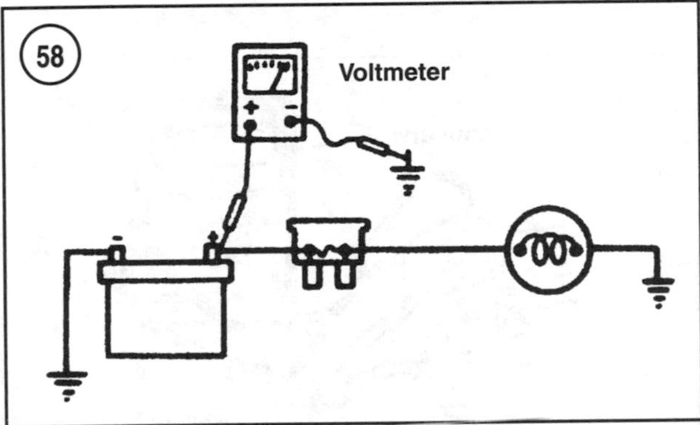

58

voltage applied or available to various electrical components. The ohmmeter function tests circuits for continuity or lack of continuity, and measures the resistance of a circuit. The ammeter function measures current flow.

Some less expensive models contain a needle gauge and are known as analog meters. Most high-quality meters contain digital readout screens. When using an analog ohmmeter, zero or calibrate the needle according to the meter manufacturer's instructions. Some analog and almost all digital meters are self-zeroing and no manual adjustment is necessary.

Some manufacturers' specifications for electrical components are based on results using a specific test meter. Results may vary if using a meter not recommended by the manufacturer.

ELECTRICAL SYSTEM FUNDAMENTALS

A thorough study of all of the electrical systems used on the modern outboard is beyond the scope of the manual. However, the test procedures in the appropriate chapter will identify the source of most electrical problems. A basic understanding of electrical theory and terminology is necessary to perform electrical system diagnosis.

Voltage

Voltage is the electrical potential or pressure in an electrical circuit and is expressed in volts. The more pressure (voltage) in a circuit, the more work that can be performed.

Direct current (DC) describes current flowing in one direction in a circuit. All circuits powered by a battery are DC circuits.

Alternating current (AC) describes current that flows one direction in a circuit then switches to the opposite direction. The initial current produced by the charging system is an example of AC current. The current must be changed or rectified to DC to operate in a 12-volt battery powered system.

Voltage measurement

Unless directed otherwise, perform all voltage tests with the electrical connections attached.

When measuring voltage, select a meter range one scale higher than the expected voltage of the circuit to prevent damage to the meter. To determine the actual voltage in a circuit, use a voltmeter. To simply check if voltage is present, use a common test light.

NOTE
When using a test light, either lead may be attached to ground.

1. Attach the negative meter test lead to a good engine ground (bare metal). Make sure the ground is not insulated with a rubber gasket or grommet.
2. Attach the positive meter test lead to the point being tested (**Figure 58**).
3. If necessary for the circuit being tested, turn the corresponding switch to the ON position. This is only necessary for a switched circuit. The test illustrated in **Figure 58** is an example of a non-switched circuit. The meter test lead connects directly to the battery terminal and ground. The test light should illuminate or the meter should display a reading of within one volt of battery voltage. If the voltage is less, there is a problem in the circuit.

Voltage drop test

Resistance in a circuit causes voltage to drop. This resistance can be measured in an active circuit by using a multimeter to perform a voltage drop test. A voltage drop test compares the difference between the voltage available at the start of the circuit to the voltage at the end of the circuit while the circuit is operational. If the circuit has no resistance, there will be no voltage drop. The greater the resistance, the greater the voltage drop will be. A voltage drop of one volt or more usually indicates excessive resistance in the circuit.

1. Connect the positive meter test lead to the electrical source (from where the electricity is coming).
2. Connect the negative meter test lead to the electrical load (where the electricity is going). See **Figure 59**.
3. If necessary, activate the component(s) of the circuit.
4. A voltage reading of one volt or more indicates resistance in the circuit. A reading equal to battery voltage indicates an open circuit or very low resistance.

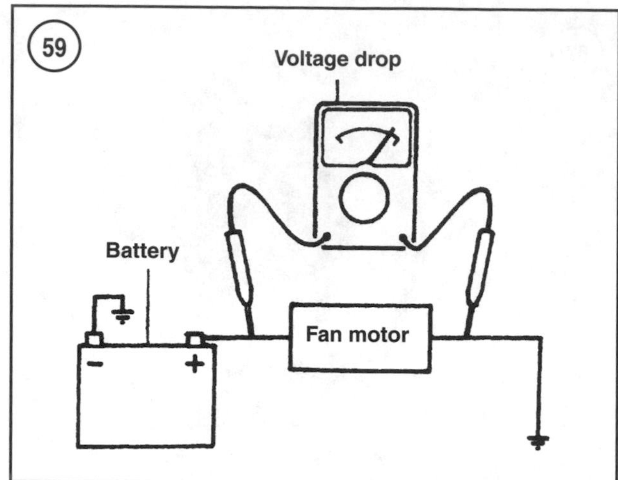

Resistance

Resistance is the opposition to the flow of electricity within a circuit or components and is measured in ohms. Resistance causes a reduction in available current voltage.

A resistance test, although useful, is not always a good indicator of the circuit's actual ability under operating conditions. This is due to the low voltage (6-9 volts) that the meter uses to test the circuit. The operating voltage in an ignition coil secondary winding can be several thousand volts. Such high voltage can cause the coil to malfunction, even though it may test acceptable during a resistance test.

Resistance generally increases with temperature. Perform all testing with the components or circuits at a room temperature of approximately 68° F (20° C). Performing resistance testing at higher temperatures will usually indicate higher resistance readings and result in unnecessary parts replacement.

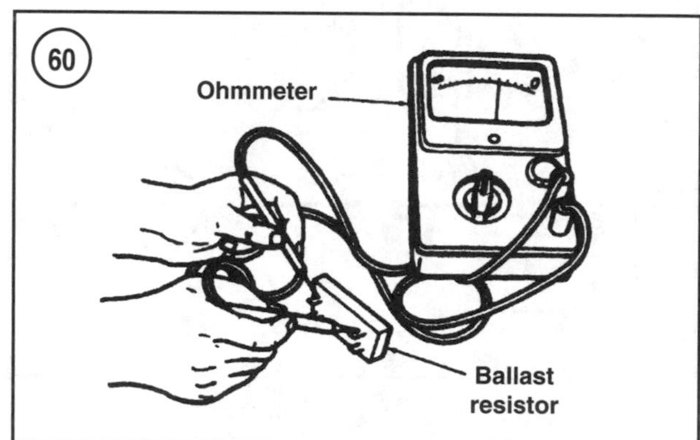

Resistance and continuity measurement test

CAUTION

Do not test for resistance in a live circuit. The meter will suffer damage if it is connected onto a live circuit. Remember, if using and analog meter, it must normally by calibrated each time it is used or the scale is changed.

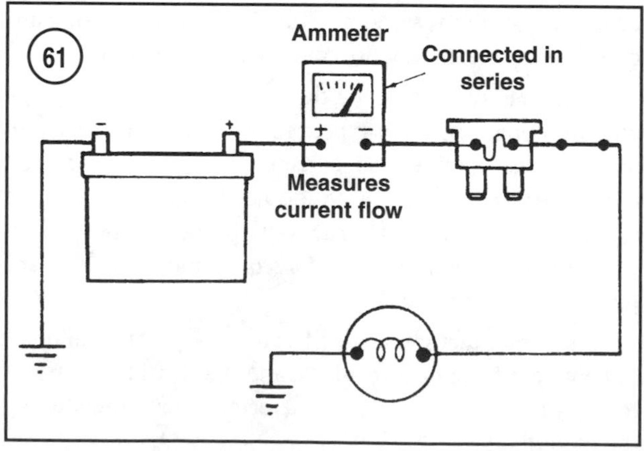

A continuity test can determine if the circuit is complete. Perform this type of test with a multimeter or a self-powered test light.

1. Disconnect the negative battery cable. Disconnect all wires or other components from the component terminals.
2. Attach one test lead (ohmmeter or test light) to one end of the component or circuit.
3. Attach the other test lead to the opposite end of the component or circuit (**Figure 60**).
4. A self-powered test light will illuminate if the circuit is complete or has continuity. An ohmmeter will indicate either low or no resistance if the circuit has continuity. An open circuit is indicated if the meter displays infinite resistance.

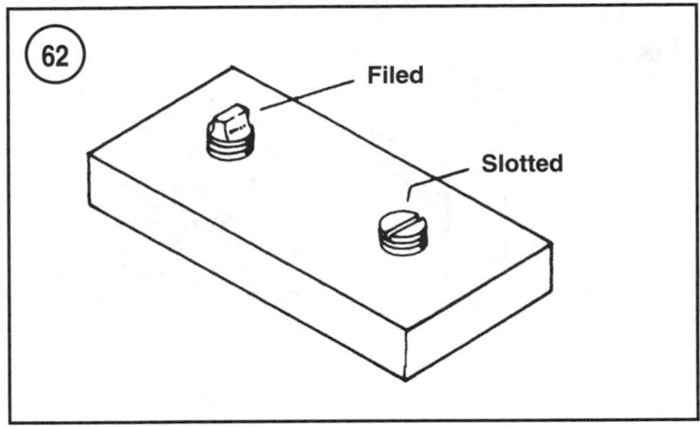

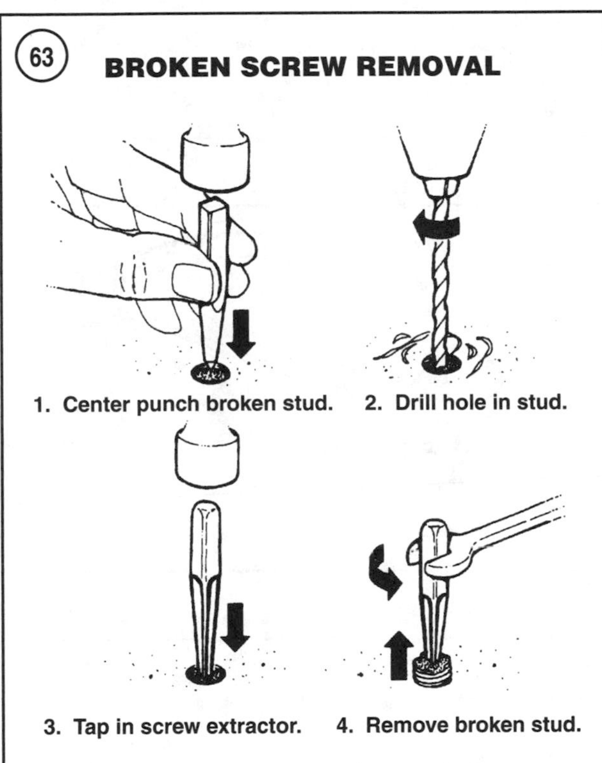

Amperage

Amperage (amp) is the unit of measure for the amount of current (flow of electricity) within a circuit. The higher the current, the more work can be performed up to a given point. If the current flow exceeds the circuit or components capacity, the system is damaged.

Amperage measurement

The ammeter function of a multimeter measures current flow or amp of a circuit (**Figure 61**). Amperage measurement requires that the circuit is disconnected and the ammeter is connected in series into the circuit. Always use an ammeter that can read higher than the anticipated current flow to prevent damage to the meter. Connect the positive test lead onto the electrical source and the negative test lead onto the electrical load.

BASIC MECHANICAL SKILLS

Along with the information in *Safety* and *Service Hints* in this chapter, there are a few common mechanic's skills that an outboard owner needs to perform service and repair procedures.

Frozen Nuts and Screws Removal

When a fastener corrodes and cannot be removed, several methods may be used to loosen it. First, apply penetrating oil such as Liquid Wrench or WD-40. Apply it liberally and let it penetrate for 10-15 minutes. Rap the fastener several times with a small hammer. Do not hit it hard enough to cause damage. Attempt to remove the fastener. If unsuccessful, repeat the process.

For difficult or frozen screws, apply penetrating oil as described, then insert a screwdriver in the slot and rap the top of the screwdriver with a hammer. This loosens the corrosion so the screw can be removed in the normal way. If the screw head is too damaged to use this method, grip the head with locking pliers and twist the screw out.

Avoid applying heat unless specifically instructed, as it may melt, warp or remove temper from parts.

Broken Fastener Removal

If the head breaks off a screw or bolt, several methods are available for removing the remaining portions. If a large portion of the remainder projects out, try gripping it with locking pliers. If the projection is too small (or a sufficient grip cannot be obtained on the protruding piece), file it to fit a wrench or cut a slot in it to fit a screwdriver. See **Figure 62**.

If the head breaks off flush, which often happens in this situation, use a screw extractor. To do this, center punch the exact center of the remaining portion of the screw or bolt. Drill a small hole in the screw and tap the extractor into the hole. Back the screw out with a wrench on the extractor. See **Figure 63**.

NOTE

If the screw is drilled off-center and the threaded opening is damaged, a threaded insert will be necessary to repair the bore.

Threaded insert kits are available at local marine and automotive supply stores. Follow the manufacturer's instructions for installation.

CAUTION

Never exert excessive force upon a screw extractor. They may break under stress, leaving little protruding material to grip for removal. Extractors are manufactured of a very hard material that is almost impossible to drill out. If the extractor breaks and cannot be removed, have a reputable machine or welding shop remove the remnant.

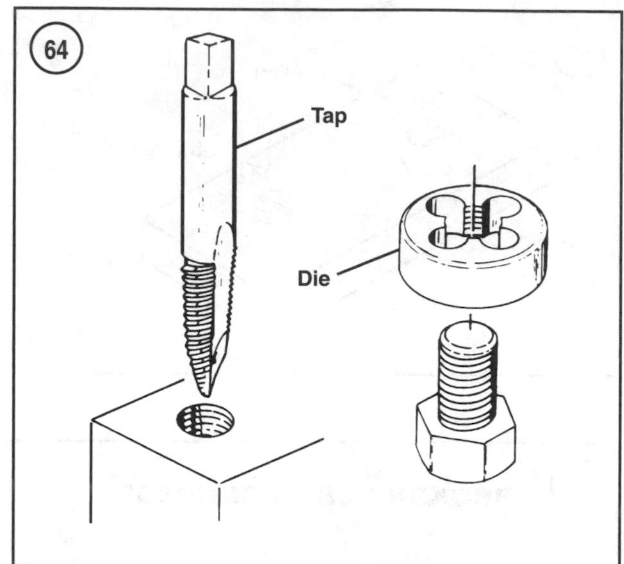

Damaged Threads Repair

Occasionally, threads are stripped through carelessness or impact damage. Often the threads can be renewed by running a tap (for internal threads or nuts) or die (for external threads on bolts) through the threads (**Figure 64**). Use only a specially designed spark plug tap to clean or renew spark plug threads.

If an internal thread is damaged, it might be necessary to install a Helicoil or some other type of threaded insert. Follow the manufacturer's instructions when installing the insert.

If it is necessary to drill and tap a hole, refer to **Table 3** for U.S. Standard and metric tap drill sizes.

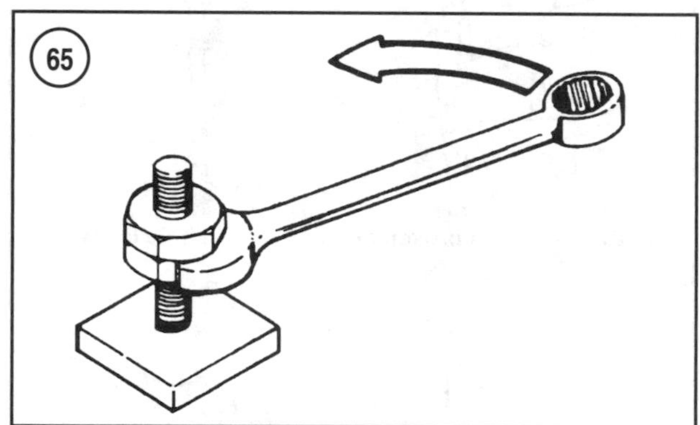

Stud Removal and Installation

A stud removal tool that makes removal and installation of studs easier is available from most tool suppliers. If this tool is not available, thread two suitable nuts onto the stud and tighten against the other to lock them onto the stud. Remove the stud by turning the lower nut. Install the stud by turning the upper nut (**Figure 65**).

NOTE

If the threads on the damaged stud do not allow the installation of two nuts, remove the stud with a pair of locking pliers or a stud removal tool. If using locking pliers, grip the stud in an area below the threaded section or in a non-critical area (such as where the nut will not pass over the threads).

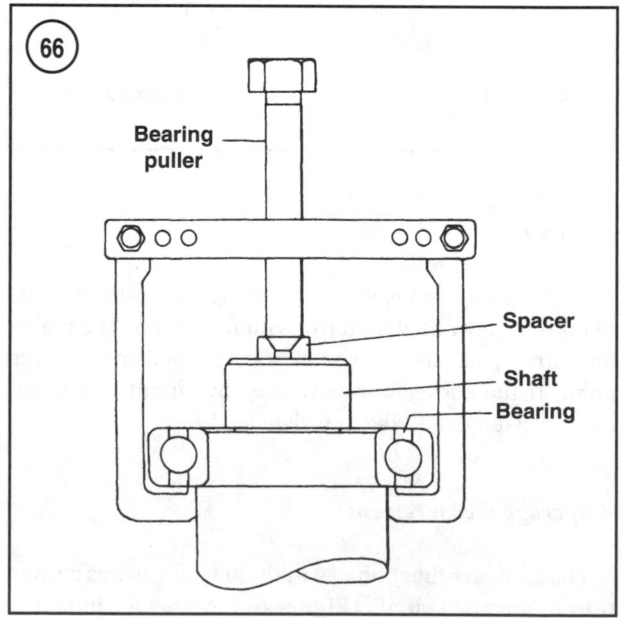

Hose Removal

When removing stubborn hoses, do not exert excessive force on the hose or fitting. Remove the hose clamp and carefully insert a small screwdriver or pick tool between

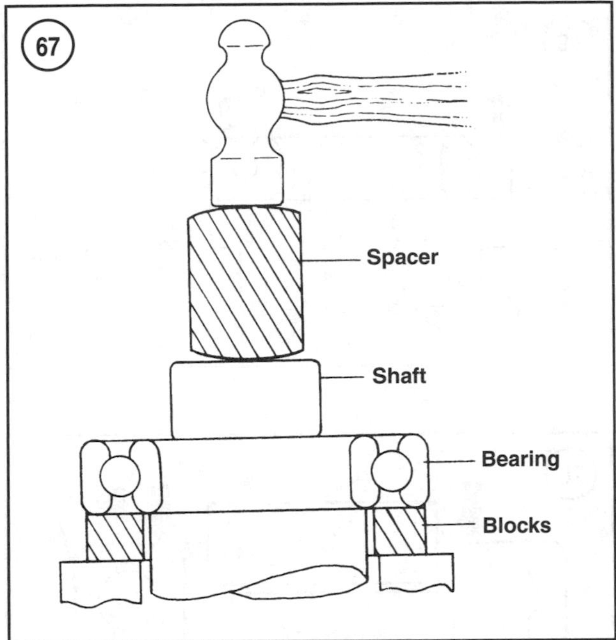

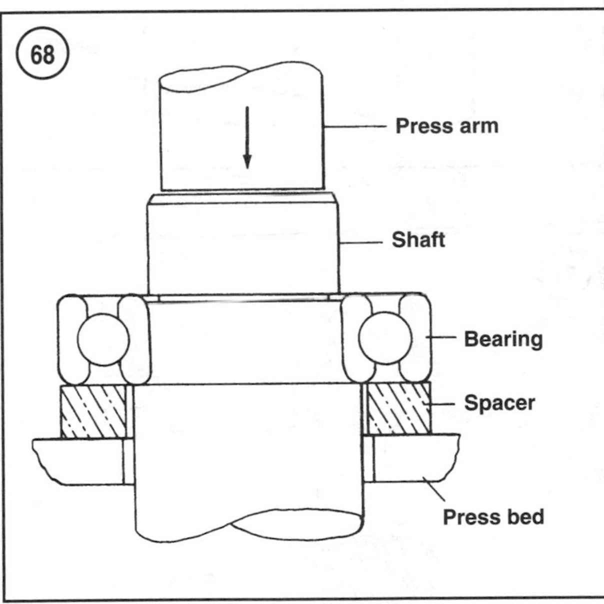

the fitting and hose. Spray lubricant under the hose and carefully twist the hose off the fitting. Remove any corrosion or rubber hose material with a wire brush. Thoroughly clean the inside of the hose. Do not use any lubricant when installing the hose (new or old). The lubricant may allow the hose to slip off the fitting, even with the clamp secure. It is usually easier to remove and install warm hoses than cool ones. Do not heat the hose with a flame. It presents a fire hazard and the hose or other components may be damaged. Simply allowing sunlight to shine on a hose heats it sufficiently to ease removal and installation.

Bearing Replacement

Ball bearings are used throughout the engine and drive system to reduce power loss and heat resulting from friction. Ball bearings are precision made parts. They must be preserved by proper lubrication and maintenance. When a damaged bearing is discovered, replace it immediately. However, when installing a new bearing, take care to prevent damage. While bearing replacement is described in the individual chapters, use the following general rules as a guideline.

NOTE
Unless directed otherwise, install bearings with the manufacturer's marking or number facing outward.

Removal

While bearings are normally removed only when damaged, there may be times when it is necessary to remove a bearing that is in good condition. However, improper bearing removal will damage the bearing and possibly the shaft or housing. Note the following when removing bearings:

1. When using a puller (**Figure 66**) to remove a bearing from a shaft, take care that the shaft is not damaged. Always place a piece of metal between the end of the shaft and the puller screw. In addition, position the ends of the puller arms to contact only on the inner bearing race.
2. When using a hammer to remove a bearing on a shaft, do not strike the hammer directly against the shaft. Instead, use a brass or aluminum rod as a spacer between the hammer and shaft (**Figure 67**). In addition, make sure to support both the inner and outer bearing races with wooden blocks as shown in **Figure 67**.
3. The ideal method of bearing removal is with a hydraulic press. In order to prevent damage to the bearing and shaft or housing, note the following when using a press:
   a. Always support the inner and outer bearing races with a suitable wood or aluminum ring (**Figure 68**). If only the outer race is supported, pressure applied against the balls and/or inner race will damage them.
   b. Always make sure the press arm (**Figure 68**) aligns with the center of the shaft. If the arm is not centered, it may damage the bearing and/or shaft.
   c. The instant the shaft is free from the bearing, it will drop. Support the shaft to prevent it from falling.

Installation

1. When installing a bearing in a housing, apply pressure to the *outer* bearing race (**Figure 69**). When installing a bearing on a shaft, apply pressure to the *inner* bearing race (**Figure 70**).
2. When installing a bearing as described in Step 1, some type of driver is required. Never strike the bearing directly with a hammer or the bearing will be damaged. Use a section of tubing or socket with an outer diameter that matches the appropriate bearing race. **Figure 71** shows the correct way to use a socket and hammer when installing a bearing on a shaft (contacting the inner race).
3. Step 1 describes how to install a bearing into a housing or over a shaft. However, when installing a bearing over a shaft *and* into a housing at the same time, a snug fit is required for both outer and inner bearing races. In this situation, install a spacer underneath the driver tool so that pressure is applied evenly across *both* races. See **Figure 72**. If the outer race is not supported as shown, the balls will push against the outer bearing track and damage the bearing assembly.

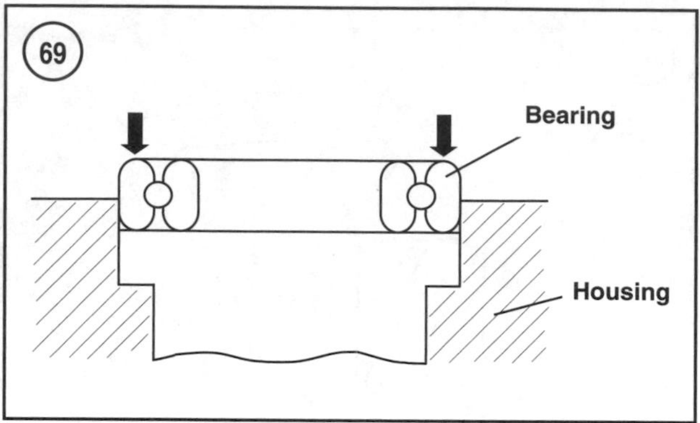

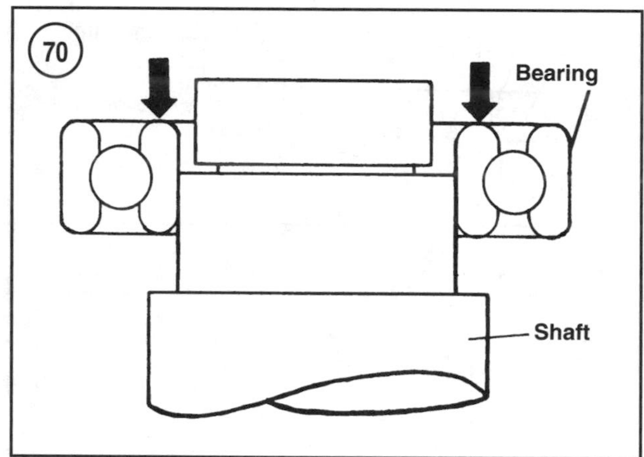

Installing an interference fit bearing over a shaft

When a tight fit is required, the bearing inside diameter will be slightly smaller than the shaft. In this case, driving the bearing onto the shaft using normal methods may damage the bearing. Instead, heat the bearing before installation.

1. Secure the shaft so that it is ready for bearing installation. Measure and gather the appropriate spacers and drivers for installation.
2. Clean the bearing surface on the shaft of all residue. Remove burrs with a file or sandpaper.
3. Fill a suitable pot or beaker with clean mineral oil. Place a thermometer rated higher than 248° F (120° C) in the oil. Support the thermometer so that it does not rest on the bottom or side of the container.
4. Remove the bearing from the wrapper and secure it with a heavy wire bent to hold it in the container. Hang the bearing so that it does not touch the bottom or side of the container.
5. Apply heat to the container while monitoring the thermometer. When the oil temperature reaches approximately 248° F (120° C), remove the bearing from the pot and quickly install it. If necessary, place a socket on the inner bearing race and tap the bearing into place. As the bearing chills, it will tighten on the shaft so work quickly. Make sure the bearing is fully seated on the shaft.

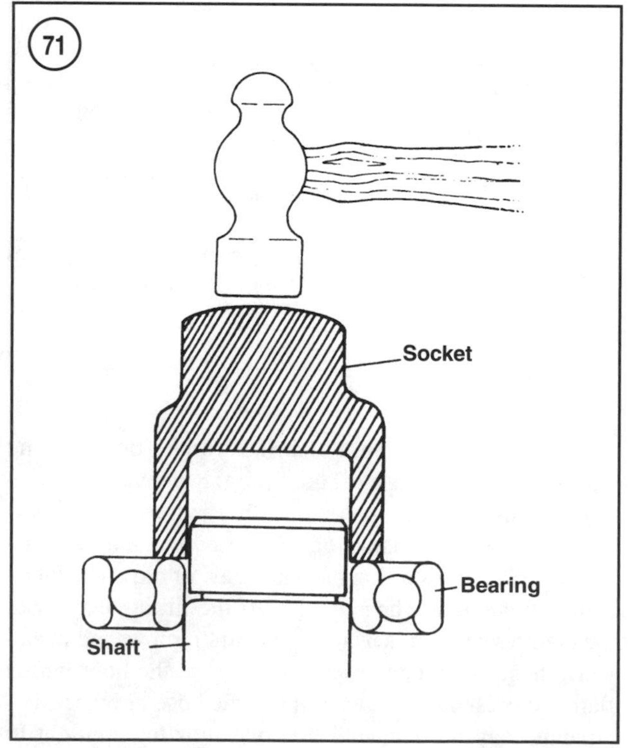

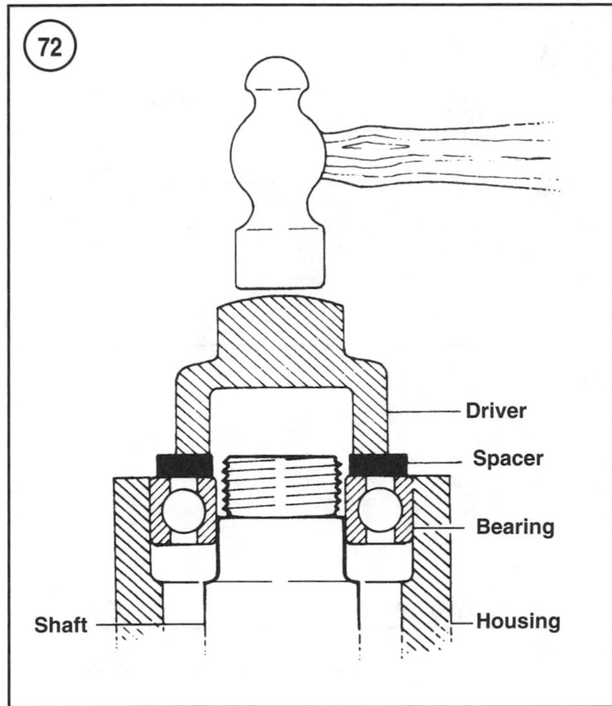

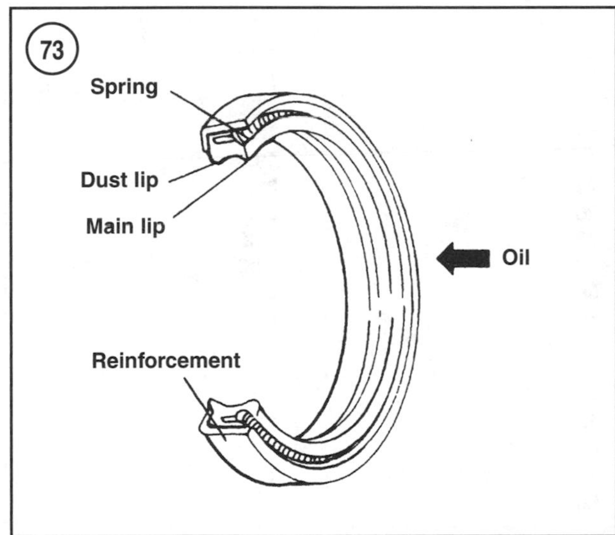

Replacing an interference fit bearing in a housing

Bearings are generally installed into a housing with a slight interference fit. Driving the bearing into the housing by normal methods may damage the housing or bearing. Instead, heat the housing to increase the bearing bore diameter and chill the bearing to decrease the bearing size before attempting installation. This will make the installation easier.

CAUTION

Before heating the housing in this procedure, wash it thoroughly with detergent and water. In order to prevent a possible fire hazard, rinse and rewash the housing as necessary to remove all traces of oil and other chemical deposits.

1. While the parts are still cold, determine the proper sizes and gather all necessary spacers and drivers for installation.
2. Place the bearing into a freezer to chill and decrease the bearing diameter.
3. Heat the housing to approximately 212°F (100° C) in an oven or hot plate. An easy way to check if the housing is hot enough is to drop tiny droplets of water on the case. If they sizzle and evaporate, the temperature is correct.

CAUTION

Do not heat the housing with a propane or acetylene torch. Never bring a flame into contact with the bearing or housing. The direct heat will destroy the case hardening of the bearing and may warp the housing.

4. Remove the housing from the oven or hot plate using a thick kitchen pot holder, heavy protective gloves or heavy shop towels.
5. Hold the housing with the bearing side down and tap the bearing(s) out.

NOTE

Unless directed otherwise, always install bearings with the manufacturer's marking facing outward.

6. While the housing is still hot, install the bearing(s) into the housing. If possible, install bearings by hand. If necessary, lightly tap the bearing(s) into the housing with a socket placed on the outer bearing race. *Never* install the bearings by driving against the inner bearing race. Drive the bearing(s) into the housing until fully seated.

Seal Replacement

Seals (**Figure 73**) are used to contain water, grease, or combustion gasses within a housing or shaft. Improper removal of a seal can damage surrounding components. Improper installation can damage the seal and surrounding components. Never reuse a seal once it has been removed. Note the following:

1. Prying is generally the easiest and most effective method of removing a seal from a housing. However, al-

ways place a shop towel under the pry tool to protect the housing.

2. Pack the seal lips with the appropriate grease after installing the seal.

3. Unless directed otherwise, install oil seals with the manufacturer's numbers facing outward.

4. Install oil seals with a socket placed against the outer diameter of the seal as shown in **Figure 74**. Make sure the seal is driven squarely into the housing. Never install the seal by driving directly against the seal with a hammer.

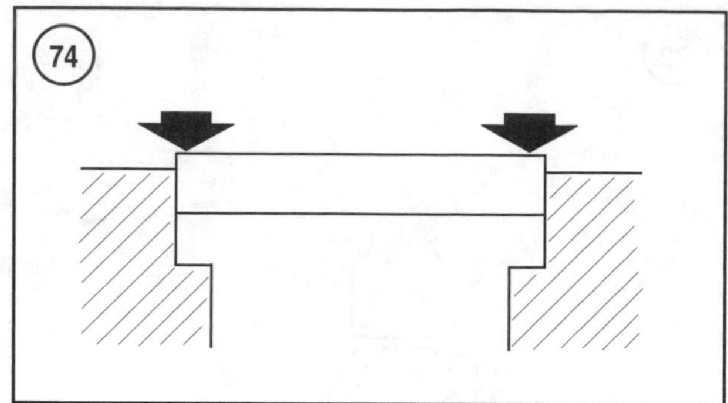

Table 1 GENERAL TORQUE SPECIFICATIONS

Screw or nut size	in.-lb.	ft.-lb.	N•m
U.S. Standard			
6-32	9	–	1.0
8-32	20	–	2.3
10-24	30	–	3.4
10-32	35	–	4.0
12-24	45	–	5.1
1/4-20	70	–	7.9
1/4-28	84	–	9.5
5/16-18	160	13	18.1
5/16-24	168	14	19.0
3/8-16	–	23	31.1
3/8-24	–	25	33.8
7/16-14	–	36	48.8
7/16-20	–	40	54.2
1/ 2-13	–	50	67.8
1/ 2-20	–	60	81.3
Metric			
M5	36	–	4.1
M6	70	–	8.1
M8	156	13	17.6
M10	–	26	35.3
M12	–	35	47.5
M14	–	60	81.3

Table 2 ENGINE CODES

Letter codes	Characteristics
M	Manual starter
E	Electric starter
L	Long drive shaft length
XL	Extra long drive shaft length
H	Tiller handle control
PT	Power trim
C	Counter rotation gearcase

Table 3 TAP DRILL SIZES

Tap size	Drill size	Decimal equivalent
Metric tap (mm)		
3 × 0.50	No. 39	0.0995
3 × 0.60	3/32	0.0937
4 × 0.70	No. 30	0.1285
4 × 0.75	1/8	0.125
5 × 0.80	No. 19	0.166
5 × 0.90	No. 20	0.161
6 × 1.00	No. 9	0.196
7 × 1.00	16/64	0.234
8 × 1.00	J	0.277
8 × 1.25	17/64	0.265
9 × 1.00	5/16	0.3125
9 × 1.25	5/16	0.3125
10 × 1.25	11/32	0.3437
10 × 1.50	R	0.339
11 × 1.50	3/8	0.375
12 × 1.50	13/32	0.406
12 × 1.75	13/32	0.406
U. S. Standard tap (in.)		
No. 0-80	3/64	0.047
No. 1-64	No. 53	0.059
No. 1-72	No. 53	0.059
No. 2-56	No. 50	0.070
No. 2-64	No. 50	0.070
No. 3-48	5/64	0.078
No. 3-56	No. 46	0.081
No. 4-40	No. 43	0.890
No. 4-48	No. 42	0.935
No. 5-40	No. 39	0.938
No. 5-44	No. 37	0.104
No. 6-32	No. 36	0.107
No. 6-40	No. 33	0.113
No. 8-32	No. 29	0.136
No. 8-36	No. 29	0.136
No. 10-24	No. 25	0.150
No. 10-32	No. 21	0.159
No. 12-24	No. 16	0.177
No. 12-28	No. 14	0.182
1/ 4-20	No. 7	0.201
1/ 4-28	No. 3	0.213
5/16-18	F	0.257
5/16-24	I	0.272
3/8-16	5/16	0.3125
3/8-24	Q	0.332
7/16-14	U	0.368
7/16-20	25/64	0.390
1/ 2-13	27/64	0.422
1/ 2-20	29-64	0.453
9/16-12	31-64	0.484
9/16-18	33/64	0.516
5/8-11	17/32	0.531
5/8-18	37/64	0.578
3/ 4-10	21/32	0.656
3/ 4-16	11/16	0.688
7/8-9	49/64	0.766
7/8-14	13/16	0.813
1-8	7/8	0.875
1-14	15/16	0.938

Table 4 CONVERSION TABLES

Multiply	By	To get equivalent of
Length		
Inches	25.4	Millimeter
Inches	2.54	Centimeter
Miles	1.609	Kilometer
Feet	0.3048	Meter
Millimeter	0.03937	Inches
Centimeter	0.3937	Inches
Kilometer	0.6214	Mile
Meter	3.281	Mile
Fluid volume		
U.S. quarts	0.9463	Liters
U.S. gallons	3.785	Liters
U.S. ounces	29.573529	Milliliters
Imperial gallons	4.54609	Liters
Imperial quarts	1.1365	Liters
Liters	0.2641721	U.S. gallons
Liters	1.0566882	U.S. quarts
Liters	33.814023	U.S. ounces
Liters	0.22	Imperial gallons
Liters	0.8799	Imperial quarts
Fluid volume (continued)		
Milliliters	0.033814	U.S. ounces
Milliliters	1.0	Cubic centimeters
Milliliters	0.001	Liters
Torque		
Foot-pounds	1.3558	Newton-meters
Foot-pounds	0.138255	Meter-kilograms
Inch-pounds	0.11299	Newton-meters
Newton-meters	0.7375622	Foot-pounds
Newton-meters	8.8507	Inch-pounds
Meters-kilograms	7.2330139	Foot-pounds
Volume		
Cubic inches	16.387064	Cubic centimeters
Cubic centimeters	0.0610237	Cubic inches
Temperature		
Fahrenheit	(F – 32) × 0.556	Centigrade
Centigrade	(C × 1.8) + 32	Fahrenheit
Weight		
Ounces	28.3495	Grams
Pounds	0.4535924	Kilograms
Grams	0.035274	Ounces
Kilograms	2.2046224	Pounds
Pressure		
Pounds per square inch	0.070307	Kilograms per square centimeter
Kilograms per square centimeter	14.223343	Pounds per square inch
Kilopascals	0.1450	Pounds per square inch
Pounds per square inch	6.895	Kilopascals
Speed		
Miles per hour	1.609344	Kilometers per hour
Kilometers per hour	0.6213712	Miles per hour

Table 5 TECHNICAL ABBREVIATIONS

ABDC	After bottom dead center
ATDC	After top dead center
BBDC	Before bottom dead center
BDC	Bottom dead center
BTDC	Before top dead center
C	Celsius (centigrade)
cc	Cubic centimeters
cid	Cubic inch displacement
CDI	Capacitor discharge ignition
cu. in.	Cubic inches
F	Fahrenheit
ft.	Feet
ft.-lb.	Foot-pounds
gal.	Gallons
H/A	High altitude
hp	Horsepower
in.	Inches
in.-lb.	Inch-pounds
I.D.	Inside diameter
kg	Kilograms
kgm	Kilogram meters
km	Kilometer
kPa	Kilopascals
L	Liter
m	Meter
MAG	Magneto
ml	Milliliter
mm	Millimeter
N•m	Newton-meters
O.D.	Outside diameter
oz.	Ounces
psi	Pounds per square inch
PTO	Power take off
pt.	Pint
qt.	Quart
rpm	Revolutions per minute

Chapter Two

Troubleshooting

This chapter provides the information required to pinpoint the source of most operational problems. If a problem occurs, perform a quick visual inspection before attempting any involved testing procedures. Look for leaking fluid, disconnected wires or damaged components. Refer to *Preliminary Inspection* in this chapter for a list of other items to check.

Troubleshooting instructions help determine which system is causing a malfunction. Additional testing pinpoints which components of the system are faulty.

Due to manufacturing variations, some wiring colors may not match the wiring colors in the manual. Always verify that the proper wires are being tested.

Related torque specifications are listed in **Table 1**. For fasteners not listed in **Table 1**, use the general torque specification in the *Quick Reference Data* section at the beginning of the manual. Other specifications are provided in **Tables 2-15**, at the end of this chapter.

ELECTRICAL COMPONENT REPLACEMENT

Most dealerships and parts suppliers will not accept the return of any electrical part. If the exact cause of any electrical system malfunction cannot be determined, have a dealership retest the specific system to verify any preliminary test results. If a new electrical component is installed and the system still does not work properly, the new component, in most cases, will not be returnable.

Consider any test results carefully before replacing a component that tests only slightly out of specification, especially resistance. A number of variables can affect test results dramatically. These include: internal circuitry of the test meter, ambient temperature, and conditions under which the machine has been operated. All instructions and specifications have been checked for accuracy; however, successful test results depend upon individual accuracy.

PRELIMINARY INSPECTION

The three basic requirements for an internal combustion engine to run (**Figure 1**) are fuel and air in the correct ratio, adequate compression, and ignition at the proper time. If any of these requirements are missing, the engine will not run. If any of these requirements are weak, the engine will not run properly. Most engine performance problems are the result of defective or improperly adjusted components affecting these three basic requirements.

Most engine malfunctions can be corrected by performing a preliminary inspection. Check all items listed in this section. If the problems persist after checking or correcting these items, refer to **Tables 2-4** and check, test or ad-

1

FUEL

COMPRESSION

SPARK

2

just the components under the applicable symptom. Check the following:

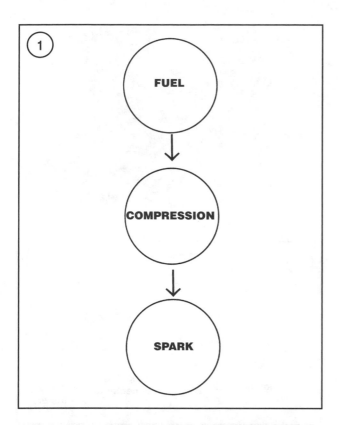

1. Ensure the fuel tank vent is opened.
2. Verify the engine has an adequate supply of fresh fuel.
3. Inspect the engine for loose, disconnected or corroded wires.
4. Check the position of the lanyard safety switch.
5. Check the battery and cable connections for tight and clean connections (Chapter Six).
6. Verify the battery is fully charged (Chapter Six).
7. Clean, inspect and re-gap the spark plugs (Chapter Three).
8. Test for spark at each cylinder. See *Spark Test* in this chapter.
9. Verify the boat hull is clean, in good condition and not water logged.
10. Verify the correct propeller is used.

STARTING DIFFICULTY

Slow starting or an inability to start the engine is usually related to an engine malfunction. First verify that proper starting procedures are followed. Starting procedures will vary by model. Review the owner's manual for starting procedures. This section provides information to help pinpoint the cause of difficult starting.

It can be difficult to determine if a starting problem is related to fuel, ignition or other causes. It is usually easiest to first verify that the ignition system is operating. Check the fuel and fuel system if the ignition system is operating but the engine will not start or starting is difficult. Refer to *Spark Test* in this chapter to determine if spark is present at the spark plugs.

WARNING

High voltage is present in the ignition system. Never touch any wires or electrical components while running the engine or performing a test. Never perform ignition system tests in wet conditions.

Spark Test

CAUTION

Perform the spark test with the spark plugs installed. Removing the spark plugs will increase the cranking speed above the speed achieved with the plugs installed. The ignition system may provide good spark at the higher cranking speed, effectively masking a fault that surfaces at the normal cranking speed.

This test checks for ignition system output at the spark plug connector. A spark gap tester (part No. 91-854009A-1) or an equivalent is required for this test.

1A. On 75-115 hp models, remove the screws (**Figure 2**) and plastic cover on the rear of the power head to access the spark plug wires. Two screws are located on the top, two screws are located on the bottom and one screw is located on the side and midway down on the cover.

1B. On 225 hp models, remove the four screws (**Figure 3**) and the plastic spark plug/coil cover on the rear of the power head.
2. Mark the cylinder number on the spark plug wires before removing them from the spark plugs. On 75-115 hp models, the top cylinder is the No. 1 cylinder. On 225 hp models, the top cylinder on the starboard bank is the No. 1 cylinder. Odd numbered cylinders are on the starboard cylinder bank and even numbered cylinders are on the port bank. Gently twist the spark plug caps to free them from the plugs, then pull the cap from the plug. Never pull on the spark plug wire to free the cap.
3. Remove the propeller as described in Chapter Eight.
4. Connect the ground lead (**Figure 4**) of the spark gap tester to a suitable engine ground such as a cylinder head or valve cover bolt.
5. Connect the spark plug connector (**Figure 4**) for one cylinder to the appropriate terminal on the spark gap tester. If the tester can accommodate multiple cylinders, connect additional spark plug wires onto the tester. On adjustable spark gap testers adjust the gap to approximately 1/4 in. (6.35 mm). Connect any remaining spark plug wires onto a suitable engine ground.

CAUTION
Never crank the engine with ungrounded spark plug wires. Make sure all spark plug wires are connected onto a spark gap tester or a good engine ground. Cranking the engine with ungrounded leads will create arcing that can damage the ignition system and other engine components.

6. Shift the engine into NEUTRAL. Position the tester away from the spark plug openings.

NOTE
The spark created by the ignition system may be difficult to detect if testing in bright sunlight or a well-lit area. Block the lighting with a piece of cardboard or other material to provide better visual verification of spark.

7. Observe the spark gap tester while cranking the engine. The presence of a blue spark at the spark gap tester during cranking indicates the ignition system is operating for that cylinder.
8. Repeat Steps 4-7 for any remaining cylinders.
9. Connect the spark plug wires to the correct spark plugs. Ensure that all leads are routed correctly.
10. Install the propeller as described in Chapter Eight.
11. Fit the plastic cover onto the rear of the power head. Install the cover screws and tighten in a crossing pattern to 65 in.-lb. (7.3 N•m) for 75-115 hp models and 71 in.-lb. (8.0 N•m) for 225 hp models.
12. Refer to *Ignition System Troubleshooting* in this chapter if spark is weak or missing any of the cylinders. Refer to *Fuel System Troubleshooting* in this chapter if the ignition system is operating properly but the engine is difficult or impossible to start.

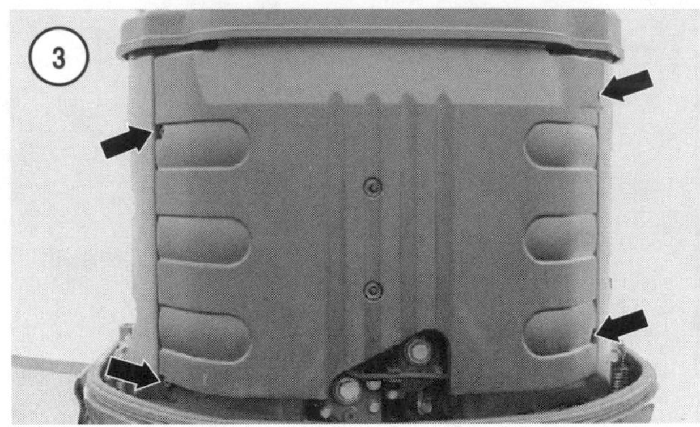

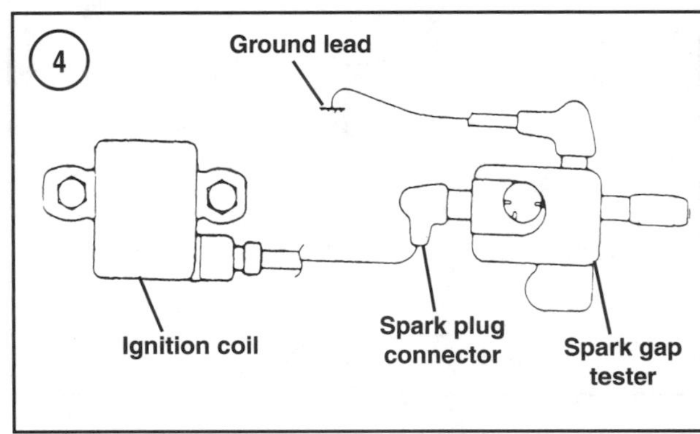

Fuel Inspection

Fuel related problems are common with most outboard engines. Gasoline has a relatively short shelf life and becomes stale within a few weeks under some conditions. Because a marine engine may not be run for several weeks at a time the gasoline often becomes stale.

As fuel evaporates, a gummy deposit usually forms in the carburetor or other fuel system components. These deposits may clog fuel filters, fuel lines, fuel pumps and small passages in the carburetor or fuel injection system.

Fuel stored in the fuel tank tends to absorb water vapor from the air. Over time, this water separates from the fuel and settles to the bottom of the fuel tank. Water in the fuel tank can lead to the formation of rust and other contaminants in the fuel tank. These contaminants block fuel filters and other fuel system passages. Inspect the fuel in the

fuel tank when the engine refuses to start and the ignition system is not at fault. An unpleasant odor usually indicates the fuel has exceeded its shelf life and should be replaced.

WARNING
Use extreme caution when working with the fuel system. Never smoke or allow sparks to occur around fuel or fuel vapor. Wipe up any spilled fuel at once with a shop towel and dispose of the shop towel in an appropriate manner. Check all fuel hoses, connections and fittings for leakage after any fuel system repair.

All models covered in this manual are equipped with either float bowl drains (**Figure 5**) on carburetor equipped models or a vapor separator tank drain screw (**Figure 6**) on electronic fuel injection (EFI) models. Refer to Chapter Five to locate the float bowl drain plugs or vapor separator tank drain screws.

To inspect the fuel slide a container under the drain plug or screw. Pump the primer bulb (**Figure 7**) until it becomes firm. Slowly remove the plug and allow all fuel to drain from the bowl. Inspect the drain plug gasket or drain screw O-ring for torn or damaged surfaces. Replace the gasket or O-ring if not found in excellent condition. Pour the fuel sample into a clear container. Install the drain plug or screw. On 75-115 hp models, securely tighten the bowl or vapor separator tank drain screw. On 225 hp models, tighten the vapor separator tank drain screw to 18 in.-lb. (2.0 N•m). Promptly clean up any spilled fuel.

Inspect the fuel. An unusual odor, debris, cloudy appearance or the presence of water indicates a problem with the fuel. If any of these conditions are noted, dispose of all the fuel in an environmentally responsible manner. Contact a local marine dealership or automotive repair facility for information on the proper disposal of the fuel. Clean and inspect the entire fuel system if water or other contamination is in the fuel.

If no fuel can be drained from the float bowl or vapor separator tank, check the fuel tank for fuel and check all hoses and connections for loose or damaged fittings. Typically the fuel inlet needle is stuck closed or plugged with debris. Clean and inspect the affected carburetor or vapor separator tank as described in Chapter Five.

ELECTRIC STARTING SYSTEM TROUBLESHOOTING

The major components of the electric starting system (**Figure 8**) include the battery, ignition switch, electric starter, starter relay, starter solenoid, neutral only start switch, fuse and associated wiring.

The electric starter (**Figure 8**) is similar in design to those commonly used on automotive applications. Its mounting location allows the starter drive (**Figure 9**) to engage the flywheel ring gear during operation. A neutral switch prevents the electric starter from operating when the engine is shifted into forward or reverse gear.

The electric starter is capable of producing substantial torque, but only for a short time without overheating. To produce the required torque, the starting system requires a fully charged battery that is in good condition. Weak or

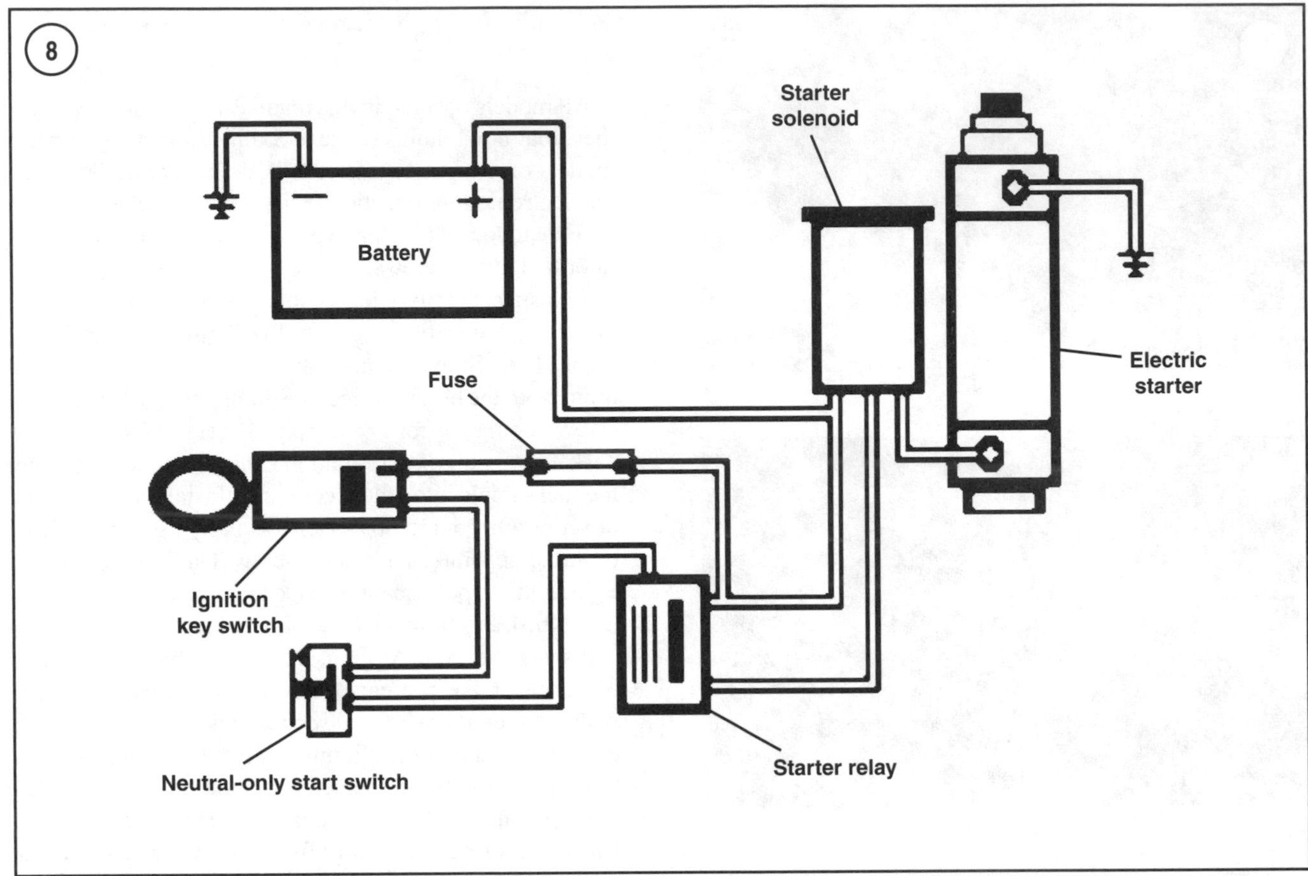

undercharged batteries are the leading cause of starting system problems. Battery maintenance and testing are covered in Chapter Six.

Electric Starter Operation

Operation of the starter circuit begins at the ignition key switch (**Figure 8**). Battery current is sent to the ignition key switch via a connection to the starter relay. The fuse protects the ignition key switch and related wiring from overloads. One large terminal on the starter relay connects to the positive battery cable wire on the starter solenoid. The other large terminal connects to the *S* terminal on the starter solenoid. The starter solenoid mounts onto the electric starter (**Figure 8**). The electric starter and solenoid are grounded to the cylinder block.

When the switch is activated, current travels from the ignition switch through the neutral start switch to the starter relay. When the starter relay is activated, current travels to the starter solenoid. When the starter solenoid is activated, current travels through internal wiring and develops a strong magnetic field. This field moves a plunger and linkage that engages the flywheel ring gear. The plunger also moves a disc that electrically connects terminals to the positive battery cable and the short cable connecting onto the electric starter. This allows remote switching of the high amperage current flow required by the electric starter using the shortest practical wire length.

Releasing the ignition key switch deactivates the starter relay. Current flow to the electric starter stops. The spring in the starter solenoid pushes the internal linkages and drive gear away from the flywheel as the electric starter stops spinning. Accumulated dirt or grease can prevent the starter drive gear from engaging or disengaging the flywheel ring gear. Clean and lubricate the armature shaft as described in Chapter Three.

The neutral start switch allows current flow to the starter relay only when the engine is in neutral. The neutral switch opens the circuit when forward or reverse gear is selected preventing activation of the starter relay.

CAUTION

Never operate the electric starter for longer than ten seconds without allowing at least a two minute cooling down period. Operating the electric starter with an undercharged

battery can result in electric starter overheating and subsequent failure.

Electric Starter Cranking Voltage Test

WARNING
Use extreme caution when working around batteries. Never smoke or allow sparks to occur in or around batteries. Batteries produce explosive hydrogen gas. Never make the final connection of a circuit to the battery terminal as an arc may occur leading to fire or explosion.

This test measures the voltage delivered to the electric starter while cranking the engine. A multimeter is required for this test. A seized gearcase or power head must be ruled out before repairing or replacing any starting system components.

1. Remove the propeller as described in Chapter Eight. Shift the engine into NEUTRAL. Reconnect the battery cable after removing the propeller.
2. Move the rubber boot away, then touch the positive meter lead to the large terminal on the starter solenoid (A, **Figure 10**).
3. Connect the negative meter lead to a suitable engine ground.
4. Activate the lanyard safety switch to prevent accidental starting. Observe the multimeter while an assistant operates the electric starter. Note the voltage reading and refer to the following:
   a. Meter indicates 9.5 volts or greater—*Starter does not crank or operates slowly*—Replace or repair the electric starter as described in Chapter Six.
   b. *Meter indicates 0 volts*—Test the starter solenoid, starter relay, neutral only start switch and ignition key switch as described in this section.
   c. *Meter indicates more than 0 volt and less than 9.5 volt*—Test the battery and inspect the terminals as described in Chapter Six.
5. Disconnect the negative battery cable and install the propeller as described in Chapter Eight.

Starter Solenoid Test

This test measures the voltage supplied to and delivered by the starter solenoid while the ignition key switch is activated.

1. Remove the propeller as described in Chapter Eight. Shift the engine into NEUTRAL. Reconnect the battery cable after removing the propeller.
2. Activate the lanyard safety switch to prevent accidental starting.
3. Move the rubber boot away, then touch the positive meter lead to the large terminal on the starter solenoid (B, **Figure 10**).
4. Touch the negative meter lead to a suitable engine ground and note the meter reading. The meter must indicate battery voltage. If not, test the battery and inspect the terminals as described in Chapter Six.
5. Move the rubber boot away, then touch the positive meter lead to the large terminal on the starter solenoid (A, **Figure 10**). Observe the multimeter while a qualified assistant operates the electric starter.

6A. *Meter indicates 9.5 volts or greater; solenoid does not click*—Remove the starter solenoid and perform the functional test as described in Chapter Six.

6B. *Meter indicates 0 volt; solenoid clicks*—Replace the starter solenoid as described in Chapter Six.

6C. *Meter indicates 9.5 volts or greater; solenoid clicks but starter does not operate*—Replace or repair the electric starter as described in Chapter Six.

6D. *Meter indicates 0 volt; solenoid does not click*—Perform the following:
   a. Touch the positive meter test lead to the brown/white wire on the starter solenoid terminal

(C, **Figure 10**). Connect the negative meter lead onto a suitable engine ground.

b. Observe the multimeter while a qualified assistant operates the ignition key switch. The meter must indicate battery voltage with the ignition key switch in the *start* position. If otherwise, test the starter relay, neutral only start switch and ignition key switch as described in this section.

7. Position all rubber boots over the respective starter solenoid terminals.
8. Disconnect the negative battery cable and install the propeller as described in Chapter Eight.

Starter Relay Test

Two separate tests are required to properly test the relay. The first test checks for voltage at the starter relay as the ignition key switch is activated.

The second test is a functional test to verify proper internal switching. Perform the functional test if correct voltage is indicated at the relay terminals. Use a multimeter, short jumper wires and a fully charged battery to perform the functional test.

Starter relay voltage test

WARNING
Use extreme caution when working around batteries. Never smoke or allow sparks to occur in or around batteries. Batteries produce explosive hydrogen gas that can explode and result in injury or death. Never make the final connection of a circuit to the battery terminal as an arc may occur and lead to fire or explosion.

1. Remove any covers and locate the starter relay as described in Chapter Six. See *Starter Relay Replacement*.
2. Activate the lanyard safety switch to prevent accidental starting.
3. Remove the propeller as described in Chapter Eight and reconnect the cables to the battery.
4. Connect the negative multimeter lead to a suitable engine ground.
5. Move the insulated wire cover aside to access the red battery current wire terminal to the starter relay (A, **Figure 11**).
   a. On 75-115 hp models, select the red wire terminal.
   b. On 225 hp models, select the brown/white wire terminal that leads to the engine wire harness. Do not select the brown/white wire terminal leading to the starter solenoid.

6. Note the multimeter and touch the positive multimeter lead to the battery cable. If the meter indicates 0 volts, a blown fuse, discharged battery, or faulty wiring is indicated. Inspect the fuses for a blown condition and wiring for disconnected, loose or corroded connections. Check the battery and terminals as described in Chapter Six.
7. Disconnect the brown wire connector (B, **Figure 11**) from the relay harness connector. Touch the positive meter lead onto the disconnected brown wire terminal. Connect the negative test lead to a suitable engine ground such as the starter mounting bolt.
8. Note the meter reading *without* activating the ignition key switch. The correct meter reading is 0 volts with the ignition key switch in the OFF or STOP position. Test the ignition key switch as described in this section and check for faulty wiring if any voltage is detected.
9. With the meter leads connected as described in Step 7, have an assistant cycle the ignition key switch to the ON or RUN position and back to the OFF or STOP position several times. Do not select the start position. Note the meter reading. The correct meter reading is 0 volt with the switch in the ON or RUN positions. Test the ignition key switch as described in this section and check for faulty wiring if any voltage is detected.
10. Note the meter reading while a qualified assistant cycles the ignition key switch several times to the START position and back to the ON or RUN positions. The correct meter reading is 12 volts or greater each time the switch is in the START position and 0 volt each time the switch is in the ON or RUN position. Test the ignition key switch and neutral-only start switch if the test results are not as specified.
11. Reconnect the brown engine wire harness connector onto the brown relay harness connector.
12. Move the insulated cover aside, then touch the positive meter lead onto the terminal (C, **Figure 11**) for the

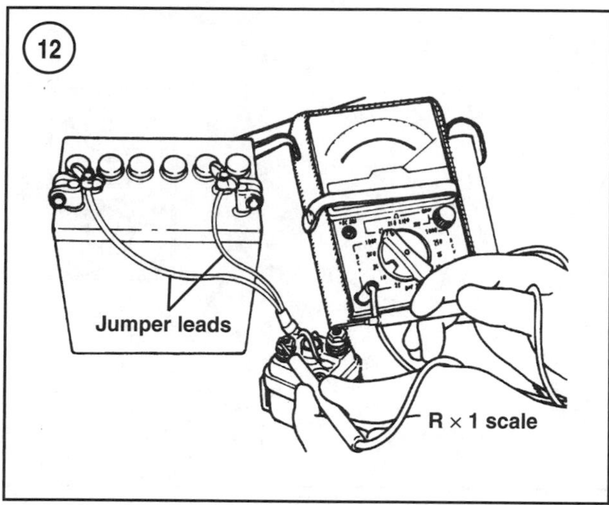

brown/white wire leading to the starter solenoid. On 225 hp models, do not inadvertently touch the lead onto the terminal for the brown/white wire leading to the fuse and engine wire harness. Touch the negative multimeter lead to the black wire terminal on the relay. The correct reading is 0 volt. Perform the starter relay functional test, as described in this section, if any voltage is present on the terminal.

13. Connect the meter test leads as described in Step 1. Note the meter reading while an assistant cycles the ignition key switch several times to the START position and back to the ON or RUN positions. The correct meter reading is 12 volts or greater each time the switch is in the START position and 0 volt each time the switch is in the ON or RUN position. Repeat the test with the negative test lead connected onto a suitable engine ground, such as the starter mounting bolt. Repair the faulty black relay ground wire or terminal if correct test results are evident only with the test lead connected onto the engine ground.

   a. *Meter indicates 0 volt in all switch positions*—Perform the starter relay functional test as described in this section.

   b. *Meter indicates 12 volts or higher in all switch positions*—A faulty starter relay, ignition key switch or wiring is indicated. Perform the starter relay functional test as described in this section. Repeat the relay voltage test if the relay passes the functional test.

14. Position all rubber boots over the starter relay terminals.

15. Disconnect the negative battery cable and install the propeller as described in Chapter Eight. Place the lanyard safety switch in the RUN position.

Starter relay functional test

A multimeter, fully charged battery and short jumper leads are required to test the starter relay. Refer to the wiring diagrams located at the back of the manual to identify the starter relay.

1. Remove the starter relay as described in Chapter Six.
2. Place the electric starter relay on a suitable work surface far away from any flammable substance.
3. Select the R × 1 scale on the multimeter. Connect the positive meter lead to one of the larger diameter terminals (**Figure 12**) on the relay. Connect the negative meter lead to the other larger diameter terminal (**Figure 12**). The correct result is *no continuity*.
4. Connect one end of a jumper lead onto the black wire or either of the smaller diameter wire terminals of the relay (**Figure 12**). Connect the other end of this jumper lead to the negative terminal of a fully charged 12 volt battery (**Figure 12**).
5. Connect one end of a jumper lead to the positive terminal of the 12-volt battery. Touch the other end of the jumper lead onto the brown wire terminal or the remaining small diameter terminal of the relay . The meter should now indicate *continuity* and an audible click should be heard.
6. Replace the starter relay if it does not perform as described.
7. Install the starter relay as described in Chapter Six.

Neutral-Only Start Switch Test

A defective neutral-only start switch can prevent electric starter operation when in neutral or allow starter operation when forward or reverse gear is selected.

Two separate tests are required to properly test the neutral-only start switch. The first test measures the voltage from the switch at all three shift positions. Removal of the switch is not required for the voltage test. The test is performed using the brown wire terminal on the starter relay.

The second test is the functional test. Removal of the switch is not required as long as the switch wires are accessible. With models using a remote control mounted ignition key switch, removal and partial disassembly of the remote control is usually required to access the wires. The wires extend from the bottom or side of the remote control on applications using a dash-mounted ignition switch.

Refer to Chapter Eleven for remote control disassembly and assembly. Refer to the wire diagrams located at the back of this manual to identify the neutral-only start switch wires.

Voltage test

1. Remove any covers and locate the starter relay as described in Chapter Six. See *Starter Relay Replacement*.
2. Activate the lanyard safety switch to prevent accidental starting.
3. Remove the propeller as described in Chapter Eight and reconnect the cables to the battery.
4. Connect the negative multimeter lead to a suitable engine ground.
5. Locate the brown wire terminal (B, **Figure 11**) on the starter relay. Trace the brown wire to the bullet connectors to the engine wire harness. Disconnect the bullet connectors.
6. Touch the positive meter lead to the brown wire terminal. Touch the negative test lead onto a suitable engine ground, such as a starter mounting bolt.
7. Shift the remote control into NEUTRAL gear. Note the multimeter while a qualified assistant cycles the ignition key switch to the START position. The meter must indicate 12 volts or greater.
8. Shift the remote control into FORWARD gear. Note the multimeter while a qualified assistant cycles the ignition key switch to the START position. The meter must indicate 0 volt.
9. Shift the remote control into REVERSE gear. Note the multimeter while a qualified assistant cycles the ignition key switch to the START position. The meter must indicate 0 volt.
10. Connect the brown engine harness wire onto the starter relay wire connector.
11. A faulty neutral-only start switch, ignition key switch or wiring is indicated if the test results are not as specified. Refer to the following:
   a. If the meter indicates 0 volt at all three shift position, test the starter relay voltage and ignition key switch as described in this section.
   b. If the meter indicates 12 volts in all three shift positions, perform the neutral-only start switch (functional test) as described in this section.
   c. If the meter indicates 12 volts in one gear and 0 volt in the other, disassemble the remote control as described in Chapter Eleven and replace the neutral-only start switch.
12. Disconnect the negative battery cable and install the propeller as described in Chapter Eight. Place the lanyard safety switch in the RUN position.

Functional test

The neutral-only start switch must be removed for this test.

13

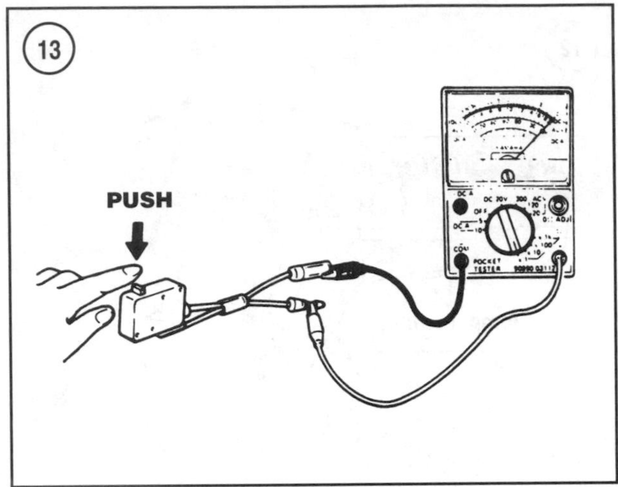

1. Disconnect the negative battery cable to prevent accidental starting.
2. Shift the remote control into NEUTRAL gear.
3. Locate the two yellow/red wires leading into the remote control. Disconnect the wires from the ignition key switch and instrument harness wires. If the ignition key switch is mounted in the remote control, refer to Chapter Eleven for disassembly procedures and remove the neutral-only start switch.
4. Calibrate the multimeter onto the R × 1 scale. Connect the meter test leads onto each of the yellow/red neutral only start switch leads and note the meter reading. The meter must indicate *continuity*. If otherwise, disassemble the remote control as described in Chapter Eleven and replace the neutral-only start switch.

5A. If the neutral-only start switch was removed for testing, note the meter reading while repeatedly pressing and releasing the switch plunger (**Figure 13**). The meter must indicated *continuity* each time the plunger is depressed and *no continuity* each time the plunger is released. If otherwise, replace the neutralonly start switch.

5B. If the neutral-only start switch remains in the remote control, note the meter reading while repeatedly shifting the remote control into the FORWARD, REVERSE, and NEUTRAL positions. The meter must indicate *continuity* each time the remote control is shifted into NEUTRAL gear and *no continuity* each time the remote control is shifted into FORWARD or REVERSE gear. If otherwise, disassemble the remote control as described in Chapter Eleven and replace the neutral-only start switch.

6A. If the neutral-only start switch was removed for testing, assemble and install the remote control as described in Chapter Eleven.

6B. If the neutral-only start switch was not removed for testing, connect the yellow/red neutral-only start switch

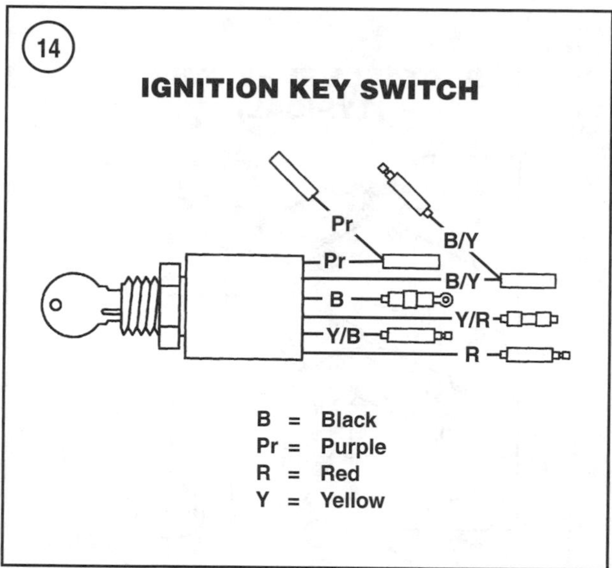

wires to the ignition key switch and instrument harness leads.

7. Connect the battery cable.

8. Verify proper operation of the neutral-only start switch before operating the engine.

Ignition Key Switch Test

The ignition switch is mounted in the remote control on most models. Some models have the ignition switch mounted in the dash of the boat. Access to the switch wires is required for testing.

If the switch is in the remote control, remove and partially disassemble the control box to access the wires. Refer to Chapter Eleven for remote control box disassembly and assembly.

If the switch is dash mounted, remove the ignition switch from the dash to allow access to the wires.

1. Disconnect the negative battery cable to prevent accidental starting. Shift the engine into NEUTRAL gear.

2A. For a remote control mounted ignition key switch, disassemble the remote control assembly enough to gain access to the ignition switch wires. Disconnect all wires leading to the ignition switch.

2B. For a dash mounted ignition key switch, remove the large retaining nut to free the switch from the dash. Disconnect each of the switch wires from the instrument harness wires.

3. Calibrate the multimeter to the R × 1 scale. Connect the *positive* meter lead to the black wire terminal leading to the ignition switch and the negative lead to the black/yellow wire key switch (**Figure 14**).

   a. With the ignition switch in the OFF or STOP position, the meter should indicate *continuity*.
   b. Place the ignition switch to the ON or RUN position. The meter should indicate *no continuity*. Push the switch inward and note the meter. The meter should indicated *no continuity*.

4. Connect the positive meter lead to the red switch wire and the negative meter lead to the yellow/black wire (**Figure 14**).

   a. With the switch in the OFF or STOP position. The meter should indicate *no continuity*.
   b. Place the switch in the ON or RUN position. The meter should indicate *no continuity*. Push inward on the switch and the meter should indicate *continuity*.
   c. Place the switch in the START position. The meter should indicate *no continuity*. Push inward on the switch and the meter should indicate *continuity*.

5. Connect the positive meter lead to the red wire and the negative lead to the purple wire (**Figure 14**). With the ignition switch in the OFF or STOP position, the meter should indicate *no continuity*. Push inward on the switch and the meter should indicate *no continuity*.

   a. Place the ignition switch in the ON or RUN position. The meter should indicate *continuity*. Push inward on the switch and the meter should indicate *continuity*.
   b. Place the ignition switch in the START position. The meter should indicate *continuity*. Push inward on the switch and the meter should indicate *continuity*.

6. Connect the positive meter lead to the red wire and the negative lead to the yellow/red wire (**Figure 14**). With the ignition switch in the OFF or STOP position, the meter should indicate *no continuity*.

   a. Place the ignition switch in the ON or RUN position. The meter should indicate *no continuity*. Push inward on the switch and the meter should indicate *no continuity*.
   b. Place the ignition switch in the START position. The meter should indicate *continuity*. Push inward on the switch and the meter should indicate *continuity*.

7. Connect the positive meter lead to the red wire and the negative lead to the black wire (**Figure 14**). With the ignition switch in the OFF or STOP position the meter should indicate *no continuity*.

   a. Place the ignition switch in the ON or RUN position. The meter should indicate *no continuity*. Push inward on the switch and the meter should indicate *no continuity*.
   b. Place the ignition switch in the START position. The meter should indicate *no continuity*. Push inward on the switch and the meter should indicate *no continuity*.

8. Replace the ignition switch if it fails to operate as described.

9A. For a remote control-mounted ignition key switch, connect the ignition key switch wires onto the remote control harness wires. Assemble the remote control as described in Chapter Eleven.

9B. On a dash-mounted ignition key switch, connect the ignition key switch wires onto the corresponding instrument harness wires. Tighten the large retaining nut to secure the switch into the dash. Route all wiring to prevent interference with moving components.

10. Connect the battery cable.

FUEL SYSTEM TROUBLESHOOTING

WARNING

Use extreme caution when working on the fuel system. Never smoke or allow sparks to occur around fuel or fuel vapors. Wipe up spilled fuel with a shop towel and dispose of the towel in an environmentally responsible manner. Check all fuel hoses, connections and fittings for leaks after any fuel system repair. Correct any fuel system leakage before operating the engine.

NOTE

Always inspect all fuel filters as described in Chapter Three before testing the fuel system.

NOTE

Refer to ***Electronic Fuel Injection*** *at the end of this chapter to test the EFI components used on 115 and 225 hp models.*

Fuel Tank, Fuel Supply Hose and Primer Bulb Inspection and Tests

A faulty fuel tank, fuel hose or related components can restrict fuel flow or allow air to enter the fuel flowing to the engine. In either case, the engine will misfire due to inadequate fuel delivery. In most instances the misfire occurs only at higher engine speeds as the fuel flow is adequate for low speed operation.

Many outboards use portable fuel tanks (**Figure 15**, typical). This arrangement allows easy tank removal for filling, cleaning and inspection. Some larger boats are equipped with built in fuel tanks (**Figure 16**) that are not easily removed for service or cleaning. Major structural components of the boat must be removed to access the tank.

The most effective method to determine if the fuel tank is faulty is to temporarily run the engine on a known-good fuel tank. Ensure the tank used for testing has good fuel hoses, fresh fuel and secure fuel hose connections. Ensure the inside diameter of the fuel hose and fuel fittings of the test fuel tank is 1/4 in. (6.4 mm) or larger. Using hose that is too small can result in a continued engine malfunction.

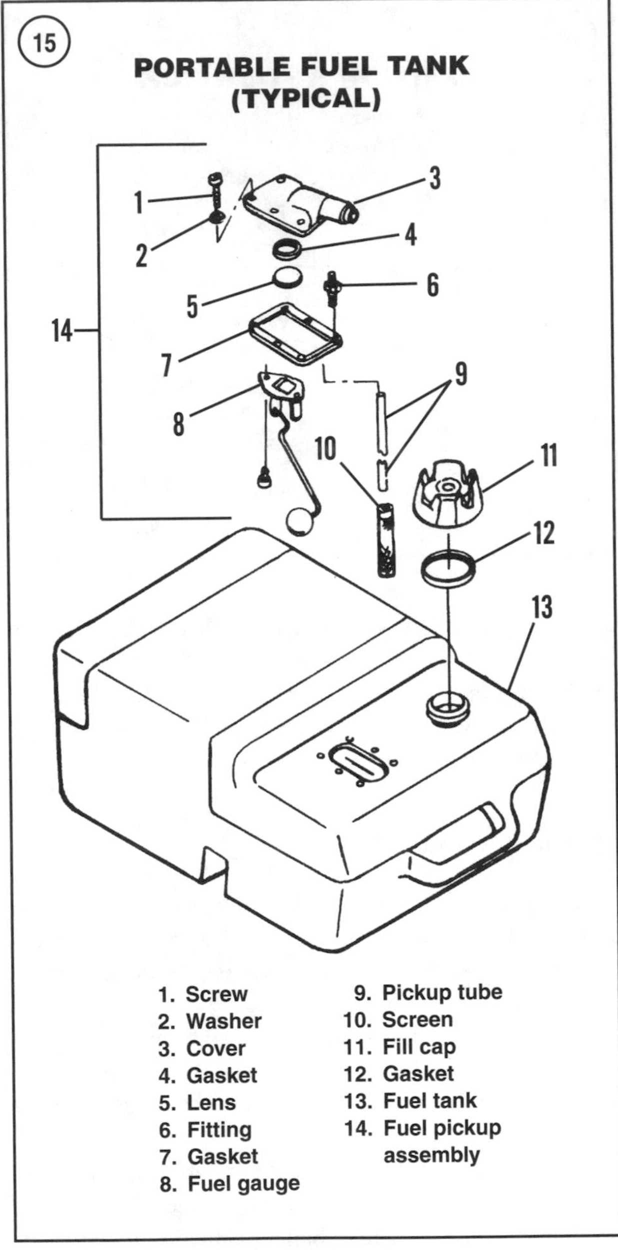

A problem with the fuel tank pickup, fuel, fuel hoses, primer bulb, fuel tank vent or anti-siphon device on built-in tanks is indicated if the engine performs properly on a known good fuel tank and hose.

A fault with the fuel system, ignition system, or other engine component is likely if the malfunction persists with the good fuel tank. Refer to **Table 3** and **Table 4** to determine which components to test, adjust or inspect.

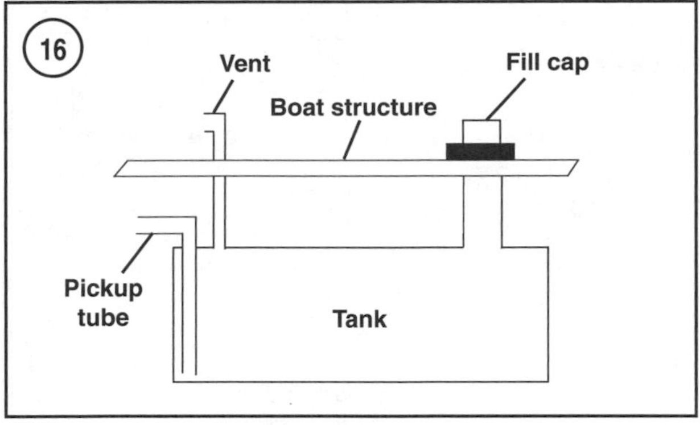

NOTE
The engine must be run at full throttle for several minutes to accurately check for a fuel tank related fault.

Checking the fuel tank pickup

The fuel tank pickup (14, **Figure 15**) draws fuel from near the bottom of the fuel tank. Most applications use a simple tube extending from the cover (3, **Figure 15**) to near the bottom of the fuel tank. Some fuel tanks are equipped with a screen or filter (10, **Figure 15**) to capture debris present in the fuel tank. This filter may become obstructed with debris restricting fuel flow. Debris can block the tube type fuel tank pickup as well.

Partial disassembly of the fuel tank is necessary to inspect the fuel tank pickup. Refer to Chapter Five for portable fuel tank cleaning and inspection instructions.

When a built-in fuel tank is used, inspection of the fuel tank pickup is more difficult. Accessibility to the fuel tank and components may be limited. On some boats, seating, storage areas and even the structure of the boat must be removed to access the fuel tank.

Contact the boat manufacturer for information on the repair and a source for replacement parts of a built-in fuel tank.

Checking the fuel tank vent

Fuel tank venting is required for fuel to flow from the fuel tank to the engine. Inadequate venting allows a vacuum to form in the tank as fuel is drawn from the tank. With continued running, the vacuum becomes strong enough to prevent the fuel pump from drawing fuel from the tank. Fuel starvation occurs when the supply of fuel is less than the engine demands. Fuel starvation usually results in decreased power or surging at higher engine speeds. Fuel starvation can also occur at lower speeds causing the engine to stall and not restart.

The vent for a portable tank is incorporated into the fill cap. This allows closing of the vent to prevent fuel spillage when carrying the fuel tank. On some tanks the vent is incorporated into the fuel gauge cover (3, **Figure 15**). A special valve opens to allow venting only when the quick-connector is attached onto the fuel tank.

The vent system for a built-in fuel tank includes a vent opening at the fuel tank, the vent hose, and the hull mounted vent fitting (**Figure 16**). This type of venting system is always open. Insects may obstruct the vent passages.

If inadequate fuel tank venting is suspected, loosen the fuel tank fill cap slightly to allow the tank to vent. Clean and inspect the fuel tank vent hose and all fittings on a built-in fuel tank if the fuel starvation symptoms disappear after the cap is loosened.

Check the position of the vent screw on the fill cap when using a portable fuel tank. Replace the fill cap if the screw is fully open but fuel starvation still occurs.

Anti-siphon devices

An anti-siphon device prevents fuel from siphoning from the tank if a leak occurs in the fuel line between the tank and engine. An anti-siphon valve is generally used on a built-in fuel tank. The most common type is a spring loaded check valve located at the fuel pickup hose fitting. Other types are the manual valve and solenoid activated valve. Anti-siphon devices are an important safety feature and should not be bypassed.

CAUTION
Never run an outboard without providing cooling water. Use either a test tank or flush/test device. Always remove the propeller before running the engine on a flush/test device.

The most effective way to test for a faulty anti-siphon device if so equipped is by using a process of elimination. Run the engine on a portable fuel tank connected directly to the engine fuel pump. Perform this test under actual running conditions. A fault is indicated with the fuel tank pickup, fuel hoses, primer bulb, fuel tank vent or anti-siphon device if the engine performs properly while connected to the portable fuel tank. If all fuel hose components are in good condition, the malfunction is likely caused by a blocked or faulty anti-siphon device. Remove and replace the anti-siphon device following the instructions provided with the new component.

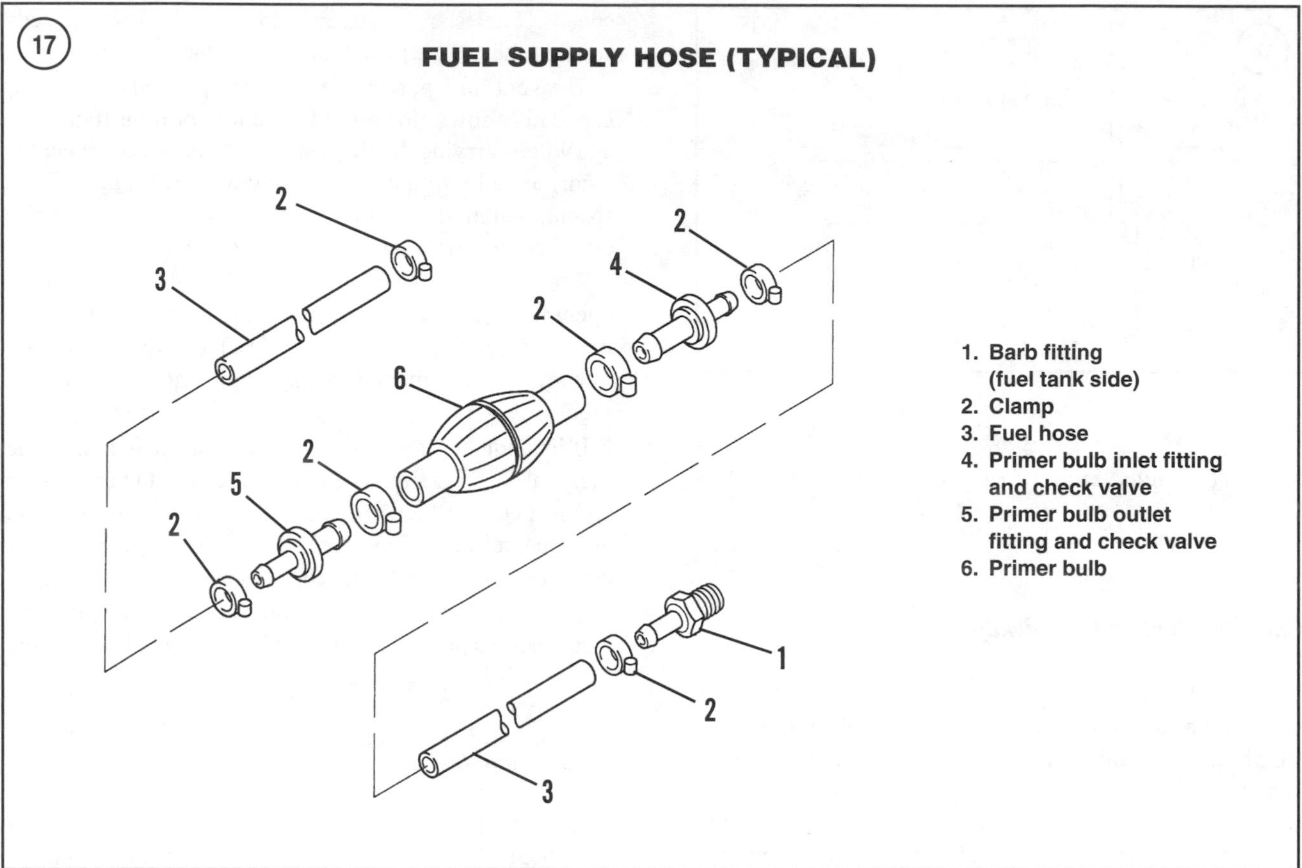

Replacement of the anti-siphon device requires removal of the fuel hose and possibly the fuel tank pickup. Inspect the faulty valve prior to installing the new one. Clean the fuel tank if a significant amount of debris is found in the anti-siphon device or fuel tank pickup. Debris in the fuel tank will usually cause a repeat failure. Inspect all fuel system hoses and filters for blockage if debris is in the fuel tank, fuel tank pickup or anti-siphon device. Always correct any fuel system leakage prior to returning the engine to service.

NOTE

Some anti-siphon devices can be cleaned instead of replaced. Thoroughly inspect the device for worn, damaged or corroded components. Replace the valve if in questionable condition.

Testing the fuel supply hose

A faulty fuel supply hose (**Figure 17**, typical) can result in fuel leakage, cause a fuel restriction, or allow air to enter the fuel supply. Visually inspect all fuel hoses for cracks or a weathered appearance. Pinch the fuel hose until it collapses and release it. Replace the fuel hose if it is difficult to squeeze, excessively soft or sticks together on the internal surfaces. Replace the fuel hose if any leakage is detected.

CAUTION

Avoid using couplings or other patching methods to repair a damaged fuel hose. The coupling or patch may result in restricted fuel flow and lead to fuel starvation. A temporary repair usually fails and results in a fuel or air leak.

The fuel supply hose must be connected to a fitting on the hose exiting from the front and lower engine covers.

Refer to **Figure 17**.

1. Remove the fuel hose clamp, then carefully pull the fuel hose from the connector leading into the lower engine cover.
2. Remove the clamp, then carefully pull the fuel hose from the tank fitting (1, **Figure 17**). Remove the clamps and pull the primer bulb and check valves (4-6, **Figure 17**) as an assembly from the fuel line. Inspect and pressure test the primer bulb as described in this section.

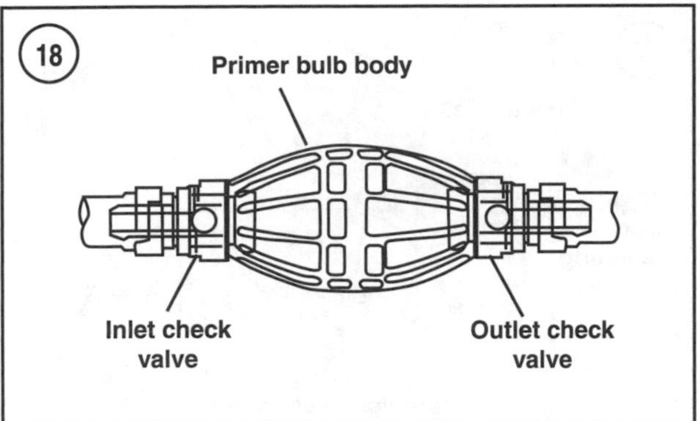

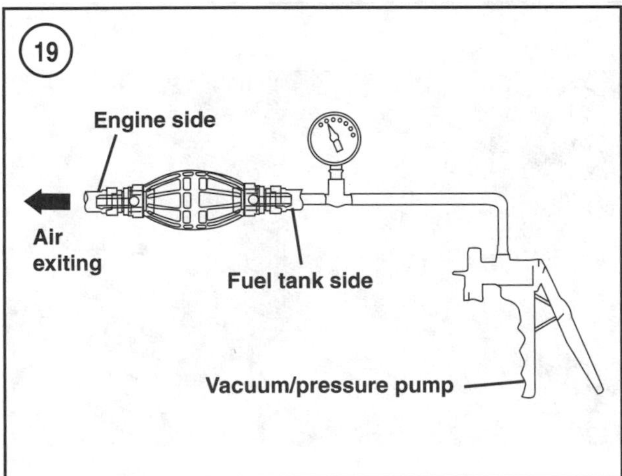

3. Direct one end of the disconnected hose to a clear area and use compressed air to blow through the hose. Replace the hose if air does not flow freely through it. An internal restriction is usually caused by deteriorated internal surfaces.
4. Inspect all fuel hoses from the tank to the carburetors if debris is found in the hose.
5. Replace all fuel hose clamps during assembly. Check the entire fuel system for fuel leaks and correct them before operating the engine. Refer to Chapter Five for primer bulb installation instructions.

Inspecting the primer bulb

The primer bulb (6, **Figure 17**) is a hand operated fuel pump integrated into the fuel supply hose. It serves as a means to fill the carburetor float bowls or vapor separator tank with fuel prior to starting the engine.

Pump the primer bulb only if the engine has not been used for several hours. Excessive pumping can create a potential flooding condition.

Never use excessive force when pumping the primer bulb. Gently squeeze the primer bulb until it becomes firm indicating that the carburetor float bowl or vapor separator tank is filled.

The major components of the primer bulb assembly (**Figure 18**) include the body, inlet check valve (tank side) and outlet check valve (engine side).

A malfunctioning primer bulb can lead to an inability to prime the fuel system or cause a restriction in the fuel system. Hard starting, poor performance or engine stalling are the typical symptoms. Most failures of the primer bulb are the result of defective check valves at the engine or fuel tank side of the bulb.

A blocked check valve will cause insufficient fuel delivery to the engine. If the restriction is on the tank side, the bulb will collapse during engine operation. If a check valve fails to seat properly, the bulb will not become firm when the float bowls or vapor separator tank are full.

Fuels available today may contain ingredients that cause deterioration of fuel system components, including the primer bulb. Squeeze the primer bulb until fully compressed then release it. Replace the primer bulb if it tends to stick together on the internal surfaces when released. Thoroughly inspect the fuel hose and other fuel system components if this condition is noted. Prior to replacing the primer bulb, pressure test it as described in this section.

WARNING
Use extreme caution when working with the fuel system. Never smoke or allow sparks to occur around fuel or fuel vapor. Wipe up any spilled fuel at once with a shop towel and dispose of the shop towel in an appropriate manner. Check all fuel hoses, connections and fittings for leakage after any fuel system repair. Correct all fuel leakage before returning the engine to service.

Primer bulb pressure test

Test the primer bulb check valves using a hand operated vacuum pump available at most automotive parts stores and through most tool suppliers.
1. Disconnect both ends of the fuel line connecting the fuel tank to the engine. Remove and discard the clamps (2, **Figure 17**) at both fuel line connections to the primer bulb. Position the primer bulb over a container and pull both fuel lines from the primer bulb.
2. Squeeze the primer bulb until fully collapsed. Replace the primer bulb if it does not freely expand when released. Replace the primer bulb if it is cracked, weathered or is hard to squeeze.
3. The arrow molded into the primer bulb body points toward the engine. Connect a hand operated pressure pump (**Figure 19**) onto the fuel tank side fitting. Clamp the hose

to the primer bulb hose fitting. Gently squeeze the hand operated pump. Air must exit the engine side (**Figure 19**) as the pressure pump is operated. Replace the primer bulb assembly or check valves if it does not operate as specified.

4. Connect the hand operated vacuum pump to the engine side fitting (**Figure 20**). Clamp the pump hose securely to the primer bulb fuel fitting. Gently pump the vacuum pump lever. Air must enter the fuel tank side hose fitting (**Figure 20**) as the pump is operated. Replace the primer bulb assembly or check valves if it does not operate as specified.
5. Connect the pressure pump hose to the fuel tank side fitting (**Figure 19**). Block the engine side fitting with a finger. Submerge the primer bulb in water. Gently pump the hand operated pressure pump enough to achieve a few pounds of air pressure inside the bulb. Replace the primer bulb assembly if air bubbles are detected. Thoroughly dry the primer bulb after testing.
6. Install the primer bulb as described in Chapter Six.

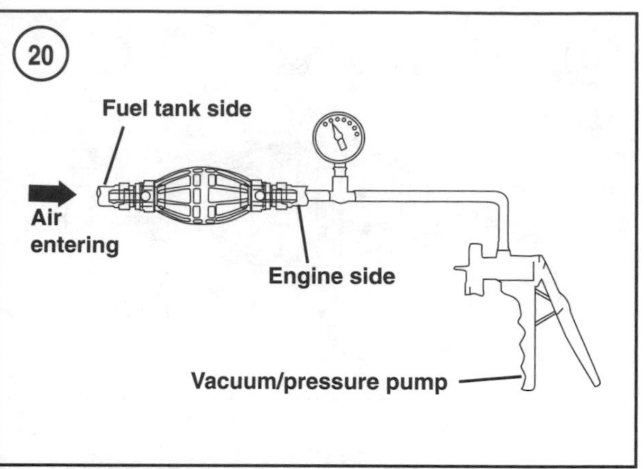

Mechanical Low-Pressure Fuel Pump Test

The mechanical low-pressure fuel pump supplies fuel to the carburetors on 75 and 90 hp models and the vapor separator tank on 115 hp model. Two fuel pumps (**Figure 21**) are used on 2001 and 2002, 75 and 90 hp models. A single pump is used on 2003, 75 and 90 hp and all 115 hp models. An electric low-pressure fuel pump is used to supply fuel to the vapor separator tank on 225 hp models. Refer to *Electronic Fuel Injection* in this chapter.

Failure of the fuel pump can result in inadequate fuel delivery to the engine (fuel starvation), fuel leakage or in some rare cases excessive fuel pressure.

Testing the fuel pump using a fuel pressure gauge, a graduated container suitable for holding fuel, and a stopwatch to check the volume of fuel delivered during a specific time frame is accurate but time consuming, and the potential for dangerous fuel leakage is always present.

A more effective way to check the fuel pump is to have an assistant operate the engine under actual running conditions. Vigorously pump the primer bulb when fuel starvation symptoms occur. Inspect the fuel pump if the symptoms disappear when the primer bulb is pumped. Refer to Chapter Six for fuel pump removal, inspection and repair.

WARNING

On-water testing or adjustments require two people: one to operate the boat, the other to monitor the gauges or test equipment and make necessary adjustments. All personnel must remain seated inside the boat at all times. Do not lean over the transom while the boat is under way. Use extensions to allow all gauges and test equipment to be located in normal seating areas.

Carburetor Malfunction Test

Four carburetors (**Figure 22**) are used on 75 and 90 hp models. All 115 and 225 hp models use an electronic fuel injection (EFI) system instead of a conventional carburetor type fuel system. The carburetors meters air and fuel to the engine. Movement of the throttle plate in the carburetor controls the air flow into the engine. Air flowing through the carburetor causes fuel flow from the carburetor into the engine. Sized passages in the carburetor control the rate of fuel flow at a given engine speed and throttle opening.

A problem with the carburetor can result in hard starting, rough idle, or an inability to run at idle speed. Other symptoms include rough operation hesitation during acceleration. Poor performance at higher engine speeds and spark plug fouling are other common symptoms.

CAUTION

Always correct problems with the fuel, fuel tank and the fuel pump before troubleshooting the carburetor(s).

This section provides troubleshooting tips and instructions to help isolate the cause of most carburetor related problems. Refer to the following symptoms for a list of possible causes.

Hard starting, rough idle or stalling at idle

Check for the following:

1. Electrothermal valve malfunction.
2. Flooding carburetor.
3. Incorrect carburetor adjustment or synchronization.
4. Plugged carburetor passages.

Rough operation at various engine speeds

Check for the following:

1. Incorrect carburetor adjustment or synchronization.
2. Electrothermal valve malfunction.
3. Plugged carburetor passages.
4. Incorrectly adjusted float.

Hesitation during acceleration

Check for the following:

1. Faulty dashpot/accelerator pump.
2. Improper carburetor adjustment or synchronization.
3. Plugged carburetor passages.
4. Incorrectly adjusted float.
5. Flooding carburetor.
6. Electrothermal valve malfunction.
7. Incorrect propeller.

Spark plug fouling or excessive exhaust smoke

Check for the following:

1. Electrothermal valve malfunction.
2. Incorrect carburetor adjustment or synchronization.
3. Flooding carburetor.
4. Incorrectly adjusted float.
5. Plugged carburetor passages.

Poor performance at higher engine speed

1. Plugged carburetor passages.
2. Incorrect carburetor adjustments or synchronization.

Engine stalls during rapid decelleration

1. Faulty dashpot/accelerator pump.
2. Improper carburetor adjustment or synchronization.

WARNING

Use extreme caution when working with the fuel system. Never smoke or allow sparks to occur around fuel or fuel vapors. Wipe up spilled fuel at once and dispose of shop towels in an appropriate manner. Check all fuel hoses, connections and fittings for leaks after any fuel system repair. Correct any fuel system leaks before returning the engine to service.

Checking for a flooding carburetor

A flooded carburetor is generally the result of debris in the needle valve or possibly a worn or damaged needle valve and seat. An improperly adjusted, damaged or fuel saturated float can also cause carburetor flooding. The result allows excessive amounts of fuel to enter the engine causing stalling or poor low speed operation. In many cases the engine performs satisfactory at higher engine speeds as the engine is able to burn the excess fuel.

1. Remove the silencer cover (**Figure 23**) as described in Chapter Five.

2. Look into the front opening of the carburetor (**Figure 24**) while gently squeezing the primer bulb. The presence of fuel flowing from the carburetor opening indicates a flooding condition for that carburetor.
3. If flooding is evident, remove and repair the affected carburetor as described in Chapter Five.
4. Clean all spilled fuel with shop towels. Install the silencer cover as described in Chapter Five. Correct any fuel leakage before operating the engine.

Checking for incorrect carburetor adjustment or synchronization

Improper carburetor adjustment can result in stalling at idle speed, rough running at idle and/or mid range engine speeds, hesitation during acceleration and excessive exhaust smoke.

Adjustment to the carburetors is limited to idle speed, carburetor synchronization and dashpot adjustments.

CAUTION
If the engine is later operated at a lower altitude, the carburetor adjustment or jet changes for operation at high altitude must be returned to their original settings. Internal engine damage can occur if the engine is run at lower altitudes with the higher altitude fuel adjustments.

CAUTION
*The pilot screws adjust the amount of fuel flowing into the low speed passages. These screws are covered with an aluminum plug and adjustment is not recommended. The factory adjustment places the screws a precise number of turns out from the lightly seated position. The screws should not be rotated unless they must be removed for carburetor cleaning. See **Pilot Screw Adjustment** in Chapter Four.*

Improper pilot screw adjustment results in hard starting, stalling at idle, excessive exhaust smoke, hesitation/bogging on acceleration or rough idle. In most cases the symptoms are present at lower engine speeds only. Do not adjust the pilot screws to a different number of turns out from the original factory setting.

The carburetor throttle plates must open and close at exactly the same time. If not, the engine will idle and run roughly. Carburetor synchronization screws are used to precisely adjust the throttle plate openings. Carburetor synchronization is described in Chapter Four. Refer to **Table 3** and **Table 4** for other items to check if rough operation continues after carburetor synchronization.

Checking for a faulty dashpot/accelerator pump

A faulty dashpot/accelerator pump (**Figure 25**) usually causes hesitation during rapid acceleration or stalling during rapid decelleration. Typically the engine performs properly during slow acceleration or decelleration. Rapid acceleration causes an instantaneous pressure change within the intake manifold. This pressure change causes a momentary decrease in fuel delivery from the carburetor(s) and a potential for hesitation or stalling. The dashpot/accelerator pump provides additional fuel to the engine during rapid acceleration. The dashpot/accelerator pump also prevents stalling during rapid decelleration by slowing the closing of the throttle plates.

Failure of the dashpot is usually caused by binding linkages or a leaking diaphragm. Check for a binding linkage and correct if needed. If the linkages are not binding, check for a leaking diaphragms as follows:

1. Disconnect the negative battery cable to prevent accidental starting. Locate the dashpot/accelerator pump on the lower port side of the power head.
2. Disconnect the hose from the dashpot/accelerator pump fitting. Connect a length of hose to the fitting to monitor air flow into and out of the diaphragm cavity. The hose must fit properly onto the fitting.

3. Place a finger over the end of the hose. Have an assistant rapidly move the throttle to the full open position. Air pressure must be detected at the hose.
4. Remove the finger to allow the air pressure escape.
5. Again place a finger of the end of the hose. Have the assistant rapidly move the throttle to the idle position. A slight vacuum must form at the hose.
6. Observe the linkages, then remove the finger. The dashpot/accelerator pump linkage must extend as air flows into the hose.
7. Replace the dashpot/accelerator pump (Chapter Five) if the pressure and vacuum fail to form at the hose as specified.
8. Reconnect the hose onto the dashpot/accelerator pump fitting. Connect the battery cable. Route the hose to prevent interference with moving components.

Checking for plugged carburetor passages

Plugged jets, passages, orifices or vents in the carburetor can result in a rich condition if it involves an air passage, or a lean condition delivery if it involves a fuel passage. Typical symptoms of plugged carburetor passages include difficult starting, surging or misfiring at higher engine speeds or hesitation during acceleration. The symptoms can occur at any engine speed depending on the location and extent of the blockage. With plugged low speed passages the engine may run roughly or stall at idle speed yet run good at higher engine speeds.

Remove, clean and inspect the carburetors if all other fuel system components such as fuel, fuel tank and fuel pump are in good condition, but these symptoms are present. Complete carburetor removal, cleaning, inspection and assembly are covered in Chapter Five.

CAUTION

Continued operation with a lean fuel condition can lead to piston damage and power head failure.

Checking for an improperly adjusted carburetor float

An improperly adjusted float can cause carburetor flooding, rough idle, hesitation during acceleration, and spark plug fouling. Disassemble the carburetors and check the float adjustment if these symptoms cannot be corrected by carburetor adjustment and synchronization.

Checking for air leakage at the carburetor mounting surfaces

Air leakage at the carburetor mounting surface (**Figure 26**) causes air to be drawn into the engine along with the air/fuel mixture. The resulting dilution of the air/fuel mixture causes the engine to operate under an excessively lean condition.

Typical symptoms of an air leak include:

1. A hissing or squealing noise emanating from the engine.
2. Rough idle characteristics.
3. Hesitation during acceleration.
4. Poor high speed performance.
5. Spark plug overheating (See Chapter Three).

A common method to locate the leakage is using a spray type lubricant such as WD 40. With the engine running at idle speed, carefully spray the lubricant onto the carburetor mating surface (**Figure 26**). If a leak is present the lubricant will be drawn into the engine at the point of leakage. Any change in the idle characteristic indicates leakage at the carburetor mounting surfaces.

If leakage is evident, remove the carburetor, the spacer if so equipped, and gaskets as described in Chapter Five. Inspect the gasket surfaces. Replace any seals, gaskets or O-rings in the carburetor or intake manifold when they are disturbed. Even small tears or nicks allow sufficient air leakage to cause an engine malfunction.

Altitude Adjustments

When operating the outboard engine at high elevation, it is usually necessary to change the carburetor main jets and readjust the carburetors. Higher elevation generally requires less fuel for proper operation. Contact a Mercury or Mariner outboard dealer in the area where the engine is operated for jet change or adjustment recommendations. Be aware that carburetor adjustments beyond the factory recommendation may cause damage to the engine.

All models covered in this manual have an emissions information decal (**Figure 27**) on the flywheel cover or valve cover. The information on this decal supersedes other adjustment specifications. Unless specifically recommended by the engine manufacture, do not adjust the outboard outside of the specifications listed on this decal.

CAUTION
Carburetor adjustment or jet changes for operation at high altitude must be returned to original settings if the engine is later operated at a lower altitude. Internal engine damage can occur if the engine is run at lower altitudes with the higher altitude fuel adjustments.

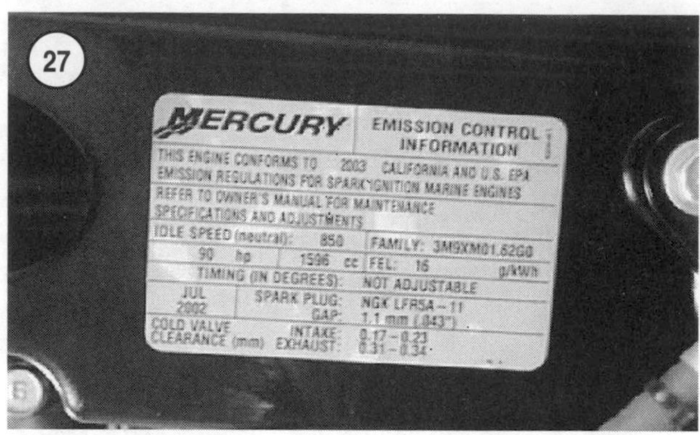

Electrothermal Valve Malfunction

NOTE
The electrothermal valve will not operate properly unless the throttle is ***closed*** *during engine start-up. Refer to the owner's manual for the engine starting procedure.*

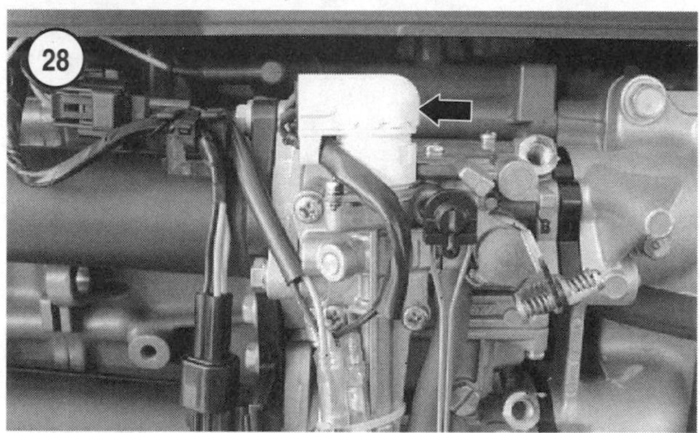

The two electrothermal valves **(Figure 28)** mount onto the sides of the top of the No. 3 carburetor. The valves provides additional fuel to the engine during cold start and warm up using a connection of the valve to passages within the carburetor. The additional fuel helps prevent stalling and allows for quicker warm up. Circuits within the ignition system advance the ignition timing during cold running conditions to enhance cold running characteristics.

A malfunction of this component can cause hard starting, stalling or excessive exhaust smoke.

Current to operate the electrothermal valves is supplied by the battery charging coil via wires connected to the engine control unit.

Heat is produced as this current passes through a coil inside the electrothermal valve. This heat is conducted to a wax pellet in the valve. When heated, the wax pellet expands and moves the plunger portion of the valve outward. Movement of the plunger causes the additional fuel or higher idle speed to gradually decrease. The amount of heat produced in the electrothermal valve is directly related to run time, engine speed and the engine temperature gain during warm up. After switching the engine off, the electrothermal valve cools along with the engine. When cool, the plunger moves to a position providing additional fuel or faster idle speed. This allows for automatic temperature compensation and smoother cold engine operation.

Failure of the electrothermal valve can be caused by a failure of the battery charging coil, failure of the internal heat producing coil or failure to generate plunger movement. Testing of the valve involves checking for coil heating, coil resistance testing and checking for plunger movement. Check for coil heating then perform the additional testing as indicated.

Checking for electrothermal valve coil heating

This test requires running the engine on a test tank or under actual running conditions. Perform this test only on a cold engine using a flush/test device or a suitable test tank.

1. Attach a flushing device to the gearcase as described in Chapter Three under *Cooling system flush*.

2. Have an assistant start the engine. Touch the body of the electrothermal valve and note the presence of heat as the engine runs.

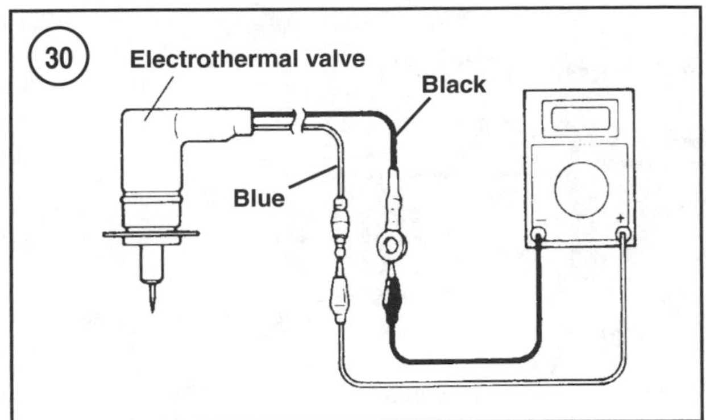

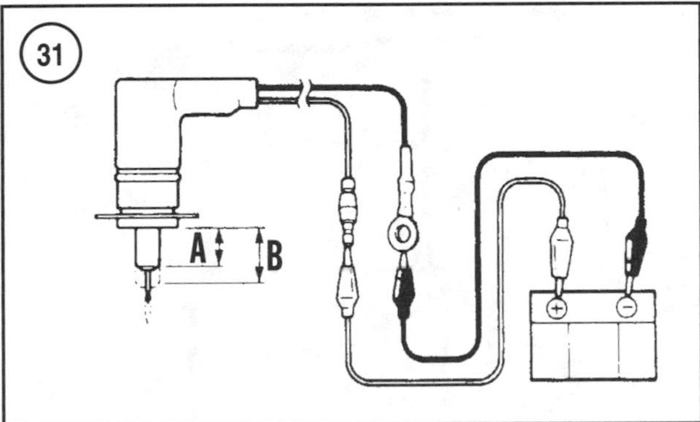

3. A gradual increase in valve temperature should occur as the engine runs. It make take a few minutes before noticing increasing heat.

4. Test the coil resistance and charging system if heating is not detected. Coil resistance and charging system test instructions are provided in this section.

5. Check for plunger movement if symptoms persist and coil heating is detected.

Testing the electrothermal valve coil resistance

Removal of the electrothermal valve is not required for testing provided there is access to the wire connectors for the valve. For accurate test results, use a digital multimeter for this test.

1. Disconnect the negative battery cable to prevent accidental starting.

2. Note the wire routing and connection points. Disconnect the engine harness wires (**Figure 29**) from the upper electrothermal valve. Do not inadvertently disconnect the throttle position sensor wires. The electrothermal valve wires are blue and black. The throttle position sensor wires are red, pink and orange.

3. Connect the positive meter lead onto the blue electrothermal valve wire and the negative meter lead onto the black valve wire (**Figure 30**).

4. The meter must indicate 15-25 ohms. If otherwise, the internal coil is shorted or open and the electrothermal valve must be replaced.

5. Reconnect the blue and black valve wires onto the corresponding engine harness wire connectors. Route the wiring to prevent interference with moving components.

6. Repeat Steps 2-5 for the lower electrothermal valve.

7. Connect the battery cable.

8. Clean the terminals. Connect the cables to the battery if so equipped.

Checking for electrothermal valve plunger movement

WARNING

Use extreme caution when working around batteries. Never smoke or allow sparks to occur in or around a battery. Batteries produce hydrogen gas. Never make the final connection of a circuit to the battery terminal as an arc may occur leading to fire or explosion.

This test checks for electrothermal valve movement when applying a dedicated power source. A fully charged battery, jumper wires, and a small ruler are required to perform this test.

1. Remove the electrothermal valves as described in Chapter Five.

2. Measure the plunger extension at the points indicated (A, **Figure 31**). Record the measurement.

3. Using a jumper lead connect one lead of the electrothermal valve to the positive terminal of a fully charged battery (**Figure 31**).

4. Using a jumper lead connect other lead of the electrothermal valve to the negative terminal of a fully charged battery (**Figure 31**).

5. Maintain the connections for 5-7 minutes.

6. With all leads connected to the battery measure and record the plunger extension at the points indicated in B, **Figure 31**.

7. Compare the measurement in Step 2 with measurement in Step 6. Replace the electrothermal valve if no difference in measurement is indicated.

8. Install the electrothermal valve as described in Chapter Five.

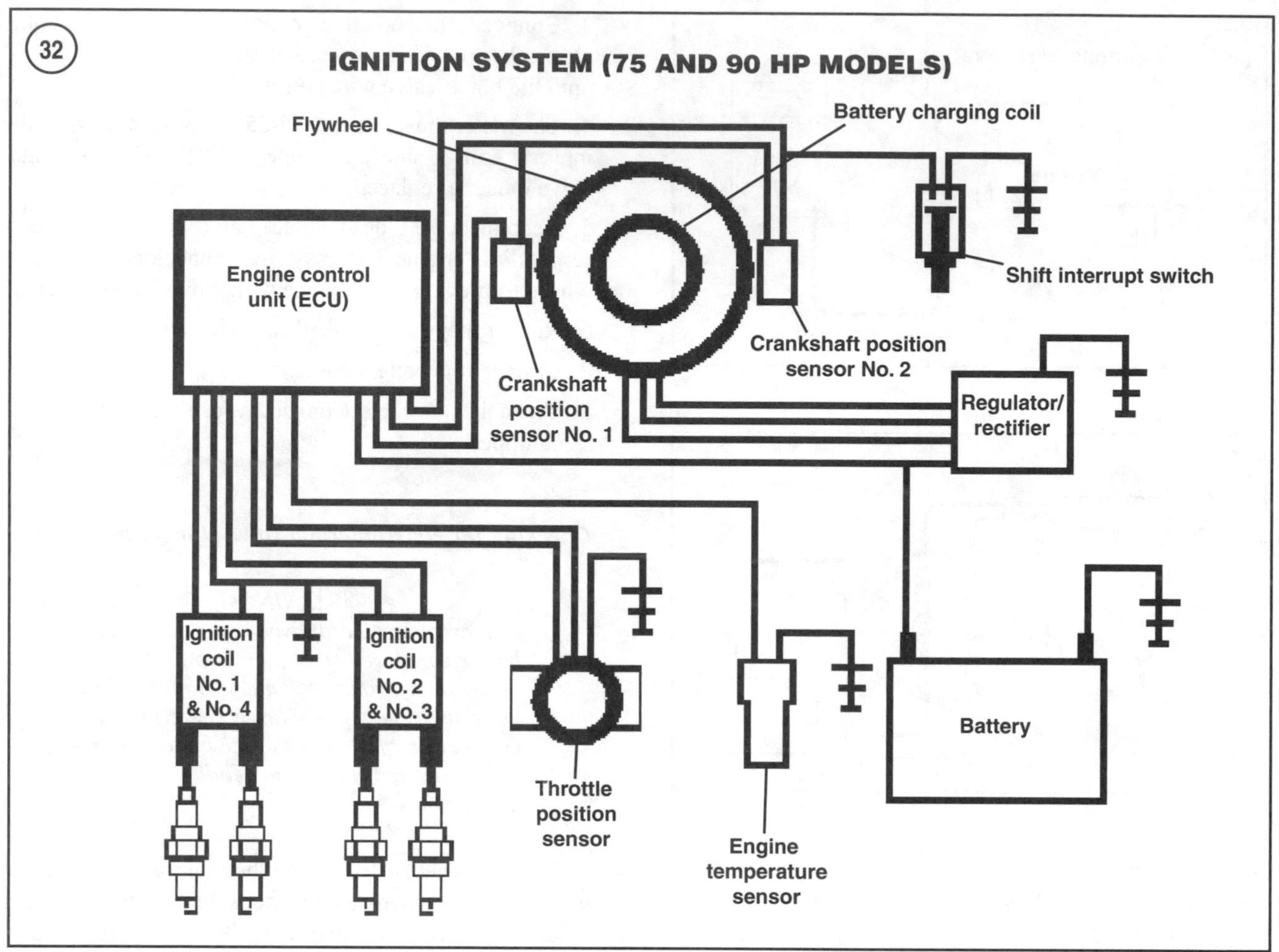

IGNITION SYSTEM TROUBLESHOOTING

Outboard engines consistently run at a higher speed than most internal combustion engines. This places a greater burden on the ignition system and other engine systems. Proper engine operation is only possible when the ignition system is operating correctly. Spark must be generated at the plugs several thousand times per minute and each spark must occur at exactly the right time.

This section provides a brief description on the various systems used on Mercury and Mariner four-stroke outboards followed by testing instructions for the various components.

Ignition System Operation (75 and 90 hp Models)

An ignition system wiring diagram is provided in **Figure 32**. These models utilize a direct current (DC) powered capacitor discharge type ignition system. The battery and charging system provides the electric current to operate the system. Two separate wires supply battery voltage to the system. A red wire connects the battery positive (+) terminal to the rectifier/regulator and a terminal on the engine control unit (ECU). Battery voltage is continuously supplied to the ECU using this wire. A white wire connects the ignition switch stop circuit to the ECU. This wire is connected to engine ground when the ignition switch is in the *off* position.

Electrical current from the red wire powers special circuits increasing the battery voltage to 165-200 volts. This current is stored in an internal capacitor for later release.

Low voltage pulses are developed as the raised bosses on the flywheel pass near the two crankshaft position sensors. These pulses are directed to the ECU (**Figure 32**).

Using the input from the crankshaft position sensors, the ECU determines which plugs to fire and the correct time to initiate a spark. Timing adjustment is not required on this model.

At the correct time, the ECU signal activates a silicon controlled rectifier (SCR) within the unit, which causes

the voltage stored in the capacitor to release into the ignition coil primary winding. As the voltage flows through the primary winding, a much higher voltage develops in the coil secondary winding. This voltage is directed to the spark plugs.

This type of ignition system is commonly referred to as a double fire system. Cylinders 1 and 4 fire simultaneously and cylinders 2 and 3 fire simultaneously. When one piston is nearing the top of its compression stroke the other piston is nearing the top of its exhaust stroke. The second spark occurs during the exhaust stroke, burning any unburned fuel.

These models are equipped with a throttle position sensor (**Figure 33**). The sensor is mounted to the port side of the bottom carburetor and couples to the carburetor throttle shaft. This allows the sensor shaft to rotate as the throttle opens and closes. A varying voltage signal from the throttle position sensor allows the ECU to accurately determine the position of the throttle. The ECU uses this information to calculate the optimum ignition timing settings for all throttle settings.

A temperature sensor is incorporated into the ECU. It provides input to the ECU, indicating the approximate ambient temperature within the engine cover. This feature allows changes in ignition timing to enhance cold engine running characteristics. This feature provides a faster idle (approximately 1100 rpm) during cold engine operation. Depending on the ambient temperature, this faster idle speed can occur for up to 5 minutes after starting the engine.

The engine temperature sensor (**Figure 34**) provides a varying resistance value based upon the temperature of the engine cooling water. Input from the sensor is used by the ECU to compute the optimum ignition timing. This input is also used by the ECU to activate the overheat warning system.

The shift interrupt switch connects to the red/white wire leading to the No. 2 crankshaft position sensor. The switch mounts onto the shift cable and linkage bracket on the lower port side of the power head. The normal shifting loads that occur when shifting out of forward gear will cause the linkages to momentarily depress the plunger. Depressing the plunger grounds the red/white wire leading to the No. 2 crankshaft position sensor; causing ignition to cease on cylinders No. 1 and No. 4. This reduces the load on the sliding clutch to allow easier shifting to neutral gear. The switch must reset after shifting. Otherwise the red/white wire will remain grounded, preventing ignition on cylinders No. 1 and No. 4.

Low oil pressure and overspeed protection circuits are also integrated into the ECU. Refer to *Warning Systems Troubleshooting* in this chapter for additional information. When activated, the ignition key switch or lanyard safety switch grounds the stop circuit. Grounding the stop circuit causes the ECU to ground the circuit that charges the capacitor, which disables the ignition system and stops the engine.

The ECU provides a limp-home feature in the event of sensor failure. The ignition timing is set at 10° BTDC if the input from the throttle position or engine temperature sensor extends beyond the normal operating ranges. This feature allows for continued engine operation at reduced power output.

Ignition System Test Sequence (75 and 90 hp Models)

Refer to **Tables 5-8** for test specifications. Wiring diagrams are at the end of the manual. Always refer to *Preliminary Inspection* in this chapter before performing any testing. Many times ignition problems are the result of dirty, loose, corroded or damaged wire connections. Wasted time and the replacement of good components results from not performing these preliminary steps. The recommended general troubleshooting procedure is listed below.

1. Stop circuit test.
2. Engine control unit (ECU) output test.

3. Rectifier/regulator output test.
4. Battery charging coil output test.
5. Battery charging coil resistance test.
6. Crankshaft position sensor output test.
7. Crankshaft position sensor resistance test.
8. Ignition coil resistance test.
9. Spark plug wire resistance test.
10. Throttle position sensor voltage test.
11. Engine temperature sensor resistance test.
12. Shift interrupt switch test.

Stop circuit test (75 and 90 hp models)

A faulty stop circuit usually results in an inability to start the engine. Starting is difficult as the fault prevents proper charging of the capacitor in the engine control unit (ECU).

In some cases the engine will start yet suffer an ignition misfire at various engine speeds. A partial short to ground in this circuit prevents the capacitor from being fully charged. This fault prevents adequate voltage to the ignition coil and spark plug. This fault is usually evident at higher engine speeds. Generally a higher voltage is required to fire the plugs at higher engine speeds.

A faulty stop circuit can also result in an inability to switch the engine off.

The stop circuit includes the ignition switch, lanyard safety switch and associated wiring.

Refer to *Spark Test* in this chapter to determine if spark is present prior to testing the stop circuit. A problem with the stop circuit is unlikely if spark is present at the spark plug(s), however testing may indicate a partial short or intermittent problem. Perform all tests without running the engine.

1. Disconnect the negative battery cable to prevent accidental starting.
2. Disconnect the engine wire harness from the instrument harness adapter (**Figure 35**). Refer to **Figure 36** to locate the terminal for the white wire. Make sure to select the terminal in the adapter harness instead of the engine wire harness connector.
3. Calibrate the multimeter to the R × 1 scale. Connect the negative meter lead onto a suitable engine ground. Touch the positive meter lead onto the adapter harness terminal for the white wire in the harness adapter (**Figure 36**).
4. Place the ignition key switch in the ON or RUN position. Make sure the lanyard safety switch is in the normal or RUN position. Note the meter reading and place the ignition key switch in the START position. The meter must indicate *no continuity* in the ON or RUN and START positions. If otherwise, a fault is present in the ignition key switch, lanyard safety switch or wiring. Test the ignition key switch as described in this chapter. See *Electric Starting System Troubleshooting* in this chapter. Proceed with testing if no fault is found with the ignition key switch.

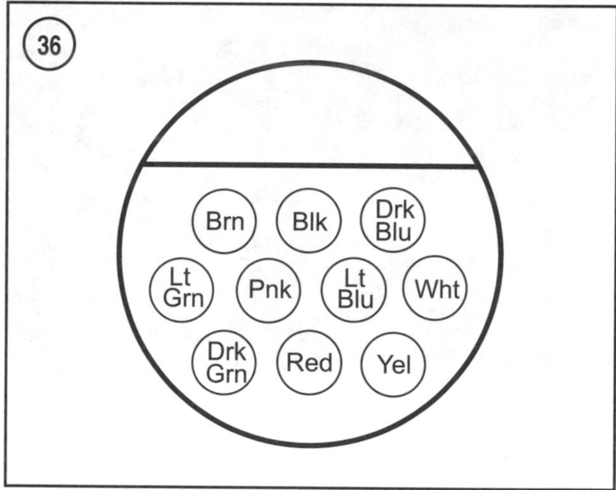

5. Connect the meter test leads as described in Step 3. Place the ignition key switch in the ON or RUN position. Observe the meter and pull the cord from the lanyard safety switch. The meter must change from *no continuity* to *continuity* when the lanyard safety switch is activated. If not, the lanyard safety switch or related wiring is faulty and must be replaced.

6. With the meter leads attached as described in Step 3, place the ignition key switch in the OFF or STOP position. The meter must indicate *continuity*. If otherwise, the ignition key switch or wiring is faulty. Test the ignition key switch as described in this chapter. Repair or replace the instrument wire harness if no fault is found with the ignition key switch.

7. If all stop circuit components function correctly, but the ignition system does not produce spark, perform the engine control unit output test as described in this section.

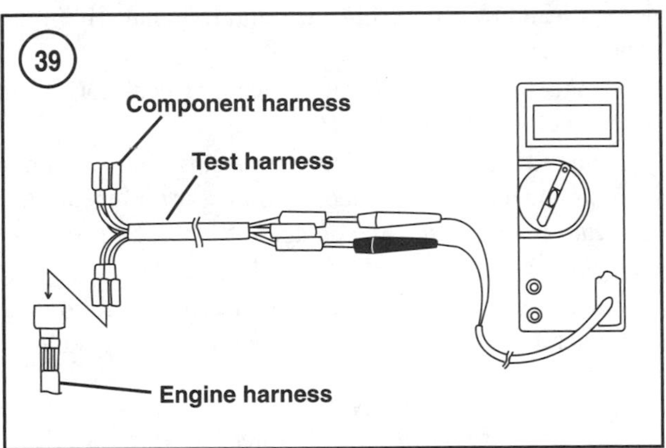

Engine control (ECU) unit output test
(75 and 90 hp models)

Perform the engine control unit peak output test if spark is missing or weak on all or a pair of cylinders. A faulty ignition coil or spark plug wire is likely if spark is missing or weak on a single cylinder.

This test measures the peak voltage delivered to the ignition coils. An accurate tachometer, test harness (part No. 91-804771) and a multimeter capable of measuring peak voltage are required for this procedure.

This test must be performed under actual operating conditions.

WARNING
On-water testing or adjustments require two people. One person to operate the boat, the other to monitor the gauges or test equipment and make necessary adjustments. All personnel must remain seated inside the boat at all times. Do not lean over the transom while the boat is under way. Use extensions to allow all gauges and test equipment to be located in normal seating areas.

1. Disconnect the negative battery cable. Push up and in on the locking tabs, then remove the electrical component cover (**Figure 37**).
2. Disconnect the engine upper harness connector from the engine control unit (**Figure 38**).
3. Connect the test harness to the engine wire harness plug and to the engine control unit as shown in **Figure 39**.
4. Connect the positive meter lead to the white/blue wire terminal of the test harness. Connect the negative lead to the white wire terminal of the test harness.
5. Select the peak DC volts function on the meter.
6. Route the test leads and harness away from any moving components. Clamp them as necessary to ensure the test leads maintain secure contact to the test harness during engine operation.
7. Attach the shop tachometer to the engine following the manufacturer's instructions. Connect the battery cable.

NOTE
*Some tests must be performed at cranking speed. Disconnect and ground all spark plug wires to allow electric starter operation without starting the engine or disabling the ignition system. Refer to **Spark Test** in this chapter for spark plug wire removal and installation instructions.*

8. Observe the meter readings while an assistant operates the engine at the speeds indicated in **Table 5**. Record the voltage readings for each speed range.
9. Stop the engine. Connect the positive meter lead to the white/green wire terminal of the test harness and the negative lead to the white wire terminal of the test harness.
10. Have an assistant operate the engine at the speeds indicated in **Table 5**. Record the voltage readings for each speed range.
11. Stop the engine and compare the meter readings with the specifications listed in **Table 5**. Refer to the following:
    a. Test the ignition coil for cylinders No. 2 and No. 3 if the voltage readings in Step 8 are above the specifi-

cation in **Table 5**. Follow the test instructions provided in this section.

b. Test the ignition coil for cylinders No. 1 and No. 4 if the voltage readings in Step 10 are above the specification listed in **Table 5**. Follow the test instructions provided in this section.

c. Test the crankshaft position sensor resistance and crankshaft position sensor peak output and the shift interrupt switch if the voltage readings in Step 8 or Step 10 are below the specification in **Table 5**. Follow the test instructions provided in this section.

12. Perform the rectifier/regulator output test if the crankshaft position sensor tests correctly but incorrect test results are noted in Step 8 and Step 10. Follow the test instructions provided in this section.

13. A faulty fuse, wire harness or engine control unit is indicated if the crankshaft position sensor, ignition coil and charging system test correctly but the misfire persists. Check the fuses and wire harness before replacing the engine control unit. Refer to *Engine Control Unit* in this section for additional information.

14. Disconnect the negative battery cable. Disconnect the test leads and test harness from the engine. Connect the engine harness connector to the engine control unit connector (**Figure 38**).

15. Carefully snap the electrical component cover onto the retaining slots. Ensure the locking tabs fully engage the slots. Connect the battery cable.

Rectifier/regulator output test (75 and 90 hp models)

Perform the rectifier/regulator output test if spark is missing or weak on all cylinders. A faulty crankshaft position sensor, shift interrupt switch or ignition coil is likely if spark is missing or weak on a pair of cylinders. A faulty ignition coil or spark plug wire is likely if spark is missing or weak on a single cylinder.

This test measures the peak voltage delivered by the rectifier/regulator. An accurate tachometer and a multimeter capable of measuring peak voltage are required for this procedure.

This test must be performed under actual operating conditions.

WARNING

On-water testing or adjustments require two people: one person to operate the boat, the other to monitor the gauges or test equipment and make necessary adjustments. All personnel must remain seated inside the boat at all times. Do not lean over the transom while the boat is under way. Use extensions to allow all gauges and test equipment to be located in normal seating areas.

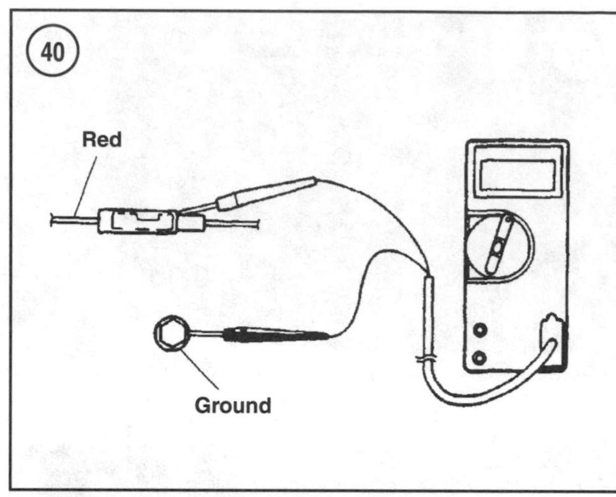

1. Disconnect the negative battery cable. Push up and in on the locking tabs, then remove the electrical component cover (**Figure 37**).

2. Ground the negative meter lead. Insert the positive meter lead between the bullet connector (**Figure 40**) for the red wire leading into the rectifier/regulator (A, **Figure 41**). Do not disconnect the red wire for this test. Make sure the test lead probe contacts the metal terminal within the connector.

3. Connect the battery cable. Select the peak DC volts function on the meter.

4. Route the test leads and harness away from any moving components. Clamp them as necessary to ensure the test leads maintain secure contact to the test harness during engine operation.

5. Attach the shop tachometer to the engine following manufacturer's instructions. Connect the battery cable.

NOTE

*Some tests must be performed at cranking speed. Disconnect and ground all spark plug wires to allow electric starter operation without starting the engine or disabling the ignition system. Refer to **Spark Test** in this chapter for spark plug wire removal and installation instructions.*

6. Observe the meter readings while an assistant operates the engine at the speeds indicated in **Table 5**. Record the voltage readings for each speed range.

7. Stop the engine. Disconnect the negative battery cable, then remove the test leads.

8. Connect the battery cable.

9. Compare the meter readings with the specifications in **Table 5**. Refer to the following:
   a. Output voltage is below the specification at any engine speed—Perform the battery charging coil output test as described in this section. Perform the rectifier/regulator resistance test (see *Charging System Troubleshooting*) if the ignition coil output test correctly.
   b. Output is above the specification—Perform the rectifier/regulator resistance test as described in this chapter under *Charging System Troubleshooting*.
10. Disconnect the test leads.

Battery charging coil output test (75 and 90 hp models)

Perform the battery charging coil output test if spark is missing or weak on all cylinders and low output voltage is measured at the rectifier/regulator.

This test measures the peak voltage delivered by the battery charging coil. An accurate tachometer, test harness (part No. 91-804772) and a multimeter capable of measuring peak voltage are required for this procedure. This test must be performed under actual operating conditions.

WARNING

On-water testing or adjustments require two people: one to operate the boat, the other to monitor the gauges or test equipment and make necessary adjustments. All personnel must remain seated inside the boat at all times. Do not lean over the transom while the boat is under way. Use extensions to allow all gauges and test equipment to be located in normal seating areas.

1. Disconnect the negative battery cable. Push up and in on the locking tabs, then remove the electrical component cover (**Figure 37**).
2. Disconnect the battery charging coil harness connector (B, **Figure 41**) from the rectifier/regulator harness.
3. Connect the test harness to the battery charging coil harness connector and to rectifier/regulator harness connector as shown in **Figure 39**.
4. Select the peak DC volts function on the meter.
5. Attach the shop tachometer to the engine following the manufacturer's instructions.
6. Connect the positive meter lead to the red wire terminal of the test harness. Connect the negative lead to the white wire test terminal of the test harness. Route the test leads and harness away from any moving components. Clamp them as necessary to ensure the test leads maintain secure contact to the test harness during engine operation. Connect the battery cable.

NOTE

*Some tests must be performed at cranking speed. Disconnect and ground all spark plug wires to allow electric starter operation without starting the engine or disabling the ignition system. Refer to **Spark Test** in this chapter for spark plug wire removal and installation instructions.*

7. Observe the meter readings while an assistant operates the engine at the speeds indicated in **Table 5**. Record the voltage readings for each speed range.
8. Stop the engine. Connect the positive meter lead to the red wire terminal of the test harness and the negative lead to the black wire terminal of the test harness.
9. Have an assistant operate the engine at the speeds indicated in **Table 5**. Record the voltage readings for each speed range.
10. Stop the engine. Connect the positive meter lead to the white wire terminal of the test harness and the negative lead to the black wire terminal of the test harness.
11. Have an assistant operate the engine at the speeds indicated in **Table 5**. Record the voltage readings for each speed range.
12. Stop the engine. Disconnect the negative battery cable.
13. Remove the test harness and connect the battery charging coil harness connector onto the rectifier/regulator harness connector.
14. Compare the meter readings with the specifications listed in **Table 5**. Refer to the following:
   a. If meter reading is below the specification at any speed range, perform the battery charging coil resistance test as described in this section and inspect the

flywheel for damaged magnets. See *Flywheel Removal and Installation* in Chapter Seven. Replace the battery charging coil if it fails the resistance test or if low output voltage is evident and no defect is found with the flywheel.

b. If meter reading is above the specification, perform the engine control unit output test as described in this section.

15. Snap the electrical component cover onto the retaining slots. Make sure the locking tabs fully engage the slots. Connect the battery cable.

Battery charging coil resistance test (75 and 90 hp models)

Perform the battery charging coil resistance test if the battery charging coil output voltage is below the specification. A test harness (part No. 91-804772) and an accurate digital multimeter are required for this procedure.

1. Disconnect the negative battery cable. Push up and in on the locking tabs, then remove the electrical component cover (**Figure 37**).
2. Disconnect the battery charging coil harness connector (B, **Figure 41**) from the rectifier/regulator harness.
3. Plug the test harness onto the battery charging coil harness connector. Do not plug the test harness onto the rectifier/regulator harness connector for this procedure.
4. Select the R × 1 scale on the meter. Touch the meter test leads to the test harness wire colors specified in **Table 6**. Test lead polarity is not important for this test. The meter must indicate 0.32-0.48 ohm at each pair of connection points. If otherwise, replace the battery charging coil as described in Chapter Six.
5. Remove the test harness and connect the battery charging coil harness connector onto the rectifier/regulator harness connector.
6. Connect the battery cable.
7. Carefully snap the electrical component cover onto the retaining slots. Make sure the locking tabs fully engage the slots. Connect the battery cable.

Crankshaft position sensor output test (75 and 90 hp models)

Perform the crankshaft position sensor output test if spark is missing or weak on cylinders 1 and 4 or cylinders 2 and 3. The No. 1 crankshaft position sensor triggers ignition on cylinders No. 1 and No. 4. The No. 2 crankshaft position sensor triggers ignition on cylinders No. 2 and No. 3 (**Figure 32**).

At times a sensor malfunction can occur randomly and result in intermittent ignition misfire. A buildup of oil, grease or other contamination can cause the crankshaft position sensor to malfunction. If allowed to build to a sufficient thickness the deposits prevent the sensor from detecting the passing of the flywheel bosses. Clean excessive oil, grease or other deposits from the crankshaft position sensor and the flywheel bosses with a light solvent.

This test measures the peak voltage delivered by the crankshaft position sensors. An accurate tachometer, test harness (part No. 91-804771) and a multimeter capable of measuring peak voltage are required for this procedure. This test must be performed under actual operating conditions.

WARNING

On-water testing or adjustments require two people: one to operate the boat, the other to monitor the gauges or test equipment and make necessary adjustments. All personnel must remain seated inside the boat at all times. Do not lean over the transom while the boat is under way. Use extensions to allow all gauges and test equipment to be located in normal seating areas.

1. Disconnect the negative battery cable. Push up and in on the locking tabs, then remove the electrical component cover (**Figure 37**).
2. Disconnect the engine upper harness connector from the engine control unit (**Figure 38**).
3. Connect the test harness to the engine wire harness plug and to the engine control unit as shown in **Figure 39**.
4. Select the peak DC volts function on the meter.
5. Connect the positive meter lead to the white/yellow wire terminal of the test harness. Connect the negative lead to the white wire terminal of the test harness.
6. Route the test leads and harness away from any moving components. Clamp them as necessary to ensure the test leads maintain secure contact to the test harness during engine operation.
7. Attach the shop tachometer to the engine following manufacturer's instructions. Connect the battery cable.

NOTE

*Some tests must be performed at cranking speed. Disconnect and ground all spark plug wires to allow electric starter operation without starting the engine or disabling the ignition system. Refer to **Spark Test** in this chapter for spark plug wire removal and installation instructions.*

8. Observe the meter readings while an assistant operates the engine at the speeds indicated in **Table 5**. Record the voltage readings for each speed range.

9. Stop the engine. Connect the positive meter lead to the white/red wire terminal of the test harness and the negative lead to the white wire terminal of the test harness.

10. Have an assistant operate the engine at the speeds indicated in **Table 5**. Record the voltage readings for each speed range.

11. Stop the engine and compare the meter readings with the specifications listed in **Table 5**. Refer to the following:

   a. If the voltage recorded in Step 8 or Step 10 is above the specification at any engine speed, replace the engine control unit (ECU) as described in Chapter Six.

   b. If the voltage recorded in Step 8 is below the specification at any engine speed, the crankshaft position sensor for cylinders No. 2 and No. 3 or the flywheel is faulty. Perform the crankshaft position sensor resistance test as described in this section and inspect the flywheel for damaged magnets. See *Flywheel Removal and Installation* in Chapter Seven. Replace the crankshaft position sensor if it fails the resistance test or if low output voltage is evident and no defect is found with the flywheel.

   c. If the voltage recorded in Step 10 is below the specification at any engine speed, the crankshaft position sensor for cylinders No. 1 and No. 4 or the flywheel is faulty. Perform the crankshaft position sensor resistance test as described in this section and inspect the flywheel for damaged magnets. See *Flywheel Removal and Installation* in Chapter Seven. Replace the crankshaft position sensor if it fails the resistance test or if low output voltage is evident and no defect is found with the flywheel.

12. Disconnect the negative battery cable.

13. Disconnect the test leads and test harness from the engine. Connect the engine harness connector onto the engine control unit connector (**Figure 38**).

14. Carefully snap the electrical component cover onto the retaining slots. Ensure the locking tabs fully engage the slots. Connect the battery cable.

Crankshaft position sensor resistance test (75 and 90 hp models)

Perform the crankshaft position sensor resistance test if the crankshaft position sensor output voltage is below the specification. A test harness (part No. 91-804771) and an accurate digital multimeter are required for this procedure.

1. Disconnect the negative battery cable. Push up and in on the locking tabs, then remove the electrical component cover (**Figure 37**).

2. Disconnect the engine upper harness connector from the engine control unit (ECU) (**Figure 38**).

3. Connect the test harness onto the engine wire harness connector. Do not plug the test harness onto the ECU for this test.

4. Select the R × 100 scale on the meter. Touch the meter test leads to the test harness wire colors specified in **Table 6**. Test lead polarity is not important for this test. The meter must indicate 445-545 ohm at each pair of connection points. If otherwise, replace the faulty crankshaft position sensor(s) as described in Chapter Six.

5. Remove the test harness and connect the engine harness connector onto the ECU connector (**Figure 38**).

6. Connect the battery cable.

7. Snap the electrical component cover onto the retaining slots. Ensure the locking tabs fully engage the slots. Connect the battery cable.

Ignition coil resistance test (75 and 90 hp models)

Resistance testing checks for open circuits or short circuits in the primary and secondary windings of the ignition coil.

The wire length used for the primary winding of the ignition coil is relatively short and the resistance readings are fairly low. A much longer length of wire is used in the secondary winding and the resistance readings are relatively high. Use a digital multimeter for the most accurate test results. Usually, a fault within the ignition coil surfaces when the resistance is tested. Ignition coil test specifications are listed in **Table 6**. Make all resistance tests at approximately 68° F (20° C) to ensure accurate test results.

Bear in mind that a resistance test only indicates a short or open circuit. Faults within the coil may result in internal arcing that prevents a strong blue spark at the spark plug. If an internal short is present a clicking noise emanates from the coil while attempting to start the engine. Use a spark test tool to check for a good strong blue spark as the engine is cranked. Refer to *Spark Test* in this chapter for instructions on using a spark test tool. Test both the primary and secondary resistance for each coil on the engine. Removal of the ignition coil is not required for testing provided there is access to the wire terminals. Refer to Chapter Six if coil removal is required. An accurate digital multimeter is required for this procedure.

1. Disconnect the negative battery cable to prevent accidental starting.

2. Remove the screws (**Figure 42**) and plastic cover on the rear of the power head to access the spark plug wires.

Two screws are located on the top, two screws are located on the bottom and one screw is located on the side and midway down on the cover.

3. Mark the cylinder number on the spark plug wires before removing them from the spark plugs. The top cylinder is the No. 1 cylinder. Gently twist the spark plug caps to free them from the plugs, then pull the cap from the plug. Never pull on the spark plug wire to free the cap.

4. Remove the screw, then disconnect the black coil wires from the engine ground. Note the wire routing and connection points, then unplug the black/white ignition coil wires from the black/white and black/orange engine harness wires.

5. To test the primary coil resistance, calibrate the meter to the R × 1 scale. Then touch the meter test leads onto the black/white and black coil wire terminals (**Figure 43**). Polarity is not important for this test. The meter must indicate 0.078-0.106 ohm. If otherwise, the primary winding is shorted or open and the coil must be replaced.

6. To test the secondary coil resistance, calibrate the meter to the R × 1K scale. Unthread the two spark plug wires from the coil. Touch the meter test leads to the spark plug wire terminals in the coil (**Figure 44**). Polarity is not important for this test. The meter must indicate 3500-4700 ohms. If otherwise the secondary coil winding is shorted or open and the coil must be replaced.

7. Test the remaining ignition coil as described in Step 5 and Step 6.

8. Before installation, test the spark plug wire resistance as described in this section.

9. Carefully thread the spark plug wires onto the ignition coil terminals.

10. Secure the ignition coil black ground wires and the engine wire harness black wire onto the ground with the screw.

11. Connect the ignition coil black/white wires onto the respective black/white and black/orange engine harness wires.

12. Connect the spark plug wires onto the correct spark plugs. Ensure that all leads are routed correctly.

13. Fit the plastic cover onto the rear of the power head. Install the cover screws and tighten in a crossing pattern to 65 in.-lb. (7.3 N•m).

14. Connect the battery cable.

Spark plug wire resistance test (75 and 90 hp models)

Inspect the spark plug wires for cracks in the insulation, abraded surfaces or a weathered appearance. Defective insulation allows arcing to the cylinder block or other surfaces. This condition results in an ignition misfire and creates a potentially hazardous condition. The spark plug wires thread into the ignition coil to allow individual replacement. The amount of wire resistance varies by the cylinder in which the wire connects. Always mark the cylinder number on the wire and coil prior to removal.

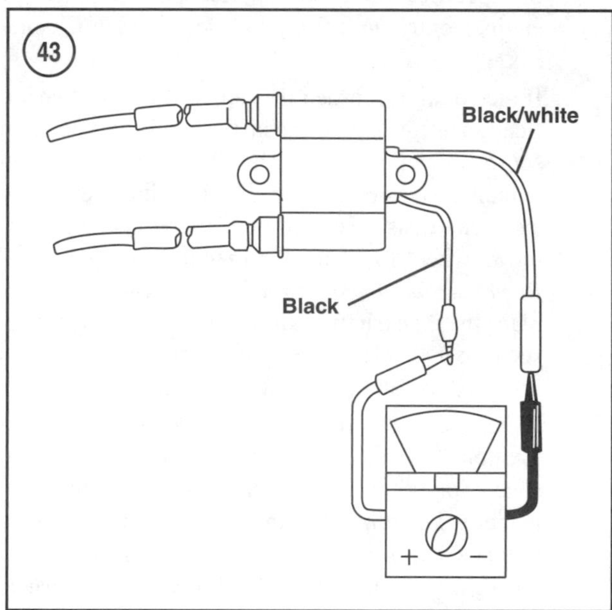

1. Disconnect the negative battery cable to prevent accidental starting.

2. Remove the screws (**Figure 42**) and plastic cover on the rear of the power head to access the spark plug wires. Two screws are located on the top, two screws are located on the bottom and one screw is located on the side and midway down on the cover.

3. Mark the cylinder number on the spark plug wires before removing them from the spark plugs. The top cylinder is the No. 1 cylinder. Gently twist the spark plug caps to free them from the plugs, then pull the cap from the plug. Never pull on the spark plug wire to free the cap.

4. Carefully unthread the two spark plug wires from the coil.

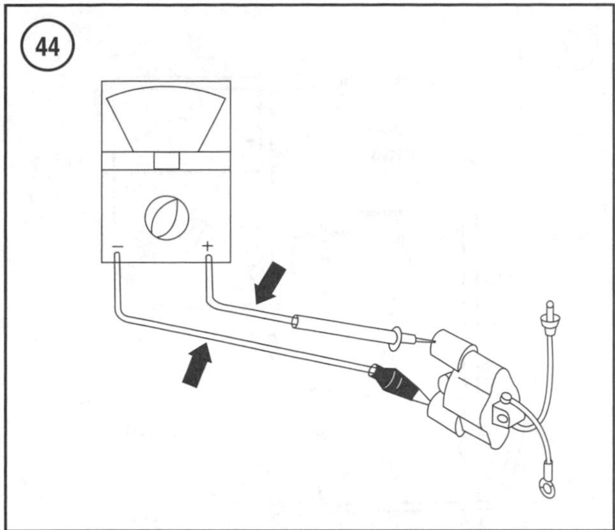

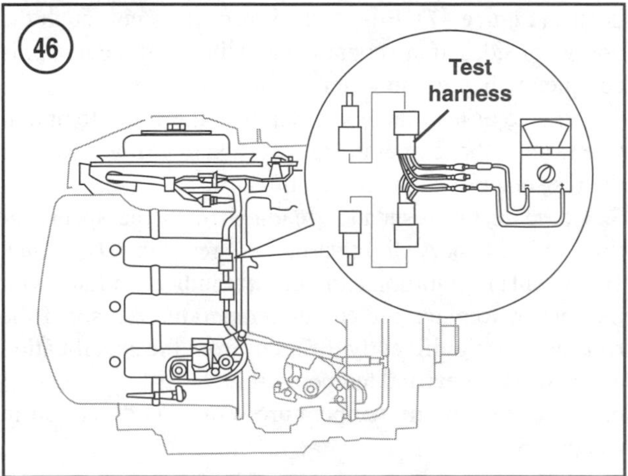

5. Calibrate the multimeter onto the R × 1K scale then connect the test leads to each end of the spark plug wire. Note the resistance and the cylinder from which the lead was removed. Test lead polarity is not important for this test. Replace the spark plug wire if the resistance is not as specified in **Table 6**.
6. Repeat Step 5 for the remaining three spark plug wires.
7. Carefully thread the spark plug wires onto the ignition coils.
8. Connect the spark plug wires onto the correct spark plugs. Ensure that all leads are routed correctly.
9. Fit the plastic cover onto the rear of the power head. Install the cover screws and tighten in a crossing pattern to 65 in.-lb. (7.3 N•m).
10. Connect the battery cable.

Throttle position sensor voltage test (75 and 90 hp models)

A defective throttle position sensor (**Figure 33**) can cause poor performance at higher throttle settings, hesitation during acceleration or excessively fast idle speed. The engine control unit (ECU) will fix the ignition timing at 10° BTDC if it detects a fault with the throttle position sensor.

Improper throttle position sensor adjustment can cause the same symptoms as a faulty one. Always adjust the throttle position sensor (Chapter Four) prior to performing any testing. This test measures the input voltage supplied to the sensor by the ECU and then measures the output voltage supplied to the ECU by the sensor.

A digital multimeter, shop tachometer and test harness (part No. 91-805773) are required for this test. Testing requires running the engine under actual operating conditions.

WARNING

On-water testing or adjustments require two people: one to operate the boat, the other to monitor the gauges or test equipment and make necessary adjustments. All personnel must remain seated inside the boat at all times. Do not lean over the transom while the boat is under way. Use extensions to allow all gauges and test equipment to be located in normal seating areas.

1. Disconnect the negative battery cable.
2. Disconnect the throttle position sensor harness connector from the engine wire harness connector (**Figure 45**).
3. Connect the test harness to the engine wire harness plug and to the throttle position sensor harness as shown in **Figure 46**.
4. Select the DC volts function on the meter.
5. Connect the positive meter lead to the red wire terminal of the test harness. Connect the negative lead to the orange wire terminal of the test harness.

6. Route the test leads and harness away from any moving components. Clamp them as necessary to ensure the test leads maintain secure contact to the test harness during engine operation.
7. Attach the shop tachometer to the engine following manufacturer's instructions. Connect the battery cable.
8. Observe the meter readings while an assistant operates the engine at the 850 rpm in FORWARD gear. The meter must indicate 4.75-5.25 volts. A faulty ECU or wiring is indicated if the input voltage is not within the specification. Inspect the wires which connect the throttle position sensor to the ECU for damaged insulation, broken wires or faulty terminals. Replace the ECU if the input voltage is incorrect and no fault is found with the wiring.
9. Stop the engine. Connect the positive meter lead to the pink wire terminal of the test harness. Connect the negative lead to the orange wire terminal of the test harness.
10. Observe the meter readings while an assistant operates the engine at the 850 rpm in FORWARD gear. The meter must indicate 0.68-0.82 volt. A faulty or improperly adjusted throttle position sensor is indicated if the voltage is not within the specification. If necessary, readjust the sensor as described in Chapter Four and repeat the test. Replace the sensor if the output voltage is not within the specification after adjustment.
11. Connect the meter test leads to the test harness as described in Step 9. Have an assistant start the engine and shift into FORWARD gear. Monitor the meter while the assistant *slowly* advances the throttle to full-open. Then, monitor the meter while the assistant *slowly* closes the throttle to the idle position. The meter must indicate a steady increase in voltage as the throttle advances and a steady decrease as the throttle closes. Replace the throttle position sensor as described in Chapter Five if the voltage reading is erratic or does not increase and decrease as described.
12. Stop the engine and disconnect the negative battery cable.
13. Remove the test harness and connect the engine wire harness connector to the throttle position sensor harness connector. To prevent potential interference with the throttle linkages, secure the connector with a plastic locking clamp as shown in **Figure 45**.
14. Connect the battery cable.

Engine temperature sensor resistance test (75 and 90 hp models)

A fault with the engine temperature sensor can cause poor cold engine operating characteristics, excessively high idle speed on a fully warmed engine, or improper activation of the overheat warning system. The engine control unit (ECU) will fix the ignition timing at 10° BTDC if it detects a fault with the engine temperature sensor.

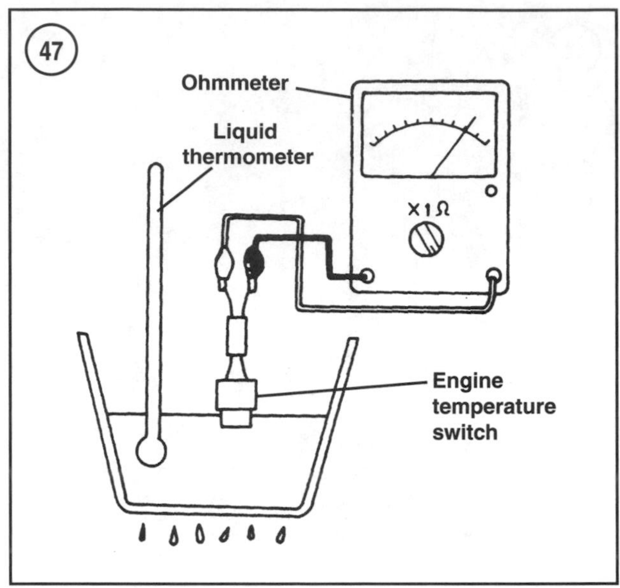

This test requires an accurate digital or analog multimeter, a liquid thermometer and a container of water that can be heated.

1. Remove the engine temperature sensor as described in Chapter Six.
2. Calibrate the meter onto the appropriate ohms scale for the resistance specification in **Table 8**. Connect the meter leads between the two sensor terminals. Test lead polarity is not important for this test.
3. Suspend the sensor in a container of water that can be heated (**Figure 47**). Ensure the sensor does not touch the bottom or sides of the container and the tip of the sensor is completely below the water surface.
4. Add ice or heat the container until the water temperature reaches the temperatures specified in **Table 8**. Record the resistance at each temperature.
5. Compare the resistance readings with the specifications in **Table 8**. A slight variance is resistance (less than 10 percent) is common and does not indicate a fault with the sensor. Replace the engine temperature sensor if the resistance is significantly different from the specification at any of the specified temperatures.
6. Install the engine temperature sensor as described in Chapter Six.

Shift interrupt switch test (75 and 90 hp models).

Perform this test if spark is missing only on cylinder No. 1 and No. 4 and the crankshaft position sensors and ignition coils test correctly. The shift interrupt switch

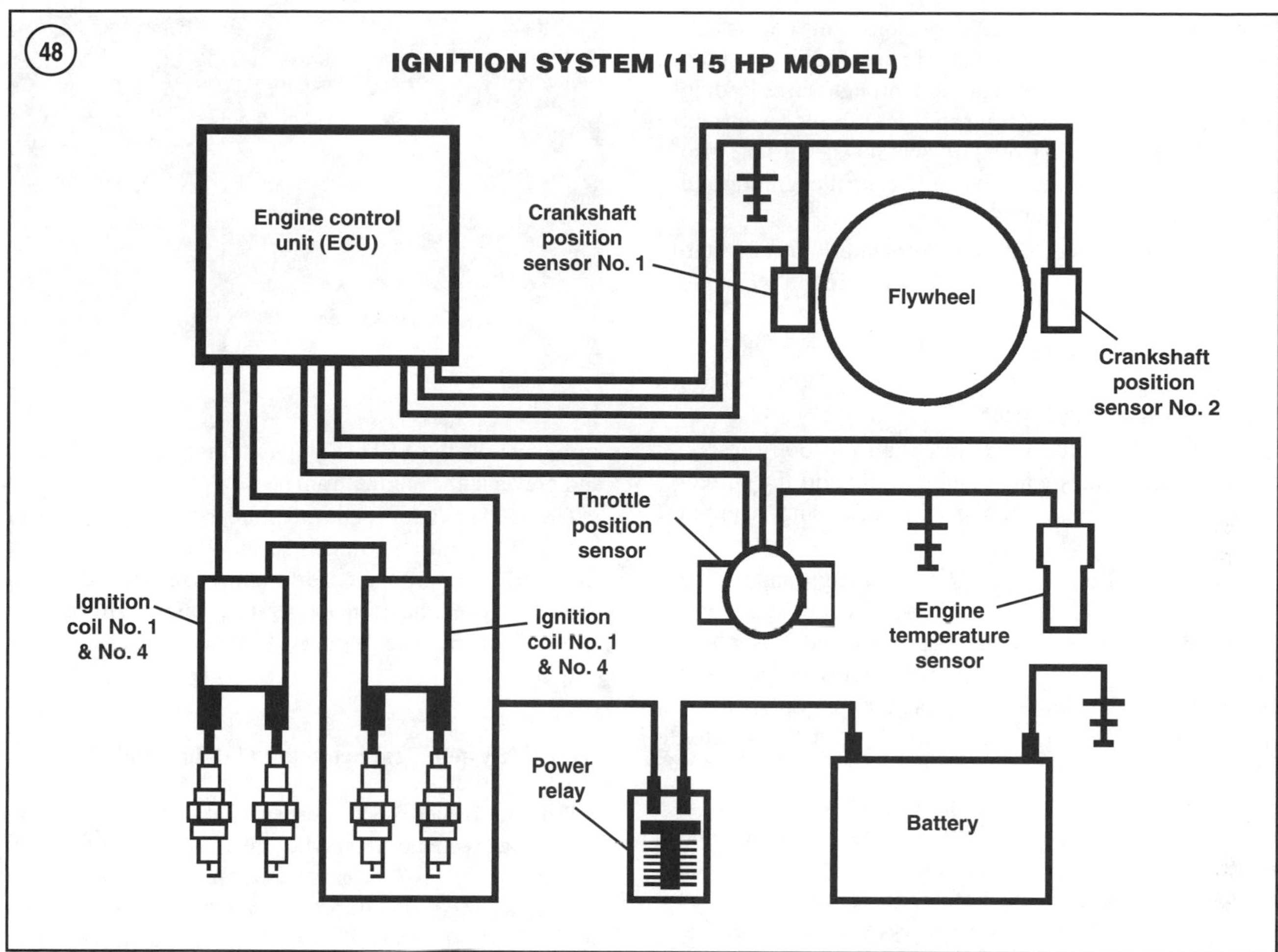

mounts onto the shift cable bracket on the lower port side of the power head. The switch operates momentarily while shifting from FORWARD gear to NEUTRAL gear. A multimeter is required for this test. The switch should be removed for testing as the momentary switching that occurs during shifting may occur too rapidly to be detected by the meter.

1. Remove the shift interrupt switch as described in Chapter Six.

2. Calibrate the meter to the R × 1 scale.

3. Connect the meter test leads onto the white/red and black switch wire terminals. Polarity is not important for this test.

4. Observe the meter while repeatedly depressing and releasing the switch plunger. The meter must indicate *continuity* each time the plunger is depressed and *no continuity* each time the plunger is released. Replace the switch if it fails to perform as specified.

NOTE
Improper installation of the shift interrupt switch may cause no spark on cylinders No. 1 and No. 4. If the test indicates no fault with the switch, the fault is usually corrected after installing the switch as described in Chapter Six.

5. Install the shift interrupt switch as described in Chapter Six.

Ignition System Operation (115 hp Models)

An ignition system wiring diagram is provided in **Figure 48**. This model utilizes a direct current (DC) powered ground interrupt ignition system. The battery and charging system provides the electric current to operate the system. The power relay supplies battery current to the engine control unit (ECU) and both ignition coils. The relay activates when the ignition key switch is placed in the ON or RUN and START positions. This allows battery current to flow through the primary windings in both ignition coils and returns to ground through wires leading into the ECU. A strong magnetic field forms as current flows through the coil primary windings. Current also flows into the ECU causing it to power up the ignition and fuel system control circuits.

A white wire connects the ignition switch stop circuit to the ECU. This wire connects to engine ground when the ignition switch is in the OFF position.

The raised bosses on the flywheel pass near the two crankshaft position sensors, generating low voltage pulses which are read by the ECU.

Using the input from the crankshaft position sensors, the ECU determines which plugs to fire and the correct time to initiate a spark. Timing adjustment is not required on this model.

At the correct time, the ECU opens the ground for the correct ignition coil. This causes the magnetic field to collapse. The collapsing field passes through and causes high voltage to form in the both secondary coil windings. The secondary coil voltage is directed to the spark plug and is high enough to create spark under all normal operating conditions.

This type of ignition system is commonly referred to as a double fire system. Cylinders 1 and 4 fire simultaneously and cylinders 2 and 3 fire simultaneously. When one piston is nearing the top of its compression stroke the other piston is nearing the top of its exhaust stroke. The second spark occurs during the exhaust stroke, burning any unburned fuel.

These model are equipped with a throttle position sensor (**Figure 49**) which mounts onto the upper throttle body on the port side of the power head. This allows the sensor shaft to rotate as the throttle opens and closes. A varying voltage signal from the throttle position sensor allows the ECU to accurately determine the position of the throttle. The ECU uses this information to calculate the optimum ignition timing settings and fuel delivery for all throttle settings.

The engine temperature sensor (**Figure 34**) provides a varying resistance value based upon the temperature of the engine cooling water. Input from the sensor is used by the ECU to compute the optimum ignition timing. This input is also used by the ECU to control fuel delivery and activate the overheat warning system.

Low oil pressure and overspeed protection circuits are also integrated into the ECU. Refer to *Warning Systems* in this chapter for additional information.

When activated, the ignition key switch or lanyard safety switch grounds the stop circuit. Grounding the stop circuit causes the ECU to stop initiating spark at the coil and prevents the engine from starting.

The ECU has a limp-home feature in the event of sensor failure. The ignition timing is set at 10° BTDC if the input from the throttle position or engine temperature sensor extends beyond the normal operating ranges. This feature allows for continued engine operation at reduced power output.

Ignition System Test Sequence (115 hp Model)

Refer to **Tables 5-8** for test specifications. Wiring diagrams are located at the end of the manual. Always refer to *Preliminary Inspection* in this chapter prior to performing any testing. Many times ignition problems are the result of dirty, loose, corroded or damaged wire connections. The recommended general troubleshooting sequence is as follows:

1. Stop circuit test.
2. Power relay test.
3. Rectifier/regulator output test.
4. Battery charging coil output test.
5. Battery charging coil resistance test.
6. Crankshaft position sensor output test.
7. Crankshaft position sensor resistance test.
8. Ignition coil resistance test.
9. Throttle position sensor voltage test.
10. Engine temperature sensor resistance test.

Stop circuit test (115 hp model)

A faulty stop circuit will signal the engine control unit (ECU) to stop initiating spark at the coil and prevents the engine from starting. A faulty stop circuit usually will not result in an inability to switch the engine off as the ignition key switch will deactivate the power relay when in the OFF or STOP position. This removes the power

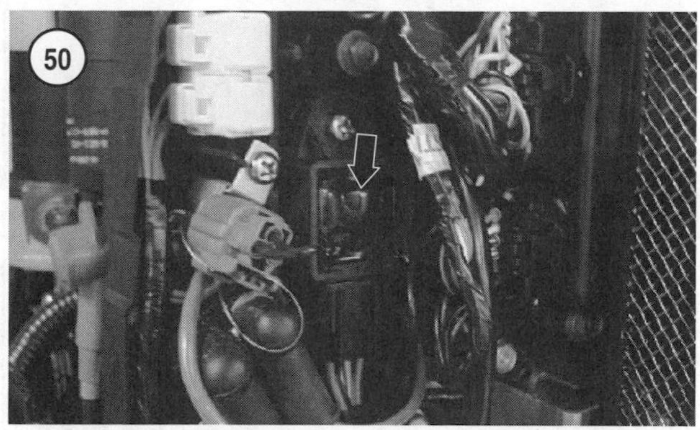

50

51

source from the ignition coils and ECU, preventing ignition system operation.

The stop circuit includes the ignition switch, lanyard safety switch and associated wiring.

Refer to *Spark Test* in this chapter to determine if spark is present prior to testing the stop circuit. A problem with the stop circuit is unlikely if spark is present at the spark plug(s), however testing may indicate a partial short or intermittent problem. Perform all tests without running the engine.

1. Disconnect the negative battery cable to prevent accidental starting.
2. Disconnect the engine wire harness from the instrument harness adapter (**Figure 35**). Refer to **Figure 36** to locate the terminal for the white wire. Make sure to select the terminal in the adapter harness instead of the engine wire harness connector.
3. Calibrate the multimeter to the R × 1 scale. Ground the negative meter lead. Touch the positive meter lead to the adapter harness terminal for the white wire in the harness adapter (**Figure 36**).
4. Place the ignition key switch in the ON or RUN position. Make sure the lanyard safety switch is in the normal or RUN position. Note the meter reading and place the ignition key switch in the start position. The meter must indicate *no continuity* in the ON or RUN and START positions. If otherwise, a fault is present in the ignition key switch, lanyard safety switch or wiring. Test the ignition key switch as described in this chapter. See *Electric Starting System Troubleshooting*. Proceed with testing if no fault is found with the ignition key switch.
5. Connect the meter test leads as described in Step 3. Place the ignition key switch in the ON or RUN position. Observe the meter and pull the cord from the lanyard safety switch. The meter must change from *no continuity* to *continuity* when the lanyard safety switch is activated. If not, the lanyard safety switch or related wiring is faulty and must be replaced.
6. With the meter leads attached as described in Step 3, place the ignition key switch in the OFF or STOP position. The meter must indicate *continuity.* If otherwise, the ignition key switch or wiring is faulty. Test the ignition key switch as described in this chapter. Repair or replace the instrument wire harness if no fault is found with the ignition key switch.
7. If all stop circuit components function correctly, but the ignition system does not produce spark, test the power relay and the remaining ignition system components as described in this section.

Power relay test (115 hp model)

A fault with the power relay (**Figure 50**) will result in loss of power to the ignition coils and the engine control unit (ECU). A multimeter is required for this test.

1. Activate the lanyard safety switch to prevent accidental starting. Place the ignition key switch in the OFF or STOP position.
2. Unplug the engine wire harness connectors from the ignition coil harness connectors (**Figure 51**).
3. Calibrate the meter to the 20 or 40 VDC scale. Ground the negative meter lead. Touch the positive meter lead to the red/white wire terminal in the engine harness plug that connects onto the upper ignition coil. Then, touch the meter lead to the red/white terminal in the connector that connects onto the lower ignition coil. Do not inadvertently connect the test lead to the coil harness connector terminals. The meter must indicate 0 volt at the terminal in each harness connector. Test the ignition key switch as described in this chapter if voltage is present at either connection point. Proceed with the test procedures if no fault is found with the ignition key switch.
4. Connect the meter test leads as described in Step 3. Observe the meter while placing the ignition key switch in the ON or RUN position. The meter must indicate battery voltage at each test point. Refer to the following:

a. If the meter readings in Step 3 and Step 4 are correct, the power relay is operating correctly. Proceed to Step 12.

b. If the meter reading in Step 3 is correct, but the reading in Step 4 is incorrect, proceed to Step 6.

c. If the meter readings on the two connector terminals are different from each other, repair or replace the faulty engine harness wiring or terminals that connect to the ignition coils.

5. Connect the engine wire harness connectors onto the ignition coil harness connectors. Route the wiring to prevent interference with moving components.

6. Remove the power relay as described in Chapter Six. Place the ignition key switch in the OFF or STOP position. Connect the battery cables.

7. Connect the negative battery cable to a suitable engine ground. Refer to **Figure 52** to identify the wire color terminals, then touch the positive meter lead to the red wire terminal in the engine harness connector for the power relay. The meter must indicate battery voltage. If otherwise, inspect the 20 amp power relay fuse. Repair or replace the faulty wiring or terminals if no fault is found with the fuse.

8. Connect the positive meter lead to the red wire terminal in the engine harness connector (**Figure 52**). Touch the negative meter lead to the black wire terminal in the connector. The meter must indicate battery voltage. If not, repair or replace the black wire or terminal connecting the harness connector to the engine ground.

9. Connect the negative battery cable to a suitable engine ground. Refer to **Figure 52** to identify the wire color terminals, then touch the positive meter lead to the yellow wire terminal in the engine harness connector for the power relay. The meter must indicate 0 volt. If voltage is present on the terminals, test the ignition key switch as described in this chapter.

10. Connect the meter test leads as described in Step 8. Observe the meter while placing the ignition key switch in the ON or RUN position. Refer to the following:

a. If the meter indicates 0 volt, test the ignition key switch as described in this chapter.

b. If the meter indicates battery voltage, the voltage supply to the relay is correct. Replace the relay if incorrect test results were evident in Step 3 or Step 4.

11. Install the power relay as described in Chapter Six.

12. Place the ignition key switch in the OFF or STOP position. Place the lanyard safety switch in the normal RUN position.

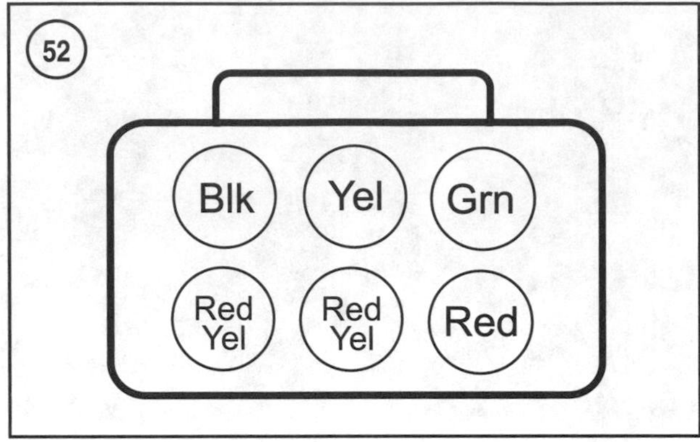

Rectifier/regulator output test (115 hp model)

Perform the rectifier/regulator output test if an ignition misfire is occurring at higher engine speeds. A fault with the charging system can cause an ignition system malfunction, particularly at higher engine speeds.

This test measures the peak voltage delivered by the rectifier/regulator. An accurate tachometer, test harness (part No. 91-881824) and a multimeter capable of measuring peak voltage are required for this procedure.

This test must be performed under actual operating conditions.

WARNING

On-water testing or adjustments require two people: one person to operate the boat, the other to monitor the gauges or test equipment and make necessary adjustments. All personnel must remain seated inside the boat at all times. Do not lean over the transom while the boat is under way. Use extensions to allow all gauges and test equipment to be located in normal seating areas.

1. Disconnect the negative battery cable. Push up and in on the locking tabs, then remove the electrical component cover (**Figure 37**).

2. Refer to the wire diagrams at the end of the manual to identify wire colors for the battery charging coil. Trace the wires from the charging coil to the rectifier/regulator. Disconnect the battery charging coil harness connector from the rectifier/regulator.

3. Connect the test harness to the battery charging coil harness connector and to rectifier/regulator harness connector as shown in **Figure 39**.

4. Select the peak DC volts function on the meter.

5. Connect the positive meter lead to the red wire terminal of the test harness. Connect the negative meter lead to the black wire terminal of the test harness.

6. Connect the battery cable.
7. Route the test leads and harness away from any moving components. Clamp them as necessary to ensure the test leads maintain secure contact to the test harness during engine operation.
8. Attach the shop tachometer to the engine following manufacturer's instructions. Connect the battery cable.

NOTE
*Some tests must be performed at cranking speed. Disconnect and ground all spark plug wires to allow electric starter operation without starting the engine or disabling the ignition system. Refer to **Spark Test** in this chapter for spark plug wire removal and installation instructions.*

9. Observe the meter readings while an assistant operates the engine at the speeds indicated in **Table 5**. Record the voltage readings for each speed range.
10. Stop the engine. Disconnect the negative battery cable, then remove the test leads.
11. Disconnect the test harness, then connect the battery charging coil harness connector to the rectifier/regulator.
12. Compare the meter readings with the specifications in **Table 5**.
    a. If output voltage is below the specification at any engine speed, perform the *Battery charging coil output test* as described in this section. Perform the *Rectifier/regulator resistance test* (see *Charging System Troubleshooting*) if the ignition coil output test correctly.
    b. If output is above the specification, perform the rectifier/regulator resistance test as described in this chapter under *Charging System Troubleshooting.*
13. Install the electrical component cover. Ensure the locking tabs fully engage the slots.
14. Connect the battery cable.

Battery charging coil output test (115 hp model)

Perform the battery charging coil output test if output is low at the rectifier/regulator. This test measures the peak voltage delivered by the battery charging coil. An accurate tachometer, test harness (part No. 91-881824) and a multimeter capable of measuring peak voltage are required for this procedure. This test must be performed under actual operating conditions.

WARNING
On-water testing or adjustments require two people: one to operate the boat, the other to monitor the gauges or test equipment and make necessary adjustments. All personnel must remain seated inside the boat at all times. Do not lean over the transom while the boat is under way. Use extensions to allow all gauges and test equipment to be located in normal seating areas.

1. Disconnect the negative battery cable. Push up and in on the locking tabs, then remove the electrical component cover (**Figure 37**).
2. Attach the shop tachometer to the engine following manufacturer's instructions. Connect the battery cable.
3. Refer to the wiring diagrams at the end of this manual to identify wire colors for the battery charging coil. Trace the wires from the charging coil to the rectifier/regulator. Disconnect the battery charging coil harness connector from the rectifier/regulator.
4. Connect the test harness to the battery charging coil harness connector and to the rectifier/regulator harness connector as shown in **Figure 39**.
5. Mark a *1, 2 or 3* on each of the three green test harness wires. This is to ensure all wires are tested.
6. Connect the positive meter lead onto the No. 1 green wire terminal of the test harness. Connect the negative meter lead onto the No. 2 green wire terminal of the test harness.
7. Connect the battery cable. Select the peak DC volts function on the meter. Route the test leads and harness away from any moving components. Clamp them as necessary to ensure the test leads maintain secure contact with the test harness during engine operation.

NOTE
*Some tests must be performed at cranking speed. Disconnect and ground all spark plug wires to allow electric starter operation without starting the engine or disabling the ignition system. Refer to **Spark Test** in this chapter for spark plug wire removal and installation instructions.*

8. Observe the meter readings while an assistant operates the engine at the speeds indicated in **Table 5**. Record the voltage readings for each speed range.
9. Repeat Steps 6-8 with the positive meter lead connected onto the No. 1 green wire terminal of the test harness and the negative meter lead connected onto the No. 3 green wire terminal of the test harness.
10. Repeat Steps 6-8 with the positive meter lead connected onto the No. 2 green wire terminal of the test harness and the negative meter lead connected onto the No. 3 green wire terminal of the test harness.

11. Stop the engine. Disconnect the negative battery cable, then remove the test leads.
12. Disconnect the test harness, then connect the battery charging coil harness connector onto the rectifier/regulator. Connect the battery cable.
13. Compare the meter readings with the specifications in **Table 5**. If any of the meter readings are below the specifications, perform the battery charging coil resistance test as described in this section and inspect the flywheel for damaged magnets. See *Flywheel Removal and Installation* in Chapter Seven. Replace the battery charging coil if it fails the resistance test or if low output voltage is evident and no defect is found with the flywheel.
14. Install the electrical component cover. Ensure the locking tabs fully engage the slots.
15. Connect the battery cable.

Battery charging coil resistance test (115 hp model)

Perform the battery charging coil resistance test if the battery charging coil output voltage is below the specification. A test harness (part No. 91-881824) and an accurate digital multimeter are required for this procedure.

1. Disconnect the negative battery cable. Push up and in on the locking tabs, then remove the electrical component cover (**Figure 37**).
2. Refer to the wiring diagrams at the end of the manual to identify wire colors for the battery charging coil. Trace the wires from the charging coil to the rectifier/regulator. Disconnect the battery charging coil harness connector from the rectifier/regulator.
3. Connect the test harness to the battery charging coil harness connector. Do not connect the test harness onto the rectifier/regulator for this test.
4. Mark a 1, 2 or 3 on each of the three green test harness wires. This is to ensure all wires are selected during the test procedures.
5. Select the R × 1 scale on the meter.
6. Connect the positive meter lead to the No. 1 green wire terminal and the No. 2 green wire terminal of the test harness. Record the resistance reading.
7. Connect the positive meter lead onto the No. 1 green wire terminal and the No. 3 green wire terminal of the test harness. Record the resistance reading.
8. Connect the positive meter lead onto the No. 2 green wire terminal and the No. 3 green wire terminal of the test harness. Record the resistance reading.
9. The meter must indicate 0.2-0.8 ohm for each connection point indicated in Steps 6-8. If otherwise, replace the battery charging coil as described in Chapter Six.
10. Remove the test harness and connect the battery charging coil harness connector onto the rectifier/regulator.
11. Connect the battery cable.
12. Install the electrical component cover. Ensure the locking tabs fully engage the slots. Connect the battery cable.

Crankshaft position sensor output test (115 hp model)

Perform the crankshaft position sensor output test if spark is missing or weak. The No. 1 crankshaft position sensor crontrols ignition for cylinders No. 1 and No. 4. The No. 2 crankshaft position sensor controls ignition for cylinders No. 2 and No. 3.

At times a sensor malfunction can occur randomly and result in intermittent ignition misfire. A buildup of oil, grease or other contamination can cause the crankshaft position sensor to malfunction. If allowed to build to a sufficient thickness the deposits prevent the sensor from detecting the passing of the flywheel bosses. Clean excessive oil, grease or other deposits from the crankshaft position sensor and the flywheel bosses with a light solvent.

This test measures the peak voltage delivered by the crankshaft position sensors. An accurate tachometer, test harness (part No. 91-881825) and a multimeter capable of measuring peak voltage are required for this procedure. This test must be performed under actual operating conditions.

WARNING

On-water testing or adjustments require two people: one to operate the boat, the other to monitor the gauges or test equipment and make necessary adjustments. All personnel must remain seated inside the boat at all times. Do not lean over the transom while the boat is under way. Use extensions to allow all gauges and test equipment to be located in normal seating areas.

1. Disconnect the negative battery cable. Push up and in on the locking tabs, then remove the electrical component cover (**Figure 37**).
2. Refer to the wire diagrams at the end of the manual to identify wire colors for the crankshaft position sensor harness. Trace the wires from the crankshaft position sensor, located under the flywheel, to the engine wire harness connector. Disconnect the crankshaft position sensor harness connector from the engine wire harness connector.
3. Connect the test harness to the engine wire harness plug and the crankshaft position sensor harness connector as shown in **Figure 39**.

4. Select the peak DC volts function on the meter.
5. Connect the positive meter lead to the white/red wire terminal of the test harness. Connect the negative lead to the black wire terminal of the test harness.
6. Route the test leads and harness away from any moving components. Clamp them as necessary to ensure the test leads maintain secure contact with the test harness during engine operation.
7. Attach the shop tachometer to the engine following manufacturer's instructions. Connect the battery cable.

NOTE
*Some tests must be performed at cranking speed. Disconnect and ground all spark plug wires to allow electric starter operation without starting the engine or disabling the ignition system. Refer to **Spark Test** in this chapter for spark plug wire removal and installation instructions.*

8. Observe the meter readings while an assistant operates the engine at the speeds indicated in **Table 5**. Record the voltage readings for each speed range.
9. Stop the engine. Connect the positive meter lead to the white/black wire terminal of the test harness and the negative lead to the black wire terminal of the test harness.
10. Have an assistant operate the engine at the speeds indicated in **Table 5**. Record the voltage readings for each speed range.
11. Stop the engine and compare the meter readings with the specifications listed in **Table 5**. Refer to the following:
   a. If the voltage recorded in Step 8 or Step 10 is above specification at any engine speed, replace the engine control unit (ECU) as described in Chapter Six.
   b. If the voltage recorded in Step 8 is below specification at any engine speed, the crankshaft position sensor for cylinders No. 1 and No. 4 or the flywheel is faulty. Perform the crankshaft position sensor resistance test as described in this section and inspect the flywheel for damaged magnets. See *Flywheel Removal and Installation* in Chapter Seven. Replace the crankshaft position sensor if it fails the resistance test or if low output voltage is evident and no defect is found with the flywheel.
   c. If the voltage recorded in Step 10 is below specification at any engine speed, the crankshaft position sensor for cylinders No. 2 and No. 3 or the flywheel is faulty. Perform the crankshaft position sensor resistance test as described in this section and inspect the flywheel for damaged magnets. See *Flywheel Removal and Installation* in Chapter Seven. Replace the crankshaft position sensor if it fails the resistance test or if low output voltage is evident and no defect is found with the flywheel.
12. Disconnect the negative battery cable.
13. Disconnect the test leads and test harness from the engine. Connect the crankshaft position sensor harness connector onto the engine wire harness connector.
14. Install the electrical component cover. Ensure the locking tabs fully engage the slots. Connect the battery cable.

Crankshaft position sensor resistance test (115 hp model)

Perform the crankshaft position sensor resistance test if the crankshaft position sensor output voltage is below the specification. A test harness (part No. 91-881825) and a digital multimeter are required for this procedure.

1. Disconnect the negative battery cable. Push up and in on the locking tabs, then remove the electrical component cover (**Figure 37**).
2. Refer to the wire diagrams at the end of the manual to identify wire colors for the crankshaft position sensor harness. Trace the wires from the crankshaft position sensor, located under the flywheel, to the engine wire harness connector. Disconnect the crankshaft position sensor harness connector from the engine wire harness connector.
3. Connect the test harness to the crankshaft position sensor harness connector. Do not connect the test harness to the engine harness connector for this test.
4. Select the R × 100 scale on the meter. Touch the meter test leads to the test harness wire colors specified in **Table 6**. Test lead polarity is not important for this test. The meter must indicate 445-565 ohm at each pair of connection points. If otherwise, replace the faulty crankshaft position sensor(s) as described in Chapter Six.
5. Remove the test harness and connect the crankshaft position sensor harness connector to the engine harness connector.
6. Connect the battery cable.
7. Install the electrical component cover. Ensure the locking tabs fully engage the slots. Connect the battery cable.

Ignition coil resistance test (115 hp model)

Resistance testing checks for open circuits or short circuits in the primary and secondary windings of the ignition coil.

The wire length used for the primary winding of the ignition coil is relatively short and the resistance readings are fairly low. A much longer length of wire is used in the secondary winding and the resistance readings are relatively high. Use a digital multimeter for the most accurate results. Usually, a fault within the ignition coil surfaces when the resistance is tested. Ignition coil test specifications are listed in **Table 6**. Make all resistance tests at approximately 68° F (20° C) to ensure accurate test results.

Bear in mind that a resistance test only indicates a short or open circuit. Faults within the coil may result in internal arcing that prevents a strong blue spark at the spark plug. If an internal short is present a clicking noise usually emanates from the coil while attempting to start the engine. Use a spark test tool to check for a good strong blue spark as the engine is cranked. Refer to *Spark Test* in this chapter for instructions on using a spark test tool. Test both the primary and secondary resistance for each coil on the engine. Removal of the ignition coil is not required for testing provided there is access to the wire terminals. Refer to Chapter Six if coil removal is required. A test harness (part No. 91-881826) and a digital multimeter are required for this procedure.

1. Disconnect the negative battery cable to prevent accidental starting.
2. Remove the screws (**Figure 42**) and plastic cover on the rear of the power head to access the spark plug wires. Two screws are located on the top, two screws are located on the bottom and one screw is located on the side and midway down on the cover.
3. Mark the cylinder number on the spark plug wires before removing them from the spark plugs. The top cylinder is the No. 1 cylinder. Gently twist the spark plug caps to free them from the plugs, then pull the cap from the plug. Never pull on the spark plug wire to free the cap.
4. Unplug the engine wire harness connectors from the ignition coil harness connectors (**Figure 51**).
5. To test the primary coil resistance, proceed as follows:
   a. Calibrate the meter to the R × 1 scale.
   b. Connect the test harness (part No. 91-881826) to the upper ignition coil harness connector. Do not connect the test harness onto the engine wire harness for this test.
   c. Touch the meter test leads to the black/white and red/yellow test harness wire terminals. Polarity is not important for this test. The meter must indicate 1.8-2.6 ohms. If otherwise, the primary winding is shorted or open and the coil must be replaced.
6. To test the secondary coil resistance, calibrate the meter to the R × 1K scale. Touch the meter test leads to the terminals in the spark plug wire caps. Polarity is not important for this test. The meter must indicate 18.97K-35.23K ohms for the No. 1 and No. 4 ignition coil and 18.55K-34.35K ohms for the No. 2 and No. 3 ignition coil. If otherwise the secondary coil winding is shorted or open and the coil must be replaced.

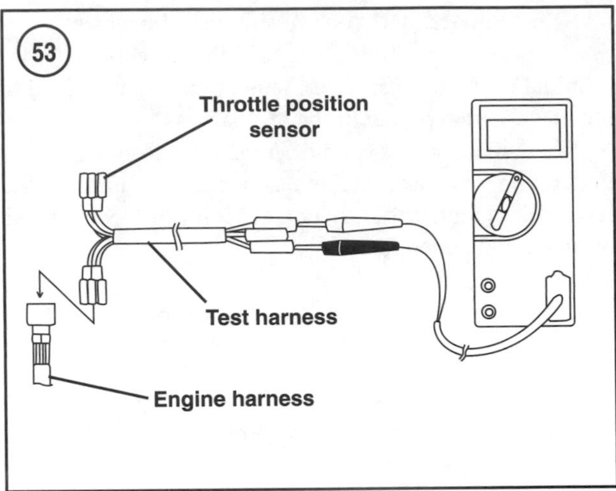

7. Test the remaining ignition coil as described in Step 5 and Step 6.
8. Remove the test harness. Attach the engine wire harness connectors to the ignition coil harness connectors.
9. Connect the spark plug wires onto the correct spark plugs. Ensure that all leads are routed correctly.
10. Fit the plastic cover onto the rear of the power head. Install the cover screws and tighten in a crossing pattern to 65 in.-lb. (7.3 N•m).
11. Connect the battery cable.

Throttle position sensor voltage test (115 hp model)

A defective throttle position sensor (**Figure 49**) can cause poor performance at higher throttle settings, hesitation during acceleration or excessively fast idle speed. The engine control unit (ECU) will fix the ignition timing at 10° BTDC if it detects a fault with the throttle position sensor.

Improper throttle position sensor adjustment can cause the same symptoms as a faulty sensor. Always adjust the throttle position sensor (Chapter Four) prior to performing any testing. This test measures the input voltage supplied to the sensor by the ECU and measures the output voltage supplied to the ECU by the sensor.

A digital multimeter, shop tachometer and test harness (part No. 91-881827) are required for this test. Testing requires running the engine under actual operating conditions.

WARNING

On-water testing or adjustments require two people: one to operate the boat, the other to monitor the gauges or test equipment and make necessary adjustments. All personnel must remain seated inside the boat at all times. Do not lean over the transom while the boat is under way. Use extensions to allow all gauges and test equipment to be located in normal seating areas.

1. Disconnect the negative battery cable.
2. Disconnect the throttle position sensor harness connector from the engine wire harness connector.
3. Connect the test harness to the engine wire harness plug and to the throttle position sensor as shown in **Figure 53**.
4. Select the DC volts function on the meter.
5. Connect the positive meter lead to the orange wire terminal of the test harness. Connect the negative lead to the black wire terminal of the test harness.
6. Route the test leads and harness away from any moving components. Clamp them as necessary to ensure the test leads maintain secure contact to the test harness during engine operation.
7. Attach the shop tachometer to the engine following manufacturer's instructions. Connect the battery cable.
8. Observe the meter readings while an assistant operates the engine at 750 rpm in FORWARD gear. The meter must indicate 4.75-5.25 volts. A faulty ECU or wiring is indicated if the input voltage is not within the specification. Inspect the wiring connecting the throttle position sensor to the ECU for damaged insulation, broken wiring or faulty terminals. Replace the ECU if the input voltage is incorrect and no fault is found with the wiring.
9. Stop the engine. Connect the positive meter lead to the pink wire terminal of the test harness. Connect the negative lead to the black wire terminal of the test harness.
10. Observe the meter readings while an assistant operates the engine at 750 rpm in FORWARD gear. The meter must indicate 0.718-0.746 volt. A faulty or improperly adjusted throttle position sensor is indicated if the voltage is not within the specification. If necessary, readjust the sensor as described in Chapter Four and repeat the test. Replace the sensor if it cannot be adjusted to within the specification.
11. Connect the meter test leads to the test harness as described in Step 9. Have an assistant start the engine and shift into FORWARD gear. Monitor the meter while the assistant *slowly* advances the throttle to full-open. Then, monitor the meter while the assistant *slowly* closes the throttle to the idle position. The meter must indicate a steady increase in voltage as the throttle advances and a steady decrease as the throttle closes. Replace the throttle position sensor as described in Chapter Five if the voltage reading is erratic or does not increase and decrease as described.
12. Stop the engine and disconnect the negative battery cable.
13. Remove the test harness and connect the engine wire harness connector onto the throttle position sensor. To prevent potential interference with the throttle linkages, secure the wiring with a plastic locking clamp.
14. Connect the battery cable.

Engine temperature sensor resistance test (115 hp model)

A fault with the engine temperature sensor can cause poor cold engine operating characteristics, too high of an idle speed on a fully warmed engine or improper activation of the overheat warning system. The engine control unit (ECU) will fix the ignition timing at 10° BTDC if it detects a fault with the engine temperature sensor.

This test requires an accurate digital or analog multimeter, a liquid thermometer and a container of water that can be heated.

1. Remove the engine temperature sensor as described in Chapter Six.
2. Calibrate the multimeter to the appropriate ohms scale for the test specification in **Table 8**. Connect the meter leads between the two sensor terminals. Test lead polarity is not important for this test.
3. Suspend the sensor in a container of water that can be heated (**Figure 47**, typical). Ensure the sensor does not touch the bottom or sides of the container and the tip of the sensor is completely below the water surface.
4. Add ice or heat the container until the water temperature reaches the temperatures specified in **Table 8**. Record the resistance at each temperature.
5. Compare the resistance readings with the specifications in **Table 8**. A slight variation in resistance (less than 10 percent) is common and does not indicate a fault with the sensor. Replace the engine temperature sensor if the resistance is significantly different from the specification at any of the specified temperatures.
6. Install the engine temperature sensor as described in Chapter Six.

Ignition System Operation (225 hp Model)

An ignition system wiring diagram is provided in **Figure 54**. This model uses a direct current (DC) powered ground-interrupt ignition system. The battery and charging system provides the electric current to operate the system. The power relay supplies battery current to the three ignition coils, high-pressure electric fuel pump relay and the low-pressure electric fuel pump driver. The

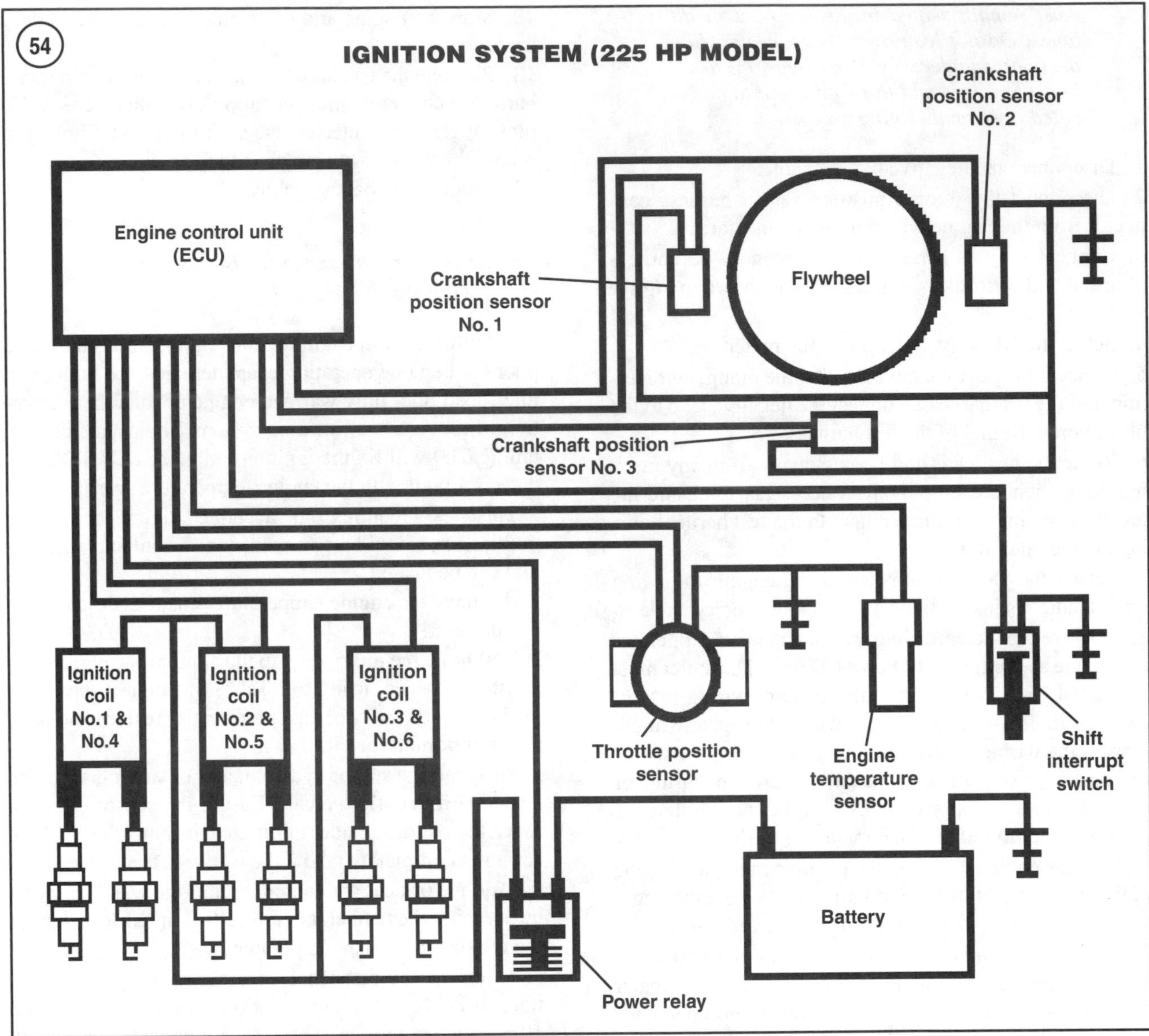

relay activates when the engine control unit (ECU) provides the ground circuit for the relay. The ECU activates the relay when the ignition key switch is placed in the ON or RUN and START position and the ECU receives input from the crankshaft position sensors. Activating the relay allows battery current to flow through the primary windings in the three ignition coils and returns to ground through wires leading into the ECU. Each coil contains a single primary winding and two secondary windings. A strong magnetic field forms as current flows through the coil primary windings.

A white wire connects the ignition switch stop circuit to the ECU. This wire is connected to engine ground when the ignition switch is in the OFF position.

Low voltage pulses are developed as the raised bosses on the flywheel pass near the two crankshaft position sensors. These pulses are directed to the ECU.

Using the input from the crankshaft position sensors, the ECU determines which plugs to fire and the correct time to initiate a spark. Timing adjustment is not required on this model.

At the correct time, the ECU opens the ground for the correct ignition coil. This causes the magnetic field to rapidly collapse. The collapsing field passes through and causes high voltage to form in the secondary coil windings. The secondary coil voltage is directed to the spark plug and is high enough to create spark under all normal operating conditions.

55

56

This type of ignition system is commonly referred to as a double fire system. Cylinders 1 and 4 fire simultaneously, cylinders 2 and 5 fire simultaneously and cylinders 3 and 6 fire simultaneously. When one piston is nearing the top of its compression stroke the other piston is nearing the top of its exhaust stroke. The second park occurs during the exhaust stroke, burning any unburned fuel.

This model is equipped with a throttle position sensor (**Figure 55**). The throttle position sensor mounts onto the upper throttle body on the starboard side of the power head. This allows the sensor shaft to rotate as the throttle opens and closes. A varying voltage signal from the throttle position sensor allows the ECU to accurately determine the position of the throttle. The ECU uses this information to calculate the optimum ignition timing settings and fuel delivery for all throttle settings.

The engine temperature sensor (**Figure 56**) mounts onto the upper port side of the power head. It provides a varying resistance value based upon the temperature of the engine cooling water. Input from the sensor is used by the ECU to compute the optimum ignition timing. This input is also used by the ECU to control fuel delivery.

Low oil pressure and overspeed protection circuits are also integrated into the ECU. Refer to *Warning Systems* in this chapter for additional information. When activated, the ignition key switch or lanyard safety switch grounds the stop circuit. Grounding the stop circuit causes the ECU to stop initiating spark at the coil and prevents the engine from starting.

The ECU has a limp-home feature in case of sensor failure. The ignition timing is set at 10° BTDC if the input from the throttle position or engine temperature sensor extends beyond the normal operating ranges. This feature allows for continued engine operation at reduced power output.

The shift interrupt switch, when activated, grounds the blue/yellow wire leading to the ECU. The switch mounts onto the shift cable and linkage bracket on the lower starboard side of the power head. The normal shifting loads that occur when shifting out of forward or reverse gear will cause the linkages to momentarily depress the plunger. Depressing the plunger grounds the blue/yellow wire, causing the ECU to stop ignition on one or more cylinders. This reduces the load on the sliding clutch to allow easier shifting to neutral gear. The switch must reset after shifting, or the blue/yellow wire will remain grounded and the engine will misfire. The ECU stops ignition on cylinders 1 and 4 if the switch activates at engine speeds less than 850 rpm. The ECU stops ignition on cylinders 1and 2 or cylinders 4 and 5 if the switch activates at engine speeds above 850 rpm but less than 2000 rpm. The ECU does not stop ignition if the switch activates at engine speeds of 2000 rpm and higher.

Ignition System Test Sequence (225 hp Model)

Refer to **Tables 5-8** for test specifications. Wiring diagrams are at the end of this manual. Always refer to *Preliminary Inspection* in this chapter prior to performing any testing. Many times ignition problems are the result of dirty, loose, corroded or damaged wire connections. Wasted time and the replacement of good components results from not performing these preliminary steps. The recommended general troubleshooting procedure is as follows:

1. Stop circuit test.
2. Power relay test.
3. Rectifier/regulator output test.
4. Battery charging coil output test.
5. Battery charging coil resistance test.
6. Crankshaft position sensor output test.
7. Crankshaft position sensor resistance test.
8. Ignition coil resistance test.
9. Throttle position sensor voltage test.

10. Engine temperature sensor resistance test.
11. Shift interrupt switch test.

Stop circuit test (225 hp model)

A faulty stop circuit will signal the engine control unit (ECU) to stop initiating spark at the coil, preventing the engine from starting. A faulty stop circuit will usually not result in an inability to switch the engine off as the ignition key switch will cause the ECU to deactivate the power relay when in the *off* or *stop* position. This removes the power source from the ignition coils and prevents ignition system operation.

The stop circuit includes the ignition switch, lanyard safety switch and associated wiring.

Refer to *Spark Test* in this chapter to determine if spark is present before testing the stop circuit. A problem with the stop circuit is unlikely if spark is present at the spark plug(s), however testing may indicate a partial short or intermittent problem. Perform all tests without running the engine.

1. Disconnect the negative battery cable to prevent accidental starting.
2. Disconnect the engine wire harness from the instrument harness adapter (**Figure 35**). Refer to **Figure 36** to locate the terminal for the white wire. Make sure to select the terminal in the adapter harness instead engine wire harness connector.
3. Calibrate the multimeter onto the R × 1 scale. Ground the negative meter lead. Touch the positive meter lead onto the adapter harness terminal for the white wire in the harness adapter (**Figure 36**).
4. Place the ignition key switch in the ON or RUN position. Make sure the lanyard safety switch is in the normal or RUN position. Note the meter reading and place the ignition key switch in the start position. The meter must indicate *no continuity* in the ON or RUN and START positions. If otherwise, a fault is present in the ignition key switch, lanyard safety switch or wiring. Test the ignition key switch as described in this chapter. See *Electric Starting System Troubleshooting*. Proceed with testing if no fault is found with the ignition key switch.
5. Connect the meter test leads as described in Step 3. Place the ignition key switch in the ON or RUN position. Observe the meter and pull the cord from the lanyard safety switch. The meter must change from *no continuity* to *continuity* when the lanyard safety switch is activated. If not, the lanyard safety switch or related wiring is faulty and must be replaced.
6. With the meter leads attached as described in Step 3, place the ignition key switch in the OFF or STOP position. The meter must indicate *continuity*. If otherwise, the ignition key switch or wiring is faulty. Test the ignition key switch as described in this chapter. Repair or replace the instrument wire harness if no fault is found with the ignition key switch.
7. If all stop circuit components function correctly, but the ignition system does not produce spark, test the power relay, then the remaining ignition system components as described in this section.

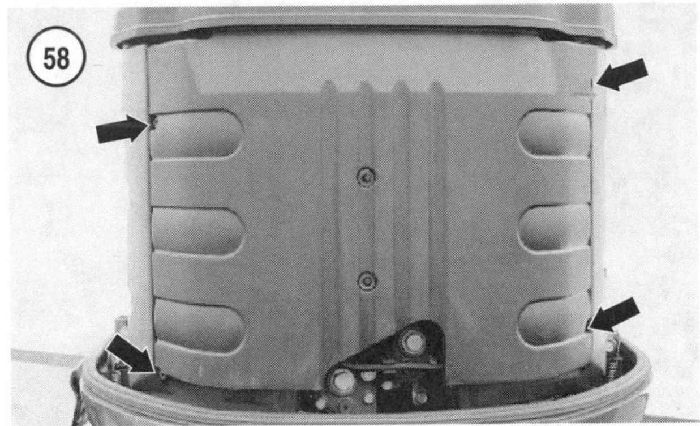

Power relay test (225 hp model)

A fault with the power relay (**Figure 57**) will result in no power being supplied to the ignition coils and the engine control unit (ECU). A multimeter is required for this test. Fuses are beneath the starboard electric component cover.

1. Disconnect the negative battery cable to prevent accidental starting.
2. Remove the four screws (**Figure 58**) and the plastic spark plug/coil cover on the rear of the power head to access the spark plugs.
3. Mark the cylinder number on the spark plug wires before removing them from the spark plugs. The top cylinder on the starboard bank is the No. 1 cylinder. Odd numbered cylinders are on the starboard cylinder bank

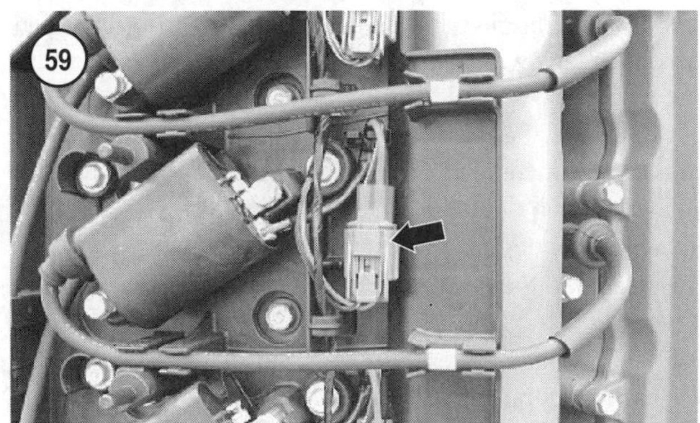

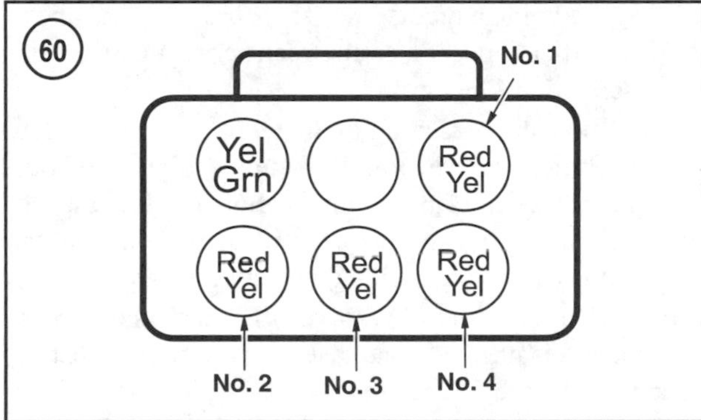

and even numbered cylinders are on the port bank. Gently twist the spark plug caps to free them from the plugs, then pull the cap from the plug. Never pull on the spark plug wire to free the cap.

4. Remove the propeller as described in Chapter Eight. Shift the engine into NEUTRAL gear.

5. Connect each of the spark plug wires onto a suitable engine ground.

CAUTION
Never crank the engine with ungrounded spark plug wires. Cranking the engine with ungrounded leads will create arcing that can damage the ignition system and other engine components.

6. Disconnect one of the engine wire harness connectors from the ignition coil harness connector (**Figure 59**).

7. Connect the battery cable.

8. Calibrate the meter to the 20 or 40 VDC scale.

9. Connect the negative meter lead onto a suitable engine ground. Touch the positive meter lead to the red/yellow wire terminal in the engine harness plug that connects to the upper ignition coil.

10. The meter must indicate 0 volt. If voltage is detected, replace the power relay as described in Chapter Six.

NOTE
*Some tests must be performed at cranking speed. Disconnect and ground all spark plug wires to allow electric starter operation without starting the engine or disabling the ignition system. Refer to **Spark Test** in this chapter for spark plug wire removal and installation instructions.*

11. Observe the meter while an assistant places the ignition key switch in the START position.
   a. If the meter indicates battery voltage, the power relay is functioning properly. Proceed to Step 16.
   b. If the meter indicates 0-10.5 volts, proceed to Step 12.

12. Perform the crankshaft position sensor output test as described in this section. If the sensors test correctly, proceed to Step 13.

13. Remove the power relay as described in Chapter Six.

14. Connect the negative meter lead onto a suitable engine ground. Refer to **Figure 60**, then touch the positive meter lead onto the red/yellow No 3. terminal in the engine harness connector for the power relay. Then, touch the meter test lead onto the red/yellow No. 4 terminal in the connector. The meter must indicate battery voltage at both connection points. Refer to the following:
   a. If there is battery voltage at both connection points, and 0-10.5 volts in Step 11, replace the power relay as described in Chapter Six and repeat the test. Faulty wiring or terminals is indicated if incorrect test results are evident with the replacement relay.
   b. If there is battery voltage only at the red/yellow No. 3, replace the No. 2, 20 amp (yellow) fuse.
   c. If there is battery voltage only at red/yellow No. 4, replace the No. 1, 20 amp (yellow) fuse.

15. Install the power relay as described in Chapter Six.

16. Disconnect the negative battery cable.

17. Connect the engine harness connector onto the ignition coil harness connector. Route the wiring to prevent pinching or interference with moving components.

18. Connect the spark plug wires to the correct spark plugs. Ensure that all leads are routed correctly.

19. Install the propeller as described in Chapter Eight.

20. Fit the plastic cover onto the rear of the power head. Install the cover screws and tighten in a crossing pattern to 71 in.-lb. (8.0 N•m).

Rectifier/regulator output test (225 hp model)

Perform the rectifier/regulator output test if an ignition misfire is occurring at higher engine speeds. A fault with the charging system can cause an ignition system malfunction, particularly at higher engine speeds.

This test measures the peak voltage delivered by the rectifier/regulator. An accurate tachometer, test harness (part No. 91-888862) and a multimeter capable of measuring peak volts are required for this procedure.

This test must be performed under actual operating conditions.

WARNING

On-water testing or adjustments require two people: one to operate the boat, the other to monitor the gauges or test equipment and make necessary adjustments. All personnel must remain seated inside the boat at all times. Do not lean over the transom while the boat is under way. Use extensions to allow all gauges and test equipment to be located in normal seating areas.

1. Disconnect the negative battery cable to prevent accidental starting.
2. Remove the silencer cover as described in Chapter Five. Remove the four screws and the plastic cover on the bottom of the mounting plate.
3. Disconnect the rectifier/regulator harness connector from the engine harness connector. Connect the test harness to the rectifier/regulator harness connector.
4. Install the silencer cover as described in Chapter Five. Route the test harness to prevent interference and allow access to the test points.
5. Select the peak DC volts function on the meter.
6. Ground the negative meter lead. Connect the positive meter lead to the red wire terminal of the test harness.
7. Route the test leads and harness away from any moving components. Clamp them as necessary to ensure the test leads maintain secure contact to the test harness during engine operation.
8. Attach the shop tachometer to the engine following manufacturer's instructions. Connect the battery cable.

NOTE

*Some tests must be performed at cranking speed. Disconnect and ground all spark plug wires to allow electric starter operation without starting the engine or disabling the ignition system. Refer to **Spark Test** in this chapter for spark plug wire removal and installation instructions.*

9. Observe the meter readings while an assistant operates the engine at the speeds indicated in **Table 5**. Record the voltage readings for each speed range.
10. Stop the engine, then connect the positive meter lead onto the black wire terminal of the test harness. Make sure the negative test lead is grounded.
11. Observe the meter readings while an assistant operates the engine at the speeds indicated in **Table 5**. Record the voltage readings for each speed range.
12. Stop the engine and disconnect the test leads.
13. Remove the silencer cover as described in Chapter Five.
14. Disconnect the test harness from the rectifier/regulator harness connector.
15. Compare the meter readings with the specifications in **Table 5** and refer to the following:
    a. If the voltage reading in Step 9 or Step 11 is above specification, replace the rectifier/regulator as described in Chapter Six.
    b. If the voltage reading in Step 9 or Step 11 is below specification, perform the battery charging coil output test as described in this section. Replace the rectifier/regulator if low output is evident and the battery charging coil output test correctly.
16. Install the plastic cover over the relay and harness connector. Seat the cover against the mounting plate, then thread the four screws into the cover and mounting plate. Securely tighten the screws.
17. Install the silencer cover as described in Chapter Five.
18. Remove the shop tachometer, then connect the battery cable.

Battery charging coil output test (225 hp model)

Perform the battery charging coil output test if low output is measured at the rectifier/regulator. This test measures the voltage delivered by the unloaded battery charging coil. An accurate tachometer, test harness (part No. 91-804772) and a multimeter capable of measuring peak volts are required for this procedure. This test must be performed under actual operating conditions.

WARNING

On-water testing or adjustments require two people: one to operate the boat, the other to monitor the gauges or test equipment and make necessary adjustments. All personnel must remain seated inside the boat at all times. Do not lean over the transom while the boat is under way. Use extensions to allow all gauges and test equipment to be located in normal seating areas.

1. Disconnect the negative battery cable.

2. Remove the silencer cover as described in Chapter Five.
3. Locate the connectors for the three green and three green/white battery charging coil wires. The connectors are located directly above the fuel filter bracket.
4. Unplug the connector for the green coil wires. Connect the female test harness connector onto the connector for the green coil wires.
5. Install the silencer cover as described in Chapter Five. Route the test harness to prevent interference and allow access to the test points.
6. Select the peak DC volts function on the meter.
7. Attach the shop tachometer to the engine following manufacturer's instructions. Connect the battery cable.

CAUTION
To prevent damage to the meter or leads and inaccurate test results, route the test leads and harness away from any moving components. Clamp them as necessary to ensure the test leads maintain secure contact to the test harness during engine operation.

NOTE
Some tests must be performed at cranking speed. Disconnect and ground all spark plug wires to allow electric starter operation without starting the engine or disabling the ignition system. Refer to ***Spark Test*** *in this chapter for spark plug wire removal and installation instructions.*

8. Connect the positive meter lead onto the red wire terminal of the test harness. Connect the negative meter lead onto the black wire of the test harness. Observe the meter readings while an assistant operates the engine at the speeds indicated in **Table 5**. Record the voltage readings for each speed range.
9. Stop the engine, then connect the positive meter lead onto the red wire terminal of the test harness. Connect the negative meter lead to the white wire of the test harness. Observe the meter readings while an assistant operates the engine at the speeds indicated in **Table 5**. Record the voltage readings for each speed range.
10. Stop the engine, then connect the positive meter lead to the black wire terminal of the test harness. Connect the negative meter lead to the white wire of the test harness. Observe the meter readings while an assistant operates the engine at the speeds indicated in **Table 5**. Record the voltage readings for each speed range.
11. Stop the engine and disconnect the negative battery cable.
12. Remove the silencer cover as described in Chapter Five.
13. Remove the test harness from the green coil wire connector. Plug the green wire connector onto the corresponding rectifier/regulator connector.
14. Unplug the connector for the green/white coil wires. Connect the female test harness connector onto the connector for the green/white coil wires.
15. Install the silencer cover as described in Chapter Five. Route the test harness to prevent interference and allow access to the test points.
16. Connect the positive meter lead to the red wire terminal of the test harness. Connect the negative meter lead to the black wire of the test harness. Observe the meter readings while an assistant operates the engine at the speeds indicated in **Table 5**. Record the voltage readings for each speed range.
17. Stop the engine. Connect the positive meter lead to the red wire terminal of the test harness. Connect the negative meter lead to the white wire of the test harness. Observe the meter readings while an assistant operates the engine at the speeds indicated in **Table 5**. Record the voltage readings for each speed range.
18. Stop the engine. Connect the positive meter lead to the black wire terminal of the test harness. Connect the negative meter lead to the white wire of the test harness. Observe the meter readings while an assistant operates the engine at the speeds indicated in **Table 5**. Record the voltage readings for each speed range.
19. Stop the engine and disconnect the test leads.
20. Compare the meter readings with the specifications in **Table 5**. If any of the meter readings are below the minimum specifications, perform the battery charging coil resistance test as described in this section and inspect the flywheel for damaged magnets. See *Flywheel Removal and Installation* in Chapter Seven. Replace the battery charging coil if it fails the resistance test or if low output voltage is evident and no defect is found with the flywheel.
21. Disconnect the negative battery cable.
22. Remove the test harness from the green/white coil wire connector. Plug the green/white wire connector onto the corresponding rectifier/regulator connector. Route the wiring to prevent pinching or interference with moving components.
23. Install the silencer cover as described in Chapter Five.
24. Connect the battery cable.

Battery charging coil resistance test (225 hp model)

Perform the battery charging coil resistance test if the battery charging coil output voltage is below the specification. A test harness (part No. 91-804772) and an accurate digital multimeter are required for this procedure.

1. Disconnect the negative battery cable.
2. Remove the silencer cover as described in Chapter Five.
3. Locate the connectors for the three green and three green white battery charging coil wires. The connectors are located directly above the fuel filter bracket.
4. Unplug the connector for the green coil wires. Do not unplug the green/white coil wires at this time. Connect the female test harness connector onto the connector for the green coil wires. Do not connect the test harness onto the rectifier/regulator connector for this test.
5. Select the R × 1 scale on the meter. Touch the meter test leads to the test harness wire colors specified in **Table 6**. Test lead polarity is not important for this test. The meter must indicate 0.10-0.60 ohm at each pair of connection points. If otherwise, replace the battery charging coil as described in Chapter Six.
6. Remove the test harness from the green coil wire connector. Plug the green wire connector onto the corresponding rectifier/regulator connector.
7. Unplug the connector for the green/white coil wires. Connect the female test harness connector onto the connector for the green/white coil wires.
8. Touch the meter test leads to the test harness wire colors specified in **Table 6**. Test lead polarity is not important for this test. The meter must indicate 0.10-0.50 ohm at each pair of connection points. If otherwise, replace the battery charging coil as described in Chapter Six.
9. Remove the test harness from the green/white coil wire connector. Plug the green/white wire connector onto the corresponding rectifier/regulator connector. Route the wiring to prevent pinching or interference with moving components.
10. Install the silencer cover as described in Chapter Five.
11. Connect the battery cable.

Crankshaft position sensor output test (225 hp model)

Perform the crankshaft position sensor output test if spark is missing or weak on cylinders 1 and 4, 2 and 5 or 3 and 6. A fault on two or all three sensors will cause missing or weak spark on four or possibly all six cylinders.

A sensor malfunction can occur randomly and result in intermittent ignition misfire. A buildup of oil, grease or other contamination can cause the crankshaft position sensor to malfunction. If allowed to build to a sufficient thickness the deposits prevent the sensor from detecting the passing of the flywheel bosses. Clean excessive oil, grease or other deposits from the crankshaft position sensor and the flywheel bosses with a light solvent.

This test measures the peak voltage delivered by the crankshaft position sensors. An accurate tachometer, test harness (part No. 91-888863) and a multimeter capable of measuring peak voltage are required for this procedure. This test must be performed under actual operating conditions.

WARNING

On-water testing or adjustments require two people: one person to operate the boat, the other to monitor the gauges or test equipment and make necessary adjustments. All personnel must remain seated inside the boat at all times. Do not lean over the transom while the boat is under way. Use extensions to allow all gauges and test equipment to be located in normal seating areas.

1. Disconnect the negative battery cable.
2. Refer to the wiring diagrams at the end of the manual to identify wire colors for the crankshaft position sensor harness. Trace the wires from the crankshaft position sensor, located under the flywheel, to the engine wire harness connector (**Figure 61**). The connector is located on the upper port side of the power head and directly above the No. 2 intake runner in the silencer cover. Disconnect the crankshaft position sensor harness connector from the engine wire harness connector.
3. Connect the test harness to the engine wire harness plug and the crankshaft position sensor harness connector as shown in **Figure 39**.
4. Select the peak DC volts function on the meter.
5. Attach the shop tachometer to the engine following manufacturer's instructions. Connect the battery cable.

CAUTION
To prevent damage to the meter test leads and inaccurate test results, route the test leads and harness away from any moving components. Clamp them as necessary to ensure the test leads maintain secure contact to the test harness during engine operation.

NOTE
Some tests must be performed at cranking speed. Disconnect and ground all spark plug wires to allow electric starter operation without starting the engine or disabling the ignition system. Refer to ***Spark Test*** *in this chapter for spark plug wire removal and installation instructions.*

6. Connect the positive meter lead to the red wire terminal of the test harness. Connect the negative lead to the blue wire terminal of the test harness. Observe the meter readings while an assistant operates the engine at the speeds indicated in **Table 5**. Record the voltage readings for each speed range.
7. Stop the engine. Connect the positive meter lead to the black/red wire terminal of the test harness. Connect the negative lead to the blue wire terminal of the test harness. Observe the meter readings while an assistant operates the engine at the speeds indicated in **Table 5**. Record the voltage readings for each speed range.
8. Stop the engine. Connect the positive meter lead to the brown wire terminal of the test harness. Connect the negative lead to the blue wire terminal of the test harness. Observe the meter readings while an assistant operates the engine at the speeds indicated in **Table 5**. Record the voltage readings for each speed range.
9. Stop the engine and compare the meter readings with the specifications listed in **Table 5**. Refer to the following:
   a. Voltage recorded in Step 6, Step 7 or Step 8 is above the specification at any engine speed—Replace the engine control unit (ECU) as described in Chapter Six.
   b. Voltage recorded in Step 6, Step 7 or Step 8 is below the specification at any engine speed—Perform the crankshaft position sensor resistance test as described in this section and inspect the flywheel for damaged magnets. See *Flywheel Removal and Installation* in Chapter Seven. Replace the crankshaft position sensor assembly if it fails the resistance test or if low output voltage is evident and no defect is found with the flywheel.
10. Disconnect the negative battery cable. Remove the shop tachometer.
11. Disconnect the test leads and test harness from the engine. Connect the crankshaft position sensor harness connector onto the engine wire harness connector.
12. Connect the battery cable.

Crankshaft position sensor resistance test (225 hp model)

Perform the crankshaft position sensor resistance test if the crankshaft position sensor output voltage is below the specification. A test harness (part No. 91-888863) and an accurate digital multimeter are required for this procedure.

1. Disconnect the negative battery cable.
2. Refer to the wire diagrams at the end of the manual to identify wire colors for the crankshaft position sensor harness. Trace the wires from the crankshaft position sensor, located under the flywheel, to the engine wire harness connector (**Figure 61**). The connector is located on the upper port side of the power head and directly above the No. 2 intake runner in the silencer cover. Disconnect the crankshaft position sensor harness connector from the engine wire harness connector.
3. Connect the test harness onto the crankshaft position sensor harness connector. Do not connect the test harness onto the engine wire harness connector for this test.
4. Select the R × 100 scale on the meter. Touch the meter test leads to the test harness wire colors specified in **Table 6**. Test lead polarity is not important for this test. The meter must indicate 459-561 ohms at each pair of connection points. If otherwise, replace the crankshaft position sensor assembly as described in Chapter Six.
5. Disconnect the test leads and test harness from the engine. Connect the crankshaft position sensor harness connector onto the engine wire harness connector.
6. Connect the battery cable.

Ignition coil resistance test (225 hp model)

Resistance testing checks for open circuits or short circuits in the primary and secondary windings of the ignition coil.

The wire length used for the primary winding of the ignition coil is relatively short and the resistance readings are fairly low. A much longer length of wire is used in the secondary winding and the resistance readings are relatively high. Use a digital multimeter for the most accurate test results. Usually, a fault within the ignition coil surfaces when the resistance is tested. Ignition coil test specifications are listed in **Table 6**. Make all resistance tests at approximately 68° F (20° C) to ensure accurate test results.

Bear in mind that a resistance test only indicates a short or open circuit. Faults within the coil may result in internal arcing that prevents a strong blue spark at the spark plug. If an internal short is present a clicking noise usually emanates from the coil while attempting to start the engine. Use a spark test tool to check for a good strong blue spark as the engine is cranked. Refer to *Spark Test* in this chapter for instructions on using a spark test tool. Test both the primary and secondary resistance for each coil on the engine. Removal of the ignition coil is not required if the wire terminals are accessible. Refer to Chapter Six if coil removal is required. An accurate digital multimeter is required for this procedure.

1. Disconnect the negative battery cable to prevent accidental starting.
2. Remove the four screws (**Figure 58**) and the plastic spark plug/coil cover on the rear of the power head to access the spark plugs.
3. Mark the cylinder number on the spark plug wires before removing them from the spark plugs. The top cylinder on the starboard bank is the No. 1 cylinder. Odd numbered cylinders are on the starboard cylinder bank and even numbered cylinders are on the port bank. Gently twist the spark plug caps to free them from the plugs, then pull the cap from the plug. Never pull on the spark plug wire to free the cap.
4. Carefully unplug the three engine wire harness connectors from the ignition coil harness connectors (**Figure 59**).
5. To test the primary coil resistance, proceed as follows:
   a. Calibrate the meter to the R × 1 scale.
   b. Touch the meter test leads to the red and black wire terminals in the coil harness connector. Polarity is not important for this test. The meter must indicate 1.5-1.9 ohms. If otherwise, the primary winding is shorted or open and the coil must be replaced.
6. To test the secondary coil resistance, calibrate the meter to the R × 1K scale. Touch the meter test leads to the terminals in the spark plug wire caps. Polarity is not important for this test. The meter must indicate 19.60K-35.00K ohms. If otherwise the secondary coil winding is shorted or open and the coil must be replaced.
7. Test the remaining two ignition coils as described in Step 5 and Step 6.
8. Connect the engine wire harness connectors onto the ignition coil harness connectors.
9. Connect the spark plug wires onto the correct spark plugs. Ensure that all leads are routed correctly.
10. Fit the plastic cover onto the rear of the power head. Install the cover screws and tighten in a crossing pattern to 71 in.-lb. (8.0 N•m).

Throttle position sensor voltage test (225 hp model)

A defective throttle position sensor (**Figure 55**) can cause poor performance at higher throttle settings, hesitation during acceleration or excessively fast idle speed. The engine control unit (ECU) will fix the ignition timing at 10° BTDC if it detects a fault with the throttle position sensor.

Improper throttle position sensor adjustment can cause the same symptoms as a faulty sensor. Always adjust the throttle position sensor (Chapter Four) prior to performing any testing. This test measures the input voltage supplied to the sensor by the ECU and measures the output voltage supplied to the ECU by the sensor. A digital multimeter, shop tachometer and test harness (part No. 91-881827) are required for this test.

Testing requires running the engine under actual operating conditions.

WARNING

On-water testing or adjustments require two people: one to operate the boat, the other to monitor the gauges or test equipment and make necessary adjustments. All personnel must remain seated inside the boat at all times. Do not lean over the transom while the boat is under way. Use extensions to allow all gauges and test equipment to be located in normal seating areas.

1. Disconnect the negative battery cable.
2. Disconnect the throttle position sensor harness connector from the engine wire harness connector. The sensor mounts on top of the upper throttle body on the starboard side of the power head.
3. Connect the test harness to the engine wire harness plug and to the throttle position sensor as shown in **Figure 53**.
4. Select the DC volts function on the meter.
5. Connect the positive meter lead to the orange wire terminal of the test harness. Connect the negative lead to the black wire terminal of the test harness.
6. Route the test leads and harness away from any moving components. Clamp them as necessary to ensure the test leads maintain secure contact to the test harness during engine operation.
7. Attach the shop tachometer to the engine following manufacturer's instructions. Connect the battery cable.

8. Observe the meter readings while an assistant operates the engine at the idle speed (750 rpm) in FORWARD gear. The meter must indicate 4.75-5.25 volts. A faulty ECU or wiring is indicated if the input voltage is not within the specification. Inspect the wiring connecting the throttle position sensor to the ECU for damaged insulation, broken wiring or faulty terminals. Replace the ECU if the input voltage is incorrect and no fault is found with the wiring.
9. Stop the engine. Connect the positive meter lead to the pink wire terminal of the test harness. Connect the negative lead to the black wire terminal of the test harness.
10. Observe the meter readings while an assistant operates the engine at the idle speed (750 rpm) in FORWARD gear. The meter must indicate 0.695-0.705 volt. A faulty or improperly adjusted throttle position sensor is indicated if the voltage is not within the specification. If necessary, readjust the sensor as described in Chapter Four and repeat the test. Replace the sensor if it cannot be adjusted to within the specification.
11. Connect the meter test leads to the test harness as described in Step 9. Have an assistant start the engine and shift into FORWARD gear. Monitor the meter while the assistant *slowly* advances the throttle to full-open. Then, monitor the meter while the assistant *slowly* closes the throttle to the idle position. The meter must indicate a steady increase in voltage as the throttle advances and a steady decrease as the throttle closes. Replace the throttle position sensor as described in Chapter Five if the voltage reading is erratic or does not increase and decrease as described.
12. Stop the engine and disconnect the negative battery cable.
13. Remove the test harness and connect the engine wire harness connector to the throttle position sensor. To prevent potential interference with the throttle linkages, secure the wiring with a plastic locking clamp.
14. Connect the battery cable.

Engine temperature sensor resistance test (225 hp model)

A fault with the engine temperature sensor can cause poor cold engine operating characteristics, excessive idle speed on a fully warmed engine or improper activation of the overheat warning system. The engine control unit (ECU) will fix the ignition timing at 10° BTDC if it detects a fault with the engine temperature sensor.

This test requires an accurate digital or analog multimeter, a liquid thermometer and a container of water that can be heated.

1. Remove the engine temperature sensor as described in Chapter Six.
2. Calibrate the multimeter onto the appropriate scale for the test specification in **Table 8**. Connect the meter leads between the two sensor terminals. Test lead polarity is not important for this test.
3. Suspend the sensor in a container of water that can be heated (**Figure 47**, typical). Ensure the sensor does not touch the bottom or sides of the container and the tip of the sensor is completely below the water surface.
4. Add ice or heat to the container until the water temperature reaches the temperatures specified in **Table 8**. Record the resistance at each temperature.
5. Compare the resistance readings with the specifications in **Table 8**. Replace the engine temperature sensor if the resistance at any specified temperature is not within the specification.
6. Install the engine temperature sensor as described in Chapter Six.

Shift interrupt switch test (225 hp model)

Perform this test if spark is missing on two or four cylinders only at engine speeds less than 2000 rpm. The shift interrupt switch mounts onto the shift cable bracket on the lower starboard side of the power head. The switch operates momentarily while shifting from *forward* or *reverse* gear into *neutral* gear. A multimeter is required for this test. The switch should be removed for testing as the momentary switching that occurs during shifting may occur too rapidly to be detected by the meter.

1. Remove the shift interrupt switch as described in Chapter Six.
2. Calibrate the meter to the R × 1 scale.
3. Connect the meter test leads onto the blue/yellow and black switch wire terminals. Polarity is not important for this test.
4. Observe the meter while repeatedly depressing and releasing the switch arm. The meter must indicate *no continuity* each time the switch arm is depressed and *continuity* each time the switch arm is released. Replace the switch if it fails to perform as specified.

NOTE

Improper installation of the shift interrupt switch may cause no spark on two or four cylinders at engine speeds less than 2000 rpm. If the test indicates no fault with the switch, the fault is usually corrected after installing the switch as described in Chapter Six.

5. Install the shift interrupt switch as described in Chapter Six.

Engine Control Unit (ECU) Test (Ignition System Operation)

A faulty engine control unit (ECU) can cause a no start condition, irregular idle, ignition misfire or incorrect speed limiting. In some rare cases a fault can cause incorrect warning system operation. Refer to *Warning System Troubleshooting* in this chapter for additional information on warning system operation and test instructions.

Testing the ECU is a process of elimination. Test all other components of the ignition system as described in this chapter. Replace the ECU only after ruling out all other components. Faulty wires or connectors cause far more ignition problems than a defective ECU.

Flywheel Inspection

A fault with the flywheel can cause an ignition misfire or erratic ignition timing. These faults are generally caused by a buildup of grease or other contamination on the flywheel surfaces. A cracked or damaged flywheel magnet can cause similar symptoms. Inspection of the flywheel magnets requires removal from the power head. Flywheel removal and installation are described in Chapter Seven.

Clean debris or contamination from the flywheel using a mild solvent. The use of strong solvents can damage the adhesive bonding the magnets to the flywheel on some models. Wipe iron dust or small metallic particles from the magnets using a lightly oiled shop towel.

Inspect the flywheel for corrosion or cracks in the magnets and other surfaces. Carefully sand corrosion from the surfaces. Replace the flywheel if cracks are found in the magnets or other surfaces.

WARNING SYSTEM TROUBLESHOOTING

The warning system alerts the operator in the event of a cooling or lubrication system failure.

Another feature of the warning system provides engine overspeed control. Should the engine reach or exceed a designated engine speed, the engine control unit (ECU) initiates an ignition misfire or shuts off the fuel injectors to reduce the engine speed.

Continued operation with the warning system activated can lead to serious and expensive engine damage. Refer to *Warning System Operation* in this section befure testing any components. This section provides a brief description of system components and operation, followed by test instructions for the warning system components.

Warning System Operation

75 and 90 hp models

If low oil pressure or engine overheating, the warning system alerts the operator by sounding the warning horn and initiating the power reduction circuits. Power to the warning system is provided by the battery and charging system.

Components of the warning system include the oil pressure switch, engine temperature sensor, engine control unit (ECU) and the warning horn. Power to operate the warning horn is provided by the ignition key switch.The ECU sounds the warning horn by grounding the tan/blue wire in the instrument harness and grounding the pink wire in the engine harness. An optional warning light kit is available to provide a visual warning.

Control of the low oil pressure warning system is provided by the oil pressure switch (**Figure 62**). The oil pressure switch remains open as long as the oil pressure is 21.75 psi (150 kPa) or higher. If the oil pressure drops below this value, the oil pressure switch closes and grounds the pink/white wire connecting the switch to the ECU. The ECU then sounds the warning horn, interrupts ignition on cylinders No. 1 and No. 4 and retards the ignition timing to *gradually* reduce the engine speed to a maximum of 3000 rpm. A delay feature prevents the system from activating during the first two seconds after starting the engine. This allows time for the lubrication system to build pressure. Normal operation returns only after reducing the throttle to the idle position, stopping the engine and correcting the condition causing low oil pressure.

The ECU relies on input from the engine temperature sensor (**Figure 63**) to control the overheat warning system. If the engine temperature sensor input indicates over-

heating, the ECU sounds the warning horn, interrupts ignition on cylinders No. 1 and No. 4, and retards the ignition timing to *gradually* reduce the engine speed to a maximum of 3000 rpm. A delay feature prevents activation of the overheat warning system for either 24 or 75 seconds after starting the engine to allow normal residual heat to disperse. The system delays the warning for 24 seconds if the engine speed is 2000 rpm and higher and 75 seconds if the engine speed is less than 2000 rpm. Normal operation returns only after reducing the throttle to the idle position, stopping the engine and correcting the cause of overheating.

Never operate the engine with the warning horn sounding. Continued operation results in costly damage to the power head and other engine components.

Overspeed protection is provided automatically by the ECU. A controlled misfire occurs at preset values based upon engine speed. Normal ignition system operation resumes when the throttle is reduced enough to drop the engine speed below the preset value. Note the following:

1. If the engine speed exceeds 6200 rpm, the ECU interrupts ignition to cylinder No. 1 *or* cylinder No. 4.
2. If the engine speed exceeds 6250 rpm, the ECU interrupts ignition on cylinder No. 1 *and* cylinder No. 4.
3. If the engine speed exceeds 6300 rpm, the ECU interrupts ignition on cylinder No. 1, cylinder No. 4 *and* cylinder No. 2 *or* cylinder No. 3.
4. If the engine speed exceeds 6350 rpm, the ECU interrupts ignition on all four cylinders.

115 hp model

The warning system alerts the operator if low oil pressure or engine overheating occurs. The warning horn and initiation of the power reduction circuits alert the operator if either condition occurs. Electrical current to operate the system is provided by the battery and charging system.

Components of the warning system include the oil pressure switch, engine temperature sensor, engine control unit (ECU) and the warning horn. Power to operate the warning horn is provided by the ignition key switch. The ECU sounds the warning horn by grounding the tan/blue wire in the instrument harness and grounding the pink wire in the engine harness. An optional warning light kit is available to provide a visual warning.

Control of the low oil pressure warning system is provided by the oil pressure switch (**Figure 62**). The oil pressure switch remains open as long as the oil pressure is 21.75 psi (150 kPa) or higher. If the oil pressure drops below this value, the oil pressure switch closes and grounds pink/white wire connecting the switch to the ECU. The ECU then sounds the warning horn, interrupts ignition and fuel injector operation on cylinders No. 1 and No. 4 and retards the ignition timing to *gradually* reduce the engine speed to a maximum of 2000 rpm. A delay feature prevents the system from activating during the first two seconds after starting the engine. This allows time for the lubrication system to build pressure. If the oil pressure drops below switch value, the warning system circuits in the ECU sounds the warning horn. Normal operation occurs only after reducing the throttle to the idle position, stopping the engine and correcting the condition causing low oil pressure.

The ECU relies on input from the engine temperature sensor (**Figure 63**) to control the overheat warning system. If the engine temperature sensor input indicates engine heat increasing at a faster than normal rate after starting or if the engine temperature exceeds 194°F (90°C), the ECU sounds the warning horn, interrupts ignition and fuel injector operation on cylinders No. 1 and No. 4 and retards the ignition timing to *gradually* reduce the engine speed to a maximum of 2000 rpm. A delay feature prevents activation of the overheat warning for either 20 or 60 seconds after starting the engine to allow normal residual heat to disperse. The system delays the warning for 20 seconds if the engine speed is 2000 rpm and higher and 60 seconds if the engine speed is less than 2000 rpm. Normal operation occurs only after reducing the throttle to the idle position, stopping the engine and allowing the temperature to drop below 167° F (75°C).

Never operate the engine with the warning horn sounding. Continued operation results in costly damage to the power head and other engine components.

Overspeed protection is provided automatically by the ECU. A controlled misfire occurs at preset values based upon engine speed. Normal ignition system operation resumes when the throttle is reduced enough to drop the engine speed below the preset value. Note the following:

1. If the engine speed exceeds 6200 rpm, the ECU interrupts ignition to cylinder No. 1 *or* cylinder No. 4.
2. If the engine speed exceeds 6250 rpm, the ECU interrupts ignition on cylinder No. 1 *and* cylinder No. 4.
3. If the engine speed exceeds 6350 rpm, the ECU interrupts ignition on cylinder No. 1, cylinder No. 4 *and* cylinder No. 2 *or* cylinder No. 3.
4. If the engine speed exceeds 6450 rpm, the ECU interrupts ignition on all four cylinders.

225 hp model

The warning system alerts the operator if low oil pressure or engine overheating occurs. The warning horn and initiation of the power reduction circuits alert the operator if either condition occurs. Electrical current to operate the system is provided by the battery and charging system.

Components of the warning system include the oil pressure sender, engine temperature switches, engine control unit (ECU), shift position switch and the warning horn. Power to operate the warning horn is provided by the ignition key switch. The ECU sounds the warning horn by grounding the tan/blue wire in the instrument harness and grounding the pink wire in the engine harness. An optional warning light kit is available to provide a visual warning.

Control of the low oil pressure warning system is provided by the oil pressure sender (**Figure 62**). The oil pressure sender provides a varying value to the ECU that indicates the oil pressure. Under normal conditions, oil pressure will be lowest at idle speeds and increases as engine speed increases. The ECU continuously monitors the sender input. If the sender indicates the oil pressure has dropped below the lower limit for the given engine speed, the ECU then sounds the warning horn and progressively interrupts ignition and fuel injector operation on cylinders No. 2, No. 5, No. 3, and No. 6 to *gradually* reduce the engine speed to a maximum of 2000 rpm. A delay feature prevents the system from activating during the first two seconds after starting the engine. This allows time for the lubrication system to build pressure. Normal operation occurs only after reducing the throttle to the idle position, stopping the engine and correcting the condition causing low oil pressure.

The ECU relies on input from the two engine temperature switches (**Figure 64**) to control the overheat warning system. The pink wire connects both switches to the ECU. Either switch activates if the cooling water it contacts exceeds 183° F (84°C). When activated, the switch grounds the pink wire. The switches reset and the pink wire is ungrounded when the cooling water temperature drops to approximately 167° F (75° C). If either switch activates,

the ECU progressively interrupts ignition and fuel injector operation on cylinders No. 2, No. 5, No. 3, and No. 6 to *gradually* reduce the engine speed to a maximum of 2000 rpm. A delay feature prevents activation of the overheat warning system for either 25 or 75 seconds after starting the engine to allow normal residual heat to disperse. The system delays the warning for 25 seconds if the engine speed is 2000 rpm or higher and 75 seconds if the engine speed is less than 2000 rpm. Normal operation occurs only after reducing the throttle to the idle position, stopping the engine and allowing the engine temperature to drop enough to reset the engine temperature switches.

Never operate the engine with the warning horn sounding. Continued operation results in costly damage to the power head and other engine components.

Overspeed protection is provided automatically by the ECU. A controlled misfire occurs at preset values based upon engine speed and gear position. The shift position switch mounts onto the shift cable bracket on the lower starboard side of the power head. A brown wire connects one shift position switch terminal to the ECU. A black wire connects the other terminal to the engine ground. The shift linkages depresses the shift arm when the gearcase is shifted into neutral gear, grounding the brown wire and signaling the ECU that the engine is in neutral gear. Note

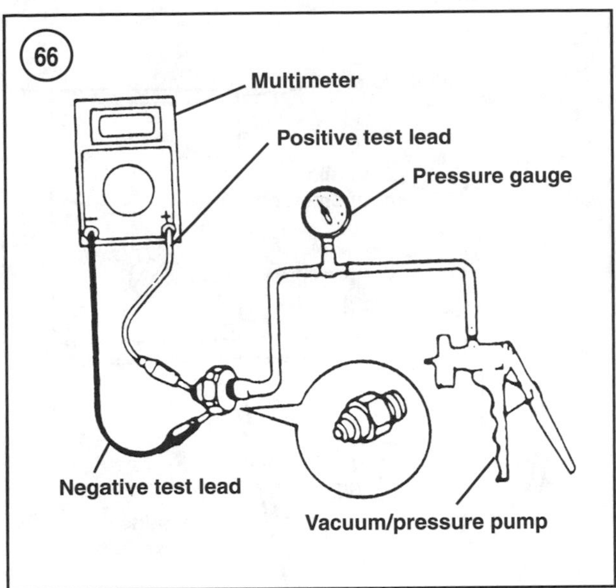

the following to determine the overspeed protection system operation:

1. If the engine speed exceeds 4500 rpm in neutral gear, the ECU interrupts ignition on cylinder No. 1 *or* cylinder No. 4.
2. If the engine speed exceeds 4750 in neutral gear, the ECU interrupts ignition on all six cylinders.
3. If the engine speed exceeds 6200 rpm in forward or reverse gear, the ECU interrupts ignition to cylinder No. 1 *or* cylinder No. 4.
4. If the engine speed exceeds 6350 rpm in forward or reverse gear, the ECU interrupts ignition on the No. 1, No. 4, No. 2, and No. 5 cylinders.
5. If the engine speed exceeds 6450 rpm in forward or reverse gear, the ECU interrupts ignition on all six cylinders. Normal ignition system operation resumes after the throttle is reduced enough to drop the engine speed below the preset value for the gear position.

Cooling or Lubrication System Fault Evaluation

The warning horn tone and power reduction feature is the same for overheating and low oil pressure. If the warning horn sounds, check for the presence of the water stream (**Figure 65**) exiting the lower back area of the engine before stopping the engine. Refer to *Cooling System Troubleshooting* in this chapter if the water stream is not present. If the water stream is present, the warning is likely due to low oil pressure. Refer to *Power Head Troubleshooting* in this chapter to check the engine oil pressure.

Test all applicable warning system components if a warning alarm occurs and a cooling or lubrication system fault has been ruled out. Refer to *Warning System Operation* in this section to determine which components are used.

Oil Pressure Switch Test

The oil pressure switch is used on 75-115 hp models. This test measures the pressure in which the switch activates. This test requires a multimeter and a vacuum/pressure pump. Purchase the vacuum/pressure pump from an automotive parts or tool supply store. Test the switch as follows:

1. Remove the oil pressure switch as described in Chapter Six.
2. Slide an appropriately sized hose over the threaded fitting of the oil pressure switch (**Figure 66**). Apply a clamp over the connection to ensure an air tight connection. Do not apply pressure at this time.
3. Calibrate the meter to the R × 1 scale.
4. Connect the meter leads onto the switch terminals and the body of the switch (**Figure 66**). Polarity is not important for this test. If necessary, use a clamp to secure the test lead to the switch body. The meter must indicate *continuity*. If otherwise the switch has failed open and must be replaced.
5. Observe the meter and the pressure gauge while *slowly* applying pressure to the switch. Note the pressure gauge reading when the meter reading changes to *no continuity*.
6. Observe the meter and pressure gauge while *slowly* relieving the pressure. Note the pressure gauge reading when the reading changes to *continuity*.
7. Repeat Step 5 and Step 6 several times to check for an intermittent switch failure. The meter must change to a *no continuity* each time the pressure reaches approximately 22 psi (150 kPa) and *continuity* each time the pressure drops below the specification. Replace the oil pressure switch if it fails to perform as specified.
8. Remove the test leads and pressure/vacuum pump from the oil pressure switch. Clean all hose material from the threaded section of the switch.
9. Install the oil pressure switch as described in Chapter Six.

Oil Pressure Sender Test

WARNING

On-water testing or adjustments require two people: one to operate the boat, the other to monitor the gauges or test equipment and make necessary adjustments. All personnel must remain seated inside the boat at all times. Do not lean over the transom while the boat is under way. Use extensions to allow all gauges and test equipment to be located in normal seating areas.

The oil pressure sender is used on 225 hp models. This test measures the sender output voltage at a specified oil pressure. This test requires an oil pressure gauge with a suitable adapter, multimeter and the test harness (part No. 91-888860). This test must be performed with the engine running under actual operating conditions on a flush/test device.

1. Test the oil pressure as described in this chapter. See *Oil Pressure Test*. The engine oil pressure must be correct to accurately test the sender.
2. Disconnect the negative battery cable.
3. Locate the oil pressure sender on the front starboard side of the power head and to the rear of the oil filter.
4. Disconnect the engine wire harness connector from the oil pressure sender. Connect the test harness to the engine wire harness plug and the oil pressure sender.
5. Select the DC volts function on the meter.
6. Connect the positive meter lead to the green wire terminal of the test harness. Connect the negative lead to the black wire terminal of the test harness.
7. Route the test leads and harness away from any moving components. Clamp them as necessary to ensure good contact during engine operation.
8. Attach the shop tachometer to the engine following manufacturer's instructions. Connect the battery cable.
9. Observe the meter readings while an assistant operates the engine at the idle speed (700 rpm) in FORWARD gear. The meter must indicate 4.75-5.25 volts. A faulty engine control unit (ECU) or wiring is indicated if the input voltage is not within the specification. Inspect the wiring connecting the oil pressure sender to the ECU for damaged insulation, broken wiring or faulty terminals. Replace the ECU if the input voltage is incorrect and no fault is found with the wiring.
10. Stop the engine. Connect the positive meter lead to the green/white wire terminal of the test harness. Connect the negative lead to the black wire terminal of the test harness.
11. Observe the meter readings while an assistant operates the engine at the idle speed (700 rpm) in NEUTRAL gear. The meter must indicate approximately 3.8 volts. The engine and oil temperature has a significant effect on oil pressure, and the output from the sensor will vary accordingly. This value is representative of the normal reading with the engine and oil at normal operating temperature. The output voltage may vary by 1 volt or more if operating the engine in very cold or warm climates. Replace the oil pressure sender as described in Chapter Six if the output voltage is significantly different from the specification.
12. Stop the engine. Disconnect the negative battery cable.
13. Remove the test harness and connect the engine wire harness connector onto the oil pressure sender. To prevent potential interference with the throttle linkages, secure the wiring with a plastic locking clamp.
14. Connect the battery cable.

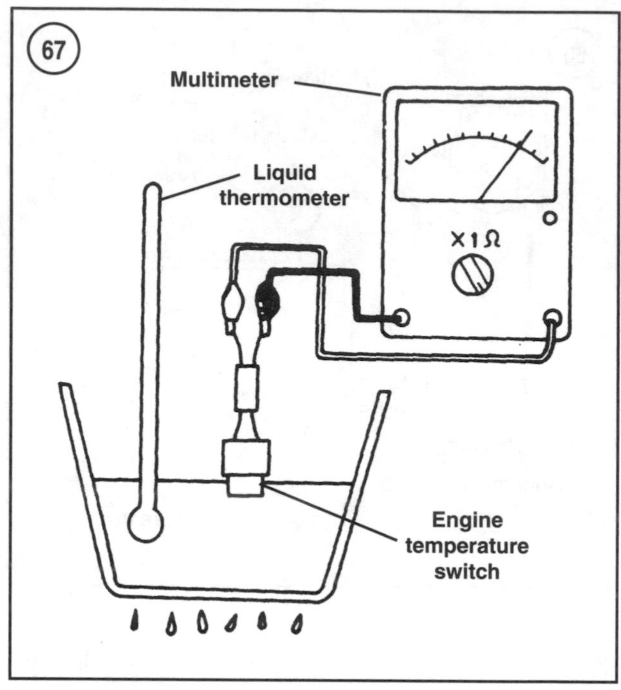

Engine Temperature Switch Test

CAUTION

Suspend the engine temperature switch so only the sensor is below the surface of the water. An inaccurate reading will occur if the test leads contact the water.

The engine temperature switch is used on 225 hp models. The switch is designed to switch ON at a predetermined temperature and switch OFF at a lower temperature. This switch signals the engine control unit (ECU) that overheating is occurring. The switch (**Figure 64**) mounts into the thermostat housings on each side of the cylinder block.

One switch lead is connected to the engine ground. This switch will not operate correctly if this connection is faulty. The other lead is connected to the pink wire leading to the ECU.

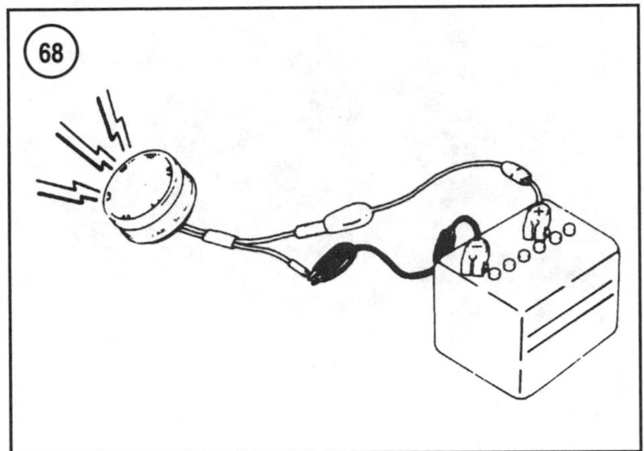

68

This test requires a multimeter, liquid thermometer and a container of water that can be heated.

1. Disconnect both cables from the battery.
2. Remove the two engine temperature switches as described in Chapter Six.
3. Fill thc container with cool tap water and suspend the tip of one of the overheat switches in the water (**Figure 67**). Ensure the switch does not contact the bottom or sides of the container. Place a liquid thermometer in the container with the overheat switch as shown in **Figure 67**.
4. Calibrate the multimeter onto the R × 1 scale. Connect the meter leads between the two overheat switch wires. Polarity is not important for this test. The meter must indicate *no continuity* if placed in cool water. If the meter indicates continuity, the switch is shorted and must be replaced. If the switch fails, no further testing is required.
5. Heat and gently stir the water while observing the meter. Note the temperature when the meter switches from *no continuity* to *continuity*. This should occur at a temperature of approximately 183° F (84°C). Discontinue the test if the water boils before the meter reading changes.
6. Allow the water to cool and note the temperature at which the meter changes from *continuity* to *no continuity*. This should occur at a temperature of 154-179° F (68-82° C).
7. Replace the overheat switch if it does not perform as specified.
8. Test the other engine temperature switch as described in Steps 3-7.
9. Install the two engine temperature switches as described in Chapter Six.

Engine Temperature Sensor Test

On 75-115 hp models, the engine temperature sensor provides input for both the ignition and warning systems. If suspected of causing a malfunction of the warning system, test the engine temperature sensor as described under *Ignition System Troubleshooting* in this chapter.

Warning Horn Test

A warning horn is mounted inside the remote control or behind the dashboard. Access to both wires is required to test the warning horn. Refer to Chapter Eleven to access the horn wires if mounted inside the remote control. Connect the wires of the horn to a battery using jumper leads (**Figure 68**). Replace the warning horn if it fails to emit a loud tone.

Shift Position Switch Test (225 hp Model)

Perform this test if an ignition misfire occurs only at 4500 rpm or higher in FORWARD gear and no faults are found with the ignition and fuel system. The shift position switch mounts onto the shift cable bracket on the lower starboard side of the power head. The switch operates when the engine is shifted into *neutral*. A multimeter is required for this test.

1. Disconnect the negative battery cable to prevent accidental starting.
2. Locate the shift position switch on the lower engine cover. Identify the switch by wire color. The shift position switch wires are brown and black. The shift interrupt switch wires are blue/yellow and black. The switches are similar in appearance and mount onto the same bracket.
3. Disconnect the shift position switch wire harness connector from the engine wire harness connector.
4. Calibrate the meter to the R × 1 scale. Connect the meter test leads to brown and black wire terminals in the connector. Polarity is not important for this test.
5. Observe the meter while repeatedly shifting the engine into FORWARD gear and returning to NEUTRAL gear. The meter must indicate *no continuity* each time the engine is shifted into *forward* gear and *continuity* each time the engine is shifted into *reverse* gear. Replace the switch as described in Chapter Six if it fails to perform as specified.

NOTE

Improper installation of the shift position switch may cause an ignition misfire at 4500 rpm or higher in forward gear. Check for improper switch installation if the ignition misfire persists with the replacement switch.

Engine Control Unit (ECU) Test (Warning System Operation)

Check all wire and connections if the switches or sensors are in good condition. Replace the engine control unit (ECU) if all other warning system components operate correctly but a false alarm persists. Bear in mind that far more false alarms are caused by faulty wire connections than a defective ECU. Replacing the ECU seldom corrects the condition. Thoroughly inspect all applicable wires and terminals before replacing the ECU. ECU removal and installation are described in Chapter Six.

Overspeed Protection System Test

WARNING
On-water testing or adjustments require two people: one to operate the boat, the other to monitor the gauges or test equipment and make necessary adjustments. All personnel must remain seated inside the boat at all times. Do not lean over the transom while the boat is under way. Use extensions to allow all gauges and test equipment to be located in normal seating areas.

The engine control unit (ECU) controls the overspeed protection system. It initiates an ignition misfire to prevent power head damage from excessive engine speed.

A malfunctioning overspeed protection system can cause a misfire to occur while the engine is running within the recommended speed range. Conversely, a malfunction may allow engine speed above the recommended range without activating the system. **Table 10** lists the recommended engine speeds for all models and the speed at which overspeed control should activate.

To test the system, connect an accurate tachometer and run the engine at wide-open throttle under actual operating conditions. Replace the ECU if the engine speed exceeds the maximum limit without activating the overspeed protection system. If a misfire occurs while running within the recommended speed range, first test all fuel and ignition system components. If all fuel and ignition system components are functioning correctly, replace the ECU.

CHARGING SYSTEM TROUBLESHOOTING

The battery charging systems provide electric current to operate the ignition system and other engine components such as the trim and electronic fuel injection system. It also provides current to operate electric devices on the boat such as navigational lighting, radios, depth finders and live well pumps. Another duty of the charging system is charging the onboard batteries. Charging system components include the flywheel, battery charging coil, rectifier/regulator, fuses, wiring and the battery.

This section describes charging system activation and test procedures.

69

70

Charging System Operation and Testing

When the engine is running, the magnets located along the inner ring of the flywheel (**Figure 69**) pass next to the battery charging coil (**Figure 70**). Alternating current (AC) is created as the magnetic lines of force from the flywheel mounted magnets pass through the battery charging coil windings. This alternating current is not suitable for charging the battery or operating many engine electrical components. The rectifier/regulator (**Figure 71**, typical) converts the AC to direct current (DC) providing battery charging capability. The rectifier/regulator limits the output of the charging system to prevent overcharging the battery. Overcharging can damage the battery and some electrical component on the engine.

71

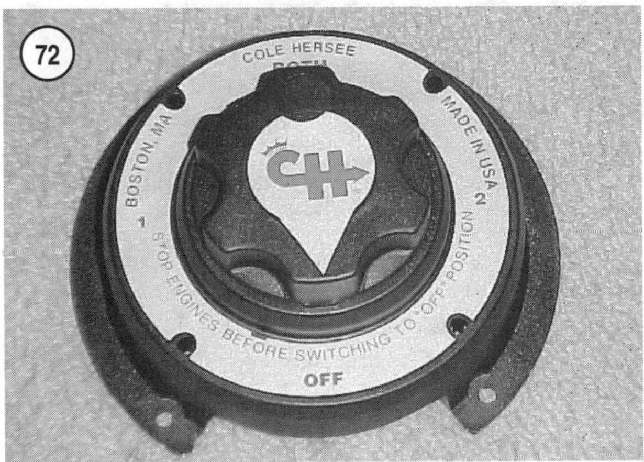

72

A malfunctioning charging system generally results in an undercharged battery. Many newer boats are equipped with numerous electrical components including electric trolling motors, depth finders, communication radios, stereo systems, live well pumps, lighting and other electrical accessories. Many times the current required to operate these accessories exceeds the output of the charging system resulting in an undercharged battery.

The installation of an auxiliary battery and a switching device (**Figure 72**) may be required to power these accessories. These devices separate the batteries and prevent electrical accessories from discharging the engine cranking battery. They also allow charging of multiple batteries while underway. Follow the manufacturer's instructions when installing these switching devices.

On 75 and 90 hp models, the signal to operate the tachometer is provided by the charging system. In almost all instances the charging system is providing some battery charging capacity if the tachometer registers engine speed. However a fault can allow tachometer operation even though the charging system is performing well below its maximum efficiency.

On 115 and 225 hp models, the tachometer signal is generated by the engine control unit (ECU) and unlike the 75 and 90 hp models does not depend on the charging system to operate.

Overcharging is almost always the result of a faulty rectifier/regulator. An overcharge condition can also result from a faulty battery or corroded terminals and wiring. Refer to *Battery care and cleaning* in Chapter Six if the rectifier/regulator operates correctly but overcharging is occurring. Always clean the terminals and correct any problems with wiring or connections prior to testing the charging system.

Perform the *Charging System Output Test* in this section to determine if the charging system is operating. Testing the individual components of the charging system should identify the faulty components.

Because the charging system operation can adversely affect the ignition system operation, many of the charging system test procedures are performed during ignition system troubleshooting. The charging system output test procedures indicate when to perform the designated ignition system test procedure(s).

WARNING

Use extreme caution when working around batteries. Never smoke or allow sparks to occur around batteries. Batteries produce explosive hydrogen gas that can explode and result in injury or death. Never make the final connection of a circuit to the battery terminal as an arc may occur and lead to fire or explosion.

WARNING

Stay clear of the propeller shaft while running an outboard on a flush/test device. Remove the propeller before running the engine to help avoid serious injury. Disconnect all spark plug wires and both battery cables before removing or installing the propeller.

CAUTION

Never remove or disconnect the battery cables or any lead of the charging system while the engine is running. Permanent damage to the charging system components usually occurs when these cables or leads are disconnected.

Charging System Output Test

Always inspect the battery terminals, all wire terminals, plugs and other charging system connections for corrosion, debris or damaged terminals. Correct all defects prior to performing this test. This test must be performed with the engine running. An accurate digital multimeter is required for this test.

1. Switch all electrical accessories OFF. With the engine not running, connect the multimeter to the battery terminals. Record the battery voltage.
2. Start the engine, run at idle speed and note the voltage. The voltage should be at least 0.2 volt greater than the voltage recorded in Step 1.
3. Next, throttle up to approximately 2000 rpm and note the multimeter. The voltage should again be at least 0.2 volt greater than the voltage recorded in Step 1.
4. Repeat Step 3 and Step 4 with all onboard accessories turned ON one at a time. If the voltage drops below 0.2 volt more than the voltage recorded in Step 1, the charging system is likely functioning correctly; however, the accessory load may exceed the capacity of the charging system.
   a. If the voltage increase is more than 0.2 volts above the voltage recorded in Steps 2 and 3, the charging system output is correct, as long as the voltage does not exceed 13.8 volts.
   b. If the voltage increase in Step 2 or Step 4 is less than 0.2 volts above the voltage in Step 1 (accessories on), perform the battery charging coil output test as described in this chapter (see *Ignition System Troubleshooting*) and the rectifier/regulator resistance test (75-115 hp models only). Replace the rectifier/regulator if it fails the resistance test or if low output is evident and the battery charging coil tests correctly.
   c. If the charging voltage exceeds 13.8 volts, the charging system is overcharging. First, check the charging system wiring for damaged wires or loose or corroded connections. If the wiring and connections are in acceptable condition, replace the rectifier/regulator as described in Chapter Six.

Rectifier/Regulator Resistance Test (75 and 90 hp Models)

This test measures the resistance on the rectifier/regulator used on 75 and 90 hp models. Perform this test if the rectifier/regulator fails the output test and no fault is found with the battery charging coil.

An accurate multimeter is required for this procedure.

1. Remove the rectifier/regulator as described in Chapter Six.
2. Calibrate the meter to the R × 10 scale. Connect the *positive* meter lead to the red rectifier/regulator wire terminal. Connect the *negative* meter lead to the green, then

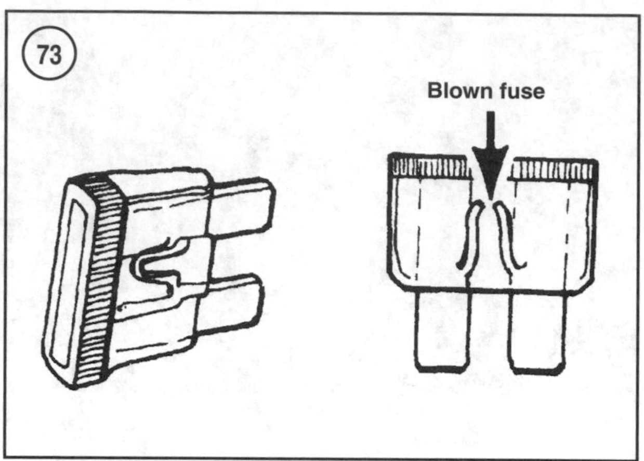

both green/white wire terminals. The meter must indicate 100-300 ohms at each connection point.
3. Calibrate the meter to the R × 1k scale. Connect the *negative* meter lead to the red rectifier/regulator wire terminal. Connect the *positive* meter lead to the green, then both green/white wire terminals. The meter must indicate *no continuity* at each connection point.
4. Calibrate the meter to the R × 1k scale. Connect the *positive* meter lead to the black rectifier/regulator wire terminal. Connect the *negative* meter lead to the green, then both green/white wire terminals. The meter must indicate *no continuity* at each connection point.
5. Calibrate the meter to the R × 10 scale. Connect the *negative* meter lead to the black rectifier/regulator wire terminal. Connect the *positive* meter lead to the green, then both green/white wire terminals. The meter must indicate 100-300 ohms at each connection point.
6. Replace the rectifier/regulator if it fails to perform as specified.
7. Install the rectifier/regulator as described in Chapter Six.

Rectifier/Regulator Resistance Test (115 hp Model)

This test measures the resistance on the rectifier/regulator used on the 115 hp model. Perform this test if the rectifier/regulator fails the output test and no fault is found with the battery charging coil. An accurate multimeter and test harness (part No. 91-881824) are required for this procedure.

1. Disconnect the negative battery cable. Push up and in on the locking tabs, then remove the electrical component cover.
2. Refer to the wire diagrams at the end of the manual to identify wire colors for the battery charging coil. Trace the wires from the charging coil to the rectifier/regulator. Dis-

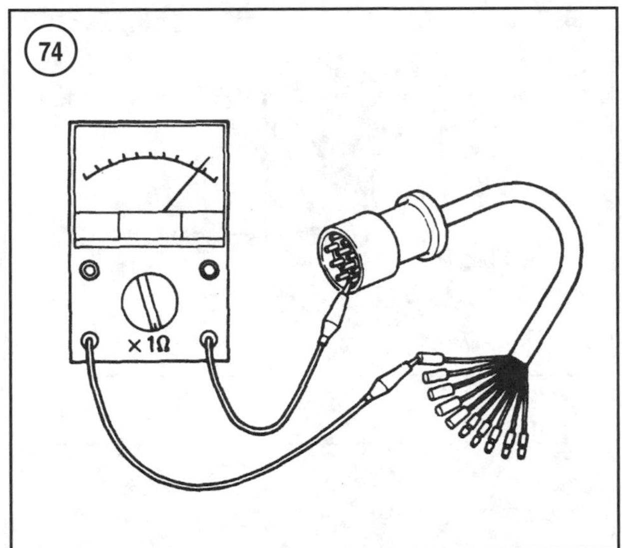

connect the battery charging coil harness connector from the rectifier/regulator.

3. Connect the test harness onto rectifier/regulator harness connector.

4. Calibrate the meter to the R × 10 scale. Connect the *positive* meter lead onto the red test harness wire. Connect the *negative* meter lead onto each of the three green test harness wires. The meter must indicate 100-300 ohms at each connection point.

5. Calibrate the meter to the R × 1k scale. Connect the *negative* meter lead onto the red test harness wire. Connect the *positive* meter lead onto each of the three green test harness wires. The meter must indicate *no continuity* at each connection point.

6. Calibrate the meter to the R × 1k scale. Connect the *positive* meter lead to the black test harness wire. Connect the *negative* test lead to each of the three green test harness wires. The meter must indicate *no continuity* at each connection point.

7. Calibrate the meter to the R × 10 scale. Connect the *negative* meter lead to the black test harness wire. Connect the *positive* meter lead to each of the three green test harness wires. The meter must indicate 100-300 ohms at each connection point.

8. Disconnect the test harness, then connect the battery charging coil harness connector onto the rectifier/regulator.

9. Install the electrical component cover. Ensure the locking tabs fully engage the slots.

10. Connect the battery cable.

Fuse Test

Fuses protect the wiring harness and electric components from damage if a circuit overloads or shorts. Refer to the wire diagrams located at the end of the manual to determine fuse usage for all models. A fault with the fuse can prevent the electric starter from operating, prevent trim and tilt system from operating, or prevent the electronic fuel system from operating.

WARNING
Never replace a fuse without thoroughly checking the wire harness for defects. Never install a fuse with a capacity greater than the original fuse.

All models covered in this manual use the plug-in type fuse (**Figure 73**). A blown fuse can usually be identified with a visual inspection (**Figure 73**). However, a fuse can appear to be in good condition, but still have no continuity. Check the continuity of all fuses using a multimeter in the event of an electrical problem.

Refer to the wiring diagrams at the back of this manual to determine which wires connect to the fuses. If an electric system or component fails to operate, always test all fuses in the connecting wiring before performing further troubleshooting. A multimeter is required for fuse testing.

1. Disconnect both cables from the battery.
2. Grasp the back of the fuse and pull it out of the fuse holder. Some fuse holders are located under the plastic electrical component cover.
3. Calibrate the meter to the R × 1 scale. Connect to both fuse terminals and note the meter.
4. If the fuse is good, the meter will indicate *continuity. No continuity* means the fuse has failed and must be replaced. Note that a fuse failure is usually the result of a shorted or overloaded circuit. Inspect all engine and instrument wires for damaged insulation, chafing, loose or corroded connections or other damage. Repair damaged wiring or poor connections before replacing the fuse.

Wire Harness Test

Due to the harsh marine environment that boats operate in, wiring harness problems are common. Corroded or damaged wires or connections can cause electrical or ignition system components to malfunction. Electrical problems can also occur intermittently, making troubleshooting extremely difficult.

If an electrical malfunction occurs and testing indicates that all individual components are functioning properly, inspect the wiring harness. Disconnect all components from the harness and test for continuity using a multimeter (**Figure 74**).

Most wiring harness problems occur at the connectors and plugs. Inspect the connectors for bent pins (**Figure 75**) and loose terminals (**Figure 76**). Make sure the connectors lock together securely (**Figure 77**). Loose connectors are a major cause of intermittent electrical problems. To test the wiring harness, proceed as follows:

1. Disconnect both cables from the battery.
2. Mark all wire terminals connected to the wire harness. Note the wire routing then disconnect all wires from the harness.
3. Refer to the wire diagrams located at the end of the manual to identify the wire color to connector pin locations.
4. Calibrate the multimeter to the R × 1 scale. Connect the meter test leads to the pins as indicated in **Figure 74**. Polarity is not important for this test.
5. The meter should show *continuity.*
6. Observe the meter reading while twisting, bending and pulling on the wire harness. A fault is indicated if the meter reading changes to *no continuity*. Often intermittent faults are found this way.
7. Repeat Steps 3-6 for the remaining wires in the harness.
8. Connect all components to the engine wire harness. Route all wires in a manner preventing them from contacting any moving components. Prior to connecting them ensure all ground terminals for the wire harness are clean and securely attached to the wire harness.
9. Clean the terminals. Connect the cables to the battery.

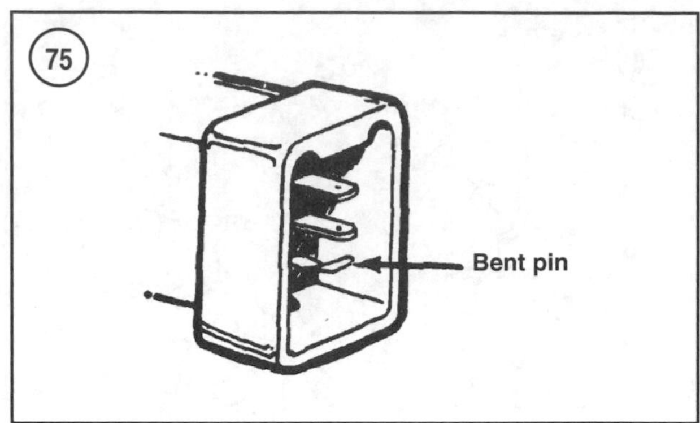

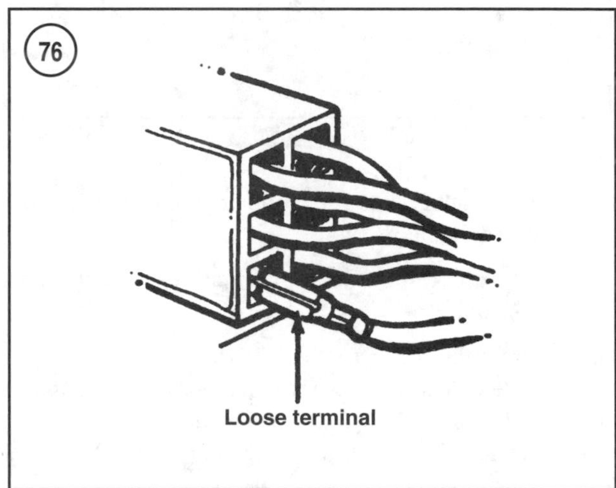

POWER HEAD TROUBLESHOOTING

All models covered in this manual use a four-stroke power head with an overhead camshaft design. The use of an overhead camshaft reduces engine weight compared to a cylinder block mounted camshaft. The overhead camshaft design provides a less complex valve train and allows for easier adjustments and repairs.

This section provides troubleshooting tips and testing instructions to pinpoint most power head related failures. Compression and oil pressure testing are also provided in this section.

Engine Noises

Some power head noise is generated during normal engine operation. A ticking or heavy knocking noise that intensifies during acceleration is a reason for concern.

If suspecting a worn or damaged component is the cause of an engine noise, consider having a professional technician listen to the engine. In many cases only the trained ear of the technician can determine what component has failed.

Power head repairs can be costly and time consuming. Investigate all noises thoroughly before disassembling the power head.

A broken or loose bracket or fastener can cause a noise that is easily mistaken for an internal power head failure.

Ticking noise

Ticking is common when valve adjustment is required or a valve train component has failed. Adjust the valves as described in Chapter Four, then listen to the engine.

Ticking can also result from a damaged piston. Inspect the spark plugs for damage or aluminum deposits (**Figure 78**). Complete power head disassembly and repair is required if metal deposits are found on the spark plug. Perform a compression test as described in this chapter. Remove the cylinder head and inspect the valves, gaskets,

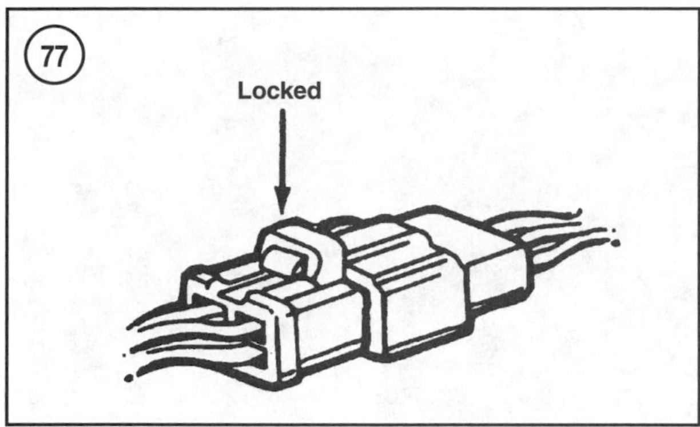

pistons and cylinders if low compression is revealed. Cylinder head removal and installation are provided in Chapter Seven.

See *Valve Train Failure* in this section for additional information if the spark plugs and compression are good, but the ticking noise persists.

CAUTION

Running the engine with an abnormal noise may result in increased damage dramatically increasing the cost of repairs.

Whirring or squealing noise

A whirring or squealing noise is usually related to a problem with main or connecting rod bearings. Often the noise becomes louder if the throttle is abruptly reduced to idle from a higher speed.

Sometimes the cylinder creating the noise can be identified using a mechanic's stethoscope. Touch the tip of the probe to the power head while listening. Compare the noise emanating from one area of the power head, cylinder head or crankcase, with the noise from the same area but on a different cylinder. A noise confined to one cylinder indicates a problem with its connecting rod bearing. A noise common to all cylinders indicates a problem with crankshaft main bearings. Test the oil pressure as described in this chapter to determine if the noise is caused by insufficient lubrication. Be aware that the timing belt, timing chains and pulleys can generate a fair amount of noise. Use the stethoscope to be certain the noise is emanating from the power head before proceeding with a power head repair.

WARNING

Use extreme caution when working on or around a running engine. Tie back long hair and do not wear loose clothing. Avoid the flywheel and drive belts. Never allow anyone near the propeller or propeller shaft while the engine is running.

Knocking noise

Use a mechanic's stethoscope to determine if the noise is emanating from the power head or elsewhere. The noise will be more pronounced in the crankcase area if a problem exists in the crankshaft and connecting rods. Special insulated pliers allow spark plug wire removal while the engine is running. The noise may lessen when the spark plug wire is removed on the suspected cylinder. This procedure is difficult to do and may result in damage to the electrical system. Ground the spark plug promptly to reduce the chance of damage to ignition system. Another method of isolating the cylinder is to remove one spark plug wire and attach it to an engine ground. Start the engine and listen to the noise. Install the spark lead and repeat the process for another cylinder. If the noise is less when one lead is grounded compared to another, that cylinder is suspect.

Always perform an oil pressure test if a knocking noise is detected. Knocking noise combined with low or unstable oil pressure generally indicates fault with the crankshaft main and/or connecting rod bearings. Refer to *Oil Pressure Test* in this chapter.

Bearing failure causes metal particles to accumulate in the oil pan. These particles are picked up by the oil pump where they are deposited in the oil filter. Inspect the oil filter if bearing failure is suspected. Remove the filter as described in Chapter Three. Cut open the filter and inspect the filter element. Bearing failure is likely if a significant amount of metal debris is found.

Lubrication System Failure

A lubrication system failure can lead to catastrophic power head failure. Lubrication system failure leads to scuffed pistons (**Figure 79**), excessive wear of valve train components (**Figure 80**) and eventual power head failure.

Failure of the lubrication system results from the following common causes:

1. Incorrect oil level.
2. Oil leakage or high oil consumption.
3. Contaminated, diluted or wrong type of oil.
4. Oil pump system failure.

CAUTION
Damage can occur in a matter of seconds if the lubrication system fails. To help prevent serious engine damage, slow down and stop the engine at once if low oil pressure is indicated by the warning system.

Incorrect oil level

Incorrect oil level can result from improperly filling the engine or improperly checking the engine oil level.

An excessive oil level allows the crankshaft and other components to agitate the oil and cause the formation of bubbles or foam. This foamy oil may cause a drop in oil pressure and lead to activation of the low oil pressure warning system. In some cases the oil pressure can remain above the low oil pressure activation point yet the engine will still suffer from inadequate lubrication.

Oil level check and oil filling instructions are provided in Chapter Three.

Oil leakage or high oil consumption

A rapid drop in oil level can result from oil leakage or from high oil consumption. In most cases oil leakage is easily detected and corrected. Common leakage points are at the rocker cover area, oil filter mounting surface, fuel pump mounting surface or crankcase mating surfaces. Air flowing around the power head often distributes a thin film of oil on all external surfaces. To locate the point of leakage:

1. Clean the engine with a degreasing agent.
2. Run the engine until it reaches operating temperature.
3. Turn the engine off. Wipe a white towel across all surfaces of the power head. Oil leakage is readily detected on the towel when the leakage point is contacted.

Pinholes or casting flaws may cause leakage to occur at other points on the power head. Many times simply tightening fasteners corrects oil leakage. Replace gaskets, seals or other effected components if the leakage continues.

All engines consume some oil while running. Some of the oil lubricating the cylinders and valves is drawn into the combustion chamber and subsequently burned. Oil consumption rates vary by model, condition of the engine, and how the engine is used. Engines with high operating hours or engines with worn internal components generally burn more oil than new or low hour engines. Damage to the piston and cylinders from detonation or preignition can cause increased oil consumption. New or recently rebuilt engines generally consume oil during the break-in period. After the break-in period the oil consumption should return to normal.

A typical symptom of excessive oil consumption is blue smoke in the exhaust during hard acceleration or high speed operation. Inspection of the spark plug usually reveals fouling or an oily film on the spark plug.

Perform a compression test if smoking or an oil fouled plug is noted. Worn or damaged components will generally cause a low compression reading. Compression test instructions are provided in this section. On all models covered in this manual, the oil pan is located in the drive shaft housing. Oil leakage from the gearcase or the presence of water in the oil can also occur if the oil pan is leaking. Power head removal is required to access the oil pan and the power head mounting adapter. Refer to Chapter Seven for power head removal and installation. Oil pan and drive shaft housing removal and installation is covered in Chapter Ten.

Contaminated, diluted or wrong type of oil

Contaminants enter the engine oil during normal operation. Dirt or dust enters the engine along with the air used during normal operation. Other particles form during the combustion process. Dirt, dust and other particles are captured by the lubricating oil and circulated throughout the engine. Most of the larger particles are captured in the oil filter. Smaller particles circulate through the engine with the lubricating oil. Frequent oil changes flush these particles from the oil before they reach high concentrations.

High concentrations of these particles cause increased wear of internal power head components.

During normal operation, unburned fuel and water vapor accumulate in the lubricating oil. Oil also absorbs heat from the engine during operation. This heating causes the unburned fuel and water to evaporate from the oil and form crankcase vapor. The crankcase ventilation system returns the vapor to the combustion chamber where it burns or exits through the exhaust.

A faulty fuel system can dramatically increase the amount of unburned fuel in the oil. High levels of unburned fuel may not evaporate quickly enough to prevent oil dilution.

Failure to reach normal engine operating temperature prevents the fuel and water vapor from evaporating. Failure to reach normal operating temperature is generally caused by a faulty or improperly installed thermostat or water pressure relief valve.

Wipe a sample of the oil from the dipstick between your finger and thumb. Compare the thickness of the oil with a sample of new oil. Smell the oil then check for a white or light color residue.

A very thin feel, fuel smell in the oil or white residue indicates oil dilution. Test the cooling and fuel system, as described in this chapter, if oil dilution is indicated.

Using the wrong grade, type or weight of oil can lead to increased engine wear and/or complete power head failure. Poor quality oil may not provide the level of protection required by the engine. Using the wrong type of oil usually leads to serious power head damage. Never use two-stroke outboard oil in a four-stroke outboard. Using the improper weight of oil can prevent correct oil circulation during cold engine operation or allow excessive thinning of the oil at higher temperatures. Oil recommendations are provided in Chapter Three.

Oil pump system failure

Failure of the lubrication system causes rapid wear of internal components and eventual power head seizure. Causes of oil pumping system failure include:

1. Worn, damaged or broken oil pump components.
2. Worn or damaged crankshaft or connecting rod bearings.
3. A blocked, damaged or loose oil pickup tube or screen.
4. A faulty or stuck oil pressure relief valve.

Failure of the lubrication system causes a loss of oil pressure and activation of the low oil pressure warning system. Continued operation results in rapid wear of internal components followed by eventual power head seizure. Check the oil pressure if the warning system activates and low oil level is ruled out as the cause. Refer to *Oil Pressure Test* in this section.

Detonation

Detonation damage is due to heat and pressure in the combustion chamber becoming too great for the fuel that is used. Fuel burns at a controlled rate during normal combustion. If heat and pressure become too high, the fuel explodes violently. These explosions in the combustion chamber cause serious damage to internal engine components. The piston typically suffers the brunt of the damage. Detonation usually occurs only at higher engine speeds or during heavy acceleration. A pinging noise from the power head accompanied by a loss of power is often noted when detonation is occurring. Inspect the spark plug if detonation damage is suspected. Aluminum deposits or a melted electrode indicate probable detonation damage. Perform a compression test to determine the extent of damage to the power head. Repair the power head if low compression is indicated. Correct the causes of detonation to prevent additional power head damage or repeat failures.

Conditions that promote detonation include:

1. Using a fuel with an excessively low octane rating.
2. Excessive carbon deposits in the combustion chamber.
3. Overheating of the engine.
4. Using the incorrect propeller or overloading the engine.
5. Excessively lean fuel delivery.
6. Over-advanced ignition timing.

Preignition

Preignition is caused by an overheated object inside the combustion chamber triggering early ignition. The flame from the early ignition collides with the flame front initiated by the spark plug. An explosion occurs as these flame fronts collide. The piston suffers the brunt of the damage caused by this explosion. Inspect the spark plug and perform a compression test if pre-ignition is suspected. Aluminum deposits on the spark plug are likely when preignition has occurred. Repair the power head if low compression is revealed. Correct the causes of preignition to prevent additional power head damage or repeat failures.

Conditions that promote pre-ignition include:

1. Excessive carbon deposits in the combustion chamber.
2. Using the wrong heat range of spark plug.
3. Overheating of the engine.

Engine Seizure

Power head seizure results from failure of internal power head components. This can occur at any engine speed. If the failure occurs at higher engine speeds the engine may abruptly stop or gradually slow down and stall. Typically the seizure is caused by a crankshaft, connecting rod or piston failure. Although not as common, power head seizure also occurs from a failure of the valve train components. Power head seizure prevents the electric starter from cranking the engine. Major repair is almost always required after power head seizure.

Failure of the gearcase can also prevent flywheel rotation. Before suspecting the power head, remove the gearcase. Gearcase removal and installation are provided in Chapter Eight.

Oil in the cylinders can hydraulically lock the cylinders and prevent flywheel rotation. Refer to *Oil Entering the Cylinders* in this section if the engine is seized after storage or transport. Manually attempt to rotate the flywheel with the gearcase removed. Repair the gearcase if the flywheel can be rotated. Remove then repair the power head if the seizure persists. Power head removal, repair and installation instructions are provided in Chapter Seven.

Water Entering the Cylinder

Water can enter the cylinder from a number of areas including:

1. Water entering the carburetor or throttle body openings.
2. Water in the fuel.
3. Leaking exhaust covers or gaskets.
4. Leaking cylinder head gaskets.

The typical symptom is rough running particularly at idle. The engine may run correctly at higher speed as a small amount of water may not prevent normal combustion at higher speeds.

Water in the cylinder is almost always verified upon removal and inspection of the spark plug. Water remaining on the plug, a white deposit or very clean appearance indicates water is entering the cylinder.

Water marks or the presence of water in the silencer cover indicates water is entering the engine through the carburetor openings. This condition results from submersion, mounting the engine too low on the boat or a mounting location subjecting the engine to a considerable amount of water spray.

Water in the fuel allows water to enter the cylinders along with the incoming air. Inspect the fuel in the carburetor bowl, vapor separator tank or fuel filter for the presence of water as described this chapter.

Leaking exhaust covers and/or gaskets allow water to enter the cylinders from the exhaust passages. High performance four stroke engines typically have an aggressive camshaft lift and duration creating a fair amount of valve overlap. Valve overlap allows reverse exhaust flow under certain conditions. Reverse exhaust flow may increase the chance of water entering the cylinder through the exhaust valve if water is present in the exhaust passages. Leaking exhaust cover gaskets allow water into the exhaust passages. Correct leaking exhaust cover gaskets if external leakage is detected or water is found in the cylinder. Exhaust cover removal, inspection and installation are provided in Chapter Seven.

Head Gasket Failure

A leaking cylinder head gasket results from a failure of the gasket that seals the cylinder head to the cylinder block. Damage to the gasket is likely if the engine has overheated. Symptoms of a leaking head gasket include:

1. Water in the oil.
2. Water entering the cylinder(s).
3. Overheating (particularly at higher engine speeds).
4. Rough running (particularly at lower engine speeds).
5. External water or exhaust leakage at the cylinder head-to-cylinder block mating surfaces.

Perform a compression test if any of these symptoms are noted. Bear in mind that cylinder head gasket leakage is not always verified by a compression test. Typically, slightly lower compression is noted on two adjoining cylinders. Only removal and inspection of the gasket and mating surfaces verifies a gasket failure.

Remove the cylinder head and inspect the cylinders and piston domes if water is entering the cylinders and external causes such as water in the fuel or silencer cover are ruled out. Compare the appearance of the affected cylinder with other cylinders on the engine. Cylinders suffering from water intrusion usually have significantly less carbon deposit on the piston and cylinders. Rusting or corrosion of the valves, valve seats, cylinders and piston dome is common when this condition is occurring. A complete power head repair is required if rusting or pitting is noted on the cylinders or piston domes. Refer to Chapter Seven for cylinder head removal and installation instructions.

Leaking water jackets in the cylinder block or cylinder head are difficult to find. Casting flaws, pinholes and cracks may or may not be visible. Replacement of the cylinder block and/or cylinder head is required if water is entering the cylinder and no visible defects in the gaskets are found. Continued operation with water intrusion results in eventual power head failure.

Oil Entering the Cylinders

Oil entering the cylinders is almost always the result of improper storage of the engine. When positioned improperly, oil from the crankcase or oil pan can flow past the piston rings and enter the combustion chambers. This can lead to a seized or hydraulically locked engine, fouled spark plugs, low oil level and high oil consumption. The preferred position for the engine is in the upright position. If the engine must be stored on its side, make sure the carburetor or throttle body openings face upward.

1. If oil in the cylinders is suspected, remove and inspect the spark plugs.
2. Ground the spark plug wires.
3. Place a shop towel over the spark plug holes.
4. Slowly rotate the flywheel to blow the oil from the cylinders.
5. Correct the oil level as described in Chapter Three.
6. Install the spark plugs and connect the wire.
7. Run the engine to check for proper operation.

Inspect the spark plugs after running the engine, as subsequent spark plug fouling is likely. Refer to Chapter Three for spark plug maintenance.

Valve Train Failure

Failure of the valve train can cause low compression, excessive power head noise or an inability to start the engine. Components comprising the valve train include the timing belt, timing chain (225 hp models), valves, valve springs, lifter and valve pad and the cylinder head. This section describes common causes of valve train failure.

Timing belt failure

CAUTION
Attempts to start the engine with improper valve timing or a broken timing belt can lead to damaged valves, pistons and other power head components.

Failure of the timing belt will result in an inability to start the engine, rough running or poor performance.

On 75-115 hp models, a broken timing belt prevents valve operation and operation of the mechanical fuel pump. This prevents engine starting.

An excessively worn timing belt may allow the belt to jump over one or more of the teeth on the crankshaft pulley. This results in improper valve timing causing rough operation and poor performance.

Inspect the camshaft timing marks for proper alignment as described in Chapter Four. Perform a compression test if poor performance continues after correcting the broken timing belt or incorrect valve timing. Inspect the condition of the timing belt as described in Chapter Three.

Timing chain failure

CAUTION
Attempts to start the engine with a broken or jammed timing chain can lead to damaged valves, pistons and other power head components.

Timing chains are used only on 225 hp models. The timing chains connect onto the two camshafts in each cylinder head. Failure of the timing chain can cause one of the camshafts to not rotate or possibly jam and prevent rotation of both camshafts. The timing chain is very durable and failure is quite rare unless the chain is excessively worn. Timing chain failure generally occurs only on engines with high operating hours.

Sticking, worn or damaged valves

Sticking, worn or damaged valves cause low compression, rough operation, poor performance and/or backfiring.

Corrosion or heavy carbon deposits can cause valves to stick in the open position. Valves can become bent or damaged from contacting the top of the piston or foreign objects in the combustion chamber.

Any of these conditions result in an inability to fully close the affected valve. Rough operation at lower engine speed is common with a sticking, worn or damaged valve. Backfiring occurs when a leaking valve allows the burning fuel to enter the intake manifold or exhaust passages. Backfiring or a popping noise coming from the intake usually is the result of a stuck, worn or damaged intake valve. Backfiring or a popping noise coming from the exhaust is usually the result of a stuck, worn or damaged exhaust valve.

Perform a compression test if any of the listed symptoms are noted.

Improper valve adjustments can cause the same symptoms as sticking, worn or damaged valves. Check the valve adjustment before disassembling the power head. Valve adjustment is described in Chapter Four.

If backfiring is noted, run the engine with one spark plug wire at a time grounded. The backfire will stop when the spark plug wire is grounded on the affected cylinder. Remove the cylinder head and inspect the valves when backfiring and low compression are evident on the same cylinder and improper valve adjustment is ruled out.

Sticking valves are often the result of improper long term storage, water entering the cylinders or submersion of the engine. Using the wrong type of oil, improper fuel system operation or lugging the engine all contribute to increased deposits or wear of the valve and seat area.

Oil recommendations are provided in Chapter Three. Prevent lugging by selecting the correct propeller for the given engine and boat combination. Refer to Chapter One for propeller selection.

Worn valve guides

Worn valve guides prevent consistent closing of the valves. A compression test usually does not verify an excessively worn valve guide because the valve tends to seat normally at cranking speed. Continued operation with worn valve guides will cause the valve seats to wear unevenly and eventually cause low compression and poor performance.

High oil consumption, fouled spark plugs and blue exhaust smoke during deceleration are typical symptoms of excessively worn valve guides and valve stem seals. Only disassembly of the cylinder head and subsequent measurement can confirm excessively worn valve guides. Refer to Chapter Seven.

Camshaft failure

Failure of any of the camshaft lobes (**Figure 80**) can cause the same symptoms as a sticking or damaged valve. Removal of the valve arm cover allows inspection of the camshaft lobes. Rocker arm cover removal and installation is covered in Chapter Seven. Inspect the camshaft lobes for excessive wear as described in Chapter Seven.

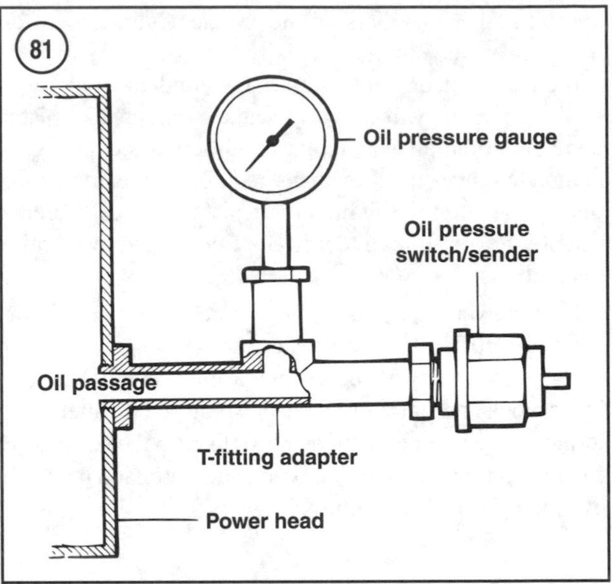

Excessively worn camshaft lobes are generally the result of improper valve adjustment, using the incorrect type, grade or weight of oil, a high number or operating hours and/or oil dilution. Valve adjustment is covered in Chapter Four. Refer to *Lubrication System Failure* in this section for additional information on oil dilution.

Oil Pressure Test

An oil pressure gauge, T-fitting adapter and a shop tachometer are required to perform an oil pressure test. This test must be performed under actual operating conditions.

Test the oil pressure at the threaded opening for the oil pressure switch on 75-115 hp models and the oil pressure sender on 225 hp models. Mounting locations, removal and installation instructions for the oil pressure switch or oil pressure sender are provided in Chapter Six.

Use a T-fitting adapter with the same threads as the oil pressure switch on the male and female ends. One of the female ends must have the same thread size and pitch as the oil pressure gauge. Oil pressure gauges and threaded adapters are available from most automotive parts stores. Tighten the adapters securely before running the engine.

WARNING

On-water testing or adjustments require two people: one to operate the boat, the other to monitor the gauges or test equipment and make necessary adjustments. All personnel must remain seated inside the boat at all times. Do not lean over the transom while the boat is under way. Use extensions to allow

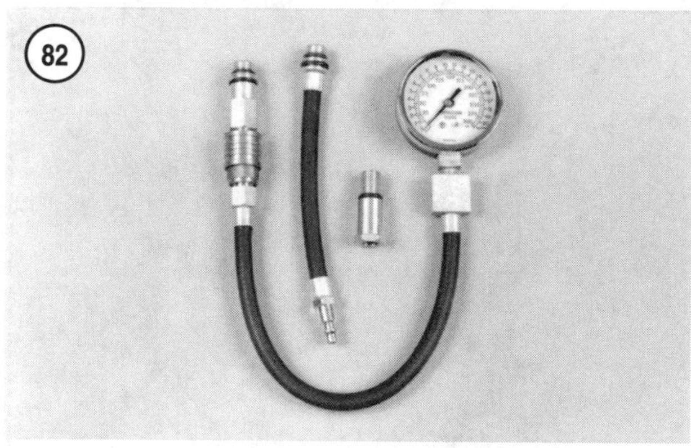

82

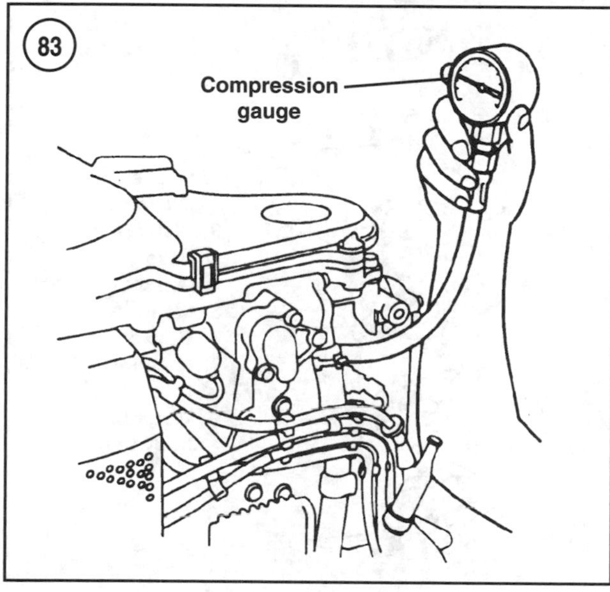

83

all gauges and test equipment to be located in normal seating areas.

Test the oil pressure as follows:

1. Run the engine until it reaches normal operating temperature.
2. Refer to Chapter Six and remove the oil pressure switch or sender.
3. Install the male end of the adapter into the oil pressure switch opening. Securely tighten the adapter.
4. Install the oil pressure switch into one of the female openings of the adapter. Securely tighten the oil pressure switch.
5. Connect the engine wire harness connector to the oil pressure switch or oil pressure sender.
6. Install the threaded adapter of the oil pressure gauge (**Figure 81**) into the remaining female opening of the adapter. Securely tighten all fittings. Secure the oil pressure gauge hose to prevent it from contacting any moving components.
7. Following the manufacturer's instructions, attach the shop tachometer to the engine.
8. Start the engine and immediately check for and correct any oil leakage at the gauge and adapter fittings.
9. Shift the engine into FORWARD gear. Observe the oil pressure gauge while an assistant operates the throttle to run the engine at the lower speed specified in **Table 12**. The lower speed range checks for conditions causing low oil pressure. Record the pressure at the lower speed.
10. Observe the pressure gauge while an assistant advances the throttle to achieve 5000 rpm. The upper speed range checks the operation of the oil pressure relief valve. Record the pressure at each speed then stop the engine.
11. Compare the oil pressure reading with the specification in **Table 12**. Oil pressure below or above the listed specification indicates a problem with the oil pumping system.
    a. Low oil pressure at the lower speed range indicates low oil level, damaged or blocked pickup tube, worn or broken oil pump components or worn crankshaft or connecting rod bearings. Inspect the oil pump and related components as described in Chapter Seven.
    b. Oil pressure exceeding the specification at the upper speed range indicates a stuck or faulty oil pressure relief valve. On 75-115 hp models, the oil pressure relief valve is incorporated into the oil pump and cannot be replaced separately. The oil pump assembly is mounted onto the mid-section of the engine. On 225 hp models, the oil pressure relief valve threads into the power head adapter on the mid-section of the engine and can be replaced separately. Replace the oil pump (75-115 hp models) or oil pressure relief valve (225 hp models) as described in Chapter Ten.
12. Remove the shop tachometer, oil pressure gauge and adapter. Install the oil pressure switch or oil pressure sender as described in Chapter Six.

Compression Test

A good quality compression gauge and adapters (**Figure 82**) are required for accurate compression testing. They are available at automotive parts stores and from tool suppliers. A small can of engine oil may also be required.

1. Remove all of the spark plugs as described in Chapter Three. (See *Spark plug removal*.) Connect the spark plug leads onto a suitable engine ground such as a clean cylinder head bolt. Activate the lanyard safety switch to further disable the ignition system.
2. Install the compression gauge into the No. 1 spark plug hole (**Figure 83**). On 75-115 hp models, the top cylinder is the No. 1 cylinder. On 225 hp models, the top cylinder on the starboard bank is the No. 1 cylinder. Odd numbered cylinders are on the starboard cylinder bank and even

numbered cylinders are on the port bank. Securely tighten the hose adapter. Position the throttle in the wide-open position during testing.

3. Stand clear of the remaining spark plug openings during testing. Observe the compression gauge and operate the electric starter. Crank the engine a minimum of five revolutions at normal cranking speeds. Record the compression reading.

4. Repeat Step 2 and Step 3 for the remaining cylinders. Record all compression readings.

5. The compression must meet or exceed the minimum specification in **Table 13**. In addition, the compression must not vary more than 10 percent between cylinders.

6. If low compression is noted, squirt approximately 1 teaspoon of clean engine oil into the suspect cylinder through the spark plug hole. Rotate the engine several revolutions to distribute the oil in the cylinder, then repeat Step 2 and Step 3.

   a. If the compression increases significantly, the piston rings and cylinder are excessively worn.

   b. If the compression does not increase, the compression leakage is the result of a worn valve face or seat.

7. Remove the compression gauge.

8. Install the spark plugs as described in Chapter Three. (See *Spark plug installation.*) Place the lanyard safety switch in the normal RUN position.

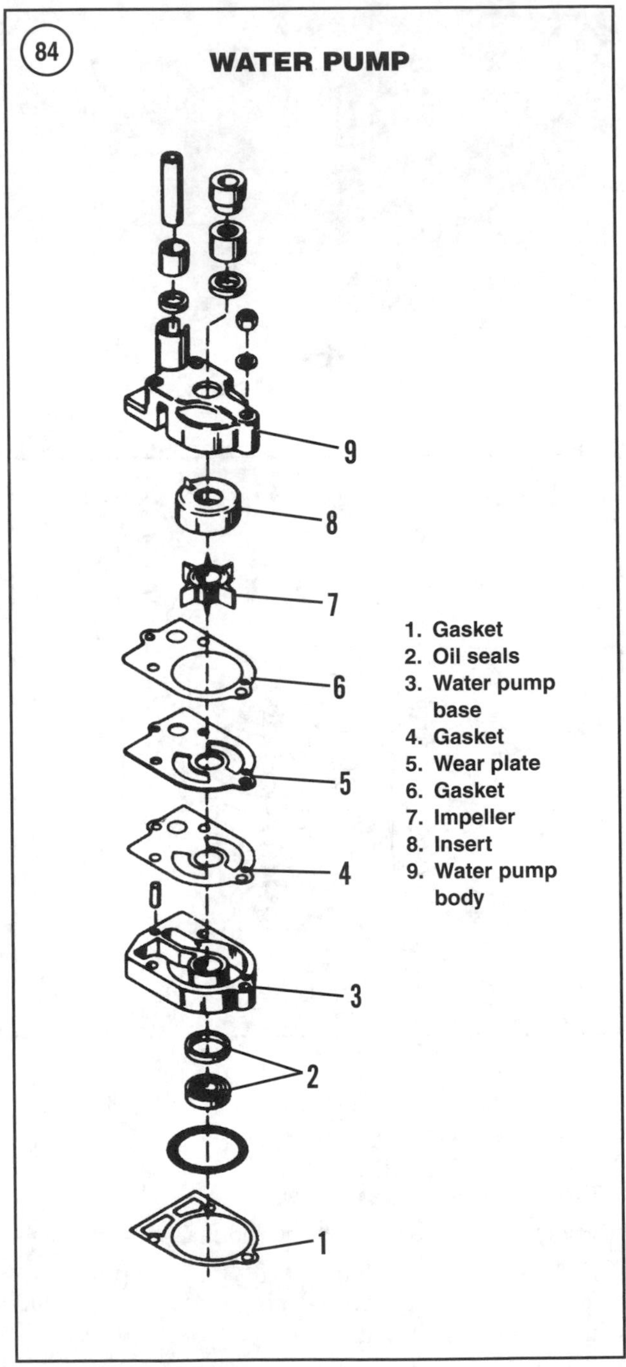

COOLING SYSTEM TROUBLESHOOTING

Water is pumped into the power head by the gearcase mounted water pump (**Figure 84**, typical). The water is pumped to the exhaust area of the power head, then into the cylinder block and heads, where it absorbs heat from the power head. The water exits the power head near the power head mounting surface and travels out through the drive shaft housing. As it exits through the drive shaft housing it absorbs heat from the oil pan. All models are equipped with a thermostat (**Figure 85**). Two thermostats are used on 225 hp models. They help maintain a minimum power head temperature by restricting exiting water until the minimum temperature is reached. All 75-115 hp models are equipped with a water pressure relief valve. This valve allows additional water to exit when the cylinder block pressure reaches a set value. Cylinder block water pressure increases with increasing water pump speed. This valve allows for additional water flow through the power head at higher engine speeds. Because two thermostats are used, the water pressure relief valve is not needed on 225 hp models.

A stream is visible at the rear of the lower engine cover when water is exiting the power head. The fitting for the stream commonly becomes blocked with debris and ceases flowing. Clean the passage with a stiff wire. Inspect the cooling system if the water stream is still not present.

Cooling System Inspection

Inspect the cooling system if the gauge indicates overheating, the warning horn sounds or the water stream is not exiting the rear of the engine. Overheating is the result

85

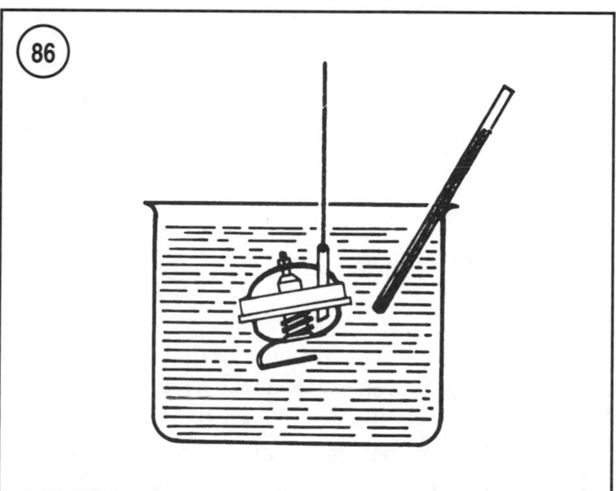

86

of insufficient water flow through the power heads or failure to absorb heat as it flows. Overheating causes activation of the warning system on 75-90 hp models. The lack of a water stream, unusual odors or the presence of steam from the exhaust indicates overheating. Poor idle quality or stalling at idle may also occur with overheating.

Most overheating problems are directly related to excessive wear or failure of water pump components. Inspect and correct any faults found in the water pump prior to inspecting any other cooling system components. Refer to Chapter Eight for water pump inspection and repair instructions.

Inspect the water pressure relief valve on 75-115 hp models and test the thermostat if overheating persists after water pump inspection. Thermostat testing is provided in this section.

Remove the water jacket and exhaust covers as described in Chapter Seven and inspect the cooling system passages for debris and deposit buildup if no faults are found with the water pump, thermostat and water pressure valve. Water flow may be restricted by rocks, pieces of the water pump, sand, shells or other debris. Salt, calcium or other deposits can form in the cooling passages and restrict water flow. Deposit buildup can also insulate the water passages, preventing the water from absorbing heat from the power head. Use a cleaner specifically designed to dissolve these of deposits. Make sure the cleaner used is suitable for use on aluminum material. Always follow the manufacturer's instructions when using these products.

Leakage at the power head-to-mounting adapter can allow water to exit to the drive shaft housing instead of flowing through the power head. Remove the power head as described in Chapter Seven, and inspect the gasket if overheating is occurring and no faults are found with the water pump, thermostat(s), water pressure relief valve or cooling water passages.

Engine Temperature Test

Always verify the actual temperature of the engine using thermomelt sticks before testing other cooling system components. Thermomelt sticks resemble crayons and are designed to melt at a specific temperature. The melting temperatures are listed on the side of the stick or the label.

Hold the sticks against the cylinder head near the temperature sender or overheat switch. Check the temperature immediately after or during the suspected overheat condition. Hold different temperature sticks to the power head to determine the temperature range. Stop the engine if the temperature exceeds 195° F (90°C). Normal water temperature is 140-190° F (60-88° C). Perform a cooling system inspection if the temperature is higher than normal. Test the temperature sender or switch if an alarm or gauge is indicating overheating but the thermomelt sticks indicate normal temperature. Perform this test with the engine in the water under actual operating conditions. Water supplied by the flushing adapter tends to mask problems with the cooling system.

Thermostat Test

Test the thermostat if the engine overheats or is running too cool. A thermometer, piece of string and a container of water that can be heated are required.

1. Remove the thermostat as described in Chapter Seven. Suspend the thermostat into the container of water with the string tied to the thermostat as shown in **Figure 86**.
2. Place the thermometer in the container and begin heating the water. Observe the temperature of the water and the thermostat while the water heats.

3. Note the temperature at which the thermostat begins to open. Record the start to open temperature. Replace the thermostat if the water begins to boil prior to the thermostat opening.
4. Continue heating the water while observing the thermostat. Note the temperature when the plunger reaches the full open position. Remove the thermostat and *quickly* measure the plunger opening height.
5. Compare the plunger opening height, start-to-open temperature, and full-open temperatures with the specifications in **Table 14**. Replace the thermostat if it fails to open at the specified temperature or if the plunger opening width is less than the minimum specification.
6. Install the thermostat as described in Chapter Seven.

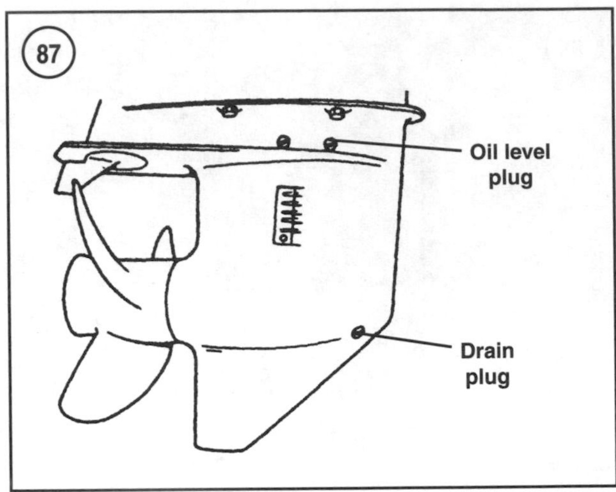

GEARCASE TROUBLESHOOTING

Gearcase problems are generally leakage and/or component failure and usually result from striking underwater objects or insufficient maintenance.

Gearcase Lubricant Contamination

Refer to Chapter Eight to locate the gearcase oil level and drain plugs. Position the gearcase in a vertical position. Do not remove the oil level plug (**Figure 87**). Remove the drain plug and allow a thimble full of gearcase lubricant to flow onto a small piece of cardboard. Quickly install the drain plug. Refer to Chapter Three to check and correct the gearcase lubricant level.

Metal contamination in the lubricant

Fine metal particles form in the gearcase during normal usage. The gearcase lubricant may have a *metal flake* appearance when inspected during routine maintenance. The fine metal particles tend to cling to the end of the drain plug. Carefully apply some of the material to the forefinger and thumb and rub them together. If any of the material is large enough to feel between the finger and thumb, disassemble and repair the gearcase as described in Chapter Eight.

Water in the gearcase lubricant

Under certain conditions a small amount of water may mix with the gearcase lubricant. Pressure test the gearcase to determine the source of water intrusion. Refer to *Gearcase Pressure Testing* in Chapter Eight. Failure to correct the leakage eventually leads to extensive damage to the internal components. Continued neglect will cause complete failure of the gearcase. Partial disassembly of the gearcase is needed to inspect the internal components for damage. Refer to Chapter Eight for gearcase disassembly, inspection and assembly.

Lubricant Leakage

The presence of gearcase lubricant on the exterior or around the gearcase indicates a need to pressure test and find the source of leakage. Refer to *Gearcase Pressure Test* in Chapter Eight. Failure to correct the leakage results in gear and bearing damage. Continued neglect will cause complete gearcase failure. Refer to Chapter Eight for gearcase disassembly, inspection and assembly.

Gearcase Vibration or Noise

Normal gearcase noise is barely noticeable over normal engine noise. The presence of rough growling noises or a loud high pitched whine is reason for concern. These noises usually are caused by failed or damaged internal components. Inspect the gearcase lubricant for metal contamination if abnormal noises are noted. In almost all cases, inspection of the gearcase lubricant will determine if gearcase components have failed.

Knocking or grinding noise

A knocking or grinding noise coming from the gearcase is usually caused by damaged gears or other components in the gearcase. Damaged gears typically create a substantial amount of larger metal particles. This type of failure usually results in damage to most internal components

and complete repair is needed. Refer to Chapter Eight for gearcase repair.

High pitched whine

A high-pitched whine usually indicates a bearing problem or misaligned gears. The only way to verify a faulty gear or bearing is to disassemble the gearcase and inspect all components. Refer to Chapter Eight for gearcase repair.

Gearcase vibration

Vibration in the engine can originate in the gearcase. In almost all cases the vibration is due to a bent propeller shaft or damaged propeller. The propeller can appear to be in perfect condition yet be out of balance. The best way to solve propeller vibration is to have the propeller checked at a reputable propeller repair shop. Another option is to simply try a different propeller.

Always check for a bent propeller shaft if vibration is present. Check the propeller shaft as described in Chapter Eight. A bent propeller shaft is usually caused by impacting underwater objects while underway. In many cases other damage occurs to the gearcase.

Never operate the engine if severe vibration is present. Vibrating or out of balance components place added stress on the gears, bearings and other engine components. Operating the engine with excessive gearcase vibration can seriously compromise the durability of the entire outboard.

WARNING
Remove all spark plug wires and disconnect both battery cables before working around the propeller.

Propeller Hub Slippage

The prop hub is installed in the propeller to cushion the shifting action and help absorb the shock of minor impact. When the propeller hub fails it spins inside the bore. Make a reference mark on the propeller shaft aligned with a reference mark on the prop. Operate the boat to verify the slippage. After removing the engine from the water, compare the reference marks. Have the prop repaired if the reference marks are not aligned after running the engine.

Shifting Difficulty

Hard shifting or difficulty when engaging the gear is usually the result of improper shift cable adjustment. Refer to Chapter Four and adjust the shift cables and linkage. Gearcase removal, disassembly and inspection is required if shifting problems are not corrected by adjustments. Refer to Chapter Eight for gearcase repair.

TRIM/TILT SYSTEM TROUBLESHOOTING

Operating the boat with the engine tilted out tends to raise the bow of the boat. This bow-up trim may increase boat speed by reducing the amount of water contacting the hull. Tilting the engine out may also cause excessive bow lift and result in reduced visibility for the driver during acceleration. The propeller is positioned progressively closer to the water surface as the engine is tilted out and may allow the propeller to draw in surface air (ventilate). Ventilation causes the propeller to lose grip to the water and causes the engine speed to increase without thrust increase.

Operating the boat with the engine tilted in tends to lower the bow of the boat. This bow-down trim tends to improve rough water ride and reduces ventilation during acceleration. Be aware that tilting the engine in generally reduces boat speed and can contribute to a dangerous handling condition (bow steer) on some boats.

The correct trim angle is a compromise between the best handling and top speed. The angle chosen must not be high enough to cause a rough ride or low enough that handling suffers. Correct trim angle positions the engine tilted out 3-5° from the water line on most applications.

Trim System Operation (75-115 hp Models)

A single hydraulic cylinder system (**Figure 88**) is used on all 75-115 hp models. The single cylinder system is commonly referred to as the *yellow cap* system due to the color of the fluid fill cap.

75-90 hp models use a pair of relays (**Figure 89**) and 115 hp models use a single relay unit (**Figure 90**) to control electric motor/pump rotational direction and fluid movement within the system. Switch the relays by operating the remote control-mounted trim switch (**Figure 91**). Internal relief valves limit the hydraulic pump pressure to 540-990 psi (3723-6826 kPa) of up pressure and 505-850 psi (3482-5860 kPa) of down pressure.

Operating the trim in the up direction causes fluid to flow into the up side or up cavity of the single trim cylinder (A, **Figure 88**) by the hydraulic pump (B). The pressure exerted onto the piston in the cylinder causes it to tilt the engine outward. Valves in the trim system prevent the engine from tilting beyond a set amount unless the engine speed is below approximately 2000 rpm. This is accomplished by limiting the pressure in the hydraulic cylinder at higher tilt ranges. The pressure is limited to the point at which the hydraulic cylinder cannot offset the propeller thrust created at higher engine speeds. The pressure is high enough to allow full outward tilting at lower engine speeds. This feature helps prevent over trimming of the engine at higher speeds yet allow full outward tilting for shallow water operation or placing the engine into the trailer position.

Operating the trim system in the down direction causes fluid to flow to the down side or cavity of the hydraulic cylinder. The pressure exerted on the piston in the cylinder pulls the engine inward. Tilt-in limit bolts installed in both sides of the clamp bracket prevent an excessive tilt-in angle. An excessive tilt-in angle can cause handling problems on some boats. Move the bolts closer to the transom different if additional tilt in is desired. Move the bolts to holes away from the transom if handling become difficult when the engine is operated in the full-in position. Install the bolts in the same holes on each clamp bracket.

Fluid remaining in the cylinders after stopping the pump effectively locks the cylinder in position. This helps the engine maintain the trim setting and holds the engine down when running in reverse.

A pressure relief valve located in the piston in the hydraulic cylinder provides a shock control system in the event of underwater impact. It allows fluid to move from the down to the up side of the cylinder during the impact. This controlled fluid flow allows outward engine movement at a much slower and safer rate. Bear in mind this system only helps minimize impact damage and cannot totally prevent damage to the outboard.

The manual relief valve, located through an opening in the starboard clamp bracket (**Figure 92**), allows manual tilting or lowering of the engine. To activate the manual relief valve slowly rotate the valve three complete turns counterclockwise. Manually raise or lower the engine to the desired position, while an assistant securely tightens the manual relied valve.

The fluid fill/level check plug (C, **Figure 88**) is located on the rear side of the fluid reservoir. This mounting location allows access only with the engine in the full tilt up/out position. Never try to remove the fluid fill/level check plug with the engine lowered. Fluid filling and level check instructions are provided in Chapter Nine.

Trim System Operation (225 hp Model)

A three hydraulic cylinder system (**Figure 93**) is used on all 225 hp models.

The relay unit (**Figure 90**) control electric motor/pump rotational direction and fluid movement within the system. Switch the relays by operating the remote control-mounted trim switch (**Figure 91**). Internal relief valves limit the hydraulic pump pressure to 1770-2060 psi (12,204-14,204 kPa) of up pressure and 970-1260 psi (6688-8688 kPa) of down pressure.

Operating the trim motor (C, **Figure 93**) in the up direction causes fluid to flow into the up side or up cavity of all three hydraulic cylinders. The pressure exerted onto the pistons in the cylinders causes it to tilt the engine outward. The trim rams (A, **Figure 93**) push against thrust pads on

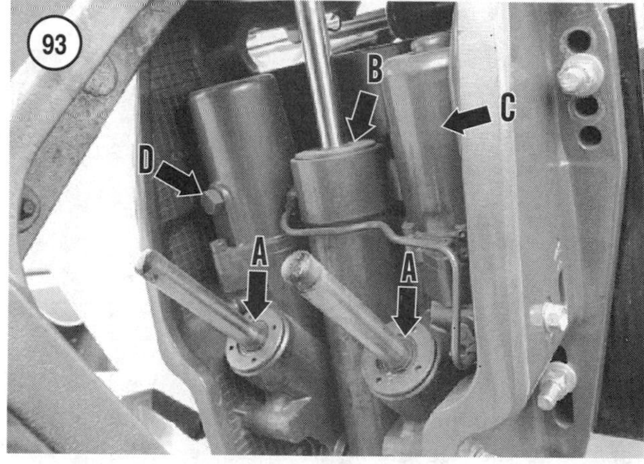

the swivel bracket, whereas a pivot pin connects the tilt cylinder (B) ram onto the swivel bracket. The engine reaches the limit of the trim range when the two trim rams reach their limit of travel. Any additional outward trim must then be provided by the single tilt cylinder. Since only a single cylinder actually moves the engine, the system produces considerably less working force. The working force is high enough to offset propeller thrust and allow full outward tilting at lower engine speeds. The working force from the single cylinder is not high enough to offset propeller thrust at higher engine speeds. This feature helps prevent over-trimming of the engine at higher speeds, yet allows full outward tilting for shallow water operation or placing the engine into the trailer position.

Operating the trim system in the down direction causes fluid to flow to the down side or cavity of the three hydraulic cylinders. The pressure exerted on the piston in the cylinder causes it to pull the engine inward. Since the trim rams do not connect to the swivel bracket, only the single tilt cylinder moves the engine down or inward. The tilt pin installed in the clamp bracket openings prevents an excessive tilt-in angle. An excessive tilt-in angle can cause handling problems on some boats. Move the pin to holes closer to the transom if additional tilt-in is desired. Move the pin to holes further away from the transom if handling problems develop when the engine is operated in the full-in position.

Fluid remaining in the cylinders after stopping the pump effectively locks the cylinders in position. This helps the engine maintain the trim setting and holds the engine down when running in reverse.

A pressure relief valve located in the piston in the tilt cylinder provides a shock control system in the event of underwater impact. It allows fluid to move from the down to the up side of the cylinder during the impact. This controlled fluid flow allows outward engine movement at a much slower and safer rate. Bear in mind this system only helps minimize impact damage and cannot totally prevent damage to the engine.

The manual relief valve, located through an opening in the starboard clamp bracket (**Figure 92**), allows manual tilting or lowering of the engine. To activate the manual relief valve slowly rotate the valve three complete turns counterclockwise. Manually raise or lower the engine to the desired position while an assistant tightens the manual relief valve.

The fluid fill/level check plug (D, **Figure 93**) is located on the rear side of the fluid reservoir. This mounting location allows access only with the engine in the full tilt up/out position. Never try to remove the fluid fill/level check plug with the engine lowered. Fluid filling and level check instructions are provided in Chapter Nine.

Hydraulic System Troubleshooting

Engine will not move up or down

If the electric motor operates, but the trim system fails to operate, possible causes include low fluid level, defective manual relief valve, hydraulic pump, trim system check valve or hydraulic cylinder. Check the fluid level as described in Chapter Three. Inspect the manual relief

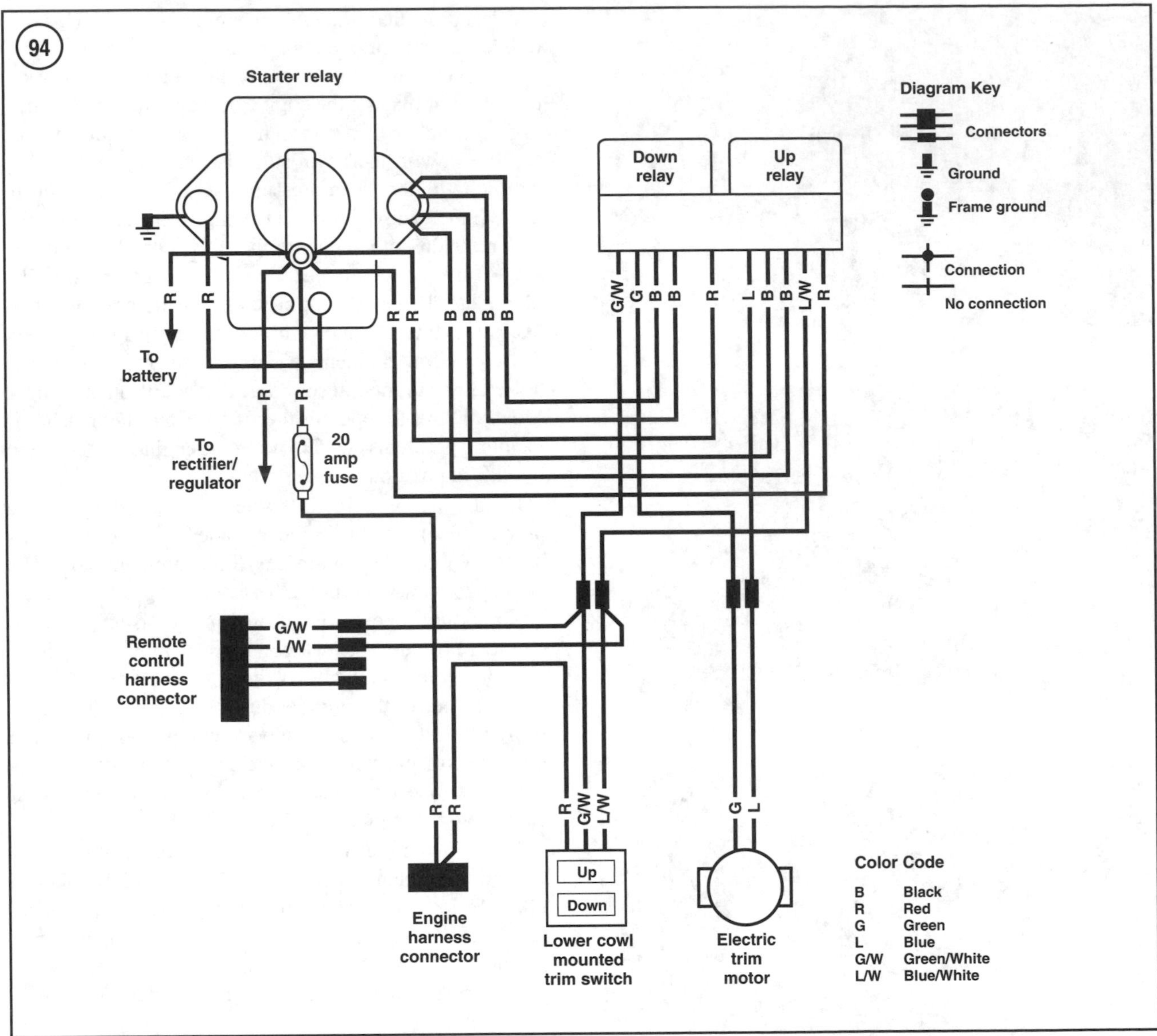

valve following the instructions provided in Chapter Nine. A faulty hydraulic pump, hydraulic cylinder or trim system check valve is likely if the fluid level is correct and manual relief valve checks correctly. Disassemble and inspect the entire trim system following the instructions in Chapter Nine. Replace the hydraulic pump if the symptoms continue.

Engine leaks down or trails out

A faulty manual relief valve, trim system check valve, hydraulic cylinder or hydraulic pump is indicated if the trim system moves up and down , but fails to maintain position. Check the manual relief valve as described in Chapter Nine. A faulty trim system check valve, hydraulic cylinder or hydraulic pump is likely if the manual relief valve is in good condition. Disassemble and inspect the entire trim system following the instructions in Chapter Nine. Replace the hydraulic pump if the symptoms continue.

Fluid leaks from the system

The presence of fluid does not always indicate a leak from the trim system. The film could be gearcase lubricant, engine oil, or other lubricants. Check the fluid level as described in Chapter Three. A film of fluid and a low fluid level indicates leakage. Clean all debris from the external surfaces of the trim system. Use pressurized water with care. Water can enter the system if pressurized water is directed against the seal surfaces.

After a thorough cleaning, operate the system through several full-up to full-down cycles. Wipe a clean shop towel over the seals and all surfaces of the trim system to check for leakage. Reseal or replace any leaking components. Trim system disassembly, repair and assembly are described in Chapter Nine.

Trim System Electrical Tests

The major electrical components of the trim system are the electric motor, trim relay(s), trim position sender and the trim switches. See **Figure 94**. This section provides test instructions for the electric trim system components.

The electric trim motor is provided with a blue and green wire. Current flow to the electric trim motor is controlled by the trim relay(s) and the trim switch.

When *up* trim or tilt direction is selected the up trim relay activates. It connects the blue trim motor wire to the positive battery terminal of the starter relay. The green wire of the electric motor is connected to the engine ground by the down relay.

When the DOWN direction is selected the down trim relay activates. It connects the green trim motor wire to the positive battery terminal of the starter relay. The blue trim motor wire is connected to the engine ground by the up relay. This switching of terminals causes the electric motor to reverse direction.

Battery voltage is supplied to the trim switch using a red/purple wire connecting the trim switch to the ignition switch or starter relay. When the switch is toggled to the *up* direction, the red/purple wire connects to the light blue or blue/white wire. This wire is connected to the wire harness to the *up* relay. When the switch is toggled to the *down* direction the red/purple wire connects to the light green or green/white wire. This wire is connected to the down relay.

Internal switching occurs when electrical current from the trim switch is applied to the selected relay. This internal switching causes this relay to supply voltage to the electric motor. The other relay remains deactivated and supplies the connection to ground for the electric motor. This connection to ground opens when a relay is activated. Both relays must make the proper internal connection for the electric motor to operate. This twin relay arrangement is used on all power trim models.

A fuse is provided in the circuit that connects the positive battery terminal to the main engine harness. One terminal of the fuse connects to the wire leading to the starter relay. The other terminal of the fuse connects to the wire leading to the ignition switch. A faulty fuse prevents battery current from reaching the trim switch. It also prevents operation of the electric starter or gauges. Refer to the wiring diagrams in the back of the manual to locate this fuse in the engine wire harness. Test this fuse if the electric trim motor fails to operate. Refer to *Fuse Test* in this chapter.

Test for correct switching at the relays if the trim pump does not operate when either the *up* or *down* direction is selected. Perform this test before testing or replacing any electrical trim system components.

Relay switch test

Perform this test before testing other trim system electrical components. An accurate multimeter is required for the procedure. Refer to **Figure 94** to assist with locating the test lead connection points.

1. Remove the propeller as described in Chapter Eight.
2. Remove the plastic electrical component cover to access the trim relays (75 and 90 hp models) or relay unit (115 and 225 hp models).
3. Set the multimeter on the 20 or 40 VDC scale. Ground the *negative* meter lead. With the *positive* meter lead, probe the red wires leading to each relay or the relay unit. Battery voltage should be present at the red wire(s). Check for a broken wire, blown fuse or loose or corroded connections if battery voltage is not noted.
4. Disconnect the blue and green trim motor wires from the trim relay wiring harness.
5. Connect the *positive* meter lead to the blue wire and *negative* meter lead to the green wire.
6. Observe the meter and toggle the trim switch to the *up* position. Battery voltage should be noted. If battery voltage is noted, the *up* relay or up circuit in the relay unit is functioning correctly.
7. Connect the *positive* meter lead to the green wire and the *negative* meter lead to the blue wire.
8. Observe the meter and toggle the trim switch in the *down* direction. Battery voltage should be noted. If battery voltage is noted, the down relay or down circuit in the relay unit is operating correctly.
9. Connect the *positive* meter lead to the blue or blue/white wire leading to the up relay or relay unit and *negative* meter lead to the black relay wire.
10. Observe the meter and toggle the trim switch to the UP direction. The meter should show battery voltage. If not, first make sure the black wire has continuity to engine ground, then test the trim switch as described in this chapter. Also inspect the trim switch connector for loose or corroded terminals.

11. Connect the *positive* meter lead to the green or green/white wire leading to the down relay or relay unit and the negative meter lead to the black relay wire.
12. Observe the meter and toggle the trim switch in the DOWN direction. The meter should read battery voltage. If not, test the trim switch as described in this chapter. Also inspect the trim switch for loose or corroded terminals.
13. Disconnect the negative battery cable from the battery.
14. Disconnect the trim motor wires from the relay harness. Calibrate the multimeter to the R × 1 scale. Connect the meter leads between the blue wire leading to the UP relay or relay unit, and a good engine ground. Polarity is not important for this test. Continuity must be present. If no continuity or very high resistance is noted, inspect the wires for loose or corroded connections. If the wiring and connections are in acceptable condition, replace the UP relay or relay unit as described in Chapter Nine.
15. Connect the meter leads between the green wire leading to the DOWN relay or relay unit and a good engine ground. Again, continuity must be noted. If no continuity or very high resistance is noted, inspect the wires for loose or corroded connections. If the wiring and connections are in acceptable condition, replace the down relay or relay unit as described in Chapter Nine.

Trim switch test

A three-position switch (**Figure 95**) mounted on the remote control handle controls the trim/tilt system. For operator convenience all models covered in this manual have an additional switch mounted on the lower engine cover. Testing instructions are similar regardless of the switch location. Use the switch to activate either the UP or DOWN relay by toggling the switch to the desired position. Battery voltage is applied to the switch by a wire from the ignition switch or starter relay. Check the fuse or wire harness if voltage is not present on the wire before replacing the switch. A multimeter is required for this procedure. Refer to **Figure 95**.

1. Disconnect both cables from the battery.
   a. When testing the remote control-mounted trim switch, disassemble the remote control as necessary to access the trim switch wires. See Chapter Eleven.
   b. When testing the lower engine cover-mounted trim switch, refer to the wiring diagrams located at the end of the manual to identify the switch wires.
   c. When testing a dash mounted trim switch, remove the switch from the dash.
2. Disconnect all three wires from the wire harness, control harness or engine harness.

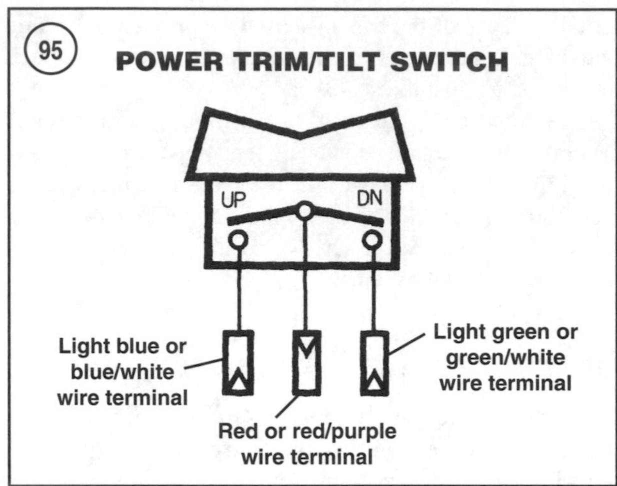

3. Calibrate the multimeter to the R × 1 scale. Connect the meter leads between the red or red/purple wire and the light blue or blue/white wire leading to the switch. Polarity is not important for this test. With the switch in the OFF position, no continuity should be noted.
4. Toggle the switch to the DOWN position. No continuity should be present. Toggle the switch to the UP position. The meter should now indicate continuity. Replace the switch if it fails to operate as described.
5. Connect the meter leads between the red or red/purple wire and the light green or green/white wire. With the switch in the OFF position, no continuity should be noted. Toggle the switch to the UP position. No continuity should be present. Toggle the switch to the DOWN position. Continuity should be now be present. Replace the switch if it fails to operate as described.

Trim position sender test

All models covered in this manual can be equipped with the optional trim gauge kit. This kit allows the operator to monitor the engine trim position at the control station. A dash mounted gauge and clamp bracket or swivel bracket mounted sender provide this feature. On 75-115 hp models, rotation of the upper pivot pin moves the rotor portion to operate the sender. On 225 hp models, the sender arm contacts the swivel bracket to operate the sender. A potentiometer in the sender sends a varying voltage signal to the gauge. Voltage supplied to the dash mounted gauge increases as the engine is trimmed up and decreases as the engine is trimmed down.

Failure to operate is due to a faulty sensor, gauge wiring or connections. Improper adjustments or installation of the upper pivot pin (75-115 hp) can also prevent correct operation of the sensor. Adjustment instructions are pro-

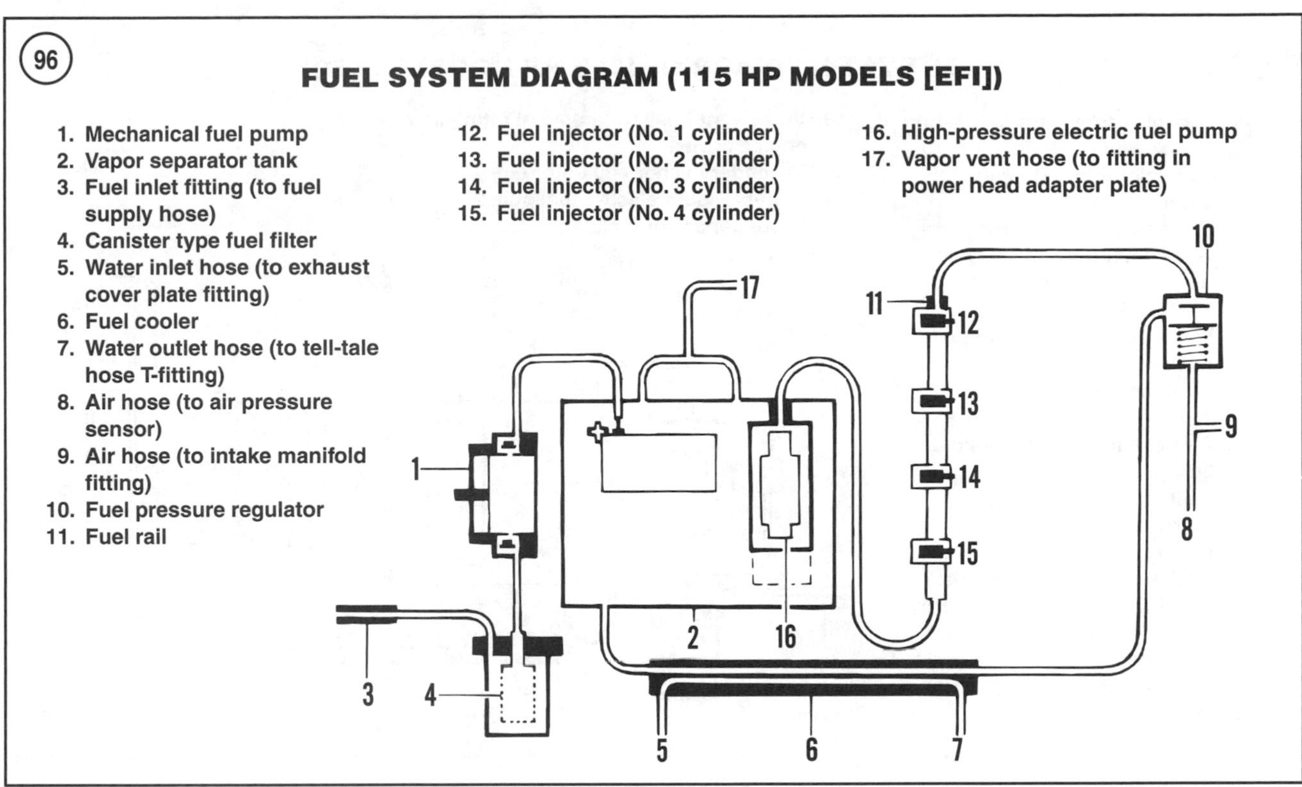

vided in Chapter Four. Upper pivot pin installation is described in Chapter Nine.

Inspect the wiring and connections before replacing the sensor or gauge. A multimeter is required for this procedure. Test the sensor as follows:

1. Disconnect the purple, black and brown/white wires from the trim gauge.
2. Select the 20 or 40 DCV scale on the multimeter.
3. Connect the positive meter lead to the purple wire. Connect the negative lead to the black wire.
4. Place the ignition key switch in the ON position. Do not start the engine. Observe the meter reading. A faulty battery, ignition key switch, wire or terminal is likely if the meter reads less than battery voltage.
5. Connect the positive lead to the brown/white wire. Connect the negative lead to the black wire.
6. Correct sender operation results in a smooth increase and decrease in voltage as the trim operates.
7. Place the ignition switch in the OFF position.
8. Replace the trim position sensor if all wiring and the trim position sensor are in good condition, but the gauge fails to operate. Replace the gauge if it fails to operate and the sender operates as specified.

ELECTRONIC FUEL INJECTION (EFI) SYSTEM TROUBLESHOOTING

This section contains procedures for testing and troubleshooting the EFI system used on 115 and 225 hp models. Before troubleshooting the fuel injection system, make sure that potential problems with other systems are eliminated as described under *Preliminary Inspection* in this chapter.

After potential problems have been eliminated, check the EFI system diagnostic codes as described in this section. If no codes are present, yet the problems persist or the engine will not start, verify operation of the fuel supply system and test the electronic control system.

Test systematically to avoid wasted time and unnecessary parts replacement. Before purchasing parts in an attempt to repair a problem, remember that most parts suppliers will not accept returns on electrical components.

System Operation

The fuel injection system is divided into the following sections:

1. The low-pressure fuel supply system.
2. The high-pressure fuel supply system.
3. The engine control system.

Refer to **Figure 96** or **Figure 97**.

FUEL SYSTEM DIAGRAM (225 HP MODELS [EFI])

1. Low-pressure electric fuel pump
2. Check valve
3. Fuel inlet fitting (to fuel supply hose)
4. Canister type fuel filter
5. Water inlet hose (from rectifier/regulator)
6. Fuel cooler
7. Water outlet hose (to tell-tale hose fitting)
8. Air hose (to air pressure sensor)
9. Air hose (to intake manifold fitting)
10. Fuel pressure regulator
11. Starboard fuel rail
12. Fuel injector (No. 1 cylinder)
13. Fuel injector (No. 3 cylinder)
14. Fuel injector (No. 5 cylinder)
15. Fuel injector (No. 6 cylinder)
16. Fuel injector (No. 4 cylinder)
17. Fuel injector (No. 2 cylinder)
18. Port fuel rail
19. Vapor vent hose (to grommet fitting in lower engine cover)
20. Secondary vapor separator tank
21. High-pressure electric fuel pump
22. Vapor separator tank

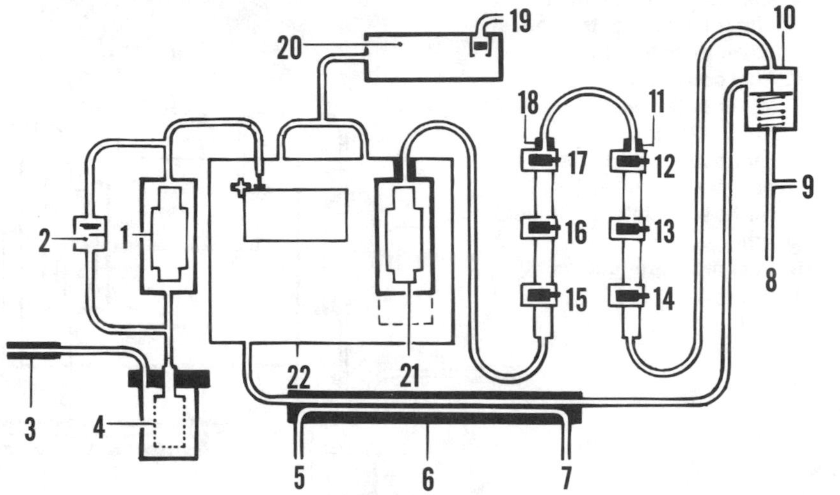

The low-pressure fuel supply system consists of the camshaft driven low-pressure fuel pump on 115 hp models or the low-pressure electric fuel pump used on 225 hp models, the fuel filter, and the vapor separator tank (**Figure 98**, typical).The system delivers fuel to the vapor separator tank from the vessel mounted fuel tank. The fuel level in the vapor separator tank is regulated by a float and needle valve. If the separator floods, excess fuel is routed to the intake manifold on 115 hp models or the secondary vapor separator tank on 225 hp models. If the secondary vapor separator tank should flood, excess fuel is routed to a fitting on the power head mounting plate. Test the mechanical low-pressure fuel pump used on 115 hp models as described in this chapter. See *Fuel System Troubleshooting*. Test instructions for the low-pressure electric fuel pump used on 225 hp models are described in this section.

The high-pressure fuel supply system consists of the vapor separator tank; high-pressure electric fuel pump, which is located in the vapor separator tank; fuel rail(s); fuel pressure regulator; and the fuel injectors. The system delivers fuel to the injectors from the vapor separator tank. Pressure is controlled by the regulator (**Figure 99**, typical), which is connected onto the fuel rail. Fuel pressure is regulated relative to intake manifold pressure and excess fuel is returned to the vapor separator tank after passing through the fuel cooler.

The engine control system consists of the engine control unit (ECU), air pressure sensor, air temperature sensor, engine temperature sensor, idle air control motor, shift position switch (115 hp models), and the throttle position sensor. Signals from these sensors combined with the engine speed and timing advance provided by the ignition system allow the ECU to compute the amount of injector-on time for maximum performance and fuel economy. Incorporated into the system is a self-diagnostic capability. A test light can be attached to the engine that blinks to indicate a malfunction or operation of normal control functions. See *Diagnostic Trouble Code Reading* in this section for test procedures.

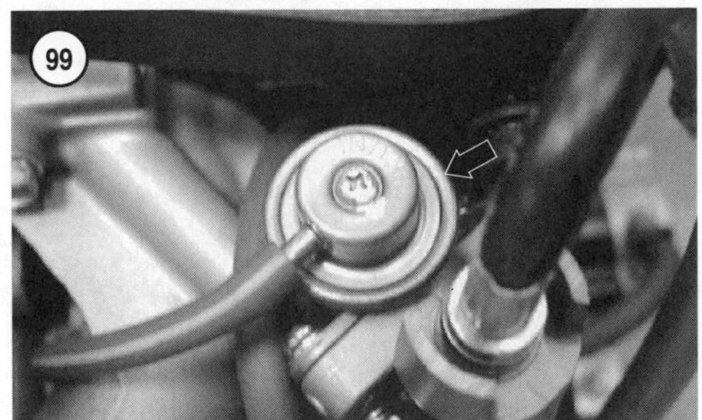

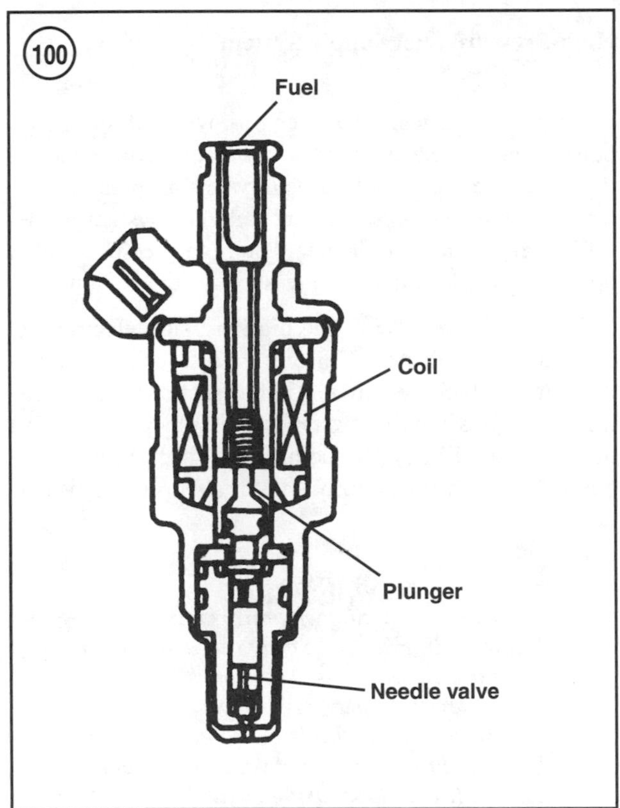

The fuel injectors (**Figure 100**) discharge fuel into the intake manifold runners and are basically solenoid-activated fuel valves that open when the ECU provides electric current.

Injector opening time or duration varies on engine and ambient conditions. For warm-up and high load conditions the injectors remain open longer. When the engine reaches operating temperature and while cruising with light loads the injectors on time is reduced.

EFI systems provide improved fuel economy, warm-up, throttle response, overall performance, reduced emissions and automatic altitude compensation.

Low-Pressure Fuel Supply System

On 115 hp models, test the fuel supply hose and fitting and the mechanical low-pressure mechanical fuel pump using the same procedures as used on the carburetor-equipped 75 and 90 hp models. See *Fuel System Troubleshooting.*

On 225 hp models, test the fuel supply hose using the same procedures used on the carburetor-equipped 75 and 90 hp models. Test the electric low-pressure fuel pump, as described in this section, if operational problems are evident and no fault is found with the fuel supply hose.

Low-pressure fuel pump operation

Operation of the low-pressure electric fuel pump is controlled by the engine control unit (ECU) and the low-pressure fuel pump driver. During normal operation, the low-pressure electric fuel pump will operate for five seconds upon placing the ignition key switch in the ON or RUN position. If the engine is not started, the pump will stop operating after the five second period. After starting the engine the pump will operate continuously for three minutes. After the three minute period, the pump will operate for ten seconds, then stop for 20 seconds. This sequence will continue as long as the engine is running and the engine speed is less than 1200 rpm. The pump operates continuously at engine speeds of 1200 rpm and higher.

Low-pressure electric fuel pump test

Test the low-pressure electric fuel pump if the engine fails to start or a fuel delivery malfunction is suspect. A multimeter, shop tachometer, stop watch and mechanic's stethoscope may be required for this test. Make sure the ignition system is operating before performing this procedure. Refer to *Spark Test* in this chapter.

1. Remove the silencer cover as described in Chapter Five.
2. Refer to *Low-pressure electric fuel pump replacement* in Chapter Five for assistance and locate the pump on the port side of the power head.
3. Listen to the pump while an assistant places the ignition key switch in the ON position. Do not start the engine in this step. The pump should operate for five seconds, then stop. Turn the ignition key switch to the OFF or STOP position. Wait approximately 30 seconds before repeating the test.
4. Repeat Step 3 several times to check for intermittent operation. The pump must operate as specified each time the ignition key switch is placed in the ON or RUN position. Refer to the following:

a. If the pump operates as specified, the electric circuits that control the pump are operational. Proceed to Step 7.
b. If the pump operates intermittently, check for faulty wiring or terminals between the electric fuel pump and pump driver and pump driver to ECU. Replace the fuel pump driver if no fault is found with the wiring or terminals.
c. If the pump does not operate, proceed to Step 5.

5. Disconnect the wire harness connector from the low-pressure electric fuel pump. Set the multimeter on the 20 or 40 VDC scale. Touch the *positive* meter lead to the terminal in the harness connector. Touch the *negative* meter lead to the blue/red terminal in the harness connector. Do not inadvertently touch the test leads to the pump harness terminals. Note the meter reading while an assistant places the ignition key switch in the ON or RUN position. The meter must indicate battery voltage for approximately 5 seconds then switch to 0 volt. Refer to the following:
a. If the meter reading is as specified, the voltage supply to the low-pressure fuel pump is operating correctly. Replace the pump as described in Chapter Five if the pump does not operate as specified in Step 3.
b. If the meter indicates 0 volt, replace the low-pressure electric fuel pump driver as described in Chapter Five and repeat the test. Look for a blown fuse, faulty wiring, wire terminals or faulty engine control unit (ECU) if the problem persists with the replacement driver. Replace the ECU only if no fault is found with the wiring or terminals.

6. Connect the wire harness connector onto the low-pressure electric fuel pump connector. Route the wiring to prevent interference with moving components.
7. Prepare the engine for operation under actual operating conditions or on a flush/test device. Connect the shop tachometer following the manufacture's instructions.
8. Have an assistant start and operate the engine at idle speed in NEUTRAL gear. Using the mechanic's stethoscope, listen to the low-pressure electric fuel pump. The pump must operate continuously for three minutes after starting the engine. After the three minute period, the pump must begin operating in a repeating 10 second on period followed by a 20 second off period sequence. Have the assistant advance the throttle to approximately 1300 rpm. The pump must operate continuously. Have the assistant reduce the speed to approximately 1100 rpm. The pump must return the repeating 10 second on 20 second off sequence.
9. Reduce the engine to idle speed, then stop the engine. Refer to the following:
a. If the pump operates continuously at idle speed, replace the fuel pump driver and repeat the test. Faulty wiring or a faulty ECU is evident if the pump runs continuously at idle speeds after the initial three minute time period. Replace the ECU only if no fault is found with the wiring.
b. If the pump continues to operate in the specified on-off sequence at speeds exceeding 1200 rpm, replace the ECU as described in Chapter Six.

10. Remove the shop tachometer. Install the silencer cover as described in Chapter Five.

High-Pressure Fuel Supply System

Perform these tests if the engine will not start, runs poorly, smokes excessively or has poor performance at higher engine speed. Before testing the high-pressure system, test the low-pressure fuel delivery system as described earlier in this chapter. The high-pressure cannot operate correctly if the low-pressure system is faulty.

Check for operation or the high-pressure electric fuel pump and fuel injectors if the engine refuses to start. Follow with the fuel pressure test in this section to determine if the high-pressure fuel system is operating properly. Test the remaining EFI system components if the engine cannot be started or runs poorly and the fuel pressure is correct.

WARNING
Use extreme caution when working with the fuel system. Fuel can spray out under high pressure. Always use appropriate safety gear. Never smoke or perform any test around and open flame or other source of ignition. Fuel and/or fuel vapor represent a serious fire and explosion hazard.

High-pressure electric fuel pump operation (115 hp models)

Operation of the high-pressure electric fuel pump is controlled by the enging control unit (ECU). During normal operation, the low-pressure electric fuel pump will operate for five seconds upon placing the ignition key switch in the ON or RUN position. If the engine is not started, the pump will stop operating after the five second period. After starting the engine the pump will operate continuously.

Testing the electric fuel pump operation (115 hp model)

Perform this test if the engine refuses to start and the ignition system is operating. See *Spark Test* in this chapter. A multimeter and mechanic's stethoscope are required for this procedure.

1. Remove all of the spark plugs as described in Chapter Three. Connect the spark plug leads onto a suitable engine ground such as a clean cylinder head bolt. Remove the propeller as described in Chapter Eight. Reconnect the battery cable after removing the spark plugs.
2. Touch a mechanic's stethoscope to the body of the vapor separator tank. Listen for fuel pump operation while an assistant places the ignition key switch in the ON or RUN position. The pump should run for approximately five seconds then stop. Then listen for fuel pump operation while the assistant activates the electric starter. The pump must operate continuously while cranking the engine. Refer to the following:
   a. If the fuel pump operates as specified, the electric fuel pump is operational. Perform the fuel pressure test as described in the section. Proceed to Step 6.
   b. If the fuel pump operates only with the ignition key switch in the ON position, check for ignition system operation as described in this section. See *Spark Test*. Correct any ignition system faults and repeat the test.
   c. If the fuel pump does not operate in either ignition key switch position, proceed to Step 3.
3. Refer to the wiring diagrams at the end of the manual to locate the wires leading to the high-pressure electric fuel pump. The electric fuel pump is located in the vapor separator tank. The vapor separator tank is located between the intake manifold and the cylinder block on the port side of the engine. Disconnect the engine wire harness connector from the electric fuel pump harness connector.
4. Set the multimeter onto the 20 or 40 VDC scale. Touch the *positive* meter lead to the red/yellow wire terminal in the harness connector. Do not inadvertently touch the leads to the fuel pump harness connector terminal. Touch the *negative* meter lead to a suitable engine ground. Turn the ignition key switch to the ON or RUN position. The meter must indicate battery voltage. Have an assistant place the ignition key switch in the START position. The meter must indicate battery voltage with the ignition key switch in the ON or RUN *and* START position. If otherwise, test the power relay as described in this chapter. See *Ignition System Troubleshooting*.
5. Touch the *positive* meter lead to the red/yellow wire terminal in the harness connector. Touch the *negative* meter lead to the blue wire terminal in the harness connector. Observe the meter while an assistant places the ignition key switch in the ON or RUN position. The meter must indicate battery voltage for a few seconds then switch off. After the pump shuts off, observe the meter while an assistant places the ignition key switch in the START position. The meter must again indicate battery voltage. Refer to the following:
   a. If the meter indicates battery voltage only with the switch in the ON or RUN position, check for ignition system operation as described in this chapter. See *Spark Test*. Correct any ignition system faults and repeat the test.
   b. If the meter indicates battery voltage as specified, but the fuel pump did not operate in Step 2, replace the high-pressure electric fuel pump as described in Chapter Five.
   c. If the meter does not indicate battery voltage in the ON, RUN or START positions, test the power relay as described in this chapter. See *Ignition System Troubleshooting*. Suspect the ECU if the relay tests correctly. ECU failure is extremely rare and replacement is recommend only if the electric fuel pump does not operate and no fault is found with the wiring or ignition system components.
6. Install the spark plugs as described in Chapter Three. Install the propeller as described in Chapter Eight.

High-pressure electric fuel pump operation (225 hp model)

Operation of the high-pressure electric fuel pump is controlled by the ECU and the fuel pump relay. During normal operation, the high-pressure electric fuel pump will operate for five seconds upon placing the ignition key switch in the ON or RUN position. If the engine is not started, the pump will stop operating after the five second period. After starting the engine the pump will operate continuously.

Testing the electric fuel pump and fuel pump relay operation (225 hp model)

Perform this test if the engine refuses to start and the ignition system is operating. See *Spark Test* in this chapter. This test checks for fuel pump operation during key-on engine cranking. A multimeter and mechanic's stethoscope are required for this procedure. Jumper leads and a fully charged battery may be required to test the fuel pump relay.

1. Remove the silencer cover as described in Chapter Five.
2. Remove all of the spark plugs as described in Chapter Three under *Spark plug removal*. Connect the spark plug leads onto a suitable engine ground such as a clean cylinder head bolt. Remove the propeller as described in Chapter Eight.
3. Reconnect the battery cable after removing the silencer cover and spark plugs.
4. Touch a mechanic's stethoscope to the body of the vapor separator tank. Listen for fuel pump operation while an assistant places the ignition key switch in the ON or RUN position. The pump should run for approximately five seconds then stop. Then listen for fuel pump operation while the assistant activates the electric starter. The pump must operate continuously while cranking the engine. Record the test results for future reference. Refer to the following:
   a. If the fuel pump operates as specified, the electric fuel pump is operational. Perform the fuel pressure test as described in the section. Proceed to Step 13.
   b. If the fuel pump operates only with the ignition key switch in the on position, check for ignition system operation as described in this chapter under *Spark Test.* Correct any ignition system faults and repeat the test.
   c. If the fuel pump does not operate in either ignition key switch position, proceed to Step 5.
5. Refer to the wiring diagrams at the end of the manual to locate the wires leading to the high-pressure electric fuel pump. The electric fuel pump is located in the vapor separator tank . The vapor separator tank is located on the port side of the power head. Disconnect the engine wire harness connector from the electric fuel pump harness connector.
6. Set the multimeter to the 20 or 40 VDC scale. Touch the *positive* meter lead to the red/yellow wire terminal in the harness connector. Touch the *negative* meter lead to a suitable engine ground. Turn the ignition key switch to the ON or RUN position. The meter must indicate battery voltage. Have an assistant place the ignition key switch in the START position. The meter must indicate battery voltage with the ignition key switch in the ON or RUN *and* START position. Record the test results for future reference. Refer to the following:
   a. If the meter indicates battery voltage as specified, but the fuel pump did not operate as described in Step 4, replace the high-pressure electric fuel pump as described in Chapter Five.
   b. If the meter indicates battery voltage only when the switch is in the ON position, check for ignition system operation as described in this chapter under *Spark Test.* Correct any ignition system faults and repeat the test.
   c. If the meter indicates 0 volt in all switch positions, proceed to Step 7.

7. Remove the fuel pump relay as described in Chapter Five. Calibrate the multimeter to the R × 1 scale.
8. Touch the meter leads to the relay terminals (A and B, **Figure 101**). The meter must indicate *no continuity.* If otherwise, the relay is shorted and must be replaced.
9. Connect the meter leads as described Step 8. Use jumper wires to connect the positive battery terminal to the relay terminal (C, **Figure 101**). Connect a second jumper wire onto the negative battery terminal. Observe the meter while alternately touching the jumper lead to the relay terminal (D, **Figure 101**) then removing the jumper wire. The meter must indicate *continuity* each time the jumper touches the relay. Replace the relay if it fails to perform as described in Step 8 and Step 9.
10. Faulty wiring or a faulty ECU is indicated if the relay test correctly in Step 8 and Step 9 and the meter indicated 0 volt in Step 6.
11. Set the multimeter onto the 20 or 40 VDC scale. Connect the *negative* test lead onto a suitable engine ground. Touch the *positive* meter lead onto the engine harness terminal for the blue/red relay wire. Observe the meter while an assistant places the ignition key switch to the ON or RUN position. The meter must indicate battery voltage for five seconds then change to 0 volt. Observe the meter while the assistant places the ignition key switch in the START position. The meter must indicate battery voltage while the electric starter operates. Refer to the following:
   a. If the meter reading is correct, the ECU is controlling the fuel pump relay correctly. Faulty wiring, fuel pump relay or fuse is indicated if the fuel pump does not operate as described in Step 4.
   b. If the meter indicates battery voltage only with the switch in the ON position, check for ignition system operation as described in this chapter under *Spark*

Test. Correct any ignition system faults and repeat the test. The ECU is suspect if the ignition system is operating correctly.

c. If the meter indicates 0 volt in all switch positions, a faulty fuse, wiring or ECU is indicated. Replace the ECU to restore fuel pump operation only if no fault is found with the fuel pump relay, ignition system, fuses or wiring.

12. Install the fuel pump relay as described in Chapter Five.

13. Install the silencer cover as described in Chapter Five.

14. Install the spark plugs as described in Chapter Three. See *Spark plug installation*. Install the propeller as described in Chapter Eight.

Fuel Pressure Test

WARNING

On-water testing or adjustments require two people: one to operate the boat, the other to monitor the gauges or test equipment and make necessary adjustments. All personnel must remain seated inside the boat at all times. Do not lean over the transom while the boat is under way. Use extensions to allow all gauges and test equipment to be located in normal seating areas.

This test measures the fuel pressure in the fuel rail(s) while cranking the engine and during operation at idle speed. A fuel pressure gauge (part No. 91-16850A7) or equivalent is required for this procedure. Perform this test if the fuel pump is operating, but the engine refuses to start or operates poorly, particularly at higher engine speed. If fuel delivery problems are suspected at certain engine speeds, operate the engine with the gauge attached to the fuel system. Leaking fuel lines, restricted passages and blocked filters can restrict fuel flow in the low-pressure and high-pressure fuel delivery systems.

If a fuel restriction is evident, the fuel pressure may be correct at slow engine speeds, but decline dramatically at higher throttle settings. If this symptom is noted, check the filters, anti-siphon valve, fuel tank pickup and low-pressure fuel pump as described in this chapter. While this test can determine whether the pump and fuel pressure regulator are operating under controlled conditions, it cannot verify that fuel pressure is adequate at all engine speeds under actual operating conditions.

1. Locate the fuel pressure test port on the engine. Refer to the following:

a. On 115 hp models, the fuel pressure test point (**Figure 102**) is located on top of the fuel rail on the rear port side of the power head.

b. On 225 hp models, the fuel pressure test point (**Figure 103**) is located on the port side fuel rail.

2. Remove the cap, then connect the fuel pressure gauge onto the test port. Route the hose to prevent interference with any moving components. Clamp the hose to a stable component to prevent excessive movement during engine operation.

3. Squeeze the primer bulb to fill the vapor separator tank with fuel. Observe the pressure gauge while switching the ignition key switch to the ON or RUN position. Do not start the engine at this time. The gauge must indicate 41-44 psi (283-303 kPa). Turn the ignition key switch to the OFF or STOP position. The gauge must hold pressure or drop slowly. Refer to the following:

a. If the gauge indicates 0 psi, test the electric high-pressure fuel pump operation as described in this section. Check for fuel in the vapor separator tank as described in this chapter. See *Fuel Inspection*. Replace the fuel pump if it operates but develops no fuel pressure.

b. If the pressure reading exceeds the specification, replace the fuel pressure regulator as described in Chapter Five.
c. If some pressure is present, but below the specification, replace the fuel pressure regulator as described in Chapter Five. Repeat the fuel pressure test. Replace the high-pressure electric fuel pump as described under *Vapor separator tank* in Chapter Five if low fuel pressure persists.
d. If pressure drops rapidly after stopping the pump, replace the fuel pressure regulator as described in Chapter Five.

4. Prepare the engine for operation under actual operating conditions. Have an assistant start the engine. Immediately check for fuel leaks and correct before proceeding. Observe the gauge while an assistant operates the engine at various throttle settings. The gauge must indicate 38-44 psi (262-303 kPa) at all operating speeds. Refer to the following:
a. If pressure exceeds the specification at lower speeds and drops at higher speeds, replace the fuel pressure regulator as described in Chapter Five.
b. If pressure is within the specification at lower speeds, but drops below the specification at higher speeds, test the fuel tank, fuel supply hose and primer bulb as described in this chapter. On 115 hp models, test the mechanical fuel pump as described in this chapter. On 225 hp models, test the low-pressure electric fuel pump as described in this section. Replace the fuel pressure regulator if no fault is found with the low-pressure pump, fuel supply hose, tank or primer bulb. Replace the high-pressure electric fuel pump, as described under *Vapor separator tank* in Chapter Five, if low fuel pressure persists with the replacement regulator.

5. Stop the engine and remove the fuel pressure gauge. Clean up any spilled fuel. Thread the cap onto the fuel pressure test port.

Vapor Separator Tank Flooding Test

1. Refer to the information in Chapter Five to locate the vapor separator tank. See *Vapor Separator Tank*. Do not remove the tank for this procedure.
2. Refer to the fuel system diagram in **Figure 96** or **Figure 97** to identify the vapor separator tank vent hoses.
a. On 115 hp models, the two vent hoses connect with a T-fitting to a single hose leading to a fitting on power head mounting adapter. The fitting is located on the front and port side of the adapter.
b. On 225 hp models, the two vent hoses connect with a T-fitting to a single hose leading to the secondary vapor separator tank. The secondary vapor separator tank is located on top of the silencer cover at the front of the engine.

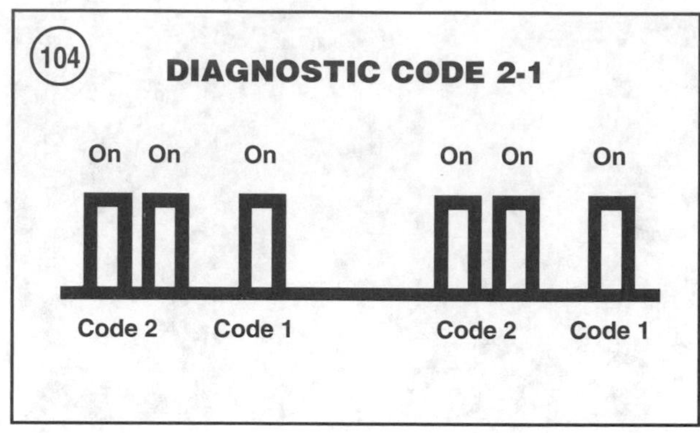

3. Disconnect the vent hose from the mounting adapter or secondary vapor separator tank fittings. Direct the hose into a container suitable for holding fuel.

4A. On 115 hp models, observe the vent hose while pumping the primer bulb. Fuel exiting the hose indicates flooding. If flooding is evident, disassemble the vapor separator tank, as described in Chapter Five, and inspect or replace the inlet needle and seat.

4B. On 225 hp models, observe the vent hose while an assistant places the ignition key switch in the ON or RUN position. Do not start the engine. After five seconds, have the assistant place the switch in the OFF or STOP position. Wait approximately 30 seconds, then repeat the procedure a minimum of three times. Fuel exiting the hose at any point in the test indicates flooding. If flooding is evident, disassemble the vapor separator tank, as described in Chapter Five, and inspect or replace the inlet needle and seat.

5. Pour any fuel in the container into the boat fuel tank or other suitable container. Reconnect the vent hose onto the mounting adapter fitting or secondary vapor separator tank fitting. Route any hoses to prevent interference with moving components.

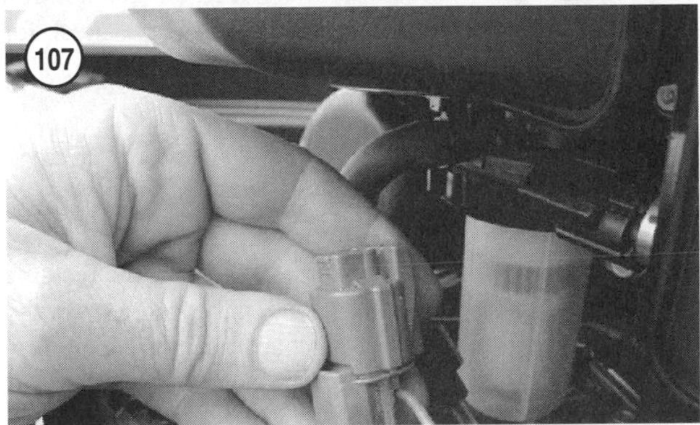

Secondary Vapor Separator Tank Flooding Test (225 hp Model)

1. Locate the vent hose for the secondary vapor separator tank. The vent hose connects to the fitting on the top of the tank and a fitting on the power head mounting adapter. Disconnect the hose from the adapter and direct the end into a container suitable for holding fuel.
2. Observe the vent hose while an assistant places the ignition key switch in the ON or RUN position. Do not start the engine. After five seconds, have the assistant place the switch in the OFF or STOP position. Wait 30 seconds, then repeat the procedure a minimum of five times. Fuel exiting the hose at any point in the test indicates flooding. If flooding is evident, replace the secondary vapor separator tank as described in Chapter Five. The secondary vapor separator tank is not serviceable.
3. Reconnect the vent hose onto the adapter plate fitting. Route the hose away from moving components.

Diagnostic Trouble Code Reading

NOTE
High-power electrical equipment such as stereos and communication radios may interfere with the electronic fuel injection system. Switch these devices off if trouble is detected with the engine. Avoid using these devices while running the engine if normal operation resumes with these devices switched off.

If the engine control unit (ECU) detects a malfunction with any of the EFI system or related ignition system sensors, it initiates the limp-home feature. This allows the engine to continue to operate, although at reduced efficiency. The ECU may limit top speed or default to a higher than normal idle speed to further compensate for the faulty sensor. After a malfunction has been corrected, the ECU returns to normal operation.

This procedure reads the trouble codes provided by the ECU to identify the malfunctioning sensor(s). A flashing malfunction indicator light sequence identifies the codes that indicate the source of the malfunction. Refer to the following example and **Figure 104** for a description of how to interpret the flashing signals.

A short duration light ON, followed by a short duration light OFF then a short duration light ON indicates a 2 for the first digit of the trouble code. The second digit of the trouble code is displayed after a short OFF period. Continuing with the example in **Figure 104**, a short light ON indicates a 1, or a trouble code of 21. A longer duration light OFF period separates individual stored codes, if there are any. Otherwise the first code repeats. If more than one code is present, they are repeated in numerical order.

The malfunction indicator light (part No. 99056A 1) and possibly the harness kit (part No. 91-884793A 1) are required to read the trouble codes.

1. On 115 hp models, depress the locking tabs (**Figure 105**), then remove the electrical component cover from the front power head.

2A. On 115 hp models (2001), locate the blue/white and red/black diagnostic wires just to the port side of the trim/tilt relay unit. Remove the rubber plugs from the wires.

2B. On 115 hp models (2002-2003), unplug the diagnostic connector (**Figure 106**) from the mounting bracket. Remove the plug from blue/white wire harness connector. The blue/white wire is located near the diagnostic connector.

2C. On 225 hp models, locate the diagnostic connector (**Figure 107**) just under the starboard side silencer cover and near the fuel filter. Remove the gray cover from the connector.

CAUTION
The green/red wire of the harness kit (part No. 91-884793A 1) is supplied with voltage when connected onto the engine wire har-

ness. Do not allow the wire terminal to come in contact with an engine ground or other engine component during testing. Cover the wire terminal with electrical tape to prevent arcing, damage to wiring or a blown fuse.

3A. On 115 hp models (2001), plug the malfunction indicator light (part No. 99056A 1) leads onto the blue/white and red/black engine harness leads. Polarity is not important for this procedure.
3B. On 115 hp models (2002-2003), plug the harness kit (part No. 91-88479A 1) onto the diagnostic connector. Plug one lead of the malfunction indicator light (part No. 99056A 1) onto the female connector of the harness kit. Plug the other indicator light lead onto the blue/white wire connector. Polarity is not important when connecting the indicator light leads.
3C. On 225 hp models, plug the harness kit (part No. 91-88479A 1) onto the diagnostic connector. Plug one lead of the malfunction indicator light (part No. 99056A 1) onto the female connector of the harness kit. Plug the other indicator light lead onto the blue/white wire connector. Polarity is not important when connecting the indicator light leads.
4. Prepare the engine for operation on a flush/test device or under actual operating conditions.

NOTE
A shorted stop circuit or other faults may prevent the engine from starting. If the engine will not start, check for codes while cranking the engine. Codes may not be displayed if the battery is discharged from excessive cranking. Fully charge the battery as needed.

5. Start the engine and immediately note the flashing light sequence. Identify the codes as described earlier in this section. Record all trouble codes until they repeat.
6. Stop the engine and remove the malfunction indicator light and harness. Replace any plugs and reinstall the diagnostic plug.
7. On 115 hp models, install the plastic electrical component cover onto the power head.
8. If codes are displayed, refer to **Table 15** to identify the code(s) and the following information for corrective action.

Code 1

A code 1 indicates the diagnostic system is operational. A repeating code 1 indicates that no malfunction is currently detected by the engine control unit.

Code 13

A code 13 indicates the engine control unit (ECU) detects a fault with the crankshaft position sensor. Test the crankshaft position sensor as described in the ignition system troubleshooting section of this chapter. Check for faulty wiring or terminals if the sensor tests correctly.

Code 15

A code 15 indicates the engine control unit (ECU) detects a fault with the engine temperature sensor. Test the engine temperature sensor as described in the ignition system troubleshooting section of this chapter. Check for faulty wiring or terminals if the sensor tests correctly.

Code 18

A code 18 indicates the engine control unit (ECU) detects a fault with the throttle position sensor. Test the throttle position sensor as described in the ignition system troubleshooting section of this chapter. Check for faulty wiring or terminals if the sensor tests correctly.

Code 19

A code 19 indicates the engine control unit (ECU) detects incorrect voltage from the battery or battery charging system. Perform the rectifier/regulator output test as describe in the ignition system troubleshooting section of this chapter. Test the battery and check the terminals as described in Chapter Six.

Code 23

A code 23 indicates the engine control unit (ECU) detects a fault with the air temperature sensor. Test the air temperature sensor as described in this section. Check for faulty wiring or terminals if the sensor tests correctly.

Code 28

A code 28 indicates the engine control unit (ECU) detects a fault with the shift position switch. On 115 hp models, test the shift position switch as described in this section. On 225 hp models test the shift position switch as described in the warning system troubleshooting section of this chapter. Check for proper shift cable adjustment if the switch tests correctly.

Code 29

A code 29 indicates the engine control unit (ECU) detects a fault with the air pressure sensor. Check for faulty wiring or connections on the wire connecting onto the sensor. If no fault is found with the wiring, replace the sensor as described in Chapter Five.

Code 33

The engine control unit (ECU) displays code 33 immediately after starting a cool engine. This indicates the ECU is delivering extra fuel to the engine and advancing the timing beyond the normal range to enhance low speed operation during warm up. If code 33 appears after the engine reaches normal operating temperature, test the thermostat(s) as described in this chapter (see *Cooling System Troubleshooting)*. Test the engine temperature sensor as described in the ignition system troubleshooting section of this chapter if the thermostat(s) test correctly.

Code 37

A code 37 indicates the engine control unit (ECU) detects unusually low manifold vacuum. Check for vacuum leaks at the throttle body to intake and intake to cylinder head mating surfaces. Perform the synchronization procedures as described in Chapter Four. If the code persists, perform a compression test as described in this chapter and adjust the valves as described in Chapter Four. Replace the air pressure sensor if the code returns and no faults are found with compression or valve adjustment.

Code 39

A code 39 indicates the engine control unit (ECU) detects a fault with the oil pressure sender. Test the oil pressure sender as described in the warning system troubleshooting section of this chapter. Check for faulty wiring or terminals if the sensor tests correctly.

Code 44

A code 44 indicates the engine control unit (ECU) detects a fault with the engine stop circuit. Test the stop circuit as described in the ignition system troubleshooting section of this chapter.

Code 45

A code 45 indicates the engine control unit (ECU) detects a fault with the shift interrupt switch. Test the shift interrupt switch as described in the ignition system troubleshooting section of this chapter. Check for proper shift cable adjustment if the switch tests correctly.

Code 46

A code 46 indicates the engine control unit (ECU) detects a fault with one or both of the engine temperature switches. Test both engine temperature switches as described in the warning system troubleshooting section of this chapter. Check for faulty wiring or terminals if both switches test correctly.

Shift Position Switch Test (115 hp Model)

Perform this test if the engine idle speed is unstable or the engine stalls at idle speed. The shift position switch mounts onto the shift cable bracket on the lower port side of the power head. The shift linkage depresses the switch plunger when the engine is shifted into neutral gear. A multimeter is required for this test.

1. Remove the shift position switch as described in Chapter Six.
2. Calibrate the meter to the R × 1 scale.
3. Connect the meter test leads onto the blue/yellow and black switch wire terminals. Polarity is not important for this test.
4. Observe the meter while repeatedly depressing and releasing the switch plunger. The meter must indicate *continuity* each time the plunger is depressed and *no continuity* each time the plunger is released. Replace the switch if it fails to perform as described.
5. Install the shift interrupt switch as described in Chapter Six.

Fuel Injector Operation Test

Test for fuel injector operation if the engine will not start or is misfiring on one or more cylinders. Use a mechanic's stethoscope or long screwdriver to amplify the noise produced by each injector. On 115 hp models, the injectors are mounted onto the intake manifold on the rear and port side of the power head. On 225 hp models, the injectors mount into the throttle bodies on the port and starboard sides of the power head.

1. On 225 hp models, remove the silencer cover as described in Chapter Five.

2. Prepare the engine for operation on a flush/test device or under actual operating conditions.

3. Start the engine and run at idle speed.

4. Place a stethoscope or long screwdriver against the body of each fuel injector (**Figure 108**). If a screwdriver is used, place the handle to your ear.

5. A clicking noise should be heard from each injector indicating that it is opening. If no clicking noise is heard or if there is a noticeably different noise from an individual injector, test the injector resistance as described in this section, and the wiring connections between the injector and the engine control unit (ECU). If the resistance is within the specification, and the connections are in good condition, install a known good injector. If the replacement injector fails to operate, a defective wiring harness, ignition system fault or ECU fault is indicated. Replace the ECU to restore injector operation only if all other components test correctly.

6. On 225 hp models, install the silencer cover as described in Chapter Five.

Fuel Injector Resistance Test

This test measures the resistance of the winding within the injector. A correct resistance reading does not indicate the injector is functional. An internal mechanical defect, foreign material or deposits can prevent the injector from operating. Injector removal is not required for this test. An accurate multimeter is required for this test.

1. Disconnect the negative battery cable to prevent accidental starting.

2. On 225 hp models, remove the silencer cover as described in Chapter Five.

3. Refer to the wiring diagrams at the end of the manual to identify the wires leading to the injectors. Trace the wires to each injector.

4. Push in on the wire clip and carefully pull the wire connector from the injector body.

5. Set the multimeter to the R × 1 scale. Touch the meter test leads to the individual terminals of the injector (**Figure 109**). The meter must indicate approximately 14.5 ohms. If not, the injector is shorted or open and must be replaced. Repeat the resistance measurement for any suspect injectors.

6. Align the tabs on the connector with the slot while connecting the harness plugs onto the injectors.

7. On 225 hp models, install the silencer cover as described in Chapter Five.

8. Connect the battery cable.

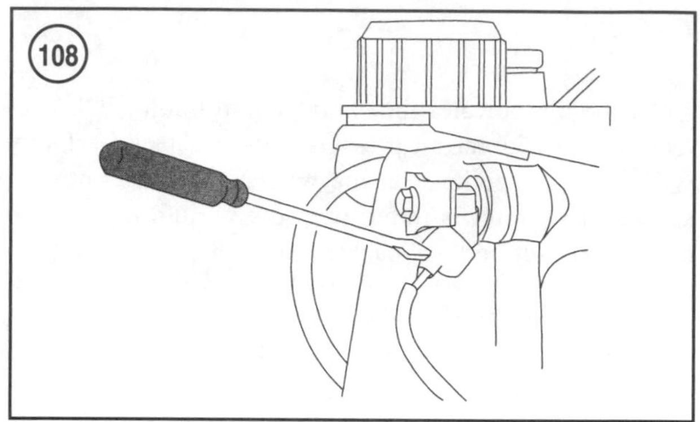

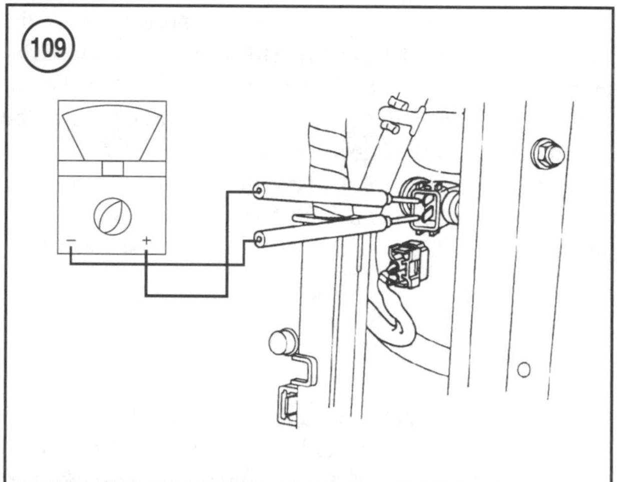

Air Temperature Sensor Resistance Test

The air temperature sensor (**Figure 110**) provides a signal to the engine control unit (ECU) indicating the temperature of the incoming air. The sensor threads into the silencer cover. Using input from the air temperature sensor, the ECU then adjusts the injector-on time to match the fuel requirements to the conditions.

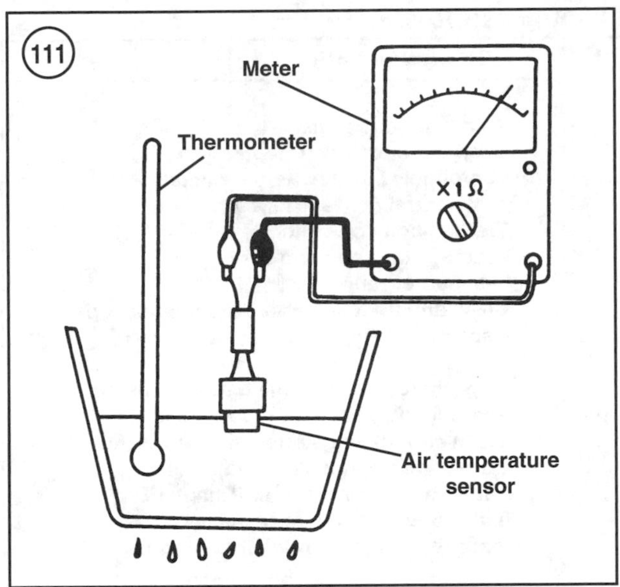

Excessive exhaust smoke, spark plug fouling and general poor performance can result from incorrect air/fuel mixture caused by a defective air temperature sensor.

Check the operation of the air temperature sensor by reading the diagnostic trouble codes. If a code 23 appears, test the sensor as follows:

This test requires an accurate digital or analog multimeter, a liquid thermometer and a container of water that can be heated.

1. Remove the air temperature sensor as described in Chapter Five.
2. Calibrate the meter onto the appropriate ohms scale for the resistance specification in **Table 8**. Connect the meter leads between the two sensor terminals. Test lead polarity is not important for this test.
3. Suspend the sensor in a container of water that can be heated (**Figure 111**). Ensure the sensor does not touch the bottom or sides of the container and the tip of the sensor is completely below the water surface.
4. Add ice or heat the container until the water temperature reaches the temperatures specified in **Table 8**. Record the resistance at each temperature.
5. Compare the resistance readings with the specifications in **Table 8**. A slight variance from the resistance specification (less than 10 percent) is common and does not indicate a fault with the sensor. Replace the air temperature sensor if the resistance is significantly different from the specification at any of the specified temperatures.
6. Install the air temperature sensor as described in Chapter Five.

Idle Air Control Motor Function Test

The engine control unit (ECU) controls idle speed using the idle air control motor. The idle air control motor varies air flowing into a dedicated passage in the intake manifold(s).

Symptoms of a faulty idle air control motor include stalling when the engine is shifted into gear, too slow or unstable idle, or excessively high idle speed. The engine usually performs correctly at higher speeds. The manufacturer does not provide procedures for testing the idle air control motor.

If these symptoms are present, first synchronize and adjust the fuel system components as described in Chapter Four. On 115 hp models, test the shift position switch as described in this section. Replace the idle air control motor as described in Chapter Five if these symptoms persist after the adjustments.

Table 1 TORQUE SPECIFICATIONS

Fastener	in.-lb.	ft.-lb.	N•m
Spark plug cover			
75-115 hp models	65	–	7.3
225 hp model	71	–	8.0
Vapor separator tank drain screw			
225 hp model	18	–	2.0

Table 2 STARTING SYSTEM TROUBLESHOOTING

Symptom	Possible causes	Corrective action
Starter does not energize		
	Engine not in neutral gear	Shift into neutral gear
	Weak or discharged battery	Charge the battery (Chapter Six)
	Dirty or corroded battery terminals	Thoroughly clean battery terminals
	Faulty neutral only start switch	Test neutral only start switch
	Faulty ignition key switch	Test ignition key switch
	Faulty starter solenoid	Test the starter solenoid
	Faulty starter relay	Test starter relay
	Loose or dirty wire connection	Clean and tighten starter wire connections
	Faulty electric starter	Repair the electric starter
Starter engages flywheel (flywheel rotates slowly)		
	Weak or discharged battery	Fully charge and test the battery (Chapter Six)
	Dirty or corroded battery terminals	Thoroughly clean battery terminals
	Loose or dirty wire connections	Clean and tighten starter wire connections
	Engine is in gear	Correct improper linkage adjustment
	Faulty electric starter	Repair the electric starter (Chapter Six)
	Internal powerhead damage	Inspect powerhead for damage
	Internal gearcase damage	Inspect gearcase lubricant for debris
Electric starter engages (flywheel does not rotate)		
	Weak or discharged battery	Fully charge and test the battery (Chapter Six)
	Dirty or corroded battery terminals	Thoroughly clean battery terminals
	Loose or dirty wire connections	Clean and tighten starter wire connections
	Water in the cylinder(s)	Inspect spark plug(s) for water contamination
	Oil in the cylinder(s)	Inspect spark plugs for oil contamination
	Damaged starter drive gear	Inspect starter drive gear
	Damaged flywheel gear teeth	Inspect flywheel gear teeth
	Faulty electric starter	Repair the electric starter
	Seized powerhead	Inspect powerhead for damage
	Seized gearcase	Inspect gearcase lubricant for debris
	Improper valve timing or adjustment	Check valve timing and adjustment
Electric starter (noisy operation)		
	Dirty or dry starter drive gear	Clean and lubricate starter drive gear
	Damaged starter drive gear teeth	Inspect starter drive gear
	Damaged or corroded flywheel gear	Inspect flywheel drive gear teeth
	Loose starter mounting bolt(s)	Tighten starter mounting bolt(s)
	Worn or dry starter bushing(s)	Repair electric starter

Table 3 FUEL SYSTEM TROUBLESHOOTING

Symptom	Possible causes	Corrective action
Engine does not start		
	Closed fuel tank vent	Open the fuel tank vent
	Old or contaminated fuel	Provide the engine with fresh fuel
	Disconnected fuel hose	Connect fuel hose
	Faulty primer bulb	Check the primer bulb
	Faulty electrothermal valve	Test the electrothermal valve
	Air or fuel leaks in hose fittings	Inspect hose fittings for leakage
	Blocked fuel filter	Inspect the filter for contaminants
	Stuck carburetor inlet needle	Repair the carburetor(s)
	Improper float level adjustment	Repair the carburetor(s)
	Blocked carburetor passages	Repair the carburetor(s)
	Faulty mechanical fuel pump	Test the mechanical fuel pump

(continued)

Table 3 FUEL SYSTEM TROUBLESHOOTING (continued)

Symptom	Possible causes	Corrective action
Engine does not start (continued)		
	Faulty electric low-pressure pump	Test the pump operation
	Faulty power relay	Test the power relay
	Low battery voltage	Check battery and charging system
	Open fuel pump fuse	Check for fuel pump operation
	Faulty electric fuel pump	Test the fuel pressure
	Low fuel pressure	Test the fuel pressure
	Faulty EFI system sensor	Check for diagnostic trouble codes
	Faulty engine temperature sensor	Test the engine temperature sensor
	Faulty air temperature sensor	Test the air temperature sensor
	Faulty throttle position sensor	Test the throttle position sensor
	Faulty fuel injector	Check fuel injector operation
	Faulty air pressure sensor	Replace the air pressure sensor
	Faulty engine control unit	Check engine control unit
Stalls or runs rough at idle		
	Old or contaminated fuel	Provide the engine with fresh fuel
	Improper idle speed adjustment	Adjust idle speed (Chapter Four)
	Improper throttle synchronization	Synchronize the throttle (Chapter Four)
	Closed or blocked fuel tank vent	Open or clear vent
	Blocked carburetor passages	Repair carburetor(s)
	Flooding carburetor	Check for carburetor flooding
	Faulty primer bulb	Check the primer bulb
	Faulty shift interrupt switch	Test shift interrupt switch
	Faulty shift position switch	Test shift position switch
	Air or fuel leaks at hose fittings	Inspect hose fittings for leakage
	Blocked fuel filter	Inspect the filter for contaminants
	Faulty mechanical fuel pump	Test the mechanical fuel pump
	Faulty electrothermal valve	Test the electrothermal valve
	Low battery voltage	Check battery and charging system
	Flooding vapor separator tank	Check for flooding
	Faulty power relay	Test the power relay
	Faulty EFI system sensor	Check for diagnostic trouble codes
	Faulty throttle position sensor	Test the throttle position sensor
	Faulty engine temperature sensor	Test the engine temperature sensor
	Faulty air temperature sensor	Test the air temperature sensor
	Faulty fuel pressure regulator	Test the fuel pressure
	Faulty electric fuel pump	Check for electric fuel pump operation
	Faulty fuel injector	Check fuel injector operation
	Faulty idle air control motor	Replace idle air control motor (Chapter Five)
	Faulty air pressure sensor	Replace air pressure sensor
	Faulty engine control unit	Check engine control unit
Idle speed too high		
	Improper throttle synchronization	Synchronize the throttle (Chapter Four)
	Improper idle speed adjustment	Adjust idle speed (Chapter Four)
	Improper throttle linkage adjustment	Adjust throttle linkages
	Binding throttle linkage(s)	Check linkage(s)
	Faulty EFI system sensor	Check for diagnostic trouble codes
	Faulty engine temperature sensor	Check engine temperature sensor
	Faulty idle air control motor	Replace idle air control motor
Hesitation during acceleration		
	Old or contaminated fuel	Supply the engine with fresh fuel
	Faulty mechanical fuel pump	Test the fuel pump
	Faulty electrothermal valve(s)	Test the electrothermal valve(s)
	Blocked carburetor passages	Repair carburetor(s)
	Faulty dashpot/accelerator pump	Test the dashpot/accellerator pump
	Blocked fuel filter	Inspect the filter(s) for contaminants
	Air or fuel leaks at hose fittings	Inspect hose fittings for leakage
	Closed or blocked fuel tank vent	Open or clear tank vent
	Flooding carburetor	Check for carburetor flooding

(continued)

Table 3 FUEL SYSTEM TROUBLESHOOTING (continued)

Symptom	Possible causes	Corrective action
Hesitation during acceleration (continued)		
	Improper valve timing	Check valve timing
	Low battery voltage	Check battery and charging system
	Flooding vapor separator tank	Check for flooding
	Faulty EFI system sensor	Check for diagnostic trouble codes
	Faulty throttle position sensor	Test throttle position sensor
	Faulty engine temperature sensor	Test the engine temperature sensor
	Faulty air temperature sensor	Test the air temperature sensor
	Faulty fuel pressure regulator	Test the fuel pressure
	Electric fuel pump failure	Test the fuel pressure
	Faulty fuel injector	Check fuel injector operation
	Faulty air pressure sensor	Replace air pressure sensor
	Faulty engine control unit	Check engine control unit
Misfire or poor high speed performance		
	Old or contaminated fuel	Supply the engine with fresh fuel
	Faulty mechanical fuel pump	Test the fuel pump
	Faulty electric low-pressure pump	Test the pump operation
	Misadjusted throttle linkages	Adjust throttle linkages
	Blocked carburetor passages	Repair carburetor(s)
	Blocked fuel filter(s)	Inspect the filter(s) for contaminants
	Air or fuel leaks at hose fittings	Inspect hose fittings for leakage
	Closed or blocked fuel tank vent	Open or clear vent
	Improper valve timing	Check valve timing
	Low battery voltage	Check battery and charging system
	Faulty EFI system sensor	Check for diagnostic trouble codes
	Faulty engine temperature sensor	Test the engine temperature sensor
	Faulty air temperature sensor	Test the air temperature sensor
	Faulty fuel pressure regulator	Test the fuel pressure
	Electric fuel pump failure	Test the fuel pressure
	Faulty fuel injector	Check fuel injector operation
	Faulty air pressure sensor	Replace the air pressure sensor
	Faulty engine control unit	Check engine control unit
Excessive exhaust smoke		
	Flooding carburetor	Check for carburetor flooding
	Blocked carburetor passages	Repair carburetor(s)
	Improper float level	Repair carburetor(s)
	Faulty electrothermal valve	Test the electrothermal valves
	Flooding vapor separator tank	Check for flooding
	Faulty EFI system sensor	Check for diagnostic trouble codes
	Faulty engine temperature sensor	Test the engine temperature sensor
	Faulty air temperature sensor	Test the air temperature sensor
	Faulty air pressure sensor	Replace the air pressure sensor
	Faulty fuel pressure regulator	Test the fuel pressure
	Stuck fuel injector	Check fuel injector operation
	Faulty air pressure sensor	Replace the air pressure sensor
	Faulty engine control unit	Check engine control unit

Table 4 IGNITION SYSTEM TROUBLESHOOTING

Symptom	Possible causes	Corrective action
Engine does not start		
	Lanyard switch activated	Check lanyard switch
	Shorted stop circuit	Test the stop circuit
	Low battery voltage	Check battery and charging system
	Faulty power relay	Test the power relay
	Faulty battery charging coil	Test the battery charging coil
	Faulty crankshaft position sensor(s)	Test crankshaft position sensor(s)

(continued)

Table 4 IGNITION SYSTEM TROUBLESHOOTING (continued)

Symptom	Possible causes	Corrective action
Engine does not start (continued)		
	Faulty shift interrupt switch	Test the shift interrupt switch
	Faulty ignition coil	Test ignition coil
	Fouled spark plug(s)	Check or replace spark plug(s)
	Faulty spark plug lead	Test spark plug lead
	Faulty engine control unit (ECU)	Perform ECU output test
Stalls or runs rough at idle		
	Fouled spark plug(s)	Check or replace spark plug(s)
	Faulty spark plug lead	Test spark plug lead
	Partially shorted stop circuit	Test the stop circuit
	Faulty shift interrupt switch	Test the shift interrupt switch
	Faulty shift position switch	Test the shift position switch
	Low battery voltage	Check battery and charging system
	Faulty power relay	Test the power relay
	Faulty battery charging coil	Test the battery charging coil
	Faulty crankshaft position sensor(s)	Test crankshaft position sensor(s)
	Faulty ignition coil	Test ignition coil
	Faulty engine control unit (ECU)	Perform ECU output test
Idle speed too high		
	Faulty engine temperature sensor	Test engine temperature sensor
	Faulty crankshaft position sensor	Test crankshaft position sensor
	Faulty throttle position sensor	Check for diagnostic trouble code(s)
	Faulty engine temperature sensor	Check for diagnostic trouble codes(s)
	Faulty engine temperature switch	Check for diagnostic trouble codes(s)
Misfire or poor high speed performance		
	Engine reaching rev limit	Check full speed engine rpm
	Fouled spark plug(s)	Check or replace spark plug(s)
	Faulty spark plug lead	Test spark plug lead
	Faulty spark plug cap	Test spark plug cap
	Fault shift interrupt switch	Test the shift interrupt switch
	Faulty shift position switch	Test the shift position switch
	Partially shorted stop circuit	Test for shorted stop circuit
	Low battery voltage	Check battery and charging system
	Faulty battery charging coil	Test the battery charging coil
	Faulty crankshaft position sensor(s)	Test crankshaft position sensor(s)
	Faulty ignition coil	Test ignition coil
	Faulty engine control unit (ECU)	Perform ECU output test

Table 5 PEAK OUTPUT VOLTAGE SPECIFICATIONS

Component	Specification (volts)
Battery charging coil	
75-115 hp models	
At cranking speed (400 rpm)	10-18
At 750 rpm	16-24
At 1500 rpm	16-24
At 3500 rpm	16-24
225 hp model	
Green coil wires	
At cranking speed (400 rpm)	8*
At 1500 rpm	42*
At 3500 rpm	93*
Green/white coil wires	
At cranking speed (400 rpm)	7*
At 1500 rpm	34*
At 3500 rpm	78*

(continued)

Table 5 PEAK OUTPUT VOLTAGE SPECIFICATIONS (continued)

Component	Specification (volts)
Crankshaft position sensor	
75 and 90 hp models	
At cranking speed (400 rpm)	2.8-3.4
At 1500 rpm	6.5-7.8
At 3500 rpm	10.5-12.0
115 hp model	
At cranking speed (400 rpm)	3.0-6.3
At 750 rpm	9-16
At 1500 rpm	18-28
At 3500 rpm	35-55
225 hp model	
At cranking speed (400 rpm)	3.8-5.3
At 1500 rpm	20-27
At 3500 rpm	43-70
Engine control unit (ECU)	
75 and 90 hp models	
At cranking speed (400 rpm)	165-190
At 1500 rpm	170-200
At 3500 rpm	170-200
Rectifier/regulator	
75 and 90 hp models	
At 1000 rpm	18-22
At 1500 rpm	19-24
At 3500 rpm	19-24
At 5000 rpm	19-24
115 hp model	
At 750 rpm	12.5-15.5
At 1500 rpm	13-16
At 3500 rpm	13-16
225 hp model	
At 1500 rpm	10.3-10.7
At 3500 rpm	10.3-10.7

*Minimum allowable voltage output.

Table 6 IGNITION AND CHARGING SYSTEM RESISTANCE SPECIFICATIONS*

Component	Specification (ohms)
Battery charging coil	
75 and 90 hp models	
Red and white test harness leads	0.32-0.48
Red and black test harness leads	0.32-0.48
White and black test harness leads	0.32-0.48
115 hp model	
Green wire No. 1 and green wire No. 2	0.2-0.8
Green wire No. 1 and green wire No. 3	0.2-0.8
Green wire No. 2 and green wire No. 3	0.2-0.8
225 hp model	
Green charging coil wires	
Red and black test harness leads	0.10-0.60
Red and black test harness leads	0.10-0.60
Black and white test harness leads	0.10-0.60
Green/white charging coil wires	
Red and black test harness leads	0.10-0.50
Red and black test harness leads	0.10-0.50
Black and white test harness leads	0.10-0.50

(continued)

Table 6 IGNITION AND CHARGING SYSTEM RESISTANCE SPECIFICATIONS* (continued)

Component	Specification (ohms)
Crankshaft position sensor	
75 and 90 hp models	
White/yellow and white test harness leads	445-545
White/red and white test harness leads	445-545
115 hp model	
White/red and black test harness leads	445-565
White/black and black test harness leads	445-565
225 hp model	
Red and blue test harness leads	459-561
Black/red and blue test harness leads	459-561
Brown and blue test harness leads	459-561
Electrothermal valve	
75 and 90 hp models	
Blue wire and black wire	15-25
Ignition coil	
75 and 90 hp models	
Primary coil resistance	
Black/white and black wire	0.078-0.106
Secondary coil resistance	
Between spark plug wire terminals	35K-47K
115 hp model	
Primary coil resistance	
Black/white and red/yellow test harness terminals	1.8-2.6
Secondary coil resistance	
Between the spark plug cap terminals	
No. 1 and No. 4 ignition coil	18.97K-35.23K
No. 2 and No. 3 ignition coil	18.55K-34.45K
225 hp models	
Primary coil resistance	
Between coil harness connector terminals	1.5-1.9
Secondary coil resistance	
Between the spark plug cap terminals	19.60K-35.00K
Spark plug wires	
75 and 90 hp models	
Cylinder No. 1	4.50K-10.70K
Cylinder No. 2	33K-8K
Cylinder No. 3	37K-89K
Cylinder No. 4	4.3K-10.2K

*Resistance specification at 68° F (20° C). Resistance readings will be greater at higher temperatures and less at lower temperatures.

Table 7 THROTTLE POSITION SENSOR TEST SPECIFICATIONS

Model	Specification (volts)
75 and 90 hp	
Input voltage	4.75-5.25
Output voltage (at 850 rpm)	0.68-0.82
115 hp models	
Input voltage	4.75-5.25
Output voltage (at 750 rpm)	0.718-0.746
225 hp models	
Input voltage	4.75-5.25
Output voltage (at 750 rpm)	0.695-0.705

Table 8 ENGINE AND AIR TEMPERATURE SENSOR RESISTANCE SPECIFICATIONS

Model	Specification (ohms)
Engine temperature sensor	
75 and 90 hp models	
At 32° F (0° C)	5.79K
At 68° F (20° C)	2.45K
At 104° F (40° C)	1.5K
At 140° F (60° C)	500
115 hp models	
At 41° F (5° C)	4.62K
At 68° F (20° C)	2.44K
At 110° F (43°C)	750
At 140° F (60° C)	500
At 212° F (100° C)	190
225 hp models	
At 68° F (20° C)	54.2K-69K
At 212° F (0° C)	3.12K-3.48K
Air temperature sensor	
At 32° F (0° C)	5.4K-6.6K
At 175° F (80° C)	290-390

Table 9 WARNING SYSTEM COMPONENT TEST SPECIFICATIONS*

Model	Specifications
75-115 hp models	
Oil pressure switch	
Switch to no continuity	22 psi (150 kPa)
225 hp models	
Oil pressure sender	
Input voltage	4.75-5.25 volts
Output voltage (700 rpm)	3.8 volts
Engine temperature switch	
Switch to continuity	183° F (84° C)
Reset to no continuity	154-179° F (68-82° C)

*Normal test specification. Temperature and normal productions will result in a higher or lower value. Replace the component if the test results vary significantly from the specification.

Table 10 OVERSPEED PROTECTION SYSTEM SPECIFICATIONS

Model	Maximum recommended engine speed (rpm)	Overspeed activation (rpm)
75 hp	4500-5500	6200
90 hp	5000-6000	6200
115 hp	5000-6000	6200
225 hp	5000-6000	6200*

*Overspeed protection activation speed in FORWARD gear. Overspeed protection activates at 4500 rpm in NEUTRAL gear.

Table 11 RECTIFIER/REGULATOR RESISTANCE SPECIFICATIONS

Model	Positive test lead	Negative test lead	Specification
75 and 90 hp	Red	Green	100-300 ohm
	Red	Green/white*	100-300 ohm
	Green	Red	No continuity
	Green/white*	Red	No continuity
	Black	Green	No continuity
	Black	Green/white*	No continuity
	Green	Black	100-300 ohm
	Green/white*	Black	100-300 ohm
115 hp	Red	Green*	100-300 ohm
	Green*	Black	No continuity
	Black	Green*	No continuity
	Red	Green	100-300 ohm

*Two green or green/white leads connect onto the rectifier/regulator or test harness. Perform the test using each green or green/white lead.

Table 12 OIL PRESSURE SPECIFICATIONS

Model	Specification
75-90 hp models	
At 850 rpm	46.5 psi (320 kPa)
At 5000 rpm	71 psi (490 kPa)
115 hp models	
At 750 rpm	50.8 psi (350 kPa)
At 5000 rpm	71 psi (490 kPa)
225 hp models	
At 700 rpm	19.6 psi (138 kPa)
At 5000 rpm	75-92 psi (517-634 kPa)

Table 13 COMPRESSION SPECIFICATIONS

Model	Specification
75 and 90 hp models	
Compression ratio	9.6 to 1
Minimum pressure at cranking speed	138 psi (950 kPa)
115 hp models	
Compression ratio	9.7 to 1
Minimum pressure at cranking speed	138 psi (950 kPa)
225 hp models	
Compression ratio	9.9 to 1
Minimum pressure at cranking speed	125 psi (860 kPa)
Maximum variance between cylinders	10 percent

Table 14 THERMOSTAT SPECIFICATIONS

Model	Specification
75 and 90 hp models	
Start to open temperature	140° F (60° C)
Full open temperature	158° F (70° C)
Minimum plunger opening height	0.12 in. (3.0 mm)

(continued)

Table 14 THERMOSTAT SPECIFICATIONS (continued)

Model	Specification
115 hp models	
Start to open temperature	122° F (50° C)
Full open temperature	140° F (60° C)
Minimum plunger opening height	0.17 in. (4.3 mm)
225 hp models	
Start to open temperature	140° F (60° C)
Full open temperature	158° F (70° C)
Minimum plunger opening height	0.17 in. (4.3 mm)

Table 15 DIAGNOSTIC TROUBLE CODES

Code	Malfunction
1	Normal (diagnostic system is operational)
13	Crankshaft position sensor fault
15	Engine temperature sensor fault
18	Throttle position sensor fault
19	Incorrect battery voltage or charging system fault
23	Air temperature sensor fault
28	Shift position switch fault
29	Air pressure sensor fault
33	Engine temperature fault or thermostat malfunction
37	Vacuum leakage at intake manifold detected
39	Oil pressure sender fault
44	Engine stop circuit fault
45	Shift interrupt switch fault
46	Engine temperature switch fault

Chapter Three

Lubrication, Maintenance and Tune-up

When operating properly, the Mercury or Mariner outboard provides smooth operation, quick starting and excellent performance. Regular maintenance and frequent tune-ups keep it in good shape and running great. This chapter provides the information necessary to perform all required lubrication, maintenance and tune-up on the Mercury or Mariner four-stroke outboard.

Table 1 lists torque specifications for maintenance related fasteners. Use the general torque specifications in the *Quick Reference Data* section at the front of the manual for fasteners not listed in **Table 1**. **Table 2** lists the maintenance requirements and intervals for all engine systems and components. Maintenance intervals are also provided in the *Quick Reference Data* at the front of the manual. **Table 3** lists lubricant capacities. **Table 4** lists spark plug recommendations. **Tables 1-4** are located at the end of this chapter.

BEFORE EACH USE

As specified in **Table 2**, check or inspect indicated items before each use. Following these recommendations help identify and correct conditions leading to a dangerous lack of control or damage to the engine.

Engine Oil Level and Condition Inspection

CAUTION
Avoid serious damage to the power head. Never run the engine with the oil level over the full mark in the dipstick. Over filling of the oil can result in foaming of the oil and inadequate lubrication of internal components.

CAUTION
Never start the engine with a low or high oil level. Low or high oil level can result in inadequate power head lubrication.

Check the oil level before and after each use. Accurate oil level measurements are only possible if the engine is switched off for thirty minutes or more and the engine is in a vertical position (**Figure 1**). The oil dipstick (**Figure 2**, typical) is located on the lower starboard side of the power head on all models covered in this manual. A metal loop-type grip is used on 75-115 hp models, whereas a plastic knob-type grip is used on 225 hp models. The grip is colored yellow for easy identification.

On 75-115 hp models, the oil fill cap is located on the valve cover (**Figure 3**). On 225 hp models, the oil fill cap is located on the upper starboard side of the power head (**Figure 4**).

1. Position the engine vertically (**Figure 1**) with the ignition switched OFF.
2. Pull the dipstick from the tube. Use a clean shop towel to wipe the dipstick clean.
3. Insert and fully seat the dipstick into the tube.
4. Pull the dipstick from the tube and note the oil level line (**Figure 5**).
   a. On 75-115 hp models, the oil level line must be within the cross hatched area between the upper and lower markings.
   b. On 225 hp models, the oil level line must be with the cross hatched area and between the *H* and *L* markings.
5. Inspect the oil on the dipstick for water (a milky appearance), fuel odor, or dark coloration. Change the oil as described in this chapter if milky or dark in color. Refer to *Power Head Troubleshooting* in Chapter Two if water or fuel odor is detected in the oil.
   a. If the oil level line is below the lower or L marking, remove the oil fill cap. Add a small amount of oil. Wait a few minutes, then recheck the oil level. Continue until the oil level just reaches or is slightly below the upper H marking on the dipstick. Do not overfill the engine with oil. If necessary, drain excess oil from the engine as described in this chapter. See *Engine Oil and Filter Replacement*. After filling, rotate the oil fill cap until locked into position.
   b. If the oil level line is above the upper or H marking, drain excess oil from the oil pan as described in this chapter. See *Engine Oil and Filter Replacement*.

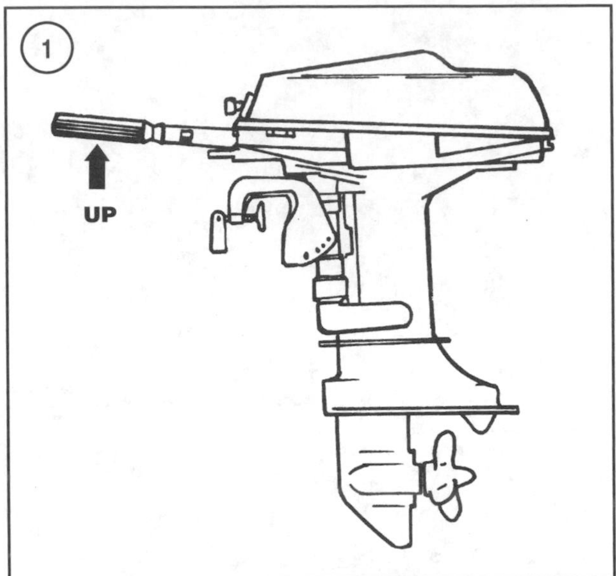

Fuel Filter Inspection

WARNING

Avoid damage to property, serious bodily injury and death. Use extreme caution when working with or around fuel. Never smoke around fuel or fuel vapor. Make sure no flame or source of ignition is present in the work area. Flame or sparks can ignite the fuel or vapor resulting in fire or explosion.

Eventually dirt, fuel deposits and other contaminants form or enter the fuel system. These contaminants are trapped by the fuel filter(s). Regular inspection and filter replacement helps prevent eventual filter blockage and

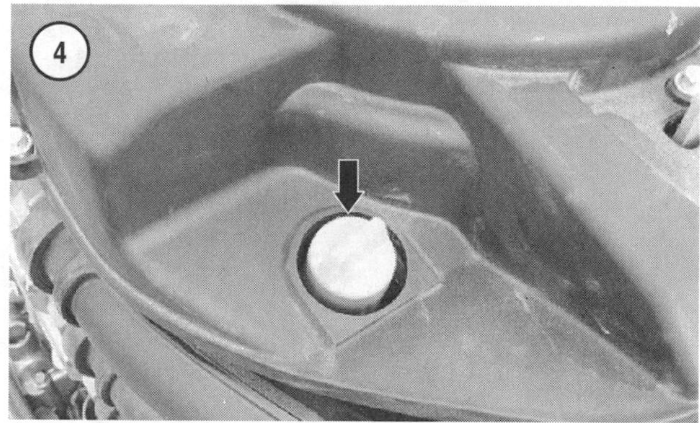

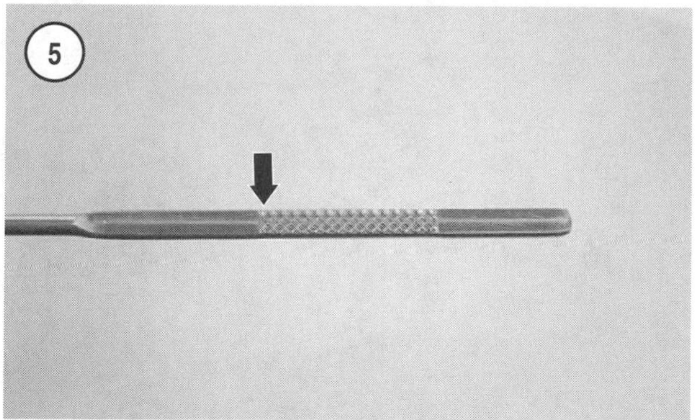

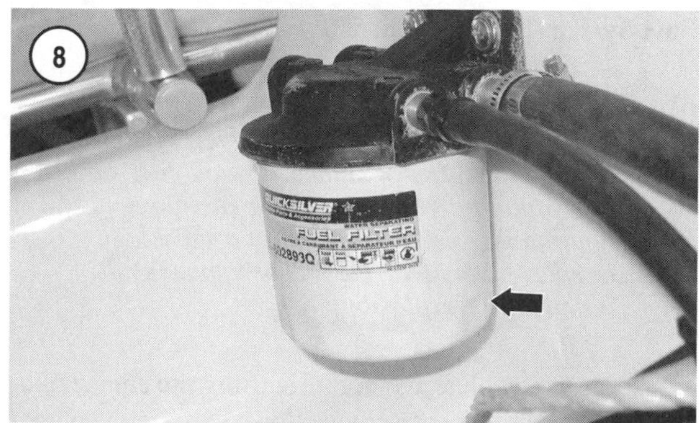

fuel starvation problems. Clean, inspect or change the fuel filter at the intervals listed in **Table 2**.

An inline fuel filter (**Figure 6**) is used on all 75 and 90 hp models. A canister fuel filter (**Figure 7**) is used on 115 and 225 hp models. The filter is located along the fuel hose connecting the fuel supply tank to the fuel pump. The filter body or canister is constructed of translucent material allowing visual detection of contamination. Direct a beam of light into the filter body or canister to check for sediment or contamination. Replace the filter or element if dark staining or a significant amount of sediment is detected within the filter.

The canister filter used on 115 and 225 hp models contains a float to indicate water in the canister. The float is constructed of a material that floats on water but sinks in fuel. The float remains at the bottom of the canister if no or very little water is in the canister. If the float appears suspended or lifted from the bottom of the canister, replace the filter element as described in Chapter Five.

Fuel injected 115 and 225 hp models are equipped with an additional fuel filter to protect the high-pressure fuel system components. The high-pressure fuel filter cannot be visually inspected as it is located within the vapor separator tank. Inspect the high-pressure filter when a contaminated filter is suspected of causing fuel starvation. Fuel filter replacement is described in Chapter Five.

NOTE

*Some boats are equipped with large spin-on type fuel filters (**Figure 8**). Most of these provide water separating capabilities for added protection for the fuel system. They are located between the primer bulb and fuel tank on most applications. Service these units when servicing other fuel filters on the engine. Replacement filter elements for this type of filter are available from marine dealerships and marine supply stores. Follow the filter manufactures instructions to remove or install this type of filter.*

Fuel System Leakage Check

WARNING
Use extreme caution when working with or around fuel. Never smoke around fuel or fuel vapor. Make sure no flame or source of ignition is present in the work area. Flame or sparks can ignite the fuel or vapor resulting in fire or explosion.

Inspect for fuel leakage before starting the engine. Observe all fuel hoses, hose connections, carburetors, vapor separator tank and other fuel system components while squeezing the primer bulb. If fuel leakage is noted, tighten clamps or replace defective hoses. Correct the source of any fuel leakage before starting the engine.

After starting the engine check for fuel odor or a an oily sheen on the water surface around the engine. Stop the engine immediately and inspect the fuel system for leakage if either of these conditions are noted. Fuel system repair is covered in Chapter Five.

Oil Leakage Check

Inspect for oil leakage prior to starting the engine. Visually inspect the power head and inner part of the lower engine cover for the presence of oil residue. Wipe the power head surfaces with a clean white shop towel to help identify the point of leakage. Usually, oil leakage will occur at the valve cover, at the rear of the power head, at the oil filter-to-cylinder block mating surface, or at the breather hose connections. Tighten loose fasteners/filters or replace hoses and gaskets to correct the oil leakage before operating the engine.

Engine Mounting Bolt Check

WARNING
Operating the engine with loose clamp screws or engine mounting bolts can result in serious bodily injury, death and/or loss of the engine. Always check and tighten all mounting bolts before operating the engine.

Four mounting bolts, washers and nuts (**Figure 9**), two on each side, secure the engine clamp brackets to the boat transom. Check the bolts, washers and nuts and tighten as necessary before operating the engine. Replace all four self-locking nuts if they loosen again during engine operation.

Steering System Inspection

WARNING
Never operate the engine if binding or excessive slack is present in the steering or other control system. The steering or other control system may unexpectedly fail and prevent the operator from controlling the vessel.

Check the operation of the steering components prior to starting the engine. Rotate the steering wheel to the clock-

wise and counterclockwise limits. Note the presence of binding or excessive slack as the wheel changes direction.

Binding is usually caused by inadequate lubrication, a faulty steering cable, a faulty helm or damaged midsection components. If binding is noted, lubricate the steering system components as described in this chapter. If the binding persists after lubrication, disassemble and inspect the midsection components as described in Chapter Ten.

Excessive slack is usually caused by loose steering linkage fasteners, worn or damaged engine mounts, a worn or faulty steering cable, a worn or faulty helm, or worn or damaged midsection components. If excessive slack is detected, inspect all of the midsection components for visual defects as described in Chapter Ten. Replace the steering cable or helm if the midsection and steering linkages are ruled out as the cause of excessive steering slack.

Propeller Inspection

CAUTION

Never operate the engine with significant propeller damage. Damage to the propeller can result in a significant decrease in performance, increased wear from excessive vibration, unusual handling characteristics and/or excessive engine speed.

Before starting the engine, inspect the propeller for cracked, damaged or missing blade sections. File out small imperfections, but avoid removing too much material or an imbalance can occur. Straighten small bends with locking pliers. Have the propeller repaired at a reputable propeller repair shop if significant damage is noted (**Figure 10**).

Inspect the propeller shaft if the propeller has suffered significant damage. To check for a bent propeller shaft, disconnect the battery cables and spark plug leads, then shift the engine in NEUTRAL. Spin the propeller while observing the end of the propeller shaft (**Figure 11**). If the shaft wobbles noticeably, the propeller shaft is bent and must be replaced. See Chapter Eight.

Lanyard Switch Operation Check

Always check the operation of the lanyard switch before getting underway. Start the engine then pull the cord from the lanyard switch (**Figure 12**). If the engine fails to stop, turn the ignition switch OFF, operate the choke, disconnect or squeeze shut the fuel line until the engine stalls. Repair the faulty stop circuit before restarting the engine. Test instructions for the stop circuit are provided in Chapter Two. *Never* operate an engine with a faulty lanyard switch.

Cooling System Operation Check

NOTE

Inspect the cooling system for proper operation every time the engine is run. A stream of water exiting from the rear of the engine cover indicates that the water pump is operating. Never run the engine if it overheats or if the water stream is absent.

Check for the presence of the water stream immediately after starting the engine. A stream of water (**Figure 13**) exiting the lower back area of the engine indicates the water pump is operating. This stream may not appear for the first few seconds of operation especially at idle speed. Stop the engine and check for cooling system if the stream fails to appear within the normal time frame. Refer to *Cooling System Troubleshooting* in Chapter Two. Never run the engine if it is overheating or the water stream fails to appear.

AFTER EACH USE

As specified in **Table 2**, certain maintenance items must be performed after each usage. Observing these requirements can dramatically reduce corrosion of engine components and extend the life of the engine.

Cooling System Flush

Flush the cooling system after each use to prevent corrosion and deposit buildup in the cooling passages. Operating the engine in salt, polluted, silt- or sand-laden water increases the need to flush the cooling system. Operating the engine in silt- or sand-laden water substantially reduces the life of water pump components. Inspect the water pump and other cooling system components frequently if operating under these conditions.

Some models are equipped with a power head flush fitting (**Figure 14**) on the rear (75-115 hp) or starboard side (225 hp) of the lower motor cover. This fitting allows connection of a garden hose for flushing the power head cooling passages without removing the boat from the water.

On engines stored on a trailer or boat lift, flush the engine using a flush/test adapter (**Figure 15**). These adapters are available from marine dealerships or marine supply stores. This method is preferable as it flushes the entire cooling system. Use the slide-on flush/test adapter (**Figure 15**) or a two-piece flush/test adapter (**Figure 16**) on all models covered in this manual. The two-piece design is preferred over the slide-on type because it will not slip out of position during engine operation. Purchase the two-piece adapter (part number 44357A 2) from a Mercury or Mariner dealership.

The engine can also be flushed by operating it in a test tank filled with clean water.

Using the power head flush fitting

CAUTION

Never run the engine while using the power head flush fitting. The flush port does not supply adequate water flow to cool the water pump components with the gearcase out of the water. If the gearcase is immersed in the water with the engine running, salt, brackish or polluted water will flow into the power head along with the clean water from the flush fitting, preventing a thorough flushing of the system.

CAUTION

The engine must be in the vertical position to flush the cooling system with the power head flush fitting. Otherwise, water can enter the combustion chamber through the exhaust passages and damage the internal power head components.

1. Place the engine in the vertical position (**Figure 1**).
2. Remove the plug and thread the hose into the fitting.
3. Turn the water valve fully open. Continue flushing the power head for a minimum of five minutes, until the exiting water is clear.
4. Remove the hose and replace the plug.
5. Keep the engine in a vertical position for a few minutes to drain water from the cooling system.

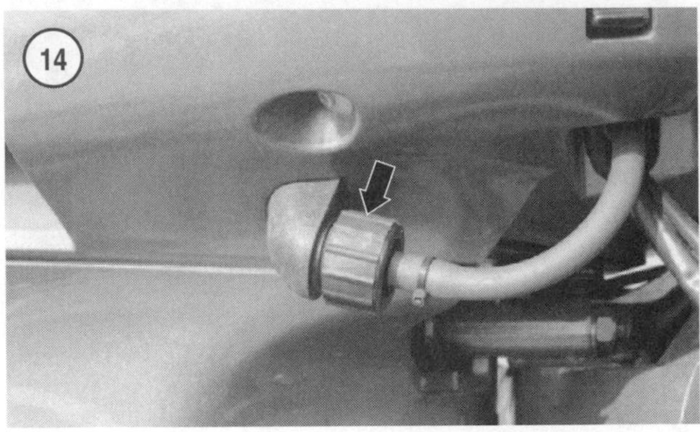

14

15

Using a flush/test adapter

1. To attach the flush/test adapter onto the gearcase, install the rubber sealing washer, then thread the garden hose fitting onto the flush/test adapter fitting.
   a. If using a slide-on adapter, starting at the front edge of the gearcase, slide the cups onto each side of the gearcase. Position the cups over the water inlets (**Figure 15**).
   b. If using a two-piece adapter, squeeze the clamp plate on the opposite side from the hose connection then

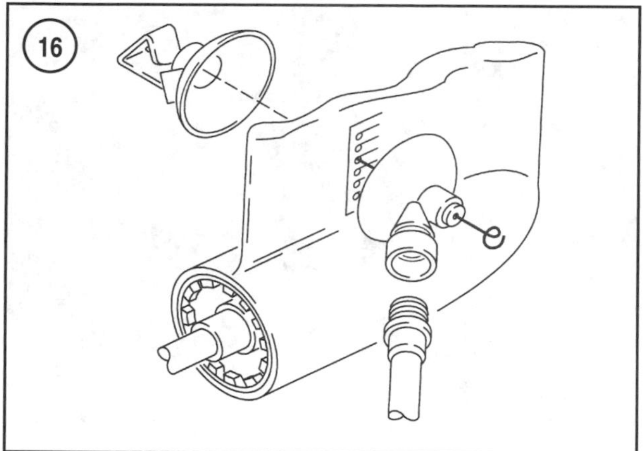

16

17

pull the cup from the wire. Slide the wire with the cup attached through the water screen openings (**Figure 16**). Squeeze the clamp plate enough to pass the wire through the cup and both sides of the clamp plate. Press both cups and the wire loop firmly against the gearcase. Release the clamp plate.

2. Route the water hose to avoid contact with the propeller. If necessary, remove the propeller (Chapter Eight) or secure the hose with tie straps.
3. Turn on the water. Make sure the adapter cups are positioned directly over the water inlets.
4. Start the engine and run at fast idle in NEUTRAL until it reaches normal operating temperature.
5. Continue to run the engine for a minimum of five minutes, until the exiting water is clear. Monitor the engine temperature and water stream (**Figure 13**). Stop the engine immediately if the stream is absent, or if the engine steams or overheats.
6. Throttle the engine back to normal idle speed for a few minutes then stop the engine. Remove the flush adapter.
7. Place the engine in a vertical position (**Figure 1**) to drain water from the cooling system.

Using a test tank

1. Remove the propeller as described in Chapter Eight.
2. Place the engine into the test tank. Ensure the water level is well above the water inlets on the sides of the gearcase.
3. Securely tighten the engine mounting bolts before starting the engine.
4. Start the engine and run at fast idle in NEUTRAL until it reaches normal operating temperature.
5. Continue to run the engine for a minimum of five minutes, until the exiting water is clear. Monitor the engine temperature and water stream (**Figure 13**). Stop the engine immediately if the stream is absent, or if the engine steams or overheats.
6. Throttle the engine back to normal idle speed for a few minutes then stop the engine. Wait a few minutes before removing the engine from the test tank. This is especially important if the engine must be tilted for removal from the tank.
7. Place the engine in a vertical position (**Figure 1**) for a few minutes to fully drain the cooling system.

Engine Cleaning

Clean all dirt or vegetation from all external engine surfaces after each use. This helps reduce corrosion, reduces wear on gearcase and trim system seals, and allows easier inspection for worn or damaged components.

Never use strong cleaning solutions or solvent to clean the outboard motor. Mild dish soap and pressurized water does an adequate job of cleaning most debris from the engine. To prevent damage or contamination of power head components, never direct water towards any openings on the engine cover. Avoid directing the spray from a high-pressure nozzle or pressure washer directly at any opening, seals, plugs, wiring or wire grommets. The water may bypass seals and contaminate the trim system, electric trim motor, or trim fluid reservoir.

Rinse the external surfaces with clean water to remove any soap residue. Wipe the engine with a soft cloth to prevent water spots.

ROUTINE MAINTENANCE

A maintenance log is provided at the end of this manual. Always keep a log of maintenance items performed and when they were done. Try to log the number of running hours after each use. Without a maintenance/running hours log or a dash mounted hour meter (**Figure 17**) it is almost impossible to accurately determine the hours of usage. Be aware that a dash mounted hour meter may run when the key switch is ON and the engine not running. Note this event in the maintenance log should it occur.

Perform all applicable maintenance items listed in **Table 2**. Some maintenance items do not apply to all models. The type of fuel system used determines the engine maintenance requirements.

FUEL REQUIREMENTS

WARNING
Use extreme caution when working with or around fuel. Never smoke around fuel or fuel vapors. Make sure no flame or source of ignition is present in the work area. Flame or sparks can ignite the fuel or vapor resulting in fire or explosion.

NOTE
Fuel has a relatively short shelf life. Fuel begins to lose some desirable characteristics in as little as 14 days. Always use a major brand fuel from a facility that sells a large amount of fuel, and use the fuel within a few weeks of purchase.

All models covered in this manual are designed to use regular grade unleaded fuel with an average octane rating of 87 or higher. This fuel should meet the requirements for the engine when operated under normal operating conditions. Premium fuel is not recommended by the manufacturer for use in all models covered in this manual.

CAUTION
Engine damage can result from using deteriorated fuel. Varnish-like deposits form in the fuel system as fuel deteriorates. These deposits block fuel passages and result in decreased fuel delivery. Decreased fuel delivery causes a lean condition in the combustion chamber. Damage to the pistons, valves and other power head components result from operating the engine with an excessively lean fuel mixture.

LUBRICANTS

Lubrication for the power head, midsection, gearcase and other areas helps prevent wear, guards against corrosion and provides smooth operation of turning or sliding surfaces.

Outboards operate in a corrosive environment and often require special types of lubricants. Using the wrong type of lubricant can cause serious engine damage or substantially shorten the life of the engine.

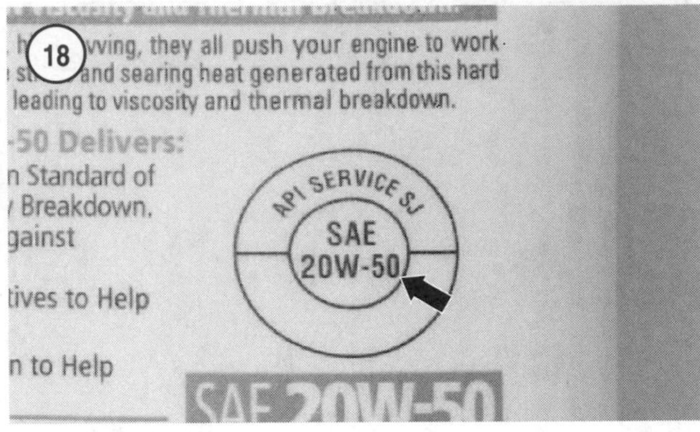

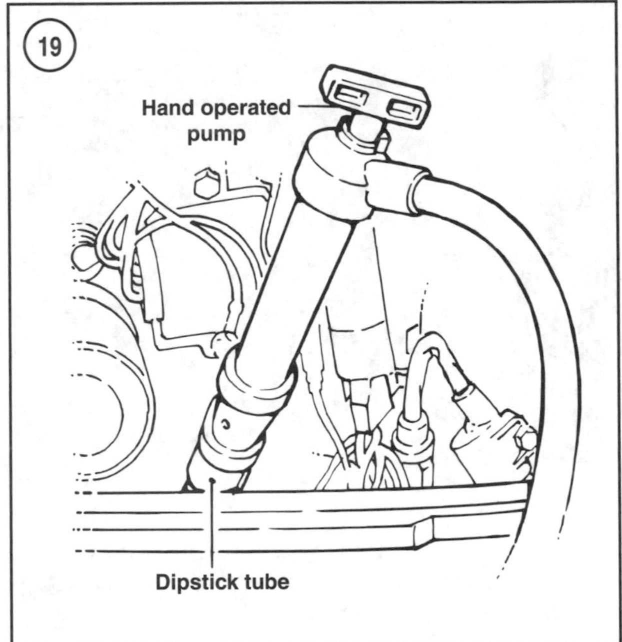

Engine Oil Recommendations

CAUTION
Never use non-detergent oil or two stroke outboard motor oil in a four stroke outboard. It will not adequatly lubrication the internal engine components, resulting in severe power head damage or engine seizure.

Mercury/Marine recommends using Quicksilver 4-cycle marine oil or a premium quality four-stroke oil in all Mercury or Mariner four stroke outboards. Quicksilver oil is available at a local Mercury or Mariner dealership. Premium quality four-stroke is available from automotive parts stores and many other sources.

Always use a good grade of oil in the four stroke outboard. Look for the API classification emblem on the oil

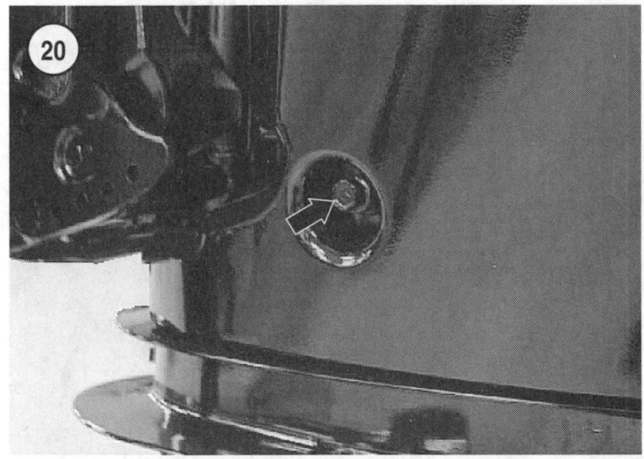

container (**Figure 18**) when selecting oil for the engine. This label lists the American Petroleum Institute (API) service classification of the oil. Use only oil meeting or exceeding one the following service classifications: SH, SG, SF, CF-4, CE, CD or CDII.

Oils with a 10W-30 viscosity rating are recommended for use in all air temperature operating ranges. Oils with a 25W-40 viscosity rating are acceptable for use provided the air temperature exceeds 40° F (4° C). The oil viscosity rating is listed on the API classification emblem (**Figure 18**). Engine oil capacities are listed in **Table 3**.

The oil filter traps dirt, debris and other contaminants during engine operation. Always replace the filter when changing the oil. If the filter is not changed, contaminated oil remaining in the filter will immediately flow into the fresh oil upon starting. Oil filter change instructions are provided under *Power Head Maintenance* in this chapter.

Gearcase Lubricant Recommendations

CAUTION

Never use automotive gearcase or transmission lubricant in the gearcase. These types of lubricants are usually not suitable for marine applications. The use of other than recommended lubricants can lead to increased wear and corrosion of internal components.

Use Mercury or Mariner gearcase lubricant or a good quality SAE 90 marine gearcase lubricant that meets GL5 specifications. **Table 3** lists the *approximate* gearcase lubricant capacity for the Mercury or Mariner four stroke outboards.

Other Lubrication Points

Refer to the maintenance procedures described in this chapter for the recommended grease to use on the midsection components and other lubrication points. If the recommended grease is not available, use a good quality water-resistant marine grease. Avoid using greases with graphite or other metallic additives.

POWER HEAD MAINTENANCE

This section describes routine maintenance for the power head and related components.

Engine Oil and Filter Replacement

Performing regular oil changes is the most effective way to ensure engine durability. Always change the oil filter when changing the engine oil. Otherwise, the residual oil remaining in the used filter will mix with the new oil.

Two methods may be used to remove the oil from the engine. The oil can be pumped from the oil pan or crankcase if the boat is stored in the water or if the drain plug is difficult to access. Hand operated pumps (**Figure 19**) or electric motor operated pumps are available from most marine dealerships or marine supply stores. The oil can also be drained using the drive shaft housing mounted drain plug (**Figure 20**). On 225 hp models, the starboard side drive shaft housing cover must be removed to access the drain plug.

Engine oil removal (pump method)

1. Disconnect the negative battery cable to prevent accidental starting.
2. Remove the oil fill cap to allow quicker oil removal.
3. Place the engine in the vertical position. Remove the dipstick from the engine (see *Engine Oil Level and Condition Inspection*).
4. Install the sealing washer onto the threaded adapter of the oil pump. Carefully thread the adapter onto the dipstick (**Figure 19**).
5. Operate the pump until all oil is removed. Stop the oil pump for a few minutes to allow any remaining oil to drain to the bottom of the oil pan. Operate the pump again to remove any remaining oil.
6. Remove the oil pump from the dipstick. Wipe up any spilled oil. Dispose of the used oil in an environmentally responsible manner.
7. Refill the engine oil and change the oil filter as described in this section.

Draining the engine oil

1A. On 75-115 hp models, use the power trim to position the engine into the full tilt position. Engage the tilt lock lever (**Figure 21**) to secure the engine. Position the engine toward the port direction enough to direct the oil drain fitting downward.

1B. On 225 hp models, use the power trim to position the engine in the vertical position.

2. Disconnect the negative battery cable to prevent accidental starting. Remove the oil fill cap to allow quicker oil draining.

3. On 225 hp models, remove the 12 screws that secure the starboard side cover (**Figure 22**) onto the drive shaft housing. The eleven shorter screws thread into the starboard side cover openings. The longer screw threads into the port side cover opening. Carefully pull the cover away from the housing.

4. Refer to **Table 3** to determine the engine oil capacity. Place a container under the drain plug (**Figure 20**). Hold the container tightly against the engine to capture dripping oil.

5. Remove the oil drain plug. Retrieve the seal from the opening if not found on the drain plug. Allow the pan to drain completely. Wipe up any spilled oil. Dispose of the used oil in an environmentally responsible manner.

6. Inspect the drain plug seal for worn, torn or damaged surfaces. Replace if any defects are noted.

7. Wipe all debris and residual oil from the drain plug and drain. Apply a light coat of clean engine oil onto the seal, then fit the seal onto the drain plug.

8. Thread the drain plug into the oil pan. Tighten the plug to 17.5 ft.-lb. (23.7 N•m) for 75-115 hp models and 20 ft.-lb. (27.1 N•m) for 225 hp models.

9. On 225 hp models, fit the starboard side cover onto the drive shaft housing. Thread the 12 screws into the cover and drive shaft housing. The 11 shorter screws thread into the starboard side cover openings. The longer screw threads into the port side cover opening. Tighten the screws evenly to 70 in.-lb. (7.9 N•m).

10. Connect the negative battery cable.

11. On 75-115 hp models, disengage the tilt lock lever. Use the power trim to place the engine in the vertical position.

12. Refill the engine oil and change the oil filter as described in this section.

21

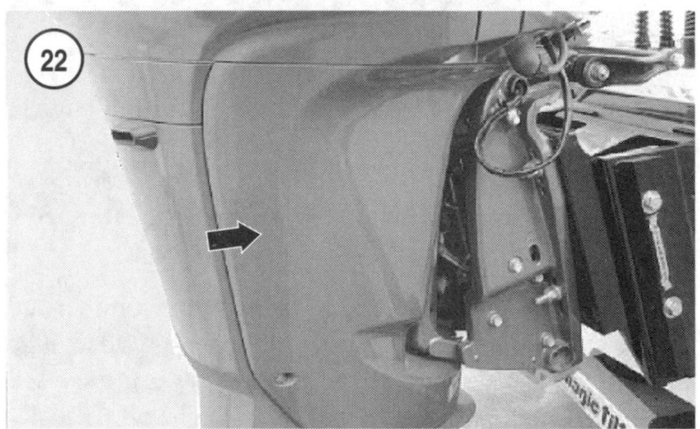
22

23

Refilling the engine oil

Use oil that meets or exceeds one of the following service classifications: SH, SG, SF, CF-4, CE, CD or CDII. Use oil with a 10W-30 viscosity rating for all air temperature operating ranges. Oil with a 25W-40 viscosity rating is acceptable for use provided the air temperature exceeds 40° F (4° C).

WARNING

Never use two-stroke outboard engine oil in a four-stroke outboard. Using the wrong type of oil will cause significant engine wear and possibly power head failure.

1. Refer to **Table 3** to determine the quantity of oil required.

24

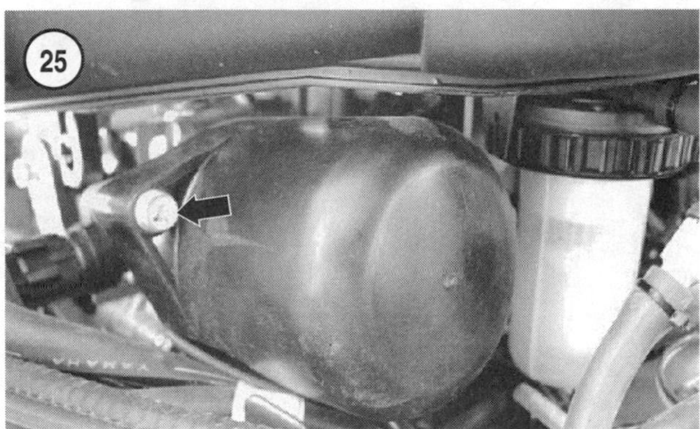
25

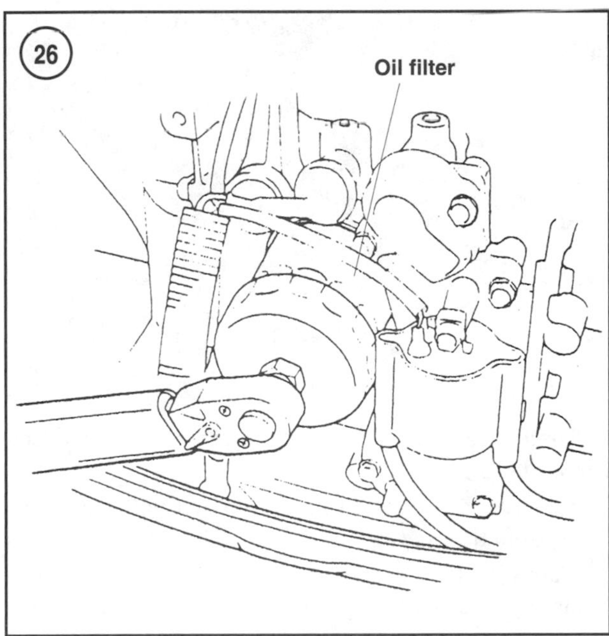

26

2. Disconnect the negative battery cable to prevent accidental starting.

3. Using a funnel, slowly pour approximately 75 percent of the oil capacity into the oil fill opening.

4. Check the engine oil level as described in this chapter. Add oil to the opening in small quantities until the oil level is at or just below the full marking on the dipstick. Do not overfill the engine oil. Drain excess oil if necessary.

5. Install the oil fill cap.

Changing the oil filter

All models covered in this manual use a spin-on type oil filter (**Figure 23**). Purchase a new filter from a Mercury or Mariner dealership prior to starting this operation. An oil filter removal tool as shown in **Figure 24** (75-115 hp models: part No. 91-802653 Q1; *225 hp models:* part No. 91-888734) is required to remove the oil filter. This tool is available from most automotive parts stores and tool suppliers. The tool must properly match the oil filter. Otherwise, the tool will slip on the filter during removal or the tool may damage the new filter during installation.

Residual oil will drain from the engine when the filter is removed. Fashion a suitable oil filter drain pan from a used plastic oil container. Cut the container to a depth allowing it to slide directly under the filter.

On 75 and 90 hp models, the oil filter (**Figure 23**) threads onto the lower starboard side of the power head below the electric starter. On 225 hp models, the filter is located under a plastic cover on the lower front and starboard side of the power head.

1. Disconnect the negative battery cable to prevent accidental starting.

2. On 225 hp models, remove the screw (**Figure 25**) then pull the plastic filter cover from the power head. Use soap and water to thoroughly clean the filter cover.

3. Using compressed air, blow all debris from around the oil filter. Place a small container under the oil filter. Place a shop towel under the oil filter if unable to fit a container under the filter.

4. Fit the oil filter removal tool onto the filter. Engage a socket driver into the tool (**Figure 26**). Loosen the oil filter one turn counterclockwise. Remove the tool, then unthread the filter.

5. Make sure the filter sealing ring is not stuck to the cylinder block. Dispose of the oil filter in an environmentally responsible manner.

6. Carefully clean the oil filter mating surface. Apply a light coating of engine oil onto the sealing ring on the new oil filter (**Figure 27**). Thread the oil filter onto the cylinder block fitting until a slight resistance is felt and the sealing ring just contacts the mating surface.

7. Use white correction fluid or a felt tip marker to make reference markings on the cylinder block and the filter

body (**Figure 28**). This is necessary to determine the amount of rotation during final filter tightening.

8A. On 75-115 hp models, using the oil filter removal tool (**Figure 26**), tighten the filter an additional 3/4 to 1 turn. Do not over-tighten the filter.

8B. On 225 hp models, using the oil filter removal tool, tighten the filter (**Figure 26**) to 156 in.-lb. (17.6 N•m). The filter must make a minimum 3/ 4 turn clockwise after the sealing ring contacts the mating surface. Tighten the filter an additional amount as necessary.

9. Connect the negative battery cable. Prepare the engine for starting in the water or on a flush/test device (see *Cooling System Flush*).

10. Start the engine and immediately check for oil leakage from the filter area. Oil leakage from the filter is generally the result of inadequate tightening, debris under the sealing ring, a damaged sealing ring, using the wrong type of filter or a faulty filter. Correct any leakage before operating the engine.

11. Stop the engine. Check and correct the oil level as described in this chapter (see *Engine Oil Level and Condition Inspection*).

12. On 225 hp models, fit the plastic cover over the oil filter. Thread the screw into the cover and cylinder block. Securely tighten the screw.

Power Head Anodes

Anodes are used to help counteract corrosion damage to the power head cooling passages. The anode is constructed of a material more corrosively active than the cylinder head or cylinder block material. Essentially the anodes sacrifice themselves to protect the power head. Regular inspection and replacement helps ensure continued protection against corrosion damage.

Anode cleaning, inspection and replacement (75-115 hp)

CAUTION

Remove the anode cover before removing the anode attaching screw. Otherwise, the anode may fall from the cover and become lodged in the cooling water passages. The center mounted screw attaches the anode onto the cover. The two side mounted screws attach the cover onto the cylinder head or exhaust cover.

All 75-115 hp models are equipped with a pair of anodes mounted onto special covers (**Figure 29**) beneath the spark plug cover. A third anode is mounted on the starboard side exhaust cover (**Figure 30**).

27

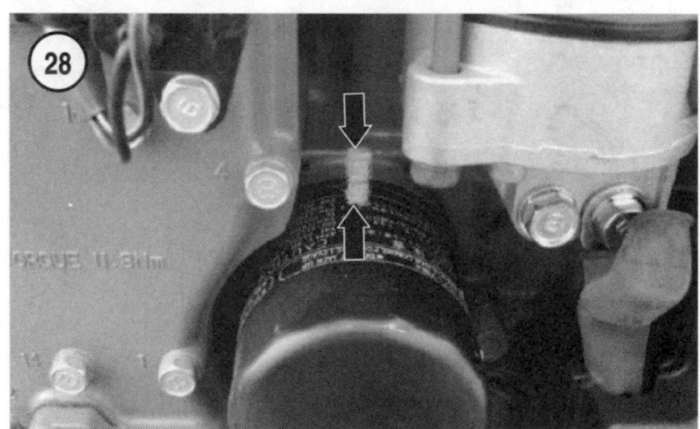
28

29

1. Disconnect the negative battery cable to prevent accidental starting.

2. Remove the screws (**Figure 31**) and pull the plastic cover from the cylinder head.

3. Carefully loosen and remove the two anode cover mounting screws (A, **Figure 32**). Do not remove the anode attaching screw (B, **Figure 32**) at this time. Otherwise, the anode may fall from the cover and become lodged in the cooling water passages.

4. Carefully pry the cover loose, then lift it and the rubber grommet from the cylinder head. Use the same method to remove the remaining two anode/cover assemblies.

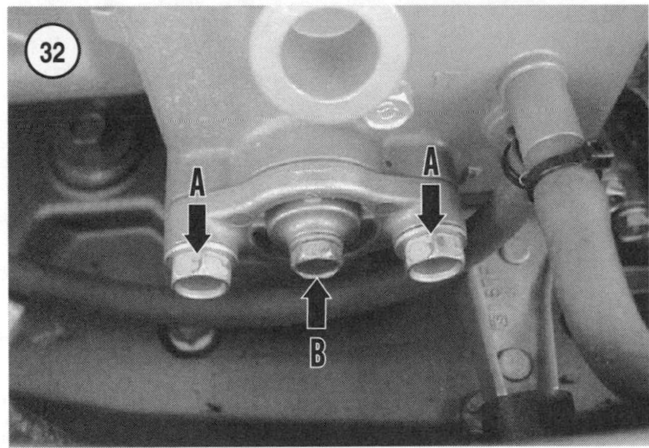

5. Use a stiff brush to clean all corrosion or contaminants from the anode opening and cover mating surfaces. Do not damage the rubber grommet contact surfaces. Use a tap or thread chaser to remove deposits from the threaded openings.

6. Remove the anode screw (B, **Figure 32**) then pull the anode and rubber grommet from the cover.

7. Use a stiff brush to remove corrosion and other deposits from the anode, screw threads and anode cover. Do not damage the rubber grommet contact surfaces.

8. Inspect the anodes for deep pitting or cracked surfaces. Replace any anode with deep pitting or if 50 percent or more of the anode has corroded away.

9. Inspect the rubber grommet for worn or damaged areas. Replace the rubber grommet if damaged.

10. Fit the anode onto the cover. Make sure the projection on the anode fits into the recess in the cover. Thread the anode attaching screw into the cover and anode. Tighten the screw to 70 in.-lb. (7.9 N•m).

11. Slide the rubber grommet over the anode and seat against the cover. Apply a very light coating of Quicksilver 2-4-C grease onto the grommet and cover mating surfaces only. To maintain corrosion protection, do not apply any paint or protective coatings to the anode or mounting bolts. Do not allow grease to enter the threaded openings.

12. Guide the anode into the opening then seat the cover and anode assembly against the cylinder head or exhaust cover surface. Rotate the cover to align the screw openings. Thread the two screws into the cover and cylinder head or exhaust cover. Tighten the screws evenly to 156 in.-lb. (17.6 N•m).

13. Assemble and install the remaining two anode covers as described in Steps 10-12.

14. Connect the negative battery cables. Prepare the engine for starting in the water or on a flush/test device (see *Cooling system flush* in this chapter).

15. Start the engine and immediately check for water leakage from the anode cover. Replace the rubber grommet if leakage is noted.

16. Stop the engine then install the plastic cover onto the rear of the cylinder head. Thread the five screws into the cover and cylinder head. Tighten the screws evenly to 65 in.-lb. (7.3 N•m).

Anode cleaning, inspection and replacement (225 hp)

CAUTION

Remove the cover and anode as an assembly before removing the anode attaching screw. Otherwise, the anode may fall from the cover and become lodged in the cooling water passages. The larger screw attaches the anode cover on to the cylinder head. The smaller screw attaches the anode to the cover.

All 225 hp models are equipped with four anodes. The anodes attach to special covers (**Figure 33**) mounted onto each cylinder head. The plastic cover (**Figure 34**) must be removed to access the anode covers.

1. Disconnect the negative battery cable to prevent accidental starting.
2. Remove the four screws (**Figure 34**), then pull the plastic cover from the rear of the power head. Locate the four anode covers near the spark plug openings.
3. Carefully loosen and remove the anode cover screw. Do not remove the anode attaching screw. Otherwise, the anode may fall from the cover and become lodged in the cooling water passage. The anode cover screw is the larger of the two screws. The anode attaching screw is a smaller washer headed screw.
4. Carefully pry the cover loose then lift it and the rubber grommet from the cylinder head. Use the same method to remove the remaining three anode/cover assemblies.
5. Use a stiff brush to clean all corrosion and contaminants from the anode opening and cover mating surfaces. Do not damage the rubber grommet contact surfaces. Use a tap or thread chaser to remove deposits from the threaded openings.
6. Remove the anode screw then pull the anode and rubber grommet from the cover.
7. Use a stiff brush to remove corrosion and other deposits from the anode, screw threads and anode cover. Do not damage the rubber grommet contact surfaces.
8. Inspect the anodes for deep pitting and cracked surfaces. Replace any anode with deep pitting or if 50 percent or more of the anode has corroded away.
9. Inspect the rubber grommet for worn or damaged areas. Replace the rubber grommet if damaged.
10. Fit the anode onto the cover. Make sure the projection on the anode fits into the recess in the cover. Thread the anode attaching screw into the cover and anode. Tighten the screw to 70 in.-lb. (7.9 N•m).
11. Slide the rubber grommet over the anode and seat against the cover. Apply a very light coat of Quicksilver 2-4-C grease to the grommet and cover mating surfaces only. To maintain corrosion protection, do not apply any paint or protective coatings to the anode or mounting bolts. Do not allow grease to enter the threaded openings.
12. Guide the anode into the opening. Seat the cover and anode assembly against the cylinder head or exhaust cover surface. Rotate the cover to align the screw opening. Thread the screw into the cover and cylinder head. Tighten the screw to 150 in.-lb. (16.9 N•m).
13. Assemble and install the remaining three anode covers as described in Steps 10-12.
14. Connect the negative battery cables. Prepare the engine for starting in the water or on a flush/test device (see *Cooling system flush* in this chapter).
15. Start the engine and immediately check for water leakage from the anode cover. Replace the rubber grommet if leakage is noted.

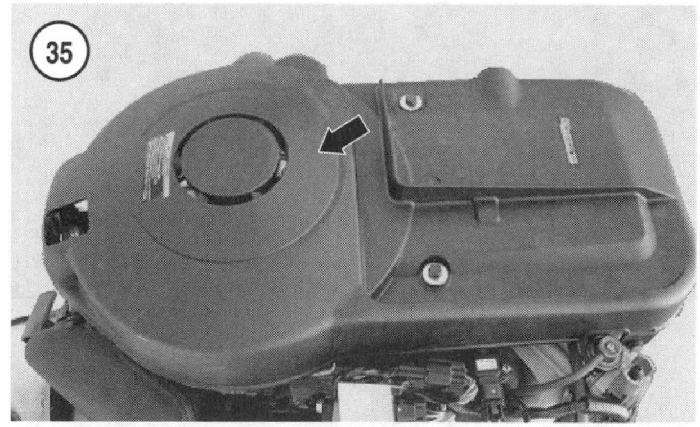

16. Stop the engine. Install the plastic cover onto the rear of the power head. Tighten the screws in a crossing pattern to 71 in.-lb. (8.0 N•m).

Timing Belt and Tensioner Pulleys

Inspect the timing belt, pulleys and tensioner for damage or excessive wear at the intervals listed in **Table 2**. The flywheel cover (**Figure 35**, typical) must be removed to access the timing belt and pulleys. Flywheel cover removal is described in Chapter Seven.

1. Disconnect the negative battery cable to prevent accidental starting.

2. Remove the flywheel cover as described in Chapter Seven.

3. Using compressed air, blow all dust or loose material from the timing belt and pulleys.

4. Manually rotate the flywheel while inspecting the entire length and both sides of the timing belt (**Figure 36**). Replace the timing belt as described in Chapter Seven if any of the following conditions are noted:

   a. Oil soaked surfaces.

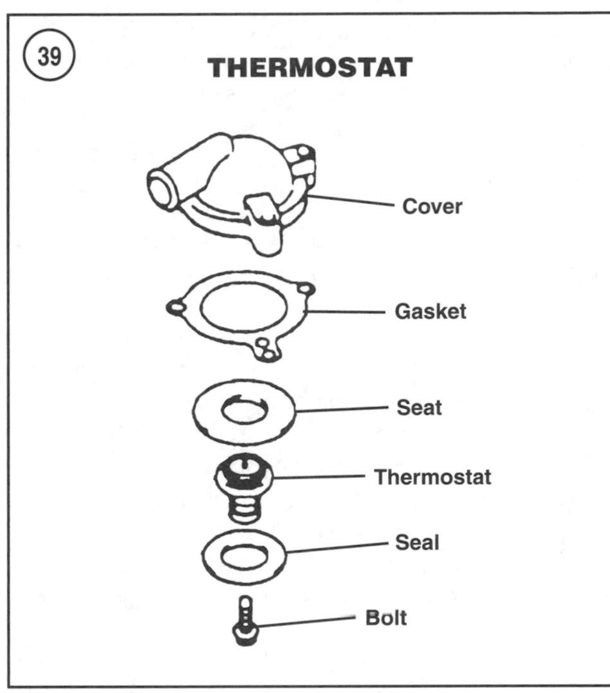

   b. Deformed or bulging areas.
   c. Worm timing belt cogs.
   d. Cracks or wear on the flat side of the belt.
   e. Cracked or missing timing belt cogs.
   f. Worn edges on the top or bottom side of the timing belt.

5. Inspect the crankshaft and camshaft pulleys for corroded, worn or damaged cogs (**Figure 37**). Replace the pulleys if worn or damaged. Replace the pulleys if corroded surfaces cannot be cleaned by polishing them with crocus cloth. Pulley removal and installation is described in Chapter Seven.

6. Inspect the tensioner pulley (**Figure 38**) for wear in the belt contact surfaces. Visually inspect the pulley for tilting on its axis. Tilting indicates possible wear of the pulley bearing or bending of the pulley bracket. Remove and inspect the tensioner pulley assembly if tilting is evident. Replace the tensioner pulley if wear is noted on the belt contact surfaces. Tensioner pulley replacement is described in Chapter Seven.

7. Install the flywheel cover as described in Chapter Seven.

8. Connect the battery cable.

Thermostat Inspection

Inspect the thermostat (**Figure 39**, typical) at the intervals listed in **Table 2**. Thermostat removal, inspection and installation is described in Chapter Seven. While removed, test the thermostat as described in Chapter Two. To prevent overheating or oil dilution problems, always replace a faulty or damaged thermostat.

Hoses and Clamps

Heat and pressure combined with exposure to fuel, oil and vapor will result in deterioration and eventual failure of hoses and clamps. To prevent leakage and possible engine damage, inspect all hoses and clamps at the intervals listed in **Table 2**. Perform the inspection on a frequent basis if the engine is used for commercial or heavy usage. Replace hoses every few years. The cost of the hoses is far less than the cost of the repair if they should fail.

Squeeze all hoses to check flexibility. Inspect the entire length of all fuel, water and breather hoses. Note the presence of leakage, weathered, burned or cracked surfaces.

Replace any hoses that are hard or brittle, cracked, leaking or have a spongy feel. Use only the recommended hose available from a Mercury or Mariner dealership. Other hoses available at auto parts stores may not meet the demands placed upon them or may not meet coast guard requirements.

Inspect the spring clamps (**Figure 40**) for corrosion or damage. Squeeze the clamp ends with pliers to check the spring tension. Replace spring hose clamps that are damaged, corroded or have lost spring tension. Inspect plastic locking hose clamps (**Figure 41**) for damaged, weathered or deteriorated surfaces. Grasp the clamp and rotate it on the fitting to check for a snug fit. Remove and replace damaged or loose fitting plastic tie clamps.

Carefully tug on the fuel lines to ensure a tight fit at all connections. Replace the clamp and/or hose if the hose can be easily pulled from the fitting.

40

41

42

Electric Starter Maintenance

Inspect the battery-to-electric starter terminals (**Figure 42**) and lubricate the starter drive (**Figure 43**) at regular intervals. These maintenance items are especially important if the engine operates in salt water, brackish or polluted water.

Electric starter terminal inspection

1. Disconnect the negative battery cable to prevent arcing and accidental starting.
2. Move the insulating boots away from the electric starter terminals. Inspect the terminals for corrosion.
3. If corrosion is evident perform the following:
   a. Remove the nut and cables from the starter solenoid terminals. Use a stiff brush to thoroughly clean the cable and solenoid terminals.
   b. Attach the electric starter cable to the closest solenoid terminal. Tighten the starter solenoid-to-electric starter nut to 78 in.-lb. (8.8 N•m).
   c. Attach the battery cable terminal to the starter solenoid terminal furthest from the electric starter body. Route the cable to prevent interference with other components. Make sure the cable terminal does not contact the electric starter terminal or other compo-

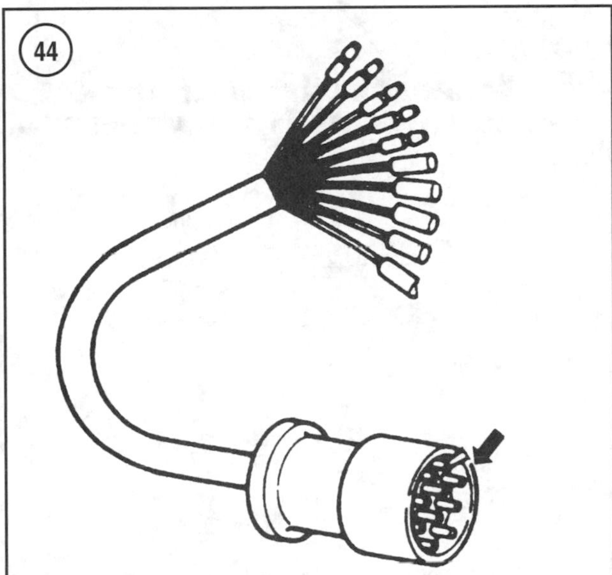

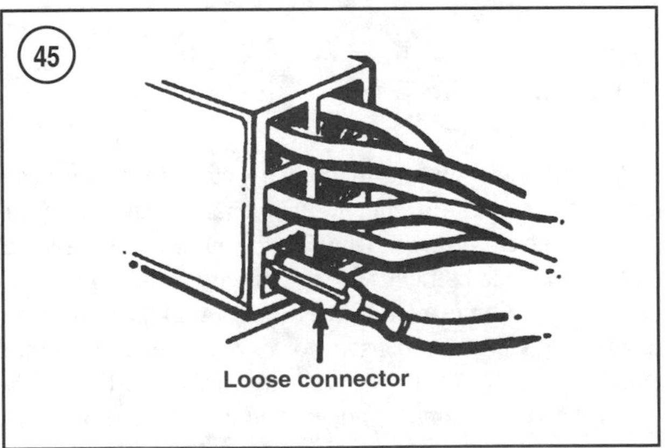

nents. Tighten the battery cable terminal nut to 70 in.-lb. (7.9 N•m). Do not overtighten the terminal nuts, which will crack or damage the starter solenoid.

4. Apply a light coat of Quicksilver 2-4-C grease to the electric starter terminals. Position the insulating boots fully over the terminals.
5. Connect the negative battery cables.

Starter drive lubrication

CAUTION
Do not apply an excessive amount of lubricant onto the electric starter drive. Excess lubricant may sling onto the timing belt during electric starter operation. Exposure to oil will cause deterioration and premature failure of the timing belt.

1. Disconnect the negative battery cable to prevent accidental starting.
2. Remove the flywheel cover as described in Chapter Seven.
3. Apply a few drops of engine oil to the splined section of starter drive (**Figure 43**). Excess oil may contaminate and damage the timing belt.
4. Install the flywheel cover as described in Chapter Seven.
5. Connect the battery cable.

Wiring and Connector Inspection

Periodically inspect the main harness connector (**Figure 44**) for contaminated or faulty pin connections (**Figure 45**). Carefully scrape contamination from the contacts. Apply a light coat of water-resistant marine grease to the main harness plug and terminals to seal out moisture and prevent corrosion.

Inspect the entire length of all wires and harness for worn, burnt, damaged or bare insulation. Repair or replace faulty wiring or connectors before operating the engine.

Battery Inspection

Unlike automobiles, boats may sit idle for weeks without running. Without proper maintenance the battery loses charge and begins to deteriorate. Marine engines are exposed to a great deal more moisture than automobiles resulting in more corrosion on the battery terminals. Clean the terminals and charge the battery at no more than 30 day intervals. Refer to Chapter Six for complete battery testing, maintenance and charging instructions.

Engine Carbon Deposit Removal

Excessive carbon deposits can increase engine compression and promote detonation. To help prevent serious power head damage, decarbon the engine at the intervals listed in **Table 2**.

Special fuel additives and sprays (**Figure 46**), used regularly, are very effective at removing most carbon deposits. They are available from most marine dealerships and marine supply stores. These products are either added to the fuel or sprayed into the carburetor opening during engine operation. Always follow the manufacturer's instructions when using these products.

Prevent heavy carbon deposits by using good quality fuel and oil. Use the correct propeller for the engine and boat combination (Chapter One). Check and correct all applicable fuel system adjustments to minimize carbon deposits.

Throttle and Shift Linkage Lubrication

Apply water-resistant grease to all pivot points of the throttle and shift linkages (**Figure 47**, typical) at the intervals listed in **Table 2**. Regular lubrication prevents corrosion and helps ensure smooth operation. Refer to Chapter Four and Chapter Five to assist with locating all throttle and shift pivot points.

NOTE
To assist with locating all of the throttle and shift linkage pivot point, disconnect the negative battery terminal to prevent accidental starting. Observe the linkages while an assistant moves the shift and throttle levers.

Apply a light coat of Quicksilver 2-4-C or other water resistant grease to all pivot points and sliding surfaces. Excess lubrication provides no additional benefit and may attract dirt and debris. Use penetrating oil if difficult access prevents the application of grease at a particular point.

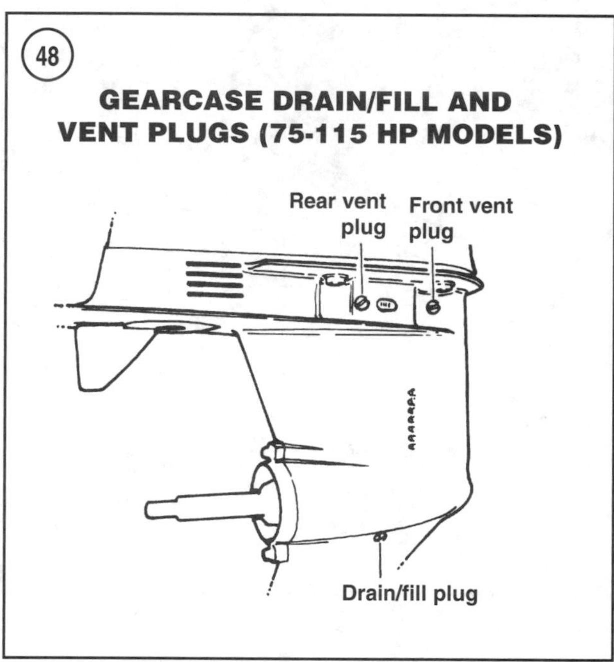

Valve Adjustment

Normal engine wear will gradually cause the valve clearance to change. Infrequent maintenance can cause increased valve train wear. Running the engine with incorrect valve clearance can cause rough engine operation, excessive valve train noise and excessive wear to the valve train components. To compensate for normal wear, check and correct the valve clearance at the intervals specified in **Table 2**. Valve adjustment is described in Chapter Four.

GEARCASE MAINTENANCE

This section describes routine maintenance for the gearcase and related components.

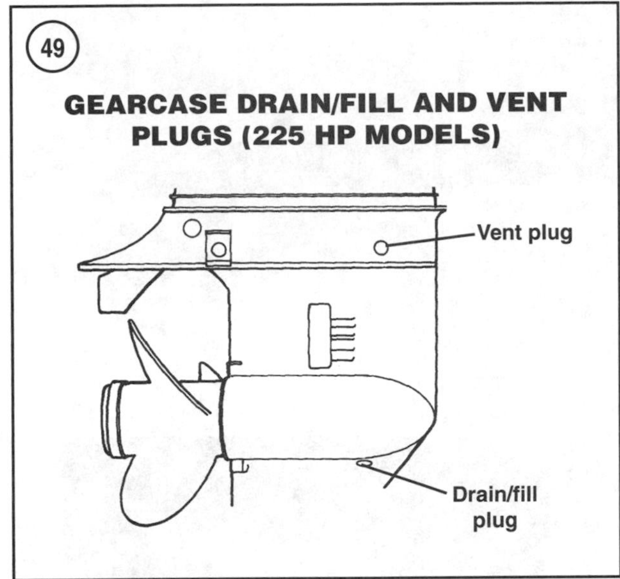

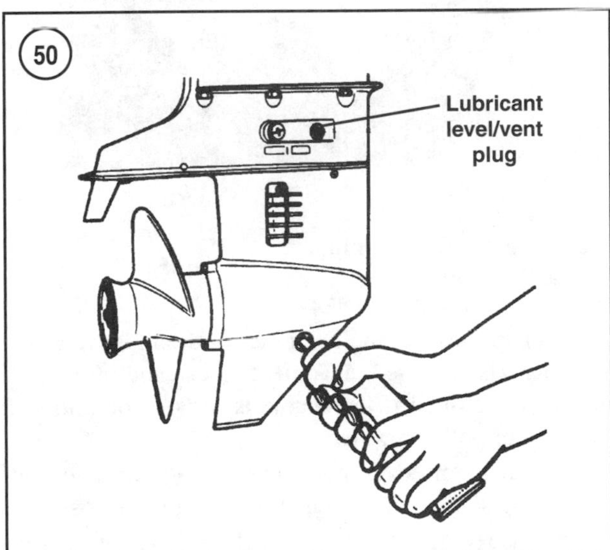

Gearcase Lubricant Check

Checking the gearcase lubricant at periodic intervals may make it possible to detect potential gearcase problems and correct the cause before more extensive damage occurs. Normal gearcase operation contaminates the gearcase lubricant; by changing the lubricant at the specified intervals (**Table 2**) additional wear caused by the contamination can be significantly reduced.

Note that all 75-115 hp models have two oil vent plugs (**Figure 48**). Both vent plugs must be removed when checking the gearcase lubricant. All 225 hp models have a single vent plug (**Figure 49**).

CAUTION
Inspect the sealing washers on all gearcase plugs. Replace missing or damaged sealing washers to prevent water or lubricant leakage.

NOTE
A small amount of very fine particles are usually present in the gear lubricant. These fine particles form during normal gearcase operation. The presence of large particles indicates a potential problem within the gearcase.

Inspect the gearcase lubricant as follows:

1. Disconnect the negative battery cable to prevent accidental starting.
2. Position the engine in the vertical position for at least a hour before checking the lubricant.
3. Position a suitable container under the gearcase. Slowly remove the fill/drain plug (**Figure 48** or **Figure 49**) and allow a small sample, a teaspoon or less, of fluid to drain from the gearcase. Quickly replace the fill/drain plug and tighten it to 60 in.-lb. (6.8 N•m).
4. Rub a small amount of the fluid sample between finger and thumb. Refer to Chapter Two (see *Gearcase Troubleshooting*) if the lubricant feels gritty or metal particles are present in the fluid sample, or if water or a milky appearance is noted.
5. Slowly remove the vent plug(s) (**Figure 48** or **Figure 49**). The lubricant level should be even with the bottom of the threaded vent plug opening(s).
6. Perform the following if the lubricant level is low:
   a. Remove the lubricant drain/fill plug and quickly install the lubricant pump hose or tube into the opening.
   b. Pump lubricant into the fill/drain plug opening (**Figure 50**) until fluid flows from the vent plug (s).
   c. A leak is likely if over 1 oz. (30 mL) of lubricant is required to fill the gearcase. If a leak is suspected, pressure test the unit as described in Chapter Eight.
   d. Install the vent plug(s) and tighten to 60 in.-lb. (6.8 N•m).
   e. Remove the lubricant pump hose or tube and quickly install the lubricant drain/fill plug.
7. Tighten the lubricant drain/fill plug to 60 in.-lb. (6.8 N•m).
8. Allow the gearcase to remain undisturbed in a shaded area for one hour, then recheck the lubricant level. Top off the lubricant as necessary.
9. Connect the battery cable.

Gearcase Lubricant Change

CAUTION
Inspect the sealing washers on all gearcase plugs. Replace missing or damaged sealing washers to prevent water or lubricant leakage.

NOTE
225 hp models are available with a standard RH rotation gearcase or with an optional LH counter rotation gearcase. Except for the gearcase lubricant capacities, the maintenance requirements are very similar. Refer to ***Outboard Engine Identification*** *in Chapter One to determine which gearcase is used on the engine. Then, refer to* ***Table 3*** *in this chapter to determine the amount of gearcase lubricant required.*

All 75-115 hp models have two oil vent plugs (**Figure 48**). Both vent plugs must be removed when checking the gearcase lubricant. All 225 hp models have a single vent plug (**Figure 49**).

1. Disconnect the negative battery cable to prevent accidental starting.
2. Refer to **Table 3** to determine the amount of gearcase lubricant required.
3. Place a suitable container under the gearcase. Remove the drain/fill and vent plugs from the gearcase (**Figure 48** or **Figure 49**).
4. Take a small sample of the gearcase lubricant and inspect as described under *Gearcase lubricant check* in this section. Refer to Chapter Two (see *Gearcase Troubleshooting*) if any problems are noted with the fluid.
5. Allow the gearcase to drain completely. Tilt the engine to position the fill/drain opening at the lowest point to ensure the gearcase drains completely. After draining, place the engine in the upright position.
6. Use a pump dispenser or a squeeze tube to *slowly* pump gearcase lubricant into the drain plug opening (**Figure 50**). Continue to fill the gearcase until lubricant flows out the vent plug opening(s). Without removing the pump or tube from the fill/drain opening, install the vent plug(s) into the opening.
7. Remove the pump from the fill/drain opening then quickly install the drain/fill plug.
8. Tighten the drain/fill and vent plugs to 60 in.-lb. (6.8 N·m).
9. Allow the engine to remain upright in a shaded location for one hour. Recheck the gearcase lubricant level as described in this section. Top off the lubricant as necessary.
10. Connect the battery cable.

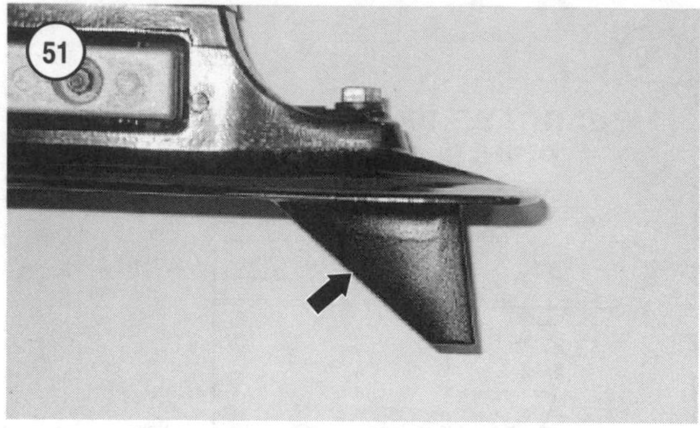

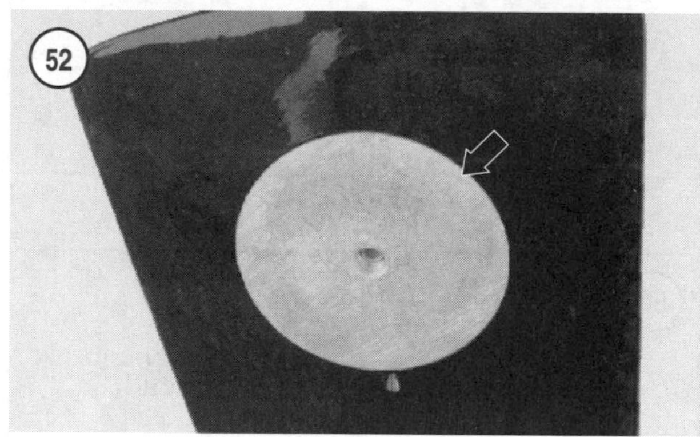

Gearcase Anode Cleaning, Inspection and Replacement

Clean and inspect the gearcase anodes (**Figure 51**) at the intervals specified in **Table 2**. Clean and inspect the anodes more often if the engine is run or stored in salt, brackish or polluted water.

Never paint or cover the anode with a protective coating. Doing so dramatically increases engine corrosion.

A trim tab (**Figure 51**) is used on all models covered in this manual. It serves two functions for the engine. The fin portion projects into the thrust of water from the propeller. The force of the water against the fin imparts side force on the gearcase. When properly adjusted, the trim tab offsets steering torque created by the rotating propeller, reducing the tendency of the steering wheel to pull or steer easier in one direction. *Trim Tab Adjustment* is described in Chapter Four.

On 225 hp models, the trim tab also functions as a sacrificial anode. Note that as the trim deteriorates and looses material, offset steering torque diminishes. For this reason, inspect the trim tab frequently.

The use of some high-performance propellers will result in physical interference with the tab. On such applications a flat anodic plate (**Figure 52**) must be installed in place of the trim tab. Do not install the flat plate unless

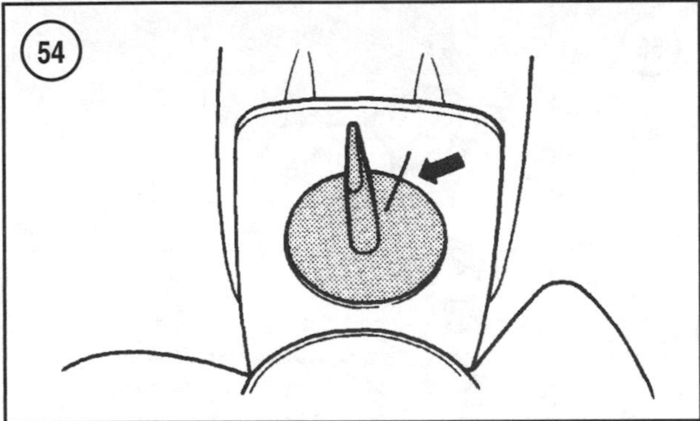

necessary. The benefit of reduced steering torque is lost and the flat plate has less surface area of anodic protection. Furthermore, the slightly reduced hydrodynamic drag from using the plate rarely provides any noticeable increase in boat speed.

Side mounted gearcase anodes (**Figure 53**) are used on all 75-115 hp models. A single screw and locknut secures the anodes into the gearcase openings.

NOTE

Some 75-115 hp models are factory equipped with a black painted trim tab. This tab is not made of aluminum and is not designed to provide sacrificial protection. The other gearcase anodes provide the needed protection when used in freshwater. If the engine is used in saltwater, brackish or polluted water, replace the painted trim tab with a tab made of unpainted zinc or aluminum/indium for increased corrosion protection.

Trim Tab/Anode Cleaning and Inspection

1. Disconnect the negative battery cable to prevent accidental starting.
2. Use a stiff blush to clean deposits and other material from the trim tab/anode.
3. Inspect the trim tab/anode for deep pitting, lost material and a loose fit onto the gearcase. Also, inspect the gearcase surfaces for corrosion damage.
4. Replace the trim tab/anode if it has deep pitting or has lost 40 percent or more of its material. This is especially important for the trim tab.
5. If the trim tab/anode has loosened on the mounting surface, remove, clean and reinstall it. Replace the trim tab/anode if the mating surface has deteriorated. If the trim tab loosens, it may adversely affect the boat handling or contact the propeller, possibly damaging the propeller and other gearcase components.
6. Connect the battery cable.
7. If corrosion is noted on the gearcase surfaces, but the trim tab/anode is not experiencing corrosion, corrosion or contamination may be preventing the anode from grounding to the mounting surface. Check for proper grounding as follows:
   a. Calibrate a multimeter to the R × 1 scale.
   b. Connect the negative meter test lead onto the negative battery terminal.
   c. Note the meter reading while touching the positive test lead to the mounting screws/bolts and the trim tab/anode surfaces.
   d. If the meter does not read *continuity* at all test lead connection points, remove the trim tab/anode and thoroughly clean the mounting surfaces, mounting screws/bolts and the threaded openings. Repeat the test after cleaning and reinstalling the trim tab/anode. Check for faulty ground wiring or terminals if incorrect meter readings persists.

CAUTION

Never paint or apply any coating to the sacrificial anode or anode mounting surfaces. Anodes must be grounded to the housing and cleaned of all foreign material to provide maximum corrosion protection.

Trim Tab/Anode Replacement

Clean the mounting area thoroughly before installing a new trim tab. The trim tab must contact a bare metal surface to ensure proper grounding to the gearcase.

1. Disconnect the battery cable to prevent accidental starting.
2. Use a marker to reference the trim tab setting (**Figure 54**). Do not use a scribe as the gearcase will corrode where the paint is scratched.

3A. On 75-115 hp models, remove the trim tab bolt from the rear of the drive shaft housing (**Figure 55**).
3B. On 225 hp models, locate and remove the bolt access cover (**Figure 56**). Use a socket and extension to remove the trim tab bolt.
4. Carefully tap the trim tab loose, then remove it from the gearcase.
5. Use a stiff brush to thoroughly clean the bolt, bolt holes and the trim tab mounting surface. Continue cleaning until the surface is shiny.
6. Use a stiff brush and file to clean all contaminants or casting slag from the mounting surfaces of the trim tab. The mounting surfaces must be clean and true to ensure proper grounding and a flush fit to the gearcase. Do not apply any paint or other material to the trim tab mounting surface.
7. Install the trim tab onto the gearcase and hold in position. Align with the reference marking (**Figure 54**) made prior to removal. Tighten the trim tab bolt to 22 ft.-lb. (29.8 N•m) for 75-15 hp models and 31 ft.-lb. (42.0 N•m) for 225 hp models.
8. Slowly rotate and pull rearward on the propeller while checking for adequate clearance between the trim tab and the propeller blade. A minimum of 0.100 in. (2.5 mm) is required. If necessary, file material from the trim tab to achieve adequate clearance.
9. Connect the battery cable.

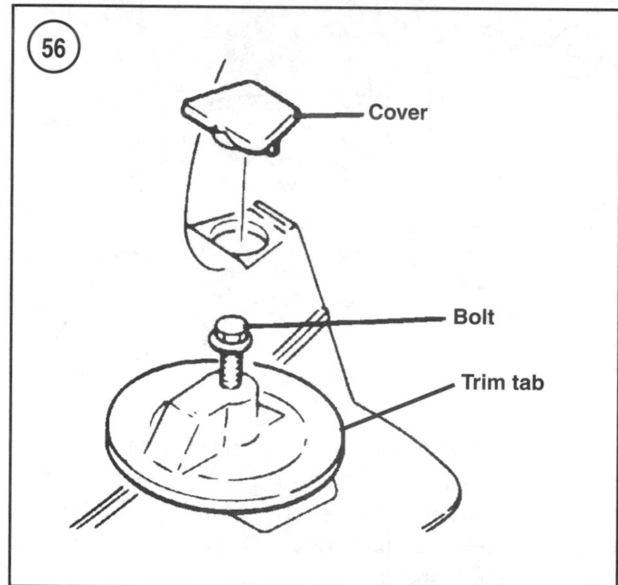

Side Mounted Anode Replacement (75-115 hp Models)

1. Disconnect the battery cable to prevent accidental starting.
2. Remove the bolt and locknut, then tap the anode free from the gearcase. If necessary, carefully pry the anode from the gearcase. Use padding on the pry bar to avoid damaging the gearcase finish.
3. Use a stiff brush to thoroughly clean the bolt, bolt holes and the anode mounting surfaces. Continue cleaning until the surface is shiny.
4. Use a stiff brush and file to clean all contaminants or casting slag from the mounting surfaces of the anode. The anode mounting surfaces must be clean and true to ensure proper grounding and a flush fit to the gearcase. Do not apply any paint or other material to the trim tab mounting surface.
5. Fit the replacement anodes into the respective openings in the gearcase. The thicker end of the anodes face toward the front of the gearcase and the bolt/nut recesses face outward.
6. Hold the anodes in position while guiding the bolt through the opening in the port side anode. Fit the locknut into the recess in the starboard side anode. Thread the locknut onto the bolt.
7. Hold the bolt while tightening the nut to 60 in.-lb. (6.8 N•m).
8. Use a pry bar to center the anodes in the openings. If the anodes contact the sides of the openings, the anode surface area is reduced, resulting in a reduction in corrosion protection. Retighten the bolt and nut after centering the anode.
9. Connect the battery cable.

Water Pump and Impeller Inspection

Certain components of the water pump (**Figure 57**, typical), wear and result in reduced water pump capacity. To ensure reliable operation of the cooling system, replace the water pump impeller and inspect the related water pump components at the intervals listed in **Table 2**. Replace or inspect the water pump components more fre-

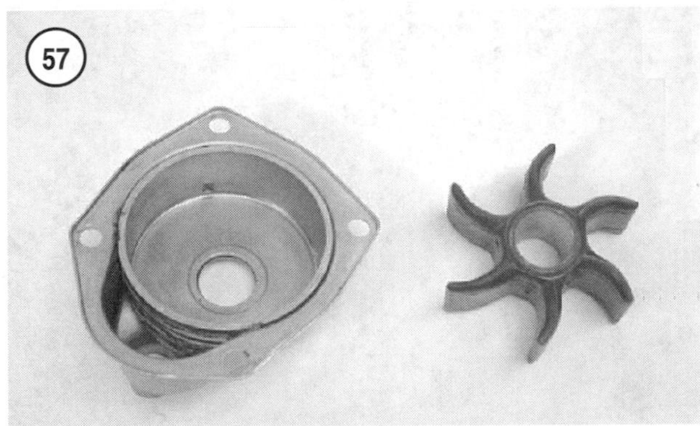
57

58

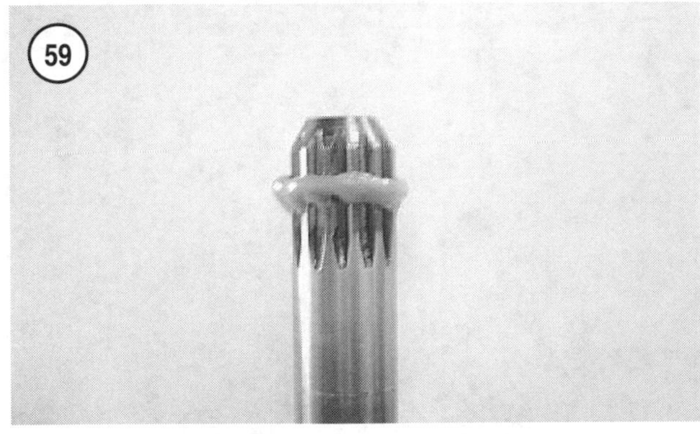
59

quently if the engine operates in saltwater, sandy or silt laden water. Water pump disassembly, inspection and assembly is described in Chapter Eight.

Propeller Shaft Lubrication and Inspection

Lubricate and inspect the propeller shaft at the interval listed in **Table 2**.

1. Remove the propeller as described in Chapter Eight.
2. Observe the propeller shaft for wobbling while spinning the propeller shaft. Replace the propeller shaft (Chapter Eight) if any wobbling is detected.
3. Using a suitable solvent and a shop towel, clean the propeller shaft splined section, propeller nut threads and tapered section.
4. Inspect the propeller nut, thrust washer and spacers for wear, cracks or damage. Replace all defective or worn components.
5. Apply a two generous beads of Quicksilver 2-4-C grease or other equivalent water-resistant grease to the splined section of the propeller shaft (**Figure 58**).
6. Install the propeller as described in Chapter Eight.

Drive Shaft Lubrication

To prevent corrosion and reduce wear, lubricate the upper splined section of the drive shaft (**Figure 59**) at the intervals listed in **Table 2**. Lubricate the splines more frequently if the engine operates in saltwater, brackish or polluted water. If neglected, the upper splined section of the drive shaft may seize into the lower end of the crankshaft, preventing removal of the gearcase without damage to engine components.

The gearcase must be removed to access the splined connection. Refer to *Gearcase Removal and Installation* in Chapter Eight for instructions and lubricant recommendations.

MIDSECTION MAINTENANCE

Midsection maintenance involves lubricating the pivoting surfaces, checking the trim fluid level and inspection of the sacrificial anode. These maintenance items reduce corrosion damage, reduce wear to bushings and pins and help ensure smooth tilting and steering movement.

Swivel and Tilt Tube Lubrication

Lubricate the pivot points of the swivel and tilt tubes at the intervals listed in **Table 2**.

Pump Quicksilver 2-4-C or another suitable water resistant marine grease into the fittings on the swivel tube (**Figure 60**) and tilt tube (**Figure 61**). Continue to pump until the old grease is expelled from between the pivot points.

Steering System Lubrication

CAUTION
The steering cable must be in the retracted position before grease is injected into the fitting. The cable can become hydraulically locked when grease is injected with the cable extended. Refer to the cable manufacturer's instructions for the type and frequency of lubrication

Some steering cables are provided with a grease fitting. Regular lubrication of the steering cable and linkage dramatically increases service life. Pump water-resistant grease into the grease fitting until a slight resistance is felt. Avoid overfilling the steering cable with grease. Apply grease to the sliding surfaces and pivot points of the steering linkage. Cycle the steering to full port and full starboard several times to distribute the lubricant.

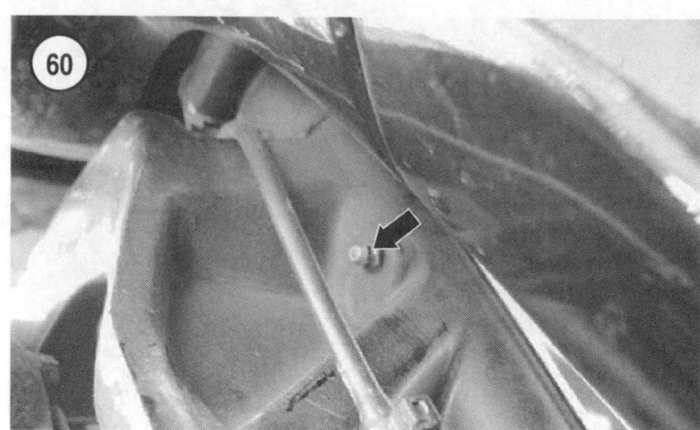

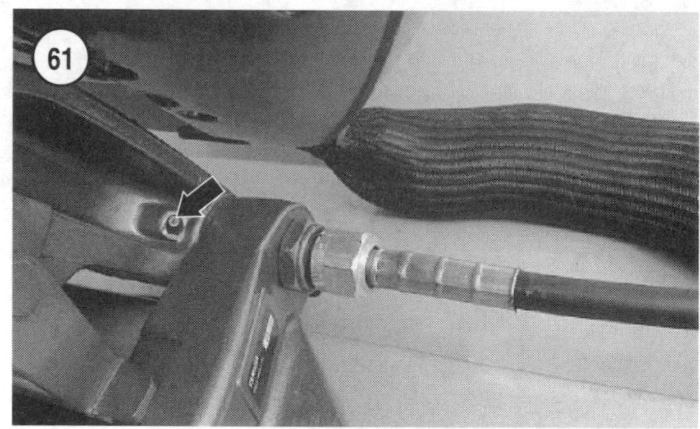

Trim System Fluid Level Check

WARNING
Always wear eye protection, gloves and protective clothing when working around the power trim/tilt system. The fluid in the trim system is under pressure. Loosen all valves and reservoir plugs slowly to allow internal pressure to subside.

Check the trim fluid level at the intervals specified in **Table 2** or if a low fluid level is suspected of causing a trim system malfunction.

Use Quicksilver power trim and steering fluid (part No. 92-190100A12) in all power trim systems. If this fluid is not available, use Dexron III automatic transmission fluid (ATF). The engine must be secured in the full tilt position to access the trim system fill plug. Use an overhead lift (**Figure 62**) or use other methods to support the engine while checking and filling the fluid level. Do not rely solely on the tilt lock mechanism to support the engine.

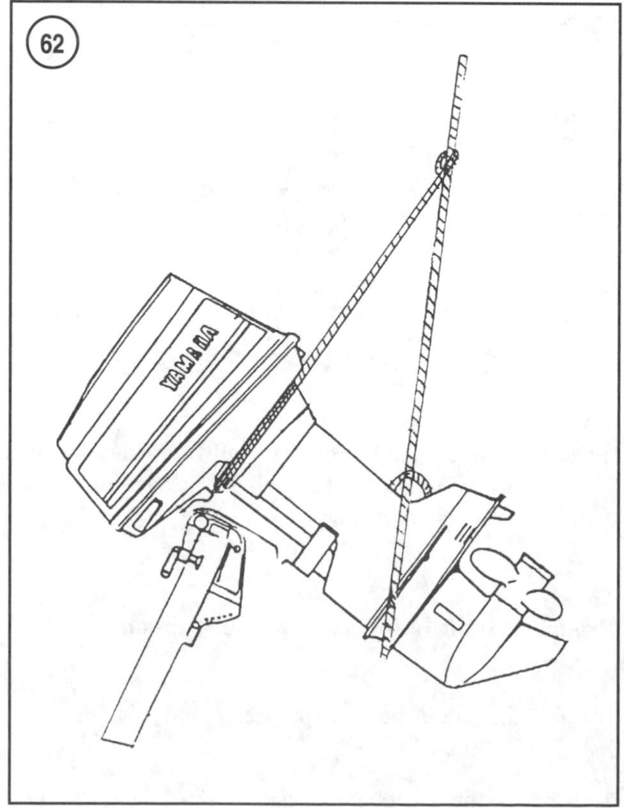

On 75-115 hp models, the yellow colored fill cap is located on the aft side of the hydraulic pump and reservoir assembly (**Figure 63**). The pump reservoir is closest to the starboard side clamp bracket. On 225 hp models, the fill cap is located on the aft side of the fluid reservoir (**Figure 64**). The fluid reservoir is closest to the port side clamp bracket. The fluid in the reservoir may be under pressure. Always remove the reservoir plug slowly and allow the pressure to gradually subside.

If the trim system is not operational due to low fluid level or failure of the electric motor or pump, the engine must be tilted by using the manual relief valve. The valve

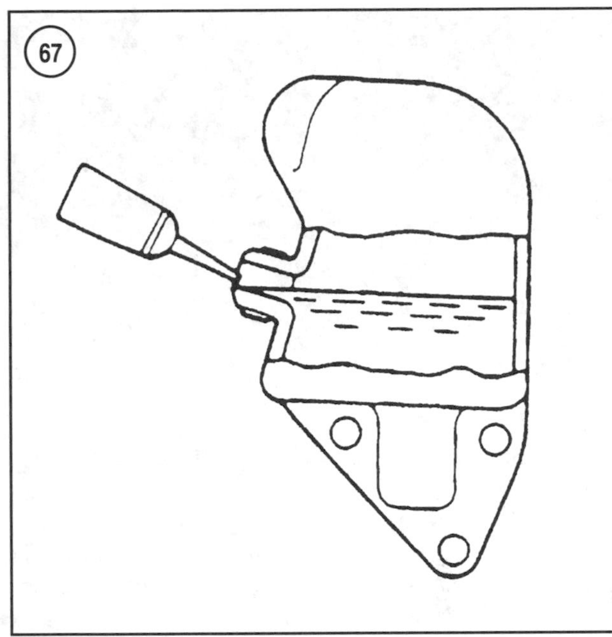

is accessible through the opening in the starboard side clamp bracket (**Figure 65**). To use the manual relief valve, use a screwdriver to rotate the valve 3-4 turns counterclockwise. With assistance, move the engine to the full tilt position. Engage the tilt/lock lever (**Figure 66**), then turn the valve clockwise until fully seated. Do not over-tighten the valve.

1. Operate the trim/tilt system or use the manual relief valve to move the engine to the full up position.

2. Secure the engine in position with an overhead cable or other reliable method (**Figure 62**). Use compressed air to clean the fill cap area. Place a suitable container under the trim system to capture any spilled fluid.

3. Slowly remove the fill cap from the trim system pump or reservoir. Clean the fill cap and inspect the cap seal. Replace the seal if torn, deteriorated or otherwise defective.

4. The fluid level should be even with the fill cap opening. Use a toothpick or other suitable tool to gauge the depth of the fluid.

5. Add fluid until level with the bottom of the fill cap opening (**Figure 67**). Wipe any spilled oil or debris from the fill opening area. Carefully thread the fill cap onto the reservoir. Tighten the fill cap to 60 in.-lb. (6.9 N•m) for 75-115 hp models and 62 in.-lb. (7.0 N•m) for 225 hp models.

6. Remove the overhead cable or supporting blocks and lower the engine. Run the trim system to the full up and full down position several times to purge air from the internal passages.

68

69

Midsection Anode Cleaning, Inspection and Replacement

All models covered in this manual incorporate a large sacrificial anode mounted to the bottom of the clamp brackets (**Figure 68**). Clean and inspect this anode at the intervals specified in **Table 2**.

Cleaning and inspection

1. Operate the trim/tilt system or use the manual relief valve to move the engine to the full up position.
2. Disconnect the negative battery cable to prevent accidental starting.
3. Secure the engine in position with an overhead cable or other reliable method (**Figure 62**).
4. Use a stiff blush to clean deposits and other material from the anode. Remove the anode as necessary to access the surface next to the boat transom.
5. Inspect the anode for deep pitting, lost material and a loose fit onto the clamp brackets. Also, inspect the midsection component surfaces for corrosion damage.
6. Replace the anode if it has deep pitting or has lost 40 percent or more of its material.
7. If the anode has loosened on the mounting surface, remove, clean and reinstall the anode as described in this section. Replace the anode if the mating surface has deteriorated.
8. Connect the battery cable. Remove the overhead cable or supporting blocks and lower the engine.
9. If corrosion is noted on the gearcase surfaces, but the anode is not experiencing corrosion, corrosion may be preventing the anode from grounding to the mounting surface. Check for proper anode grounding as follows:
   a. Calibrate a multimeter to the R × 1 scale.
   b. Connect the negative meter test lead onto the negative battery terminal.
   c. Note the meter reading while touching the positive test lead onto the mounting screws and the exposed anode surfaces.
   d. If the meter does not read continuity at all test lead connection points, disassemble and thoroughly clean the anode, mounting surfaces, mounting screws and the threaded openings. Repeat the test after cleaning and reinstalling the anode. Check for faulty ground wiring or terminals if incorrect meter readings persist.

CAUTION
Never paint or apply any coating to the sacrificial anode or anode mounting surfaces. Anodes must be grounded to the housing and cleaned of all foreign material to provide maximum corrosion protection.

Replacement

1. Operate the trim/tilt system or use the manual relief valve to move the engine to the full up position.
2. Disconnect the negative battery cable to prevent accidental starting.
3. Secure the engine in position with an overhead cable or other reliable method (**Figure 62**).
4A. On 75-115 hp models, support the anode, then remove the two screws (**Figure 68**) that secure the anode onto the clamp bracket spacer.
4B. On 225 hp models, note the routing and connection point for the ground wire. Support the anode (**Figure 69**), then remove the four screws and washers and the two brackets that secure the anode onto the clamp brackets.
5. Pull the anode from the spacer (75-115 hp) or clamp brackets (225 hp). If stuck, lightly tap on the anode until free. If necessary, carefully pry the anode from the midsection. Use padding on the pry bar to avoid damaging other surfaces.
6. Use a stiff brush to thoroughly clean the screws, screw holes and the anode mounting surfaces.

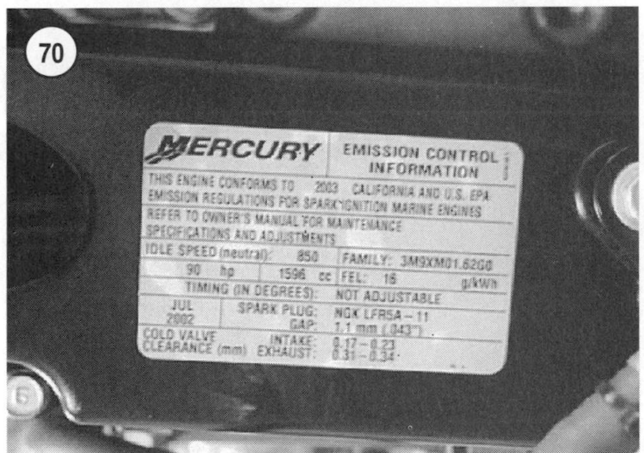

7. Use a stiff brush and file to clean all contaminants or casting slag from the mounting surfaces of the anode. The anode mounting surfaces must be clean and true to ensure proper grounding and a flush fit. Do not apply any paint or other material to the anode.

8. Fit the replacement anodes into the spacer or clamp brackets. On 75-115 hp models, the flat side must contact the clamp bracket spacer. On 225 hp models, the curved side must drop down or away from the clamp brackets.

9A. On 75-115 hp models, hold the anode in position while threading the two screws and washers into the anode and spacer. Tighten the two screws evenly to 60 in.-lb. (6.8 N•m).

9B. On 225 hp models, hold the anode in position, then fit one of the brackets onto the starboard end of the anode. Align the openings, then thread one of the screws through the bracket, anode and clamp bracket. Install the other bracket and the remaining three screws. Do not forget to connect the ground wire terminal onto the rear and port side anode screw. Route the ground wire to avoid interference with moving components, then tighten the four screws evenly to 70 in.-lb. (7.9 N•m).

10. Connect the battery cable. Remove the overhead cable or supporting blocks and lower the engine.

TUNE UP

A complete tune up involves a series of adjustments, tests, inspections and parts replacements to return the engine to original factory specifications. Only a complete tune up delivers the expected performance, economy and durability. Perform the following operations for a complete engine tune up.

1. Perform a compression test.
2. Replace the spark plug.
3. Perform all applicable synchronization, linkage and idle speed adjustment.
4. Check the ignition timing.
5. Test run the outboard.

Compression Test

No tune up is complete without a compression test. An engine with low compression on one or more cylinders cannot be properly tuned. Correct the cause of low compression before proceeding with the tune-up. Compression test instructions are provided in Chapter Two.

Spark Plugs

No other component affects engine performance more than the spark plugs. Always replace the spark plugs when performing a complete tune-up. Cleaned and regapped plugs will not provide the durability of new spark plugs. Inspect used plugs as described in *Spark plug inspection*. Correct any plug identified condition before proceeding with the tune-up.

Replacement spark plugs must be the correct size, reach and heat range to operate properly. The recommended spark plug and gap specification is listed on emission control information decal (**Figure 70**). The decal is affixed to the rocker arm cover or flywheel cover. Refer to the spark plug recommendations in **Table 4** if unable to locate or read this decal.

Removal

On 75-115 hp models the spark plugs are positioned deep within the rocker arm cover. Remove the screws (**Figure 71**) and plastic cover on the rear of the power head to access them. Two screws are located on the top, two screws are located on the bottom and one screw is located on the side and midway down on the cover. A long extension and thin-walled socket is required to remove or install the spark plugs. On 225 hp models, the spark plugs thread into valleys in the rocker arm covers. Remove the four screws (**Figure 72**) and the plastic ignition coil cover on the rear of the power head to access the spark plugs.

On occasion the aluminum threads in the cylinder heads are damaged during spark plug removal. This condition can be repaired without removing the cylinder head by installing a special threaded insert. Have a reputable marine repair shop perform this repair unless familiar with this operation and have access to the necessary tools.

CAUTION
Use special insulated pliers to remove the spark plug cap from the spark plugs. The caps are easily perforated by the gripping surfaces of standard pliers. A damaged cap may cause arcing and an ignition misfire.

NOTE
Mark the cylinder number on each spark plug lead as it is removed.

1. Disconnect the negative battery cable to prevent accidental starting.

2. Mark the cylinder number on the spark plug leads before removing them from the spark plugs. On 75-115 hp models, the top cylinder is the No. 1 cylinder. On 225 hp models, the top cylinder on the starboard bank is the No. 1 cylinder. Odd numbered cylinders are on the starboard cylinder bank and even numbered cylinders are on the port bank. Gently twist the spark plug caps to free them from the plugs, then pull the cap from the plug. Never pull on the spark plug lead to free the cap.

3. Use compressed air to blow debris from around the spark plugs before removing them. If the plug is corroded at the threads, apply a penetrating oil to the threaded section and allow it to soak.

4. Using an appropriate socket, remove the spark plugs. Mark the cylinder number on the plug or arrange them to identify the plug from each cylinder.

5. Clean the spark plug holes in the cylinder head with a thread chaser (**Figure 73**). These are available at most automotive parts stores. Make sure the thread chaser matches the spark plug threads. Thread the chaser by hand into each spark plug hole. Several passes may be required to remove all carbon or corrosion deposits from the threaded hole. Blow all debris from the holes with compressed air.

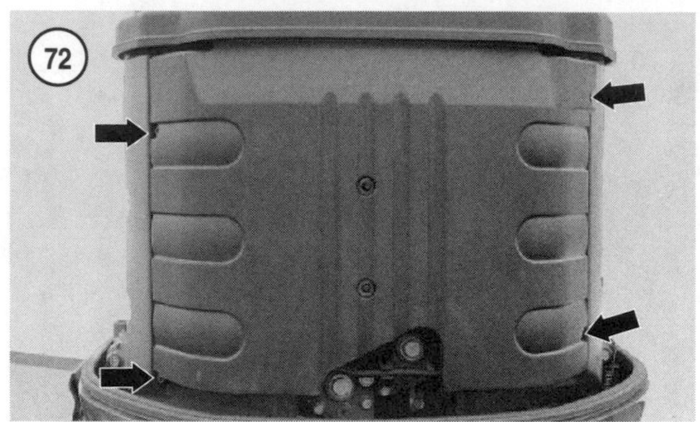
72

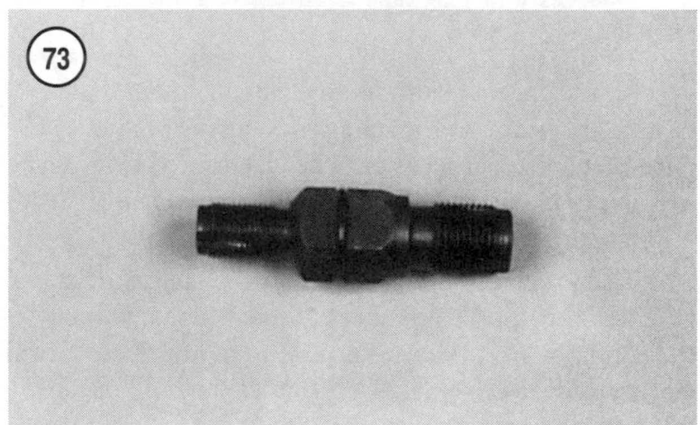
73

Inspection

Remove the plugs and compare them to the plugs shown in **Figure 74**. Spark plugs can give a clear indication of problems in the engine before the symptoms occur. Additional inspection and testing may be required if an abnormal spark plug condition is noted. Refer to Chapter Two for troubleshooting instructions.

Cleaning

Although cleaning and adjusting the gap on the plugs usually corrects most spark plug related problems, replacement is highly recommended. Spark plugs are inexpensive and new ones offer a considerably longer life than a cleaned and gapped plug.

If the spark plugs must be reused, clean the plug using a wire brush and solvent to dissolve the deposits. Special spark plug cleaning devices are available that use a forced abrasive blast to remove stubborn deposits.

Remove all debris from the plug with compressed air prior to installation.

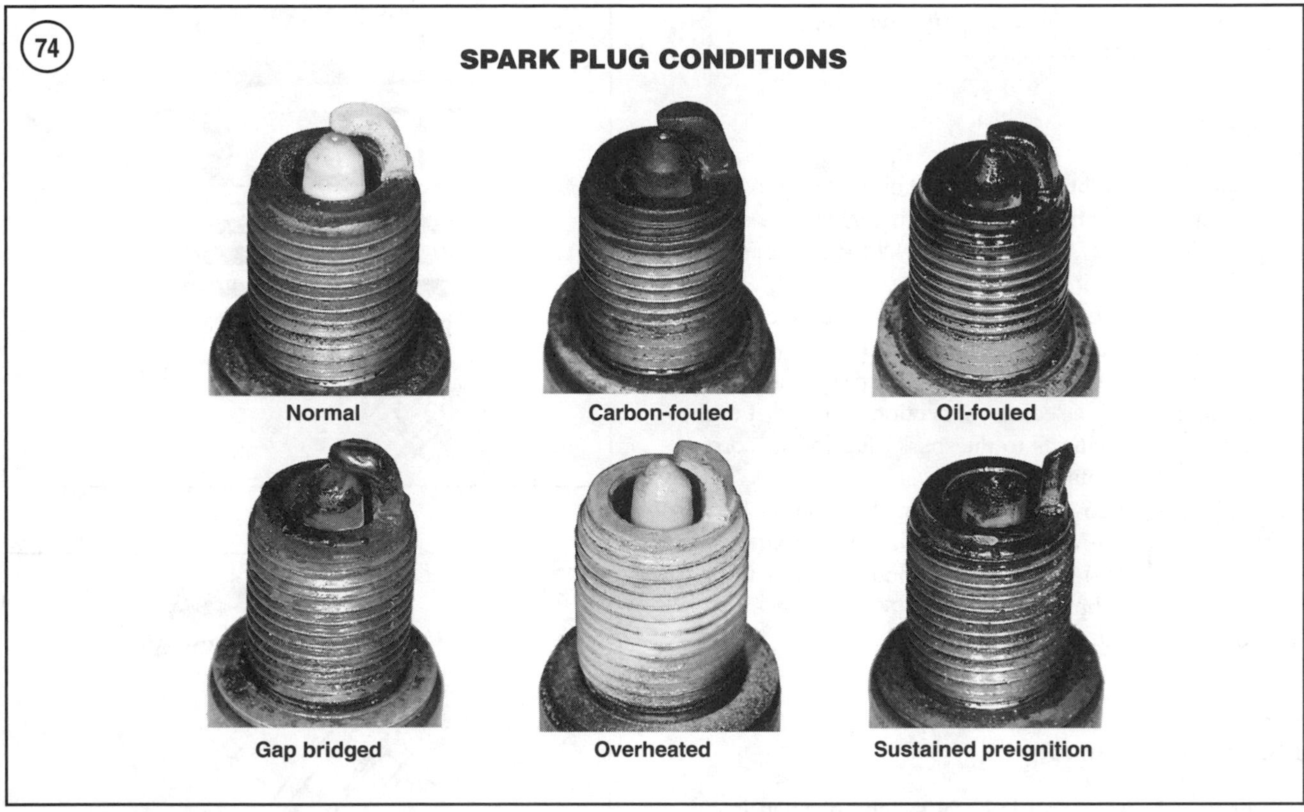

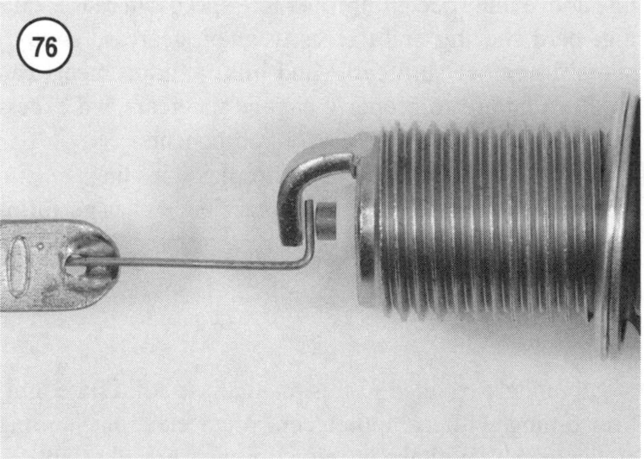

Gap adjustment

Use a gap adjusting tool (**Figure 75**) to adjust the spark plug gap. Never tap the plug against a hard object to close the gap. The ceramic insulator can crack and break away. Gapping tools are available at most auto parts stores. They allow correction of the gap without damaging the plug.

1. Refer to the emissions control information decal (**Figure 70**) or **Table 4** to determine the correct spark plug gap.
2. Check the gap using a wire feeler gauge (**Figure 76**) of the same thickness as the recommended gap. The gauge should pass between the electrodes with a slight drag.
3. Inspect the spark plug for parallel electrode surfaces (**Figure 77**). Carefully bend the electrode until the surfaces are parallel and the gap is correct.

NOTE
Some spark plug brands require that the terminal end be installed prior to installation.

*Thread the terminal onto the spark plug as indicated in **Figure 78**.*

Installation

1. Apply a very light coat of engine oil to the spark plug threads and thread them in by hand. Tighten the spark plugs to 20 ft.-lb. (27.1 N•m) for 75-115 hp models and 18 ft.-lb. (24.4 N•m) for 225 hp models.
2. Apply a light coat of corrosion preventative oil (silicone lubricant) to the inner surfaces of the spark plug cap. Snap the cap fully onto the correct spark plug. Tug lightly on the cap to verify a secure connection. Verify that each spark plug lead connects to the spark plug for the corresponding cylinder number.
3. Fit the plastic cover onto the rear of the power head. Install the cover screws and tighten in a crossing pattern to 65 in.-lb. (7.3 N•m) for 75-115 hp models and 71 in.-lb. (8.0 N•m) for 225 hp models.
4. Connect the battery cable.

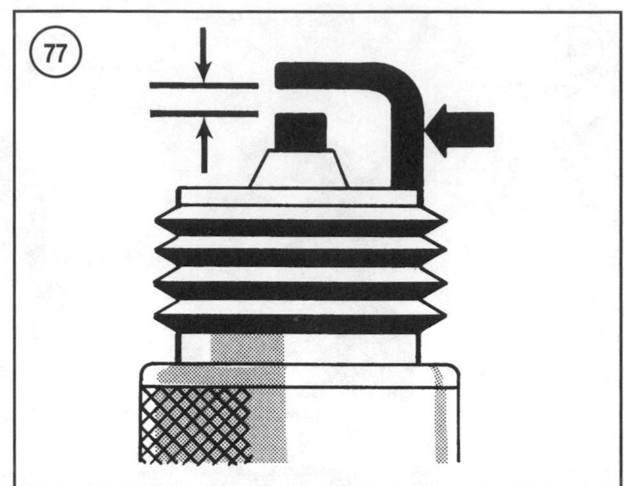

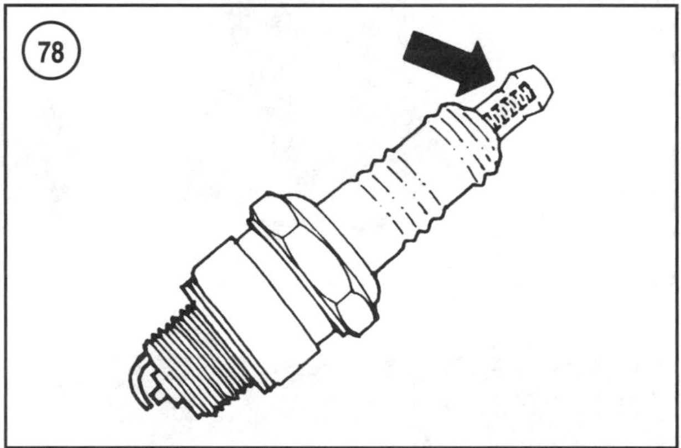

Synchronization, Linkage and Idle Speed Adjustments

Proper carburetor/throttle body synchronization is essential for smooth and efficient operation, particularly at just above idle speed. Improper idle speed can cause stalling, hard shifting and excess wear on gearcase components. Improper shift cable and linkage adjustments can result in failure to properly engage the gears and excessive wear or failure of gearcase components.

Perform all applicable synchronization, linkage and idle speed adjustments (see Chapter Four) when performing a complete tune-up.

Timing Check

All models covered in this manual use solid state ignition timing with computer controlled electronic timing advance. Although the ignition timing is not adjustable, it should be checked periodically to ensure proper timing control. Improper timing advance indicates a fault with the engine control unit (ECU) or other ignition system component. Check the ignition timing as described in Chapter Four when performing a complete tune-up.

Test Running the Outboard

Operate the engine on a flush/test device or in a test tank to ensure correct starting and idling prior to water testing the boat. Connect a shop tachometer to the engine. Follow the manufacturer's instructions when attaching the tachometer to the engine. Have an assistant operate the boat while noting the idle speed. Refer to Chapter Four to adjust the idle speed.

Note the tachometer reading at wide-open throttle. Perform this test with the average load in the boat. Operate the trim/tilt system, if so equipped, to the correct trim position. Record the maximum engine speed then refer to Chapter Four to determine the correct engine operating range for the engine (see *Ignition Timing Check)*. Check the propeller for damage or incorrect pitch if the engine speed is not within the recommended speed range. Refer to Chapter Two for troubleshooting procedures if the correct propeller is installed but the engine fails to reach the recommended speed range. Check the mechanical integrity of the engine and all fuel and ignition system components.

Try a rapid acceleration and run the engine at various speed ranges. Refer to Chapter Two for troubleshooting procedures if rough operation is noted at any speed range or hesitation occurs during rapid acceleration.

STORAGE PREPARATION AND RE-COMMISSIONING

Except for some commercial application, outboard engines seldom operate year round. Special preparation is required if the engine requires either short- or long- term storage.

The objective when preparing the engine for storage is to prevent corrosion or deterioration during the storage period. Re-commissioning prepares the engine for operation after storage.

All major systems require some preparation before storage. If done correctly the engine should operate properly after recommissioning.

Storage Preparation

Perform any maintenance that becomes due during the storage period. Maintenance requirements are listed in **Table 2**. These requirements generally include the following:

1. Change the gearcase lubricant.
2. Check the fluid in the hydraulic tilt or trim system.
3. Lubricate the propeller shaft.
4. Remove and maintain the battery as described in Chapter Six.
5. Check all electrical harnesses for corrosion or faulty connections.
6. Lubricate all steering, throttle and control linkage.
7. Lubricate all pivot and swivel shafts on the midsection of the engine.
8. Change the engine oil and clean or replace the oil filter.
9. Check the condition and clean all sacrificial anodes.

Serious problems can be avoided if the fuel system is properly prepared for storage. Drain as much fuel from the fuel tank as possible. Clean or change all fuel filters on the engine prior to storage.

Clean the exterior of the gearcase, drive shaft housing and swivel brackets to remove vegetation, dirt or deposit buildup.

Wipe down the components under the cover and apply a good corrosion preventative spray. Corrosive preventative sprays are available from most marine dealerships and marine supply stores. Flush the cooling system following the instructions in this chapter.

Treat the internal power head components with a storage sealing agent (**Figure 79**) as described in this section. This step can prevent corrosion inside the power head during the storage period.

Storage sealing agent application

Use a fuel stabilizer to help prevent the formation of gum or varnish in the fuel system during the storage period. Be aware some additives may adversely affect some fuel system components if mixed incorrectly. Deterioration of hoses, check valves and other nonmetallic components may occur. Never mix these additives at a ratio greater than that specified on the label.

1. Remove the silencer cover from the carburetors or throttle bodies as outlined in Chapter Five.
2. Run the engine at idle speed in a test tank or on a flush/test adapter for 10 minutes or until the engine reaches operating temperature.
3. Raise the engine speed to approximately 1500 rpm. Spray the storage sealing agent into all carburetor or throttle body openings. Spray the agent evenly into all openings. Spray in 5-10 second intervals. Continue to spray the agent into the engine until heavy smoking from the exhaust is noted. This indicates the agent has passed through the engine. Stop the engine at this point. Continued operation will burn away the fogging agent and eliminate the protective coating on the intake and exhaust passages.
4. Remove the engine from the test tank or remove the flush/test adapter. Remove each spark plug and spray the sealing agent into each spark plug hole. Crank the engine a few times to distribute the sealing agent.
5. Check the engine oil level and correct as required. Drain each carburetor float bowl or the vapor separator tank as described in Chapter Five (see *Fuel System Service*). Disconnect the fuel hose from the fuel tank and route it to a container suitable for holding fuel. Slowly pump the primer bulb to move residual fuel in the fuel hoses to the float bowl or vapor separator tank for drainage. Install the drain plugs and securely tighten them. Disconnect the fuel hose from the engine. Treat any remaining fuel in the fuel tank with fuel stabilizer.

6. Apply a light coat of engine oil to the threads and install the spark plugs. Store the engine in the upright position. Check the speedometer opening at the leading edge of the gearcase (**Figure 80**), and other water drains on the gearcase, for the presence of debris. They must be clear to ensure water is not trapped in the cooling system. Clean them with a small piece of wire and compressed air.
7. Inspect the water stream fitting on the lower engine cover (**Figure 81**, typical) for blockage. Blow through the opening with compressed air to ensure it is clear. Remove stubborn debris with a small piece of stiff wire.
8. Disconnect the battery cables. Refer to Chapter Six for battery storage instructions.

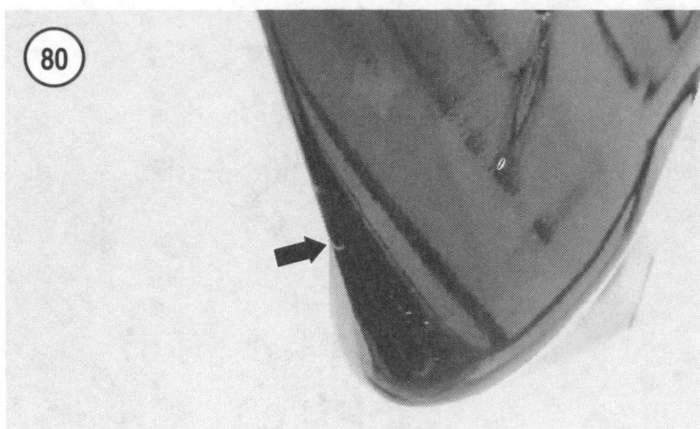

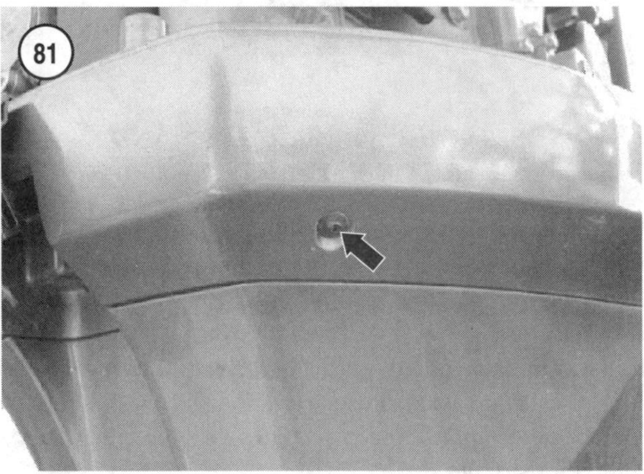

Re-commissioning the Engine

Perform all required maintenance as listed in **Table 2**. It is wise to service the water pump and replace the impeller as described in Chapter Eight. This vital component may deteriorate during extended storage.

Change or correct all lubricant levels. Supply the engine with fresh fuel.

Service the battery as instructed in Chapter Six. Supply cooling water and then start the engine. Run the engine at low speed until the engine reaches operating temperature. Check for proper operation of the cooling, electrical and warning systems and correct as required. If the engine will not start or runs incorrectly, refer to Chapter Two for troubleshooting procedures.

SUBMERSION

Complete disassembly and inspection of the power head is required if the engine was submerged when running. Internal damage to the power head (bent connecting rod) is likely. Refer to Chapter Seven for power head repair instructions.

Many components of the engine suffer the corrosive effects of submersion in salt, brackish or polluted water. The symptoms may not occur for some time after the event. Salt crystals form in many areas of the engine and promote intense corrosion in that area. Corrosion and subsequent failure of the wire harness and its connections usually occurs fairly quickly. It is difficult to remove all of the salt crystals from the harness connectors. Replace the wire harness and clean all electrical connections to ensure a reliable repair. The electric starter, relays and any switch on the engine usually fail if not thoroughly cleaned of all salt residue.

Retrieve and service the engine as soon as possible. Vigorously wash all debris from the engine with freshwater after retrieval. Complete power head disassembly and inspection is required when sand, silt or other gritty material is found inside the engine cover. If these contaminants enter the power head, they will cause rapid wear or complete failure of the internal engine components. Refer to Chapter Seven for power head repair instructions.

Service the engine quickly to ensure it is running within two hours after retrieval. Submerge in a tank of clean freshwater if the engine cannot be serviced within a two hour time frame. This is especially important if the engine was submerged in salt, brackish or polluted water. This protective submersion prevents exposure to air and decreases the potential for corrosion. This will not preserve the engine indefinitely. Service the engine within a few days after beginning protective submersion.

Completely disassemble and inspect the power head internal components if the engine was not serviced in a timely manner.

Perform the following steps as soon as the engine is retrieved from the water.

1. Remove the engine cover and vigorously wash all material from the engine with freshwater. Completely disas-

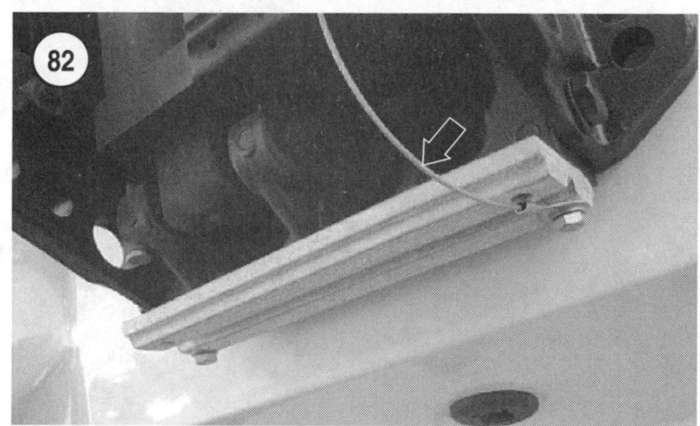

semble and inspect the power head if sand, silt or gritty material is present inside the engine cover.

2. Dry the exterior of the engine with compressed air. Remove the spark plugs and ground all spark plug leads. Remove the propeller as described in Chapter Eight.

3. Drain all water and residual fuel from the fuel system. Remove any water from the silencer cover. Replace all fuel filters on the engine. See Chapter Five.

4. Drain the oil from oil pan. Position the engine with the spark plugs openings facing down. Remove the rocker arm cover as described in Chapter Seven.

5. Slowly rotate the flywheel clockwise as viewed from the flywheel end by the recoil starter or manually on electric start models to force the water from the cylinders. Rotate the flywheel several times noting if the engine is turning freely. Completely disassemble and inspect power head if interference is noted.

6. Position the engine with the spark plug openings facing up. Pour approximately one teaspoon of engine oil into each spark plug opening. Repeat Step 5 to distribute the oil in the cylinders.

7. Disconnect all electrical connections and inspect the terminals. Dry all exterior surfaces and wire connectors with compressed air. Remove, disassemble and inspect the electric starter as described in Chapter Six.

8. Clean the rocker arms and rocker arm covers. Install the rocker arm cover (Chapter Seven).

9. Replace the oil filter and fill the engine with fresh oil. Clean and install the spark plugs. Reconnect all wire harnesses and battery terminals.

10. Provide the engine with a fresh supply of fuel. Start the engine and run it at a low speed for a few minutes. Refer to Chapter Two for troubleshooting instructions if the engine cannot be started. Stop the engine immediately and investigate if unusual noises are noted. Allow the engine to run at low speed for a minimum of 30 minutes to dry any residual water from the engine. Promptly investigate any unusual noises or running conditions.

11. Change the engine oil again and clean or replace the oil filter. Perform all maintenance items listed in **Table 2**.

CORROSION PREVENTION

Reducing corrosion damage is a very effective way to increase the life and reliability of an outboard. Corrosion damage can affect virtually every component of the engine.

Corrosion is far more prevalent if the engine is operated in salt or heavily polluted water. Serious damage to the engine is certain if steps are not taken to protect the engine. A simple and effective way to reduce corrosion in the power head cooling passages is to always flush the cooling system after running the engine. Refer to *After Each Use* in this chapter.

Use a corrosion preventative spray on the external engine components to substantially reduce corrosion damage to engine wiring, terminals, exposed fasteners and other components. Regular use is highly recommended if the engine is operated in salt laden or polluted water. Corrosion preventative sprays are available from most marine dealerships or marine supply stores.

Clean and inspect all power head, gearcase and midsection anodes at more frequent intervals if the engine is operated in a corrosive environment. Refer to the instructions provided in the chapter. Special electronic equipment is available using current from the battery to offset galvanic corrosion (see *Galvanic Corrosion Protection* in Chapter One). The current draw from these systems is relatively low. Consider installing this type of system if the boat is stored in the water for extended periods of time. The cost of the system may very well be less than the cost of repairing corrosion damage. These systems are available from most marine dealerships and marine supply stores.

Never connect the boat accessories to AC shore power without using some type of galvanic isolator or isolation transformer. Engine components can corrode extremely rapidly without an isolator in place. Disconnect the cables from the battery or remove the battery from the boat for charging.

Special isolators are available that allow charging the battery or connections to shore power without promoting rapid corrosion. Contact a marine dealership or marine supply store for information on isolators.

Ensure all grounding wires (**Figure 82**) on the gearcase, midsection and power head are attached and have a good terminal connection. Failure to maintain the ground connections prevents the sacrificial anodes from protecting the ungrounded components.

Table 1 LUBRICATION, MAINTENANCE, AND TUNE-UP TORQUE SPECIFICATIONS

	in.-lb.	ft.-lb.	N•m
Battery cable terminal nut	70	–	7.9
Clamp bracket anode			
75-115 hp models	60	–	6.8
225 hp models	70	–	7.9
Drive shaft housing cover			
75-115 hp models	65	–	7.3
225 hp models	70	–	7.9
Gearcase drain/fill plug	60	–	6.8
Oil filter			
75-115 hp models	(see text)		
225 hp models	–	13	17.6
Oil drain plug			
75-115 hp models	–	17.5	23.7
225 hp models	240	20	27.1
Power head anode cover			
75-115 hp models	–	13	17.6
225 hp models	150	–	16.9
Power head anode to cover	70	–	7.9
Solenoid-to-electric starter nut	78	–	8.8
Spark plug			
75-115 hp models	–	20	27.1
225 hp models	–	18	24.4
Spark plug cover			
75-115 hp models	65	–	7.3
Spark plug/coil cover			
225 hp models	71	–	8.0
Transom bracket anode	70	–	7.9
Trim fluid fill cap			
75-115 hp models	60	–	6.8
225 hp models	62	–	7.0
Trim tab bolt			
75-115 hp models	–	22	29.8
225 hp models	–	31	42.0

Table 2 MAINTENANCE SCHEDULE

Before each use	Check the engine oil level and condition
	Inspect the fuel filter
	Inspect the fuel system for leakage
	Check for oil leakage
	Check the engine mounting bolts
	Check the steering system
	Inspect the propeller
	Check the lanyard switch operation
	Check the cooling system operation
After each use	Flush the cooling system
	Clean external engine surfaces

(continued)

Table 2 MAINTENANCE REQUIREMENTS AND INTERVALS (continued)

Interval	Maintenance
Initial 20 hours of operation (225 hp model only)	Change the engine oil and filter
	Change the gearcase lubricant
	Inspect the fuel filter
	Clean and inspect the spark plugs
	Check for oil leakage
	Inspect hoses and clamps
	Inspect the wiring
	Check for loose fasteners
	Adjust the throttle and shift cables
	Check the flywheel nut tightening torque
	Check or adjust the idle speed
Every 180 days or 100 hours usage (225 hp model only)	Adjust and lubricate throttle and shift linkages
	Lubricate steering cable and pivot points
	Lubricate the tilt tube and swivel tube
	Lubricate the propeller shaft
	Change the engine oil and filter
	Change the gearcase lubricant
	Clean and inspect the spark plugs
	Check for loose fasteners
	Inspect hoses and clamps
	Inspect the fuel filter
	Clean and inspect the sacrificial anodes
	Inspect the battery-to-electric starter terminals
	Inspect the timing belt, pulleys and tensioner
	Lubricate the drive shaft splines
	Lubricate starter drive
	Visually inspect the thermostat for damage
	Check the power trim fluid level
	Inspect the battery
	Remove carbon deposits from the power head
Once a year or 100 hours of use (75-115 hp models only)	Adjust and lubricate throttle and shift linkages
	Lubricate steering cable and pivot points
	Lubricate the tilt tube and swivel tube
	Lubricate the propeller shaft
	Change the engine oil and filter
	Change the gearcase lubricant
	Clean and inspect the spark plugs
	Check for loose fasteners
	Inspect hoses and clamps
	Inspect the fuel filter
	Clean and inspect the sacrificial anodes
	Inspect the timing belt, pulleys and tensioner
	Lubricate the drive shaft splines
	Inspect the battery-to-electric starter terminals
	Visually inspect the thermostat for damage
	Check the power trim fluid level
	Inspect the battery
	Remove carbon deposits from the power head
	Adjust the carburetors*
	Lubricate starter drive
	Check ignition timing and synchronization
Every 3 years or 300 hours of use	Replace the water pump impeller
Every 4 years or 400 hours of use (75-115 hp models)	Adjust the valves
Every 4 years or 400 hours of use (225 hp model only)	Check the oil pump pressure
	Inspect the timing chain tensioners*
	Adjust the valves
Every 5 years or 1000 hours of usage (225 hp model only)	Replace the timing belt
	Replace the timing chains*

*This maintenance item may not apply to all models

Table 3 LUBRICANT CAPACITIES

Model	Capacity
75-115 hp	
Engine oil	5.0 qt. (4.7 L)
Gearcase lubricant	24 oz. (0.71 L)
225 hp	
Engine oil	
With filter change	6.3 qt. (6.0 L)
Without oil filter change	6.1 qt. (5.8 L)
Gearcase lubricant	
Standard RH rotation gearcase	39 oz. (1.15 L)
Counter rotation LH gearcase	34 oz. (1.0 L)

Table 4 SPARK PLUG RECOMMENDATIONS

Model	Recommended plug	Spark plug gap
75 and 90 hp	NGK LFR5A-11	0.039-0.043 in. (1.0-1.1 mm)
115 hp	NGK LFR6A-11	0.039-0.043 in. (1.0-1.1 mm)
225 hp	NGK LFR5A-11	0.039-0.043 in. (1.0-1.1 mm)

Chapter Four

4

Synchronization and Adjustments

This chapter covers adjustment for all systems on the outboard.

NOTE
The throttle position sensor and idle speed are adjusted during the throttle linkage and synchronization adjustment procedures. Attempts to adjust the throttle position sensor without first adjusting the linkages may result in incorrect synchronization of the throttle position sensor to the throttle linkages; causing rough engine operation and hesitation upon rapid acceleration.

Because one adjustment may affect other adjustments, the throttle linkage adjustment, synchronization and idle speed adjustment procedures are combined in model specific sections. Although the throttle position sensor does not usually require adjustment unless removed or disturbed, the adjustment instructions are included in the linkage adjustment and synchronization procedures. The linkage adjustments, and on some models the synchronization adjustments, must be performed before adjusting the throttle position sensor.

Table 1 provides tightening specifications for applicable fasteners. Use the general torque specification listed in the *Quick Reference Data* section at the front of the manual for fasteners not listed in **Table 1**. **Tables 2-5** provide adjustment and operating specifications. **Tables 1-5** are located at the end of this chapter.

PILOT SCREW ADJUSTMENT (75-90 HP MODELS)

The pilot screws are covered with an aluminum plug and adjustment beyond the original factory setting is not recommended. Remove the plug and pilot screw only if necessary for cleaning the carburetor passage.

1. Drill a small hole into the aluminum cover (**Figure 1**). Insert the tip of a scribe into the hole and carefully pry the cover out of the opening. Discard the cover.
2. Before removing the pilot screw, count the turns while turning the screw clockwise until lightly seated.

3. Record the number of turns, then remove the screw from the carburetor.
4. After cleaning the passage, thread the screw in until lightly seated. Back the screw out the number of turns recorded prior to removal. The screw should be 2-3 turns out from the lightly seated position.
5. Install a new plug into the screw opening.

LINKAGE, THROTTLE POSITION SENSOR, CARBURETOR SYNCHRONIZATION AND IDLE SPEED ADJUSTMENTS

75-90 hp Models

An accurate shop tachometer and carburetor synchronization gauge set (part No. 91-809871) or a commonly available carburetor tuner (**Figure 2**) is required for the synchronization adjustment. Adapters included with the gauge set usually fit the plug openings in the intake runner. Remove one of the synchronization port plugs (**Figure 3**) from the intake runner and compare the plug diameter and thread pitch with the adapters. Purchase the correct size adapters from a tool supplier as required.
1. Disconnect the negative battery cable to prevent accidental starting.
2. Locate the throttle cam and roller on the lower port side of the power head. See **Figure 4**.
3. Move the throttle arm (A, **Figure 4**) toward the idle position until it contacts the stop (B).
4. With the throttle arm against the stop, the tip of the throttle cam (C, **Figure 4**) must align with the center of the throttle lever for the bottom carburetor. If otherwise, carefully pry the throttle linkage off of the throttle arm post (D). Loosen the jam nut and rotate the connector on the linkage to achieve the length necessary for proper cam tip-to-lever alignment. Turning the connector clockwise moves the tip down and turning the connector counterclockwise moves the tip up.
5. Carefully snap the linkage connector onto the throttle cam post and check the tip-to-lever alignment. Readjust the link as needed.
6. Adjust the throttle cable as described in this chapter.
7. Locate the sensor (**Figure 5**) on the lower port side of the engine.
8. Move the throttle arm (A, **Figure 4**) toward the idle position until it contacts the stop (B). Hold the arm in this position during the throttle position sensor adjustment.
9. Loosen both sensor screws (A, **Figure 5**) just enough to allow rotation of the sensor body. Rotate the sensor body (B, **Figure 5**) in the clockwise direction until the screws reach the end of the adjusting slot. Hold the sensor

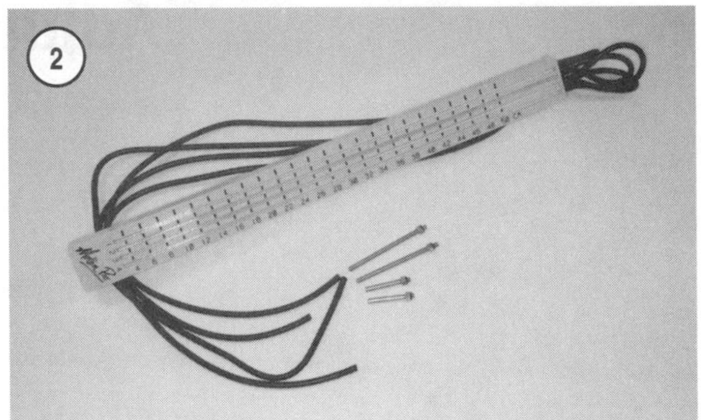

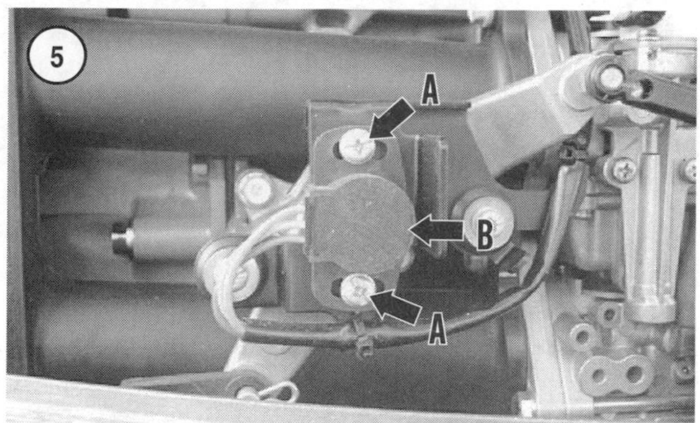

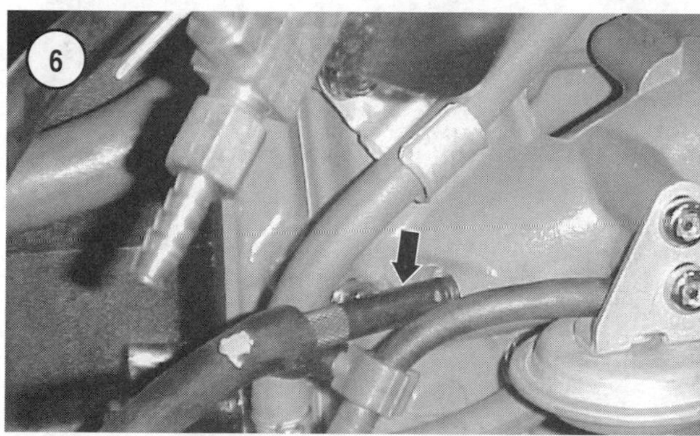

in this position, then tighten both screws evenly to 15 in.-lb. (1.7 N•m).

10. Connect the battery cable. Prepare the engine for operation under actual running conditions.

NOTE
Perform the synchronization adjustments only under actual running conditions. Attempts to perform these adjustments using a flush/test device will result in less than ideal running characteristics under actual running conditions.

11. Remove all four synchronization port plugs (**Figure 3**) from the intake runners. Thread the adapters (**Figure 6**) into all four ports. Connect the gauge set hoses onto the adapters. Mark the cylinder number for the corresponding intake runner number on the hose and gauge set.

12. Attach an accurate shop tachometer to the engine following the manufacturer's instructions.

WARNING
Use extreme caution if working on or around a running engine. Stay clear of the flywheel, timing belt and pulleys.

WARNING
Safely performing on-water testing or adjustments requires two people: one person to operate the boat, the other to monitor the gauges or test equipment and make necessary adjustments. All personnel must remain seated inside the boat at all times. Do not lean over the transom while the boat is under way. Use extensions to allow all gauges and test equipment to be located in normal seating areas.

13. Start the engine and allow it to run at fast idle, in NEUTRAL gear, for approximately ten minutes or until the engine reaches normal operating temperature. In cold operating conditions, this may take as long as 20 minutes.

14. Place the throttle in the idle position and wait a few minutes for the idle speed to stabilize.

15. Rotate the idle speed screw (**Figure 7**) until the engine reaches exactly 1000 rpm. The idle speed adjusting screw is located on the No. 4 (bottom) carburetor. Clockwise screw rotation increases idle speed and counterclockwise rotation decreases idle speed.

16. Locate the synchronization screw (**Figure 8**) on the No. 3 carburetor. Observe the reading on the gauge for the No. 3 and No. 4 carburetors along with the tachometer. *Slowly* turn the synchronization screw until the vacuum gauge readings for the No. 3 and No. 4 carburetors are equal. The actual vacuum readings are not relevant for the

4

adjustment; they must simply be equal. Stop immediately and adjust the idle speed (Step 15) if the engine speed changes during adjustment. Continue adjusting the screw until equal gauge readings are attained with the engine at 1000 rpm.

17. Locate the synchronization screw (**Figure 8**) on the No. 2 carburetor. Observe the gauge readings for carburetors 2, 3, 4 and the tachometer while adjusting the screw for the No. 2 carburetor. *Slowly* turn the synchronization screw until the vacuum readings for cylinders 2-4 are equal. The actual vacuum readings are not relevant for the adjustment. They simply must be equal. Stop immediately and adjust the idle speed (Step 15) if the engine speed changes during adjustment. Continue adjusting until all three gauge readings are equal with an engine speed of 1000 rpm.

18. Locate the synchronization screw (**Figure 8**) on the No. 1 (top) carburetor. Observe the gauge readings for carburetors 1, 2, 3, 4 and the tachometer while adjusting the screw for the No. 1 carburetor. *Slowly* turn the synchronization screw until all four vacuum readings are equal. The actual vacuum readings are not relevant for the adjustment; they must simply be equal. Stop immediately and adjust the idle speed (Step 15) if the engine speed changes during adjustments. Continue adjusting until all four gauge readings are equal with an engine speed of 1000 rpm.

19. Advance the engine speed to 2500 rpm, in NEUTRAL gear, then slowly return to idle. Check the gauge and tachometer readings. Readjust the synchronization and idle speeds screws if required.

20. Adjust the idle speed screw (**Figure 7**) to achieve an idle speed of 825-875 rpm in NEUTRAL gear. Have an assistant shift the engine into FORWARD gear. Allow the engine speed to stabilize then check the in-gear idle speed. The engine should idle at 775-800 rpm in FORWARD gear. If necessary, adjust the idle speed in NEUTRAL gear to the higher or lower side of the specification to attain the correct in-gear idle speed.

21. Turn the engine OFF.

22. Remove the adapters from the intake runners. Inspect the sealing washers on the plugs for damaged surfaces. Replace the washers if damaged. Install the plugs (**Figure 3**) and tighten to 70 in.-lb. (7.9 N•m). Remove the shop tachometer.

115 hp Model

An accurate shop tachometer, digital multimeter meter and carburetor synchronization gauge set (part No. 91-809871) or a carburetor tuner (**Figure 2**) are required for the synchronization adjustment. Adapters included

with the gauge set usually fit the plug openings in the intake runner. Remove one of the synchronization port plugs (**Figure 3**) from the intake runner and compare the plug diameter and thread pitch with the adapters. Purchase the correct size adapters from a tool supplier as required.

Do not adjust the throttle position sensor unless it was removed from the throttle body or moved on the mount. The throttle position sensor is secured with tamper-proof screws that require a special driver tool (part No. 91-881828). If the sensor must be adjusted, use the test harness part (No. 91-881827) to connect the test meter onto the engine and sensor harnesses. Purchase the tamper-proof driver tools from a tool supplier or from a Mercury or Mariner dealership. Purchase the test harness from a Mercury or Mariner dealership.

1. Disconnect the negative battery cable to prevent accidental starting.

2. Remove the silencer cover as described in Chapter Five.

3. Hold the throttle arm (A, **Figure 9**) against the throttle stop (B). Check for proper alignment of the throttle roller with the marking on the throttle cam (C). The center of the

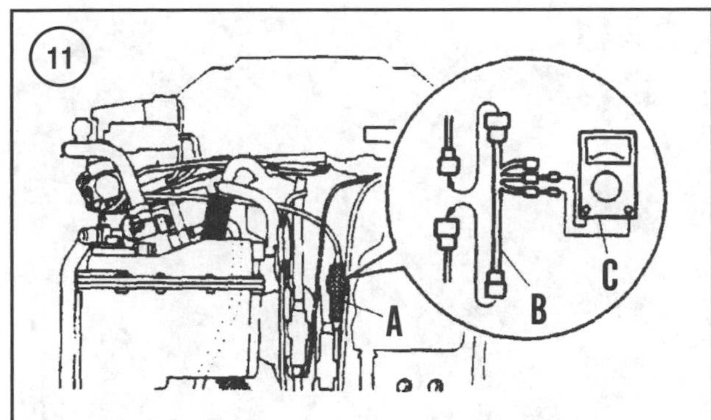

roller must align with the marking and have a 0.020 in. (0.51 mm) clearance between the roller and cam at the marking. If otherwise, perform the following:

a. Carefully pry the link rod (D, **Figure 9**) off the throttle cam post.
b. Loosen the jam nut, then rotate the link rod connector to achieve the link rod length necessary for proper throttle roller to cam alignment.
c. Carefully snap the link rod onto the throttle cam post and securely tighten the jam nut.
d. Check the roller and cam alignment. Perform additional adjustment as needed.

4. Adjust the throttle cable as described in this chapter.

NOTE
Throttle position sensor adjustment is not required unless the sensor was moved on the mount or removed to replace the sensor or upper throttle body.

5. If the throttle position sensor was removed, disturbed or changed from the original factory adjustment, perform the following:

a. Remove the flywheel cover as described in Chapter Seven.
b. Locate the throttle position sensor (**Figure 10**) on top of the upper throttle body on the port side of the power head.
c. Trace the sensor wiring to the connection onto the engine wire harness (A, **Figure 11**, typical). Disconnect the sensor wiring from the engine harness. Attach the test harness (part No. 91-881827) to the engine harness and throttle position sensor harness connectors (B, **Figure 11**, typical). Connect the positive test lead of a meter (C, **Figure 11**, typical) onto the pink test harness wire. Connect the negative meter test lead onto the black test harness wire.
d. Rotate the synchronization screws (A, **Figure 12**) counterclockwise until the No. 3 and No. 4 throttle plates just start to open. Loosen the throttle plate screw (B, **Figure 12**) until the No. 1 and No. 2 throttle plates are fully closed.
e. Set the meter onto the 1 or 2 VDC scale. Connect the battery cable. Turn the ignition key switch to the RUN or ON position. Do not start the engine.
f. Loosen the tamper-proof screws and rotate the sensor on the mount until the meter indicates 0.69-0.71 volt. Tighten the tamper-proof screws evenly to 43 in.-lb. (4.9 N•m).
g. Move the throttle several times to the full throttle position and back to idle. Record the voltage for future reference.
h. Rotate the synchronization screw (A, **Figure 12**) until the No. 3 and No. 4 throttle plates just reach the closed position.
i. Observe the voltage displayed on the meter while *slowly* rotating the throttle plate screw (B, **Figure 4**). Stop when the voltage displayed is 0.028-0.036 volt or higher than the voltage recorded in Step 5g. Record the voltage for later reference.
j. Turn the ignition key switch to the OFF or STOP position. Disconnect the negative battery cable to prevent accidental starting.

6. Move the throttle several times to the full throttle position and back to idle. Repeat the throttle cam-to-roller check and adjustment described in Step 3.

NOTE
Any adjustments to the throttle cam and roller may change the adjustment on a throttle position sensor that has been removed, rotated on the mount or otherwise changed from the original factory adjustment. Always check and readjust the throttle position sensor if the cam and roller require adjustment and the sensor was removed, rotated on the mount or otherwise changed

from the original factory adjustment. If the sensor was not disturbed it does not require additional adjustment after cam and roller adjustments.

7. If the throttle cam and roller required adjustment for Step 5 and the throttle position sensor was previously adjusted, perform the following:
   a. Connect the battery cable. Turn the ignition key switch to the ON or RUN position and check the voltage displayed on the meter. Repeat Step 5 if the meter reading is different from the final reading recorded in Step 5i.
   b. Turn the ignition key switch to the OFF or STOP position.
   c. Disconnect the meter and test harness. Connect the throttle position sensor harness onto the engine wire harness connector. Route the wiring to prevent interference with moving components.
   d. Install the silencer cover as described in Chapter Five.
   e. Install the flywheel cover as described in Chapter Seven.
8. Connect the battery cable. Prepare the engine for operation under actual running conditions.

NOTE
Synchronization adjustments must be made under actual running conditions. Attempts to perform these adjustments using a flush/test device will result in less than ideal running characteristics.

9. Remove all synchronization port plugs (**Figure 13**) from the intake runners. Reposition the wiring and hoses as necessary to access the plugs. Thread the adapters (**Figure 6**) into all four ports. Connect the gauge set hoses onto the adapters. Mark the cylinder number for the corresponding intake runner number on the hose and gauge set.
10. Attach an accurate shop tachometer to the engine following the manufacturer's instructions.

WARNING
Use extreme caution if working on or around a running engine. Stay clear from the flywheel, timing belt and pulleys.

WARNING
Safely performing on-water testing or adjustments requires two people: one person to operate the boat, the other to monitor the gauges or test equipment and make necessary adjustments. All personnel must remain seated inside the boat at all times. Do not lean over the transom while the boat is under way. Use extensions to allow all gauges and test equipment to be located in normal seating areas.

11. Start the engine and allow it to run at fast idle, in NEUTRAL gear, for approximately ten minutes or until the engine reaches normal operating temperature. In cold operating conditions, this may take as long as 20 minutes.

12. Place the throttle in the idle position and allow a few minutes for the idle speed to stabilize.

NOTE
Due to different engine combustion and intake air flow dynamics, the vacuum readings for the No. 1 and No. 2 cylinders will vary slightly from the readings for the No. 4 and No. 3 cylinders. Proper adjustment will result in vacuum readings that vary 1-3 cm Hg from the cylinder with the highest vacuum to the cylinder with the lowest vacuum. This variation is acceptable and does not affect the engine provided the readings are within the specified variance.

13. Use the access slot in the silencer cover (**Figure 14**) to access the synchronization screw. Observe the vacuum readings while *slowly* turning the synchronization screw until vacuum readings for the No. 3 and No. 4 cylinders are within 1-3 cm Hg of the highest and lowest vacuum readings for the No. 1 and No. 2 cylinders. This slight variance is normal and does not affect the engine. Attempts to adjust the screw to attain the same vacuum readings for all four cylinders is not required and usually not successful. Record all four vacuum readings for future reference.

14. Advance the throttle to approximately 2000 rpm then *slowly* return the idle a minimum of five cycles. Return the throttle to the idle position.

15. Allow one minute for the idle to stabilize, then note the vacuum reading for each cylinder. The vacuum readings must not vary more than 3 cm Hg from the readings recorded in Step 13. If otherwise, readjust the throttle synchronization as described in Steps 12-15.

16. Note the highest and lowest idle speed in NEUTRAL gear. The idle speed must be 700-800 rpm. If not, stop the engine and adjust the throttle position sensor as described in Ste 5. Repeat the throttle cam, roller and synchronization adjustments described in Steps 7-16.

17. Stop the engine. Remove the adapters from the intake runners. Inspect the sealing washers on the plugs for damaged surfaces. Replace the washers if damage is noted. Install the plugs (**Figure 13**) and tighten to 70 in.-lb. (7.9 N•m). Remove the shop tachometer.

225 hp Model

An accurate shop tachometer, digital multimeter and carburetor synchronization gauge set (part No. 91-809871) or a commonly available carburetor tuner (**Figure 2**) are required for the synchronization adjustment. Adapters included with the gauge set usually fit the plug openings in the intake runner. Remove one of the synchronization port plugs (**Figure 3**) from the intake runner and compare the plug diameter and thread pitch with the adapters. Purchase the correct size adapters from a tool supplier as required.

The throttle position sensor is secured onto the mounting bracket with tamper-proof screws that requires a special driver tool (part No. 91-881828). If the sensor must be adjusted, use the test harness (part No. 91-881827) to connect the test meter to the engine and sensor harnesses. Purchase the tamper-proof driver tools from a tool supplier or from a Mercury or Mariner dealership. Purchase the test harness from a Mercury or Mariner dealership.

1. Disconnect the negative battery cable to prevent accidental starting.

2. Remove the flywheel cover as described in Chapter Seven.

3. Remove the silencer cover as described in Chapter Five.

4. Loosen the screw (A, **Figure 15**) on the port side throttle body lever. Remove the nut (B, **Figure 15**) and lift the linkage from the lever.

5. Remove the nut (A, **Figure 16**) and lift the linkage from the starboard side throttle body lever. Rotate the starboard side throttle stop screw (B, **Figure 16**) counterclockwise to achieve a small gap between the screw tip and the throttle body lever.

6. Rotate the *starboard* side synchronization screws (A and B, **Figure 17**) counterclockwise until the throttle

plates for the No. 3 (middle) and No. 5 (bottom) cylinders just begin to open.

7. Rotate the *port* side throttle stop screw (C, **Figure 15**) counterclockwise to achieve a small gap between the screw tip and the throttle body lever.

8. Rotate the *port* side synchronization screws (A and B, **Figure 18**) counterclockwise until the throttle plates for the No. 4 (middle) and No. 6 (bottom) cylinders just begin to open.

9. Locate the sensor throttle position sensor (**Figure 19**) on top of the upper throttle body on the starboard side of the power head. Trace the sensor wiring to the connection onto the engine wire harness (A, **Figure 11**, typical). Disconnect the sensor wiring from the engine harness. Attach the test harness to the engine harness and throttle position sensor harness connectors (B, **Figure 11**, typical). Connect the positive test lead of a digital meter (C, **Figure 11**, typical) to the pink test harness wire. Connect the negative meter test lead to the orange test harness wire. Set the meter on the 1 or 2 VDC scale.

10. Connect the battery cable then turn the ignition key switch to the ON or RUN position. Do not start the engine. The meter must indicate 0.645-0.655 volt. If not, adjust the throttle position sensor as follows:

a. Loosen the two throttle position sensor mounting screws. Do not inadvertently loosen the sensor mounting bracket screws.
b. Rotate the throttle position sensor on the mounting bracket to achieve the specified voltage. Rotate the sensor clockwise to decrease the voltage and counterclockwise to increase the voltage.
c. Tighten the tamper-proof screws to 44.0 in.-lb. (5.0 N•m).
d. After tightening the screws, check the meter to verify proper sensor voltage. Readjust the sensor as needed.
e. Turn the ignition key switch to the OFF or STOP position. Disconnect the meter test leads. Do not disconnect the test harness at this time.

11. Record the corrected throttle position sensor voltage for future reference.

12. Observe the meter while *slowly* rotating the No. 3 (middle) synchronization screw (A, **Figure 17**) until the meter reading is exactly 0.001 volt higher than the voltage recorded in Step 11.

13. Observe the meter while *slowly* rotating the No. 5 (bottom) synchronization screw (B, **Figure 17**) until the meter reading is exactly 0.002 volt higher than the voltage recorded in Step 11.

14. Observe the meter while *slowly* rotating the starboard side throttle stop screw (B, **Figure 16**) until the meter reading is exactly 0.040 volt higher than the voltage recorded in Step 11.

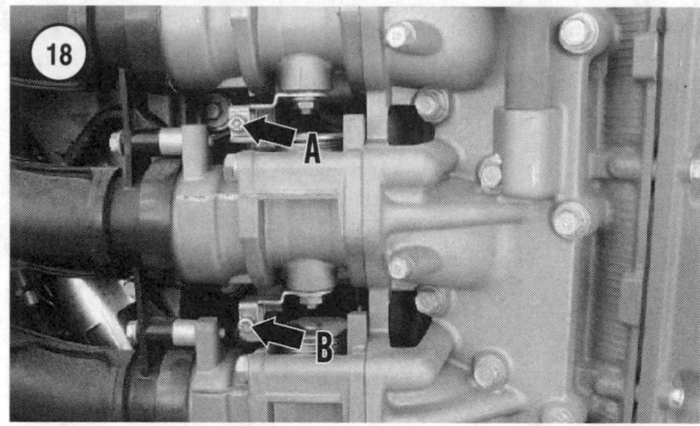

15. Observe the tip on the port side throttle lever while *slowly* rotating the No. 4 (middle) synchronization screw (A, **Figure 18**) in the clockwise direction. Stop when any movement of lever tip is detected.

16. Observe the tip on the port side throttle lever while *slowly* rotating the No. 6 (bottom) synchronization screw (B, **Figure 18**) in the clockwise direction. Stop when any additional movement of lever tip is detected.

17. Rotate the port side throttle stop screw (C, **Figure 15**) clockwise until the screw tip just contacts the throttle lever. Then turn the screw exactly one turn clockwise.

NOTE

Synchronization adjustments must be made under actual running conditions. Attempts to perform these adjustments using a flush/test device will result in poor operation under actual running conditions.

18. Prepare the engine for operation under actual running conditions.

19. Remove the three synchronization port plugs (**Figure 20**) from the starboard side intake runners. Thread the adapters (**Figure 6**) into all three ports. Mark the cylinder

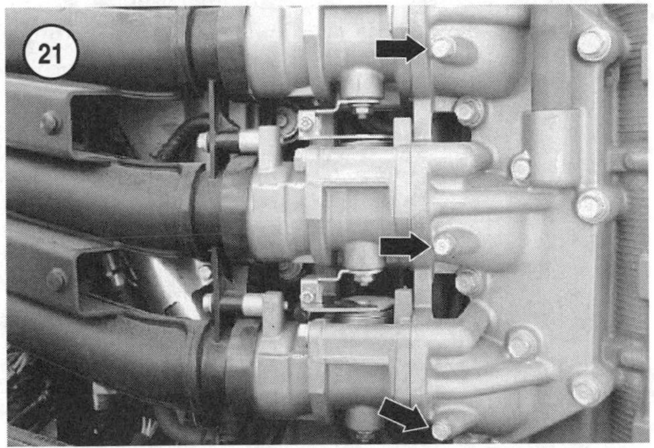

number for the corresponding intake runner number on the hose and gauge set.

20. Attach an accurate shop tachometer to the engine following the manufacturer's instructions.

WARNING
Use extreme caution if working on or around a running engine. Stay clear from the flywheel, timing belt and pulleys.

WARNING
Safely performing on-water testing or adjustments requires two people: one person to operate the boat, the other to monitor the gauges or test equipment and make necessary adjustments. All personnel must remain seated inside the boat at all times. Do not lean over the transom while the boat is under way. Use extensions to allow all gauges and test equipment to be located in normal seating areas.

21. Start the engine and allow it to run at idle speed, in NEUTRAL gear, for approximately ten minutes or until the engine reaches normal operating temperature. In cold operating conditions, this may take as long as 20 minutes. The idle speed will stabilize at 650-750 rpm in neutral gear after the engine reaches normal operating temperature.

22. Slowly rotate the starboard side No. 3 cylinder (middle) synchronization screw (A, **Figure 17**) until the vacuum reading for the No. 3 cylinder is within 2 cm Hg of the vacuum reading for the No. 1 cylinder. The actual vacuum readings are not relevant for this adjustment. They simply must be within the specified difference between the two cylinders.

23. *Slowly* rotate the starboard side No. 5 cylinder (bottom) synchronization screw (B, **Figure 17**) until the vacuum reading for the No. 5 cylinder is within 2 cm of the vacuum reading for the No. 1 and No. 3 cylinders. The actual vacuum readings are not relevant for this adjustment. They simply must be within the specified difference from one cylinder to the next. Do not adjust the throttle stop screw (B, **Figure 16**) to equalize the vacuum readings.

24. Allow a few minutes for the idle speed to stabilize then check the three vacuum readings. Readjust the synchronization screws if necessary.

25. Record the vacuum readings for the No. 1, No. 3 and No. 5 cylinders. Add the three vacuum readings together, then divide the sum by three. Record the results as the *average vacuum reading* for the starboard cylinder bank.

26. Stop the engine. Remove the adapters from the No. 3 and No. 5 intake runners. Do not remove the adapter from the No. 1 intake runner at this time. Inspect the sealing washers on the plugs for damaged surfaces. Replace the washers if damaged. Install the plugs (**Figure 20**) into the ports and tighten to 71 in.-lb. (8.0 N•m).

27. Remove the three synchronization port plugs (**Figure 21**) from the port side intake runners. Thread the adapters (**Figure 6**) into all three ports. The fourth hose and adapter must remain connected to the No. 1 cylinder synchronization port in the starboard manifold during the remaining synchronization procedures. Mark the cylinder number for the corresponding intake runner number on the hose and gauge set.

28. Start the engine and allow it to run at idle speed, in NEUTRAL gear, for approximately ten minutes or until the engine reaches normal operating temperature. In cold operating conditions, this may take as long as 20 minutes. The idle speed will stabilize at 650-750 rpm in neutral gear after the engine reaches normal operating temperature.

29. *Slowly* rotate the port side No. 4 cylinder (middle) synchronization screw (A, **Figure 18**) until the vacuum reading for the No. 4 cylinder is within 2 cm Hg of the vacuum reading for the No. 2 cylinder. The actual vacuum readings are not relevant for this adjustment. They simply

must be within the specified difference between the two cylinders.

30. *Slowly* rotate the port side No. 6 cylinder (bottom) synchronization screw (B, **Figure 18**) until the vacuum reading for the No. 6 cylinder is within 2 cm of the vacuum reading for the No. 2 and No. 4 cylinders. The actual vacuum readings are not relevant for this adjustment. They simply must be within the specified difference from one cylinder to the next. Do not adjust the throttle stop screw (C, **Figure 15**) to equalize the vacuum readings.

31. Allow a few minutes for the idle speed to stabilize, then check the three vacuum readings. Readjust the synchronization screws if necessary.

32. Record the vacuum readings for the No. 2, No. 4 and No. 6 cylinders. Add the three vacuum readings together, then divide the sum by three. Record the results as the *average vacuum reading* for the port cylinder bank.

33. The average vacuum reading for the port cylinder bank (Step 32) must be within 4 cm Hg of the average reading for the starboard cylinder bank (Step 25). If the average difference exceeds the specification as follows:

a. If the average vacuum reading is within specification continue to Step 34.

b. Observe the four vacuum readings while *slowly* rotating the port side throttle stop screw (C, **Figure 15**) until the average vacuum readings for the No. 2, No. 4 and No. 6 cylinders are within 4 cm Hg of the vacuum reading for the No. 1 cylinder. The No. 1 cylinder reading represents the average vacuum for the starboard cylinder bank. Do not adjust the starboard throttle stop screw (B, **Figure 16**) to equalize the readings.

34. Connect the positive test lead of a digital multimeter (C, **Figure 11**, typical) onto the pink test harness wire. Connect the negative meter test lead onto the orange test harness wire. Set the meter on the 1 or 2 VDC scale. The meter should indicate 0.695-0.705 volt after performing the synchronization adjustments. If otherwise, adjust the sensor as follows:

a. Loosen the two throttle position sensor mounting screws. Do not inadvertently loosen the sensor mounting bracket screws.

b. Rotate the throttle position sensor on the mounting bracket to achieve the specified voltage. Rotate the sensor clockwise to decrease the voltage and counterclockwise to increase the voltage.

c. Tighten the tamper-proof screws to 44.0 in.-lb. (5.0 N•m).

d. After tightening the screws, check the meter to verify proper sensor voltage. Readjust the sensor as needed.

35. Stop the engine. Disconnect the meter and test harness. Connect the throttle position sensor harness to the engine wire harness connector. Route the wiring to prevent interference with moving components. Do not disconnect the vacuum hoses and gages at this time.

36. Fit the linkage connector to the post on the port side throttle body lever. Thread the nut (B, **Figure 15**) onto the post. Tighten the nut to 35 in.-lb. (4.0 N•m). Do not tighten the throttle body lever screw (A, **Figure 15**) at this time.

37. Fit the linkage connector onto post on starboard side throttle body lever. Thread the nut (A, **Figure 16**) onto the post. Tighten the nut to 35 in.-lb. (4.0 N•m).

38. Start the engine and allow it to run at idle speed, in NEUTRAL gear, for approximately ten minutes or until the engine reaches normal operating temperature. In cold operating conditions, this may take as long as 20 minutes.

39. Without moving the port side throttle body lever, tighten the screws (A, **Figure 15**) to 35 in.-lb. (4.0 N•m). If the engine speed increases during or after the tightening process, the lever is moving. Loosen the screw and repeat the tightening process if any change in engine speed is detected.

40. Check for a gap between the tip of the port side (C, **Figure 15**) and starboard side (B, **Figure 16**) stop screws (C, **Figure 15** and B, **Figure 16**) and the throttle body levers. Repeat Step 39 and Step 40 if any gap is evident.

41. Compare the vacuum reading for the No. 1 cylinder with the vacuum readings for cylinders No. 2, No. 4 and No. 6. The reading for the No. 1 cylinder must be within 4 cm Hg of the average vacuum readings for the ports cylinder bank. If the difference exceeds 4 cm Hg, readjust the bank synchronization as described in Step 33.

42. Check the idle speed indicated on the tachometer. The engine idle speed must be 650-750 rpm in neutral gear with the engine at normal operating temperature. If otherwise, adjust the idle speed as follows:

a. Carefully pry the throttle link connector (A, **Figure 22**) from the throttle arm lever (B).

b. Rotate the port side throttle stop screw (C, **Figure 15**) clockwise to achieve a 0.125 in. (3.2 mm) gap between the screw tip and the throttle body lever.

c. Rotate the starboard side throttle stop screw (B, **Figure 16**) until the tachometer indicates an idle speed of 650-750 rpm. Clockwise rotation increases idle speed and counterclockwise rotation decreases idle speed.

d. *Slowly* rotate the port side throttle stop screw (C, **Figure 15**) until the screw tip just touches the throttle body lever. Do not rotate the screw enough to move the lever.

e. Move the throttle arm lever (B, **Figure 22**) toward the flywheel until resistance is felt.

f. Loosen the jam nut on the disconnected throttle link, then rotate the connector until the pocket aligns perfectly with the post on the lever.

g. Carefully snap the connector onto the post. Make sure the throttle body levers did not move after connecting the link. If they moved, remove and readjust the link.

h. Securely tighten the link jam nut.

43. Stop the engine. Remove the shop tachometer from the engine. Disconnect the negative battery cable to prevent accidental starting.

44. Remove the adapters from the No. 1, No. 2, No. 4 and No. 6 intake runners. Inspect the sealing washers on the plugs for damaged surfaces. Replace the washers if damage is noted. Install the plugs (**Figure 21**) into the ports and tighten to 71 in.-lb. (8.0 N•m).

45. Check the alignment of the marking on the throttle cam (B, **Figure 23**) with the throttle roller (A). The center of the roller must align with the marking on the cam with a 0.039 in. (1.0 mm) gap between the roller and the throttle cam surfaces. Adjust the linkages if the marking and cam do not align as specified as follows:

a. Remove the locking pin and carefully pull the throttle cable end off of the throttle cam post.

b. Carefully pry the throttle link connector (A, **Figure 22**) from the throttle arm lever (B). Loosen the jam nut on the disconnected throttle link

c. Move the throttle arm lever until the throttle cam marking and roller align as specified. Maintain the lever in this position during the adjustment.

d. Rotate the connector until the pocket aligns perfectly with the post on the lever. Do not inadvertently move the throttle body levers.

e. Carefully snap the connector onto the post and check the cam and roller alignment. Disconnect the link and repeat the adjustment as needed.

f. Verify a secure link connection, then securely tighten the jam nut.

g. Adjust the throttle cable as described in this chapter.

46. Install the silencer cover as described in Chapter Five.

47. Install the flywheel cover as described in Chapter Seven.

IGNITION TIMING CHECK

The ignition timing is electronically controlled by the engine control unit (ECU) on all models covered in this manual and is not adjustable. The ignition timing check verifies proper timing advance under actual operating conditions. The engine must be operated at the maximum recommended engine speed range to accurately read the ignition timing. The maximum recommended engine speed ranges are listed in **Table 3**. A shop tachometer and strobe timing light are required for this procedure.

WARNING
Use extreme caution if working on or around a running engine. Stay clear from the flywheel, timing belt and pulleys.

WARNING
Safely performing on-water testing or adjustments requires two people: one person to operate the boat, the other to monitor the gauges or test equipment and make necessary adjustments. All personnel must remain seated inside the boat at all times. Do not lean over the transom while the boat is under way. Use extensions to allow all gauges and test equipment to be located in normal seating areas.

1. Remove the spark plug cover as described in Chapter Three. See *Spark plug removal*.

2. Attach an accurate shop tachometer following the manufacturer's instructions.

3. Attach a strobe timing light onto the No. 1 spark plug lead engine following the manufacturer's instructions.
4. Prepare the engine for operation under actual operating conditions.
5. Start the engine and allow it to warm to normal operating temperature.
6. Have a qualified assistant reduce the engine speed to idle, then shift the engine into FORWARD gear. Allow the idle to stabilize to the normal range specified in **Table 2**.
7. Point the timing light at the flywheel and timing pointer (**Figure 24**). Note the reading.
8. Have the assistant advance the throttle to full-open. Allow the engine to reach the maximum recommended speed range specified in **Table 3**, then point the timing light at the flywheel and pointer. Note the reading.
9. Reduce the engine speed and return to port.
10. Remove the timing light and shop tachometer.
11. Install the spark plug cover as described in Chapter Three. See *Spark plug installation*.
12. The idle and at maximum engine speed ignition timing readings must be within the specifications in **Table 4**. If incorrect timing is evident, test the crankshaft position sensor as described in Chapter 2. If the crankshaft position sensor tests correctly, remove the flywheel as described in Chapter Seven and inspect the flywheel key. Consider replacing the engine control unit to correct improper ignition timing advance only after ruling out a fault with all other ignition system components. Failure of the engine control unit is extremely rare and replacement seldom corrects an ignition problem.

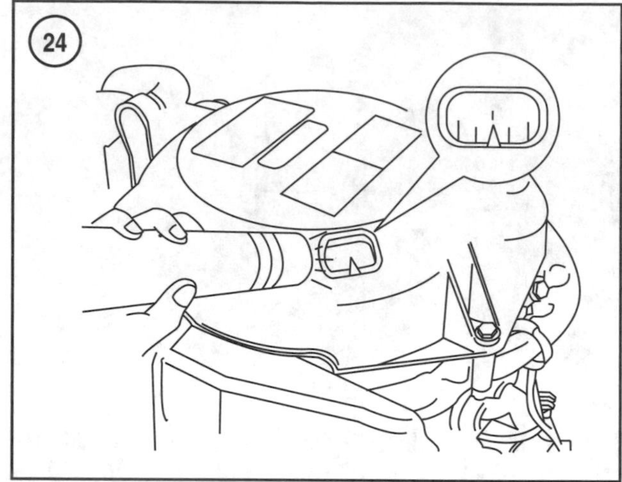

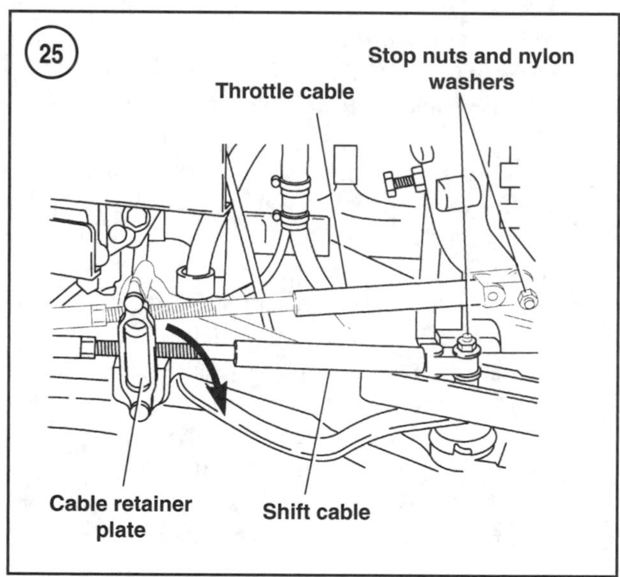

THROTTLE CABLE ADJUSTMENT

75-115 hp Models

1. Disconnect the negative battery cable to prevent accidental starting.
2. Pivot the cable barrel retainer (**Figure 25**) to release the throttle cable barrel.
3. Remove the locking pin from the post (**Figure 25**) on the throttle arm, then lift the throttle cable from the post and barrel opening.
4. Push the throttle arm rearward, until it reaches the closed throttle stop.
5. Grasp the cable barrel and plastic cable end. Lightly push the cable end toward the cable barrel to remove any slack in the cable. Maintain light pressure on the cable end during the cable barrel adjustments.
6. Rotate the cable barrel until the cable barrel can be inserted into the opening and the plastic cable end fits over the post without moving the throttle arm away from the stop. Do not adjust the barrel to excessively pre-load the throttle arm against the stop. Doing so may cause the remote control to malfunction. The throttle arm must contact the stop with light pressure.

7. Insert the locking pin into the post (**Figure 25**) to secure the cable end onto the throttle arm. To secure the barrel, pivot the cable barrel retainer (**Figure 25**) until it snaps over the post.

8. Move the remote control to the full-throttle position and back to idle several times. The throttle arm must return back to trough the full thhe stop each time. Also the remote control must move throttle range without binding. Readjust the cable if the throttle arm does not return to the stop each time or if binding is evident.

9. Connect the battery cable.

5. Rotate the cable barrel until it can be inserted into the barrel recess without disturbing the cam marking-to-roller alignment and roller-to-cam gap.
6. Fit the barrel into the recess. Pivot the clamp plate over the barrels. Securely tighten the clamp plate screw.
7. Move the remote control to the full-throttle position and back to idle several times. The throttle arm must return to the correct throttle cam-to-roller alignment and gap each time. Also, the remote control must move through the full throttle range without binding. Readjust the cable if incorrect cam-to-roller alignment or binding is evident.
8. Connect the battery cable.

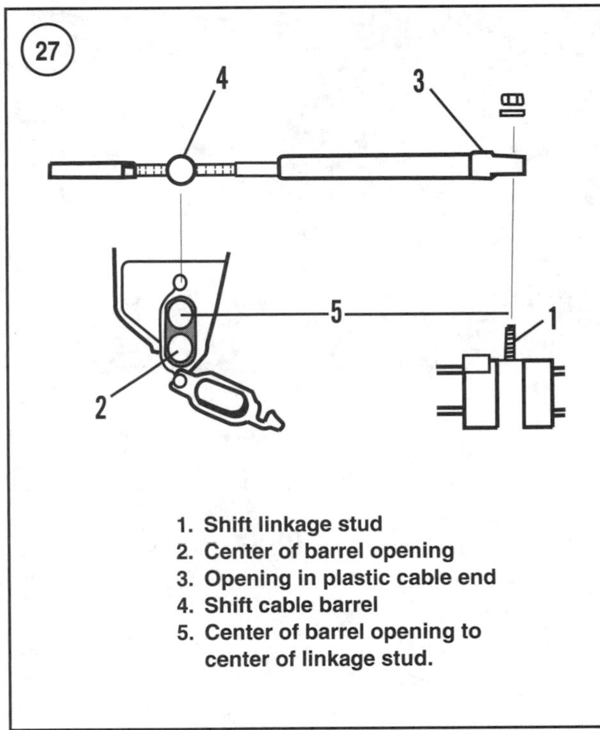

1. Shift linkage stud
2. Center of barrel opening
3. Opening in plastic cable end
4. Shift cable barrel
5. Center of barrel opening to center of linkage stud.

225 hp Model

1. Disconnect the battery cable to prevent accidental starting.
2. Loosen the hex screw, then pivot the clamp plate (**Figure 26**) away from the cable barrels.
3. Lift the throttle cable barrel out of the recess. The throttle cable is on the port side. The shift cable is on the starboard side.
4. Move the plastic cable end until the marking on the throttle cam (B, **Figure 23**) aligns with the center of the throttle roller (A) with a 0.039 in. (1.0 mm) gap between the roller and cam surface. Hold the cam in this position during the cable adjustment.

SHIFT CABLE ADJUSTMENT

75-115 hp Models

1. Disconnect the negative battery cable to prevent accidental starting.
2. Place the remote control in the NEUTRAL gear position.
3. Pivot the cable barrel retainer to release the cable barrel (4, **Figure 27**) from the opening (2).
4. Remove the locking nut and washer, then lift the plastic cable end off of the shift linkage stud (1, **Figure 27**).
5. Make sure the gearcase is in neutral gear by rotating the propeller. If the propeller does not rotate freely in the clockwise and counterclockwise directions, move the shift linkage stud forward or rearward until the neutral detent is felt and the propeller rotates freely.
6. Lightly push the shift linkage stud forward and rearward to locate the points at which resistance is felt. Do not push on the stud with enough effort to shift into gear. Position the shift linkage stud at the midway point between the points where resistance is felt. This is the center of neutral gear position.
7. Measure the distance between the center of the barrel opening and the center of the shift linkage stud (5, **Figure 27**). Record the measurement for future reference.
8. Grasp the cable barrel and plastic cable end. Lightly push the cable end toward the cable barrel to remove any slack in the cable. Maintain light pressure on the cable end during the cable barrel adjustments.
9. Rotate the shift cable barrel (4, **Figure 27**) until the distance from the center of the barrel to the center of the opening in the plastic cable end (3) is equal to the distance recorded in Step 7.
10. Rotate the cable barrel three complete turns away from the cable end. This should increase the distance from the center of the barrel to the center of the opening in the cable end. This provides a slight pre-load towards reverse

gear and reduces the chance of unintentional shifting into forward gear.

11. Fit the opening in the plastic cable end over the shift linkage stud. Secure the cable end with the washer and locknut. Tighten the nut then back it off enough to allow the washer to rotate on the stud. Do not over-tighten the nut. Doing so will cause the cable to bind and increase shifting effort.

12. Insert the cable barrel into the opening. If necessary rotate the cable barrel slightly to align with the opening.

13. Pivot the cable retainer until it snaps over the post.

14. Check for proper adjustment as follows:

   a. Place the remote control lever in the FORWARD gear position while rotating the propeller counterclockwise. Correct adjustment results in no counterclockwise rotation as forward is selected.
   b. Have an assistant place the remote control lever in the NEUTRAL gear position. Correct adjustment results in free propeller rotation in either direction as neutral gear is selected.
   c. Have an assistant place the remote control lever in the REVERSE gear position while rotating the propeller in the clockwise direction. Correct adjustment results in no clockwise rotation as reverse gear is selected.

15. Readjust the shift linkage if incorrect clutch engagement or disengagement is evident.

16. Connect the battery cable. Check for correct and predictable shift selection when the engine is started. Correct faulty adjustments before operating the engine.

225 hp Model

1. Disconnect the negative battery cable to prevent accidental starting.

2. Loosen the hex screw, then pivot the clamp plate (**Figure 26**) away from the cable barrels.

3. Lift the throttle cable barrel out of the recess. The shift cable is on the starboard side. The throttle cable is on the port side.

4. Remove the locking clip, then lift the plastic cable end off of the shift linkage post (A, **Figure 28**).

5. Move the shift linkage post until the center aligns with the marking on the bracket (B, **Figure 28**).

6. Grasp the cable barrel and plastic cable end. Lightly push the cable end toward the cable barrel to remove any slack in the cable. Maintain light pressure on the cable end during the cable barrel adjustments.

7. Rotate the cable barrel until it can be inserted into the barrel recess and the cable end can be installed onto the linkage post without disturbing the post-to-marking alignment.

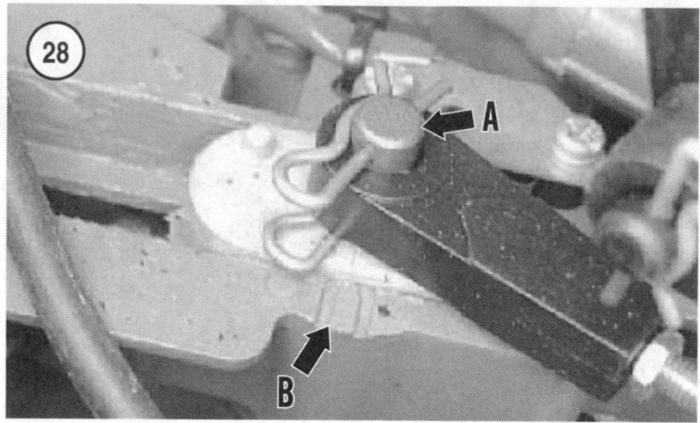

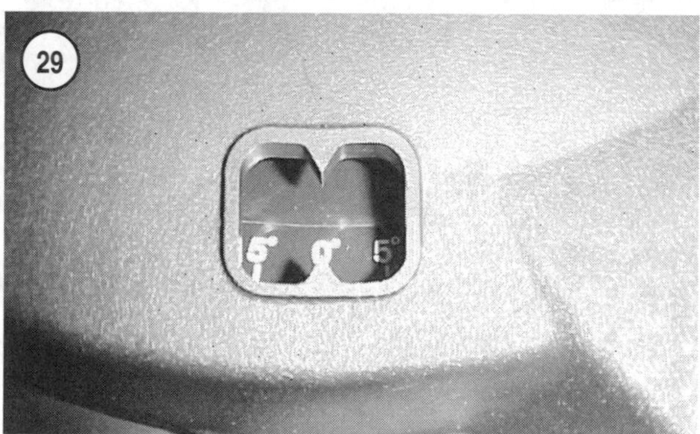

8. Fit the barrel into the recess and the cable end over the post. Check for proper post-to-marking alignment and correct if necessary.

9. Pivot the clamp plate over the barrels. Securely tighten the clamp plate screw. Install the locking clip onto the shift linkage post to secure the cable end.

10A. On standard rotation (RH) gearcase, check for proper adjustment as follows:

   a. Place the remote control lever in the FORWARD gear position while rotating the propeller counterclockwise. Correct adjustment results in no counterclockwise rotation as forward is selected.
   b. Have an assistant place the remote control lever in the neutral gear position. Correct adjustment results in free propeller rotation in either direction as NEUTRAL gear is selected.
   c. Have an assistant place the remote control lever in the REVERSE gear position while rotating the propeller in the clockwise direction. Correct adjustment results in no clockwise rotation as reverse gear is selected.

10B. On counter rotation (LH) gearcase, check for proper adjustment as follows:

   a. Place the remote control lever in the FORWARD gear position while rotating the propeller clock-

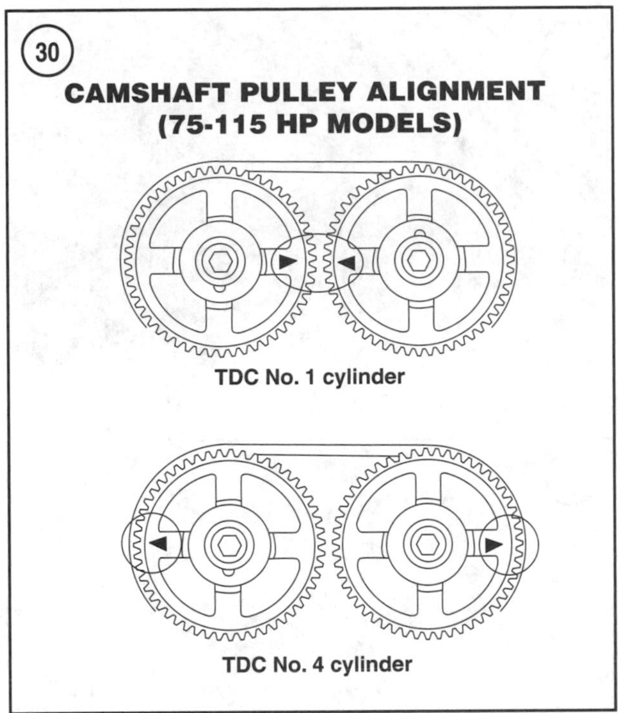

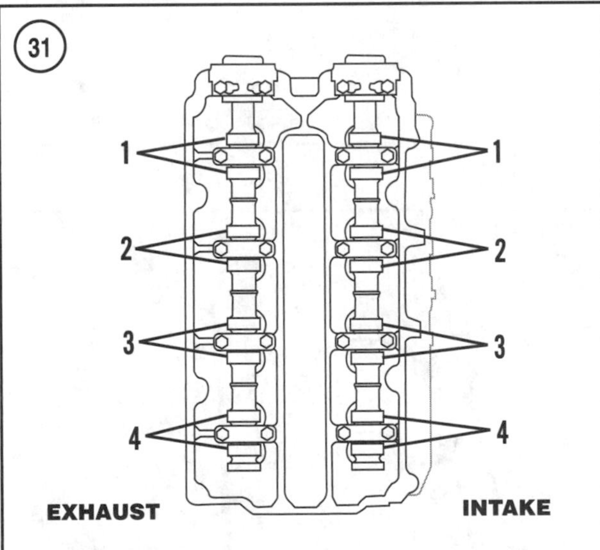

wise. Correct adjustment results in no clockwise rotation as forward is selected.

b. Have an assistant place the remote control lever in the NEUTRAL gear position. Correct adjustment results in free propeller rotation in either direction as neutral gear is selected.

c. Have an assistant place the remote control lever in the REVERSE gear position while rotating the propeller in the counterclockwise direction. Correct adjustment results in no counterclockwise rotation as reverse gear is selected.

11. Readjust the shift linkage if incorrect clutch engagement or disengagement is evident.

12. Connect the battery cable. Check for correct and predictable shift selection when the engine is started. Correct faulty adjustments before operating the engine.

4

VALVE ADJUSTMENT

75-115 hp Models

NOTE

The valve clearance measurements must be performed with the engine at normal room temperature. If necessary, place the engine in a room cooled or warmed to a normal room temperature of 68° F (20° C) for several hours prior to measuring the valve clearances.

1. Allow the engine to cool or warm to room temperature. This may take several hours if the engine has been recently started.

2. Disconnect the negative battery cables to prevent accidental starting.

3. Remove the spark plugs to allow easier crankshaft rotation. See *Spark plug removal* in Chapter Three.

4. Remove the flywheel cover and valve cover as described in Chapter Seven.

5. Place the crankshaft and camshaft at top dead center (TDC) for the No. 1 (top) cylinder as follows:

   a. Rotate the flywheel clockwise and temporarily place the flywheel cover on the power head to allow use of the timing pointer.

   b. Continue rotating the flywheel until the *0* mark aligns with the pointer (**Figure 29**).

   c. Remove the flywheel cover.

6. Place the camshaft pulleys in the No. 1 TDC position as follows:

   a. Inspect the alignment of the marks on the camshaft pulleys (**Figure 30**). The marks should directly align with the camshafts at TDC for No. 1 cylinder.

   b. Rotate the flywheel exactly one revolution if the marks point in opposite directions (**Figure 30**). Rotate the flywheel just enough to correct camshaft mark alignment. Remove and reinstall the timing belt if unable to align the camshaft mark and the flywheel timing pointer at the same time. Refer to Chapter Seven for timing belt removal and installation instructions.

7. Refer to **Figure 31** and **Figure 32** to locate the following valve pads and camshaft lobes.

a. Both No. 1 intake valve pads and lobes.
b. Both No. 2 intake valve pads and lobes.
c. Both No. 1 exhaust valve pads and lobes.
d. Both No. 3 exhaust valve pads and lobes.

8. Measure the valve clearance (**Figure 33**) for the lobes and cams specified in Step 7 by inserting a feeler gauge between the valve pad and the camshaft lobe (**Figure 34**). The valve clearance equals the thickness of the feeler gauge that passes between the lobe and pad with a slight drag. Record each camshaft lobe-to-valve pad clearance.

9. Rotate the flywheel exactly one revolution until the camshaft pulley markings face in opposite directions (**Figure 30**). This places the crankshaft and camshafts in the No. 4 TDC position.

10. Refer to **Figure 31** and **Figure 32** to locate the following valve pads and camshaft lobes.

a. Both No. 3 intake valve pads and lobes.
b. Both No. 4 intake valve pads and lobes.
c. Both No. 2 exhaust valve pads and lobes.
d. Both No. 4 exhaust valve pads and lobes.

11. Measure the valve clearance (**Figure 33**) for the lobes and cams specified in Step 9 by inserting a feeler gauge between the valve pad and the camshaft lobe (**Figure 34**). The valve clearance equals the thickness of the feeler gauge that passes between the lobe and pad with a slight drag. Record each camshaft lobe-to-valve pad clearance.

12. Rotate the flywheel exactly one revolution clockwise to place the engine in the No. 1 cylinder TDC position.

13. Compare the measured valve clearances with the specifications provided in **Table 5**. If any of the clearances are incorrect, change the valve pad thickness for that location. Instructions follow:

a. Remove the camshaft and pulleys as described in Chapter Seven.
b. Using the notch (**Figure 35**) for access, carefully remove the valve pad requiring a change.
c. Using an outside micrometer, measure the thickness of the valve pad near the outer edge (**Figure 36**).
d. Select a pad of the thickness required to correct the clearance. Pads are available in varying thicknesses from a Mercury or Mariner dealership. Install a thicker pad to decrease or thinner pad to increase the valve clearance.
e. Perform these steps for each valve with an incorrect clearance.
f. Install the camshafts and pulleys as described in Chapter Seven.

14. Install the flywheel cover and valve cover as described in Chapter Seven.

15. Install the spark plug as described in Chapter Three. See *Spark plug installation*.

16. Connect the battery cable.

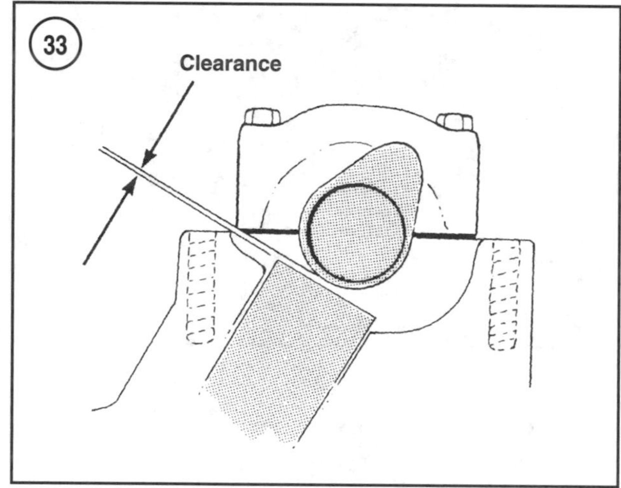

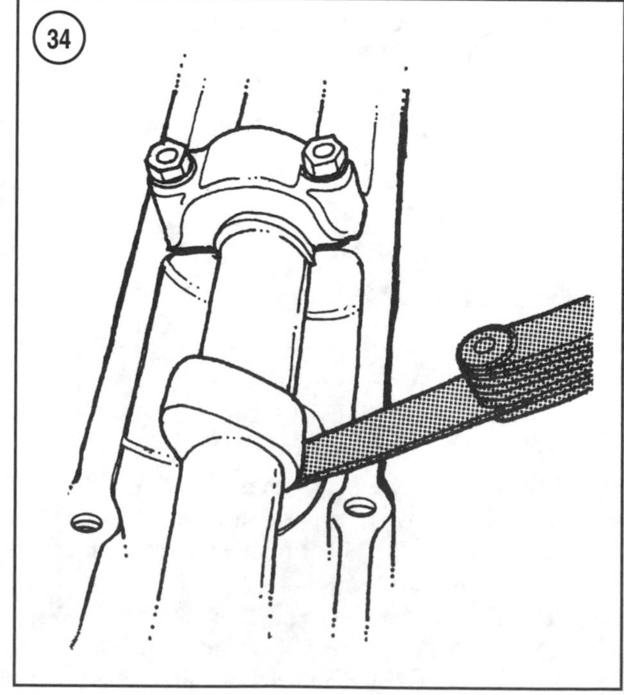

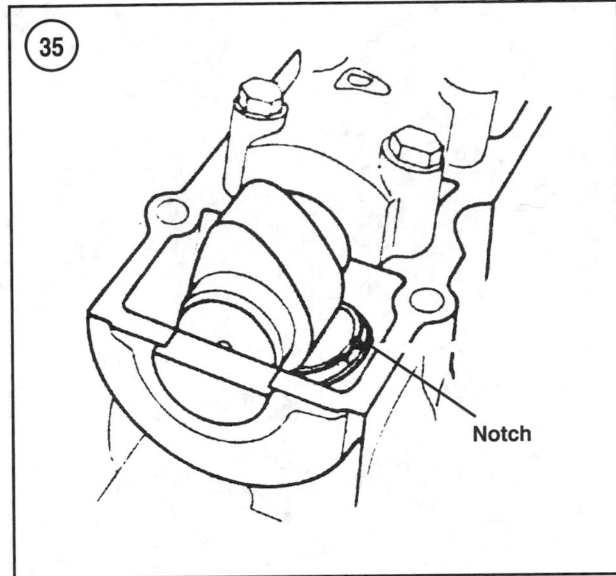

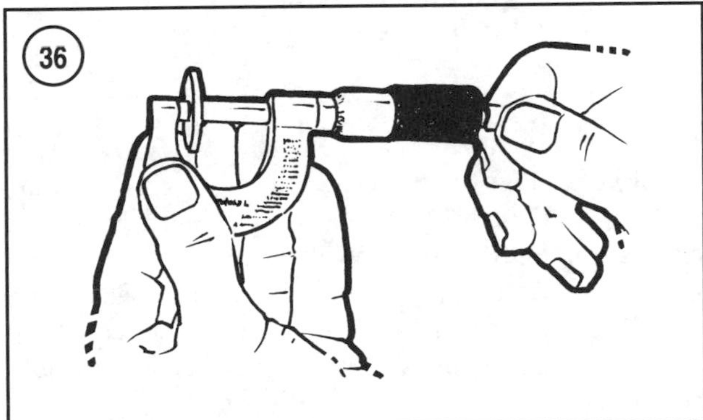

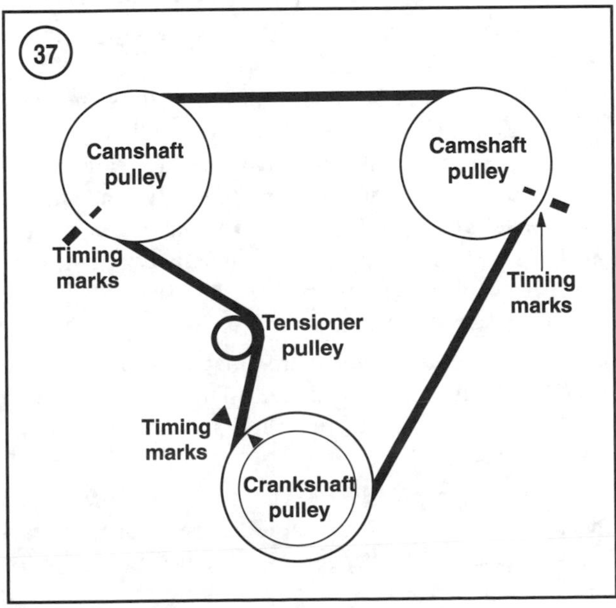

225 hp Model

NOTE

The valve clearance measurements must be performed with the engine at normal room temperature. If necessary, place the engine in a room cooled or warmed to 68° F (20° C) for several hours before measuring the valve clearances.

1. Allow the engine to cool or warm to room temperature. This may take several hours if the engine has been recently started.
2. Disconnect the negative battery cables to prevent accidental starting.
3. Remove the spark plugs to allow easier crankshaft rotation. See *Spark plug removal* in Chapter Three.
4. Remove the flywheel cover and valve covers as described in Chapter Seven.
5. Rotate the flywheel clockwise until the top dead center (TDC) marking on the flywheel aligns with the timing pointer (**Figure 29**).
6. Place the camshaft pulleys in the No. 1 cylinder TDC position as follows:
   a. Inspect the alignment of the cast in marks on the camshaft pulleys with the marks on the cylinder heads (**Figure 37**). The marks should align if the camshafts are at TDC for the No. 1 cylinder.
   b. Rotate the flywheel exactly one revolution if the camshaft marks are 180° from the cylinder head marks. Rotate the flywheel just enough to correct camshaft mark alignment. Remove and reinstall the timing belt if unable to align the camshaft mark and the flywheel timing pointer at the same time. Refer to Chapter Seven for timing belt removal and installation instructions.
7. Refer to **Figure 38**. Locate the valve pads and camshaft lobes (**Figure 32**) for the No. 4 cylinder intake and exhaust valves. Measure the valve clearance (**Figure 33**) by inserting feeler gauges between the valve pad and the camshaft lobe (**Figure 34**). The valve clearance equals the thickness of the feeler gauge that passes between the lobe and pad with a slight drag. Record each camshaft lobe-to-valve pad clearance.
8. Rotate the flywheel approximately 120° until the *2TDC* marking on the flywheel aligns with the timing pointer.
9. Refer to **Figure 38**. Locate the valve pads and camshaft lobes (**Figure 32**) for the No. 5 cylinder intake and exhaust valves. Measure the valve clearance (**Figure 33**) by inserting feeler gauges between the valve pad and the camshaft lobe (**Figure 34**). The valve clearance equals the thickness of the feeler gauge that passes between the lobe

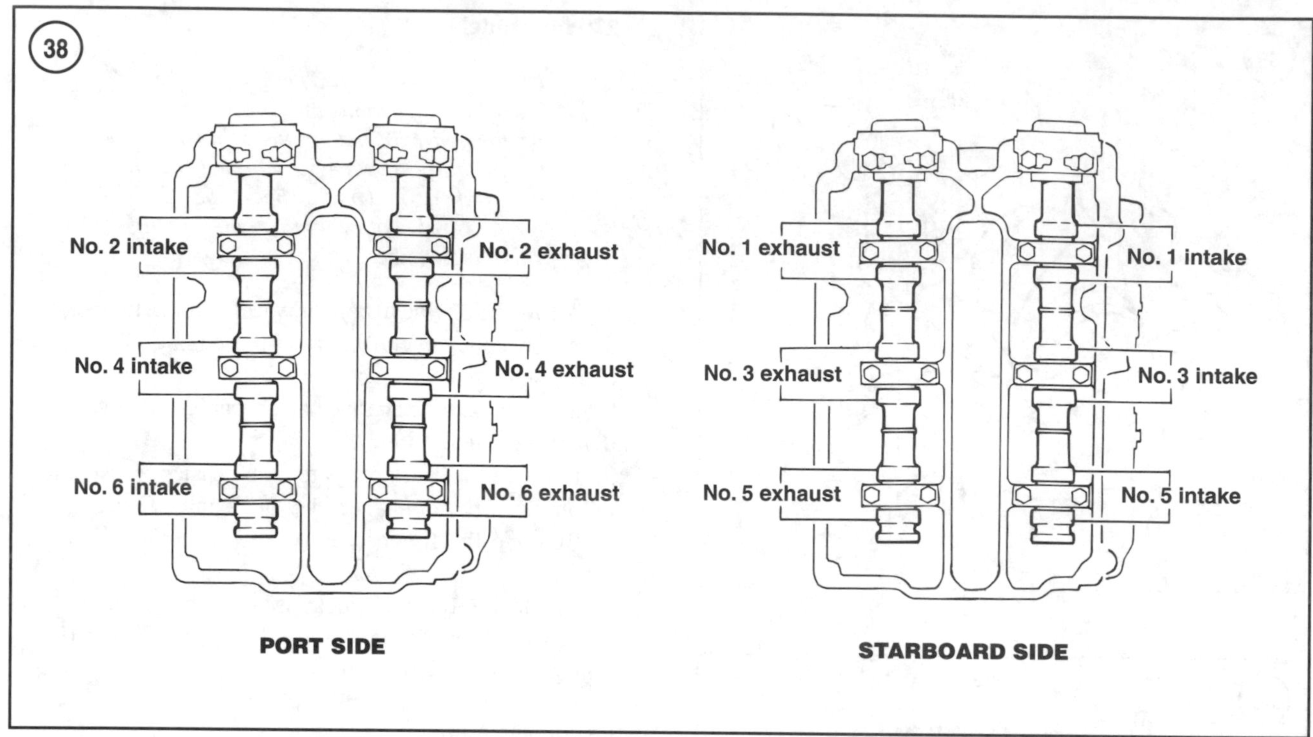

and pad with a slight drag. Record each camshaft lobe-to-valve pad clearance.

10. Rotate the flywheel approximately 120° until the *3TDC* marking on the flywheel aligns with the timing pointer.

11. Refer to **Figure 38**. Locate the valve pads and camshaft lobes (**Figure 32**) for the No. 6 cylinder intake and exhaust valves. Measure the valve clearance (**Figure 33**) by inserting feeler gauges between the valve pad and the camshaft lobe (**Figure 34**). The valve clearance equals the thickness of the feeler gauge that passes between the lobe and pad with a slight drag. Record each camshaft lobe-to-valve pad clearance.

12. Rotate the flywheel approximately 120° and until the *1TDC* marking on the flywheel aligns with the timing pointer.

13. Refer to **Figure 38**. Locate the valve pads and camshaft lobes (**Figure 32**) for the No. 1 cylinder intake and exhaust valves. Measure the valve clearance (**Figure 33**) by inserting feeler gauges between the valve pad and the camshaft lobe (**Figure 34**). The valve clearance equals the thickness of the feeler gauge that passes between the lobe and pad with a slight drag. Record each camshaft lobe-to-valve pad clearance.

14. Rotate the flywheel approximately 120° and until the *2TDC* marking on the flywheel aligns with the timing pointer.

15. Refer to **Figure 38**. Locate the valve pads and camshaft lobes (**Figure 32**) for the No. 2 cylinder intake and exhaust valves. Measure the valve clearance (**Figure 33**) by inserting feeler gauges between the valve pad and the camshaft lobe (**Figure 34**). The valve clearance equals the thickness of the feeler gauge that passes between the lobe and pad with a slight drag. Record each camshaft lobe-to-valve pad clearance.

16. Rotate the flywheel approximately 120° until the *3TDC* marking on the flywheel aligns with the timing pointer.

17. Refer to **Figure 38**. Locate the valve pads and camshaft lobes (**Figure 32**) for the No. 3 cylinder intake and exhaust valves. Measure the valve clearance (**Figure 33**) by inserting feeler gauges between the valve pad and the camshaft lobe (**Figure 34**). The valve clearance equals the thickness of the feeler gauge that passes between the lobe and pad with a slight drag. Record each camshaft lobe-to-valve pad clearance.

18. Rotate the flywheel approximately 120° until the *1TDC* marking on the flywheel aligns with the timing pointer. This returns the crankshaft and camshafts to the No. 1 cylinder TDC position.

19. Compare the measured valve clearances with the specifications provided in **Table 5**. If any of the clearances are incorrect, change the valve pad thickness for that location. Instructions follow:

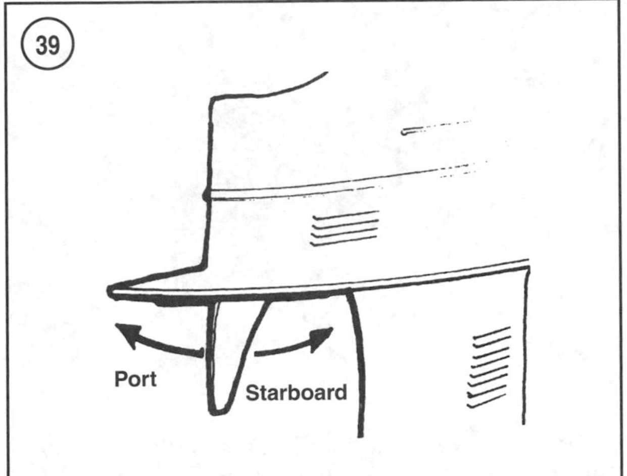

a. Remove the camshaft and pulleys as described in Chapter Seven.
b. Using the notch (**Figure 35**) for access, carefully remove the valve pad requiring a change.
c. Using an outside micrometer, measure the thickness of the valve pad near the outer edge (**Figure 36**).
d. Select a pad of the thickness required to correct the clearance. Pads are available in varying thickness from a Mercury or Mariner dealership. Install a thicker pad to decrease or thinner pad to increase the valve clearance.
e. Perform these steps for each valve with an incorrect clearance.
f. Install the camshafts and pulleys as described in Chapter Seven.

20. Install the flywheel cover and valve covers as described in Chapter Seven.
21. Install the spark plugs as described in Chapter Three. See *Spark plug installation*.
22. Connect the battery cable.

TRIM TAB ADJUSTMENT

Water test the boat with an average load onboard. When running at planing speed, note if the boat tends to steer in one direction or the other. If so, the steering effort can be neutralized by adjusting the trim tab.

1. Disconnect the negative battery cable to prevent accidental starting.
2. Loosen but do not remove the trim tab attaching bolt. Refer to Chapter Three to locate and access the bolt. See *Trim tab replacement*.
3. If the engine steers or pulls in the port direction, pivot the rear trailing edge of the trim tab slightly toward the port side (**Figure 39**) . If the engine steers or pulls in the starboard direction, pivot the rear trailing edge of the trim tab slightly toward the starboard side (**Figure 39**).
4. Hold the trim tab in position and tighten the trim tab bolt as described in Chapter Three. See *Trim tab replacement*.
5. Connect the battery cable.
6. Additional adjustment may be required to further reduce steering pull.

TRIM POSITION SENDER ADJUSTMENT

NOTE

Gauge resistance, battery voltage, wire length and sender resistance may prevent the gauge from reaching both the fully up and down readings. Synchronize the sender to the fully down position only.

1. Observe the trim gauge while trimming the engine to the fully down position. The gauge should indicate that the engine is fully DOWN just as the engine reaches the fully down position.
2. To adjust the trim position sender, tilt the engine to the fully UP/OUT position. Engage the tilt lock lever and use blocks or an overhead cable to prevent the engine from falling.
3. Turn the ignition key switch to the ON or RUN position. Do not start the engine. To prevent accidental starting, pull the lanyard cord until it trips the lanyard safety switch.

4A. On 75-115 hp models, adjust the sender as follows:

a. Loosen both trim sender screws until the sender (**Figure 40**) can be rotated on the mount. Do not remove the mounting screws.
b. Have an assistant observe the gauge. Rotate the sender body in the direction required for proper gauge readings. Clockwise rotation increases the gauge reading and counterclockwise rotation decreases the gauge reading.

4

c. Tighten the two sender mounting screws to 70 in.-lb. (7.9 N•m).

4B. On 225 hp models, adjust the sender as follows:

a. Loosen both trim sender mounting screws (**Figure 41**). Do not remove the mounting screws.

b. Pivot the sender arm away from the swivel bracket to prevent it from moving the sender while the screws are loose. Hold the arm away from the bracket until the screws are re-tightened.

c. Have an assistant observe the gauge. Rotate the sender body in the direction required for proper gauge readings. Clockwise rotation increases the gauge reading and counterclockwise rotation decreases the gauge reading.

d. Tighten the two sender mounting screws to 71 in.-lb. (8.0 N•m).

e. Release the sender arm.

5. Remove the supports then disengage the tilt lock lever.

6. Observe the trim gauge while trimming the engine to the fully down position. Repeat the adjustment if necessary.

7. Turn the ignition key switch to the OFF or STOP position. Connect the lanyard cord onto the lanyard safety switch.

Table 1 SYNCHRONIZATION AND ADJUSTMENT TORQUE SPECIFICATIONS

Fastener	in.-lb.	ft.-lb.	N•m
Synchronization port plugs			
75-115 hp models	70	–	7.9
225 hp models	71	–	8.0
Throttle body lever screw	35	–	4.0
Throttle link nut			
225 hp models	35	–	4.0
Throttle position sensor			
75 and 90 hp models	15	–	1.7
115 hp models	43	–	4.9
225 hp models	44	–	5.0
Trim position sender			
75-115 hp models	70	–	7.9
225 hp models	71	–	8.0

Table 2 IDLE SPEED SPECIFICATIONS

Model	Specification (rpm)
75 and 90 hp models	
Neutral gear	825-875
Forward gear	775-800
115 hp models	
Neutral gear	700-800
225 hp models	
Neutral gear	650-750

Table 3 MAXIMUM RECOMMENDED ENGINE SPEED SPECIFICATIONS

Model	Maximum recommended speed (rpm)
75 hp models	4500-5500
90 hp models	5000-6000
115 hp models	5000-6000
225 hp models	5000-6000

Table 4 IGNITION TIMING SPECIFICATIONS

Model	Timing specification
75 and 90 hp models	
At idle speed	5° ATDC
At maximum recommended engine speed	18° BTDC
115 hp models	
At idle speed	5° ATDC
At maximum recommended engine speed	18° BTDC
225 hp models	
At idle speed	0° TDC
At maximum recommended engine speed	24° BTDC

Table 5 VALVE CLEARANCE SPECIFICATIONS

Model	Specification
All models	
Intake valve	0.007-0.009 in. (0.17-0.23 mm)
Exhaust valve	0.012-0.014 in. (0.31-0.37 mm)

Chapter Five

Fuel System

This chapter covers removal, repair and installation of all fuel system components.

Before removal and disassembly of any fuel system component, refer to *Fuel System Service* in this chapter for information needed to perform a safe, reliable and effective repair.

Torque specifications are listed in **Table 1** at the end of this chapter. Torque specifications not listed in **Table 1** are in the *Quick Reference Data* at the beginning of this manual.

WARNING

Use caution when working with the fuel system. Never smoke around fuel or fuel vapors. Make sure no flame or source of ignition is present in the work area. Flame or sparks can ignite fuel or vapor resulting in a fire or explosion.

FUEL SYSTEM SERVICE

Always use gloves and eye protection when working with the fuel system. Take all necessary precautions against fire or explosion. To prevent arcing or accidental starting, always disconnect the negative battery cable *before* servicing any outboard.

Pay close attention when removing and installing components especially carburetors to avoid installing them in the wrong location during assembly.

Capture fuel from disconnected hoses or fittings using a small container or clean shop towel. Try to use a clear container as it allows a visual inspection of the fuel. Clean the fuel tank and all other fuel delivery components if water or other contamination is noted in the fuel.

Drain all fuel from the carburetors using the float bowl drain screws (**Figure 1**). On EFI models, drain fuel from the vapor separator tank using the drain screw opening (**Figure 2**) at the bottom of the tank. Refer to *Carburetor* or *Vapor Separator Tank* for specific instructions.

Inspect all hoses for leakage or deterioration when servicing the fuel system. Damaged fuel hoses pose a safety hazard. In addition, pieces of deteriorated or damaged hoses can break free and block fuel passages in the system. Refer to *Fuel Hoses* in this chapter.

On carburetor equipped engines (75 and 90 hp models), disassemble and assemble *one* carburetor at a time. Some models have fuel and air jet sizes calibrated to the cylinder. Refer to *Carburetor* in this chapter for additional instructions.

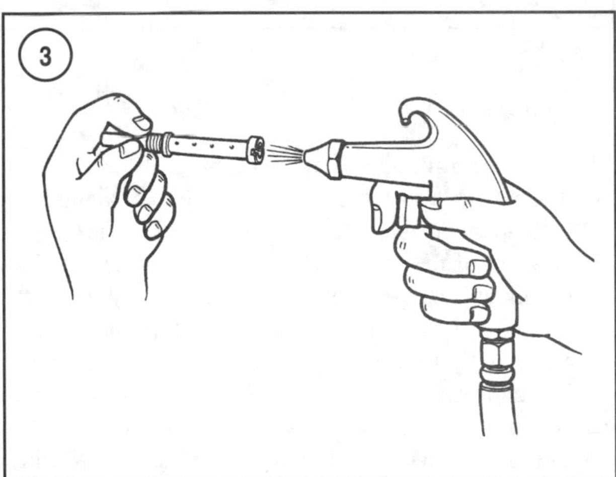

Gaskets, Seals and O-rings

To ensure a safe and reliable repair use only factory recommended replacement parts. Some commonly available seals or O-rings are not suitable for contact with fuel.

To avoid potential fuel or air leakage, replace all seals and O-rings anytime a fuel system component is removed from the engine. Consider reusing a seal or O-ring only if a replacement in not available and the original is found to be in excellent condition.

To help avoid the potential for contamination during a lengthy down time, have the required gasket or repair kit on hand prior to removal and disassembly of the component(s).

Fuel System Component Cleaning

The most important step in carburetor, fuel pump or vapor separator tank repair is the cleaning process. Use only solvents suitable for use on carburetors. Some cleaning agents can damage fuel system components. Aerosal carburetor cleaners are available at most auto parts stores. They effectively remove most stubborn deposits. Avoid using any solvents not suitable for aluminum.

Remove all plastics or rubber components from the assembly before cleaning them with solvent. Gently scrape away gasket material with a scraper. Never scrape away any metal from the component. Use a stiff cleaning brush and solvent to remove deposits from the carburetor bowl. Never use a wire brush as the sealing surfaces can quickly become damaged. Blow out all passages and orifices with compressed air (**Figure 3**). A piece of straw from a broom works well to clean small passages. Never use stiff wire for this purpose as the wire may enlarge the size of the passage, altering the fuel system calibration. Allow components to soak in the solvent for several hours if the deposits are particularly difficult to remove.

Use care and patience when removing fuel jets and other threaded or pressed in components. Clean the passage without removing the jet if it cannot be removed without causing damage. Carburetor fuel jets are easily damaged.

One small particle in the carburetor or fuel injection system can compromise the cleaning process. Continue to clean until *all* deposits and debris are removed.

Fuel System Component Inspection

Place all components on a clean surface as they are removed from the carburetor or vapor separator tank and cleaned. Arrange these components in a manner consistent with the provided illustrations. This saves time and helps ensure the parts are installed in the correct location.

Inspect the inlet needle for wear or deterioration (**Figure 4**). Replace the inlet needle unless the tip is perfectly cone shaped.

Inspect the inlet needle seat for grooved or damaged surfaces. Carburetor flooding is likely if a worn or faulty inlet needle or seat is used.

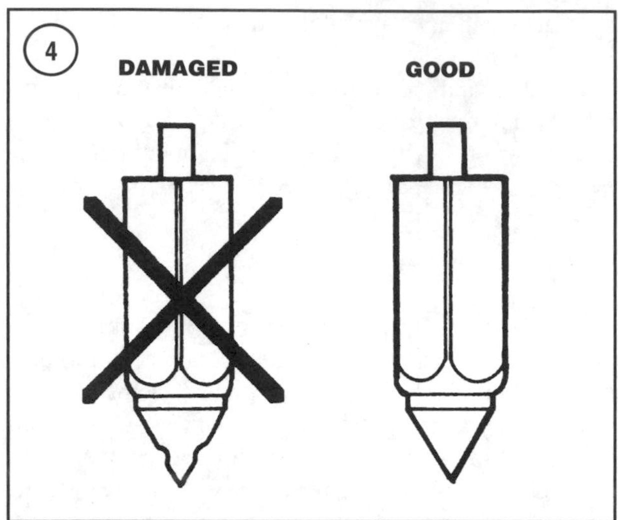

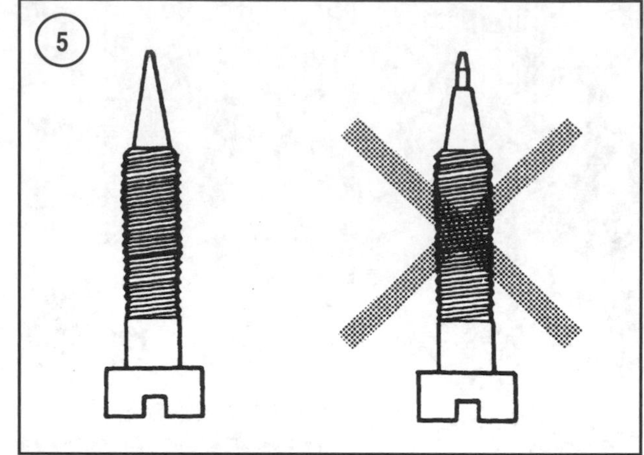

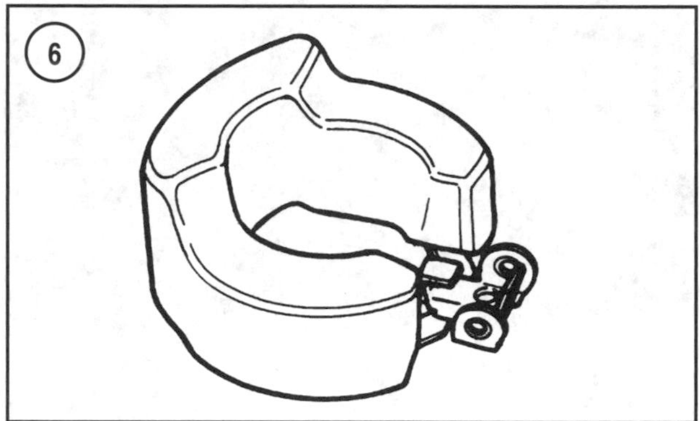

Inspect the tip of the pilot screw on carburetor equipped models (75 and 90 hp) for wear or damage (**Figure 5**). Damage to the tip usually occurs from improper seating of the screw during adjustment. In many instances the seat is also damaged. Damage to the screw or seat will cause rough idle or improper off-idle engine operation. Replace the screw or carburetor when worn or faulty components are noted.

Inspect the float (**Figure 6**, typical) for wear or damage. Some floats are made of a translucent material allowing visual detection of fuel within the float.

Push a thumbnail gently against the material on non-translucent floats. A leaking or saturated float is indicated if fuel appears at the thumbnail contact area. Replace the float if visibly damaged, leaking or saturated. Check the float for free movement while moving on the float pin. Replace the float if it does not move freely.

Check and correct float level settings (**Figure 7**) prior to assembling the carburetor or vapor separator tank. Use an accurate ruler or a caliper with depth reading capability. Set the float *exactly* as specified to help ensure proper carburetor or vapor separator tank operation. Specific instructions are provided in the assembly instructions.

When servicing the carburetor or throttle body, move the throttle lever (**Figure 8**, typical) from closed to wide-open throttle. Remove the throttle plate and repeat this step if binding or rough operation is noted. Continued binding indicates a bent throttle shaft. If free movement is noted with the plate removed, an improperly aligned or damaged throttle plate is evident. Replace the throttle shaft, carburetor or throttle body as necessary to eliminate binding. Apply a suitable thread locking compound and stake all throttle plate retaining screws to prevent loosening.

Fuel Jet Inspection

Fuel jets (**Figure 9**, typical) meter the fuel flow through various passages in the carburetor. The jets, along with other components allow the carburetor to deliver the precise amount of fuel needed for the engine. Fuel jet sizes vary by model and carburetor location on the engine. Fuel jets normally have a number stamped on the side or end. Note the fuel jet number and location in the carburetor prior to removal. Always reinstall the fuel jets and other carburetor components to the correct location.

Purchase replacement jets at a Mercury or Mariner dealership or a carburetor specialty shop. For proper engine operation, replacement jets must have the same size and shape of opening as the original fuel jets. Improper engine operation, increased exhaust emissions or potentially serious power head damage can result from using incorrect or damaged fuel jets.

Using the engine at an elevation higher than 5000 ft. (1524 m) may require alternate fuel jets to achieve optimal engine operation. If necessary, contact a Mercury or Mariner dealership in the area with a similar elevation for recommended jet changes.

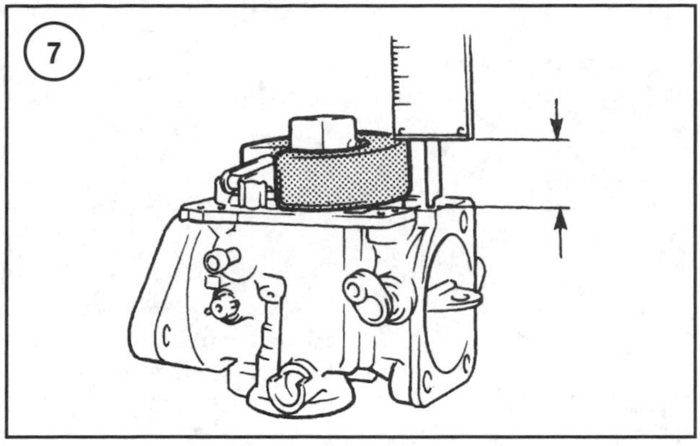

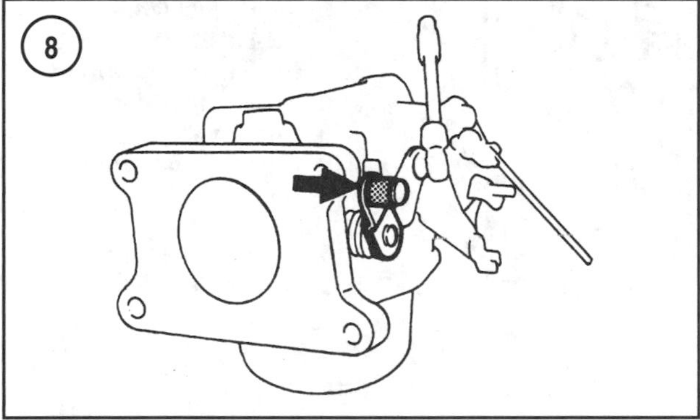

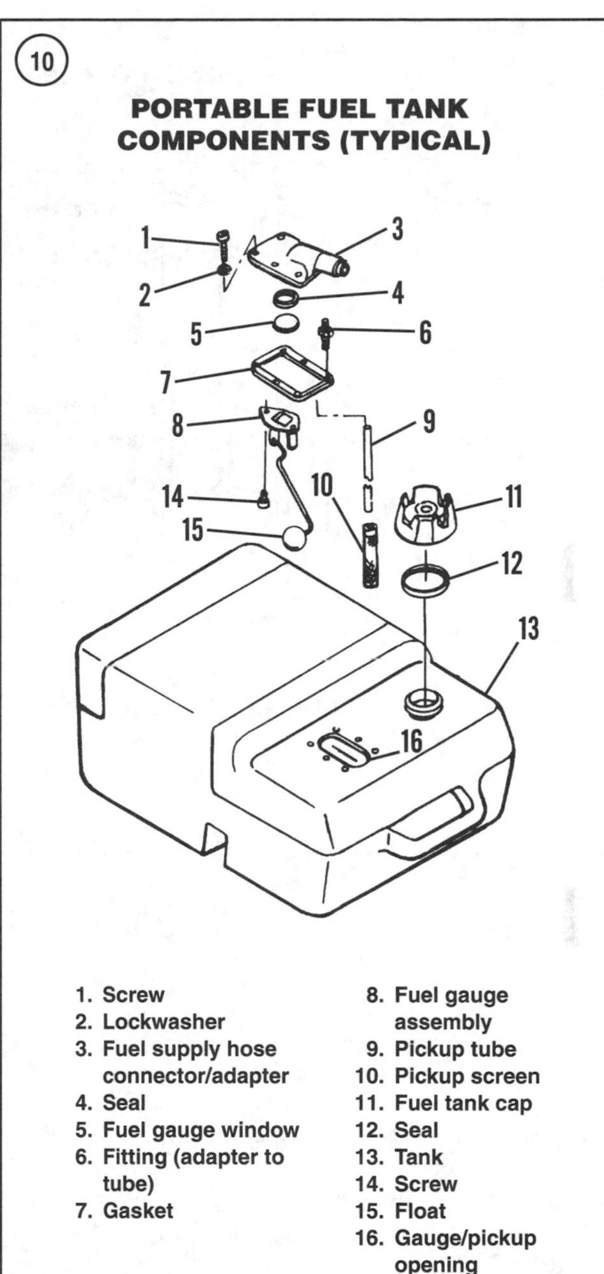

PORTABLE FUEL TANK COMPONENTS (TYPICAL)

1. Screw
2. Lockwasher
3. Fuel supply hose connector/adapter
4. Seal
5. Fuel gauge window
6. Fitting (adapter to tube)
7. Gasket
8. Fuel gauge assembly
9. Pickup tube
10. Pickup screen
11. Fuel tank cap
12. Seal
13. Tank
14. Screw
15. Float
16. Gauge/pickup opening

FUEL TANK CLEANING AND INSPECTION

WARNING
Fuel leakage can lead to fire and explosion. Check for and correct fuel leaks after any repair to the fuel system.

Two types of fuel tanks are used with Mercury and Mariner four stroke outboards. They include portable fuel tanks (**Figure 10**, typical) and built-in fuel tanks.

Refer to a marine repair shop or marine dealership if parts are needed for fuel tanks.

Built-in fuel tanks are usually located slightly forward of the boat transom. On some boats the fuel tank is mounted further forward or under the deck or floor. Fortunately, tank access panels are installed in most boats. These panels allow access to fuel line fittings and the fuel level sender assembly. Removal of upholstery or major boat structures may be required if the tank requires removal. Proper long term storage and fuel system inspection are more important with built in fuel tanks. Long term

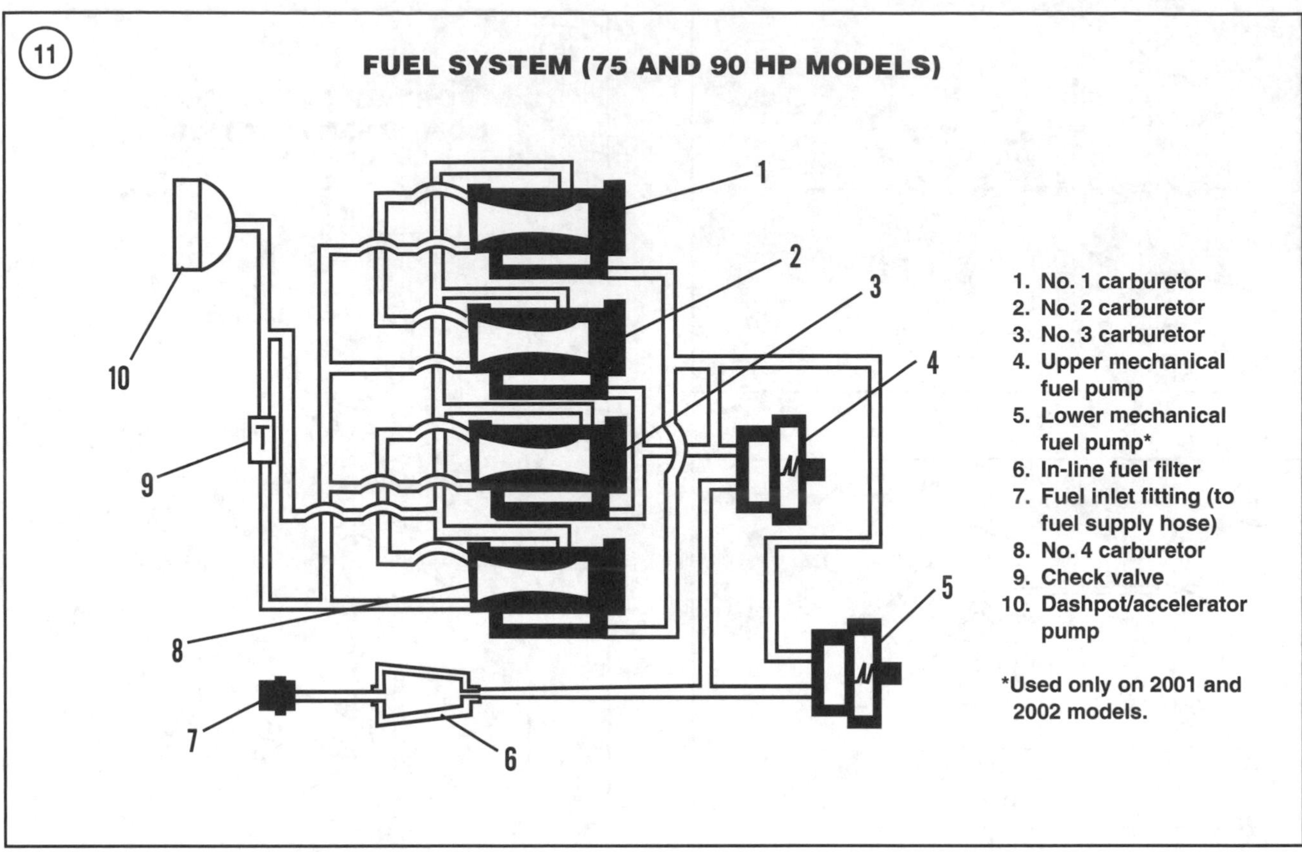

storage and fuel system inspection are described in Chapter Three.

Portable Fuel Tank

Portable remote fuel tanks require periodic cleaning and inspection. Inspect the remainder of the fuel system for potential contamination if water is found in the tank. The tank used on the engine may differ in appearance and component usage from the illustration (**Figure 10**).

1. Remove the fuel tank cap and seal (11 and 12, **Figure 10**) from the fuel tank. Carefully pour the fuel from the tank into a suitable container.
2. Remove the screws (1, **Figure 10**) retaining the connector/adapter (3) to the fuel tank. Carefully lift the fuel gauge and float (8 and 15, **Figure 10**) from the tank. Never force the assembly as damage may occur. Rotate or tilt the assembly as required for removal. Remove and discard the gasket (7, **Figure 10**) located between the connector/adapter and fuel tank.
3. Check for free movement of the float arm on the fuel gauge assembly (8, **Figure 10**). Replace the assembly if binding cannot be corrected by bending the float arm into the correct position.
4. Inspect the float (15, **Figure 10**). Replace the float if any physical damage is noted or it appears to be saturated with fuel.
5. Pull the screen and pickup tube (9 and 10, **Figure 10**) from the fitting (6). Clean the tube and screen using a suitable solvent. Dry them with compressed air. Inspect the screen for torn or damaged surfaces. Inspect the pickup tube for cracks or deterioration. Replace the screen or tube if defects are noted.
6. Remove the fitting (6, **Figure 10**) from the connector/adapter (3). Carefully push the window and seal (4 and 5, **Figure 10**) from the connector/adapter. Clean the fitting and all passages of the connector/adapter using a suitable solvent.
7. Add a small amount of solvent to the fuel tank. Block the gauge/pickup opening (16, **Figure 10**) with a shop towel. Install the fuel tank cap. Shake the tank to distribute the solvent throughout the tank. Empty the solvent and dry the tank with compressed air.
8. Inspect the internal and external tank surfaces. Repeat Step 7 if debris remains in the tank. Inspect the tank for cracks, damage or softened surfaces. Replace the tank if any defects are noted or leakage is suspected.

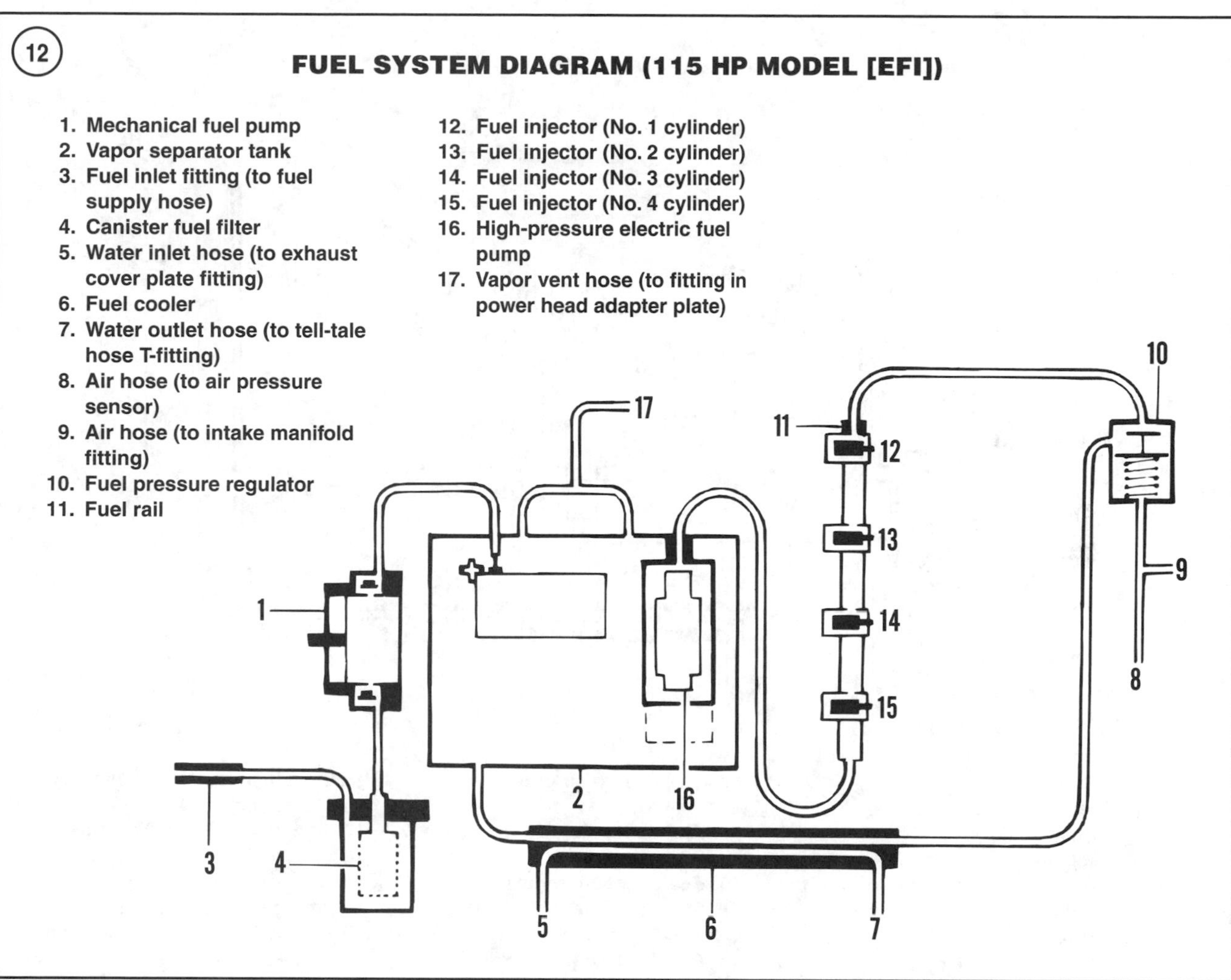

9. Assembly is the reverse of disassembly. Note the following:
   a. Clean all debris from the gasket surfaces.
   b. Install a new gasket (7, **Figure 10**) between the connector/adapter and the fuel tank.
   c. Install a new seal (4, **Figure 10**) between the window and the connector/adapter.
   d. Do not bend the fuel gauge rod during installation into the fuel tank.
10. Check for and correct any fuel leakage.

Built-In Fuel Tanks

The only components that can be serviced without major disassembly of the boat are the fuel pickup, fuel level sender and antisiphon device. These components are available from most marine dealerships and marine supply stores. Removal and inspection instructions vary by the model and brand of fuel tank. Contact the tank manufacturer or boat manufacturer for specific instructions. Correct any fuel leakage before filling the tank or operating the engine.

FUEL HOSE INSPECTION AND REPLACEMENT

Refer to **Figures 11-13** for fuel system diagrams and hose connection points.

Use only Mercury or Mariner replacement hoses or hoses that meet US Coast Guard requirements for marine applications. Never install a fuel hose with a smaller diameter than the original hose.

Inspect all fuel hoses and replace hoses that are sticky, spongy, hard and brittle, or have surface cracks. Replace hoses that are split on the ends. Do not cut off the split end and reconnect the hose. The hose will split again and

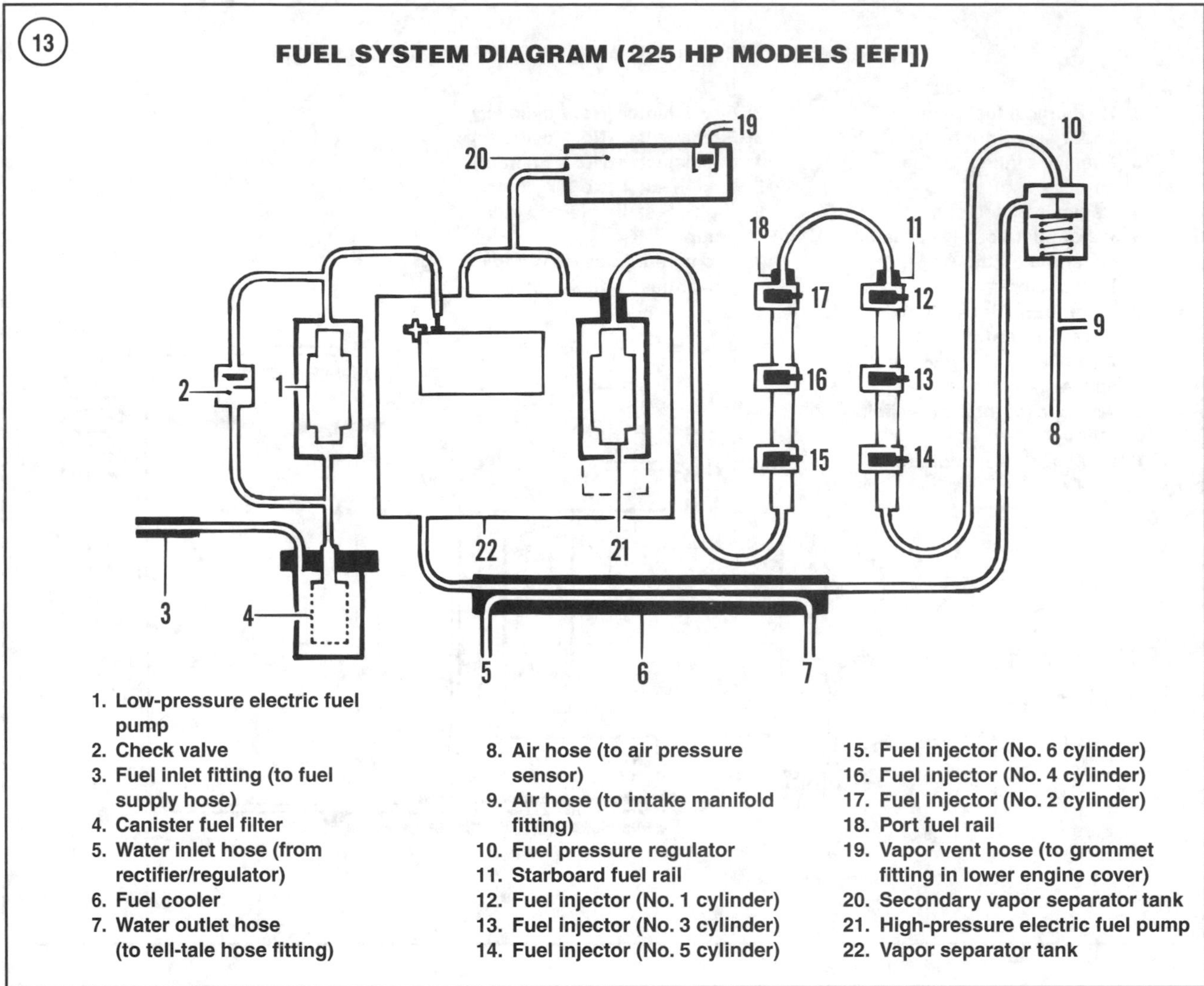

1. Low-pressure electric fuel pump
2. Check valve
3. Fuel inlet fitting (to fuel supply hose)
4. Canister fuel filter
5. Water inlet hose (from rectifier/regulator)
6. Fuel cooler
7. Water outlet hose (to tell-tale hose fitting)
8. Air hose (to air pressure sensor)
9. Air hose (to intake manifold fitting)
10. Fuel pressure regulator
11. Starboard fuel rail
12. Fuel injector (No. 1 cylinder)
13. Fuel injector (No. 3 cylinder)
14. Fuel injector (No. 5 cylinder)
15. Fuel injector (No. 6 cylinder)
16. Fuel injector (No. 4 cylinder)
17. Fuel injector (No. 2 cylinder)
18. Port fuel rail
19. Vapor vent hose (to grommet fitting in lower engine cover)
20. Secondary vapor separator tank
21. High-pressure electric fuel pump
22. Vapor separator tank

cause a potentially dangerous fuel leak. To avoid hose failure or interference with other components, never install a shorter or longer hose than the original. When one fuel hose on the engine requires replacement others likely have similar defects. Replace all fuel hoses on the engine to ensure a reliable repair.

FUEL HOSE CONNECTORS REPLACEMENT

WARNING
Fuel leakage can lead to fire or explosion. Correct fuel leakage after any repair is made to the fuel system.

The clamps used to secure fuel hoses include the spring clamp (**Figure 14**), plastic locking clamp (**Figure 15**), and full-circle crimp clamp (**Figure 16**). Spring clamps can be reused if in good condition. Plastic locking and full-circle crimp clamps must be replaced if removed. Always replace clamps with the same type. The wrong clamp can cause fuel leakage or physical interference with other components.

CAUTION
Do not replace spring, plastic locking fuel-circle hose clamps with screw type hose clamps. Screw clamps may loosen or damage the fuel hoses and cause dangerous fuel leakage.

Spring Clamps

Remove spring clamps (**Figure 14**) by squeezing the bent ends together with pliers while carefully moving the clamp away from the fitting. Replace the clamp if corroded, bent, deformed or if it has lost spring tension.

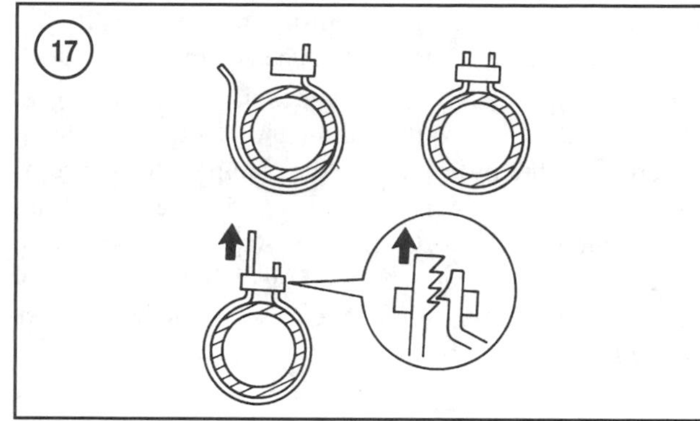

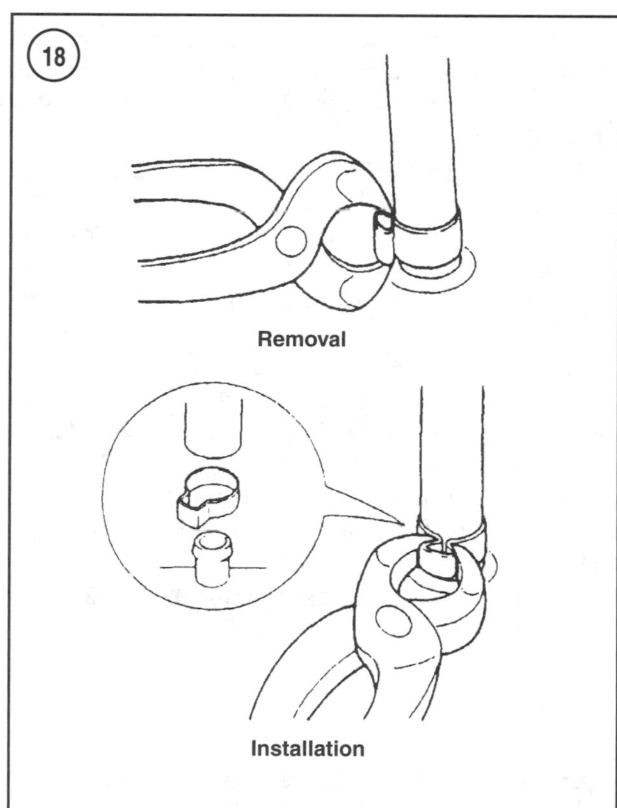

Plastic Locking Clamps

The plastic locking clamp (**Figure 15**) must be cut to be removed. Some plastic tie clamps are not suitable for fuel system applications and may fail. Use only Mercury or Mariner parts for hose clamps. After placing the clamp into position, pull the end through the clamp (**Figure 17**) until the hose is securely fastened and will not rotate on the fitting. Avoid pulling the clamp too tight as the clamp may be damaged, then loosen or fail. Cut any excess length of clamp with side cutters or scissors.

Full-Circle Crimp Clamps

Full-circle crimp clamps (**Figure 16**) must be cut to be removed. Use only the manufacturer recommended crimping pliers (Mercury part No 91-803146T or equivalent) to tighten the clamp. Using other types of pliers may damage the hose or clamp, and result in over-or under-tightening.

To remove the clamp, grip the clamp at the crimped section with a sharp side cutter or nipper as shown in **Figure 18**. Squeeze and pull lightly on the crimp until the clamp loosens. Remove the hose from the fitting then slip the clamp from the end. Discard the used clamp.

To install the clamp, slip the new clamp over the hose. Fit the hose fully onto the fitting and position the clamp directly over the fitting. Crimp the clamp with the recommended crimping pliers as shown in **Figure 18**. Do not over-tighten the clamp. Over-tightening damages the hose and may cause the clamp to fail. Tug on the hose to verify a secure connection. Tighten the clamp if the hose moves on the fitting.

FUEL FILTER REPLACEMENT

With normal usage, debris and deposits form in the fuel system. Fuel filters capture these contaminants to prevent them from blocking small passages or damaging fuel system components.

Unless the filter is periodically inspected and replaced as needed, the blockage builds and fuel delivery to the engine decreases. The resulting lean fuel-to-air ratio will cause poor performance and possibly power head damage. Refer to Chapter Three to determine the filter replacement intervals.

This section describes replacement for in-line (**Figure 19**) and canister-type (**Figure 20**) fuel filters. These are the primary filters that require periodic inspection. Filters are sometimes incorporated into some fuel system components. Replacement for these types of filters is described in the replacement instructions for the applicable components.

Refer to the appropriate diagram (**Figures 11-13**) to determine the type of filters used.

In-Line Fuel Filter

An in-line fuel filter (**Figure 19**) is used on 75 and 90 hp models. The filter is located on the lower rear and starboard side of the power head. A protective sleeve covers the filter. The in-line filter is non-serviceable and must be replaced if contaminated.

1. Slide the protective sleeve toward the front of the engine to expose the filter.
2. Carefully cut the plastic locking clamps from the hoses at each end of the fuel filter. Do not inadvertently cut the fuel hose or filter fitting.
3. Use a flat blade screwdriver to push each hose off of the fuel filter fittings. Drain any residual fuel from the hoses. Promptly clean up any spilled fuel.
4. Note the arrow on the body of the replacement filter. Carefully slide each fuel hose fully over the filter fitting. Ensure the arrow on the filter body faces rearward, toward the hose leading to the fuel pump.
5. Install a new plastic locking clamp onto each fuel hose. Position the clamps directly over the filter fittings, then securely tighten the clamps.
6. Install the filter in the original location. Route the hoses away from any moving components.
7. Observe the fuel filter and other fuel system components for fuel leakage while pumping the primer bulb. Correct any fuel leakage before proceeding.
8. Slide the protective sleeve over the fuel hose and position it over the fuel filter.
9. Connect the battery cable.

Canister Fuel Filter

115 hp model

The filter is located on the rear of the power head. Replace the filter element if contaminated. Attempts to clean the element usually damage the filter surfaces.

Refer to **Figure 21**.

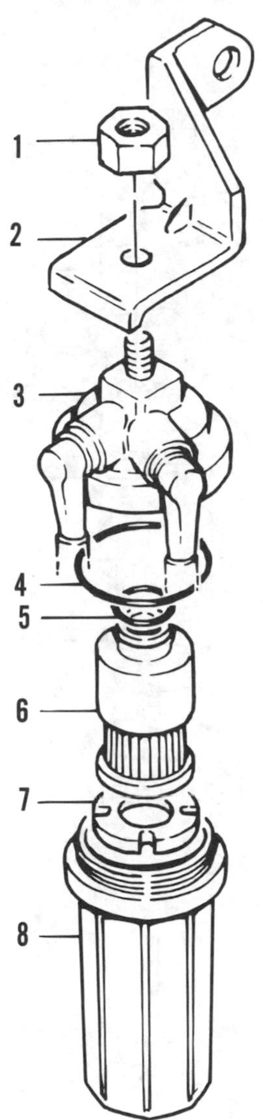

1. Use compressed air to blow all dirt and debris from the filter and surrounding areas.
2. Place a container or shop towel under the filter to capture any spilled fuel.
3. Grip the canister (8, **Figure 21**) with a shop towel. Fuel will spill during canister removal. Rotate the canister counterclockwise, as viewed from the bottom, until free from the filter body. Empty the canister into a suitable container.
4. Remove the float (7, **Figure 21**) from the canister.
5. Grip the filter element (6, **Figure 21**) and pull straight down to remove it from the filter body.
6. Remove the O-rings (4 and 5, **Figure 21**) from the filter body, filter element or canister. Inspect the O-rings for torn, flattened or deteriorated surfaces. Replace the O-rings if any defects are evident.
7. Use a suitable solvent to clean the float and canister. Dry the float and canister with compressed air.
8. Use compressed air to remove debris and residual fuel from the canister mating surface on the filter body.
9. Inspect the float for cracks, damaged surfaces and fuel saturation. Replace the float if these or other defects are evident.
10. Apply a light coat of four-cycle outboard engine oil onto the surfaces, then fit the O-ring (4, **Figure 21**) onto the step at the top of the canister.
11. Align the notches in the float with the ribs in the canister, then drop the float into the canister.
12. Apply a light coat of oil to the O-ring (5, **Figure 21**), then install into the groove in the top of the replacement filter element (6).
13. Insert the filter element into the filter body. Rotate the element slightly to allow proper seating of the O-ring, then seat the element fully into the body.
14. Without dislodging the element, guide the canister and float over the element. Make sure the mating surfaces are parallel, then carefully thread the canister onto the filter body. Work carefully to avoid cross-threading. Securely tighten the canister.
15. Observe the fuel filter and other fuel system components for fuel leakage while pumping the primer bulb. Correct any signs of fuel leakage before proceeding. Replace the canister O-ring if fuel leakage from the mating surface to the filter body cannot be eliminated by tightening the canister.
16. Connect the battery cable.

225 hp model

The filter is located on the front of the power head. The silencer cover must be removed to access the filter. Replace the filter element if contaminated. Attempts to clean the element usually damage the filter surfaces.

Refer to **Figure 22**.

1. Remove the silencer cover as described in this chapter.
2. Use compressed air to blow all dirt and debris from the filter and surrounding areas.
3. Place a suitable container or shop towel under the filter to capture any spilled fuel.
4. Grip the retaining ring (12, **Figure 22**) with a shop towel to capture spilled fuel. Rotate the retaining ring counterclockwise, as viewed from the bottom, while supporting the canister (11, **Figure 22**). When free, remove the retaining ring.
5. Carefully pull down on the canister until free from the filter body. Remove the red float (8, **Figure 22**) from the filter element or canister. Use needlenose pliers to remove the spring (9, **Figure 22**) from the canister. Empty the canister into a suitable container.
6. Grip the filter element (7, **Figure 22**) and pull straight down to remove it from the filter body.
7. Remove the O-rings (6 and 10, **Figure 22**) from the filter body, filter element or canister. Inspect the O-rings for torn, flattened or deteriorated surfaces. Replace the O-rings if these or other defects are evident.
8. Use a suitable solvent to clean the float and canister. Dry the float and canister with compressed air.
9. Use compressed air to remove debris and residual fuel from the canister mating surface on the filter body.
10. Inspect the float for cracks, damaged surfaces and fuel saturation. Replace the float if these or other defects are evident.
11. Inspect the spring for corrosion damage and lack of spring tension. Replace the spring if these or other defects are evident.
12. Apply a light coat of four-cycle outboard engine oil to the O-ring (10, **Figure 22**) and fit it onto the step at the top of the canister.
13. Use needlenose pliers to insert the spring into the recess in the bottom of the canister.
14. Apply a light coating of oil onto the surfaces then place the O-ring (6, **Figure 22**) onto the top of the replacement filter element (7). Make sure the opening in the O-ring aligns with the opening of the filter element.
15. Insert the filter element into the opening in the filter body. Rotate the element slightly to allow proper seating of the O-ring, then seat the element fully into the body.
16. Guide the float (8, **Figure 22**) over the body of the element. Without dislodging the element or float, guide the canister and float over the element. Make sure the mating surfaces are parallel, then carefully seat the canister into the opening in the filter body.

CANISTER FUEL FILTER (255 HP MODEL)

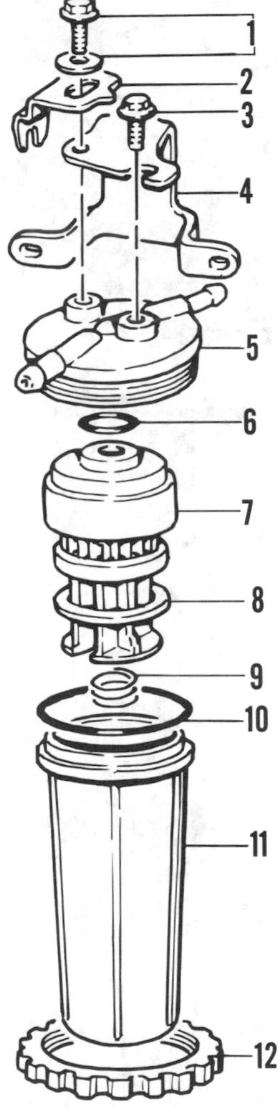

1. Screw and washer
2. Bracket
3. Screw
4. Bracket
5. Filter body
6. O-ring
7. Filter element
8. Float (red)
9. Spring
10. O-ring
11. Canister
12. Retaining ring

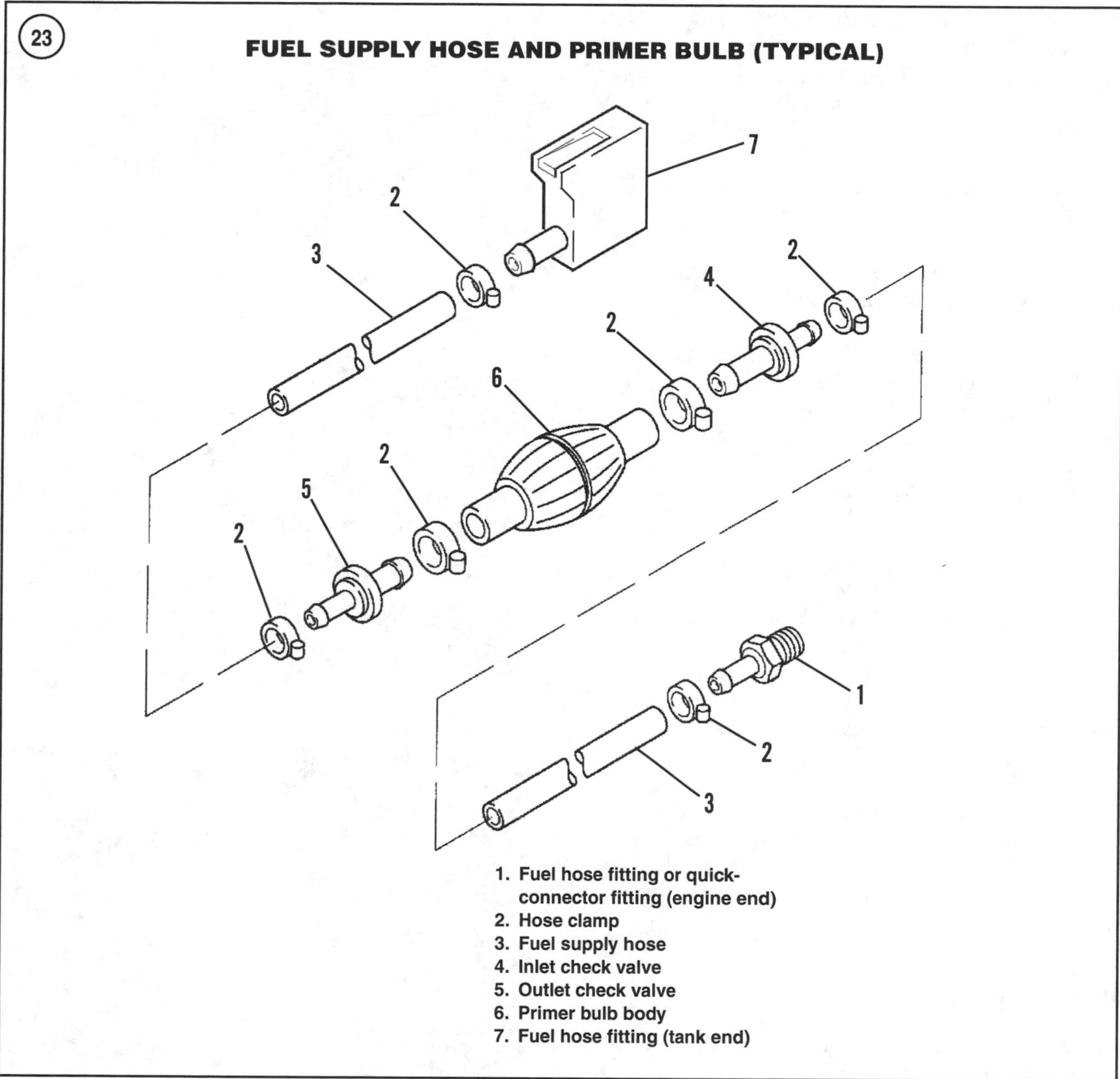

17. Support the canister while guiding the retaining ring over the canister. Carefully thread the retaining ring onto the filter body. Work carefully to avoid cross-threading. Securely tighten the retaining ring.

18. Inspect the fuel filter and other fuel system components for fuel leakage while pumping the primer bulb. Correct any signs of fuel leakage before proceeding. Replace the canister O-ring if fuel leakage from the mating surface to the filter body cannot be eliminated by tightening the retaining ring.

19. Connect the battery cable.

PRIMER BULB REPLACEMENT

The primer bulb (6, **Figure 23**) is located in the fuel hose connecting the fuel tank to the engine. Primer bulb testing instructions are provided in Chapter Three.

1. Remove the clamp. Slide the fuel tank hose from the coupling in the fuel hose leading into the engine cover. Drain any residual fuel into a container. Remove and discard the hose clamps at both ends of the primer bulb.

2. Note the direction of the arrow on the primer bulb body, then remove the primer bulb from the fuel hoses.

Drain any fuel remaining in the primer bulb into a suitable container.

3. Squeeze the primer bulb until fully collapsed. Replace the bulb if it does not freely expand when released. Replace the bulb if it is weathered, cracked or hard to squeeze.

4. Inspect the fuel hoses for wear, damage, weathered appearance or the presence of leakage. Replace both fuel hoses if defects are evident.

5. Installation is the reverse of removal. Note the direction of flow (**Figure 24**) while installing the new primer bulb. Arrows on the new bulb must align with the direction of fuel flow *toward the engine*. Carefully slide the fuel hoses onto the fittings of the primer bulb.

6. Install new fuel clamps on the primer bulb hose fittings. Ensure the fuel clamps fit tightly.

7. Squeeze the primer bulb while checking for fuel leakage. Correct any fuel leaks before operating the engine.

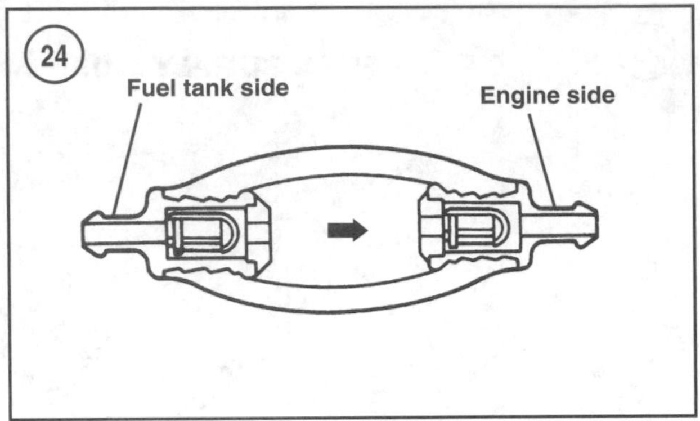

MECHANICAL FUEL PUMP

This section describes removal, repair and replacement of the mechanical fuel pump.

Two pumps (**Figure 25**) are used on 2001 and 2002, 75 and 90 hp models. One fuel pump (**Figure 26**) is used on 2003, 75 and 90 hp models and all 115 hp models. The pump(s) mount onto the valve covers at the rear of the power head. Replace all gaskets, O-rings and seals anytime the fuel pump is disassembled. It is a good practice to also replace the diaphragm when repairing the fuel pump(s). Always service both pumps on models so equipped. The condition causing one pump to malfunction is usually affecting the other.

Removal and Installation

1. Remove the plastic spark plug cover as described in Chapter Three (see *Spark plug removal*).

2. Place a shop towel under the fuel pump to capture any spilled fuel. Mark each hose and the fuel pump to help ensure correct connections upon installation.

3. Move each spring hose clamp away from the hose fittings. Using a flat blade screwdriver, carefully push each hose off of the fittings. Capture any residual fuel in a suitable container.

4. Support the fuel pump. Loosen and remove both mounting screws (**Figure 25** or **Figure 26**) from the fuel pump. Pull the fuel pump away from the cylinder block. Direct the fittings into a container and drain all fuel from the pump. Place the pump on a clean work surface. Remove the O-ring from the valve cover or fuel pump.

5. Inspect the O-ring for crushed, cut, deteriorated or damaged surfaces. Replace the O-ring if any defects are evident. Clean all debris or contaminants from the mounting surfaces and stuff a small shop towel into the opening to prevent contamination of the crankcase.

6. On 75 and 90 hp models (2001 and 2002), remove the remaining fuel pump as described in Steps 2-5.

7. Disassemble and repair the fuel pump(s) as described in this section.

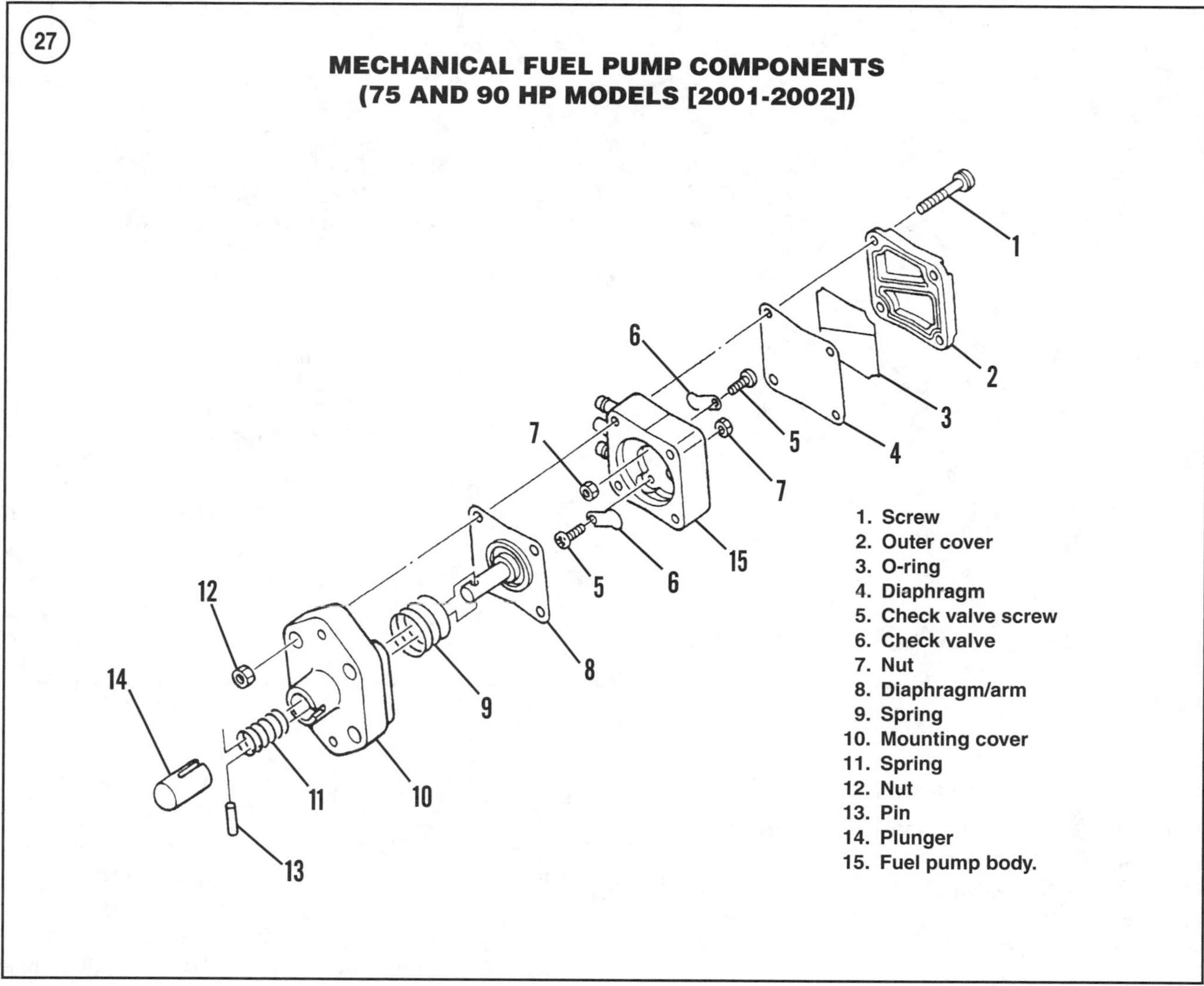

8. Lubricate the O-ring with four-cycle outboard engine oil and slide it over the plunger boss on the pump body. Seat the O-ring against the mounting cover.

9. Remove the shop towel from the opening. Guide the plunger into the opening while installing the fuel pump onto the valve cover. Hold the pump in firm contact with the cover while threading both mounting screws (**Figure 25** or **Figure 26**) into the pump and valve cover. Evenly tighten both screws to 70 in.-lb. (7.9 N•m).

10. Slide both fuel hoses onto the fittings. Make sure the inlet hose connects onto the fitting marked *in* and the outlet hose connects onto the fitting marked *out*. The inlet hose always leads to the fuel filter. The outlet hose always leads to the carburetors or vapor separator tank. Position the clamps over the hoses and fittings.

11. On 75 and 90 hp models (2001 and 2002), install the remaining fuel pump as described in Steps 8 -10.

12. Inspect all hose connections and the fuel pump assembly for evidence of fuel leakage while squeezing the primer bulb. Correct any fuel leakage before proceeding.

13. Install the plastic spark plug cover as described in Chapter Three (see *Spark plug installation*).

14. Connect the battery cable.

Fuel Pump Repair

75 and 90 hp models (2001 and 2002)

Refer to **Figure 27**.

1. Remove the mechanical fuel pump as described in this section.

2. Remove the four screws (1, **Figure 27**) retaining the outer cover (2) and mounting cover (10) onto the fuel

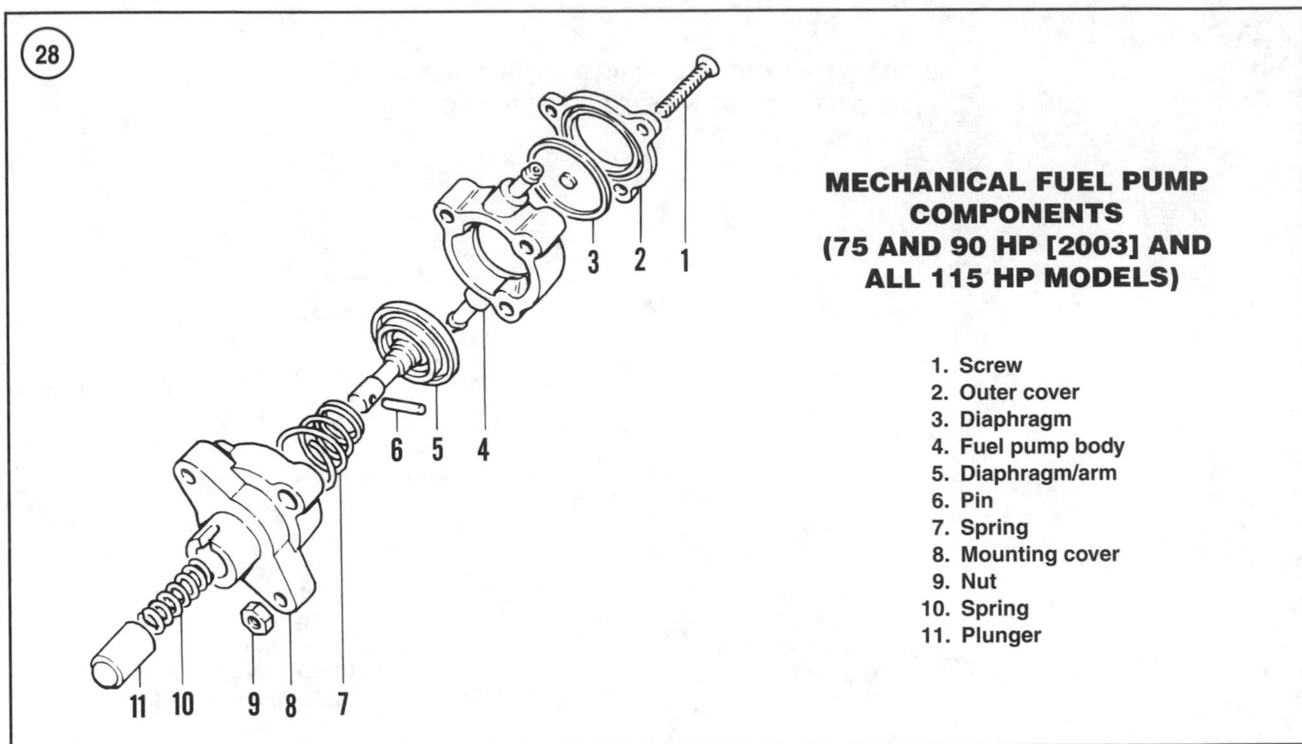

pump body (15). Remove all four nuts (12, **Figure 27**) from the recesses in the mounting cover.

3. Lift the outer cover from the fuel pump body. Remove the O-ring (3, **Figure 27**) from the groove in the outer cover. Inspect the O-ring for worn, pinched or deteriorated surfaces. Replace the O-ring if these or other defects are evident.

4. Lift the diaphragm (4, **Figure 27**) from the fuel pump body.

5. Carefully separate the fuel pump body from the mounting cover and diaphragm/arm (8, **Figure 27**).

6. Collapse the springs (9 and 11, **Figure 27**) by pushing in on the plunger (14) and the metal portion of the diaphragm/arm. With the springs collapsed, rotate the diaphragm/arm until the pin (13, **Figure 27**) aligns with the notch in the mounting cover. Pull the pin from the plunger and diaphragm arm opening, then carefully pull the diaphragm, plunger and springs from the mounting cover.

7. Remove the two check screws (5, **Figure 27**), then lift both check valves (6) from the fuel pump body. Remove both nuts (7, **Figure 27**) from the recesses in the fuel pump body.

8. Inspect both diaphragms for ripped, creased, stretched or deteriorated surfaces. Replace the diaphragms if any defects are evident.

9. Inspect the check valve for worn, cracked or broken surfaces. Replace the check valves if any defects are evident.

10. Inspect the springs for corrosion damage and lost spring tension. Replace the spring(s) if any defects are evident.

11. Clean the fuel pump body, springs, plunger, check valves and covers using a suitable solvent. Dry all components using compressed air. Direct air through all passages to clear debris.

12. Inspect the covers and fuel pump body for surface warping, cracking and deteriorated or worn surfaces. Replace any faulty, damaged or questionable component(s).

13. Place both nuts (7, **Figure 27**) into the recesses in the fuel pump body (15). Place each check valve in position on the fuel pump body.

14. Thread the screws into the check valves and nuts. Securely tighten the screws.

15. Install the smaller spring (11, **Figure 27**) into the opening in the mounting cover (10). Install the plunger (14, **Figure 27**) into the mounting cover with the smaller diameter side facing outward.

16. Install the larger spring (9, **Figure 27**) onto the mounting cover with the larger diameter side facing the cover. Insert the arm of the diaphragm (8, **Figure 27**) through the spring (9) and the opening in the mounting cover.

17. Collapse the springs (9 and 11, **Figure 27**) by pushing in on the plunger (14) and the metal portion of the diaphragm/arm. Rotate the diaphragm and plunger until the pin openings in the diaphragm arm and plunger align with the notch in the mounting cover. Insert the pin (13, **Figure 27**) through the notch and into the openings in the diaphragm arm and plunger.
18. Rotate the diaphragm approximately 90° and until the screw holes align with the screw holes in the mounting cover. Release the plunger and diaphragm.
19. Place the fuel pump body (15, **Figure 27**) on the mounting cover. Align the screw holes in the fuel pump body with the holes in the mounting cover and diaphragm.
20. Install the outer diaphragm (4, **Figure 27**) onto the fuel pump body. Install the O-ring (3, **Figure 27**) into the groove in the outer cover (2). Install the cover onto the outer diaphragm. Align the screw holes in the diaphragm and cover. Correct any pinching, misalignment or creasing of the diaphragms.
21. Insert the four nuts (11, **Figure 27**) into the recesses in the mounting cover. Hold the cover against the fuel pump body and mounting cover while threading the four screws (1, **Figure 27**) into the cover, pump body and nuts. Tighten the cover screws in a crossing pattern to 25 in.-lb. (2.8 N•m).
22. Install the fuel pumps as described in this section.

75 and 90 hp (2003) and all 115 hp models

Refer to **Figure 28**.
1. Remove the mechanical fuel pump as described in this section.
2. Remove the three screws (1, **Figure 28**) retaining the outer cover (2) and mounting cover (8) onto the fuel pump body (4). Remove three nuts (9, **Figure 28**) from the recesses in the mounting cover.
3. Lift the outer cover (2, **Figure 28**) from the diaphragm (3) and fuel pump body.
4. Remove the diaphragm from the fuel pump body or cover.
5. Carefully separate the fuel pump body from the mounting cover and diaphragm/arm (5, **Figure 28**).
6. Collapse the springs (7 and 10, **Figure 28**) by pushing in the plunger (11) and the metal portion of the diaphragm/arm. With the springs collapsed, rotate the diaphragm/arm until the pin (6, **Figure 28**) aligns with the notch in the mounting cover. Pull the pin from the diaphragm arm and plunger, then carefully pull the diaphragm, plunger and springs from the mounting cover.
7. Inspect both diaphragms for ripped, creased, stretched or deteriorated surfaces. Replace the diaphragms if any defects are evident.
8. Inspect the metal check valves in the pump body for worn, cracked or broken surfaces. Replace the fuel pump assembly if these or other defects are evident. The check valves are not available separately.
9. Inspect the springs for corrosion damage and lost spring tension. Replace the spring(s) if these or other defects are evident.
10. Clean the fuel pump body, springs, plunger, and covers using a suitable solvent. Dry all components using compressed air. Direct air through all passages to clear debris.
11. Inspect the covers and fuel pump body for surface warping, cracking and deteriorated or worn surfaces. Replace any faulty, damaged or questionable component(s).
12. Install the smaller spring (10, **Figure 28**) into the opening in the mounting cover (8). Install the plunger (11, **Figure 28**) into the mounting cover with the smaller diameter side facing outward.
13. Install the larger spring (7, **Figure 28**) onto the mounting cover with the larger diameter side facing the cover. Insert the arm of the diaphragm/arm (5, **Figure 28**) through the spring and into the opening in the mounting cover.
14. Collapse the springs (7 and 10, **Figure 28**) by pushing in on the plunger (11) and the metal portion of the diaphragm/arm. Rotate the diaphragm and plunger until the pin openings in the diaphragm/arm and plunger align with the notch in the mounting cover. Insert the pin (6, **Figure 28**) through the notch and the openings in the diaphragm/arm and plunger.
15. Rotate the diaphragm approximately 90°, then release the plunger and diaphragm. The pin and corresponding openings in the plunger and arm must be approximately 90° from the notch in the mounting cover.
16. Align the mark on the side of the mounting cover (**Figure 29**) with the corresponding mark on the pump

body, then seat the body against the diaphragm and cover. Make sure the raised lip on the outer diameter of the diaphragm enters the corresponding groove in the mounting cover and pump body.

17. Install the outer diaphragm (3, **Figure 28**) onto the fuel pump body with the raised tip in the center facing the pump body. Make sure the raised lip on the outer diameter of the diaphragm enters the corresponding groove in the pump body.

18. Align the marking on the side of the outer cover (**Figure 29**) with the corresponding marking on the pump body, then seat the cover against the diaphragm and pump body. Make sure the raised lip on the outer diameter of the diaphragm enters the corresponding groove in the cover.

19. Maintain pressure on the covers while inspecting the mating surfaces for proper seating. A gap at the mating surfaces usually indicates a pinched or improperly installed diaphragm. Remove and reinstall the covers if a gap or other indication of improper assembly is evident.

20. Insert the three nuts (9, **Figure 28**) into the recesses in the mounting cover. Apply a light coat of Loctite 242 to the threads of the three screws (1, **Figure 28**). Rotate the covers and pump body just enough to align the screw openings, then insert the screws through the covers and pump body. Thread the screws into the nuts. Do not tighten the screws at this time.

21. Check for proper seating of the pump body and cover mating surfaces. If the components are properly seated, evenly tighten the three screws to 70 in.-lb. (7.9 N•m). If otherwise, refer to Step 19.

22. Install the fuel pump as described in this section.

SILENCER COVER REMOVAL AND INSTALLATION

The silencer cover mounts on the front of the power head. The cover muffles noise while directing the incoming air into the carburetors or throttle bodies. The cover also serves as the mounting location for other fuel system components.

75 and 90 hp Models

Refer to **Figure 30**.

1. Remove the throttle position sensor as described in this chapter.

2. Disconnect the breather hose from the fitting (21, **Figure 30**) on the silencer cover.

3. Remove the eight screws (3, **Figure 30**) that secure the cover onto the adapters (5).

4. Support the silencer cover (20, **Figure 30**) while removing the three bolts (1). Carefully lift the cover from the power head.

5. Remove the four O-rings (4, **Figure 30**) from the silencer cover openings or the adapters (5). Inspect the O-rings for pinched, torn, flattened or deteriorated surfaces. Replace the O-rings if any defects are evident.

6. Wipe any debris or oily deposits from the adapters. Do not allow any contaminants to enter the intake openings in the adapter. Insert clean shop towels into the adapter openings to prevent foreign material from entering the intake openings.

7. Use a soap and water solution to clean dirt, debris and oily deposits from the silencer cover. Rinse the cover with clean water and thoroughly dry with compressed air.

8. Remove the shop towels from the adapter openings.

9. Fit the four O-rings into the grooves in the adapters. If necessary, apply a light coating of 2-4-C Marine Lubricant to the O-rings to hold them in position.

10. Without dislodging the O-rings, align the silencer cover openings with the corresponding openings in the adapter. Make sure the O-rings are in position, then seat the cover against the adapters. Hold the silencer cover against the adapters while threading the eight screws (3, **Figure 30**) into the cover and adapter openings. Do not tighten the screws at this time.

11. Align the bolt openings, then thread the three bolts (1, **Figure 30**) into the silencer cover and cylinder block openings.

12. Tighten the eight (shorter) screws to 70 in.-lb. (6.9 N•m). Tighten the three (longer) bolts to 160 in.-lb. (18.1 N•m).

13. Connect the breather hose onto the silencer cover fitting.

14. Install the throttle position sensor as described in this chapter.

115 hp Model

Refer to **Figure 31** for this procedure.

1. Cut the plastic locking clamp (55, **Figure 31**). Disconnect the breather hose (56) from the fitting on the silencer cover (62).

2. Remove the air temperature sensor as described in this chapter.

3. Disconnect the breather hose (14, **Figure 31**) from the silencer cover fitting. The hose leads to the fitting on the top of the idle air control motor (IAC).

4. Remove the six screws (63, **Figure 31**) that secure the cover onto the throttle bodies (36 and 72).

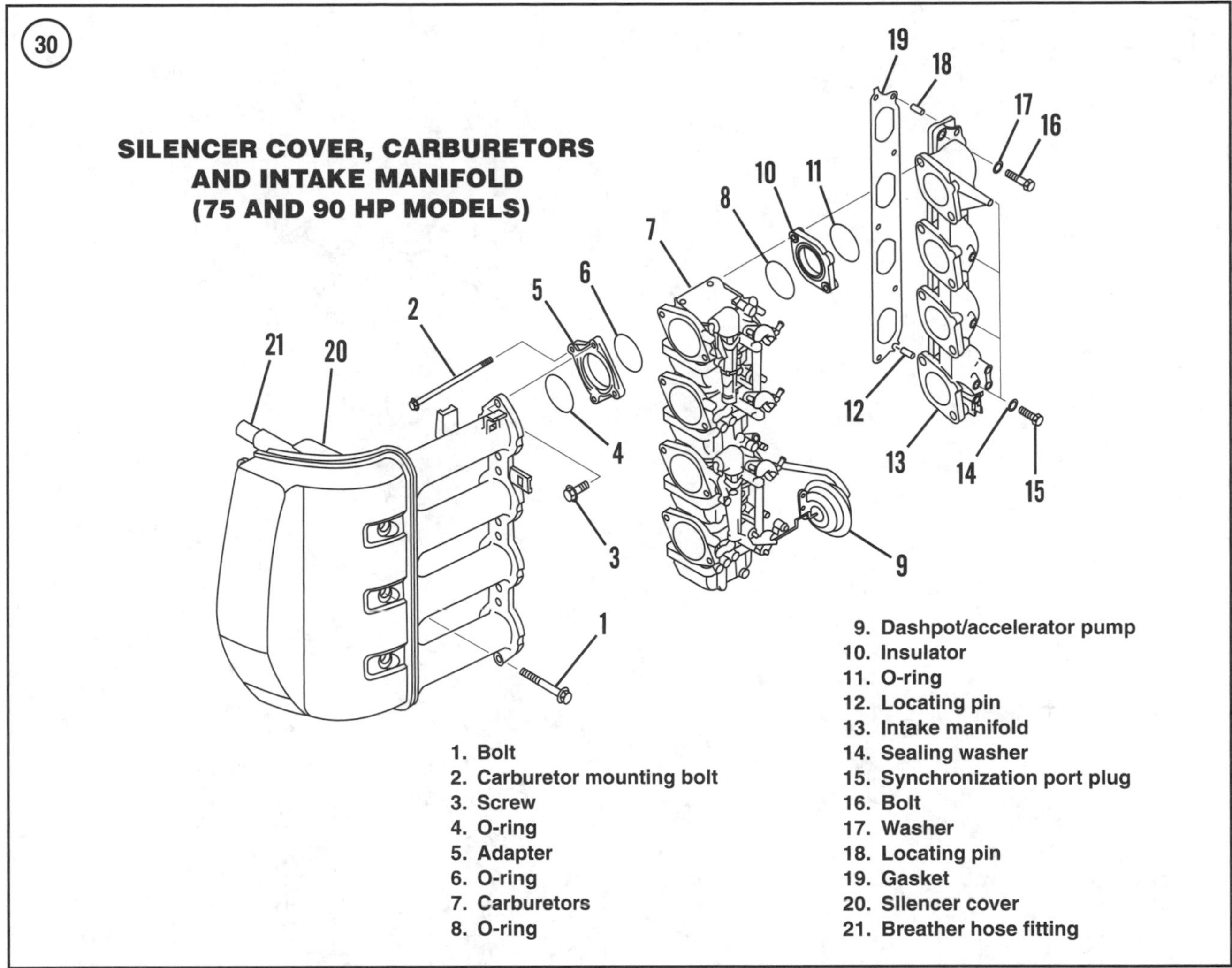

5. Support the silencer cover (62, **Figure 31**) while removing the two bolts (48). Carefully lift the cover from the power head.

6. Remove the four O-rings (46 and 47, **Figure 31**) from the silencer cover openings or throttle bodies. Inspect the O-rings for pinched, torn, flattened or deteriorated surfaces. Replace the O-rings if these or other defects are evident.

7. Wipe any debris or oily deposits from the mating surfaces of the throttle bodies. Do not allow any contaminants to enter the intake openings. Insert clean shop towels into the throttle body openings to prevent foreign material from entering the intake openings.

8. Carefully pull the screen (53, **Figure 31**) from the silencer tube. If necessary, pry the tab sections to release the screen.

9. Remove the screw (52, **Figure 31**) and retainer (54), then pull the silencer tube (51) from the cover opening.

10. Use a soap and water solution to clean dirt, debris and oily deposits from the silencer tube, cover and screen. Rinse the components with clean water and thoroughly dry with compressed air.

11. Insert the silencer into the cover opening. Seat the silencer, then position the retainer (54, **Figure 31**) onto the cover and silencer tube. Thread the screw (52, **Figure 31**) into the retainer and tighten to 70 in.-lb. (7.9 N•m). Carefully snap the screen (53, **Figure 31**) onto the silencer tube. Make sure the tabs on the screen fit over the lip on the silencer.

12. Fit the four O-rings into the grooves in the silencer cover. If necessary, apply a light coat of 2-4-C Marine Lubricant to the O-rings to hold them in position.

13. Remove the shop towels from the adapter openings.

14. Without dislodging the O-rings, align the silencer cover openings with the corresponding openings in the throttle bodies. Make sure the O-rings are in position, then

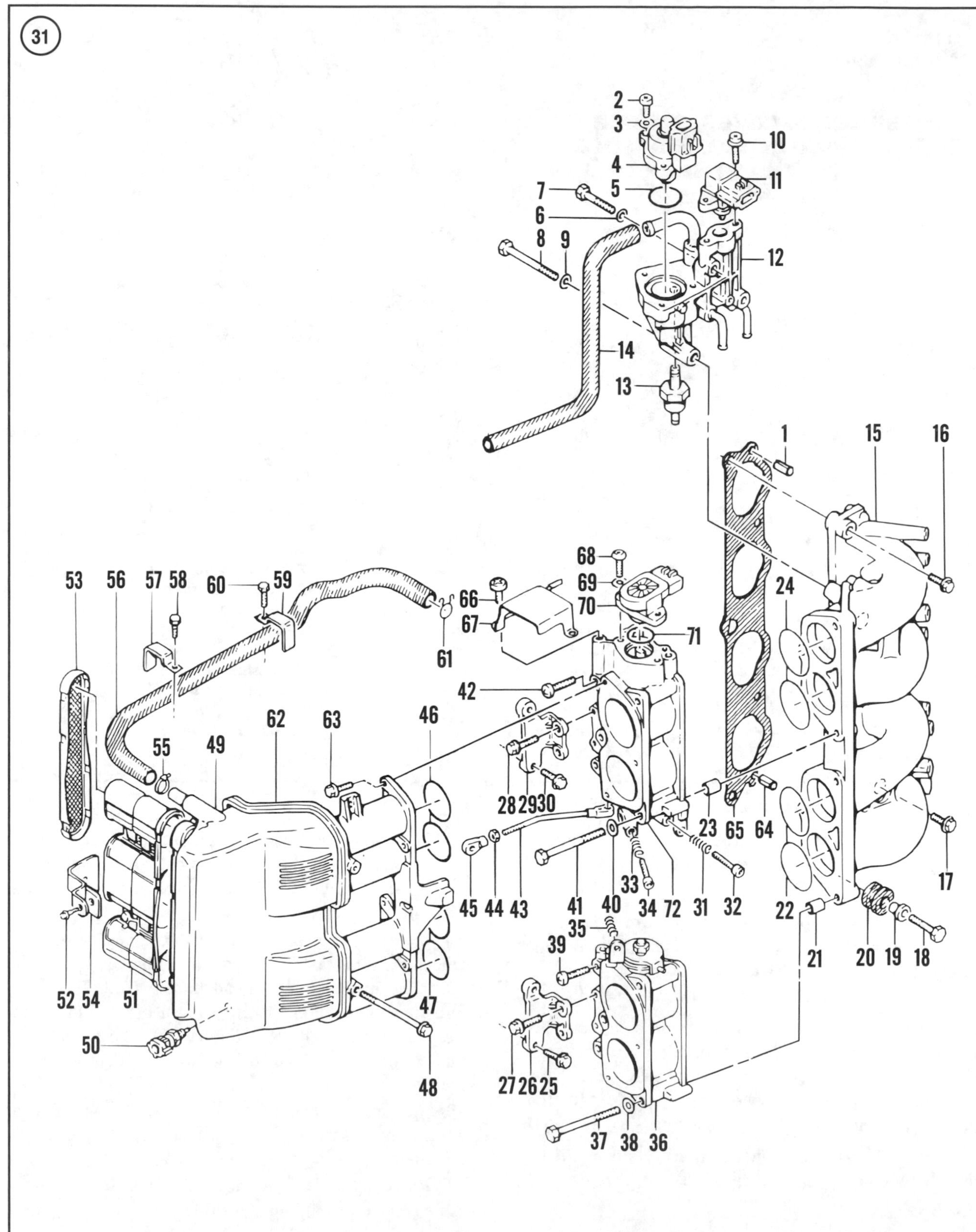
31
1
2
3
4
5
6
7
8
9
10
11
12
13
14
15
16
17
18
19
20
21
22
23
24
25
26
27
28
29
30
31
32
33
34
35
36
37
38
39
40
41
42
43
44
45
46
47
48
49
50
51
52
53
54
55
56
57
58
59
60
61
62
63
64
65
66
67
68
69
70
71
72

SILENCER COVER, THROTTLE BODIES AND INTAKE MANIFOLD (115 HP MODEL)

1. Roll pin
2. Screw
3. Washer
4. Idle air control motor
5. O-ring
6. Washer
7. Screw
8. Screw
9. Washer
10. Screw
11. Air pressure sensor
12. Housing
13. Filter
14. Breather hose
15. Intake manifold
16. Screw
17. Screw
18. Bolt
19. Sleeve
20. Grommet
21. Dowel pin
22. O-rings
23. Dowel pin
24. O-rings
25. Screw
26. Support bracket
27. Screw
28. Screw
29. Support bracket
30. Screw
31. Spring
32. Screw
33. Spring
34. Screw
35. Spring
36. Lower throttle body
37. Bolt
38. Washer
39. Screw
40. Washer
41. Bolt
42. Screw
43. Throttle linkage
44. Jam nut
45. Connector
46. O-rings
47. O-rings
48. Bolt
49. Breather hose fitting
50. Air temperature sensor
51. Silencer tube
52. Screw
53. Screen
54. Retainer
55. Plastic locking clamp
56. Breather hose
57. Clamp
58. Screw
59. Clamp
60. Screw
61. Spring clamp
62. Silencer cover
63. Screw
64. Roll pin
65. Gasket
66. Screw
67. Cover
68. Screw
69. Washer
70. Throttle position sensor
71. O-ring
72. Upper throttle body

seat the cover against the throttle bodies. Hold the silencer cover in firm contact with the throttle bodies, then thread the six screws (63, **Figure 31**) into the cover and throttle body openings. Do not tighten the screws at this time.

15. Align the threaded openings, then thread the two bolts (48, **Figure 31**) into the silencer cover and cover mounting bracket on the power head.

16. Tighten the six screws and two bolts to 70 in.-lb. (6.9 N•m).

17. Connect the IAC breather hose (14, **Figure 31**) to the silencer cover fitting. Route the hose to prevent interference with moving components.

18. Connect the breather hose (56, **Figure 31**) to the fitting (49) on the silencer cover. Secure the hose onto the fitting with a plastic locking clamp (55, **Figure 31**).

19. Install the air temperature sensor as described in this chapter.

20. Connect the battery cable.

5

225 hp Model

Refer to **Figure 32**.

1. Remove the flywheel cover as described in Chapter Seven.

2. Unplug the engine wire harness connector from the air temperature sensor (10, **Figure 32**).

3. Remove the screw then carefully lift the secondary vapor separator tank (26, **Figure 32**) until the two mounting posts are throttle position sensor free from the openings at the top of the cover.

4. Remove the four bolts (7, **Figure 32**) and bushings (8) that secure the silencer cover onto the power head.

5. Remove the four nuts (5, **Figure 32**) that secure the silencer cover onto the throttle body studs (25).

6. Pull the cover away from the power head just enough to access the breather hose fitting (4, **Figure 32**). Disconnect the breather hose (3, **Figure 32**) from the fitting, then pull the cover assembly free from the power head.

7. Remove the four sleeves (18, **Figure 32**) and bushings (19) from the openings at the back of the assembly.

8. Remove the six seals (24, **Figure 32**) from the silencer cover tubes (15). Inspect the seals for cut, deformed or deteriorated surfaces. Replace the seals if any defects are evident.

9. Wipe any debris or oily deposits from the seal mating surfaces in the throttle bodies. Do not allow any contaminants to enter the intake openings. Insert clean shop towels into the throttle body openings to prevent foreign material from entering the intake openings.

10. Remove the air temperature sensor as described in this chapter.

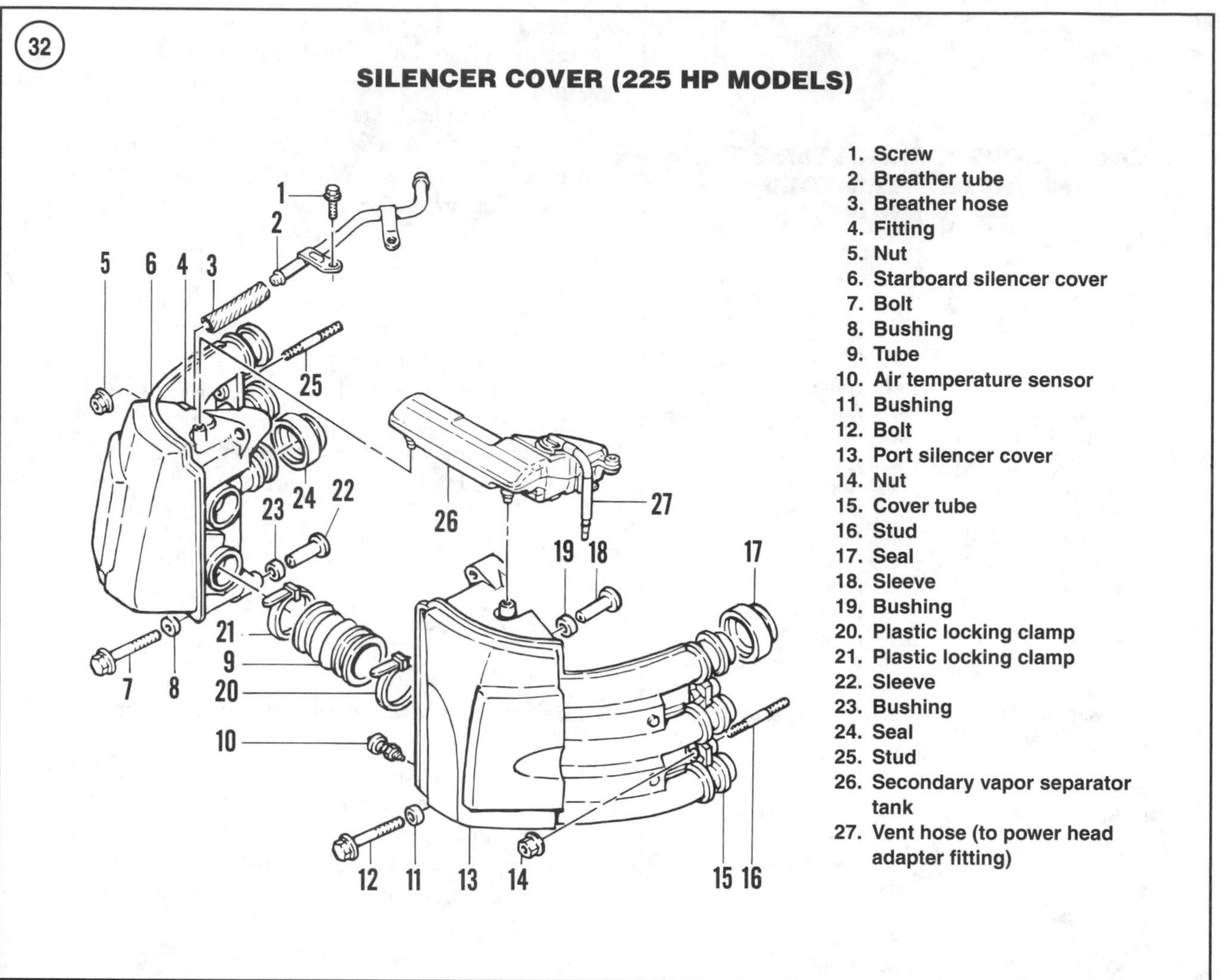

11. Cut the four plastic locking clamps (21, **Figure 32**), then separate the port and starboard silencer cover halves. Remove both tubes (9, **Figure 32**) from the covers. Inspect the tubes for cut, deformed or deteriorated surfaces. Replace the tubes if any defects are evident.
12. Use a soap and water solution to clean dirt, debris and oily deposits from the silencer covers and tubes. Rinse the components with clean water and thoroughly dry with compressed air.
13. Fit the two tubes (9, **Figure 32**) onto the fittings of the starboard silencer cover (6). Push on the tubes until fully seated on the fittings, then secure the tubes with plastic locking clamps.
14. Guide the tubes onto the corresponding fittings on the port silencer cover (13, **Figure 32**). Push the two halves together until the tubes fully seat on the port side fittings. Secure the tubes onto the port cover with plastic locking clamps.

15. Insert the four bushings (23, **Figure 32**) and sleeves (22) into the openings in the back of the silencer cover. The larger diameter side of the sleeves must face outward.

16. Install the air temperature sensor as described in this chapter.

17. Position the secondary vapor separator tank (26, **Figure 32**) on the flywheel to prevent interference during cover installation.

18. Fit the six seals (24, **Figure 32**) over the silencer cover tubes (15). The larger diameter opening must face toward the silencer cover. Make sure the lip on the seals fit into the groove in the tubes. To ease installation, lubricate the mating surfaces with a soap and water solution.

19. Remove the shop towels from the throttle body openings.

33

34

35

20. Connect the breather hose (3, **Figure 32**) onto the silencer cover fitting (4). Connect the engine wire harness connector onto the air temperature sensor.

21. Without dislodging the sleeves and bushings, guide the six cover tube openings (15, **Figure 32**) into the corresponding throttle body seals (17). Inspect all six seals to ensure proper installation. Remove the cover and reposition the seals as necessary.

22. Guide the silencer cover over the four studs (16, **Figure 32**), then seat the cover against the power head.

23. Thread the four nuts (14, **Figure 32**) onto the studs. Do not tighten the nuts at this time.

24. Fit the bushings (8, **Figure 32**) over the silencer cover bolts (7). Thread the bolts and bushings into the silencer cover and power head openings. Tighten the four bolts and four nuts in a crossing pattern to 71 in.-lb. (8.0 N•m).

25. Install the flywheel cover as described in Chapter Seven.

26. Guide the mounting pins on the bottom of the secondary vapor separator tank into the corresponding openings in the silencer cover. Seat the tank onto the cover. If inadvertently disconnected, connect the vent hose (27, **Figure 32**) onto the power head adapter plate fitting. Thread the screw into the secondary vapor separator tank. Tighten the screw to 71 in.-lb. (8.0 N•m).

27. Route the breather and vent hoses to prevent interference with moving components. Secure the hoses with plastic locking clamps as needed.

28. Connect the battery cable.

INTAKE MANIFOLD REMOVAL AND INSTALLATION

The intake manifold mounts directly onto the cylinder head and directs the air and fuel mixture into the intake ports. The manifold also serves as the mounting location for the carburetors, throttle bodies, fuel injectors, vapor separator tank and other components. The intake manifold, carburetors or throttle bodies and vapor separator tank (if so equipped) are removed as an assembly. The assembly must be removed to access the vapor separator tank and some other fuel system components.

CAUTION

Always replace the intake manifold gaskets anytime the manifold is removed. Air leaks occur if the gasket is reused. Leakage at the manifold-to-cylinder head mating surface will result in a rough idle and lean fuel/air ratio on the affected cylinder(s). Operating the engine with a lean fuel/air mixture may result in high combustion chamber temperatures and subsequent damage to the valves and piston.

75 and 90 hp Models

Refer to **Figure 30.**

1. Remove the silencer cover as described in this chapter.
2. Cut the plastic locking clamps, then disconnect the fuel hose from the fuel pump outlet fitting (**Figure 33**). Drain the hoses into a suitable container.
3. Disconnect the engine wire harness from the throttle position sensor connector harness (**Figure 34**).
4. Disconnect the electrothermal valve harness from the engine wire harness connector (**Figure 35**).

5. Carefully pry the throttle linkage connector (**Figure 36**) off of the throttle cap post.
6. Remove the five bolts (16, **Figure 30**) and washers (17) that retain the intake manifold onto the cylinder head. Do not inadvertently remove the four synchronization port plugs (15, **Figure 30**). The mounting bolts thread into the manifold flange. The plugs thread directly into the ports.
7. Pull the manifold assembly away from the cylinder head. If necessary, carefully pry the manifold loose with a blunt tip pry bar. Avoid damaging the aluminum mating surfaces.
8. Remove the gasket (19, **Figure 30**) from the cylinder head or manifold surfaces. Carefully scrape all of the residual gasket material from the mating surfaces. Do not allow loose material or other contaminants to enter the intake ports. Use a razor scraper to remove residual gasket material from the surfaces surrounding the locating pins (12 and 18, **Figure 30**). Residual material may prevent proper seating of the mating surfaces; possibly warping the intake manifold.
9. Insert clean shop towels into the cylinder head intake ports to prevent foreign material from entering the openings while the intake is removed.
10. Remove and install any applicable fuel system components from the intake manifold as described in this chapter.
11. Remove the shop towels from the cylinder head intake ports.
12. Fit the corresponding gasket openings over the locating pins (12 and 18, **Figure 30**), then seat the gasket onto the cylinder head.
13. Align the locating pin openings in the intake manifold with the pin in the cylinder head, then seat the manifold assembly against the gasket.
14. Hold the manifold in position while threading the five bolts (15, **Figure 30**) and washer (14) into the manifold flange and cylinder head openings. Evenly tighten the five screws to 159 in.-lb. (18.0 N•m).
15. Rotate the throttle cam until it contacts the throttle roller. Carefully snap the throttle linkage connector (**Figure 36**) onto the post on the throttle cam.
16. Connect the electrothermal valve harness connector (**Figure 35**) onto the engine wire harness connector.
17. Connect the throttle position sensor harness connector onto the engine wire harness connector.
18. Route the wire harnesses to prevent interference with moving components. Secure the harness onto the intake manifold runners with plastic locking clamps.
19. Route the fuel hoses to the mechanical fuel pump fittings. Push the hoses fully onto the outlet fittings, then secure the connections with plastic locking clamps.

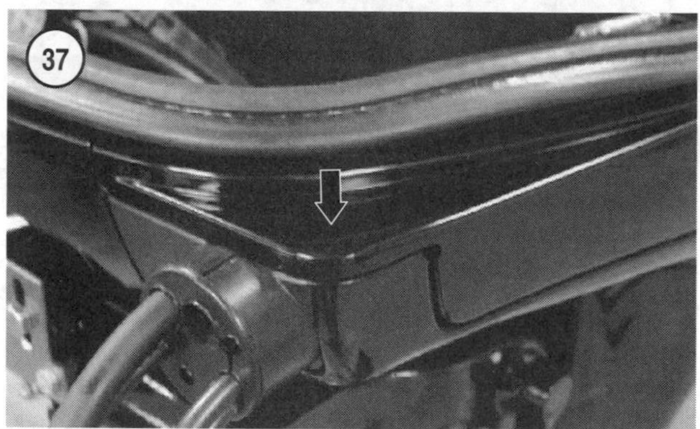

20. Inspect all hose connections and the fuel pump assembly for evidence of fuel leakage while squeezing the primer bulb. Correct any fuel leakage before proceeding.
21. Install the silencer cover as described in this chapter.
22. Connect the battery cable.
23. Perform all applicable throttle linkage and fuel system adjustments as described in Chapter Four.

115 hp Model

Refer to **Figure 31.**

1. Remove the two screws, then lift the cover (**Figure 37**) that retains the cable and hose grommet into the lower engine cover. Remove the eight screws, then pull the port side cover from the drive shaft housing. The screws thread into openings in the front and rear mating surfaces to the starboard side cover. Five are in the front and three are in the back.
2. Remove the silencer cover as described in this chapter.
3. Disconnect the vapor separator tank vent hose from the fitting on the lower engine cover. The fitting is located directly below the silencer cover when installed.
4. Disconnect the throttle cable from the throttle linkage post.

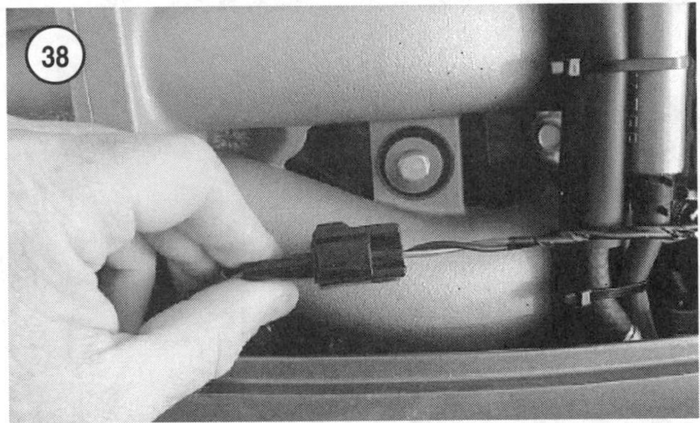

5. Disconnect the engine wire harness connectors from the throttle position sensor (70, **Figure 31**), air pressure sensor (11) and the idle air control motor (4). Reach behind the manifold runners and disconnect the engine wire harness connector from the top of the vapor separator tank.

6. Trace the fuel outlet hose from the mechanical fuel pump to the fitting on the vapor separator tank. Remove the clamp, then use a flat blade screwdriver to push the hose from the fitting. Drain the hose into a suitable container.

7. Remove the clamps, then use a flat blade screwdriver to push the water hoses from the upper and lower fuel cooler fittings. The water hose fittings are located furthest from the manifold and the hoses lead to the exhaust cover and power head adapter fittings. The fuel hoses are located closest to the manifold and the hoses lead to the vapor separator tank and the fuel pressure regulator fittings.

8. Disconnect the engine wire harness connector from the shift position switch harness connector (**Figure 38**).

9. Disconnect the engine wire harness connectors from the four fuel injectors.

10. Cut the plastic locking clamps that secure the wire harness onto the fuel rail. Route the harness away from the manifold to prevent interference during removal.

11. Remove the five screws (16, **Figure 31**) that retain the intake manifold onto the cylinder head. Support the manifold assembly while removing the four screws (25 and 30, **Figure 31**) that secure the support brackets (26 and 29) onto the cylinder block.

12. Carefully pull the manifold assembly away from the cylinder head. If necessary, carefully pry the manifold loose. Use a blunt tip pry bar and work carefully to avoid damaging the aluminum mating surfaces.

13. Remove the gasket (65, **Figure 31**) from the cylinder head or manifold surfaces. Carefully scrape all of the residual gasket material from the mating surfaces. Do not allow loose material or other contaminants to enter the intake ports. Use a razor scraper to remove the gasket material from the surfaces surrounding the roll pins (1 and 64, **Figure 31**). Residual material may prevent proper seating of the mating surfaces, or possibly warp the intake manifold.

14. Insert clean shop towels into the cylinder head intake ports to prevent foreign material from entering the openings while the intake is removed.

15. Remove and install any applicable fuel system components from the intake manifold as described in this chapter.

16. Remove the shop towels from the cylinder head ports.

17. Fit the corresponding gasket openings over the locating pins (1 and 64, **Figure 31**), then seat the gasket (65) onto the cylinder head.

18. Align the roll pin openings in the intake manifold with the pins in the cylinder head, then seat the manifold assembly (15, **Figure 31**) against the gasket.

19. Hold the manifold in position while threading the five screws (16, **Figure 31**) into the manifold and cylinder head openings. Do not tighten the screws at this time. Thread the four screws (25 and 30, **Figure 31**) into the support brackets and cylinder block openings. Tighten the four support bracket bolts to 70 in.-lb. (7.9 N•m). Tighten the five intake to cylinder head screws to 159 in.-lb. (18.0 N•m).

20. Connect the vapor separator tank vent hose to the fitting on the lower engine cover. The fitting is located directly below the silencer cover when installed.

21. Connect the shift position switch connector (**Figure 38**) onto the engine wire harness connector.

22. Connect the four engine wire harness connectors onto the fuel injector connectors.

23. Route the injector and shift position switch wiring along the length of the fuel rail. Secure the wiring onto the rail with plastic locking clamps.

24. Connect the water hoses onto the upper and lower water fittings on the fuel cooler. Do not inadvertently connect the hoses onto the fuel fittings on the cooler. The water hose fittings are located furthest from the manifold and the hoses lead to the exhaust cover and power head adapter fittings. The fuel hoses are located closest to the manifold and the hoses lead to the vapor separator tank and the fuel pressure regulator fittings. Secure the water hoses onto the fittings with spring clamps.

25. Route the fuel hose from the mechanical fuel pump to the fitting on the vapor separator tank. Push the hoses fully onto the vapor separator tank fitting, then secure the connection with a spring clamp.

26. Inspect all hose connections and the fuel pump assembly for evidence of fuel leakage while squeezing the primer bulb. Correct any fuel leaks before proceeding.

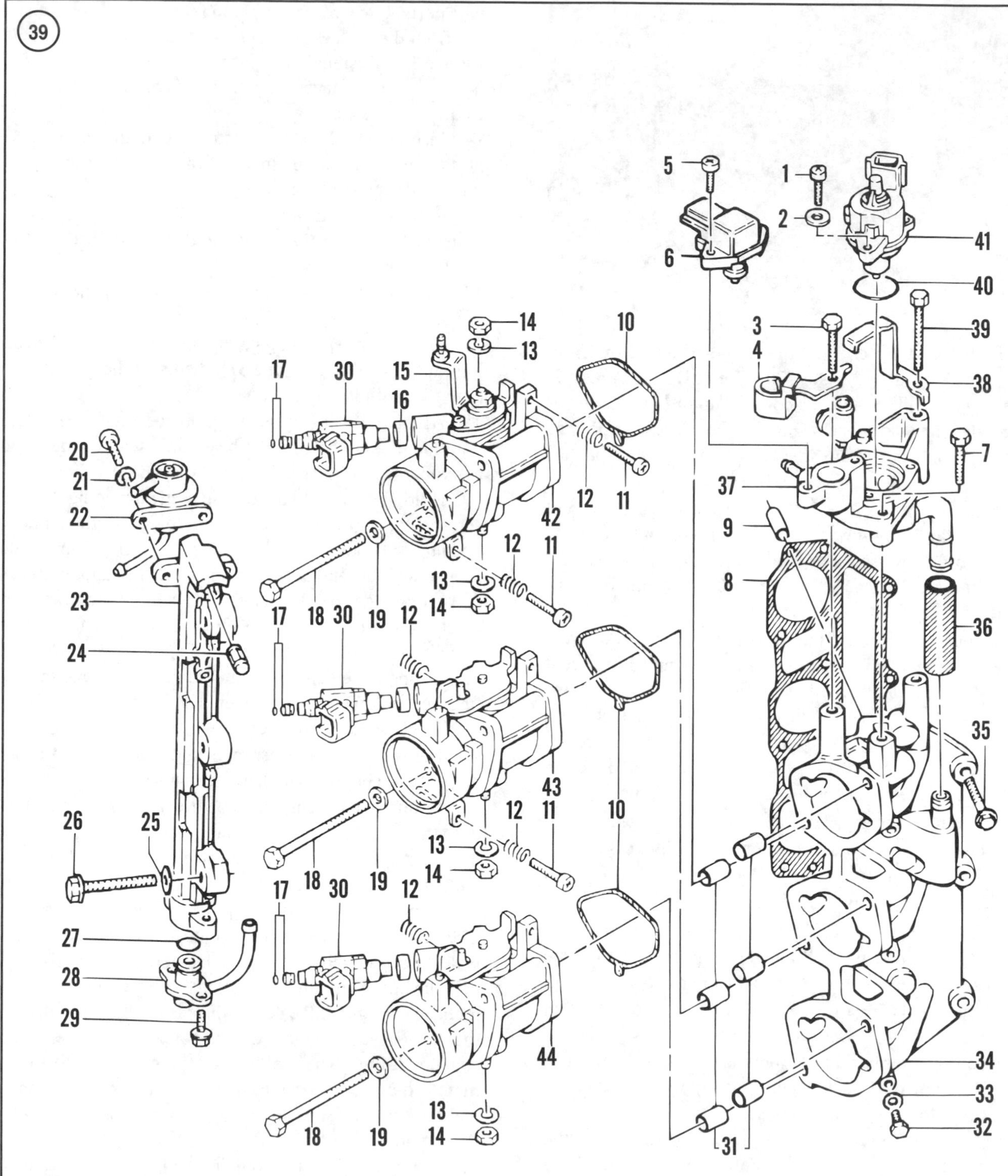

PORT SIDE INTAKE MANIFOLD, THROTTLE BODIES AND FUEL RAIL (225 HP MODEL)

1. Screw
2. Washer
3. Screw
4. Bracket
5. Screw
6. Air pressure sensor
7. Screw
8. Gasket
9. Locating pin
10. Seal
11. Screw
12. Spring
13. Washer
14. Nut
15. Throttle body lever
16. Seal
17. Grommet and O-ring
18. Bolt
19. Washer
20. Screw
21. Washer
22. Fuel pressure regulator
23. Port fuel rail
24. Cap
25. Washer
26. Screw
27. O-ring
28. Fitting
29. Screw
30. Fuel injector
31. Dowel pins
32. Plug
33. Sealing washer
34. Intake manifold
35. Bolt
36. Air hose
37. Idle air control motor housing
38. Bracket
39. Screw
40. O-ring
41. Idle air control motor
42. Throttle body (No. 2 cylinder)
43. Throttle body (No. 4 cylinder)
44. Throttle body (No. 6 cylinder)

27. Connect the engine wire harness connectors to the throttle position sensor (70, **Figure 31**), air pressure sensor (11) and the idle air control motor (4). Reach behind the manifold runners and connect the engine wire harness to the electric fuel pump connector on the top of the vapor separator tank. Route the wiring to prevent interference with moving components.
28. Connect the throttle cable to the throttle linkage post.
29. Install the silencer cover as described in this chapter.
30. Align the seal on the power head adapter with the corresponding groove in the port side drive shaft housing cover, then install the cover onto the drive shaft housing. Seat the port cover against the starboard cover. Make sure that hoses, cables, wiring or other components are not pinched between the covers, then thread the eight screws into the port side cover openings. Five are in the front and three are in the back. Tighten the eight screws evenly to 65 in.-lb. (7.3 N•m).
31. Guide the cable and hose grommet into the opening in the port side lower engine cover. Fit the cover (**Figure 37**) onto the grommet and lower engine cover. Thread the two screws into the cover and tighten to 65 in.-lb. (7.3 N•m).
32. Connect the battery cable.
33. Perform all applicable throttle linkage and fuel system adjustments as described in Chapter Four.

225 hp Model

Port intake manifold

A fuel pressure test gauge (part No. 91-166850A7 or equivalent) is required for these procedures.

Refer to **Figure 39**.

1. Remove the flywheel cover as described in Chapter Seven.
2. Remove the silencer cover as described in this chapter.
3. Locate the fuel pressure test port (**Figure 40**) on the port side fuel rail. Remove the cap (24, **Figure 39**) from the top of the fuel rail, then connect the fuel pressure test

gauge onto the fitting (**Figure 41**, typical). Direct the gauge drain hose into a suitable container, then depress the drain valve to relieve the fuel pressure. Disconnect the gauge. Drain all of the fuel from the gauge hoses.

4. Remove the rubber plug from the top of the vapor separator tank (**Figure 42**). Depress the valve in the plug opening to relieve the vapor pressure. Replace the plug after relieving the pressure.

5. Locate the quick-connect fitting (**Figure 43**) along the fuel line that runs to the rear of the flywheel. Push the two halves of the connector together, then push the collar toward the tapered end of the fitting. Maintain pressure on the collar while separating the fittings. Drain the hoses into a container suitable for holding fuel.

6. Remove the nut and disconnect the throttle linkage from the upper throttle body lever (15, **Figure 39**).

7. Disconnect the return hose and pressure reference hoses from the fuel pressure regulator (22, **Figure 39**). The air reference hose leads to a fitting on the idle air control motor housing (37, **Figure 39**). The return hose leads to the fuel cooler. Drain the return hose into a container suitable for holding fuel.

8. Disconnect the engine wire harness connectors from the air pressure sensor (6, **Figure 39**) and the idle air control motor (41).

9. Support the intake manifold assembly while removing the nine intake mounting bolts (35, **Figure 39**). Pull the manifold assembly away from the cylinder head. If necessary, carefully pry the manifold slightly away from the cylinder head. Use a blunt tip pry bar and work carefully to avoid damaging the aluminum mating surfaces.

10. Reach behind the manifold assembly to disconnect the engine wire harness connectors from the three fuel injectors (30, **Figure 39**). Pull the manifold assembly off of the power head.

11. Remove the gasket (8, **Figure 39**) from the cylinder head or manifold surfaces. Carefully scrape all residual gasket material from the mating surfaces. Do not allow loose material or other contaminants to enter the intake ports. Use a razor scraper to remove the gasket material from the surfaces surrounding the locating pins (9, **Figure 39**). Residual material may prevent proper seating of the mating surfaces; possibly warping the intake manifold.

12. Insert clean shop towels into the cylinder head intake ports to prevent foreign material from entering the openings while the intake is removed.

13. Remove and install any applicable fuel system components from the intake manifold as described in this chapter.

14. Remove the shop towels from the cylinder head ports.

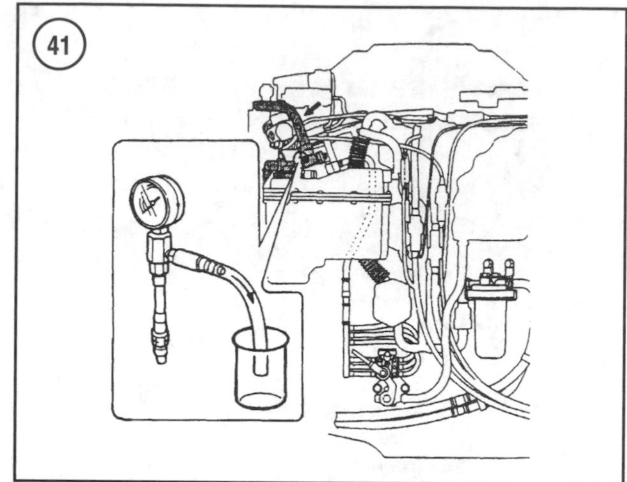

15. Fit the corresponding gasket openings over the locating pins (9, **Figure 39**), then seat the gasket (8) onto the cylinder head.

16. Align the intake manifold assembly with the cylinder head. Do not seat the manifold against the gasket at this time. Connect the engine wire harness connectors onto the three fuel injectors.

17. Align the locating pin openings in the intake manifold (34, **Figure 39**) with the pins in the cylinder head, then seat the manifold assembly against the gasket.

18. Hold the manifold in position while threading the nine bolts (35, **Figure 39**) into the manifold and cylinder head openings. Evenly tighten the nine bolts to 159 in.-lb. (18.0 N•m).

19. Connect the engine wire harness connectors to the idle air control motor and air pressure connectors. Route the wiring to prevent interference with moving components.

20. Connect the throttle linkage onto the post on the upper throttle body lever (15, **Figure 39**). Secure the linkage

to the post with the nut. Tighten the nut to 35 in.-lb. (4.0 N•m).

21. Route the fuel hose with the female quick-connect fitting over the upper rear of the power head until aligned with male fitting. Push the collar on the female fitting toward the fitting, then insert the male fitting fully into the opening. Push the collar away from the female fitting to secure the connection. Tug on the fittings to verify a secure connection.

22. Connect the fuel return hose and reference pressure hoses onto the fuel pressure regulator fittings. The air reference hose leads to a fitting on the idle air control motor housing (37, **Figure 39**). The return hose leads to the fuel cooler. Secure the fuel return hose with a spring clamp. Route the hoses to prevent interference with moving components.

23. Install the silencer cover as described in this chapter.

24. Connect the negative battery cable.

25. Perform all applicable linkage and fuel system adjustments as described in Chapter Four.

26. Start the engine and immediately check for fuel leaks. Immediately stop the engine if leakage is evident. Correct the source of the leakage before operating the engine.

27. Stop the engine, then install the flywheel cover as described in Chapter Seven.

Starboard intake manifold

Refer to **Figure 44**.

1. Remove the flywheel cover as described in Chapter Seven.

2. Remove the silencer cover as described in this chapter.

3. Locate the fuel pressure test port (**Figure 40**) on the port side fuel rail. Remove the cap (24, **Figure 39**) from the top of the fuel rail, then connect the fuel pressure test gauge onto the fitting (**Figure 41**, typical). Direct the gauge drain hose into a suitable container, then depress the drain valve to relieve the fuel pressure. Disconnect the gauge. Drain all of the fuel from the gauge hoses.

4. Remove the rubber plug from the top of the vapor separator tank (**Figure 42**). Depress the valve in the plug opening to relieve the vapor pressure. Replace the plug after relieving the pressure.

5. Locate the quick-connect fitting (**Figure 43**) along the fuel line that runs to the rear of the flywheel. Push the two halves of the connector together, then push the collar toward the tapered end of the fitting. Maintain pressure on the collar while separating the fittings. Drain the hoses into a container suitable for holding fuel.

6. Remove the nut then disconnect the throttle linkage from the upper throttle body lever.

7. Place a shop towel or suitable container under the starboard fuel rail. Remove the clamp (30, **Figure 44**), then disconnect the fuel hose (43) from the lower fuel rail fitting (28). Drain the hose into a container suitable for holding fuel.

8. Disconnect the engine wire harness connector from the throttle position sensor (3, **Figure 44**).

9. Disconnect the hose from the fitting on the side of the intake manifold (11, **Figure 44**). The hose leads to the idle air control motor housing on the top of the port side intake manifold.

10. Disconnect the engine wire harness connectors from the three fuel injectors (25, **Figure 44**).

11. Support the intake manifold assembly while removing the nine intake mounting bolts (8, **Figure 44**). Pull the manifold assembly off of the cylinder head. If necessary, carefully pry the manifold assembly away from the cylinder head. Use a blunt tip pry bar and work carefully to avoid damaging the aluminum mating surfaces.

12. Remove the gasket (9, **Figure 44**) from the cylinder head or manifold surfaces. Carefully scrape all of the residual gasket material from the mating surfaces. Do not allow loose material or other contaminants to enter the intake ports. Use a razor scraper to remove the gasket material from the surfaces surrounding the locating pins (10, **Figure 44**). Residual material may prevent proper seating of the mating surfaces or possibly warp the intake manifold.

13. Insert clean shop towels into the cylinder head intake ports to prevent foreign material from entering the openings while the intake manifold is removed.

14. Remove and install any applicable fuel system components from the intake manifold as described in this chapter.

15. Remove the shop towels from the cylinder head ports.

5

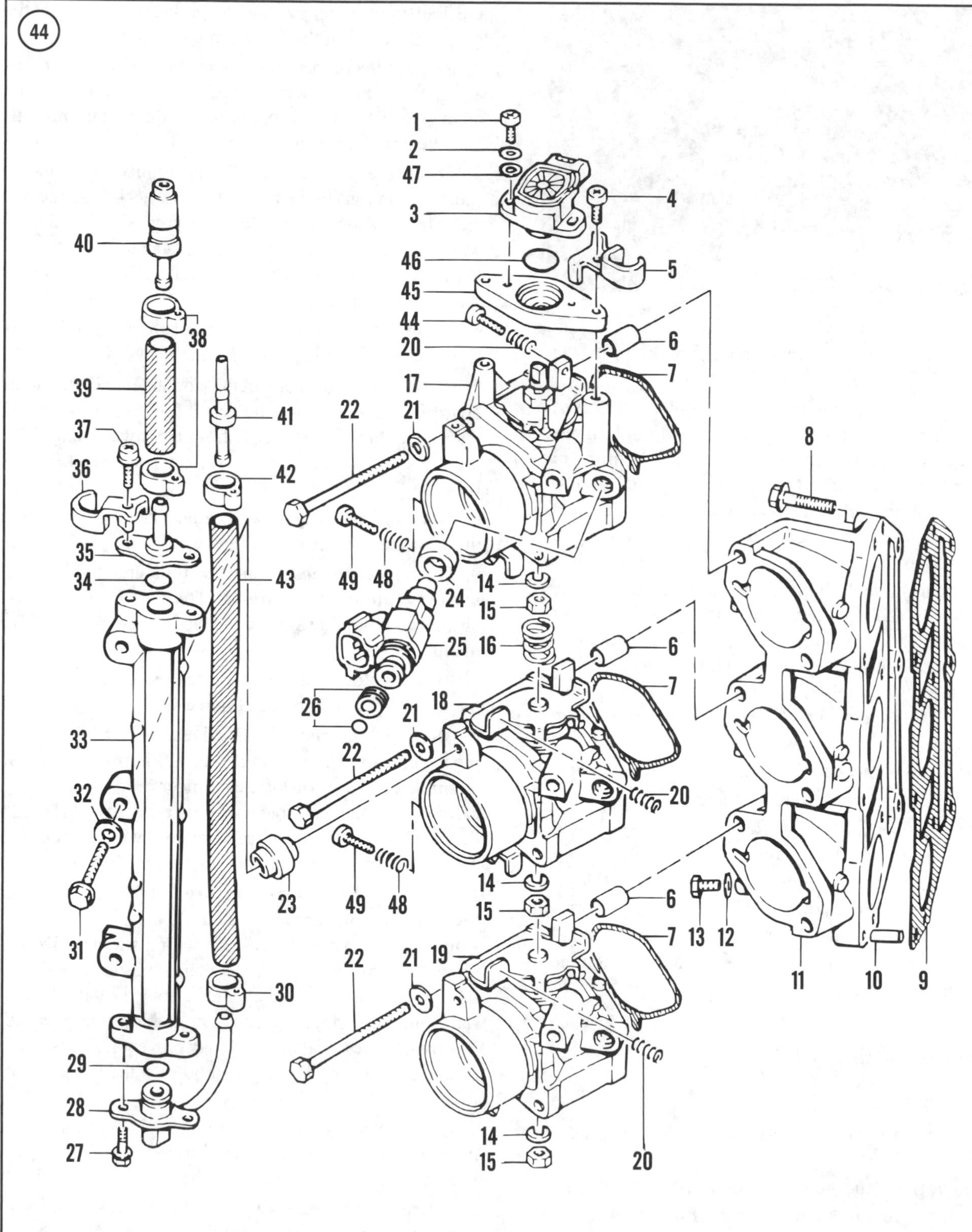
44
1
2
47
3
4
40
46
5
45
38
44
6
20
39
17
7
22
21
37
41
8
36
42
35
49
48
34
43
14
24
15
25
16
6
26
18
21
7
33
22
20
32
23
49
48
14
6
15
13
12
7
31
22
21
19
11
10
9
30
29
28
14
27
15
20

STARBOARD SIDE INTAKE MANIFOLD, THROTTLE BODIES AND FUEL RAIL (225 HP MODEL)

1. Screw
2. Lockwasher
3. Throttle position sensor
4. Screw
5. Bracket
6. Dowel pin
7. Seal
8. Bolt
9. Gasket
10. Locating pin
11. Intake manifold
12. Sealing washer
13. Plug
14. Lockwasher
15. Nut
16. Spring
17. Throttle body (No. 1 cylinder)
18. Throttle body (No. 3 cylinder)
19. Throttle body (No. 5 cylinder)
20. Spring
21. Washer
22. Bolt
23. Collar
24. Seal
25. Fuel injector
26. Grommet and O-ring
27. Screw
28. Fitting
29. O-ring
30. Full-circle crimp clamp
31. Screw
32. Washer
33. Starboard fuel rail
34. O-ring
35. Fitting
36. Bracket
37. Screw
38. Full-circle crimp clamp
39. Fuel hose (to starboard fuel rail)
40. Quick-connector fitting
41. Fitting
42. Full-circle crimp clamp
43. Fuel hose (to vapor separator tank)
44. Screw
45. Adapter plate
46. O-ring
47. Washer
48. Spring
49. Screw

16. Fit the corresponding gasket openings over the locating pins (10, **Figure 44**), then seat the gasket (9) onto the cylinder head.
17. Align the intake manifold assembly with the cylinder head. Align the locating pin openings in the intake manifold (11, **Figure 44**) with the pins in the cylinder head, then seat the manifold assembly against the gasket. Hold the manifold in position while threading the nine bolts (35, **Figure 39**) into the manifold and cylinder head openings. Evenly tighten the nine bolts to 159 in.-lb. (18.0 N•m).
18. Connect the engine wire harness connectors to the three fuel injectors.
19. Connect the engine wire harness connector to the throttle position (3, **Figure 44**). Route the wiring to prevent interference with moving components.
20. Connect the hose onto the fitting on the side of the intake manifold (11, **Figure 44**). The hose leads to the idle air control motor housing on the top of the port side intake manifold.
21. Connect the throttle linkage to the post on the upper throttle body lever (15, **Figure 39**). Secure the linkage to the post with the nut. Tighten the nut to 35 in.-lb. (4.0 N•m).
22. Route the fuel hose with the male quick-connect fitting (40, **Figure 44**) over the upper rear of the power head until aligned with male fitting. Push the collar on the female fitting toward the fitting, then insert the male fitting fully into the opening. Push the collar away from the female fitting to secure the connection. Tug on the fittings to verify a secure connection.
23. Slip a new full-circle clamp (30, **Figure 44**) over the end of the fuel hose (43). The hose leads to a fitting on the top of the vapor separator tank. Push the hose fully onto the fitting (28, **Figure 44**) at the bottom of the fuel rail. Slide the clamp over the hose until positioned over the fitting. Tighten the full-circle clamp as described in this chapter (see *Replacing Fuel Hose Connectors*).
24. Install the silencer cover as described in this chapter.
25. Connect the negative battery cable.
26. Perform all applicable linkage and fuel system adjustments as described in Chapter Four.
27. Start the engine and immediately check for fuel leaks. Immediately stop the engine if leakage is evident. Correct the source of the leakage before operating the engine.
28. Stop the engine, then install the flywheel cover as described in Chapter Seven.

DASHPOT REPLACEMENT

The dashpot is used only on 75 and 90 hp models. It is located on the lower rear port side of the power head (**Figure 45**). The dashpot also functions as the accelerator pump.

1. Use a flat blade screwdriver to push the hose off the dashpot fitting. The hose leads to fittings on all four carburetors.
2. Remove the two screws from the dashpot bracket, then swing the assembly away from the intake to disengage the dashpot link arm from the carburetor throttle lever.
3. Insert the end of the dashpot link arm into the bushing in the lower carburetor throttle lever.
4. Swing the dashpot assembly back toward the intake manifold. Align the screw openings, then thread the two screws into the dashpot bracket and intake manifold openings. Evenly tighten the two screws to 70 in.-lb. (7.9 N•m).
5. Push the hose fully onto the dashpot fitting. Route the hose to prevent interference with moving components.
6. Connect the battery cable.

ELECTROTHERMAL VALVE REPLACEMENT

The electrothermal valve is used only on 75 and 90 hp models. The valves (**Figure 46**) mount onto the No. 1 and No. 3 carburetors. The top valve connects to the No. 1 and No. 2 carburetors and the bottom valve connects onto the No. 3 and No. 4 carburetors. The valves can be replaced without removing the carburetors.

Refer to **Figure 47**.

1. Cut the plastic locking clamp that secures the electrothermal valve wiring onto the housing (19, **Figure 47**).
2. Disconnect the electrothermal valve wire connectors from the engine wire harness connectors.
3. Remove the two screws (13, **Figure 47**) and retainer (14), then carefully lift the electrothermal valve (12) from the housing. If necessary, pry between the housing and the area below where the wires enter the valve to free the valve.
4. Remove the O-ring from the valve or the valve opening in the housing. Discard the O-ring.
5. Remove the remaining electrothermal valve as described in Steps 1-4.
6. Test the electrothermal valves as described in Chapter Two.
7. Use a light and inspection mirror to look into the electrothermal valve openings in the housings. If debris or contaminants are present, remove and repair the four carburetors as described in this chapter.
8. Fit a new O-ring onto the body of the electrothermal valve. Seat the O-ring against the step on the bottom side of the valve.
9. Guide the needle of the electrothermal valve into the housing (19, **Figure 47**). Make sure the mating surfaces are parallel, then rotate the valve slightly while seating the valve into the housing.
10. Rotate the valve to position the wiring facing forward, then fit the retainer (14, **Figure 47**) onto the valve and housing. Rotate the retainer to align the screw openings, then thread the two screws (13, **Figure 47**) into the retainer and housing. Securely tighten the screws.
11. Connect the electrothermal valve wire connectors onto the engine wire harness connectors. Secure the wiring onto the valve housing (19, **Figure 47**) with a plastic locking clamp.
12. Install the remaining valve as described in Steps 8-11.
13. Inspect all hose connections and the electrothermal valves for evidence of fuel leakage while squeezing the primer bulb. Correct any fuel leakage before proceeding.
14. Connect the battery cable.

CARBURETOR

Draining the Carburetor Bowls

1. Locate the bowl drain screws (**Figure 48**) on the port side of each carburetor float bowl.

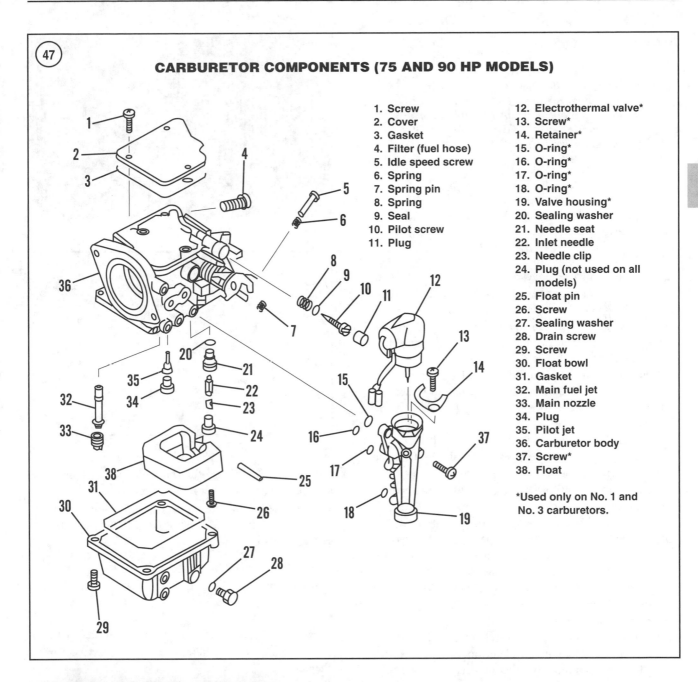

47

CARBURETOR COMPONENTS (75 AND 90 HP MODELS)

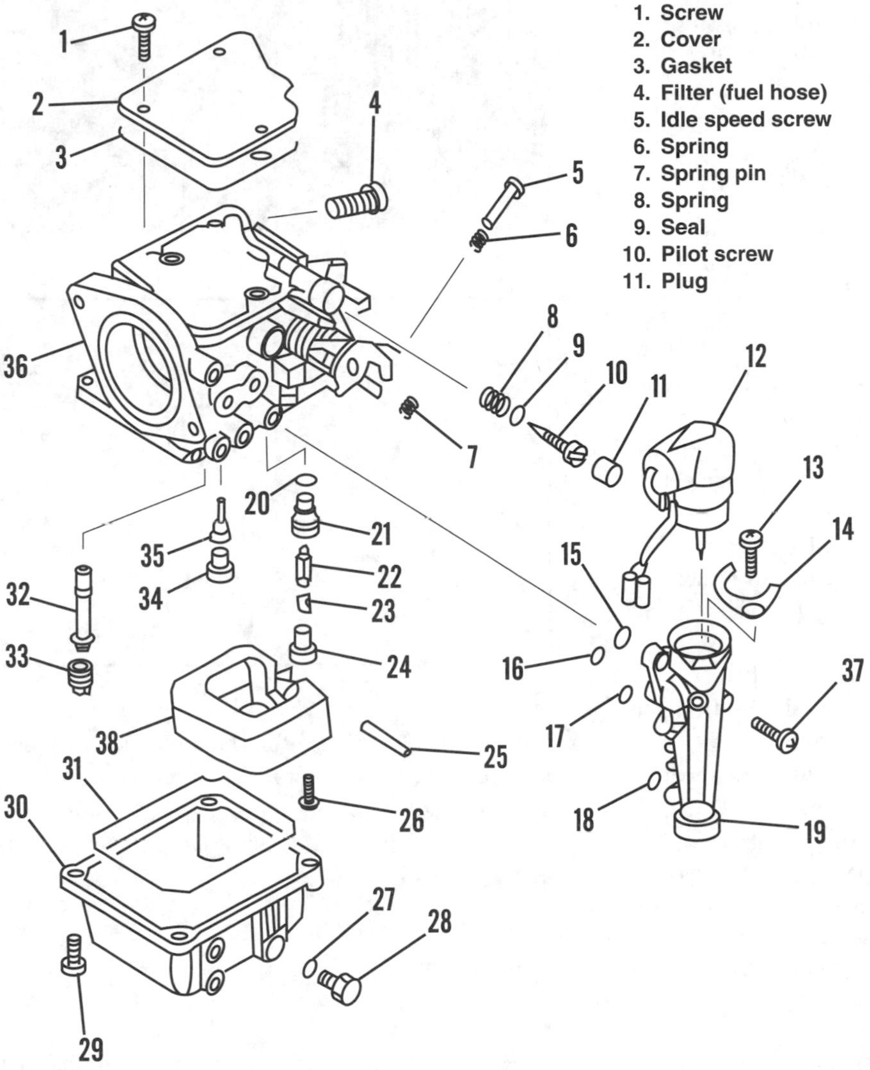

1. Screw
2. Cover
3. Gasket
4. Filter (fuel hose)
5. Idle speed screw
6. Spring
7. Spring pin
8. Spring
9. Seal
10. Pilot screw
11. Plug
12. Electrothermal valve*
13. Screw*
14. Retainer*
15. O-ring*
16. O-ring*
17. O-ring*
18. O-ring*
19. Valve housing*
20. Sealing washer
21. Needle seat
22. Inlet needle
23. Needle clip
24. Plug (not used on all models)
25. Float pin
26. Screw
27. Sealing washer
28. Drain screw
29. Screw
30. Float bowl
31. Gasket
32. Main fuel jet
33. Main nozzle
34. Plug
35. Pilot jet
36. Carburetor body
37. Screw*
38. Float

*Used only on No. 1 and No. 3 carburetors.

2. Place a shop towel under the drain screw for the top carburetor bowl.

3. *Slowly* loosen and remove the bowl drain screw (28, **Figure 47**). Allow the bowl to drain completely.

4. Inspect the sealing washer (27, **Figure 47**) for torn, crushed or damaged surfaces. Replace the sealing washer if it shows any signs of wear.

5. After draining is complete, thread the drain screw and washer into the bowl opening. Securely tighten the screw.

6. Drain the remaining three carburetor bowls, one at a time and working down, as described in Steps 2-5.

Removal

CAUTION
Mark the mounting location on each carburetor prior to removal. Improper fuel calibration or problems with linkage or hose connections are likely if carburetors are installed in the wrong location.

NOTE
Although it is possible to remove the carburetors individually, it is usually easier and quicker to first remove the intake manifold assembly.

Refer to **Figure 30.**

1. Remove the silencer cover as described in this chapter.
2. Drain the carburetor bowls as described in this section.
3. Cut the plastic locking clamp that secures the electrothermal valve wiring onto the housings (19, **Figure 47**). Disconnect the electrothermal valve wire connectors from the engine wire harness connectors.
4. Remove the intake manifold assembly as described in this chapter. Place the assembly on a clean work surface with the intake-to-cylinder head mating surface facing downward.
5. Remove the dashpot as described in this chapter.
6. Carefully pry the throttle linkage (**Figure 49**) from the post on the carburetor throttle levers.
7. Remove the eight bolts (2, **Figure 30**) then separate the four adapters (5) from the carburetors.
8. Remove the four O-rings (6, **Figure 30**) from the adapters (5) or carburetors. Inspect the O-rings for pinched, torn, flattened or deteriorated surfaces. Replace the O-rings if these or other defects are evident.
9. Separate the four insulators (10, **Figure 30**) from the carburetors (7) and the intake manifold (13).
10. Remove the O-rings (8 and 11, **Figure 30**) from the adapters or intake manifold surfaces. Inspect the O-rings for pinched, torn, flattened or deteriorated surfaces. Replace the O-rings if these or other defects are evident.
11. Mark the carburetor number on each carburetor before disconnecting the hoses.
12. Note the routing and connection points, then disconnect the fuel supply and dashpot air hoses from the carburetor fittings.
13. Separate the four carburetors. Repair one carburetor at a time. Remark the carburetor if the mounting location markings are removed during the cleaning process.
14. Remove the small filters from the openings in the fuel supply fittings. Remove the filter from the fuel hose (**Figure 50**) if not found in the fitting. If necessary, use a piece of stiff wire to push the filters out from the other end of the hose. Inspect the filters for contamination or a damaged screen. Replace the filter if contaminated or damaged.
15. Use a solvent to clean the adapters, insulators and intake manifold mating surfaces. Dry all components with compressed air.

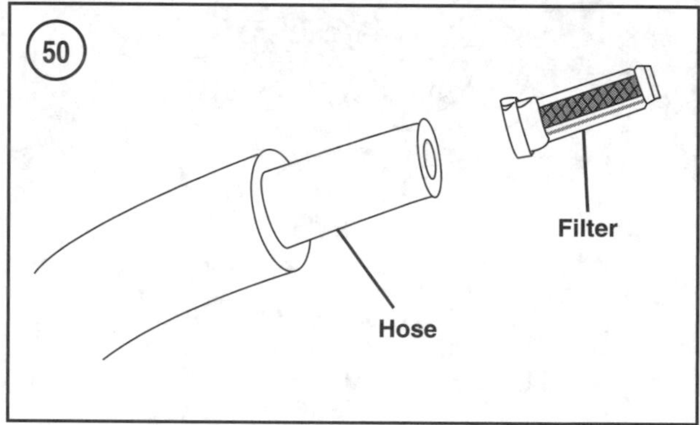

Disassembly

Refer to **Figure 47**.

1. Remove the carburetors as described in this chapter.
2. Remove the electrothermal valves as described in this chapter.
3. Remove the drain screw (28, **Figure 47**) and drain all residual fuel from the carburetor. Remove and discard the sealing washer (27, **Figure 47**).
4. On the No. 1 and No. 3 carburetors, remove the three screws (13, **Figure 47**), then pull the housing (19) from the side of the carburetor. Remove and discard the four O-rings (15-18, **Figure 47**).
5. Place the carburetor on a clean work surface with the float bowl side facing upward. Remove the four screws (29, **Figure 47**), then lift the float bowl (30) from the carburetor. Remove the gasket (31, **Figure 47**) from the carburetor or float bowl. Discard the gasket.

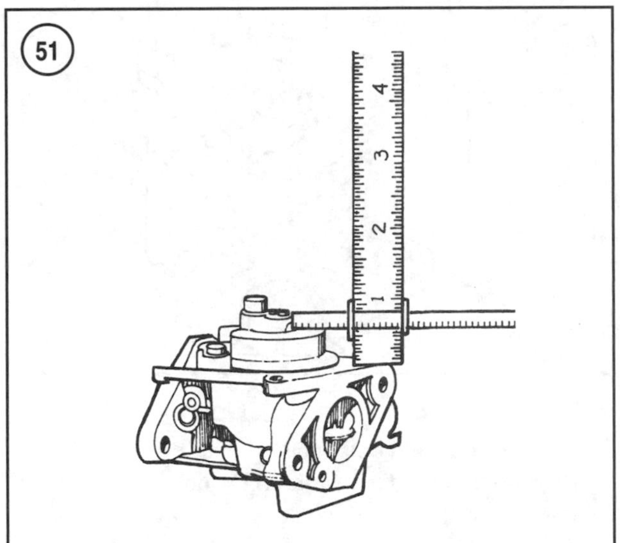

6. Remove the screw (26, **Figure 47**) then lift the float (38), float pin (25) and inlet needle (22) from the carburetor. Using a large screwdriver, remove the inlet needle seat (21, **Figure 47**) and sealing washer (20). Remove and discard the sealing washer.
7. Use an appropriately sized screwdriver to remove the main fuel jet (32, **Figure 47**) from the carburetor. Insert a screwdriver into the throttle bore opening and push the main nozzle down and out of the carburetor.
8. Pull the plug (34, **Figure 47**) from the carburetor then remove the pilot jet (35) from the opening.
9. Remove thc three screws (1, **Figure 47**) and lift the cover (2) and gasket (3) from the carburetor.
10. Remove the idle speed screw and spring (5 and 6, **Figure 47**).

CAUTION
The pilot screws are covered with an aluminum plug and the plug and screw should be removed only if necessary for cleaning the carburetor passage. Before removing the pilot screw, count the turns while turning the screw clockwise until lightly seated. Record the number of turns, then remove the screw from the carburetor. After cleaning the passage, thread the screw in until lightly seated. Back the screw out the number of turns recorded prior to removal. The screw should be 2-3 turns out from the lightly seated position.

NOTE
To remove the aluminum cover to access the pilot screws, first drill a small hole into the aluminum cover. Insert the tip of a scribe into the hole and carefully pry the cover out of the opening. After installing the pilot screw, tap a new plug into the screw opening.

11. Clean and inspect the carburetor components as described in this chapter (see *Fuel System Service*).

CAUTION
Always replace damaged carburetor fuel jets. Seemingly insignificant damage to a jet can have a profound effect on fuel delivery. Adverse effects to performance, emissions and engine durability can result from using of damaged carburetor fuel jets.

5

Assembly

Refer to **Figure 47**.
1. Fit the gasket (3, **Figure 47**) and cover (2) onto the top of the carburetor. Align the openings, then thread the three screws into the cover, gasket and carburetor body. Securely tighten the screws.
2. Install a new sealing washer (20, **Figure 47**) over the threaded end of the needle seat (21). Seat the washer against the step on the seat, then thread the seat into the carburetor body. Make sure the sealing washer remains on the seat during installation. Use a large screwdriver to securely tighten the seat.
3. Insert the smaller step side of the main nozzle (33, **Figure 47**) into the opening in the bottom of the carburetor body. Seat the nozzle in the opening, then thread the main fuel jet (32, **Figure 47**) into the nozzle opening. Use an appropriately sized screwdriver to securely tighten the fuel jet.
4. Insert the smaller diameter side of the pilot jet (35, **Figure 47**) into the opening in the bottom of the carburetor body. Seat the jet then push the plug (34, **Figure 47**) into the opening.
5. Fit the needle clip (23, **Figure 47**) onto the round end of the inlet needle. Guide the needle clip over the tab on the top of the float (38, **Figure 47**). Insert the float pin (25, **Figure 47**) through the opening in the float arm.
6. Guide the inlet needle into the seat while lowering the float onto the carburetor body. Fit the float pin into the recess in the carburetor body. Hold the pin in position while threading the screw (26, **Figure 47**) into the opening next to the recess. Carefully tighten the screw. Over-tightening will damage the threaded opening.
7. Make sure the needle clip is hooked over the tab on the float. If otherwise, remove the float and reposition the clip before proceeding.
8. Adjust the float level as follows:
   a. Place the carburetor on a level work surface with the float side facing upward (**Figure 51**).

b. Allow the tab on the float (**Figure 52**) to just rest on the inlet needle.
c. Measure the distance from the carburetor body to the bottom surface of the float (**Figure 51**). The distance must be 0.51-0.59 in. (13.0-15.0 mm). If otherwise, bend the metal tab (**Figure 52**) up or down to achieve the correct float level.

9. Fit a new gasket (31, **Figure 47**) onto the bottom of the carburetor body. The gasket must align with the float bowl mating surfaces.
10. Carefully guide the float bowl over the float, then seat the bowl onto the carburetor body. The bowl drain screw openings must be on the port side of the carburetor upon assembly. Thread the four screws (29, **Figure 47**) into the bowl and carburetor body openings. Securely tighten the screws using a crossing pattern.
11. Fit the new sealing washer (27, **Figure 47**) onto the drain screw (28). Thread the screw and washer into the carburetor bowl opening and securely tighten.
12. Fit the seal (9, **Figure 47**) and spring (8) over the pilot screw (10). Thread the pilot screw into the opening until lightly seated. Back the screw out 2-1/2 turns for 75 hp models and 2 turns for 90 hp models. Push the plug (11, **Figure 47**) into the pilot screw opening.
13. Fit the spring (6, **Figure 47**) over the idle speed screw (5). Thread the screw into the opening until it just contacts the throttle lever. Then turn the screw 1/4 additional turn.
14. *No. 1 and No. 3 carburetor only*—Install four new O-rings (15-18, **Figure 47**) into the recesses in the valve housing (19). Without dislodging the O-rings, fit the housing onto the side of the carburetor and float bowl. Hold the housing in position while threading the three screws into the housing and carburetor. Securely tighten the three screws.
15. Install the electrothermal valves as described in this chapter.
16. Install the carburetors as described in this chapter.

Installation

Refer to **Figure 30**.

1. Place the intake manifold (13, **Figure 30**) on a work surface with the carburetor openings facing upward.
2. Fit the O-ring (11, **Figure 30**) into the recess on the intake side of one of the insulators (10).
3. Without dislodging the O-ring, place the insulators on the intake manifold. Align the port opening in the insulator with the corresponding opening in the manifold. Rotate the insulator to align the insulator and manifold bolt openings.
4. Fit the O-ring (8, **Figure 30**) into the recess in the insulator. Work carefully to avoid dislodging the O-rings.

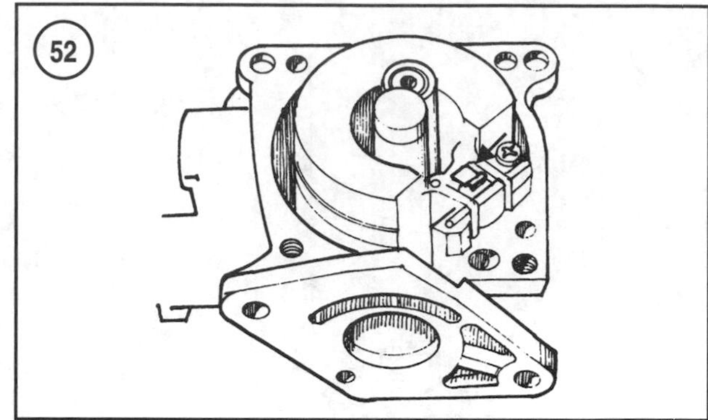

5. Align the port and bolt openings while placing the bottom carburetor onto the insulator. Do not dislodge the insulator or O-rings.
6. Place the O-ring (6, **Figure 30**) in the recess in the carburetor side of the adapter (5). Place the adapter on the carburetor.
7. Rotate the carburetor to align the bolt openings, then thread the two bolts (2, **Figure 30**) into the adapter, carburetor, insulator and manifold openings. Evenly tighten the two bolts to 70 in.-lb. (7.9 N•m).
8. Install the No. 3, No. 2, and No. 1 carburetors onto the intake manifold as described in Steps 2-7.
9. Insert the smaller-diameter end of the filters (**Figure 50**) into each of the carburetor fuel inlet fittings. Push lightly on the filter to seat in the openings.
10. Connect the fuel supply onto the corresponding carburetor fittings. The fuel supply hoses are the larger of the two fittings on each carburetor. The hoses lead to the mechanical fuel pump fittings. Secure the fuel supply hoses onto the fittings with plastic locking clamps.
11. Connect the dashpot air hoses onto the smaller of the two fittings on each carburetor.
12. Install the dashpot and electrothermal valves as described in this chapter.
13. Carefully snap the throttle linkage (**Figure 49**) onto each throttle lever post.
14. Install the intake manifold as described in this chapter.

THROTTLE BODY REMOVAL/INSTALLATION

This section describes removal and installation for the throttle body used on models with electronic fuel injection (EFI). Replace all O-rings and seals unless they are found in excellent condition.

115 hp Model

Refer to **Figure 31**.

1. Remove the silencer cover and intake manifold as described in this chapter.
2. Disconnect the air hoses from the throttle body fittings. The hoses lead to the two fittings on the idle air control motor housing (12, **Figure 31**).
3. Remove the throttle position sensor as described in this chapter.
4. Remove the four screws (27, **Figure 31**) that secure the support brackets (26 and 29) onto the throttle bodies. Remove the brackets.
5. Secure the intake manifold in a vise with the throttle bodies positioned in the normal vertical position. Remove the six bolts (41, **Figure 31**) and washers (40), then carefully pull both throttle bodies away from the intake manifold. Lift the upper throttle body (72, **Figure 31**) straight up to separate it from the lower throttle body (36). Work carefully to avoid dislodging the spring in the throttle shaft coupling.
6. Remove the O-rings (22 and 24, **Figure 31**) from the throttle bodies or intake manifold surfaces. Inspect the O-rings for crushed, cut or deteriorated surfaces. Replace the O-rings if these or other defects are evident.
7. Use an aerosol carburetor cleaner to clean all debris and oily deposits from the throttle bodies and the mating surfaces on the intake manifold. Dry the surfaces with compressed air.
8. Place the throttle bodies on a clean work surface with the intake manifold side facing upward.
9. Align the throttle shafts and guide the tab on the lower throttle body shaft between the screw tip and the spring on the upper throttle body shaft. Maintain this alignment during throttle body installation.
10. Place the O-rings (22 and 24, **Figure 31**) into the recesses in the throttle bodies.
11. Align the openings in the intake manifold with the openings in the throttle bodies. Align the dowel pins (21 and 23, **Figure 31**) with the corresponding openings in the throttle bodies, then seat the intake fully onto the throttle bodies.
12. Hold the throttle bodies in firm contact with the intake, then turn the entire assembly over. Verify proper alignment of the throttle shaft coupling and proper seating of the O-rings in the grooves. Correct improper alignment or seating before proceeding.
13. Without dislodging the throttle bodies, thread the six bolts (41, **Figure 31**) and washers (40) into the throttle body and intake manifold openings. Evenly tighten the bolts to 159 in.-lb. (18.0 N•m).
14. Install the support brackets (26 and 29, **Figure 31**) onto the throttle bodies. Align the openings, then thread the screws (27, **Figure 31**) into the bracket and throttle body openings. Tighten the four screws to 70 in.-lb. (7.9 N•m).
15. Install the throttle position sensor as described in this chapter.
16. Connect the two hoses onto the corresponding fittings on the throttle bodies. The hoses lead to fittings on the idle air control motor housing (12, **Figure 31**).
17. Install the intake manifold assembly and silencer cover as described in this chapter.

225 hp Model

Port side

Refer to **Figure 39**.

1. Remove the silencer cover and port side intake manifold as described in this chapter.
2. Remove the port fuel rail and injectors as described in this chapter.
3. Remove the two bolts (18, **Figure 39**) and washers (19) from the top throttle body (42).
4. Carefully pull the throttle body away from the intake manifold. Work carefully to avoid dislodging the spring (12, **Figure 39**) from the throttle shaft couplings.
5. Remove the seal (10, **Figure 39**) from the throttle body or the intake manifold surface. Inspect the seal for crushed, cut or deteriorated surfaces. Replace the seal if these or other defects are evident.
6. Repeat Steps 3-5 for the middle and bottom throttle bodies.
7. Use an aerosol carburetor cleaner to clean all debris and oily deposits from the throttle bodies and the mating surfaces on the intake manifold. Dry the surfaces with compressed air.
8. Fit the seal (10, **Figure 39**) into the recess in the upper throttle body (42). Align the dowel pins (31, **Figure 39**) with the openings in the throttle body, then seat the throttle body against the intake manifold.
9. Verify proper seating of the mating surfaces, then thread the two bolts (18, **Figure 39**) and washers (19) into the throttle body and intake openings. Evenly tighten the bolts to 159 in.-lb. (18.0 N•m).
10. Fit the seal (10, **Figure 39**) into the recess in the middle throttle body. Guide the tab on the throttle shaft of the throttle body between the screw tip (11, **Figure 39**) and the spring (12) in the upper throttle body shaft. Then, align the dowel pins (31, **Figure 39**) with the corresponding openings in the throttle body. When perfectly aligned, seat the throttle body against the intake manifold.

11. Verify proper seating of the mating surfaces, then thread the two bolts (18, **Figure 39**) and washers (19) into the throttle body and intake openings. Evenly tighten the bolts to 159 in.-lb. (18.0 N•m).
12. Install the lower throttle body (42, **Figure 39**) as described in Steps 10 and 11.
13. Install the fuel injectors and fuel rail as described in this chapter.
14. Install the port side intake manifold and silencer cover as described in this chapter.

Starboard side

Refer to **Figure 44**.

1. Remove the silencer cover and starboard side intake manifold as described in this chapter.
2. Remove the starboard fuel rail and injectors as described in this chapter.
3. Remove the two bolts (22, **Figure 44**) and washers (21) from the top throttle body (17).
4. Carefully pull the throttle body away from the intake manifold. Avoid dislodging the spring (20, **Figure 44**) from the throttle shaft couplings.
5. Remove the seal (7, **Figure 44**) from the throttle body or the intake manifold surface. Inspect the seal for crushed, cut or deteriorated surfaces. Replace the seal if these or other defects are evident.
6. Repeat Steps 4-6 for the middle and bottom throttle bodies.
7. Use an aerosol carburetor cleaner to clean all debris and oily deposits from the throttle bodies and the mating surfaces on the intake manifold. Dry the surfaces with compressed air.
8. Fit the seal (7, **Figure 44**) into the recess in the upper throttle body (17). Align the dowel pins (6, **Figure 44**) with the corresponding openings in the throttle body, then seat the throttle body against the intake manifold.
9. Verify proper seating of the mating surfaces, then thread the two bolts (22, **Figure 44**) and washers (21) into the throttle body and intake openings. Evenly tighten the bolts to 159 in.-lb. (18.0 N•m).
10. Fit the seal (7, **Figure 44**) into the recess in the middle throttle body (18). Guide the tab on the throttle shaft of the throttle body between the screw tip (49, **Figure 44**) and the spring (20) in the upper throttle body shaft. Align the dowel pins (6, **Figure 44**) with the corresponding openings in the throttle body. Seat the throttle body against the intake manifold.
11. Verify proper seating of the mating surfaces, then thread the two bolts (22, **Figure 44**) and washers (21) into the throttle body and intake openings. Evenly tighten the bolts to 159 in.-lb. (18.0 N•m).
12. Install the lower throttle body (19, **Figure 44**) as described in Steps 10 and 11.
13. Install the fuel injectors and starboard fuel rail as described in this chapter.
14. Install the starboard side intake manifold and silencer cover as described in this chapter.

VAPOR SEPARATOR TANK

This section describes draining, removal, disassembly, assembly and installation of the vapor separator tank. Replace the O-rings and filter anytime the vapor separator tank is disassembled. The top cover O-ring increases in length after removal and is very difficult to reposition into the groove in the mating surface.

115 hp Model

Draining

Refer to **Figure 53**.

1. Place a container or a number of shop towels under the drain screw opening.
2. *Slowly* loosen and remove the drain screw (14, **Figure 53**). Allow the tank to completely drain.
3. Inspect the O-ring (13, **Figure 53**) on the drain screw for crushed, cut or deteriorated surfaces. Replace the O-ring if these or other defects are evident.
4. Thread the drain screw into the opening. Securely tighten the screw.
5. Connect the battery cable unless the vapor separator tank must be removed.

Removal and installation

Refer to **Figure 53**.

1. Drain the vapor separator tank as described in this section.
2. Remove the intake manifold as described in this chapter.
3. Remove the spring clamp, then disconnect the fuel return hose from the reservoir fitting (12, **Figure 53**). The hose leads to the fuel cooler. Drain the hose into a container suitable for holding fuel.
4. Remove the full-circle crimp clamp from the fitting, then disconnect the fuel outlet hose from the cover fitting (2, **Figure 53**). The hose leads to the fuel rail. Drain the hose into a container suitable for holding fuel.
5. Support the vapor separator tank while removing the three screws (8, **Figure 53**) and sleeves (9). Lift the tank from the manifold. Remove the three sleeves (11, **Figure 53**) and grommets (10) from the intake manifold open-

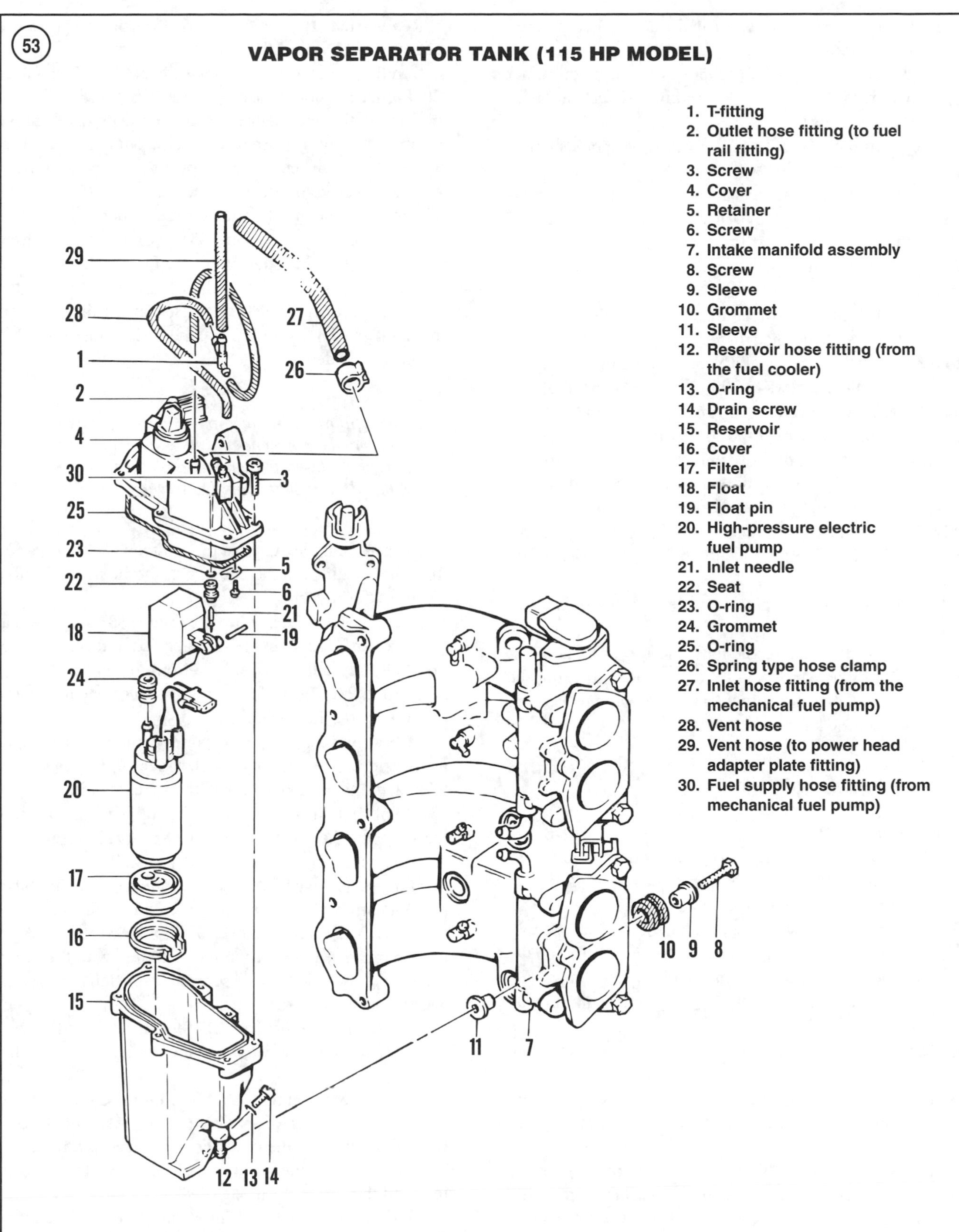

1. T-fitting
2. Outlet hose fitting (to fuel rail fitting)
3. Screw
4. Cover
5. Retainer
6. Screw
7. Intake manifold assembly
8. Screw
9. Sleeve
10. Grommet
11. Sleeve
12. Reservoir hose fitting (from the fuel cooler)
13. O-ring
14. Drain screw
15. Reservoir
16. Cover
17. Filter
18. Float
19. Float pin
20. High-pressure electric fuel pump
21. Inlet needle
22. Seat
23. O-ring
24. Grommet
25. O-ring
26. Spring type hose clamp
27. Inlet hose fitting (from the mechanical fuel pump)
28. Vent hose
29. Vent hose (to power head adapter plate fitting)
30. Fuel supply hose fitting (from mechanical fuel pump)

ings. Inspect the grommets for deformed or deteriorated surfaces and replace as needed.

6. Clean any debris or oily deposits from the grommet openings in the manifold. Oil promotes deterioration of the grommet material.

7. Disassemble, clean, and assemble the vapor separator tank as described in this section.

8. Insert the three grommets into the openings in the manifold. Make sure the groove in the grommets fit over the lip in the openings. Insert the sleeves (9 and 11, **Figure 53**) into the grommets with the larger diameter side facing outward.

9. Align the threaded openings in the vapor separator tank with the sleeves, then thread the three screws (8, **Figure 53**) into the sleeves and vapor separator tank openings. Tighten the screws to 70 in.-lb. (7.9 N•m).

10. Slip a new full-circle clamp over the end and push the fuel outlet hose fully over the cover fitting (2, **Figure 53**). Slide the clamp over the hose until positioned over the fitting. Tighten the full-circle clamp as described in this chapter (see *Replacing Fuel Hose Connectors*).

11. Push the fuel return hose fully over the reservoir fitting (12, **Figure 53**), then secure the hose with the spring clamp.

12. Install the intake manifold as described in this chapter.

13. Inspect all hose connections and the fuel pump assembly for evidence of fuel leakage while squeezing the primer bulb. Correct any fuel leakage before proceeding.

14. Connect the battery cable.

Disassembly and assembly

Refer to **Figure 53**.

1. Remove the vapor separator tank as described in this section. Clamp the assembly into a vise with protective jaws. Do not over-tighten the vise.

2. Loosen the clamp, then disconnect the fuel supply hose from the fitting on the cover. When assembled on the engine, the hose leads to the mechanical fuel pump.

3. Remove the drain screw (14, **Figure 53**) and O-ring (13). Discard the O-ring.

4. Disconnect the vent hose (28, **Figure 53**) from the two fittings on the cover.

5. Remove the seven cover screws (3, **Figure 53**). If necessary, use an impact driver to loosen the screws. Replace any screws damaged during the removal process.

6. Lift the cover assembly from the reservoir. Do not pry the cover loose. The delicate mating surfaces are easily damaged with a pry bar. If necessary, tap the cover loose with a rubber mallet.

7. Remove the O-ring (25, **Figure 53**) from the groove in the reservoir. Discard the O-ring.

8. Carefully pull the high-pressure electric fuel pump (20, **Figure 53**) out of the cover to access the wire connector. Unplug the wire connector to free the pump. Remove the grommet (24, **Figure 53**) from the pump outlet fitting or the opening in the cover. Inspect the grommet for deformed, cracked or deteriorated surfaces. Replace the grommet if these or other defects are evident.

9. Pull the cover (16, **Figure 53**) from the bottom of the pump. Carefully pull the filter (17, **Figure 53**) from the pump. If necessary, twist on the filter until free from the pump. Inspect the filter for debris, varnish-like deposits and damaged surfaces. Replace the filter if these or other defects are evident.

NOTE

The float pin in the vapor separator tank is rounded on one end and square on the other. Push on the rounded end to remove the pin. Install the rounded end first when installing the pin.

10. Use a small pick to push the float pin (19, **Figure 53**) from the openings in the cover. Lift the float (18, **Figure 53**) from the cover.

11. Remove the inlet needle (21, **Figure 53**) from the seat (22). Remove the screw (6, **Figure 53**) and retainer (5), then carefully pull the seat (22) from the cover. Remove the O-ring (23, **Figure 53**) from the seat or opening in the cover. Discard the O-ring.

12. Clean and inspect the vapor separator tank components as described in this chapter (see *Fuel System Service*). Dry the components with compressed air.

13. Apply a light coat of four-cycle outboard engine oil to the surfaces, then install the new O-ring (23, **Figure 53**) onto the needle seat (22). Carefully push the seat into the opening in the cover. Rotate the seat during installation to prevent damage to the O-ring. Make sure the tapered seat faces outward. Fit the retainer (5, **Figure 53**) arms into the groove in the seat, then secure the retainer with the screw (6). Do not over-tighten the screws. Over-tightening damages the screw threads.

14. Insert the inlet needle (21, **Figure 53**) into the seat. The tapered tip of the valve must contact the taper in the seat.

15. Align the tab on the float (18, **Figure 53**) with the inlet needle, then align the pin bore in the float with the corresponding bore in the cover bosses. Insert the float pin, rounded end first, into the mounted bosses and float opening until the end is flush with the boss.

16. Install the filter (17, **Figure 53**) onto the bottom of the pump (20). Push the cover (16, **Figure 53**) onto the fil-

ter. The slot in the cover must face toward the opposite side of the pump as the fuel outlet passage at the top of the pump. Rotate the cover as needed.

17. Apply a light coat of engine oil to the grommet (24, **Figure 53**) then install it into the fuel pump outlet opening in the top cover. Align the grommet opening with the fuel passage, then seat the grommet in the opening.

18. Plug the fuel pump wiring onto the connector in the cover. Align the fuel outlet on the pump with the opening in the grommet, then fully seat the pump against the grommet.

19. Fit the new O-ring (25, **Figure 53**) into the corresponding groove in the reservoir (15). Do not apply any sealant onto the O-ring.

20. Guide the tabs on the fuel pump filter into the notches in the reservoir while carefully lowering the cover onto the reservoir. Do not pinch the pump wiring between the cover and reservoir or cover and pump body. Reposition the wiring as needed. Verify correct alignment, then seat the cover onto the reservoir.

21. Thread the seven screws (3, **Figure 53**) into the cover and reservoir openings. Tighten the screws in a crossing pattern to 18.0 in.-lb. (2.0 N•m).

22. Install a new O-ring (13, **Figure 53**) onto the drain screw (14). Thread the screw into the reservoir. Securely tighten the screw.

23. Connect the vent hoses (28, **Figure 53**) to the two smaller fittings on the top cover.

24. Connect the fuel supply hose to the fitting (30, **Figure 53**). Secure the hose with a spring clamp.

25. Install the vapor separator tank as described in this section.

225 hp model

Draining

Refer to **Figure 54**.

1. Remove the silencer cover as described in this chapter.
2. Place a suitable container or a number of shop towels under the drain screw opening.
3. *Slowly* loosen and remove the drain screw (25, **Figure 54**). Allow the tank to completely drain.
4. Inspect the sealing washer (24, **Figure 54**) on the drain screw for crushed, cut or deteriorated surfaces. Replace the washer if any defects are evident.
5. Thread the drain screw into the opening. Tighten the drain screw to 18 in.-lb. (2.0 N•m).
6. Unless the vapor separator tank must be removed, install the silencer cover as described in this chapter and connect the battery cable.

Removal and installation

Refer to **Figure 54**.

1. Remove the silencer cover as described in this chapter.
2. Drain the vapor separator tank as described in this section.
3. Disconnect the vent hose (45, **Figure 54**) from the T-fitting (3).
4. Loosen the clamps, then use a flat blade screwdriver to push the water hoses off the fittings on the fuel cooler (16, **Figure 54**). The water hoses are on the upper and lower starboard side fittings. Drain the hoses.
5. Loosen the clamp, then push the fuel return hose from the fuel cooler fitting. The return hose fitting is on the top and port side fitting. Drain the hose into a container suitable for holding fuel.
6. Locate the quick-connect fitting (**Figure 43**) along the fuel line that runs to the rear of the flywheel. Push the two halves of the connector together, then push the collar toward the tapered end of the fitting. Maintain pressure on the collar while separating the fittings. Drain the hoses into a container suitable for holding fuel.
7. Locate the high-pressure electric fuel pump harness extending out of the top of the vapor separator tank. Trace the harness to the connection on the engine wire harness. Unplug the connectors.
8. Remove the screw from the hose retaining bracket. The screw is located directly below the fuel cooler.
9. Trace the wire harness for the low-pressure electric fuel pump (20, **Figure 54**) to the connection onto the engine wire harness. Unplug the connectors.
10. Trace the wire harness for the fuel pump relay (15, **Figure 54**) to the connection onto the engine wire harness. The connector is located just below the low-pressure fuel pump connector. Unplug the connector.
11. Support the vapor separator tank assembly while removing the four screws (26, **Figure 54**) that retain the tank and mounting bracket onto the power head. Disconnect the assembly from the power head. Place the assembly on a clean work surface with the mounting bracket facing upward.
12. Remove the sleeves (27 and 29, **Figure 54**) and grommets (28) from the tank openings. Inspect the grommets for deformed or deteriorated surfaces and replace as needed. Clean any debris or oily deposits from the grommet openings in the manifold. Oil promotes deterioration of the grommet.
13. Pinch the end together, then push the wire retainer clips from the opening in the mounting plate (10, **Figure 54**).

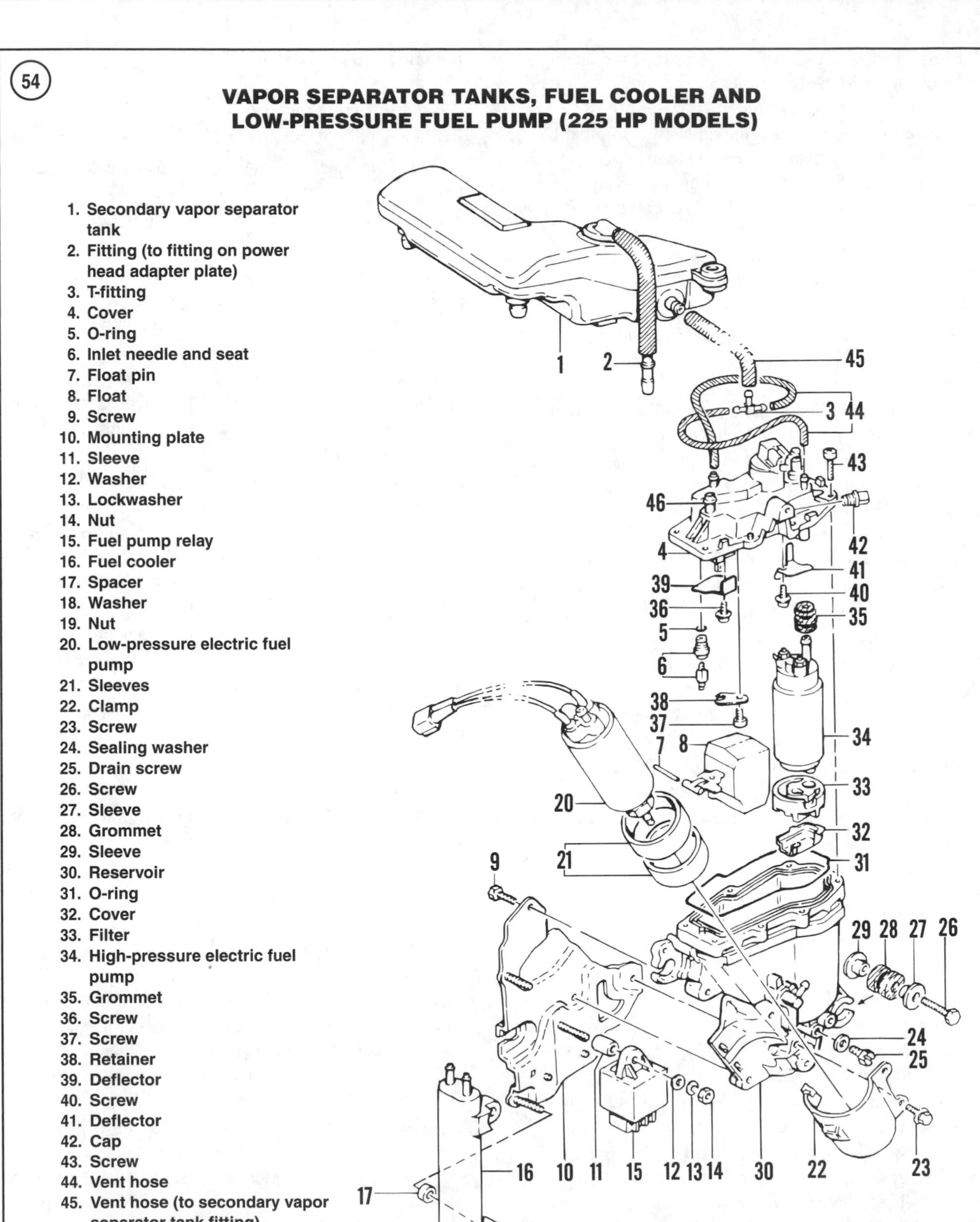
54
VAPOR SEPARATOR TANKS, FUEL COOLER AND LOW-PRESSURE FUEL PUMP (225 HP MODELS)
1. Secondary vapor separator tank
2. Fitting (to fitting on power head adapter plate)
3. T-fitting
4. Cover
5. O-ring
6. Inlet needle and seat
7. Float pin
8. Float
9. Screw
10. Mounting plate
11. Sleeve
12. Washer
13. Lockwasher
14. Nut
15. Fuel pump relay
16. Fuel cooler
17. Spacer
18. Washer
19. Nut
20. Low-pressure electric fuel pump
21. Sleeves
22. Clamp
23. Screw
24. Sealing washer
25. Drain screw
26. Screw
27. Sleeve
28. Grommet
29. Sleeve
30. Reservoir
31. O-ring
32. Cover
33. Filter
34. High-pressure electric fuel pump
35. Grommet
36. Screw
37. Screw
38. Retainer
39. Deflector
40. Screw
41. Deflector
42. Cap
43. Screw
44. Vent hose
45. Vent hose (to secondary vapor separator tank fitting)
46. Fuel supply hose fitting

14. Remove the three screws (9, **Figure 54**), then separate the mounting plate (10) from the vapor separator tank.

15. Insert the three grommets (28, **Figure 54**) into the openings in the tank. Make sure the groove in the grommets fits over the lip in the openings. Insert the sleeves (27 and 29, **Figure 54**) into the grommets with the larger diameter side facing outward.

16. Insert the locking tabs of the wire retaining clips into the openings in the mounting plate. Push on the clips until the tabs lock into the openings.

17. Align the three screw openings, then seat the vapor separator tank onto the mounting bracket. Thread the three screws (9, **Figure 54**) into the mounting plate and tank openings. Tighten the screws to 159 in.-lb. (18.0 N•m).

18. Route the fuel hoses to the connection points, then install the tank and mounting plate assembly onto the power head. Align the screw openings, then thread the four mounting screws (26, **Figure 54**) into the sleeves and threaded opening in the power head. Check for hoses or wiring pinched between the mounting plate and the power head. Reposition wiring or hoses to eliminate pinching, then tighten the four screws to 159 in.-lb. (18.0 N•m).

19. Reconnect the low-pressure electric fuel pump, high-pressure electric fuel pump and fuel pump relay harness connectors onto the engine wire harness connectors. Route the wiring to prevent interference with moving components.

20. Secure the hose retaining bracket with the screw. The bracket is located directly below the fuel cooler.

21. Push the water hoses fully onto the fuel cooler fittings. The water hoses are on the upper and lower starboard side fittings.

22. Push the fuel return hose fully onto the fitting on the top and port side fuel cooler fitting. Secure the hose with a spring clamp.

23. Route the fuel hose with the female quick-connect fitting over the upper rear of the power head until aligned with male fitting. Push the collar on the female fitting toward the fitting, then insert the male fitting fully into the opening. Push the collar away from the female fitting to secure the connection. Tug on the fittings to verify a secure connection.

24. Connect the vent hose (45, **Figure 54**) onto the T-fitting (3). Route the hoses to prevent interference with moving components.

25. Connect the battery cable.

26. Start the engine and immediately check for fuel leaks. Immediately stop the engine if leakage is evident. Correct the leaks before operating the engine.

27. Stop the engine. Install the silencer cover as described in this chapter.

Disassembly and assembly

Refer to **Figure 54**.

1. Remove the vapor separator tank as described in this section. Clamp the assembly into a vise with protective jaws. Do not over-tighten the vise.

2. Loosen the clamp, then disconnect the fuel supply hose from the fitting on the cover (4, **Figure 54**). When assembled on the engine, the hose leads to the mechanical fuel pump.

3. Remove the clamp, then use a flat blade screwdriver to push the fuel outlet hose off of the outlet fitting (46, **Figure 54**). When assembled on the engine, the hose leads to the fuel rails.

4. Loosen the clamp, then push the fuel return hose from the fitting on the reservoir (30, **Figure 54**). When assembled on the engine, the hose connects to the fuel cooler.

5. Remove the drain screw (25, **Figure 54**) and sealing washer (24). Discard the sealing washer.

6. Disconnect the vent hoses (44, **Figure 54**) from the two fittings on the cover.

7. Remove the seven cover screws (43, **Figure 54**). If necessary, use an impact driver to loosen the screws. Replace any screws damaged during the removal process.

8. Lift the cover assembly from the reservoir. Do not pry the cover loose. The delicate mating surfaces are easily damaged with a pry bar. If necessary, tap the cover loose with a rubber mallet.

9. Remove the O-ring (31, **Figure 54**) from the groove in the reservoir. Discard the O-ring.

10. Carefully pull the high-pressure electric fuel pump (34, **Figure 54**) out of the cover to access the wire connector. Unplug the wire connector to free the pump. Remove the grommet (35, **Figure 54**) from the pump or opening in the cover. Inspect the grommet for deformed, cracked or deteriorated surfaces. Replace the grommet if these or other defects are evident.

11. Pull the cover (32, **Figure 54**) from the bottom of the pump. Carefully pull the filter (33, **Figure 54**) from the pump. If necessary, twist the filter until free from the pump. Inspect the filter for debris, varnish-like deposits and damaged surfaces. Replace the filter if any defects are evident.

NOTE

The float pin in the vapor separator tank is rounded on one end and square on the other. Push on the rounded end to remove the pin.

5

Install the rounded end first when installing the pin.

12. Use a small pick to push the float pin (7, **Figure 54**) from the cover. Lift the float (8, **Figure 54**) from the cover.
13. Remove the screw (37, **Figure 54**) and retainer (38), then carefully pull the inlet needle and seat (6) from the cover. Remove and discard the O-ring (5, **Figure 55**) from the seat or opening in the cover.
14. Remove the screws (36 and 40, **Figure 54**) then lift the deflectors (39 and 41) from the cover. Inspect the deflectors for cracking or corroded surfaces and replace as needed.
15. Clean and inspect the vapor separator tank components as described in this chapter (see *Fuel System Service*). Dry the components with compressed air.
16. Fit the deflectors onto the cover and secure with the two screws (36 and 40, **Figure 54**). Tighten the screws to 18 in.-lb. (2.0 N•m).
17. Apply a light coat of engine oil to a new O-ring (5, **Figure 54**) and install it onto the needle seat. Install the seat into the opening in the cover. Rotate the seat during installation to prevent damage to the O-ring. Make sure the tapered seat faces outward. Fit the retainer (38, **Figure 54**) arms into the groove in the seat, then secure the retainer with the screw (37). Tighten the screw to 18 in.-lb. (2.0 N•m).
18. Insert the inlet needle into the seat. The tapered tip of the valve must contact the taper in the seat.
19. Align the tab on the float (8, **Figure 54**) with the inlet needle, then align the pin bore in the float with the corresponding openings in the cover bosses. Insert the float pin, rounded end first, into the mounted bosses and float opening until the end is flush with the boss.
20. Install the filter (33, **Figure 54**) onto the bottom of the pump (34). Push the cover (32, **Figure 54**) onto the filter. The slot in the cover must face toward the opposite side of the pump as the fuel outlet passage at the top of the pump. Rotate the cover as needed.
21. Apply a light coat of engine oil to the grommet (35, **Figure 54**) and install it into the fuel pump outlet opening in the top cover. Align the grommet opening with the fuel passage, then seat the grommet in the opening.
22. Plug the fuel pump wiring onto the connector in the cover. Align the fuel outlet on the pump with the opening in the grommet, then fully seat the pump against the grommet.
23. Fit the new O-ring (31, **Figure 54**) into the groove in the reservoir (30). Do not apply any sealant to the O-ring.
24. Guide the tabs on the fuel pump filter with the notches in the reservoir while carefully lowering cover onto the reservoir. Do not pinch the pump wiring between the cover and reservoir or pump body. Reposition the wiring as needed. Verify correct alignment, then seat the cover onto the reservoir.
25. Thread the seven screws (43, **Figure 54**) into the cover and reservoir openings. Tighten the screws in a crossing pattern to 35 in.-lb. (4.0 N•m).
26. Install a new sealing washer (24, **Figure 54**) onto the drain screw (25). Thread the screw into the reservoir and tighten to 18 in.-lb. (2.0 N•m).
27. Connect the vent hoses (44, **Figure 54**) onto the two smaller fittings on the top cover.
28. Push the fuel supply hose fully onto the fitting on the cover (46, **Figure 54**). Secure the hose with a spring clamp.
29. Slip a new full-circle clamp over the end push the fuel outlet hose fully onto the cover fitting. Slide the clamp over the hose until positioned over the fitting. Tighten the full-circle clamp as described in this chapter (see *Fuel Hose Connector Replacement*).
30. Push the fuel return hose onto the fitting on the reservoir. Secure the hose with a spring clamp.
31. Install the vapor separator tank as described in this section.

SECONDARY VAPOR SEPARATOR TANK REMOVAL AND INSTALLATION

This component is used only on 225 hp models. The tank is located on top of the silencer cover. The tank is non-serviceable.

Refer to **Figure 54.**

1. Disconnect the vent hose (45, **Figure 54**) from the fitting on the side of the reservoir.
2. Carefully disconnect the vent hose fitting (2, **Figure 54**) from the fitting on the power head adapter plate. Route the disconnected hose to the tank to prevent the hose from snagging other components during removal.
3. Remove the screw from the top of the tank. Lift out the tank until the mounting posts are free from the openings in the flywheel cover.
4. Clean the external surfaces with a suitable solvent and dry with compressed air. Do not direct air into the fittings. The air pressure may rupture or damage the check valve.
5. Guide the mounting pins on the bottom of the secondary vapor separator tank into the corresponding openings in the silencer cover. Seat the tank onto the cover. Thread the screw into the secondary vapor separator tank. Tighten the screw to 71 in.-lb. (8.0 N•m).
6. Route the vent hose and fitting (2, **Figure 54**) to the power head adapter and connect to the adapter fitting.

7. Connect the vent hose (45, **Figure 54**) onto the fitting on the side of the reservoir. Route the vent hoses to prevent interference with moving components. Secure the hoses with plastic locking clamps as needed.
8. Connect the battery cable.

LOW-PRESSURE ELECTRIC FUEL PUMP REPLACEMENT

The low-pressure electric fuel pump is used on 225 hp models. The pump mounts onto the vapor separator tank on the port side of the power head. The silencer cover must be removed to access the pump. The pump is non-serviceable.

Refer to **Figure 54**.

1. Remove the silencer cover as described in this chapter.
2. Remove the rubber plug from the top of the vapor separator tank (**Figure 42**). Depress the valve in the plug opening to relieve the vapor pressure. Install the plug after relieving the pressure.
3. Disconnect the engine wire harness connector from the low-pressure electric fuel pump harness.
4. Cut the plastic locking clamp to free the fuel hose and check valve from the fuel pump clamp (22, **Figure 54**).
5. Remove the spring clamps, then use a flat blade screwdriver to push the hoses off of the upper and lower fuel pump fittings. Drain the hoses into a suitable container.
6. Remove the two screws (23, **Figure 54**), then swing the clamp (22) away from the fuel pump (20). Disengage the hooks on the clamp from the recesses in the reservoir, then remove the clamp.
7. Pull the pump out of the recess in the reservoir. Remove the sleeves (21, **Figure 54**) from the pump.
8. Slip the sleeves over the replacement pump and position them equal amounts from the top and bottom ends of the pump. Make sure to leave a gap between the sleeves.
9. Carefully fit the replacement pump into the recess in the reservoir. Reposition the sleeves as necessary.
10. Engage the hooks on the clamp (22, **Figure 54**) into the recesses in the reservoir. Swing the clamp over the low-pressure pump. Seat the pump into the recess and push the clamp firmly against the reservoir. Thread the two screws (23, **Figure 54**) into the clamp and reservoir openings. Evenly tighten the two screws to 44 in.-lb. (5.0 N•m).
11. Connect the engine wire harness connector onto the low-pressure electric fuel pump harness. Route the wiring to prevent interference with moving components. Secure the wiring with plastic locking clamps as needed.
12. Insert a plastic locking clamp into the slot in the fuel pump clamp (22, **Figure 54**). Tighten the clamp to secure the fuel hose and check valve. Make sure the arrow on the check valve body faces downward.
13. Push the fuel hoses fully onto the upper and lower fittings of the low-pressure electric fuel pump (20, **Figure 54**). Secure the hoses with spring clamps.
14. Inspect all hose connections and the fuel pump assembly for evidence of fuel leakage while squeezing the primer bulb. Correct any fuel leakage before proceeding.
15. Connect the battery cable.
16. Start the engine and check for fuel leaks. Immediately stop the engine if leakage is evident. Correct the leak before operating the engine. 5
17. Stop the engine. Install the silencer cover as described in this chapter.

FUEL PUMP RELAY REPLACEMENT

The fuel pump relay mounts onto the vapor separator mounting bracket on the port side of the power head. This component is used on 225 hp models. The silencer cover and vapor separator tank must be removed to access the relay.

Refer to **Figure 54**.

1. Remove the vapor separator tank assembly as described in this chapter.
2. Push in on the tab, then unplug the harness from the relay.
3. Remove the nut (14, **Figure 54**), lockwasher (13) and washer (12), then pull the relay from the stud.
4. Pull the relay (15, **Figure 54**) and sleeve (11) from the stud.
5. Slide the sleeve over the mounting stud. Slide the opening in the replacement relay over the mounting stud, then seat the relay against the sleeve. Install the washer, lockwasher and nut onto the stud. Hold the relay in position while tightening the nut to 27 in.-lb. (3.0 N•m).
6. Plug the harness onto the relay. Tug on the harness to verify a secure connection.
7. Install the vapor separator tank as described in the chapter.

FUEL PUMP DRIVER REPLACEMENT

The fuel pump driver mounts onto a bracket on the port side lower engine cover. The driver controls the operation of the low-pressure electric fuel pump. This component is used on 225 hp models.

1. Remove the silencer cover as describe in this chapter.
2. Trace the blue/red wire from the low-pressure electric fuel pump to the fuel pump driver.

3. Depress the locking tab, then carefully unplug the four-wire connector from the driver harness connector.
4. Remove the screw to free the driver from the bracket.
5. Depress the locking tab, then push the four-wire connector onto the driver harness connector. Release the locking tab, then tug on the harness to verify a secure connection.
6. Fit the driver onto the mounting bracket, then thread the screw into the drive and mounting bracket openings. Tighten the screw to 71 in.-lb. (8.0 N•m).
7. Route the wiring to prevent pinching or interference with moving components.
8. Install the silencer cover as described in this chapter.

FUEL COOLER REPLACEMENT

115 hp Model

The fuel cooler mounts onto the side of the intake manifold on the port side of the engine.

Refer to **Figure 55**.

1. Locate the cooling water hoses, fuel hoses and corresponding fittings on the fuel cooler (19, **Figure 55**). The cooling water hoses connect onto the upper and lower fittings furthest from the intake manifold. The fuel hoses connect to the closer fittings.
2. Loosen the clamps (16, **Figure 55**), then use a flat blade screwdriver to push the two cooling water hoses from the cooler fittings. Drain all water from the hoses.
3. Place a shop towel under the cooler to capture spilled fuel. Loosen the clamps (6, **Figure 55**), then disconnect the two hoses from the fuel cooler fittings. Drain the hoses into a container suitable for holding fuel.
4. Cut the plastic locking clamps (15, **Figure 55**) from the fuel cooler and the lower water and fuel hoses.
5. Support the cooler while fully loosening the two screws (18, **Figure 55**) and washers (17). Do not pull the screws from the cooler at this time.
6. Carefully pull the cooler away from the intake manifold. Remove the two spacers (9, **Figure 55**), then remove the screws and washers.
7. Use a suitable solvent to clean the external surfaces and internal cooler passages. Direct compressed air into the fittings to remove debris and contaminants. Dry the cooler with compressed air prior to installation. Cover the fitting with tape or a cap to prevent contamination while the cooler is removed.
8. Insert the mounting screws and washers into the openings in the cooler. Make sure the screw heads are on the same side of the cooler as the cooling water fittings. Slip the two spacers onto the other end of the screws.
9. Install the cooler onto the intake manifold. Align the openings and thread the mounting screws (18, **Figure 55**) into the intake manifold. Tighten the screws to 70 in.-lb. (7.9 N•m).
10. Push the cooling water and fuel hoses onto the cooler fittings. The cooling water hoses connect onto the upper and lower fittings furthest from the intake manifold. The fuel hoses connect onto the closer fittings. Secure the hoses with the four spring clamps (6 and 16, **Figure 55**).
11. Route the cooling water and fuel hoses to prevent interference with moving components. Install the plastic locking clamps (15, **Figure 55**) onto the fuel cooler and lower water and fuel hoses.
12. Inspect all hose connections and the fuel pump assembly for evidence of fuel leakage while squeezing the primer bulb. Correct any fuel leakage before proceeding.
13. Connect the battery cable.
14. Start the engine and immediately check for fuel leaks. Immediately stop the engine if leakage is evident. Correct the source of the leakage before operating the engine.

225 hp Model

The fuel cooler mounts onto the vapor separator mounting bracket on the port side of the power head. The silencer cover and vapor separator tank must be removed to access the relay.

Refer to **Figure 54**.

1. Remove the vapor separator tank as described in this chapter.
2. Loosen the clamp and use a flat blade screwdriver to push the remaining fuel hose from the cooler fitting. The hose leads to the return fitting on the vapor separator tank. Drain the hose into a container suitable for holding fuel.
3. Remove the two nuts (19, **Figure 54**) and washers (18), then pull the fuel cooler (16) away from the mounting plate (10). Remove the two spacers (17, **Figure 54**) from the cooler mounting bosses or the studs on the mounting plate.
4. Use a suitable solvent to clean the external surfaces and internal cooler passages. Direct compressed air into the fittings to remove debris and contaminants. Dry the cooler with compressed air prior to installation. Cover the fitting with tape or a cap to prevent contamination while the cooler is removed.
5. Fit the spacers (17, **Figure 54**) over the studs on the mounting plate. Guide the cooler over the studs and seat the cooler bosses against the spacers. Install the two washers (18, **Figure 54**), then thread the two nuts (19) onto the studs. Tighten the nuts to 44 in.-lb. (5.0 N•m).
6. Push the fuel hose onto the lower port side fitting on the fuel cooler. The cooling water hoses connect onto the

FUEL COOLER, FUEL PRESSURE REGULATOR, FUEL RAIL AND INJECTORS (115 HP MODEL)

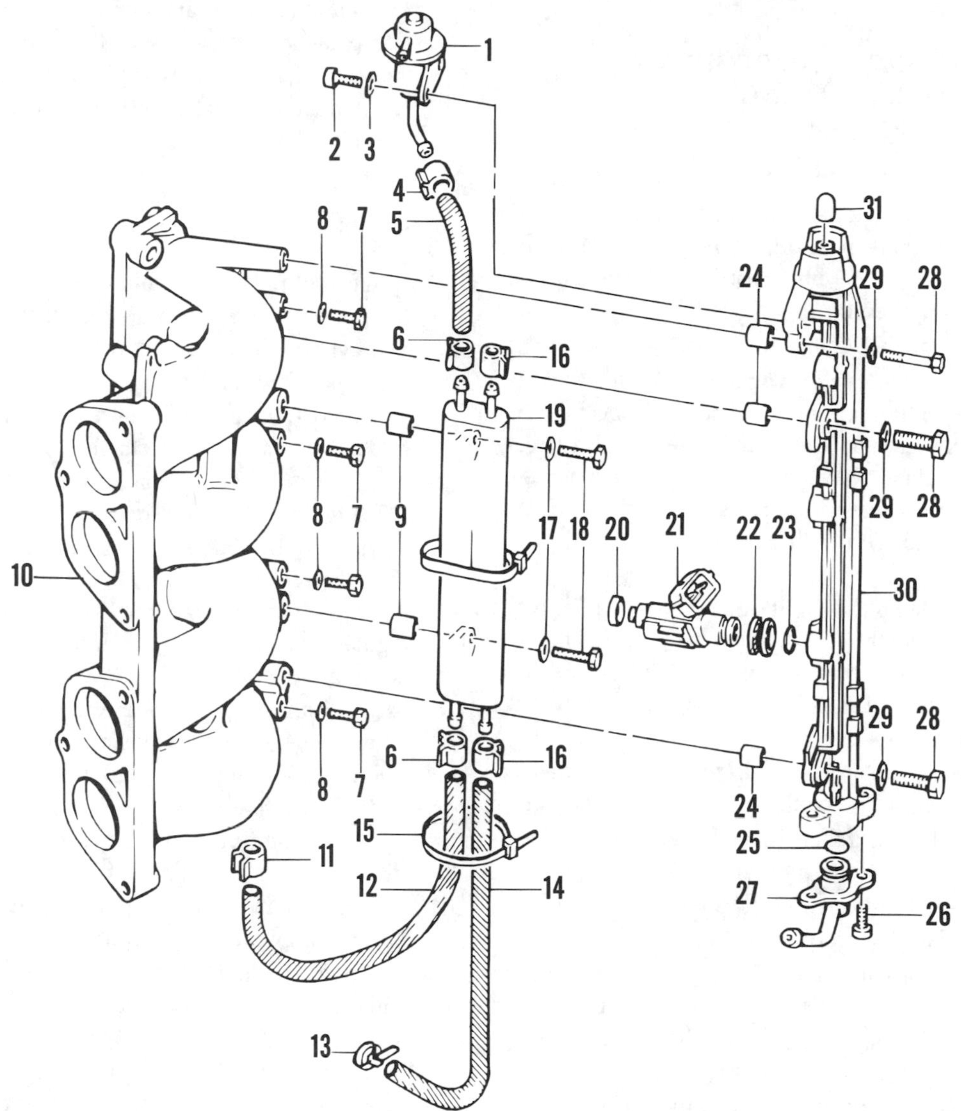

1. Fuel pressure regulator
2. Screw
3. Washer
4. Spring clamp
5. Fuel return hose
6. Spring clamps
7. Plug
8. Sealing washer
9. Spacer
10. Intake manifold
11. Spring clamp
12. Fuel return hose (to vapor separator tank)
13. Plastic locking clamp
14. Cooling water hose (from exhaust cover fitting)
15. Plastic locking clamp
16. Spring clamps
17. Washer
18. Screw
19. Fuel cooler
20. Seal
21. Fuel injector
22. Grommet
23. O-ring
24. Spacer
25. O-ring
26. Screw
27. Fitting
28. Screw
29. Washer
30. Fuel rail
31. Cap

starboard side fittings. Secure the hose with a spring clamp.

7. Install the vapor separator tank as described in this chapter.

FUEL PRESSURE REGULATOR REPLACEMENT

115 hp Model

The fuel pressure regulator mounts onto the top of the fuel rail on the rear and port side of the power head. A fuel pressure test gauge (Mercury part No. 91-166850A7 or equivalent) is required for this procedure.

Refer to **Figure 55.**

1. Remove the cap (31, **Figure 55**) on the top of the fuel rail to access the fuel pressure test port. Connect the fuel pressure test gauge onto the fitting (**Figure 41**, typical). Direct the gauge drain hose into a suitable container, then depress the drain valve to relieve the fuel pressure. Disconnect the gauge. Drain all of the fuel from the gauge hoses.
2. Loosen the clamp (4, **Figure 55**) then use a flat blade screwdriver to push the fuel return hose (5) off of the regulator fitting. Disconnect the pressure reference hose from the regulator fitting. The hose leads to the intake manifold fitting.
3. Remove the two screws (2, **Figure 55**) and washers (3), then disconnect the regulator (1) from the fuel rail.
4. Remove and discard the small O-ring from the regulator or the opening into the fuel rail.
5. Cover the fuel rail opening to prevent contamination while the regulator is removed.
6. Use an aerosol carburetor cleaner to clean debris or oily deposits from the regulator. Dry the regulator with compressed air. Do not direct air into the fittings. Pressurized air may damage the regulator.
7. Apply a light coat of four-cycle outboard engine oil to a new O-ring and install it onto the mating surface of the fuel pressure regulator.
8. Guide the tube on the regulator into the fuel rail opening, then seat the regulator onto the fuel rail. Rotate the regulator to align the regulator and rail screw openings. The smaller air hose fitting must be on the top side of the regulator. Thread the two screws (2, **Figure 55**) and washers (3) into the regulator flange and fuel rail. Tighten the screws to 70 in.-lb. (7.9 N•m).
9. Push the fuel return hose (5, **Figure 55**) fully onto the larger of the two regulator fittings. Secure the hose with the spring clamp. Push the air hose onto the smaller fitting. This hose does not require a clamp.
10. Inspect all hose connections and the fuel pump assembly for evidence of fuel leakage while squeezing the primer bulb. Correct any fuel leakage before proceeding.
11. Connect the battery cable.
12. Start the engine and immediately check for fuel leaks. Immediately stop the engine if leakage is evident. Correct the source of the leakage before operating the engine.
13. Thread the cap (31, **Figure 55**) onto the fuel pressure test port.

225 hp Model

The fuel pressure regulator mounts onto the port side fuel rail. The port side intake manifold must be removed to access the fuel pressure regulator.

Refer to **Figure 39.**

1. Remove the silencer cover and port side intake manifold as described in this chapter.
2. Place a shop towel under the fuel pressure regulator (22, **Figure 39**) to capture spilled fuel.
3. Loosen the clamp then use a flat blade screwdriver to push the fuel return hose off the regulator fitting. The return hose is the larger of the two hoses connecting onto the regulator. Drain the hose into a container suitable for holding fuel.
4. Disconnect the pressure reference hose from the regulator fitting. The hose leads to a fitting on the idle air control motor housing (37, **Figure 39**).
5. Remove the two screws (20, **Figure 39**) and washers (21), then carefully pull the regulator (22) from the fuel rail.
6. Remove and discard the O-ring from the regulator or the opening into the fuel rail.
7. Cover the fuel rail opening to prevent contamination while the regulator is removed.
8. Use an aerosol carburetor cleaner to clean debris or oily deposits from the regulator. Dry the regulator with compressed air. Do not direct air into the fittings. Pressurized air may damage the regulator.
9. Apply a light coat of four-cycle outboard engine oil to a new O-ring and install it onto the mating surface of the fuel pressure regulator.
10. Guide the tube on the regulator into the fuel rail opening, then seat the regulator onto the fuel rail. Rotate the regulator to align the regulator and rail screw openings. The smaller air hose fitting must be on the top side of the regulator. Thread the two screws (20, **Figure 39**) and washers (21) into the regulator flange and fuel rail. Tighten the screws to 71 in.-lb. (8.0 N•m).
11. Push the fuel return hose fully onto the larger of the two regulator fittings. The fuel return hose leads to the

fuel cooler when assembled onto the engine. Secure the hose with the spring clamp.

12. Push the air hose onto the smaller fitting. This hose does not require a clamp.

13. Install the port side intake manifold as described in this chapter.

14. Connect the battery cable.

15. Start the engine and immediately check for fuel leaks. Immediately stop the engine if leakage is evident. Correct the leak before operating the engine.

16. Stop the engine, then install the silencer cover as described in this chapter.

FUEL RAIL AND INJECTORS REMOVAL AND INSTALLATION

WARNING

Wear safety goggles to protect the eyes when working with the fuel system. The fuel rails contain fuel under high pressure. Fuel may unexpectedly spray out. Always relieve the fuel pressure before removing the fuel rails.

To prevent dangerous fuel leakage, always replace all seals, grommets and O-rings when removed from the fuel rail or injectors.

Replace the injector filters if debris or contaminants are found in the fuel rail or connecting hoses. Blockage in the injector filters can cause symptoms that mimic a faulty injector.

To reduce down time and the chance for contamination, have all replacement seals, grommets, O-rings and other needed parts on-hand before removing the fuel rails.

The fuel injectors are essentially non-serviceable. However, professional cleaning can renew the injectors by purging deposits and debris from the internal passages. Contact an automotive repair shop that performs this service. Replace the injector if testing reveals an electrical failure.

115 hp Model

The fuel rail mounts to the side of the intake manifold on the rear and port side of the power head.

Refer to **Figure 55**.

1. Remove the cap (31, **Figure 55**) on the top of the fuel rail to access the fuel pressure test port. Connect the fuel pressure test gauge onto the fitting (**Figure 41**, typical). Direct the gauge drain hose into a suitable container, then depress the drain valve to relieve the fuel pressure. Disconnect the gauge. Drain all of the fuel from the gauge hoses.

2. Cut the plastic locking clamps that secure the wiring to the fuel rail.

3. Disconnect the engine wire harness connectors from the four fuel injectors. Push on the wire clip to release the connectors from the injectors.

4. Place a shop towel under the fuel rail to capture spilled fuel.

5. Remove the clamp and use a flat blade screwdriver to push the fuel hose off of the fuel rail fitting (27, **Figure 55**). The hose leads to the outlet fitting on the vapor separator tank. Drain the hose into a container suitable for holding fuel.

6. Loosen the clamp (4, **Figure 55**) and use a flat blade screwdriver to push the fuel return hose (5) off of the regulator fitting. Disconnect the pressure reference hose from the regulator fitting. The hose leads to the intake manifold fitting.

7. Support the fuel rail (30, **Figure 55**) while fully loosening the three screws (28, **Figure 55**) and washers (29). Do not pull the screws from the fuel rail at this time.

8. Carefully pull the fuel rail from the intake manifold. Remove the spacers (24, **Figure 55**), screws, and washers.

9. Remove the four fuel injectors (21, **Figure 55**) from the intake manifold or fuel rail openings. For easier removal, gently twist the injectors while pulling them from the openings.

10. Remove the seals (20, **Figure 55**) from the injector tips or the openings in the intake manifold. Discard the seals.

11. Remove the grommets and O-rings from the injectors (**Figure 56**). Discard the grommets and O-rings. Carefully pull the filters (**Figure 56**) from the fuel injector inlets. Replace the filter if debris, deposits or damaged surfaces are evident.

12. Remove the two screws (26, **Figure 55**), then pull the fitting (27) from the bottom of the fuel rail. Remove the O-ring (25, **Figure 55**) from the fitting or fuel rail opening.

13. Remove the fuel pressure regulator as described in this chapter.

14. Use a suitable solvent to clean the external surfaces and internal rail passages. Direct compressed air into the openings to remove debris and contaminants. Dry the rail with compressed air, then cover the openings to prevent contamination.

15. Install the fuel pressure regulator onto the fuel rail as described in this chapter.

16. Fit a new grommet (**Figure 56**) over the inlet end of the fuel injectors. Seat the grommet against the plastic body of the injector.

17. Lubricate a new O-ring with four-cycle outboard engine oil, then install it into the grooves in the fuel injectors.

18. Push the filters (**Figure 56**) into the injector openings until the flange contacts the injector inlet.

19. Insert the inlet end of the injectors into the four openings into the fuel rail. Gently rotate the injectors during installation to prevent damage to the O-rings. Seat the injectors into the openings. The grommet must contact the fuel rail.

20. Lubricate a new O-ring (25, **Figure 55**) with four-cycle outboard engine oil and install it onto the fitting (27). Guide the fitting into the opening at the bottom of the rail. Gently rotate the fitting during installation to prevent damage to the O-ring. Seat the fitting onto the rail. Rotate the fitting to direct the hose fitting facing forward, then thread the two screws (26, **Figure 55**) into the fitting flange and fuel rail openings. Tighten the screws to 43 in.-lb. (4.9 N•m).

21. Lubricate the new seals (20, **Figure 55**) with four-cycle outboard engine oil, then install them into the four injector openings in the intake manifold.

22. Insert the three screws (28, **Figure 55**) and washers (29) into the openings in the fuel rail. The 6 mm screw fits into the upper opening. The two 8 mm screws fit into the middle and lower openings. Slip the spacers (24, **Figure 55**) over the threaded ends of the screws, then seat them against the fuel rail.

23. Carefully guide the four fuel injector tips into the corresponding seals in the intake manifold. Verify proper alignment with the openings, then seat the fuel rail against the intake manifold. Move the fuel rail as necessary to align the screw openings, then thread the three screws into the intake manifold. Do not tighten the screws at this time.

24. *Slowly* rotate the injectors to position the harness connector terminals facing rearward.

25. Tighten the single 6 mm screw to 70 in.-lb. (7.9 N•m). Tighten the two 8 mm screws to 159 in.-lb. (18.0 N•m).

26. Push the fuel return hose (5, **Figure 55**) fully onto the fuel pressure regulator fitting. The return hose fitting is the larger of the two regulator fittings. Secure the hose with a spring clamp.

27. Slip a new full-circle clamp over the hose and seat the fuel hose fully onto the fitting (27, **Figure 55**). The hose leads to the fuel outlet fitting on the vapor separator tank. Slide the clamp over the fitting and tighten as described in this chapter (see *Fuel Hose Connector Replacement*).

28. Connect the pressure reference hose onto the smaller regulator fitting. The hose leads to the intake manifold fitting.

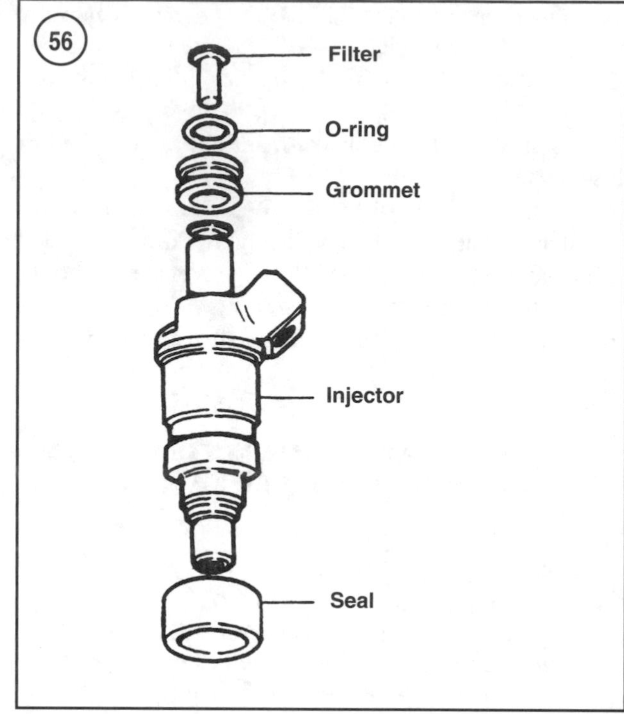

29. Connect the engine wire harness connectors to the four fuel injectors. Secure the wiring to the fuel rail with plastic locking clamps.

30. Route all hoses and wiring to prevent pinching or interference with moving components.

31. Inspect all hose connections and the fuel pump assembly for evidence of fuel leakage while squeezing the primer bulb. Correct any fuel leak before proceeding.

32. Connect the battery cable.

33. Start the engine and immediately check for fuel leaks. Immediately stop the engine if leakage is evident. Correct the leak before operating the engine.

34. Thread the cap (31, **Figure 55**) onto the fuel pressure test port.

225 hp model

Port side

The fuel rail mounts onto the starboard side of the port side throttle bodies. The port intake manifold must be removed to access the fuel rail.

Refer to **Figure 39**.

1. Cut the full-circle clamp, then use a flat blade screwdriver to push the fuel hose off of the fitting (28, **Figure 39**).

2. Loosen the clamp then push the fuel return hose off the regulator fitting. The fuel return hose is the larger of the

two regulator fittings. The return hose leads to the fuel cooler. Disconnect the pressure reference hose from the smaller regulator fitting. The hose leads to the intake manifold fitting.

3. Support the fuel rail (23, **Figure 39**) while fully loosening the three screws (26, **Figure 39**) and washers (25). Do not pull the screws from the fuel rail at this time.

4. Carefully pull the fuel rail from the throttle bodies. Remove the three alignment collars from the screws or throttle body openings, then remove the screws and washers.

5. Remove the three fuel injectors (30, **Figure 39**) from the throttle body or fuel rail openings. For easier removal, carefully twist the injectors while pulling them from the openings.

6. Remove the seals (16, **Figure 39**) from the injector tips or the openings in the throttle bodies. Discard the seals.

7. Remove the grommets and O-rings from the injectors (**Figure 56**). Discard the grommets and O-rings. Carefully pull the filters (**Figure 56**) from the fuel injector inlets. Replace the filter if debris, deposits or damaged surfaces are evident.

8. Remove the two screws (29, **Figure 39**), then pull the fitting (28) from the bottom of the fuel rail. Remove the O-ring (27, **Figure 39**) from the fitting or fuel rail opening. Discard the O-ring.

9. Remove the fuel pressure regulator as described in this chapter.

10. Use a suitable solvent to clean the external surfaces and internal rail passages. Direct compressed air into the openings to remove debris and contaminants. Dry the rail with compressed air, then cover the openings to prevent contamination.

11. Install the fuel pressure regulator onto the fuel rail as described in this chapter.

12. Fit a new grommet (**Figure 56**) over the inlet end of the fuel injectors. Seat the grommet against the plastic body of the injector.

13. Lubricate the a new O-ring with four-cycle outboard engine oil, and install it into the grooves in the fuel injectors.

14. Carefully push the filters (**Figure 56**) into the injector openings until the flange contacts the injector inlet.

15. Carefully insert the inlet end of the injectors into the three openings into the fuel rail. Gently rotate the injectors to align the injector body with the recesses in the fuel rail, then seat the injectors into the openings. The grommet must contact the fuel rail.

16. Lubricate the surfaces with four-cycle outboard engine oil, then install a new O-ring (27, **Figure 39**) onto the fitting (28). Carefully guide the fitting into the opening at the bottom of the rail. Gently rotate the fitting during installation to prevent damage to the O-ring. Seat the fitting onto the rail. Rotate the fitting to direct the hose fitting facing toward the injectors. Align the openings, then thread the two screws (29, **Figure 39**) into the fitting flange and fuel rail openings. Tighten the screws to 44 in.-lb. (5.0 N•m).

17. Lubricate the surfaces with four-cycle outboard engine oil, then insert the new seals (16, **Figure 39**) into the openings in the throttle bodies.

18. Insert the three alignment collars into the openings in the throttle bodies. Carefully guide the three fuel injector tips into the corresponding seals in the throttle bodies. Verify proper alignment with the openings and the alignment collars, then seat the fuel rail against the intake manifold.

19. Support the fuel rail while threading the three screws (26, **Figure 39**) and washers (25) into the throttle bodies. Verify proper seating of the rail and injectors, then tighten the screws to 159 in.-lb. (18.0 N•m).

20. Push the fuel return hose completely onto the fuel pressure regulator fitting. The return hose fitting is the larger of the two regulator fittings. Secure the hose with a spring clamp.

21. Slip a new full-circle clamp over the end then push the fuel hose fully onto the fitting (28, **Figure 39**). The hose leads to the fuel outlet fitting on the vapor separator tank. Slide the clamp over the hose until positioned over the fitting. Tighten the full-circle clamp as described in this chapter (see *Fuel Hose Connector Replacement*).

22. Install the port intake manifold as described in this chapter.

Starboard side

The fuel rail mounts onto the port side of the starboard side throttle bodies. The starboard intake manifold must be removed to access the fuel rail.

Refer to **Figure 44.**

1. Cut the full-circle clamps (30 and 38, **Figure 44**), then use a flat blade screwdriver to push the fuel hoses off of the fittings (28 and 35).

2. Support the fuel rail (33, **Figure 44**) while fully loosening the three screws (31, **Figure 44**) and washers (32). Do not pull the screws from the fuel rail at this time.

3. Carefully pull the fuel rail from the throttle bodies. Remove the three alignment collars (23, **Figure 44**) from the screws or throttle body openings, then remove the screws and washers.

4. Remove the three fuel injectors (25, **Figure 44**) from the throttle body or fuel rail openings. For easier removal, carefully twist the injectors while pulling them from the openings.

5. Remove the seals (24, **Figure 44**) from the injector tips or the openings in the throttle bodies. Discard the seals.

6. Remove the grommets and O-rings from the injectors (**Figure 56**). Discard the grommets and O-rings. Carefully pull the filters (**Figure 56**) from the fuel injector inlets. Replace the filter if debris, deposits or damaged surfaces are evident.

7. Remove the two screws (27, **Figure 44**), then pull the fitting (28) from the bottom of the fuel rail. Remove and discard the O-ring (29, **Figure 44**) from the fitting or fuel rail opening.

8. Remove the two screws (37, **Figure 44**) and the bracket (36), then pull the fitting (35) from the top of the fuel rail. Remove and discard the O-ring (34, **Figure 44**) from the fitting or fuel rail opening.

9. Use a suitable solvent to clean the external surfaces and internal rail passages. Direct compressed air into the openings to remove debris and contaminants. Dry the rail with compressed air, then cover the openings to prevent contamination.

10. Fit a new grommet (**Figure 56**) over the inlet end of the fuel injectors. Seat the grommet against the plastic body of the injector.

11. Lubricate a new O-ring with four-cycle outboard engine oil, and install it into the grooves in the fuel injectors.

12. Carefully push the filters (**Figure 56**) into the injector openings until the flange contacts the injector inlet.

13. Carefully insert the inlet end of the injectors into the three openings into the fuel rail. Gently rotate the injectors to align the injector body with the recesses in the fuel rail, then seat the injectors into the openings. The grommet must contact the fuel rail.

14. Lubricate the surfaces with four-cycle outboard engine oil, then install a new O-ring (29, **Figure 44**) onto the lower fitting (28). Carefully guide the fitting into the opening at the bottom of the rail. Gently rotate the fitting during installation to prevent damage to the O-ring. Seat the fitting onto the rail. Rotate the fitting until the hose fitting faces the injectors. Align the openings and thread the two screws (27, **Figure 44**) into the fitting flange and fuel rail openings. Tighten the screws to 44 in.-lb. (5.0 N•m).

15. Lubricate the surfaces with four-cycle outboard engine oil, then install a new O-ring (34, **Figure 44**) onto the upper fitting (35). Guide the fitting into the opening at the top of the rail. Gently rotate the fitting during installation to prevent damage to the O-ring. Seat the fitting onto the rail. Rotate the fitting to align the screw openings. Fit the bracket (36, **Figure 44**) onto the fitting, then thread the two screws (37, **Figure 44**) into the fitting flange and fuel rail openings. Tighten the screws to 44 in.-lb. (5.0 N•m).

16. Lubricate the surfaces with four-cycle outboard engine oil, then insert the new seals (24, **Figure 44**) into the openings in the throttle bodies.

17. Insert the three alignment collars (23, **Figure 44**) into the openings in the throttle bodies. Carefully guide the three fuel injector tips into the corresponding seals in the throttle bodies. Verify proper alignment with the openings and the alignment collars, then seat the fuel rail against the intake manifold.

18. Support the fuel rail while threading the three screws (31, **Figure 44**) and washers (32) into the throttle bodies. Verify proper seating of the rail and injectors, then tighten the screws to 159 in.-lb. (18.0 N•m).

19. Slip new full-circle clamps (30 and 38, **Figure 44**) over the ends then push the fuel hoses (43 and 39) fully onto the fittings (28 and 35). Slide the clamps over the hoses until positioned over the fittings. Tighten the full-circle clamps as described in this chapter (see *Fuel Hose Connector Replacement*).

20. Install the starboard intake manifold as described in this chapter.

IDLE AIR CONTROL MOTOR

The idle air control motor (IAC) is non-serviceable. However, blockage in the connecting hoses and passages leading to the IAC can cause symptoms that mimic failure of the component. Removing the blockage will usually correct the malfunction without the need to replace the IAC.

115 hp Model

The idle air control motor mounts into a housing on the intake manifold.

Refer to **Figure 31**.

1. Remove the intake manifold as described in this chapter.

2. Disconnect the hose from the filter (13, **Figure 31**). The hose connects to a T-fitting, which connects the fuel pressure regulator and air pressure sensor to the intake manifold.

3. Loosen the clamps then disconnect the two hoses from the fittings on the bottom of the housing (12, **Figure 31**). The hoses lead to fittings on the throttle bodies.

4. Disconnect the breather hose (14, **Figure 31**) from the fitting on top of the housing. The hose leads to a fitting on the silencer cover.

5. Support the housing while removing the two screws (7 and 8, **Figure 31**) and washers (6 and 9). Pull the housing assembly off of the manifold (15, **Figure 31**).

6. Remove the three screws (2, **Figure 31**) and washers (3), then carefully pull the idle air control motor (IAC) from the housing.
7. Remove the air pressure sensor (11, **Figure 31**) as described in this chapter.
8. Remove and discard the O-ring (5, **Figure 31**) from the IAC or opening in the housing.
9. Unthread the filter (13, **Figure 31**) from the housing. Blow through the filter to check for blockage. Replace the filter if blocked or contaminated.
10. Use a suitable solvent to clean oily deposits or debris from the housing. Direct air into the passages to remove debris, then dry the housing with compressed air.
11. Thread the filter into the opening in the bottom of the housing. Securely tighten the filter.
12. Install the air pressure sensor as described in this chapter.
13. Lubricate the surfaces with four-cycle outboard engine oil, then install the new O-ring (5, **Figure 31**) onto the IAC. Seat the O-ring against the mounting flange.
14. Guide the IAC into the opening in the housing. Verify that the O-ring is in position, then seat the IAC against the housing. Rotate the IAC to align the openings, then thread the three screws and washers into the IAC and housing. Tighten the screws to 18 in.-lb. (2.0 N•m).
15. Align the screw openings, then seat the housing (12, **Figure 31**) onto the intake manifold (15). Thread the two mounting screws and washers (6-9, **Figure 31**) into the housing and intake manifold. Tighten the screws to 159 in.-lb. (18.0 N•m).
16. Connect the two hoses to the fittings on the bottom of the housing. The hoses lead to fittings on the side of the throttle bodies. Secure the hoses with spring clamps.
17. Connect the breather hose (14, **Figure 31**) to the fitting on the top of the housing.
18. Connect the hose to the filter (13, **Figure 31**).
19. Install the intake manifold as described in this chapter.

225 hp Model

The idle air control motor (IAC) mounts into a housing on the top of the port side intake manifold.

Refer to **Figure 39**.

1. Disconnect the engine wire harness connector from the IAC (41, **Figure 39**).
2. Remove the three screws (1, **Figure 39**) and washers (2) , then carefully pull the IAC from the housing.
3. Remove and discard the O-ring (40, **Figure 39**) from the IAC or opening in the housing.
4. Remove the screw (39, **Figure 39**) and bracket (38).
5. Remove the air pressure sensor (6, **Figure 39**) as described in this chapter.
6. Remove the two screws (7, **Figure 39**), and disconnect the hose (36) from the housing (37). Lift the housing from the intake manifold (34).
7. Use a suitable solvent to clean oily deposits or debris from the housing. Direct air into the passages to remove debris, then dry the housing with compressed air.
8. Guide the fitting into the hose (36, **Figure 39**) then seat the housing (37) onto the intake manifold. Fit the bracket (38, **Figure 39**) onto the housing. Align the openings, then thread the screws (7 and 39) into the bracket, housing and manifold. Tighten the screws to 71 in.-lb. (8.0 N•m).
9. Install the air pressure sensor as described in this chapter.
10. Lubricate the surfaces with four-cycle outboard engine oil, then install the new O-ring (40, **Figure 39**) onto the IAC. Seat the O-ring against the mounting flange.
11. Guide the IAC into the opening in the housing. Verify that the O-ring is in position, then seat the IAC against the housing. Rotate the IAC to align the openings, then thread the three screws and washers into IAC and housing. Tighten the screws to 18 in.-lb. (2.0 N•m).
12. Connect the engine wire harness connector onto the IAC. Route the wiring and hoses to prevent contact with moving components. Secure the hoses and wiring with plastic locking clamps as needed.

AIR TEMPERATURE SENSOR

The air temperature sensor threads into the silencer cover at the front of the power head.

Refer to **Figure 31** or **Figure 32**.

1. Carefully unplug the engine wire harness connector from the air temperature sensor (50, **Figure 31** or 10, **Figure 32**).
2. Engage a wrench onto the hex-shaped section, then unthread the sensor from the silencer cover. Do not engage the wrench or exert pressure against the plastic harness connector section of the sensor.
3. Use compressed air to remove debris or oily deposits from the sensor and the threaded opening in the silencer cover. Do not apply cleaning solvent onto the sensor.
4. Thread the replacement sensor into the opening. Do not apply sealant onto the threads. Tighten the sensor to 35 in.-lb. (4.0 N•m).
5. Connect the engine wire harness connector onto the sensor. Route the wiring to prevent interference with moving components.
6. Connect the battery cable.

AIR PRESSURE SENSOR

115 hp Model

The air pressure sensor mounts onto the idle air control motor housing on the intake manifold. The intake manifold is located on the rear and port side of the power head.

Refer to **Figure 31.**

1. Carefully unplug the engine wire harness connector from the air pressure sensor (11, **Figure 31**).
2. Remove the two screws (10, **Figure 31**), then lift the sensor from the housing (12). In necessary, gently twist the sensor to free it from the opening.
3. Remove the O-ring from the sensor or the opening into the housing. Discard the O-ring.
4. Use compressed air to remove debris from the external surfaces of the sensor and the opening in the housing. Do not apply solvent to the sensor or direct air into the sensor opening. Solvent or pressurized air will damage the sensor.
5. Apply a light coat or four-cycle outboard engine oil, then fit the new O-ring onto the sensor fitting. Seat the O-ring against the sensor body.
6. Guide the sensor fitting into the opening, then seat the sensor onto the housing. Rotate the sensor to position the wire terminal end directly over the two fittings on the bottom of the housing.
7. Rotate the sensor to align the openings. Thread the two screws (10, **Figure 31**) into the sensor and housing. Tighten the screws to 43 in.-lb. (4.9 N•m).
8. Plug the engine wire harness connector onto the sensor. Route the wiring to prevent contact with moving components.
9. Connect the battery cable.

225 hp Model

The air pressure sensor mounts onto the idle air control motor housing on the port side intake manifold.

Refer to **Figure 39**.

1. Carefully unplug the engine wire harness connector from the air pressure sensor (6, **Figure 39**).
2. Remove the two screws (5, **Figure 39**), then lift the sensor from the housing (37). If necessary, gently twist the sensor to free it from the opening.
3. Remove and discard the O-ring from the sensor or the opening into the housing.
4. Use compressed air to remove debris from the external surfaces of the sensor and the opening in the housing. Do not apply solvent to the sensor or direct air into the sensor opening. Solvent or pressurized air will damage the sensor.

5. Apply a light coat of four-cycle outboard engine oil, then fit the new O-ring onto the sensor fitting. Seat the O-ring against the sensor body.
6. Guide the sensor fitting into the opening, then seat the sensor onto the housing. Rotate the sensor to position the wire terminal end facing starboard.
7. Rotate the sensor as necessary to align the openings then thread the two screws (5, **Figure 39**) into the sensor and housing. Tighten the screws to 44 in.-lb. (5.0 N•m).
8. Plug the engine wire harness connector onto the sensor. Route the wiring to prevent contact with moving components.
9. Connect the battery cable.

THROTTLE POSITION SENSOR

75 and 90 hp Models

The throttle position sensor (**Figure 57**) mounts to the lower port side of the power head and is operated by the throttle linkage.

1. Place the remote control in the idle position.
2. Carefully unplug the engine wire harness connector from the sensor harness. Cut the plastic tie clamps as required.
3. Remove the two sensor mounting screws. Pull the sensor away from the mounting bracket.
4. Disconnect the sensor shaft from the coupler. If dislodged during sensor removal, align the pin with the slot and fit the coupler onto the throttle shaft.
5. Position the throttle position sensor on the mounting bracket with the wires exiting toward the front of the engine. Rotate the throttle position sensor until the pin in the sensor aligns with the slot in the coupler.
6. Support the sensor while threading the two mounting screws into the sensor and mounting bracket. Rotate the throttle position sensor clockwise until it reaches the limit

of its adjusting slot, then tighten the mounting screws to 15 in.-lb. (1.7 N•m).

7. Plug the engine wire harness connector onto the sensor wire harness. Route the wiring to prevent interference with moving components. Install plastic locking clamps as needed to secure the wiring.

8. Connect the battery cable.

9. Adjust the throttle position sensor as described in Chapter Four.

115 hp Model

Remove the throttle position sensor only if it or the upper throttle body must be replaced. The throttle position sensor mounts onto the upper throttle body on the port side of the power head. The cover and throttle position sensor are secured with tamper-proof screws that require special driver tools. Purchase the tamper-proof driver tools from a tool supplier or from a Mercury/Mariner dealership (part No. 91-881828).

Refer to **Figure 31**.

1. Carefully unplug the engine wire harness connector from the throttle position sensor.

2. Use the special driver tool to remove the three tamper-proof screws (66, **Figure 31**), sleeves, and washers, then lift the cover (67) from the throttle body.

3. Remove the two tamper-proof screws (68, **Figure 31**) and washers (69), then lift the sensor (70) off of the throttle body (72).

4. Remove and discard the O-ring (71, **Figure 31**) from the sensor or the opening in the throttle body.

5. Use compressed air to remove debris or contaminants from the sensor body and the opening in the throttle body. Do not apply solvent to the sensor. The solvent may seep into and damage the sensor.

6. Apply a light coat of four-cycle outboard engine oil, then fit the new O-ring (71, **Figure 31**) onto the sensor. Fit the O-ring over the sensor shaft boss and seat it against the sensor body.

7. Align the flat surface on the sensor rotor with the flat surface in the throttle body shaft. Guide the boss into the opening in the throttle body. Avoid dislodging the O-ring. Rotate the sensor slightly to verify engagement of the sensor rotor onto the throttle body shaft, then seat the sensor onto the throttle body.

8. Rotate the sensor to align the screw openings. The harness connector on the sensor must face rearward. Thread the two tamper-proof screws (68, **Figure 31**) and washers (69) into the sensor and throttle body. Use the special driver tool to tighten the screws to 43 in.-lb. (4.9 N•m).

9. Plug the engine wire harness connector onto the sensor. Route the wiring to prevent contact with moving components.

10. Connect the battery cable.

11. Adjust the throttle position sensor as described in Chapter Four.

12. Fit the cover (67, **Figure 31**) over the sensor and seat on the throttle body. Align the openings, then thread the three tamper-proof screws (66, **Figure 31**), sleeves and washer into the cover and throttle body. Use the special driver tool to tighten the screws to 40 in.-lb. (4.5 N•m).

225 hp Model

The throttle position sensor mounts onto the upper throttle body on the starboard side of the power head. The throttle position sensor is secured with tamper-proof screws that require special driver tools. Purchase the tamper-proof driver tools from a tool supplier or from a Mercury/Mariner dealership (part No. 91-881828).

Refer to **Figure 44**.

1. Carefully unplug the engine wire harness connector from the throttle position sensor.

2. Remove the two tamper-proof screws (1, **Figure 44**) and washers (2 and 47), then lift the sensor (3) off the adapter plate (45).

3. Remove and discard the O-ring (46, **Figure 44**) from the sensor or the opening in the throttle body.

4. Use compressed air to remove debris or contaminants from the sensor body, throttle body shaft, and adapter plate. Do not apply solvent to the sensor. The solvent may seep into and damage the sensor.

5. Apply a light coating or four-cycle outboard engine oil, then fit the new O-ring (46, **Figure 44**) onto the sensor. Fit the O-ring over the sensor shaft boss then seat it against the sensor body.

6. Align the flat surface on the sensor rotor with the flat surface in the throttle body shaft. Guide the boss into the opening in the adapter plate. Avoid dislodging the O-ring. Rotate the sensor slightly to verify engagement of the sensor rotor to the throttle body shaft, then seat the sensor onto the adapter plate.

7. Rotate the sensor to align the screw openings. The harness connector on the sensor must face rearward. Thread the two tamper-proof screws (1, **Figure 44**) and washers (2 and 47) into the sensor and adapter plate (45). Use the special driver tool to tighten the screws to 44 in.-lb. (5.0 N•m).

8. Plug the engine wire harness connector onto the sensor. Route the wiring to prevent contact with moving components.

9. Connect the battery cable.

10. Adjust the throttle position sensor as described in Chapter Four.

Table 1 FUEL SYSTEM TORQUE SPECIFICATIONS

Fastener	in.-lb.	N•m
Air pressure sensor		
115 hp models	43	4.9
225 hp models	44	5.0
Air temperature sensor		
115 and 225 hp models	35	4.0
Carburetor mounting bolts		
75 and 90 hp	70	7.9
Dashpot		
75 and 90 hp models	70	7.9
Fuel cooler		
115 hp models	70	7.9
225 hp models	44	5.0
Fuel filter mounting bracket	71	8.0
Fuel pressure regulator		
115 hp models	70	7.9
225 hp models	71	8.0
Fuel rail mounting screws		
115 hp models		
6 mm screws	70	7.9
8 mm screws	159	18.0
225 hp models	159	18.0
Fuel rail fitting screws		
115 hp models	43	4.9
225 hp models	44	5.0
Fuel pump relay		
225 hp models	27	3.0
Fuel pump driver		
225 hp models	71	8.0
Idle air control motor (IAC)		
115 and 225 hp models	18	2.0
Idle air control motor housing		
115 hp models	159	18.0
225 hp models	71	8.0
Hose and cable grommet retainer		
75-115 hp models	65	7.3
Intake manifold to cylinder head	159	18.0
Intake support bracket-to-cylinder block	70	7.9
Drive shaft housing cover screws		
115 hp models	65	7.3
225 hp models	70	7.9
Low-pressure electric fuel pump bracket		
225 hp models	44	5.0
Mechanical fuel pump		
Cover screws		
75 and 90 hp models (2001-2002)	25	2.8
75 and 90 hp (2003) and 115 hp models	70	7.9
Mounting screws		
75-115 hp models	70	7.9
Secondary vapor separator tank	71	8.0
Silencer cover fasteners		
75 and 90 hp		
Shorter screws	70	7.9
Longer bolts	160	18.1
115 hp models		
Screws	70	7.9
Bolts	70	7.9
225 hp models	71	8.0

(continued)

Table 1 FUEL SYSTEM TORQUE SPECIFICATIONS (continued)

Fastener	in.-lb.	N•m
Silencer tube retainer screw		
115 hp models	70	7.9
Throttle body mounting bolt		
115 and 225 hp models	159	18.0
Throttle linkage ball joint		
225 hp models	35	4.0
Throttle linkage pivot bolts		
225 hp models	71	8.0
Throttle position sensor		
75 and 90 hp	15	1.7
115 hp models	43	4.9
225 hp models	44	5.0
Throttle position sensor cover		
115 hp models	40	4.5
Vapor separator tank		
Drain screw		
225 hp models	18	2.0
Inlet needle seat retainer		
225 hp models	18	2.0
Mounting screws to intake manifold		
115 hp models	70	7.9
Mounting screws to power head		
225 hp models	159	18.0
Mounting plate screws		
225 hp models	159	18.0
Top cover screws		
115 hp models	18	2.0
225 hp models	35	4.0

5

Chapter Six

Electrical and Ignition Systems

This chapter provides service procedures for the battery, charging system, starting system and ignition system components. Wiring diagrams are located at the end of the manual. Torque specifications are listed in **Table 1**. Use the general tightening torque specifications listed in the *Quick Reference Data* section at the front of the manual for fasteners not listed in **Table 1**. Battery capacity, battery cable size recommendations, battery charge percentage and electric starter specifications are listed in **Tables 2-5**. **Tables 1-5** are located at the end of this chapter.

NOTE
Due to manufacturing variations, wire colors called out in this manual may not match the wire colors in the wiring diagram or the actual wiring on the outboard. Always verify wire colors before beginning a procedure.

ELECTRICAL COMPONENT REPLACEMENT

Most dealerships and parts suppliers will not accept the return of any electrical part. If the exact cause of any electrical system malfunction cannot be determiend, have a dealership retest the specific system to verify any preliminary test results. If a new electrical component is installed and the system still does not work properly, the new component, in most cases, will not be returnable.

Consider any test results carefully before replacing a component that tests only slightly out of specification, especially resistance. A number of variables can affect test results dramatically. These include: internal circuitry of the test meter, ambient temperature, and conditions under which the machine has been operated. All instructions and specifications have been checked for accuracy; however, successful test results depend upon individual accuracy.

BATTERY

Batteries used in marine applications endure far more rigorous treatment than those used in automotive electrical systems. Marine batteries (**Figure 1**) have a thicker exterior case to cushion the plates during tight turns and rough water operation. Spill-proof caps on the battery cells prevent electrolyte from spilling into the bilge.

Automotive batteries should be used in a boat *only* during an emergency situation when a suitable marine battery is not available.

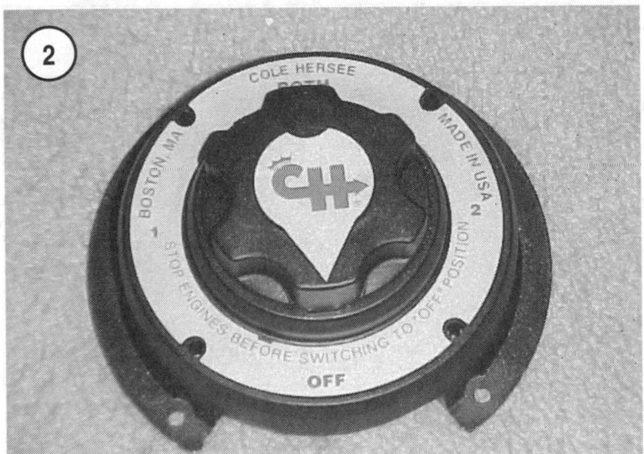

Rating Methods

The battery industry has developed specifications and performance standards to evaluate battery energy potential. Several rating methods are available to provide information on battery selection.

Cold cranking amps (CCA)

The cold cranking amps rating is the amperage the battery can deliver for 30 seconds at 0° F (-17° C) without dropping below 1.2 volts per cell (7.2 volts on a standard 12 volt battery). The higher the number, the more amps the battery can deliver to crank the engine. CCA times 1.3 equals MCA.

Marine cranking amps (MCA)

The marine cranking amps rating is similar to the CCA rating, except the test is run at 32° F (0° C) instead of 0° F (-17° C). This is closer to actual boat operating environments. MCA times 0.77 equals CCA.

Reserve capacity

Reserve capacity represents the time in minutes that a fully charged battery at 80°F (27° C) can deliver 25 amps, without dropping below 1.75 volts per cell (10.5 volts on a standard 12 volt battery). The reserve capacity rating defines the length of time that a typical vehicle can be operated after the charging system fails. The 25 amp figure takes into account the power required by the ignition system, lighting and other accessories. The higher the reserve capacity, the longer the vehicle could be operated after a charging system failure.

Amp-hour rating

The ampere hour rating is also called the 20 hour rating. This rating represents the steady current flow that the battery will deliver for 20 hours while at 80° F (27° C) without dropping below 1.75 volts per cell (10.5 volts on a standard 12 volt battery). To calculate the amp-hour rating, multiply the current flow by 20 hours. Example: A 60 amp-hour battery will deliver 3 amps continuously for 20 hours.

This rating method has been largely discontinued by the battery industry. Cold cranking amps or marine cranking amps and reserve capacity are now the most common battery rating methods.

Recommendations

A battery with inadequate capacity can cause hard starting or an inability to start the engine. Use a battery with a minimum rating of 350 cold cranking amps (CCA) or 465 marine cranking amps (MCA) for operation at air temperatures 32° F (0° C) and higher. Use a battery with a minimum rating of 775 CCA or 1000 MCA for operation at temperatures below 32° F (0° C).

A battery with a capacity exceeding the minimum requirement is acceptable and is highly recommended if the boat is equipped with numerous electrical accessories. Consider adding an additional battery and installing a battery switch (**Figure 2**) on such applications. The switch allows starting and charging operations to use one or both batteries. The switch can be turned off if the boat is at rest or in storage to prevent discharge that occurs from some on-board accessories.

Usage

Separate batteries may be used to provide power for accessories such as lighting, fish finders, depth finders and radios. To determine the required capacity of such batteries, calculate the accessory current amperage draw and refer to **Table 2**.

Two batteries may be connected in parallel to double the ampere-hour capacity while maintaining the required 12 volts. See **Figure 3**. For accessories that require 24 volts, batteries may be connected in series (**Figure 4**), but only accessories specifically requiring 24 volts should be connected to the system. If charging becomes necessary, individually disconnect and charge batteries connected in a parallel or series circuit.

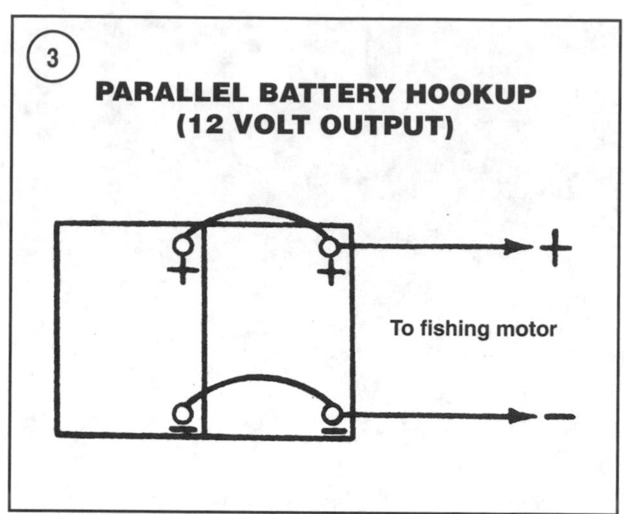

Mounting

The battery must be securely fastened in the boat to prevent the battery from shifting or moving in the bilge area. The positive battery terminal or the entire top of the battery must be covered with nonconductive shield or boot.

An improperly secured battery can contact the hull or metal fuel tank in rough water or while trailering the boat. If the battery terminals shorts against the metal hull or fuel tank, it can create sparks and cause an electrical fire. An explosion could occur if the fuel tank or battery case is compromised.

If the battery is not properly grounded and the battery contacts the metal hull, the battery will seek a ground through the control cables or the boat wiring harness. The short circuit can create sparks and an electrical fire. The control cables and boat wiring can be irreparably damaged.

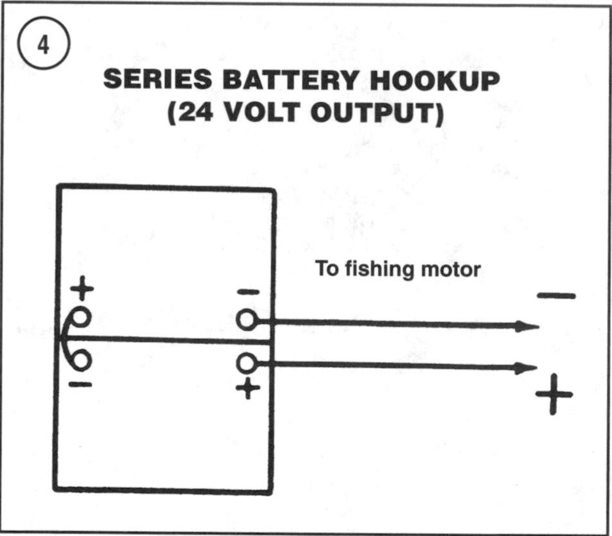

Observe the following preventive steps when installing a battery in a boat, especially a metal boat or a boat with a metal fuel tank.

1. Choose a mounting location that provides good access to the battery for maintenance and is as far as practical from the fuel tank. If possible, choose a location that is close enough to the engine to use the original equipment battery cable. If longer cables are required, refer to the battery cable recommendations in **Table 3**. Use the shortest practical cable.
2. Secure the battery to the hull with a plastic battery box and tie-down strap (**Figure 5**), or a battery tray with a nonconductive shield or boot covering the positive battery terminal (**Figure 6**). Install an additional shield or boot onto the negative battery terminal for added protection against arcing between the terminals.

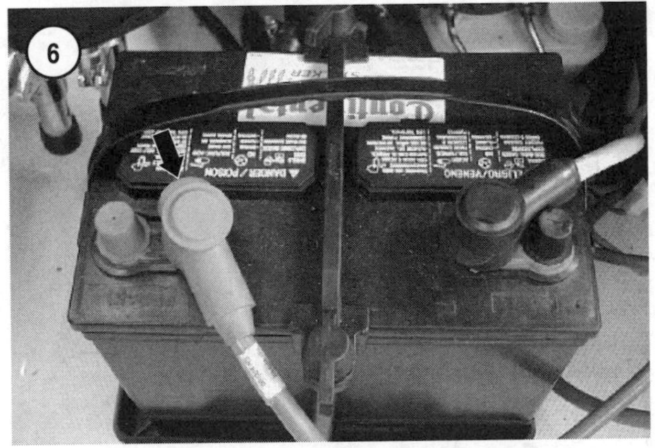

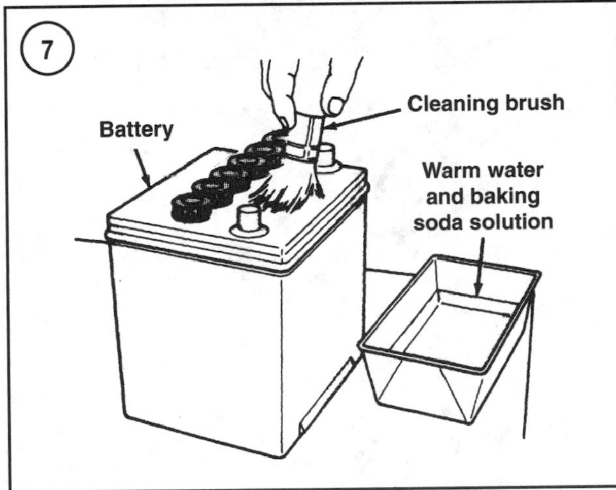

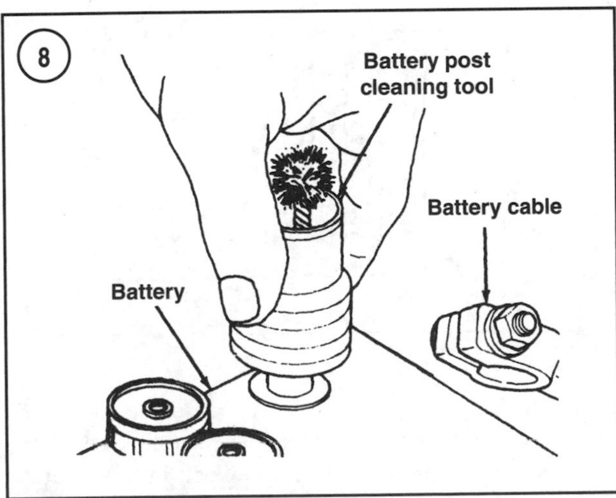

3. Make sure all battery cable connections (two at the battery and two at the engine) are clean and tight. *Do not* use wing nuts to secure battery cables. If wing nuts are present, discard and replace them with corrosion resistant hex nuts and lock washers to ensure good electrical connections. Loose or dirty battery connections can cause engine malfunction and failure of expensive components.
4. Periodically inspect the installation to make sure the battery is physically secured to the hull and the battery cable connections are clean and tight.

Care and Inspection

For reliable starting and maximum battery life, inspect the battery case and terminals on a frequent basis.

1. Remove the battery box cover or battery tray cover. See **Figure 5** or **Figure 6**.
2. Disconnect the negative battery cable, then the positive battery cable.

NOTE

*Some batteries have a built-in lifting strap (**Figure 1**).*

3. Attach a battery carry strap to the terminal post. Remove the battery from the boat.
4. Inspect the entire battery case for cracks, holes, deep abrasion or other damage. Replace the battery if these or other defects are evident.
5. Inspect the battery box or tray for cracks, corrosion, deterioration or other damage. Replace the box or tray if any defects are evident.

NOTE

When cleaning the battery, do not allow the baking soda solution to enter the battery cells or the electrolyte will be severely weakened.

6. Clean the top of the battery with a stiff bristle brush using a baking soda and water solution (**Figure 7**). Rinse the battery case with clear water and wipe it dry with a clean cloth or paper towel.
7. Clean the battery terminal post with a stiff wire brush or battery terminal cleaning tool (**Figure 8**).

NOTE

Do not overfill the battery cells. The electrolyte expands due to heat from the charging system and will overflow if the level is more that 3/16 in. (4.8 mm) above the battery plates.

8. Remove the filler caps and check the electrolyte level. Add distilled water, if needed, to bring the level up to 3/16 in. (4.8 mm) above the plates in the battery case (**Figure 9**).

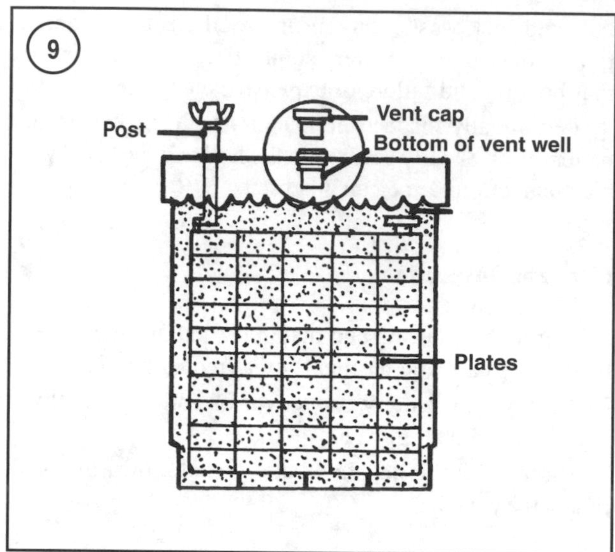

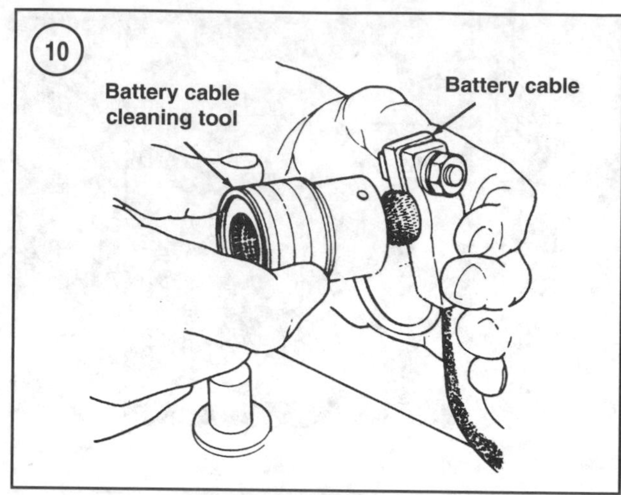

9. Clean the battery cable clamps with a stiff wire brush (**Figure 10**).

10. Place the battery back into the boat and into the battery box or tray. When using a battery tray, install and secure the retaining bracket.

11. Connect the positive battery cable first, then connect the negative cable.

12. Securely tighten the battery connections. Coat the connections with petroleum jelly or a light grease to minimize corrosion. When using a battery box, install the cover and secure the assembly with a tie down strap.

Testing

Hydrometer test

On batteries with removable vent caps, the best way to check the battery state of charge is to check the specific gravity of the electrolyte with a hydrometer. Use a hydrometer with numbered graduations from 1.100-1.300 points rather than one with color-coded bands. To use the hydrometer, squeeze the rubber bulb, insert the tip fully into the cell, then release the bulb to fill the hydrometer. See **Figure 11**.

NOTE

Do not test specific gravity immediately after adding water into the battery cells, as the water will dilute the electrolyte and lower the specific gravity. To obtain an accurate hydrometer reading, charge the battery after adding water and before testing with a hydrometer.

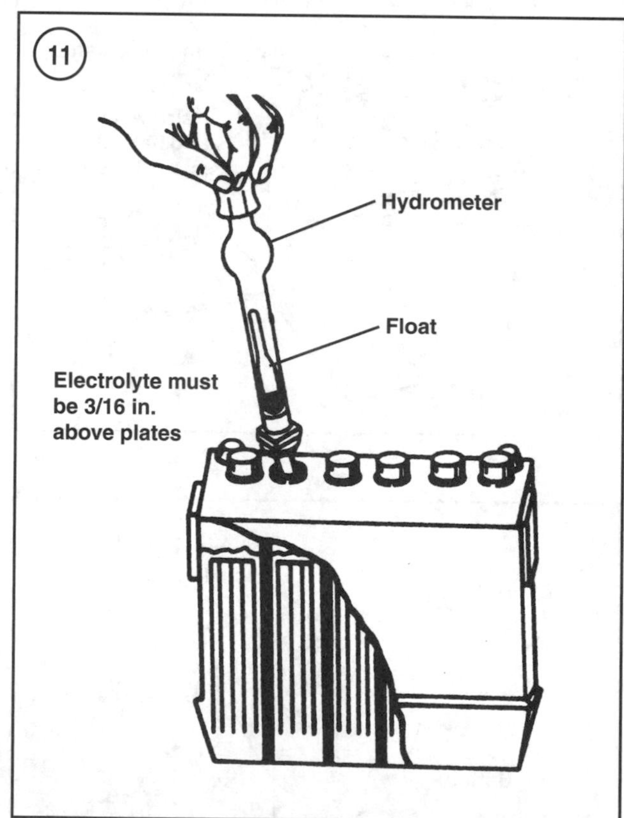

Draw enough electrolyte to raise the float inside the hydrometer. When using a temperature-compensated hydrometer, discharge the electrolyte back into the battery cell and repeat the process several times to adjust the temperature of the hydrometer to the electrolyte.

Hold the hydrometer upright and note the number on the float that is even with the surface of the electrolyte (**Figure 12**). This number is the specific gravity for the

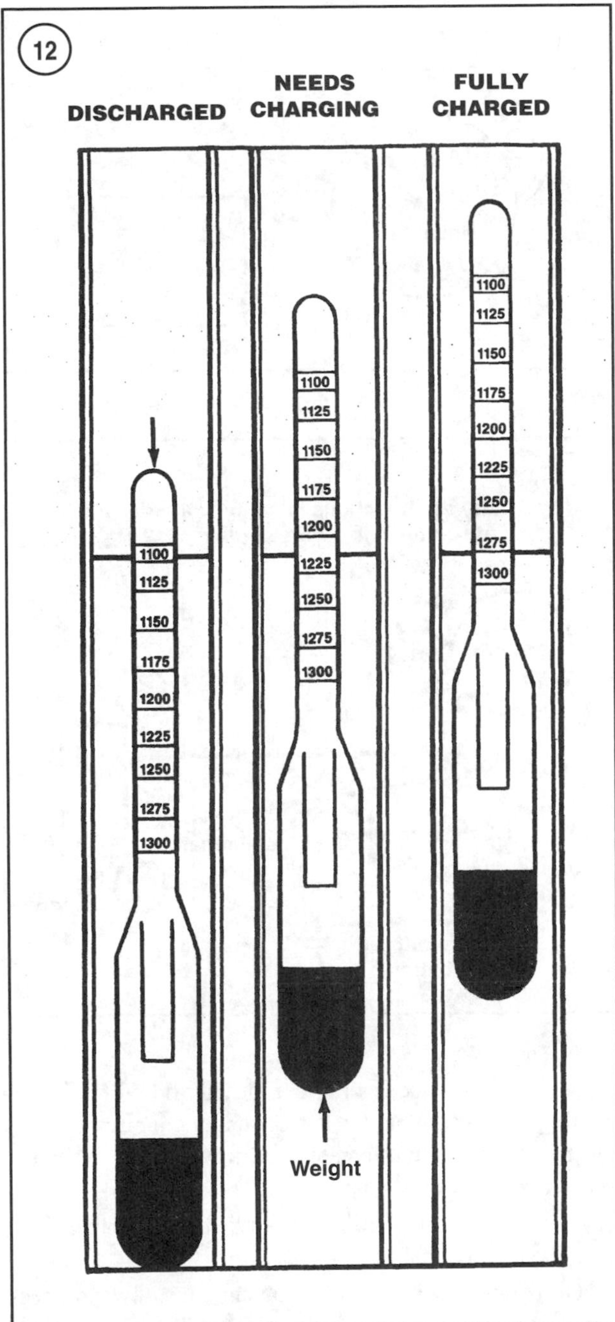

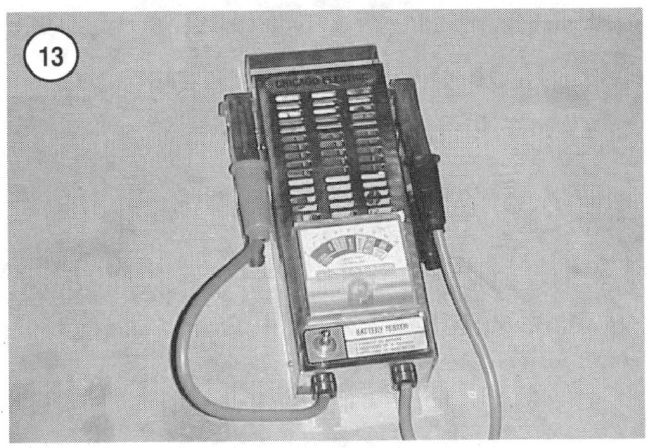

cell. Discharge the electrolyte into the cell from which it came.

The specific gravity of a cell is the indicator of the cell's state of charge. A fully charged cell will read 1.260 or higher at 80° F (27° C). A cell that is 75 percent charged will read from 1.220-1.230. A cell with a 50 percent charge will read from 1.170-1.180. A cell reading 1.120 or lower is discharged. All cells should be within 30 points specific gravity of each other. If there is more than 30 points variation, the battery condition is questionable. Charge the battery and recheck the specific gravity. If 30 points or more variation remains between the cells after charging, the battery has failed and must be replaced. Refer to **Table 4** for battery charge level based on specific gravity readings.

NOTE

*If a temperature-compensated hydrometer is **not** used, add four points specific gravity to the actual reading for every 10° above 80° F (27° C). Subtract four points specific gravity for every 10° below 80° F (27° C).*

Open-circuit voltage test

On sealed or maintenance-free batteries, check the state of charge by measuring the open-circuit (no load) voltage of the battery. Use a digital multimeter for best results. For the most accurate results, allow the battery to rest for at least 30 minutes to allow the battery to stabilize. Then, observing the correct polarity, connect the meter onto the battery terminals and note the meter reading. If the open-circuit voltage is 12.7 volts or higher, the battery is fully charged. A reading of 12.4 volts means the battery is approximately 75 percent charged, a reading of 12.2 means the battery is approximately 50 percent charged and a reading of 12.1 means the battery is approximately 25 percent charged.

Load test

Two common methods are used to load test batteries. A commercially available load tester (**Figure 13**) measures the battery voltage as it applies a load across the terminals. Measure the cranking voltage following the instructions in this section if a load tester is not available.

1. Attach a multimeter onto the battery terminals as shown in **Figure 14**.
2. Remove and ground the spark plug lead to the power head to prevent accidental starting.
3. Crank the engine for approximately 15 seconds while noting the meter reading. Note the voltage reading at the end of the 15 second period.

4A. If the voltage is 9.5 volts or higher, the battery is sufficiently charged and of sufficient capacity for the outboard.

4B. If the voltage is below 9.5 volts, one of the following conditions is present:

a. The battery is discharged or defective. Charge the battery and retest.

b. The battery capacity is too small for the outboard. Refer to *Battery Recommendations* in this chapter.

c. The starting system is drawing excessive current and causing the battery voltage to drop. Refer to Chapter Two for starting system troubleshooting procedures.

d. A mechanical defect is present in the power head or gearcase, creating excessive load and current draw on the starting system. Inspect the power head and gearcase for defects.

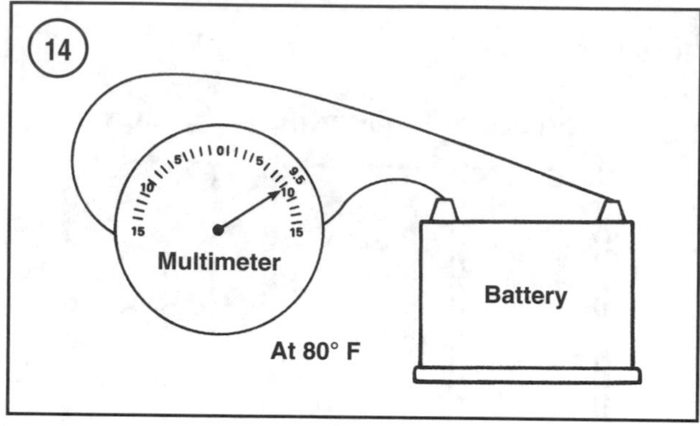

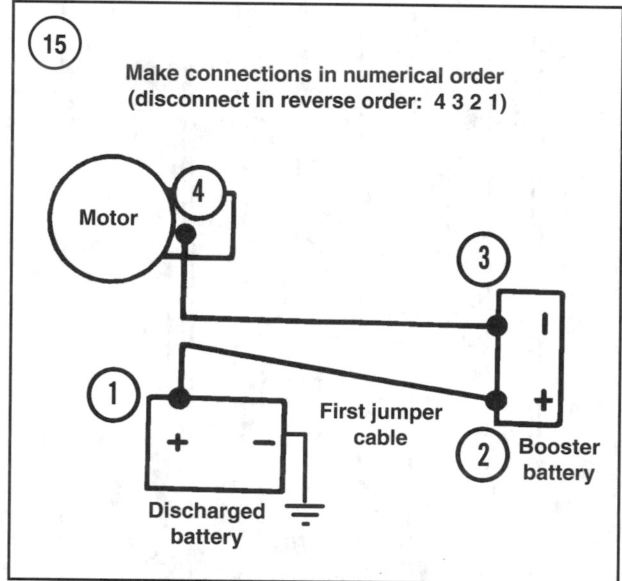

Storage

Wet cell batteries slowly discharge when stored. Before storing a battery, clean the case with a solution of baking soda and water. Rinse it with clear water and wipe dry. Fully charge the battery, then store it in a cool, dry location. Check the electrolyte and state of charge frequently during storage. If the specific gravity falls to 40 points or more below full charge (1.260), or the open circuit voltage falls below 12.4 volts, recharge the battery.

Charging

Check the state of charge with a hydrometer or digital multimeter as described in the previous section.

Remove the battery from the boat for charging. A charging battery releases highly explosive hydrogen gas. In many boats, the area around the battery is not well ventilated unless the vessel is moving and the gas may remain in the area for hours after the charging process has been completed. Sparks or flames occurring near the battery can cause it to explode and spray battery acid over a wide area.

If the battery cannot be removed for charging, make sure the bilge access hatches, doors or vents are fully open to allow adequate ventilation. Observe the following precautions when charging batteries:

1. Never smoke is close proximity to a battery.
2. Make sure all accessories are turned off before disconnecting the battery cables. Disconnecting a circuit that is electrically active will create a spark which can ignite explosive gas that may be present.
3. Always disconnect the negative battery cable first, then the positive cable.
4. On batteries with removable vent caps, always check the electrolyte level before charging the battery. Maintain the correct level throughout the charging process.
5. Never attempt to charge a battery that is frozen.

WARNING
Be extremely careful not to create any sparks around the battery when connecting the battery charger.

6. Connect the negative charger lead onto the negative battery terminal and the positive charger lead onto the positive terminal. If the charger output is variable, select a

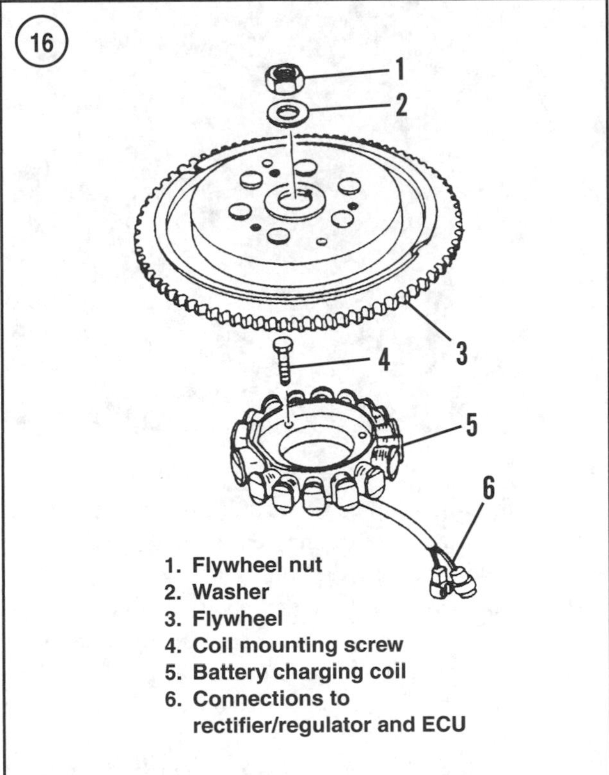

1. Flywheel nut
2. Washer
3. Flywheel
4. Coil mounting screw
5. Battery charging coil
6. Connections to rectifier/regulator and ECU

setting of approximately 4 amps. Charge the battery slowly at low amp settings, rather than quickly at high amp settings.

7. If the charger has a dual voltage setting, set the voltage to 12 volts, then switch the charger ON.
8. If the battery is severely discharged, allow it to charge for at least eight hours. Check the charging process with a hydrometer.

Jump Starting

If the battery becomes severely discharged, the engine can be jump started from another battery in or out of the boat. Jump starting can be dangerous if the proper procedure is not followed.

Check the electrolyte level of the discharged battery before attempting the jump start. If the electrolyte is not visible or it appears to be frozen, do not jump start the discharged battery.

WARNING
To lessen the chance of injury or damage to the electrical system, use extreme caution when connecting the booster battery to the discharged battery. ***Make sure*** *the jumper cables are connected to the correct polarity.*

1. Connect the jumper cables in the order shown in **Figure 15**.

WARNING
An electrical arc can occur when the final connection is made. This could cause an explosion if it occurs near the battery. For this reason, make the final connection to a good engine ground, away from the battery and not on the battery itself.

2. Make sure all jumper cables are out of the way of moving engine parts.

CAUTION
Do not run the engine without an adequate water supply and do not exceed 3000 rpm without an adequate load.

3. Start the engine. Once it starts, run it at a fast idle.

CAUTION
Running the engine at high speed with a discharged battery can damage the charging system.

4. Remove the jumper cables in the exact reverse of the order shown in **Figure 15**.

CHARGING SYSTEM

This section describes replacement procedures for the battery charging coil and rectifier/regulator.

WARNING
Avoid accidental starting or arcing. Always disconnect the negative battery cable before servicing any outboard.

Battery Charging Coil Replacement

CAUTION
It may be necessary to use an impact driver to remove the battery charging coil mounting screws. Do no use excessive force. The cylinder block or mounting base can sustain damage if excessive force is used.

1. Remove the flywheel as described in Chapter Seven.
2. On 225 hp models, remove the silencer cover as described in Chapter Five.
3. Refer to the wiring diagrams at the back of the manual to identify the wire coloring for the battery charging coil (5, **Figure 16**, typical).

4A. On 75 and 90 hp models, disconnect the coil wiring as follows:

a. Remove the three screws, then the plastic electrical component cover (**Figure 17**).
b. Locate the three-wire connector for the harness connecting the battery charging coil to the rectifier/regulator harness. The harness contains two green wires and one green/white wire.
c. Depress the locking tab, then unplug the connectors.

4B. On 115 hp models, disconnect the coil wiring as follows:

a. Depress the three locking tabs, then remove the plastic electrical component cover.
b. Pull up on the locking tab, then disconnect the battery charging coil harness from the rectifier/regulator. The wire harness contains three white wires, one red wire and one black wire.
c. Trace the red wire to the engine wire harness. Depress the locking tab, then unplug the connectors.
d. Trace the black wire to the ground terminal. Remover the screw to disconnect the coil ground.

4C. On 225 hp models, disconnect the coil wiring as follows:

a. Trace both charging coil harnesses to the rectifier/regulator harness. The harness passes behind the electric starter. One harness contains three green wires. The other harness contains three green/white wires.
b. Cut the plastic locking clamps to free the connectors from the mounting bracket.
c. Depress the locking tabs, then unplug both connectors.

5A. On 75-115 hp models, locate and remove the clamp that secures the charging coil harness onto the mounting base. The clamp is located on the front and starboard side of the coil mounting base.

5B. On 225 hp models, remove the plastic locking clamps that secure the coil harnesses onto the oil fill tube and support.

6. Use a permanent marker to make reference marks on the coil and mounting base. This is necessary to ensure correct orientation of the wiring during installation. Transfer the marking onto the replacement coil.

7. Remove the screws (4, **Figure 16**, typical) that secure the battery charging coil onto the mounting base. Three screws are used on 75-115 hp models and four screws are used on 225 hp models. Use an impact driver as needed to remove the screws. Replace the screws if damaged during the removal process.

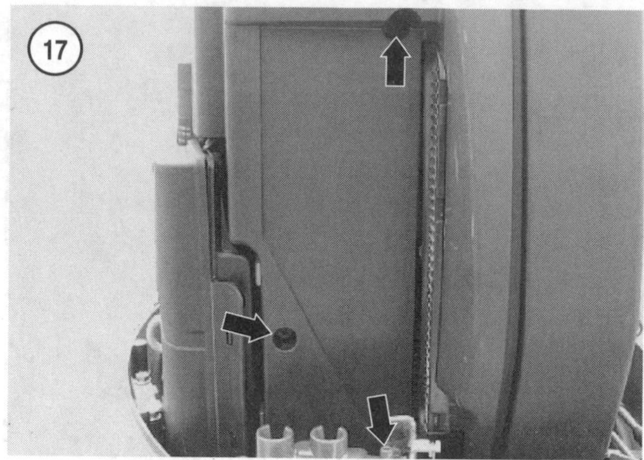

8. Note the wire routing, then carefully remove the coil. Route the wiring through the various passages to avoid snagging and damaging the connectors.

9. Use compressed air to remove belt material and other debris from the coil mounting base. Use a wire brush to clean corrosion from the mounting surfaces, screw openings and mounting screws. Corrosion commonly occurs in these areas.

10. Install the replacement coil onto the mounting plate. Align the match markings made in Step 5 and the mounting screw openings.

11. Thread the screws into the coil and mounting base openings. Tighten the screw to 70 in.-lb. (7.9 N•m) for 75-115 hp models and 71 in.-lb. (8.0 N•m) for 225 hp models.

12. Route the coil wiring to the connection points onto the rectifier/regulator, engine wire harness or engine ground.

13A. On 75-115 hp models, install the clamp to secure the charging coil harness onto the mounting base. Securely tighten the clamp screw.

13B. On 225 hp models, use plastic locking clamps to secure the coil harnesses onto the oil fill tube and support.

14A. On 75 and 90 hp models, plug the coil harness connector onto rectifier/regulator harness connector. Route the wiring to prevent pinching or interference with moving components. Install the electrical component cover and securely tighten the three mounting screws.

14B. On 115 hp models, connect the coil wiring as follows:

a. Connect the black wire onto the engine ground terminal. Securely tighten the screw.
b. Connect the coil wire harness connector onto the rectifier/regulator harness connector.
c. Connect the red wire to the engine wire harness. Depress the locking tab to push the connector to-

gether. Release the tab, then tug on the harnesses to verify a secure connection.

d. Route the wiring to prevent pinching or interference with moving components, then install the electrical component cover.

14C. On 225 hp models, connect the two charging coil harness connectors to the rectifier/regulator harness. Secure the harness onto the mounting bracket with plastic locking clamps.

15. Install the flywheel as described in Chapter Seven.

16. On 225 hp models, install the silencer cover as described in Chapter Five.

Rectifier/Regulator Replacement

75-115 hp models

1. Disconnect the negative battery cable to prevent accidental starting and arcing at the rectifier/regulator terminals. Arcing can damage the rectifier/regulator and other engine components.

2. On 75 and 90 hp models, remove the silencer cover as described in Chapter Five.

3A. On 75 and 90 hp models, disconnect the rectifier/regulator wiring as follows:

a. Locate the rectifier/regulator (**Figure 18**, typical) on the electrical components mounting plate at the front of the power head.

b. Locate the three-wire connector for the harness connecting the battery charging coil to the rectifier/regulator harness. The harness contains two green wires and one green/white wire. Depress the locking tab, then unplug the connectors.

c. Trace the black rectifier/regulator wire to the ground wire terminal. Remove the screw to disconnect the wire. Temporarily replace the screw to retain the other grounding wires on the terminal.

d. Trace the red rectifier/regulator wire to the engine wire harness. Unplug the connectors.

e. Unplug the gray tachometer wire from the green/white rectifier wire terminal.

3B. On 115 hp models, disconnect the rectifier/regulator wiring as follows:

a. Locate the rectifier/regulator (**Figure 18**, typical) on the front of the power head. The component is located between the electrical component cover and the silencer cover.

b. Depress the locking tab, then unplug the harness connector from the bottom of the rectifier/regulator.

4. Remove the two mounting screws and lift the component from the mounting plate.

5. Install the rectifier/regulator onto the mounting plate with the wire harness or harness connector end facing downward.

6. Thread the two mounting screws into the rectifier/regulator and mounting plate. Tighten the screws to 70 in.-lb. (79 N•m).

7A. On 75 and 90 hp models, connect the rectifier/regulator wiring as follows:

a. Depress the locking tab, then plug the rectifier/regulator wire harness connector onto the engine wire harness connector. Release the locking tab and tug on the wiring to verify a secure connection.

b. Connect the black rectifier/regulator wire onto the ground wire terminal. Securely tighten the ground wire screw.

c. Connect the red rectifier/regulator wire terminal to the corresponding engine wire harness connector. Make sure the red wire connectors lock together securely. A loose connection on the red wire will cause failure of the rectifier/regulator.

d. Connect the gray tachometer wire terminal onto the green/white rectifier/regulator wire terminal.

7B. On 115 hp models, depress the locking tab, then plug the harness connector onto the connector on the bottom of the rectifier/regulator. Release the locking tab and tug on the harness to verify a secure connection.

8. Route the wiring to prevent pinching or interference with moving components. Secure the wiring with plastic locking clamps as needed.

9. On 75 and 90 hp models, install the silencer cover as described in Chapter Five.

10. Connect the battery cable.

225 hp model

Refer to **Figure 19**.

6

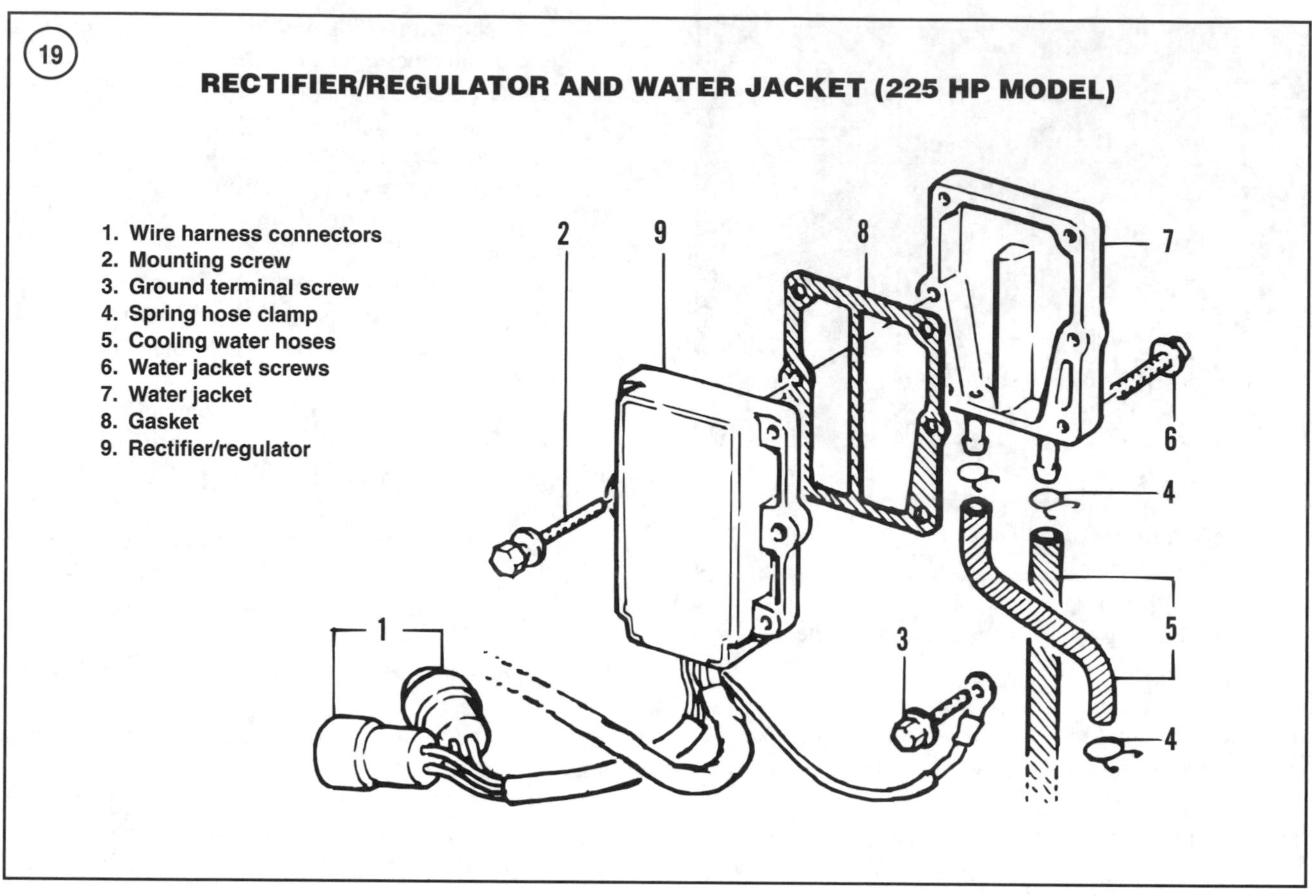

1. Remove the silencer cover as described in Chapter Five.

2. Remove the power trim/tilt relay unit as described in Chapter Nine.

3. Disconnect the oil pressure sender harness as described in this chapter (See *Oil Pressure Sender Replacement*).

4. Disconnect the instrument harness from the engine wire harness.

5. Disconnect the battery cables from the terminal on the mounting plate and the electric starter.

6. Disconnect the trim position sender harness as described in Chapter Nine (See *Trim Position Sender Replacement*).

7. Remove the fuel filter mounting bracket. Refer to Chapter Five to locate the fuel filter. Do not disconnect the fuel hoses.

8. Trace both charging coil harnesses to the rectifier/regulator harness connectors (1, **Figure 19**). One harness contains three green wires. The other harness contains three green/white wires. Cut the plastic locking clamps to free the connectors from the mounting bracket. Depress the locking tabs, then unplug both connectors.

9. Disconnect the brown/white wire from the starter relay. Refer to *Starter Relay Replacement* in this chapter to locate the component.

10. Remove the screw that secures the black ground wires onto the electrical component mounting plate. The screw is located to the port side of the electric starter and just above the trim/tilt relay.

11. Remove the six screws that secure the electrical component mounting plate onto the power head. Pull the plate away from the front of the power head to access the rectifier/regulator.

12. Loosen the clamps, then use a flat blade screwdriver to push the cooling water hoses (5, **Figure 19**) off of the rectifier/regulator water jacket.

13. Trace the black rectifier/regulator wire to the ground terminal on the power head. Remove the screw (3, **Figure 19**) to disconnect the ground wire.

14. Remove the two mounting screws (2, **Figure 19**), then remove the rectifier/regulator and water jacket assembly.

15. Remove the four screws (6, **Figure 19**) and the water jacket (7) from the rectifier/regulator. If necessary, use a

blunt tip pry bar to remove the water jacket. Work carefully to avoid damaging the mating surfaces.

16. Remove the gasket (8, **Figure 19**) from the rectifier/regulator or water jacket. Discard the gasket.

17. Remove any debris from the water jacket. Blow compressed air through the cooling water hose to purge debris from the hoses. Blockage in the hoses or jacket will cause overheating and subsequent failure of the rectifier/regulator. Also, blockage may prevent water from draining from the jacket and cause freeze damage to the components if subjected to freezing temperatures.

18. Install a new gasket onto the water jacket, then fit the jacket onto the back of the rectifier. The open side of the jacket must face toward the rectifier/regulator. Thread the four screws (6, **Figure 19**) into the water jacket and rectifier/regulator openings. Tighten the screws in a crossing pattern to an initial torque of 53 in.-lb. (6.0 N•m). Then, tighten the screws in a crossing pattern to a final torque of 106 in.-lb. (12.0 N•m).

19. Install the rectifier/regulator and water jacket assembly onto the power head with the wiring and hose fittings facing downward. Thread the two mounting screws (2, **Figure 19**) into the assembly and the power head openings. Tighten the screws evenly to an initial torque of 53 in.-lb. (6.0 N•m). Then, tighten the screws evenly to a final torque of 106 in.-lb. (12.0 N•m).

20. Connect the black rectifier/regulator wire terminal onto the power head ground terminal. Securely tighten the screw (3, **Figure 19**).

21. Push the cooling water hoses (5, **Figure 19**) fully onto the water jacket fittings. Secure the hoses with the spring clamps.

22. Position the electrical component mounting plate onto the front of the power head. Align the openings, then thread the six screws into the plate and threaded openings in the power head. Make sure the other two wires are connected onto the terminal, then tighten the six screws to 71 in.-lb. (8.0 N•m).

23. Connect the ground wire onto the ground terminal screw on the mounting bracket. The screw is located to the port side of the electric starter and just above the trim/tilt relay. Tighten the ground wire screw to 71 in.-lb. (8.0 N•m).

24. Connect the brown/white wire to the starter relay terminal.

25. Depress the locking tab then plug the charging coil harness connectors onto the rectifier/regulator connectors (1, **Figure 19**). Release the tab, then tug on the harness to verify a secure connection.

26. Install the mounting bracket with fuel filter onto the power head. Tighten the mounting bracket screws to 71 in.-lb. (8.0 N•m).

27. Connect the trim position sender harness to the engine harness as described in Chapter Nine (See *Trim Position Sender Replacement*).

28. Connect the battery cables to the appropriate terminals on the mounting plate and electric starter.

29. Plug the engine harness connector to the oil pressure sender.

30. Install the power trim/tilt relay unit as described in Chapter Nine.

31. Plug the instrument harness connector into the engine harness connector.

32. Route all wiring and hoses to prevent pinching or interference with moving components. Secure the wiring and hoses with plastic locking clamps as needed.

33. Install the silencer cover as described in Chapter Five.

STARTING SYSTEM

This section describes removal, inspection, and installation of the starter relay, electric starter and starter solenoid. This section also describes electric starter repair.

Starter Relay Replacement

Two different starter relays (**Figure 20**, typical) are used. All 75 and 90 hp models utilize a rubber-mounted starter relay (**Figure 21**). This relay is retained by a snug fit in the rubber mount. The rubber mount is secured by a snug fit of the arms (7, **Figure 21**) in the mounting bracket (1).

On 115 and 225 hp models, a clamp secures the rigid mounted starter relay onto the electrical component mounting bracket.

Refer to the wiring diagrams at the end of the manual to identify the wiring coloring for the starter relay. Use the wire coloring to identify the starter relay from other components on the mounting plate.

75 and 90 hp models

The relay is located on the front starboard side of the power head and directly above the trim/tilt relays.

Refer to **Figure 21** for this procedure.

1. Disconnect the negative battery cable to prevent accidental starting and arcing at the terminals. Arcing can damage the rectifier/regulator and other engine components.

2. Remove the three screws, then the plastic electrical component cover (**Figure 17**).

3. Remove the terminal nuts, then disconnect the larger black and black/white wires from the relay terminals. Disconnect the brown relay wire from the engine wire harness connector. Trace the smaller diameter black relay wire to the ground terminal on the up trim/tilt relay. Remove the nut to disconnect the black wire. Temporarily thread the nut onto the terminal to retain the other two black wire terminals.

4. Carefully pull the starter relay (4, **Figure 21**) from the rubber mount (3).

5. Inspect the mount for damage or deterioration. Remove the mount by pulling it from the mounting bracket. Replace the mount by slipping the elongated openings (8, **Figure 21**) over the mounting arms (7). Ensure the arms pass completely through the elongated openings and the hooked ends engage the openings.

6. Slide the relay (4, **Figure 21**) fully into the opening in the rubber mount. Fit the lip on the opening over the outer edge of the relay.

7. Connect the larger diameter black and black/white wires onto the two large relay terminals. Ensure the wire terminals do not touch the other terminals or components. Install and tighten the terminal nuts to 25 in.-lb. (2.8 N•m).

8. Connect the brown relay wire onto the brown engine wire harness connector. Remove the nut, then connect the smaller diameter black relay wire onto the up relay terminal along with the other two black wires. Securely tighten the terminal nut.

9. Route the wiring to prevent pinching or interference with moving components. Install the electrical component cover and securely tighten the three mounting screws.

10. Connect the cable to the battery. Check for proper starting system operation.

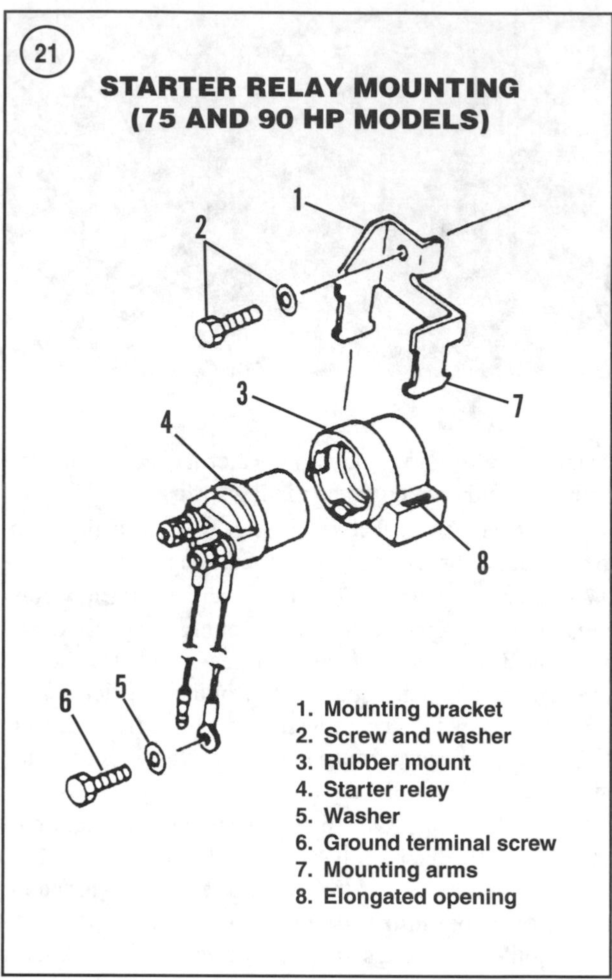

115 and 225 hp models

On 115 hp models, the bracket and relay are located on the front starboard side of the power head. On 225 hp models, the bracket and relay are located on the lower front and port side of the power head.

1. Disconnect the negative battery cable to prevent accidental starting and arcing at the terminals. Arcing can damage the rectifier/regulator and other engine components.

2. On 115 hp models, depress the three locking tabs, then remove the plastic electrical component cover.

3. On 225 hp models, remove the silencer cover as described in Chapter Five. Remove the plastic cover to access the relays. The cover is located on the lower port side of the mounting plate.

4. Remove the screws, then disconnect the red and brown/white (115 hp) or two brown/white (225 hp) wires from the relay terminals.

5. Disconnect the brown relay wire from the engine harness connector.

6A. On 115 hp models, trace the black relay wire to the ground terminal. Remove the screw to disconnect the relay ground.

6B. On 225 hp models, trace the black relay wire to the ground terminal on the trim/tilt relay. Remove the screw to disconnect the black wire.

7. Loosen the screw, then swing the relay clamp arm away from the relay. Pull the relay from the mounting bracket.

8. Fit the replacement starter relay into the recess in the mounting bracket. Make sure the black/brown wire faces downward. Position the clamp arm over the plastic body of the relay. Make sure the arm does not contact any of the relay terminals. Hold the clamp in position and tighten the screw.

9. Connect the brown relay wire terminal onto the brown engine harness terminal.

10A. On 115 hp models, route the black relay wire to the ground terminal. Connect the black wire terminal to ground with the screw.

10B. On 225 hp models, route the black relay wire to the ground terminal on the trim/tilt relay unit. Connect the black wire terminal onto the relay terminal with the screw.

11. Connect the red and brown/white (115 hp) or two brown/white wires onto the two larger terminals on the relay and secure with the screws and washers. Ensure the wire terminals do not touch the other terminal or other components.

12. Position the insulating boots over the red and brown/white or two brown/white wire terminals.

13. On 115 hp models, install the plastic electrical component cover onto the power head. Make sure the locking tabs engage properly.

14. On 225 hp models, install the silencer cover as described in Chapter Five.

15. Connect the cable to the battery. Check for proper starting system operation.

Starter Removal and Installation

Three bolts (A, **Figure 22**) secure the electric starter onto the power head. On 75-115 hp models, the starter is located on the starboard side of the power head. On 225 hp models, the starter is located on the front of the power head.

1. Disconnect the negative battery cable to prevent accidental starting and arcing at the terminals. Arcing can damage the rectifier/regulator and other engine components.

2. Remove the flywheel cover as described in Chapter Seven.

3A. On 75 and 90 hp models, remove the three screws, then the plastic electrical component cover (**Figure 17**).

3B. On 115 hp models, depress the three locking tabs, then remove the plastic electrical component cover.

4. On 225 hp models, remove the silencer cover as described in Chapter Five.

5. Move the insulating boot away from the wire terminal (B, **Figure 22**), then remove the nut from the starter solenoid terminal. Disconnect the positive battery cable from the starter solenoid terminal.

6. On 75 and 90 hp models, remove the bolt (C, **Figure 22**) then disconnect the negative battery cable from the starter housing.

7A. On 75 and 90 hp models, trace the black and black/white wires from the electric starter to the starter relay terminals. Remove the nuts, then disconnect the wires from the starter relay terminals.

7B. On 115 and 225 hp models, trace the red and brown/white (115 hp) or two brown/white (225 hp) wires from the electric starter to the starter relay terminals. Remove the screws and washers, then disconnect the wires from the relay terminals.

8. Support the electric starter while removing the three mounting bolts (A, **Figure 22**) and washers. Lift the electric starter from the engine.

9. Clean the starter mounting surfaces and mounting bolt openings in the power head.

10. Install the replacement electric starter onto the power head. Align the openings, then thread the three bolts and washers into the starter housing and power head openings. Do not apply sealant or thread locking agents onto the bolt threads. On some models, the starter grounds through the mounting bolts. Tighten the three bolts to 159 in.-lb. (18.0 N•m).

11A. Connect the larger diameter black and black/white wires onto the two large relay terminals. Ensure the wire terminals do not touch the other terminal or other components. Install and tighten the terminals nuts to 25 in.-lb. (2.8 N•m).
11B. Connect the red and brown/white (115 hp) or two brown/white wires onto the two larger terminals on the relay and secure with the screws and washers. Ensure the wire terminals do not touch the other terminal or other components. Position the insulating boots over the red and brown/white or two brown/white wire terminals.
12. Connect the positive battery cable terminal onto the starter solenoid terminal. Install the terminal nut and tighten to 120 in.-lb. (13.6 N•m) for 75 and 90 hp models and 70 in.-lb. (7.9 N•m) for 115 and 225 hp models.
13. On 75 and 90 hp models, connect the negative battery cable onto the starter housing terminal with the bolt. Tighten the terminal bolt to 120 in.-lb. (13.6 N•m).
14. Slip the insulating boot over the cable and position over the battery cable terminals.
15. Route the wiring and hoses to prevent pinching or interference with moving components. Secure the wiring and hoses with plastic locking clamps as needed.
16A. On 75 and 90 hp models, install the electrical component cover and securely tighten the three mounting screws.
16B. On 115 hp models, install the plastic electrical component cover onto the power head. Make sure the locking tabs engage properly.
17. On 225 hp models, install the silencer cover as described in Chapter Five.
18. Install the flywheel cover as described in Chapter Seven.
19. Connect the negative battery cable to the battery. Check for proper starting system operation.

Starter Solenoid Replacement

Refer to **Figure 23**.
1. Remove the electric starter as described in this chapter.
2. Remove the larger nut retaining the short cable to the starter solenoid. Disconnect the cable from the starter solenoid.
3. Remove both screws (1, **Figure 23**) and lift the starter solenoid (9) from the electric starter housing (2).
4. Pull the starter lever (4, **Figure 23**) from the electric starter housing. Pull the lever spring (5, **Figure 23**) from the mounting holes in the starter solenoid.
5. Remove both screws (6, **Figure 23**) and lift the cover (7) from the starter solenoid.
6. Test the starter solenoid as described in this section (see *Electric Starter Component Inspection*).

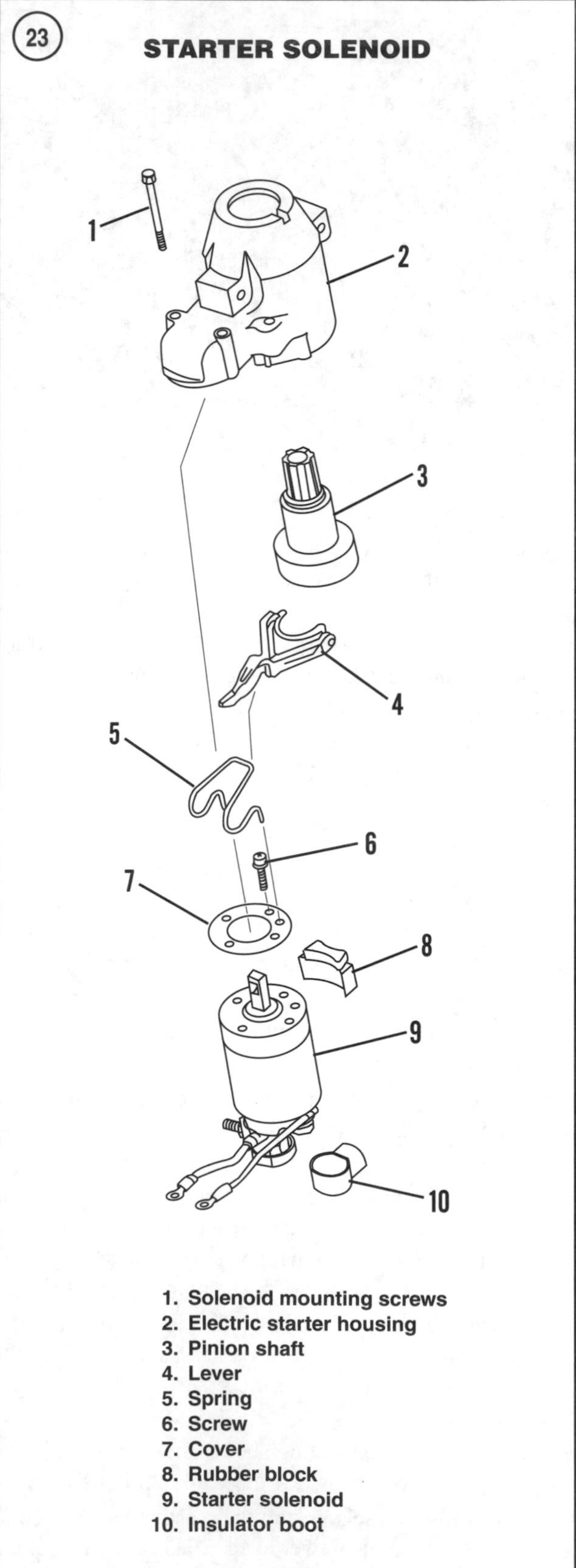

7. Align the screw and spring holes in the cover (7, **Figure 23**) with the matching holes in the solenoid (9). Install and securely tighten both screws (6, **Figure 23**). Install both ends of the spring into the cover and solenoid as indicated in **Figure 23**.
8. Install the lever (4, **Figure 23**) into the electric starter housing (2). Orient the lever with the spring notch facing outward.
9. Position the rubber block (8, **Figure 23**) within the starter relay opening. Carefully insert the relay into the opening in the electric starter housing. Ensure the spring (5, **Figure 23**) contacts the notch and the tip of the lever passes through the opening in the solenoid shaft.
10. Hold the solenoid in position and install the mounting screws (1, **Figure 23**). Tighten the mounting screws to 70 in.-lb. (7.9 N•m).
11. Connect the short cable to the starter solenoid terminal. Tighten the terminal nut to 78 in.-lb. (8.8 N•m).
12. Install the electric starter as described in this chapter.

Starter Disassembly and Assembly

Refer to **Figure 24**.

1. Remove the starter solenoid (26, **Figure 24**) as described in this chapter.
2. For reference during assembly, place match marks on the starter frame, upper and lower covers (**Figure 25**).
3. Secure the electric starter into a vice with soft jaws. Do not over-tighten the vice. Pry the starter pinion (3, **Figure 24**) downward. Tap the edge of the pinion stopper (2, **Figure 24**) down with a small hammer until the locking clip (1) is exposed. Carefully pry the locking clip from the pinion stopper.
4. Rotate the starter pinion counterclockwise to remove it from the pinion shaft (11, **Figure 24**). Pull the spring (4, **Figure 24**) from the shaft.
5. Remove both screws (39, **Figure 24**) from the lower cover (38). Remove both throughbolts (40, **Figure 24**) then carefully tap the lower cover (38) free from the frame (28). Pull the lower cover off the starter.
6. Using a small punch, tap the plate (35, **Figure 24**) from the groove on the lower end of the armature (29). Pull the brush plate (34, **Figure 24**) from the commutator.
7. Pull the frame and armature (28 and 29, **Figure 24**) from the starter housing (9). Mark the armature side and remove the plate (20, **Figure 24**) from the starter housing or frame. Remove the three planetary gears (19, **Figure 24**) from the planetary shaft (18).
8. Remove the planetary assembly from the starter housing by tapping lightly on the pinion shaft (11, **Figure 24**) with a plastic hammer. Pull the pinion shaft from the planetary assembly.
9. Carefully pry the E-clip (12, **Figure 24**) from the planetary shaft (18). Lift the washer and cover (13 and 14, **Figure 24**) from the planetary shaft. Pull the locating ring and gear (15 and 16, **Figure 24**) from the planetary. Slide the bushing off the planetary shaft.
10. Clean the upper cover, lower cover, armature and frame assembly using a mild solvent. Dry all components with compressed air.
11. Inspect all parts for worn, damaged or shorted components as described in this section.
12. Lubricate the entire planetary shaft (18, **Figure 24**) with a light coat of Quicksilver 2-4-C Maine Lubricant. Slide the bushing (17, **Figure 24**) over the planetary shaft (18). Place the gear (16, **Figure 24**), locating ring (15) and cover (14) over the planetary shaft as indicated in **Figure 24**.
13. Install the washer (13, **Figure 24**) over the planetary shaft. Carefully snap the E-clip (12) into the groove on the planetary shaft.
14. Apply a light coating of Quicksilver 2-4-C Maine Lubricant onto the upper end of the planetary shaft. Guide the planetary shaft into the pinion shaft.
15. Lubricate the bearing surfaces of the pinion shaft then guide the pinion assembly into the starter housing. Align the locating tabs on the locating ring (15, **Figure 24**), cover (14) and gear (16) with the notch in the starter housing (9).
16. Lubricate the planetary gears (19, **Figure 24**) with Quicksilver 2-4-C Maine Lubricant and mesh them with the larger gear (16). Install the plate (20, **Figure 24**) onto the starter housing (9).
17. Ensure all brushes and springs are in position prior to installing the brush plate (34, **Figure 24**). Hold the brushes fully retracted in the brush plate while sliding the brush plate over the commutator. Release the brushes only after the brush plate slides into position.
18. Carefully tap the plate (35, **Figure 24**) onto the groove at the lower end of the armature (29). Apply a light coating of Quicksilver 2-4-C Maine Lubricant onto the gear teeth and bearing surfaces of armature.
19. Install the frame (28, **Figure 24**). Hold the armature in the planetary while cautiously guiding the frame assembly over the armature.
20. Rotate the armature (29, **Figure 24**) while inserting the upper end into the planetary assembly. The armature will drop into the opening as the gear teeth on the armature mesh with the planetary gears.
21. Apply a drop or two of engine oil to the bushing in the lower cover. Align the screw opening in the brush plate (34, **Figure 24**), plate (35) and lower cover (38) while carefully guiding the lower cover over the brush plate. Fit

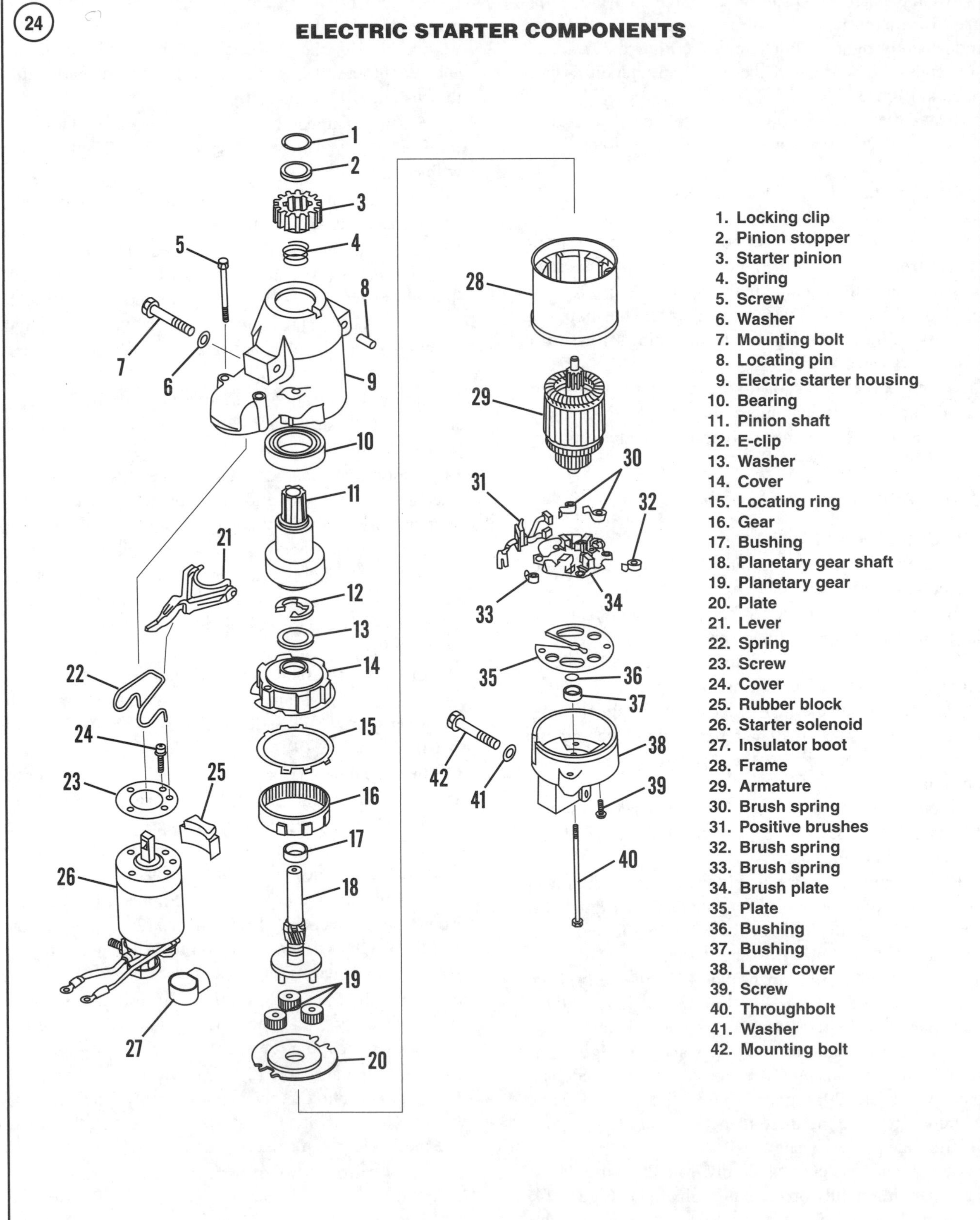
24
ELECTRIC STARTER COMPONENTS
1
2
3
4
5
6
7
8
9
10
11
12
13
14
15
16
17
18
19
20
21
22
23
24
25
26
27
28
29
30
31
32
33
34
35
36
37
38
39
40
41
42
1. Locking clip
2. Pinion stopper
3. Starter pinion
4. Spring
5. Screw
6. Washer
7. Mounting bolt
8. Locating pin
9. Electric starter housing
10. Bearing
11. Pinion shaft
12. E-clip
13. Washer
14. Cover
15. Locating ring
16. Gear
17. Bushing
18. Planetary gear shaft
19. Planetary gear
20. Plate
21. Lever
22. Spring
23. Screw
24. Cover
25. Rubber block
26. Starter solenoid
27. Insulator boot
28. Frame
29. Armature
30. Brush spring
31. Positive brushes
32. Brush spring
33. Brush spring
34. Brush plate
35. Plate
36. Bushing
37. Bushing
38. Lower cover
39. Screw
40. Throughbolt
41. Washer
42. Mounting bolt

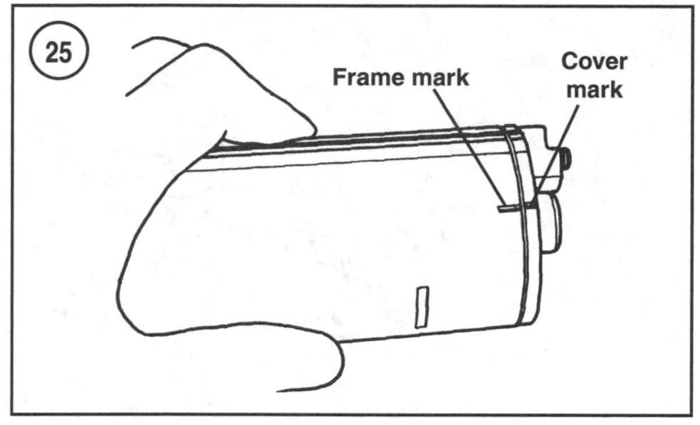

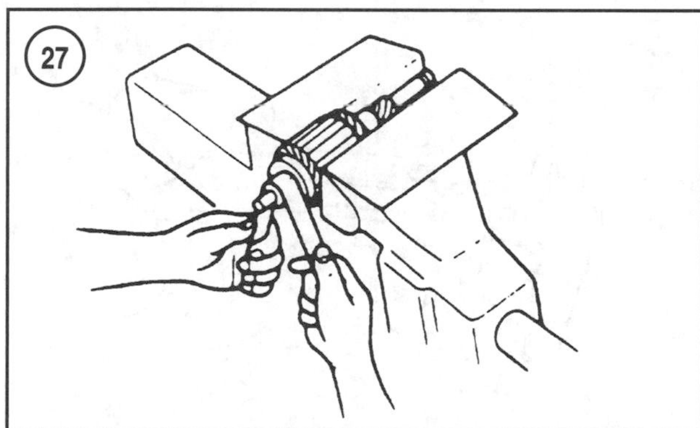

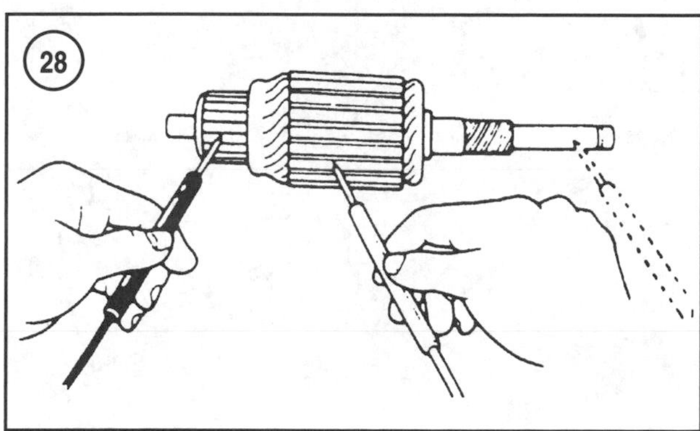

the insulator portion of the positive brush (31, **Figure 24**) into the groove in the lower cover (38).

22. Thread both screws (39, **Figure 24**) into the lower cover and brush plate. Tighten the screws to 18 in.-lb. (2.0 N•m). Align all reference marks (**Figure 25**) and aligning structures, then install both throughbolts (40, **Figure 24**). Tighten the throughbolts to 70 in.-lb. (7.9 N•m).

23. Slide the spring (4, **Figure 24**) and starter pinion (3) onto the planetary shaft. Place the stopper (2, **Figure 24**) onto the planetary shaft with the open end up.

24. Push the washer down until the locking clip groove is exposed. Insert the clip into the groove, then pull the stopper up and over the locking clip. The stopper must completely cover the sides of the clip.

25. Install the starter solenoid as described in this section.

Starter Component Inspection

1. Inspect the pinion for chipped, cracked or worn teeth (**Figure 26**). Replace the pinion if any defects are evident. Inspect the splines at the pinion end of the shaft. Replace the shaft if corroded, damaged or excessively worn.

2. Repeatedly thread the pinion drive onto and off the armature shaft. Replace the pinion drive or armature if the pinion drive does not turn smoothly on the shaft.

3. Carefully secure the armature in a vise with protective jaws (**Figure 27**). Tighten the vise only enough to secure the armature. Carefully polish away any corrosion deposits and glazed surfaces from the commutator using 600 grit Carborundum cloth (**Figure 27**). Avoid removing too much material. Rotate the armature often to polish the surfaces evenly.

4. Check the armature for a shorted or open circuit as follows:

   a. Calibrate a multimeter to the R × 1 scale.

   b. Connect the multimeter between any commutator segment and the armature lamination (**Figure 28**). The meter must indicate *no continuity*. If otherwise, the armature is shorted and must be replaced.

   c. Connect the multimeter between any commutator segment and the armature shaft (**Figure 28**). The meter should indicate *no continuity*. If otherwise, the armature is shorted and must be replaced.

   d. Connect the multimeter between two of the commutator segments (**Figure 29**). Repeat this test with the meter connected to each of commutator segments. The meter must indicate *continuity* for each connection point. If otherwise, the commutator has failed to open and the armature must be replaced.

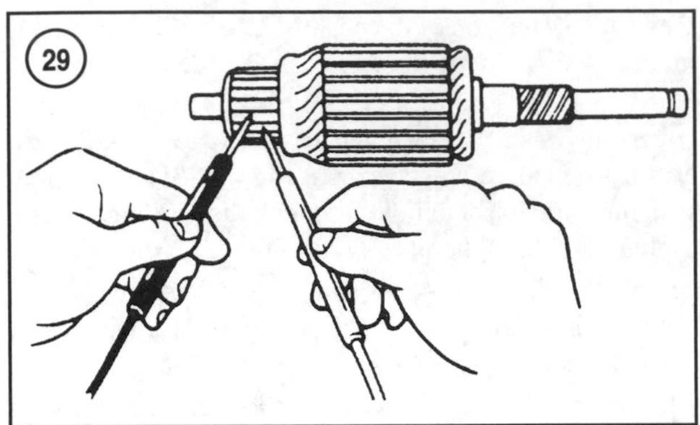

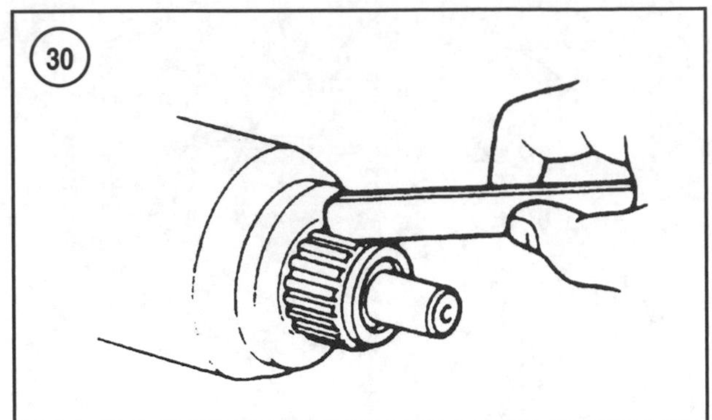

5. Use a small jewelers file to remove the mica particles from the undercut between the commutator segments (**Figure 30**).

6. Blow away any loose particles using compressed air. Use a depth micrometer to measure the depth of each undercut (**Figure 31**) in the commutator. Replace the armature if any of the undercut measurements are less than 0.008 in. (0.20 mm).

7. Measure the commutator diameter (**Figure 32**) at several locations around the circumference. Replace the armature if the commutator diameter is less than 1.102 in. (28.0 mm) at any point.

8. Use a vernier caliper or micrometer to measure the brush length (**Figure 33**). Replace all of the brushes if any of the measurements are less than 0.374 in. (9.5 mm).

9. Replace the complete brush plate if corroded, contaminated, chipped or broken. Inspect the brush springs for corrosion damage or weak spring tension. Replace the springs if these or other defects are evident.

10. Inspect the magnets in the frame assembly for corrosion or other contamination and clean as required. Inspect the frame assembly for cracked or loose magnets. Replace the frame assembly if it cannot be adequately cleaned or if the magnets are damaged.

11. Inspect the bearing surfaces on the armature and the bushings for discoloration and excessive or uneven wear. Remove and replace any questionable bearings or bushings using a suitable pulling tool and driver. Replace the armature if the bearing surfaces are rough or uneven.

12. Test the starter solenoid as follows:

   a. Calibrate a multimeter onto the R × 1 scale.
   b. Connect the meter test leads onto the two large solenoid terminals. The meter should indicate *no continuity*.
   c. Clamp the solenoid into a vise with soft jaws. Using a jumper wire, connect the black/white or brown/white solenoid terminal onto the positive terminal of a 12-volt battery.

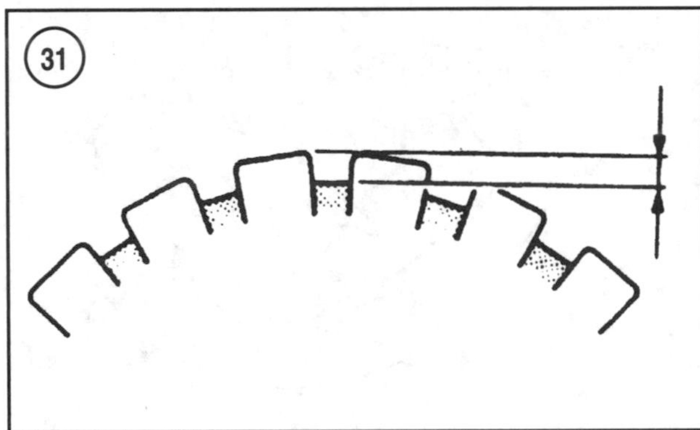

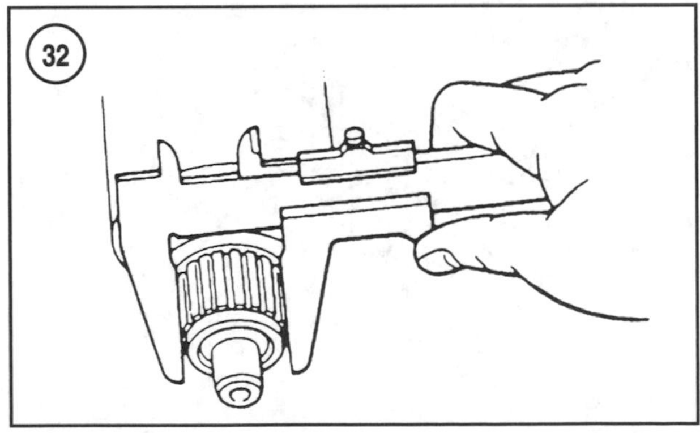

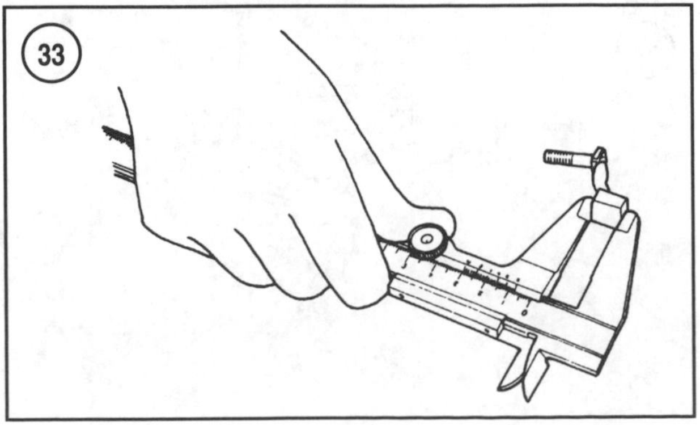

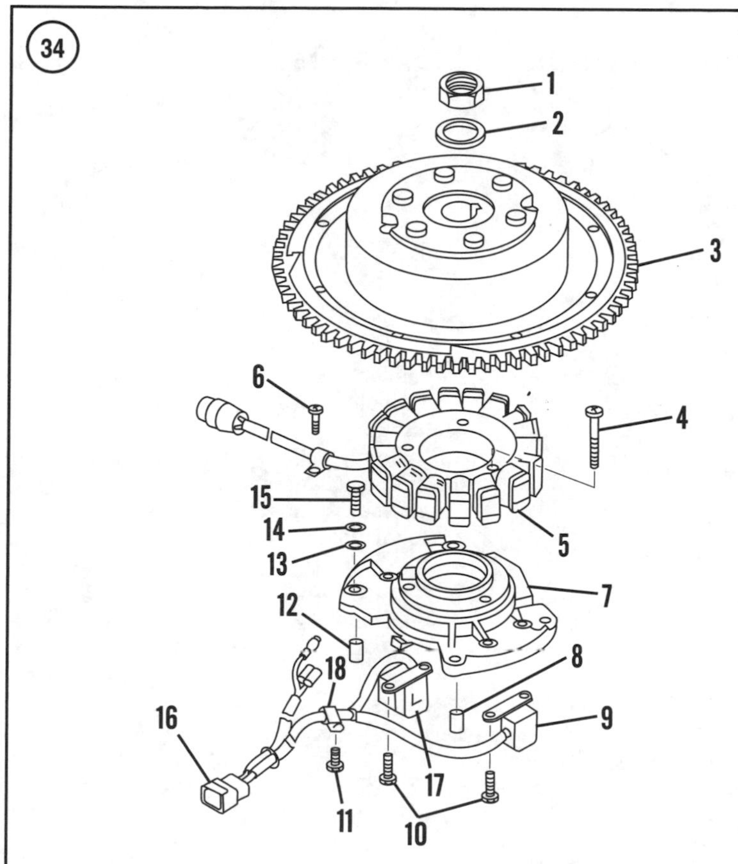

CRANKSHAFT POSITION SENSOR MOUNTING (75-115 HP MODELS)

1. Flywheel nut
2. Washer
3. Flywheel
4. Screw
5. Battery charging coil
6. Screw
7. Charge coil/sensor mounting base
8. Locating pin
9. Crankshaft position sensor (longer wiring)
10. Screw
11. Screw
12. Locating pin
13. Flat washer
14. Lockwasher
15. Screw
16. Connector
17. Crankshaft position sensor (shorter wiring)
18. Wire clamp

d. Observe the meter while attaching a jumper wire from the negative terminal of the battery to an unpainted surface of the solenoid. Continuity should be present and the solenoid shaft should extend rapidly when the jumper wire is attached.

e. Replace the solenoid if it fails to operate as described.

IGNITION SYSTEM

This section describes replacement for the following ignition system components:

1. Crankshaft position sensor.
2. Engine control unit.
3. Engine temperature sensor.
4. Engine temperature switch.
5. Ignition coil.
6. Oil pressure switch.
7. Oil pressure sender.
8. Power relay.
9. Shift interrupt switch.
10. Shift position switch.

CAUTION

To prevent arcing or accidental starting, disconnect the negative battery cable before removing any ignition system component. Arcing can damage the rectifier/regulator and other engine components.

Crankshaft Position Sensor Replacement

The crankshaft position sensors are located on the battery charging coil mounting base. The sensors utilize a common wire harness and cannot be replaced individually. On 225 hp models, the sensors are integrated into the battery charging coil mounting base and the assembly must be replaced if the sensors are faulty.

The flywheel and battery charging coil must be removed to access the sensors.

75-115 hp models

Refer to **Figure 34**.

1. Remove the flywheel as described in Chapter Seven.

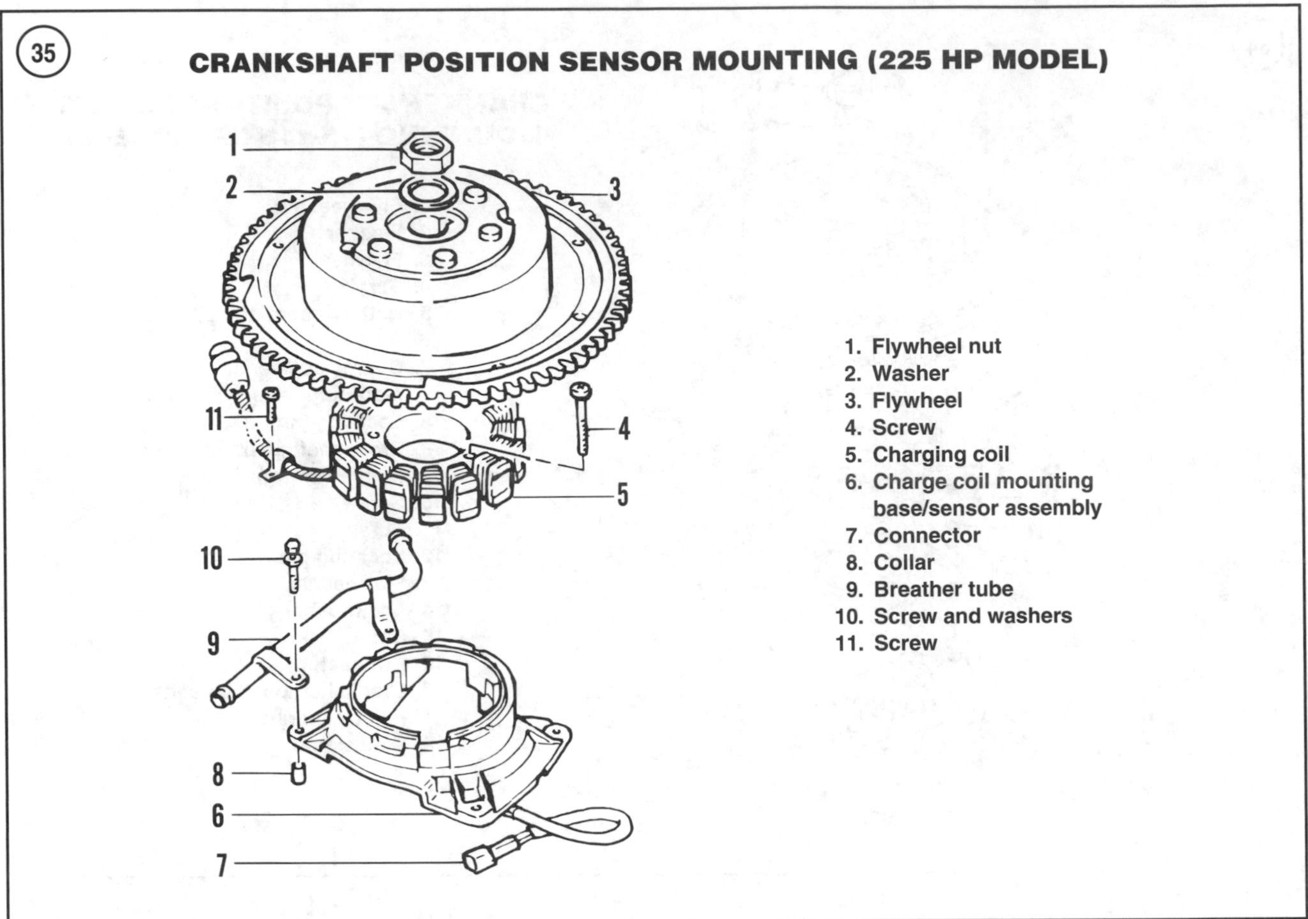

2. Remove the battery charging coil as described in this chapter.

3. Disconnect the engine wire harness from the sensor harness connector (16, **Figure 34**).

4. Mark the mounting base relative to the orientation on the power head. This helps ensure correct wire routing and phasing of the coils during installation.

5. Remove the four screws (15, **Figure 34**) and washers (13 and 14), then lift the mounting base (7) from the power head.

6. If dislodged, install the locating pins (8 and 12, **Figure 34**) into the openings in the power head.

7. Remove the screw (11, **Figure 34**) to release the wire clamp (18).

8. Remove the four screws (10, **Figure 34**) and the sensors (9 and 17) from the mounting plate.

9. Use compressed air to remove debris from the mounting plate, power head and threaded openings.

10. Select the sensor (17, **Figure 34**) with the shorter wire length to the clamp (18). Install this sensor at the location closest to the clamp screw. Fit the sensor onto the mounting base with the protrusion facing outward or toward the flywheel when assembled onto the power head. Thread the two screws (10, **Figure 34**) into the sensor and mounting base opening. Tighten the screws to 43 in.-lb. (4.9 N•m).

11. Install the sensor (9, **Figure 34**) with the longer wire length onto the mounting base as described in Step 10.

12. Fit the wire clamp (18, **Figure 34**) onto the mounting base. Secure the clamp with the screw and tighten to 18 in.-lb. (2.0 N•m).

13. Align the markings made in Step 4 with the locating pin opening. Seat the mounting base onto the power head. Do not pinch the wire harness between the power head and mounting base.

14. Thread the four screws (15, **Figure 34**) and washers (13 and 14) into the mounting base and power head. Tighten the screws in a crossing pattern to 70 in.-lb. (7.9 N•m).

15. Plug the sensor harness connector (16, **Figure 34**) onto the engine wire harness connector. Route all wiring and hoses to prevent pinching or interference with moving components.

16. Install the battery charging coil as described in this chapter.
17. Install the flywheel as described in Chapter Seven.

225 hp model

Refer to **Figure 35**.

1. Remove the flywheel as described in Chapter Seven.
2. Remove the battery charging coil as described in this chapter.
3. Disconnect the engine wire harness from the sensor harness connector (7, **Figure 35**).
4. Mark the mounting base relative to the orientation on the power head. This helps ensure correct wire routing and phasing of the coils during installation.
5. Remove the four screws and washers (10, **Figure 35**), then lift the mounting base (6) from the power head. Retrieve the two collars (8, **Figure 35**) from the top of the power head.
6. Use compressed air to remove debris from the mounting plate, power head and threaded openings.
7. Align the markings (Step 4) and threaded openings, then seat the mounting base onto the power head. Do not pinch the wire harness between the power head and mounting base.
8. Insert the two collars between the mounting base and the threaded openings in the power head. The openings in the collars must align with the starboard side mounting screw openings.
9. Align the screw openings in the breather tube (9, **Figure 35**) flanges with the mounting screw openings. Thread two of the mounting screws and washers (10, **Figure 35**) into the breather tube flanges, mounting base, collars and power head openings. Make sure the screws pass through both collars. Thread the remaining two screws into the port side openings. Tighten the four mounting screws in a crossing pattern to 71 in.-lb. (8.0 N•m).
10. Plug the sensor harness connector (7, **Figure 35**) onto the engine wire harness connector. Route all wiring and hoses to prevent pinching or interference with moving components.
11. Install the battery charging coil as described in this chapter.
12. Install the flywheel as described in Chapter Seven.

Engine Control Unit (ECU) Replacement

CAUTION
The engine control unit (ECU) can be damaged from electrostatic discharge. Touch an engine ground to dissipate any static charge in the body before touching the ECU or related wire connectors.

6

The engine control unit (ECU) (**Figure 36**, typical) mounts onto the electrical component mounting plate. On 75-115 hp models, the mounting plate is located on the front and starboard side on the power head and the plastic cover must be removed for access. On 225 hp models, the mounting plate is located on the front and port side of the power head and the silencer cover must be removed for access.

1A. On 75 and 90 hp models, remove the three screws, then the plastic electrical component cover (**Figure 17**).
1B. On 115 hp models, depress the three locking tabs, then remove the plastic electrical component cover.
1C. On 225 hp models, remove the silencer cover as described in Chapter Five.
2. Refer to the wire diagrams at the end of the manual to identify the wire colors connecting onto the ECU. Identify the ECU from other components on the mounting plate by connecting wire coloring.
3. Depress the locking tab then unplug the engine wire harness connector(s) from the ECU. Three connectors are used on 75 and 90 hp models, two connectors are used on 115 hp models and a single connector is used on 225 hp models.
4. Remove the four mounting screws and carefully pull the ECU from the mounting plate. Use compressed air to remove debris from the ECU and mounting surfaces. Wipe any oil deposits from the mounting surfaces.
5. Install the ECU onto the mounting plate. Refer to the following to assist with orientation.
   a. On 75-115 hp models, the connector openings must face toward the starboard side.
   b. On 225 hp models, the wire connector opening must face downward.
6. Support the ECU while threading the four mounting screws into the ECU and mounting plate. Tighten the

screws in a crossing pattern to 70 in.-lb. (7.9 N•m) for 75-115 hp models and 71 in.-lb. (8.0 N•m) for 225 hp models.

7. Depress the locking tab then plug the engine harness connector(s) onto the ECU. Release the tab then tug on the harness to verify a secure connection. Refer to the following to assist with connector plug locations.

   a. On 75 and 90 hp models, the six-pin connector plugs into the upper ECU opening, the eight-pin connector plugs into the middle ECU opening and the four-pin connector plugs into the lower opening.

   b. On 115 hp models, the 24-pin connector plugs into the upper ECU opening and the 12-pin connector plugs into the lower opening.

8. Route the wiring and hoses to prevent pinching or interference with moving components. Secure the wiring and hoses with plastic locking clamps as needed.

9A. On 75 and 90 hp models, install the electrical component cover and securely tighten the three mounting screws.

9B. On 115 hp models, install the plastic electrical component cover onto the power head. Make sure the locking tabs engage properly.

9C. On 225 hp models, install the silencer cover as described in Chapter Five.

Engine Temperature Sensor Replacement

NOTE

*The engine temperature sensor (**Figure 37**, typical) and the engine temperature switches used on some models are similar in appearance and mount in similar locations. Refer to the wiring diagrams at the end of the manual to identify the wire colors connected to the sensor.*

75-115 hp models

On 75 and 90 hp models, the engine temperature sensor (**Figure 37**, typical) mounts onto the lower end of exhaust cover on the starboard side of the power head. The sensor is located just to the rear of the dipstick grip. On 115 hp models, the engine temperature sensor mounts onto the upper end of the exhaust cover on the starboard side of the power head. The sensor is located just to the rear of the electric starter.

1. Pinch the sides of the connector then pull it from the sensor.

2. Remove the two screws on each side of the plug connector, then pull the retainer and sensor from the exhaust cover.

3. Remove the rubber seal from the sensor body or opening in the exhaust cover. Replace the seal if it is cut, deformed or has deteriorated surfaces.

4. Wipe all corrosion deposits or debris from the mating surfaces and the opening in the plate. The opening must be completely clean for accurate sensor readings.

5. Install the rubber seal over the sensor tip and seat against the sensor body.

6. Install the sensor into the opening with the square boss on the sensor body facing upward on 75 and 90 hp models, or facing forward on 115 hp models. *Do not* apply any grease or sealing agent to the sensor. Seat the sensor into the opening.

7. Fit the retainer into the groove in the sensor body with the open end facing upward for 75 and 90 hp models and facing forward for 115 hp models. Align the openings, then thread the two screws into the retainer and cover openings. Tighten the two screws to 70 in.-lb. (7.9 N•m).

8. Align the recess in the harness connector with the square boss on the sensor body, then squeeze the side of the connector and plug it onto the sensor. Release the connector, then tug on the harness to verify a secure connection.

9. Route the sensor wiring to prevent interference with moving components.

225 hp model

The engine temperature sensor threads into the upper port side of the cylinder block just above the upper throttle body.

1. Remove the flywheel cover as described in Chapter Seven.

2. Remove the silencer cover as described in Chapter Five.

38

39

3. Trace the sensor harness to the engine harness connector located just above the engine control unit (ECU) on the electrical component mounting plate. Unplug the connector.

4. Unthread and remove the sensor from the cylinder block.

5. Remove the sealing washer from the sensor or cylinder block. Discard the washer.

6. Clean all corrosion or other contaminants from the threaded opening. The opening must be clean for accurate sensor readings.

7. Install a new gasket onto the sensor tip and seat it against the sensor body.

8. Thread the sensor into the opening and tighten to 133 in.-lb. (15.0 N•m).

9. Route the sensor harness to the connector on the electrical component mounting plate. Route the wiring to prevent pinching or interference with the flywheel or other moving components. Plug the sensor harness onto the engine harness.

10. Install the silencer cover as described in Chapter Five.

11. Install the flywheel cover as described in Chapter Seven.

Engine Temperature Switch Replacement

NOTE

*The engine temperature switches (**Figure 38**) and the engine temperature sensor (**Figure 37**) are similar in appearance and mount in similar locations. Refer to the wiring diagrams at the end of the manual to identify the wire colors connected onto the switches.*

The engine temperature switch (**Figure 38**, typical) is used only on 225 hp models. Two switches are used. They mount onto the thermostat housings on the upper port and upper starboard sides of the power head.

1. Remove the flywheel cover as described in Chapter Seven.

2. Trace the starboard side switch wires to the connectors on the engine wire harness. Cut the plastic locking clamp then disconnect the switch wires from the engine harness.

3. To access the starboard side switch, push the plastic wire harness support toward the flywheel.

4. Remove the screw and retainer. Lift the switch from the thermostat housing.

5. Remove the port side engine temperature switch using the methods described in Steps 2-4.

6. Clean all corrosion deposits and debris from the switch openings. The openings must be clean for proper switch operation.

7. Carefully guide the switch into the opening in the starboard side thermostat housing. Seat the switch, then fit the retainer onto the switch and thermostat housing. Rotate the switch to align the switch wiring with the open end of the retainer. Thread the screw into the retainer and thermostat housing, then tighten to 71 in.-lb. (8.0 N•m).

8. Connect the switch wires to the corresponding engine harness connectors. Route the wiring to prevent pinching and interference with the flywheel and other moving components. Secure the wiring and connectors with plastic locking clamps.

9. Install the port side temperature switch using the method described in Step 7 and Step 8.

10. Install the flywheel cover as described in Chapter Seven.

Ignition Coil Replacement

Each ignition coil unit (**Figure 39**, typical) houses a single common primary and two independent secondary coil windings. Each coil provides the spark for two cylinders. Two coils are used on 75-115 hp models and three coils are used on 225 hp models. Although they differ in appearance and mounting location, the ignition coil replacement procedures are very similar.

1. Disconnect the negative battery cable to prevent accidental electric starter operation.

2A. On 75-115 hp models, remove the screws (**Figure 40**) and plastic cover on the rear of the power head. Two screws are located on the top, two screws are located on the bottom and one screw is located on the side and midway down on the cover.

2B. On 225 hp models, remove the four screws (**Figure 41**) and the plastic ignition coil cover on the rear of the power head.

NOTE
Mark the cylinder number on each spark plug lead as it is removed.

3. Mark the cylinder number on the spark plug leads before removing them from the spark plugs. On 75-115 hp models, the top cylinder is the No. 1 cylinder. On 225 hp models, the top cylinder on the starboard bank is the No. 1 cylinder. Odd numbered cylinders are on the starboard cylinder bank and even numbered cylinders are on the port bank. Gently twist the spark plug caps to free them from the plugs, then pull the cap from the plug. Never pull on the spark plug lead to free the cap.

4A. On 75 and 90 hp models, unplug the black/white coil wire from the engine harness connector. Remove the screw to disconnect the black coil wire from the ground terminal. Temporarily replace the screw to retain other wires that may be connected onto the terminal.

4B. On 115 hp models, depress the locking tab, then unplug the red and black/white or red and black/red coil wire harness connector from the engine harness connector.

4C. On 225 hp models, depress the locking tab, then unplug the red/yellow and black/red, red/yellow and black/yellow, or red/yellow and black/white coil wire harness connector from the engine harness connector.

5. Remove the two mounting screws (**Figure 39**, typical) and lift the coil from the power head.

6. Clean all corrosion deposits, belt material or oily deposits from the coil mating surfaces.

7. Install the coil onto the power head and secure with the two mounting screws. Tighten the screws to 70 in.-lb. (7.9 N•m) for 75-115 hp models and 71 in.-lb. (8.0 N•m) for 225 hp models.

8A. On 75 and 90 hp models, plug the black/white coil wire connector onto black/orange or black/white engine harness connector. Remove the screw, then connect the black ignition coil wire onto the ground terminal. Make sure to connect any other wires that were originally connected onto the terminal. Tighten the ground terminal screw to 70 in.-lb. (6.9 N•m).

40

41

8B. On 115 and 225 hp models, depress the tab, then plug the ignition coil wire harness connector onto the engine harness connector. Release the tab, then tug on the harness to verify a secure connection.

9. Apply a light coating of corrosion preventative oil (silicone lubricant) to the inner surfaces of the spark plug cap. Carefully slide the cap over the correct spark plug. Snap the cap fully onto the spark plug. Tug lightly on the cap to verify a secure connection. Verify that each spark plug lead connects to the spark plug for the corresponding cylinder number.

10. Remove and install any other ignition coils requiring replacements as described in Steps 3-9.

11. Fit the plastic cover (**Figure 40** or **Figure 41**) onto the rear of the power head. Install the screws and tighten in a crossing pattern to 65 in.-lb. (7.3 N•m) for 75-115 hp models and 71 in.-lb. (8.0 N•m) for 225 hp models.

12. Connect the battery cable.

Oil Pressure Switch

The oil pressure switch (**Figure 42**) is only used on 75-115 hp models. The oil pressure switch threads into the upper port side of the power head.

1. Remove the flywheel cover as described in Chapter Seven.
2. Pull the rubber insulating boot away from the terminal. Remove the nut and disconnect the pink/white from the switch.
3. Use a deep socket to unthread the switch from the power head.
4. Clean all foreign material from the switch threads and the threaded opening in the power head. Do not allow foreign material to enter the opening. The opening must be clean for proper switch operation.
5. Apply a very light coat of Loctite Pipe Sealant to the threaded section of the switch. Do not allow the sealant to enter the passage into the switch body. Excess sealant may prevent the switch from grounding to the power head and cause it to malfunction.
6. Thread the switch into the power head opening by hand. Use a deep socket to tighten the switch to 70 in.-lb. (7.9 N•m).
7. Connect the pink/white wire onto the switch terminal. Securely tighten the terminal nut. Position the rubber insulating boot over the terminal and sensor body. Route the wiring to prevent pinching or interference with the flywheel, timing belt and other moving components. Secure the wiring with plastic locking clamps as needed.
8. Install the flywheel cover as described in Chapter Seven.
9. Start the engine and immediately check for oil leaks at the switch. Replace or retighten the switch as necessary to correct any oil leakage.

Oil Pressure Sender Replacement

The oil pressure sender (**Figure 43**) is used on 225 hp models. The oil pressure sender is located on front starboard side of the power head and to the rear of the oil filter.

6

1. Remove the oil filter as described in Chapter Three (see *Oil filter replacement*).
2. Squeeze the sides, then carefully unplug the engine harness connector from the sender.
3. Engage a wrench onto the hex-shaped section, then unthread and remove the sender.
4. Clean all foreign material from the sender threads and the threaded opening in the power head. Do not allow foreign material to enter the opening. The opening must be clean for proper sealing upon installation.
5. Apply a very light coat of Loctite Pipe Sealant to the threaded section of the sender. Do not allow the sealant to enter the passage into the sender body. Excess sealant may prevent the sender from grounding to the power head and cause it to malfunction.
6. Thread the sender into the opening by hand. Engage a wrench onto the hex-shaped section and tighten the sender to 159 in.-lb. (18.0 N•m).
7. Squeeze the sides of the engine harness connector and plug it into the sender. Tug on the harness to verify a secure connection. Route the wiring to prevent pinching or interference with the linkages and other moving components. Secure the wiring with plastic locking clamps as needed.
8. Install the oil filter as described in Chapter Three.
9. Start the engine and immediately check for oil leaks at the sender. Replace or retighten the sender as necessary to correct any oil leakage.

Power Relay Replacement

The power relay (**Figure 44**, typical) is used on 115 and 225 hp models. A single screw secures the relay onto the electrical component mounting plate.

On 115 hp models, the mounting plate is located on the front and starboard side on the power head. The plastic cover must be removed for access. On 225 hp models, the mounting plate is located on the front and port side of the power head and the silencer cover must be removed for access.

1. Disconnect the negative battery cable to prevent arcing and accidental starting. Arcing can damage the rectifier/regulator and other engine components.

2A. On 115 hp models, depress the three locking tabs, then remove the plastic electrical component cover.

2B. On 225 hp models, remove the silencer cover as described in Chapter Five. Remove the four screws and the plastic cover on the bottom of the mounting plate.

3. Refer to the wire diagrams at the end of the manual to identify the wire colors connecting onto the power relay. Identify the relay from other components on the mounting plate by wire color.

4. Depress the locking tab and unplug the engine wire harness connector from the relay.

5. Remove the screw and pull the relay off the mounting plate. Use compressed air to remove debris from the mounting plate. Wipe any oil deposits from the mounting surfaces.

6. Depress the locking tab, then plug the engine harness connector onto the relay. Release the tab, then tug on the harness and relay to verify a secure connection.

7. Insert the relay into the recess in the mounting plate. Make sure no wiring is pinched between the relay and the plate. Thread the screw into the relay and mounting plate. Securely tighten the screw.

8. Route the wiring to prevent pinching or interference with moving components. Secure the wiring with plastic locking clamps as needed.

9. On 225 hp models, install the plastic cover over the relay and seat against the mounting plate. Thread the four screws into the cover and mounting plate. Securely tighten the screws.

10A. On 115 hp models, install the plastic electrical component cover onto the power head. Make sure the locking tabs engage properly.

10B. On 225 hp models, install the silencer cover as described in Chapter Five.

11. Connect the battery cable.

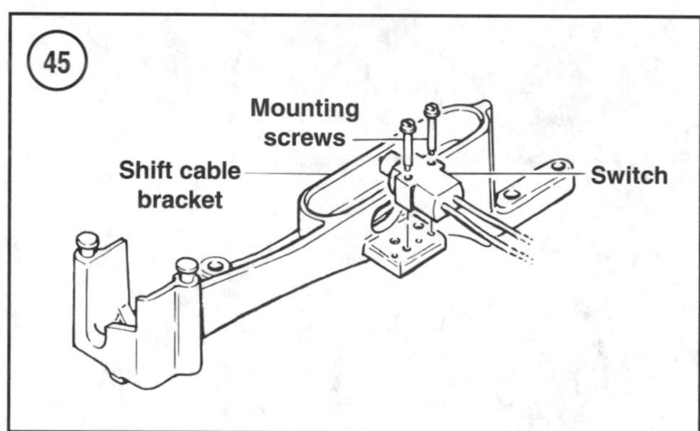

Shift Interrupt Switch Replacement

The shift interrupt switch is used on 75, 90 and 225 hp models. The interrupt switch is similar in appearance and mounts in a similar location as the shift position switch used on 115 and 225 hp models. The switches perform different functions and are not interchangeable.

NOTE
The shift interrupt switch and shift position switch are similar in appearance and mount in similar locations. Refer to the wiring diagrams at the end of the manual to identify the wire colors connected onto the switches.

75 and 90 hp models

The shift interrupt switch mounts onto the shift cable bracket on the lower port side of the power head. The drive shaft housing cover must be removed to access the switch.

Refer to **Figure 45**.

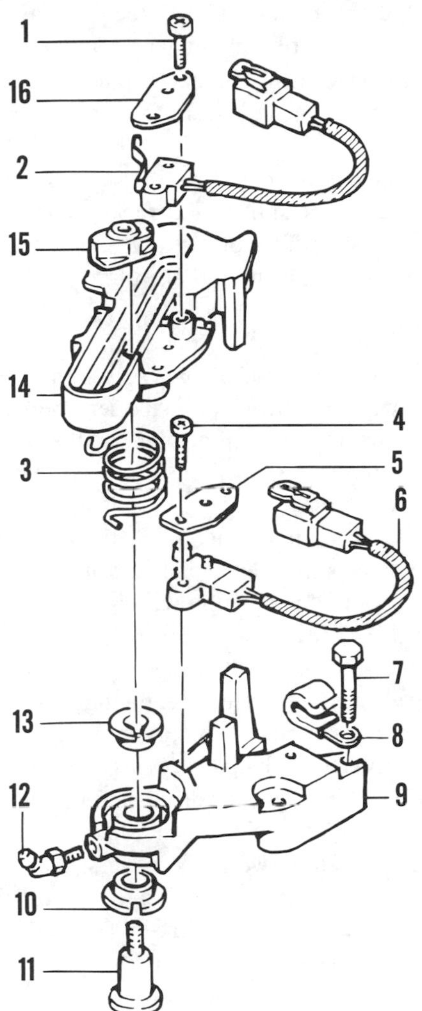

1. Disconnect the negative battery cables to prevent accidental starting.
2. Remove the eight screws that secure the port drive shaft housing cover (**Figure 46**, typical). Carefully pull the port side cover from the drive shaft housing. The cover should pull easily from the housing. If any resistance is noted, check for overlooked screws. Let the cover hang on the cable bundle. It is not necessary to remove the cable clamp unless replacing the cable(s) or cover.
3. Disconnect the white/red and black interrupt switch wires from the engine wire harness connectors.
4. Remove the two mounting screws (**Figure 45**) and lift the switch from the shift cable bracket. Use compressed air to blow debris off the bracket. Debris on the mounting surfaces may prevent proper seating of the switch and cause it to malfunction.
5. Guide the plunger of the replacement switch into the opening in the cable bracket, then seat the switch onto the mount. Move the switch to align the screw openings with the rear mounting screw openings in the bracket. The front mounting screw openings are used on some engines to correct improper switch operation.
6. Hold the switch in position while threading the switch mounting screws into the switch and mounting bracket. Securely tighten the mounting screws.
7. Plug the white/red and black switch wires onto the corresponding engine wire harness connectors. Route the wiring to prevent pinching or interference with the shift linkages or other moving components. Secure the wiring with plastic locking clamps as needed.
8. Fit the port cover onto the drive shaft housing and mate against the starboard side cover. Make sure no wiring or hoses are pinched between the covers, then thread the eight screws (**Figure 46**, typical) into the port side openings. Tighten the screws to 65 in.-lb. (7.3 N•m).
9. Connect the battery cable.
10. Prepare the engine for operation under actual running conditions. Start the engine and allow it to reach normal operating temperature. Shift the engine into FORWARD gear and back to NEUTRAL several times. Note if the engine runs significantly rougher when in neutral gear. If this condition is evident, remove the switch and reinstall using the front mounting screw openings.

225 hp model

The shift interrupt switch mounts onto the pivot bracket on the lower starboard side of the power head.

Refer to **Figure 47** for this procedure.

1. Disconnect the negative battery cable to prevent accidental starting. Shift the engine into NEUTRAL gear.

6

2. Pull up on the locking tab, then disconnect the shift interrupt switch (6, **Figure 47**) harness connector from the engine harness connector. Do not inadvertently disconnect the shift position switch. The shift interrupt switch uses a blue/yellow and black wire. The shift position switch uses a brown and black wire.
3. Remove the screw (7, **Figure 47**) and wire clamp (8) from the switch harness.
4. Remove the two mounting screws (4, **Figure 47**) and cover (5) from the switch. Carefully lift the switch from the pivot bracket (9, **Figure 47**).
5. Use compressed air to remove debris from the brackets. Debris on the mounting surfaces may prevent proper seating of the switch and cause it to malfunction.
6. Align the screw openings, then install the replacement interrupt switch onto the pivot bracket. Fit the cover (5, **Figure 47**) onto the switch, then thread the two screws into the cover, switch and pivot bracket openings. Tighten the screws to 18 in.-lb. (2.0 N•m).
7. Pull up on the locking tab, then connect the shift interrupt switch harness onto the engine harness connector.
8. Route the wiring to prevent interference with the shift linkages and other moving components. Secure the switch harness onto the bracket with the wire clamp (8, **Figure 47**) and screw (7). Tighten the clamp screw to 71 in.-lb. (8.0 N•m).
9. Connect the battery cable.

Shift Position Switch Replacement

The shift position switch is used on 115 and 225 hp models. The shift position switch is similar in appearance and mounts in a similar location as the shift interrupt switch used on 75, 90 and 225 hp models. The switches perform different functions and are not interchangeable.

NOTE
Refer to the wiring diagrams at the end of the manual to identify the wire colors connected to the shift position switch.

115 hp model

The shift position switch mounts onto the shift cable bracket on the lower port side of the power head. The drive shaft housing cover must be removed to access the switch.

Refer to **Figure 45**.

1. Disconnect the negative battery cables to prevent accidental starting.
2. Remove the eight screws that secure the port drive shaft housing cover (**Figure 46**, typical). Carefully pull the port side cover from the drive shaft housing. The cover should pull easily from the housing. If any resistance is noted, check for overlooked screws. Let the cover hang on the cable bundle. It is not necessary to remove the cable clamp unless replacing the cable(s) or cover.
3. Depress the locking tab, then unplug the shift position switch harness connector from the engine harness connector.
4. Remove the two mounting screws (**Figure 45**) and lift the switch from the shift cable bracket. Use compressed air to blow debris off the bracket. Debris on the mounting surfaces may prevent proper seating of the switch and cause it to malfunction.
5. Guide the plunger of the replacement switch into the opening in the cable bracket, then seat the switch onto the mount. Move the switch to align the screw openings with the rear mounting screw openings in the bracket. The front mounting screw openings are used to correct improper switch operation.
6. Hold the switch in position while threading the switch mounting screws into the switch and mounting bracket. Securely tighten the mounting screws.
7. Depress the locking tab, then plug the position with harness connector onto the engine harness connector. Route the wiring to prevent pinching or interference with the shift linkages or other moving components. Secure the wiring with plastic locking clamps as needed.
8. Fit the port cover onto the drive shaft housing and mate it against the starboard side cover. Make sure no wires or hoses are pinched between the covers, then thread the eight screws (**Figure 46**, typical) into the port side openings. Tighten the screws to 65 in.-lb. (7.3 N•m).
9. Connect the battery cables.

225 hp model

The shift position switch mounts onto the shift cable bracket on the lower starboard side of the power head.

Refer to **Figure 47**.

1. Disconnect the negative battery cable to prevent accidental starting. Shift the engine into NEUTRAL gear.
2. Pull up on the locking tab, then disconnect the shift position switch (2, **Figure 47**) harness connector from the engine harness connector. Do not inadvertently disconnect the shift interrupt switch. The shift position switch uses a brown and black wire. The shift interrupt switch uses a blue/yellow and black wire.
3. Remove the screw (7, **Figure 47**) and wire clamp (8) from the switch harness.

4. Remove the two mounting screws (1, **Figure 47**) and cover (16) from the switch. Carefully lift the switch from the shift cable bracket (14, **Figure 47**).

5. Use compressed air to blow debris off the brackets. Debris on the mounting surfaces may prevent proper seating of the switch and cause it to malfunction.

6. Align the screw openings, then install the replacement position switch onto the cable bracket. Fit the cover (16, **Figure 47**) onto the switch, then thread the two screws into the cover, switch, and pivot bracket openings. Tighten the screws to 18 in.-lb. (2.0 N•m).

7. Pull up on the locking tab, then connect the shift position switch harness onto the engine harness connector.

8. Route the wiring to prevent interference with the shift linkages and other moving components. Secure the switch harness onto the bracket with the wire clamp (8, **Figure 47**) and screw (7). Tighten the clamp screw to 71 in.-lb. (8.0 N•m).

9. Connect the battery cable.

Table 1 ELECTRICAL AND IGNITION SYSTEM TORQUE SPECIFICATIONS

Fastener	in.-lb.	N•m
Battery charge coil		
75-115 hp models	70	7.9
225 hp models	71	8.0
Charge coil/sensor mounting base		
75-115 hp models	70	7.9
225 hp models	71	8.0
Drive shaft housing cover		
75-115 hp models	65	7.3
225 hp models	70	7.9
Crankshaft position sensor screws		
75-115 hp models	43	4.9
Electrical component mounting bracket		
225 hp models	71	8.0
Engine control unit (ECU) mounting		
75-115 hp models	70	7.9
225 hp models	71	8.0
Engine temperature sensor		
75-115 hp models	70	7.9
225 hp models	133	15.0
Engine temperature switch		
225 hp models	71	8.0
Fuel filter mounting bracket		
225 hp models	71	8.0
Grounding terminal screw		
225 hp models	71	8.0
Ignition coil mounting screws		
75-115 hp models	70	7.9
225 hp models	71	8.0
Ignition coil ground wire screw		
75 and 90 hp models	70	7.9
Negative battery cable to power head		
115 hp models	70	7.9
225 hp models	160	18.1
Negative battery cable to starter		
75 and 90 hp models	120	13.6
Oil pressure sender		
225 hp models	159	18.0
Oil pressure switch		
75-115 hp models	70	7.9
Port side cover		
75 and 90 hp models	65	7.3

(continued)

Table 1 ELECTRICAL AND IGNITION SYSTEM TORQUE SPECIFICATIONS (continued)

Fastener	in.-lb.	N•m
Positive battery cable to solenoid		
75 and 90 hp models	120	13.6
115 and 225 hp models	70	7.9
Rectifier/regulator mounting screws		
75 and 90 hp models	70	7.9
225 hp models		
Mounting screws		
Initial step	53	6.0
Final step	106	12.0
Water jacket		
Initial step	53	6.0
Final step	106	12.0
Shift interrupt switch		
225 hp models	18	2.0
Shift position switch		
225 hp models	18	2.0
Spark plug cover		
75-115 hp models	65	7.3
Spark plug/coil cover		
225 hp models	71	8.0
Starter bush plate screws	18	2.0
Starter mounting bolts	159	18.0
Starter throughbolts	70	7.9
Starter solenoid to electric starter	70	7.9
Starter solenoid terminal nut		
(short cable)	78	8.8
Starter relay terminal nuts		
75 and 90 hp models	25	2.8
Wire clamp screw		
Mounting plate	18	2.0
Shift interrupt/position		
switch harness	71	8.0

Table 2 BATTERY CAPACITY (HOURS)

Accessory	Draw	Provides continuous power for:	Approximate recharge time
80 amp-hour battery	5 amps	13.5 hours	16 hours
	15 amps	3.5 hours	13 hours
	25 amps	1.6 hours	12 hours
105 amp-hour battery			
	5 amps	15.8 hours	16 hours
	15 amps	4.2 hours	13 hours
	25 amps	2.4 hours	12 hours

Table 3 BATTERY CABLE RECOMMENDATIONS

Cable length	Minimum cable gauge size (AWG)
To 3-1/2 ft.	4
3-1/2 to 6 ft.	2
6 to 7-1/2 ft.	1
7-1/2 to 9-1/2 ft.	0
9-1/2 to 12 ft.	00
12 to 15 ft.	000
15 to 19 ft.	0000

Table 4 BATTERY STATE OF CHARGE

Specific gravity reading	Percentage of charge remaining
1.120-1.140	0
1.135-1.155	10
1.150-1.170	20
1.160-1.180	30
1.175-1.195	40
1.190-1.210	50
1.205-1.225	60
1.215-1.235	70
1.230-1.250	80
1.245-1.265	90
1.260-1.280	100

Table 5 ELECTRIC STARTER SPECIFICATIONS

Measurement	Specification
Brush length	0.374-0.610 in. (9.5-15.5 mm)
Commutator diameter	1.102-1.142 in. (28.0-29.0 mm)
Commutator undercut	0.008-0.020 in. (0.2-0.5 mm)

Chapter Seven

Power Head

This chapter provides complete power head repair instructions. Flywheel removal and installation along with break-in procedures are also included in this chapter.

Table 1 provides tightening specifications for most power head fasteners. Use the general torque specification listed in the *Quick Reference Data* section at the front of the manual for fasteners not listed in **Table 1**. **Tables 2-11** list tolerances and dimensions for power head components. **Tables 1-11** are located at the end of this chapter.

The power head can be removed without removing the entire outboard from the boat.

The power heads covered in this chapter differ in construction and require different service procedures. The chapter is arranged in a normal disassembly/assembly sequence. When only partial repair is required, follow the procedure(s) to the point where the faulty parts can be replaced, then jump ahead to the assembly procedures to reassemble the power head.

FLYWHEEL/COVER REMOVAL AND INSTALLATION

Securely mount the engine to the boat or mount the power head to a sturdy work bench before removing or installing the flywheel. If removing both the flywheel and power head, remove the flywheel before loosening the power head mounting bolts and nuts.

WARNING
Wear safety glasses when removing or installing the flywheel or other components of the engine. Never use a hammer, press or puller without eye protection.

WARNING
Disconnect the negative battery cable before removing or installing the flywheel.

CAUTION
Never strike the flywheel with a hard object. The flywheel magnets may break and result in poor charging system performance and/or potential damage to other engine components.

Refer to **Figure 1** or **Figure 2**. A flywheel holding toll (part No. 91-83163M) and puller (part No. 91-83164M) are required for this procedure.

1. Disconnect both cables from the battery. Remove the spark plugs and connect the spark plug leads to a suitable engine ground.

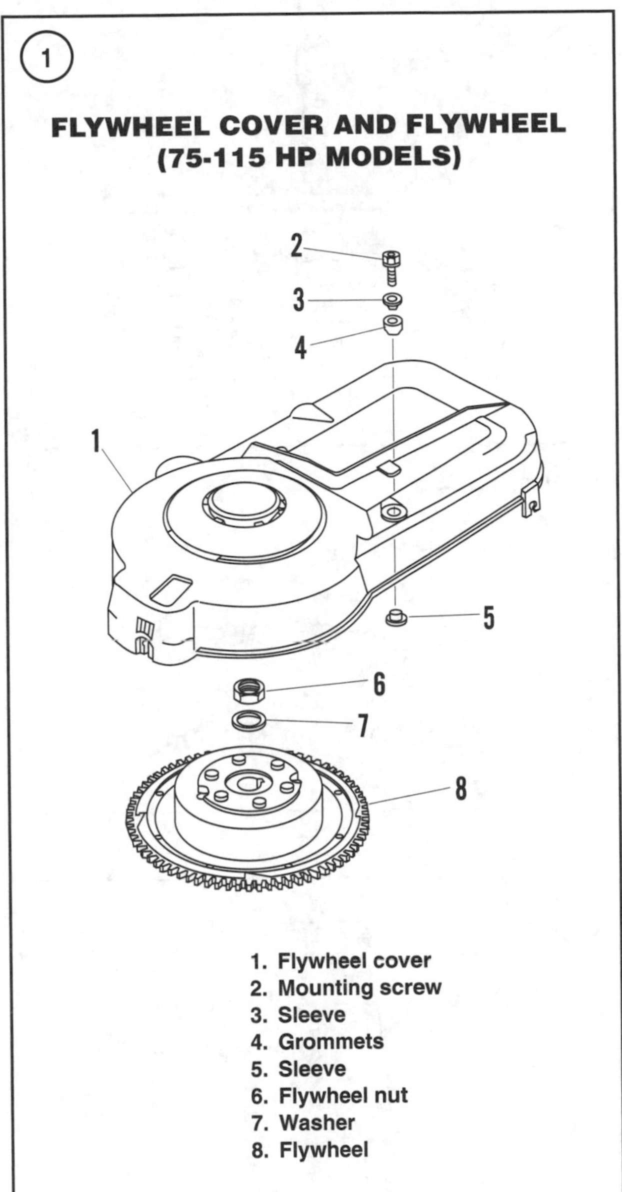

2A. On 75-115 hp models, remove the two screws (2, **Figure 1**) and carefully pull the slots at the rear of the cover from the mounting posts. Lift the flywheel cover (1, **Figure 1**) from the power head.

2B. On 225 hp models, remove the single screw at the front (2, **Figure 2**) and the two screws on the side, then carefully pull up on the rear of the cover to free the grommet (8) from the mounting post. Lift the flywheel cover (1, **Figure 2**) from the power head.

3. Use dish washing soap and water to clean oily deposits and belt material from the cover. Dry the cover with compressed air.

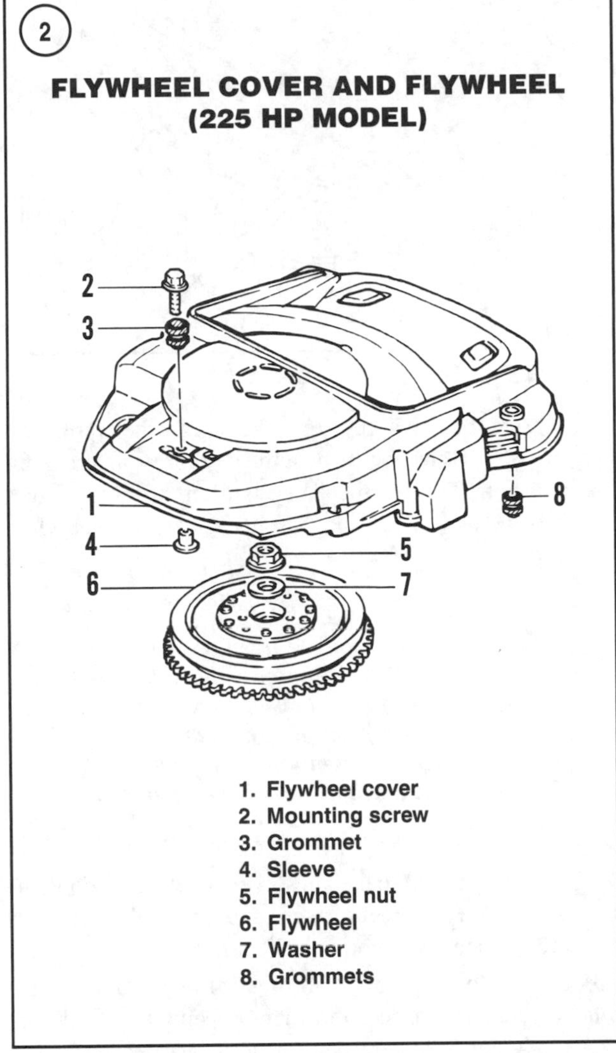

4. Insert the pins of the flywheel holding tool (part No. 91-83163M) into the holes in the flywheel as indicated in **Figure 3**. Using a breaker bar and socket, loosen the flywheel nut until the top surface is flush with the upper end of the crankshaft.

5. Thread the three bolts of the puller (part No. 91-83164M) through the puller plate and into the flywheel as indicated in **Figure 4**. Ensure the center (larger) puller bolt is in direct contact with the crankshaft and the surfaces of the puller and flywheel are parallel before tightening the puller bolt.

6. Hold the flywheel with the holding tool while tightening the puller bolt. See **Figure 5**. Tighten the center puller bolt until the flywheel pops free from the crankshaft taper.

7. Remove the flywheel nut and washer, then lift the flywheel from the crankshaft.

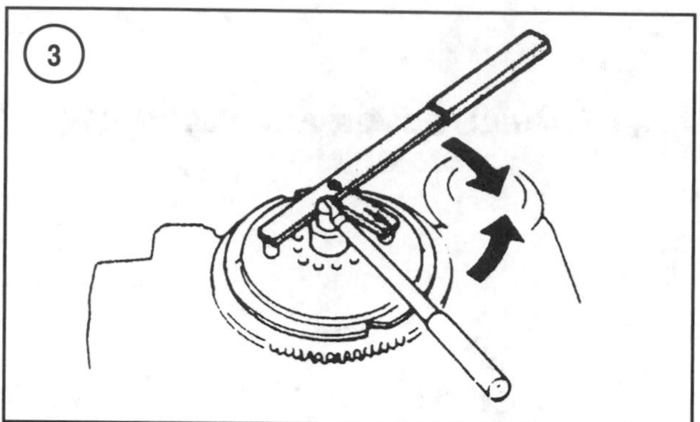

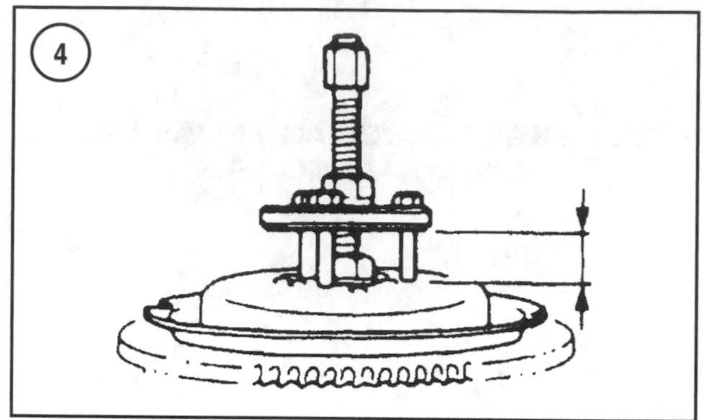

8. Remove the drive key from the slot in the crankshaft (**Figure 6**) or flywheel. Inspect the key for wear, cracking or distortion. The flywheel key is often sheared or distorted if the propeller strikes an underwater object while underway.

CAUTION
Never reuse a damaged flywheel drive key. Operating with a worn or damaged key can cause damage to the flywheel or crankshaft. A distorted or partially sheared key may change the actual ignition timing and cause poor performance or possible engine damage.

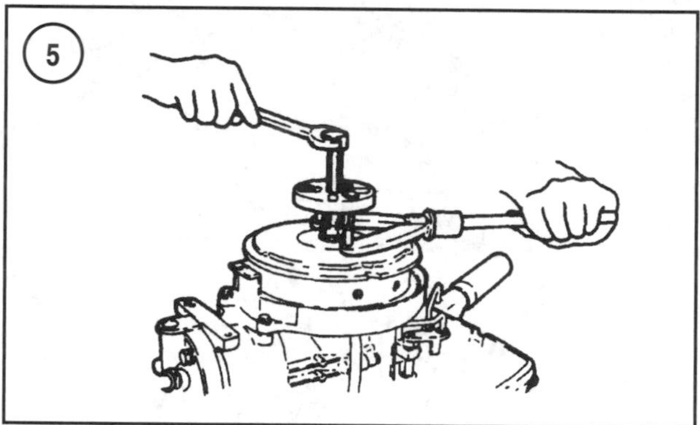

9. Use a shop towel soaked in solvent to clean all contaminants from the flywheel surfaces and the crankshaft taper. Dry the surfaces with compressed air.

10. Using gloves, remove all metal filings from the flywheel magnets. Inspect the magnets and flywheel surfaces for cracked or corroded surfaces. Remove corrosion with fine sandpaper. Replace the flywheel if deep pitting, cracks or damaged magnets are noted.

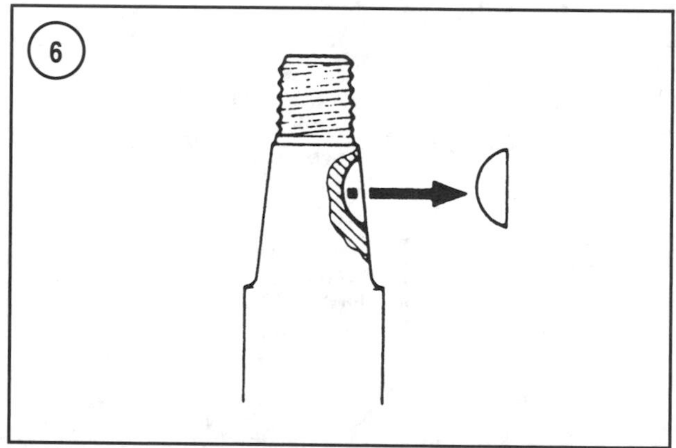

11. Place the flywheel key into the crankshaft slot with the rounded side facing inward (**Figure 6**). Place the flywheel over the end of the crankshaft. Align the flywheel key slot with the flywheel key. Lower the flywheel onto the crankshaft taper. Ensure the key enters the slot.

12. Place the washer over the crankshaft and seat it against the flywheel. Apply a light coat of four-stroke outboard engine oil onto the threads, then thread the flywheel nut onto the crankshaft.

13. Insert the pins of the flywheel holding tool (part No. 91-83163M) into the holes in the flywheel as indicated in **Figure 3**. Hold the flywheel with the tool then tighten the flywheel nut to 140 ft.-lb. (190.0 N•m) for 75-115 hp models and 177 ft.-lb. (240.0 N•m) for 225 hp models.

14A. On 75-115 hp models, install the flywheel cover as follows:

a. Insert the grommets (4, **Figure 1**) and sleeves (3 and 5) into the screw opening in the flywheel cover.
b. Align the screw openings while placing the flywheel cover onto the power head. Thread the two screws (2, **Figure 1**) into the cover and power head openings. Do not tighten the screws at this time.
c. Snap the two slots at the rear of the cover onto the mounting post on the power head.
d. Tighten the two cover screws to 65 in.-lb. (7.3 N•m).

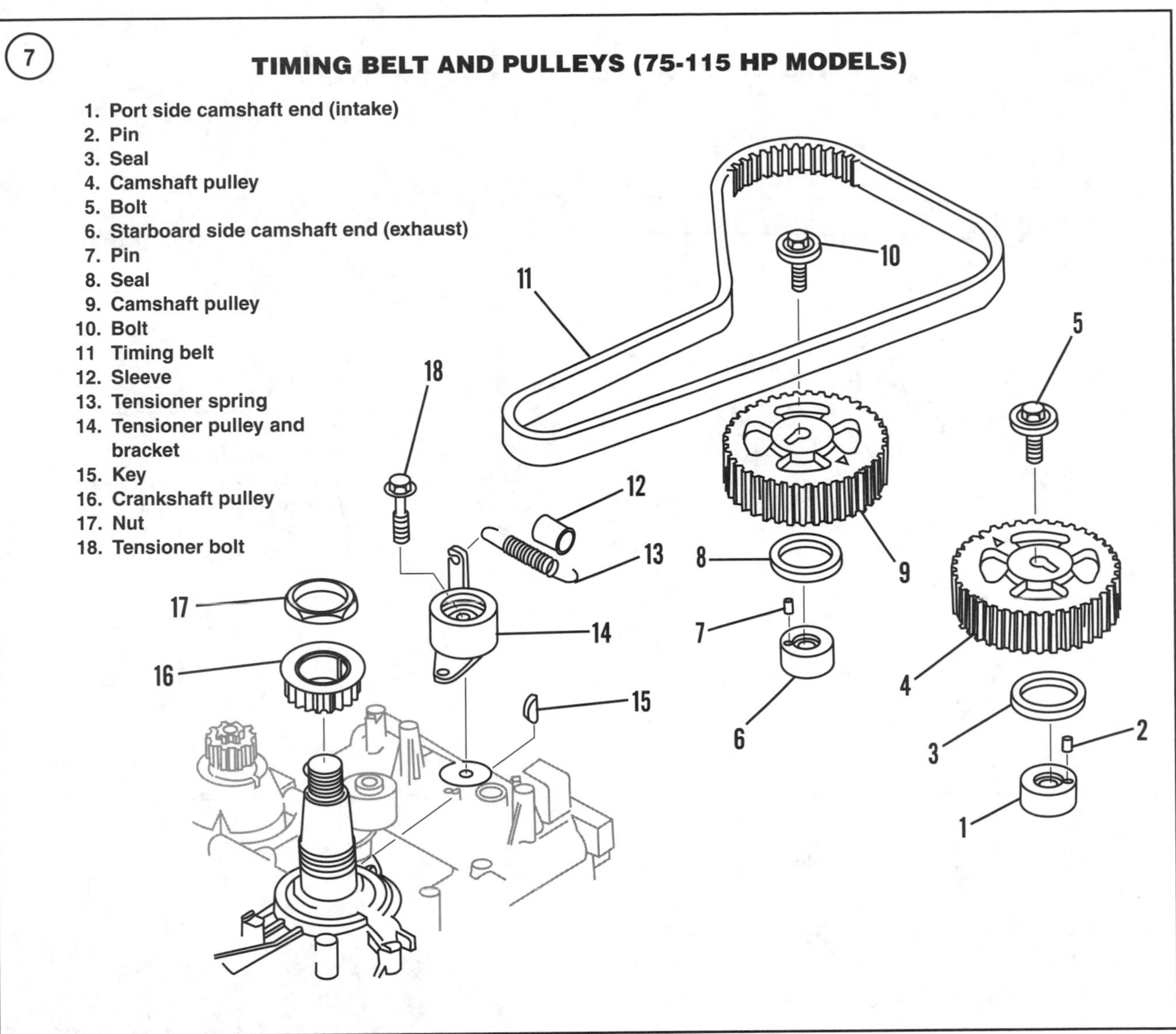

14B. *225 hp models*—Install the flywheel cover as follows:

a. Fit the two larger grommets (8, **Figure 2**) into the two openings at the rear of the cover.

b. Fit the three smaller grommets (3, **Figure 2**) into the screw openings at the front and sides of the cover. Insert the three sleeves (4, **Figure 2**) into the three grommets with the flange facing down.

c. Align the two rear mounted grommets with the corresponding mounting post on the power head, while placing the cover onto the power head.

d. Thread the three screws (2, **Figure 2**) into the cover grommets and power head openings.

e. Carefully push down on the rear of the cover until the rear mounted grommets seat fully on the mounting post.

f. Tighten the three screws to 71 in.-lb. (8.0 N•m).

15. Visually inspect the cover to ensure adequate clearance is present between the belt, flywheel and cover. Remove the cover and check for missing or improperly installed fasteners or grommets if interference is evident.

16. Connect the cable onto the battery.

TIMING BELT AND TENSIONER REMOVAL AND INSTALLATION

Refer to **Figure 7** or **Figure 8**.

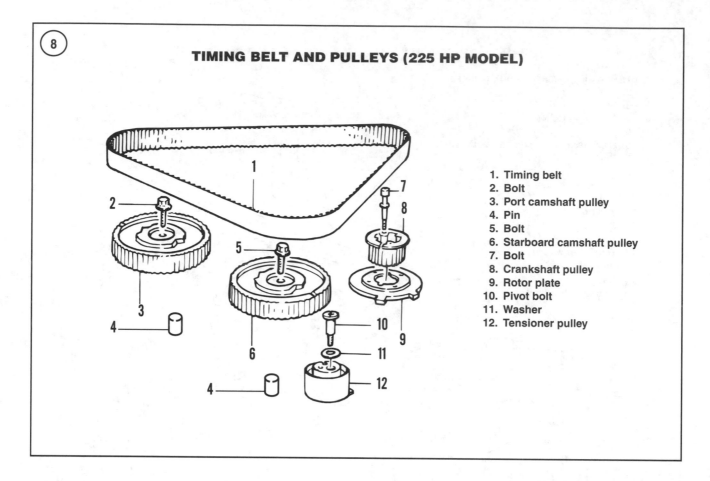

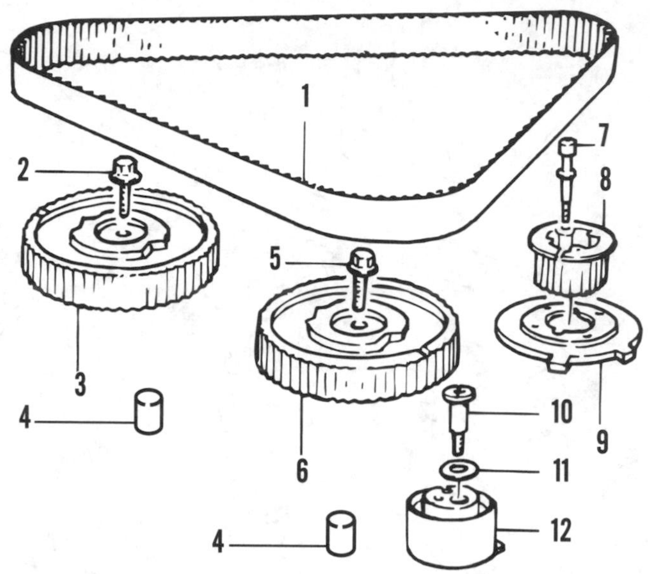

8

TIMING BELT AND PULLEYS (225 HP MODEL)

1. Timing belt
2. Bolt
3. Port camshaft pulley
4. Pin
5. Bolt
6. Starboard camshaft pulley
7. Bolt
8. Crankshaft pulley
9. Rotor plate
10. Pivot bolt
11. Washer
12. Tensioner pulley

1. Disconnect the negative battery cables to prevent accidental starting.

2. Remove the flywheel cover and flywheel as described in this chapter.

3. Remove the battery charging coil and crankshaft position sensor as described in Chapter Six.

4. Note the orientation of the lettering on the side of the timing belt (**Figure 9**). If the belt is installed with the lettering upside down, the belt must be reinstalled.

5. Remove the spark plugs to allow easier rotation of the flywheel. See *Spark Plugs* in Chapter Three.

6A. On 75-115 hp models, temporarily install the flywheel onto the crankshaft. It is not necessary to install the flywheel nut or washer. Rotate the flywheel until the cast-in markings on the camshaft pulleys align (**Figure 10**). This places the engine at TDC for the No. 1 cylinder. Remove the flywheel.

6B. On 225 hp models, temporarily install the flywheel onto the crankshaft. It is not necessary to install the flywheel nut or washer. Rotate the flywheel until the cast-in markings on the camshaft pulleys align with the raised timing marks on the cylinder heads (**Figure 11**). This places the engine at TDC for the No. 1 cylinder. Remove the flywheel as desribed in this chapter.

CAUTION

Never rotate the flywheel or camshaft pulley with the timing belt removed or the valves and pistons will be damaged.

NOTE

Not the orientation of the lettering on the side of the timing belt before removing the

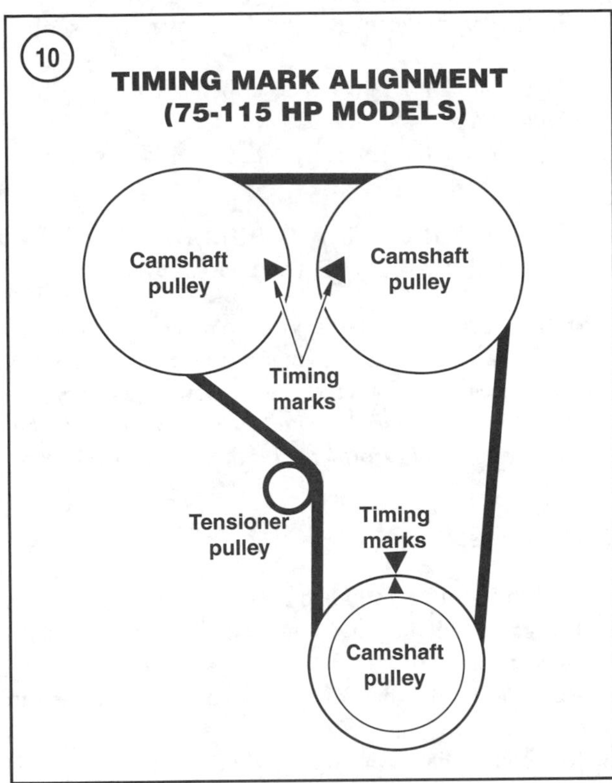

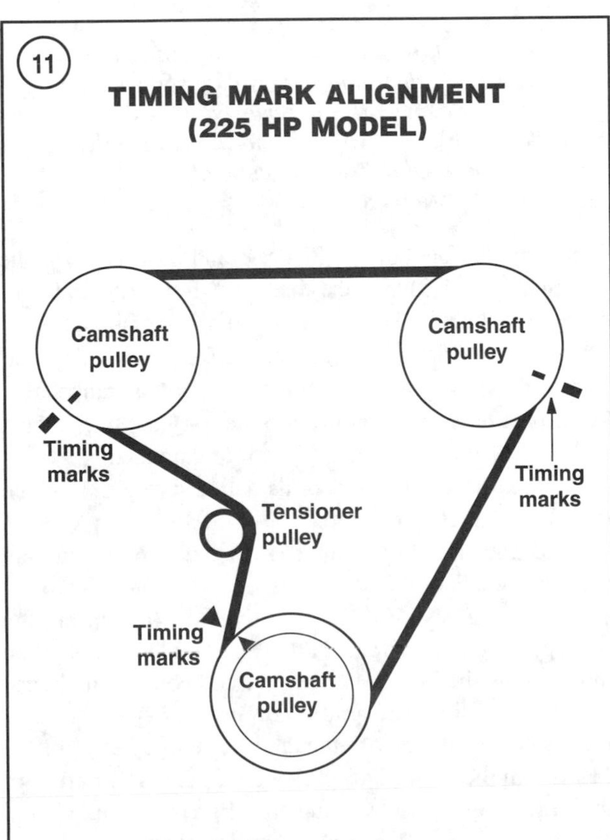

timing belt. If the timing belt must be reused, install the belt with the lettering facing in the original direction. Operating the engine with the used belt lettering facing in a different direction will cause belt to wear out quicker or fail.

7A. On 75-115 hp models, remove the tensioner and timing belt as follows:

a. Carefully unhook the spring (13, **Figure 7**) from the tensioner pulley and bracket (14) and the cylinder block bracket.
d. Remover the bolt (18, **Figure 7**) and lift the tensioner and bracket from the cylinder block.
c. Without rotating the pulleys, remove the timing belt.

7B. On 225 hp models, remove the timing belt and tensioner as follows:

a. Insert a hex wrench into the hex-shaped opening in the tensioner pulley (12, **Figure 8**). Turn the hex wrench clockwise against the spring tension to align the remaining opening in the tensioner pulley with the corresponding opening in the cylinder block. Insert a 0.200 in. (5 mm) diameter steel rod into the pulley and cylinder block openings, then *slowly* release the spring tension onto the rod.
b. Without rotating the pulleys, remove the timing belt.
c. Turn the hex wrench clockwise against the spring tension to remove the rod from the pulley and cylinder block openings. Then *slowly* release the spring tension. Remove the hex wrench.
d. Remove the bolt (10, **Figure 8**) and washer (11), then lift the tensioner pulley from the cylinder block.

8. Inspect the timing belt as described in Chapter Three. See *Timing belt and tensioner pulleys*.

9A. On 75-115 hp models, install the tensioner pulley and bracket (14, **Figure 7**) onto the cylinder block. Thread the bolt (18, **Figure 7**) into the pulley, bracket and cylinder block openings. Do not tighten the bolt or install the spring at this time.

9B. On 225 hp models, install the tensioner pulley (12, **Figure 8**) onto the cylinder block with the hex wrench opening facing up. Thread the bolt (10, **Figure 8**) and washer (11) into the pulley and cylinder block openings. Tighten the bolt to 29.0 ft.-lb. (39.3 N•m).

10A. On 75-115 hp models, rotate the crankshaft pulley to align the round opening in the crankshaft pulley plate with the raised timing mark on the cylinder block (**Figure 10**). The flywheel key aligns with the opening in the pulley.

10B. On 225 hp models, rotate the crankshaft pulley to align the timing mark on the crankshaft pulley plate with the raised timing mark on the cylinder block (**Figure 11**).

The mark on the crankshaft pulley casting aligns with the pulley plate mark.

11. Verify proper alignment of the camshaft pulley markings as described in Step 6A or Step 6B. Correct the alignment before proceeding.

12. Place the timing belt onto the crankshaft pulley. The belt must be oriented so the lettering is right side up if new, or in the original orientation if reusing the belt.

13. Take up the slack on the port side opposite the tensioner while wrapping the timing belt around the camshaft pulleys. Do not rotate the camshaft pulleys. Ensure timing belt properly engages the pulley teeth.

14. Inspect the timing marks on the camshaft pulley and the flywheel for correct alignment. Correct misalignment before proceeding.

15A. On 75-115 hp models, complete the tensioner installation as follows:

a. Route the back side of the belt on the port side of the tensioner pulley.
b. Tighten the tensioner pulley bolt (18, **Figure 7**) to 29 ft.-lb. (39.3 N•m).
c. Fit the sleeve (12, **Figure 7**) over the spring (13). Then hook the spring into the slots in the tensioner pulley pivot bracket and the cylinder block bracket.

15B. On 225 hp models, install the tensioner as follows:

a. Fit the opening of the spring arm on the bottom of the tensioner pulley, onto the corresponding pin on the cylinder block while mounting the pulley onto the cylinder block. Align the openings, then thread the pivot bolt (10, **Figure 8**) and washer (11) into the pulley and cylinder block. Tighten the bolt to 29 ft.-lb. (39.3 N•m).
b. Insert a hex wrench into the hex-shaped opening in the tensioner pulley (12, **Figure 8**). Turn the hex wrench clockwise against the spring tension to align the remaining opening in the tensioner pulley with the corresponding opening in the cylinder block. Insert a 0.200 in. (5 mm) diameter steel rod into the pulley and cylinder block openings, then *slowly* release the spring tension onto the rod.
c. Route the back side of the belt on the port side of the tensioner pulley.
d. Turn the hex wrench clockwise against the spring tension to remove the rod from the pulley and cylinder block openings. *Slowly* release the pulley against the timing belt.
e. Remove the hex wrench.

16. Verify proper timing mark alignment before installing other components.

17. Install the crankshaft position sensor and battery charging coil as described in Chapter Six.

18. Install the flywheel and flywheel cover as described in this chapter.

19. Install the spark plugs as described in Chapter Three. See *Spark Plugs*.

20. Connect the battery cable.

CRANKSHAFT PULLEY REMOVAL AND INSTALLATION

The power head must be removed to replace the pulley on 75-115 hp models. On 225 hp models, the crankshaft pulley can be replaced without removing the power head from the engine. Refer to *Crankshaft Pulley Removal (75-115 hp)* under *Power Head Removal and Installation* in this chapter.

225 hp Model

Refer to **Figure 8** for this procedure.

1. Disconnect the negative battery cable to prevent accidental starting.
2. Remove the flywheel and timing belt as described in this chapter.
3. Remove the battery charging coil and crankshaft position sensor as described in Chapter Six.

CAUTION
Do not allow the crankshaft to rotate while loosening the crankshaft pulley screws unless the camshafts are removed. Rotation of the crankshaft with the camshafts installed may allow the pistons to contact the valves, causing damage.

4. Remove the four bolts (7, **Figure 8**) and washers and lift the crankshaft pulley (8) from the crankshaft. Tap the pulley with a rubber mallet if it will not lift freely from the crankshaft.
5. Remove the drive key from the crankshaft or pulley slot.
6. Lift the rotor plate (9, **Figure 8**) from the crankshaft.
7. Inspect the pulley and rotor plate for wear or damage. Replace the pulley or plate if worn or damaged.
8. Inspect the key for bent or damaged surfaces. Replace the key if defects are noted.
9. Place the drive key into the crankshaft groove with the rounded side facing inward.
10. Align the key slot with the drive key, then install the rotor plate onto the crankshaft. The two tabs on the plate must follow the key slot or be oriented counterclockwise from the key slot. The ignition timing will be incorrect if the plate is installed with the tab leading the key slot.
11. Install the crankshaft pulley over the crankshaft with the larger diameter side facing up. Align the key slot in the pulley with the key, then seat the pulley against the plate.

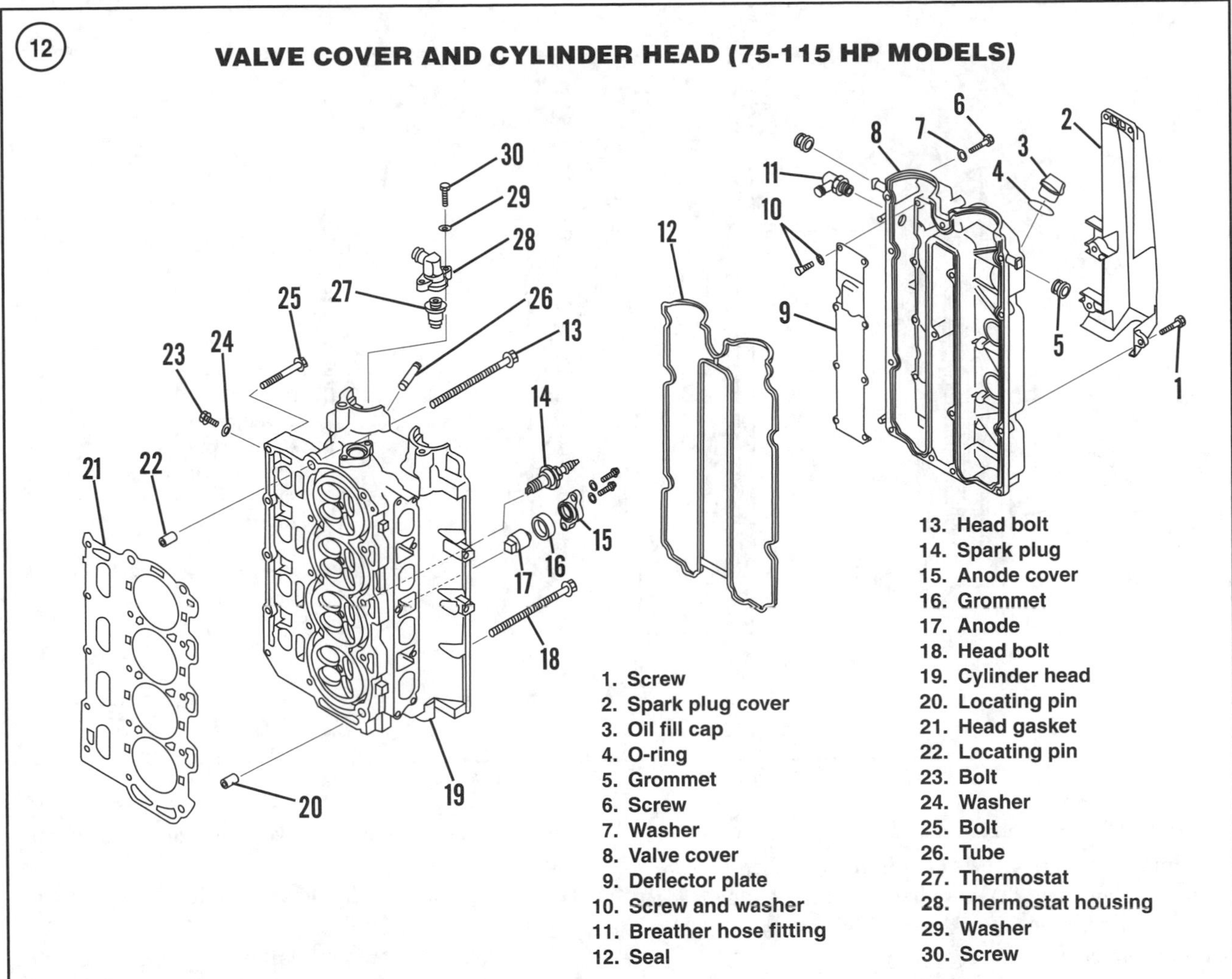

7

CAUTION
Do not allow the crankshaft to rotate while tightening the crankshaft pulley screws unless the camshafts are first removed. Rotation of the crankshaft with the camshafts installed may allow the pistons to contact the valves,causing damage.

12. Apply RTV 587 sealer onto the threads then thread the four bolts (7, **Figure 8**) and washers into the pulley and crankshaft openings. Tighten the screws in a crossing pattern to 62 in.-lb. (7.0 N•m).
13. Install the battery charging coil and crankshaft position sensor as described in Chapter Six.
14. Install the flywheel and timing belt as described in this chapter.
15. Connect the battery cable.

VALVE COVER REMOVAL AND INSTALLATION

The valve cover can be removed without removing the power head from the engine. However, access to the fasteners is far easier with the power head removed. If the cover will be removed during major power head repair, remove the cover after removing the power head. Consider removing the cover with the power head installed when adjusting the valves or for minor repairs such as replacing a damaged cover, gasket or seal.

75-115 hp Models

Refer to **Figure 12**.

1. Disconnect the negative battery cable to prevent accidental starting.

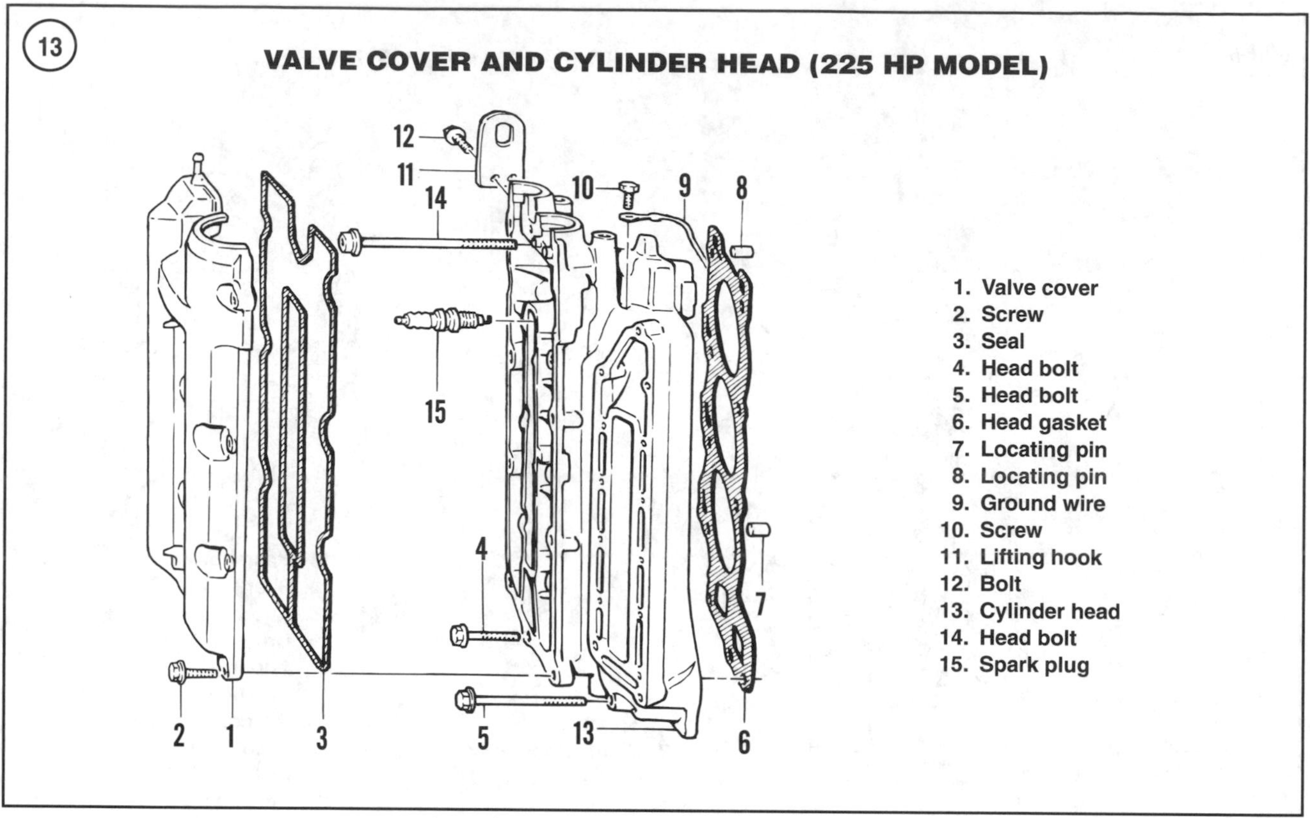

2. Remove the flywheel cover as described in this chapter.

3. Remove the five screws (1, **Figure 12**), then remove the spark plug cover (2). Disconnect the spark plug leads from the spark plugs. Mark the cylinder number on the lead for reference during assembly.

4. Remove the fuel pump(s) as described in Chapter Five.

5. Pull the breather hose from the fitting (11, **Figure 12**) on the cover. Remove the fourteen screws (6, **Figure 12**) and pull the valve cover from the cylinder head.

6. Remove and discard the seal (12, **Figure 12**) from the rocker arm cover.

7. Remove the eight screws and washer (10, **Figure 12**) and lift the deflector plate (9) from the cover.

8. Using a suitable solvent, thoroughly clean the cover and deflector plate.

9. Place the deflector plate onto the cover. Install the eight screws and washer. Tighten the eight screws evenly to 17 in.-lb. (1.9 N•m).

10. Apply GM Silicone Sealer (part No. 92-91600-1) onto the seal and the areas around the upper camshaft retainers. Fit the seal into the groove in the cover.

11. Without dislodging the seal, install the valve cover onto the cylinder head. Thread the fourteen screws and washers into the cover and cylinder head. Tighten the screws in a crossing pattern, working from the center outward, to 70 in.-lb. (7.9 N•m).

12. Connect the breather hose onto the cover fitting (11, **Figure 12**).

13. Install the fuel pump(s) as described in Chapter Five.

14. Install the spark plug cover (2, **Figure 12**) onto the cover. Install the five cover screws (1, **Figure 12**) and tighten them evenly to 65 in. lb. (7.3 N•m). Connect the spark plug leads onto their corresponding spark plug.

15. Install the flywheel cover as described in this chapter.

16. Connect the battery cable.

225 hp Model

Refer to **Figure 13**.

1. Disconnect the negative battery cable to prevent accidental starting.

2. Remove the four screws and the plastic cover (**Figure 14**) from the rear of the power head.

3. Note the wire routing and connection points, then disconnect the engine harness connectors from the three ignition coils.

4. Disconnect the spark plug leads from the spark plugs. Mark the cylinder numbers on the leads for reference during assembly.

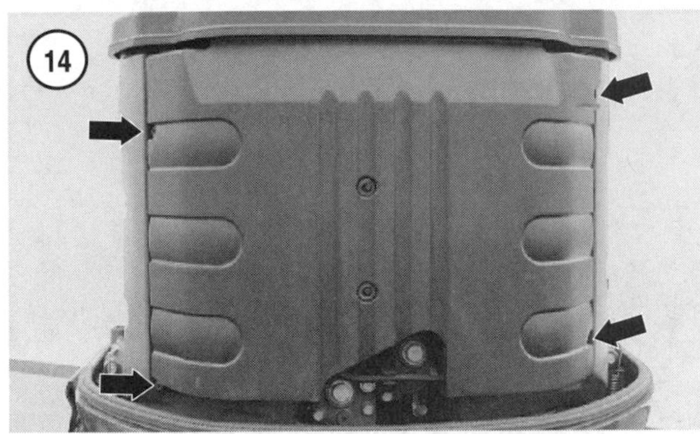

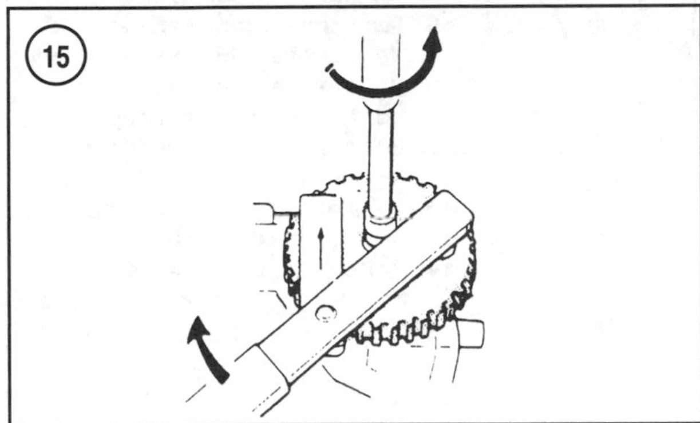

5. Remove the six screws, then pull the coil mounting plate and coils from the rear of the power head.
6. Remove the 14 screws (2, **Figure 13**) and pull the port valve cover (1) from the cylinder head (13).
7. Remove and discard the seal (3, **Figure 13**) from the valve cover.
8. Remove the starboard valve cover as described in Step 6 and Step 7.
9. On the starboard valve cover, remove the eight screws and the deflector plate from the valve cover.
10. Using a suitable solvent, thoroughly clean the cover and deflector plate.
11. On the starboard valve cover, place the deflector plate onto the cover. Thread the eight screws into the deflector plate and cover. Tighten the screws evenly to 18 in.-lb. (2.0 N•m).
12. Apply GM Silicone Sealer (part No. 92-91600-1) to the seals and the areas around the upper camshaft retainers. Fit the seal into the grooves in the covers.
13. Without dislodging the seal, install the starboard valve cover onto the cylinder head. Thread the fourteen screws into the cover and cylinder head. Tighten the screws in a crossing pattern, working from the center outward, to 70 in.-lb. (7.9 N•m). Wait a few minutes, then retorque the screws to the same specification.
14. Install the port valve cover onto the cylinder head as described in Step 13.
15. Install the coil mounting plate onto the rear of the power head. Thread the six screws into the plate and power head openings. Tighten the screw to 71 in.-lb. (8.0 N•m).
16. Connect the engine wire harness connectors to the ignition coil connectors. Connect the spark plug leads onto the corresponding spark plugs.
17. Install the plastic cover onto the rear of the power head. Thread the four screws into the cover and power head openings. Tighten the screws to 35 in.-lb. (4.0 N•m).
18. Connect the battery cable.

CAMSHAFT, TIMING CHAIN AND CAMSHAFT PULLEY REMOVAL AND INSTALLATION

The camshafts can be removed without removing the power head from the engine. However, access to the fasteners is far easier with the power head removed. If the camshafts or pulleys will be removed during major power head repair, remove them after removing the power head. Consider removing the camshafts with the power head installed when replacing valve adjusting shims or other external valve train components.

75-115 hp Models

A flywheel holding tool (part No. 91-83163M) is required for this procedure.

1. Disconnect the negative battery cables to prevent accidental starting.
2. Remove the flywheel cover described in this chapter.
3. Remove the valve cover as described in this chapter.
4. Remove the spark plugs to allow easier rotation of the flywheel. See *Spark Plugs* in Chapter Three.
5. Rotate the flywheel until the cast-in markings on the camshaft pulleys align as shown in **Figure 10**. This places the engine at TDC for the No. 1 cylinder.

CAUTION
Unless instructed otherwise, never rotate the flywheel or camshaft pulley with the timing belt removed or the valves and pistons will be damaged.

6. Remove the timing belt tensioner as described in this chapter. Without rotating the pulleys or flywheel, carefully slip the timing belt off of the camshaft pulleys.
7. Engage the lugs of the flywheel holding tool (part No. 91-83163M) to the openings in the camshaft pulleys to prevent camshaft rotation. See **Figure 15**. Remove the

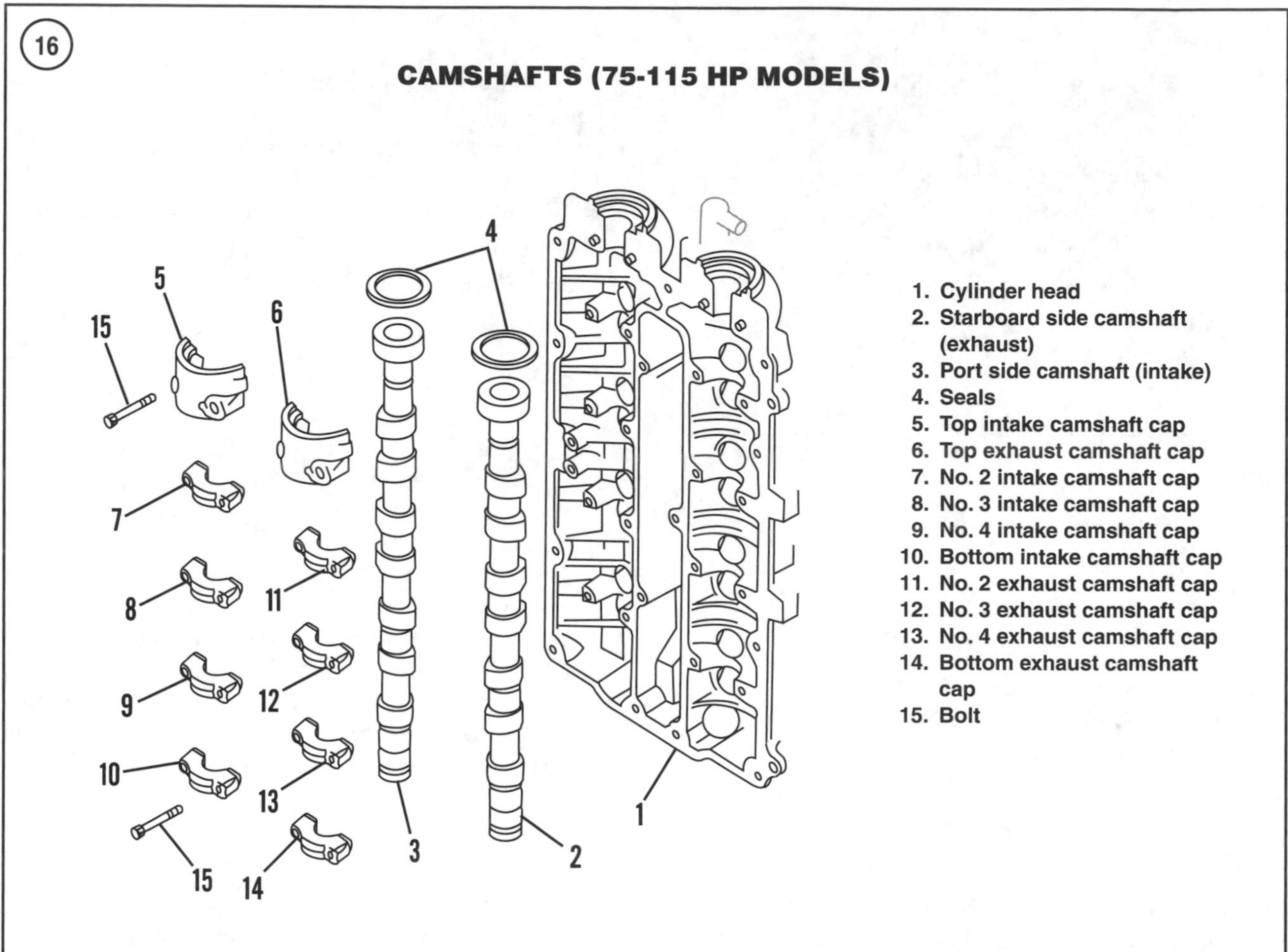

bolts (5 and 10, **Figure 7**) and lift the pulleys (4 and 9) from the camshafts ends (1 and 6).

8. Mark the location and the up side of each camshaft bearing cap (**Figure 16**). Loosen the bolts (15, **Figure 16**) 1/4 turn at a time in the opposite of the tightening sequence indicated in **Figure 17**.

9. Support the camshafts while removing each camshaft bearing cap.

10. Mark the location (port or starboard), then pull each camshaft from the cylinder head. Remove the seals (3 and 8, **Figure 7**) from the camshafts. Discard the seals.

11. Inspect the camshafts for worn or damaged surfaces as described in this chapter.

12. Rotate the flywheel as necessary to position the timing pointer to 0° TDC. Then rotate the flywheel exactly 90° clockwise. This step is necessary to prevent possible valve interference during camshaft installation.

13. Apply molybdenum disulfide grease to each camshaft lobe. Identify the exhaust cam by locating the tang (**Figure 18**) or the pink mark.

14. Install the exhaust cam into the cradle on the starboard side on the cylinder head. Position the threaded opening and locating pin hole on the top side.

15. Apply engine oil onto the camshaft contact surfaces, then place the camshaft caps (6 and 11-14, **Figure 16**) onto the camshaft and cylinder head. Ensure the up side of each cap is facing up. Stamped numbers on the caps usually face down. Thread the bolts for each cap into the cylinder head until finger tight. Tighten the bolts following the sequence (11-20, **Figure 17**) until the caps just contact the cylinder head.

16. Install the intake camshaft into the cradle on the port side of the cylinder head. Position the threaded opening and pin hole on the top side. Apply engine oil to the camshaft contact surfaces then place the camshaft caps (5 and 7-10, **Figure 16**) onto the camshaft and cylinder head. Ensure the up side of each cap is facing up. Stamped numbers on the caps usually face down. Thread the bolts for each cap into the cylinder head until finger tight. Tighten

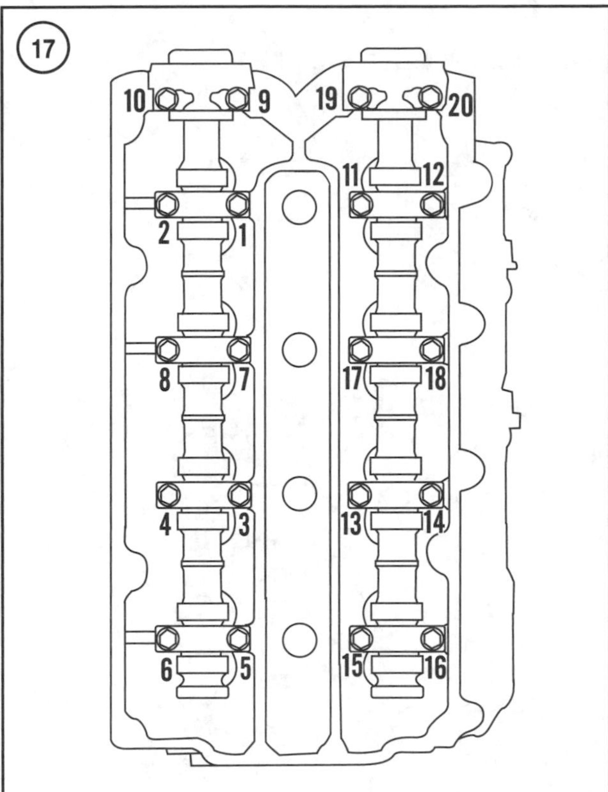

the bolts in the sequence (1-10, **Figure 17**) until the caps just contact the cylinder head.

17. Tighten all camshaft cap bolts (15, **Figure 16**) in sequence (**Figure 17**) to 70 in.-lb. (7.9 N•m). Next, tighten the bolts a second time in sequence to 150 in.-lb. (16.9 N•m).

18. Fit the new seals (3 and 8, **Figure 7**) over the top of the camshafts with the seal lip facing inward. Push the seals in until they bottom in the bore.

19. Insert the pin (2, **Figure 7**) into the opening in the port camshaft (1). Guide the pin into the opening in the bottom of the port side pulley while lowering the pulley to the camshaft. Install and hand tighten the bolts (5, **Figure 7**). Rotate the pulley until the timing mark faces toward the starboard side.

20. Insert the pin (7, **Figure 7**) into the opening in the starboard camshaft (6). Rotate the starboard camshaft until the pulley (9) can be installed with the timing marks aligned as shown in **Figure 10**. Guide the pin into the opening on the pulley while lowering the pulley onto the camshaft. Ensure the timing marks perfectly align.

21. Rotate the flywheel 90° counterclockwise until it just reaches TDC for the No. 1 cylinder.

22. Install the timing belt and tensioner as described in this chapter.

23. Engage the lugs of the flywheel holding tool (Mercury part No. 91-83163M) with the openings in the camshaft pulleys to prevent any camshaft rotation (**Figure 15**). Tighten each camshaft pulley bolt to 44 ft. lb. (60.0 N•m).

24. Install the valve cover and flywheel cover as described in this chapter.

25. Install the spark plugs as described in Chapter Three.

26. Connect the battery cable.

225 hp Model

Refer to **Figure 19**.

1. Disconnect the negative battery cables to prevent accidental starting.
2. Remove the flywheel cover described in this chapter.
3. Remove the valve cover as described in this chapter.
4. Remove the spark plugs to allow easier rotation of the flywheel. See *Spark Plugs* in Chapter Three.
5. Rotate the flywheel until the cast-in markings on the camshaft pulleys align with the marks on the cylinder heads as shown in **Figure 11**. This places the engine at TDC for the No. 1 cylinder.

CAUTION

Unless instructed otherwise, never rotate the flywheel or camshaft pulley with the timing belt removed or the valves and pistons will be damaged.

6. Remove the timing belt tensioner as described in this chapter. Without rotating the pulleys or flywheel, carefully slip the timing belt off of the camshaft pulleys.
7. Engage an adjustable wrench onto the hex shaped section (17, **Figure 19**) on the port side exhaust camshaft. Hold the wrench to prevent any camshaft rotation, then remove the bolt (1, **Figure 19**) from the pulley (2). Care-

19

CAMSHAFTS AND CAMSHAFT PULLEYS (225 HP MODEL)

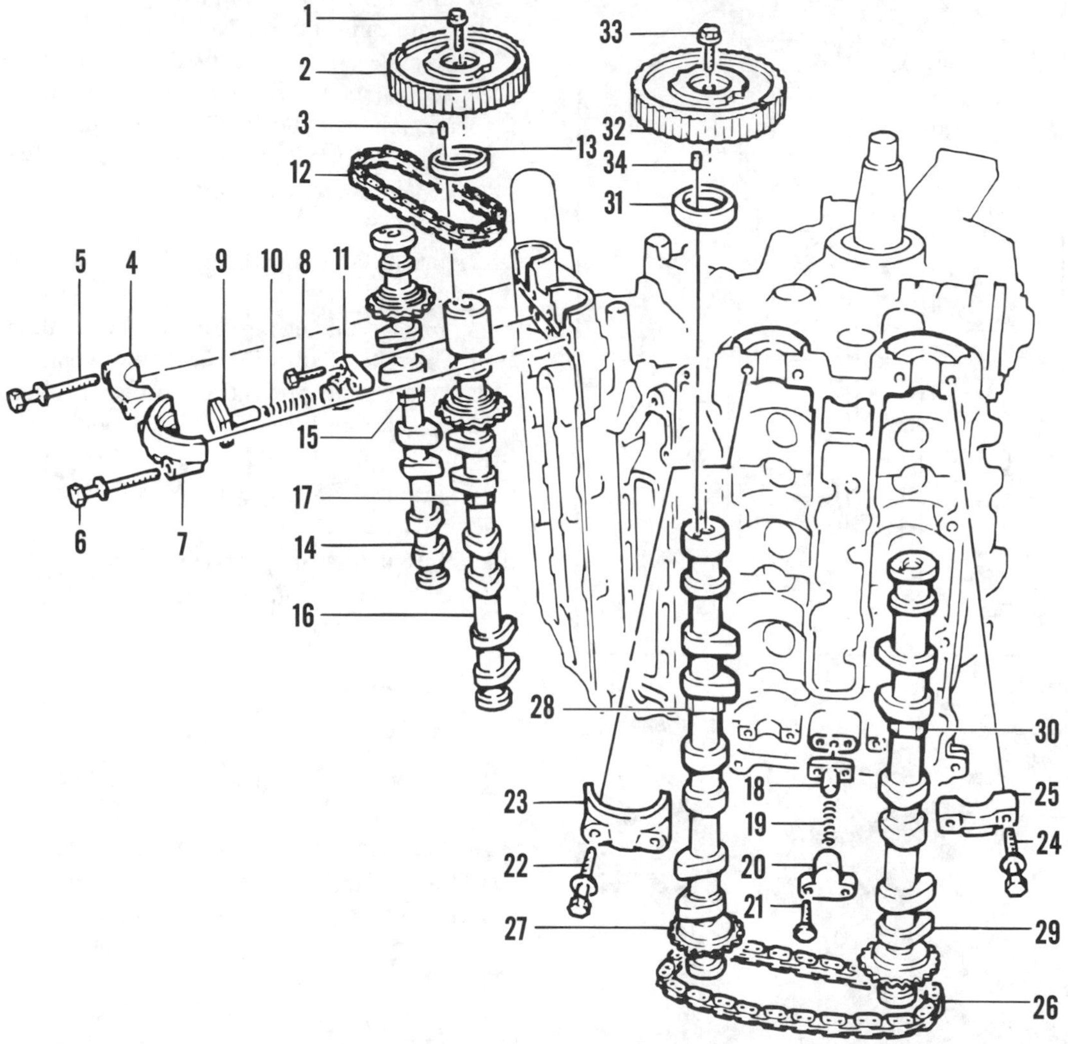

1. Bolt
2. Port side pulley
3. Pin
4. Camshaft cap
5. Bolt and washer
6. Bolt and washer
7. Camshaft cap
8. Screw
9. Tensioner plunger
10. Spring
11. Tensioner body
12. Timing chain
13. Seal
14. Port side intake camshaft (69JP marking [without tang])
15. Hex shaped section
16. Port side exhaust camshaft (69JP marking [with tang])
17. Hex shaped section
18. Tensioner plunger
19. Spring
20. Tensioner body
21. Screw
22. Bolt and washer
23. Camshaft cap
24. Bolt and washer
25. Camshaft cap
26. Timing chain
27. Starboard side exhaust camshaft (69JS marking [with tang])
28. Hex shaped section
29. Starboard side intake camshaft (69JS marking [without tang])
30. Hex shaped section
31. Seal
32. Starboard side pulley
33. Bolt
34. Pin

fully lift the pulley from the camshaft. Remove the pin (3, **Figure 19**) from the camshaft or pulley opening.

8. Remove the two screws (8, **Figure 19**), then lift the timing chain tensioner body (11) from the cylinder head. Remove the plunger (9, **Figure 19**) and spring (10) from the body.

9. Mark the location and the up side of the port camshaft bearing caps (4 and 7, **Figure 19**). Loosen the bolts (5 and 6, **Figure 19**) 1/4 turn at a time in the opposite of the tightening sequence (16-1, **Figure 20**).

10. Support the camshafts while removing each camshaft bearing cap.

11. Mark the location on the camshaft and cylinder head, then pull the port side camshafts and timing chain (12, **Figure 19**) from the cylinder head. Remove the seal (13, **Figure 19**) from the exhaust camshaft. Discard the seal.

12. Note the tang on the exhaust camshaft (**Figure 18**) for reference during assembly, then remove the timing chain from the camshafts.

13. Engage an adjustable wrench onto the hex shaped section (28, **Figure 19**) on the starboard side exhaust camshaft. Hold the wrench to prevent any camshaft rotation, then remove the bolt (33, **Figure 19**) from the pulley (32). Carefully lift the pulley from the camshaft. Remove the pin (34, **Figure 19**) from the camshaft or pulley opening.

14. Remove the two screws (21, **Figure 19**), then lift the timing chain tensioner body (20) from the cylinder head. Remove the plunger (18, **Figure 19**) and spring (19) from the body.

15. Mark the location and the upward orientation of the starboard side camshaft bearing caps (23 and 25, **Figure 19**). Loosen the bolts (22 and 24, **Figure 18**) 1/4 turn at a time in the opposite of the tightening sequence (16-1, **Figure 20**).

16. Support the camshafts while removing each camshaft bearing cap.

17. Mark the location on the camshaft and cylinder head, then pull the starboard side camshafts and timing chain (26, **Figure 19**) from the cylinder head. Remove the seals (31, **Figure 19**) from the exhaust camshaft. Discard the seal.

18. Note the tang on the exhaust camshaft (**Figure 18**) for reference during assembly, then remove the timing chain from the camshafts.

19. Inspect the camshafts and related components for worn or damaged surfaces as described in this chapter.

20. Rotate the flywheel to position the timing pointer at 0° TDC. Then rotate the flywheel exactly 60° clockwise. This step is necessary to prevent possible valve interference during camshaft installation.

21. Locate the wider notches with the larger protrusions in the starboard side camshaft sprockets (**Figure 21**). Align the two gold colored links on the timing chain with the wider notches while fitting the chain onto the starboard side camshaft sprockets. Identify the starboard side camshafts by the *69JS* markings. The exhaust camshaft (27, **Figure 19**) must be on the left and the intake camshaft must be on the right. Identify the exhaust camshaft by the tang on the casting (**Figure 18**). Apply molybdenum disulfide grease to each camshaft lobe.

22. Without disturbing the gold link-to-notch alignments, guide the two camshafts into the cradles in the starboard side cylinder head. The timing chain ends of the camshafts must face down.

23. Apply engine oil to the camshaft contact surfaces, then place the camshaft caps (23 and 25, **Figure 19**) onto the camshaft and cylinder head. Ensure the up side of each cap is facing up. Stamped numbers on the caps usually face down. Thread the bolts for each cap into the cylinder head until the caps just contact the cylinder head. Tighten the cap bolts finger tight.

24. Insert the spring (19, **Figure 19**) into the tensioner body (20), then insert the plunger (18) into the body. Install the tensioner assembly onto the cylinder head. The shoe portion of the plunger must align with and contact the timing chain. Thread the two screws (21, **Figure 19**) into the tensioner body and cylinder head openings. Tighten the screws finger tight at this time.

25. Tighten the starboard side cap bolts (22 and 24, **Figure 19**) in sequence (1-16, **Figure 20**) to an initial torque of 70 in.-lb. (7.9 N•m). Tighten the starboard side cap bolts in sequence to a final torque of 150 in.-lb. (16.9 N•m).

26. Tighten the timing chain tensioner screws (21, **Figure 19**) to 105 in.-lb. (11.9 N•m).

27. Locate the wider notches with the larger protrusions in the port side camshaft sprockets (**Figure 21**). Align the two gold colored links on the timing chain with the wider notches while fitting the chain onto the starboard side camshaft sprockets. Identify the port side camshafts by the *69JP* markings. The exhaust camshaft (16, **Figure 19**) must be on the right and the intake camshaft must be on the left. Identify the exhaust camshaft by the tang on the casting (**Figure 18**). Apply molybdenum disulfide grease to each camshaft lobe.

28. Without disturbing the gold link-to-notch alignments, guide the two camshafts into the cradles in the port side cylinder head. The timing chain ends of the camshafts must face up.

29. Apply engine oil onto the camshaft contact surfaces, then place the camshaft caps (4 and 7, **Figure 19**) onto the camshaft and cylinder head. Ensure the up side of each cap is facing up. Stamped numbers on the caps usually face down. Thread the bolts for each cap into the cap and

7

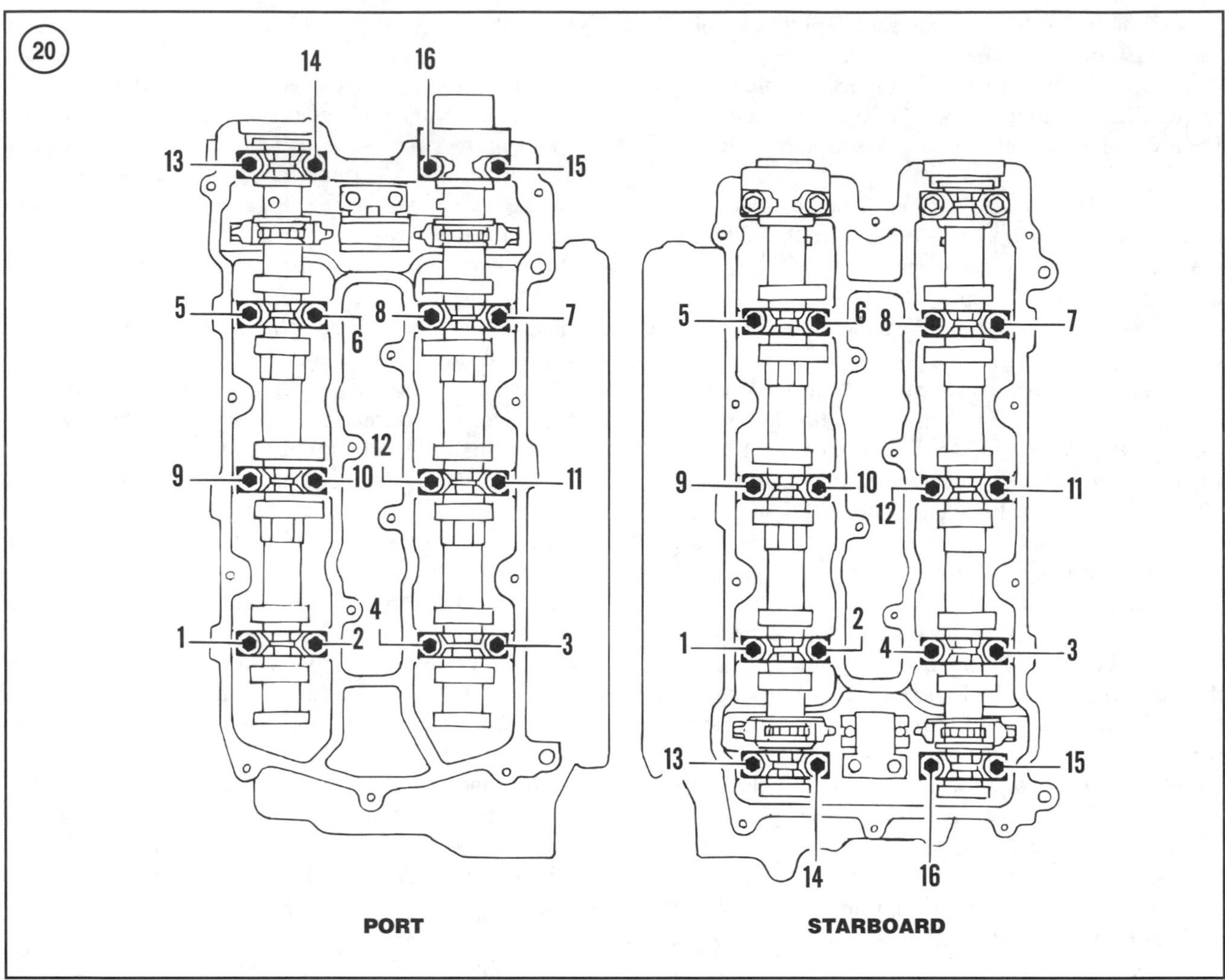

cylinder head until the cap just contacts the cylinder head. Tighten the bolts finger tight at this time.

30. Insert the spring (10, **Figure 19**) into the tensioner body (11), then insert the plunger (9) into the body. Install the tensioner assembly onto the cylinder head. The shoe portion of the plunger must align with and contact the timing chain. Thread the two screws (8, **Figure 19**) into the tensioner body and cylinder head openings. Tighten the screws finger tight at this time.

31. Tighten the starboard side cap bolts (5 and 6, **Figure 19**) in sequence (1-16, **Figure 20**) to an initial torque of 70 in.-lb. (7.9 N•m). Tighten the starboard side cap bolts in sequence to a final torque of 150 in.-lb. (16.9 N•m).

32. Tighten the timing chain tensioner screws (8, **Figure 19**) to 105 in.-lb. (11.9 N•m).

33. Fit the new seals (13 and 31, **Figure 19**) over the top of the camshafts with the seal lip facing inward. Push the seals in until they bottom in the bore.

34. Insert the pin (34, **Figure 19**) into the opening in the starboard side exhaust camshaft. Guide the pin into the opening in the bottom of the starboard side pulley (32, **Figure 19**) while lowering the pulley to the camshaft. Install and hand tighten the bolt (33, **Figure 19**). Rotate the pulley until the timing mark aligns with the cylinder head mark indicated in **Figure 11**.

35. Insert the pin (3, **Figure 19**) into the opening in the port side exhaust camshaft. Guide the pin into the opening in the bottom of the port side pulley (2, **Figure 19**) while lowering the pulley to the camshaft. Install and hand tighten the bolt (1, **Figure 19**). Rotate the pulley until the timing mark aligns with the cylinder head mark indicated in **Figure 11**.

36. Rotate the flywheel 60° counterclockwise until it just reaches TDC for No. 1 cylinder.

37. Install the timing belt and tensioner as described in this chapter.

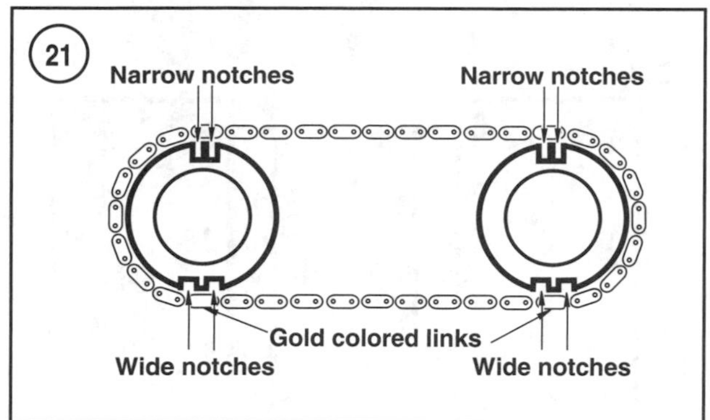

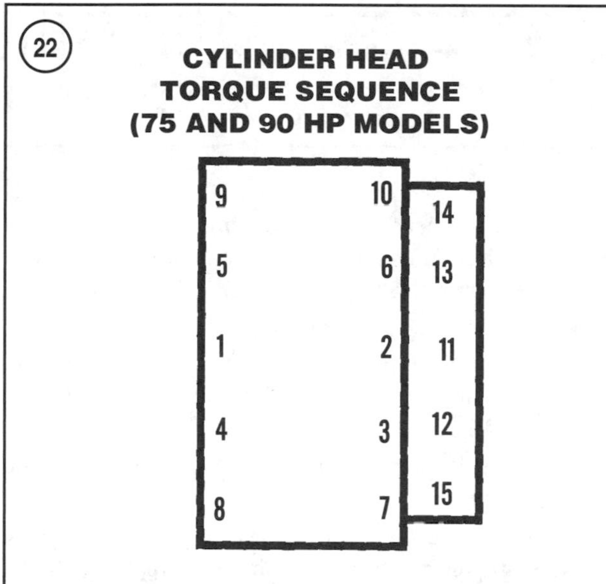

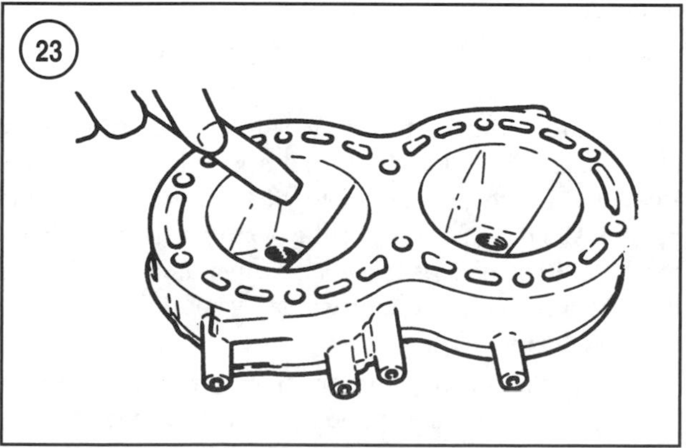

38. Engage an adjustable wrench onto the hex shaped section (28, **Figure 19**) on the starboard side exhaust camshaft. Hold the wrench to prevent any camshaft rotation, then tighten the bolt (33, **Figure 19**) for the starboard side pulley to 44 ft.-lb. (60 N•m). Use the same method to tighten the port side pulley bolt (1, **Figure 19**) to the same specification.
39. Install the spark plugs as described in Chapter Three.
40. Install the valve cover and flywheel cover as described in this chapter.
41. Connect the battery cable.

CYLINDER HEAD REMOVAL AND INSTALLATION

CAUTION
To prevent cylinder head warpage, loosen the cylinder head bolts in the opposite order of the tightening sequence.

75-115 hp Models

Refer to **Figure 12**.

1. Disconnect the negative battery cable to prevent accidental starting.
2A. On 75 and 90 hp models, remove the carburetor and intake manifold assembly as described in Chapter Five.
2B. On 115 hp models, remove the intake manifold and throttle body assembly as described in Chapter Five.
3. Remove the flywheel cover and valve cover as described in this chapter.
4. Remove the timing belt and tensioner as described in this chapter.
5. Remove the camshafts and camshaft pulleys as described in this chapter.
6. Loosen the fifteen cylinder head bolts (13, 18 and 25, **Figure 12**) 1/4 turn at a time in the opposite order of the tightening sequence (**Figure 22**) until the bolts turn freely.
7. Support the head while removing all cylinder head bolts. Pull the cylinder head away from the cylinder block and place it on a clean work surface.
8. Remove and discard the head gasket (21, **Figure 12**).
9. Remove and reposition the locating pins (20 and 22, **Figure 12**) into the cylinder block openings if found in the cylinder head openings.
10. Use a wooden or plastic scraper to carefully remove all head gasket material and carbon from the cylinder block and cylinder head mating surfaces (**Figure 23**). Do not gouge or scratch any surface. All gasket surfaces must be absolutely clean.
11. Inspect the cylinder head for surface warpage and other defects as describe in this chapter. See *Cylinder Head Component Inspection*.
12. Ensure all gasket mating surfaces are absolutely clean and free of defects. Install a new head gasket (21, **Figure 12**) onto the cylinder head. Ensure the openings in the gasket match the openings in the cylinder head. All

7

four pistons must be down in the bores. Rotate the flywheel clockwise approximately 90° if the No. 1 piston is at the top of its stroke.

13. Align the locating pin openings, then seat the cylinder head onto the cylinder block. Hold the cylinder head in position until all bolts are installed.

14. Apply a light coat of four-stroke outboard engine oil onto the threads, then thread the bolts through the head and into the block. Do not tighten the bolts at this time. Note the locations of the 10 mm bolts for reference during the tightening process. Mark the bolt heads as needed.

15. Tighten the bolts in sequence (**Figure 22**) to 120 in.-lb. (13.6 N•m) for the 8 mm bolts and 132 in.-lb. (14.9 N•m) for the 10 mm bolts.

16. Tighten the bolts in sequence a second time to 20 ft.-lb. (27.1 N•m) for the 8 mm bolts and 24 ft.-lb. (32.5 N•m) for the 10 mm bolts.

17. Tighten the 10 mm bolts in sequence an additional 90°. Do not tighten the 8 mm bolts.

18. Install the camshafts and camshaft pulleys as described in this chapter.

19. Install the timing belt and tensioner as described in this chapter.

20. Install the valve cover and flywheel cover as described in this chapter.

21A. On 75 and 90 hp models, install the carburetor and intake manifold assembly as described in Chapter Five.

21B. On 115 hp models, install the intake manifold and throttle body assembly as described in Chapter Five.

22. Check the valve adjustment as described in Chapter Four.

23. Connect the battery cable.

225 hp Model

Refer to **Figure 13**.

1. Disconnect the negative battery cable to prevent accidental starting.
2. Remove the intake manifold and throttle body assemblies as described in Chapter Five.
3. Remove the flywheel cover and valve cover as described in this chapter.
4. Remove the timing belt and tensioner as described in this chapter.
5. Remove the camshafts, timing chains and camshaft pulleys as described in this chapter.
6. Remove the exhaust/water jacket covers from the cylinder heads as described in this chapter.
7. Loosen the starboard side cylinder head bolts (4, 5 and 14, **Figure 13**) 1/4 turn at a time in the opposite order of the tightening sequence (**Figure 24**) until the bolts turn freely.

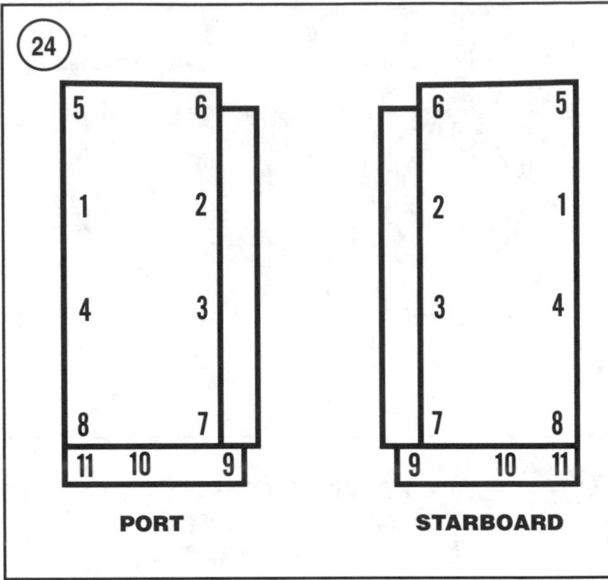

8. Support the head while removing all cylinder head bolts. Pull the cylinder head away from the cylinder block and place it on a clean work surface.
9. Remove and discard the head gasket (6, **Figure 13**).
10. Remove and reposition the locating pins (7 and 8, **Figure 13**) into the cylinder block openings if found in the cylinder head openings.
11. Remove the port side cylinder head using the method described in Steps 7-10.
12. Use a wooden or plastic scraper to carefully remove all head gasket material and carbon from the cylinder block and cylinder head mating surfaces (**Figure 23**). Do not gouge or scratch any surface. All gasket surfaces must be absolutely clean.
13. Inspect the cylinder head for warp as described in this chapter.
14. Ensure all gasket mating surfaces are absolutely clean and free of defects. Install a new head gasket (6, **Figure 13**) onto the port side cylinder head. Ensure the openings in the gasket match the openings in the cylinder head. All three pistons must be down in the bores. Rotate the flywheel clockwise approximately 60° if the No. 1 piston is at the top of its stroke.
15. Align the locating pin openings, then seat the port cylinder head onto the cylinder block. Hold the cylinder head in position until all bolts are installed.
16. Apply a light coat of four-stroke outboard engine oil to the threads, then thread the bolts through the head and into the block. Do not tighten the bolts at this time. Note the locations of the 10 mm bolts for reference during the tightening process. Mark the bolt heads as needed.

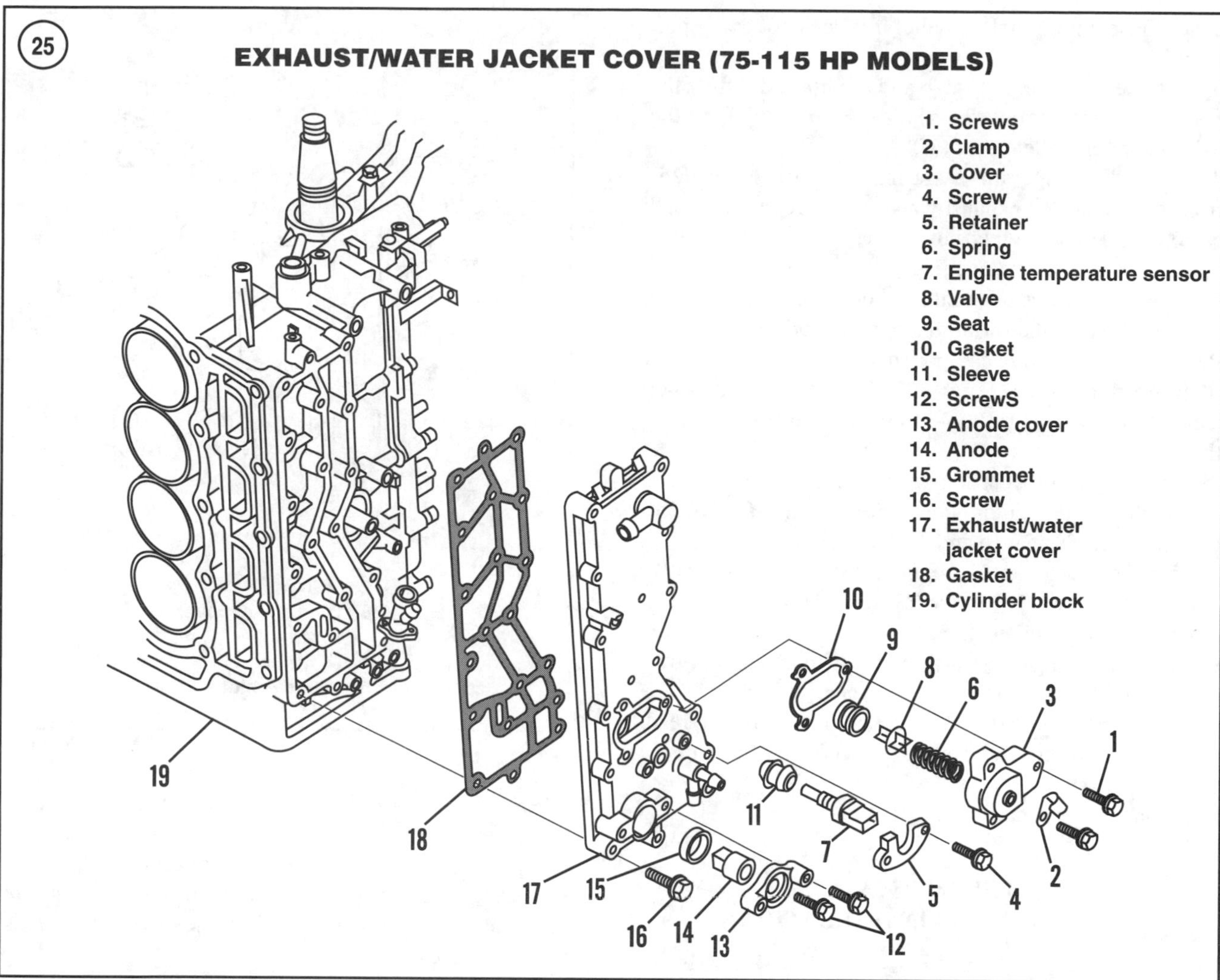

17. Tighten the bolts in sequence (**Figure 24**) to 124 in.-lb. (14.0 N•m) for the 8 mm bolts and 168 in.-lb. (19.0 N•m) for the 10 mm bolts.

18. Tighten the bolts in sequence a second time to 248 in.-lb. (28.0 N•m) for the 8 mm bolts and 27 ft.-lb. (37.0 N•m) for the 10 mm bolts.

19. Tighten the 10 mm bolts in sequence an additional 90°. Do not tighten the 8 mm bolts.

20. Install the starboard cylinder head and tighten the fasteners using the method described in Steps 14-19.

21. Install the exhaust/water jacket covers onto the cylinder heads as described in this chapter.

22. Install the camshafts, timing chains and camshaft pulleys as described in this chapter.

23. Install the timing belt and tensioner as described in this chapter.

24. Install the valve cover and flywheel cover as described in this chapter.

25. Install the intake manifold and throttle body assemblies as described in Chapter Five.

26. Check the valve adjustment as described in Chapter Four.

27. Connect the battery cable.

WATER PRESSURE RELIEF VALVE REMOVAL AND INSTALLATION (75-115 HP MODELS)

The water pressure relief valve mounts into the exhaust/water jacket cover on the starboard side of the cylinder block. The valve can be removed without removing the power head from the engine.

Refer to **Figure 25**.

1. Disconnect the negative battery cable to prevent accidental starting.

2. Remove the two screws (1, **Figure 25**) and clamp (2), then pull the cover (3) away from the power head. Tap the

cover loose with a rubber mallet if it does not easily pull away.
3. Pull the spring and valve (6 and 8, **Figure 25**) from the opening. Carefully pull the seat (9, **Figure 25**) from the exhaust/water jacket cover (17).
4. Carefully scrape all gasket material (10, **Figure 25**) from the cover and exhaust/water jacket cover. Clean all corrosion, scale or other contamination from the cover, valve, spring, seat and opening.
5. Inspect the valve and seat for worn, broken or missing sections. Inspect the spring for corroded or broken loops. Replace any defective components.
6. Insert the seat (9, **Figure 25**) into the exhaust/water jacket cover opening. Push on the seat until it locks into the opening.
7. Insert one of the X shaped ends of the valve (8, **Figure 25**) into the seat opening. Place the spring (6, **Figure 25**) over the other X shaped end.
8. Install a new gasket (10, **Figure 25**) onto the cover (3). Insert the screws (1, **Figure 25**) and clamp (2) into the cover to help retain the gasket.
9. Align the spring recess in the cover with the spring while pushing the cover onto the exhaust/water jacket cover.
10. Inspect the gasket for correct alignment then thread the screws into covers. Tighten the screws evenly to 70 in.-lb. (7.9 N•m).
11. Connect the battery cable.

THERMOSTAT REMOVAL AND INSTALLATION

75-115 hp Models

The thermostat is located beneath a cover on the top side of the cylinder head. The thermostat can be replaced without removing the power head from the engine.

Refer to **Figure 12**.

1. Disconnect the negative battery cable to prevent accidental starting.
2. Remove the flywheel cover as described in this chapter.
3. Loosen the clamp, then pull the water hose off the thermostat cover fitting (28, **Figure 12**).
4. Remove the two screws (30, **Figure 12**) and washers (29).
5. Lift the thermostat cover from the power head. Carefully tap the cover loose with a rubber mallet if it does not easily pull free.
6. Use needlenose pliers to pull the thermostat (27, **Figure 12**) from the opening.
7. Carefully scrape all gasket material from the thermostat cover and power head. Clean all corrosion, scale or other contamination from the thermostat cover, thermostat and thermostat opening.
8. Test the thermostat as described in Chapter Two.
9. Carefully guide the thermostat into the opening with the spring side facing inward. Seat the thermostat against the step in the opening.
10. Place a new gasket on the thermostat cover. Insert the screws with washers through the holes to help retain the gasket.
11. Install the cover over the thermostat with the water hose fitting facing starboard. Thread the two screws into the cover and cylinder head openings until hand tight.
12. Inspect the gasket for correct alignment, then tighten the two screws to 70 in.-lb. (7.9 N•m).
13. Connect the water hose onto the thermostat cover fitting and secure with the spring clamp.
14. Install the flywheel cover as described in this chapter.
15. Connect the battery cable.

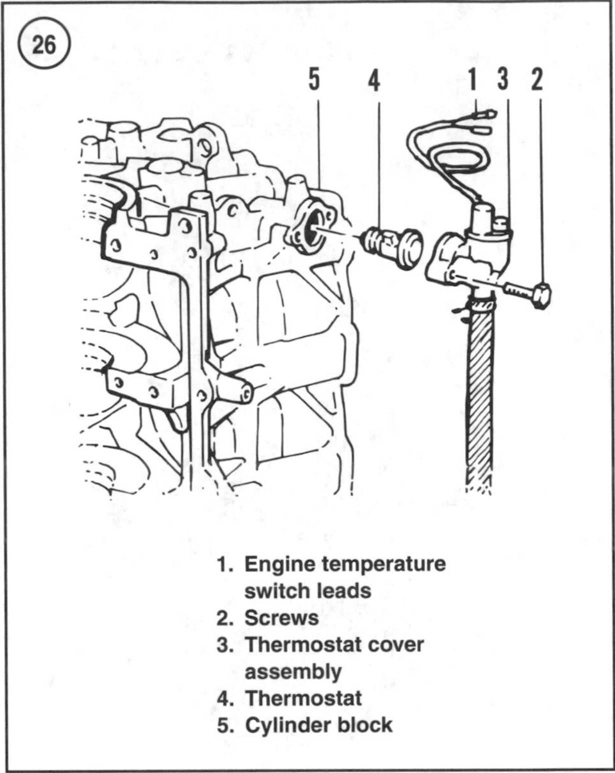

1. Engine temperature switch leads
2. Screws
3. Thermostat cover assembly
4. Thermostat
5. Cylinder block

225 hp Model

The thermostats are located beneath covers on the upper port and upper starboard sides of the cylinder block. The thermostats can be replaced without removing the power head from the engine.

Refer to **Figure 26**.

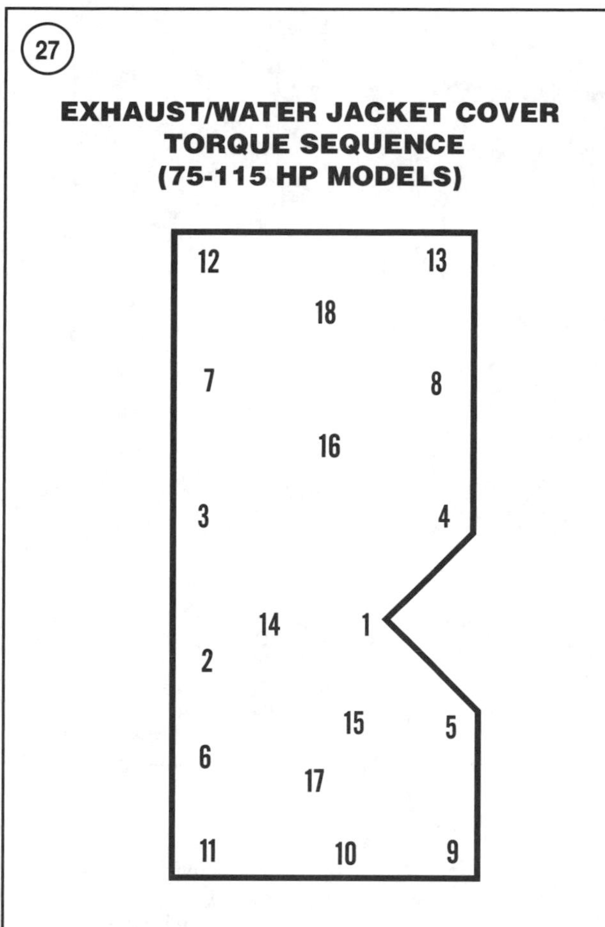

1. Disconnect the negative battery cable to prevent accidental starting.
2. Remove the flywheel cover as described in this chapter.
3. Locate the thermostat cover assembly (3, **Figure 26**) on the upper port side of the cylinder block.
4. Disconnect the engine temperature switch leads from the engine wire harness connectors.
5. Remove the two screws (2, **Figure 26**), then carefully pull the thermostat cover assembly away from the cylinder block. Carefully tap the cover loose with a rubber mallet if it does not easily pull free.
6. Use needlenose pliers to pull the thermostat (4, **Figure 26**) from the opening.
7. Clean all corrosion, scale or other contamination from the thermostat cover, thermostat and thermostat opening.
8. If required, remove the thermostat from the port side of the cylinder block using the method described in Steps 3-7.
9. Test the thermostat(s) as described in Chapter Two.
10. Carefully guide the thermostat into the port side cylinder block opening with the spring side facing inward. Seat the thermostat against the step in the opening.
11. Install the cover over the thermostat with the water hose fitting facing down. Thread the two screws into the cover and cylinder head openings until hand tight.
12. Inspect the cover for correct alignment, then securely tighten the two screws (2, **Figure 26**).
13. Connect the engine temperature switch leads onto the engine wire harness connectors. Route the wiring to prevent interference with moving components.
14. If removed, install the thermostat into the starboard side cylinder block opening using the method described in Steps 10-13.
15. Install the flywheel cover as described in this chapter.
16. Connect the battery cable.

EXHAUST/WATER JACKET COVER REMOVAL AND INSTALLATION

75-115 hp Models

The exhaust/water jacket cover mounts onto the starboard side of the cylinder block. The cover can be replaced without removing the power head from the engine.

Refer to **Figure 25**.

1. Disconnect the negative battery cable to prevent accidental starting.
2. Remove the engine temperature sensor as described in Chapter Six.
3. Remove the water pressure relief valve as described in this chapter.
4. Remove the anode from the cover as described in Chapter Three.
5. Loosen the clamps, then disconnect the water hoses from the fittings on the upper and lower ends of the cover.
6. Loosen the cover screws (16, **Figure 25**) 1/4 turn at a time in the opposite order of the tightening sequence (**Figure 27**) until the screws turn freely.
7. Mark the mounting location for each screws then remove them from the cover.
8. Locate the pry points at the top and bottom of the cover. Use a blunt tip pry bar to carefully pry the cover loose. Then pull the cover off of the cylinder block.
9. Carefully scrape all carbon and gasket material from the cover mating surfaces and exhaust passages. Clean all corrosion, scale or other contaminants from the exposed water passages.
10. Inspect the cover for holes or other signs of leakage and distorted or damaged surfaces. Replace the cover if any defects are evident. Defects can allow water to enter the exhaust ports and seriously damage the internal power head components.

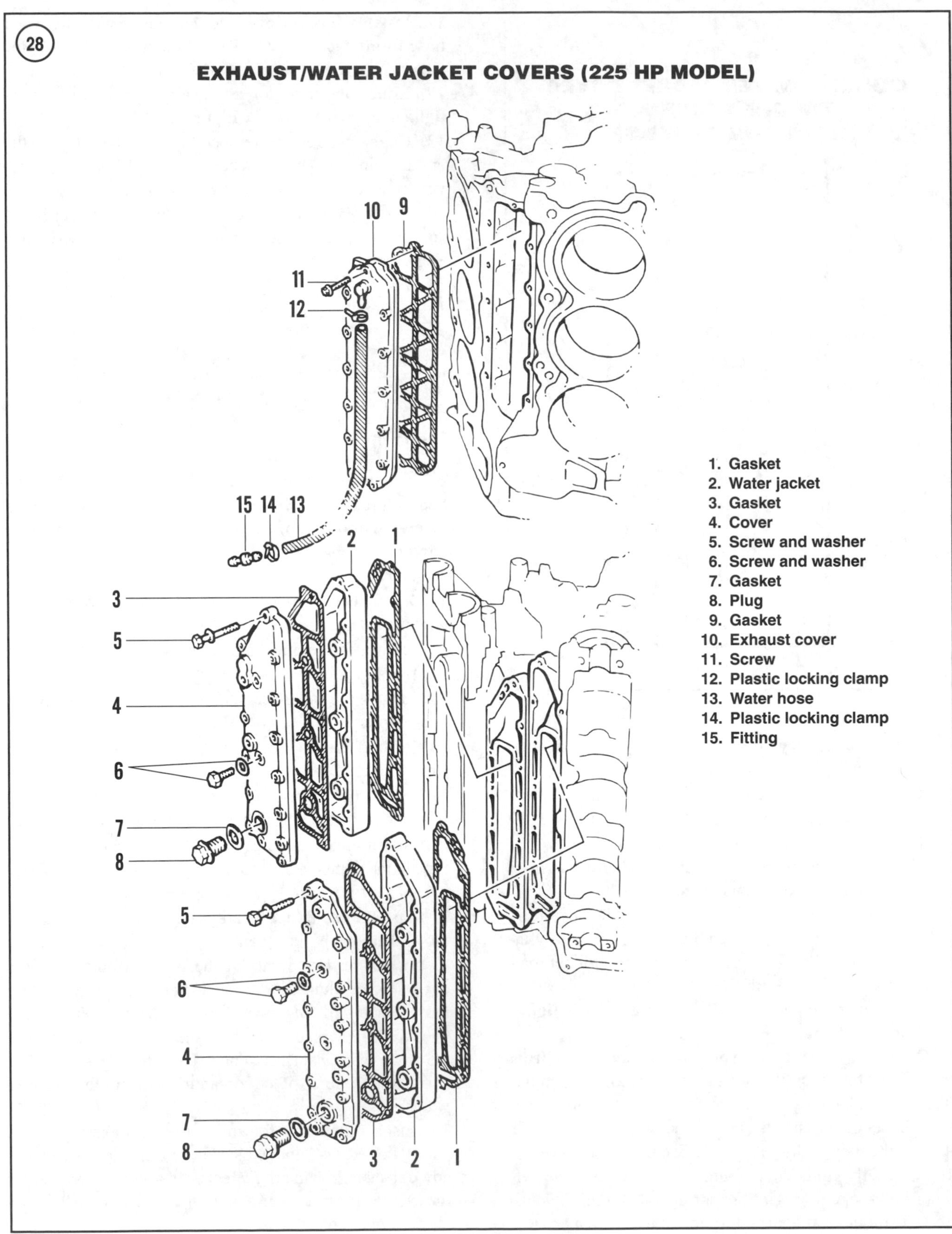
28
EXHAUST/WATER JACKET COVERS (225 HP MODEL)
10
9
11
12
15
14
13
2
1
3
5
4
6
7
8
5
6
4
7
8
3
2
1
1. Gasket
2. Water jacket
3. Gasket
4. Cover
5. Screw and washer
6. Screw and washer
7. Gasket
8. Plug
9. Gasket
10. Exhaust cover
11. Screw
12. Plastic locking clamp
13. Water hose
14. Plastic locking clamp
15. Fitting

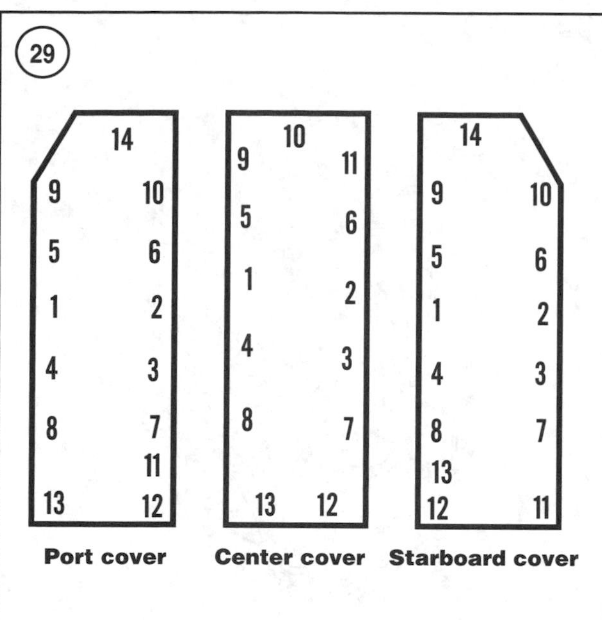

11. Use a properly sized thread chaser to clean all corrosion or contaminants from the threaded holes for the cover mounting bolts. Inspect the threaded holes for damaged threads. Install a thread insert if damaged threads will not clean up with the chaser.
12. Carefully place the cover and new gasket onto the cylinder block.
13. Thread the screws into the cover and cylinder block openings. Tighten the screws finger-tight.
14. Inspect the gasket and cover for proper alignment. Loosen the screws and realign the cover if necessary.
15. Tighten the screws in the sequence (**Figure 27**) to 53.0 in.-lb. (6.0 N•m). Tighten the screws a final time and in sequence to 106 in.-lb. (12.0 N•m).
16. Connect the water hoses onto the upper and lower cover fittings. Secure the hoses with spring clamps.
17. Install the anode into the cover as described in Chapter Three.
18. Install the water pressure relief valve as described in this chapter.
19. Install the engine temperature sensor as described in Chapter Six.
20. Connect the battery cable.
21. Start the engine and inspect the cover for water or exhaust leakage.

225 hp Model

The exhaust/water jacket covers mount onto the rear of the power head. The center exhaust cover mounts between the cylinder heads. The two exhaust/water jacket covers mount onto the cylinder heads. The exhaust/water jacket covers can be replace without removing the power head from the engine.

Refer to **Figure 28**.

1. Disconnect the negative battery cable to prevent accidental starting.
2. Remove the four screws and the plastic cover (**Figure 14**) from the rear of the power head.
3. Note the wire routing and connection points, then disconnect the engine harness connectors from the three ignition coils.
4. Disconnect the spark plug leads from the spark plugs. Mark the cylinder numbers on the leads for reference during assembly.
5. Remove the screws, then pull the coil mounting plate and coils from the rear of the power head.
6. Loosen the starboard side exhaust/water jacket cover screws (5 and 6, **Figure 28**) 1/4 turn at a time in the opposite order of the tightening sequence (**Figure 29**) until the screws turn freely.
7. Mark the mounting location for each screw, then remove them from the cover.
8. Locate the pry points at the top and bottom of the cover (4, **Figure 28**). Use a blunt tip pry bar to carefully pry the cover loose. Then pull the cover off of the water jacket (2).
9. Tap on the water jacket with a rubber mallet until free from the cylinder block.
10. Remove the gasket (1 and 3, **Figure 28**) from the cover, water jacket and cylinder block surfaces.
11. If required, remove the port side exhaust/water jacket cover using the method described in Steps 5-10.
12. Remove the plastic locking clamp (12, **Figure 28**), then pull the water hose (13) off of the exhaust cover fitting.
13. Loosen the center exhaust cover screws (11, **Figure 28**) 1/4 turn at a time in the opposite order of the tightening sequence (**Figure 29**) until the screws turn freely.
14. Mark the mounting location for each screws then remove them from the cover.
15. Locate the pry points at the top and bottom of the cover (10, **Figure 28**). Use a blunt pry bar to carefully pry the cover loose. Then pull the cover off of the cylinder block.
16. Carefully scrape all carbon and gasket material from the cover and water jacket mating surfaces and exhaust passages. Clean all corrosion, scale or other contaminants from the exposed water passages.
17. Inspect the covers and water jackets for holes or other signs of leakage and distorted or damaged surfaces. Replace the cover if any defects are evident. Defects can al-

low water to enter the exhaust ports and seriously damage the internal power head components.

18. Use a thread chaser to clean all corrosion or contaminants from the threaded holes for the cover mounting bolts. Inspect the threaded holes for damaged threads. Install a thread insert if damaged threads will not clean up with the chaser.

19. Carefully place the center exhaust cover (10, **Figure 28**) and new gasket (9) onto the cylinder block.

20. Thread the screws into the cover and cylinder block openings. Tighten the screws finger tight.

21. Inspect the gasket and cover for proper alignment. Loosen the screws and realign the cover if necessary.

22. Tighten the screws in the sequence (**Figure 29**) to 53.0 in.-lb. (6.0 N•m). Tighten the screws a final time and in sequence to 106 in.-lb. (12.0 N•m).

23. Install the new gaskets (1 and 3, **Figure 28**) onto each side of the port side water jacket (2). Fit the cover (4, **Figure 28**) onto the cover.

24. Apply a light coating of four-stroke outboard engine oil onto the threads, then insert the screws and washers into the cover, water jacket and gasket openings to retain the gasket during installation.

25. Carefully place the cover, water jacket and gaskets in position on the port side cylinder head. Thread the screws into the cylinder head openings until finger tight.

26. Inspect the cover, gaskets and water jacket alignment. Loosen the screws and realign the cover and water jacket if necessary.

27. Tighten the screws in the sequence (**Figure 29**) to 53.0 in.-lb. (6.0 N•m). Tighten the screws a final time and in sequence to 106 in.-lb. (12.0 N•m).

28. If removed, install the starboard side exhaust/water jacket cover onto the cylinder head using the method described in Steps 23-27.

29. Push the water hose (13, **Figure 28**) onto the exhaust cover (10) fitting. Secure the hose onto the fitting with a plastic locking clamp.

30. Install the coil mounting plate onto the rear of the power head. Thread the screws into the plate and power head openings. Tighten the screw to 71 in.-lb. (8.0 N•m).

31. Connect the engine wire harness connectors onto the ignition coil connectors. Connect the spark plug leads to the spark plugs.

32. Install the plastic cover onto the rear of the power head. Thread the screws into the cover and power head openings. Tighten the screws to 35 in.-lb. (4.0 N•m).

33. Connect the battery cable.

34. Start the engine and inspect the covers for water or exhaust leakage.

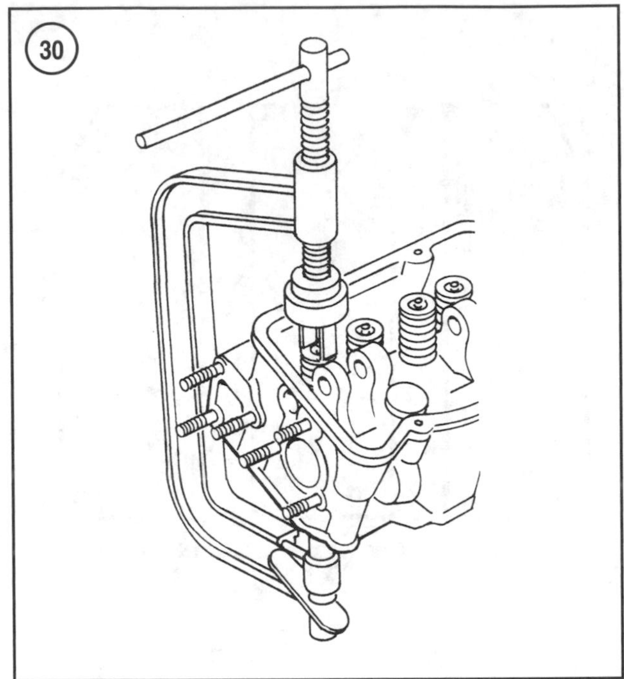

CYLINDER HEAD

Disassembly

A valve spring compressor tool (**Figure 30**) (part No. 91-809494A1 or equivalent) is required for cylinder head disassembly on models covered in this manual.

CAUTION

Arrange the valve lifter and valve pads on a clean work surface as they are removed from the cylinder head. Mark the work surface next to the lifter and pads indicating the location for each component.

Mark the location of each component prior to removal from the cylinder head. Refer to **Figure 31**.

1. Using pliers, carefully pull each lifter (8, **Figure 31**) and valve pad (9) from the cylinder head.

2. Engage the valve spring compressor tool (part No. 91-809494A1 or equivalent) with the valve and spring cap (**Figure 30**). Tighten the clamp just enough to remove the keepers from the grooved portion of the valve stem (**Figure 32**).

3. Slowly loosen the clamp and remove the spring cap (6, **Figure 31**), spring (5) and spring base (3) from the cylinder head.

4. Repeat Steps 2 and 3 for the remaining valves.

5. Inspect the cylinder head components as described in this chapter.

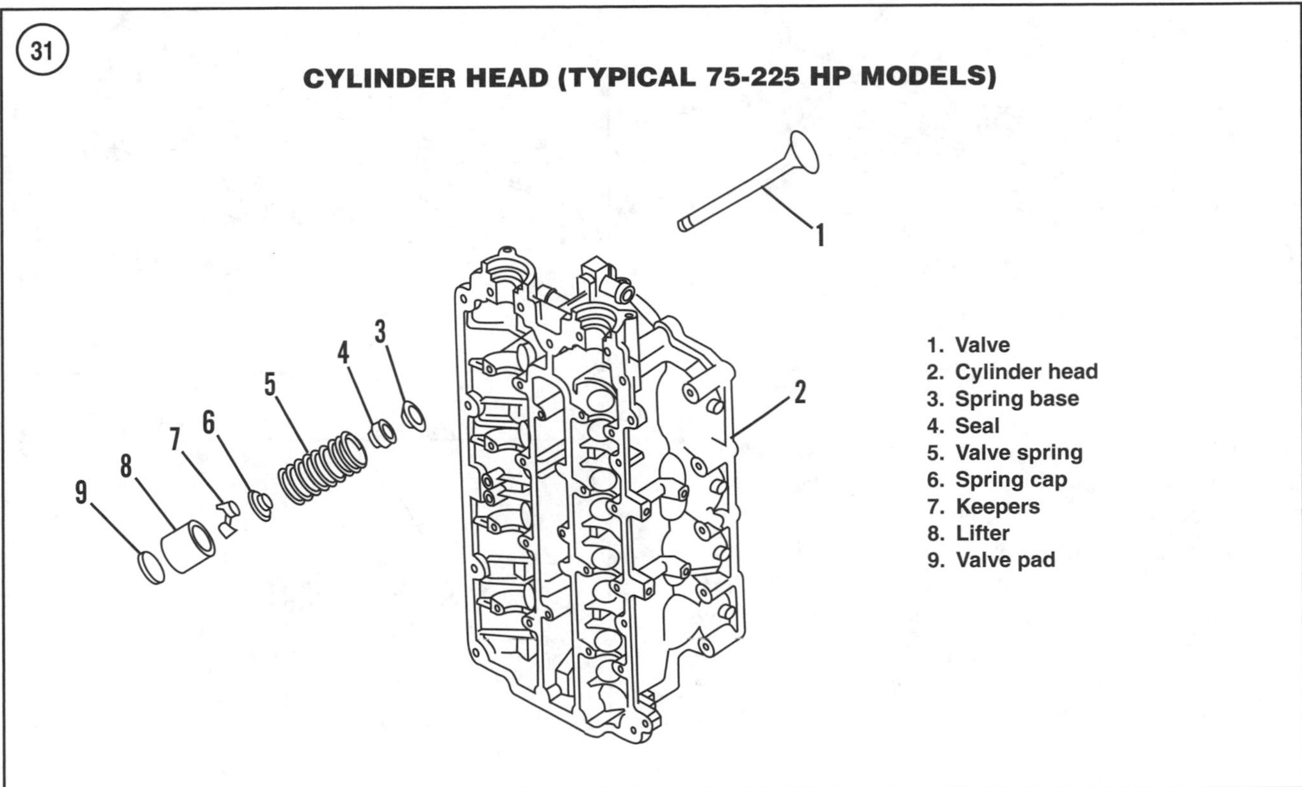

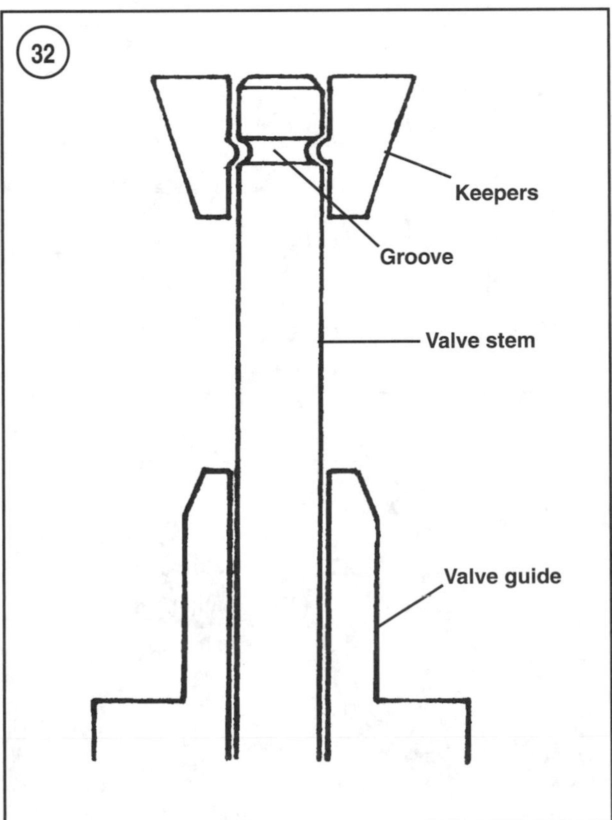

Inspection and Measurement

Check the cylinder head for surface warp any time the cylinder head is removed. The surfaces can be checked without disassembling the cylinder head. Disassemble, inspect and measure the cylinder head components if a fault with the cylinder head is suspected of causing an engine malfunction.

1. Scrape all carbon deposits from the combustion chamber using a blunt scraper (**Figure 23**). Avoid scraping aluminum material from the cylinder head.
2. Pull the valve stem seals (4, **Figure 31**) from the spring side of the valve guides.
3. Remove the cylinder head anodes as described in Chapter Three.
4. Thoroughly clean all grease or corrosion from the cylinder head using a solvent suitable for aluminum material.
5. Check for surface warpage by placing a straightedge at various points (**Figure 33**) on the cylinder head mating surface. Hold the straightedge firmly against the head and check the gap at various points along the straightedge (**Figure 34**) using a feeler gauge. The thickness of the feeler gauge that can be passed under the straightedge indicates the surface warpage. Have a reputable machine shop perform this operation if a surfacing plate is not available. Replace the cylinder head if the warpage ex-

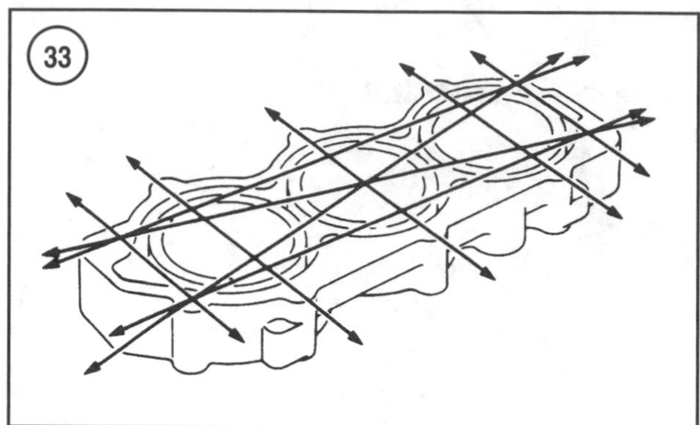

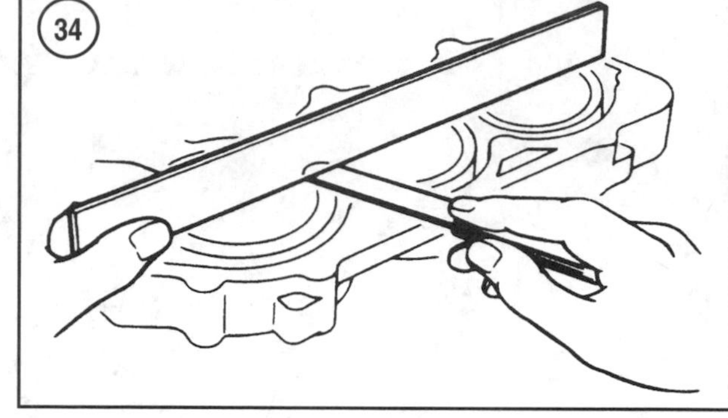

ceeds 0.004 in. (0.10 mm). Do not machine the gasket surface as it can lead to increased compression and difficulty adjusting the valves on some models.

6. Remove minor warp of less than 0.004 in. (0.010 mm), by placing a sheet of 600 grit wet or dry abrasive paper on a surfacing plate. Use slight downward pressure and move the cylinder head in a figure eight motion (**Figure 35**). Stop periodically and check the warpage. Remove only the material necessary to true the surface. Thoroughly clean the cylinder head using hot soapy water and dry with compressed air.

7. Inspect the cylinder head surfaces for cracks or other visual defects. Pay particular attention to the surfaces that separate the water jacket from the combustion chamber.

Valve Inspection and Measurement

A micrometer and a dial indicator are required for this procedure.

1. Using a solvent and parts cleaning brush, clean all carbon deposits from the valves. Inspect the valve stem (**Figure 36**) for wear, roughness, cracks, corrosion or damage. Inspect the valve face (**Figure 36**) for cracked, corroded, damaged or pitted surfaces. Correct valve seating causes a light shiny surface on the valve and valve seats. Replace the valve if any defects are visible.

2. Using an accurate micrometer, measure each valve stem (**Figure 37**) along the valve guide contact area. Rotate the valve 90° and repeat the measurement. Record the highest and lowest measurements. Repeat these measurements for the remaining valves. Compare the measurements with the valve stem specification in **Table 2**. Replace the valve if the diameter is below the minimum specification.

3. Mount the valve on V-blocks and position the tip of a dial indicator against the valve stem (**Figure 38**). Observe the amount of needle movement when rotating the valve.

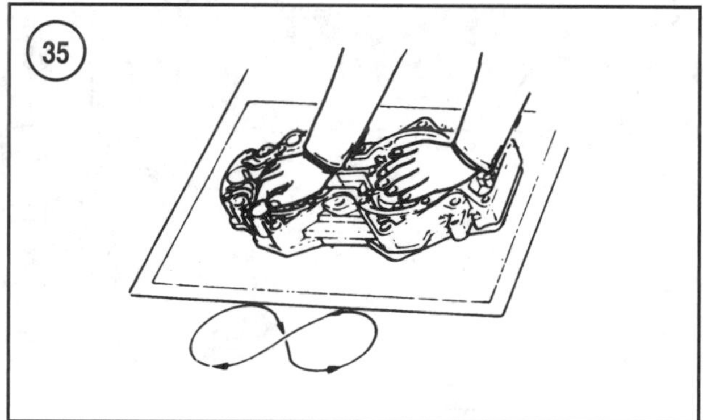

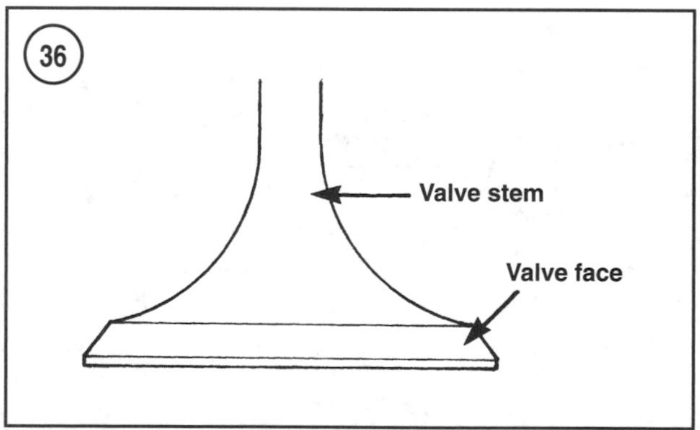

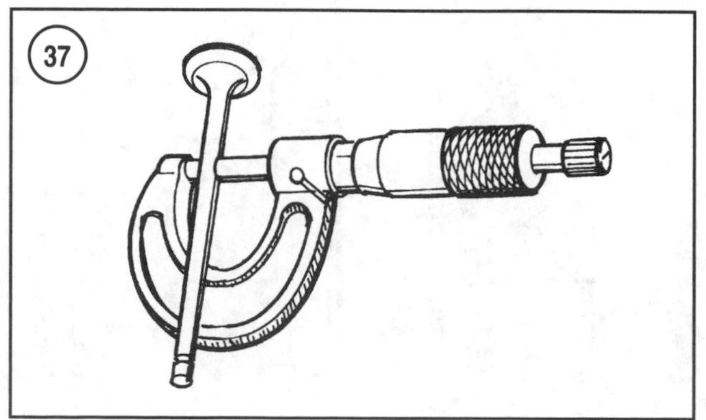

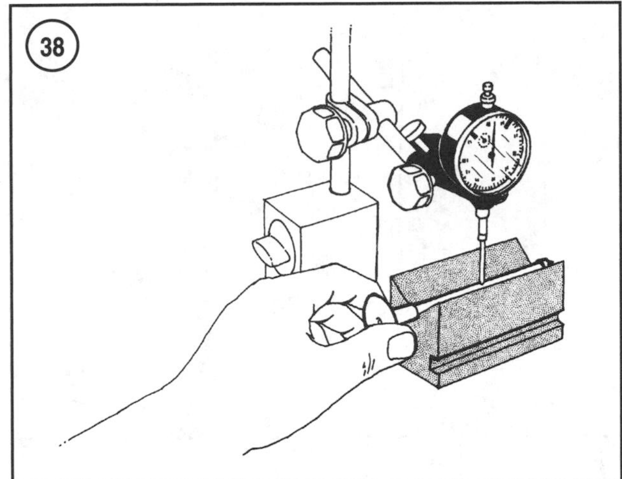

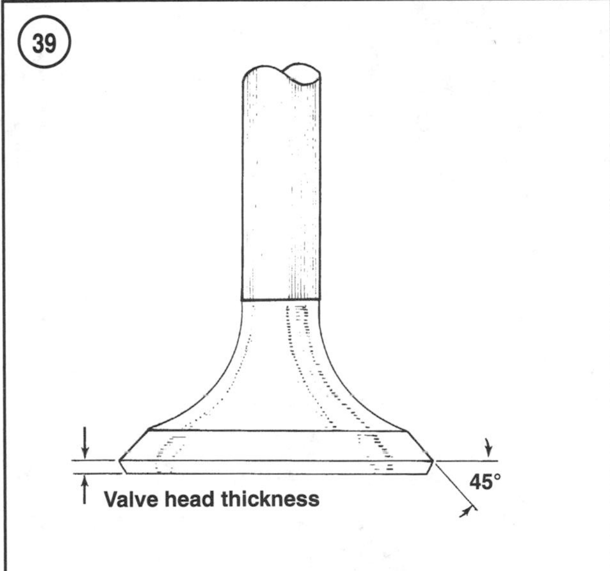

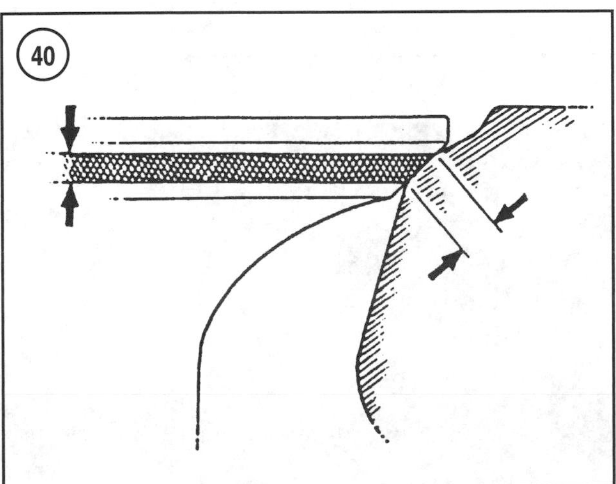

Replace the valve if the runout exceeds 0.001 in. (0.025 mm).

4. Measure the valve margin at the points indicated in **Figure 39**. Replace the valve if the margin is less than the minimum specification in **Table 2**.

Valve Seats Inspection and Measurement

1. Inspect the valve seats in the cylinder head for worn, rough, cracked or damaged surfaces. Have the seats reconditioned or replaced if defects are visible.
2. Use a vernier caliper to measure the width of the valve seating surfaces on the cylinder head (**Figure 40**). Have the valve seat reconditioned at a machine shop if the seat width is not within the specification in **Table 2**.

Valve Guides Inspection and Measurement

1. Inspect the valve guide bore for cracked, discolored or damaged surfaces. Have the valve guides replaced at a machine shop if these or other visual defects are evident.
2. Measure the inner diameter of the valve guides along the entire length of the bore. Rotate the gauge 90° and repeat the measurements. Record the largest and smallest measurements. Have the valve guide replaced at a qualified machine shop if any of the measurements are not within the specification in **Table 2**.

CAUTION

Improper valve guide installation can lead to poor valve sealing, increased valve wear and potential failure. Ensure that the replacement valve guides are installed to a depth of 0.45 in. (11.4 mm) on 75-115 hp models. Use only a valve guide installation tool (part No. 91-888864) to install the valve guides on 225 hp models. On 225 hp models, the guide reaches the proper depth when the installation tool contacts the cylinder head.

3. Subtract the largest valve stem measurement from the smallest valve guide measurement to determine the lowest valve stem clearance (**Figure 41**).
4. Subtract the smallest valve stem diameter from the largest valve guide diameter to determine the highest valve stem clearance.
5. Compare the results with the specification in **Table 2**. A worn valve stem or valve guide is indicated if excessive clearance is noted. A damaged or improperly installed valve guide is indicated if the stem clearance is insufficient. Replace the valve and/or valve guide to correct the clearance.

7

Valve Springs Inspection and Measurement

1. Inspect each valve spring for discoloration, excessive wear, cracks or other damage. Never switch the intake and exhaust valve springs as the spring tension may differ. Damage to the valve and other components can occur when valve springs are installed onto the wrong valve.
2. Use an accurate caliper to measure the free length of each spring (**Figure 42**). Replace any spring with free length measurement that is less than the minimum specification in **Table 3**.
3. Using a square, measure each spring for an out of square condition (**Figure 43**). Replace any spring that exceeds the out of square specification in **Table 3**.

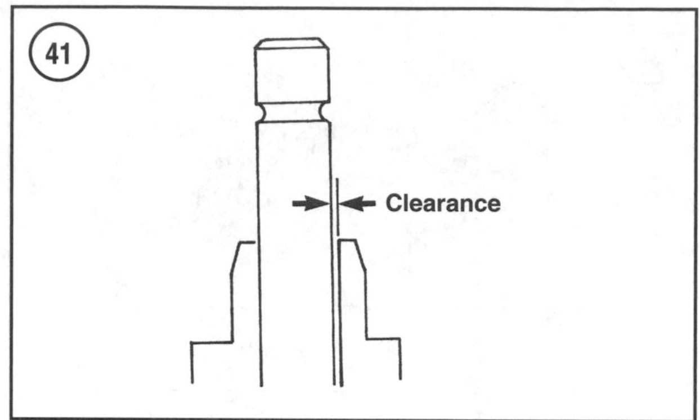

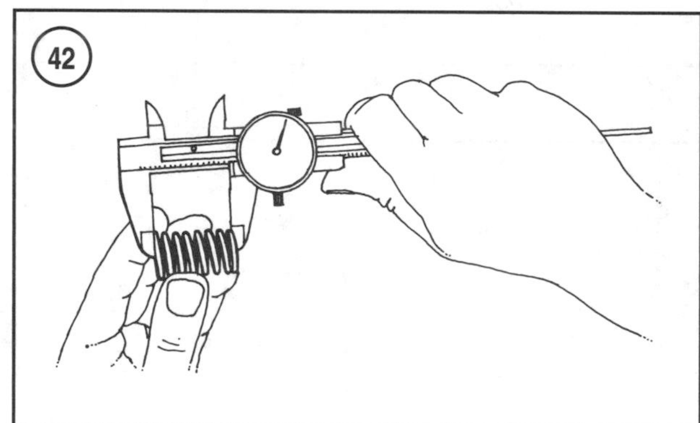

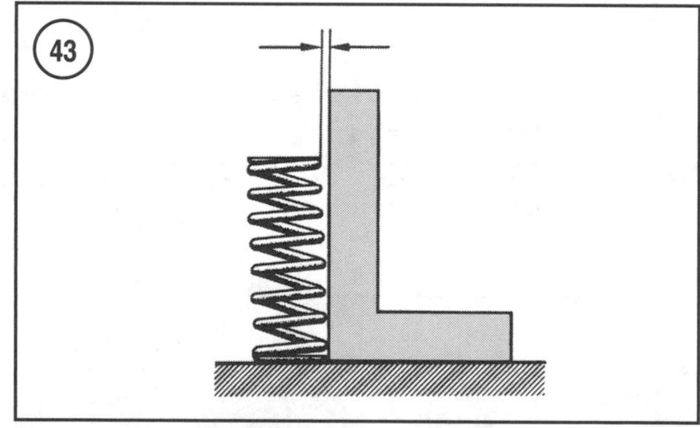

Camshaft Inspection and Measurement

An inside micrometer and a dial indicator are required for this procedure.

1. Inspect the camshaft surfaces (**Figure 44**) for wear, cracks or corrosion. Replace the camshaft if these or other visual defects are noted.
2. Measure the length of each camshaft lobe as indicated in **Figure 45**. Replace the camshaft if any of the lobe length measurements are less than the minimum specification in **Table 4**.
3. Measure each lobe width at a point 90° from the lobe length measuring points. Replace the camshaft if any of the lobe width measurements are less than the minimum specification in **Table 4**.
4. Measure the camshaft bearing journals (**Figure 46**). Compare the journal measurements with the specification in **Table 4**. Replace the camshaft if any of your measurements are less than the minimum specification.
5. Use an inside micrometer to measure the diameter of the lifter bores in the cylinder head. Replace the cylinder head if any of the lifter bore measurements exceed the specification in **Table 4**.
6. Install all camshaft caps, without the camshafts, onto the cylinder head as described in this chapter under *Camshaft, Timing Chain and Camshaft Pulley.* Use an inside micrometer to measure the diameter of each camshaft bore (**Figure 47**). Replace the cylinder head if any of the camshaft bore measurements exceed the specification in **Table 4**. Remove the caps after the measurements. Make sure to arrange the caps in the order in which they mount onto the cylinder head.
7. Subtract the camshaft bearing journal measurement (Step 4) from the corresponding camshaft bore measurement (Step 6) to determine the camshaft-to-bearing journal clearance. Compare the results with the specification in **Table 4**. Excess clearance indicates a worn journal,

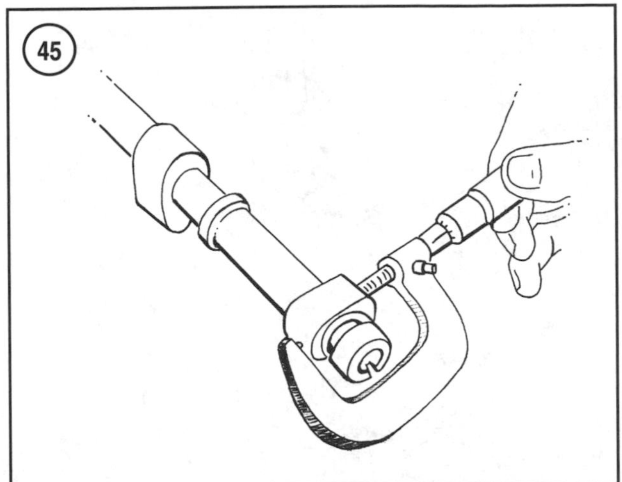

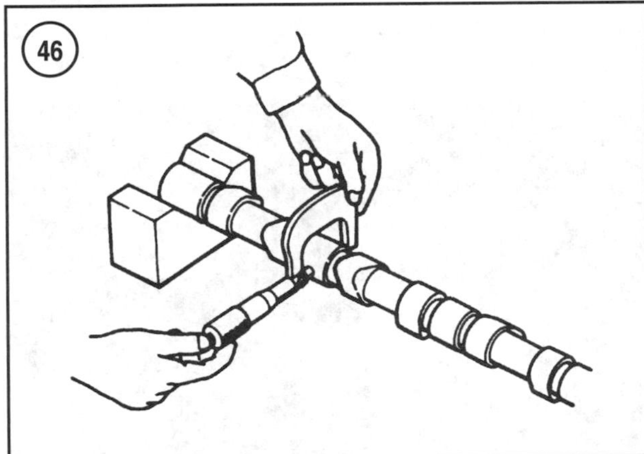

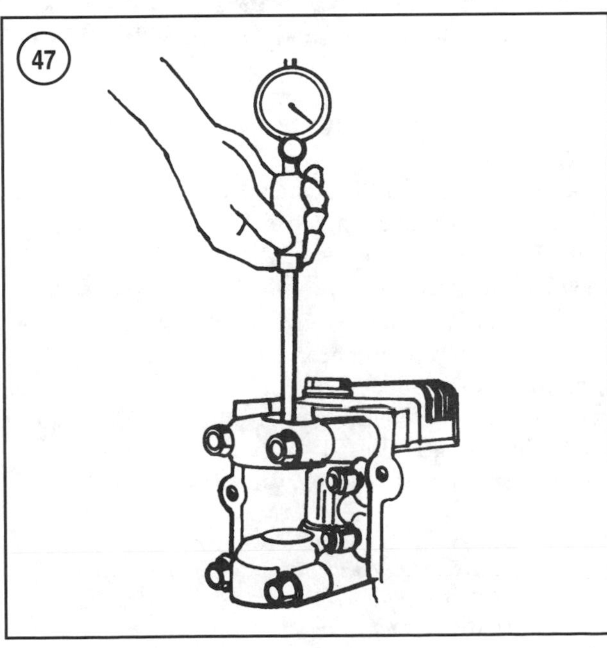

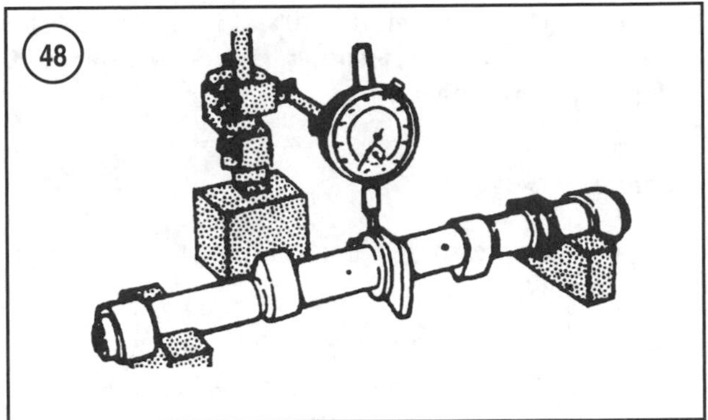

worn bore or inaccurate measurement. Insufficient clearance indicates inaccurate measurements. Repeat the measurements or replace the camshaft or cylinder head to correct excessive clearance.

8. Place the camshaft on blocks positioned under the top and bottom journals (**Figure 48**). Securely mount a dial indicator with the plunger contacting one of the middle camshaft journals. Observe the dial indicator while slowly rotating the camshaft. Repeat the measurement on all journals. The amount of needle movement on the dial indicator indicates the camshaft runout. Replace the camshaft if the amount of runout on any journal is exceeds the specification in **Table 4**.

9. Inspect the lifters (8, **Figure 31**) and valve pads (9) for discoloration, worn or damaged surfaces. Replace any lifter or valve pad with visible defects.

Timing Chain and Tensioner Inspection

1. Check each of the timing chain links for looseness or binding at the pivot pints. Inspect the timing chain surfaces that contact the sprockets and tensioner for worn or highly polished surfaces. Replace the timing chain(s) (12 and 26, **Figure 19**) if any links feel loose or bind, or if the surfaces are worn or highly polished.

2. Inspect the tensioner plungers (9 and 18, **Figure 19**) for discoloration and unevenly worn surfaces. Replace the plunger(s) if the chain contact surface is discolored, unevenly worn or if the wear groove in the plunger face exceed 0.039 in. (1.0 mm) in depth.

3. Inspect the tensioner plungers for wear in the surfaces that fit into the tensioner bodies. Replace the bodies and plungers if wear is evident.

4. Inspect the tensioner bodies (11 and 20, **Figure 19**) for wear in the plunger opening. Replace the bodies and plungers if wear is evident.

5. Inspect the plunger springs (10 and 19, **Figure 19**) for damaged loops and lost spring tension. Replace the springs if these or other defects are evident.

Assembly

A spring compressor toll (part No. 91-809494A1) is required for this procedure.

CAUTION
Install the valve lifter and pads into the same cylinder bore as noted prior to removal.

Refer to **Figure 31**.

1. Press the new valve stem seal (4, **Figure 31**) onto the end of the valve guide. Lubricate the stem with four-stroke outboard engine oil, then insert the No. 1 intake valve into the valve guide and seat it against the valve seat.
2. Place the spring base (3, **Figure 31**) over the valve spring with the larger diameter side facing the cylinder head. Guide the valve spring (5, **Figure 31**) over the valve stem and seat the spring and base against the head. Place the spring cap (6, **Figure 31**) onto the valve spring with the keeper recess facing outward.
3. Fit the valve spring compressor tool (part No. 91-809494A1 or equivalent) onto the valve and spring cap (**Figure 30**). Tighten the clamp just enough to expose the grooved portion of the valve stem and allow installation of the keepers (7, **Figure 31**). Install both keepers into the cap and fit them into the valve stem groove (**Figure 32**).
4. Slowly loosen the clamp and inspect the spring cap and stem for proper seating of the keepers.
5. Repeat Steps 1-4 for the remaining valves.
6. Install the valve pad (9, **Figure 31**) into the opening in the lifter (8). Lubricate the lifter with four-stroke outboard engine oil and guide it over the valve stem. Carefully push the lifter and pad into the bore until the back side of the pad just contacts the valve stem. Repeat this step for the remaining pads and lifters.

POWER HEAD REMOVAL AND INSTALLATION

Inspect the engine to locate the fuel supply hose, throttle and shift cable connections, battery cable connections and trim system connections. Most hoses and wires must be removed if performing a complete power head disassembly. Disconnect only the hoses, wires and linkage required for power head removal. Disconnect the remaining hoses and wires after removing the power head.

Use the diagrams of the fuel and electrical systems to assist with hose and wire routing. Take pictures or make a drawing of all wire and hose connections *before* beginning the removal process.

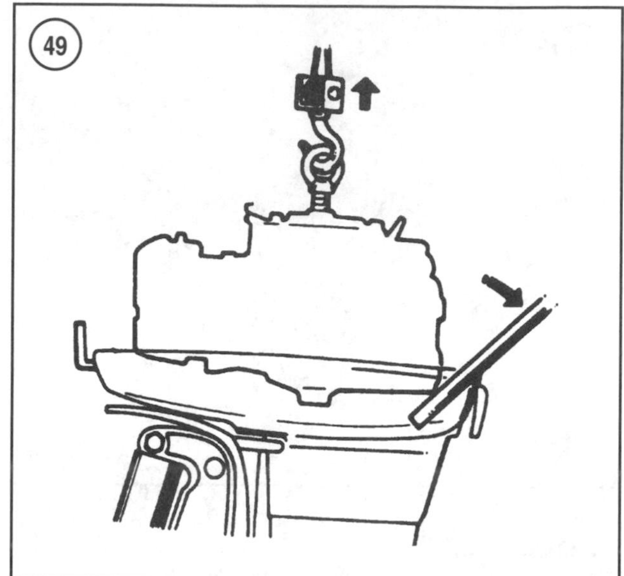

Secure the proper lifting equipment (**Figure 49**) before attempting to remove the power head. A completely assembled power head may weigh over 200 lb. (90 kg). Always use an assistant to lift or move the power head.

A special lifting tool (part No. 91-83164M) is required to lift 75-115 hp power heads. Use a three-point lifting strap (part No. 91-883705T or equivalent) and the three power head-mounted lifting eyes to lift the 225 hp power head. The lifting tool used on 75-115 hp models can be used if the lifting strap is not available.

WARNING
The power head may abruptly separate from the midsection during removal. Avoid using excessive lifting force.

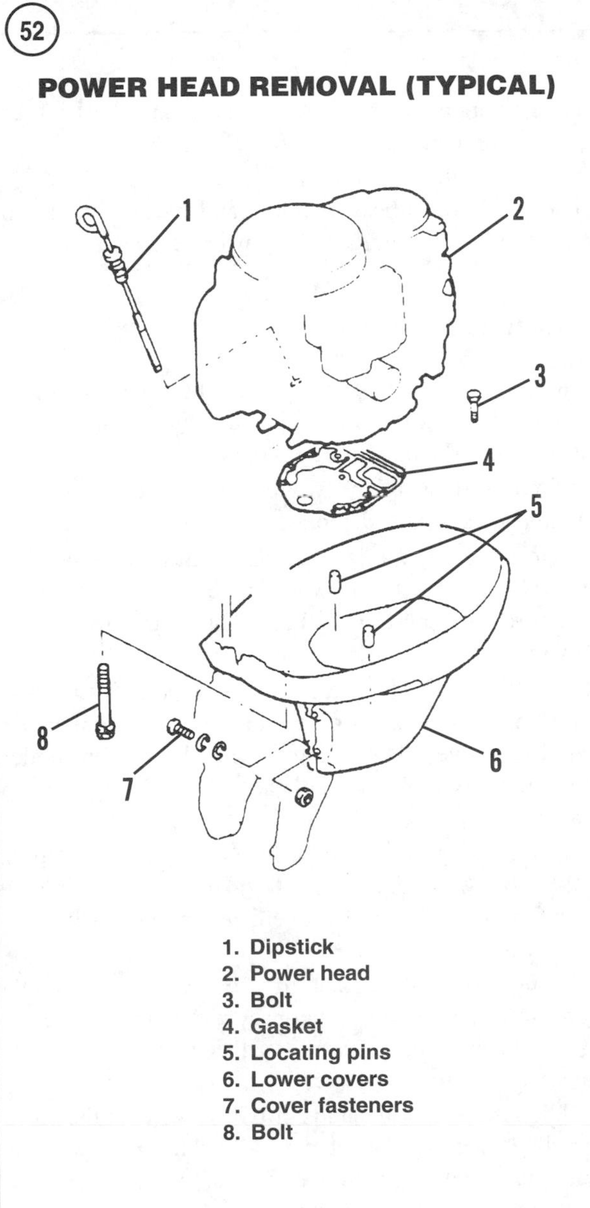

7

CAUTION

Use care when lifting the power head from the midsection. Corrosion may form at the power head and midsection mating surfaces and prevent easy removal. To help prevent damage to the mating surfaces, avoid using sharp objects to pry the assemblies apart.

Power Head Removal

1. Remove the flywheel cover as described in this chapter.
2. Disconnect the electric trim motor wires from the relay harness or engine wire harness. Refer to Chapter Nine to assist with locating the trim relays and related wiring. See *Trim/Tilt Relay Replacement.*
3. Disconnect the engine cover mounted trim switch wiring (**Figure 50**, typical) from the relay harness or engine wire harness.
4. On 225 hp models, disconnect the engine harness connectors from the low-pressure electric fuel pump driver. Refer to Chapter Five to assist with locating the driver and leads.

5A. On 75-115 hp models, remove the two screws, then lift the cover (**Figure 51**) that retains the cable and hose grommet into the port side lower engine cover. Remove the eight screws, then pull the port and starboard side lower engine covers (6, **Figure 52**, typical) from the drive shaft housing. The screws thread into openings in the front and rear mating surfaces to the starboard side cover. Five are in the front and three are in the back.

5B. On 225 hp models, remove the two screws, then lift the cable retaining bracket (**Figure 53**) from the starboard side lower engine cover. Remove the 12 screws then pull the port and starboard lower engine covers (6, **Figure 52**, typical) from the drive shaft housing. The eleven shorter screws thread into the starboard side openings. The longer screw threads into the port side opening.

6. Drain the engine oil as described in Chapter Four.

7. Remove the dipstick (1, **Figure 52**).
8. Disconnect both battery cables from the battery and engine.
9. On 115 hp models, disconnect the vapor separator tank vent hose from the fitting on the front and port side of the lower engine cover.
10. Disconnect the throttle and shift cables. Disconnect the remote control harness from the engine harness.
11. Remove the gearcase as described in Chapter Eight.
12. Disconnect the fuel supply hose.
13. Disconnect the freshwater flush hose from the power head fitting.
14. Disconnect the shift interrupt switch and shift position switch (if so equipped) leads from the engine wire harness.
15. Disconnect the tell-tale hose from the power head or lower engine cover mounted fitting.
16A. On 75-115 hp models, attach the lifting tool (part No. 91-83164M or equivalent) onto the flywheel using the included bolts. Do not remove the flywheel nut. Thread the lifting hook fully into the threaded opening of the tool.
16B. On 225 hp models, hook the three-point lifting strap (part No. 91-883705T or equivalent) onto the three power head lifting eyes. The lifting tool for 75-115 hp models can be used to lift the power head if the lifting strap is not available.
17A. On 75-115 hp models, remove the two bolts and six nuts and washers that secure the power head onto the adapter. The two bolts are located at the back and the three nuts and washers are located on each side of the drive shaft housing.
17B. On 225 hp models, remove the 13 bolts that secure the power head onto the adapter. Seven 9 mm bolts and Six 10 mm bolts are used.
18. Pry the power head loose from the midsection (**Figure 54**).
19. Attach a suitable overhead hoist to the lifting eye or lifting strap. Using a block of wood, keep the power head and midsection mating surfaces parallel while slowly lifting the power head from the midsection (**Figure 49**).
20. Remove the power head gasket (4, **Figure 52**, typical) from the midsection or bottom of the power head. Discard the gasket.
21. Mount the power head onto a power head stand (**Figure 55**) or a sturdy work surface.
22. Place clean shop towels in the midsection openings to prevent contaminants from entering the oil pan and cooling water passages. Carefully scrape all gasket material from the power head mating surfaces.
23. Inspect the mating surfaces on the midsection and power head for pits or damage. Replace damaged or defective components. Oil or water leakage is likely if these surfaces are damaged.

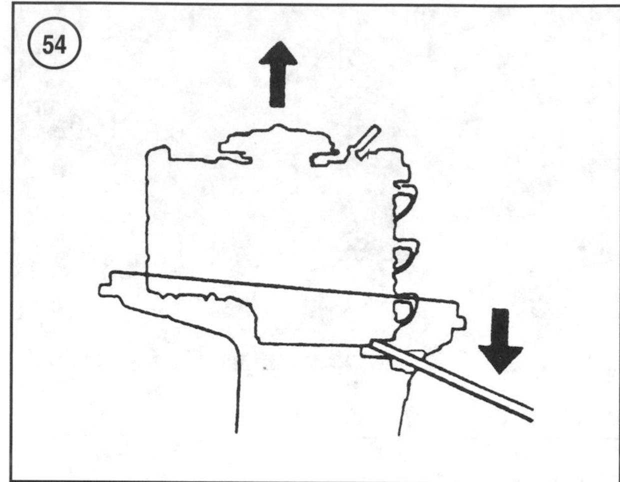

24. Remove the locating pins (5, **Figure 52**, typical) if found in the power head openings and insert them into the corresponding openings in the power head adapter.

Power Head Installation

1. Remove the shop towels from the openings in the midsection. Look into the oil pan and check for contamination. Flush the pan as required.
2. If removed, install the two locating pins (5, **Figure 52**) into the holes in the adapter.
3A. On 75-115 hp models, attach the lifting tool (part No. 91-83164M) onto the flywheel with the included bolts. Do not remove the flywheel nut. Thread the lifting hook fully into the threaded opening.
3B. On 225 hp models, hook the three-point lifting strap (part No. 91-883705T or equivalent) to the three power head lifting eyes. The lifting tool for 75-115 hp models can be used to lift the power head if the lifting strap is not available.
4. Fit the new power head gasket (4, **Figure 52**) onto the midsection. Align the pins (5, **Figure 52**) with their holes in the gasket. Align the openings in the gasket and midsection.
5. Using an overhead hoist, lift the power head from the work surface. Keep the power head mounting surface parallel to the midsection mating surface while lowering the power head onto the adapter.
6. Align the mounting studs or bolt holes with the corresponding holes in the adapter. Align the pins with the holes in the bottom of the power head, then seat the power head onto the gasket and adapter.

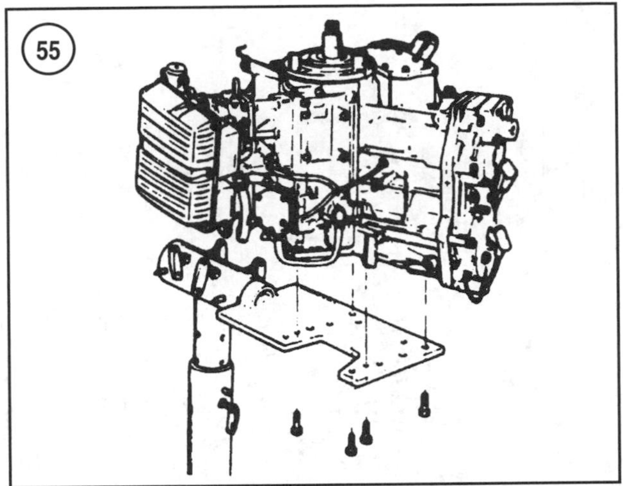

7A. On 75-225 hp models, thread the six washers and nut onto the studs on the side of the drive shaft housing. Tighten the six nuts in a crossing pattern to 40 ft.-lb. (54.2 N•m). Thread the two bolts into the opening at the rear of the adapter. Tighten the two bolts to 20 ft.-lb. (27.1 N•m).

7B. On 225 hp models, thread the 13 bolts into the adapter plate and power head openings. Tighten the bolts in a crossing pattern to 31 ft.-lb. (42.0 N•m).

8. On 115 hp models, connect the vapor separator tank vent hose onto the fitting on the front and port side of the lower engine cover. Secure the hose onto the fitting with a plastic locking clamp.

9A. On 75-115 hp models, align the seal on the power head adapter with the corresponding groove in the port and starboard side drive shaft housing covers, then install the covers onto the drive shaft housing. Seat the port cover against the starboard cover. Make sure that no hoses, cables, wiring or other components are pinched between the covers, then thread the eight screws into the port side cover openings. Five are in the front and three are in the back. Tighten the eight screws evenly to 65 in.-lb. (7.3 N•m).

9B. On 225 hp models, align the seal on the power head adapter with the corresponding groove in the port and starboard side drive shaft housing covers, then install the covers onto the drive shaft housing. Seat the port cover against the starboard cover. Make sure that no hoses, cables, wiring or other components are pinched between the covers, then thread the 12 screws into the port side cover openings. The eleven shorter screws thread into the starboard side opening. The longer screw threads into the port side opening. Tighten the screws evenly to 70 in.-lb. (7.9 N•m).

10. Connect the throttle and shift cables onto the throttle and shift linkage attaching points.

11. Plug the remote control harness onto the engine harness connector.

12A. On 75-115 hp models, guide the cable and hose grommet into the opening in the port side lower engine cover. Fit the cover (**Figure 51**) onto the grommet and lower engine cover. Thread the two screws into the cover and tighten to 65 in.-lb. (7.3 N•m).

12B. On 225 hp models, install the cable retaining plate (**Figure 53**) onto starboard side lower engine cover. Fit the cover (**Figure 51**) onto the grommet and lower engine cover. Thread the two screws into the bracket and lower engine cover. Securely tighten the screws.

13. Connect the tell-tale hose onto the power head or lower engine cover mounted fitting. Secure the hose onto the fitting with a plastic locking clamp.

14. Connect the shift interrupt switch and shift position switch (if so equipped) leads onto the engine wire harness connectors.

15. On 225 hp models, connect the engine harness connectors onto the low-pressure electric fuel pump driver. Refer to Chapter Five to assist with locating the driver and leads.

16. Connect the fuel supply hose onto the fuel filter fitting. Secure the hose with a suitable clamp. See Chapter Five.

17. Connect the freshwater flush hose onto the power head fitting. Secure the hose onto the fitting with a plastic locking clamp.

18. Connect the electric trim motor wires onto the relay harness or engine wire harness connectors. Refer to *Trim/Tilt Relay Replacement* in Chapter Nine to assist with locating the trim relays and related wiring.

19. Connect the engine cover-mounted trim switch wiring (**Figure 50**, typical) onto the relay harness or engine wire harness connectors.

20. Fill the oil pan with the recommended oil as described in Chapter Three.

21. Install the dipstick (1, **Figure 52**, typical).

22. Install the gearcase as described in Chapter Eight.

23. Install the flywheel cover as described in this chapter.

24. Connect the battery cables to the engine and battery terminals.

25. Route all wiring and hoses to prevent interference with moving components. Secure the hoses and wiring with plastic locking clamps as needed.

26. Perform all applicable adjustments as described in Chapter Four.

OIL PUMP REMOVAL AND INSTALLATION

On 225 hp models, the oil pump mounts onto the bottom of the power head and is driven by the drive shaft. On 75-115 hp models, the oil pump mounts onto the power head adapter on the mid section of the engine. Refer to Chapter Ten for oil pump removal and installation for 75-115 hp models.

225 hp Model

Refer to **Figure 56**.

1. Remove the power head as described in this chapter.
2. Remove the four screws (**Figure 56**) and remove the oil pump from the power head.
3. Remove the O-rings (**Figure 56**) from the power head or top side of the oil pump. Discard the O-rings.
4. Inspect the oil pump for as described in this chapter.
5. Lubricate the new O-rings (**Figure 56**) with four-stroke outboard engine oil and place them into the grooves in the oil pump mating surface.
6. Pour engine oil into the two openings on the bottom of the oil pump. Rotate the pump shaft to distribute oil throughout the pump. Apply a light coating of Quicksilver 2-4-C Marine Lubricant onto the splines in the pump rotor and seal lips.
7. Align the oil pump drive and crankshaft splines and the oil passages openings while installing the oil pump onto the power head. Do not dislodge the O-rings during the installation.
8. Rotate pump to align the screw openings, then thread the four screw (**Figure 56**) into the oil pump and power head openings. Tighten the four screws in a crossing pattern to 71 in.-lb. (8.0 N•m).
9. Install the power head as described in this chapter.

OIL PUMP INSPECTION

The oil pump is non-serviceable. Replace the oil pump if low oil pressure is occurring and other causes such as a faulty pressure relief valve or worn bearing are ruled out.

1. Clean the external oil pump surfaces with solvent and dry them with compressed air.
2. Immerse the oil pump in solvent. Rotate the splined drive shaft bore to purge all engine oil from the pump. Dry the pump using compressed air. Do not allow the splined section to rotate while directing compressed air into the oil passages.
3. Inspect the oil pump mating surfaces for corrosion or cracks and replace as required.
4. Manually rotate the splined drive shaft bore while checking for binding or roughness. Binding or roughness is caused by mechanical damage or debris in the pump. Replace the pump if binding, roughness is noted or if debris was purged from the passages during the cleaning process.

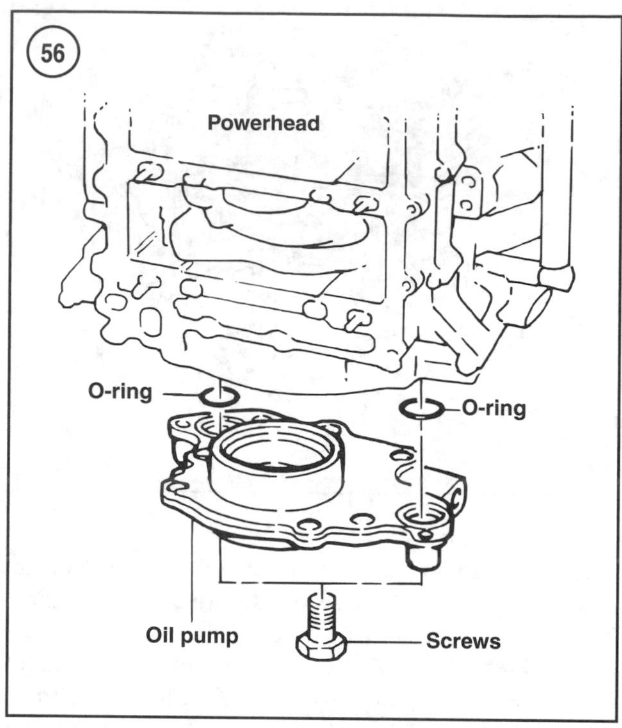

CRANKSHAFT PULLEY REMOVAL (75-115 HP MODELS)

The power head must be removed to replace the crankshaft pulley on 75-115 hp models. A crankshaft adapter (part no. 91-904776A1 or equivalent) and a 46 mm deep socket (or part No. 91-881847) are required for this procedure.

Refer to **Figure 57**.

1. Remove the power head as described in this chapter.
2. Remove the flywheel and timing belt as described in this chapter.
3. Remove the battery charging coil and crankshaft position sensor as described in Chapter Six.
4. Insert the crankshaft splined adapter (part No. 91-904776A1 or equivalent) into the crankshaft splines to prevent crankshaft rotation while loosening the 46 mm nut.

CAUTION
Do not allow the crankshaft to rotate while loosening the crankshaft pulley nut unless the camshafts are first removed. Rotation of the crankshaft with the camshafts installed may allow the pistons to contact the valves resulting in damage to the valves and pistons.

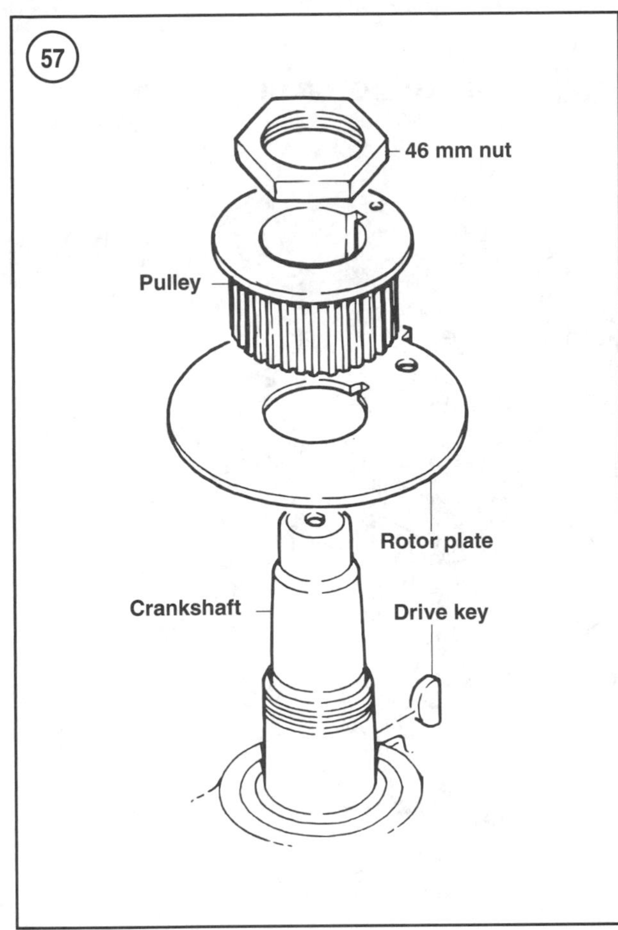

5. Engage a 46 mm deep socket (or part No. 91-881847) onto the large nut (**Figure 57**) on the upper end of the crankshaft.

6. Hold the splined adapter to prevent crankshaft rotation, then loosen and remove the 46 mm nut.

7. Lift the crankshaft pulley (**Figure 57**) from the crankshaft. Tap the pulley with a rubber mallet if it will not lift freely from the crankshaft. Remove the drive key (**Figure 57**) from the crankshaft or pulley slot.

8. Lift the rotor plate (**Figure 57**) from the crankshaft.

9. Inspect the pulley and rotor plate for wear or damage. Replace the pulley or plate if worn or damaged.

10. Inspect the key for bent or damaged surfaces. Replace the key if defects are noted.

11. Place the drive key into the crankshaft groove with the rounded side facing inward.

12. Align the key slot with the drive key, then install the rotor plate onto the crankshaft. The tab on the plate must follow the key slot or be oriented counterclockwise from the key slot. The ignition timing will be incorrect if the plate is installed with the tab leading the key slot.

13. Install the crankshaft pulley over the crankshaft with the larger diameter side facing up. Align the key slot in the pulley with the key, then seat the pulley against the plate.

14. Thread the crankshaft pulley nut onto the crankshaft until it just contacts the pulley.

15. Insert the crankshaft splined adapter into the crankshaft splines to prevent crankshaft rotation while tightening the 46 mm nut.

CAUTION

Do not allow the crankshaft to rotate while tightening the crankshaft pulley nut unless the camshafts are first removed. Rotation of the crankshaft with the camshafts installed may allow the pistons to contact the valves resulting in damage to the valves and pistons.

16. Engage a 46 mm deep socket to the large nut (**Figure 57**) on the upper end of the crankshaft.

17. Hold the splined adapter to prevent crankshaft rotation, then tighten the crankshaft pulley nut to 195 ft.-lb. (264 N•m).

18. Install the battery charging coil and crankshaft position sensor as described in Chapter Six.

19. Install the flywheel and timing belt as described in this chapter.

20. Install the power head as described in this chapter.

POWER HEAD DISASSEMBLY AND ASSEMBLY

Always make notes, drawings and photographs of all external power head components *before* beginning disassembly.

Correct hose and wire routing is important for proper engine operation. An incorrectly routed hose or wire may interfere with linkage movement and result in a dangerous lack of throttle control. Hoses or wires may chafe and short or leak when allowed to contact sharp or moving parts. Other components such as fuel pumps can be mounted in two or more positions.

Mark the up and forward direction before removing any components. If possible remove a cluster of components sharing common wires or hoses. This will reduce the time required to disassemble and assemble the power head. This method also reduces the chance of improper connections during assembly.

Use muffin tins or egg cartons to organize the fasteners as they are removed. Mark all fasteners to ensure they are installed in the correct location during assembly.

58

CYLINDER BLOCK COMPONENTS (75-115 HP MODELS)

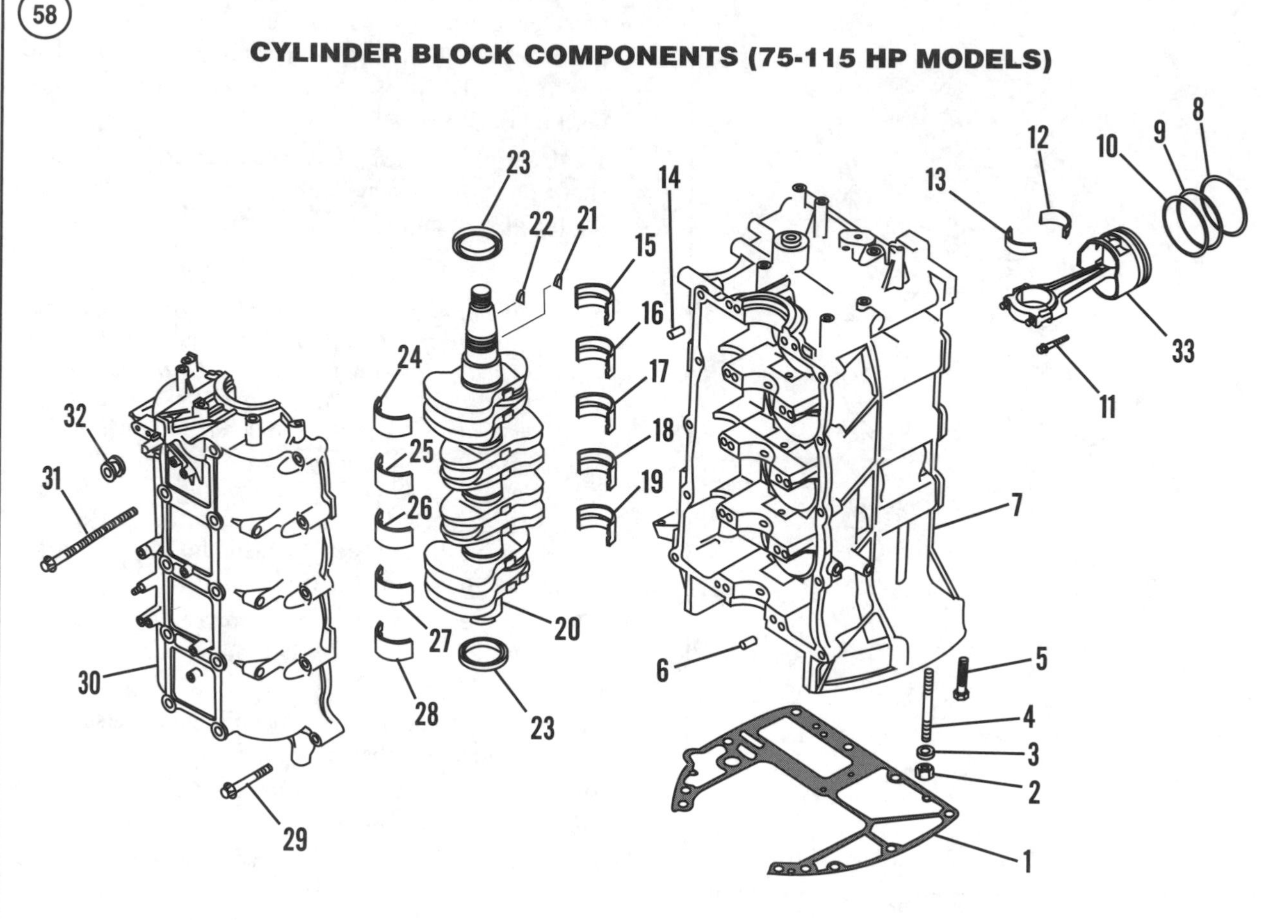

1. Mounting gasket
2. Nut
3. Washer
4. Stud
5. Bolt
6. Locating pin
7. Cylinder block
8. Top compression ring
9. Second compression ring
10. Oil control ring
11. Rod bolt
12. Rod bearing (connecting rod side)
13. Rod bearing (rod cap side)
14. Locating pin
15. Top main bearing (cylinder block side)
16. No. 2 main bearing (cylinder block side)
17. No. 3 main bearing (cylinder block side)
18. No. 4 main bearing (cylinder block side)
19. Bottom main bearing (cylinder block side)
20. Crankshaft
21. Drive key
22. Drive key
23. Crankshaft seal
24. Top main bearing (crankcase cover side)
25. No. 2 main bearing (crankcase cover side)
26. No. 3 main bearing (crankcase cover side)
27. No. 4 main bearing (crankcase cover side)
28. Bottom main bearing (crankcase cover side)
29. Bolt
30. Crankcase cover
31. Bolt
32. Grommet
33. Piston

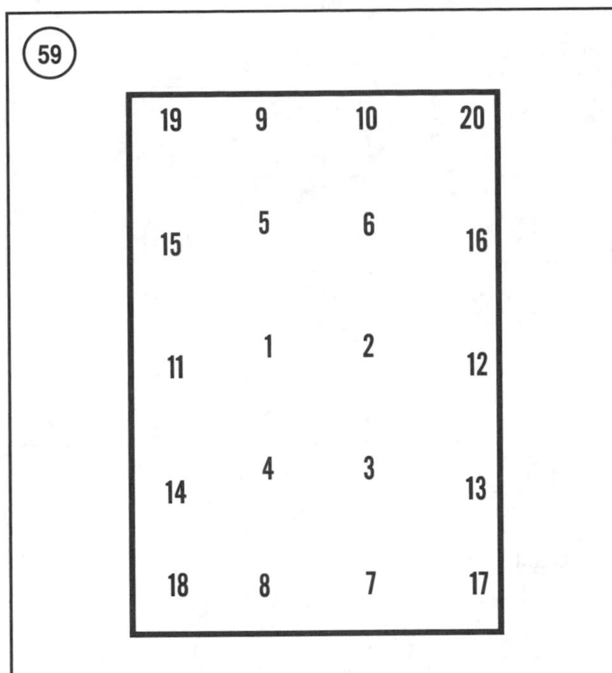

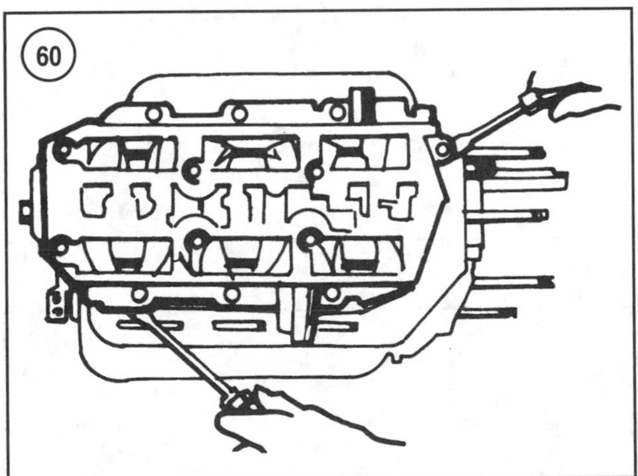

75-115 hp Models

External component removal

1. Remove the power head as described in this chapter.
2. Remove all applicable fuel system components as described in Chapter Five.
3. Remove all electrical and ignition system components as described in Chapter Six.
4. Remove the flywheel, timing belt and tensioner as described in this chapter.
5. Remove the camshaft pulleys, camshafts, cylinder head and crankshaft pulley as described in this chapter.
6. Remove the exhaust/water jacket cover, thermostat and water pressure relief valve as described in this chapter.
7. Remove the oil filter as described in Chapter Three.

Cylinder block disassembly

Refer to **Figure 58**.

1. Place the cylinder block assembly on a clean work surface with the crankcase cover side facing up.
2. Loosen the crankcase cover bolts (31, **Figure 58**) 1/4 turn at a time in the opposite order of the tightening sequence (**Figure 59**) until the screws turn freely.
3. Locate the pry points at the top and bottom corners of the cover. Carefully pry the cover from the crankcase (**Figure 60**). Check for overlooked bolts if removal is difficult. If dislodged, place the locating pins (6 and 14, **Figure 58**) into the corresponding openings in the cylinder block mating surface.
4. Note the seal lip direction then remove the oil seals from the top and bottom of the crankshaft (**Figure 61**).
5. Note the location and up side of each of the outer main bearing inserts (24-28, **Figure 58**), then remove them from the crankshaft or crankcase cover. Arrange the bearing inserts so they will not become switched with other bearing inserts.
6. Remove one piston and rod assembly at a time.
   a. Use a scribe to mark the cylinder number on the side of the connecting rod and rod cap (**Figure 62**).
   b. Using white paint, highlight the UP mark on each piston dome (**Figure 63**).
   c. Evenly loosen, 1/4 turn at a time, the connecting rod bolts (**Figure 64**) until they spin freely. Lightly tap the rod cap to free it from the crankshaft and connecting rod (**Figure 65**). Remove the insert type bearing from the crankshaft or connecting rod cap.
   d. Scrape the carbon ridge from the top of the cylinder bore with a small knife. Work carefully and avoid scratching the cylinder wall. Using a wooden

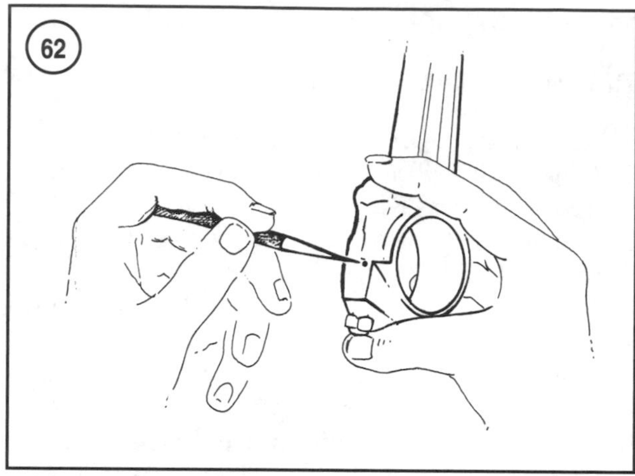

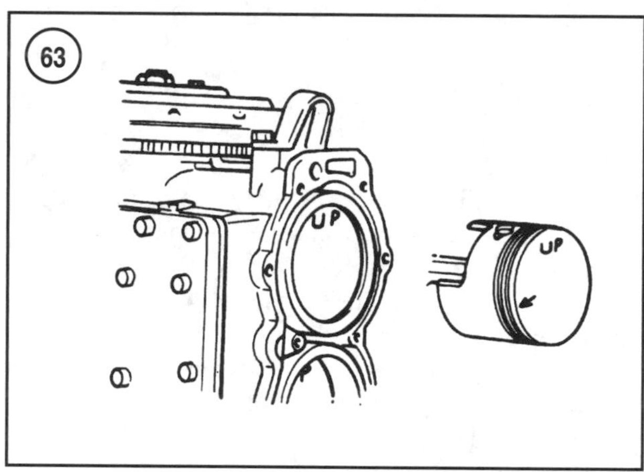

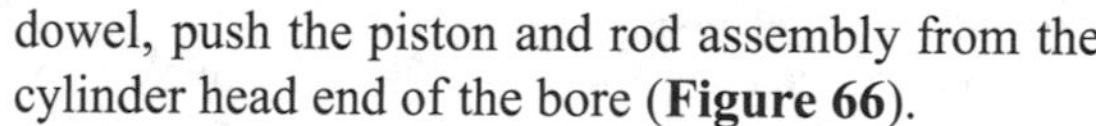

dowel, push the piston and rod assembly from the cylinder head end of the bore (**Figure 66**).

e. Align the tabs on the back side of the bearings with the notches, then install the insert bearings into the connecting rod and rod cap (**Figure 67**). Align the markings made prior to removal (**Figure 62**), then install the cap onto the rod. Install the rod bolts (1, **Figure 68**) to retain the cap and bearings.

7. Repeat Step 6 to remove the remaining three piston and rod assemblies.

8. Using a ring expander, remove the upper two compression rings from the pistons (**Figure 69**). Carefully unwind the oil control ring (lower rails and spacer) from the piston skirts. Work carefully to prevent damage to the piston.

CAUTION

Do not remove the connecting rod from the piston 75-115 hp models. The piston and rod assembly must be replaced as an assembly if either the connecting rod or piston is defective or excessively worn.

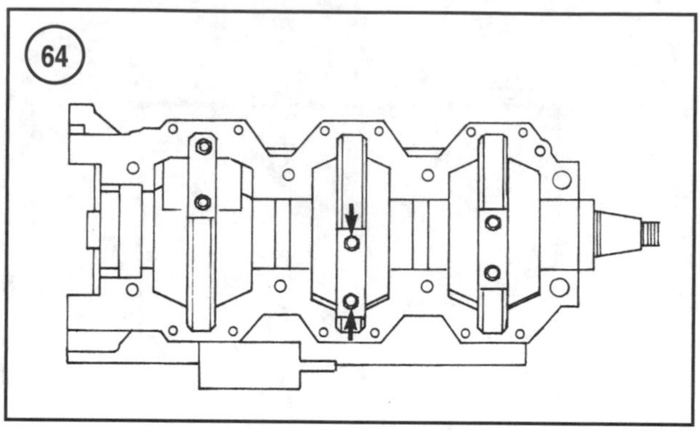

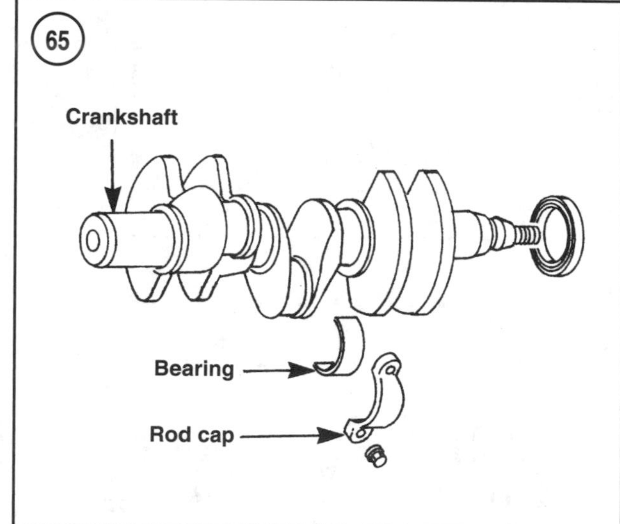

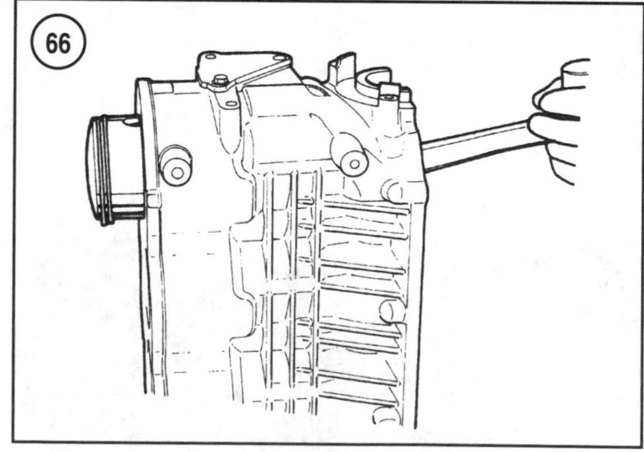

9. Carefully lift the crankshaft (20, **Figure 58**) out of the cylinder block. Note the location of each of the main bearing inserts (15-19, **Figure 58**), then remove them from the cylinder block. Arrange the insert bearings so they cannot become switched with other bearings.

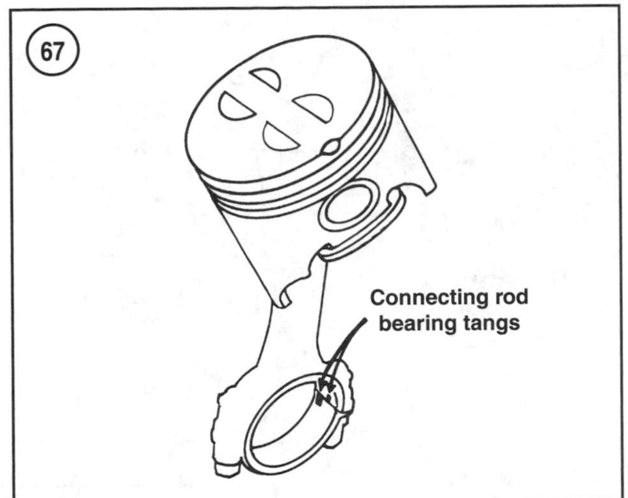

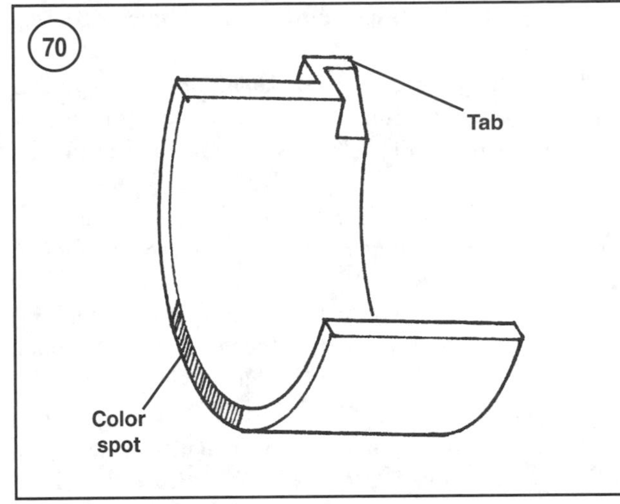

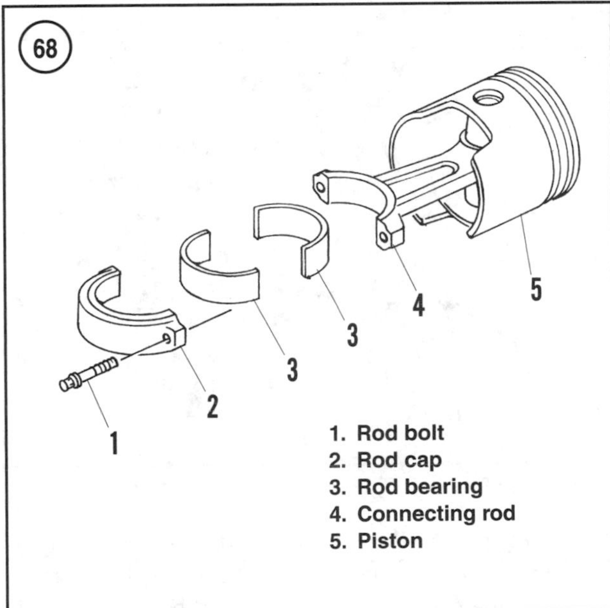

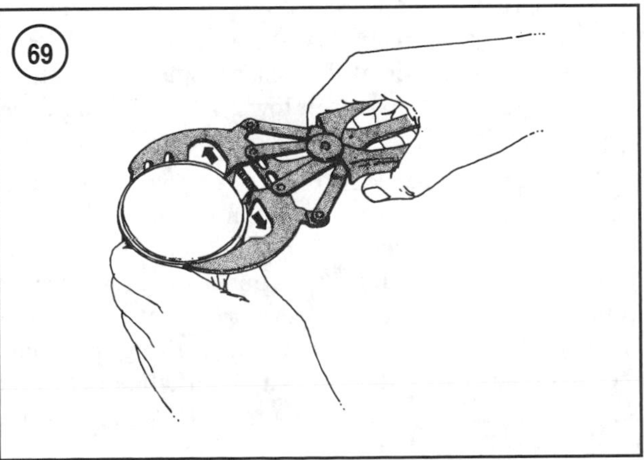

10. Thoroughly clean the cylinder block with hot soapy water. Clean other components with clean solvent. Clean carbon from the piston dome with a non-metallic parts cleaning brush and solvent. Dry all components with compressed air. Apply a light coat of oil to the piston, piston pin, cylinder bore, bearings, connecting rod and crankshaft to prevent corrosion.
11. Inspect all cylinder block components as described in this chapter.
12. Note the color spot on the side of each insert bearing (**Figure 70**) for each main and pair of connecting rod bearings. If reusing the original cylinder block, connecting rods and crankshaft, order replacement bearings with the same color code as the original. If replacing the cylinder block, connecting rod or crankshaft, refer to *Bearing Selection* in this chapter to determine the color code for the replacement bearings.

Cylinder block assembly

Refer to **Figure 58**. A ring compressor tool (part No. FT2997) is required for this procedure.

1. Run a white shop cloth through the cylinder to check for debris. Repeat the cleaning process until the cloth passes through clean.
2. Check main bearing clearance as follows:
   a. Clean all oil from the main bearings, cylinder block and crankcase cover prior to installing the bearings. Install the bearings (15-19, **Figure 58**) into the cylinder block and crankcase cover. Align the tabs on the bearings (**Figure 70**) with the notches in the cylinder block and crankcase cover. Make sure the correct color bearing is installed at each position in the cylinder block and crankcase cover. Install the

larger thrust bearing into the third or middle bearing position.

b. Carefully lower the crankshaft into the cylinder block and rest it on the bearings. Make sure the tapered flywheel end faces the top of the cylinder block.

c. Place a section of Plastigage across each main bearing journal (**Figure 71**). Align the locating pins (6 and 14, **Figure 58**) with the corresponding openings then install the crankcase cover (30, **Figure 58**) onto the cylinder block. Thread all crankcase bolts into the cover and cylinder block. Do not rotate the crankshaft.

d. Tighten the crankcase cover bolts in sequence (1-20, **Figure 59**) to 120 in.-lb. (13.6 N•m) for the ten 8 mm bolts and 168 in.-lb. (19.0 N•m) for the ten 10 mm bolts. Tighten the ten 10 mm bolts a second time in sequence (1-10, **Figure 59**) an additional 60° of rotation. The points on the hex heads are 60° apart and can be used for reference during the tightening process. Tighten the ten 8 mm bolts in sequence (11-20, **Figure 59**) to 240 in.-lb. (27.1 N•m).

e. Loosen the crank case bolts 1/4 turn at a time in the reverse order of the tightening sequence (20-1, **Figure 59**) until they rotate freely. Remove the bolts then lift the cover from the cylinder block.

f. Measure each main bearing clearance by comparing the width of the Plastigage to the markings on the Plastigage envelope (**Figure 72**). The main bearing clearance must be 0.0009-0.0017 in. (0.024-0.044 mm). Incorrect clearance indicates improper bearing selection or excessive bearing or crankshaft wear. Repeat the bearing selection procedure to ensure the proper bearings are installed. See *Bearing Selection* in this chapter. Measure the crankshaft for excessive wear as described in the chapter. See *Cylinder Block Component Inspection and Measurement*. Install new main bearings and measure the clearance if the correct bearings are installed and the crankshaft is not excessively worn.

g. Lift the crankshaft from the cylinder block and clean the Plastigage from the crankshaft and bearing surfaces.

3. Install the crankshaft as follows:

a. Apply four-stroke outboard engine oil onto the crankshaft main bearings.

b. Carefully lower the crankshaft into the cylinder block and rest it on the bearings. Make sure the tapered flywheel end faces the top of the cylinder block.

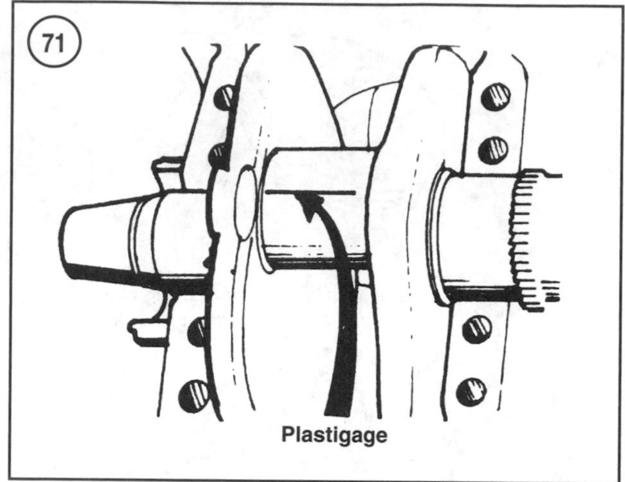

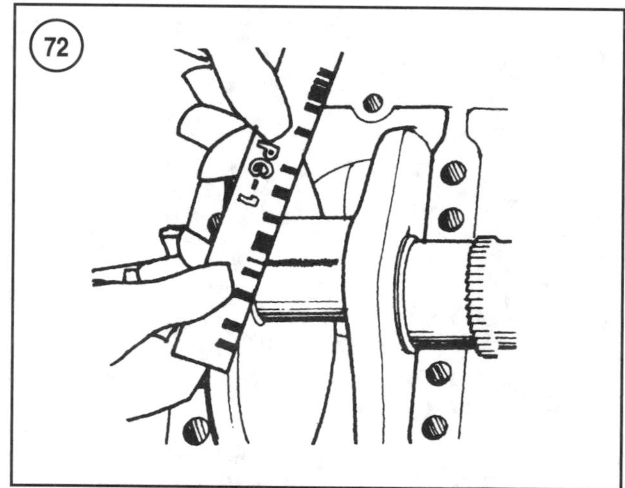

c. *Slowly* rotate the crankshaft to check for free movement. Remove the crankshaft and check for proper bearing seating and installation if binding or rough movement is detected.

d. Apply four-stroke outboard engine oil onto the seals lips and carefully slide the upper and lower seals onto the crankshaft ends (**Figure 61**) with the lip side facing inward or toward the crankcase. Seat the seals fully in the cylinder block bores.

4. Using a ring expander (**Figure 69**), open the new rings just enough to pass over the piston crown. Release the rings into the correct groove on the piston. The top compression ring (8, **Figure 58**) is thinner than the second compression ring (9). Identify the top side of each ring by the *T* marking near the end gap. The markings must face the top of the piston after installation. Install both oil rails and the spacer into the bottom groove. Make sure the spacer separates the rails.

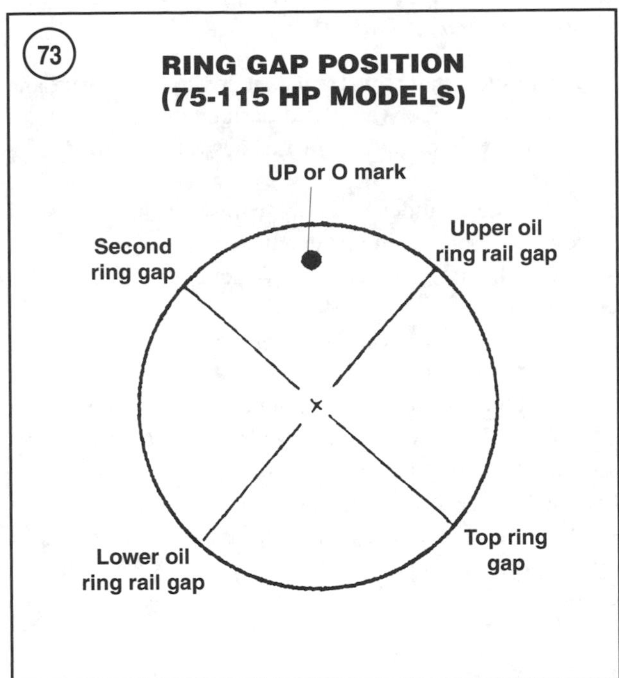

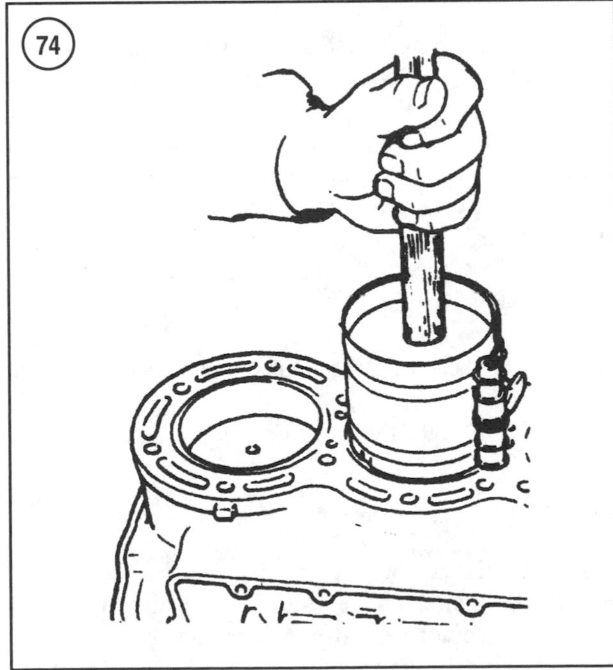

5. Rotate the second compression ring so the gap is approximately 45° starboard of the *up* marking on the piston crown. Rotate the top compression ring so the gap is 180° from the gap in the second ring. Rotate the upper oil rail so the gap is 45° to the port side of the *up* mark on the piston crown. Rotate the lower oil rail until the gap is 180° degrees from the upper rail (**Figure 73**).

6. Apply four-stroke outboard engine oil onto the piston, piston rings and cylinder wall.
7. Install the piston and rods onto the crankshaft as follows:
   a. Fit a ring compressor (part No. FT2997 or equivalent) over the No. 1 piston and rings. Tighten the compressor enough to fully compress the rings yet still allow the piston to slide through the compressor.
   b. Have an assistant help retain the crankshaft in the cylinder block during piston installation. Rest the power head on the side to allow access to the cylinder head and crankcase cover mating surfaces. Carefully rotate the crankshaft until the No. 1 crankpin is at the bottom of its stroke.
   c. Insert the No. 1 piston and rod assembly into the cylinder block from the cylinder head side. Ensure the *up* marks on the piston and rod face toward the flywheel side of the crankshaft (**Figure 63**). Guide the connecting rod toward the crankshaft during piston installation.
   d. Hold the ring compressor firmly against the cylinder block and gently drive the piston into the bore until the piston dome is slightly below the cylinder head mating surface (**Figure 74**). Stop and check for adequate ring compression and/or improper ring alignment if any resistance is detected.
   e. Install the bearing inserts into the connecting rods and rod caps. Make sure the bearing tabs (**Figure 67**) are properly aligned with the notches in the connecting rods and rod caps.
8. Check the connecting rod bearing clearance as follows:
   a. Place a section of Plastigage onto the crankpin (**Figure 71**). Install the rod cap and bolts.
   b. Align the markings on the connecting rod and rod cap (**Figure 62**) install the cap on the rod. On 75 and 90 hp models, the flat side on the rod cap must face toward the flywheel. On 115 hp models, the small dimples on the connecting rod and rod cap must face toward the flywheel. Install the rod bolts and tighten finger-tight.
   c. Tighten the rod bolts to an initial torque of 132 in.-lb. (14.9 N•m). Tighten each rod bolt an additional 60° of rotation. Do not rotate the crankshaft.
   d. Loosen the rod bolts and remove the rod cap.
   e. Measure the connecting rod bearing clearance by comparing the width of the Plastigage to the markings on the Plastigage envelope (**Figure 72**). The rod bearing clearance must be 0.0010-0.0012 in. (0.025-0.030 mm). Incorrect clearance indicates improper bearing selection or excessive bearing or

7

crankshaft wear. Repeat the bearing selection procedure to ensure the proper bearings are installed. See *Bearing Selection* in this chapter. Measure the crankshaft for excessive wear as described in this chapter. Replace worn or damaged components and check the clearance again.

9. Clean the Plastigage material from the crankshaft and connecting rod bearing. Apply engine oil to the crankshaft, bearings and the rod bolts. Align the rod cap and install it onto the connecting rod. Install the new connecting rod bolts finger-tight. Check for proper rod cap-to-connecting rod alignment. Correct as required. Tighten the rod bolts to an initial torque of 132 in.-lb. (14.9 N•m.). Tighten each rod bolt an additional 60° of rotation.
10. Repeat Steps 4-9 for the remaining three piston and connecting rod assemblies. Rotate the flywheel to position the crankpin at the bottom of its stroke for the corresponding cylinder.
11. Install the crankcase cover as follows:
    a. Clean all oil residue or other contamination from the crankcase cover and cylinder block mating surface. Make sure the locating pins (6 and 14, **Figure 58**) are in position in the openings on the cylinder block mating surfaces.
    b. Apply a light even coat of Loctite Master Gasket 514 (part No. 92-12654-2) onto the mating surface of the crankcase cover. Coat the entire mating surface, but do not allow sealant to flow into the bolts holes.
    c. Inspect the crankshaft main bearings inserts for proper alignment. Inspect the crankshaft seals for correct placement then place the crankcase cover onto the cylinder block.
    d. Apply a light coat of four-stroke outboard engine oil to the threads, then install the crankcase cover bolts finger-tight.
    e. Tighten the crankcase cover bolts in sequence (1-20, **Figure 59**) to 120 in.-lb. (13.6 N•m) for the ten 8 mm bolts and 168 in.-lb. (19.0 N•m) for the ten 10 mm bolts. Tighten the ten 10 mm bolts a second time in sequence (1-10, **Figure 59**) an additional 60° or rotation. The points on the hex heads are 60° apart and can be used for reference during the tightening process. Tighten the ten 8 mm bolts in sequence (11-20, **Figure 59**) to 240 in.-lb. (27.1 N•m).
    f. Rotate the crankshaft while checking for smooth rotation. Disassemble the cylinder block and check for an incorrectly installed rod cap or bearing if binding is evident. Recheck the bearing clearances if binding is evident, but the bearing and rod caps were installed correctly.

External component installation

1. Install the exhaust/water jacket cover, thermostat and water pressure relief valve as described in this chapter.
2. Install the crankshaft pulley as described in this chapter.
3. Install the cylinder head, the camshafts and camshaft pulleys as described in this chapter.
4. Install the timing belt and tensioner as described in this chapter.
5. Install all electrical and ignition system components as described in Chapter Six.
6. Install the flywheel as described in this chapter.
7. Install all applicable fuel system components as described in Chapter Five.
8. Install a new oil filter as described in Chapter Three.
9. Install the power head as described in this chapter.
10. Perform the break-in procedures as described in this chapter.

225 hp Model

External component removal

1. Remove the power head as described in this chapter.
2. Remove all applicable fuel system components as described in Chapter Five.
3. Remove all electrical and ignition system components as described in Chapter Six.
4. Remove the exhaust/water jacket covers and thermostats as described in this chapter.
5. Remove the flywheel, tensioner and timing belt as described in this chapter.
6. Remove both camshaft pulleys, the four camshafts, both cylinder heads and the crankshaft pulley as described in this chapter.
7. Remove the oil filter as described in Chapter Three.

Cylinder block disassembly

Refer to **Figure 75**.

1. Place the cylinder block assembly on a clean work surface with the crankcase cover side facing up.
2. Loosen the 17 crankcase cover bolts (41, **Figure 75**) 1/4 turn at a time in the opposite order of the tightening sequence (**Figure 76**) until the screws turn freely.
3. Locate the pry points at the top and bottom corners of the cover. Carefully pry the cover from the crankcase (**Figure 60**). Check for overlooked bolts if difficult removal is encountered.
4. Remove the gasket (37, **Figure 75**) from the crankcase cover or crankcase (28). Discard the gasket.

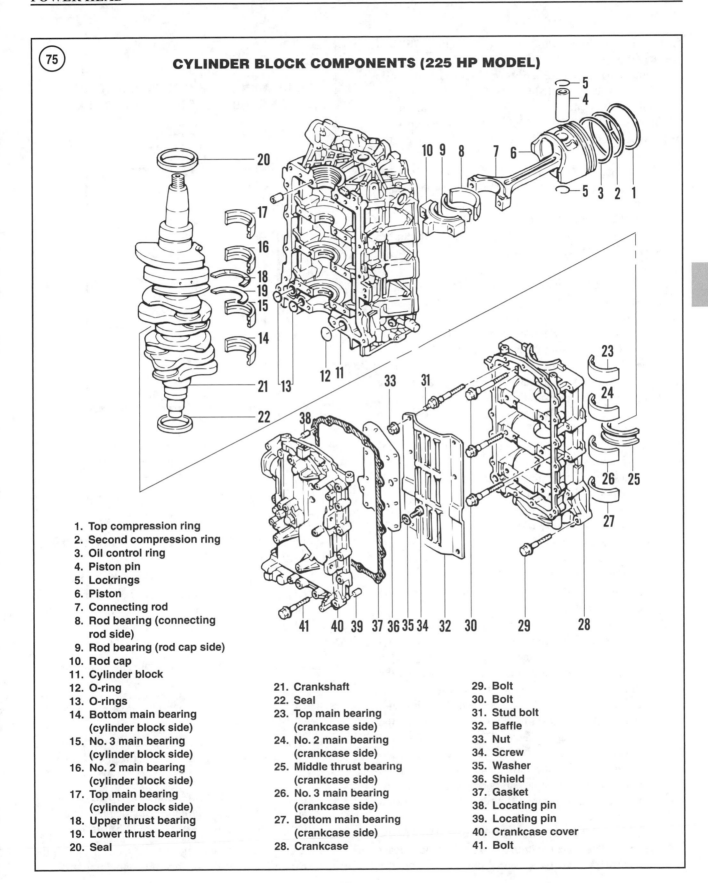

(75)

CYLINDER BLOCK COMPONENTS (225 HP MODEL)

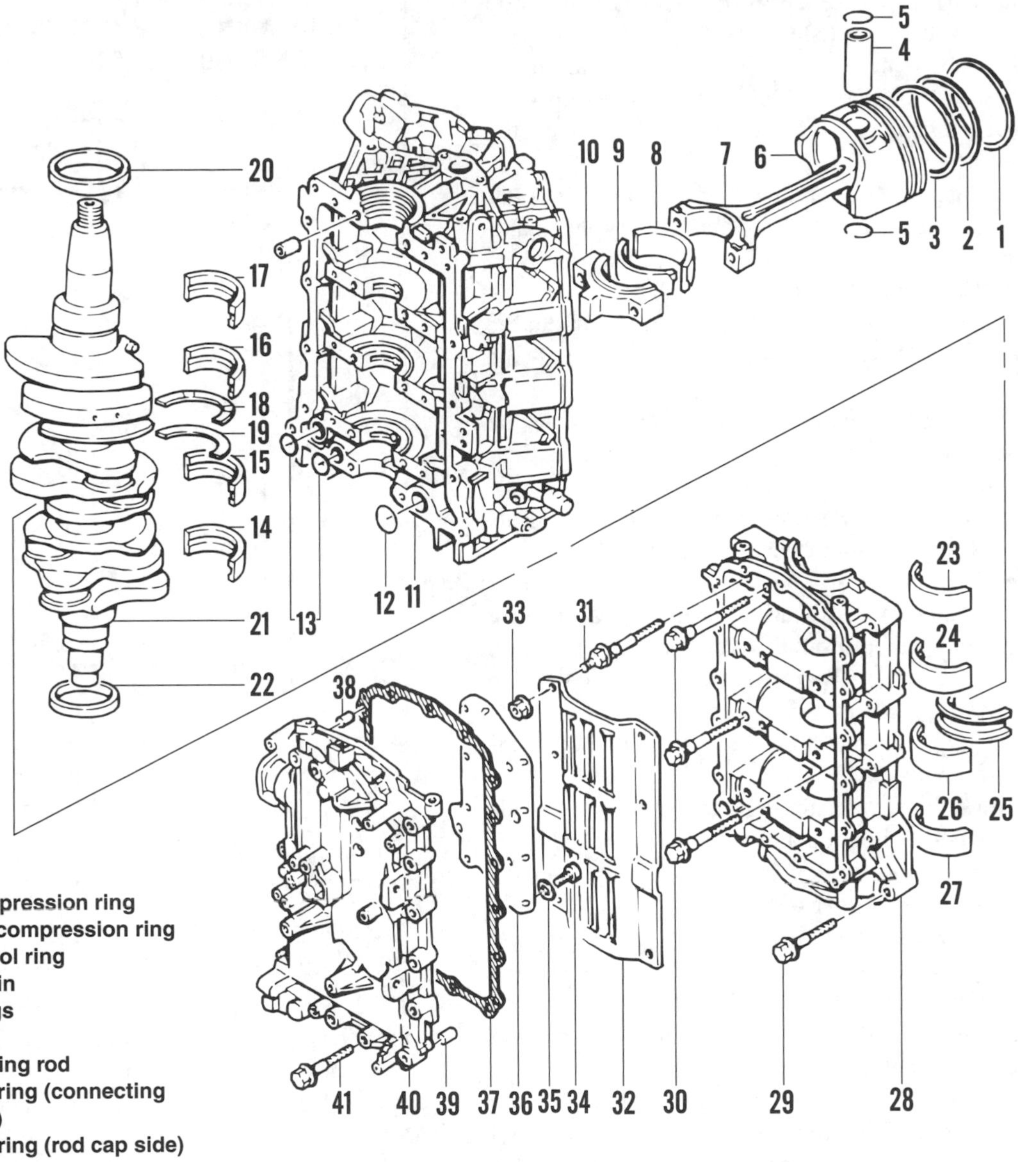

1. Top compression ring
2. Second compression ring
3. Oil control ring
4. Piston pin
5. Lockrings
6. Piston
7. Connecting rod
8. Rod bearing (connecting rod side)
9. Rod bearing (rod cap side)
10. Rod cap
11. Cylinder block
12. O-ring
13. O-rings
14. Bottom main bearing (cylinder block side)
15. No. 3 main bearing (cylinder block side)
16. No. 2 main bearing (cylinder block side)
17. Top main bearing (cylinder block side)
18. Upper thrust bearing
19. Lower thrust bearing
20. Seal
21. Crankshaft
22. Seal
23. Top main bearing (crankcase side)
24. No. 2 main bearing (crankcase side)
25. Middle thrust bearing (crankcase side)
26. No. 3 main bearing (crankcase side)
27. Bottom main bearing (crankcase side)
28. Crankcase
29. Bolt
30. Bolt
31. Stud bolt
32. Baffle
33. Nut
34. Screw
35. Washer
36. Shield
37. Gasket
38. Locating pin
39. Locating pin
40. Crankcase cover
41. Bolt

5. Remove the fourteen screws (34, **Figure 75**) and washers (35), then lift the shield (36) from the cover.
6. Remove the six nuts (33, **Figure 75**) then lift the baffle (32) from the stud bolts (31).
7. Loosen the twenty-three crankcase bolts (30, **Figure 75**) and six stud bolts (31) 1/4 turn at a time in the opposite order of the tightening sequence (**Figure 77**) until the screws turn freely.
8. Locate the pry points at the top and bottom corners of the crankcase (28, **Figure 75**). Carefully pry the crankcase from the cylinder block (**Figure 60**). Check for overlooked bolts if difficult removal is encountered.
9. Remove the O-rings (12 and 13, **Figure 75**) from the crankcase or cylinder block openings. Discard the O-rings.
10. If the locating pins are dislodged or found in the crankcase opening, return them to the corresponding openings in the cylinder block.
11. Note the seal lip direction then remove the oil seals from the top and bottom of the crankshaft (**Figure 61**).
12. Note the location and up side of each of the outer main bearings and thrust bearing inserts (23-27, **Figure 75**), then remove them from the crankshaft or crankcase. Arrange the bearing inserts so they will not become switched with other bearing inserts.
13. Remove one piston and rod assembly at a time. Instructions follow:

a. Use a scribe to mark the cylinder number on the side of the connecting rod and rod cap (**Figure 62**).
b. Using white paint, highlight the UP mark on each piston dome (**Figure 63**).
c. Evenly loosen, 1/4 turn at a time, the connecting rod bolts (**Figure 64**) until they spin freely. Lightly tap the rod cap to free it from the crankshaft and connecting rod (**Figure 65**). Remove the insert bearing from the crankshaft or connecting rod cap.
d. Scrape the carbon ridge from the top of the cylinder bore with a small knife. Work carefully and avoid scratching the cylinder wall. Using a wooden dowel, push the piston and rod assembly from the cylinder head end of the bore (**Figure 66**).
e. Align the tabs on the back side of the bearings with the notches, then install the insert bearings into the connecting rod and rod cap (**Figure 67**). Align the marks made prior to removal (**Figure 62**) then install the cap onto the rod. Install the rod bolts (1, **Figure 68**) to retain the cap and bearings.

14. Repeat Step 13 to remove the remaining five piston and rod assemblies.
15. Carefully lift the crankshaft (21, **Figure 75**) out of the cylinder block. Note the location of each of the main bearing inserts (14-17, **Figure 75**), then remove them from the cylinder block. Arrange the insert bearings so they cannot become switched with other bearings.

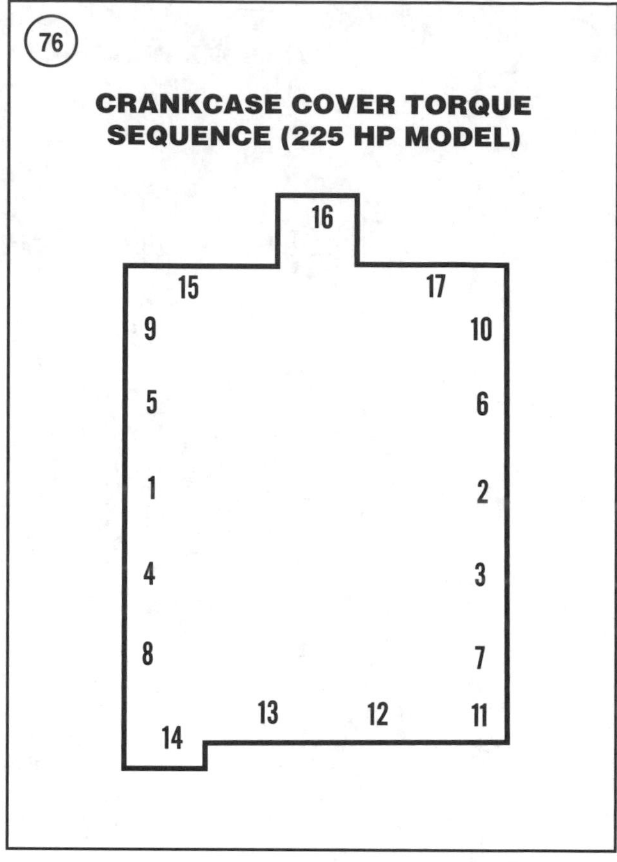

16. Remove the thrust bearings (18 and 19, **Figure 75**) from the recesses in the cylinder block.

17. Using a ring expander, remove the upper two compression rings from the pistons (**Figure 69**). Carefully unwind the oil control ring (lower rails and spacer) from the piston skirts. Work carefully to prevent damage to the piston.

18. Disassemble the connecting rod and piston as follows:

a. Mark the cylinder number on top side of the piston and connecting rod.
b. Using a suitable pick or scribe, pry the lock rings (**Figure 78**) from the grooves in the piston pin bore.
c. Use a deep socket or section of tubing as a piston pin removal-and-installation tool. The tool must be slightly smaller in diameter than the piston pin. Piston pin specifications are listed in **Table 7**.
d. Support the connecting rod and carefully push the piston pin from the piston and connecting rod.

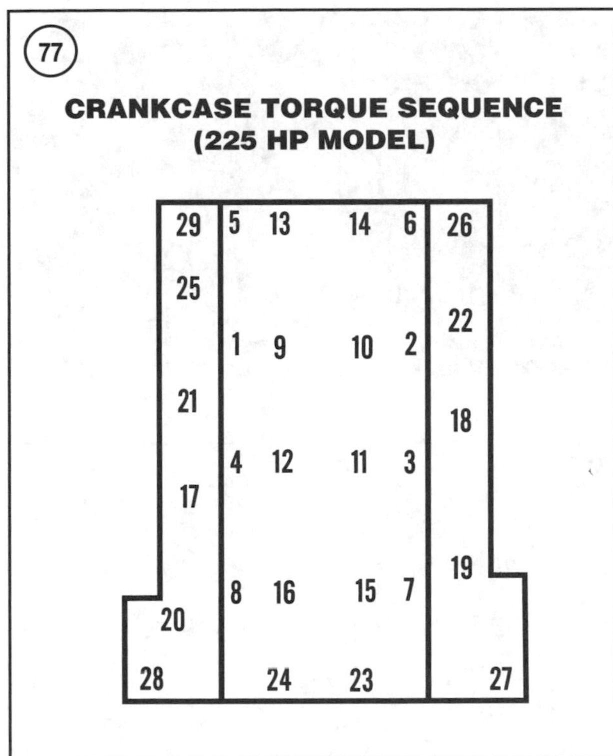

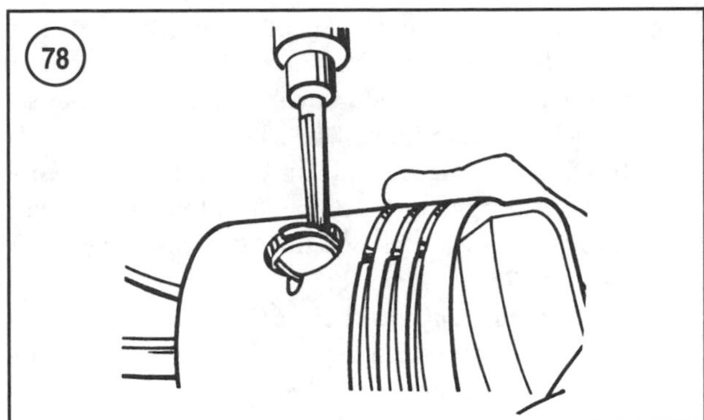

e. Separate the piston and connecting rod. Make sure the cylinder number is marked on the piston and connecting rod.

19. Thoroughly clean the cylinder block with hot soapy water. Clean other components with solvent. Clean carbon from the piston dome with a non metallic parts cleaning brush and solvent. Dry all components with compressed air. Apply a light coat of oil to the piston, piston pin, cylinder bore, bearings, connecting rod and crankshaft to prevent corrosion.

20. Inspect all cylinder block components as described in this chapter.

21. Note the number stamped into the insert bearing faces for each main and the color on the side of each pair of connecting rod bearings (**Figure 70**).

22. If reusing the original cylinder block, connecting rods and crankshaft, order replacement bearings with the same number stamping or color code as the original. If replacing the cylinder block, connecting rod or crankshaft, refer to *Bearing Selection* in this chapter to determine the number or color code for the replacement bearings.

Cylinder block assembly

Refer to **Figure 75.** A ring compressor tool (part No. FT2997) is required for this procedure.

1. Run a white shop cloth through the cylinder to check for debris. Repeat the cleaning process until the cloth passes through clean.

2. Check main bearing clearance as follows:
   a. Clean all oil from the main bearings, cylinder block and crankcase.
   b. Install the bearings (14-17, **Figure 75**) into the cylinder block (11). Align the tabs on the bearings (**Figure 70**) with the notches in the cylinder block. Make sure the correct bearing number is installed at each position in the cylinder block. It is not necessary to install the two thrust bearings (18 and 19, **Figure 75**) into the cylinder block at this time.
   c. Install the bearings (23-27, **Figure 75**) into the crankcase (28). Align the tabs on the bearings (**Figure 70**) with the notches in the cylinder block. Make sure the correct number bearing is installed at each position in the cylinder block. Install the larger thrust bearing (25, **Figure 75**) into the middle bearing position in the crankcase (28).
   d. Carefully lower the crankshaft into the cylinder block and rest it on the bearings. Make sure the tapered flywheel end faces the top of the cylinder block.
   e. Place a section of Plastigage across each main bearing journal (**Figure 71**). Align the locating pins with the corresponding openings then install the crankcase (28, **Figure 75**) onto the cylinder block. Thread all crankcase bolts into the cover and cylinder block. Do not rotate the crankshaft.
   f. Tighten the six 8 mm crankcase stud bolts (31, **Figure 75**) and the two 8 × 95 mm bolts that align with the stud bolts in sequence (1-8, **Figure 77**) to 221 in.-lb. (25.0 N•m). Tighten the eight 10 mm inner crankcase bolts in sequence (9-16, **Figure 77**) to 30 ft.-lb. (40.0 Nm.). Tighten the thirteen 8 mm outer crankcase bolts in sequence (17-29, **Figure 77**) to 124 in.-lb. (14.0 N•m).

7

g. Tighten the six 8 mm stud bolts, the two 8 × 95 mm bolts that align with the stud bolts and the eight 10 mm inner bolts an additional 90° of rotation in sequence (1-16, **Figure 77**). The points on the hex heads are 60° apart and can be used for reference during the tightening process. Tighten the thirteen 8 mm outer bolts a second time in sequence (17-29, **Figure 77**) to 248 in.-lb. (28.0 N•m).
h. Loosen the crank case bolts 1/4 turn at a time in the reverse order of the tightening sequence (29-1, **Figure 77**) until they rotate freely. Remove the bolts then lift the crankcase from the cylinder block.
i. Measure each main bearing clearance by comparing the width of the Plastigage to the markings on the Plastigage envelope (**Figure 72**). The main bearing clearance must be 0.001-0.002 in. (0.025-0.050 mm). Incorrect clearance indicates improper bearing selection or excessive bearing or crankshaft wear. Repeat the bearing selection procedure to ensure the proper bearings are installed. See *Bearing Selection* in this chapter. Measure the crankshaft for excessive wear as described in this chapter. See *Cylinder Block Component Inspection and Measurement.* Install new main bearings and measure the clearance if the correct bearings are installed and the crankshaft is not excessively worn.
j. Lift the crankshaft from the cylinder block and clean the Plastigage from the crankshaft and bearing surfaces.

3. Install the crankshaft as follows:
   a. Apply four-stroke outboard engine oil onto the surfaces and install the two thrust bearings (18 and 19, **Figure 75**) into their recesses in the cylinder block (11). The grooved sides of the thrust bearings (**Figure 79**) must face toward the crankshaft surfaces when assembled.
   b. Apply four-stroke outboard engine oil onto the crankshaft main bearings.
   c. Carefully lower the crankshaft into the cylinder block and rest it on the bearings. Make sure the tapered flywheel end faces the top of the cylinder block.
   d. *Slowly* rotate the crankshaft to check for free movement. Remove the crankshaft and check for proper bearing seating and installation if binding or rough movement is detected.
   e. Apply four-stroke outboard engine oil onto the seals lips and carefully slide the upper and lower seals onto the crankshaft ends (**Figure 61**) with the lip side facing inward or toward the crankcase. Seat the seals fully in the cylinder block bores.
4. Install the crankcase as follows:

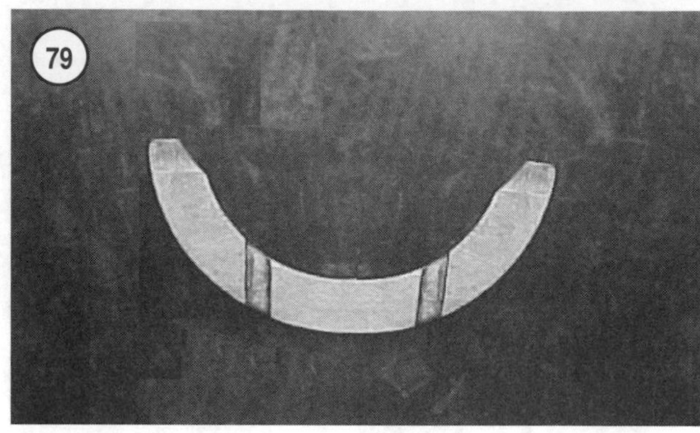

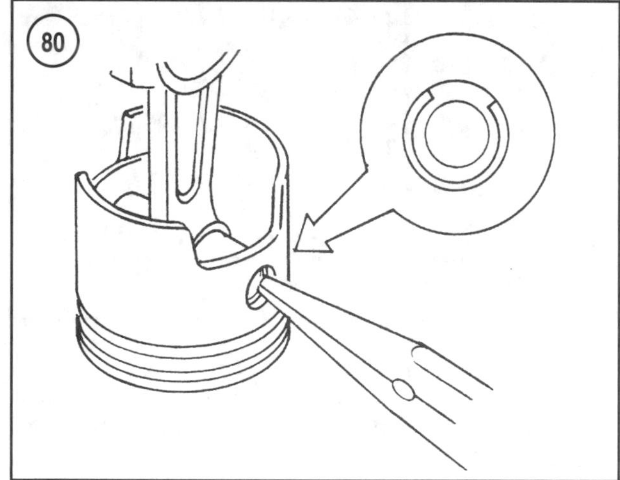

   a. Clean all oil residue or other contamination from the crankcase cover and cylinder block mating surface. Make sure the locating pins are in position in the openings on the cylinder block mating surfaces.
   b. Apply a light even coat of Loctite Master Gasket 514 (part No. 92-12654-2) onto the mating surface of the crankcase cover. Coat the entire mating surface, but do not allow sealant to flow into the bolt holes.
   c. Inspect the crankshaft main bearings inserts and thrust bearings for proper alignment.
   d. Apply four-stroke outboard engine oil onto the surfaces, then install the new O-rings (12 and 13, **Figure 75**) into the recesses in the cylinder block. Make sure the O-rings fit around the oil passage openings.
   e. Inspect the crankshaft seals for correct placement then place the crankcase cover onto the cylinder block. Apply a light coat of four-stroke outboard engine oil to the threads, then install the crankcase cover bolts finger tight.

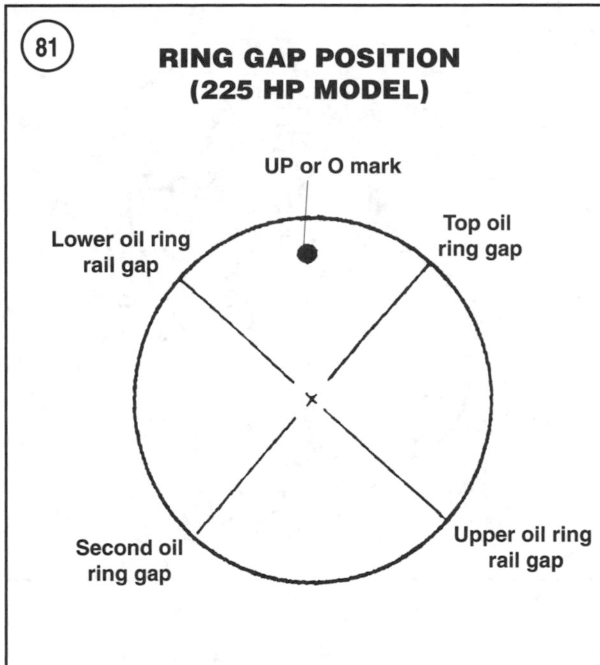

f. Tighten the six 8 mm crankcase stud bolts (31, **Figure 75**) and the two 8 × 95 mm bolts that align with the stud bolts in sequence (1-8, **Figure 77**) to 221 in.-lb. (25.0 N•m). Tighten the eight 10 mm inner crankcase bolts in sequence (9-16, **Figure 77**) to 30 ft.-lb. (40.0 Nm.). Tighten the thirteen 8 mm outer crankcase bolts in sequence (17-29, **Figure 77**) to 124 in.-lb. (14.0 N•m).

g. Tighten the six 8 mm stud bolts, the two 8 × 95 mm bolts that align with the stud bolts and the eight 10 mm inner bolts an additional 90° of rotation in sequence (1-16, **Figure 77**). The points on the hex heads are 60° apart and can be used for reference during the tightening process. Tighten the thirteen 8 mm outer bolts a second time in sequence (17-29, **Figure 77**) to 248 in.-lb. (28.0 N•m).

h. Rotate the crankshaft while checking for smooth rotation. Disassemble the cylinder block and check for and incorrectly installed bearing if binding is evident. Recheck the bearing clearances if binding is evident but the bearings were installed correctly.

5. Assemble the piston and rod assembly as follows:

a. Align the piston pin bores in the piston and connecting rod. Make sure the UP marking on the big end of the connecting rod faces the same direction as the UP marking on the dome of the piston.

b. Lubricate the piston pin bores with engine oil, then push the piston pin (4, **Figure 75**) into the piston and connecting rod bores.

c. Using needlenose pliers, install a new lockrings (5, **Figure 75**) into the groove on each side of the piston pin bore (**Figure 80**). Ensure the lock rings span the notched part of the groove and firmly seat in the groove.

6. Using a ring expander (**Figure 69**), open the new rings just enough to pass over the piston crown. Release the rings into the correct groove on the piston. The top compression ring (1, **Figure 75**) is thinner than the second compression ring (2). Identify the top side of each ring by the RN or T marking near the end gap. The markings must face the top of the piston after installation. Install both oil rails and the spacer into the bottom groove. Ensure the spacer separates the rails.

7. Rotate the lower oil rail so the gap is approximately 45° to the port side of the UP marking on the piston crown. Rotate the top compression ring so the gap is 45° to the starboard side of the UP mark on the piston crown. Rotate the second compression ring so the gap is 180° from the gap in the top compression ring gap. Rotate the upper oil rail to the gap is 180° degrees from the upper rail gap (**Figure 81**).

7

8. Apply four-stroke outboard engine oil onto the piston, piston rings and cylinder wall.

9. Install the piston and rods onto the crankshaft as follows:

a. Fit a ring compressor part No. FT2997 or equivalent over the No. 1 piston and rings. Tighten the compressor enough to fully compress the rings yet still allow the piston to slide through the compressor.

b. Have an assistant help retain the crankshaft in the cylinder block during piston installation. Rest the power head on the side to allow access to the cylinder head and crankcase cover mating surfaces. Carefully rotate the crankshaft until the No. 1 crankpin is at the bottom of its stroke.

c. Insert the No. 1 piston and rod assembly into the cylinder block from the cylinder head side. Ensure the UP marks on the piston and rod face toward the flywheel side of the crankshaft (**Figure 63**). Guide the connecting rod toward the crankshaft during piston installation.

d. Hold the ring compressor firmly against the cylinder block and gently drive the piston into the bore until the piston dome is slightly below the cylinder head mating surface (**Figure 74**). Stop and check for adequate ring compression and/or improper ring alignment if any resistance is detected.

e. Install the bearing inserts into the connecting rods and rod caps. Make sure the bearing tabs (**Figure 67**) are properly aligned with the notches in the connecting rods and rod caps.

10. Check the connecting rod bearing clearance as follows:

a. Place a section of Plastigage onto the crankpin (**Figure 71**).

b. Align the markings on the connecting rod and rod cap (**Figure 62**) then install the rod cap and bearing onto the connecting rod. Install the rod bolts and tighten finger tight only.

c. Tighten both rod bolts to an initial torque of 204 in.-lb. (23.0 N•m). Tighten both bolts a second time to 36 ft.-lb. (48.8 N•m). Tighten each rod bolt an additional 90° of rotation. Do not rotate the crankshaft.

d. Loosen the rod bolts and remove the rod cap.

e. Measure the connecting rod bearing clearance by comparing the width of the Plastigage to the markings on the Plastigage envelope (**Figure 72**). The rod bearing clearance must be 0.0014-0.0028 in. (0.035-0.071 mm). Incorrect clearance indicates improper bearing selection or excessive bearing or crankshaft wear. Repeat the bearing selection procedure to ensure the proper bearings are installed. Measure the crankshaft for excessive wear as described in this chapter. Replace worn or damaged components and check the clearance again.

11. Clean the Plastigage material from the crankshaft and connecting rod bearing. Apply engine oil to the crankshaft and bearings and install the rod cap and new connecting rod bolts. Check for proper rod cap-to-connecting rod alignment. Correct as required. Tighten both rod bolts to an initial torque of 204 in.-lb. (23.0 N•m). Tighten both bolts a second time to 36 ft.-lb. (48.8 N•m). Tighten each rod bolt an additional 90° of rotation.

12. Rotate the crankshaft while checking for smooth rotation. If binding is evident, disassemble the cylinder block and check for an incorrectly installed rod cap or bearing. Recheck the bearing clearances if binding is evident but the bearing and rod caps were installed correctly.

13. Repeat Steps 4-12 for the remaining five piston-and-rod assemblies. Rotate the flywheel to position the crankpin at the bottom of its stroke for the corresponding cylinder.

14. Align the openings, then fit the baffle (32, **Figure 75**) onto the stud bolts (31) with the curved side away from the cylinder block. Apply a light coat of Loctite 242 to the threads, then thread the nuts (33, **Figure 75**) onto the stud bolts. Tighten the nuts evenly to 106 in.-lb. (12.0 N•m).

15. Install the shield (36, **Figure 75**) onto the crankcase cover (40). Apply a light coating of Loctite 242 onto the threads, then thread the screws (34, **Figure 75**) and washers (35) into the shield and crankcase cover openings. Tighten the screws evenly to 18.0 in.-lb. (2.0 N•m).

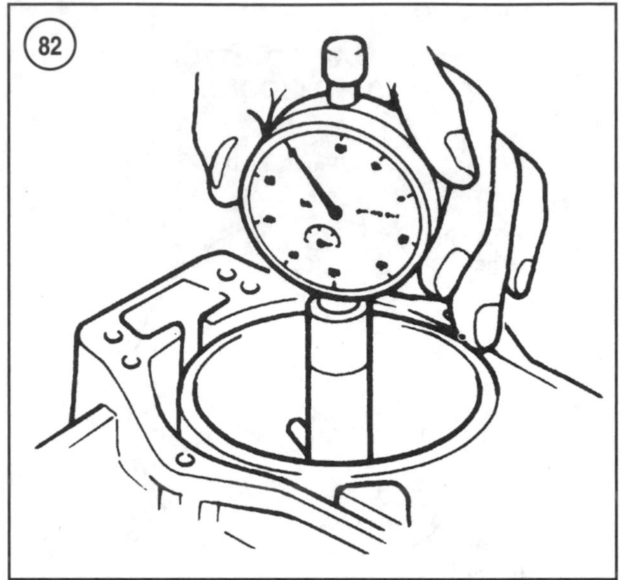

16. If dislodged, install the locating pins (38 and 39, **Figure 75**) into the openings in the crankcase cover (40). Align the locating pin openings, then install a new gasket (37, **Figure 75**) onto the crankcase cover.

17. Align the locating pins with the corresponding openings on the crankcase (28), then seat the crankcase cover onto the crankcase. Apply a light coat of four-stroke outboard engine oil to the threads, then thread the crankcase cover bolts (41, **Figure 75**) into the crankcase cover and crankcase and tighten finger tight.

18. Check for proper gasket and cover alignment. Loosen the bolts and correct the alignment as needed. Tighten the crankcase cover bolts in sequence (1-17, **Figure 76**) to 124 in.-lb. (14.0 N•m). Tighten the bolts a second time in sequence (1-17, **Figure 76**) to 248 in.-lb. (28.0 N•m).

External component installation

1. Install the crankshaft pulley as described in this chapter.
2. Install both cylinder heads, the four camshafts and both camshaft pulleys as described in this chapter.
3. Install the timing belt and tensioner as described in this chapter.
4. Install the exhaust/water jacket covers and thermostats as described in this chapter.
5. Install all electrical and ignition system components as described in Chapter Six.
6. Install the flywheel as described in this chapter.

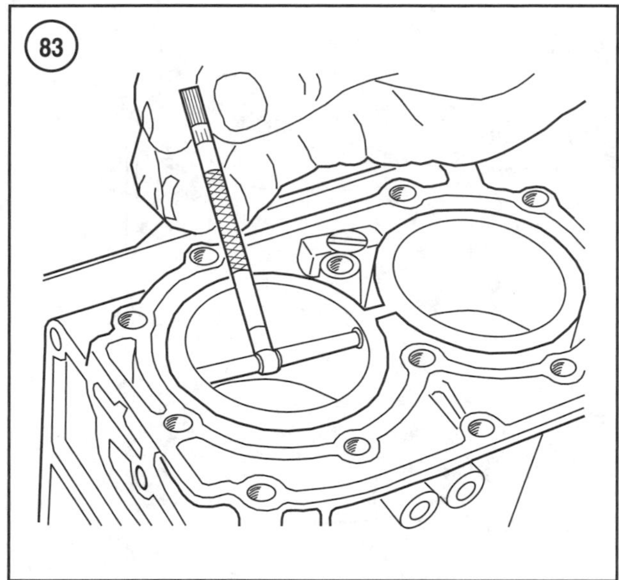

7. Install all fuel system components as described in Chapter Five.

8. Install a new oil filter as described in Chapter Three.

9. Install the power head as described in this chapter.

10. Perform the break-in procedures as described in this chapter.

CYLINDER BLOCK COMPONENT INSPECTION AND MEASUREMENT

Measurement of the power head components requires precision measuring equipment. Have a marine repair shop or machine shop perform the measurements if access is unavailable or you are unfamiliar using with the equipment.

All components must be clean and dry before measuring. Keep the components at room temperature for several hours before measuring them.

Cylinder Bore Inspection and Measurement

1. Inspect the cylinder bores for cracks or deep grooves. Deep grooves or cracks in the cylinder bores indicate damage that cannot be repaired by boring and installing oversize pistons. Replace the cylinder block or have a sleeve installed if the cylinder bore is cracked or deeply scratched. Contact a qualified marine dealership or machine shop to locate a source for block sleeving.

2. Inspect the mounting surfaces for the power head, exhaust/water jacket cover and crankcase cover for cracks or damage. Replace the cylinder block if cracks, deep scratches or gouging is noted.

3. White powder-like deposits in the combustion chamber usually indicate water is entering the combustion chamber. Inspect the cylinder walls and cylinder head thoroughly for cracks if this type of deposit is noted. Inspect the used head gasket and mating surfaces for discolored areas. Discolored or corroded sealing surfaces indicate a likely source of leakage. Replace any defective or suspect components.

4. Inspect all bolt holes for cracks, corrosion or damaged threads. Use a thread chaser to clean the threads of corrosion or sealant. Pay particular attention to the cylinder head bolt holes. Damaged threads can often be repaired by installing a threaded insert. Have a machine shop or qualified professional install the insert if you do not have the required equipment or are unfamiliar with its use.

5. Clean and inspect all bolts, nuts and washers. Replace any bolts or nuts with damaged threads or a stretched appearance. Replace damaged or cup-shaped washers.

6. Inspect the locating pins and pin holes for bent pins or damaged openings. Replace damaged pins or components with damaged pin holes.

NOTE
The cylinder block and crankcase or crankcase cover (75-115 hp models) are a matched assembly. Replace the entire assembly if either portion requires replacement.

7. Have the cylinder bore lightly honed at a marine repair shop or machine shop before taking any measurements. A heavier honing is required if the cylinder bore is glazed or aluminum deposits are present.

8. Use either a dial (**Figure 82**) or telescoping type (**Figure 83**) cylinder bore gauge to measure the cylinder bore.
   a. For 75-115 hp models, measure the cylinder bore diameter at 0.8 in. (20 mm), 2.8 in. (70 mm) and 4.7 in. (120 mm) down from the cylinder head mating surface.
   b. For 225 hp models, measure the cylinder bore diameter at 0.8 in. (20 mm), 2.4 in. (60 mm) and 3.9 in. (100 mm) down from the cylinder head mating surface.

9. Take the measurements at 90° (**Figure 84**) apart at all three depths. Record all six measurements for each cylinder.

10. Compare the measurements with specification in **Table 6**. A prior repair to the power head may have required boring and the installation of a 0.010 in. (0.25 mm) oversize piston. Measure the pistons to determine if the cylin-

der has been bored. Add this amount to the standard bore specification for bored cylinders.

Refer to the following recommendations:

a. If the cylinder bore is within the standard bore diameter specification, use a standard size piston in that location.
b. If the cylinder has not be previously bored, but bore diameter exceeds standard bore diameter specification, have the cylinder bored to the oversize specification and install an 0.010 in. (0.25 mm) oversize piston in that location.
c. If the cylinder bore is within the oversize bore diameter specification, use an 0.010 in. (0.25 mm) oversize piston in that location.
d. If the cylinder bore diameter exceeds the oversize specification, replace the cylinder block or have a sleeve installed and use a standard piston in that location.

CAUTION
Always check the availability of oversize pistons before having the cylinder bored.

11. Subtract the smallest cylinder diameter from the largest diameter to determine the cylinder taper from the top to the bottom of the bore. Compare the result with the maximum cylinder taper specification in **Table 6**.
12. Subtract the smallest cylinder bore diameter at a given depth with the diameter at the same depth 90° apart to determine the out-of-round measurement. Compare the result with the maximum out-of-round specification in **Table 6**.
13. Have the cylinder bored and install an oversize piston in that location if the taper or out-of-round exceeds the specification. Replace the cylinder block or have a sleeve installed if the taper or out of round exceeds the specification and the cylinder has been previously bored.
14. Repeat the cylinder bore measurements for all cylinders.

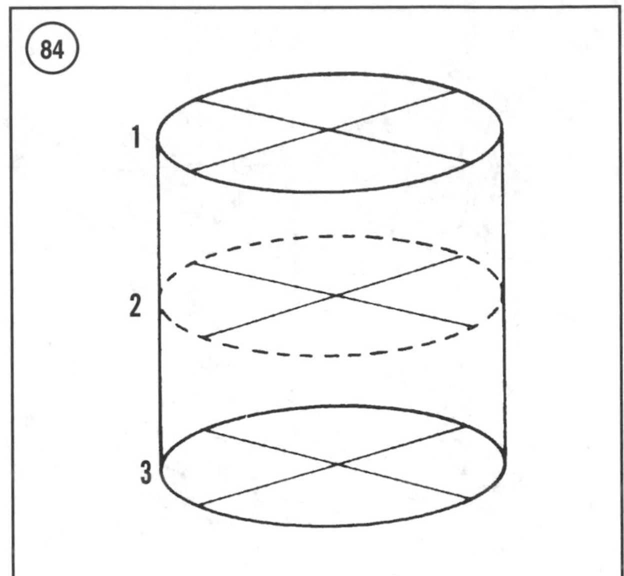

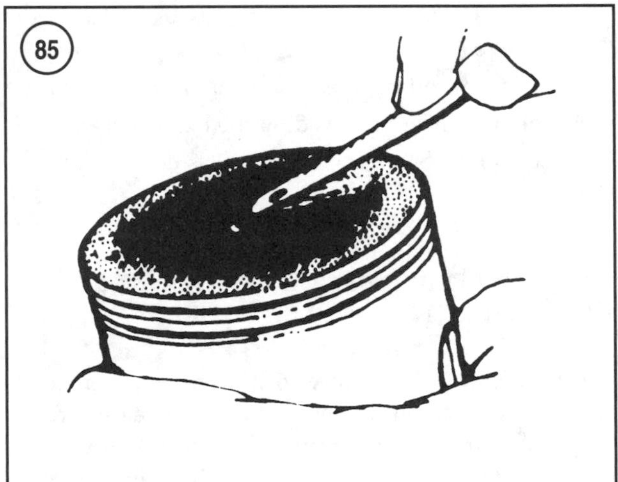

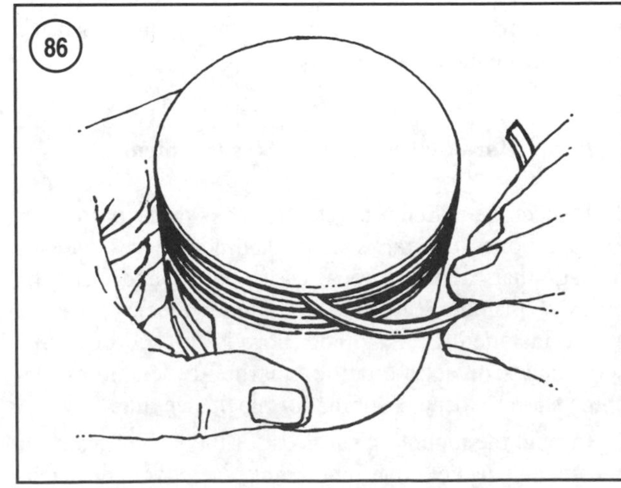

Piston and Rings Inspection and Measurement

1. Use a blunt scraper to remove carbon deposits from the piston dome (**Figure 85**).
2. Clean the piston ring grooves using a piece of broken ring (**Figure 86**). Use only the ring originally installed on the piston.
3. Use solvent and a bristle brush to clean all remaining deposits from the piston surfaces. Dry the piston with compressed air.
4. Inspect the piston for eroded surfaces at the edge of the dome, cracks near the ring grooves, cracks or missing por-

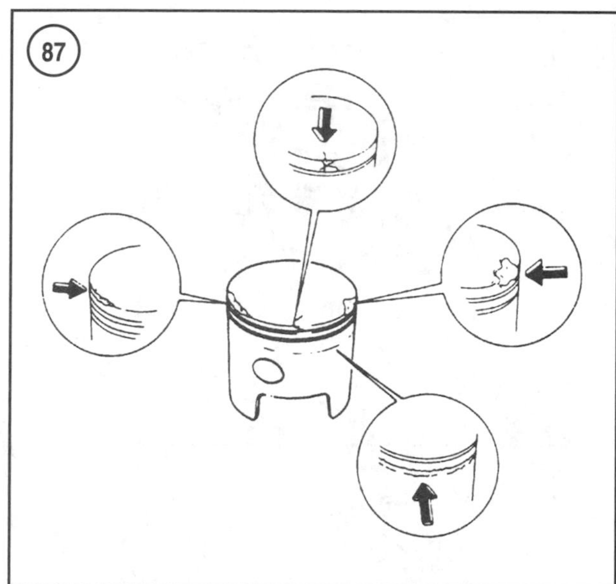

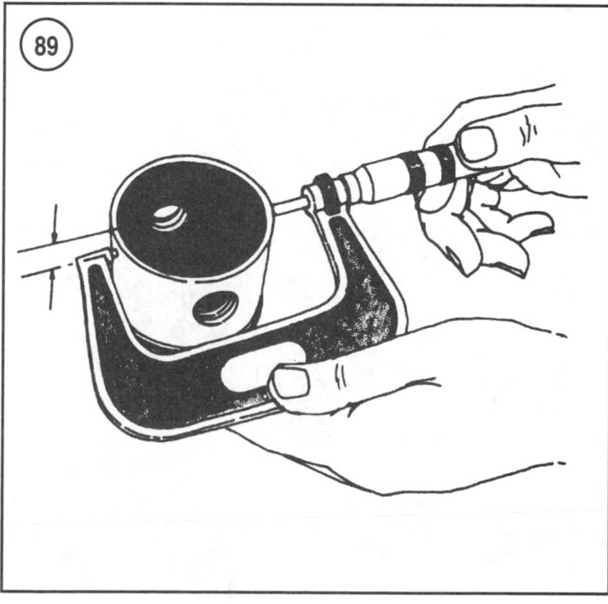

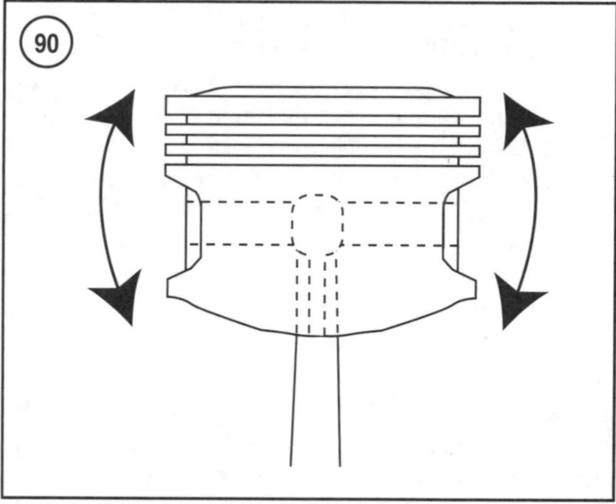

7

tions in the piston dome (**Figure 87**). Inspect for erosion in the ring groove and scoring or scuffing on the piston skirt (**Figure 88**).

5. Inspect the piston pin for wear, discoloration or a scrubbed appearance. Inspect the lockring groove for damage or erosion. Replace the piston if any of these defects are noted.

6. Replace the rings if the piston is removed from the cylinder. Low compression, high oil consumption and other problems may surface if used rings are installed.

7. Using an outside micrometer, measure and record the diameter of the piston at a point 90° from the piston pin bore and 0.51 in. (13.0 mm) from the bottom of the skirt. (**Figure 89**). Compare the diameter to the specification in **Table 7**.

   a. On 75-115 hp models, replace the piston and rod assembly if the piston diameter is less than the minimum specification.
   b. On 225 hp models, replace the piston if the diameter is less than the minimum specification.

8. Measure and record the piston diameter for the remaining pistons.

9A. On 75-115 hp models, pivot the piston on the piston pin and connecting rod to check for binding or play. The piston should pivot on the pin without detectable looseness or play. Rock the piston side to side (**Figure 90**) to check for play in the piston pin bore, piston pin or connecting rod bore. Normal wear results in barely any play in this area. Replace the piston and connecting rod assembly if binding or excessive play is evident.

9B. On 225 hp models, measure the piston pin and pin bores for excessive wear. Instructions follow:

   a. Using an inside micrometer measure the piston pin bore diameter at both openings (**Figure 91**). Replace the piston and piston pin if either diameter exceeds 0.8280 in. (21.03 mm).

b. Use an outside micrometer to measure the pin bore diameter along the entire length of the pin (**Figure 92**). Replace the piston and piston pin if the diameter is less than 0.8268 in. (21.00 mm) at any point on the pin.

c. Use an inside micrometer to measure the pin bore diameter in the connecting rod (**Figure 93**). Replace the connecting rod if the bore exceeds 0.8268 in. (21.00 mm).

10. Temporarily install new rings into the piston ring grooves as described in the cylinder block assembly instructions in this chapter. Using a feeler gauge, measure the clearance between the side of the ring and the side of the ring groove (**Figure 94**). The ring side clearance equals the thickness of the feeler gauge that passes between the ring and the ring groove with a light drag. Record the side clearance measurements for all rings on all of the pistons. Remove the piston rings and compare the measurements with the specifications in **Table 7**. Refer the following recommendations.

a. On 75-115 hp models, replace the piston if the clearance is not within the specification in **Table 7**.

b. On 225 hp models, if the ring side clearance is not within the specification, use feeler gauges to measure the width of the ring grooves. The ring groove width equals the thickness of feeler gauges that pass through the groove with a slight drag. Replace the piston if the ring groove width is not within the specification in **Table 7**. If the ring groove is within the specification yet the side clearance is not correct, try another new ring in the groove and repeat the side clearance measurement.

Piston-to-Cylinder Clearance Measurement

1. Perform this calculation for each cylinder using the recorded piston and cylinder bore diameters. Subtract the piston diameter from the largest measured cylinder bore diameter for the given cylinder. The results indicate the largest clearance (**Figure 95**).

2. Subtract the piston diameter from the smallest cylinder bore diameter for the given cylinder. The results indicate the smallest clearance. Compare the largest and smallest clearance with the specification in **Table 7**.

3. Excessive clearance indicates excessive cylinder bore diameter or below minimum piston diameter. Inadequate clearance indicates a bore diameter that is too small or a piston that is too large. Replace the piston or bore the cylinder to the next oversize to correct the clearance.

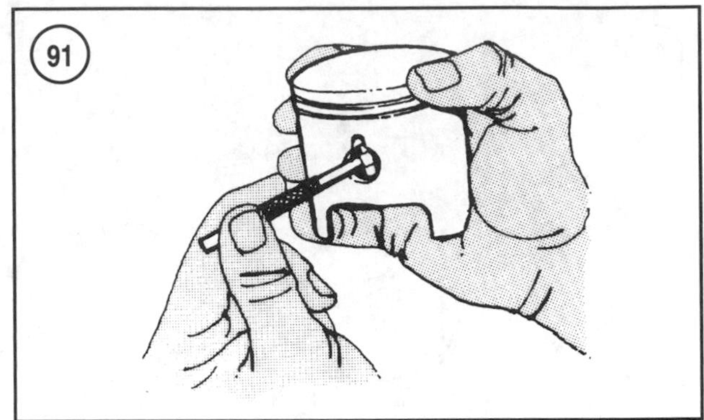
91

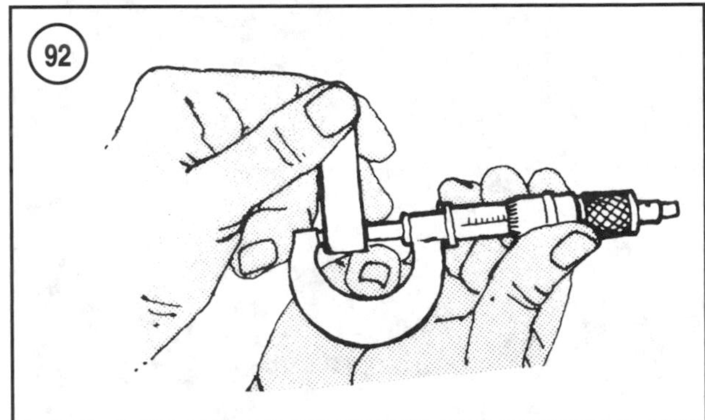
92

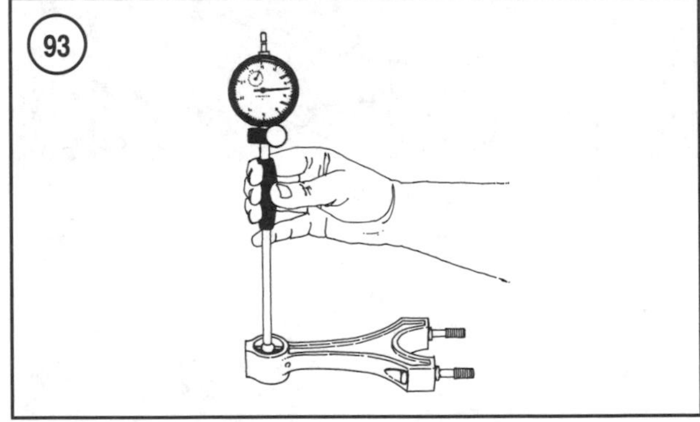
93

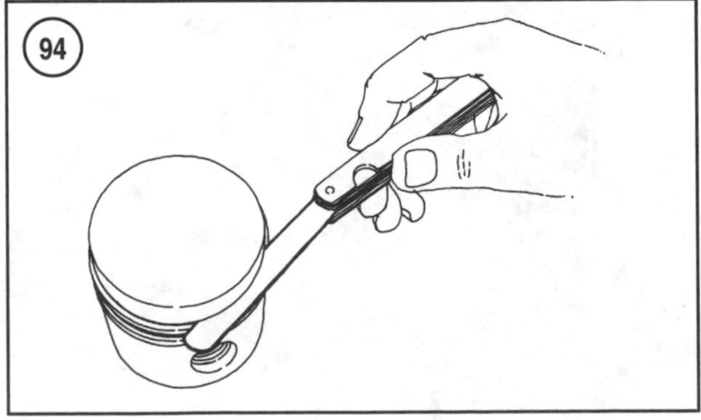
94

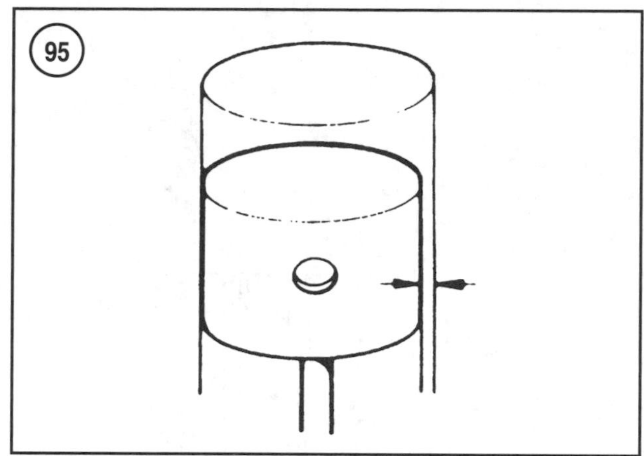

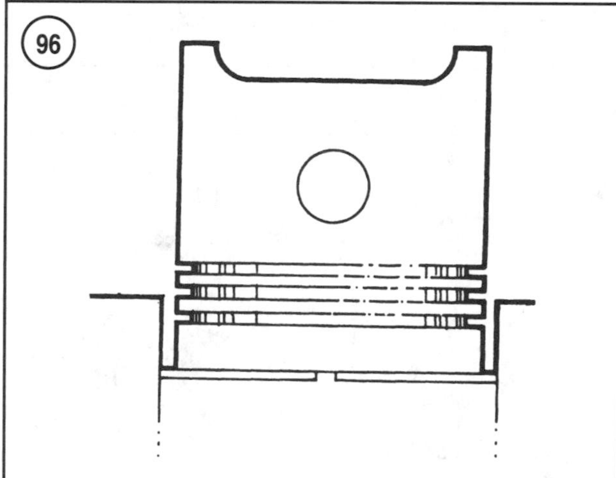

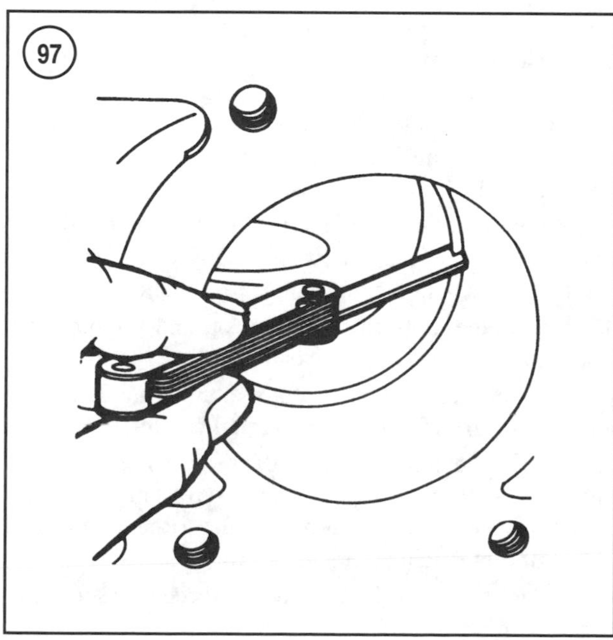

Ring End Gap Measurement

1. Using a piston without rings (**Figure 96**), push a new piston ring into the No. 1 cylinder bore to a depth of 0.8 in. (20 mm) from the cylinder head side of the cylinder block surface.
2. Using feeler gauges, measure the width of the ring gap (**Figure 97**). The ring gap equals the width of the feeler gauge that passes through the gap with a slight drag.
3. Compare the ring gap measurement with the specification in **Table 7** then refer to the following:
    a. If the ring end gap is within the specification, use the new ring in the cylinder during the assembly.
    b. If the ring gap is not within the specification, measure the cylinder bore as described in this section. If the cylinder bore diameter is within the specification, repeat the ring gap measurement using another new piston ring. Continue until a ring with the correct gap is selected for the cylinder and piston ring position.
4. Repeat Steps 1-3 until rings with correct gap measurements are selected for all piston ring positions for each cylinder. Tag the rings to ensure they are installed onto the correct piston and into the correct cylinder bore.

7

Connecting Rod Inspection

Use solvent and a bristle brush to thoroughly clean the connecting rod surfaces. Dry the connecting rods with compressed air.

NOTE
Some minor surface corrosion, glaze-like deposits or minor scratches can be removed with crocus cloth or 320 grit Carburundum. Polish the surfaces enough to remove the deposits.

Inspect each connecting rod for a bent condition, discoloration and worn or damaged bearing surfaces (**Figure 98**). Replace the connecting rod if these or other defects are evident.

Connecting Rod Side Clearance Measurement

Perform this operation on 225 hp models. The manufacture does not provide side clearance specifications for 75-115 hp models.

1. Install the No. 1 connecting rod, with the bearings installed, onto the crankshaft as described in the cylinder block assembly instructions in this chapter. It is not necessary to install the crankshaft into the cylinder block to perform this measurement.
2. Using feeler gauges, measure the clearance between the connecting rod and the side of the crankshaft journal (**Figure 99**). The connecting rod side clearance equals the thickness of the feeler gauge that passes between the side of the connecting rod and crankshaft surface with a slight drag.
3. Record the side clearance, then remove the connecting rod from the crankshaft.
4. Repeat Steps 1-3 for the each of the connecting rods.
5. The connecting rod side clearance must be 0.008-0.010 in. (0.20-0.25 mm) for each connecting rod. Refer to the following recommendations:
    a. If side clearance is within the specification, use the connecting rod in the corresponding location on the crankshaft.
    b. If side clearance is less than the specification, improper rod cap to connecting rod alignment is indicated. Verify proper alignment and repeat the measurement.
    c. If side clearance exceeds the specification, replace the connecting rod and repeat the measurement. Replace the crankshaft if the clearance exceeds the specification with the new connecting rod.

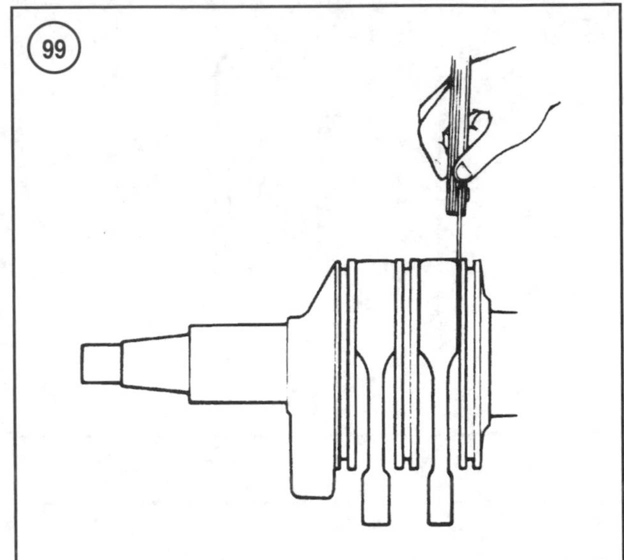

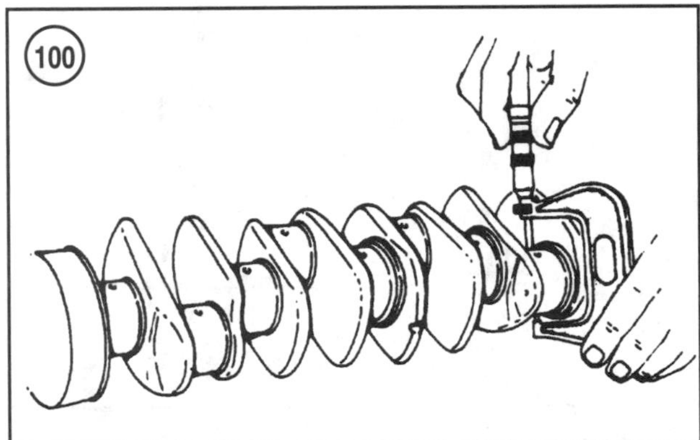

Crankshaft and Bearing Inspection

Inspect the crankshaft for cracks, corrosion etching, bluing or discoloration. Also check for rough or irregular surfaces or transferred bearing material. Replace the crankshaft if these or other defects are evident. Grinding the crankshaft and installing undersize bearings is not recommended.

Inspect the insert bearings and thrust bearings (**Figure 79**) for corrosion, discoloration and rough surfaces. Replace the bearings if not found in excellent condition.

NOTE

Some minor surface corrosion, deposits or minor scratches can be removed with crocus cloth or 320 grit Carburundum. Polish the surfaces only enough to remove the deposits. Excessive polishing can remove excessive material and damage the crankshaft surfaces.

Crankshaft Measurement

1. Using an outside micrometer, measure each of the crankpin and main bearing journal diameters (**Figure 100**). Record each of the measurements.
2. Compare the measurements with the specification in **Table 5**. Replace the crankshaft if any of the measurements are less than the minimum specification.
3. Support the crankshaft on the top and bottom main bearing journals with V-blocks or a balance wheel.
4. Position a dial indicator at a remaining main bearing journal (**Figure 101**) or other parallel bearing surface.
5. Observe the dial indicator movement while slowly rotating the crankshaft. Repeat the measurement with the indicator at each main bearing surface. Record the dial indicator movement as crankshaft runout.
6. Replace the crankshaft if runout exceeds the specification in **Table 5**.

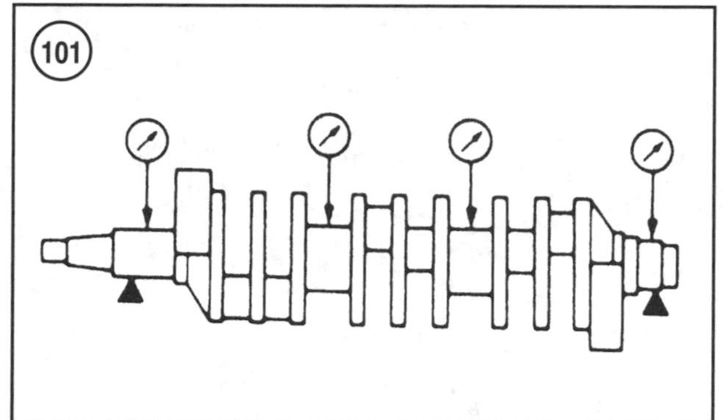

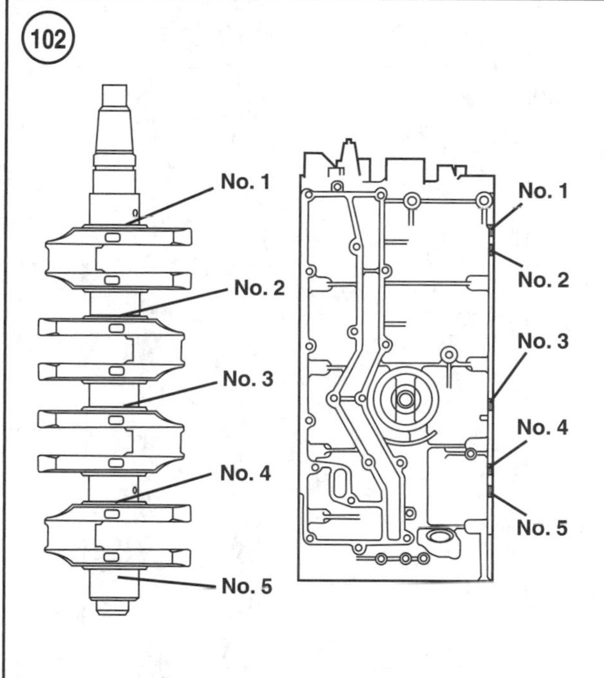

BEARING SELECTION

Perform the bearing selection procedures if replacing the crankshaft, cylinder block or connecting rod(s). Use the same color or number code bearing as the original if using the original crankshaft, cylinder block and connecting rod(s).

Main Bearing Selection

75-115 hp models

Perform this procedure if replacing the cylinder block or crankshaft. If using the original components, use the same bearing color code in all locations as the original bearing. Select the main bearings by reading number codes stamped into the crankshaft and cylinder block (**Figure 102**).

1. Determine the crankshaft main journal diameter for the top main bearing by reading the code for the No. 1 (top) journal (**Figure 102**).
   a. Multiply the number stamped into the crankshaft by 0.001. Add the results to the base measurement of 47.9.
   b. Record the results as the *crankshaft main journal diameter.*
   c. Read the codes and perform the calculation for the remaining four main bearing surfaces. Record all results.
2. Determine the main bearing bore diameter by reading the codes stamped in starboard side of the cylinder block (**Figure 102**). Read the code for the top or No. 1 main bearing bore.
   a. Multiply this number by 0.001. Add the results to a base measurement of 54.0.
   b. Record the results as the main bearing bore diameter.
   c. Read the codes and perform the calculations for the remaining four main bearing bores. Record all results.
3. Subtract the calculated crankshaft main journal diameter from the calculated main bearing bore diameter and refer to **Table 8**.
4. Install bearings with the indicated color code in the specified location. Install the bearing with the oil groove only in the cylinder block side. Repeat the calculation and bearing selection for the remaining locations.
5. Measure the bearing clearance as described in the assembly procedures. Excessive main bearing clearance with new and correct color bearings indicates excessive crankshaft wear. Measure the crankshaft and check all calculations before replacing the crankshaft. Inadequate oil clearance indicates incorrect bearing selection or improperly installed components.

225 hp model

Perform this procedure if replacing the cylinder block or crankshaft. If using the original components, use the same bearing number in all location as the original bearing. Select the main bearings by reading number codes stamped into the crankshaft and cylinder block (**Figure 103**).

1. Read and record the No. 1 main bearing code on the port side of the cylinder block (**Figure 103**).
2. Read and record the No. 1 main bearing code on the bottom crankshaft flyweight (**Figure 103**).

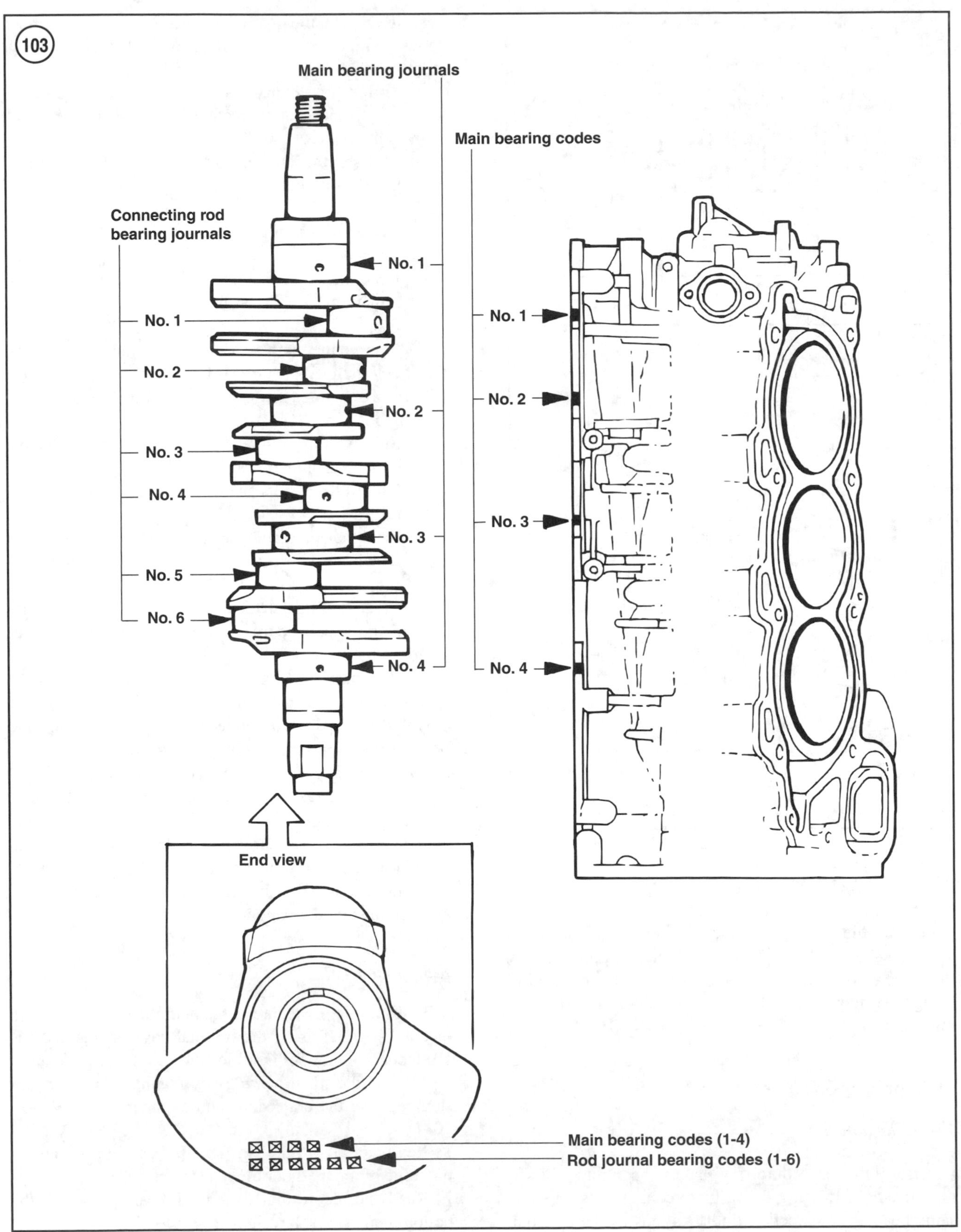
103
Main bearing journals
Main bearing codes
Connecting rod bearing journals
No. 1
No. 1
No. 2
No. 2
No. 3
No. 4
No. 3
No. 5
No. 6
No. 4
No. 1
No. 2
No. 3
No. 4
End view
Main bearing codes (1-4)
Rod journal bearing codes (1-6)

3. Refer to **Table 9** to determine which bearing number to select for the specified main bearing.
4. Repeat Steps 1-3 for each of the remaining four main bearing locations.
5. Assemble the cylinder block using the specified bearing number for the individual locations.
6. Measure the clearance as described in the assembly procedures. Excessive main bearing clearance with new and correct number bearings indicates excessive crankshaft wear. Measure the crankshaft and check all calculations before replacing the crankshaft. Inadequate oil clearance indicates incorrect bearing selection or improperly installed components.

Connecting Rod Bearing Selection

75 and 90 hp models

Perform this procedure when replacing the crankshaft or connecting rod(s). If using the original components, use the same bearing color code in all locations as the original bearing. A pair of yellow code connecting rod bearings are required for this procedure.
1. Install the crankshaft into the cylinder block as described in the assembly procedures. See *Cylinder Block Assembly (75-115 hp Models)*. Install the piston and connecting rod assembly into the No. 1 cylinder using two yellow code bearings in the connecting rod.
2. Measure the connecting rod bearing clearance as described in the assembly procedures. Record the clearance, then remove the bearing from the connecting rod. Remove the piston and rod assembly from the cylinder bore.
3. Repeat Step 1 and 2 for the remaining piston and rod assemblies.
4. Refer to **Table 10** to determine the correct color bearings to use in each location for the clearance measured with the yellow code bearings.
5. Assemble the cylinder block using the specified bearings and measure the bearing clearance as described in the assembly procedures. Excessive rod bearing clearance with new and correct number bearings indicates excessive crankshaft wear. Measure the crankshaft and check all calculations before replacing the crankshaft. Inadequate oil clearance indicates incorrect bearing selection or improperly installed components.

225 hp model

Perform this procedure if replacing the crankshaft. If using the original crankshaft, use the same bearing color code in all locations as the original bearing. Select new main bearings by reading rod journal bearing codes on the bottom crankshaft flyweight (**Figure 103**).

1. Read the rod journal bearing codes for cylinders 1-6. The codes read left to right starting with the code for the No. 1 journal.

2. Refer to **Table 11** to determine the bearing color codes to use for the number code. Record the specified number code for all six rod journal locations.

3. Assemble the cylinder block using the specified bearings in all locations and measure the bearing clearance as described in the assembly procedures. Excessive rod bearing clearance with new and correct number bearings indicates excessive crankshaft wear. Measure the crankshaft and check all calculations before replacing the crankshaft. Inadequate oil clearance indicates incorrect bearing selection or improperly installed components.

ENGINE BREAK-IN PROCEDURES

Perform the break-in procedure any time internal components of the power head are replaced. During the first few hours of running, many of the components of the power head must avoid full load until fully seated. Failure to properly break in the engine can result in power head failure, decreased performance, shorter engine life and increased oil consumption.

Full break-in is requires approximately 10 hours of running time. Increased oil consumption can be expected during this period. Check the oil level *frequently* during break-in. Check and correct the tightness of all external fasteners during the break-in period.

1. During the first hour of the break-in period, do not exceed 3500 rpm or half throttle. Do not run more than a few minutes at a given throttle setting.

2. During the second hour of operation, advance the engine to full throttle for a period of one- to two-minute intervals. Otherwise run the engine at 3/4 throttle or 4500 rpm or less during the second hour.

3. During the next eight hours, operate the engine at full throttle for a maximum of five minutes at a time. Otherwise run the engine at any throttle settings below full throttle.

Table 1 POWER HEAD TORQUE SPECIFICATIONS

Fastener	in.-lb.	ft.-lb.	N•m
Baffle plate nuts			
225 hp models	106	–	12.0
Camshaft caps			
Initial torque	70	–	7.9
Final torque	150	–	16.9
Camshaft pulley			
75-115 hp models	–	44	60.0
Connecting rod bolts			
75-115 hp models			
Initial torque*	132*	–	14.9*
225 hp models			
Initial torque*	204*	17*	23.0*
Second torque*	–	36*	48.8*
Crankcase bolts			
225 hp models			
Stud bolts			
Initial torque*	221*	–	25.0*
8 × 95 mm bolts*			
Initial torque*	221*	–	25.0*
10 mm inner bolts			
Initial torque*	–	30*	40.0*
8 mm outer bolts			
Initial torque	124	–	14.0
Final torque	248	–	28.0
Crankcase cover bolts			
75-115 hp models			
8 mm bolts			
Initial torque	120	–	13.6
Final torque	240	20	27.1
10 mm bolts			
Initial torque*	168*	–	19.0*
225 hp models			
Initial torque	124	–	14.0
Final torque	248	–	28.0
Crankcase cover shield			
225 hp models	18	–	2.0
Crankshaft pulley nut			
75-115 hp models	–	195	264
Crankshaft pulley screws			
225 hp models	62	–	7.0
Cylinder head bolts			
75-115 hp models			
8 mm bolts			
Initial torque	120	–	13.6
Final torque	240	20	27.1
10 mm bolts			
Initial torque	132	–	14.9
Second torque*	–	24*	32.5*
225 hp models			
8 mm bolts			
Initial torque	124	–	14.0
Final torque	248	21	28.0
10 mm bolts			
Initial torque	168	–	19.0
Second torque*	–	27*	37.0*

(continued)

Table 1 POWER HEAD TORQUE SPECIFICATIONS (continued)

Fastener	in.-lb.	ft.-lb.	N•m
Exhaust/water jacket cover			
Initial torque	53	–	6.0
Final torque	106	–	12.0
Flywheel cover			
75-115 hp models	65	–	7.3
225 hp models	71	–	8.0
Flywheel nut			
75-115 hp models	–	140	190.0
225 hp models	–	177	240.0
Hose and cable grommet cover			
75-115 hp models	65	–	7.3
Ignition coil mounting plate			
225 hp models	71	–	8.0
Drive shaft housing cover screws			
115 hp models	65	–	7.3
225 hp models	70	–	7.9
Oil pump mounting			
225 hp models	71	–	8.0
Power head mounting fasteners			
75-115 hp models			
Nuts and washers	–	40	54.2
Bolts	240	20	27.1
225 hp models			
Bolts	–	31	42.0
Spark plug cover			
75-115 hp models	65	–	7.3
Spark plug/coil cover			
225 hp models	35	–	4.0
Tensioner pulley bolt	–	29	39.3
Thermostat cover			
75-115 hp models	70	–	7.9
Timing chain tensioner			
225 hp models	105	–	11.9
Valve cover	70	–	7.9
Valve cover deflector plate			
75-115 hp models	17	–	1.9
225 hp models	18	–	2.0
Water pressure relief valve cover			
75-115 hp models	70	–	7.9

*Not the final tightening torque. Refer to the text for specific tightening instructions.

Table 2 VALVE SERVICE SPECIFICATIONS

Measurement	Specification
Margin thickness	
75-90 hp models	
Intake valve	0.018-0.026 in. (0.46-0.66 mm)
Exhaust valve	0.026-0.033 in. (0.66-0.84 mm)
115 hp models	
Intake valve	0.031-0.047 in. (0.79-1.19 mm)
Exhaust valve	0.039-0.055 in. (0.99-1.40 mm)
225 hp models	
Intake valve	0.028 in. (0.71 mm)*
Exhaust valve	0.039 in. (0.99 mm)*

(continued)

7

Table 2 VALVE SERVICE SPECIFICATIONS (continued)

Measurement	Specification
Maximum valve stem runout	0.001 in. (0.025 mm)
Valve seat width	
75 and 90 hp models	
Intake valve	0.014-0.022 in. (0.36-0.56 mm)
Exhaust valve	0.014-0.022 in. (0.36-0.56 mm)
115 hp models	
Intake valve	0.062-0.076 in. (1.57-1.93 mm)
Exhaust valve	0.071-0.080 in. (1.80-2.03 mm)
225 hp models	
Intake valve	0.043-0.055 in. (1.09-1.40 mm)
Exhaust valve	0.055-0.067 in. (1.40-1.70 mm)
Stem diameter	
75-115 hp models	
Intake valve	0.2352-0.2358 in. (5.974-5.989 mm)
Exhaust valve	0.2346-0.2352 in. (5.959-5.974 mm)
225 hp models	
Intake valve	0.2156-0.2162 in. (5.476-5.491 mm)
Exhaust valve	0.2151-0.2157 in. (5.464-5.479 mm)
Stem to guide clearance	
75-115 hp models	
Intake valve	0.0006-0.0017 in. (0.015-0.043 mm)
Exhaust valve	0.0012-0.0023 in. (0.030-0.058 mm)
225 hp models	
Intake valve	
Exhaust valve	0.0004-0.0008 in. (0.010-0.020 mm)
Valve guide bore	
75-115 hp models	0.2364-0.2369 in. (6.004-6.017 mm)
225 hp models	0.2169-0.2173 in. (5.509-5.519 mm)

*Replace the valve if the margin is less than the specification.

Table 3 VALVE SPRING SERVICE SPECIFICATIONS

Measurement	Specification
Maximum out of square	
75-115 hp models	0.099 in. (2.51 mm)
225 hp models	0.059 in. (1.50 mm)
Free length	
75 and 90 hp models	2.057 in. (52.25 mm)*
115 hp models	2.094 in. (53.19 mm)*
225 hp models	1.677-1.740 in. (42.60-44.20 mm)

*Replace the valve spring if the free length is less than the specification.

Table 4 CAMSHAFT SERVICE SPECIFICATIONS

Measurement	Specification
Bearing journals	0.9827-0.9835 in. (24.961-24.981 mm)
Camshaft bore (cylinder head)	0.9843-0.9850 in. (25.00-25.019 mm)
Camshaft bearing journal to bore clearance	0.0008-0.0024 in. (0.020-0.061 mm)
Lobe length	
75-115 hp models	
Intake	1.465-1.472 in. (37.21-37.39 mm)
Exhaust	1.453-1.459 in. (36.91-37.06 mm)

(continued)

Table 4 CAMSHAFT SERVICE SPECIFICATIONS (continued)

Measurement	Specification
Lobe length (continued)	
225 hp models	
Intake	1.7835-1.7874 in. (35.301-45.400 mm)
Exhaust	1.7854-1.7894 in. (45.349-45.451 mm)
Lobe width	
75-115 hp models	
Intake	1.178-1.184 in. (29.92-30.07 mm)
Exhaust	1.178-1.184 in. (29.92-30.07 mm)
225 hp models	
Intake	1.4154-1.4193 in. (35.951-36.050 mm)
Exhaust	1.4154-1.4193 in. (35.951-36.050 mm)
Maximum camshaft runout	0.0039 in. (0.099 mm)
Valve lifter bore (cylinder head)	
75-115 hp models	1.102-1.103 in. (27.991-28.016 mm)
225 hp models	1.2984-1.2992 in. (32.979-33.000 mm)

7

Table 5 CRANKSHAFT SERVICE SPECIFICATIONS

Measurement	Specification
Connecting rod bearing clearance	
75 and 90 hp models	0.0009-0.0014 in. (0.023-0.035 mm)
115 hp models	0.0010-0.0012 in. (0.025-0.031 mm)
225 hp models	0.0014-0.0028 in. (0.035-0.071 mm)
Connecting rod side clearance	
225 hp models	0.008-0.010 in. (0.20-0.25 mm)
Main bearing clearance	
75-115 hp models	0.0009-0.0017 in. (0.24-0.44 mm)
225 hp models	0.0010-0.0020 in. (0.025-0.050 mm)
Crankpin journal diameter	
75-115 hp models	1.7311 in. (43.971 mm)*
225 hp models	1.9676-1.9685 in. (49.976-50.000 mm)
Main bearing journal diameter	
75-115 hp models	1.8887 in. (47.972 mm)*
225 hp models	2.4791-2.4800 in. (62.968-62.992 mm)
Maximum crankshaft runout	0.001 in. (0.03 mm)

*Minimum specification. Replace the crankshaft if the measurement is less than the specification.

Table 6 CYLINDER BORE SERVICE SPECIFICATIONS

Measurement	Specification
Cylinder bore diameter	
75-115 hp models	
Standard bore diameter	3.1102-3.1110 in. (79.000-79.020 mm)
Oversize bore diameter	3.1201-3.1209 in. (79.250-79.272 mm)
225 hp models	
Standard bore diameter	3.7008-3.7016 in. (94.000-94.020 mm)

(continued)

Table 6 CYLINDER BORE SERVICE SPECIFICATIONS (continued)

Measurement	Specification
Maximum cylinder bore taper	
75-115 hp models	0.003 in. (0.076 mm)
225 hp models	0.002 in. (0.051 mm)
Maximum cylinder bore out-of-round	
75-115 hp models	0.003 in. (0.076 mm)
225 hp models	0.002 in. (0.051 mm)

Table 7 PISTON SERVICE SPECIFICATIONS

Measurement	Specification
Connecting rod pin bore diameter	
225 hp models	0.8268 in. (21.00 mm)
Piston diameter	
75-115 hp models	
Standard piston	3.1074-3.1082 in. (78.928-78-949 mm)
Oversize piston	3.1174-3.1182 in. (79.178-79.199 mm)
Piston pin bore diameter	
225 hp models	0.8276-0.8280 in. (21.02-21.03 mm)
Piston pin diameter	
225 hp models	0.8268 in. (21.00 mm)
Piston ring end gap	
75-115 hp models	
Top compression ring	0.006-0.012 in. (0.15-0.30 mm)
Second compression ring	0.028-0.035 in. (0.70-0.90 mm)
Oil control ring	0.008-0.028 in. (0.02-0.70 mm)
225 hp models	
Top compression ring	0.006-0.012 in. (0.15-0.30 mm)
Second compression ring	0.012-0.018 in. (0.30-0.45 mm)
Oil control ring	0.006-0.024 in. (0.15-0.60 mm)
Piston ring side clearance	
75-115 hp models	
Top compression ring	0.001-0.003 in. (0.02-0.08 mm)
Second compression ring	0.001-0.003 in. (0.03-0.08 mm)
Oil control ring	0.001-0.006 in. (0.03-0.15 mm)
225 hp models	
Top compression ring	0.002-0.003 in. (0.05-0.08 mm)
Second compression ring	0.001-0.003 in. (0.03-0.08 mm)
Oil control ring	0.002-0.005 in. (0.05-0.13 mm)
Piston to cylinder clearance	
75-115 hp models	0.0028-0.0031 in. (0.070-0.080 mm)
225 hp models	0.0030-0.0031 in. (0.075-0.080 mm)
Ring groove width	
225 hp models	
Top ring groove	0.0484-0.0492 in. (1.23-1.25 mm)
Second ring groove	0.0480-0.0488 in. (1.22-1.24 mm)
Bottom ring groove	0.0988-0.0996 in. (2.51-2.53 mm)

Table 8 MAIN BEARING SELECTION (75-115 HP MODELS)

Calculated diameter (mm)	Cylinder side bearing color (with oil groove)	Crankcase side bearing color (without oil groove)
6.023-6.026	Green	Yellow
6.027-6.034	Blue	Green
6.035-6.042	Blue	Blue
6.043-6.049	Red	Blue
6.050-6.058	Red	Red

Table 9 MAIN BEARING SELECTION (225 HP MODELS)

Cylinder block main bearing code	Crankshaft main bearing code	Bearing No.
00-04	68-76	2
00-03	80-83	1
00	77	1
00-01	78-79	1
00-07	84-92	1
01	77	2
02	77-78	2
02	79	1
03-04	77-79	2
04	80	2
04	81	1
04-05	82-83	1
05	68	3
05	69	2
05-06	70-81	2
06	68-69	3
06	82	2
06	83	1
07-09	68-70	3
07-10	74-83	2
07	71	2
07-08	72-73	2
08-11	88-92	1
08	71	3
08	84	2
08	85-87	1
09	71-71	3
09	73	2
09	86-87	1
09-10	84-85	2
10	86	2
10	87	1
10-22	68-73	3
11	74	3
11	75	2
11-12	76	2
11-13	77-78	2
11-15	79-87	2
12	88	2
12	89	1
12-13	90-92	1
12-13	74-75	3
13	76	3
13	88-89	2
14	78	2
14	91-92	1
14-15	88-90	2
14-16	74-77	3
15	78	3
15	91	2
15	92	1
16	78-79	3
16	80	2
16-17	81-84	2
16-21	85-92	2
17-22	74-80	3
18	81	3
18	82	2

(continued)

7

Table 9 MAIN BEARING SELECTION (225 HP MODELS) (continued)

Cylinder block main bearing code	Crankshaft main bearing code	Bearing No.
18-19	83-84	2
19	81-82	3
20	84	2
20-22	81-83	3
21	84	3
22	84-85	3
22	86-92	2
98-99	76-92	1
98-99	68-74	2
98	75	1
99	75	2

Table 10 CONNECTING ROD BEARING SELECTION (75-115 HP MODELS)

Measured clearance	Piston side bearing color	Rod cap side bearing color
75 and 90 hp models		
0.0026-0.0028 in. (0.066-0.071 mm)	Blue	Red
0.0023-0.0025 in. (0.058-0.065 mm)	Blue	Blue
0.0020-0.0022 in. (0.050-0.057 mm)	Green	Blue
0.0017-0.0019 in. (0.043-0.049 mm)	Green	Green
0.0014-0.0016 in. (0.036-0.042 mm)	Yellow	Green
0.0009-0.0013 in. (0.023-0.035 mm)	Yellow	Yellow
115 hp models		
0.0024-0.0025 in. (0.059-0.063 mm)	Blue	Red
0.0021-0.0023 in. (0.053-0.058 mm)	Blue	Blue
0.0019-0.0020 in. (0.049-0.050 mm)	Green	Blue
0.0016-0.0018 in. (0.036-0.046 mm)	Green	Green
0.0013-0.0015 in. (0.035-0.039 mm)	Yellow	Green
0.0010-0.0012 in. (0.025-0.031 mm)	Yellow	Yellow

Table 11 CONNECTING ROD BEARING SELECTION (225 HP MODELS)

Crankshaft rod bearing code	Bearing color
00	Yellow
76-83	Blue
84-91	Green
92-99	Yellow

Chapter Eight

Gearcase

This chapter provides lower gearcase removal, repair and installation instructions. Water pump maintenance and repair instructions are also included in this chapter.

Table 1 lists torque specifications for most gearcase fasteners. Use the general torque specifications listed in the *Quick Reference Data* at the front of the manual for fasteners not listed in **Table 1**. **Table 2** lists gearcase backlash specifications. **Table 1** and **Table 2** are located at the end of this chapter.

The lower gearcase can be removed from the outboard without removing the entire outboard from the boat.

The gearcases covered in this chapter differ in construction and require different service procedures. The chapter is arranged in a normal disassembly/assembly sequence. When only partial repair is required, follow the procedure(s) to the point where the faulty parts can be replaced, then jump ahead to reassemble the gearcase.

GEARCASE OPERATION

The gearcase transfers the rotation of a vertical drive shaft to a horizontal propeller shaft (**Figure 1**). A pinion (drive) gear on the drive shaft is in constant mesh with forward and reverse (driven) gears in the lower gearcase housing. These gears are spiral bevel cut to change the vertical power flow into the horizontal flow required by the propeller shaft. The spiral bevel design also provides quiet operation.

All gearcases use precision shimmed gears. This means that the gears are precisely located in the gear housing by the use of very thin metal spacers, called shims (**Figure 2**). After assembly, correct shimming of the gears is verified by measuring the *gear lash*, also referred to as *backlash*. Gear lash is the measurement of the clearance (or air gap) between a tooth on the pinion gear and two teeth on the forward or reverse gear.

Excessive gear lash indicates that the gear teeth are too far apart. This will cause excessive gear noise (whine) and a reduction in gear strength and durability since the gear teeth are not sufficiently overlapping.

Insufficient gear lash indicates that the gear teeth are too close together. Operation with insufficient gear lash leads to gear failure since there will not be enough clearance to maintain a film of lubricant. Heat expansion only compounds the problem.

All lower gearcases incorporate a water pump to supply cooling water to the power head. All models require gearcase removal to service the water pump. Water pump disassembly, inspection and assembly procedures are covered in this chapter.

Standard Rotation (RH) Gearcase

A sliding clutch, splined to the propeller shaft, engages the spinning forward or reverse gear (**Figure 3**). This creates a direct coupling of the drive shaft to the propeller shaft. Since this is a straight mechanical engagement, shifting should only be done at idle speed. Shifting at higher speeds results in gearcase failure.

When neutral is selected (**Figure 3**), the shift mechanism positions the clutch midway between the driven gears. This allows the propeller shaft to freewheel or remain stationary. No propeller thrust is delivered.

When forward is selected (**Figure 3**), the shift mechanism moves the clutch to engage the front mounted gear. This mechanical engagement results in clockwise rotation of the propeller.

When reverse is selected (**Figure 3**), the shift mechanism moves the clutch to engage the rear mounted gear. This mechanical engagement results in counterclockwise rotation of the propeller.

NOTE

Models with a C in the model designation have a counter rotation gearcase. The gearcase is designed to provide forward thrust when the propeller shaft rotates in the left-hand, or counterclockwise, direction (as viewed from the rear). A left-hand propeller must be used on these models.

CAUTION

Never use a left-hand propeller on a gearcase designed to use only a right-hand propeller. Gearcase component failure may occur from continued operation in the wrong direction for forward thrust.

Counter Rotation (LH) Gearcase

Left-hand, or counterclockwise, propeller shaft rotation is used for forward thrust on models with an *L* in the model designation code. Left-hand units are fused along with a right-hand unit on dual engine applications. The use of the left-hand unit allows for balanced propeller torque from the two engines. A control box is used that provides the opposite direction of shift cable movement versus right-hand units.

A sliding clutch, splined to the propeller shaft, engages the spinning forward or reverse gear (**Figure 3**). This couples the drive shaft to the propeller shaft. Since this is a straight mechanical engagement, shifting should only be done at idle speed. Shifting at higher speeds results in gearcase failure.

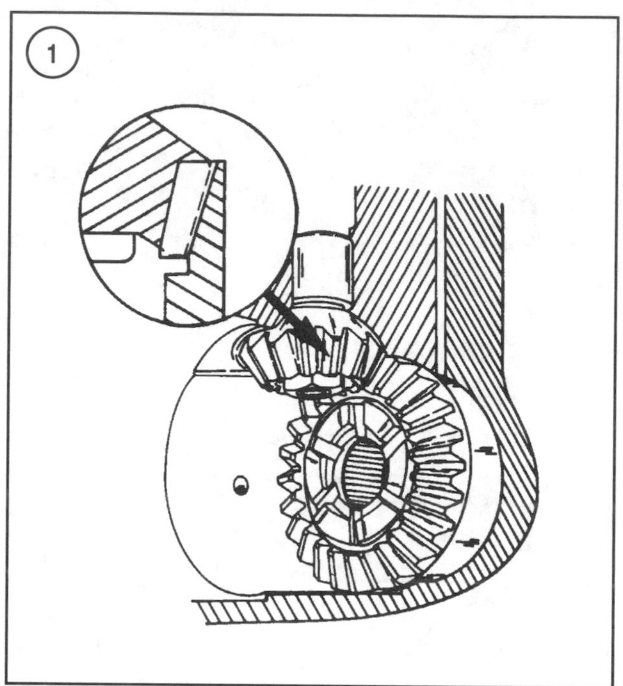

When neutral is selected (**Figure 3**), the shift mechanism positions the clutch midway between the driven gears. This allows the propeller shaft to freewheel or remain stationary. No propeller thrust is delivered.

When forward is selected (**Figure 3**), the shift mechanism moves the clutch to engage the rear mounted gear. This mechanical engagement results in counterclockwise rotation of the propeller.

When reverse is selected (**Figure 3**), the shift mechanism moves the clutch to engage the front mounted gear. This me-

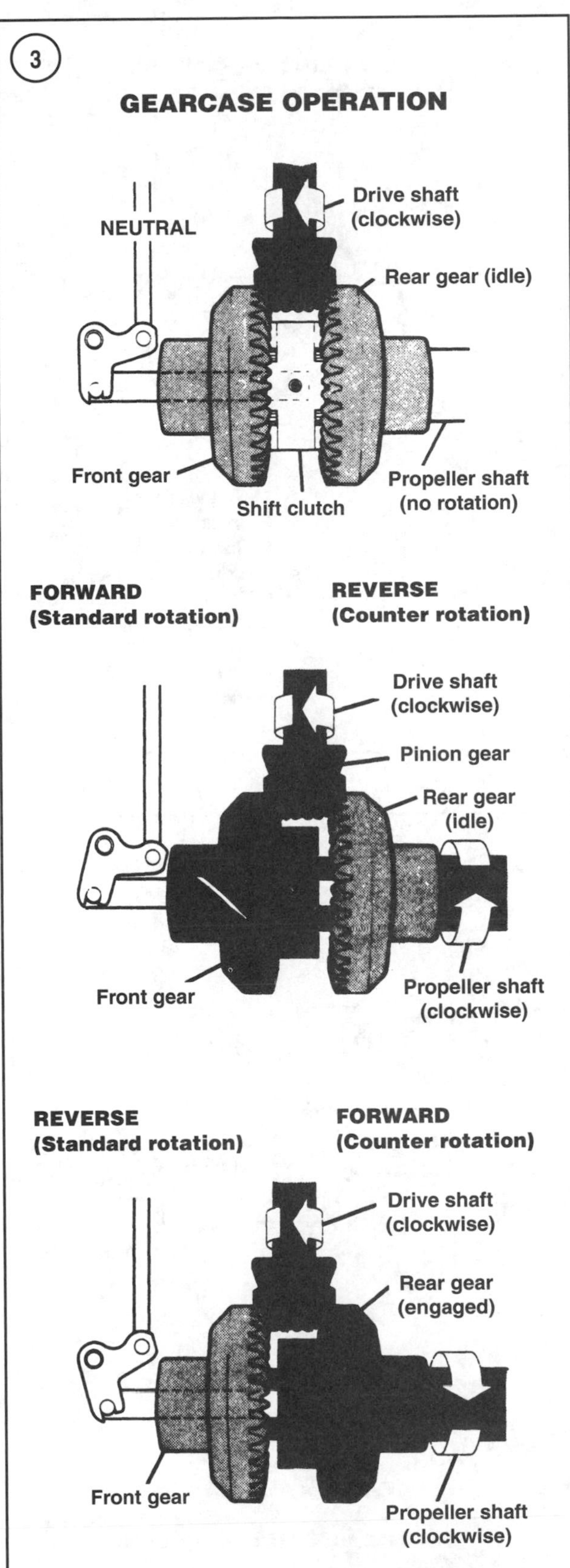

chanical engagement results in clockwise rotation of the propeller.

GEARCASE SERVICE PRECAUTIONS

When working on a gearcase, keep the following precautions in mind to make the work easier, faster and more accurate.

1. Replace elastic locknuts each time they are removed.

2. Use special tools where noted. The use of makeshift tools can damage components and cause injury.

3. Use an appropriate fixture to the hold the gearcase whenever possible. Use a vise with protective jaws to hold individual components. If protective jaws are not available, insert blocks of wood or similar padding on each side of the housing or component before clamping.

4. Remove and install pressed-on parts with an appropriate mandrel, support an arbor, or hydraulic press. Do not attempt to pry or hammer press-fit components on or off.

5. Tighten all fasteners to the torque specification in **Table 1**. Proper tightening is essential to ensure long life and satisfactory service from the gearcase.

6. To help reduce corrosion, especially in saltwater areas, apply Quicksilver Perfect Seal (part No. 92-34227-1) or equivalent to all external surfaces of bearing carriers, housing mating surfaces, and fasteners when no other sealant, adhesive or lubricant is recommended. Never apply sealing compound onto surfaces where it can get into gears or bearings.

7. Replace all O-rings, seals and gaskets when removed. Apply Quicksilver 2-4-C Marine Lubricant (part No. 92-825407) or equivalent to new O-rings and seal lips to provide initial lubrication.

8. Tag all shims (**Figure 2**) with the location and thickness of each shim as removed from the gearcase. Shims are reusable as long as they are not damaged or corroded. Follow shimming instructions closely and carefully. Shims control gear location and/or bearing preload. Incorrectly shimming a gearcase can cause failure of the gears and/or bearings, or greatly reduce service life.

9. Whenever a threadlocking adhesive is specified, first spray the threads of the threaded opening or nut and screw with Locquic Primer (part No. 92-809824). Allow the primer to air dry before proceeding. Locquic primer will clean the surfaces for better adhesion and leaves behind a catalyst that significantly accellerates the curing rate of the threadlocking adhesive.

PROPELLER REMOVAL/INSTALLATION

All models covered in this manual use either a rubber thrust hub design (**Figure 4**) or the Flo-Torq II design propeller (**Figure 5**).

With the rubber thrust hub design, the propeller is driven via a splined connection of the propeller shaft to the rubber thrust hub. The rubber thrust hub is pressed into a bore in the propeller (**Figure 6**) and provides a cushion effect when shifting. It also provides some protection for the gearcase components in the event of underwater impact. The front mounted thrust washer (1, **Figure 4**) directs the propeller thrust to a tapered area on the propeller shaft.

With the Flo-Torq II design, the propeller is driven via a splined connection of the propeller to the splined hub (3, **Figure 5**) and the Delrin drive hub (2). Similar to the thrust hub design, the front mounted thrust washer (1, **Figure 5**) directs the propeller thrust to a tapered area on the propeller shaft. Unlike the thrust hub design, the Delrin drive hub can be replaced by the operator, without the use of a hydraulic or arbor press.

On 75-115 hp models, a tab washer and elastic nut secure the propeller onto the propeller shaft. A castellated nut and cotter pin are used to secure the propeller on 225 hp models.

WARNING
To prevent accidental engine starting during propeller service, disconnect the negative battery cable. Remove the ignition key and the lanyard safety switch from models so equipped.

CAUTION
Use light force to remove the propeller from the propeller shaft. The use of excessive force will result in damage to the propeller, propeller shaft and internal components of the gearcase. If the propeller cannot be removed by normal means, have a reputable marine repair shop or propeller repair shop remove the propeller.

NOTE
Because the components are contained within the propeller, the drive hub design may not be evident until the propeller is removed. The propeller removal and installation procedures are very similar for both designs.

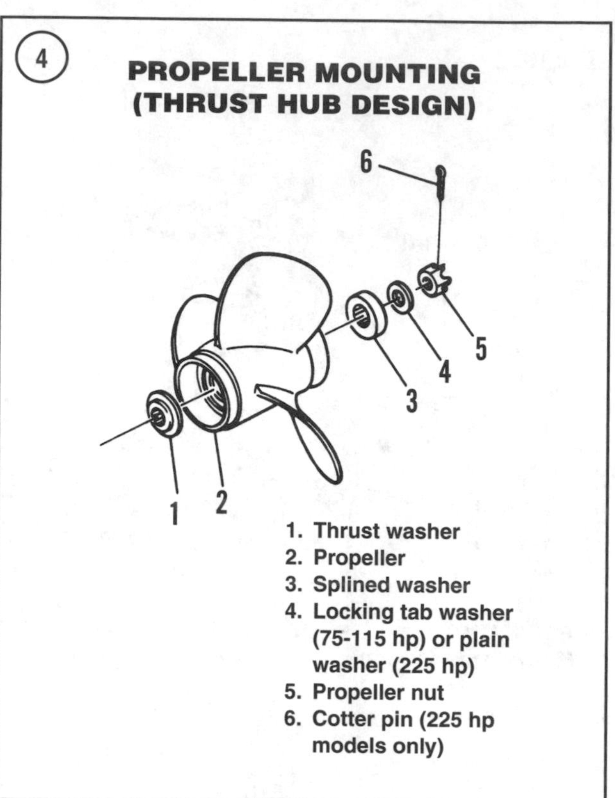

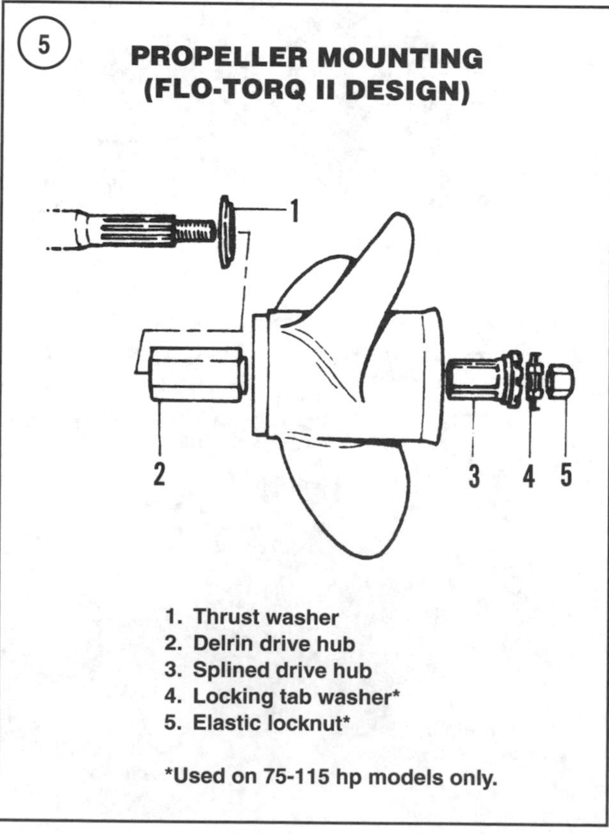

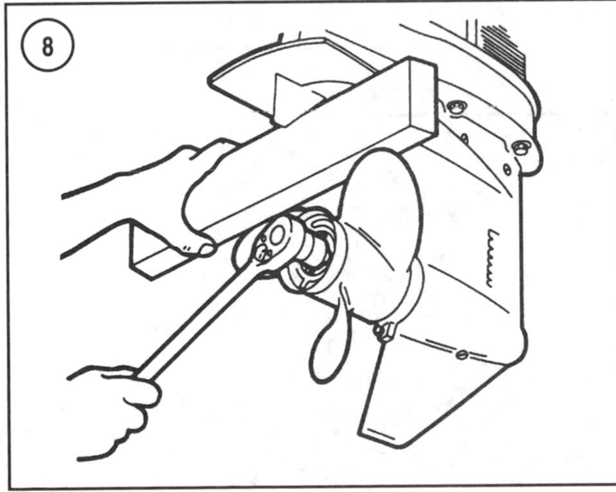

Propeller Removal

After removal, inspect the propeller for the presence of loose black rubber material in the drive hub area (**Figure 6**) or a cracked or damaged Delrin drive hub (**Figure 7**). Have rubber thrust hub design propellers inspected or replaced at a propeller repair facility if loose black rubber material is evident. It normally indicates the hub has spun in the propeller bore. Replace the Delrin drive hub used on Flo-Torq II propellers if cracked, deformed or worn surfaces are evident. Satisfactory performance is not possible with a spun or damaged propeller hub.

1. Disconnect the negative battery cable to prevent accidental starting.

2A. On 75-115 hp models, pry the locking tab(s) up from the notches in the propeller or splined drive hub (3, **Figure 5**).

2B. On 225 hp models, use pliers to straighten and remove the cotter pin (6, **Figure 4**).

3. Place a suitable block of wood between the propeller and the antiventilation plate to prevent propeller rotation (**Figure 8**).

4. Remove the propeller nut with an appropriate socket. Turn the propeller nut counterclockwise for removal. Replace the elastic propeller nut, used on 75-115 hp models, if it can be unthreaded by hand.

5. On 225 hp models, remove the washer (4, **Figure 4**) from the propeller shaft.

6. Slide the propeller and all related hardware from the propeller shaft. Use a block of wood as a cushion and carefully drive the propeller from the shaft if necessary. Use light force only to avoid damaging the propeller or gearcase components.

7. Remove the thrust washer (1, **Figure 4**) or (1, **Figure 5**) from the shaft. If the thrust washer is seized, tap lightly around the perimeter of the washer until free from the shaft. Inspect the thrust washer for cracks or excessively worn surfaces. Replace the thrust washer if cracks or excessive wear are evident.

CAUTION

Never reuse a damaged, worn or cracked propeller thrust washer. An excessively worn hub may allow the propeller to contact the gearcase during operation and damage the propeller and gearcase housing.

8. On the Flo-Torq II design, pull the splined drive hub (3, **Figure 5**) from the aft propeller shaft bore. Working from the aft bore, carefully push the Delrin drive hub out of the forward propeller bore.

9. Clean the propeller shaft thoroughly. Inspect the propeller shaft for cracked, worn or damaged surfaces. Pay particular attention to the tapered surface that contacts the thrust washer. Inspect the propeller shaft for twisted splines (**Figure 9**). Visually check for deflection while rotating the propeller shaft. Twisted splines and propeller shaft bending occur when the propeller contacts underwater objects while underway. Replace the propeller shaft if worn surfaces, twisted splines or shaft deflection is evident.

Propeller Installation

1. Lubricate the propeller shaft liberally with Quicksilver 2-4-C Marine Lubricant, Special Lubricant 101 or an equivalent.
2. Slide the thrust washer (1, **Figure 4**) onto the propeller shaft. The tapered bore of the thrust washer must face toward the tapered section of the propeller shaft. Seat the thrust washer against the propeller shaft taper.
3A. On a rubber thrust hub design propeller, slide the propeller onto the propeller shaft. Align the splines and seat the propeller against the thrust washer.
3B. On a Flo-Torq II propeller, install the propeller and drive hubs onto the propeller shaft as follows:

   a. Align the flat sections, then insert the Delrin drive hub (2, **Figure 5**) into the front propeller bore. The open end of the drive hub must face outward.
   b. Slide the propeller over the propeller shaft and seat against the thrust washer.
   c. Fit the smaller end of the splined drive hub over the end of the propeller shaft. Rotate the propeller to align the slots in the Delrin drive hub with the runners on the splined hub. The splined hub will drop slightly into the hub when aligned.
   d. Rotate the propeller and splined drive hub to align the hub splines with the propeller shaft splines. The splined hub will drop fully into Delrin hub when aligned.

4A. On 75-115 hp models, install the locking tab washer (4, **Figure 5**) onto the propeller shaft and seat against the propeller or splined drive hub. The protruding side must fit into the recess in the propeller or splined drive hub.
4B. On 225 hp models, install the washer (4, **Figure 4**) onto the propeller shaft and seat against the propeller or splined drive hub.
5. Thread the propeller nut onto the propeller shaft. The elastic or castellated side must face outward.

CAUTION
Rotate the locking tab washer, used on 75-115 hp models, to align the hexagon-shaped recess with the propeller nut before tightening. Improper alignment will cause damage to the locking tab washer.

6. Place a suitable block of wood between the propeller and the antiventilation plate to prevent propeller rotation. See **Figure 8**.
7. Tighten the propeller nut to 55 ft.-lb. (75.0 N•m). Secure the propeller nut as follows:

   a. On 75-115 hp models, select three locking tabs that align with the notches in the propeller or splined drive hub. Drive the tabs into the notches with a

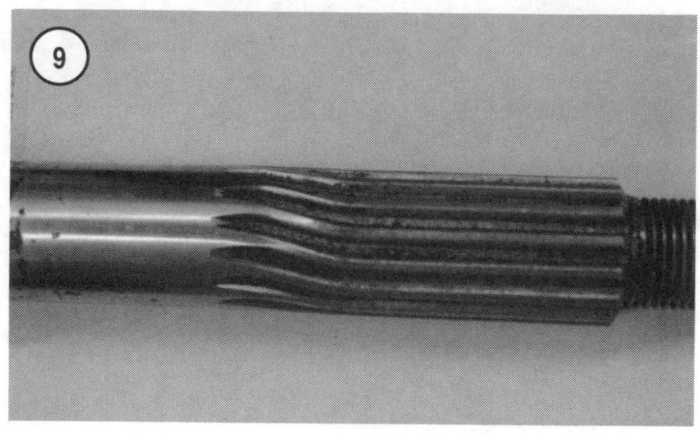

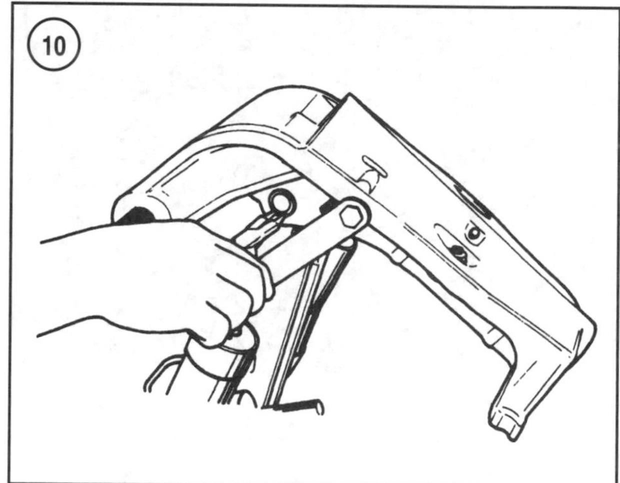

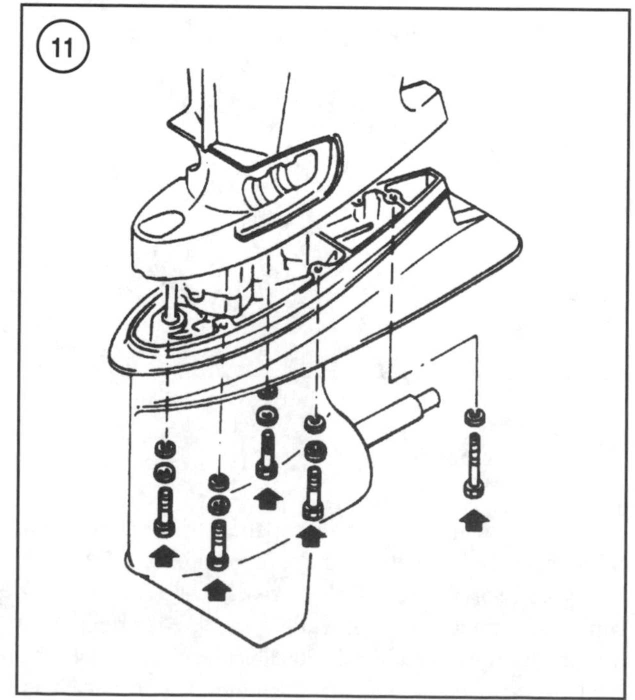

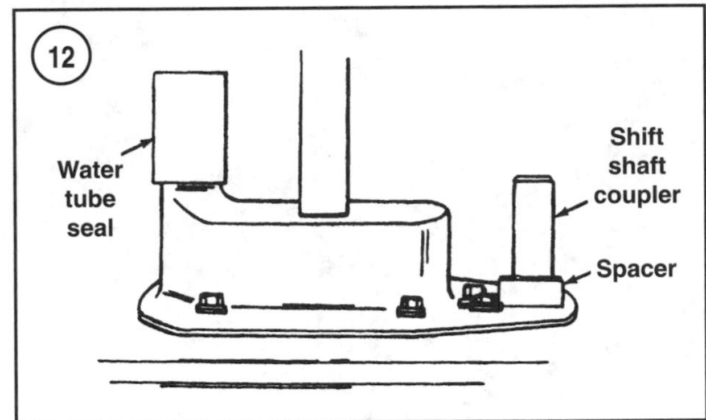

hammer and punch. If necessary, tighten the propeller nut slightly to align the tabs. *Never* loosen the nut to align the tabs.

b. On 225 hp models, insert the cotter pin (6, **Figure 4**) through the opposing pair of slots in the castellated propeller nut that align with the hole in the propeller shaft. Then, bend over the ends of the pin. If necessary, tighten the propeller nut slightly to align the slots with the hole. *Never* loosen the nut to align the slots.

8. Push forward and *slowly* rotate the propeller to check for rubbing at the propeller to gearcase mating surfaces. Very light contact is common and does not indicate a problem. Binding or heavy contact indicates improper propeller installation, a bent propeller shaft or a misaligned or damaged propeller drive hub. Remove the propeller and inspect the components as necessary.
9. Connect the battery cable.

GEARCASE REMOVAL/INSTALLATION

Always remove the propeller prior to removing or installing the gearcase. Refer to the procedures described in this chapter. To prevent accidental starting or starter engagement, disconnect the negative battery cable prior to gearcase removal.

Drain the gearcase lubricant prior to removal if the gearcase will require disassembly. Refer to Chapter Three for procedures.

Gearcase removal and installation procedures vary by model. Refer to the procedures specified for the model requiring service.

CAUTION

Work carefully if using a pry bar to separate the gearcase from the drive shaft housing. Always ensure that all fasteners are removed before attempting to pry the housings apart. Use a blunt tip pry bar and locate a pry point near the front and rear mating surfaces.

NOTE

Apply moderate heat to the gearcase and drive shaft housing mating surfaces if corrosion prevents easy removal of the gearcase.

75-115 hp Models

Removal

1. Use the power trim system to place the engine in the full tilt position. Engage the tilt lock lever (**Figure 10**).
2. Disconnect the negative battery cable to prevent accidental starting.
3. Remove the propeller as described in this chapter.
4. Shift the engine into FORWARD gear. Rotate the propeller shaft counterclockwise to assist full gear engagement.
5. Support the gearcase while removing the four bolts and washers (two on each side) and washer and locknut located just forward for the trim tab (**Figure 11**).
6. Pull the gearcase straight down and away from the drive shaft housing.
7. Place the gearcase in a suitable holding fixture or on a clean work surface.
8. If the water tube seal (**Figure 12**) remains on the water tube in the drive shaft housing, remove it and install it onto the water pump outlet before installing the gearcase.
9. If the shift shaft coupler or nylon spacer (**Figure 12**) remains on the upper shift shaft in the drive shaft housing, remove the components and install them before installing the gearcase.
10. Inspect the trim tab as described in Chapter Three. Replace the trim tab as required.
11. Thoroughly clean the exposed surfaces of the drive shaft. Make sure to remove all of the grease residue from the splined section at the top.

Installation

1. Make sure the water tube seal is securely attached to the water pump body. If the seal is loose, glue the seal onto the water pump outlet with Loctite 405 adhesive (**Figure 12**).

CAUTION

Do not apply grease to the top of the drive shaft in Step 2. Excess grease between the top of the drive shaft and the power head crankshaft can create a hydraulic lock, pre-

8

venting the drive shaft from fully engaging the crankshaft. Operating the engine with the hydraulic lock can damage the power head and gearcase components.

2. Apply a light coat of Quicksilver 2-4-C Marine Lubricant to the drive shaft splines. Coat the shift shaft coupler splines and the inner diameter of the water tube seal with the same grease (**Figure 12**).

3. Rotate the shift shaft to shift the gearcase into FORWARD gear. Rotate the propeller shaft to assist gear engagement. When forward gear is engaged and the propeller shaft is rotated clockwise, the sliding clutch will ratchet.

4. Install the nylon spacer on the shift shaft coupler onto the shift shaft. Rotate the coupler clockwise to align the splines, then seat the coupler on the spacer (**Figure 13**).

5. Place the remote control in the FORWARD gear full throttle position. If the control cables are disconnected, push the shift cable linkage connector (**Figure 14**) forward in the bracket until it reaches the end of the slot.

6. Run a 1/4 in. (6.4 mm) bead of RTV sealant (part No. 92-903113-2) along the water dam at the rear of the water pump base (**Figure 15**).

7. Position the gearcase under the drive shaft housing. Align the water tube with the seal on the water pump, the drive shaft with the crankshaft and the shift shaft with the shift shaft coupler.

8. Guide the drive shaft straight into the bushing in the drive shaft housing. Make sure the water tube is perfectly aligned with the seal on the water pump, then push the gearcase toward the drive shaft housing. If the gearcase will not seat against the drive shaft housing, perform the following steps:

   a. Temporarily install the propeller onto the propeller shaft. It is not necessary to install the propeller nut for this procedure.

   b. Rotate the propeller counterclockwise *slightly* to align the drive shaft splines with the oil pump and crankshaft splines. In addition, move the control lever or cable linkage connector *slightly* to align the upper shift shaft and coupler splines. Repeat this step until the gearcase seats against the drive shaft housing.

   c. Remove the propeller from the propeller shaft.

9. Apply a light coat of Loctite 271 (part No. 92-809819) onto the threads, then thread the four bolts (**Figure 11**) into the gearcase and drive shaft housing. Thread the nut and lockwasher onto the stud located just forward of the trim tab. Tighten the fasteners hand-tight at this time.

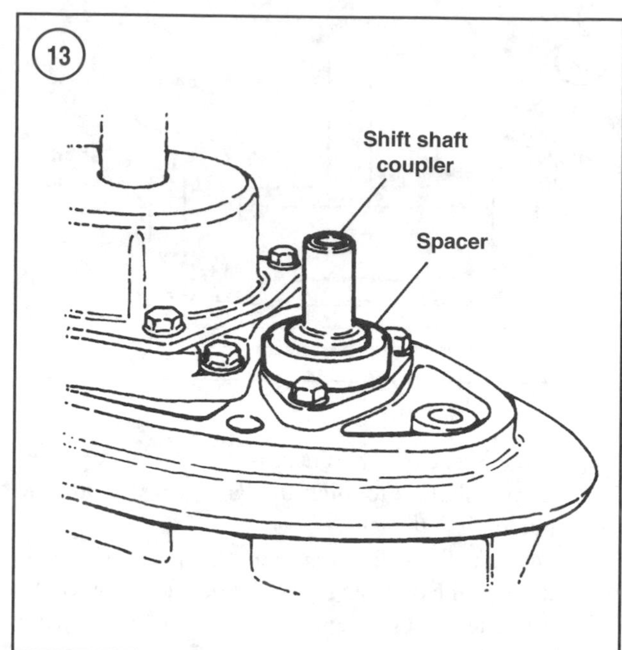

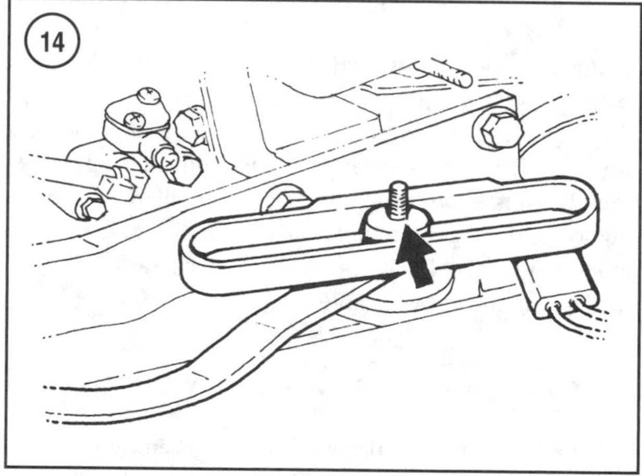

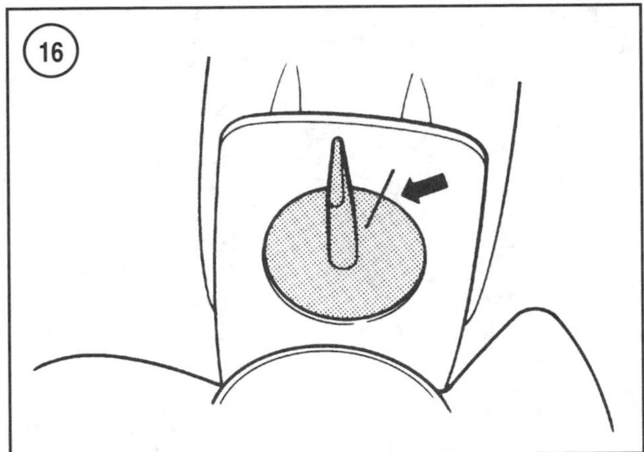

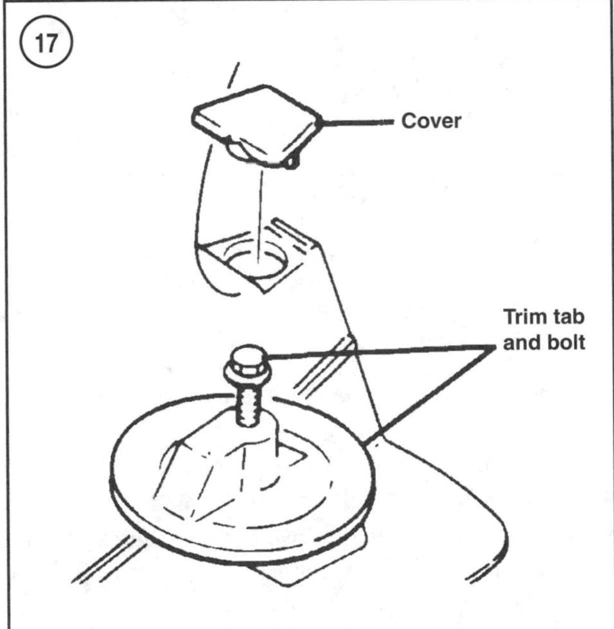

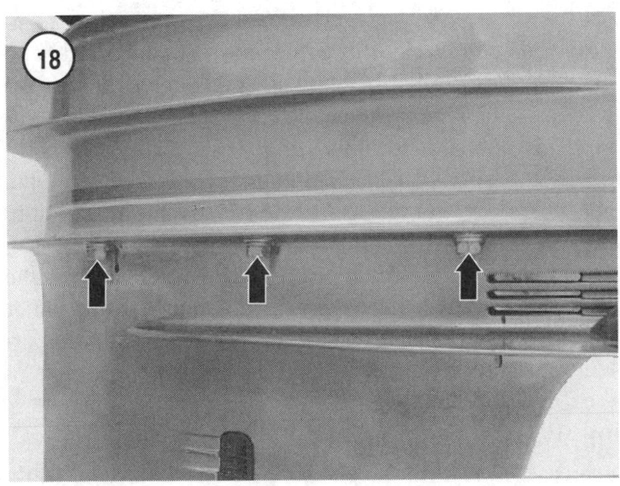

NOTE
If the gearcase does not shift as described in Step 10, the shift shafts are incorrectly indexed. Remove the gearcase and repeat Steps 3-9.

10. Shift the engine into FORWARD gear; the propeller shaft must lock when rotated counterclockwise. Shift into NEUTRAL; the propeller must rotate freely in both directions. Shift into REVERSE; the propeller should lock when rotated in the clockwise direction. If the shift operation is not as specified, remove the gearcase and re-index the upper shift shaft and shift shaft coupler.
11. Once the shift function is correct, tighten the gearcase mounting fasteners to 40 ft.-lb. (54.2 N•m).
12. Install the propeller as described in this chapter.
13. Connect the battery cable.
14. Release the tilt lock lever and return the engine to the upright position.
15. Check and correct the gearcase lubricant level as described in Chapter Three.
16. Adjust the shift cables as described in Chapter Four.

8

225 hp Model

Removal

1. Use the power trim system to place the engine in the full tilt position. Engage the tilt lock lever (**Figure 10**).
2. Disconnect the negative battery cable to prevent accidental starting.
3. Remove the propeller as described in this chapter.
4. Make index markings on the trim tab and housing with a white grease pencil or china marker (**Figure 16**). Do not use a scribe as the gearcase will corrode where the paint is scratched.
5. Place the remote control into the NEUTRAL gear position.
6. Locate and remove the bolt access cover (**Figure 17**). Use a socket and extension to remove the trim tab bolt. Carefully tap the trim tab loose, then remove it from the gearcase.
7. Remove the bolt from the trim tab mounting cavity. Support the gearcase while removing the three bolts and washers (**Figure 18**) from each side of the gearcase.
8. Verify that all bolts are removed, then lower the gearcase from the drive shaft housing. If necessary, carefully tug or pry the gearcase from the housing. Pry at points near the front and rear of the gearcase to drive shaft housing mating surface.
9. Reposition the water tube grommet into the water pump body if dislodged during gearcase removal.

10. Clean corrosion and other contaminants from the gearcase mating surfaces, shift shafts and drive shaft.
11. Inspect the grommet that connects the water tube onto the water pump and the exhaust passage seal for damage or deterioration. Replace the grommet or seal if faulty or in questionable condition.

Installation

1. Make sure the water tube seal is in position in the water pump opening.
2. Fit the seal into the exhaust passage opening in the gearcase.
3. Shift the remote control into NEUTRAL gear.

CAUTION
Do not apply grease to the top of the drive shaft in Step 4. Excess grease between the top of the driveshaft and the power head crankshaft can create a hydraulic lock, preventing the drive shaft from fully engaging the crankshaft. Operating the engine with the hydraulic lock can damage the power head and gearcase components.

4. Apply a light coat of Quicksilver 2-4-C Marine Lubricant or equivalent onto the splined section at the upper end of the drive shaft and the grommet that connects the water tube into the water pump (**Figure 19**).
5. Install the shift handle (part No. 888877) onto the lower shift shaft (**Figure 20**). If this tool is not available, grip the lower shift shaft with pliers and a shop towel. (**Figure 21**).
6. Rotate the drive shaft in the clockwise direction (**Figure 20**) while observing the propeller shaft. Rotate the lower shift shaft until the propeller shaft rotates in the clockwise then counterclockwise direction. Note the shift shaft position for each gear. Position the shift shaft at the point midway between the location where clockwise and counterclockwise rotation occurs. Rotate the drive shaft to verify the gearcase is in NEUTRAL gear. Remove the shift handle.

CAUTION
Never rotate the propeller shaft to align the drive shaft splined connection with the crankshaft splines. The water pump impeller can suffer damage that leads to overheating of the engine.

CAUTION
Work carefully when installing the upper end of the drive shaft into the crankshaft. The lower seal on the crankshaft can be dislodged or damaged by the drive shaft. Ensure the shafts are properly aligned before inserting the drive shaft into the crankshaft. Never attempt to force the gearcase into position. Rotate the drive slightly and again attempt to install the gearcase if necessary.

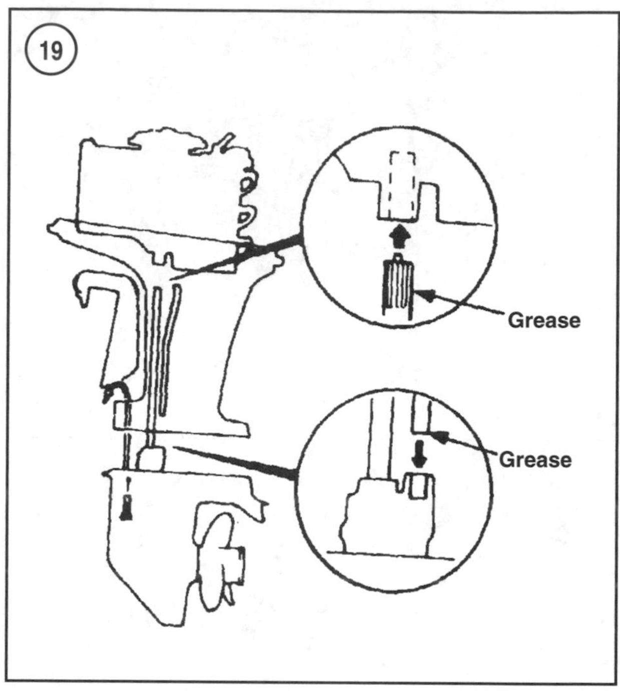

7. Ensure all locating pins are in the respective bores within the gearcase and drive shaft housings.
8. Align the lower end of the water tube (**Figure 19**) with the opening in the water pump while guiding the drive shaft into the drive shaft housing.
9. Align the drive shaft with the crankshaft and both shift shafts while attempting to seat the gearcase against the drive shaft housing. Never force the gearcase into position. This could result in damage to the shift shafts and drive shaft seal. If difficulty is encountered, lower the gearcase and *slightly* rotate the drive shaft clockwise. Repeat this step until the splined drive shaft connection engages the splined opening in the crankshaft and the gearcase seats against the drive shaft housing. If difficulty is encountered with shift shaft alignment, have an assistant slightly toggle the remote control lever to align the shift shaft splines. Verify proper alignment of the water tube-to-water pump opening during each installation attempt. Make sure the locating pins enter the openings in the drive shaft housing.
10. Apply Loctite 242 to the threads of the seven gearcase mounting bolts. Support the gearcase while

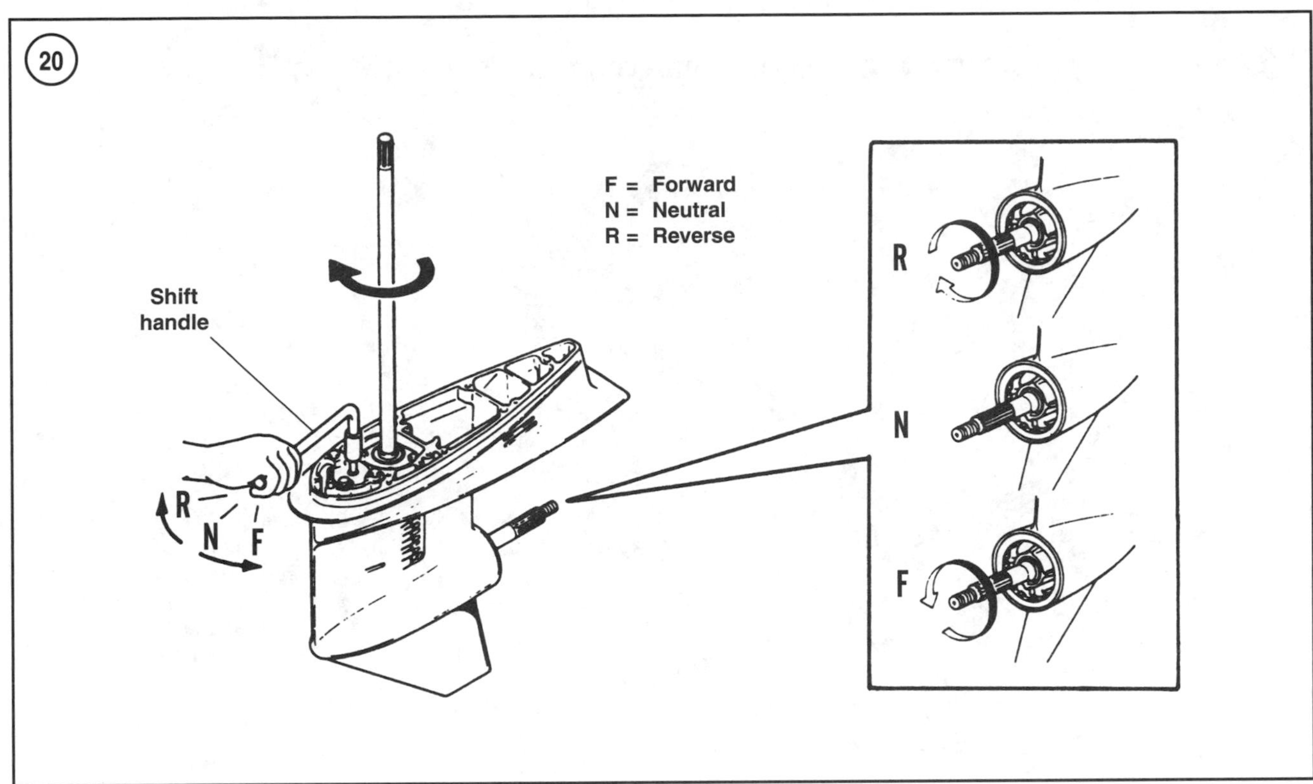

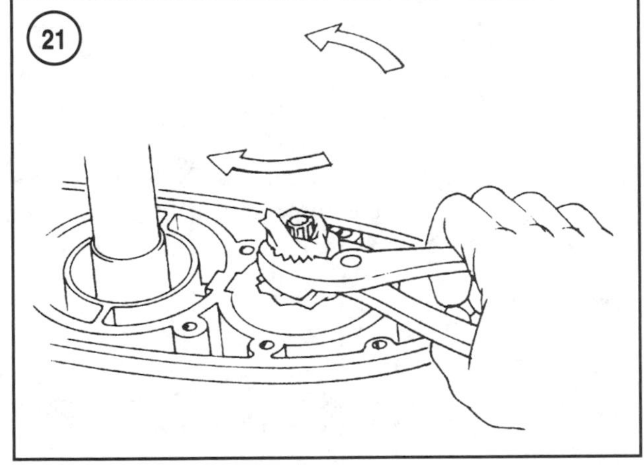

threading the bolts into the gearcase and drive shaft housing. Tighten the mounting bolts to 37 ft.-lb. (50.0 N•m).

11. Install the trim tab onto the gearcase and hold in position. Align the reference marking (**Figure 16**) made prior to removal. Use a socket and extension to install and tighten the trim tab bolt to 32 ft.-lb. (43.4 N•m). Fit the bolt access cover (**Figure 17**) into the opening in the drive shaft housing. Apply a soap and water solution to the cover to assist with installation.

12. Install the propeller as described in this chapter.

13. Connect the battery cable.

14. Release the tilt lock lever and return the engine to the upright position.

15. Check and correct the gearcase lubricant level as described in Chapter Three.

16. Adjust the shift cables as described in Chapter Four.

WATER PUMP DISASSEMBLY AND ASSEMBLY

Disassemble and inspect the water pump components at the intervals listed in Chapter Three and if the engine is running warmer than normal.

Always replace the impeller, seals, O-rings and all gaskets anytime the water pump is disassembled. Never compromise the operation of this vital component. Overheating and extensive power head damage can result from operation with faulty water pump components.

75-115 hp Models

Disassembly

Refer to **Figure 22**.

1. Drain the gearcase lubricant as described in Chapter Three.

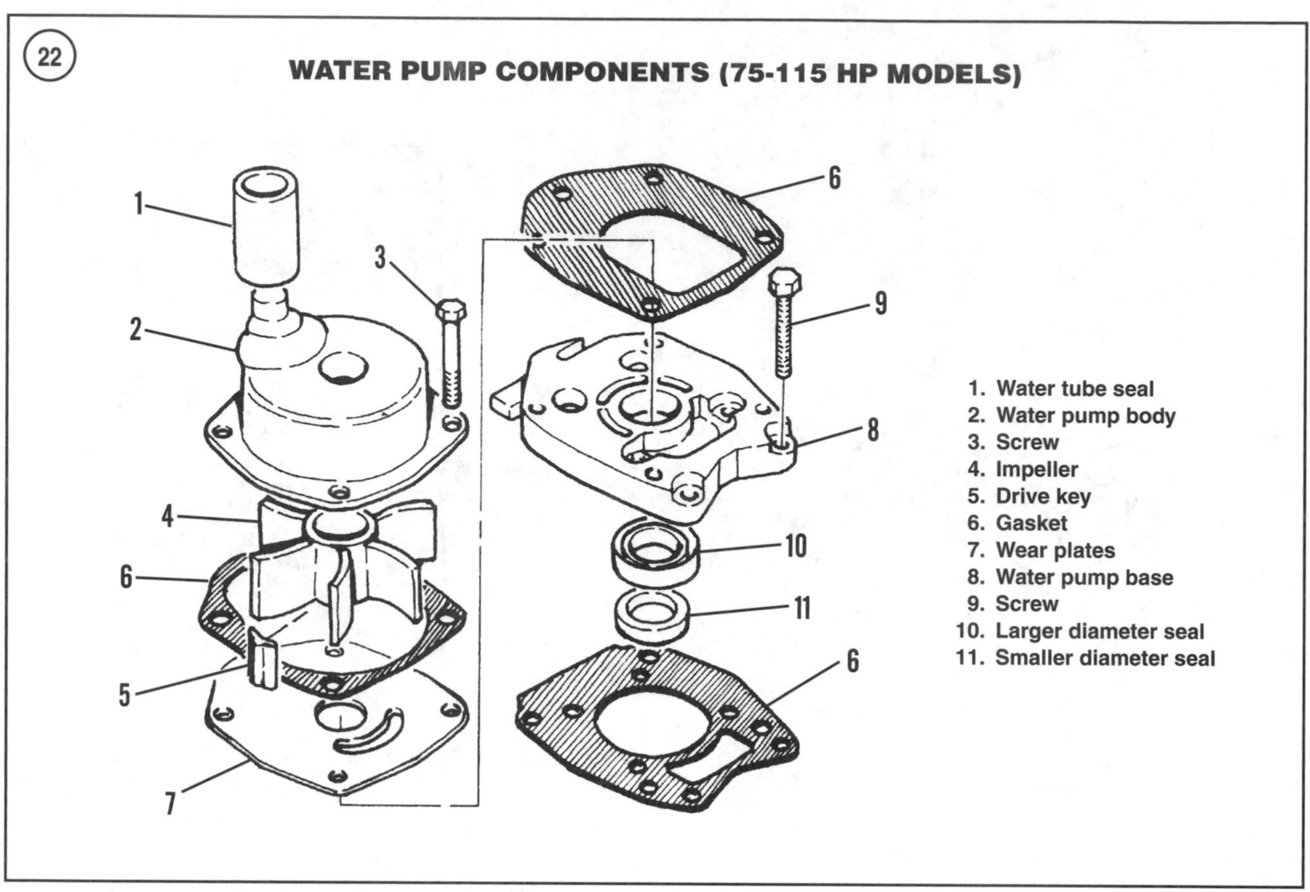

2. Remove the gearcase as described in this chapter.
3. Pull the water tube seal (1, **Figure 22**) from the water pump body (2). Remove the four screws (3, **Figure 22**) and lift the water pump body from the wear plate (7).
4. Carefully pry the water pump impeller (4, **Figure 22**) away from the wear plate, then slide the impeller up and over the drive shaft. Pull the drive key (5, **Figure 22**) from the drive shaft.
5. Lift the wear plate (7, **Figure 22**) from the water pump base (8). Carefully scrape the gaskets (6, **Figure 22**) from the wear plate, water pump base and water pump body.
6. Remove the water pump base only if removing the drive shaft, replacing the seals or if it is damaged. Remove the six screws (9, **Figure 22**) and carefully pry the water pump base (8) away from the gearcase. Remove the gasket from the gearcase or water pump base.
7. Working carefully to avoid damaging the water pump base, pry the drive shaft seals (10 and 11, **Figure 22**) from the water pump base.
8. Clean all water pump components with solvent and dry with compressed air. Use a suitable solvent along with an abrasive cleaning pad to remove all carbon and salt or mineral deposits from the exposed portions of the drive shaft. The shaft must be clean enough to allow the impeller to slide freely along the entire length.
9. Carefully scrape gasket remnants from all components. Inspect all water pump components for wear or damage as described in this chapter.

Assembly

CAUTION
To prevent water and gear lubricant leakage replace all gaskets, seals and O-rings when they are removed or disturbed.

NOTE
Thoroughly clean all corrosion or other deposits from the exposed portions of the drive shaft prior to installing any water pump components. The impeller must slide freely along the length of the shaft.

Refer to **Figure 22**.

1. Use a socket or section of tubing as a seal installation tool. The tool must contact the outer diameter of the seal, but not the seal bore in the water pump base.

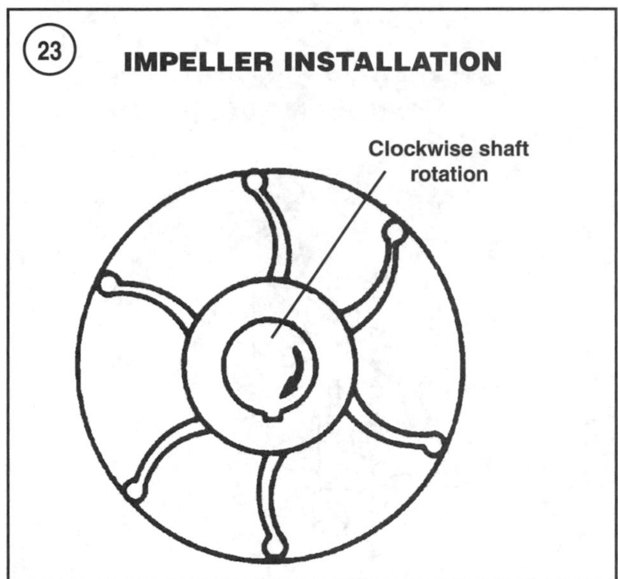

2. Apply Loctite 271 (Mercury part No. 92-809819) onto the outer diameter of both seals prior to installing them into the water pump base. Position the smaller diameter seal (11, **Figure 22**) into the opening at the bottom of the water pump base with the lip side facing inward. Push the seal into the bore until it bottoms. Place the second seal into the opening with the seal lip or spring side facing outward. Push the seal into the bore until it contacts the first seal. Apply a bead of Quicksilver 2-4-C Marine Lubricant onto the lips of the seals.

3. Place the new gasket (6, **Figure 22**) on the gearcase with the sealing bead side facing up. Gasket sealing compound is not required. Guide the water pump base over the drive shaft, seal side down, and place the base onto the gearcase. Position the base with the protruding side facing the rear of the gearcase.

4. Seat the water pump base against the gearcase. Apply Loctite 271 onto the threads of the six mounting screws (9, **Figure 22**). Install the screws then tighten them in a crossing pattern to 60 in.-lb. (6.8 N•m).

5. Slide the gasket (6, **Figure 22**) and wear plate (7) over the drive shaft. Align these components with the water pump base.

6. Apply 2-4-C Marine Lubricant to the drive key (5, **Figure 22**) and install it into position on the flat surface of the drive shaft.

7. Slide the impeller (4, **Figure 22**) over the drive shaft. Align the slot in the impeller hub with the drive key and push the impeller down against wear plate. If reusing the original impeller the vanes must curl in a counterclockwise direction (**Figure 23**). Flip the impeller if required.

8. Apply a light coat of 2-4-C Marine Lubricant to the inner surface of the water pump body (2, **Figure 22**).
9. Install a new gasket (6, **Figure 22**) onto the water pump body (2) with the sealing bead facing the body.
10. Place the water pump body over the drive shaft and slide it down until it contacts the impeller vanes. Rotate the drive shaft clockwise while pushing down on the water pump body.
11. Continue rotating the drive shaft until the impeller fully enters the water pump body and the body seats against the wear plate. Ensure the gaskets (6, **Figure 22**) remain in position.
12. Apply Loctite 271 to the threads then install the four screws (3, **Figure 22**) into the water pump body and base. Tighten the screws in a crossing pattern to 60 in.-lb. (6.8 N•m).
13. Glue the water tube seal onto outlet on the water pump body with Loctite 405 adhesive. Apply grease into the seal opening before installing the gearcase.
14. Install the gearcase as described in this chapter.
15. Fill the gearcase with lubricant as described in Chapter Three.
16. Check for proper cooling system operation and correct any problems before putting the engine into service.

225 hp Model

Disassembly

Refer to **Figure 24**.
1. Drain the gearcase lubricant as described in Chapter Three.
2. Remove the gearcase as described in this chapter. To ease impeller removal and reduce the chance of contaminating the gearcase, clean all corrosion and debris from the exposed surfaces of the drive shaft prior to disassembly.
3. Carefully pry the water tube guide (4, **Figure 24**) and grommet (5) from the water pump body.
4. Remove the four screws (3, **Figure 24**) and washers (2) from the pump body (6). Carefully pry the water pump body away from the wear plate (16, **Figure 24**). Work carefully to avoid damaging mating surfaces. Slide the body up and over the drive shaft.
5. Remove the O-ring (8, **Figure 24**) from the pump body or wear plate. Discard the O-ring.
6. Carefully pry the collar (9, **Figure 24**), spacer (10) and washers (11-13) away from the water pump impeller (14), then slide them up and over the drive shaft. If removal is difficult, carefully split the collar with a chisel and slide it from the shaft. Work carefully to avoid damaging the drive shaft.

7. Mark the UP side of the impeller if it must be reused. Carefully pry the impeller away from the wear plate using a blunt tip pry bar. Work carefully to avoid damaging the wear plate. Remove the impeller by sliding it up and over the drive shaft. If the impeller is seized on the drive shaft, carefully split the inner hub of the impeller with a sharp chisel. Work carefully to avoid damaging the drive shaft surfaces. To help prevent drive shaft damage, cut the impeller hub at the area aligned with the drive key slot. Remove the drive key (15, **Figure 24**) from the slot in the drive shaft.
8. Remove the water pump insert (7, **Figure 24**) only if it must be replaced. Refer to *Water Pump Component Inspection* in this chapter to determine the need for replacement. The removal process damages the insert. Use a punch to drive the insert from the water pump body through the drive shaft bore. Remove the O-ring (1, **Figure 24**) from the water pump body. Discard the insert and O-ring after removal.
9. If the wear plate must be reused, mark the impeller side of the wear plate with a permanent marker. Do not scratch the plate. Carefully pry the wear plate (16, **Figure 24**) loose from the gearcase and drive shaft bearing and seal housing. Work carefully to avoid damaging mating surfaces or dislodging the locating pins (18, **Figure 24**). Slide the wear plate up and over the drive shaft. Remove the gasket (17, **Figure 24**) from the wear plate or gearcase housing. Discard the gasket. If dislodged, insert the locating pins into the respective opening(s) in the gearcase housing.
10. Clean all corrosion and contaminants from the water pump body, wear plate and mating surface on the gearcase. Use a suitable solvent along with a Scotch-Brite pad to remove all carbon and salt or mineral deposits from the exposed portions of the drive shaft. The shaft must be clean enough to allow the impeller to slide freely along the entire length.
11. Inspect the seal protector in the drive shaft bearing and seal housing for melted or damaged surfaces. If melted or damaged, replace the protector as described in this chapter.
12. Inspect all water pump components as described in this chapter. See *Water Pump Component Inspection*.

Assembly

Refer to **Figure 24.**

1. Install a new gasket (17, **Figure 24**) and the wear plate (16) onto the gearcase housing. The openings in the gasket and wear plate must fit over the locating pins (18, **Figure 24**). Seat the gasket and wear plate against the housing.

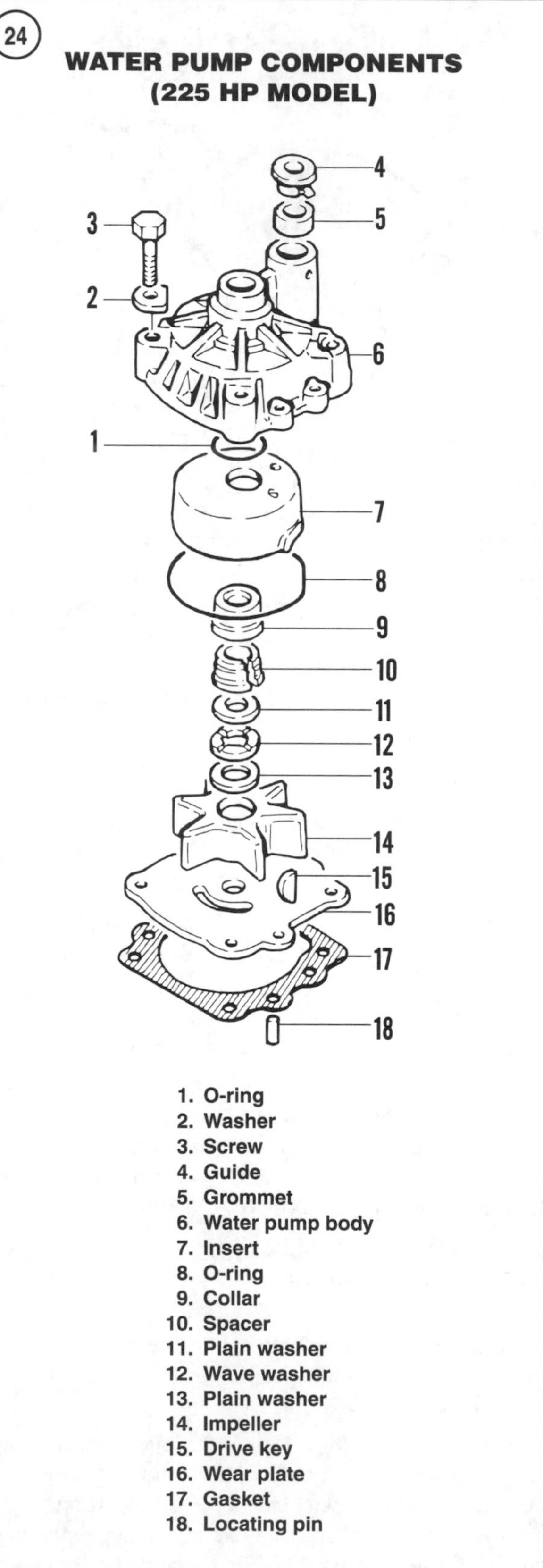

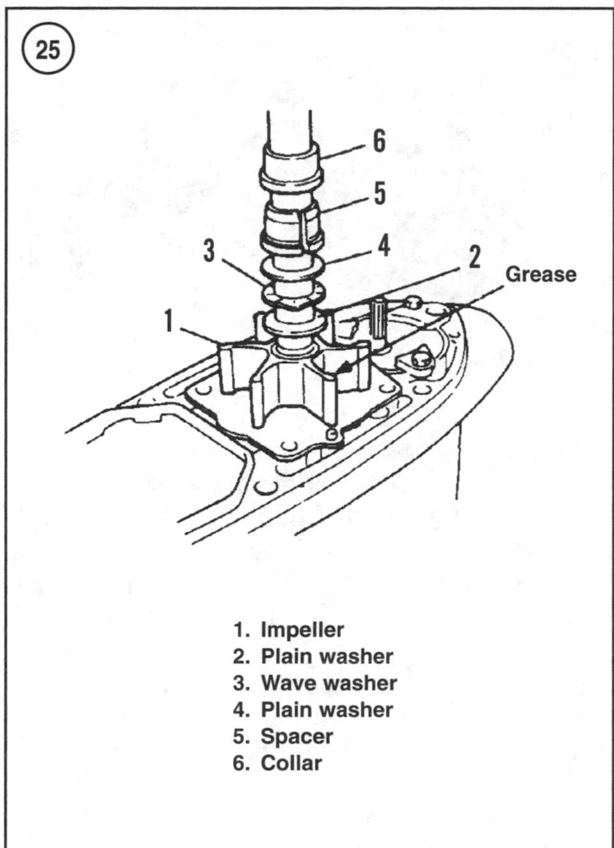

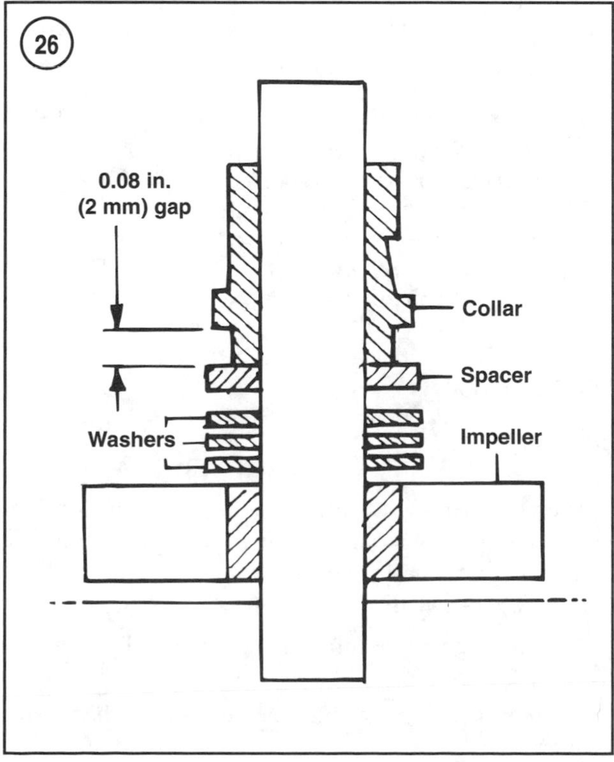

2. Apply a light coat of Quicksilver 2-4-C Marine Lubricant or an equivalent into the slot (**Figure 15**), then insert the rounded side of the drive key into the drive shaft. Apply a light coat of the same grease onto the exposed surfaces of the wear plate and the impeller contacting area of the drive shaft.

3. Slide the impeller over the drive shaft. Align the impeller drive key slot with the drive key, then seat the impeller against the wear plate. If reusing the original impeller the vanes must curl in a counterclockwise direction (**Figure 23**). Flip the impeller if required.

4. Install the washers, spacer and collar as follows:
   a. Slide the plain washer (2, **Figure 25**), wave washer (3) then plain washer (4) over the drive shaft and rest them on the impeller.
   b. Slide the spacer (5, **Figure 25**) over the drive shaft with the flange side facing the washers. Seat the spacer against the washers. Slide the collar over the drive shaft with the flange facing downward.
   c. Use a section of tubing that just fits over the drive shaft to push the collar over the spacer. Push on the collar to achieve a gap of approximately 0.08 in. (2.0 mm) between the collar and spacer flanges (**Figure 26**).

5. If removed, install the water pump insert as follows:
   a. Install a new O-ring (1, **Figure 24**) into the water pump body. Make sure the O-ring fits into the groove surrounding the drive shaft opening.
   b. Apply a light coat of Quicksilver 2-4-C Marine Lubricant onto the O-ring and the insert bore in the pump body.
   c. Align the two locating tabs on the insert with the corresponding openings in the pump body, then push the insert into the body. Rotate the insert if necessary to align the tabs and openings, then seat the insert into the body. The insert surface must be flush with the mating surface of the pump body.

6. Install a new O-ring (8, **Figure 24**) into the groove in the water pump body. Use a very light coat of 3M Weather-strip Adhesive to hold the O-ring in position. Apply a light coat of Quicksilver2-4-C Marine Grease onto the inner surfaces of the insert. Slide the water pump body over the drive shaft. Align the bolt and locating pin openings, then rest the body on the impeller vanes.

7. Rotate the drive shaft in the clockwise direction as viewed from the top while lightly pressing down on the water pump body. Continue until the impeller vanes enter the insert in the water pump body. Rotate the water pump body counterclockwise as needed to align the screw and locating pin openings, then seat the body against the wear plate.

8. Apply Loctite 242 onto the threads of the four screws and washers, then thread them into the water pump body and gearcase housing. Tighten the four bolts in a crossing pattern to 159 in.-lb. (18.0 N•m).
9. Apply grease, then insert the grommet (5, **Figure 24**) and guide (4) into the water tube opening in the water pump body.
10. Install the gearcase as described in this chapter.
11. Fill the gearcase with lubricant as described in Chapter Three.
12. Check for proper cooling system operation and correct any problems before putting the engine into service.

WATER PUMP COMPONENT INSPECTION

Inspect the impeller (A, **Figure 27**) for brittle, missing, burnt or tightly curled vanes. Replace the impeller if these or other defects are evident. Squeeze the vanes toward the hub and release the vanes. The vanes must spring back to the extended position when released. If otherwise the impeller material has lost flexibility and must be replaced.

Inspect the water pump insert (B, **Figure 27**) for worn or damaged surfaces. Remove and replace the insert or water pump body if not found in excellent condition. Operating the engine with rough insert surfaces will quickly wear the impeller.

Inspect the water pump body for melted plastic or indications of impeller material transfer onto the insert. Replace the water pump body and wear plate if either defect is evident.

Inspect the water tube guide and grommet for cracked, brittle or distorted surfaces and replace as required.

Inspect the wear plate for grooved, worn or rough surfaces. Replace the wear plate if these or other defects are evident. Operating the engine with a worn, grooved or damaged wear plate will quickly wear the impeller.

GEARCASE DISASSEMBLY/ASSEMBLY

This section covers complete gearcase disassembly, inspection and re-assembly for the standard RH rotation gearcases used on all models covered in this manual. Instructions specific to the counter rotation gearcase used on 225 hp models are included in the disassembly and assembly procedures along with the procedures for the standard rotation gearcase.

Once the gearcase is disassembled, refer to *Gearcase Component Inspection* to determine the need to replace gearcase components.

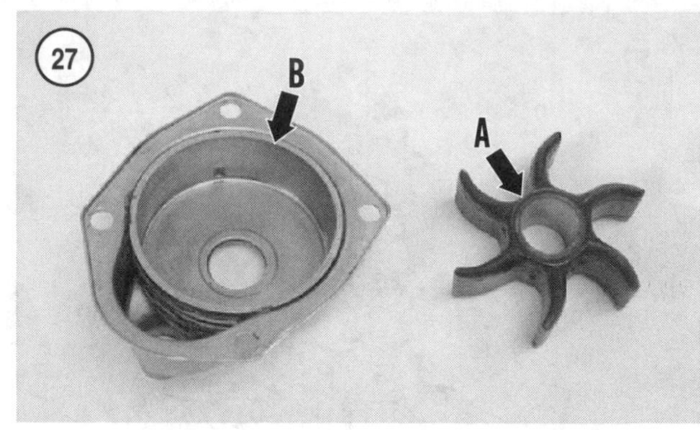

The gears must be shimmed and the gear lash (clearance) between forward gear and the pinion gear must be verified before completing the assembly.

A number of the disassembly and assembly operations require special service tools. The Mercury part numbers of required tools are listed in the disassembly/assembly procedures.

Special gauging fixtures and precision measuring instruments are required to select shims for the gearcase. Have the measurements performed by a qualified technician if you do not have access to the special tools or are unfamiliar with their use. The cost of the special tools may exceed the expense of having a professional perform the measurements.

Note the mounting location and orientation of all components prior to removing them from the gearcase. Mark components that can be installed in different directions accordingly.

NOTE

If the forward gear or drive shaft roller bearings must be replaced, replace the bearing rollers and races as assemblies. Do not remove pressed-in bearings and/or races unless replacement is necessary. The removal process damages the components.

75-115 hp Models

Disassembly

The propeller shaft bearing carrier and propeller shaft can be removed without removing the gearcase from the drive shaft housing, if so desired.

Refer to **Figure 28.**

1. Drain the gearcase lubricant as described in Chapter Three.
2. Remove the propeller and gearcase as described in this chapter.

3. Remove the water pump and base as described in this chapter.

4. Remove the elastic locknuts (61, **Figure 28**) and flat washers (60) securing the propeller shaft bearing carrier into the gearcase. Use a micrometer or caliper to measure the washer thickness. Replace the washer if the measurement is less than 0.090 in. (2.29 mm) thick with the new washers (part No. 12-855941).

NOTE

The manufacture recommends to replace earlier 0.060 in. (1.53 mm) thick bearing carrier washers with 0.090 in. (2.29 mm) thick washers (part No. 12-855941) any time the bearing carrier locknuts are removed.

5. Install puller jaws (part No. 91-46086A-1) and a puller bolt (part No. 91-85716 or an equivalent) and pull the bearing carrier from the gearcase. If necessary, use a propeller thrust hub (**Figure 29**, typical) to prevent the puller jaws from sliding inward.

6. Place the bearing carrier on a clean work surface with the gear facing upward. Pull the reverse gear (54, **Figure 28**) out of the carrier, then remove the thrust bearing (**Figure 30**) and thrust bearing washer (**Figure 31**). Carefully pry the thrust bearing washer from the carrier if the lubricant film prevents easy removal. Remove the O-ring (55, **Figure 28**) from the carrier. Discard the O-ring.

7. Pull the propeller shaft assembly from the gearcase. If the shift cam follower (46, **Figure 28**) falls out of the propeller shaft, retrieve it from the gearcase and reinstall it into the propeller shaft. The pointed end must face outward.

8. Remove the pinion nut by holding the nut with a suitable socket or wrench, then turn the drive shaft counterclockwise using the spline socket (part No. 91-804776A 1) until the nut is free from the drive shaft. See **Figure 32**.

9. Support the pinion gear (39, **Figure 28**), then pull the drive shaft assembly from the gearcase.

10. Remove the pinion gear and roller bearing (32, **Figure 28**), then pull the forward gear assembly from the gearcase bore (**Figure 33**).

11. Remove the two screws (24, **Figure 28**) securing the shift shaft bushing/retainer (26) onto the gearcase. Carefully pry the retainer loose from the gearcase. Grip the splined end of the lower shift shaft (28, **Figure 28**) and pull the shaft and retainer from the gearcase. Remove the retainer from the shift shaft.

12. Remove the shift cam from the gearcase bore. See **Figure 34**.

13. Remove the O-ring (27, **Figure 28**) and seal (25) from the retainer. Do not damage the bore while prying the seal from the retainer. Discard the O-ring and seal.

NOTE

If the needle bearing inside the bearing carrier must be replaced, also remove the propeller shaft seals during the bearing removal process. If needle bearing replacement is not necessary, remove and discard both propeller shaft seals at the same time using a suitable seal puller. Do not damage the seal bore in the removal process.

14. If the bearing carrier needle and roller bearings must be replaced, remove them as follows:

a. Clamp the carrier in a vise with protective jaws or between wooden blocks. Do not clamp on the areas near the O-ring groove.
b. Pull the roller bearing (58, **Figure 28**) from the bearing carrier using a suitable slide hammer (part No. 91-34569A-1). See **Figure 35**. Discard the bearing upon removal.
c. Set the carrier in a press with the propeller end facing down.
d. Assemble the mandrel (part No. 91-26569) and driver rod (part No. 91-37323, or an equivalent). Position the mandrel and driver rod in the carrier bore on top of the needle bearing. See **Figure 36**.
e. Press the propeller shaft needle bearing and seals from the carrier. Discard the bearing and seals.

15. Remove the forward gear/bearing and clutch from the propeller shaft as follows:

a. Hook the end of a small screwdriver over an end loop of the clutch spring (**Figure 37**). Carefully wind the spring from the clutch.
b. Place the shift cam follower against a solid surface and push on the propeller shaft to relieve spring pressure on the cross pin. See **Figure 38**.
c. Use a pin punch to push the cross pin from the clutch, propeller shaft and spring guide.
d. Pull the clutch from the propeller shaft (**Figure 39**).
e. Remove the shift cam follower (46, **Figure 28**), three balls (48), spring guide (47) and spring (49) from the propeller shaft.

16. Remove the forward gear roller bearing (43, **Figure 28**), the forward gear internal needle bearing (44) and the forward gear bearing race (42) as follows:

a. Press the roller bearing from the forward gear. Support the bearing with a knife-edged bearing separator (part No. 91-37241). See **Figure 40**. Press on the gear hub using a suitable tool. Discard the bearing upon removal.

8

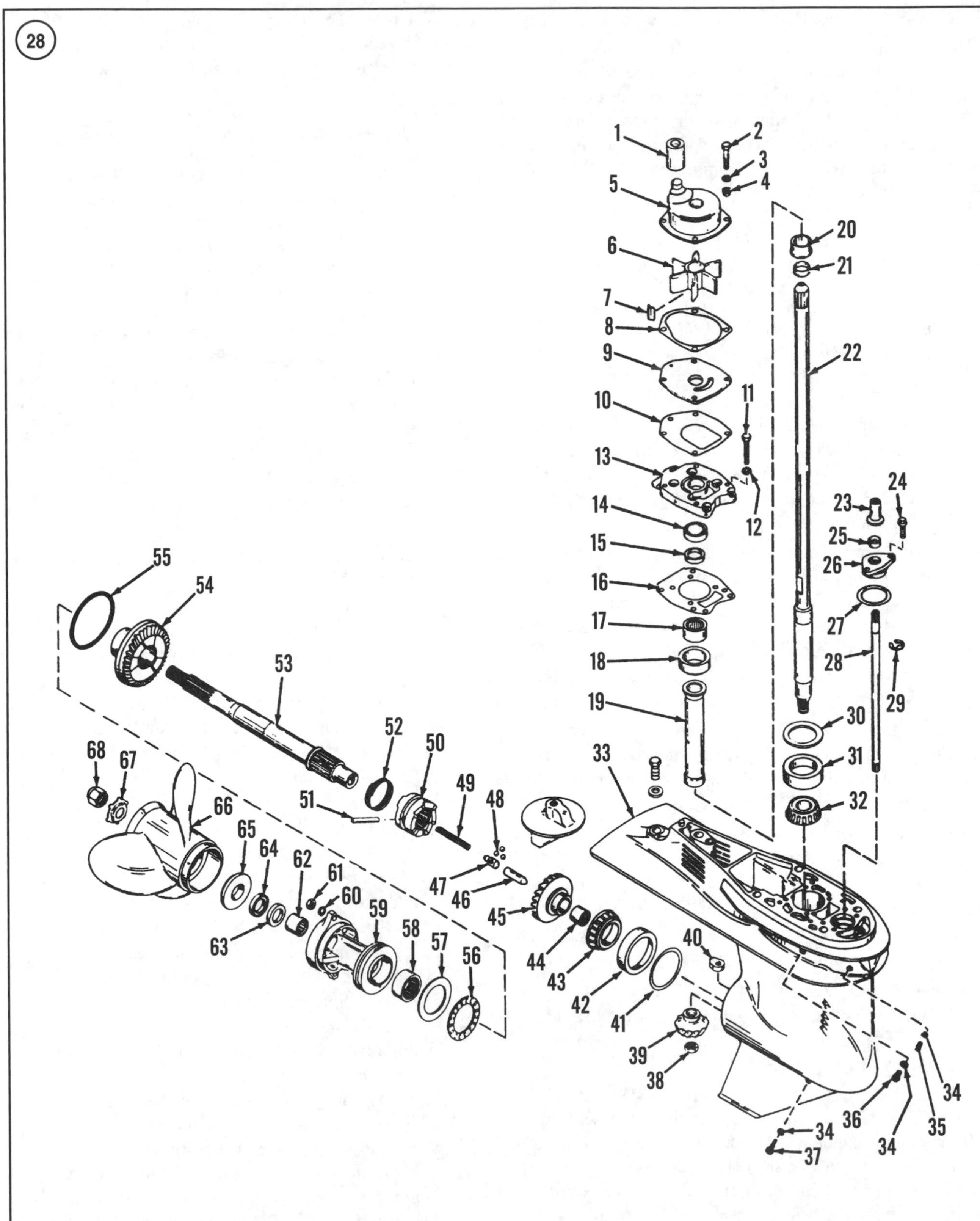
28
1
2
3
4
5
6
7
8
9
10
11
12
13
14
15
16
17
18
19
20
21
22
23
24
25
26
27
28
29
30
31
32
33
34
35
36
37
38
39
40
41
42
43
44
45
46
47
48
49
50
51
52
53
54
55
56
57
58
59
60
61
62
63
64
65
66
67
68

GEARCASE COMPONENTS (75-115 HP MODELS)

1. Water tube seal
2. Screw
3. Washer
4. Insulator*
5. Water pump body
6. Impeller
7. Impeller drive key
8. Gasket
9. Wear plate
10. Gasket
11. Screw
12. Washer
13. Water pump base
14. Seal
15. Seal
16. Gasket
17. Roller bearing
18. Bearing sleeve
19. Lubrication sleeve
20. Wear sleeve
21. Seal ring
22. Drive shaft
23. Shift shaft coupler
24. Screw
25. Seal
26. Shift shaft retainer/bushing
27. O-ring
28. Shift shaft
29. E-clip
30. Shim pack
31. Bearing race
32. Tapered roller bearing
33. Gear housing
34. Gasket
35. Plug
36. Plug
37. Plug
38. Pinion gear nut
39. Pinion gear
40. Shift cam
41. Shim pack
42. Bearing race
43. Tapered roller bearing
44. Needle bearing
45. Forward gear
46. Shift cam follower
47. Guide
48. Three balls
49. Spring
50. Clutch
51. Cross pin
52. Clutch spring
53. Propeller shaft
54. Reverse gear
55. O-ring
56. Thrust bearing
57. Thrust bearing washer
58. Roller bearing
59. Bearing carrier
60. Washer
61. Nut
62. Needle bearing
63. Seal
64. Seal
65. Thrust hub
66. Propeller
67. Tab washer
68. Propeller nut

*Not used on all models.

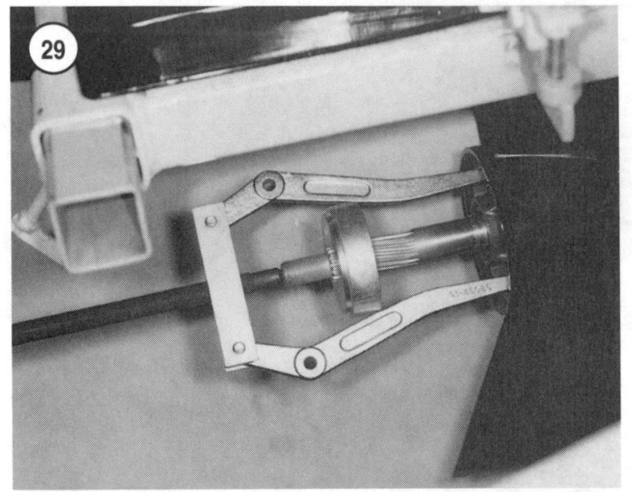

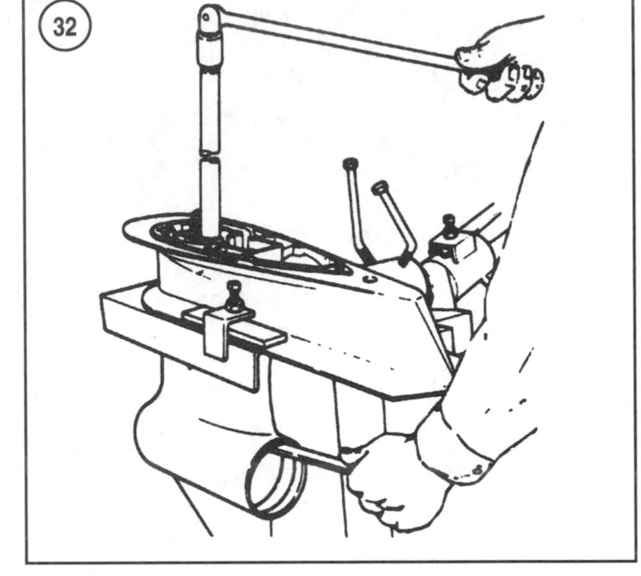

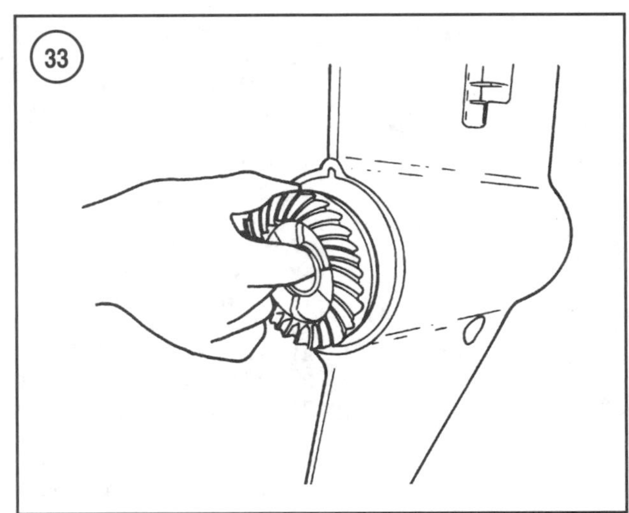

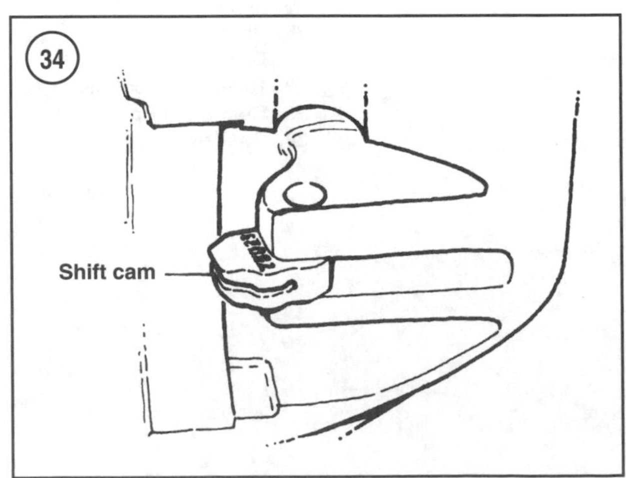
Shift cam

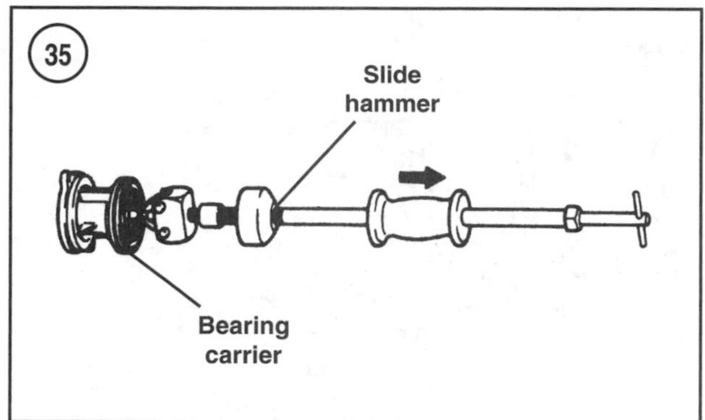
35
Slide hammer
Bearing carrier

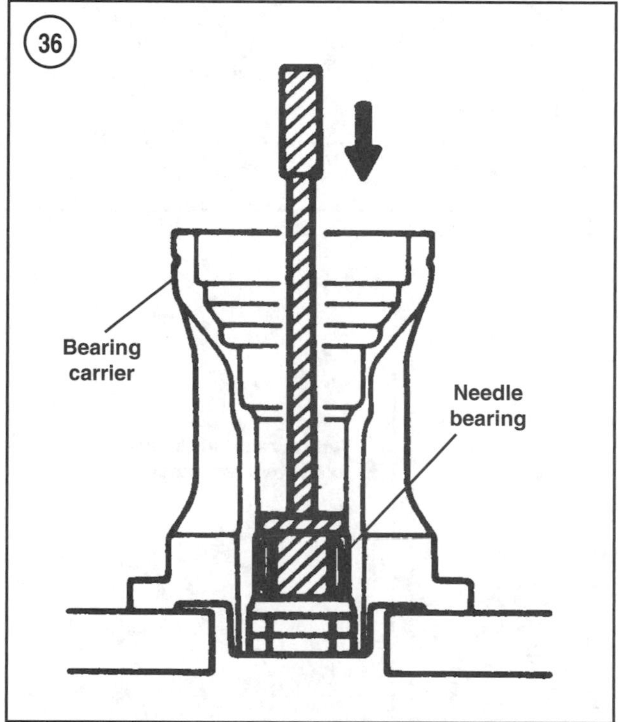
36
Bearing carrier
Needle bearing

37

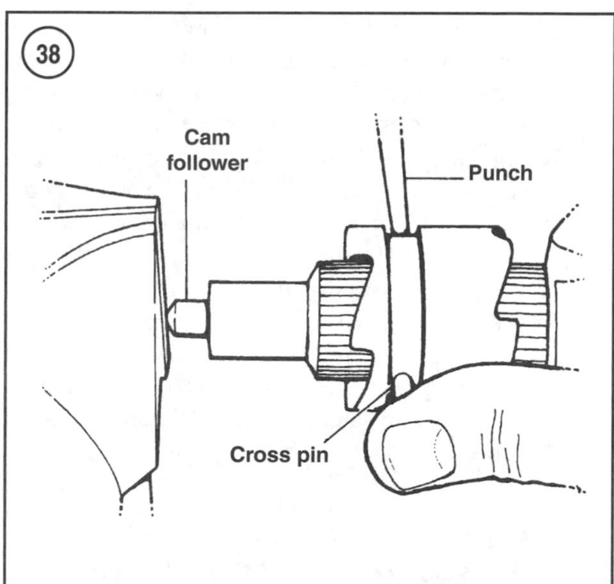
38
Cam follower
Punch
Cross pin

39

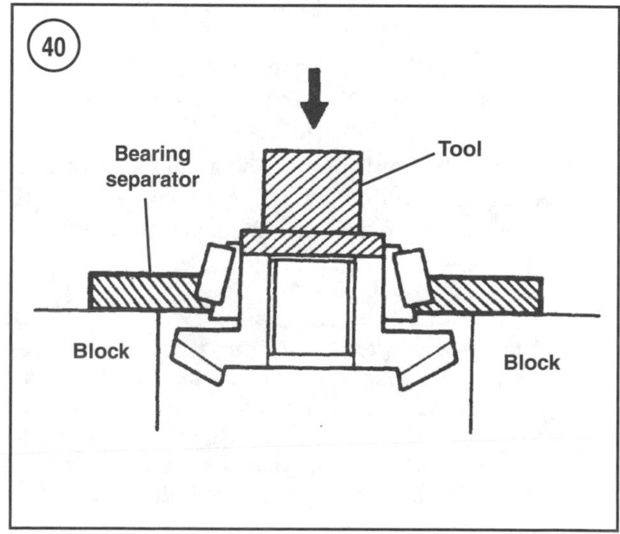
40
Bearing separator
Tool
Block
Block

b. Clamp the gear into a vise with protective jaws with the gear engagement lugs facing down. Use an awl or other suitable instrument to remove the retaining ring from the groove in the needle bearing bore.
c. Clamp the gear into the vise with the gear engagement lugs facing up. Drive the needle bearing from the gear using a punch and hammer. Discard the bearing and retainer.
d. Use a slide hammer (part No. 91-34569A-1) to remove the forward gear bearing race from the gearcase. See **Figure 41**. Remove the shim(s) from the bearing bore. Measure and record the thickness of the shims for later reference. Discard the race if the forward gear roller bearing must be replaced.

NOTE
If the forward gear bearing race was only removed so the shim(s) and forward gear lash could be changed, do not discard the bearing race.

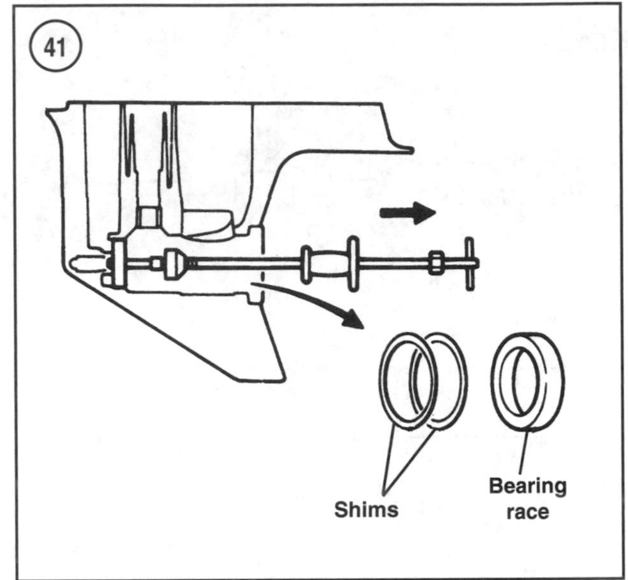

17. If the drive shaft wear sleeve (20, **Figure 28**) and seal ring (21) must be replaced, proceed as follows:
a. Support the drive shaft wear sleeve in a knife-edged bearing separator (part No. 91-37241). The pinion gear end of the shaft must face down.
b. Press on the crankshaft end of the drive shaft until the sleeve is free. See **Figure 42**. Discard the sleeve and rubber seal upon removal.

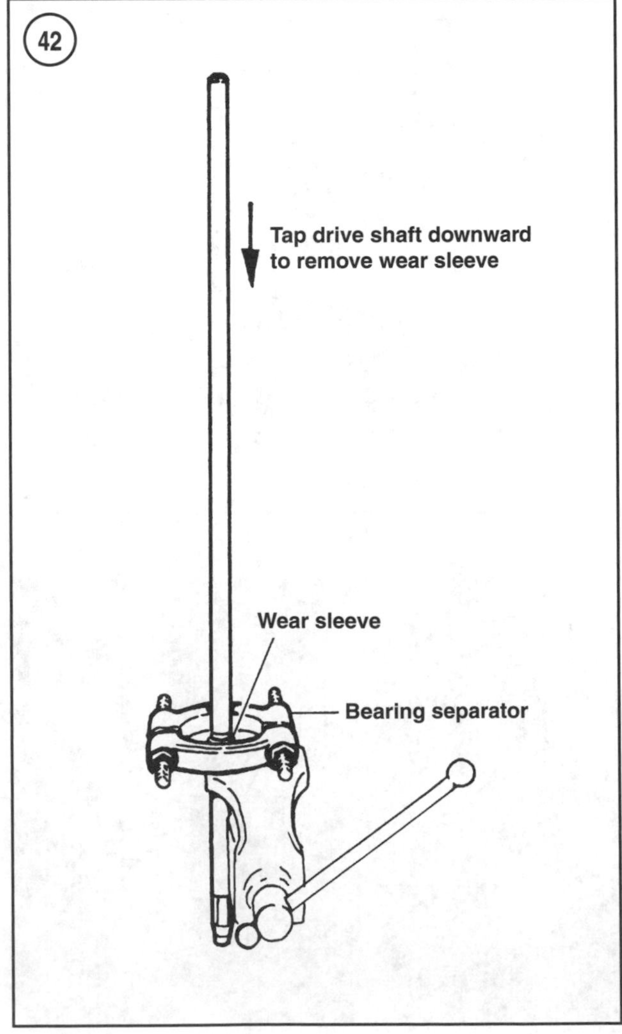

18. If the drive shaft upper bearing (17, **Figure 28**) or the lubrication sleeve (19) must be replaced, proceed as follows:
a. Remove the bearing from the drive shaft bore using a two-jaw puller (part No. 91-83165M or an equivalent) (**Figure 43**). Use a slide hammer to remove the bearing if a suitable two-jaw puller is not available. Discard the bearing.
b. Remove the bearing sleeve (18, **Figure 28**) from the drive shaft bore using the two-jaw puller or slide hammer. Discard the sleeve.
c. Remove the lubrication sleeve from the drive shaft bore using the two-jaw puller. Discard the sleeve. The removal process usually damages the lubrication sleeve.

NOTE
If the drive shaft roller bearing race was removed so the shim(s) and the pinion gear depth could be changed, do not discard the bearing race. The roller bearing race can be removed and installed without removing the drive shaft needle bearing and the lubrication sleeve.

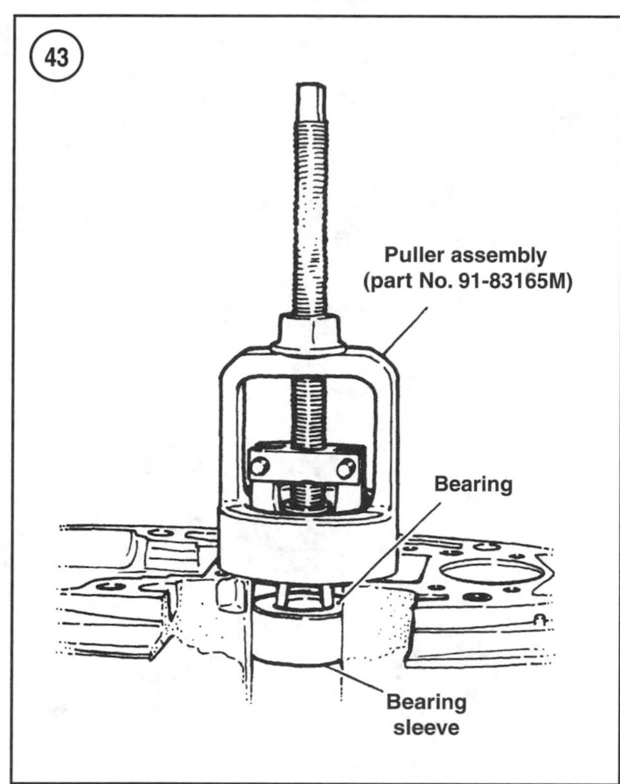

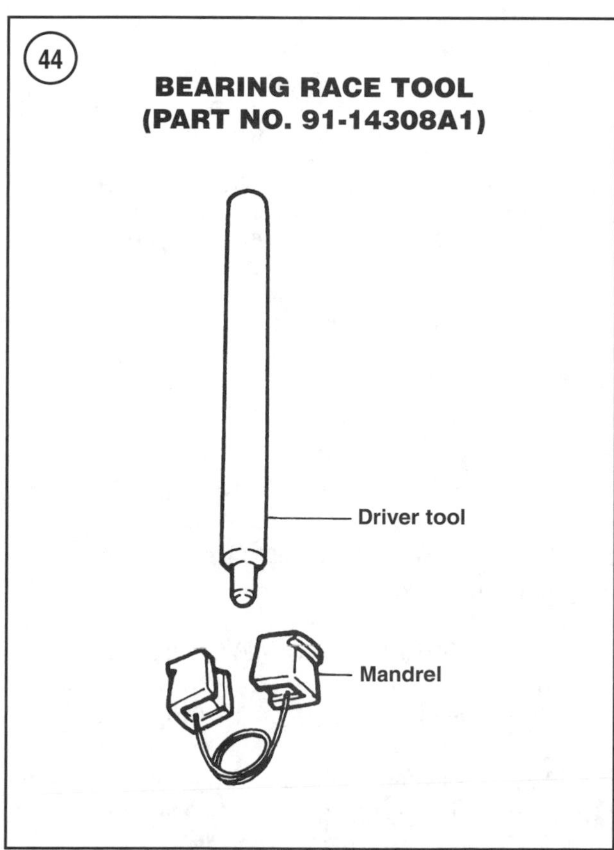

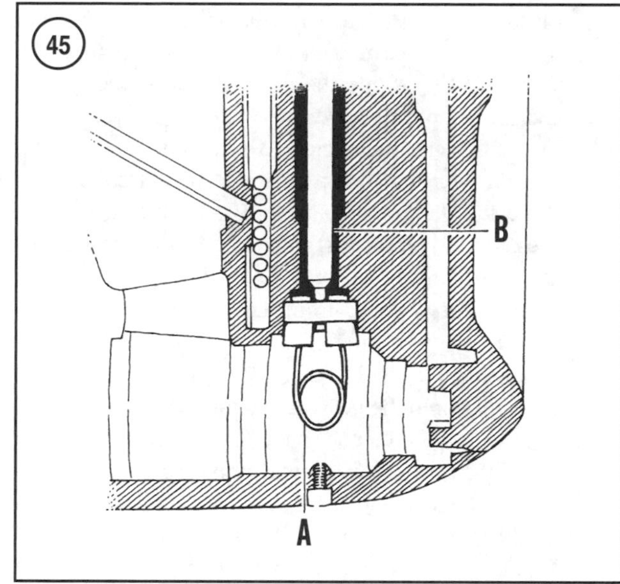

8

19. If the drive shaft roller bearing race (31, **Figure 28**) must be removed or replaced, proceed as follows:

a. Remove the bearing race from the bore by driving it down into the gearcase with a bearing remover (part No. 91-14308A-1). See **Figure 44**. Purchase or rent the tool from a Mercury or Mariner dealership. A suitable equivalent is not commonly available.
b. Insert the mandrel (A, **Figure 45**) from the propeller shaft bore and engage the slots onto the race. Insert the driver rod through the drive shaft bore. Insert the tip of the driver into the opening in the mandrel.
c. Place a shop towel under the mandrel. Use a mallet to drive the bearing race out and into the gearcase bore. Discard the bearing race if replacing the matching roller bearing.

20. Refer to *Gearcase Component Inspection*. Clean and inspect all components before beginning the reassembly procedure.

Assembly

Lubricate all internal components with Quicksilver Premium Blend gearcase lubricant or an equivalent. Do not assemble components dry. Refer to **Figure 28** for this procedure.

1. If the drive shaft wear sleeve (20, **Figure 28**) was removed, install a new sleeve and seal ring (21, **Figure 28**) as follows:

a. Position a new seal ring into the drive shaft groove. Coat the outside diameter of the seal with Loctite 271 (part No. 920809819).

b. Place a new wear sleeve into the holder (shorter piece) from the sleeve installation kit (part No. 91-14310A-1). Slide the drive shaft, double-splined end first, into the sleeve and holder.
c. Fit the driver (longer piece) from the sleeve installation kit over the pinion gear end of the drive shaft. Place the drive shaft and tool assembly in a press. Press the driver against the holder until they contact each other.
d. Wipe excess Loctite from the drive shaft and wear sleeve.

2. If the lower drive shaft bearing was removed, install the race and shim(s) into the gearcase as follows:
a. Lubricate the race and place the original shim(s) on top of the race. If the original shim(s) are lost or damaged to the point they cannot be measured, use a 0.025 in. shim.
b. Position the race into the bore with the tapered side facing down.
c. Assemble the bearing installer components as shown in **Figure 46**.
d. Tighten the nut (1, **Figure 46**) to seat the race fully in the bore. Hold the threaded rod (3, **Figure 46**) with a wrench while tightening the nut.

3. If the drive shaft lubrication sleeve (19, **Figure 28**) was removed, lubricate the new sleeve and insert it into the bore with the tapered opening facing up. Align the tab on the sleeve with the notch in the bore, then use hand pressure to push the sleeve into the bore. The sleeve will be fully seated in the bore in the next step.

NOTE
Make sure the lubrication sleeve is installed into the drive shaft bore before installing the drive shaft needle bearing and sleeve.

4. If the drive shaft needle bearing (17, **Figure 28**) and sleeve (18) were removed, install a new bearing and sleeve assembly into the drive shaft bore as follows:
a. If the new bearing is separate from the new bearing sleeve, lubricate both parts with gearcase lubricant, then set the sleeve on a press with the tapered side facing down. Position the needle bearing into the sleeve with the numbered side facing up. Using a suitable mandrel, press the bearing into the sleeve until it is flush with the sleeve.
b. Lubricate the outer diameter of the new bearing and sleeve with gearcase lubricant. Place the assembly into the drive shaft bore with the tapered side facing down.
c. Assemble the installer components as shown in **Figure 47**. Tighten the nut to seat the bearing assembly and lubrication sleeve into the drive shaft bore. Hold the threaded rod (3, **Figure 47**) with a suitable wrench while tightening the nut.

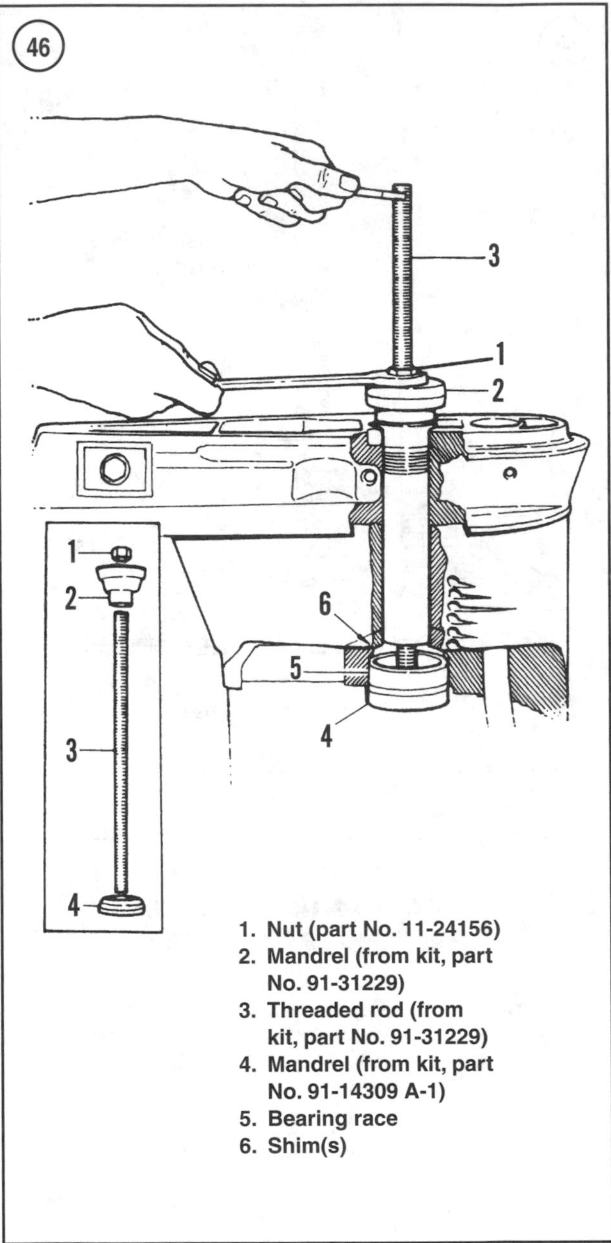

1. Nut (part No. 11-24156)
2. Mandrel (from kit, part No. 91-31229)
3. Threaded rod (from kit, part No. 91-31229)
4. Mandrel (from kit, part No. 91-14309 A-1)
5. Bearing race
6. Shim(s)

5. If the forward gear bearing race (42, **Figure 28**) was removed, install the race and shims into the gearcase as follows:
a. Position the shims (**Figure 48**) into the bearing bore. If the original shims were lost or damaged to the point they cannot be measured, use a 0.010 in. shim.
b. Lubricate the bearing race (**Figure 48**) with gearcase lubricant and insert it into the gearcase bore with the tapered side facing out. Place the mandrel (part No. 91-31106 or an equivalent) onto the race.

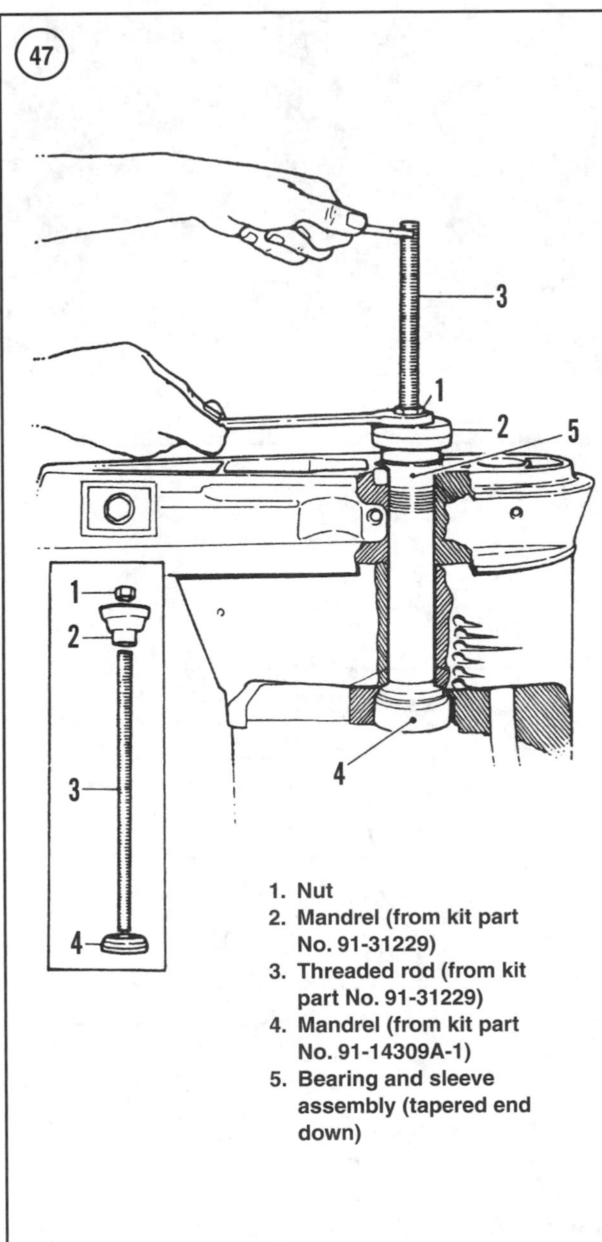

1. Nut
2. Mandrel (from kit part No. 91-31229)
3. Threaded rod (from kit part No. 91-31229)
4. Mandrel (from kit part No. 91-14309A-1)
5. Bearing and sleeve assembly (tapered end down)

c. Insert the propeller shaft into the mandrel opening. Temporarily install the empty bearing carrier over the propeller shaft and into the gearcase to keep the propeller shaft centered.

d. Thread a spare propeller nut onto the propeller shaft. Use a mallet to drive the propeller shaft against the mandrel until the bearing race fully seats in the gearcase bore.

e. Remove the propeller shaft, carrier and mandrel.

6. If the forward gear roller bearing was removed, lubricate a new bearing with gearcase lubricant and insert it onto the

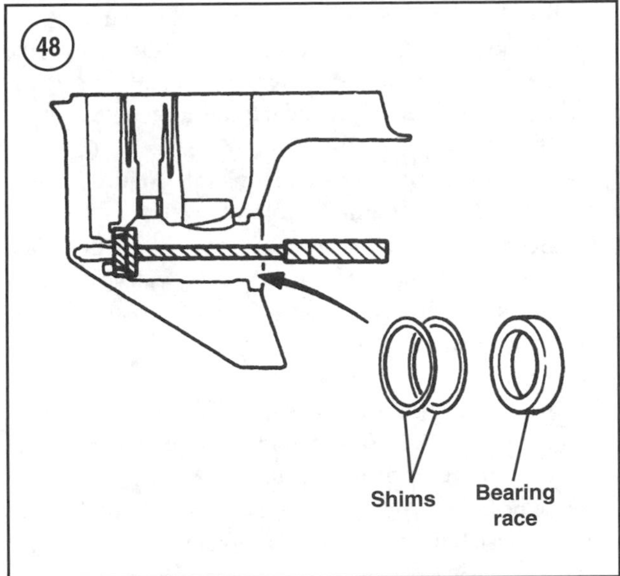

gear hub with the rollers facing up. Press the bearing fully onto the gear with a mandrel (part No. 91-37350 or equivalent). See **Figure 49**. Do not press on the roller bearing cage.

7. If the forward gear internal needle bearing (44, **Figure 28**) was removed, install the new bearing as follows:

a. Place the forward gear on a press with gear teeth facing down.

b. Lubricate the new needle bearing with gearcase lubricant, then insert the bearing into the bore with the numbered side facing up.

c. Press the bearing into the bore with a mandrel (part No. 91-877321A-1) until the bearing just bottoms in the bore. The retaining ring groove is fully exposed when the bearing bottoms in the bore. Be careful not to damage the bearing by over-pressing.

8

d. Fit the retaining ring into the groove in the needle bearing bore. If the ring cannot be installed, the needle bearing is not fully seated in the bore. Make sure the ring is fully seated around the entire circumference of the groove.

8. If the bearing carrier roller bearing (58, **Figure 28**) was removed, install the bearing as follows:

a. Set the carrier into a press with the propeller end facing down. Lubricate the new bearing with gearcase lubricant, then insert it into the carrier bore with the numbered side facing up.

b. Press the bearing into the bore with a mandrel (part No. 91-13945 or equivalent) until the bearing bottoms in the bore. See **Figure 50**. Be careful not to damage the bearing by over-pressing.

9. If the bearing carrier needle bearing (62, **Figure 28**) was removed, install the new bearing as follows:

a. Insert the carrier in a press with the propeller end facing up, and resting on the roller bearing installation tool (part No. 91-13945) or other suitable mandrel to protect the carrier and reverse gear roller bearing.

b. Lubricate the new needle bearing with gearcase lubricant, then insert it into the bore with the numbered side facing up.

c. Press the bearing into the bore with a mandrel (part No. 91-15755 or equivalent) until the bearing bottoms in the bore and the bearing is just below the seal bore. See **Figure 51**.

10. If the propeller shaft was disassembled, refer to **Figure 52** and reassemble the shaft as follows:

a. Lubricate all components with gearcase lubricant.

b. Fit the sliding clutch (6, **Figure 52**) onto the forward gear end of the propeller shaft (5) with the grooved side of the clutch facing the propeller end of the shaft. Align the cross pin hole in the sliding clutch with the slot in the propeller shaft, then slide the sliding clutch onto the propeller shaft splines.

c. Insert the spring (4, **Figure 52**) into the propeller shaft bore. Then install the spring guide (3, **Figure 52**) with the narrow end toward the spring.

d. Install the three balls (2, **Figure 52**) into the shaft bore. Make sure the balls rest against the spring guide.

e. Insert the cam follower (1, **Figure 52**) into the shaft bore with the pointed end facing out.

f. Press the cam follower against a solid object to compress the spring. Align the hole in the sliding clutch with the hole in the spring guide. If necessary, use a small punch to align the holes (**Figure 38**).

g. Insert the cross-pin into the clutch and through the spring guide hole. The cross pin must pass through the holes in the clutch, propeller shaft and spring guide.

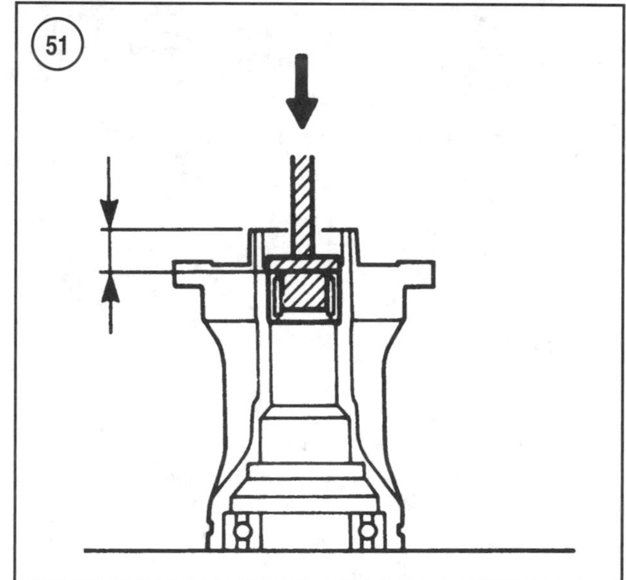

NOTE

The clutch spring must lay flat against the sliding clutch, with no overlapping coils.

h. Carefully wind the clutch spring onto the clutch (**Figure 37**). Do not open the spring any more than necessary to install it.

11. Install two new propeller shaft seals (63 and 64, **Figure 28**) as follows:

a. Coat the outer diameter of the new seals with Loctite 271.

b. Set the carrier in a press with the propeller side facing up, and resting on the roller bearing installation tool (part No. 91-13945 or an equivalent) to protect the carrier and reverse gear roller bearing.

c. Install the smaller diameter seal into the bore with the lip (spring) side facing in. Press the seal into the bore with the larger stepped end of the mandrel (part No.

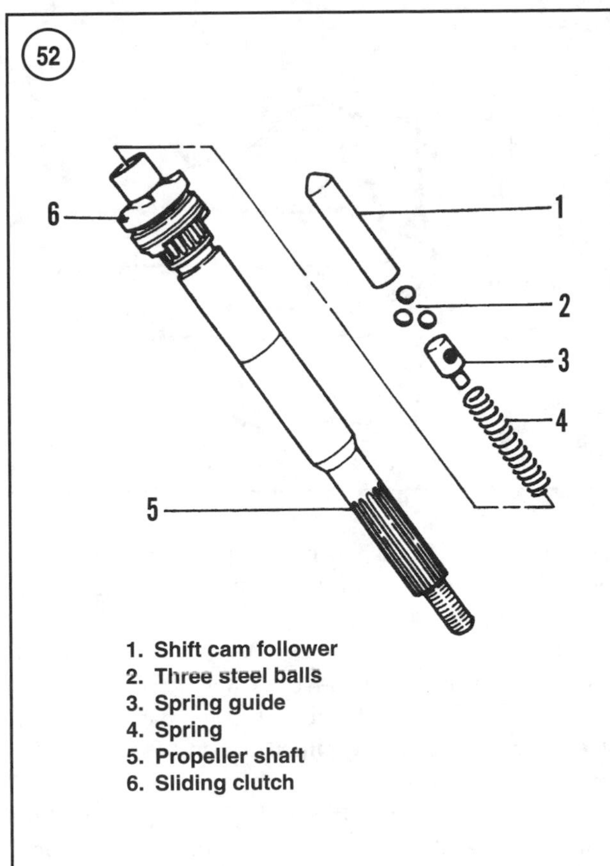

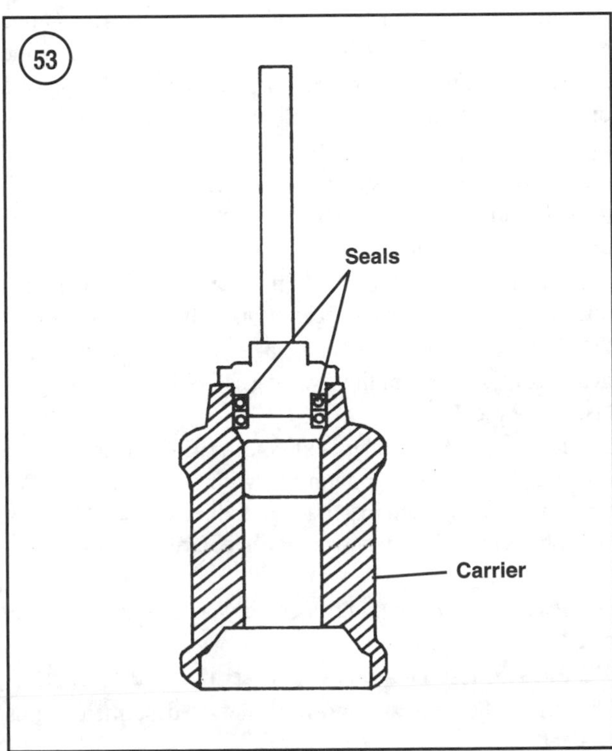

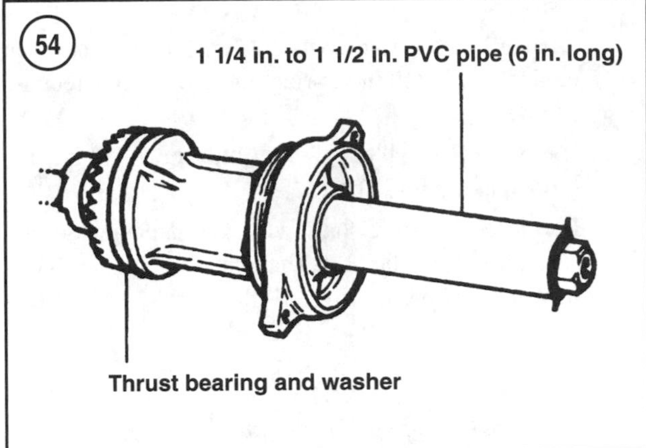

91-31108 or an equivalent) until the tool bottoms against the carrier. See **Figure 53**.

d. Install the larger diameter seal into the bore with the lip (spring) side facing out. Press the seal into the bore with the smaller stepped end of the mandrel until the tool bottoms against the carrier. See **Figure 53**.

12. Coat a new bearing carrier O-ring (55, **Figure 28**) and the propeller shaft seal lips with Quicksilver 2-4-C Marine Lubricant or an equivalent. Then install the O-ring into the groove in the bearing carrier.

13. Assemble the propeller shaft bearing carrier, reverse gear and bearings as follows:

a. Lubricate the roller bearing (58, **Figure 28**) and thrust bearing (56) with Quicksilver Needle Bearing Assembly Grease (part No. 92-825265A-1). Install the thrust bearing washer onto the bearing carrier (**Figure 31**).

b. Lubricate the thrust bearing with the same grease and place in on top of the thrust bearing washer (**Figure 30**).

c. Install the reverse gear into the bearing carrier. Be careful not to disturb the position of the thrust bearing and washer.

d. Carefully slide the propeller shaft into the bearing carrier assembly. Be careful not the damage the propeller shaft seals.

e. Obtain a section of 1 1/4 or 1 1/2 in. diameter, 6 in. long PVC pipe. Install the PVC pipe over the propeller shaft, then install the locking tab washer and propeller nut. Hand-tighten the nut to hold the propeller shaft securely in the bearing carrier (**Figure 54**).

14. Assemble and install the shift shaft components as follows:

a. Coat the outer diameter of the new shift shaft seal (25, **Figure 28**) with Loctite 271. Insert the seal into the shift shaft bushing/retainer bore with the lip (spring) side facing up. Use a suitable mandrel to press the seal into the bore until flush with the retainer bore.

8

b. Lubricate the seal lip and a new O-ring (27, **Figure 28**) with Quicksilver 2-4-C Marine Lubricant or an equivalent. Install the O-ring into the bushing/retainer groove.

c. If removed, install the E-clip (29, **Figure 28**) into the groove in the shift shaft (28).

d. Lubricate the shift shaft with the same grease and carefully insert the shift shaft into the bottom bushing/retainer bore until the E-clip contacts the assembly.

NOTE
For proper shifting, the part number (857307) stamped into the shift cam must face up on 75-115 hp models. The UP stamping in the cam is used to reference the cam position. The UP stamping may or may not be on the same side of the cam as the 857307 part No. stamping.

e. Place the shift cam into the gear housing into the gear housing with the stamped No. 857307 facing up (**Figure 55**). Guide the shift shaft into the bore and engage the shaft splines into the shift cam internal splines.

f. Align the screw openings, then seat the bushing/retainer against the gear housing. Work carefully to avoid damaging or dislodging the O-ring.

g. Apply Loctite 271 to the threads, then install the two screws (24, **Figure 28**). Tighten the screws to 60 in.-lb. (6.8 N•m).

15. Rotate the gearcase to position the propeller shaft opening facing up. Install the forward gear and bearing assembly into the opening and into the forward gear bearing race.

16. Install the drive shaft roller bearing (32, **Figure 28**) into the race at the bottom of the drive shaft bore. The tapered side of the bearing must fit into the race. Place the pinion gear (39, **Figure 28**) in position and aligned with the bearing. Rotate the pinion gear as necessary to mesh the pinion and forward gear teeth.

17. Spray the threads of the drive shaft with Loquic primer (part No. 92-809824). Guide the drive shaft into the bore while holding the pinion gear and bearing in position. Rotate the drive shaft as necessary to engage the drive shaft and pinion gear splines.

NOTE
Apply Loctite 271 onto the new pinion nut threads after the pinion gear depth and forward gear backlash have been verified. Install the original pinion nut without the threadlocking compound to check the pinion depth and gear backlash.

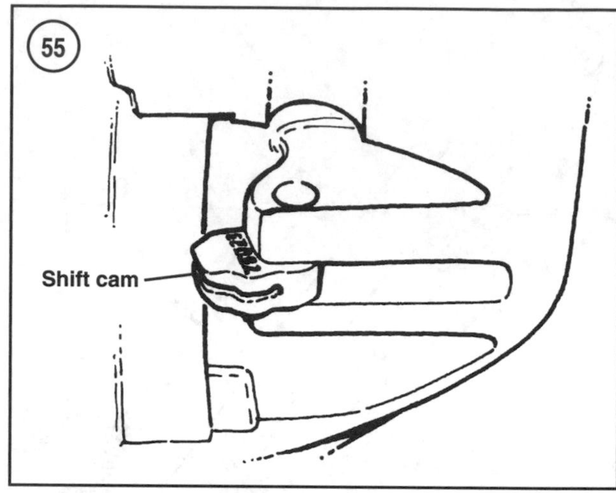

18. Thread the original pinion nut onto the drive shaft with the recessed side facing *toward* the pinion gear. Tighten the nut finger-tight at this time.

19. Hold the pinion nut with a suitable wrench or socket. Attach a spline socket (part No. 91-804776A 1) to a suitable torque wrench (**Figure 56**). Turn the drive shaft clockwise to tighten the pinion nut to 70 ft.-lb. (95.0 N•m).

20. Refer to *Gearcase Shimming* in this chapter to set the pinion gear depth. Do not continue with assembly until the pinion gear depth is correct.

21. Apply a coat of Quicksilver 2-4-C Marine lubricant onto the front and rear flanges of the bearing carrier. Guide the propeller shaft and bearing carrier assembly into the gearcase opening and into the forward gear needle bearing opening. Make sure the cam follower does not fall out during assembly.

22. Align the openings in the rear flange of the carrier with the two studs. *Slowly* rotate the drive shaft to allow the gear teeth to mesh while seating the carrier into the housing.

23. Install the washers (60, **Figure 28**) and locknuts (61) onto the studs. Tighten the locknuts to 22 ft.-lb. (30.0 N•m).

24. Refer to *Gearcase Shimming* in this chapter to set the gear lash. Do not continue with assembly until the gear lash is correct.

25. Remove the propeller shaft and bearing carrier assembly, and install a new pinion nut with Loctite 271 as described in this chapter. Install the propeller shaft and bearing assembly and tighten the locknuts as described in this chapter.

26. Install the water pump assembly as described in this chapter.

27. Pressure test the gearcase as described in this chapter.

28. Install the gearcase and propeller as described in this chapter.

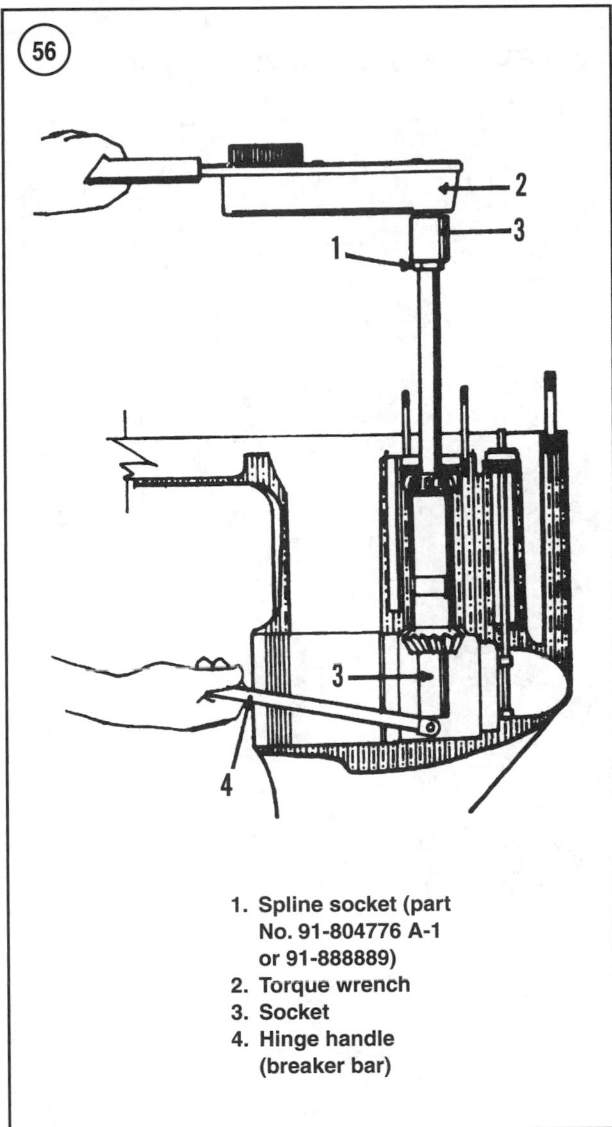

1. Spline socket (part No. 91-804776 A-1 or 91-888889)
2. Torque wrench
3. Socket
4. Hinge handle (breaker bar)

29. Fill the gearcase with the recommended lubricant as described in Chapter Three.
30. Adjust the shift cables and linkages as described in Chapter Four.

225 hp Model

Disassembly

The bearing carrier can be removed without removing the gearcase from the engine, if so desired. The propeller shaft cannot be removed without removing the gearcase.

Refer to **Figure 57** or **Figure 58**.

1. Drain the gearcase lubricant as described in Chapter Three.
2. Remove the propeller and gearcase as described in this chapter.
3. Remove the water pump and base as described in this chapter.
4. Rotate the shift shaft while rotating the drive shaft clockwise, as viewed from the top, until NEUTRAL gear is obtained.
5. Remove the three screws (**Figure 59**), then carefully pry the shift shaft bushing/retainer from the gearcase. Grip the shift shaft and carefully pull the shift shaft and bushing/retainer as an assembly from the gearcase. Do not rotate the propeller shaft after removing the shift shaft.
6. Remove the O-ring (17, **Figure 57** or 24, **Figure 58**) from the retainer. Carefully pry the shift shaft seal from the retainer. Do not damage the seal bore in the retainer during seal removal. Discard the O-rings and seal.

CAUTION
Avoid damaging the shifter and other shift components during the propeller shaft removal process. Always remove the shift shaft from the gearcase before pulling the propeller shaft from the gearcase.

7. Remove the two screws and the retaining ring (**Figure 60**). Remove the two screws (**Figure 61**) that secure the bearing carrier into the gearcase housing.

8A. On Standard rotation (RH) gearcase, install the puller jaws (part No. 91-46086A-1) and puller bolt (part No. 91-85716 or an equivalent). Tighten the puller bolt to free the assembly from the gearcase. Do not allow the propeller shaft to rotate while tightening the puller bolt. If necessary, use a propeller thrust hub (**Figure 62**, typical) to prevent the puller jaws from sliding inward. When free, grip the propeller shaft and manually pull the assembly from the gearcase.

8B. On Counter rotation (LH) gearcase, thread the adapter (part No. 91-888879) onto the propeller shaft. Thread a slide hammer (such as part No. 91-34569A-1) onto the adapter (**Figure 63**). Do not allow the propeller shaft to rotate while removing the carrier assembly. Use short hammer strokes to free the assembly from the gearcase. Remove the slide hammer and adapter. Grip the propeller shaft and manually pull the bearing carrier and propeller shaft assembly from the gearcase.

9. Remove the two large O-rings (4, **Figure 58**, typical) from the bearing carrier grooves. Discard the O-rings.

10A. On Standard rotation (RH) gearcase, remove the propeller shaft, reverse gear and bearing as follows:

a. Pull the propeller shaft assembly out of the reverse gear and bearing carrier assembly. Remove the thrust washer from the propeller shaft or reverse gear (22, **Figure 57**).

57

GEARCASE COMPONENTS (225 HP STANDARD ROTATION [RH] MODEL)

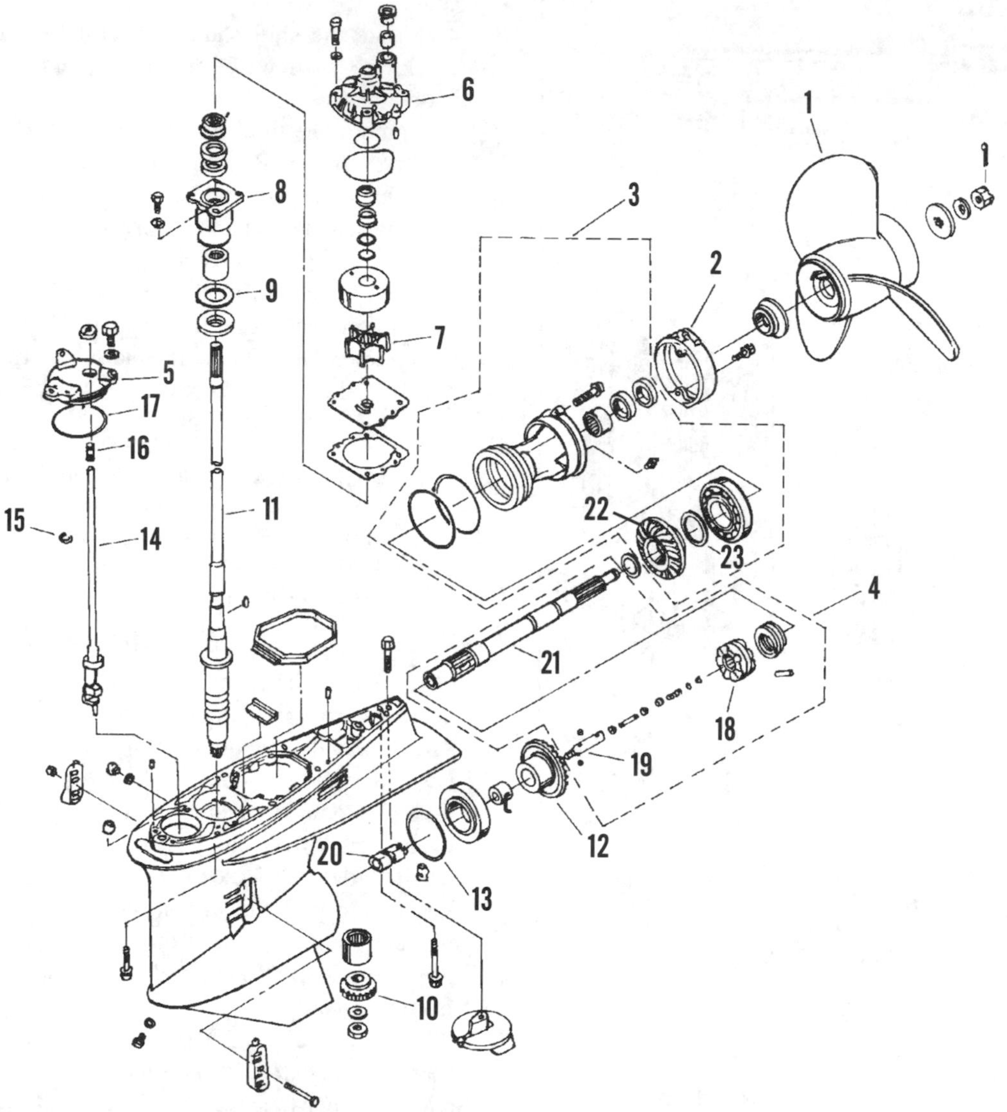

1. Propeller assembly
2. Retaining ring
3. Bearing carrier assembly
4. Shift slider and clutch assembly
5. Shift shaft retainer/bushing
6. Water pump body
7. Impeller
8. Drive shaft bearing and seal housing
9. Shim (pinion gear locating)
10. Pinion gear
11. Drive shaft
12. Forward gear
13. Shim (forward gear locating)
14. Shift shaft
15. E-clip
16. Spring
17. O-ring
18. Clutch
19. Shift slider
20. Shifter
21. Propeller shaft
22. Reverse gear
23. Shim (reverse gear locating)

58

GEARCASE COMPONENTS (225 HP COUNTER ROTATION [LH] MODEL)

1. Propeller
2. Retainer
3. Bearing carrier
4. O-rings
5. Needle bearing
6. Shim (propeller shaft end play control)
7. Thrust bearing
8. Propeller shaft
9. Roller bearing set
10. Shim (forward gear positioning)
11. Tab washer
12. Retainer
13. Forward gear
14. Clutch
15. Shift slider
16. Reverse gear
17. Needle bearings
18. Roller bearing
19. Thrust bearing
20. Reverse gear bearing sleeve
21. Shim (reverse gear positioning)
22. Shifter
23. Pinion gear
24. O-ring
25. Shift shaft retainer/bushing
26. Drive shaft
27. Drive shaft bearing and seal housing
28. Water pump body
29. Impeller

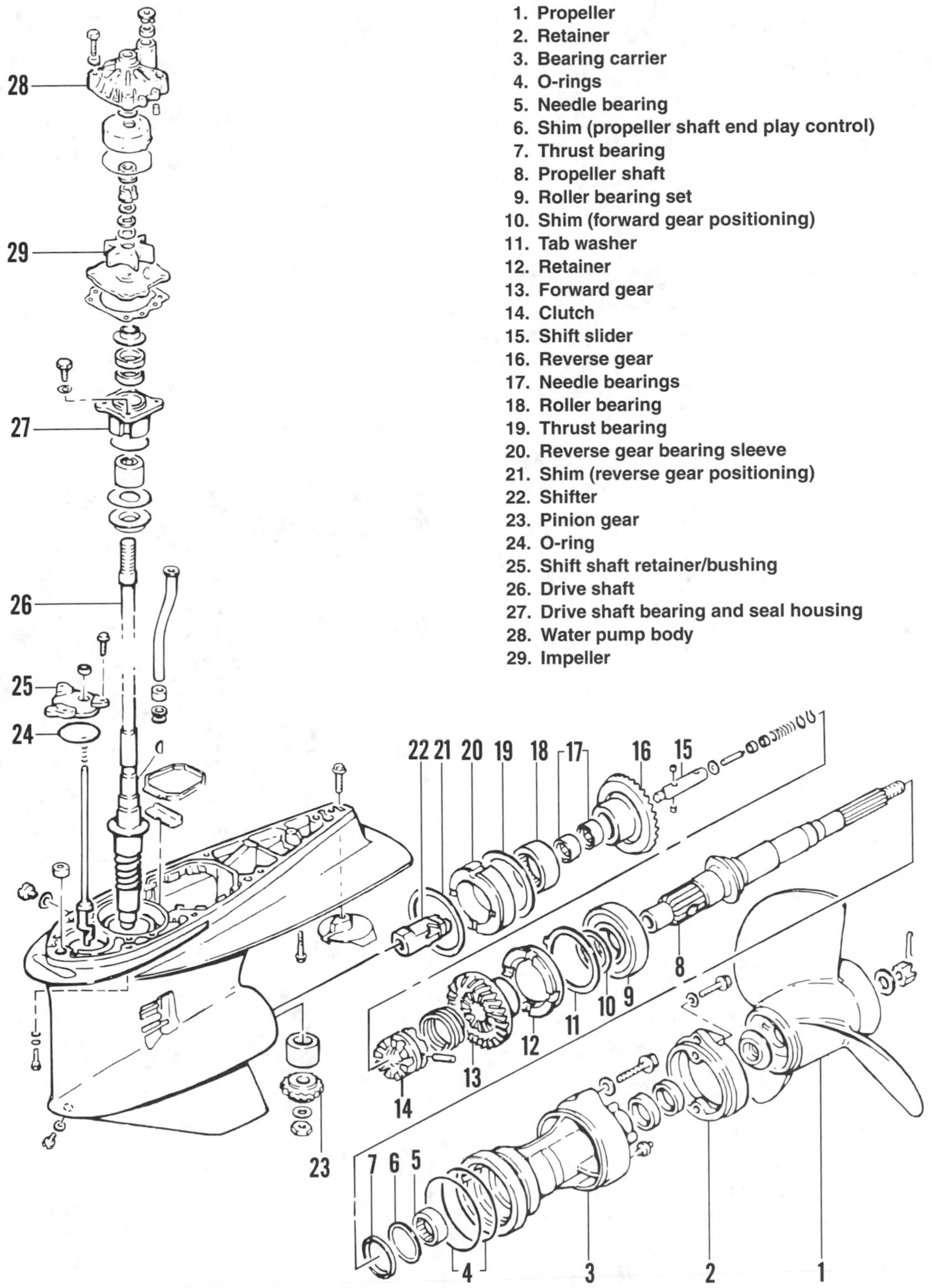

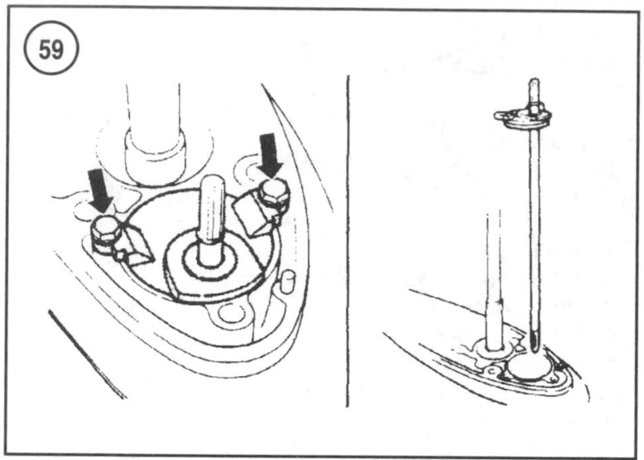

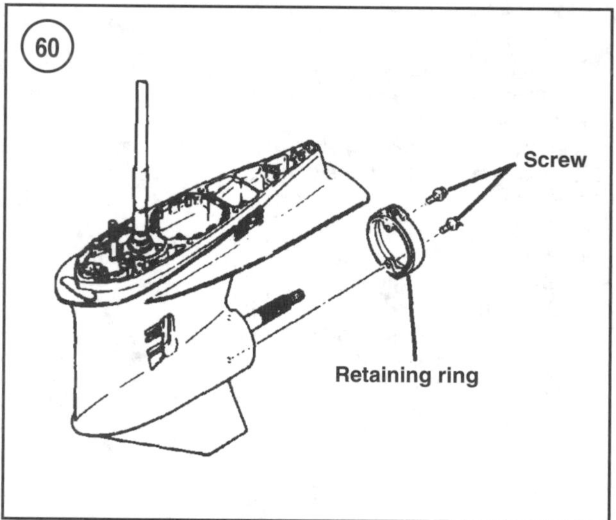

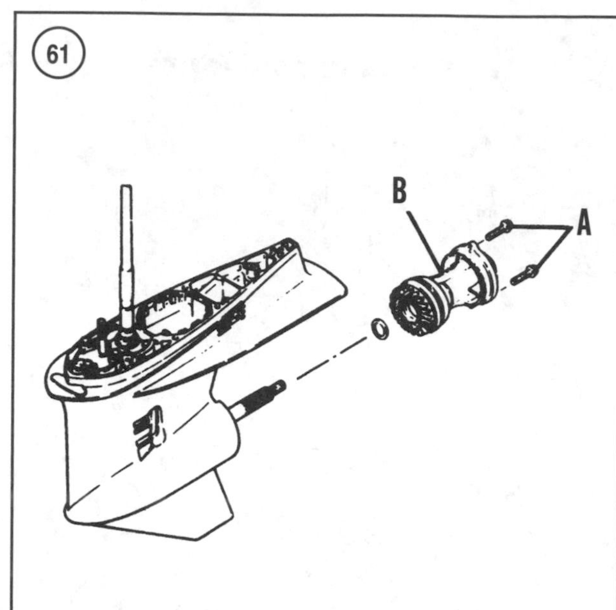

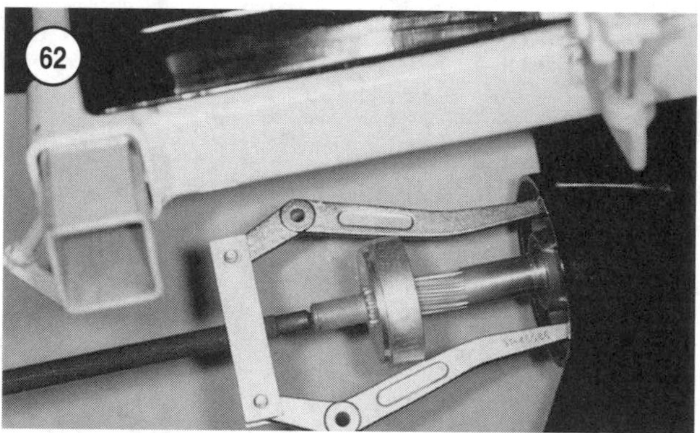

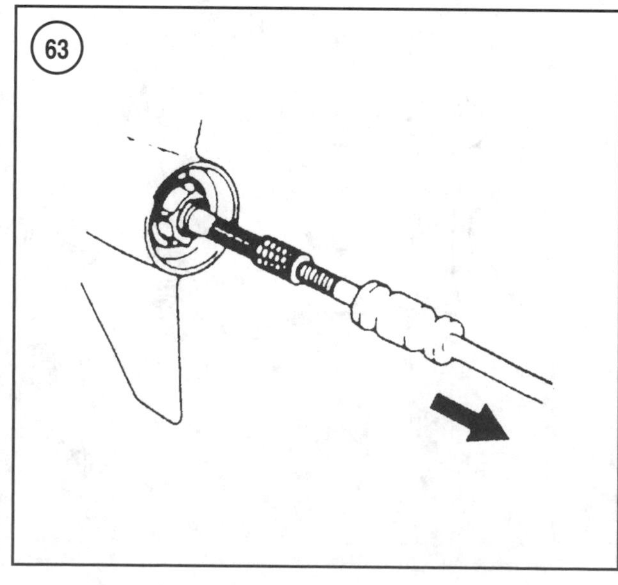

NOTE

Remove the reverse gear on standard rotation (RH) gearcases only if the reverse gear or reverse gear bearing must be replaced. The removal process damages the bearing.

b. Clamp the bearing carrier into a vise with protective jaws. Engage the jaws of a slide hammer into the hub of the reverse gear (**Figure 64**). Use short hammer strokes to remove the reverse gear from the carrier.

c. If the bearing remains on the gear, press the ball bearing from the reverse gear. Support the bearing with a knife-edged bearing separator, such as part No. 91-37241. See **Figure 65**. Press on the gear hub using a suitable tool.

d. If the bearing remains in the carrier, clamp the bearing carrier into a vise with protective jaws. Engage the jaws of a slide hammer beneath the inner bear-

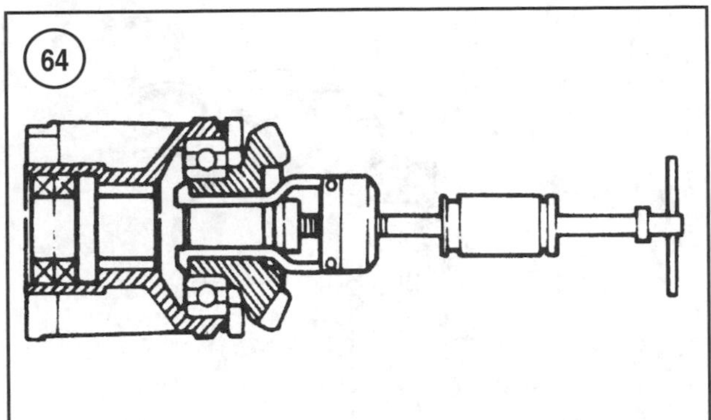

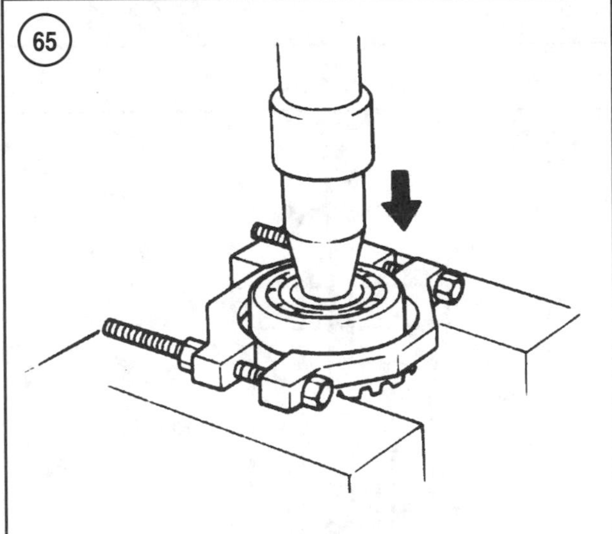

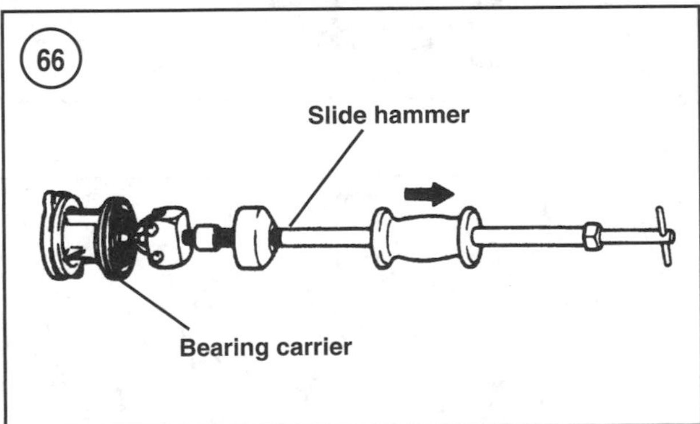

ing race (**Figure 66**). Use short hammer strokes to remove the bearing. Remove the shim (23, **Figure 57**) from the reverse gear or bearing. Discard the reverse gear bearing upon removal.

e. Hook the end of a small screwdriver over an end loop of the clutch spring (**Figure 67**). Carefully unwind the spring from the clutch. Use a pin punch to push the cross pin from the clutch, propeller shaft and shift slider (**Figure 68**).

f. Place the propeller shaft over a container suitable for capturing small objects. Pull the clutch from the propeller shaft, then pull the shifter (20, **Figure 57**) shift slider (19) and related shifter components from the propeller shaft bore.

10B. On counter rotation (LH) gearcase, remove the propeller shaft and forward gear as follows:

a. Hook the end of a small screwdriver over an end loop of the clutch spring (**Figure 67**). Carefully wind the spring from the clutch. Use a pin punch to push the cross pin from the clutch, propeller shaft and shift slider (**Figure 68**).

b. Place the propeller shaft over a container suitable for capturing small objects. Pull the clutch from the propeller shaft, then pull the shifter (22, **Figure 58**), shift slider (15) and related shifter components from the propeller shaft bore.

c. Press the propeller shaft and bearing carrier assembly out of the forward gear. Support the bearing with a knife-edged bearing separator (part No.

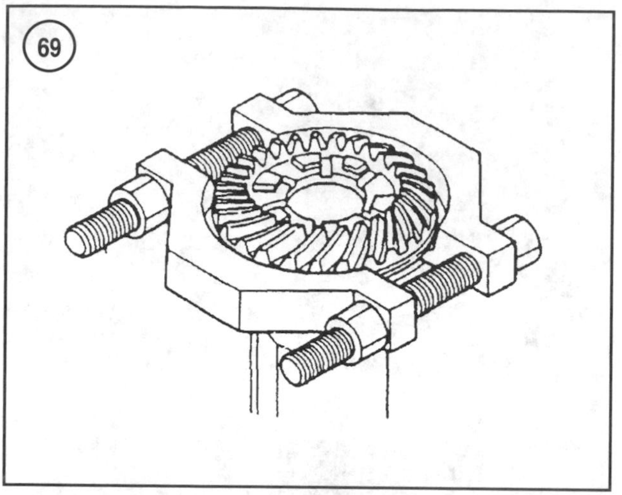

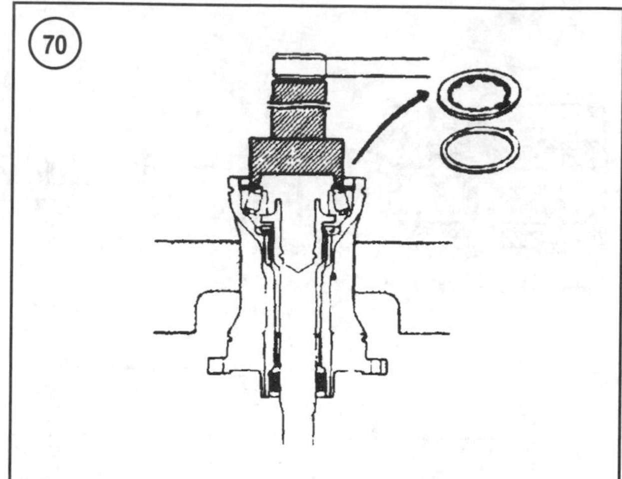

91-37241). See **Figure 69**. Press on the clutch end of the propeller shaft until the gear is free from the carrier. Remove the forward gear positioning shim (10, **Figure 58**) from the forward gear (13) or roller bearing set (9).

d. Clamp the bearing carrier firmly in a vise with protective jaws. Use the spanner tool (part No. 91-888880T) to remove the retainer and tab washer (**Figure 70**).

e. Position the bearing carrier in a press with the propeller side facing up. Thread a spare propeller nut onto the end of the propeller shaft to protect the threads. Press on the propeller shaft until free from the bearing carrier.

f. Remove the propeller shaft (8, **Figure 58**), roller bearing (9) and race, thrust bearing (7) and end play control shim (6) from the bearing carrier.

NOTE

If the needle bearing inside the bearing carrier must be replaced, also remove the propeller shaft seals during the bearing removal process. If needle bearing replacement is not necessary, remove and discard both propeller shaft seals at the same time using a suitable seal puller. Do not damage the seal bore in the process.

11. If the bearing carrier needle bearing must be replaced, remove as follows:

a. Set the carrier in a press with the propeller end facing down.

b. Assemble the mandrel (part No. 91-888881) and driver rod (part No. 91-888882, or equivalent). Position the mandrel and driver rod in the carrier bore on top of the needle bearing (**Figure 71**).

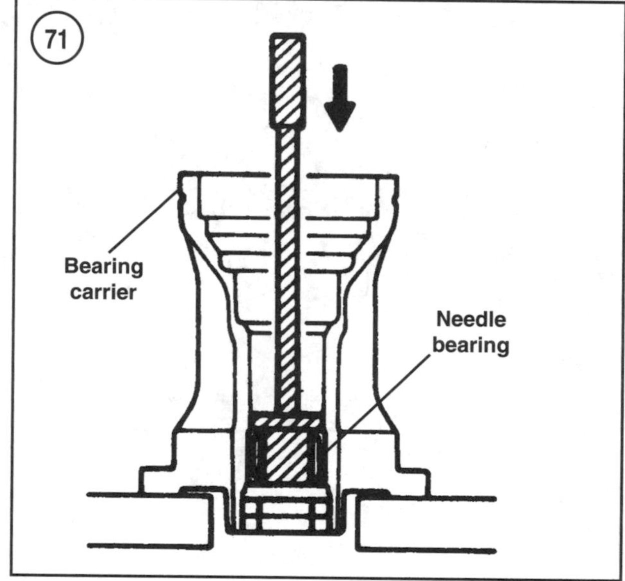

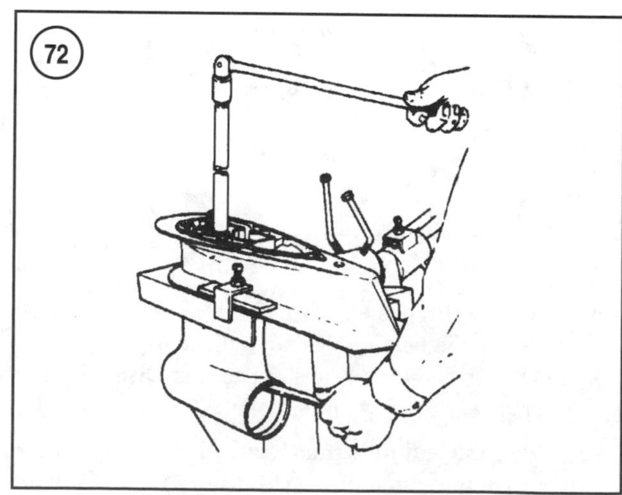

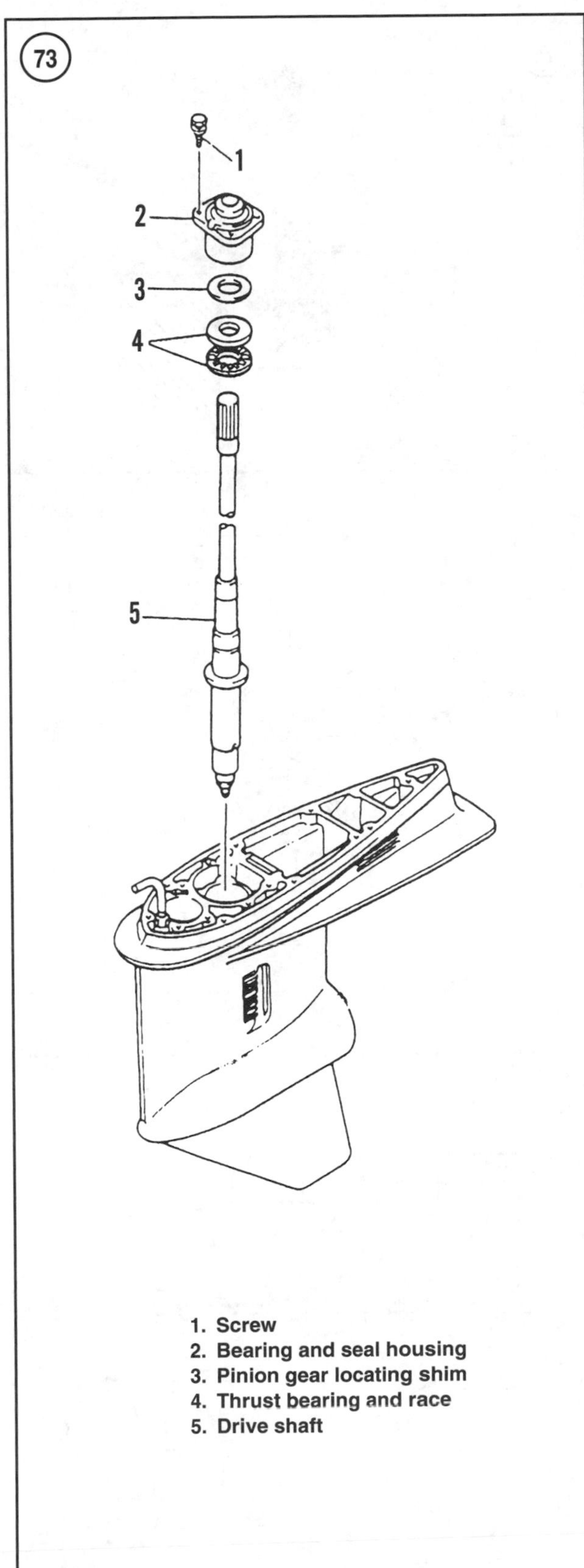

1. Screw
2. Bearing and seal housing
3. Pinion gear locating shim
4. Thrust bearing and race
5. Drive shaft

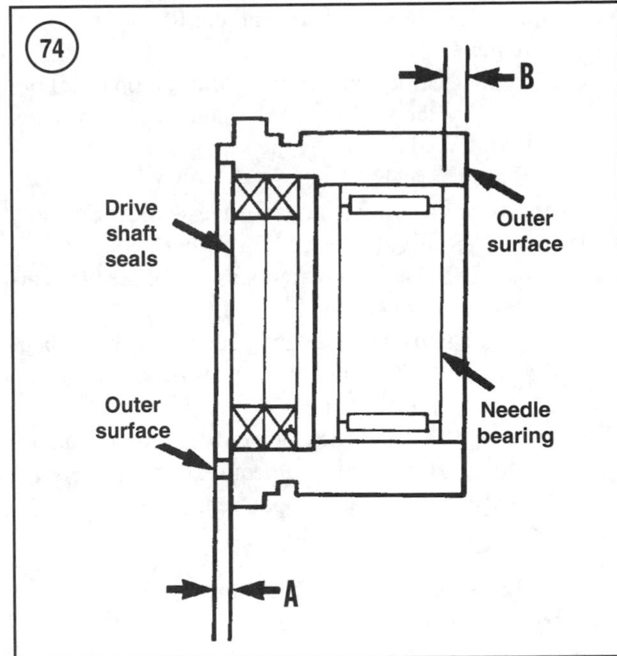

c. Press the propeller shaft needle bearing and seals from the carrier. Discard the bearing and seals.

12. Remove the pinion nut by holding the nut with a suitable socket or wrench, then turning the drive shaft counterclockwise using spline socket (part No. 91-888889) until the nut and washer are free from the drive shaft (**Figure 72**).

NOTE
Mark the up side and note the orientation of the drive shaft thrust bearing and shim prior to removal from the drive shaft or bearing and seal housing. If reused, these components must be installed in the same location and orientation as removed.

13. Remove the four screws (1, **Figure 73**), then remove the bearing and seal housing (2) from the drive shaft and gearcase. If removal is difficult, carefully pry the housing loose. Do not damage the mating surfaces. Remove the pinion gear locating shim (3, **Figure 73**) and thrust bearing (4) from the drive shaft or bearing and seal housing.

14. Replace the seals in the drive shaft bearing and seal housing (8, **Figure 57** or 27, **Figure 58**) anytime the housing requires service.

a. Carefully pry the seal protector from the top side of the housing.

b. Use a depth micrometer to measure the seal depth at the points indicated (A, **Figure 74**). This is necessary to ensure the seals contact the drive shaft at the proper location when assembled. Record the measurement.

c. Note the seal lip direction, then use a blunt tip pry bar to pry the seals from the housing. Work carefully to avoid damaging the seal bore.

d. Discard the seals.

15. Remove the bearing from the drive shaft bearing and seal housing (8, **Figure 57** or 27, **Figure 58**) only if it must be replaced. The removal process damages the bearing. Proceed as follows:

a. Place the housing on a sturdy surface with an opening below the housing that is of sufficient size to accommodate the bearing.

b. Drive the bearing from the housing with a mandrel (part No. 91-888884 or an equivalent). See **Figure 75**. Discard the bearing upon removal.

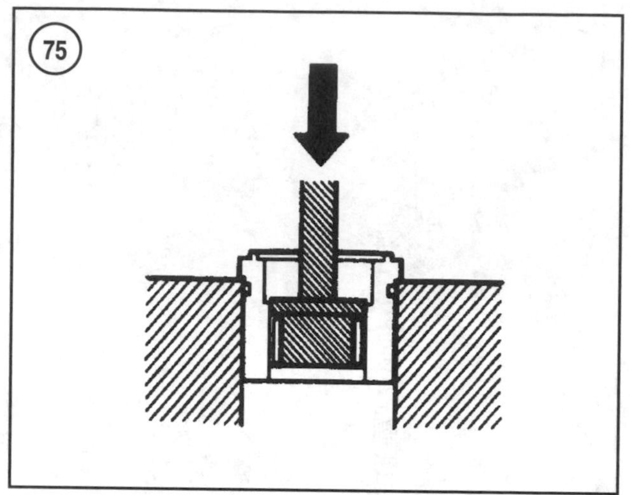

NOTE

Drive shaft removal can be difficult. When necessary, clamp the drive shaft into a vise with protective jaws. Place a large sponge into the gearcase opening to prevent components from falling from the gearcase. Support the gearcase and use a block of wood for a cushion to drive the gearcase from the drive shaft.

16. Support the pinion gear (10, **Figure 57** or 23, **Figure 58**), then pull the drive shaft from the gearcase. Remove the pinion gear from the housing.

17A. On a standard rotation (RH) gearcase, remove the forward gear from the gearcase (**Figure 76**).

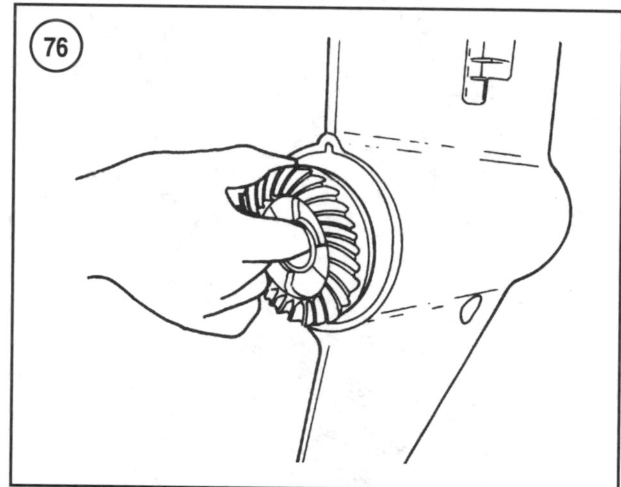

17B. On a counter rotation (LH) gearcase, remove the reverse gear from the gearcase (**Figure 76**). Then, remove the thrust bearing (19, **Figure 58**) from the forward gear or bearing carrier (20) in the gearcase. If the thrust bearing will be reused, mark the gear side for reference during assembly.

18. On a standard rotation (RH) gearcase, use a suitable slide hammer (such as part No. 91-34569A-1) to remove the forward gear bearing race from the gearcase (**Figure 77**). Remove the shim(s) from the bearing bore. Measure and record the thickness of the shims for later reference. Discard the race if the forward gear roller bearing must be replaced.

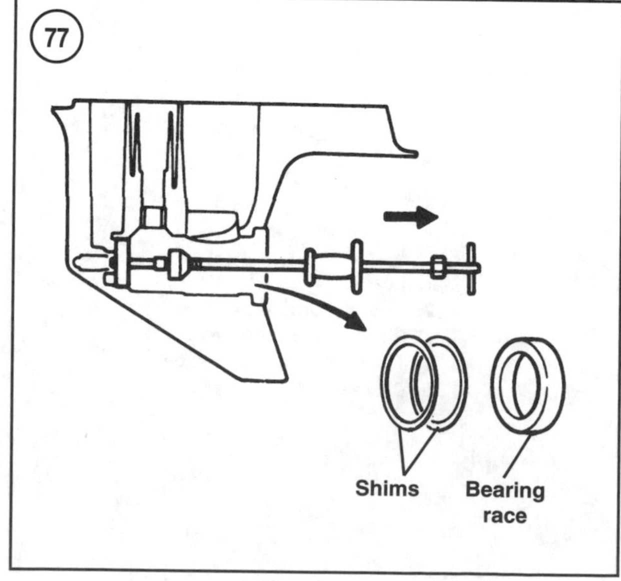

NOTE

If the forward gear bearing race was only removed so the shim(s) and forward gear lash could be changed, do not discard the bearing race.

19. On a counter rotation (LH) gearcase, remove the reverse gear bearing carrier only if replacement is required or if the reverse gear locating shims (21, **Figure 58**) must be changed to correct the gear lash. Proceed as follows:

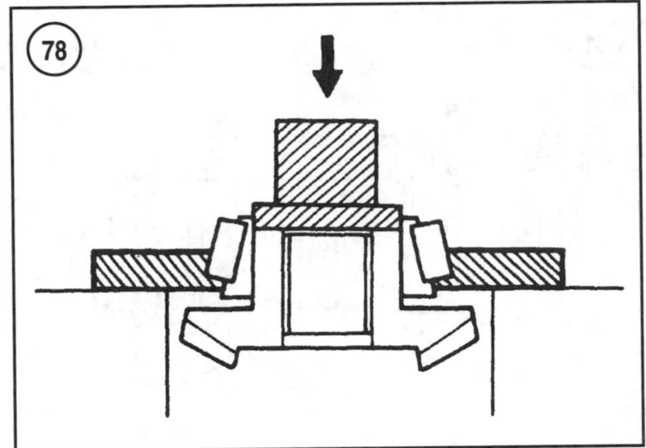

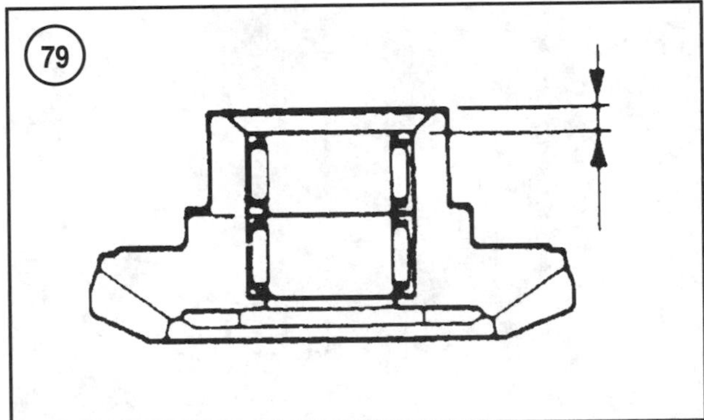

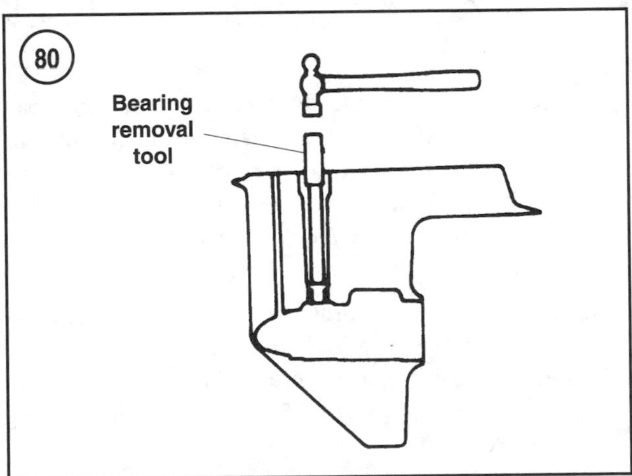

a. Insert the puller plate (part No. 91-83164M) into the gearcase with the threaded opening facing outward. Seat the puller against the bearing carrier, then thread 6 mm screws into the puller and bearing carrier threaded openings.

b. Thread the shaft of a suitable slide hammer (such as part No. 91-34569A-1) into the threaded puller opening. Use short hammer strokes to remove the carrier from the gearcase. Separate the puller and carrier. Measure and record the thickness of the shims for later reference.

20A. On a standard rotation gearcase (RH), if the forward gear roller bearing must be replaced, press the roller bearing from the forward gear using a knife-edged bearing separator (part No. 91-37241). See **Figure 78**. Press on the gear hub using a suitable tool. Discard the bearing upon removal.

20B. On a counter rotation (LH) gearcase, remove the reverse gear roller bearing (18, **Figure 58**) from the bearing sleeve (20) only if it must be replaced. The removal process damages the bearing.

a. Position the reverse gear bearing carrier assembly (20, **Figure 58**) onto a press with an opening below the carrier of ample size to accommodate the roller bearing. Place sturdy blocks under the carrier as needed.

b. Use a mandrel to press the bearing from the carrier. Discard the bearing upon removal.

8

NOTE

A single needle bearing is installed into the propeller shaft bore of the forward gear on standard rotation (RH) gearcases. Two bearings are installed into the propeller shaft bore of the reverse gear on counter rotation (LH) gearcases.

21. Remove the needle bearing(s) from the forward gear (standard rotation gearcase) or reverse gear (counter rotation gearcase) only if replacement is required. The removal process damages the bearing(s). Proceed as follows:

a. Use a depth micrometer to measure the bearing depth in the bore (**Figure 79**). This is required to ensure the bearing will contact the propeller shaft at the proper location upon assembly. Record the measurement.

b. Clamp the gear into the vise with the gear engagement lugs facing up. Do not over-tighten the vise. Drive the needle bearing(s) from the gear using a punch and hammer. Discard the bearing(s).

22. Remove the lower drive shaft bearing only if it must be replaced. The removal process damages the bearing. Proceed as follows:

a. Thread the drive rod (part No. 91-888870) onto a mandrel (part No. 91-888890) or other suitable bearing removal tool.

b. Insert the removal tool into the drive shaft bore and seat it against the bearing (**Figure 80**).

c. Carefully tap the bearing into the gearcase housing. Discard the bearing.

23. Refer to *Gearcase Component Inspection*. Clean and inspect all components before beginning the reassembly procedure.

Assembly

Lubricate all internal components with Quicksilver Premium Blend gearcase lubricant or an equivalent. Do not assemble components dry. Refer to *Gearcase Shimming* in this chapter for shim selection procedures prior to beginning the assembly process. Refer to **Figure 57** or **Figure 58**.

1. If the lower drive shaft bearing was removed, install the new bearing as follows:
   a. Apply gearcase lubricant onto the bearing surfaces and the bore in the gearcase housing.
   b. Insert the bearing into the bore with the numbered side facing down.
   c. Insert the mandrel (part No. 91-888892) into the bearing and hold in position while guiding the threaded rod into the drive shaft bore. Install the puller plate (part No. 91-29310) over the threaded rod and rest it on the gearcase (**Figure 81**). Thread the rod into the mandrel and thread the nut onto the upper end of the rod.
   d. Hold the threaded rod with a wrench, then tighten the nut to pull the bearing into the bore. Continue until the bearing just contacts the step in the bore. Do not over-tighten the nut.
   e. Remove the installation tools.

2A. On a standard rotation (RH) gearcase, if the needle bearing in the propeller shaft bore of the forward gear was removed, install the new needle bearing as follows:
   a. Place the forward gear on a press with gear teeth facing down.
   b. Lubricate the new needle bearing with gearcase lubricant, then insert the bearing into the bore with the numbered side facing up.
   c. Press the bearing into the bore with a mandrel (part No. 91-888881 or equivalent) until the bearing reaches the exact depth (**Figure 79**) recorded prior to removal.

2B. On a counter rotation (LH) gearcase, the needle bearings (17, **Figure 58**) in the propeller shaft bore of the reverse gear were removed, install the new bearings as follows:
   a. Place the reverse gear on a press with gear teeth facing down.
   b. Lubricate the new needle bearings with gearcase lubricant, then insert the first bearing into the bore with the numbered side facing up.

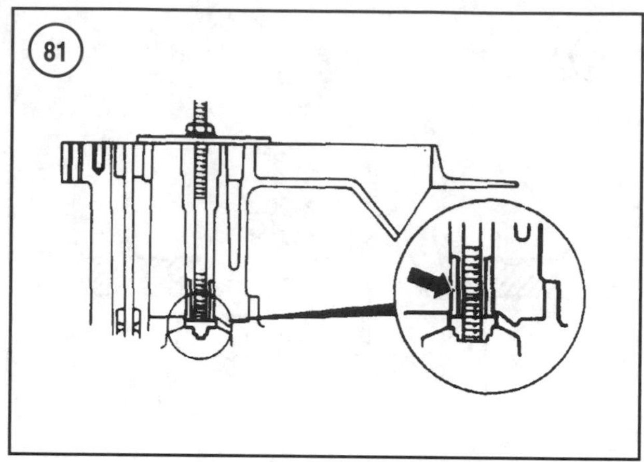

   c. Press the bearing into the bore with a mandrel (part No. 91-888881 or other suitable mandrel) until the bearing reaches a depth of 0.817-0.836 in. (20.75-21.23 mm) below the bore opening. Stop frequently and measure the depth during the installation process. Do not over-press the bearing.
   d. Insert the second bearing into the bore with the numbered side facing up. Use the same method to press the second bearing into the bore until it reaches a depth of 0.167-0.187 in. (4.24-4.75 mm) below the opening (**Figure 79**).

3A. On a standard rotation (RH) gearcase, if the forward gear roller bearing was removed, lubricate the new bearing with gearcase lubricant and set in onto the gear hub with the rollers facing up. Press the bearing fully onto the gear with a mandrel (part No. 91-888893 or equivalent). See **Figure 82**. Do not press on the roller bearing cage.

3B. On a counter rotation (LH) gearcase, if the reverse gear roller bearing (18, **Figure 58**) was removed from the sleeve (20), install the new bearing as follows:

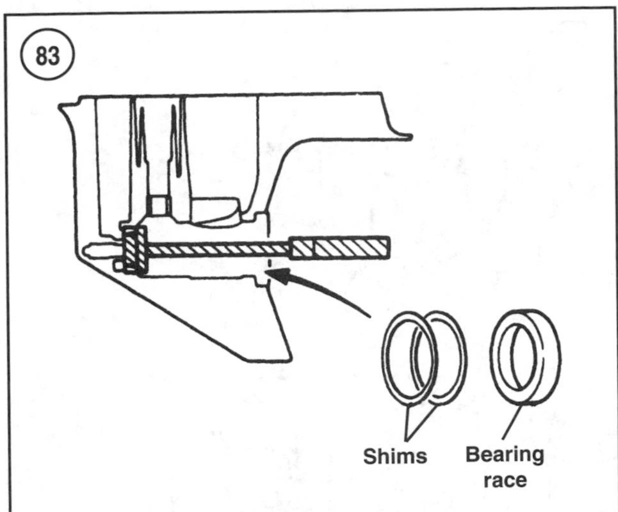

a. Place the carrier on a press with the slotted side facing up.
b. Lubricate the new bearing with gearcase lubricant. Place the new bearing into the carrier bore with the numbered side facing up.
c. Use a mandrel to press the bearing into the carrier until it reaches a depth of 0.010 in. (0.25 mm) below the bore opening. The mandrel must contact only the bearing case during installation.

NOTE

When driving a bearing race or carrier into the gearcase housing, always use very light taps and listen to the noise when the driver is struck. Strike the driver only hard enough to slightly move the race or carrier. Stop driving when the pitch changes or a sharp ring is heard as the driver is struck. This indicates the race or carrier is seated. Continued driving may bounce the bearing or race out of the bore.

4A. On a standard rotation (RH) gearcase, if the forward gear bearing race was removed, install the race and shims into the gearcase as follows:

a. Position the shims (**Figure 83**) into the bearing bore. If the original shims were lost or damaged to the point they cannot be measured, use a 0.010 in. (0.25 mm) shim.
b. Lubricate the bearing race (**Figure 83**) with gearcase lubricant and insert it into the gearcase bore with the tapered side facing out. Place the mandrel (part No. 91-8888891 or an equivalent) onto the race.
c. Insert the driver rod (part No. 91-888870) into the mandrel. Temporarily install the empty bearing carrier over the driver rod and into the gearcase to keep the driver rod centered.
d. Use a mallet to drive the rod against the mandrel until the bearing race fully seats in the gearcase bore.
e. Remove the driver rod, carrier and mandrel.

4B. On a counter rotation (LH) gearcase, if the reverse gear bearing carrier (20, **Figure 58**) was removed, install the carrier and shims as follows:

a. Position the shims (21, **Figure 58**) into the carrier bore. If the original shims were lost or damaged to the point they cannot be measured, use a 0.010 in. (0.25 mm) shim.
b. Lubricate the bearing carrier with gearcase lubricant and set it into the gearcase bore with the notched side facing in. Place the mandrel (part No. 91-8888891 or an equivalent) onto the carrier.
c. Insert the driver rod (part No. 91-888870) into the mandrel. Temporarily install the empty bearing carrier over the driver rod and into the gearcase to keep the driver rod centered.
d. Use a mallet to drive the rod against the mandrel until the carrier fully seats in the gearcase bore.
e. Remove the driver rod, carrier and mandrel.

5A. On a standard rotation (RH) gearcase, rotate the gearcase to position the propeller shaft opening facing up. Install the forward gear and bearing assembly into the opening and into the forward gear bearing race. See **Figure 76**.

5B. On a counter rotation (LH) gearcase, rotate the gearcase to position the propeller shaft opening facing up. Lubricate the surfaces with Quicksilver 2-4-C Marine Lubricant, then position the thrust bearing (19, **Figure 58**) onto the reverse gear bearing carrier (20). Install the reverse gear into the gearcase (**Figure 76**). Insert the gear hub into the bearing opening in the carrier, then seat the gear against the thrust bearing.

NOTE

The upper drive shaft bearing must be installed to the proper depth within the bearing and seal housing to ensure that the bearing contacts the drive shaft at the proper location. The housing does not provide a step or shoulder for the bearing. Slowly tap the bearing into the housing. Stop and check the depth frequently during installation.

6. If the bearing was removed from the drive shaft bearing and seal housing (8, **Figure 57** or 27, **Figure 58**), install the new bearing as follows:

a. Place the drive shaft bearing and seal housing on a press with the mounting flange side facing down.

b. Insert the new bearing into the housing bore with the numbered side facing down.
c. Press the bearing into the bore with a mandrel (part No. 91-888884 or other suitable mandrel) until the bearing reaches a depth of 0.167-0.187 in. (4.24-4.75 mm) below the opening (B, **Figure 74**). Stop frequently and measure the depth during the installation process.

7. Install the new drive shaft seals into the bearing and seal housing as follows:

a. Place the drive shaft bearing and seal housing on a press with the mounting flange facing up.
b. Coat the outer diameter of the new seals Loctite 271.
c. Install the smaller first seal into the bore with the lip (spring) side facing up. Press the seal into the bore using a mandrel (part No. 91-888887 or an equivalent) until the seal case is just below the bore opening.
d. Install the second seal into the bore with the lip (spring) side facing up. Use the same mandrel to press both seals into the bore until the second seal reaches the depth below the opening (A, **Figure 74**) that was recorded prior to removal. If a new seal housing was installed, install the seals to achieve a depth of 0.010-0.030 in. (0.25-0.76 mm).
e. Wipe excess Loctite from the seals, then apply 2-4-C Marine Lubricant or other suitable grease onto the seal lips (**Figure 84**).
f. Carefully press the seal protector into the housing and seat against the seal case.

8. Place the pinion gear (10, **Figure 57** or 23, **Figure 58**) in position and aligned with the lower drive shaft bearing. Rotate the pinion gear as necessary to mesh the pinion and forward or reverse gear teeth.

9. Spray the threads of the drive shaft with Loquic primer (part No. 92-809824). Guide the drive shaft into the bore while holding the pinion gear in position. Rotate the drive shaft as necessary to engage the drive shaft and pinion gear splines.

NOTE

Apply Loctite 271 onto the new pinion nut threads after the pinion gear depth and forward gear backlash have been verified. Install the original pinion nut without the threadlocking compound to check the pinion depth and gear backlash.

10. Install the washer then thread the original pinion nut onto the drive shaft with the recessed side facing *toward* the pinion gear. Tighten the nut finger-tight at this time.

11. Install the drive shaft bearing and seal housing as follows:

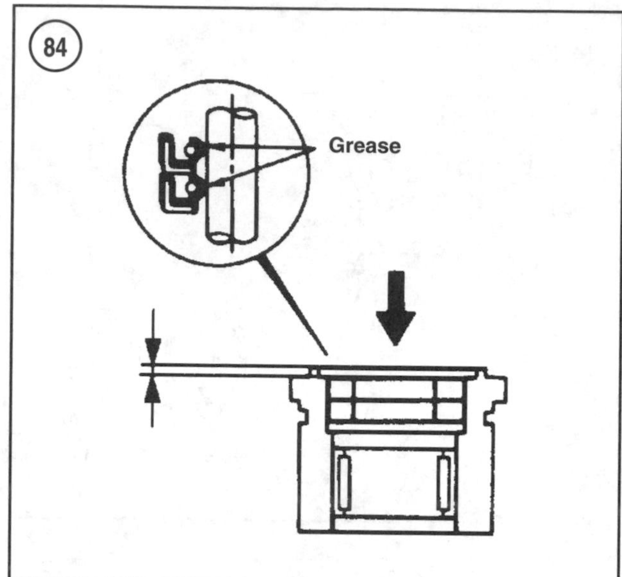

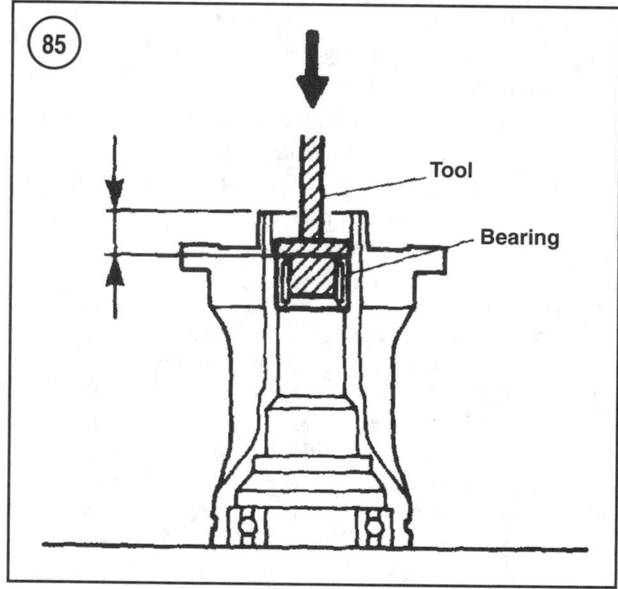

a. Apply Quicksilver 2-4-C Marine Grease onto the surfaces, then install the new O-ring onto the bearing and seal housing. Fit the O-ring onto the surface just below the mounting flange.
b. Apply gearcase lubricant onto the thrust bearing, thrust bearing race and the flange on the drive shaft.
c. Slide the thrust bearing and race (4, **Figure 73**) over the drive shaft and seat the bearing and race against the flange on the drive shaft (5).
d. Slide the pinion gear locating shim (3, **Figure 73**) over the drive shaft and seat against the thrust bearing race.

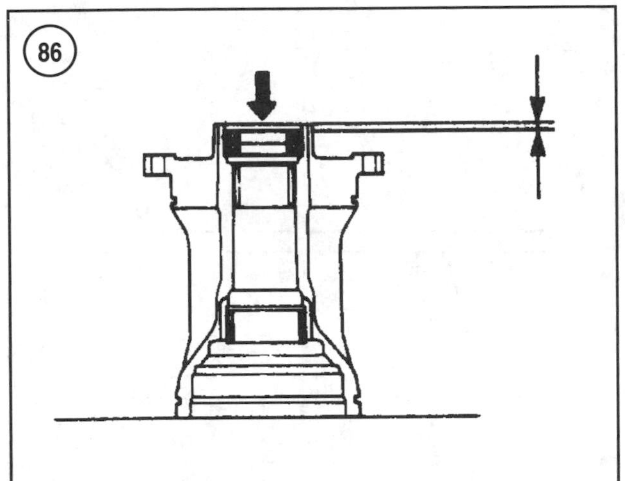

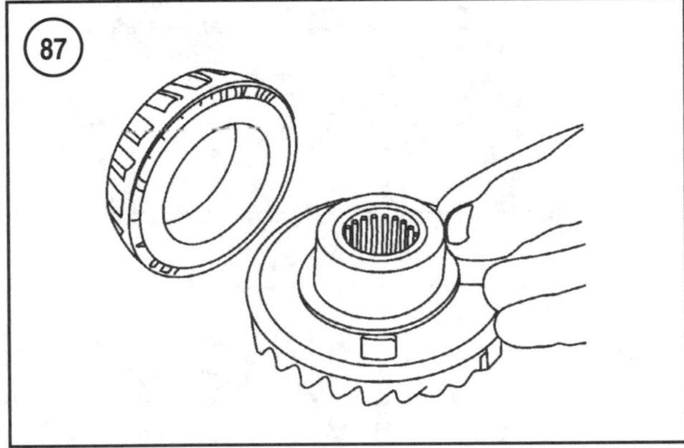

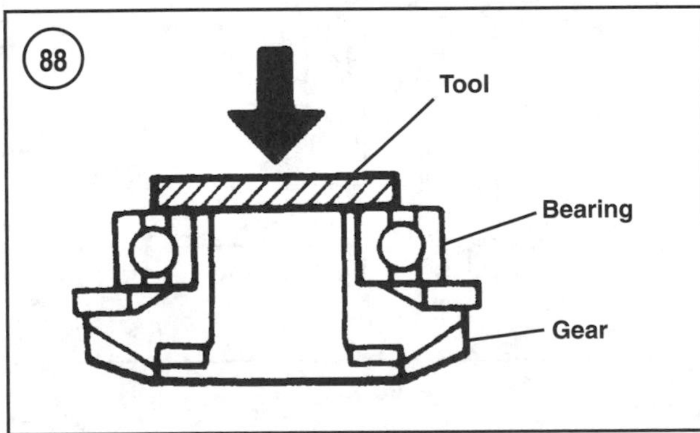

e. Apply gearcase lubricant onto the needle bearing within the drive shaft bearing and seal housing. Apply grease to the lips of the grease seals.

f. Carefully guide the drive shaft through the bearing and seals while installing the housing (2, **Figure 73**). Rotate the housing to align the screw openings, then seat the housing onto the gearcase.

g. Apply Loctite 572 onto the threads, then install the four screws (1, **Figure 73**) and washers. Tighten the screws in a crossing pattern to 18 in.-lb. (2.0 N•m).

12. Hold the pinion nut with a wrench or socket. Attach a spline socket (part No. 91-888889) to a torque wrench (**Figure 56**). Turn the drive shaft clockwise to tighten the pinion nut to 105 ft.-lb. (142.0 N•m).

13. If the bearing carrier needle bearing was removed, install the new bearing as follows:

a. Set the carrier into a press with the propeller end facing up.

b. Lubricate the new needle bearing with gearcase lubricant, then insert it into the bore with the numbered side facing up.

c. Press the bearing into the bore with a mandrel (part No. 91-888884 or an equivalent) until the bearing case reaches a depth of 0.986-1.006 in. (25.05-25.55 mm). See **Figure 85**. Stop frequently and measure the depth to prevent over-pressing and unnecessary bearing replacement.

14. Install the new propeller shaft seals into the propeller shaft bearing carrier as follows:

a. Place the bearing carrier on a press with the propeller side facing up.

b. Coat the outer diameter of the new seals with Loctite 271.

c. Install the first seal into the bore with the lip (spring) side facing up. Press the seal into the bore using a mandrel (part No. 91-825198 or an equivalent) until the seal case is just below the bore opening.

d. Install the second seal into the bore with the lip (spring) side facing up. Use the same mandrel to press both seals into the bore until the second seal reaches a depth of 0.187-0.207 in. (4.75-5.26 mm). See **Figure 86**. Stop frequently for measurement to prevent seal damage and unnecessary seal replacement.

e. Wipe excess Loctite from the seals, then apply 2-4-C Marine Lubricant or other suitable grease onto the seal lips.

15A. On a standard rotation (RH) gearcase, if removed, install the bearing and reverse gear as follows:

a. Position reverse gear on a press with the gear teeth facing down.

b. Lubricate the gear hub and ball bearing with gearcase lubricant.

c. Place the reverse gear positioning shim onto the hub of the gear (**Figure 87**).

d. Place the new bearing onto the hub of the gear with the numbered side facing up.

e. Use a suitable mandrel to press the bearing over the hub of the gear until fully seated (**Figure 88**).

f. Apply a light coat of gearcase lubricant into the bearing bore in the bearing carrier. Position the bearing carrier onto the bearing as shown in **Figure 89**.

g. Place a block onto the propeller side of the bearing carrier for protection, then press the carrier onto the reverse gear bearing until the bearing fully seats in the bore. Do not allow the carrier to tilt on the bearing.

15B. On a counter rotation (LH) gearcase, if removed, install the propeller shaft, forward gear and related bearings as follows:

a. Install the end play control shim (6, **Figure 58**) into the gear side opening in the bearing carrier (3). Align the shim opening with the propeller shaft bore and seat against the carrier.

b. Install the thrust bearing (7, **Figure 58**) into the carrier and seat against the shim. The race portion of the thrust bearing must contact the shim. Guide the threaded end of the propeller shaft into the carrier opening and seat the step on the shaft against the thrust bearing. Do not dislodge the thrust bearing or shim during the propeller shaft installation.

c. Place the carrier onto a press with the propeller side facing down. Support the propeller side of the bearing carrier with blocks as needed.

d. Install the roller bearing over the propeller shaft and into the bearing carrier with the tapered side facing up. Install the matching bearing race into the bearing carrier opening with the tapered side facing down. Use a spanner tool (part No. 91-888880T) to press the bearing race fully into the bearing carrier bore. See **Figure 90**.

e. Install the tab washer (11, **Figure 58**) into the bearing carrier. Align the tab with the recess, then seat the washer in the carrier. Thread the retainer (12, **Figure 58**) into the carrier with the recesses facing out.

f. Clamp the bearing carrier firmly in a vise with protective jaws. Use the spanner tool (part No. 91-888880T) to tighten the retainer to 80 ft.-lb. (108 N•m).

g. Lubricate the gear hub and ball bearing with gearcase lubricant. Place the forward gear positioning shim on the hub of the gear (**Figure 87**). Place the carrier on a press with the propeller side facing down. Support the propeller side of the bearing carrier with blocks as needed.

h. Fit the hub of the forward gear into the opening in the bearing. Do not dislodge the shim from the gear during installation.

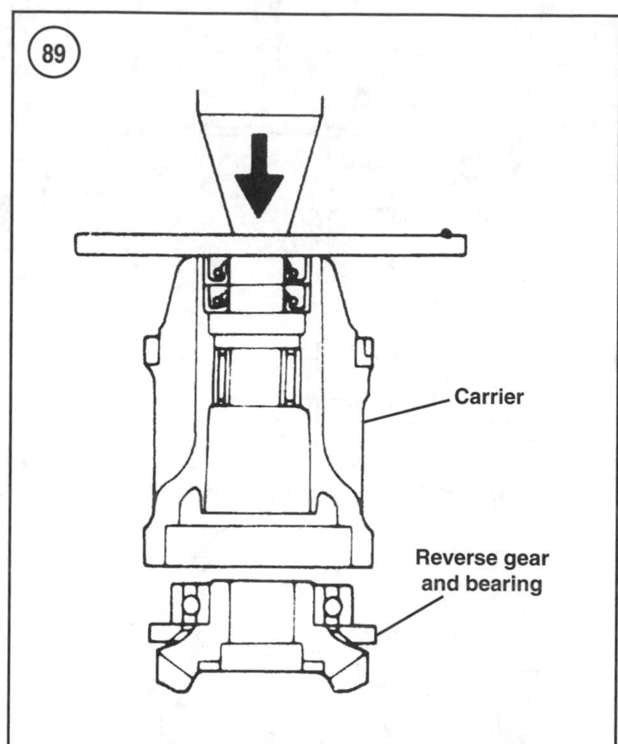

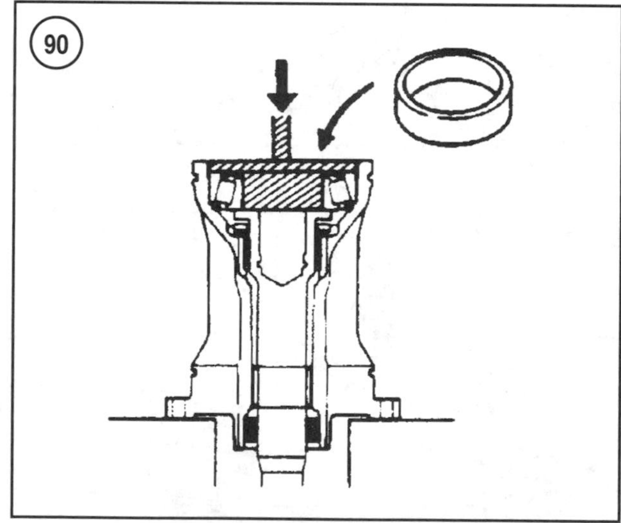

i. Temporarily install the clutch onto the propeller to protect the forward gear teeth. Make sure the *F* marking on the clutch faces the forward gear. Use the spanner tool (part No. 91-888880T) to press against the clutch and gear until the gear fully seats in the bearing. Remove the clutch.

16. Apply a coat of Quicksilver 2-4-C Marine Lubricant or other suitable grease onto the surfaces, then fit the new O-ring(s) into the groove(s) in the bearing carrier.

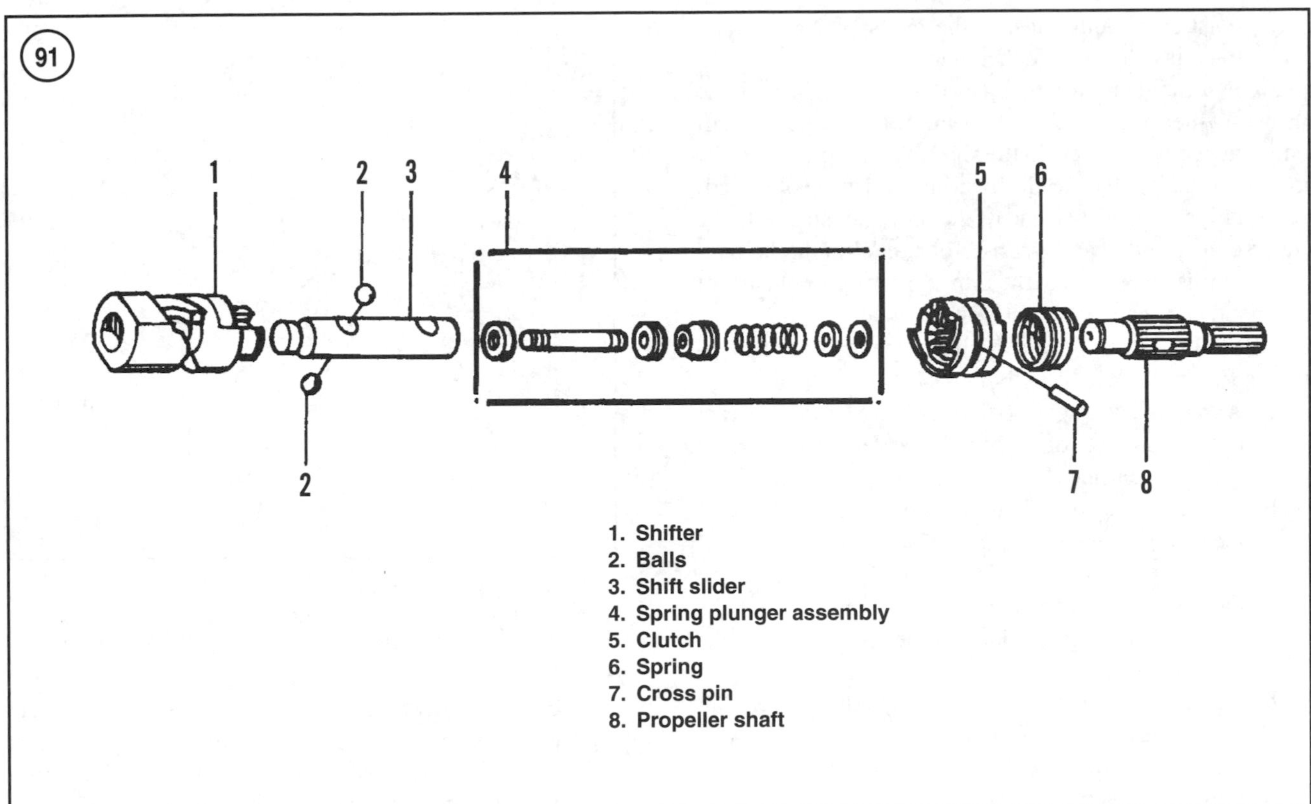

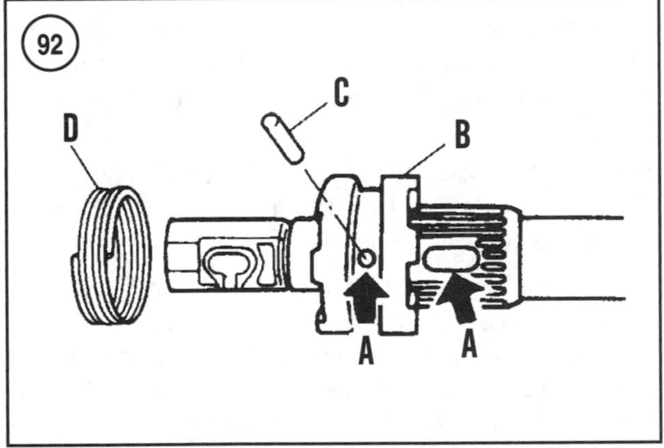

17. Install the shift slider into the propeller shaft as follows:
   a. Slide the spring plunger components (4, **Figure 91**) into the aft end of the shift slider (3). The components must be arranged as shown in **Figure 91**.
   b. Apply grease to the surfaces to help retain the ball bearings, then fit the detent balls (2, **Figure 91**) into the respective recesses in the shift slider.
   c. Fit the slot in the shifter over the protrusion on the end of the slider.
   d. Carefully insert the slider into the propeller shaft bore. Use a screwdriver or another suitable object to press the detent balls into the recesses during installation.
18. Install the sliding clutch as follows:
   a. Rotate the shift slider to align the cross pin opening in the slider with the slot in the propeller shaft (A, **Figure 92**).

NOTE
On standard rotation (RH) gearcases, the forward gear is located in the front of the gearcase. On counter rotation (LH) gearcases, the forward gear is located in the bearing carrier at the rear of the gearcase.

   b. Align the cross pin opening in the clutch (B, **Figure 92**) with the slot in the propeller shaft, then slide the clutch over the front side of the propeller shaft. The *F* marking on the clutch face must face toward the *forward* gear with the gearcase assembled.
   c. Insert the cross pin (C, **Figure 92**) through the clutch and slider openings. Carefully wind the clutch spring (D, **Figure 92**) onto the clutch. The spring must fit tightly on the clutch and the loops

must span both ends of the cross pin. Each loop must lay flat against the clutch.

19. On a standard rotation (RH) gearcase, install the thrust washer over the threaded end of the propeller shaft and seat against the step on the shaft. Working carefully to avoid damaging the needle bearing and propeller shaft seals, guide the threaded end of the propeller shaft into the reverse gear and bearing carrier bores. Without dislodging the thrust washer, seat the flange on the propeller shaft against the thrust washer and reverse gear.

20. Install the bearing carrier and propeller shaft assembly as follows:

   a. Apply a coat of Quicksilver 2-4-C Marine lubricant onto the surfaces of the bearing carrier that contact the gearcase housing.
   b. Rotate the propeller shaft to position the flat surface of the shifter facing up (**Figure 93**).
   c. Without rotating the propeller shaft, carefully guide the propeller shaft and bearing carrier into the gearcase opening and into the needle bearing in the front mounted gear.
   d. Align the mounting screw opening in the carrier with the corresponding openings in the housing, then *slowly* rotate the drive shaft to allow the gear teeth to mesh while seating the carrier into the housing. *Do not* rotate the propeller shaft until the shift shaft engages the shifter.

21. If removed, install a new seal into the shift shaft bushing/retainer (5, **Figure 57** or 25, **Figure 58**) as follows:

   a. Use Loctite primer T to clean contaminants from the seal bore and the outer diameter of the new seal.
   b. Apply a coat of Loctite 271 into the seal bore and the outer diameter of the seal casing.
   c. Fit the seal into the bore with the lip (open) side facing downward.
   d. Use an appropriately sized socket to press the seal into the bushing/retainer until seated in the bore.
   e. Apply a coat of Quicksilver 2-4-C Marine Grease onto the seal lip.

22. Slide the spring (16, **Figure 57**, typical) over the shift shaft, then insert the shift shaft through the bushing/retainer.

23. Install a new O-ring (17, **Figure 57** or 24, **Figure 58**) onto the bushing/retainer. Seat the O-ring onto the surface just below the mounting flange.

24. Guide the shift shaft through the shift shaft bore. Carefully rotate the shift shaft until the tip at the lower end of the shift shaft enters the opening in the shifter (**Figure 94**).

25. Seat the bushing/retainer onto the gearcase housing. Rotate the bushing/retainer to align the screw openings. Apply Loctite 572 onto the screws, then thread the three screws and washer into the gearcase. Tighten the screws evenly to 71 in. lb. (8.0 N•m).

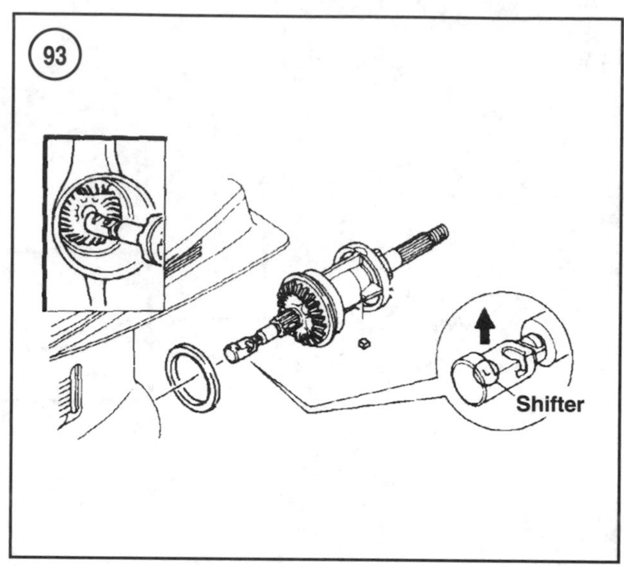

26. Rotate the bearing carrier to align the screw openings, then seat the carrier into the gearcase. Apply Loctite 572 onto the threads, then thread the two screws (**Figure 61**) into the bearing carrier and gearcase openings. Tighten the screws to 22 ft.-lb. (30.0 N•m).

27. Align the screw openings, then seat the retaining ring onto the carrier. Apply Loctite 271 onto the threads, then thread the two screws (**Figure 60**) into the ring and gearcase openings. Tighten the screws to 159 in.-lb. (18.0 N•m).

28. Refer to *Gearcase Shimming* in this chapter in this chapter to set the gear lash. Do not continue with assembly until the gear lash is correct.

29. Once the gear lash is correct, remove the propeller shaft and bearing carrier assembly, and install a new pinion nut with Loctite 271 as described in this chapter. Install the propeller shaft and bearing assembly and tighten the locknuts as described in this chapter.

30. Install the water pump assembly as described in this chapter.

31. Pressure test the gearcase as described in this chapter.

32. Install the gearcase and propeller as described in this chapter.

33. Fill the gearcase with the recommended lubricant as described in Chapter Three.

34. Adjust the shift cables and linkages as described in Chapter Four.

35. Pump 2-4-C Marine Lubricant into the bearing carrier mounted grease fitting until it flows from the housings.

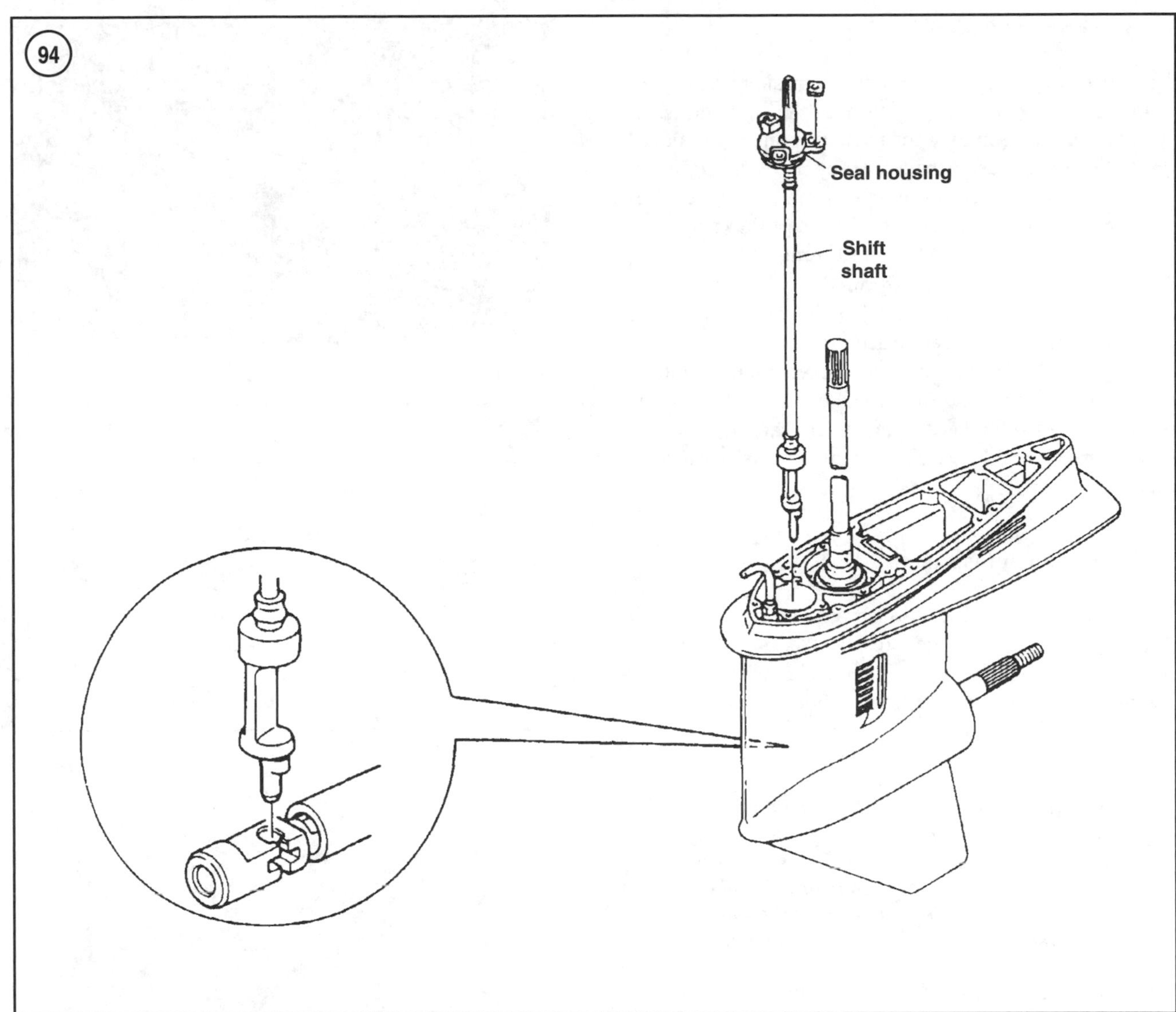

GEARCASE COMPONENT INSPECTION

Prior to inspection, thoroughly clean all components with solvent. Note component orientation prior to cleaning when necessary. Use compressed air to dry all components and arrange them in an orderly fashion on a clean work surface.

WARNING
Never allow bearings to spin when using compressed air to dry them. The bearing may fly apart or explode resulting in personal injury.

Make sure all components are removed, then use pressurized water to clean the gearcase housing. Inspect all passages and crevices for debris or contaminants. Use compressed air to thoroughly dry the gearcase.

Gearcase Housing Inspection

Inspect the gearcase for cracked, dented or excessively pitted surfaces. Damage to the skeg can be economically repaired by a reputable propeller shop. Damage to other surfaces may allow water leakage and subsequent failure of the internal components.

Make sure the locating pins are not bent or worn or have elongated openings. Replace a housing with elongated openings. Otherwise, the drive shaft may operate with improper alignment; resulting in failure of the drive shaft and other engine components.

Propeller Shaft Inspection

1. Inspect the propeller shaft for corrosion, damage or worn surfaces (**Figure 95**). Inspect the propeller shaft splines and threaded area for twisted splines or damaged propeller nut threads. Inspect the propeller shaft at the seal contact areas for deep grooves worn in the surface. Replace the propeller shaft if any of the surfaces are corroded, damaged or deeply grooved from wear.
2. Support the propeller shaft on V blocks at the points indicated in **Figure 96**. Use a dial indicator to measure the shaft deflection at the rear bearing support area. Securely mount the dial indicator. Observe the dial indicator movement and slowly rotate the propeller shaft. Replace the propeller shaft if the needle movement exceeds 0.006 in. (0.15 mm). Propeller shaft straightening is not recommended.

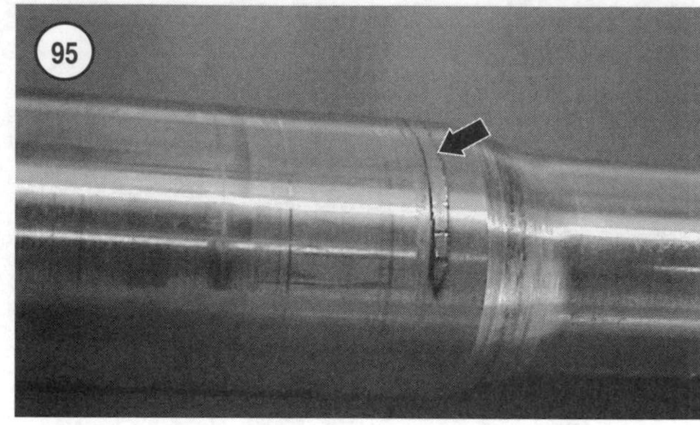

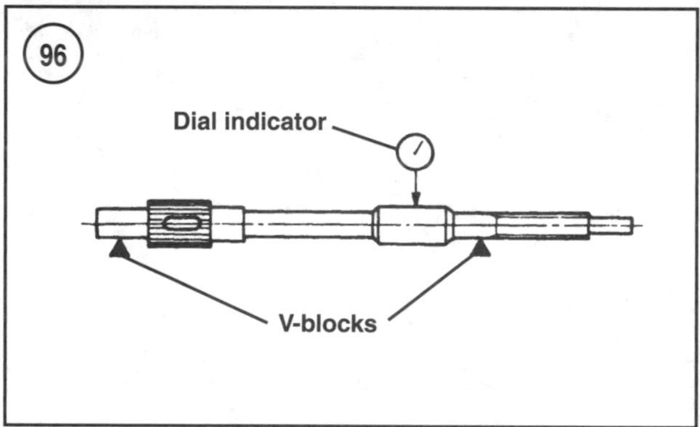

Gear and Clutch Inspection

1. Inspect the gears for worn, broken or damaged teeth (A, **Figure 97**). Note the presence of pitted, cracked, rough or excessively worn or highly polished surfaces. Replace all of the gears if these or other defects are evident.

NOTE
Replace all gears if any of the gears require replacement. A wear pattern forms on the gears in a few hours of use. The wear patterns are disturbed if a new gear is installed with used gears. This is especially important on engines with high operating hours.

2. Inspect the clutch (B, **Figure 97**) and gears for chips, damage, wear or rounded surfaces. Replace the clutch if these or other defects are evident.

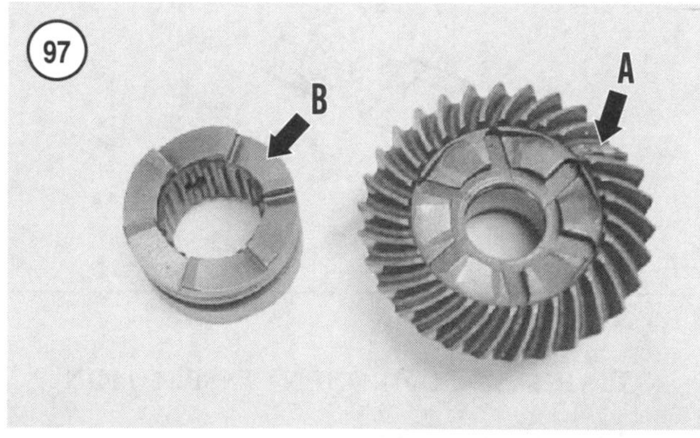

Bearing Inspection

1. Clean all bearings thoroughly in solvent and dry them with air prior to inspection. Replace bearings if the gear lubricant drained from the gearcase is heavily contaminated with metal particles. The particles tend to collect inside the bearing cases where it is difficult to remove.
2. Inspect the roller bearings and bearing races for pitting, rusting, discoloration or roughness. Inspect the bearing race for highly polished or unevenly worn surfaces. Replace the roller bearing and matching race if these or other defects are evident.
3. Rotate ball bearings and note any rough operation. Move the bearing in the directions shown in **Figure 98**. Note the presence of *axial* or *radial* looseness. Replace the bearing if rough operation or looseness is evident.
4. Inspect the needle bearings located in the bearing carrier, front mounted gear, drive shaft bore in the gear housing and drive shaft seal and bearing housing. Replace the bearing if flattened rollers, discoloration, rusting, roughness or pitting is evident.
5. Inspect the propeller shaft and drive shaft at the bearing contact area. Replace the drive shaft or propeller shaft along with the needle bearing if discoloration, pitting, transferred bearing material or roughness is evident.

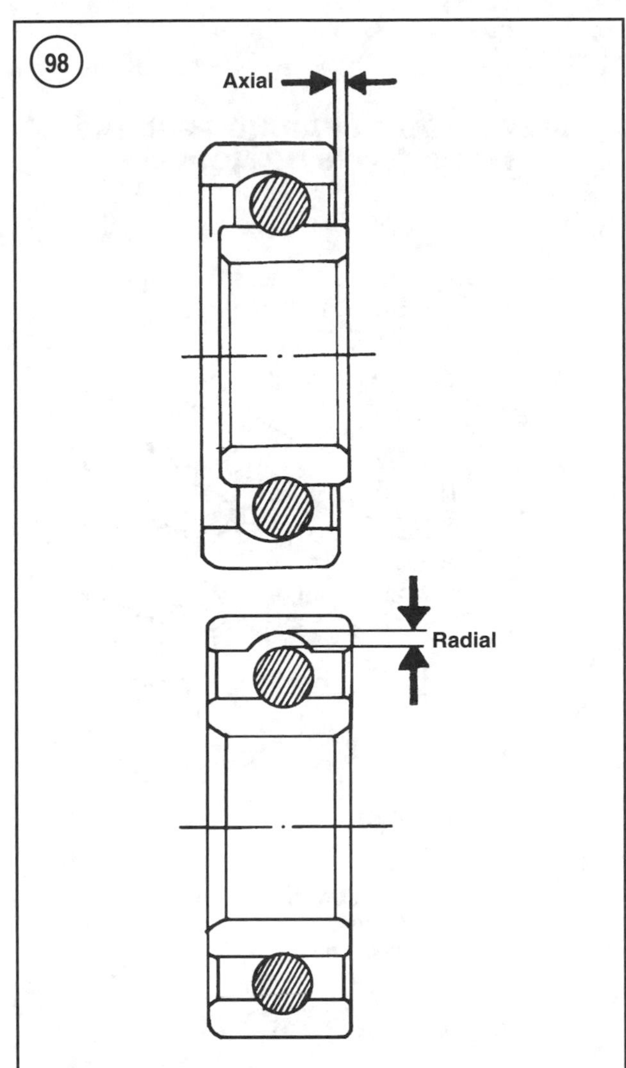

Shifting Components Inspection

1. Inspect the bore in the propeller shaft for the presence of debris, damage or excessive wear. Clean debris from the bore.
2. Inspect the clutch spring for damage, corrosion or weak spring tension and replace if defects are noted.
3. Inspect the cross pin for damage, roughness or excessive wear. Replace as required. Inspect the detent balls and spring for damage or corrosion and replace as required.
4A. On 75-115 hp models, inspect the shift cam and cam follower for worn or damaged surfaces. Replace the cam and follower if these or other defects are evident.
4B. On 225 hp models, inspect the shifter and shift slider for cracks, broken or worn areas and replace as required.
5. Inspect the shift shaft for excessive wear or a bent or twisted condition. Inspect the shift shaft bushing/retainer for cracks or a worn shift shaft bore. Replace any defective components.

Shims, Spacers, Fasteners and Washers Inspection

1. Inspect all shims for bent, rusted or damaged surfaces. Replace any shim not appearing to be in new condition.
2. Inspect the thrust washer located between the reverse gear and propeller shaft for worn, corroded or damaged surfaces and replace as required. Use only the correct part to replace the washer. In most cases it is of a certain dimension and made with a specified material.
3. Replace any locking nut unless it is in excellent condition. Always replace the pinion nut during final assembly.

Seals, O-rings and Gaskets Inspection

Replace seals anytime they are removed or if replacing a shaft that contacts the seal. If the seal must be reused, inspect it for a bent or damaged casing and a worn, weathered, cracked or damaged seal lip. Never use a damaged or questionable seal. A damaged seal will likely leak and lead to extensive damage to internal gearcase components.

Replace O-rings anytime they are removed. If an O-ring must be reused, inspect it for torn, deteriorated or flattened surfaces. Never use a damaged or questionable O-ring.

Never reuse gaskets. A gasket is made of a material that forms into small imperfections in a mating surface. With a few exceptions, gaskets are not designed to maintain a good seal after the initial installation.

GEARCASE SHIMMING

Proper pinion gear-to-forward/reverse gear engagement and the corresponding gear lash are crucial for smooth, quiet operation and long service life. Several shimming procedures must be performed to set up the gearcase properly. The pinion gear must be shimmed to the correct depth and the driven gears must be shimmed to the pinion gear for the proper backlash. A shim adjustment is usually required to achieve the proper tolerances when replacing major gearcase components such as gears, bearings, drive shaft or the gearcase housing.

The shimming procedures will vary by model and gearcase rotation used on the engine. Refer to the model specific instructions.

CAUTION
The backlash and pinion gear height adjustments must be done correctly, or it will result in a noisy gearcase as well as rapid wear of the affected gears. Do not risk dam-

age to a newly installed set of gears with an incorrect adjustment. If you feel unqualified to complete this procedure, or lack the specialized tools, have it performed by a Mercury/Mariner dealership or reputable marine repair shop.

75-115 hp Models

These models require a pinion gear depth and forward gear backlash shimming procedures. The reverse gear backlash is not adjustable on these models. Proper gearcase assembly correctly positions the reverse gear in the housing.

Setting pinion gear depth (75-115 hp models)

1. Position the gearcase with the drive shaft facing up.

NOTE

A drive shaft bearing preload tool (part No. 91-14311A-1) is required to measure pinion gear depth and gear backlash. The plate (1, ***Figure 99****) is not required on the models covered in this manual. However, the original water pump wear plate must be used to provide a mounting base for the preload tool.*

2. Temporarily install the water pump wear plate over the drive shaft and rest it on the water pump base. Do not install any gaskets for this procedure.
3. Install the bearing preload tool (part No. 91-14311A-1) onto the drive shaft in the order shown in **Figure 99**. Rest the assembly on the water pump wear plate.
   a. Make sure the thrust bearing and washer are clean and lightly oiled.
   b. Install the adjustment nut (7, **Figure 99**) completely onto the main body (6), then securely tighten the set screws (8), making sure the holes in the adapter sleeve (9) are aligned with the set screws.
   c. Measure the distance (D, **Figure 100**) between the top of the adjustment nut and the bottom of the bolt head. Then screw the adjustment nut downward to increase the distance (D, **Figure 100**) by 1 in. (25.4 mm).
   d. Rotate the drive shaft several revolutions to seat the drive shaft bearing(s).
4. Assemble the pinion gear locating tool (part No. 91-12349A-2) as shown in **Figure 101**. Face the numbered side of the gauge block out so the numbers can be seen as the tool is being used. Tighten the split collar re-

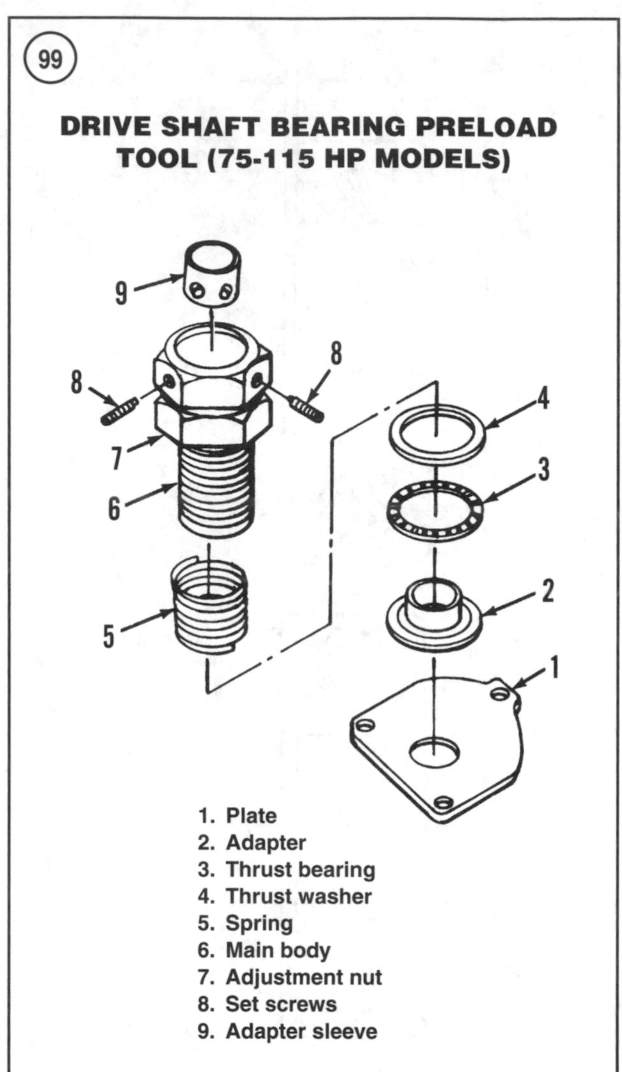

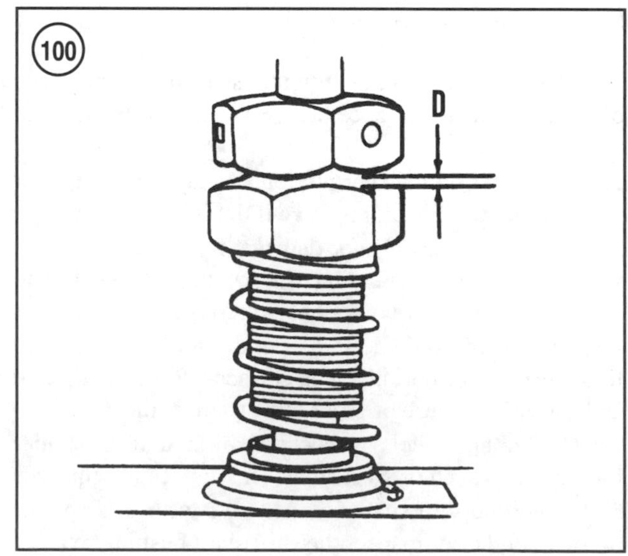

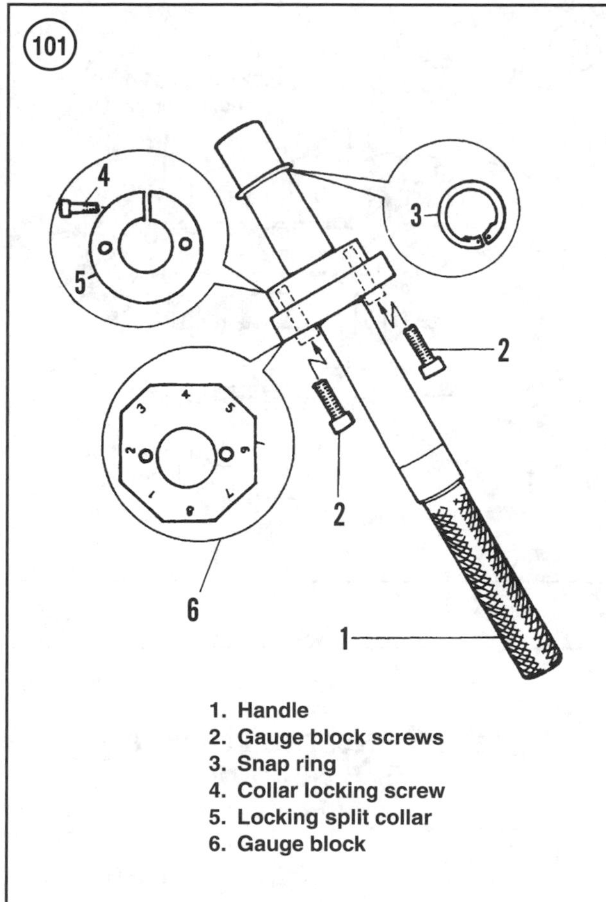

1. Handle
2. Gauge block screws
3. Snap ring
4. Collar locking screw
5. Locking split collar
6. Gauge block

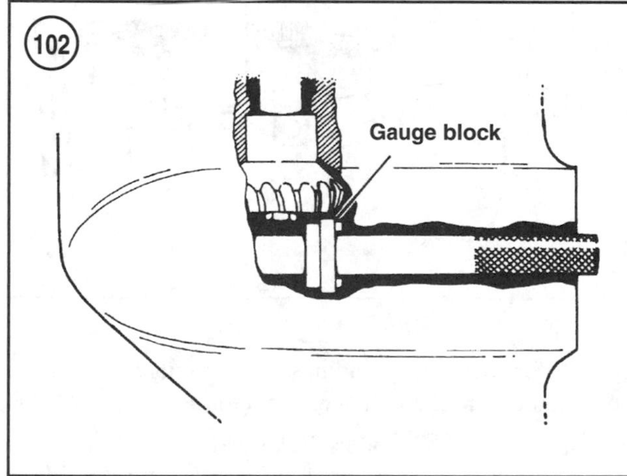

taining screw to the point where the collar can still slide back and forth on the handle with moderate hand pressure.

5. Insert the tool into the gearcase, making sure the tool passes through the forward gear needle bearing. Slide the

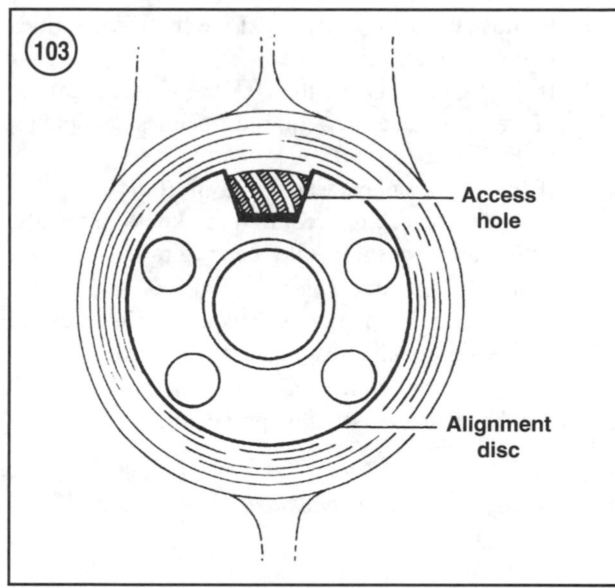

gauge block back and forth as necessary to position the gauge block directly under the teeth as shown in **Figure 102**.

6. Without disturbing the position of the gauging block, remove the tool from the gearcase and securely tighten the screw (4, **Figure 101**).

7. Reinsert the tool into the forward gear. Rotate the tool to position the specified flat gauging block surface directly under the pinion gear. Refer to the following to determine which surface to use.

   a. On 75 and 90 hp (2001 and 2002) and all 115 hp models, the flat gauging block surface next to the No. 2 stamping must be used.
   b. On 75 and 90 hp models (2003), the flat gauging block surface next to the No. 8 stamping must be used.

8. Install the No. 3 alignment disc from the tool kit over the handle. Rotate the disc to align the access hole with the pinion gear (**Figure 103**). Seat the disc against the bearing carrier shoulder in the gearcase opening.

NOTE

Rotate the drive shaft and take several readings in Step 9. Then average the feeler gauge readings.

9. Insert a 0.025 in. (0.64 mm) flat feeler gauge between the gauging block and the pinion gear (**Figure 104**). The average clearance between the gear and gauging block must be 0.025 in. (0.64 mm).

10. If the pinion gear depth measurement is not exactly 0.025 in. (0.64 mm), proceed as follows:

8

a. Remove the pinion gear and drive shaft as described in this chapter.
b. If the clearance is less than 0.025 in. (0.64 mm), remove or replace the required thickness of shim(s) under the drive shaft roller bearing race.
c. If the clearance exceeds 0.025 in. (0.64 mm), add shims or replace the required thickness of shim(s) under the drive shaft roller bearing race.
d. Reinstall the pinion gear and drive shaft as described in this chapter. Recheck the pinion depth. Make additional adjustments as required.

11. Leave the drive shaft bearing preload tool installed. Continue the gearcase assemble procedure.

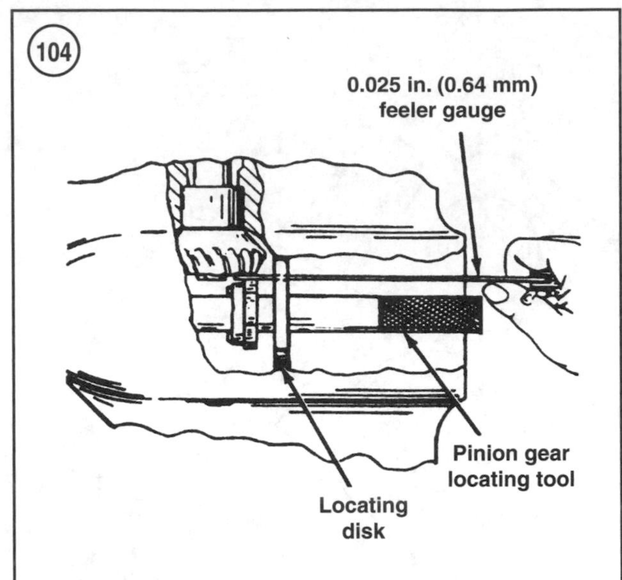

Measuring forward gear backlash (75-115 hp models)

NOTE
All water pump components must be removed prior to measuring gear backlash. The drag created by the water pump components will hinder accurate measurements.

NOTE
*Set the pinion gear depth **before** attempting to set the forward gear backlash.*

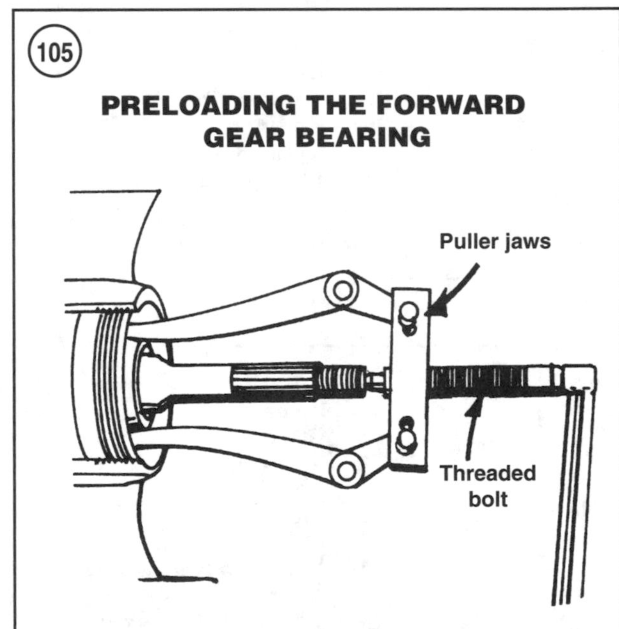

1. Install drive shaft preload tool (part No. 91-14311A-1) as described in this section (see *Setting pinion gear depth*).
2. Assemble the puller jaws (part No. 91-46086A-1) and the threaded bolt (part No. 91-85716 or an equivalent). Install the assembly onto the propeller shaft and bearing carrier as shown in **Figure 105**.
3. Tighten the puller bolt to 45 in.-lb. (5.1 N•m), then rotate the drive shaft several revolutions to the forward gear bearing roller into the race. Recheck the threaded bolt torque after rotating the drive shaft.
4. Fasten a suitable threaded rod onto the gearcase using flat washers and nuts. Install a dial indicator onto the threaded rod. See **Figure 106**.

5A. On 75 and 90 hp (2001 and 2002) and all 115 hp models, install the backlash indicator tool (part No. 91-19660-1) onto the drive shaft. Align the tool with the indictor plunger (**Figure 107**) and tighten the tool securely onto the drive shaft.

5B. On 75 and 90 hp models (2003), install the backlash indicator tool (part No. 91-78473) onto the drive shaft. Align the tool with the indictor plunger (**Figure 107**) and tighten the tool securely onto the drive shaft.

6A. On 75 and 90 hp (2001 and 2002) and all 115 hp models, adjust the dial indicator mounting so the plunger aligns with the No. 1 mark on the tool. Zero the dial indicator. For accurate readings, the plunger must be perpendicular to the indicator tool (**Figure 108**).

6B. On 75 and 90 hp models (2003), adjust the dial indicator mounting so the plunger aligns with the No. 4 mark on the tool. Zero the dial indicator. For accurate readings, the plunger must be perpendicular to the indicator tool (**Figure 108**).

NOTE
Make sure that all gearcase lubricant is drained from the gearcase prior to measur-

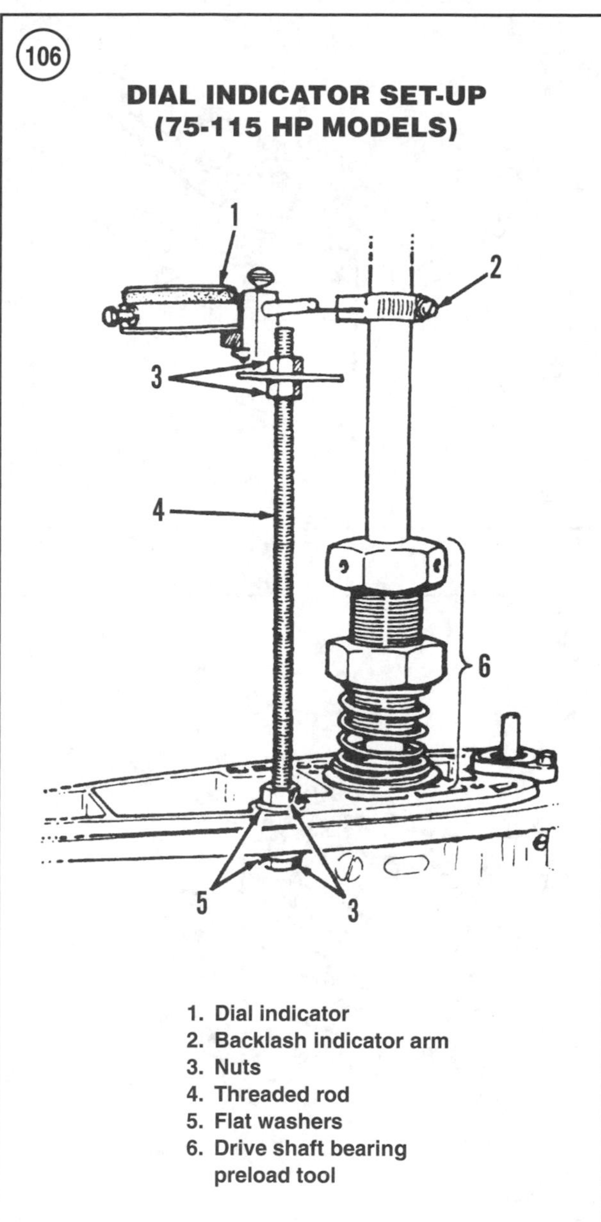

1. Dial indicator
2. Backlash indicator arm
3. Nuts
4. Threaded rod
5. Flat washers
6. Drive shaft bearing preload tool

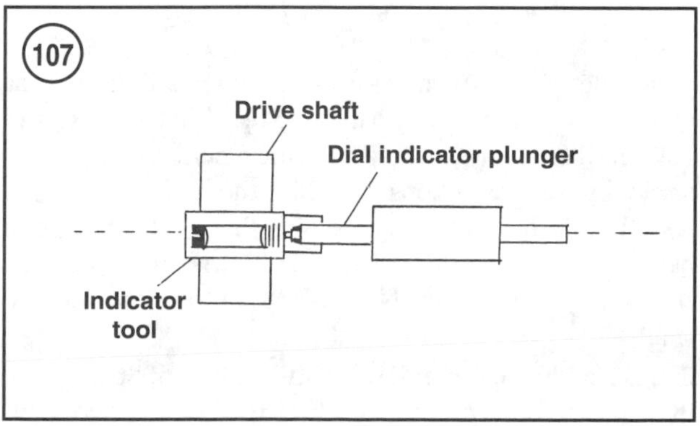

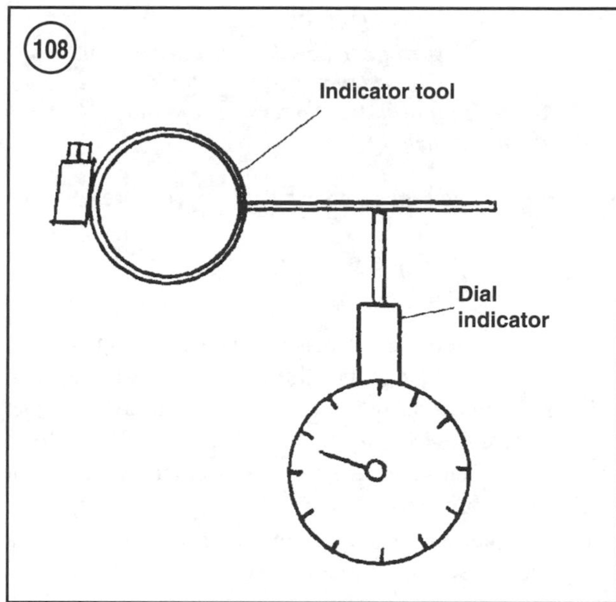

8

ing gear backlash. Inaccurate readings will result from the cushion effect of the lubricant on the gear teeth.

NOTE
The propeller shaft must not move during the gear backlash measurement. Rotate the drive shaft just enough to contact a gear tooth in one direction, then rotate the drive shaft just enough in the opposite direction to contact the opposing gear tooth.

7. Lightly rotate the drive shaft back and forth while observing the dial indicator. The dial indicator needle movement must indicate 0.015-0.022 in. (0.38-0.56 mm) for 2001 and 2002, 75 and 90 hp models and all 115 hp models. The dial indicator needle movement must indicate 0.012-0.019 in. (0.30-0.48 mm) for 2003, 75 and 90 hp models. If the backlash measurement is not as specified, proceed as follows:
   a. Disassemble the gearcase as described in this chapter to access the shims beneath the forward gear bearing race.
   b. If backlash exceeds the specification, add or replace the appropriate thickness of shim(s) behind the forward gear bearing race.
   c. If backlash is less than the specification, remove or replace the appropriate thickness of shim(s) behind the forward gear bearing race.
   d. Reassemble the gearcase and recheck the forward gear backlash. Make additional shims changes as required.

CAUTION
Once forward gear backlash is correct, the gearcase can be completely assembled. Use a new pinion nut secured with Loctite 271 during assembly.

8. Complete the remaining assembly procedure.

225 hp Model

Specialized tools and precise measuring equipment are required to select the proper shims for the bearings, gears, drive shaft and housing combination. If at all possible, have a Mercury, Mariner or Yamaha dealership perform the measurements and select shims if replacing any major gearcase components.

If these measurements cannot be performed, there is a less preferable but usually effective method of shim selection. Use the same shim thicknesses as removed from all shim locations. Assemble the gearcase, then measure the gear backlash. Gear backlash measurements will give a fairly accurate indication of what shim changes are required. On counterrotation (LH) gearcases, also measure the propeller shaft end play as described in this section.

CAUTION
If replacing the gearcase housing, do not rely solely on the gear backlash measurement to determine shim change requirements. Always have a Mercury, Mariner or Yamaha dealership select shims for the combination of components if a new or different housing will be used.

Measuring gear backlash

NOTE
All water pump components must be removed prior to measuring gear backlash. The drag created by the water pump components will hinder accurate measurements.

NOTE
Make sure that all gearcase lubricant is drained from the gearcase prior to measuring gear backlash. Inaccurate readings will result from the cushion effect of the lubricant on the gear teeth.

NOTE
The propeller shaft must not move during the gear backlash measurement. Rotate the drive shaft just enough to contact a gear tooth in one direction, then rotate the drive shaft just enough in the opposite direction to contact the opposing gear tooth.

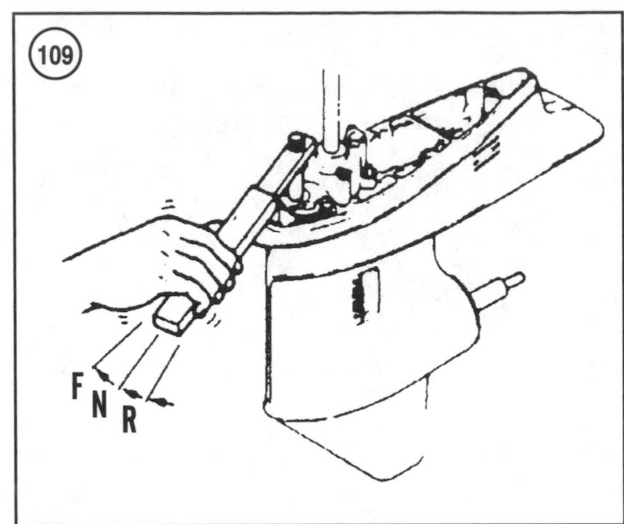

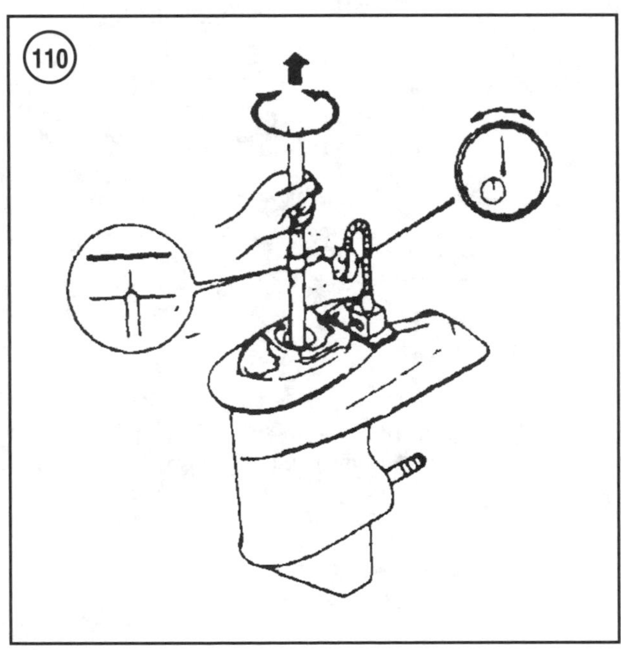

1. Rotate the drive shaft in the clockwise direction, as viewed from the top, while moving the shift shaft (**Figure 109**) until the propeller rotates in the clockwise and counterclockwise directions. Shift the gearcase into NEUTRAL by positioning the shift shaft at the mid-point between the two limits of travel (**Figure 109**). Use the shift shaft wrench (part No. 91-88877) to rotate the shift shaft.
2. Assemble the puller jaws (part No. 91-46086A-1) and the threaded bolt (part No. 91-85716) or an equivalent. In-

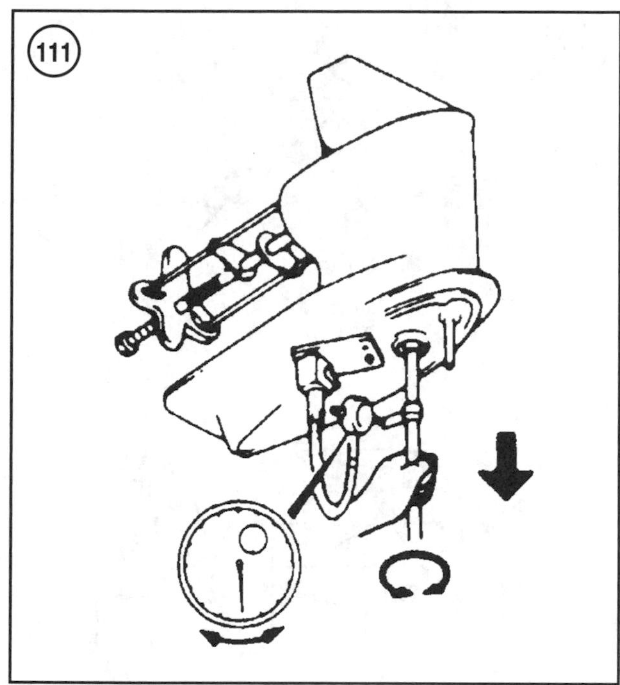

stall the assembly onto the propeller shaft and bearing carrier as shown in **Figure 105**.

3. Tighten the puller bolt to 44 in.-lb. (5.0 N•m), then rotate the drive shaft several revolutions to the forward gear bearing roller into the race. Recheck the threaded bolt torque after rotating the drive shaft.

4. Use a suitable mounting adapter (such as part No. 91-83155) to attach the dial indicator (part No. 91-58222A-1) onto the gearcase as shown in **Figure 110**.

5. Install the backlash indicator tool (part No. 91-888878) onto the drive shaft. Align the tool with the indictor plunger (**Figure 107**) and tighten the tool securely onto the drive shaft.

6. Adjust the dial indicator mounting so the plunger aligns with the marking on the tool. Then zero the dial indicator. For accurate readings, the plunger must be perpendicular to the indicator tool (**Figure 108**).

7. Rotate the gearcase to position the drive shaft facing down.

8. Lightly pull down on the drive shaft, or away from the gearcase, then gently rotate the drivc shaft in the clockwise and counterclockwise directions (**Figure 111**). Note the dial indicator readings when the drive shaft reaches free movement in each direction.

   a. On a standard rotation (RH) gearcase, record the amount of dial indictor needle movement as *forward gear backlash*.
   b. On a counter rotation (LH) gearcase, record the amount of dial indicator needle movement as *reverse gear backlash*.

9. Loosen the backlash indicator from the drive shaft. Remove the puller assembly from the propeller shaft.

10A. On a standard rotation (RH) gearcase, install the propeller onto the propeller shaft *without* the thrust washer normally located forward of the propeller. Tighten the propeller nut to 5.0 N•m (44.0 in.-lb.).

10B. On a counter rotation (LH) gearcase, rreload the rear mounted gear as follows:

   a. Temporarily remove the backlash indicator and position the gearcase with the drive shaft facing upward.
   b. Rotate the drive shaft clockwise while moving the shift shaft until the propeller shaft rotates counterclockwise.
   c. Stop rotating the drive shaft and move the shift shaft to the NEUTRAL gear position.
   d. Rotate the drive shaft counterclockwise approximately 30°.
   e. Using the shift shaft wrench, move the shift shaft in the direction necessary to achieve counterclockwise propeller shaft rotation. This pushes the clutch dogs against the dogs on the forward gear to preload the rear mounted gear. Maintain constant pressure on the shift shaft wrench during the backlash measurement. This step is necessary to prevent gear rotation and to seat the gear against the support bearings.

11. Rotate the gearcase to position the drive shaft facing down.

12. Lightly pull down on the drive shaft, or away from the gearcase, then gently rotate the drive shaft in the clockwise and counterclockwise directions (**Figure 111**). Note the dial indicator readings when the drive shaft reaches free movement in each direction.

   a. On a standard rotation (RH) gearcase, record the amount of dial indicator movement as *reverse gear backlash*.
   b. On a counter rotation (LH) gearcase, record the amount of dial indicator movement as *forward gear backlash*.

13. Remove the propeller, dial indicator, mount and the backlash indicator.

NOTE
On counter rotation (LH) gearcases, measure the propeller shaft end play and determine the need for shim changes prior to disassembling the gearcase for other shim changes. Change the end play control shims while the gearcase is disassembled for other shim changes.

14. On a counter rotation (LH) gearcase, measure the propeller shaft end play as follows:
   a. Use a suitable mount to position the dial indicator plunger in line and contacting the propeller shaft. See **Figure 112**.
   b. Zero the dial indicator, then move the propeller shaft in the fore and aft direction while observing the dial indicator. The end play must be 0.012-0.016 in. (0.25-0.40 mm). If not, disassemble the gearcase and check the orientation of the thrust bearing (7, **Figure 58**) and end play control shim (6).
   c. If all components are installed correctly, install a thinner shim to increase the end play or a thicker shim to decrease the end play.

15. Refer to *Shim Change Recommendations* in this section to identify any necessary shim changes.

CAUTION
Once forward and reverse gear backlash measurements are correct, the gearcase can be completely assembled. Use a new pinion nut secured with Loctite 271 during assembly.

16. Complete the remaining assembly procedure.

Shim Change Recommendations (225 hp Models)

Compare the backlash measurements with the specifications in **Table 2**. Shim changes are required when one or both backlash measurements are beyond the specification. Refer to the description of the backlash readings for recommended shim changes.

NOTE
Shim locations in the gearcase will vary by model. Note the location of all shims during disassembly and make sure all shims are installed in the same location.

Make all shim changes in small increments. Adjust to the mid-range of the backlash specifications anytime shim changes are required.

Partial or complete gearcase disassembly is required to access the shims. Refer to the disassembly procedures in this chapter.

After any shim change, assemble the gearcase and repeat the backlash measurements. Make required changes until both measurements are within the specifications. Several shim changes may be required.

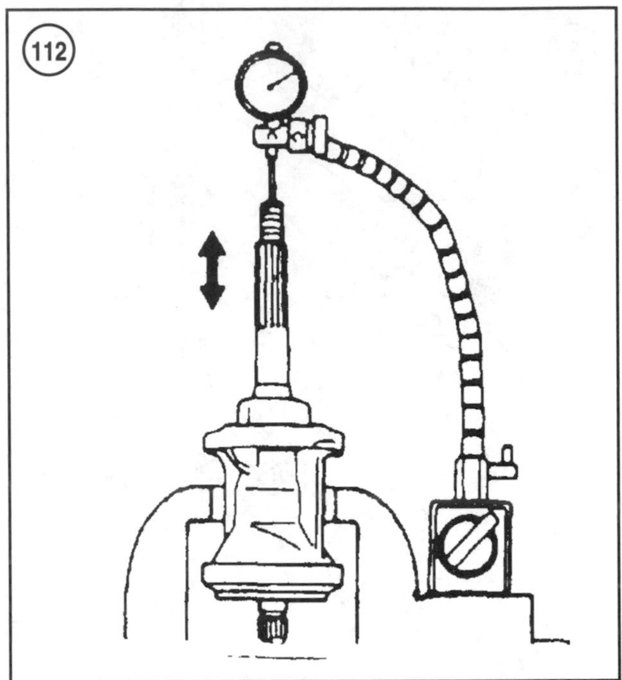

Both backlash measurements exceed the specification

When both backlash measurements exceed the maximum specification, the pinion gear is probably positioned too high in the gearcase . The pinion gear locating shim (3, **Figure 73**) is located above the thrust bearing (4) in the drive shaft bearing and seal housing. Remove the bearing and seal housing and install a thicker shim or set of shims. This positions the pinion gear closer to the forward and reverse gears and lowers both backlash readings. Measure the backlash to verify decreased backlash readings. Make further shim changes, if necessary, until both readings are within the specifications.

Both backlash measurements are less than the specification

The pinion gear is probably positioned too low in the gearcase when both backlash measurements are less than the minimum specification. The pinion gear locating shim (3, **Figure 73**) is located above the thrust bearing (4) in the drive shaft bearing and seal housing. Remove the bearing and seal housing and install a thinner shim or set of shims. This positions the pinion gear further from the forward and reverse gears and increases both backlash readings. Measure the backlash to verify increased backlash readings. Make further shim changes, if necessary, until both readings are within the specifications.

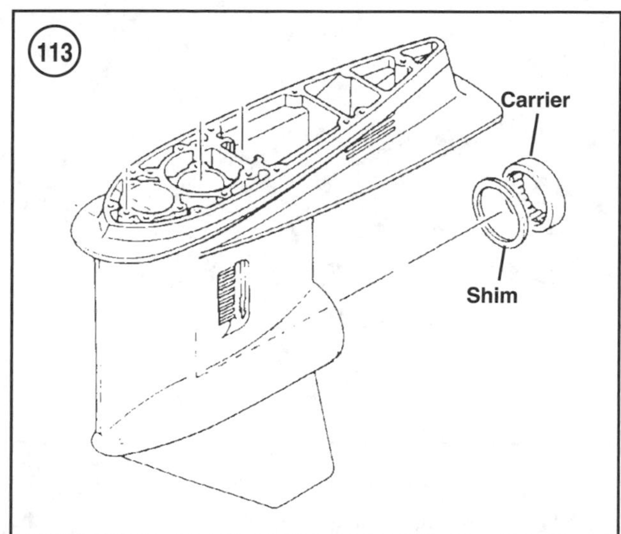

Forward gear backlash exceeds the specification (standard rotation [RH] gearcase)

The shims that set the forward gear backlash are located just forward of the bearing race (**Figure 83**) for the front mounted gear. Disassemble the gearcase and install a thicker shim or set of shims to position the forward gear closer to the pinion gear. This lowers forward gear backlash without affecting reverse gear backlash. Reassemble the gearcase and measure the backlash to verify a decreased forward gear backlash reading. Make further shim changes, if necessary, until the forward gear backlash reading is within the specification.

Forward gear backlash exceeds the specification (counter rotation [LH] gearcase)

The shim that sets the forward gear backlash (10, **Figure 58**) is located between rear mounted forward gear (13) and the bearing (9). Remove the forward gear as described in this chapter and install a thicker shim to position the forward gear closer to the pinion gear. This lowers forward gear backlash without affecting reverse gear backlash. Reassemble the gearcase and measure the backlash to verify a decreased forward gear backlash reading. Make further shim changes, if necessary, until the forward gear backlash reading is within the specification.

Forward gear backlash is less than the specification (standard rotation [RH] gearcase)

The shims that set the forward gear backlash are located just forward of the bearing race (**Figure 83**) for the front mounted gear. Disassemble the gearcase and install a thinner shim or set of shims to position the forward gear further from the pinion gear. This increases forward gear backlash without affecting reverse gear backlash. Reassemble the gearcase and measure the backlash to verify an increased forward gear backlash reading. Make further shim changes, if necessary, until the forward gear backlash reading is within the specification.

Forward gear backlash is less than the specification (counter rotation [LH] gearcase)

The shim that sets the forward gear backlash (10, **Figure 58**) is located between the rear mounted forward gear (13) and the bearing (9). Remove the forward gear as described in this chapter and install a thinner shim to position the forward gear further from the pinion gear. This increases forward gear backlash without affecting reverse gear backlash. Reassemble the gearcase and measure the backlash to verify an increased backlash reading. Make further shim changes, if necessary, until the forward gear backlash reading is within the specification.

Reverse gear backlash exceeds the specification (standard rotation [RH] gearcase)

The shim that sets the reverse gear backlash (22, **Figure 57**) is located between the reverse gear (22) and the bearing. Remove the reverse gear as described in this chapter and install a thicker shim to position the reverse gear closer to the pinion gear. This decreases reverse gear backlash without affecting forward gear backlash. Reassemble the gearcase and measure the backlash to verify a decreased backlash reading. Make further shim changes, if necessary, until the reverse gear backlash reading is within the specification.

Reverse gear backlash exceeds the specification (counter rotation [LH] gearcase)

The shims that set the reverse gear backlash are located just forward of the bearing carrier (**Figure 113**) for the front mounted gear. Disassemble the gearcase and install a thicker shim or set of shims to position the reverse gear closer to the pinion gear. This decreases reverse gear backlash without affecting forward gear backlash. Reassemble the gearcase and measure the backlash to verify a decreased reverse gear backlash reading. Make further shim changes, if necessary, until the reverse gear backlash reading is within the specification.

Reverse gear backlash is less than the specification (standard rotation [RH] gearcase)

The shim that sets the reverse gear backlash (23, **Figure 57**) is located between the reverse gear (22) and the bearing. Remove the reverse gear as described in this chapter and install a thinner shim to position the reverse gear further from to the pinion gear. This increases reverse gear backlash without affecting forward gear backlash. Reassemble the gearcase and measure the backlash to verify an increased backlash reading. Make further shim changes, if necessary, until the reverse gear backlash reading is within the specification.

Reverse gear backlash is less than the specification (counter rotation [LH] gearcase)

The shims that set the reverse gear backlash are located just forward of the bearing carrier (**Figure 113**) for the front mounted gear. Disassemble the gearcase and install a thinner shim or set of shims to position the reverse gear further from the pinion gear. This increases reverse gear backlash without affecting forward gear backlash. Reassemble the gearcase and measure the backlash to verify an increased reverse gear backlash reading. Make further shim changes, if necessary, until the reverse gear backlash reading is within the specification.

GEARCASE PRESSURE TEST

Pressure test the gearcase anytime the gearcase is disassembled. If the gearcase fails the pressure test, the source of the leakage must be found and corrected. Failure to correct any leakage will result in major gearcase damage from water entering the gearcase or lubricant leaking out.

Pressure testers are available from most tool suppliers. If necessary, a pressure tester can be fabricated using a common fuel primer bulb, air pressure gauge, fittings and hoses. If necessary, use the fittings from a gearcase lubricant pump. If using a fabricated pressure tester, clamp the hoses shut with locking pliers after applying pressure with the primer bulb. Otherwise, air may leak past the check valve in the primer bulb, giving a false indication of leakage. If at all possible, use a commercially available gearcase pressure tester.

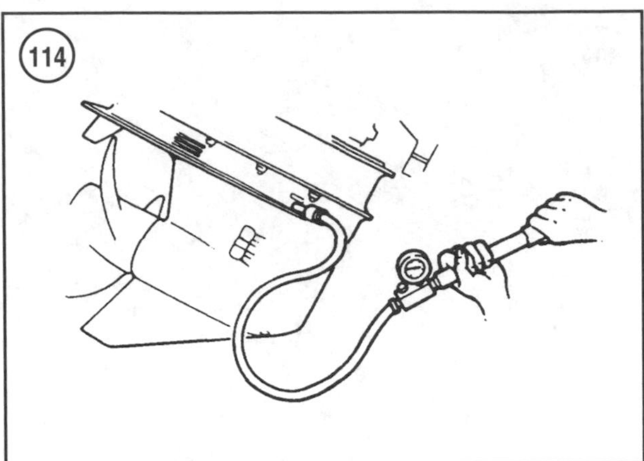

NOTE

The gearcase lubricant must be drained before pressure testing. Refer to Chapter Four if needed.

To pressure test the gearcase, proceed as follows:

1. Verify that the gearcase lubricant is completely drained. Make sure the fill/drain plug is installed and properly tightened. Always use a new sealing washer on the fill plug.
2. Remove the vent plug. Install a pressure tester into the vent hole (**Figure 114**). Tighten the tester securely. Always use a new sealing washer on the pressure tester fitting.
3. Pressurize the gearcase to 10 psi (69 kPa) for at least five minutes. During this time, periodically rotate the propeller and drive shafts and move the shift linkage through its full range of travel.
4. The gearcase must hold pressure for a minimum of five minutes. If not, pressurize the gearcase again and spray soapy water on all sealing surfaces or submerge the gearcase in water to locate the source of the leak.
5. Correct any leakage before proceeding.
6. Refer to Chapter Four and fill the gearcase with the recommended lubricant.

Table 1 GEARCASE TORQUE SPECIFICATIONS

Fastener	in.-lb.	ft.-lb.	N•m
Bearing carrier	–	22	30.0
Bearing carrier retainer ring			
225 hp models	159	–	18.0
Drive shaft bearing and seal housing			
225 hp models	18	–	2.0
Forward gear bearing retainer			
225 hp models (LH)	–	80	108
Gearcase mounting fasteners			
75-115 hp models	–	40	54.2
225 hp models	–	37	50.0
Pinion nut			
75-115 hp models	–	70	95.0
225 hp models	–	105	142.0
Propeller nut	–	55	75.0
Shift shaft bushing/retainer			
75-115 hp models	60	–	6.8
225 hp models	71	–	8.0
Trim tab bolt			
75-115 hp models	–	22	30.0
225 hp models	–	32	43.4
Water pump base			
75-115 hp models	60	–	6.8
Water pump body			
75-115 hp models	60	–	6.8
225 hp models	159	–	18.0

8

Table 2 GEARCASE BACKLASH SPECIFICATIONS

Model	Backlash specification
75 and 90 hp models (2001-2002)	
Forward gear backlash	0.015-0.022 in. (0.38-0.56 mm)
75 and 90 hp models (2003)	
Forward gear backlash	0.012-0.019 in. (0.30-0.48 mm)
115 hp models	
Forward gear backlash	0.015-0.022 in. (0.38-0.56 mm)
225 hp models	
Standard rotation (RH) gearcase	
Forward gear backlash	0.008-0.017 in. (0.21-0.44 mm)
Reverse gear backlash	0.028-0.040 in. (0.70-1.03 mm)
Counterrotation (LH) gearcase	
Forward gear backlash	0.014-0.028 in. (0.35-0.70 mm)
Reverse gear backlash	0.028-0.040 in. (0.70-1.03 mm)

Chapter Nine

Power Trim and Tilt

This chapter provides removal, repair and installation instructions for the power trim and tilt system.

Power trim and tilt are standard equipment on all models covered in this manual. A single hydraulic cylinder system (**Figure 1**) is used on all 75-115 hp models. The single cylinder system is commonly referred to as the *yellow cap* system due to the color of the fluid fill cap. A three hydraulic cylinder system (**Figure 2**) is used on all 225 hp models.

Disassembly, repair and assembly of the hydraulic part of the system require special service tools and practical experience in hydraulic system repair. Have the hydraulic system repaired at a marine repair facility if access to the required tools is not available or if you are unfamiliar with the repair operations.

Tighten all fasteners to the specifications in **Table 1**. If a fastener is not listed in **Table 1**, tighten the fastener to the general torque specification listed in the *Quick Reference Data* section at the front of the manual. **Table 1** is located at the end of this chapter.

TRIM/TILT RELAY REPLACEMENT

The models covered in this manual are equipped with either separate trim/tilt relays (**Figure 3**) or the single relay unit (**Figure 4**).

On 75 and 90 hp models, two separate trim/tilt relays are used. One relay controls the up circuit. The other controls the down circuit. The relays may be replaced individually. The relays are mounted on the lower front starboard side of the power head.

On 115 and 225 hp models, a single relay unit is used to control the up and down circuits. The single relay unit must be replaced as an assembly if either the up or down circuit has failed. On 115 hp models, the unit is mounted onto the lower front and starboard side of the power head. On 225 hp models, the unit is mounted onto the lower front and port side of the power head.

Refer to the wiring diagrams at the end of the manual and verify by wire color for the relay unit. Trace the wires to the individual relay or relay unit.

1

2

3

4

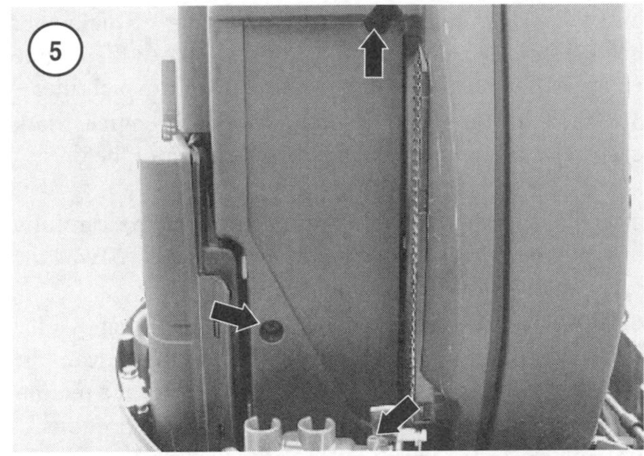
5

6

7

1. Disconnect the negative battery cable to prevent accidental starting.

2A. On 75 and 90 hp, remove the three screws (**Figure 5**), then carefully pull the plastic cover from the power head.

2B. On 115 hp, push in on the tabs (**Figure 6**), then pull the plastic cover from the power head.

2C. On 225 hp, remove the silencer cover (**Figure 7**) as described in Chapter Five. Remove the four screws, then pull the plastic relay cover from the front of the power head. The relay cover is located just below the engine control unit (ECU) and to the port side of the fuel filter.

3. Trace the wires to the component on the engine. Mark each wire connection location and orientation before removal. Disconnect all relay wires.

4A. On separate trim/tilt relays (75 and 90 hp), carefully pull the relay from the rubber mounting sleeve. Twist the relay slightly in the sleeve to ease removal.

4B. On a single relay unit (115 and 225 hp), remove the screws and lift the relay from the engine. Clean the mounting location and the threaded holes for the mounting screws. Clean and inspect all terminal connections.

5A. On separate trim/tilt relays (75 and 90 hp), apply a light film of soapy water into the relay sleeve opening. Do not allow water to contaminate other components. Carefully slide the relay into the sleeve until fully seated. Twist the relay to properly orient the wire terminal post. Reconnect the relay wires. The blue wires connect to the *up* relay and the green wires connect to the *down* relay. Route all wires to avoid interference.

5B. On single relay unit (115 and 225 hp), reconnect the relay unit wires. Tighten the relay terminal nuts to 35 in.-lb. (4.0 N•m). Reinstall the relay and secure with the two screws.

6A. On 75 and 90 hp, fit the plastic cover onto the power head and secure with the three screws.

6B. On 115 hp, align the locking tabs with the openings, then carefully snap the plastic cover onto the power head. Ensure all three tabs engage the locks.

6C. On 225 hp, install the relay cover and secure with the four screws. Tighten the screws to the general torque specification listed in the *Quick Reference Data* section at the front of the manual. Install the silencer cover as described in Chapter Five.

7. Connect the battery cable. Check for proper operation of the trim/tilt system before putting the engine into service.

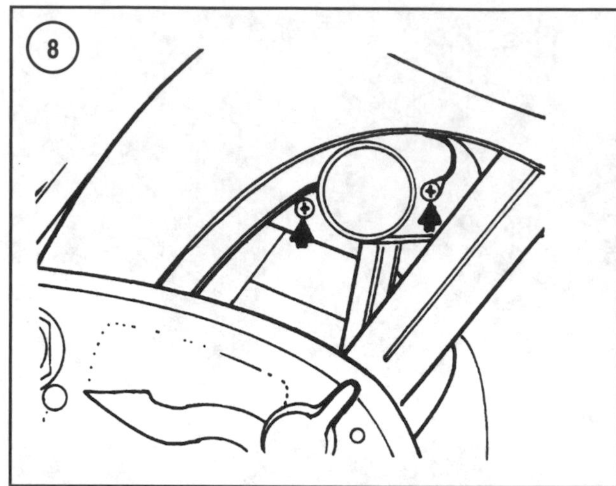

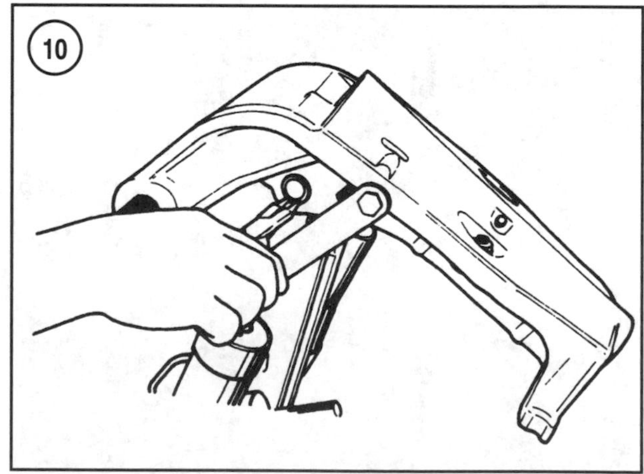

TRIM POSITION SENDER REPLACEMENT

WARNING

Never rely solely on the power trim system or tilt lock lever for support when working on the engine. Failure of the trim system or lever will allow the engine to drop unexpectedly and result in damaged property, serious injury or death.

NOTE

Always adjust the trim/tilt sender after replacement. An improperly adjusted trim/tilt sender results in inaccurate gauge readings.

The trim position sender is used on all models incorporating a dash mounted trim gauge. Two different types of senders are used.

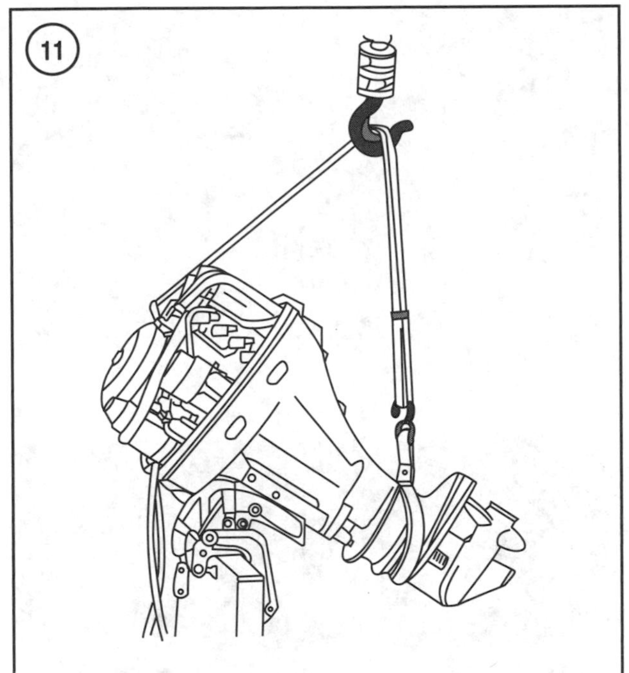

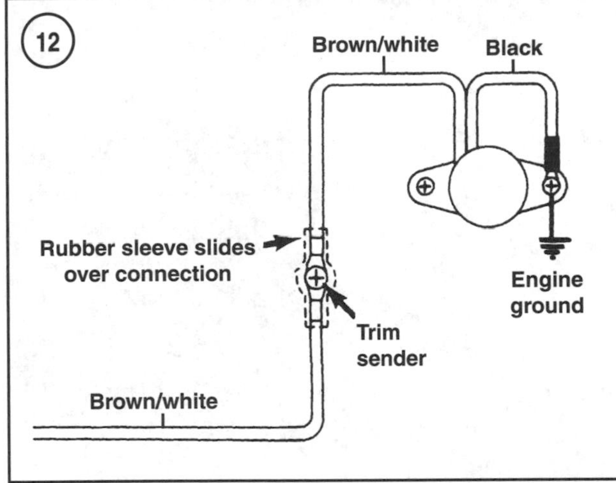

On 75-115 hp models, two screws secure the sender onto the starboard side of the swivel housing (**Figure 8**). Two tabs on the sender engage the slot in the upper pivot pin for the trim system. The tabs and rotor portion of the sender rotate as the engine tilts.

On 225 hp models, two screws secure the sender (**Figure 9**) onto the starboard bracket. The sender arm contacts the swivel bracket and moves as the engine tilts.

Make a sketch of the sender wire routing prior to removal to ensure proper routing.

1. Place the engine in the full tilt position, then engage the tilt lock lever (**Figure 10**). Support the engine with blocks or a suitable overhead cable (**Figure 11**). Disconnect the negative battery cable to prevent accidental starting or trim system operation.

2A. On 75-115 hp, trace the brown/white sender wire (**Figure 12**) to the engine wire harness connection. This wire leads to the dash mounted gauge. Loosen the screw and disconnect the wire. Trace the black sender wire to the connection to engine ground or the sender mounting screw. Disconnect the wire. Route the wires out of the lower engine cover. Remove the plastic tie clamps to allow removal of the sender.

2B. On 225 hp, trace the pink and black sender wires to the engine wire harness connection. Unplug the harness connector, then route the sender harness out of the opening in the lower engine cover.

3. Remove any plastic locking type clamps from the sender wiring to allow removal of the sender.

4. Use a felt tip marker to trace the outline of the sender on the clamp bracket or swivel housing. This step allows for quicker adjustment of the replacement sender.

5A. On 75-115 hp, note the direction in which the wires are orientated before removing the sender. Remove both mounting screws, then pull the sender from the swivel bracket. Clean the sender mounting surface and the slot in the upper pivot pin.

5B. On 225 hp, remove both mounting screws and the sender. Route the wires through the opening in the starboard clamp bracket and remove the assembly. Clean corrosion and contamination from the sender mounting location and mounting screw openings.

6A. On 75-115 hp, apply a light coat of 2-4-C Marine Lubricant into the slot in the upper pivot pin. Align the protrusion on the sender with the slot and install the replacement sender into the opening. Rotate the sender to orient the wires facing the direction noted prior to removal. Install the two mounting screws and lightly tighten. Align the sender with the traced line and securely tighten the screws.

6B. On 225 hp, pull the sender arm back then install the replacement sender onto the starboard clamp bracket. Release the arm, install and lightly tighten the mounting screws.

7. Route the sender wire through the clamp bracket and lower engine cover opening.

8A. On 75-115 hp, after connecting the terminals, coat them with liquid neoprene. Slide the sleeve over the terminals (**Figure 12**).

8B. On 225 hp, plug the pink and black sender wire connector onto the engine wire harness.

9. Route all wires so they are not pinched or stretched as the engine tilts or turns. Retain the wire with plastic locking clamps as required.

9

10. Disengage the tilt lock lever and remove the overhead support.
11. Connect the battery cable.
12. Adjust the sender and tighten the mounting screws as described in Chapter Four.

TRIM SWITCH REMOVAL AND INSTALLATION

1. Disconnect the negative battery cable to prevent accidental starting and trim system operation.
2. Locate the switch on the starboard side of the lower engine cover (**Figure 13**).

3A. On 75-115 hp, trace the wiring then disconnect the red, blue/white and green/white trim switch wires (**Figure 14**) from the engine wire harness. Do not inadvertently disconnect the trim motor or remote control harness wiring. These wires are in close proximity to the trim switch wiring.

3B. On 225 hp, trace the trim switch wire harness to the three wire connection (**Figure 15**) on the engine wire harness. Unplug the connector.

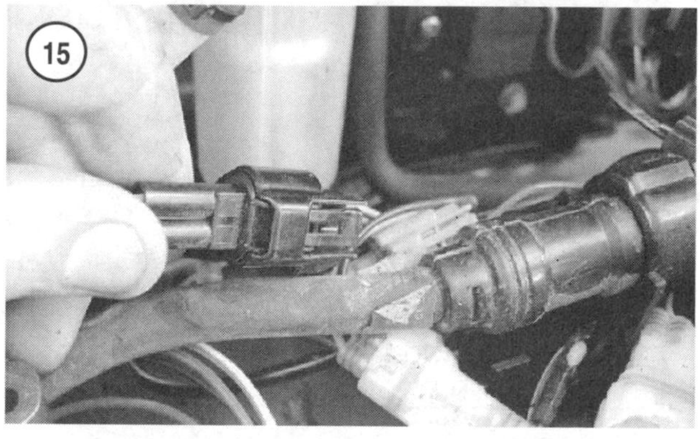

4. Carefully slide the retainer clip from the groove in the switch body. Lift the switch from the lower engine cover.
5. Slide the replacement switch into the opening with the switch harness facing downward. Press the switch fully into the opening then insert the locking clip into the switch groove.
6A. On 75-115 hp, connect the bullet connectors for the red, blue/white and green/white trim switch wires onto the corresponding engine wire harness connectors.
6B. On 225 hp, plug the engine wire harness connector onto the trim switch wire connector.
7. Route all wires away from moving components. Secure the wiring with plastic locking clamps as necessary.
8. Connect the battery cable.

MANUAL RELIEF VALVE REPLACMENT

WARNING
Never rely solely on the tilt lock lever for support when working on the engine. Failure of the lever will allow the engine to drop unexpectedly and result in damaged property, serious injury or death.

If the trim system is not operational due to low fluid level or failure of the electric motor or pump, the engine must be tilted by using the manual relief valve. The valve is accessible through the opening in the starboard side clamp bracket (**Figure 16**). To use the manual relief valve, use a screwdriver to rotate the valve 2-3 turns counterclockwise (**Figure 17**). With assistance, move the engine to the full tilt position. Engage the tilt/lock lever (**Figure 10**), then turn the valve clockwise until fully seated. Do not over-tighten the valve.

Replacement of the manual relief valve is simple if the screwdriver slot is intact. If this is not the case, the valve can usually be removed by other means. Heat the tip of a screwdriver and then hold it against the remnants of the valve. The valve material will melt into the shape of the screwdriver tip. Allow the material to fully cool, then use the same screwdriver to remove the valve. Never drill the

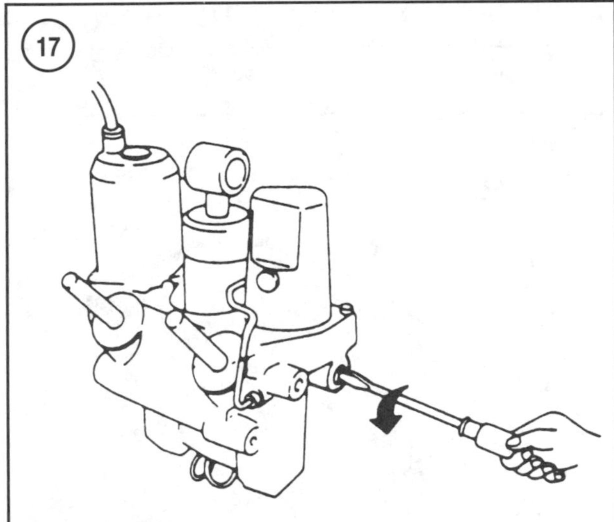

valve out or the seating surfaces. The O-ring will suffer irreparable damage.

Inspect the O-rings on the valve even though they will be discarded. If large portions are missing or torn away from the O-rings, they may migrate to a valve or other component with the trim/tilt system and cause the system to malfunction.

On 75-115 hp models, the manual relief valve can be replaced without removing the trim/tilt system from the engine. Remove the trim system for valve replacement if the original valve is damaged and the remnants cannot be removed from the opening.

On 225 hp models, the valve can be removed without removing the trim system. However, it is somewhat difficult to remove and install the relief valve snap ring through the access opening. It is usually quicker to complete the procedure by removing the trim/tilt system.

75-115 hp Models

1. Position the engine in the full up tilt position. Engage the tilt lock lever (**Figure 10**) *and* support the engine with blocks or an overhead cable (**Figure 11**).
2. Locate the manual relief valve opening on the starboard side clamp bracket (**Figure 16**). Place a suitable container under the trim system to capture any spilled fluid.
3. Slowly loosen the valve by rotating it 2-3 turns in the counterclockwise direction (**Figure 17**). Using needlenose pliers, remove the E-clip (**Figure 18**) and relief valve shaft. Rotate the valve counterclockwise until it can be pulled through the clamp bracket opening.
4. Use a light and small pick or screwdriver to remove any remnants of O-ring from the opening. Avoid damaging any of the machined surfaces in the opening.
5. Lubricate the new manual relief valve with Dexron II automatic transmission fluid and install *new* O-rings onto the valve. Lubricate the O-rings with Dexron II automatic transmission fluid and thread the valve into the opening. DO NOT tighten the valve at this time.
6. Rotate the valve clockwise until slight resistance can be felt. Rotate the valve 1/4 turn clockwise then 1/8 turn counterclockwise. Repeat this process until the manual relief valve is fully seated. DO NOT over-tighten the valve.
7. Using needlenose pliers, install the E-clip into the groove in the valve.
8. Fill the system with fluid and bleed air from the system as described in this chapter.

225 hp Model

1. Remove the power trim and tilt system as described in this chapter.
2. Slowly loosen the valve by rotating it 2-3 turns in the counterclockwise direction (**Figure 17**). Using snap ring

pliers, remove the snap ring (**Figure 19**) from the valve opening. Then, unthread the valve from the trim system.

3. Use a suitable light and small pick or screwdriver to remove any remnants of O-ring from the opening. Avoid damaging any of the machined surfaces in the opening.
4. Lubricate the new manual relief valve with Dexron II automatic transmission fluid and install *new* O-rings onto the valve. Lubricate the O-rings with Dexron II automatic transmission fluid and thread the valve into the opening. DO NOT tighten the valve at this time.
5. Rotate the valve clockwise until slight resistance can be felt. Rotate the valve 1/4 turn clockwise then 1/8 turn counterclockwise. Repeat this process until the manual relief valve is fully seated. DO NOT over-tighten the valve.
6. Using snap ring pliers, install the snap ring into the groove in the relief valve opening.
7. Install the power trim system as described in this chapter.
8. Fill the system with fluid and bleed air from the system as described in this chapter.

POWER TRIM REMOVAL AND INSTALLATION

Mark the mounting location and orientation of all components prior to removal to ensure proper assembly. Make a sketch of the trim motor wire routing before removal. Improper routing may allow the wire to become pinched during engine operation.

Unless specified otherwise, apply Quicksilver 2-4-C Marine Lubricant or equivalent onto all bushings, pivot shafts and pivot points during assembly.

WARNING
Never rely solely on the tilt lock lever for support when working on the engine. Failure of the lever will allow the engine to drop unexpectedly and result in damaged property, serious injury or death.

75-115 hp Models

Removal

1. Position the engine in the full up tilt position. Open the manual relief valve and tilt the engine if the trim system is inoperative.
2. Engage the tilt lock lever (**Figure 10**) then support the engine with an overhead cable (**Figure 11**).
3. Disconnect the negative battery cable to prevent accidental starting or trim system operation.
4. Place a suitable container under the trim system to capture any spilled fluid.

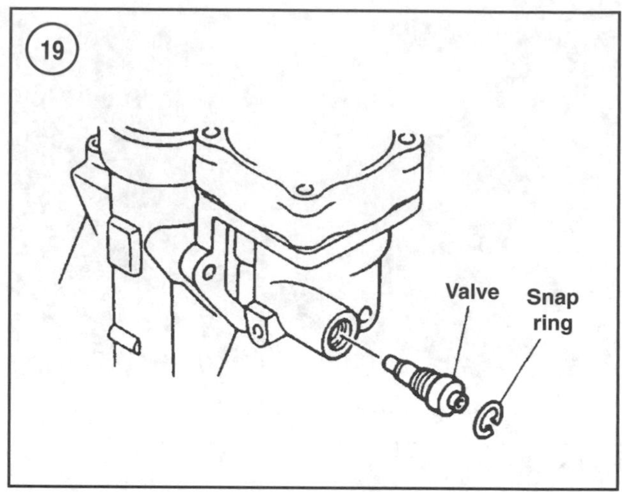

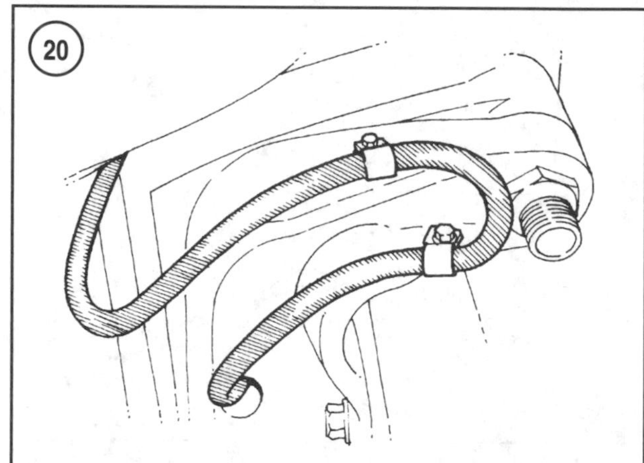

5. Remove the manual relief valve as described in this chapter. Remove the clamp for the electric motor harness from the starboard clamp bracket (**Figure 20**).
6. Trace the trim motor wire harness to locate the larger diameter bullet connectors for the blue and green wires. Disconnect the blue and green wire connectors. Route the

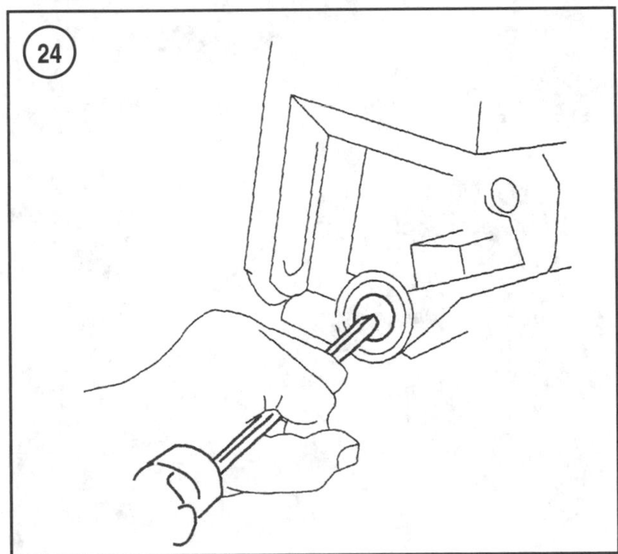

electric motor wire harness out of the engine cover and through the hole in the clamp bracket.

7. Remove the clamp bracket anode (**Figure 21**) as described in Chapter Three (see *Midsection Maintenance*).

8. Remove the retaining pin (**Figure 22**) from the upper end of the hydraulic cylinder. Using a chisel, carefully

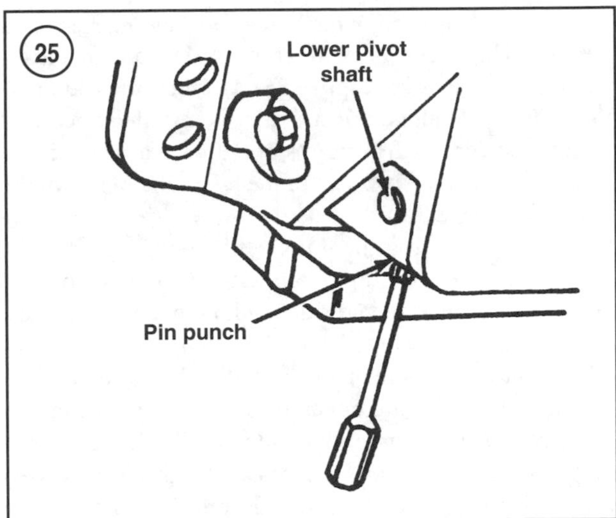

drive the pin away from the mounting surface. Pull the pin from the end of the cylinder using diagonal cutting pliers. Drive the upper pivot shaft from the swivel housing and trim ram bores.

9. Remove the retaining pin (**Figure 23**) from the lower port side of the clamp bracket.

10. Support the trim system and drive the lower pivot shaft (**Figure 24**) from the clamp bracket and trim system.

11. Swing the top side of the trim system away from the swivel bracket, then lift the system from the clamp brackets.

12. Clean the upper and lower pivot shaft openings. Inspect the pivot shafts and openings for wear or damage. Replace worn or damaged components.

Installation

1. Position the engine in the full up tilt position. Engage the tilt lock lever (**Figure 10**) then support the engine with an overhead cable (**Figure 11**). Disconnect the negative battery cable to prevent accidental starting or trim system operation.

2. Slide the lower end of the trim system into the clamp brackets, then tilt the upper end back into theupper shaft bore. Ensure the fill cap side faces outward.

3. Coat the surface of the lower pivot shaft with 2-4-C Marine Lubricant. Align the holes in the clamp brackets and trim system, then slide the lower shaft, non-grooved end first, into the port side opening until flush with the clamp bracket. Insert a pin punch into the retaining pin opening (**Figure 25**) to align the retaining pin hole with the groove in the pivot shaft. Insert the retaining pin then drive the pin into the opening until fully seated.

4. Align the upper pivot pin bores in the cylinder end and the swivel bracket. Check for correct orientation of the retaining pin openings (**Figure 26**). Correct orientation allows the pin to slope upward as it is installed. Incorrect orientation causes the pin to slope downward as it is installed. Rotate the pivot end of the hydraulic ram until the pin hole slopes upward.
5. Apply 2-4-C Marine Lubricant to the upper pivot shaft. Insert the upper pivot pin, slotted end first, into the port side bore until it enters the hydraulic ram bore. Use a screwdriver in the slotted end of the shaft to align the retaining pin bore in the pivot shaft with the corresponding opening in the hydraulic ram. Insert the retaining pin into the bores. Drive the retaining pin in until fully seated.
6. Route the electric trim motor harness through the starboard clamp bracket opening. Secure the wire harness onto the clamp bracket with the clamps as shown in **Figure 20**. Securely tighten the clamp screws.
7. Route the electric trim motor harness through the opening into the lower engine cover. Connect the blue and green wire connectors onto the corresponding engine wire harness terminals. Route the wires away from moving components. Secure the wiring with plastic locking clamps as necessary.
8. Install the manual relief valve as described in this chapter.
9. Install the clamp bracket anode as described in Chapter Three (see *Midsection Maintenance*).
10. Disengage the tilt lock lever and carefully remove the overhead support. Slowly open the manual relief valve and place the engine in the normal position. Connect the cables to the battery.
11. Correct the fluid level and bleed air from the system as described in this chapter.
12. Check for proper trim/tilt system operation before putting the engine into service.

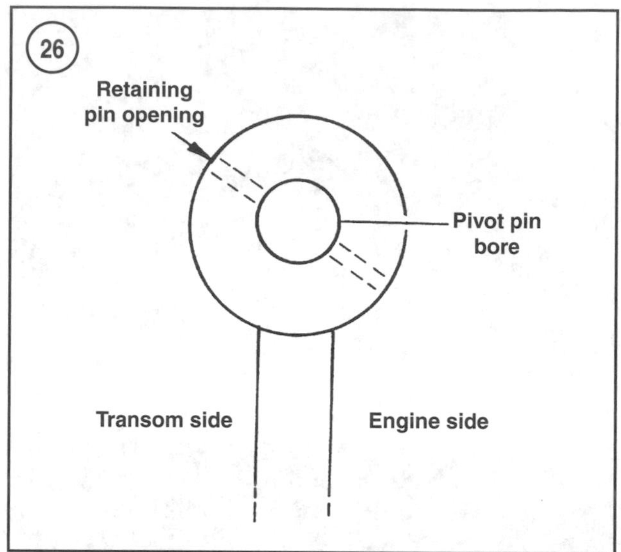

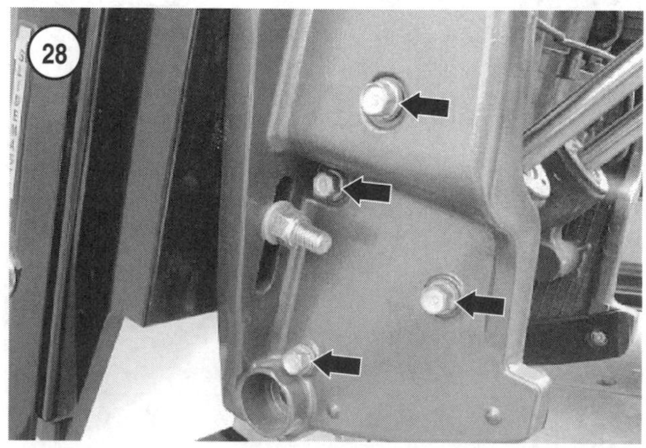

225 hp Model

Removal

1. Position the engine in the full up tilt position.
2. Engage the tilt lock lever (**Figure 10**) then support the engine with an overhead cable (**Figure 11**).
3. Disconnect the negative battery cable to prevent accidental starting or trim system operation.
4. Place a suitable container under the trim system to capture any spilled fluid.
5. Remove the clamp for the electric motor harness from the starboard clamp bracket (**Figure 20**).
6. Remove the clamp bracket anode (**Figure 27**) as described in Chapter Three (see *Midsection Maintenance*).
7. Remove any clamps securing the trim motor harness onto the starboard clamp brackets.
8. Trace the trim motor wire harness to locate the larger diameter bullet connectors for blue and green wires. Disconnect the blue and green wire connectors. Route the electric motor wire harness out of the engine cover and through the hole in the clamp bracket.

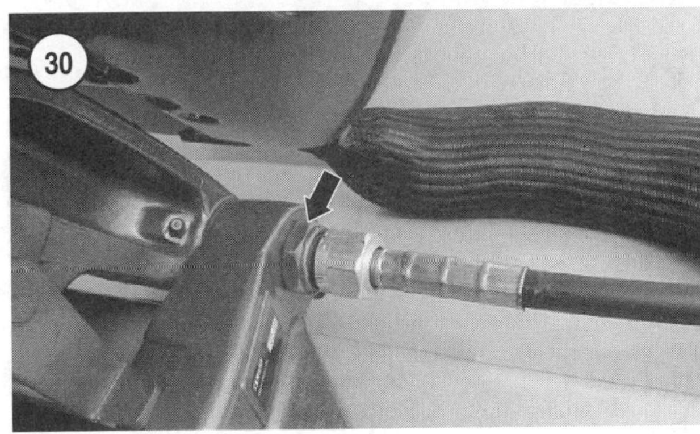

9. Remove the four trim system mounting bolts (**Figure 28**) from both the port and starboard clamp brackets.

10. Remove the snap ring (**Figure 29**) from the groove in the upper pivot shaft. Inspect the snap ring for corrosion and weak spring tension. Replace the snap ring if in questionable condition.

11. Loosen the self locking nut on the starboard side of the tilt tube (**Figure 30**).

12. Support the trim/tilt system and carefully drive the upper pivot shaft, from the starboard side, until free from the swivel housing.

13. Pull the starboard clamp bracket toward the starboard direction, then pull the trim system down and away from the clamp brackets.

14. Remove the bushings from the tilt cylinder ram. Inspect the bushings for worn or damaged surfaces. Replace the bushings if not found in excellent condition.

15. Remove the manual relief valve as described in this chapter.

16. Inspect the pivot shaft and the openings in the swivel housing and tilt cylinder ram for worn, corroded or damaged surfaces. Replace the pivot shaft if damaged. Replace the swivel housing (Chapter Ten) if the shaft bore is cracked or worn excessively.

Installation

1. Position the engine in the full up tilt position. Engage the tilt lock lever (**Figure 10**) then support the engine with an overhead cable (**Figure 11**). Disconnect the negative battery cable to prevent accidental starting or trim system operation.
2. Insert the bushings into each opening in the tilt cylinder ram. Pull on the tilt cylinder ram until fully extended. Apply a coat of Quicksilver 2-4-C Marine Lubricant into the bushing openings.
3. Install the manual relief valve as described in this chapter.
4. Pull the starboard clamp bracket toward the starboard direction, then carefully guide the trim system between the clamp brackets. Align the mounting bolts openings in the clamp bracket and trim system, then release the clamp bracket.
5. Thread the eight mounting bolts into the clamp bracket and trim system openings. Do not tighten the bolts at this time.
6. Extend or retrace the tilt cylinder ram until the pivot shaft opening in the ram aligns with the opening in the swivel housing.
7. Insert the upper pivot shaft into the port side swivel housing opening. Verify proper alignment, then push the shaft through the swivel housing and tilt cylinder ram openings until the snap ring groove is visible on the starboard side of the swivel housing. Use snap ring pliers to install the snap ring into the pivot shaft groove.
8. Route the trim motor wiring through the opening in the starboard clamp bracket. Install the clamps to secure the wiring.
9. Tighten the four trim system mounting bolts (**Figure 28**) in the port then starboard clamp brackets to 31 ft.-lb. (42.0 N•m).
10. Tighten the self locking tilt tube nut (**Figure 30**) to 16 ft.-lb. (21.7 N•m).
11. Route the electric trim motor harness through the opening into the lower engine cover. Connect the blue and green wire connectors onto the corresponding engine wire harness terminals. Route the wires away from moving components. Secure the wiring with plastic locking clamps as necessary.
12. Install the clamp bracket anode as described in Chapter Three (see *Midsection Maintenance*).
13. Disengage the tilt lock lever and carefully remove the overhead support. Slowly open the manual relief valve and place the engine in the normal position.
14. Connect the cables to the battery.
15. Correct the fluid level and bleed air from the system as described in this chapter.

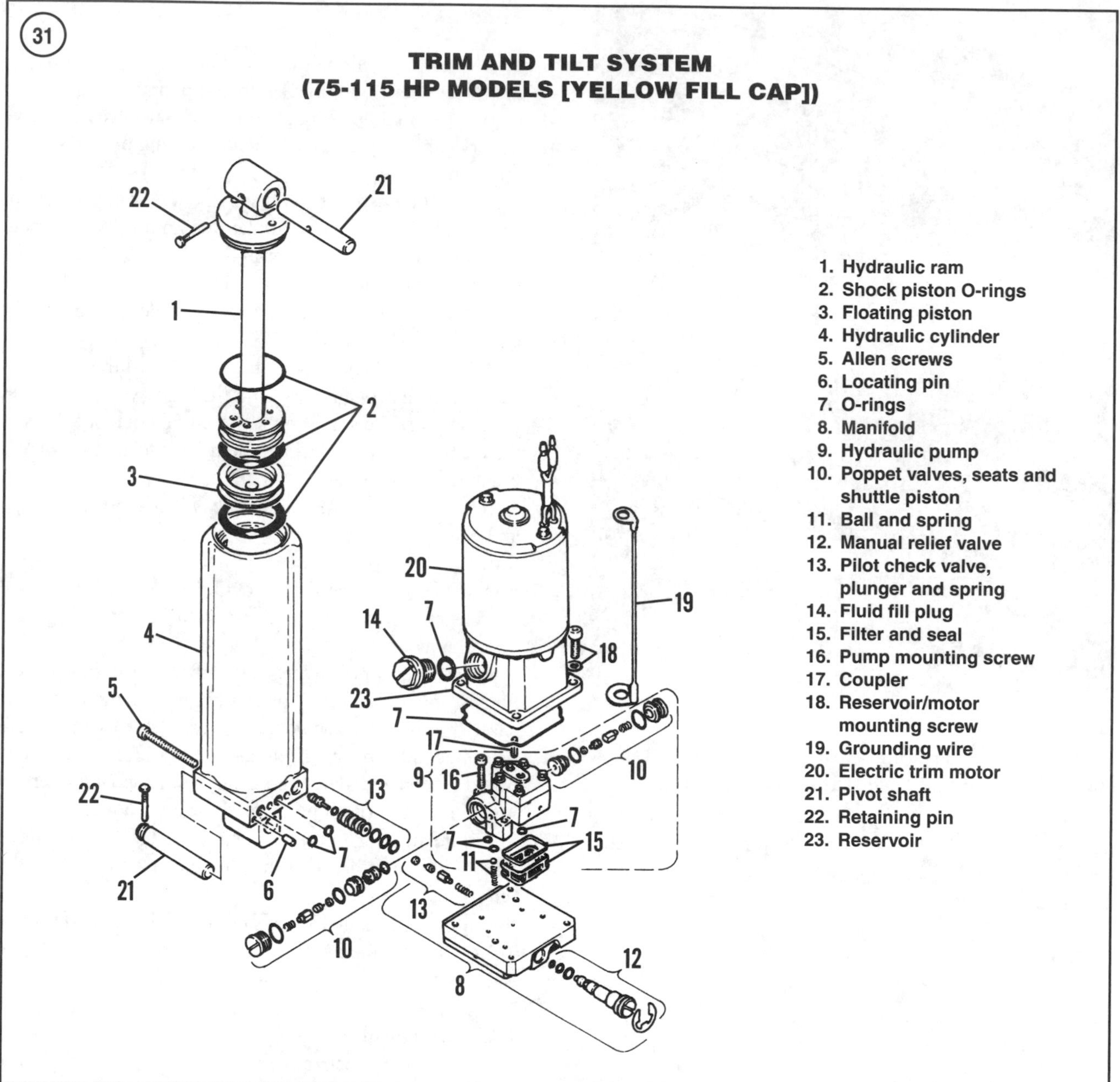

16. Check for proper trim/tilt system operation before putting the engine into service.

ELECTRIC TRIM MOTOR REMOVAL AND INSTALLATION

Proper alignment of the pump coupler, fasteners and sealing O-ring is far easier if the trim system is removed. Improper installation can result in water leakage or damage to other trim system components.

CAUTION
Never direct pressurized water at the seal surfaces when cleaning debris or contaminants from the trim system. The water may pass by the seal surface and contaminate the fluid.

The trim system must operate with clean fluid. A small amount of contaminants can wreak havoc with the trim system operation. Thoroughly clean the trim system external surfaces with soapy water prior to disassembly. Use compressed air to dry the trim system.

Work in a clean area and use lint free towels to wipe debris or fluid from the components. Cover any openings immediately after removal to prevent accidental contamination of the fluid.

CAUTION

Always note the orientation of the electric motor and wire harness prior to removing them from the engine. Use a paint dot or piece of tape to mark the wire routing. Never scratch the electric motor or trim housing as it promotes corrosion of the surface.

75-115 hp Models

Removal

The electric trim motor and fluid reservoir integrate into a single assembly. The electric trim motor is non-serviceable and must be replaced if defective.

Refer to **Figure 31**.

1. Remove the power trim and tilt system as described in this chapter.
2. Thoroughly clean the electric motor and the area surrounding the mating surface to the trim system.
3. Remove the fill plug (14, **Figure 31**) and O-ring (7) from the fluid reservoir. Place the trim system over a suitable container and pour the trim fluid from the reservoir.
4. Remove the four mounting screws (18, **Figure 31**) and lift the trim pump and reservoir assembly (23) from the trim system.
5. Remove the O-ring (7, **Figure 31**) from the trim system or reservoir. Discard the O-ring. Mark the UP facing side and remove the coupler (17, **Figure 31**) from the electric trim motor shaft or hydraulic pump shaft.
6. Wipe all debris or contaminants from the mating surfaces. Do not allow any contaminants to enter the hydraulic pump or manifold openings.

Installation

Refer to **Figure 31**.

1. Install the new O-ring (7, **Figure 31**) into the groove in the reservoir mating surface.
2. Place the coupler (17, **Figure 31**) into the hydraulic pump shaft closest to the pointed end of the pump. Align the electric motor shaft with the coupling and install the electric motor into position on the trim system.
3. Hold the electric motor slightly away from its mounting surface and turn the motor enough to align the shaft opening with the coupler. Align the pump wires to the starboard side of the system then drop the motor into position. Make sure the reservoir O-ring remains in the reservoir mating surface groove.
4. Install the mounting screws (18, **Figure 31**). Place the ground wire (19, **Figure 31**) under the front starboard mounting screw. Tighten the screws to 80 in.-lb. (9.0 N•m).
5. Install the O-ring and fill plug (7 and 14, **Figure 31**).
6. Install the trim system onto the engine as described in this chapter.

225 hp Model

Removal

The electric trim motor is fully serviceable on 225 hp models. Refer to **Figure 32**.

1. Remove the power trim and tilt system as described in this chapter.
2. Thoroughly clean the electric motor and the area surrounding the mating surface to the trim system.
3. Remove the fill plug (4, **Figure 32**) and O-ring (3) from the fluid reservoir. Place the trim system over a suitable container then pour the trim fluid from the reservoir.
4. Make reference marks on the electric motor and the corresponding mounting location on the trim system housing prior to removal. Use a paint dot or tape. Do not scratch the surfaces.
5. Remove the three mounting screws (22, **Figure 32**) and carefully lift the motor from the housing. If necessary, use a flat scraper or dull putty knife to pry the motor from the pump. Work carefully to avoid damaging the electric motor mounting surfaces. A fluid or water leak can occur if the surfaces are damaged.
6. Remove the O-ring (21, **Figure 32**) from the electric motor or trim system housing. Discard the O-ring. Retrieve the coupling (20, **Figure 32**) from the electric motor or hydraulic pump shaft. Note the top and bottom orientation of the coupling. The slot opening must face the electric motor and the protrusion must face the hydraulic pump.
7. Clean and inspect the trim motor mounting surfaces for corroded, pitted or scratched surfaces. Replace any components with scratches are deep enough to catch a fingernail.

Installation

1. Apply a light coat of Dexron II automatic transmission fluid (ATF) to the surfaces and install a new O-ring (21, **Figure 32**) on the step of the electric motor. Install the

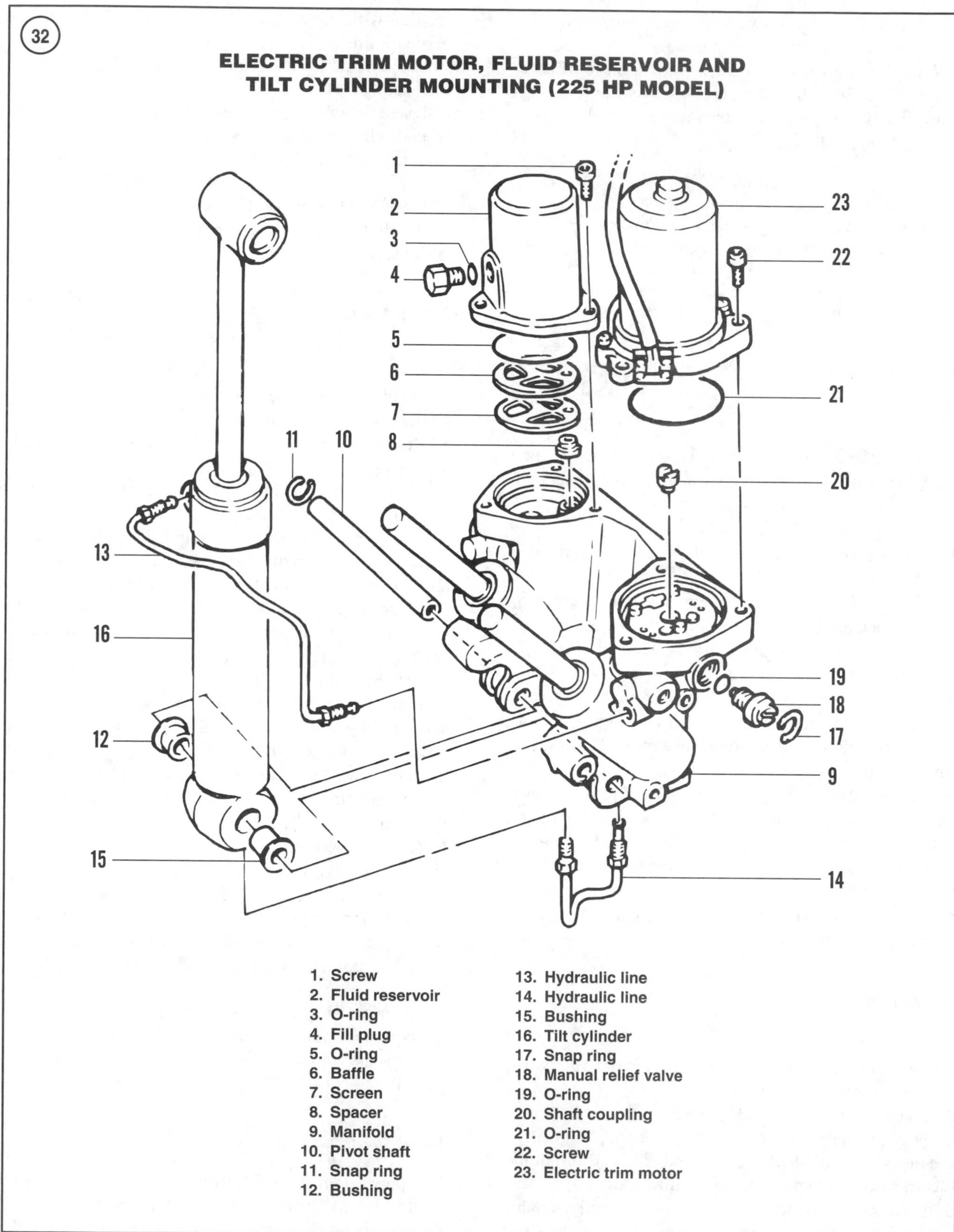

1. Screw
2. Fluid reservoir
3. O-ring
4. Fill plug
5. O-ring
6. Baffle
7. Screen
8. Spacer
9. Manifold
10. Pivot shaft
11. Snap ring
12. Bushing
13. Hydraulic line
14. Hydraulic line
15. Bushing
16. Tilt cylinder
17. Snap ring
18. Manual relief valve
19. O-ring
20. Shaft coupling
21. O-ring
22. Screw
23. Electric trim motor

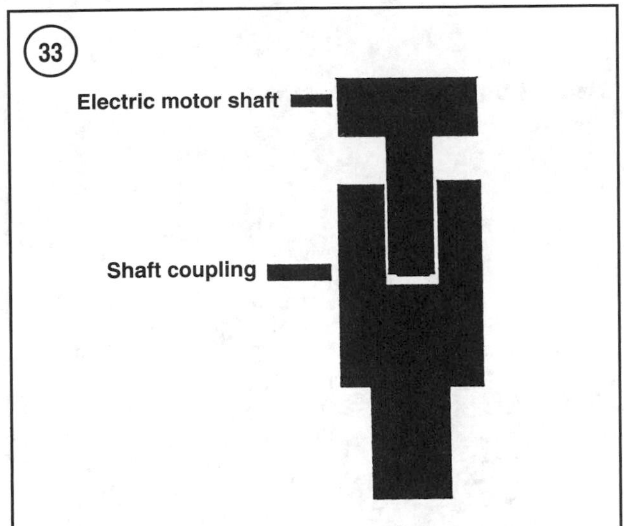

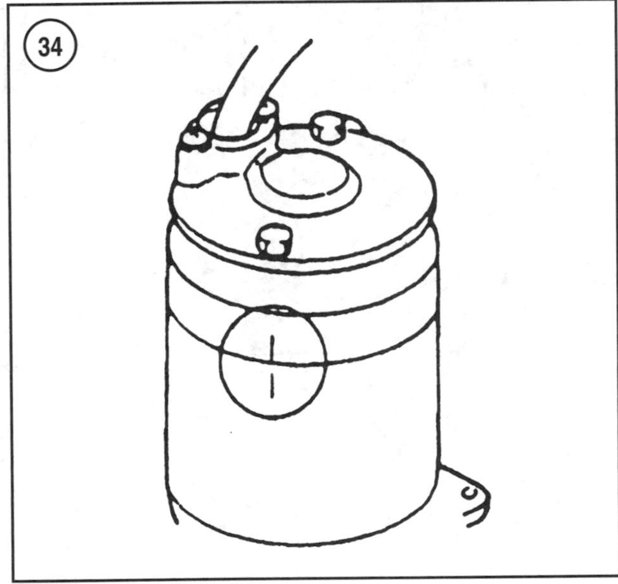

coupling onto the electric motor shaft as indicated in **Figure 33**.

2. Position the electric motor onto the pump and rotate until the protrusion on the coupling aligns with the slot in the hydraulic pump shaft. When aligned the motor drops into position. Make sure the O-ring remains in position on the electric motor step.

3. Slowly rotate the electric motor to obtain correct orientation of the wiring.

4. Install the three mounting screws (22, **Figure 32**). Tighten the screws evenly to 160 in.-lb. (18.1 N•m).

5. Install the O-ring (3, **Figure 32**) and fill plug (4).

6. Install the trim system onto the engine as described in this chapter.

7. Fill and bleed the hydraulic system as described in this chapter. Check for proper operation before putting the engine into service.

ELECTRIC TRIM MOTOR DISASSEMBLY, INSPECTION AND ASSEMBLY (225 HP MODELS)

This section describes disassembly, inspection and assembly of the trim/tilt electric motor used on 225 hp models. The electric trim motor used on 75-115 hp models is non-serviceable and must be replaced if defective.

Work in a clean environment to avoid contaminants. Use electrical cleaner to remove contaminants and debris from the motor components. Electrical contact cleaner is available at most electrical supply stores. It evaporates rapidly and leaves no residue to contaminate components. Avoid touching the brushes and commutator after cleaning. Naturally occurring oils on your fingertips will contaminate these components.

9

CAUTION
Use caution when working around the permanent magnets in the frame assembly. These magnets are quite powerful. Fingers are easily pinched between components by the magnetic force. Never drop or strike the frame assembly. The magnets may break and damage other components during operation.

NOTE
*Mark the upper cover, frame and lower cover of the electric motor (**Figure 34**) prior to repair. Use paint dots or removable tape. Never scratch the components as it will promote corrosion of the metal components.*

Disassembly

Refer to **Figure 35**.

1. Remove the electric motor as described in this chapter.
2. Mark all components (**Figure 34**) before disassembly to ensure proper orientation on assembly.
3. Remove the two screws (2, **Figure 35**) and four washers (3) that retain the frame (1) onto the lower cover (16).

NOTE
The magnets in the frame assembly are quite powerful. Considerable effort may be required to remove the frame assembly from the armature. Make sure all fasteners are removed before removing the armature.

(35)

ELECTRIC TRIM MOTOR COMPONENTS (225 HP MODEL)

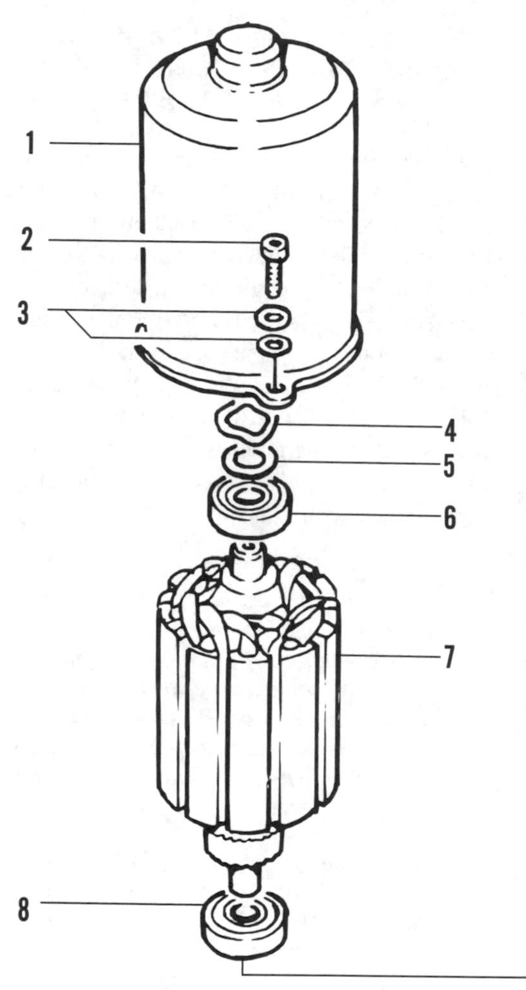

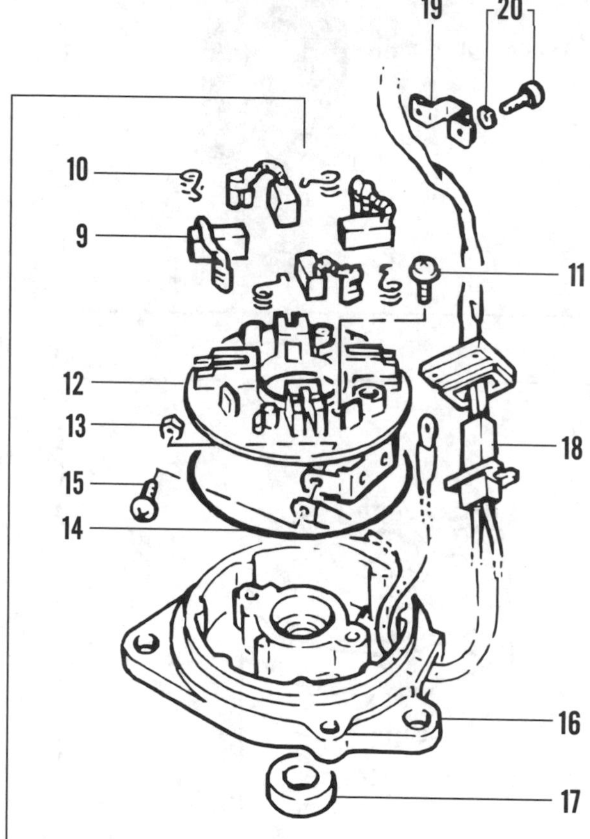

1. Frame
2. Screw
3. Washers
4. Wave washer
5. Washer
6. Bearing
7. Armature
8. Bearing
9. Brush/lead
10. Brush spring
11. Screw
12. Brush plate
13. Nut
14. O-ring
15. Screw
16. Lower cover
17. Seal
18. Wire harness
19. Wire retainer
20. Screw

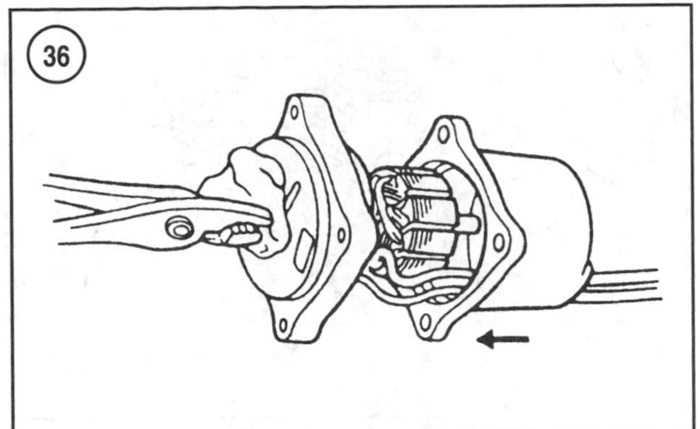
36

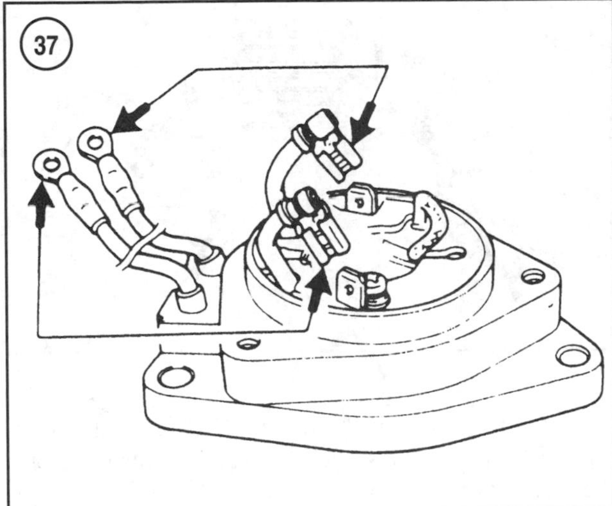
37

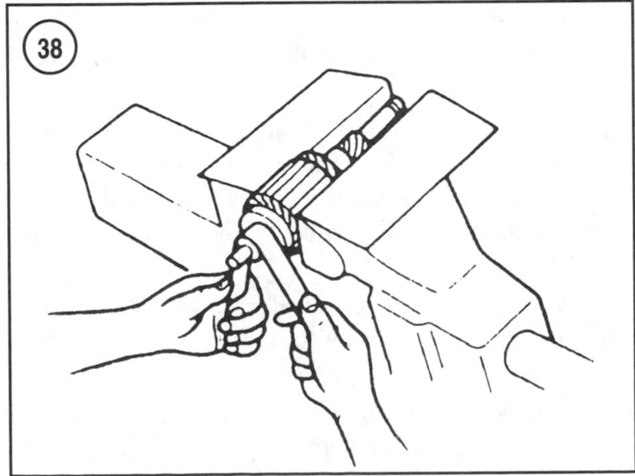
38

4. Grasp the armature shaft with pliers and a shop towel as shown in **Figure 36**. Pull the armature and lower cover from the frame. Remove the O-ring (14, **Figure 35**) from the frame or lower cover. Discard the O-ring.

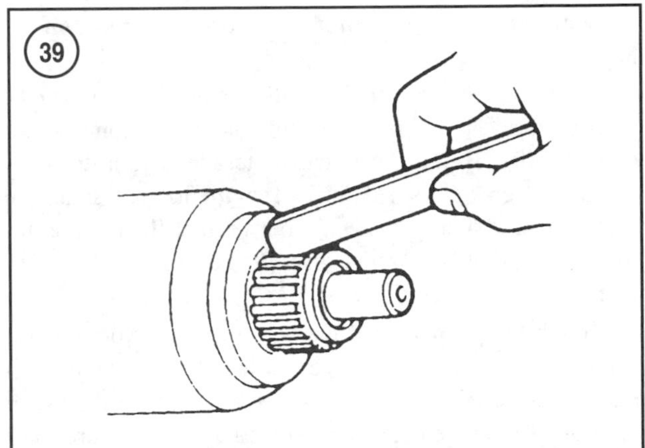
39

5. Remove the two screws (11, **Figure 35**) then pull the armature (7) and brush plate (12) out of the lower cover. Work carefully to avoid damaging the bushes or armature.
6. Note the wire connection points, then remove the two screws (15, **Figure 35**) and nuts (13).
7. Pull the brush plate from the armature.
8. Carefully pull the four brush springs (10, **Figure 35**) from the brush plate post.
9. Unplug the leads, then pull the four brush/leads (9, **Figure 35**) from the brush plate.
10. Remove the washer (5, **Figure 35**) and wave washer (4) from the armature shaft bore in the frame.
11. Carefully pry the seal (17, **Figure 35**) from the lower cover. Discard the seal.

Component Inspection and Testing

Before performing any test or measurement, clean debris and contaminants from all components. Dry the components with compressed air. Inspect the frame assembly for broken or loose magnets. Replace the frame assembly if defects are noted.

1. Calibrate the meter to the 1 ohm scale. Connect the positive test lead to the green wire connection on the cover assembly. Connect the negative test lead to the correstponding brush terminal (**Figure 37**, typical). Repeat the test with the blue wire and respective terminal. The meter must indicate *continuity* for each test. If otherwise, the lower cover is faulty and must be replaced.
2. Grip the armature in a vise with protective jaws (**Figure 38**). Use only enough force to lightly retain the component. Polish the commutator surfaces with 600 grit wet or dry Carburundum. Periodically rotate the armature to polish evenly. Avoid removing too much material.
3. Use a disposable fingernail file to remove mica and brush material from the undercut surfaces (**Figure 39**).

Use compressed air to remove all loose material from the armature.

4. Calibrate the meter to the 1 ohm scale. Touch the positive test lead to one of the segments on the commutator (**Figure 40**). Touch the negative test lead to a different segment. Repeat this test until all segments are tested. The meter must indicate *continuity* between each pair of commutator segments. If otherwise, the commutator is faulty and must be replaced.

5. Touch the positive test lead to one of the commutator segments. Touch the negative test lead to one of the laminated areas of the armature (**Figure 41**). Note the meter reading. Touch the negative test lead to the armature shaft (**Figure 41**) and note the meter reading. The meter must indicate *no continuity* for each test. If otherwise, the armature is shorted and must be replaced.

6. Using a micrometer or vernier caliper, measure the commutator diameter (**Figure 42**) at all points along the length of the segments. Replace the armature if the diameter is less than 0.984 in. (25.0 mm).

7. Inspect the bearing surfaces on the armature shaft for worn or damaged surfaces and replace as required.

8. Inspect the bearings in the lower cover and frame assembly. Replace the bearings if worn or damaged.

9. Inspect the brush spring for corrosion lost spring tension (from overheat) and other damage. Replace the springs if any doubt exist about their condition.

10. Using a vernier caliper, measure the length of the brushes (**Figure 43**). Replace all four brushes if any of them measure less than 0.157 in. (4.0 mm).

Assembly

1. Carefully press the new oil seal (17, **Figure 35**) fully into the lower cover opening. The lip side of the seal must face downward or away from the armature bearing. Apply a light coat of Quicksilver 2-4-C Marine Lubricant to the seal lip. Excess lubricant will contaminate the brushes.

2. Apply a light coat of Quicksilver 2-4-C Marine Lubricant to the lower bearing (8, **Figure 35**) and armature shaft at the bearing contact surfaces. Do not allow any grease to contact the brushes or commutator surfaces.

3. Connect the blue and green harness connectors to the respective terminals and secure with the two screws (15, **Figure 35**) and nuts (13). Securely tighten the screws and nuts.

4. Align the screw openings while carefully fitting the brush plate (12, **Figure 35**) into the lower cover (16). Install and securely tighten the two screws (11, **Figure 35**) to secure the brush plate.

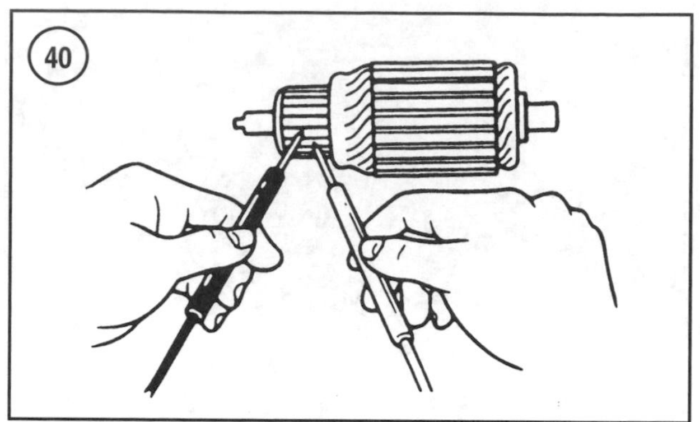

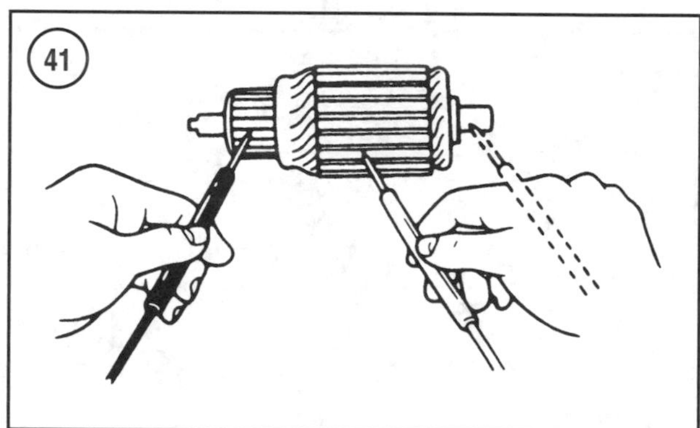

5. Install the four brush/leads (9, **Figure 35**) into the retaining slots in the brush plate. Plug each brush lead onto the brush plate terminal.

6. Push each brush spring (10, **Figure 35**) over the post on the brush plate. Make sure the internal loop fits into the slot in the post and the hook fits into the brush retaining. The hooks must push the brushes toward the commutator when assembled.

7. Collapse the brush springs and carefully slip the armature into the lower cover. The armature must seat against the bearing in the lower cover. Release the brush springs. Work carefully to avoid damaging the brushes and commutator.

8. Apply a light coat of Quicksilver 2-4-C Marine Lubricant onto the upper bearing (6, **Figure 35**) and armature shaft at the bush contact surfaces.

9. Install the wave washer (4, **Figure 35**) and washer (5) into the armature shaft opening in the frame (1).

10. Install a new O-ring (14, **Figure 35**) onto the lower cover. Use pliers and a shop towel to maintain the position of the armature and the lower cover (**Figure 36**) while guiding the armature into the frame. The upper end of the armature shaft must enter the bearing at the top of the frame.

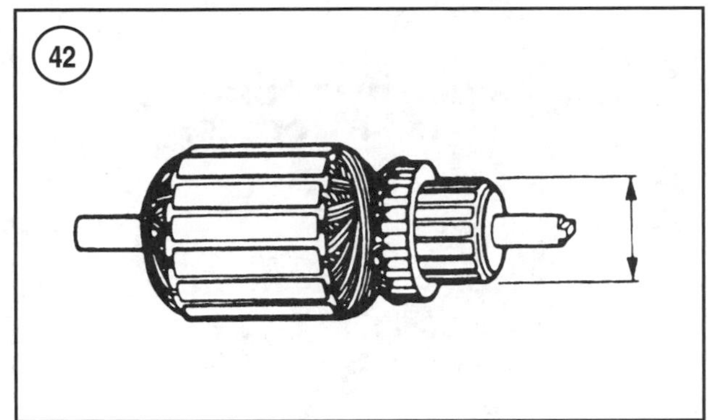

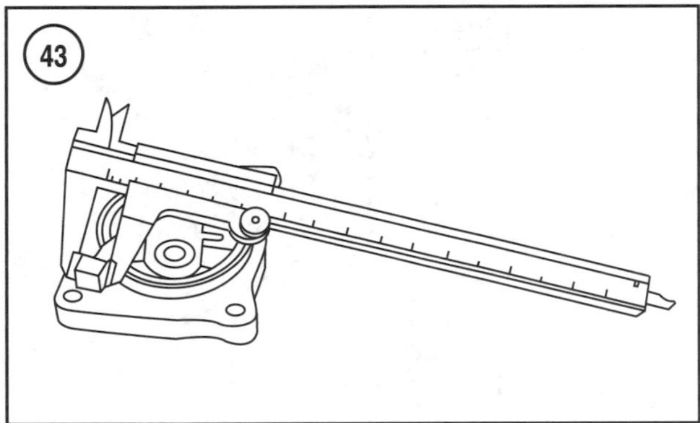

11. Seat the frame against the lower cover. Ensure the O-rings remains in position and is not damaged. Water leakage will result if the O-ring is out of position or damaged.
12. Align the marks made prior to disassembly (**Figure 34**).
13. Install the screws (2, **Figure 35**) and washers (3) that retain the lower cover onto the frame assembly. Securely tighten the screws.
14. Rotate the armature shaft and check for binding. Disassemble the motor and check for improper assembly if binding occurs.
15. Install the electric trim motor as described in this chapter.

TRIM SYSTEM DISASSEMBLY, INSPECTION AND ASSEMBLY

Problems with trim systems are almost always the result of debris in the system or damaged O-rings. Replace all O-rings and seals anytime the internal components are removed. Purchase the O-ring and seal kit for the trim system before disassembling the trim system.

Seal and O-ring kits contain numerous sizes and shapes of O-rings. Some of the O-rings have the same diameter, but have a different thickness. To help ensure correct O-ring placement, remove one O-ring at a time. Find the replacement O-ring of the exact diameter and thickness as the one removed.

Scratched or pitted hydraulic cylinder or valve seating surfaces will cause system leak-down or other hydraulic problems. Very fine scratches occur from normal operation and rarely cause hydraulic problems. Scratches deep enough to feel with a fingernail, or deep pitting on seating surfaces, indicate the need for replacing the affected component.

Cracks may form in the hydraulic cylinder or other trim system components if the engine impacts underwater objects. Replace components if cracks or other defects are evident.

Note the orientation of all springs, plugs, seats and valves as they are removed. Install all valves and springs in the original locations during assembly.

Work only in a clean environment and use lint free shop towels when cleaning all trim system components. Trim systems must operate with very clean fluid.

WARNING

The trim system contains fluid under high pressure. Always use protective eye wear and gloves when working with the trim system. Never remove any components or plugs without first bleeding the pressure off of the system. Follow the instructions carefully and loosen the manual relief valve to relieve the internal pressure.

75-115 hp Models

Disassembly

A spanner wrench (or Mercury part No. 91-74951) and heat lamp (Mercury part No. 91-63209) are required to completely disassemble the trim system. Refer to **Figure 31**.

1. Remove the trim and tilt system as described in this chapter.
2. Remove the fill plug (14, **Figure 31**) and pour all trim fluid from the reservoir.
3. Remove the electric trim motor as described in this chapter.
4. Clamp the trim system in a vice with protective jaws. Do not clamp on the hydraulic cylinder. Remove the front and rear poppet valve plugs (10, **Figure 31**). Pull the poppet assemblies from the pump openings.
5. Insert a small metal rod into the small opening in the seat for the front poppet valve. Push on the metal rod to push the shuttle valve and rear poppet valve seat from the

pump. Push the front poppet valve seat out of the pump through the rear poppet valve bore.

6. Remove the two screws (1, **Figure 44**) from the rear side of the pump and the single screw from the front side, then lift the pump from the manifold. Lift the filter (5, **Figure 44**) from the manifold.

7. Remove the seal (4, **Figure 44**) and O-rings (3) from the manifold.

8. Remove the seat (6, **Figure 44**) and O-ring (7) from the manifold opening.

9. Remove the ball then spring (8, **Figure 44**) from the manifold opening.

10. Remove both Allen screws (5, **Figure 31**) from the lower port side of the hydraulic cylinder (4), then carefully pull the manifold from the cylinder.

11. Pull the valves, seats and O-rings (13, **Figure 31**) from the cylinder and manifold openings.

12. Pull the locating pin (6, **Figure 31**) from the manifold or trim cylinder.

13. Clamp the lower end of the hydraulic cylinder in a vice with protective jaws. Fit the pins of a spanner wrench (Mercury part No. 91-74951) into the openings in the cylinder cap (**Figure 45**). Rotate the spanner wrench counterclockwise to remove the cap. Tap the spanner wrench with a plastic mallet if necessary to loosen the cap.

14. Pull the trim ram from the trim cylinder. Direct the large opening of the cylinder into a bucket of shop towels to capture the floating piston (3, **Figure 31**). Apply low pressure compressed air to the opening in the cylinder to expel the piston.

15. Clamp the pivot pin end of the hydraulic ram into a vise with protective jaws. Remove the screws retaining the shock valves to the shock piston. Lift the plate from the springs. Pull the five springs, valve seats and balls from the shock piston.

16. Wipe all hydraulic fluid from the shock piston. Using a heat lamp, apply heat to the shock piston portion of the hydraulic ram. Fit the pins of the spanner wrench into the openings in the shock valve. Rotate the spanner wrench counterclockwise to remove the shock piston. Slide the cylinder cap from the ram.

17. Carefully pry the wiper sleeve from the cylinder cap opening. Work carefully to avoid damaging the seal bore. Remove the O-rings from the ram bore and the step in the cylinder cap.

18. Clean all components using clean solvent. Dry the components with compressed air. Direct air through all passages and openings to remove all traces of solvent or debris.

19. Inspect all components for excessive wear, cracks, pitted surfaces or other defects. Replace the affected components if these or other defects are evident.

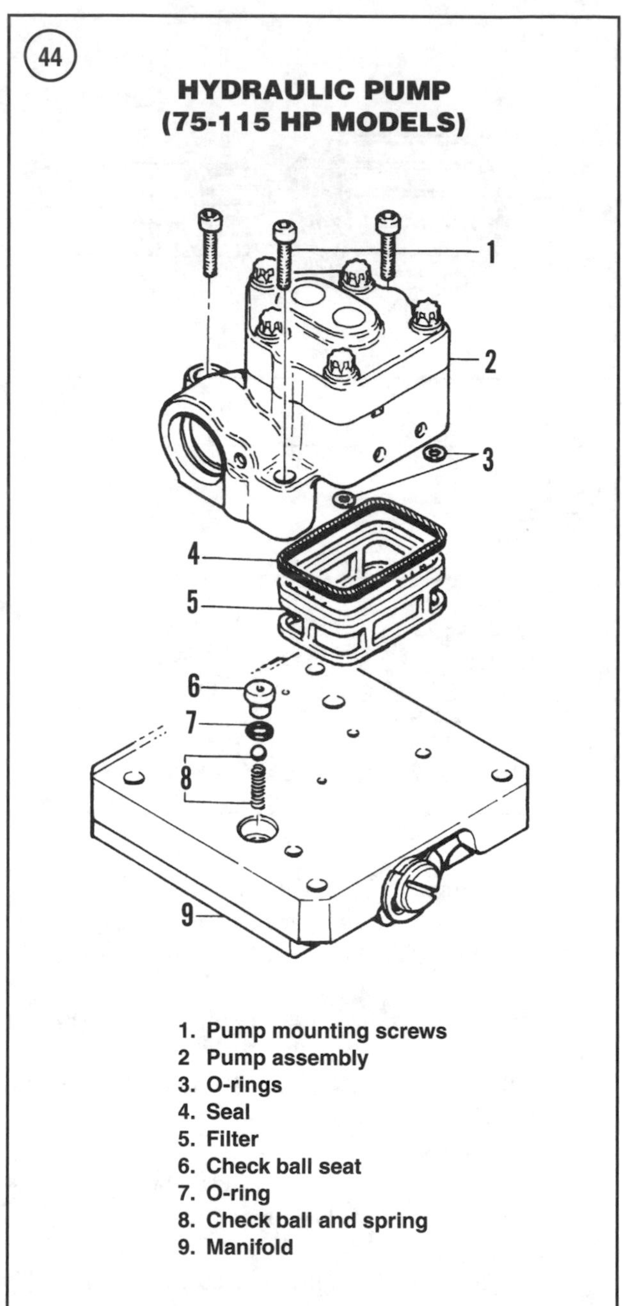

1. Pump mounting screws
2 Pump assembly
3. O-rings
4. Seal
5. Filter
6. Check ball seat
7. O-ring
8. Check ball and spring
9. Manifold

Assembly

A spanner wrench (or Mercury part No. 91-74951) is required to completely assemble the trim system. Replace all O-rings one at a time during assembly. Lubricate them and all other trim system components with Dexron II ATF before installation. Refer to **Figure 31**.

1. Press a new wiper seal into the cylinder cap bore with the smaller diameter facing outward.

2. Lubricate the surfaces with ATF then install new O-rings into the groove in the ram bore and the external step of the cylinder cap. Carefully slide the cylinder cap, wiper side first, over the cylinder ram.

3. Lubricate the surfaces with ATF then install a new O-ring into the groove in the inner bore and the groove in the outer diameter of the shock piston.

4. Apply a coat of Loctite 271 onto the cylinder ram threads. Thread the shock piston onto the ram. Clamp the pivot end of the ram into a vise with protective jaws. Fit the pins of a spanner wrench (Mercury part No. 91-74951) into the openings in the shock piston. Use the spanner wrench to tighten the shock piston to 90 ft.-lb. (122.0 N•m).

5. Install the balls, guides, and springs into the opening in the shock piston. Without dislodging the springs, guides and balls, Fit the plate onto the shock valves. Align the openings, then thread the three screws into the plate and shock valve. Tighten the shock valve plate screws to 35 in.-lb. (4.0 N•m).

6. Clamp the lower end of the hydraulic cylinder in a vice with protective jaws.

7. Lubricate the surfaces with ATF, then install the floating piston (3, **Figure 31**) into the hydraulic cylinder with the open side facing outward.

8. Insert the shock piston end of the ram into the cylinder opening. Push down on the ram until the shock piston contacts the floating piston. Hand-thread the cylinder cap into the cylinder. Fit the pins of a spanner wrench (Mercury part No. 91-74951) into the openings in the cylinder cap (**Figure 45**). Using the spanner wrench, tighten the cylinder cap to 45 ft.-lb. (61.0 N•m).

9. Fit the locating pins (6, **Figure 31**) into the trim cylinder opening.

10. Lubricate the surfaces with ATF, then insert the valve, springs, seats and O-rings (13, **Figure 31**) into the trim cylinder and manifold openings.

11. Fit the two O-rings (7, **Figure 31**) into the recessed groove in the trim cylinder mating surface.

12. Without dislodging the valves, springs, seats and O-rings, mate the trim cylinder and manifold surfaces. Make sure the locating pin in the cylinder enters the opening in the manifold.

13. Thread the two Allen screws (5, **Figure 31**) into the cylinder and manifold openings. Tighten the screws evenly to 100 in.-lb. (11.3 N•m).

14. Insert the spring and ball (8, **Figure 44**) into the manifold opening. Fit the O-ring (7, **Figure 44**) onto the seat, then insert the smaller diameter side of the seat into the opening.

15. Install the two new O-rings (3, **Figure 44**) into the recesses at the bottom of the pump.

16. Install the seal (4, **Figure 44**) then filter (5) onto the pump.

17. Without dislodging the O-rings, filter or seal, fit the hydraulic pump (2, **Figure 44**) onto the manifold (9).

18. Thread the two screws (1, **Figure 44**) into the openings at the rear side of the pump and the single screw into the opening at the front side. Tighten the three screws evenly to 70 in.-lb. (7.9 N•m).

19. Lubricate the surfaces with ATF, then insert the shuttle valve and seats (10, **Figure 31**) into the hydraulic pump openings. Use a socket or section of tubing to fully seat the poppet valve seats in the bore.

20. Insert the poppet valves into the seats with the pointed end facing inward. Fit the springs into the recesses in the poppet valve caps, then thread the caps into the seat openings. Tighten the poppet valve caps to 120 in.-lb. (13.6 N•m).

21. Install the electric trim motor as described in this chapter.

22. Install the power trim and tilt system as described in this chapter.

23. Fill and bleed the system as described in this chapter.

225 hp Model

Disassembly

A spanner wrench (or Mercury part No. 91-888867), trim ram wrench (Mercury part No. 91-88869) and shock piston clamp (Mercury part No. 91-88868) are required to completely disassemble the trim system.

1. Remove the trim and tilt system as described in this chapter.

2. Remove the fill plug (4, **Figure 32**) and pour all trim fluid from the reservoir.

3. Remove the electric trim motor as described in this chapter.

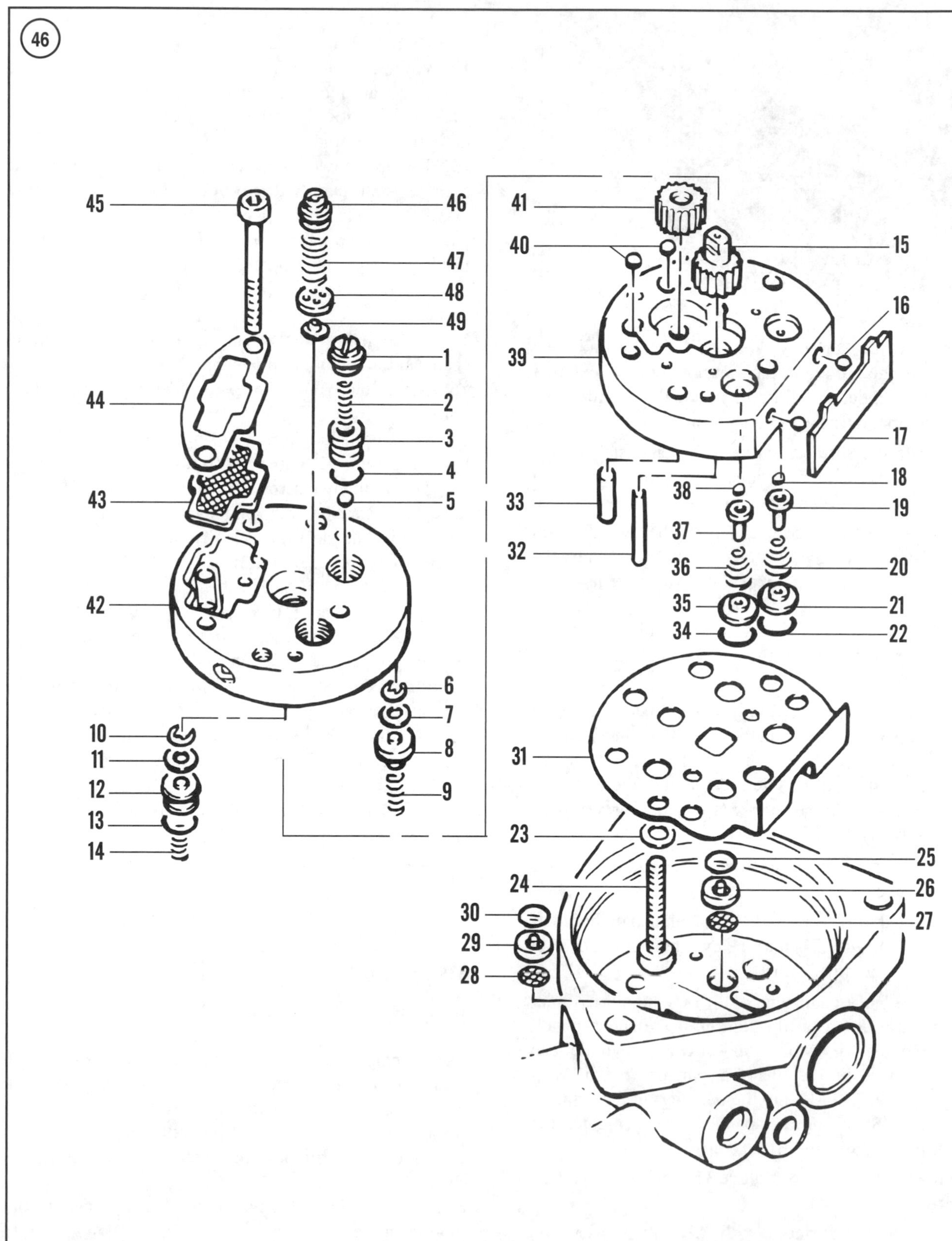
46
45
46
47
48
49
1
2
3
4
5
44
43
42
6
7
8
9
10
11
12
13
14
41
40
15
16
39
17
18
38
33
19
37
32
36
20
35
21
34
22
31
23
25
24
26
30
27
29
28

HYDRAULIC PUMP COMPONENTS (225 HP MODELS)

1. Plug
2. Spring
3. Sleeve
4. O-ring
5. Check ball
6. E-clip
7. Seal
8. Shuttle valve
9. Spring
10. E-clip
11. Seal
12. Shuttle valve
13. O-ring
14. Spring
15. Drive gear
16. Balls
17. Spring plate
18. Ball
19. Seat
20. Spring
21. Piston
22. O-ring
23. Washer
24. Allen screw
25. O-ring
26. Spacer
27. Screen
28. Screen
29. Spacer
30. O-ring
31. Bracket
32. Pin
33. Pin
34. O-ring
35. Piston
36. Spring
37. Seat
38. Ball
39. Lower pump housing
40. Balls
41. Driven gear
42. Upper pump housing
43. Screen
44. Bracket
45. Allen screw
46. Plug
47. Spring
48. Disc
49. Seal

4. Remove the three screws (1, **Figure 32**), then carefully pull the reservoir (2) from the manifold. If necessary, use a flat scraper or putty knife to pry the reservoir loose. Work carefully to avoid damaging the O-ring mating surfaces. Damage to the surfaces will allow water and oil leakage.
5. Remove the O-ring (5, **Figure 32**) from the reservoir or manifold surfaces. Discard the O-ring.
6. Remove the baffle (6, **Figure 32**) and screen (7) from the manifold. Use a mild solvent to clean all debris from the screen. Replace the screen if it is damaged or cannot be completely cleaned.
7. Pull the spacer (8, **Figure 32**) from the manifold opening.
8. Remove the three Allen screws (45, **Figure 46**), then lift the hydraulic pump assembly from the manifold. Do not separate the pump housings at this time. Place the pump on a clean work surface with the screen side facing upward.
9. Remove the O-rings (25 and 30, **Figure 46**), spacers (26 and 29) and screens (27 and 28) from the manifold opening. Remove the O-rings from the bottom of the hydraulic pump assembly if not found in the opening.
10. Lift the bracket (44, **Figure 46**) and screen (43) from the hydraulic pump. Use a mild solvent to clean all debris from the screen. Replace the screen if it is damaged or cannot be completely cleaned.
11. Remove the plug (1, **Figure 46**), then carefully pull the spring (2), sleeve (3), O-ring (4) and check ball (5).
12. Remove the plug (46, **Figure 46**), then carefully pull the spring (47), disc (48), and seal (49).
13. Invert the pump assembly, then remove the two Allen screws (24, **Figure 46**) and washers (23).
14. Lift the bracket (31, **Figure 46**) from the pump, then remove the spring plate (17) and two check balls (16).
15. Remove the O-rings (22 and 34, **Figure 46**) from the pump housing or bracket, then remove the pistons (21 and 35), springs (20 and 36), seats (19 and 37) and check balls (18 and 38).
16. Carefully separate the upper and lower pump housings.
17. Remove the drive gear (15, **Figure 46**), driven gear (41) and check balls (40) from the lower housing. Remove the pins (32 and 33, **Figure 46**) from the lower housing.
18. Remove the O-rings then lift the springs (9 and 14, **Figure 46**) and shuttle valves (8 and 12) from the upper housing. Remove the E-clips (6 and 10, **Figure 46**) then lift the seals (7 and 11) from the valves.
19. Place a suitable container under the system to capture spilled fluid. Loosen the fittings, then remove the two hydraulic lines (13 and 14, **Figure 32**).

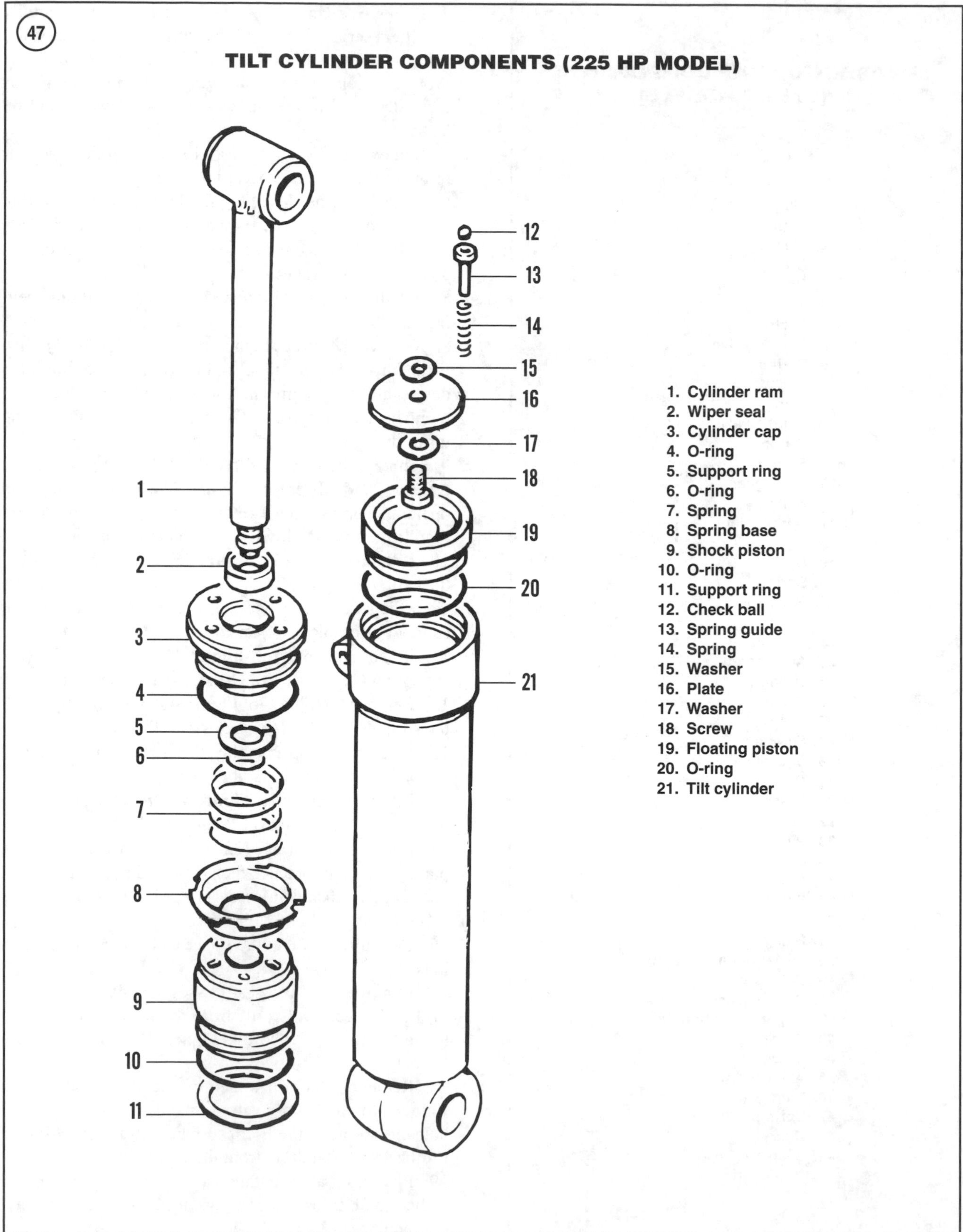
47
TILT CYLINDER COMPONENTS (225 HP MODEL)
1
2
3
4
5
6
7
8
9
10
11
12
13
14
15
16
17
18
19
20
21
1. Cylinder ram
2. Wiper seal
3. Cylinder cap
4. O-ring
5. Support ring
6. O-ring
7. Spring
8. Spring base
9. Shock piston
10. O-ring
11. Support ring
12. Check ball
13. Spring guide
14. Spring
15. Washer
16. Plate
17. Washer
18. Screw
19. Floating piston
20. O-ring
21. Tilt cylinder

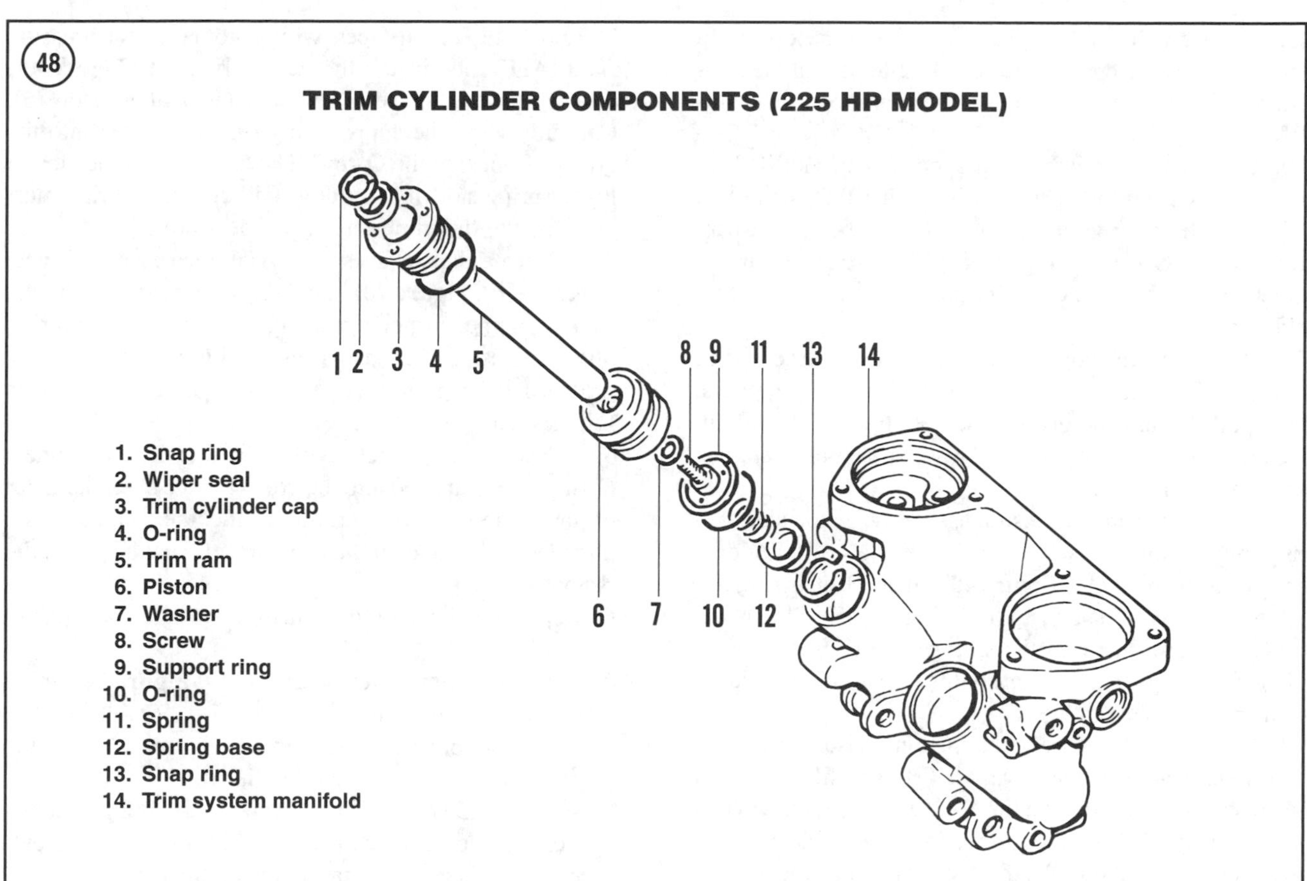

20. Remove the snap ring (11, **Figure 32**), then carefully push the port side of the pivot shaft (10) until it exits the manifold and tilt cylinder bores.

21. Clamp the lower end of the hydraulic cylinder in a vice with protective jaws. Fit the pins of a spanner wrench (Mercury part No. 91-88867) into the openings in the cylinder cap (**Figure 45**). Rotate the wrench counterclockwise to remove the cap. Tap the spanner wrench with a plastic mallet if necessary to loosen the cap.

22. Pull the trim ram from the tilt cylinder. Direct the large opening of the cylinder into a bucket of shop towels to capture the floating piston (19, **Figure 47**). Apply low pressure compressed air to the opening in the cylinder to expel the piston.

23. Remove the O-ring (20, **Figure 47**) from the piston.

24. Fit the clamp halves (Mercury part No. 91-88868) onto the side of the sides of the shock piston. Do not inadvertently clamp on the spring base (8, **Figure 47**). Secure the clamp halves and cylinder ram assembly into a vise with the pivot end of the cylinder facing upward. Fit the trim ram wrench (Mercury part No. 91-88869) onto the pivot end of the ram. Fit a socket wrench handle into the square opening in the wrench. Turn the trim ram counterclockwise until free from the shock piston. Loosen the vise, then remove the shock piston from the clamp.

25. Pull the cylinder cap (3, **Figure 47**), spring (7) and spring base from the ram. Carefully pry the wiper seal (2, **Figure 47**) from the cylinder cap. Work carefully to avoid damaging the seal bore in the cap. Use a small pick to remove the O-ring (6, **Figure 47**) and support ring from the inner bore of the cap. Remove the O-ring (4, **Figure 47**) from the groove on the outer diameter of the cap.

26. Remove the O-ring (10, **Figure 47**) and support ring (11) from the groove on the outer diameter of the shock piston (9).

27. Place the shock piston in a container with the plate and screw side facing upward. Remove the screw (18, **Figure 47**) and washer (17) then slowly lift the plate (16) and washer (15) from the piston.

28. Remove the five springs (14, **Figure 47**), guides (13) and check balls (12) from the piston.

29. Clamp the trim system manifold (14, **Figure 48**) into a vise with protective jaws. Fit the pins of a spanner wrench (Mercury part No. 91-88867) into the openings in the port side trim cylinder cap (3, **Figure 48**). Rotate the wrench counterclockwise to fully loosen the cap. Tap the

spanner wrench with a plastic mallet if necessary to loosen the cap. Repeat this procedure to loosen the starboard side cylinder cap. Remove both caps from the manifold.

30. Use snap ring pliers to remove the snap ring (1, **Figure 48**), then carefully pry the wiper seal (2) from the cap. Work carefully to avoid damaging the seal bore in the cap. Remove the O-ring (4, **Figure 48**) from the groove in the outer diameter of the cap. Repeat this step for the other cylinder cap.

31. Wrap a clean shop towel around the exposed end of one of the trim rams. Grip the ram and towel with pliers, then pull the ram and piston assembly from the manifold. Remove the remaining ram and piston assembly using the same method.

32. Clamp the ram and piston assembly, piston side facing upward, into a vise with protective jaws. Hold down on the spring base (12, **Figure 48**), then use snap ring pliers to remove the snap ring (13, **Figure 48**). Slowly release pressure then pull the spring base (12) and spring (11) from the piston (6). Repeat this step for the remaining ram and piston assembly.

33. With the ram securely clamped in a vise, remove the screw (8, **Figure 48**) and washer (7), then lift the piston (6) from the ram. Remove the O-ring (10, **Figure 48**) and support ring (9) from the groove in the outer diameter of the piston. Repeat this step for the remaining ram and piston assembly.

34. Clean all components using clean solvent. Dry the components with compressed air. Direct air through all passages and openings to remove all traces of solvent or debris.

35. Inspect all components for excessive wear, cracks, pitted surfaces or other defects. Replace the affected components if these or other defects are evident.

Assembly

1. Secure the trim ram (5, **Figure 48**) in a vise with the threaded opening facing upward. Fit the piston (6, **Figure 48**) onto the end of the ram with the tapered end facing upward. Install the washer (7, **Figure 48**) then thread the screw (8) into the piston and trim ram. Tighten the screw to 28 ft.-lb. (38 N•m).

2. Insert the spring (11, **Figure 48**) into the recess in the trim piston (6). Fit the spring base (12, **Figure 48**) onto the spring. Push down on the spring base to collapse the spring until the snap ring groove in the piston is exposed. Use snap ring pliers to install the snap ring (13, **Figure 48**) into the groove. Slowly release the spring base. Inspect the piston to verify the snap ring is fully seated into the groove.

3. Lubricate the surfaces with automatic transmission fluid (ATF) then install the new O-ring (10, **Figure 48**) into the groove in the outer diameter of the piston (6). Carefully wind the support ring (9, **Figure 48**) into the groove alongside the O-ring. The O-ring must be closest to the spring side of the groove and the support ring must be closest to the trim ram side of the groove.

4. Lubricate the surfaces with ATF, then insert the new wiper seal (2, **Figure 48**) into the cylinder cap (3) with the smaller diameter opening facing outward. Use snap ring pliers to install the snap ring (1, **Figure 48**) into the groove in the cap. Inspect the cap to verify the snap ring is fully seated into the groove.

5. Lubricate the surfaces with ATF, then install the new O-ring (4, **Figure 48**) into the groove in the outer diameter of the cylinder cap. Carefully slide the cylinder cap, threaded end first, over the trim ram and seat it against the piston.

6. Repeat Steps 1-5 for the remaining trim ram and piston assembly.

7. Clamp the trim system manifold (9, **Figure 32**) into a vise with protective jaws.

8. Install the bushings (12 and 15, **Figure 32**) into the pivot shaft openings in the tilt cylinder.

9. Apply a light coat of Quicksilver 2-4-C Marine Lubricant onto the lower pivot shaft (10, **Figure 32**), the tilt cylinder bushings and the shaft bores in the manifold.

10. Align the pivot pin bores while fitting the empty tilt cylinder (16, **Figure 32**) onto the manifold. The upper trim line opening in the cylinder must face away from the manifold. Insert the lower pivot shaft into the bore opening in the starboard side of the manifold. Align the bores, then push the lower pivot shaft through the tilt cylinder and port side manifold bore until the snap ring groove is fully exposed. Use snap ring pliers to install the snap ring into the pivot shaft groove.

11. Connect the hydraulic lines (13 and 14, **Figure 32**) onto the manifold and tilt cylinder. Thread the fittings into the openings by hand to prevent cross threading, then tighten all four fittings to 133 in.-lb. (15.0 N•m).

12. Place the lower pump housing (39, **Figure 46**) in a suitable container with the gear openings facing upward.

13. Lubricate the surfaces with ATF, then insert the pins (32 and 33, **Figure 46**) into the openings in the pump housing. The openings align with the gear recesses. Fit the driven gear (41, **Figure 46**) over the larger diameter pin then seat it in the recess in the housing. Fit the drive gear (15, **Figure 46**) over the smaller diameter pin. Manually rotate the drive gear to align the teeth with the driven gear teeth, then seat the gear into the recess in the housing.

14. Insert the check balls (40, **Figure 46**) into the openings in the pump housing.

15. Place the upper pump housing (42, **Figure 46**) in a suitable container with the filter side facing downward.
16. Fit the seals (7 and 11, **Figure 46**) over the protruding tips on each shuttle valve (8 and 12). Snap the E-clips (6 and 10, **Figure 46**) into the groove on each tip to secure the seals.
17. Lubricate the surfaces with ATF, then insert the two shuttle valve assemblies, seal side first, into the openings in the upper housing. Insert the springs (9 and 14, **Figure 46**) into both openings and seat them against the shuttle valves. Fit the O-rings (13, **Figure 46**) into the recesses in the upper housings. The recesses surround the shuttle valve openings.
18. Align the drive gear and pin openings, then carefully mate the upper and lower pump housings. Work carefully to avoid dislodging the check balls, O-rings and shuttle valve springs. If necessary, have an assistant hold the components in place with feeler gauges while mating the housing.
19. Temporarily insert the two Allen screws (45, **Figure 46**) into the openings in the upper, then the lower housings to prevent misalignment during further assembly. Place the pump assembly in a suitable container with the filter side facings downward.
20. Lubricate the surfaces with ATF, then insert the check balls (18 and 38, **Figure 46**) into the respective openings in the lower pump body. Insert the seats (19 and 37, **Figure 46**), larger end first, into the openings. Insert the springs (20 and 36, **Figure 46**), smaller end first, into the openings. Fit the pistons (21 and 35, **Figure 46**) into the openings. The tip of the seats must enter the openings in the pistons. Fit the O-rings (22 and 34, **Figure 46**) into the recesses in the lower housings. The recesses surround the piston openings.
21. Insert the two check balls (16, **Figure 46**) into the openings in the flat surface on the side of the lower housing. Insert the two tabs on the spring plate (17, **Figure 46**) into the opening in the upper housing, then seat the plate against the side of the lower housing. Fit the bracket (31, **Figure 46**) onto the lower housing with the bent over end contacting the spring plate. Work carefully to avoid dislodging the O-rings, pistons, springs and check balls. If necessary, have an assistant hold the components in place with feeler gauges while the bracket is fitted onto the pump. Fit the washers (23, **Figure 46**) onto the Allen screws (24), then thread the screws into the bracket, lower then upper pump housing. Tighten the two screws evenly to 62 in.-lb. (7.0 N•m).
22. Place the pump assembly in a container with the filter side facing upward. Remove the two Allen screws (45, **Figure 46**). Fit the screen (43, **Figure 46**) into its recess in the upper housing. Align the opening in the bracket (43, **Figure 46**) with the filter, then seat the bracket onto the housing. Insert the two Allen screws into the bracket and pump openings to help retain the components during further assembly.
23. Insert the seal (49, **Figure 46**) into the opening in the upper housing. The side with the tip in the middle must face inward. Insert the disc (48, **Figure 46**) into the opening and seat against the seal. Insert the spring (47, **Figure 46**) into the opening and seat against the disc. Thread the plug (46, **Figure 46**) into the opening. Securely tighten the plug.
24. Insert the check ball into the opening in the upper housing. Lubricate the surfaces with ATF, then install a new O-ring (4, **Figure 46**) into the groove in the sleeve (3). Insert the sleeve into the opening, with the open side facing outward. Insert the spring (2, **Figure 46**) into the open end of the sleeve. Thread the plug (1, **Figure 46**) into the opening. Securely tighten the plug.
25. Install the screens (27 and 28, **Figure 46**) into the openings in the manifold. Fit the spacers (26 and 29, **Figure 46**) into the openings. Fit the new O-rings (25 and 30, **Figure 46**) onto the spacers.
26. Align the screw openings while carefully lowering the pump assembly into the manifold opening. Work carefully to avoid dislodging the O-rings, sleeves and screens. Seat the pump assembly then thread the three Allen screws (45, **Figure 46**) into the pump and manifold. Tighten the three Allen screws evenly to 62 in.-lb. (7.0 N•m).
27. Lubricate the surfaces with automatic transmission fluid (ATF) then install the new O-ring (4, **Figure 47**) into the groove in the outer diameter of the cylinder cap (3). Carefully insert the support ring (5, **Figure 47**) into the groove in the bore of the cap. Install a new O-ring (6, **Figure 47**) into the groove alongside the support ring. The support ring must be closest to the wiper seal side of the groove.
28. Lubricate the surfaces with ATF, then press the new wiper seal (2, **Figure 47**) into the cylinder cap (3) with the smaller diameter opening facing outward. Carefully slide the cylinder cap, non-threaded end first, over the ram and seat it against the pivot end of the ram.
29. Slide the spring (7, **Figure 47**) over the ram and seat it against the cylinder cap. Slide the spring base (8, **Figure 47**) over the ram with the open side facing the spring.
30. Thread the shock piston (9, **Figure 47**) onto the ram. Fit the clamp halves (Mercury part No. 91-88868) onto the sides of the shock piston. Do not inadvertently clamp on the spring base. Secure the clamp halves and cylinder ram assembly into a vise with the pivot end of the cylinder facing upward. Fit the trim ram wrench (Mercury part No. 91-88869) onto the pivot end of the ram. Fit a socket

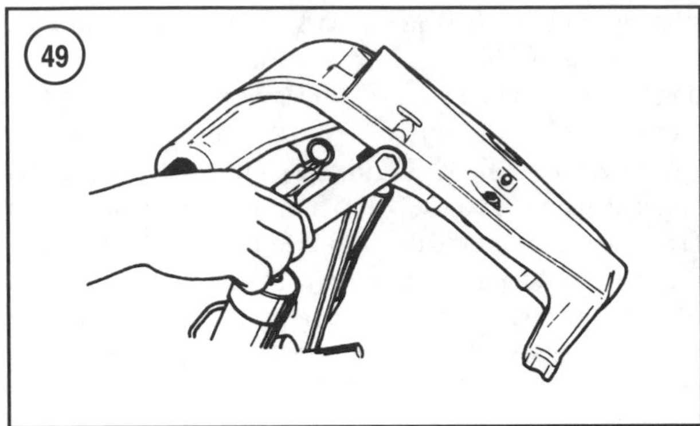

wrench handle into the square opening in the wrench. Turn the trim ram clockwise to tighten the shock piston to 41 ft.-lb. (55.5 N•m). Loosen the vise, then remove the shock piston from the clamp.

31. Clamp the pivot end of the tilt cylinder ram into a vise with protective jaws.

32. Insert the five check balls (12, **Figure 47**) into the shock piston openings. Insert the five spring guides, larger side first, into the openings and seat against the check balls. Guide the five springs (14, **Figure 47**) over the guides while inserting them into the openings.

33. Align the washer (15, **Figure 47**) with the screw opening then place it onto the shock piston. Install the plate (16, **Figure 47**) onto the shock piston and rest it on the five springs. Fit the washer (17, **Figure 47**) onto the screw (18), then thread the screw into the plate and shock piston. Tighten the screw to 62 in.-lb. (7.0 N•m).

34. Lubricate the surfaces with ATF, then install the new O-ring (10, **Figure 47**) into the groove in the outer diameter of the shock piston. Wind the support ring (11, **Figure 47**) into the groove alongside the O-ring. The support ring must be closest to the screw and spring plate side of the groove. The O-ring must be closest to the tilt cylinder ram side of the groove.

35. Lubricate the surfaces with ATF, then install the new O-ring (20, **Figure 47**) into the groove in the outer diameter of the floating piston (19). Carefully insert the floating piston into the tilt cylinder with the open side facing outward. Use an extension to push the piston to the bottom of the cylinder. Do not allow the extension to contact the bore of the cylinder during piston installation.

36. Clamp the manifold and tilt cylinder assembly into a vise with protective jaws. Make sure one of the vise jaws contacts the lower end of the tilt cylinder and the other jaw contacts the back of the manifold. Do not clamp on either of the hydraulic lines or fittings.

37. Temporarily install the manual relief valve as described in this chapter.

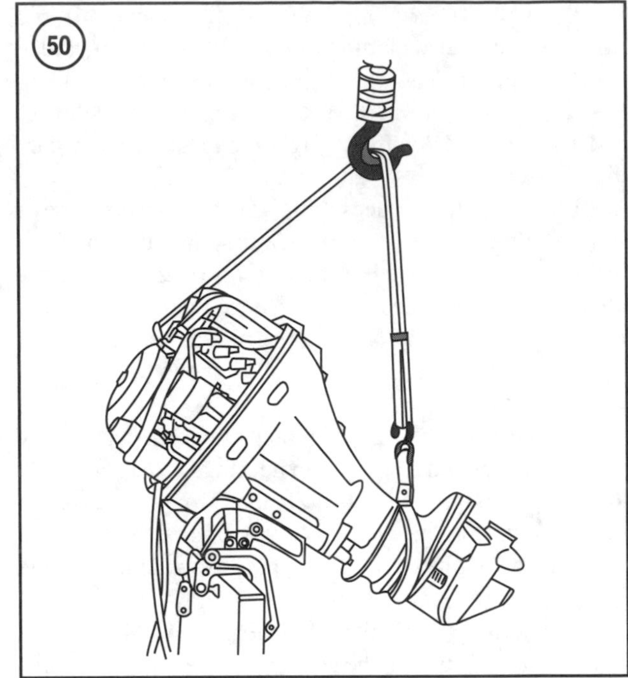

38. *Slowly* pour ATF into the trim cylinder bores until the fluid level just reaches the bottom of the threaded section.

39. Grasp the port trim ram, then *slowly* insert the piston end into the port side opening until the cylinder cap threads just contact the threaded opening. Do not push the ram into the bore more than necessary, or fluid will spill from the opposite cylinder. Avoid catching the piston O-ring on the threaded section of the opening. Install the starboard trim ram using the same method.

40. Hand-thread the cylinder caps into the manifold. Fit the pins of a spanner wrench (Mercury part No. 91-88867) into the openings in the port side trim cylinder cap (3, **Figure 48**). Rotate the wrench clockwise to tighten the cylinder cap to 118 ft.-lb. (160.0 N•m). Repeat this procedure to tighten the starboard side cylinder cap.

41. *Slowly* pour ATF into the hydraulic pump opening in the manifold until the fluid is level with the O-ring step.

42. Install the electric trim motor as described in this section. Do not install the trim system at this time.

43. Fit the larger diameter side of the spacer (8, **Figure 32**) onto the raised opening in the manifold opening. Install the screen (7, **Figure 32**) into the manifold opening. Align the round opening with the spacer, then seat the screen against the step in the opening. Install the baffle (6, **Figure 32**) into the manifold opening. Align the round opening with the spacer, then seat the baffle against the screen.

44. Lubricate the surfaces with ATF, then install the new O-ring (5, **Figure 32**) onto the step in the manifold open-

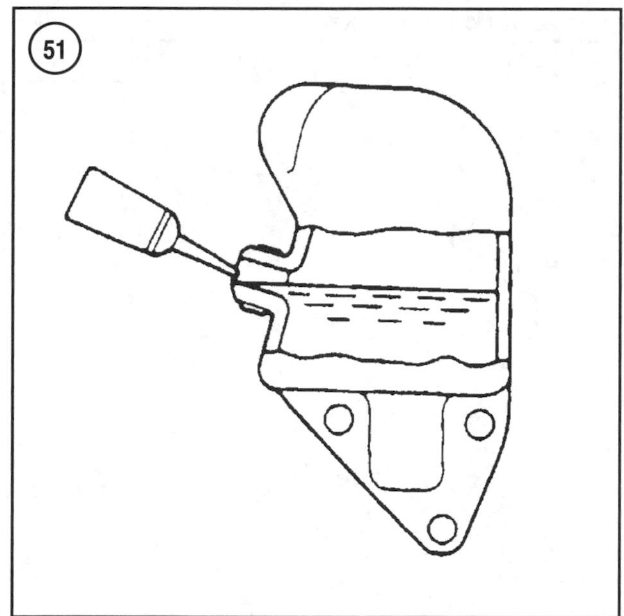

ing. Align the fill cap opening toward the rear, then seat the reservoir (2, **Figure 32**) onto the manifold. Rotate the reservoir to align the openings, then thread the three screws (1, **Figure 32**) into the reservoir and manifold. Tighten the screws evenly to 160 in.-lb. (18.1 N•m). Do not install the fluid fill cap at this time.

45. Hold the cylinder cap (3, **Figure 47**), then pull on the ram (1) until the spring (7) just contacts the cap and shock piston (9).

46. *Slowly* pour ATF into the tilt cylinder opening until the fluid level is approximately 4 in. (102 mm) below the top of the opening.

47. Carefully guide the shock piston into the tilt cylinder opening, until the threads on the cylinder cap just contact the threads in the opening. Work carefully to avoid catching the shock piston O-ring on the threaded section of the opening. Hand-thread the cylinder cap into the opening.

48. Fit the pins of a spanner wrench (Mercury part No. 91-88867) into the openings in the cylinder cap (**Figure 45**). Turn the spanner wrench clockwise to tighten the cylinder cap to 67 ft.-lb. (90.0 N•m).

49. Install the new O-ring (3, **Figure 32**) onto the fill plug (4). Thread the plug into the reservoir opening, then tighten the plug to 62 in.-lb. (7.0 N•m).

50. Rotate the manual relief valve 3-4 turns counterclockwise.

51. Install the trim system as described in this chapter.

TRIM AND TILT SYSTEM FLUID

Filling

Use Dexron II automatic transmission fluid in both types of trim systems covered in this chapter. Refer to **Figure 31** or **Figure 32** to assist with locating the fill plug and reservoir locations on the system. Refer to *Manual Relief Valve* in this chapter to assist with locating and operating the manual relief valve.

1. Open the manual relief valve and position the engine in the full UP position. Engage the tilt lock lever (**Figure 49**) and support the engine with an overhead cable (**Figure 50**). Close the manual relief valve.
2. Clean the area around the fluid fill plug. Remove the plug and inspect the O-ring on the plug. Replace the O-ring if damaged or flattened.
3. Fill the unit to the lower edge of the threaded fill plug opening (**Figure 51**). Install the fill plug. Tighten the plug to 60 in.-lb. (6.8 N•m) for 75-115 hp models and 62 in.-lb. (7.0 N•m) for 225 hp models. Remove the overhead support and disengage the tilt lock lever.
4. Cycle the trim to the full UP, then full DOWN positions several times. Stop operating the pump immediately if ventilation of the pump is heard. Ventilation causes a change in the tone of the system as the unit operates. Repeat Steps 1-4 if ventilation is detected. Continue until the unit operates to the full up position without ventilation.
5. Leave the unit in the full UP position for several minutes then check the fluid level. Add fluid if required.

9

Air Bleeding

A spongy feel or inability to hold trim under load is a common symptom when air is present in the system. If air is present the engine may tuck under when power is applied and tilt out when the throttle is reduced. Minor amounts of air in the system purge into the reservoir during normal operation. When major components have been removed, a significant amount of air can enter the system. Most air is purged during the fluid filling process. Bleeding the air takes considerably longer if the pump ventilates for more than a few seconds during the fluid fill procedure.

Allow the engine to sit for 30 minutes or longer if air remains in the system after filling with fluid. Place the engine in the full tilt position using the manual relief valve. Correct the fluid level then cycle the trim to the full UP and DOWN positions. Correct the fluid level again after 30 minutes.

Table 1 POWER TRIM AND TILT TORQUE SPECIFICATIONS

Fastener	in.-lb.	ft.-lb.	N•m
Fluid fill plug			
75-115 hp models	60	–	6.8
225 hp models	62	–	7.0
Fluid reservoir to manifold			
225 hp models	160	13.3	18.1
Hydraulic cylinder to manifold			
75-115 hp models	100	–	11.3
Hydraulic line fitting			
225 hp models	133	–	15.0
Hydraulic pump to manifold			
75-115 hp models	70	–	7.9
225 hp models	62	–	7.0
Hydraulic pump bracket screws			
225 hp models	62	–	7.0
Poppet valve plugs			
75-115 hp models	120	–	13.6
Power trim mounting bolts			
225 hp models	–	31	42.0
Relay terminal nut	35	–	4.0
Shock piston to trim/tilt ram			
75-115 hp models	–	90	122.0
Shock piston to tilt ram			
225 hp models	–	41	55.5
Shock valve plate screw			
75-115 hp models	35	–	4.0
225 hp models	62	–	7.0
Tilt cylinder cap			
225 hp models	–	67	90.0
Tilt tube nut (self locking)			
225 hp models	192	16	21.7
Trim cylinder end cap			
75-115 hp models	–	45	61.0
225 hp models	–	118	160.0
Trim motor mounting screws			
75-115 hp models	80	–	9.0
225 hp models	160	13.3	18.1
Trim piston to trim ram screw			
225 hp models	–	28	38.0
Trim position sender			
75-115 hp models	70	–	7.9
225 hp models	71	–	8.0

Chapter Ten

Midsection

This chapter describes removal and installation for all midsection components.

Repairs to the midsection typically involve replacing worn motor mounts, corrosion damaged components or components damaged because of impact with underwater objects.

Minor repairs involve replacement of easily accessible components such as the lower motor mounts, tilt tube, clamp brackets and the tilt lock lever.

Major repair may require removal of the power head and gearcase followed by complete disassembly of the midsection. Major repair also includes replacing the oil pump, power head adapter, upper motor mounts, swivel housing, swivel tube, oil pan or drive shaft housing.

Power head removal and installation are described in Chapter Seven. Gearcase removal and installation are described in Chapter Eight. Refer to Chapter Nine if it is necessary to remove the trim and tilt system components to access the midsection components.

Tighten all fasteners to the specifications in **Table 1**. If a specific fastener is not listed in **Table 1**, tighten the fastener to the general torque specification listed in the *Quick Reference Data* section at the front of the manual. **Table 1** is located at the end of this chapter.

Unless specified otherwise, apply Quicksilver 2-4-C Marine Lubricant or equivalent to all bushings, pins and pivot points during assembly.

LOWER MOTOR MOUNT REPLACEMENT

WARNING
Never rely solely on the power trim system or tilt lock lever for support when working on the engine. Failure of the trim system or lever will allow the engine to drop unexpectedly and result in damaged property, serious bodily injury or death.

1. Place the engine in the full UP position. Engage the tilt lock mechanism.
2. Use an overhead hoist to support the engine (**Figure 1**).
3. Disconnect the negative battery cable to prevent accidental starting or trim/tilt system operation.

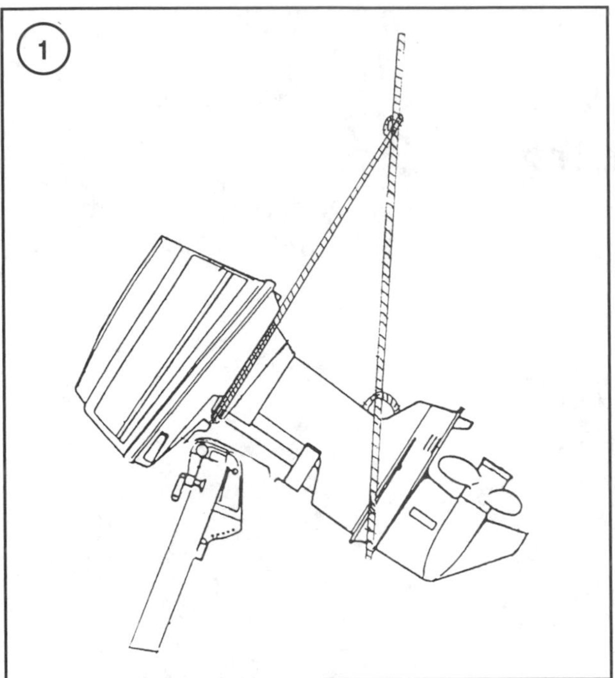
1

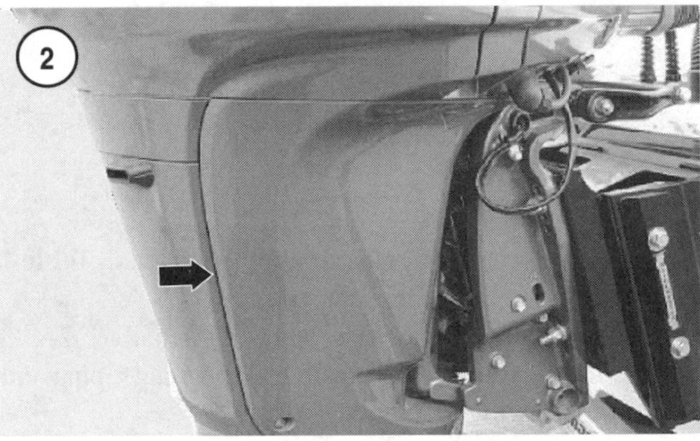
2

4. Remove the screws that secure the port and starboard covers (**Figure 2**, typical) onto the drive shaft housing. Eight screws are used on 75-115 hp models. Twelve screws are used on 225 hp models. Carefully pull the covers from the drive shaft housing. The covers should pull easily from the housing. If any resistance is noted, check for overlooked screws. Let the port cover hang on the cable bundle. It is not necessary to remove the cable clamp unless replacing the cable(s) or cover.

5A. On 75-115 hp models, remove the two screws (47, **Figure 3**) from each lower mount cover (48). Work carefully to avoid damaging the grounding wires (49, **Figure 3**) that attach to the upper screws.

5B. On the 225 hp model, remove the two screws (40, **Figure 4**) from each lower mount cover (45). Remove the

3

DRIVE SHAFT HOUSING, OIL PAN AND MOTOR MOUNTS (75-115 HP MODELS)

1. Seal
2. Screw
3. Oil pump assembly
4. Bolt
5. Nut
6. Washer
7. Washer
8. Upper motor mount/cover assembly
9. Mount bolt
10. Locating pin
11. Check valve (water drain)
12. Power head adapter
13. Coupler
14. Spacer
15. Grommet
16. Oil pan gasket
17. Dipstick
18. Oil pan
19. O-ring
20. Screw
21. Oil pickup tube
22. Grommet
23. Flange seal
24. Water tube
25. Grommet
26. Exhaust tube
27. Drive shaft housing
28. Motor mount bolt
29. Cap
30. Hose fitting
31. Roll pin
32. Cap
33. Stud
34. Washer
35. Nut
36. Drive shaft bushing
37. Stud
38. Washer
39. Nut
40. Elbow hose fitting
41. Speedometer hose
42. Straight hose fitting
43. Nut
44. Grounding wire
45. Washer
46. Lower motor mount
47. Screw
48. Mount cover/retainer
49. Grounding wire
50. Bushing
51. Shift shaft
52. Nut
53. Shift lever
54. Locking pin
55. Roller
56. Oil drain plug
57. Sealing washer
58. Seal
59. Screw

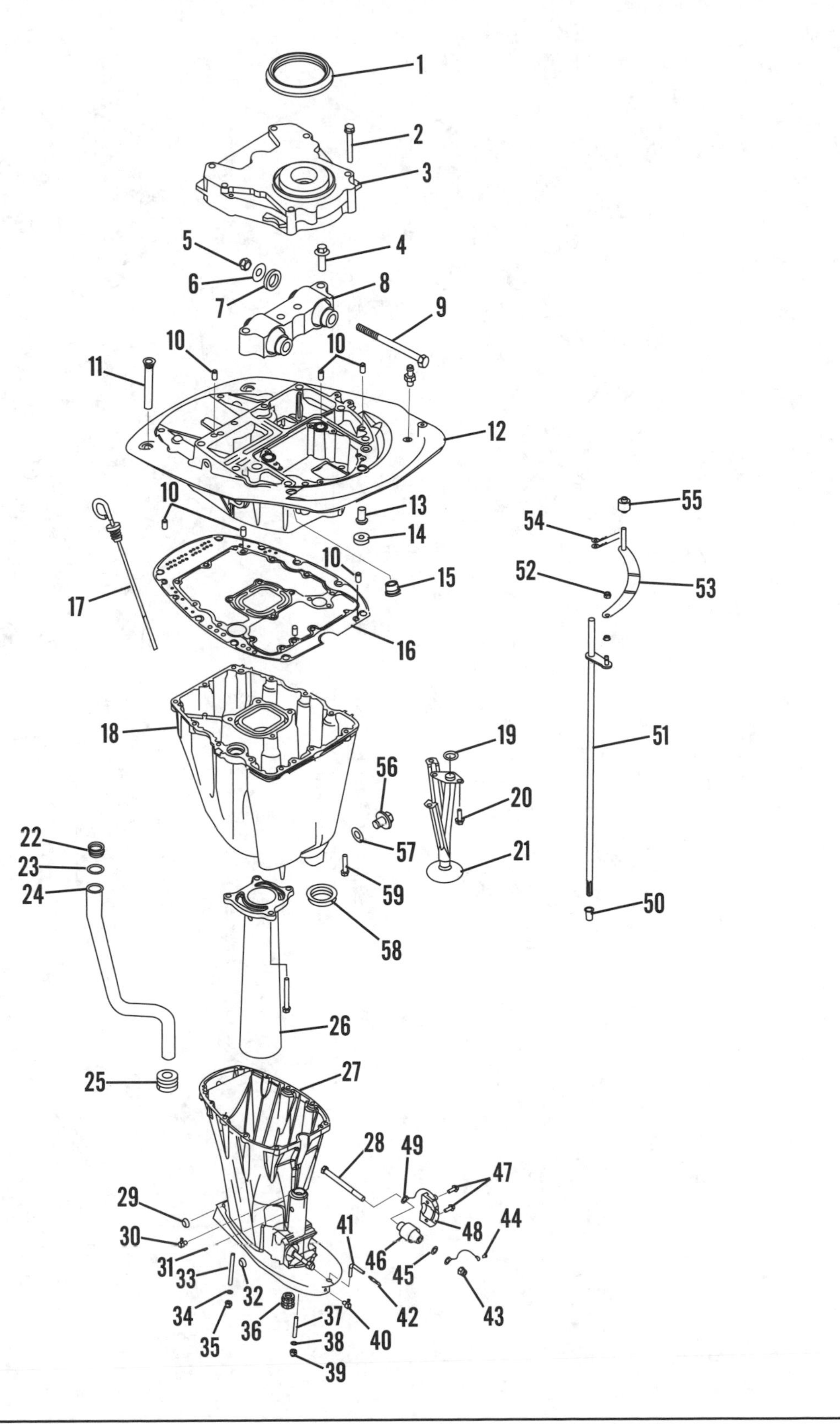
1
2
3
4
5
6
7
8
9
10
11
12
13
14
15
16
17
18
19
20
21
22
23
24
25
26
27
28
29
30
31
32
33
34
35
36
37
38
39
40
41
42
43
44
45
46
47
48
49
50
51
52
53
54
55
56
57
58
59

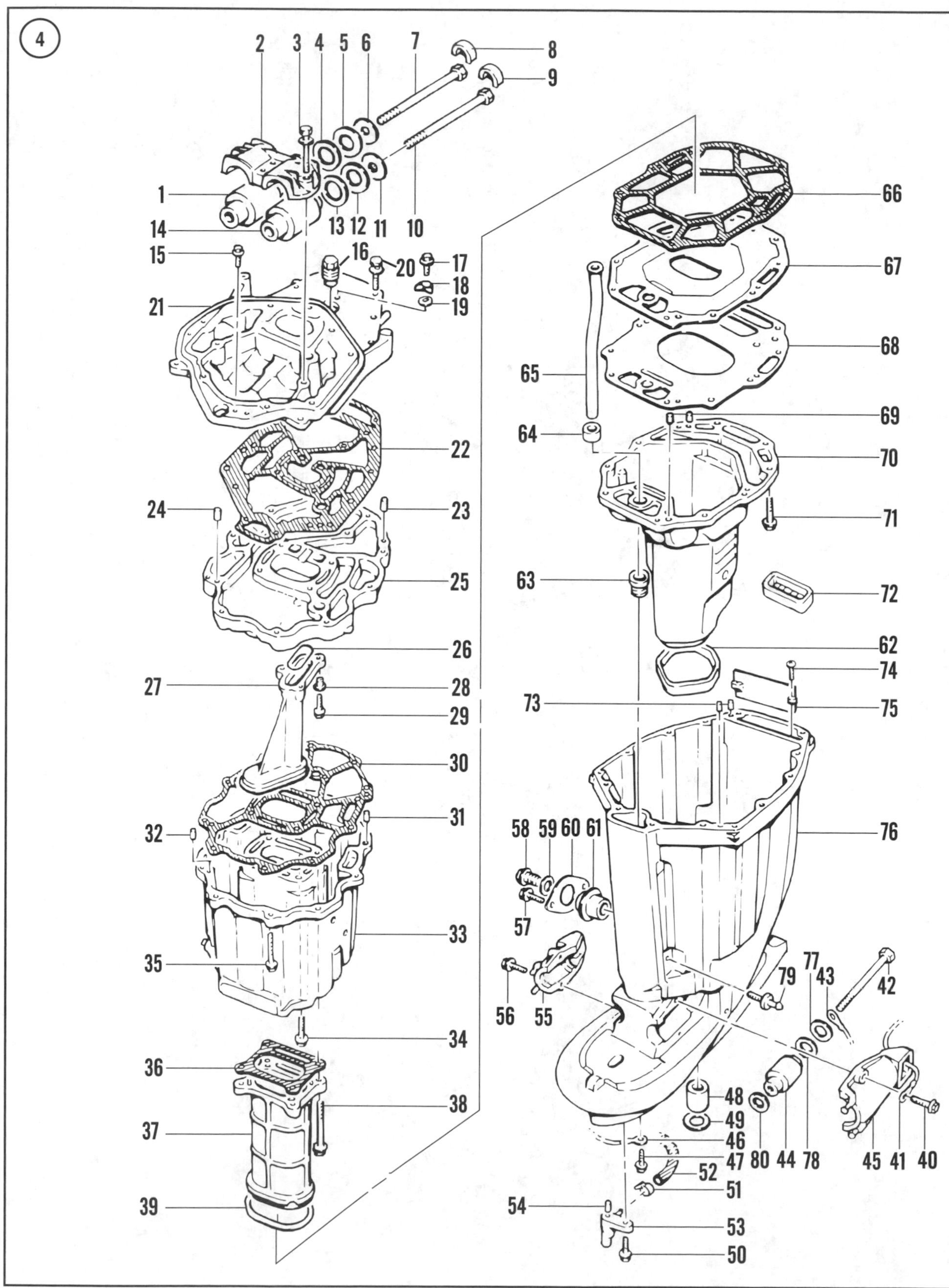
4
1
2
3
4
5
6
7
8
9
10
11
12
13
14
15
16
17
18
19
20
21
22
23
24
25
26
27
28
29
30
31
32
33
34
35
36
37
38
39
40
41
42
43
44
45
46
47
48
49
50
51
52
53
54
55
56
57
58
59
60
61
62
63
64
65
66
67
68
69
70
71
72
73
74
75
76
77
78
79
80

DRIVE SHAFT HOUSING, OIL PAN AND MOTOR MOUNTS (225 HP MODELS)

1. Upper motor mount
2. Upper mount cover/retainer
3. Mount cover screw
4. Washer
5. Washer
6. Washer
7. Upper mount bolt
8. Insulator
9. Insulator
10. Upper mount bolt
11. Washer
12. Washer
13. Washer
14. Upper motor mount
15. Bolt
16. Oil pressure relief valve
17. Screw
18. Clamp plate
19. Collar
20. Bolt
21. Power adapter plate
22. Gasket
23. Locating pin
24. Locating pin
25. Exhaust adapter plate
26. Seal
27. Oil pickup/strainer
28. Sleeve
29. Screw
30. Gasket
31. Locating pin
32. Locating pin
33. Oil pan
34. Screw (2)
35. Screw (10)
36. Gasket
37. Exhaust tube
38. Bolt
39. Seal
40. Mount cover screw
41. Grounding wire
42. Lower mount bolt
43. Grounding wire
44. Lower motor mount
45. Lower mount cover
46. Grounding wire
47. Screw
48. Bushing
49. Snap ring
50. Screw
51. Plastic locking clamp
52. Speedometer hose
53. Speedometer fitting
54. Locating pin
55. Lower mount cover
56. Screw
57. Screw
58. Oil drain plug
59. Sealing washer
60. Retainer
61. Grommet
62. Seal
63. Grommet
64. Grommet
65. Water tube
66. Gasket
67. Plate
68. Gasket
69. Locating pin
70. Silencer
71. Screw
72. Seal
73. Locating pin
74. Screw
75. Exhaust relief plate
76. Drive shaft housing
77. Washer
78. Rubber washer
79. Lower cover mounting post
80. Washer

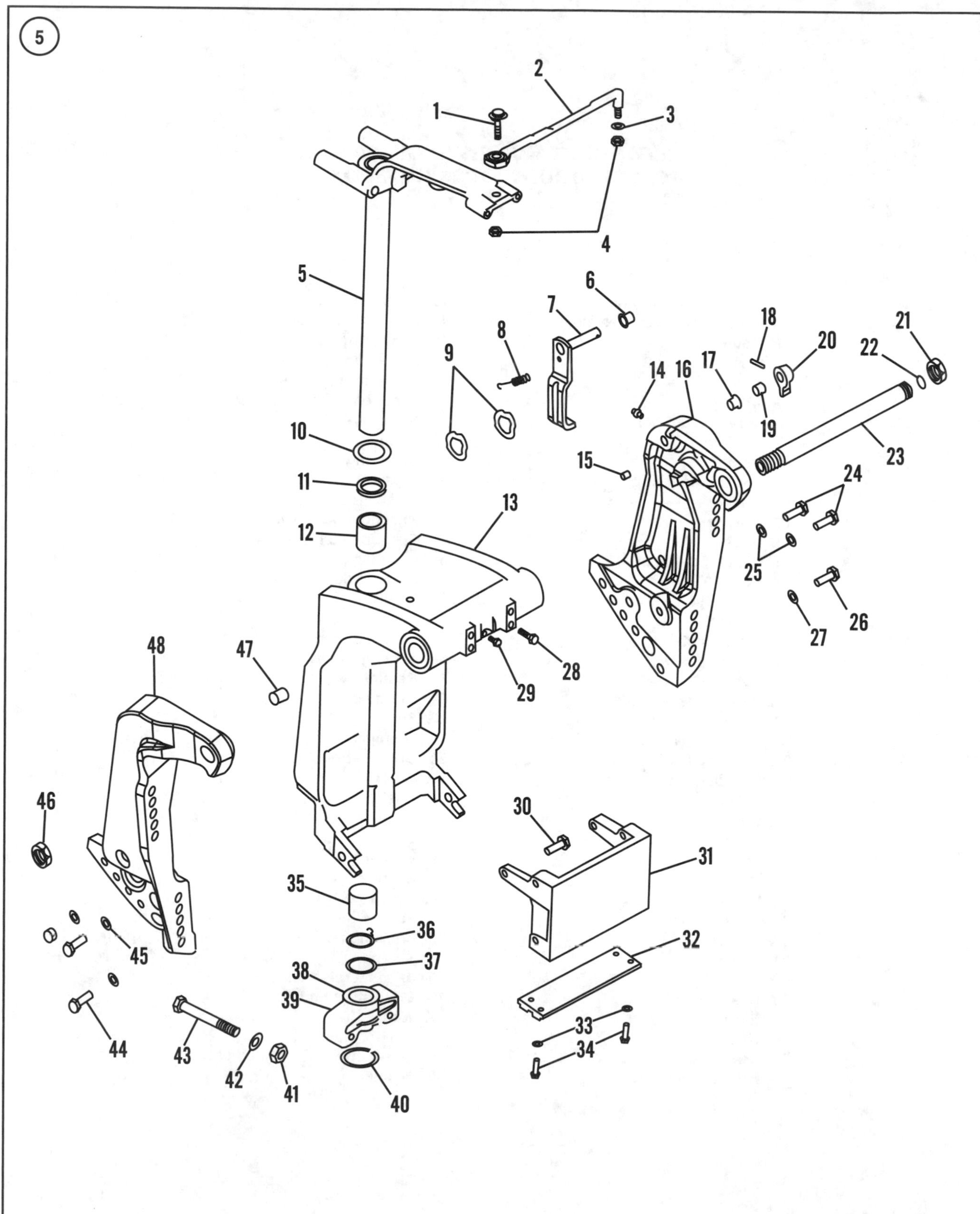
5
1
2
3
4
5
6
7
8
9
10
11
12
13
14
15
16
17
18
19
20
21
22
23
24
25
26
27
28
29
30
31
32
33
34
35
36
37
38
39
40
41
42
43
44
45
46
47
48

CLAMP BRACKETS, SWIVEL HOUSING AND SWIVEL TUBE (75-115 HP MODELS)

1. Steering linkage bolt
2. Steering linkage
3. Washer
4. Locknut
5. Swivel tube
6. Bushing
7. Tilt lock lever
8. Spring
9. Wave washers
10. Washer
11. Seal
12. Bushing
13. Swivel housing
14. Grease fitting
15. Pin
16. Port clamp bracket
17. Bushing
18. Roll pin
19. Spring
20. Knob
21. Nut
22. O-ring
23. Tilt tube
24. Bolts
25. Washers
26. Bolt
27. Washer
28. Bolt
29. Grease fitting
30. Bolt
31. Clamp bracket spacer
32. Anode
33. Washer
34. Bolt
35. Bushing
36. O-ring
37. Spacer
38. Mount bolt hole
39. Lower mount bracket
40. Retaining ring
41. Nut
42. Washer
43. Mount bolt
44. Bolt
45. Washer
46. Locknut
47. Bushing
48. Starboard clamp bracket

grounding wires (41, **Figure 4**) from the upper screws. Guide the wires through the openings in the mount covers.

6. Carefully pry the mount covers from each side of the drive shaft housing. Inspect the cover for worn, cracked or damaged surfaces. Impact with underwater objects may crack the mount cover. Operating the engine with worn or damaged lower mounts may cause wear on the cover surfaces. Replace the cover(s) if not found in excellent condition.

7A. On 75-115 hp models, hold the lower mount bolt (28, **Figure 3**) with a wrench then remove the nut (41, **Figure 5**) and washer (42) from the lower mount bracket (38). Remove the grounding wires (44, **Figure 3**) from the bolts.

7B. On 225 hp models, hold the lower mount bolt (42, **Figure 4**) with a suitable wrench then remove the nut (27, **Figure 6**) and washer (26).

8. Pry the lower mounts (46, **Figure 3** or 44, **Figure 4**) out of the recesses in the drive shaft housing. Pull the bolts, mounts and washers from the lower mount bracket. Slide the washers and bolts from the mounts.

9. Inspect the mount for excessive wear on the aluminum mount surfaces. Inspect the mount for loose rubber or separation of the metal material from the rubber material. Replace the mount if excessive wear or rubber separation is evident.

10. Clean the cover screws, mount bolts and mount contact surfaces in the covers and drive shaft housing.

11. Inspect the fasteners for wear, corrosion or damage. Replace any questionable or defective fasteners.

12. Inspect the mount contact surfaces in the drive shaft housing for pitts, cracks, wear or other damage. Replace the drive shaft housing, as described in this chapter, if the surfaces are excessively worn, cracked, deeply pitted or damaged.

13. Apply a light coat of Quicksilver 2-4-C Marine Lubricant or equivalent to the shank of the lower mount bolts (28, **Figure 3** or 42, **Figure 4**). Slide the grounding wire terminals, mounts onto the mount bolts as shown in **Figure 3** or **Figure 4**.

14. Guide the threaded ends of the mount bolts into the openings in the lower mount bracket (39, **Figure 5** or 24, **Figure 6**). Fit the mounts and large diameter washers into the respective recesses in the drive shaft housing.

15A. On 75-115 hp, install the washer (45, **Figure 3**) and ground wire terminal onto each mount bolt. Thread the nut (43, **Figure 3**) onto the bolt until the washer just contacts the lower mount bracket (39, **Figure 5**). Do not tighten the nut at this time.

15B. On 225 hp, install the washer (26, **Figure 6**) onto the mount bolt. Thread the nut (27, **Figure 6**) onto the bolt until the washer just contacts the lower mount bracket (24). Do not tighten the nut at this time.

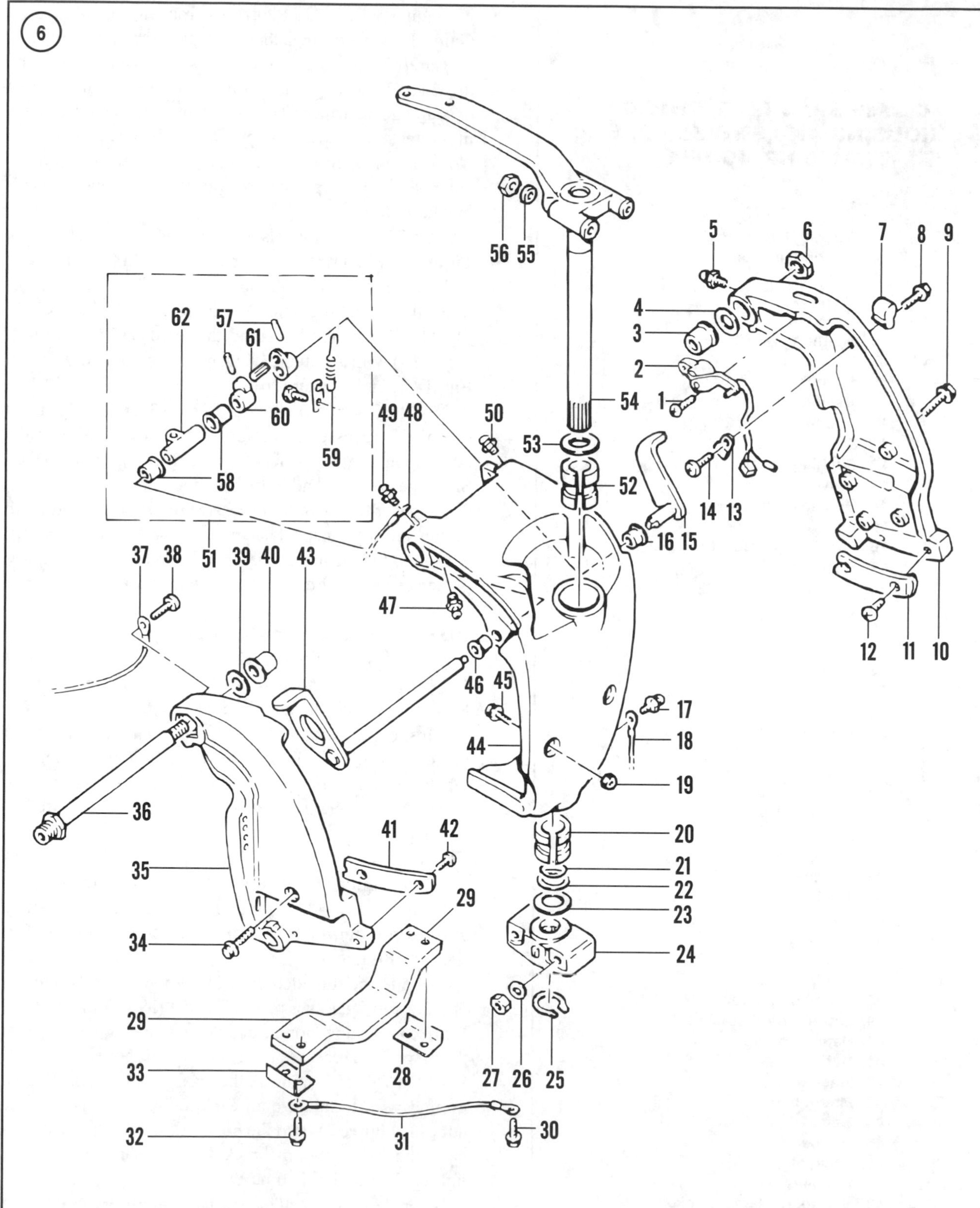
6
1
2
3
4
5
6
7
8
9
10
11
12
13
14
15
16
17
18
19
20
21
22
23
24
25
26
27
28
29
30
31
32
33
34
35
36
37
38
39
40
41
42
43
44
45
46
47
48
49
50
51
52
53
54
55
56
57
58
59
60
61
62

CLAMP BRACKETS, SWIVEL BRACKET AND SWIVEL TUBE (225 HP MODEL)

1. Screw
2. Trim position sender
3. Bushing
4. Washer
5. Grease fitting
6. Locknut
7. Clamp
8. Screw
9. Bolt
10. Starboard clamp bracket
11. Thrust pad
12. Screw
13. Clamp
14. Screw
15. Tilt lock lever
16. Bushing
17. Grease fitting
18. Grounding wire
19. Nut
20. Bushing
21. O-ring
22. Spacer
23. Washer
24. Lower mount bracket
25. Snap ring
26. Washer
27. Nut
28. Anode bracket
29. Anode
30. Screw
31. Grounding wire
32. Screw
33. Anode bracket
34. Bolt
35. Port clamp bracket
36. Tilt tube
37. Grounding wire
38. Screw
39. Washer
40. Bushing
41. Thrust pad
42. Screw
43. Tilt lock lever
44. Swivel housing
45. Trim cylinder thrust pad
46. Bushing
47. Grease fitting
48. Grounding wire
49. Grease fitting
50. Grease fitting
51. Tilt lock lever mechanism
52. Bushing
53. Washer
54. Swivel tube
55. Washer
56. Nut
57. Pins
58. Bushings
59. Spring
60. Lever crank
61. Pin
62. Collar

16A. On 75-115 hp models, fit the mount covers (48, **Figure 3**) onto the lower mounts. Verify proper alignment of the mount and washer with the recesses on the cover, then seat the cover against the drive shaft housing. Fit the grounding wire terminals onto the lower mount cover screws (47, **Figure 3**), then thread all four screws into the two mount covers and drive shaft housing. Tighten the screws evenly to 25 ft.-lb. (33.8 N•m). Hold the terminal to prevent rotation and possible damage to grounding wires.

16B. On the 225 hp model, guide the grounding wires through the opening at the rear of each mount cover. Verify proper alignment of the mount and large washers with the recesses in the mount cover, then seat the cover against the drive shaft housing. Insert the lower mount cover screws (40, **Figure 4**) through the grounding wire terminals, then thread all four screws into the mount covers and drive shaft housing. Tighten the screws evenly to 27 ft.-lb. (36.6 N•m).

17A. On 75-115 hp models, hold the lower mount bolts (28, **Figure 3**) with a wrench while tightening the nuts (43) evenly to 50 ft.-lb. (67.8 N•m).

17B. On the 225 hp model, hold the lower mount bolts (42, **Figure 4**) with a wrench while tightening the nuts evenly to 53 ft.-lb. (N•m).

18. Fit the covers onto the drive shaft housing and secure with the screws (**Figure 2**, typical). Tighten the screws evenly to 65 in.-lb. (7.3 N•m) for 75-115 hp models and 70 in.-lb. (7.9 N•m) for 225 hp models.

19. Remove the overhead support. Connect the battery cable. Operate the trim in the UP direction enough to release the tilt/lock mechanism.

20. Check for binding and listen for unusual noises while lowering the engine to the full down position. If binding or unusual noise is noted, check for improper mount or mount cover installation or loose fasteners.

TILT TUBE REPLACEMENT

WARNING

Never rely solely on the power trim system or tilt lock lever for support when working on the engine. Failure of the trim system or lever will allow the engine to drop unexpectedly and result in damaged property, serious injury or death.

Refer to **Figure 5** or **Figure 6**.

1. Place the engine in the full UP position. Engage the tilt lock mechanism.

2. Use an overhead hoist to support the engine (**Figure 1**).

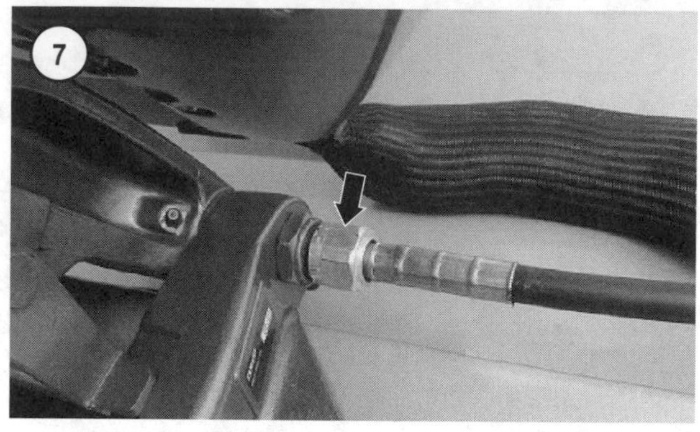

3. Disconnect the negative battery cable to prevent accidental starting or trim/tilt system operation.

4. Remove the locknut (4, **Figure 5**) and disconnect the steering link bar (2, **Figure 5**, typical) from the steering cable. Retain the two washers from the steering linkage. Discard the locknut. Always replace the steering linkage locknut when removed. Loosen the steering cable nut (**Figure 7**), and pull the steering cable out of the tilt tube.

5. Remove the large locknut (46, **Figure 5** or 6, **Figure 6**) that secures the tilt tube into the clamp brackets.

CAUTION

Provide just enough overhead support to keep the tube from binding during removal. Do not use excessive force to remove the tube. Excessive force can cause the end of the tube to flare out preventing removal from the swivel housing and clamp brackets.

6. Use a one-foot section of pipe or tubing to drive the tilt tube through the clamp brackets. The tool must be slightly smaller in diameter than the tilt tube.

7. Support the engine, and remove the driver tool. Retain the washers (9, **Figure 5** or 4 and 39, **Figure 6**) as they drop from the clamp brackets and swivel housing.

8. Thoroughly clean the tilt tube and the tilt tube bores in the swivel housing and clamp brackets.

9. Inspect the tilt tube for excessive wear, corrosion, cracking or other damage. Replace a worn or damaged tilt tube.

10. Inspect the tilt tube bore in the clamp brackets for excessive wear, corrosion damage, cracking or other defects. If the bore is worn or damaged, replace the clamp bracket(s) as described in this chapter.

11A. On 225 hp model, inspect the tilt tube bushing (3 and 40, **Figure 6**) for wear, cracks or other damage. Remove the clamp brackets as described in this chapter and replace the bushings if not in excellent condition.

11B. On 75-115 hp models, inspect the tilt tube bores in the swivel housing for wear, cracks, or corrosion. Replace the swivel housing as described in this chapter if any defects are noted.

12. Apply a generous coat of Quicksilver 2-4-C Marine Lubricant or its equivalent into the tilt tube bore in the clamp brackets and swivel housing. Apply the same grease onto the outer surfaces of the replacement tilt tube.

13. Fit the washers (9, **Figure 5** or 4 and 39, **Figure 6**) between the clamp brackets and swivel housing and aligned with the tilt tube bore.

14. Place the tilt tube into the opening in the port clamp bracket. Maintain alignment of the tube bores in the clamp brackets, washers and swivel housing bores during installation.

15. Using a block of wood for a cushion, carefully tap the tilt tube through the port clamp bracket, washers, swivel bracket and starboard clamp bracket. Continue until the threaded end fully extends from the starboard clamp bracket.

16. On 75-115 hp models, install the O-ring (22, **Figure 5**) then large nut (21) onto the tilt tube. Tighten the large nut until it seats against the shoulder of the tilt tube.

17. Thread the large locknut (46, **Figure 5** or 6, **Figure 6**) onto the starboard side of the tilt tube. Tighten the nut until the washers (9, **Figure 5** or 4 and 39, **Figure 6**) fully seat against the swivel tube and clamp bracket surfaces and all side play is removed. Do not over-tighten the nut. The swivel housing must tilt in the clamp bracket without binding or side play.

18. Apply Quicksilver 2-4-C Marine Lubricant or equivalent onto the steering cable end and the bore in the tilt tube. Insert the steering cable fully into the tilt tube. Tighten the cable nut (**Figure 7**) to 35 ft.-lb. (47.5 N•m) then engage any fastener locking devices.

19. Fit the washer onto the threaded end of the steering link bar (2, **Figure 5**, typical), then fit the threaded end into the opening in steering cable. Install the second washer over the threaded end of the linkage, then thread the new locknut (4, **Figure 5**, typical) onto the steering linkage. Tighten the locknut to 120 in.-lb. (13.6 N•m) until the cable end seats against the linkage. Back the nut off 1/4 turn. The linkage must pivot on the steering cable end.

20. Remove the overhead support. Connect the battery cable then operate the trim UP enough to release the tilt/lock mechanism.

21. Check for binding and listen for unusual noises while cycling the trim in the full up and full down positions. Check for improper tilt tube installation or over-tightening of the tilt tube nut if binding or unusual noise is present.

CLAMP BRACKET REPLACEMENT

WARNING

Never rely solely on the power trim system or tilt lock lever for support when working on the engine. Failure of the trim system or lever will allow the engine to drop unexpectedly and result in damaged property, serious bodily injury or death.

NOTE

Replace all locking or tab washers or fasteners if removed or disturbed.

NOTE

Note the connection points and routing before disconnecting the grounding wires. Clean all corrosion or contaminants from the terminals and contact surfaces during installation. Securely tighten all grounding wire screws during assembly.

If removing or installing both clamp brackets, do so one at a time. Otherwise it is difficult to maintain alignment of the tilt/tube bores and engine mounting bolt openings during installation. Refer to **Figure 5** or **Figure 6**.

1. Place the engine in the full UP position.

CAUTION

Provide just enough overhead support to support the engine during clamp bracket removal. Excessive force can cause difficult removal and possibly damage the tilt tube and/or other components.

2. Use an overhead hoist to support the engine (**Figure 1**).

3. Disconnect the negative battery cable to prevent accidental starting or trim/tilt system operation.

4. Remove the power trim/tilt system as described in Chapter Nine.

5. Remove the tilt tube as described in this chapter.

6. Remove the midsection anode as described in Chapter Three.

7. On 225 hp models, remove the trim position sender as described in Chapter Nine.

8. On 75-115 hp models, remove the bolts washers and the nuts that secure the bracket spacer (31, **Figure 5**) onto the selected clamp bracket.

9. Remove the engine mounting bolts, washers and nuts (41-43, **Figure 5**, typcial) from the selected clamp bracket. Carefully pry the clamp bracket away from the boat transom. Thoroughly clean the mounting holes in the boat transom.

10. Clean the clamp bracket, then inspect the clamp bracket and related fasteners for cracks, wear or damage. Replace any defective components.

11. Place the clamp bracket in position on the midsection. Align the bolt openings, bushings and spacers with the openings in the clamp bracket.

12. Apply high quality marine-grade sealant to all surfaces of the engine mounting bolts and the bolt holes in the boat transom. Install the mounting bolts through the clamp brackets and the boat transom. Install the washers and thread the locknuts onto the mounting bolts. Do not tighten the mounting bolts at this time. Refer to the following for mounting bolt and nut orientation:

   a. On 75-115 hp models, install the upper mounting bolts with the bolt head on the inside of the transom. Install the lower bolt with the bolt heads outside the transom. Use a suitable washer under each nut and bolt head.
   b. On 225 hp models, install all mounting bolts with the bolt heads on the outside of the transom and the nut on the inside of the transom. Use a suitable washer under each nut and bolt head.

13. On 75-115 hp models, apply a light coat of Loctite 271 (Mercury part No. 92-809820) onto the threads, then install the bolts that secure the bracket spacer onto the clamp bracket. Do not tighten the bolts at this time.

14. If removing or installing both clamp brackets, remove and replace the other clamp bracket as described in Steps 8-13.

15. Install the tilt tube as described in this chapter.

16. On 225 hp models, install the trim position sender as described in Chapter Nine.

17. Install the midsection anode as described in Chapter Three.

18. On 75-115 hp models, tighten the bolts and nuts that secure the bracket spacer onto the clamp brackets evenly to 30 ft.-lb. (40.7 N•m).

19. Install the power trim/tilt system as described in Chapter Nine.

20. Securely tighten all four engine mounting bolts.

21. Remove the overhead support. Connect the battery cable.

22. Check for binding and listen for unusual noises while cycling the trim through the full UP and full DOWN positions. Check for improper tilt tube, clamp bracket, trim system or bracket spacer installation if binding or unusual noises are present.

TILT LOCK LEVER REPLACEMENT

WARNING

Never rely solely on the power trim system or tilt lock lever for support when working on the engine. Failure of the trim system or lever will allow the engine to drop unexpectedly and result in damaged property, serious injury or death.

CAUTION

Provide just enough overhead support to support the engine during tilt lock lever replacement. Excessive force can damage the tilt tube and/or other components.

Refer to **Figure 5** or **Figure 6**.

1. Place the engine in the full UP position.
2. Use an overhead hoist to support the engine (**Figure 1**).
3. Disconnect the negative battery cable to prevent accidental starting or trim/tilt system operation.

4A. On 75-115 hp models, remove the tilt lock lever as follows:

   a. Use a suitable pin punch to drive the roll pin (18, **Figure 5**) from the knob (20).
   b. Capture the spring (19, **Figure 5**) while pulling the knob from the lever shaft.
   c. Disconnect the spring (8, **Figure 5**), then pull the tilt lock lever (7) from the port clamp bracket.
   d. Remove the bushings (6 and 17, **Figure 5**) from the clamp bracket or tilt lock lever shaft.

4B. On 225 hp models, remove the tilt lock lever as follows:

   a. Disconnect the spring (59, **Figure 6**) from the bracket and lever pin.
   b. Use a suitable pin punch to drive the roll pins (57, **Figure 6**) from the lever cranks (60).
   c. Capture the collar, bushings and lever cranks while pulling the tilt lock levers (15 and 43, **Figure 6**) from the clamp brackets.

5. Inspect all pins, levers, bushing and springs for lost spring tension, cracked, worn, corroded or damaged surfaces. Replace any worn, damaged or questionable components.
6. Install all tilt lock lever components as shown in **Figure 5** or **Figure 6**. Note the following:

   a. Lubricate all bushings and pivoting surfaces with Quicksilver 2-4-C Marine Lubricant or equivalent.
   b. Drive the roll pins into the shafts or levers until flush with the surface. Replace the roll pin or components if a roll pin does not fit snug in the bore.
   c. Connect the spring onto the tilt lock lever shaft and bracket or pin after installing the lever shafts.

7. Be sure the tilt lock lever operates smoothly. Check for improper assembly if rough operation or binding occurs. Correct any faults before removing the overhead support.
8. Connect the battery and remove the overhead support. Verify that the lever operates properly and is able to support the engine as designed.

OIL PUMP REPLACEMENT

On 75-115 hp models, the oil pump attaches onto the top side of the power head adapter. On 225 hp models, the oil pump attaches onto the bottom of the power head. Refer to Chapter Seven for oil pump replacement on 225 hp models. Refer to **Figure 3**.

75-115 hp Models

1. Remove the gearcase as described in Chapter Eight.
2. Remove the power head as described in Chapter Seven.
3. Use compressed air to remove any loose material from the exposed surfaces of the oil pump (3, **Figure 3**) and the Power head adapter (12).
4. Evenly loosen and remove the six screws (2, **Figure 3**), then lift the oil pump from the adapter. Clean screw threads and the corresponding threaded openings in the adapter.
5. Remove and discard the two O-rings from the recesses in the adapter or the bottom of the oil pump.
6. Wipe any oil or debris from the oil pump-toadapter plate mating surfaces. Do not allow any debris to enter the oil passages.
7. Inspect the two oil pump locating pins (10, **Figure 3**) for damage or loose fit in the adapter. Remove any pins that are found in the oil pump and install them into the openings in the adapter. Replace any pins that are damaged or fit loosely in the openings. Replace the adapter plate if a new pin fits loosely or if the opening is damaged or elongated.
8. Remove the seal (1, **Figure 3**) from the oil pump. Remove the seal from the bottom of the power head if not found on the oil pump.
9. Cover the oil passages in the adapter with a clean shop towel to prevent contamination of the oil system.

NOTE
The oil pump does not contain any serviceable components and should not be reused if disassembled.

10. Use a suitable solvent to thoroughly clean the oil pump. Inspect the oil pump as described in Chapter Seven.
11. Remove the cover from the oil passages in the adapter.
12. Pour a few ounces of engine oil into oil passage openings at the bottom of the oil pump. Distribute the oil by rotating the section of the pump with the splined opening.
13. Apply a light coat of Quicksilver Coupler Grease (Mercury part No. 91-816391) onto the splined opening in the pump.
14. Apply a light coat of oil onto the surfaces, then install two new O-rings into grooves surrounding the oil passages in the adapter. Ensure the O-rings fully seat in the grooves.
15. Align the drive shaft bore in the oil pump with the corresponding bore in the adapter. Align the locating pins with the corresponding opening in the oil pump body. Seat the oil pump onto the adapter. Work carefully to avoid dislodging the O-rings.
16. Thread the six screws (2, **Figure 3**) into the oil pump (3) and adapter (12). Tighten the six screws in a crossing pattern to 85 in.-lb. (9.6 N•m).
17. Apply a light coat of engine oil onto the surfaces, then fit a new seal (1, **Figure 3**) into the groove in the oil pump. The tapered side must face away from the pump body.
18. Install the power head as described in Chapter Seven.
19. Install the gearcase as described in Chapter Eight.
20. Test the oil pressure as described in Chapter Seven.

UPPER MOTOR MOUNT REPLACEMENT

1. Remove the gearcase as described in Chapter Eight.
2. Remove the power head as described in Chapter Seven.
3. On 75-115 hp models, remove the oil pump as described in this chapter.

CAUTION
Support the drive shaft housing when replacing the upper motor mounts. Otherwise the drive shaft housing will drop down and possibly damage the lower mounts or other components.

4A. On 75-115 hp models, remove the upper mount/cover assembly as follows:
a. Hold the upper mount bolts (9, **Figure 3**) with a suitable box-end wrench, then remove the two nuts and four washers (5-7).
b. Remove the two bolts (4, **Figure 3**) to free the mount and cover assembly (8) from the power head adapter (12).
c. Pull the two mount bolts (9, **Figure 3**) out of the openings in the swivel tube (5, **Figure 5**).

d. Lift the mount/cover assembly from the adapter. If necessary, tap lightly on the mount/cover to break it free from the adapter.

4B. On 225 hp models, remove the cover and upper motor mounts as follows:

a. Remove the insulators (8 and 9, **Figure 4**) from the upper mount bolts.

b. Hold the upper mount bolts (7 and 10, **Figure 4**) with a suitable box-end wrench, then remove the two nuts and lockwashers (5 and 6, **Figure 6**) from the swivel tube.

c. Remove the three mount cover screws (3, **Figure 4**), then lift the cover (2) from the mounts and adapter plate.

d. Lower the rear of the drive shaft housing slightly to pull the mount bolts (7 and 10, **Figure 4**) out of the openings in the swivel tube (54, **Figure 6**). Lift the mounts, bolts and washers out of the power head adapter. If necessary, pry the mounts from the recesses in the adapter. Avoid damaging the power head adapter.

5. Clean the cover screws, mount bolts, threaded openings and mount contact surfaces in the cover and power head adapter.

6. Inspect the mount and cover fasteners for corrosion or other damage. Replace any fastener that is not in excellent condition.

7. Inspect the mounts for excessive wear on the aluminum mount surfaces, loose rubber or separation of the metal material from the rubber material. Replace the mount if excessive wear or rubber separation is evident.

8. Inspect the mount contact surfaces in the power head adapter for deeply pitted, cracked, worn or damaged surfaces. Replace the adapter as described in this chapter if these or other defects are evident.

9A. On 75-115 hp models, install the upper mount/cover assembly onto the adapter as follows:

a. Fit the mount cover assembly into the power head adapter.

b. Thread the two bolts (4, **Figure 3**) into the mount/cover and power head adapter. Do not tighten the bolts at this time.

c. Insert the two mount bolts (9, **Figure 3**) into the swivel tube openings.

d. Move the drive shaft housing to align the bolts with the respective openings in the upper mounts, then guide the bolts through the mounts until the threaded ends exit the mounts.

e. Install the washers with the larger diameter openings (7, **Figure 3**) over the threaded ends of the bolts.

f. Install the washer with the smaller diameter opening (7, **Figure 3**) over the bolts, then thread the nuts (5) onto the bolts.

g. Tighten the two mount/cover bolts (4, **Figure 3**) evenly to 25 ft.-lb. (33.8 N•m).

h. Hold the upper mount bolts (9, **Figure 3**) with a box-end wrench. Tighten the two nuts evenly to 55 ft.-lb. (74.6 N•m).

9B. On 225 hp models, install the upper motor mounts and cover onto the adapter as follows:

a. Install the metal washers with the smaller diameter openings (6 and 11, **Figure 4**) over the upper mount bolts (7 and 10). Install the rubber washers (5 and 12, **Figure 4**), then the metal washers with the larger diameter openings (4 and 13) onto the bolts.

b. Install the upper mounts (1 and 14, **Figure 4**) onto the mount bolts and seat against the washers.

c. Guide the threaded ends of the bolts into the corresponding openings in the swivel tube (54, **Figure 6**), then move the drive shaft housing to allow the mounts to seat into the recesses in the power head adapter. Make sure the washers fit into the recesses in the power head adapter.

d. Support the drive shaft housings while installing the washers (55, **Figure 6**) and threading the nuts (56) onto the mount bolts. Do not tighten the nuts at this time.

e. Align the screw openings and fit the mount cover (2, **Figure 4**) onto the upper mounts. Make sure the washers fit into the recesses in the cover.

f. Seat the cover against the mounts and the adapter surfaces.

g. Apply Loctite 542 to the threads, then thread the screws (3, **Figure 4**) into the cover and power head adapter. Tighten the three screws evenly to 25 ft.-lb. (33.8 N•m).

h. Hold the upper mount bolts (7 and 10, **Figure 4**) with a box-end wrench, then tighten the two nuts evenly to 53 ft.-lb. (71.9 N•m).

10. On 75-115 hp models, install the oil pump as described in this chapter.

11. Install the power head as described in Chapter Seven.

12. Install the gearcase as described in Chapter Eight.

SWIVEL TUBE REPLACEMENT

1. Remove the power head as described in Chapter Seven.

2. Remove the gearcase as described in Chapter Eight.

3. Remove the locknut (4, **Figure 5**, typical), then remove the bolt (1) to release the steering linkage (2) from

the swivel tube. Discard the locknut. Always replace the steering linkage locknut when removed.

4. Remove any grounding wire terminals, hoses or wiring that connects onto the drive shaft housing and swivel bracket or clamp brackets. Refer to **Figures 3-6** to locate wires.

5. Have an assistant support the drive shaft housing, then remove the lower and upper motor mounts as described in this chapter.

6. Check for any remaining wiring, hoses or anything that may interfere with drive shaft housing removal and disconnect as required.

7. Pull the drive shaft housing assembly away from the swivel housing. Place the housing on a clean surface with the power head side facing upward. Do not lay the housing on the side or oil will spill from the pan.

8A. On 75-115 hp models, remove the swivel tube from the housing as follows:

a. Use pliers to remove the retaining ring (40, **Figure 5**) from the groove near the bottom of the swivel tube. Discard the retaining ring. Mark the forward facing side of the bracket before removal. If replaced, transfer the mark to the forward side of the replacement bracket.
b. Remove the lower mount bracket (39, **Figure 5**) from the swivel tube. Tap lightly on the bracket until free from the tube.
c. Pull the spacer (37, **Figure 5**) and O-ring (36) from the swivel tube or bracket. Discard the O-ring.
d. Pull upward on the swivel tube (5, **Figure 5**) until free from the housing.
e. Remove the washer (10, **Figure 5**) from the swivel tube or the tube opening in the housing.
f. Pry the seal (11, **Figure 5**) from the tube bore in the housing. Discard the seal.

8B. On 225 hp models, remove the swivel tube from the housing as follows:

a. Remove the snap ring (25, **Figure 6**) from the groove near the bottom of the swivel tube. Discard the snap ring.
b. Remove the lower mount bracket (24, **Figure 6**) from the swivel tube. If necessary, tap lightly on the bracket until free from the tube.
c. Remove the washer (23, **Figure 6**), spacer (22) and O-ring (21) from the swivel tube or bracket. Discard the O-ring.
d. Pull upward on the swivel tube (54, **Figure 6**) until free from the housing.
e. Remove the washer from the swivel tube or the tube opening in the housing.

9. Clean any debris, grease or other contaminants from the swivel tube and tube bore in the housing.

10. Inspect the bushings (12 and 35, **Figure 5** or 20 and 52, **Figure 6**) for excessive wear, cracks or damaged surfaces. Remove and replace the bushings if these or other defects are evident. Replacement instructions follow:

a. Clamp the swivel housing in a vise with protective jaws.
b. Use a punch or chisel to drive the bushing(s) out of the bore. Always drive from the opposite bore.
c. Lubricate the surfaces with Quicksilver 2-4-C Marine Lubricant or equivalent, then push the new bushings into each bore opening until seated in the bore.

11. On 75-115 hp models, insert the new seal (11, **Figure 5**) into the upper tube bore with the lip side facing outward. Use a washer, socket or section of tubing to seat the seal in the bore. The seal surface must be slightly below the bore opening. Apply a coat of Quicksilver 2-4-C Marine Lubricant or equivalent onto the seal lip.

12. Apply a coat of Quicksilver 2-4-C Marine Lubricant or equivalent onto the bushing bores.

13. Rest the washer (10, **Figure 5** or 53, **Figure 6**) onto the housing with the opening aligned with the tube bore.

14. Apply a coat of Quicksilver 2-4-C Marine Lubricant or equivalent onto the shaft surfaces of the swivel tube. Guide the tube into the bore. Seat the tube against the washer.

15A. On 75-115 hp models, apply a coat of Quicksilver 2-4-C Marine Lubricant or equivalent onto the surfaces then install the new O-ring (36, **Figure 5**) then spacer (37) onto the swivel shaft. Seat the spacer and O-ring against the housing.

15B. On 225 hp models, apply a coat of Quicksilver 2-4-C Marine Lubricant or equivalent onto the surfaces, then install a new O-ring (21, **Figure 6**), spacer (22) and washer (23) onto the swivel shaft. Seat the washer, spacer and O-ring against the housing.

16. Rotate the swivel tube to position the steering linkage end facing forward. This positions the motor mount bolt openings facing rearward.

17A. On 75-115 hp models, align the forward surface on the lower mount bracket (39, **Figure 5**) to face true forward, then fit the bracket over the swivel tube splines.

17B. On 225 hp models, align the lower mount bracket (24, **Figure 6**) with the recesses for the lower motor mount bolts facing forward, then fit the bracket over the swivel tube splines.

18. Verify that the lower mount bracket and swivel tube are both facing true forward. Being off by only one spline will prevent installation of the lower motor mounts. Correct improper alignment before proceeding.

19. Install the new retaining ring (40, **Figure 5**) or snap ring (25, **Figure 6**) into the groove near the bottom of the swivel tube. Make sure the ring seats fully in the groove.
20. Pivot the swivel shaft to the steering limits to check for binding or excessive side play. Binding is usually caused by improper bushing installation or improper assembly. Excessive side play is usually caused by excessively worn bushings or worn surfaces on the swivel tube. If binding or excessive side play is evident, remove the swivel tube and replace the faulty components.
21. Use an overhead cable to support the weight while aligning the drive shaft housing assembly with the swivel housing and swivel tube. When aligned, install the upper and lower motor mounts as described in this chapter.
22. Connect any grounding wire terminals, hoses or wiring that connects onto the drive shaft housing and swivel bracket or clamp brackets. Refer to **Figures 3-6** to locate wiring.
23. Align the opening in the steering linkage (2, **Figure 5**, typical) with the threaded opening in the swivel tube. Install the bolt (1, **Figure 5**, typical) as follows:
   a. On 75-115 hp models, thread the bolt into the steering linkage then the threaded opening in the swivel tube. Tighten the bolt to 20 ft.-lb. (27.1 N•m).
   b. On 225 hp models, thread the bolt into its swivel tube opening then the opening in the steering linkage. Tighten the bolt to 20 ft.-lb. (27.1 N•m).
   c. On all models, thread a new locknut onto the steering linkage bolt (1, **Figure 5**, typical). Hole the bolt to prevent rotation and tighten the nut to 20 ft.-lb. (27.1 N•m).
24. Install the power head as described in Chapter Seven.
25. Install the gearcase as described in Chapter Eight.
26. Install the power trim/tilt system as described in Chapter Nine.

SWIVEL HOUSING REPLACEMENT

1. On 225 hp models, remove the nuts (19, **Figure 6**) and pull the trim cylinder thrust pads (45) from the swivel housing. Inspect the thrust pads for uneven or excessively worn surface in the trim ram contact surfaces. Replace both thrust pads if either pad is defective.
2. Remove the power trim and tilt system as described in Chapter nine.
3. Remove the power head as described in Chapter Seven.
4. Remove the gearcase as described in Chapter Eight.
5. Remove the locknut (4, **Figure 5**, typical), then remove the bolt (1) to release the steering linkage (2) from the swivel tube. Discard the locknut. Always replace the steering linkage locknut when removed.
6. Remove any grounding wire terminals, hoses or wiring that connects onto the drive shaft housing and swivel bracket or clamp brackets. Refer to **Figures 3-6** to locate wiring.
7. Have an assistant support the drive shaft housing. Remove the lower and upper motor mounts as described in this chapter.
8. Check for any remaining wiring, hoses or anything that may interfere with drive shaft housing removal and disconnect as required.
9. Pull the drive shaft housing assembly away from the swivel housing. Place the housing on a clean surface with the power head side facing up. Do not lay the housing on the side or oil will spill from the pan.
10. Remove the port and starboard clamp brackets as described in this chapter.
11. On 225 hp models, remove the tilt lock lever as described in this chapter.
12. Remove the swivel tube and bushings from the housing as described in this chapter.
13. Inspect the swivel housing for excessive wear, cracking or deep corrosion pitting. Replace the housing if defective.
14. Install the swivel tube into the housing as described in this chapter.
15. On 225 hp models, install the tilt lock lever as described in this chapter.
16. Install the port and starboard clamp brackets as described in this chapter.
17. Insert the threaded end of the replacement cylinder thrust pads (45, **Figure 6**) into the openings in the trim system side of the housing. Seat the pads into the recesses in the housing, then thread the nuts (19, **Figure 6**) onto the pads. Tighten the nuts to 27 ft.-lb. (36.6 N•m).
18. Use an overhead cable to support the weight while aligning the drive shaft housing assembly with the swivel housing and swivel tube. When aligned, install the upper and lower motor mounts as described in this chapter.
19. Connect any grounding wire terminals, hoses or wiring that connects onto the drive shaft housing and swivel bracket or clamp brackets. Refer to **Figures 3-6** to locate connecting wiring.
20. Align the opening in the steering linkage (2, **Figure 5**, typical) with the threaded opening in the swivel tube. Install the bolt (1, **Figure 5**, typical) as follows:
   a. On 75-115 hp models, thread the bolt into the steering linkage then the threaded opening in the swivel tube. Tighten the bolt to 20 ft.-lb. (27.1 N•m).
   b. On 225 hp models, thread the bolt into the swivel tube opening then the opening in the steering linkage. Tighten the bolt to 20 ft.-lb. (27.1 N•m).

c. On all models, thread a new locknut onto the steering linkage bolt (1, **Figure 5**, typical). Hold the bolt to prevent rotation and tighten the nut to 20 ft.-lb. (27.1 N•m).

21. Install the power head as described in Chapter Seven.
22. Install the gearcase as described in Chapter Eight.
23. Install the power trim/tilt system as described in Chapter Nine.

POWER HEAD ADAPTER REPLACEMENT

75-115 hp Models

1. Drain the engine oil as described in Chapter Three. Do not reinstall the drain plug at this time.
2. Remove the gearcase as described in Chapter Eight.
3. Remove the power head as described in Chapter Seven.
4. Remove the nut (52, **Figure 3**) and disconnect the lever (53) from the shift shaft. Lift the shift shaft out of the drive shaft housing.
5. Remove the upper motor mounts as described in this chapter.
6. Pull any wiring or hoses out of the openings in the adapter plate.
7. Remove the four bolts from the top and rear of the adapter plate. Lift the adapter plate and oil pan assembly from the drive shaft housing. Remove the seal (58, **Figure 3**) from the oil pan or the opening in the drive shaft housing.
8. Pull the cooling water tube (24, **Figure 3**) from the drive shaft housing or adapter plate. Remove the flange seal (23, **Figure 3**) and grommets (22 and 25) from the water tube or adapter plate. Inspect the grommets and flange for deterioration, cracking or other defects and replace as necessary.
9. Remove the exhaust tube, then oil pan and oil pickup tube as described in this chapter.
10. Thoroughly clean the adapter plate and the mating surfaces on the drive shaft housing.
11. Inspect the adapter plate for deep corrosion pitting, cracking or worn surfaces. Replace the adapter plate if any defects are evident.
12. Install the oil pickup tube, oil pan, and exhaust tube as described in this chapter.
13. Install the water tube and grommets as follows:
    a. Apply a light coat of Quicksilver 2-4-C Marine Lubricant to the surfaces of the flange seal (23, **Figure 3**) and grommets (22 and 25).
    b. Fit the lower grommet (25, **Figure 3**) into the opening in the drive shaft housing. Make sure the groove in the grommet fits into the opening.
    c. Insert the lower end of the water tube (24, **Figure 3**) into the grommet.
    d. Fit the flange (23, **Figure 3**) onto the upper end of the water tube.
    e. Insert the upper grommet (22, **Figure 3**) into the opening in the adapter plate.
14. Fit the seal (58, **Figure 3**) over the boss for the oil pan drain. If necessary use heavy grease to hold the seal in position.
15. Guide the upper end of the water tube into the adapter plate grommet while lowering the adapter and oil pan assembly into the drive shaft housing. Rotate the water tube to align the tube end with the grommet opening. Seat the adapter and oil pan assembly against the drive shaft housing surface.
16. Move the adapter plate to align the four bolt openings at the top and the rear of the adapter. Thread the four bolts into the openings. Do not tighten the bolt at this time.
17. Install the upper motor mounts as described in this chapter.
18. Tighten the four bolts at the top and rear of the adapter plate evenly to 25 ft.-lb. (33.8 N•m).
19. Guide the shift shaft (51, **Figure 3**) into the openings in the adapter plate and drive shaft housing. Fit the opening in the shift lever (53, **Figure 3**) over the threaded post on the shift shaft. Install and securely tighten the locknut (52, **Figure 3**).
20. Route any wiring or hoses through the respective openings in the plate.
21. Install the oil pump as described in this chapter.
22. Install the power head as described in Chapter Seven.
23. Install the gearcase as described in Chapter Eight.
24. Install the oil drain plug (56, **Figure 3**) with sealing washer (57) and tighten to 210 in.-lb. (23.7 N•m). Refill the engine oil as described in Chapter Three.
25. Check for water or oil leakage after starting the engine. Correct all oil and water leaks prior to operating the engine.

225 hp Model

1. Drain the engine oil as described in Chapter Three. Do not reinstall the drain plug at this time.
2. Remove the gearcase as described in Chapter Eight.
3. Remove the power head as described in Chapter Seven.
4. Remove the upper engine mounts as described in this chapter.
5. Remove the two screws (57, **Figure 4**) then pull the retainer (60) and grommet (61) from the drive shaft housing.

6. Remove the nine bolts (15 and 20, **Figure 4**) that retain the adapter and oil pan assembly onto the drive shaft housing.
7. Carefully lift the adapter, oil pan and silencer assembly from the drive shaft housing.
8. Remove the grommet (63, **Figure 4**) from the lower end of the cooling water tube (65) or the opening in the drive shaft housing. Inspect the grommet for deterioration, cracking or other defects and replace as necessary.
9. Remove the seals (62 and 72, **Figure 4**) from the silencer (70) or openings in the drive shaft housing. Inspect the seals for burned, cracked or deteriorated surfaces and replace as necessary.
10. Remove the silencer, exhaust tube, oil pan, and pickup tube as described in this chapter.
11. Remove the oil pressure relief valve as described in this chapter.
12. Thoroughly clean the adapter plate and the mating surfaces on the drive shaft housing.
13. Inspect the adapter plate for deep corrosion pitting, cracking or worn surfaces. Replace the adapter plate if any defects are evident.
14. Install the oil pan, pickup, exhaust tube, and silencer as described in this chapter.
15. Apply a light coat of Quicksilver 2-4-C Marine Lubricant to the surfaces, then install the lower water tube grommet (63, **Figure 4**) into the drive shaft housing. Ensure the groove in the grommet fits over the opening in the housing.
16. Apply a coat of 2-4-C Marine Lubricant to the surfaces, then fit the seal (62, **Figure 4**) onto the lower end of the silencer (70).
17. Apply a coat or 2-4-C Marine Lubricant to the surfaces, then fit the exhaust relief seal (72, **Figure 4**) into the opening in the silencer.
18. Guide the lower end of the water tube into the drive shaft housing grommet while lowering the adapter and oil pan assembly into the drive shaft housing. Seat the assembly against the drive shaft housing. Rotate the adapter plate to align all of the screw openings.
19. Apply Loctite 242 onto the threads of the two 8 mm bolts (15, **Figure 4**). Thread the screws into the openings at the top and front of the adapter plate. Tighten the screw evenly to 180 in.-lb. (20.3 N•m).
20. Thread the seven 10 mm bolts into the adapter plate and drive shaft housing. Tighten the seven bolts in a crossing pattern to 31 ft.-lb. (42.0 N•m).
21. Insert the grommet (61, **Figure 4**) into the recess surrounding the drain plug opening. Fit the retainer (60, **Figure 4**) over the grommet. Apply a light coat of Loctite 242, then thread the two screws (57, **Figure 4**) into the retainer and oil pan. Tighten the screws to 70 in.-lb. (7.9 N•m).
22. Install the oil pressure relief valve as described in this chapter.
23. Install the power head as described in Chapter Seven.
24. Install the gearcase as described in Chapter Eight.
25. Install the oil drain plug (58, **Figure 4**) with sealing washer (54) and tighten to 20 ft.-lb. (27.1 N•m). Refill the engine oil as described in Chapter Three.
26. Check for water or oil leakage after starting the engine. Correct all oil and water leaks before operating the engine.

EXHAUST SILENCER REPLACEMENT (225 HP MODEL)

1. Remove the power head adapter as described in this chapter. Place the assembly on a clean work surface with the power head facing downward.
2. Remove the ten screws (71, **Figure 4**) that retain the silencer (70) onto the oil pan.
3. Lift the silencer from the oil pan. If necessary carefully pry the silencer free. Use a blunt tip pry bar and work carefully to avoid damaging the mating surfaces.
4. Remove the cooling water tube (65, **Figure 4**) and grommet (64) from the silencer.
5. Remove the gaskets (66 and 68, **Figure 4**) and plate (67) from the silencer or the oil pan. Discard the gaskets. If dislodged, fit the seal (39, **Figure 4**) onto the flange of the exhaust tube (37).
6. Carefully remove all gasket material from the silencer, plate and oil pan surfaces.
7. Use a solvent to thoroughly clean the silencer, the mating surfaces and the threaded openings in the oil pan. Be sure to remove all of the threadlocking compound from the threaded openings.
8. Inspect the silencer and plate for cracking, deep corrosion pitting or other damage. Replace the silencer and or plate if these or other defects are evident.
9. Inspect the locating pins (69, **Figure 4**) for damage or a loose fit in the oil pan. Remove any pins that are found in silencer openings and install them into the oil pan. Replace any pins that are damaged or fit loosely in the openings. Replace the oil pan if a new pin fits loosely or if the opening is damaged or elongated.
10. Fit the grommet (64, **Figure 4**) over the lower end of the water tube (65). Seat the grommet against the flange at the upper end of the water tube. Insert the non-flanged end water tube into the opening in the oil pan side of the silencer until the grommet contacts the mating surface.
11. Fit the new gaskets (66 and 68, **Figure 4**) and the plate (67) over the locating pins. Seat the gaskets against

the oil pan. The gasket with more and larger openings must contact the oil pan. The gasket with fewer and smaller openings must contact the plate and silencer.

12. Hold the water tube in position while carefully lowering the silencer cover onto the oil pan. Align the locating pin openings, then seat the silencer against the gaskets, plate and the oil pan.

13. Apply Loctite 242 onto the threads of the ten screws (71, **Figure 4**). Thread the screws into the silencer, plate and oil pan. Tighten the screws in a crossing pattern to 20 ft.-lb. (27.1 N•m).

14. Install the power head adapter as described in this chapter.

EXHAUST TUBE REPLACEMENT

75-115 hp Models

1. Remove the power head adapter/oil pan assembly from the drive shaft housing as described in this chapter.
2. Remove the four bolts, then lift the exhaust tube (26, **Figure 3**) from the oil pan. Tap lightly on the end of the tube to free it from the pan.
3. Use a suitable solvent to thoroughly clean the exhaust tube, the mating surfaces and the threaded openings in the oil pan.
4. Inspect the exhaust tube and the exhaust tube-to-oil pan mating surfaces for cracks, deep corrosion pitting, or other damage. Replace the affected components.
5. Align the bolt openings while fitting the exhaust tube (26, **Figure 3**) onto the oil pan.
6. Thread the four bolts into the exhaust tube flange and the oil pan. Tighten the fasteners in sequence as described in this chapter (see *Oil Pan Replacement*).
7. Install the power head adapter/oil pan assembly as described in this chapter.

225 hp Model

1. Remove the power head adapter/oil pan assembly from the drive shaft housing as described in this chapter.
2. Remove the exhaust silencer as described in this chapter.
3. Remove the seal (39, **Figure 4**) from the exhaust tube (37). Remove the seal from the plate (67, **Figure 4**) if not found on the tube. Inspect the seal for burning, surface cracking, deterioration or other defects and replace as necessary.
4. Remove the four bolts (38, **Figure 4**), then lift the exhaust tube from the oil pan. If necessary tap lightly on the end of the tube to free it from the pan.
5. Remove the gasket (36, **Figure 4**) from the exhaust tube or oil pan surfaces. Discard the gasket.
6. Use a solvent to thoroughly clean the exhaust tube, the mating surfaces and the threaded openings in the oil pan. Be sure to remove all threadlocking compound from the threaded openings.
7. Inspect the exhaust tube and the exhaust tube-to-oil pan mating surfaces for cracks, deep corrosion pitting, or other damage. Replace the affected components.
8. Align the bolt openings while installing a new gasket (36, **Figure 4**) and the exhaust tube (37) onto the oil pan.
9. Apply a light coat of Loctite 242 onto the threads, then thread the four bolts (38, **Figure 4**) into the exhaust tube flange and the oil pan. Tighten the four bolts in a crossing pattern to an initial torque of 90 in.-lb. (10.1 N•m). Then tighten the four bolts in a crossing pattern to a final torque of 177 in.-lb. (20 N•m).
10. Apply a light coat of 2-4-C Marine Lubricant to the surfaces, then fit the seal (39, **Figure 4**) onto the lower flange of the exhaust tube.
11. Install the exhaust silencer as described in this chapter.
12. Install the power head adapter/oil pan assembly as described in this chapter.

OIL PRESSURE RELIEF VALVE (225 HP MODEL)

1. Remove the power head as described in Chapter Seven.
2. Use compressed air to remove loose debris from the exposed surfaces of the power head adapter plate.
3. Remove the screw (17, **Figure 4**) and clamp plate (18) and collar (19) to allow removal of the valve.
4. Unthread the oil pressure relief valve (16, **Figure 4**) from the adapter plate.
5. Use solvent to thoroughly clean the valve and the threaded opening. Do not allow thread sealant or other contaminants to enter the valve or the opening in the adapter plate.
6. Thread the replacement valve into the opening. Tighten the valve to 70 in.-lb. (7.9 N•m).
7. Fit the collar (19, **Figure 4**) and clamp plate (18) onto the adapter plate. The notch in the clamp plate must align with the hex end of the valve. If necessary, tighten the valve an additional amount to achieve correct alignment.
8. Thread the screw (17, **Figure 4**) into the clamp plate, collar and adapter plate. Tighten the screw to 70 in.-lb. (7.9 N•m).
9. Install the power head as described in Chapter Seven.

OIL PAN AND OIL PICKUP TUBE REPLACEMENT

75-115 hp Models

1. Remove the power head adapter/oil pan assembly from the drive shaft housing as described in this chapter.
2. Remove the exhaust tube as described in this chapter.

CAUTION
Never pry the oil pan from the power head adapter. The gasket mating surfaces are easily damaged. Damaged surfaces may allow water, oil or exhaust leakage that may cause serious engine damage.

3. Remove the twelve screws (59, **Figure 3**), and carefully lift the oil pan (18) from the adapter. Tap lightly on the side of the pan if necessary to free the pan. Do not pry the pan from the adapter.
4. Remove the four screws (20, **Figure 3**) and lift the oil pickup tube (21) from the adapter. Remove and discard the O-ring (19, **Figure 3**) from the pickup tube or adapter.
5. Remove the gasket (16, **Figure 3**) from the oil pan or adapter plate.
6. Use a suitable solvent to clean oily residue, debris and debris from the oil pan, oil pickup tube and adapter plate surfaces. Direct solvent into the upper tube opening to clear debris from the screen.
7. Inspect the three locating pins (10, **Figure 3**) for damage or a loose fit in the power head adapter. Remove any pins that are found in the oil pan openings and install them in the power head adapter. Replace any pins that are damaged or fit loosely in the openings. Replace the power head adapter if a new pin fits loosely or if the opening is damaged or elongated.
8. Fit the openings over the locating pins while installing the new oil pan gasket (16, **Figure 3**) onto the adapter. Make sure the pickup tube screw openings in the gasket align with the corresponding openings in the adapter plate. If not, the gasket is installed with the wrong side facing the oil pan. Correct the gasket installation before proceeding.
9. Lubricate the surfaces with engine oil, then fit a new O-ring (19, **Figure 3**) onto the upper end of the tube. The O-ring must surround the tube opening and rest on the flange.
10. Guide the upper end of the pickup tube into the openings in the gasket and adapter plate. Rotate the pickup tube to align the screw openings, then seat the tube.
11. Thread the four screws into the pickup tube, gasket and adapter. Tighten the four screws evenly to 100 in.-lb. (11.3 N•m).

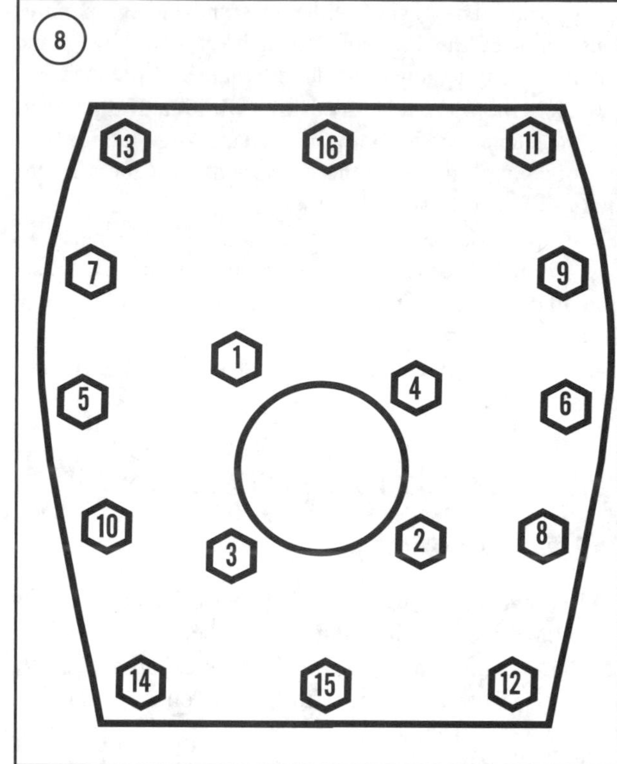

12. Guide the pickup tube into the opening while carefully lowering the oil pan onto the adapter. Align the locating pin openings, and seat the oil pan against the gasket.
13. Thread the twelve screws (59, **Figure 3**) into the oil pan and adapter. Do not tighten the screws at this time.
14. Install the exhaust tube as described in this chapter.
15. Tighten the twelve oil pan screws and the exhaust tube bolts to 100 in.-lb. (11.3 N•m) using the sequence shown in **Figure 8**.
16. Install the power head adapter/oil pan assembly as described in this chapter.

225 hp Model

1. Remove the power head adapter/oil pan assembly from the drive shaft housing as described in this chapter.
2. Remove the exhaust tube as described in this chapter.
3. Remove the two screws (34, **Figure 4**) from the area near the exhaust tube opening in the pan.

CAUTION
Never pry the oil pan from the power head adapter. The gasket mating surfaces are easily damaged. Damaged surfaces may allow water, oil or exhaust leakage that may cause serious engine damage.

4. Remove the ten screws (35, **Figure 4**) from the oil pan mounting flange. Lift the oil pan (33) from the exhaust adapter plate (25). Tap lightly on the side of the pan if necessary to free the pan. Do not pry the pan from the adapter plate.
5. Remove and discard the gasket (30, **Figure 4**) from the oil pan or exhaust adapter plate.
6. Remove the three screws (29, **Figure 4**) and sleeves (28), then lift the oil pickup tube from the exhaust adapter plate.
7. Remove the seal (26, **Figure 4**) from the pickup tube or the adapter plate. Discard the seal.
8. Inspect the two locating pins (31 and 32, **Figure 4**) for damage or a loose fit in the oil pan flange. Remove any pins that are found in the lower side of the exhaust adapter plate and install them into the oil pan. Replace any pins that are damaged or fit loosely in the openings. Replace the oil pan if a new pin fits loosely or if the opening is damaged or elongated.
9. Carefully pry the exhaust adapter plate from the power adapter plate (21, **Figure 4**). Use a blunt tip pry bar and work carefully to avoid damaging the mating surfaces. If removal is difficult, check for overlooked fasteners.
10. Remove the gasket (22, **Figure 4**) from the exhaust adapter plate or power head adapter plate. Discard the gasket.
11. Inspect the two locating pins (23 and 24, **Figure 4**) for damage or a loose fit in the exhaust adapter plate. Remove any pins that are found in the lower side of the power head adapter plate and install them in the exhaust adapter plate. Replace any pins that are damaged or fit loosely in the openings. Replace the exhaust adapter plate if a new pin fits loosely or if the opening is damaged or elongated.
12. Use a suitable solvent to clean oily residue, debris and debris from the oil pan, oil pickup tube and adapter plate surfaces. Pour solvent into the upper tube opening to clear debris from the screen.
13. Fit the openings over the locating pins while installing the new gasket (22, **Figure 4**) onto the exhaust adapter plate. The oil pan and adapter plate gaskets are similar in appearance. Make sure the gasket openings match the passages in the adapter plate. Align the locating pins with the openings, then install the power head adapter plate onto the exhaust adapter plate.
14. Install the pickup tube as follows:
   a. Lubricate the surfaces with engine oil, then fit the new seal (26, **Figure 4**) into the groove in the pickup tube (27) flange.
   b. Align the screw openings and fit the pickup tube flange onto the exhaust adapter plate. Make sure the seal is not dislodged during the installation.
   c. Install the three sleeves (28, **Figure 4**) into the screw openings. Move the pickup tube to allow the sleeves to fully enter the openings. The flange on the sleeves must contact the flange on the pickup tube.
   d. Thread the three screws (29, **Figure 4**) into the sleeves and adapter plate openings. Verify proper alignment and tighten the screws evenly to 90 in.-lb. (10.1 N•m).
15. Fit the openings over the locating pins while installing the new gasket (30, **Figure 4**) onto the oil pan. The adapter plate and oil pan gaskets are similar in appearance. Make sure the gasket openings match the passages in the oil pan.
16. Guide the pickup tube into the opening while lowering the exhaust adapter plate and power head adapter assembly onto the oil pan. Align the locating pins with the openings, then seat the adapters onto the pan.
17. Apply a light coat of Loctite 242 to the threads of the two screws (34, **Figure 4**). Thread both screws into their openings in the area near exhaust tube opening in the pan. Tighten the two screws to an initial torque of 90 in.-lb. (10.1 N•m). Tighten both screws to a final torque of 177 in.-lb. (19.9 N•m).
18. Thread the ten screws (35, **Figure 4**) into the oil pan flange and adapter plates. Tighten the ten screws in a crossing pattern to an initial torque of 90 in.-lb. (10.1 N•m). Tighten the ten screws in a crossing pattern to a final torque of 177 in.-lb. (19.9 N•m).
19. Install the exhaust tube as described in this chapter.
20. Install the power head adapter/oil pan assembly as described in this chapter.

DRIVE SHAFT HOUSING REPLACEMENT

1. Remove the power head as described in Chapter Seven.
2. Remove the gearcase as described in Chapter Eight.
3. Remove the drive shaft housing assembly from the swivel bracket as described in this chapter (see *Swivel Housing Replacement*).
4. Remove the power head adapter as described in this chapter.
5. Use pressurized water to clean debris, oily deposits and carbon buildup from the drive shaft housing. Dry the housing with compressed air.
6. Inspect the housing for cracking, deep corrosion pitting and excessively worn surfaces. Replace the housing if these or other defects are evident.
7. On 75-115 hp models, remove the hose and fitting (30, **Figure 3**) that supplies water to the drive shaft bushing.

Clean any debris or contaminants from the threaded opening, fitting and hose.

8. On 225 hp models, replace the exhaust relief plate if cracked or heat damaged. Instructions follow:

a. Remove the two screws (74, **Figure 4**) then lift the exhaust relief plate (75) from the housing.
b. Fit the replacement plate into the housing. Install the two screws to secure the plate. Tighten the two screws evenly to 35 in.-lb. (3.9 N•m).

9. On 75-115 hp models, inspect the bushing (36, **Figure 3**) in the drive shaft bore for excessive wear, rough surfaces or other damage. Replace the bushing if these or other defects are evident. Instructions follow:

a. Use a pin punch to drive the roll pin (31, **Figure 3**) into the drive shaft bushing bore.
b. Use a punch to drive the bushing out of the bore. Drive from the top side.
c. Apply a coat of Quicksilver 2-4-C Marine Lubricant or its equivalent onto the bushing bore in the drive shaft housing.
d. Use a socket and extension or section of tubing to drive the replacement bushing fully into the bore.
e. To retain the bushing, drive the roll pin into the opening until flush.

10. On 225 hp models, replace the speedometer fitting as follows:

a. Remove the clamp (51, **Figure 4**) then pull the hose from the speedometer fitting (53).
b. Remove the screw (50, **Figure 4**) then pull the speedometer fitting from the drive shaft housing.
c. Fit the replacement speedometer fitting onto the locating pin (54, **Figure 4**). Install the screw (50, **Figure 4**). Tighten the screw to 70 in.-lb. (7.9 N•m).
d. Push the speedometer hose fully over the fitting. Secure the hose with a plastic locking clamp.

11. On 75-115 hp models, thread the fitting (30, **Figure 3**) into the opening on the side of the drive shaft bore until secure. Push the water hose fully over the fitting. Secure the hose with a plastic locking clamp.

12. Install the power head adapter as described in this chapter.

13. Install the drive shaft housing assembly onto the clamp brackets as described in this chapter (see *Swivel Housing Replacement*).

14. Install the power head as described in Chapter Seven.

15. Install the gearcase as described in Chapter Eight.

Table 1 MIDSECTION TORQUE SPECIFICATIONS

Fastener	in.-lb.	ft.-lb.	N•m
Clamp bracket anode/bracket			
75-115 hp models	60	–	6.8
225 hp models	70	–	7.9
Clamp bracket to bracket spacer			
75-115 hp models	–	30	40.7
Clamp bracket thrust pad			
225 hp models	35	–	4.0
Clamp bracket to trim system			
225 hp models	–	31	42.0
Drain plug grommet retainer			
225 hp models	70	–	7.9
Drive shaft housing cover			
75-115 hp models	65	–	7.3
225 hp models	70	–	7.9
Exhaust relief plate			
225 hp models	35	–	3.9
Exhaust tube			
75-115 hp models	100	–	11.3
225 hp models			
Initial torque	90	–	10.1
Final torque	177	–	20.0

(continued)

Table 1 MIDSECTION TORQUE SPECIFICATIONS (continued)

Fastener	in.-lb.	ft.-lb.	N•m
Grounding wire			
225 hp models	70	–	7.9
Engine cover mounting post			
225 hp models	70	–	7.9
Lower motor mount cover			
75-115 hp models	–	25	33.8
225 hp models	–	27	36.6
Lower mount bolt and nut			
75-115 hp models	–	50	67.8
225 hp models	–	53	71.9
Power head adapter to drive shaft housing			
75-115 hp models	–	25	33.8
Power head adapter to oil pan			
225 hp models			
6 mm bolts	70	–	7.9
8 mm bolts	180	15	20.3
10 mm bolts	–	31	42.0
Oil pan to exhaust plate/adapter			
225 hp models			
Initial torque	90	–	10.1
Final torque	177	–	20
Oil pan to power head adapter			
75-115 hp models	100	–	11.3
Oil drain plug			
75-115 hp models	210	17.5	23.7
225 hp models	–	20	27.1
Oil pickup			
75-115 hp models	100	–	11.3
225 hp models	90	–	10.1
Oil pressure relief valve			
225 hp models	70	–	7.9
Clamp plate screw	70	–	7.9
Oil pump to power head adapter			
75-115 hp models	85	–	9.6
Silencer to oil pan			
225 hp models	–	20	27.1
Spring hook			
225 hp models	70	–	7.9
Speedometer fitting screw			
225 hp models	70	–	7.9
Steering cable nut	–	35	47.5
Steering link nut and bolt	–	20	27.1
Steering link to cable end	120*	–	13.6 *
Tilt tube grease fitting			
75-115 hp models	40	–	4.5
Trim cylinder thrust pad			
225 hp models	–	27	36.6
Trim position sender			
75-115 hp models	70	–	7.9
225 hp models	71	–	8.0
Upper mount bolt and nut			
75-115 hp models	–	55	74.6
225 hp models	–	53	71.9
Upper motor mount cover			
75-115 hp models	–	25	33.8
225 hp models	–	25	33.8
Wire clamp			
225 hp	70	–	7.9

*Tighten the fastener to this specification, then back the nut off 1/4 turn.

Chapter Eleven

Remote Control

This chapter provides instructions for the standard side mount control (**Figure 1**) and the Commander 3000 panel mount type of control (**Figure 2**). The Commander 3000 type control is also available in a binnacle mount (**Figure 3**). Contact a marine dealership for parts and information if the engine is equipped with a different brand or type of remote control.

Complete disassembly is not always required to test or replace a failed component. Perform the disassembly steps necessary to access the necessary components or wires. Reverse the steps to assemble and install the remote control. Tighten all fasteners to the general torque specifications listed in the *Quick Reference Data* section at the front of the manual.

WARNING
A malfunctioning remote control can result in a lack of shift and throttle control. Never operate an outboard with any control system malfunction. Check for proper control system operation before operating the engine or after performing any service or repair to the control system(s).

CAUTION
Always refer to the owner's manual for specific operating instructions regarding the remote control. Become familiar with the control functions before operating the engine.

CABLE REMOVAL AND INSTALLATION

Replace the cables if they arc hard to move or have excessive play. Replace both cables if either cable requires replacement. The condition causing failure or malfunction of one of the cables is almost certainly effecting the other. Mark the cable mounting points with a felt tip marker prior to removing them from the remote control. This helps ensure the throttle and shift cables are installed to the proper attaching points. To avoid confusion, remove and install one cable at a time.

NOTE
Apply Loctite 242 to the threads of the remote control handle nut or bolt during assembly.

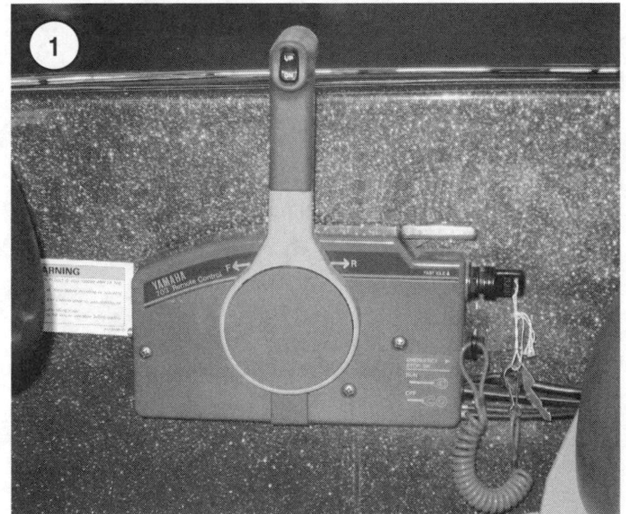

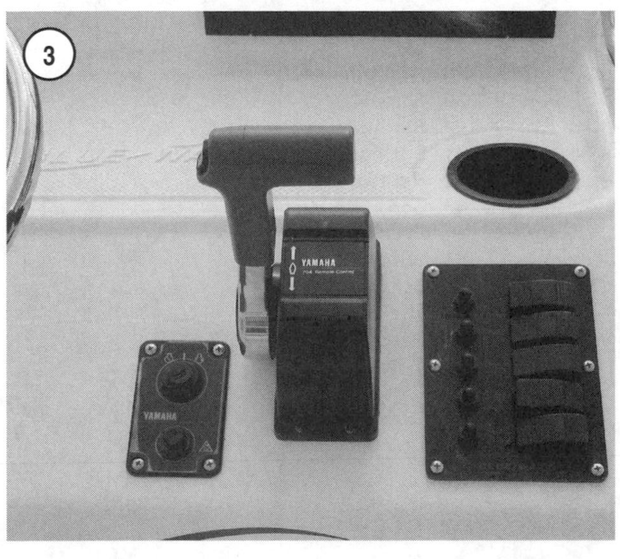

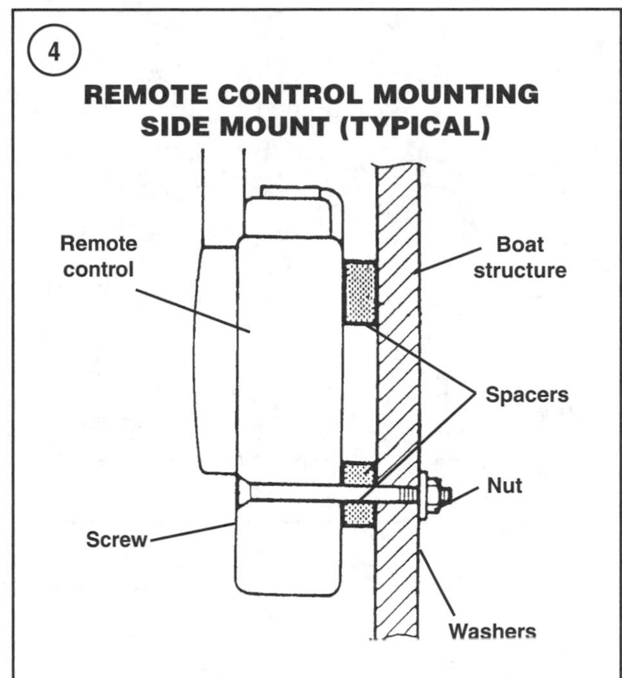

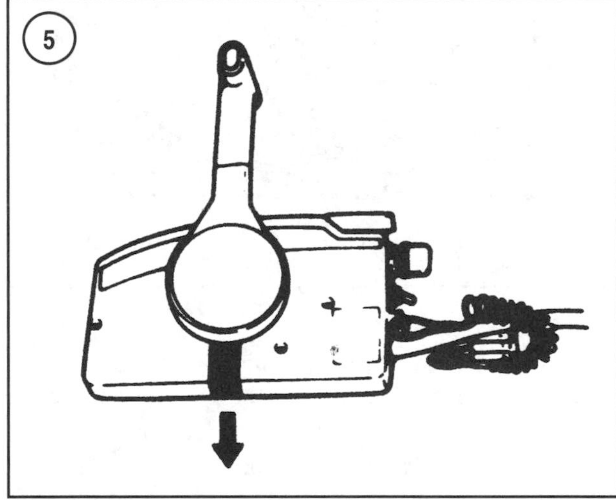

11

Side Mount Control

1. Disconnect the battery cable to prevent accidental starting.

2. Remove the screws, spacers, nuts and washers (**Figure 4**). Pull the remote control away from the boat structure.

3. Carefully pry the cover (**Figure 5**) down and away from the remote control. Slip the cover tabs from the openings while lifting it from the control.

4. Remove the two lower screws (**Figure 6**) and lift the lower back cover from the remote control.

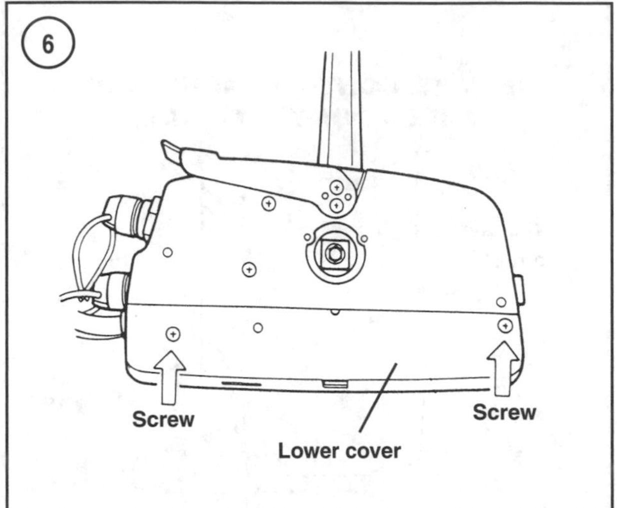

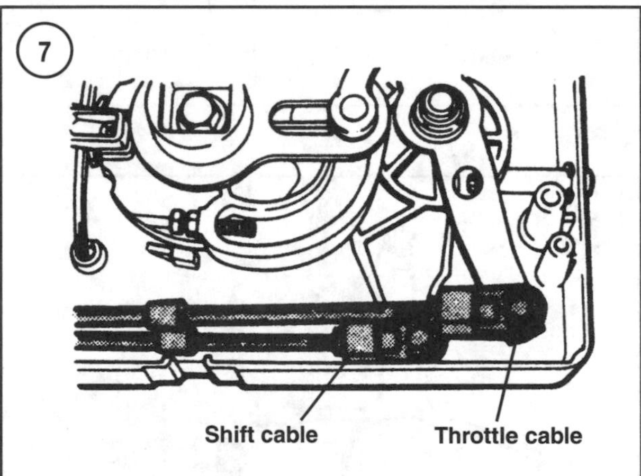

5. Mark the *throttle cable* (**Figure 7**), then remove the small nut and cable retainer from the lever. Disconnect the throttle cable from the lever.

6. Mark the *shift cable* (**Figure 7**), then remove the small nut and cable retainer from the lever. Lift the throttle cable from the lever.

7. Apply water resistant grease to the ends of the throttle cable and shift cables. Position the pin of the cable retainer (20, **Figure 8**) at the end of the shift cable. Lower the shift cable barrel into the opening at the rear of the remote control. Align the cable retainer and cable with the attaching points to the shift lever (30, **Figure 8**). Install the cable retainer (20, **Figure 8**) and nut (21). Securely tighten the nut.

8. Position the pin of the cable retainer (20, **Figure 8**) onto the end of the throttle cable. Lower the throttle cable barrel into the recess at the rear of the remote control along with the shift cable. Align the cable retainer and ca-

SIDE MOUNT CONTROL COMPONENTS

1. Control housing
2. Back cover
3. Lower cover
4. Bushing
5. Screw
6. Fast idle lever
7. Ignition key switch retaining nut
8. Wire support
9. Ignition key switch
10. Remote control harness
11. Wave washer
12. Screw
13. Fast idle cam
14. Roller
15. Spring
16. Retainer
17. Screw
18. Wire cover
19. Bolt and washer
20. Cable retainer
21. Nut
22. Cam roller
23. Control cam
24. Detent roller
25. Screw
26. Neutral switch arm
27. Spring
28. Throttle lever and linkage
29. Washer
30. Shift lever
31. Clip
32. Throttle friction lever
33. Throttle friction screw
34. Warning horn
35. Screw
36. Neutral only start switch
37. Lanyard switch
38. Trim/tilt switch
39. Grip
40. Screw
41. Spring
42. Neutral lock lever
43. Screw
44. Bracket
45. Screw
46. Screw
47. Lockwasher
48. Neutral lock bracket
49. Cover
50. Clip
51. Throttle handle
52. Cover

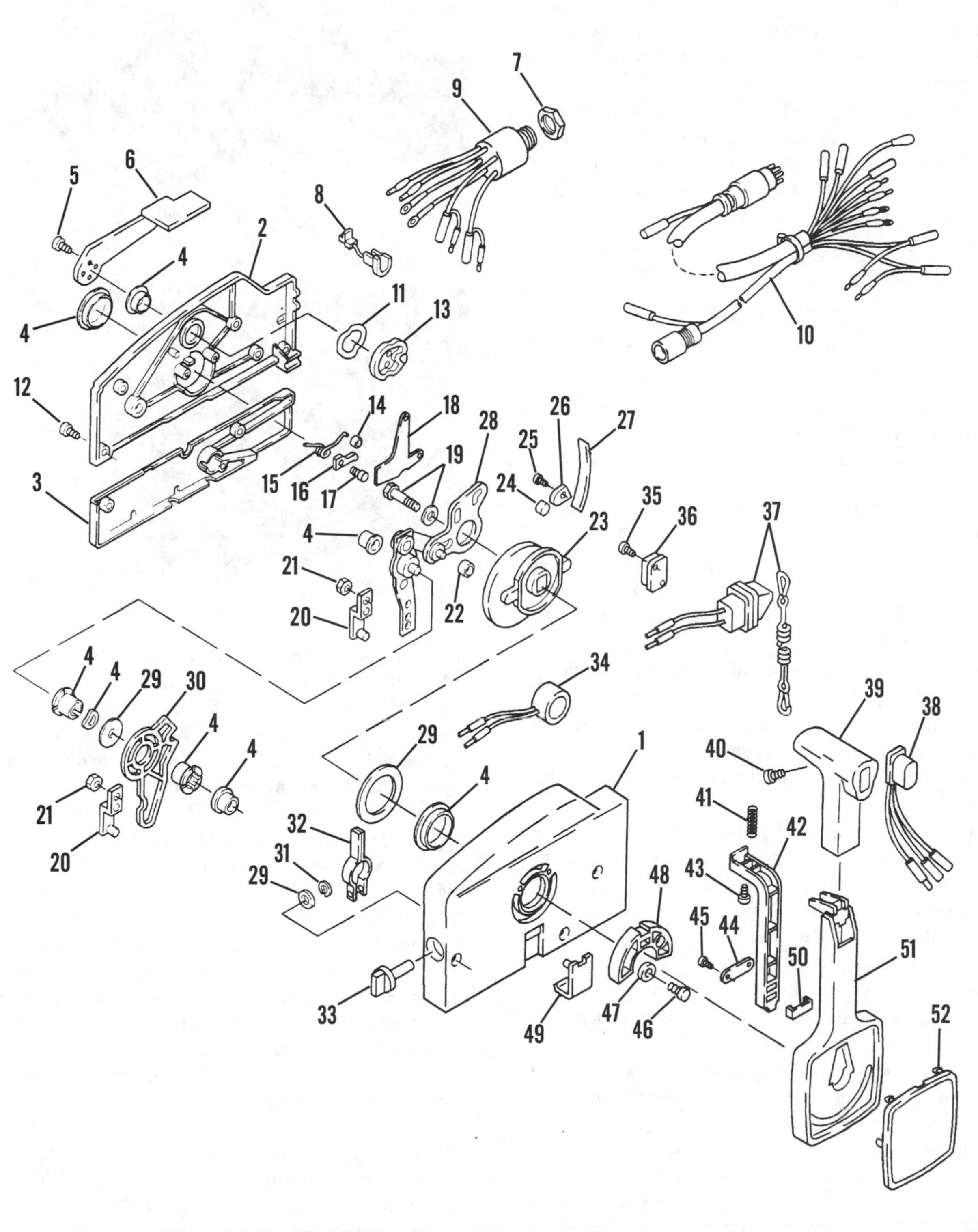
7
9
5
6
8
2
4
4
11
13
10
12
14
18
28
26
27
25
19
24
15
16
17
3
35
36
37
4
23
21
22
20
34
4
4
29
30
4
4
29
1
40
41
39
38
21
20
32
31
29
42
43
48
45
44
50
51
33
49
47
46
52

ble with its attaching points to the throttle lever (28, **Figure 8**). Install the cable retainer and nut. Securely tighten the nut.

9. Install the lower back cover and screws. Securely tighten the screws. Slip the tabs of the small cover into the opening and snap it into position.

10. Install the control and attaching screws, spacers, washers and nuts as indicated in **Figure 4**. Adjust the throttle and shift cables as described in Chapter Four.

11. Connect the battery cable. Check for proper shift and throttle operation. Correct any problems before operating the engine.

NOTE
Apply Loctite 242 to the threads of the remote control handle nut or bolt during assembly.

Commander 3000 Control (Panel or Binnacle Mount)

1. Disconnect the negative battery cable to prevent accidental starting.

2. Place the throttle handle in the FORWARD gear full-throttle position. Mark the handle location on the mounting panel to ensure correct handle orientation during installation of the control.

3. Carefully pry the neutral throttle button from the throttle handle (**Figure 9**).

4. Using an extension and socket, remove the handle retaining nut from the button opening. Guide the trim wire from the control opening while removing the handle (**Figure 10**).

5. Cut the heat shrink tubing (28, **Figure 11**) from the yellow/red wires leading into the control. Remove the screws (14, **Figure 11**) and nuts (15) to disconnect the yellow/red wires from the control. These wires lead to the dash mounted ignition key switch.

6A. For a panel mount control, pry the plastic cover from the panel mount (**Figure 12**). Outline the remote control mounting angle on the back side of the boat structure to ensure correct orientation during installation.

6B. On a binnacle mount control, remove the retaining screws on the side, then pry the plastic cover from the remote control housing.

7. Remove the four control retaining screws from the external mounting plate. Pull the control from the panel.

8. Remove the screw (26, **Figure 11**) and washer (27) then lift the rear cover (25) from the control.

9. Mark the throttle cable and attaching point. Note the position of the cable spacers (7, **Figure 11**) before removing the cable. Remove the screw (17, **Figure 11**) and lift the throttle cable from the throttle lever (20).

10. Mark the shift cable and attaching points. Note the position of the cable spacers (7, **Figure 11**) before removing the cable. Remove the screw (17, **Figure 11**) then lift the shift cable from the shift lever (16).

11. Attach the end of the shift cable to the shift lever (16, **Figure 11**). Place the cylinder shaped cable anchor into the recess at the back of the control. Install the screw (17, **Figure 11**) through the cable end and into the shift lever (16). Securely tighten the screw.

12. Install the cable spacer (7, **Figure 11**) into the recess at the back of the control if originally installed. Attach the end of the throttle cable to the throttle lever (20, **Figure 11**). Place the cylinder shaped cable anchor into the recess at the back of the control along with the shift cable or cable spacer. Install the screw (17, **Figure 11**) through the cable end and into the shift lever (16). Securely tighten the screw.

13. Slip the tab on the rear cover (25, **Figure 11**) into the notch and lower the cover into position. Position the cable anchors in the recesses, then install the screw (26, **Figure 11**) and washer (27). Securely tighten the screw.

14. Align the remote control with the outline on the mounting panel (Step 6). Install the four mounting screws

(11)

COMMANDER 3000 CONTROL COMPONENTS (PANEL OR BINACLE MOUNT)

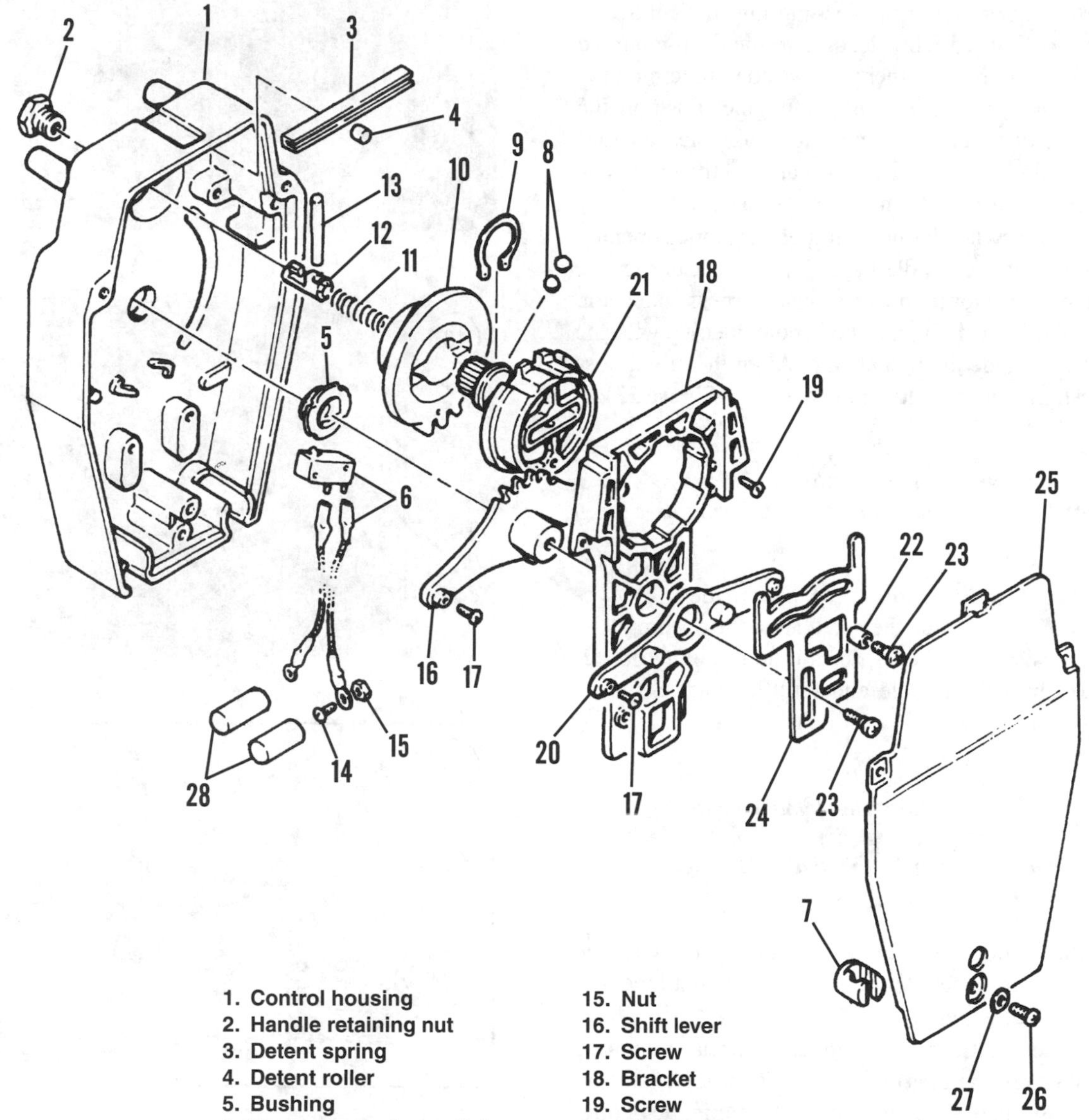

1. Control housing
2. Handle retaining nut
3. Detent spring
4. Detent roller
5. Bushing
6. Neutral-only start switch and leads
7. Cable spacer
8. Detent balls
9. Snap ring
10. Shift gear
11. Spring
12. Neutral throttle shaft
13. Pin
14. Screw
15. Nut
16. Shift lever
17. Screw
18. Bracket
19. Screw
20. Throttle lever
21. Control shaft
22. Bushing
23. Screw
24. Plate
25. Rear cover
26. Screw
27. Washer
28. Shrink tubing

through the external mounting plate and into the remote control. Securely tighten the screws.

15. Fit a section of heat-shrink tubing (28, **Figure 11**) over each disconnected yellow/red wire. Connect one of the yellow/red wire terminals leading into the control to one of the yellow/red wires leading to the dash-mounted key switch. Connect the other yellow/red wire terminal to the yellow/red wire leading to the engine. Position the shrink tubing over each terminal connection. Heat the tubing with a hair dryer until it shrinks around the terminals. Completely cover both terminals with shrink tubing.

16. Fit the trim switch harness through the slotted opening at the bottom of the handle mounting point. Connect the trim switch connector to the instrument harness connector. Place the plastic bushing into the handle opening with the larger diameter side facing outward. Align the raised boss on the bushing with the slot in the opening (**Figure 13**).

NOTE
Apply Loctite 242 to the threads of the remote control handle nut or bolt during assembly.

17. Align the throttle handle to the mark made prior to removal (Step 2), then slide the handle into the opening. Using an extension and socket, install the retaining nut (2, **Figure 11**) into the handle and throttle shaft. Securely tighten the nut.

CAUTION
*Do not over-tighten the handle retaining nut. Over-tightening may break the threaded opening in the shaft (21, **Figure 11**).*

18. Carefully slide the shaft of the neutral throttle button into the opening in the retaining nut. Push in until the button locks into the opening.

19. Snap the plastic cover onto the external mounting plate. Make sure the tabs on the cover fit into the slots in the mounting plate. Place the throttle cable in the neutral position. Adjust the shift and throttle cables as described in Chapter Four.

20. Connect the battery cable. Check for proper operation of the shift, throttle and the neutral-only start switch. Correct any faults before operating the engine.

REMOTE CONTROL DISASSEMBLY AND ASSEMBLY

Always mark the orientation of all components prior to removing them. This important step can help ensure proper remote control operation after assembly. Improper

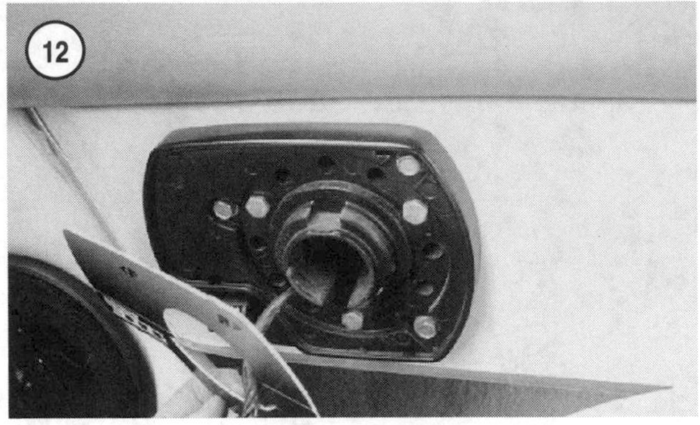

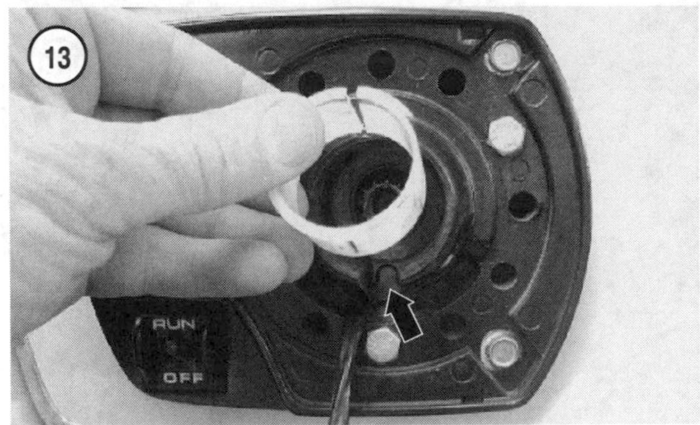

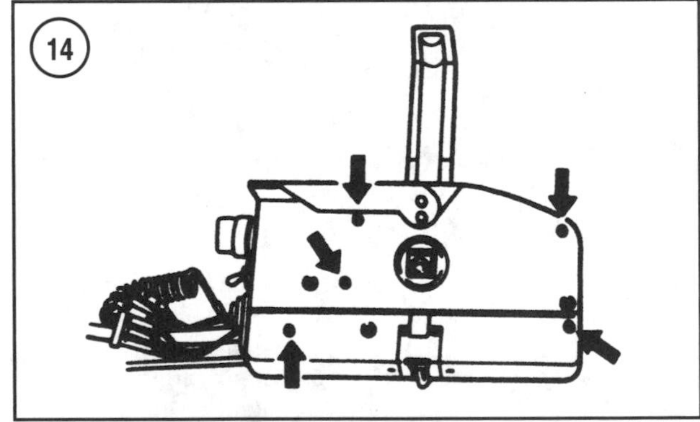

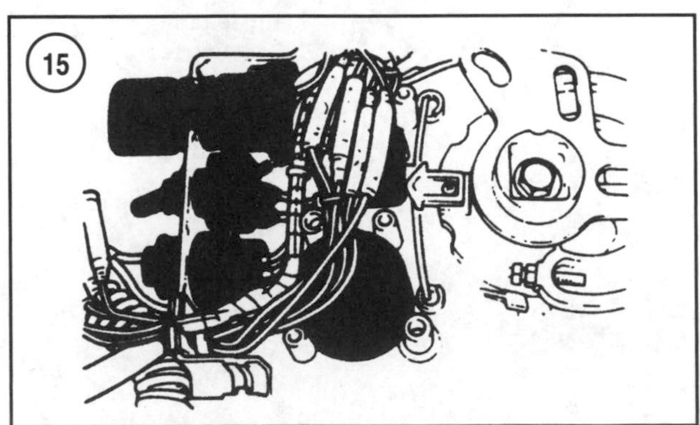

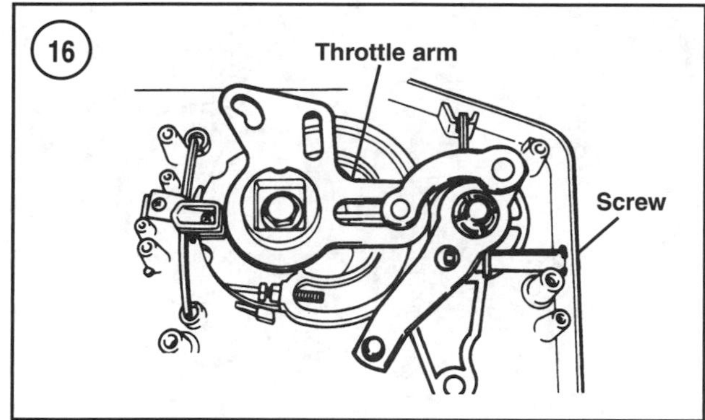

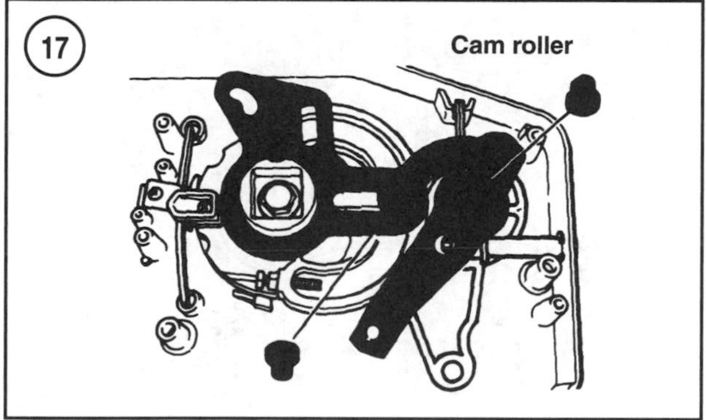

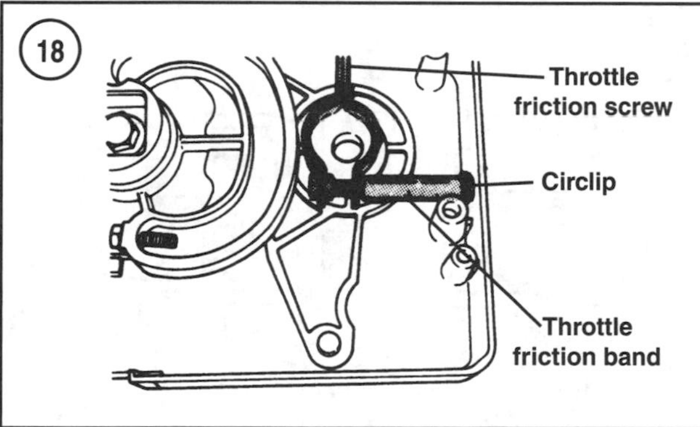

assembly can cause internal binding or reversed cable movement.

When complete disassembly is not required to access the faulty component, perform the disassembly steps until the desired component is accessible. Reverse the disassembly steps to assemble the remote control.

Use compressed air to blow debris from the external surfaces prior to disassembling the remote control. Clean all components except electric switches and the warning buzzer with solvent. Blow all components dry with compressed air. Inspect all components for damaged or excessive wear. Replace all worn, damaged or questionable components. Apply water-resistant grease to all pivot points or sliding surfaces during assembly. Test all electric components when removed to ensure proper operation upon assembly. Refer to Chapter Two to test the warning horn, trim switch and the ignition key switch.

WARNING
A remote control malfunction can lead to lack of shift and throttle control. Never operate an outboard with a control system malfunction. Check control system operation before operating the engine or after performing any service or repair to the control system(s).

CAUTION
Always refer to the owner's manual for specific operating instructions for the remote control. Become familiar with all control functions before operating the engine.

Side Mount Control

Refer to **Figure 8**.

1. Disconnect the negative battery cable to prevent accidental starting.
2. Remove the shift cables from the remote control as described in this chapter.
3. Disconnect the remote control harness from the engine. Route the wire harness away from any boat structure to allow removal of the remote control and harness from the boat.
4. Remove the remaining screws from the back cover (**Figure 14**). Lift the back cover from the control. Refer to the wiring diagrams located at the end of this manual to identify the wire colors used for the warning horn. Disconnect the wires (**Figure 15**) from the harness, then remove the warning horn from the control housing.
5. Identify the wire colors used for the lanyard safety switch and ignition key switch. Unplug the wire connectors (**Figure 15**) from the control harness. Loosen the attaching nut or remove the clip, then lift the switches from the control housing.
6. Note the wire routing, then unplug the neutral-only start switch from the control harness. Remove the mounting screws (35, **Figure 8**), then lift the neutral-only start switch (36) from the control housing.
7. Loosen the throttle friction screw (**Figure 16**). Lift the throttle arm from the control housing. Remove the cam rollers (**Figure 17**) from the control housing or throttle arm.
8. Remove the snap ring from the throttle friction screw (**Figure 18**). Lift the friction band and screw from the control housing.

9. Remove the screw, then lift the neutral switch arm (**Figure 19**) off the cam assembly. Lift the spring and detent roller (**Figure 20**) from the housing.
10. Hold the shift/throttle handle, then loosen the bolt and washer (19, **Figure 8**) until the head is just above the mechanism (**Figure 21**). Using a plastic mallet, tap the bolt head to release the shift/throttle handle from the control cam (23, **Figure 8**). Remove the bolt and washer, then remove the handle from the control.
11. Lift the control cam (**Figure 22**) and shift lever (**Figure 23**) from the housing.
12. Remove the screws (43 and 45, **Figure 8**), and lift the neutral lock lever (42) and spring (41) from the shift/throttle handle.
13. Remove the small retaining screws, then slide the trim and tilt switch from the handle (**Figure 24**).
14. Remove the two screws (46, **Figure 8**) and washers (47), then lift the neutral lock bracket (48) from the housing.
15. Slowly remove the screw from the retainer (**Figure 25**), then lift the retainer, fast idle cam, roller and spring from the housing.
16. Note the wire routing, then guide the wire harness out of the control housing.
17. Use solvent to clean all grease or contaminants from the control housing and components except electrical components.
18. Inspect all components for wear, cracks or damage. Replace any components in questionable condition. Inspect the wire harness for worn, weathered or damaged insulation. Replace the harness if any defects are noted.

NOTE
Apply Loctite 242 to the threads of the remote control handle nut or bolt during assembly.

19. Assembly is the reverse of disassembly. Note the following:
   a. Lubricate all pivot points and sliding surfaces with Quicksilver 2-4-C grease or equivalent during assembly.
   b. Attach the spring to the fast idle cam roller, then install the roller, spring and retainer as an assembly.
   c. Ensure the wire harness and connections are routed and installed in a manner that prevents them from contacting any moving components.
   d. Connect all wires to the harness at the points noted prior to removal. Refer to the wiring diagrams located at the end of the manual as necessary. Ensure that no wires become pinched between the back cover and other components on assembly.

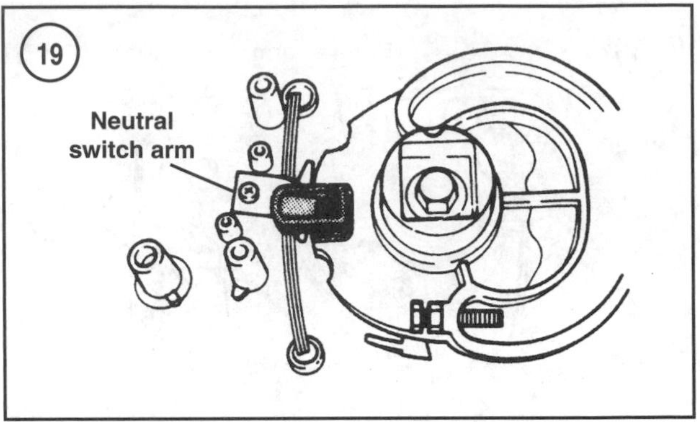

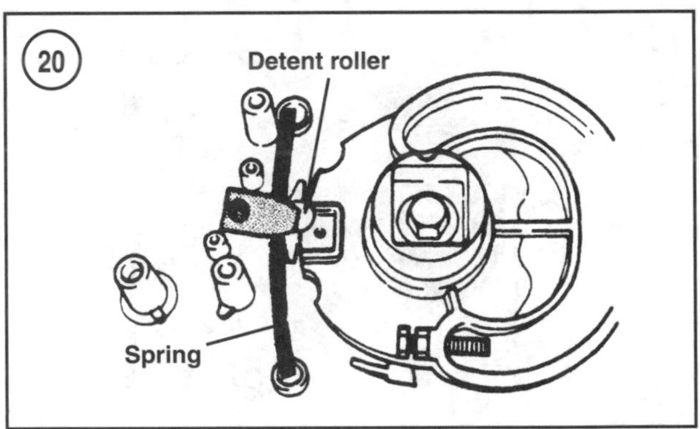

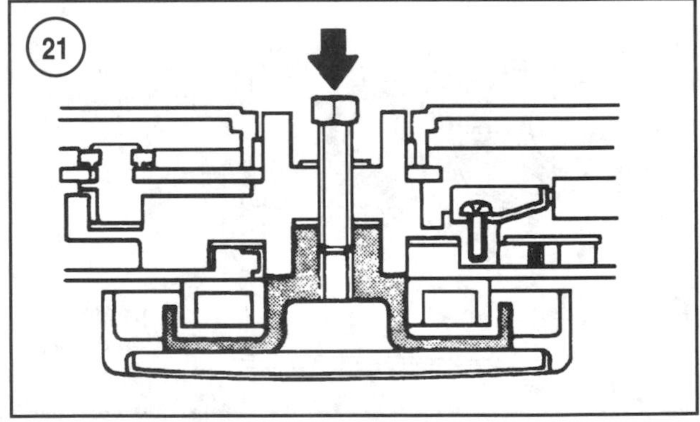

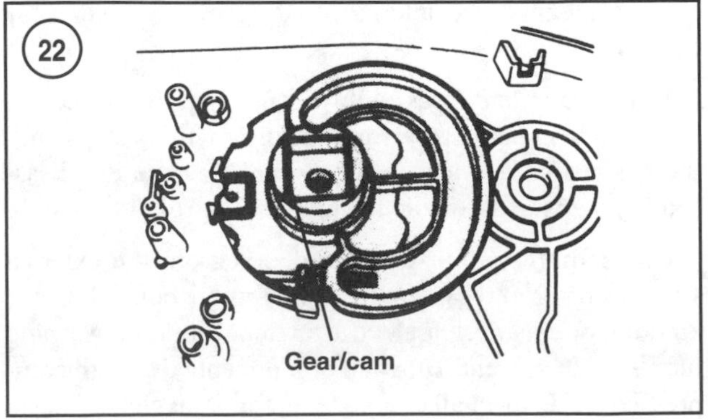

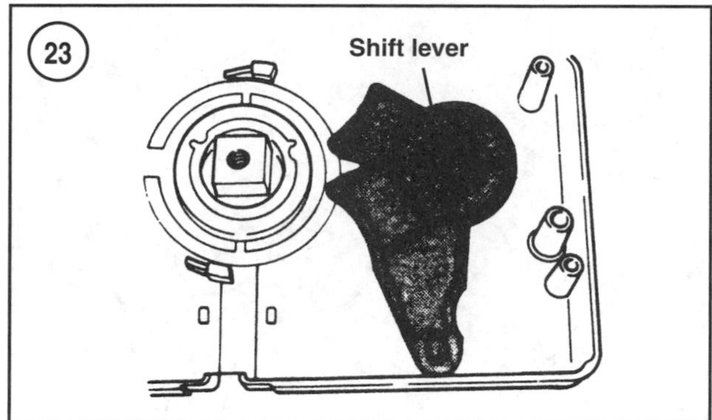

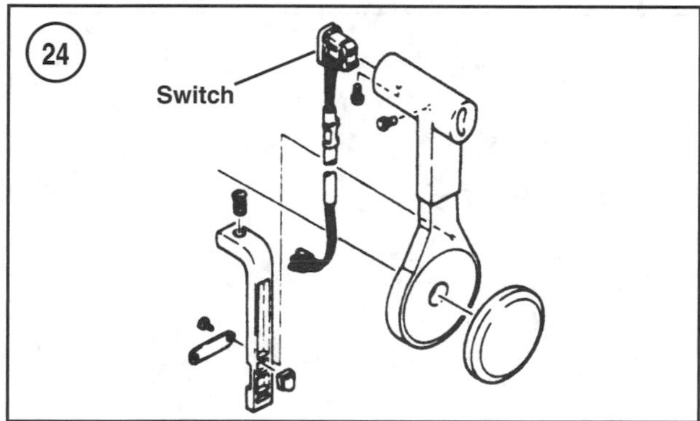

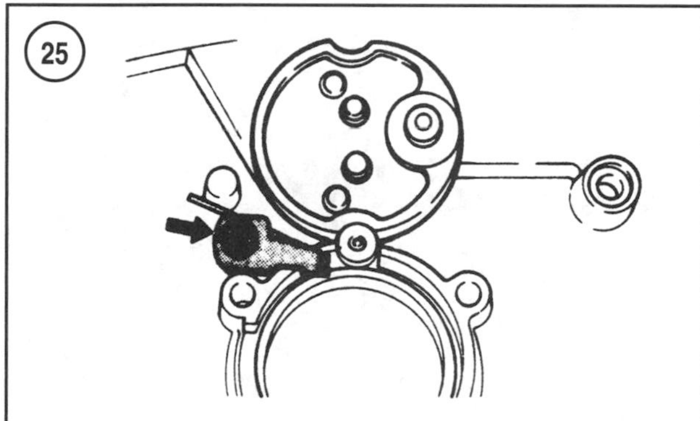

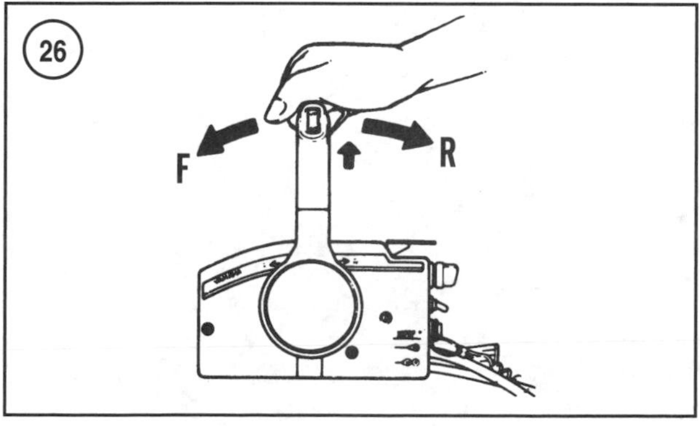

   e. Securely tighten all fasteners. Refer to the general torque specifications listed in the *Quick Reference Data* section at the front of the manual.

20. Install the shift and throttle cables then install the remote control as described in this chapter.

21. Operate the shift/throttle handle through its entire range of motion (**Figure 26**) while checking for smooth shift and throttle movement. Disassemble, clean and inspect all remote control components if binding, looseness or incorrect operation is noted.

22. Connect the battery cable.

NOTE
Apply Loctite 242 to the threads of the remote control handle nut or bolt during assembly.

Commander 3000 Type Control

Refer to **Figure 11**.

1. Remove the control and cables as described in this chapter.
2. Remove both screws (23, **Figure 11**) and the bushing (22), then lift the plate (24) from the control. Lift the throttle lever (20, **Figure 11**) from the bracket (18).
3. Remove the screws (19, **Figure 11**) and lift the bracket (18) from the control housing. Pull the control shaft (21, **Figure 11**), shift gear (10) and shift lever (16) from the control housing.
4. Separate the control shaft from the shift gear, then remove the snap ring (9, **Figure 11**) from the control shaft. Remove the detent balls (8, **Figure 11**) from the control shaft.
5. Pull the neutral throttle shaft (12, **Figure 11**) and spring (11) from the control shaft (21). Pull the pin (13, **Figure 11**) from the neutral throttle shaft. Pull the detent spring and bushing (3 and 5, **Figure 11**) from the control housing.
6. Lift the neutral-only start switch and leads (6, **Figure 11**) from the switch mounting bosses.
7. Use solvent to clean the control housing and components except electrical components.
8. Inspect all components for wear, cracks or damage. Replace any components that are worn, damaged or in questionable condition.
9. Assembly is the reverse of disassembly. Note the following:
   a. Apply Quicksilver 2-4-C grease or its equivalent to all pivot points and sliding surfaces during assembly.
   b. Align the mark on the shift lever with the mark on the shift gear (**Figure 27**) during installation.

c. Install the detent balls (8, **Figure 11**) into the openings in the control shaft.
d. Route all wires away from moving components.
e. Securely tighten all bolts and screws. Refer to the general torque specifications listed in the *Quick Reference Data* section at the front of the manual.

10. Install the shift and throttle cables. Install the remote control as described in this chapter.

11. Operate the shift/throttle handle through its entire range of motion (**Figure 26**) while checking for smooth shift and throttle movement. Disassemble, clean and inspect all remote control components if binding, looseness or incorrect operation is noted.

12. Connect the battery cable.

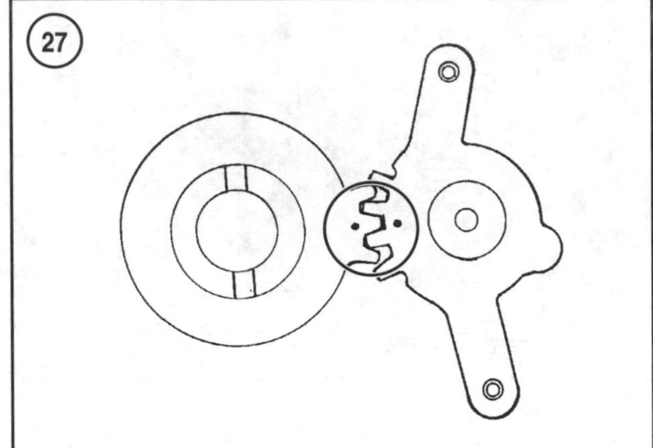

Index

A

Abbreviations, technical 41
Adjustment
  shift cable 189-191
  throttle cable 188-189
  torque specifications 196
  trim
    position sender 195-196
    tab 195
  valve 191-195
    clearance specifications 197
Air sensor
  pressure 250
  temperature 249
    sensor resistance specifications,
      troubleshooting 138
Anaerobic sealant 12

B

Battery 254-261
  cable recommendations 284
  capacity (hours) 284
  state of charge 285
Bearing selection 339-341
    connecting rod 348
    main 346-348

C

Cable adjustment
  shift 189-191
  throttle 188-189
Camshaft
  service specifications 344-345
  timing chain and pulley 295-301
Carburetor 228-232
  synchronization 178-187
Charging system 261-265
  troubleshooting 98-102
    resistance specifications 136-137
Clamp bracket 445-446
Compression specifications 139
Connecting rod bearing selection . . . 348
Conversion tables 40
Cooling system,
  troubleshooting 110-112
Corrosion, prevention 173
Crankshaft pulley 292-293, 318-319
Cylinder
  block components 333-338
  bore service specifications . . . 345-346
  head 308-314, 301-303

D

Dashpot 227-228
Diagnostic trouble codes,
  troubleshooting 140
Drive shaft housing 455-456

E

Electric starting system
  specifications 285
  troubleshooting 45-52
Electrical system
  battery 254-261
    cable recommendations 284
    capacity (hours) 284
    state of charge 285
  charging system 261-265
  component replacement 254
    troubleshooting 42
  fundamentals 31-33
  ignition system 273-283
  starter specifications 285
  starting system 265-273
  torque specifications 283-284
  wiring diagrams 472
Electronic fuel injection (EFI)
  system troubleshooting 119-131
Electrothermal valve 228
Engine temperature sensor resistance
  specifications 138
Engine
  break-in 341
  codes 38
  operation 5
  outboard identification 5-7
Exhaust
  silencer 452-453
  tube replacement 453
  water jacket cover 305-308

F

Fasteners 7-11
Flywheel/cover 286-289
Fuel requirements 148
Fuel system
  air pressure sensor 250
  air temperature sensor 249
  carburetor 228-232
  cooler 242-244
  dashpot 227-228
  electrothermal valve 228
  filter 206-209

hose 203-204
connectors 204-206
idle air control motor. 248-249
intake manifold. 219-227
mechanical pump 210-214
pressure regulator 244-245
primer bulb replacement. 209-210
pump
driver 241-242
low-pressure electric 241
relay 241
rail and injectors 245-248
service 198-200
silencer cover 214-219
tank. 201-203
throttle
body 232-234
position sensor 250-251
torque specifications. 252-253
troubleshooting 52-61, 132-134
vapor separator tank 234-240
secondary. 240-241

G

Galvanic corrosion 13-15
Gearcase 355-359
backlash specifications 405
component inspection. 393-395
disassembly/assembly 364-392
maintenance 158-163
operation. 349-351
pressure test 404
propeller 352-355
service precautions 351
shimming 395-404
torque specifications 405
troubleshooting. 112-113

I

Identification of engine. 5-7
Idle
air control motor. 248-249
speed adjustments. 178-187
Ignition system 273-283
timing check. 187-188
troubleshooting 62-92, 134-135
specifications
resistance 136-137
torque. 283-284

L

Linkage adjustment. 178-187
Lubricants. 11-12, 148-149

capacities 175
torque specifications 174

M

Main bearing selection 346-348
Maintenance
after each use 146-147
before each use 141-145
fuel requirements 148
gearcase 158-163
power head 149-158
routine 147-148
schedule 174-175
storage preparation and
recommissioning 171-172
submersion 172-173
torque specifications 174
Manifold, intake 219-227
Midsection
clamp bracket 445-446
drive shaft housing 455-456
exhaust
silencer. 452-453
tube 453
maintenance 163-167
oil
pan and pickup tube 454-455
pressure relief valve 453
pump 447
power head adapter. 451-452
swivel
housing 450-451
tube 448-450
tilt
lock lever 446-447
tube replacement 444-445
torque specifications. 456-457
Motor mount
lower. 435-444
upper. 447-448

O

Oil
pressure specifications. 139
pump. 317-318
replacement. 447
pan 454-455
pickup tube. 454-455
pressure relief valve. 453
Overspeed protection system
specifications 138

P

Peak output voltage
specifications. 135-136
Pilot screw adjustment 177-178
Piston service specifications. 346
Power head. 314-317, 319-333
adapter replacement 451-452
bearing selection. 339-341
camshaft, timing chain and
pulley 295-301
service specifications 344-345
crankshaft pulley . . . 292-293, 318-319
cylinder
block components 333-338
head. 301-303, 308-314
engine break-in procedures 341
exhaust/water jacket cover . . . 305-308
flywheel/cover 286-289
maintenance 149-158
oil pump 317-318
specifications
connecting rod bearing 348
crankshaft 345
cylinder bore 345-346
main bearing 346-348
piston. 346
torque. 342-343
valve and spring. 343-344
valve spring. 344
thermostat. 304-305
timing belt and tensioner. 289-292
troubleshooting. 102-110
valve cover 293-295
Preliminary inspection,
troubleshooting 42-43
Pressure regulator, fuel 244-245
Primer bulb 209-210
Propeller. 15-20, 352-355

R

Recommissioning 171-172
Rectifier/regulator resistance
specifications, troubleshooting. . . . 139
Remote control. 464
cable 458
RTV gasket sealant. 12

S

Sealant
anaerobic 12
RTV gasket 12
Shift cable adjustment. 189-191
Silencer cover 214-219
Spark plug recommendations 176

Specifications
camshaft 344-345
compression, troubleshooting 139
connecting rod bearings 348
crankshaft 345
cylinder bore 345-346
diagnostic trouble codes, troubleshooting 140
electric starter 285
engine and air temperature sensor resistance, troubleshooting 138
fuel system, troubleshooting . . 132-134
gearcase, backlash 405
idle speed 196
ignition and charging system resistance, troubleshooting . . 136-137
ignition
timing 197
system, troubleshooting 134-135
main bearing selection 346-348
maximum recommended engine speed 197
oil pressure, troubleshooting 139
overspeed protection system, troubleshooting 138
peak output voltage 135-136
piston 346
rectifier/regulator resistance, troubleshooting 139
starting system, troubleshooting . . 132
thermostat, troubleshooting . . 139-140
throttle position sensor test, troubleshooting 137
torque
fuel system 252-253
gearcase 405
general 38
ignition system 283-284
lubrication, maintenance, and tune-up 174
power head 342-343
synchronization and adjustment . 196
power trim and tilt 434
torque, troubleshooting 131
valve
clearance 197
service 343-344
spring 344
warning system component test, troubleshooting 138
Starting
difficulty, troubleshooting 43-45
system 265-273
troubleshooting 132
Storage preparation 171-172
Submersion 172-173
Swivel
housing replacement 450-451
tube replacement 448-450
Synchronization
carburetor 178-187
idle speed
adjustments 178-187
specifications 196
ignition timing
check 187-188
specifications 197
linkage 178-187
maximum recommended engine speed specifications 197
pilot screw adjustment 177-178
throttle position sensor 178-187
torque specifications 196

T

Tap drill sizes 39
Thermostat specifications, troubleshooting 139-140
Thermostat 304-305
Threadlocking compound 12-13
Throttle
body 232-234
cable adjustment 188-189
position sensor 250-251
adjustment 178-187
test specifications, troubleshooting 137
Tilt
lock lever 446-447
tube 444-445
Timing
belt and tensioner 289-292
check, ignition 187-188
Tools
basic hand 20-24
precision measuring 24-31
special 24
Trim and tilt system . . 412-416, 423-433
electric motor 416-423
fluid 433
manual relief valve 410-412
position sender 195-196, 408-410
relay 406-408
switch 410
tab adjustment 195
torque specifications 434
troubleshooting 113-119
Troubleshooting
charging system 98-102
compression specifications 139
cooling system 110-112
diagnostic trouble codes 140
electric starting system 45-52
electrical components 42
electronic fuel injection (EFI) system 119-131
engine and air temperature sensor resistance specifications 138
fuel system 52-61, 132-134
gearcase 112-113
ignition system 62-92, 134-135
resistance specifications 136-137
oil pressure specifications 139
overspeed protection system specifications 138
peak output voltage specifications 135-136
power head 102-110
preliminary inspection 42-43
rectifier/regulator resistance specifications 139
starting
difficulty 43-45
starting system 132
thermostat specifications 139-140
throttle position sensor test specifications 137
torque specifications 131
trim/tilt system 113-119
warning system component test specifications 138
warning system 92-98
Tune up 167-170
torque specifications 174

12

V

Valve
adjustment 191-195
cover 293-295
electrothermal valve 228
service specifications 343-344
Vapor separator tank 234-240
secondary 240-241

W

Warning system component test
specifications 138
troubleshooting 92-98
Water
pressure relief valve 303-304
pump 359-364
component inspection 364
Wiring diagrams 472

75 AND 90 HP MODELS

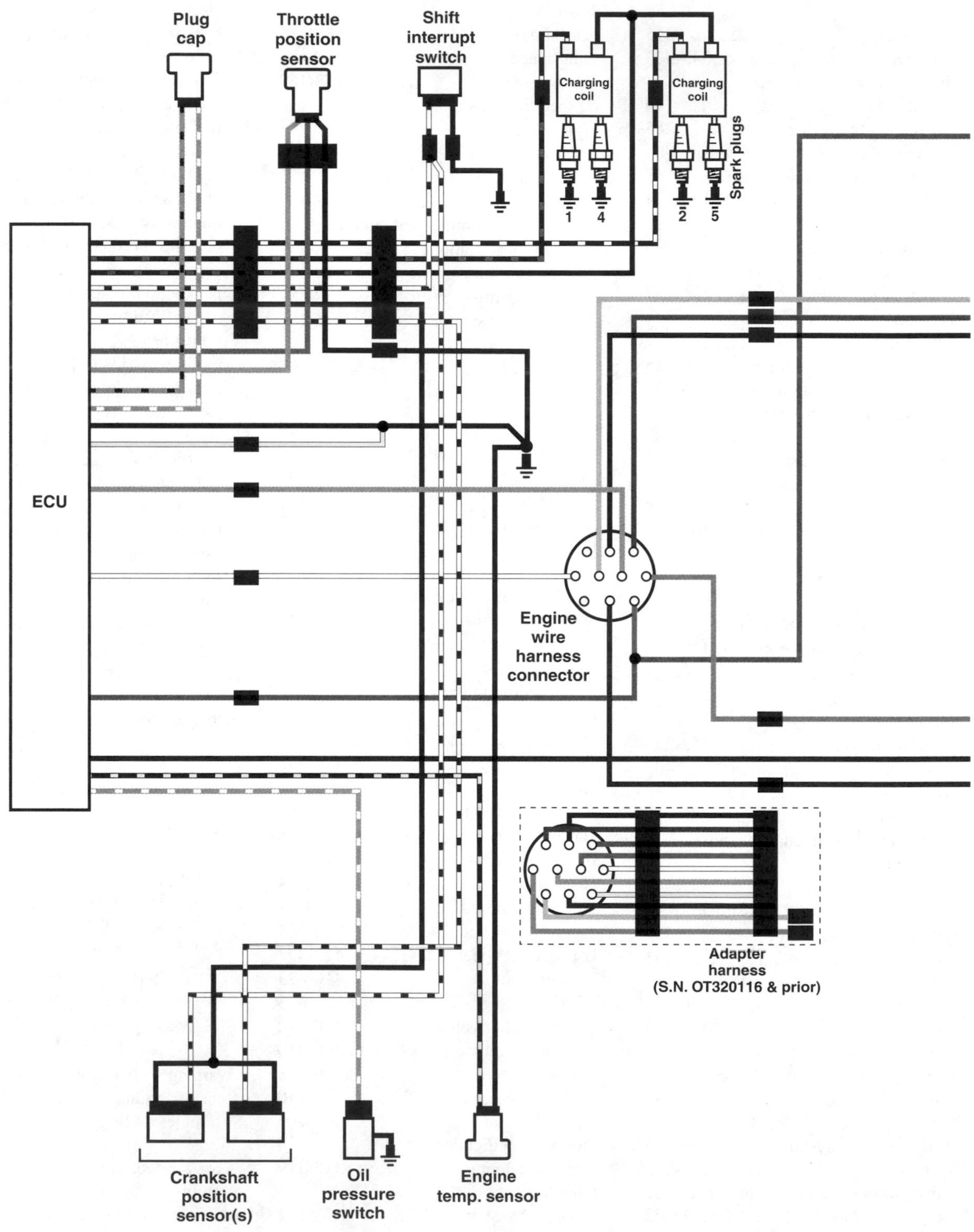

Plug cap
Throttle position sensor
Shift interrupt switch
Charging coil
Charging coil
Spark plugs
1
4
2
5
ECU
Engine wire harness connector
Adapter harness (S.N. OT320116 & prior)
Crankshaft position sensor(s)
Oil pressure switch
Engine temp. sensor

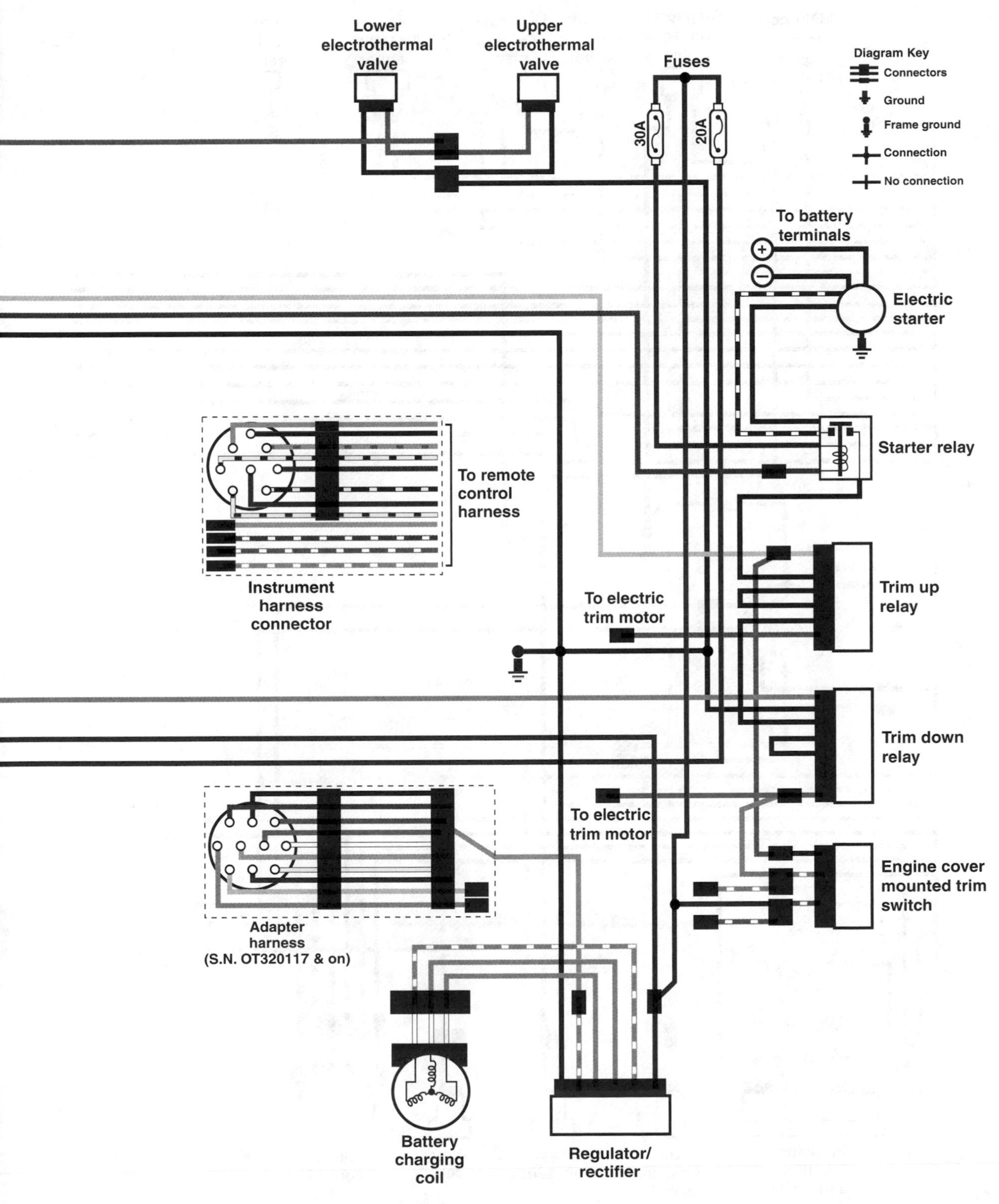
Lower electrothermal valve
Upper electrothermal valve
Fuses
30A
20A
Diagram Key
Connectors
Ground
Frame ground
Connection
No connection
To battery terminals
Electric starter
Starter relay
To remote control harness
Instrument harness connector
Trim up relay
To electric trim motor
Trim down relay
To electric trim motor
Engine cover mounted trim switch
Adapter harness (S.N. OT320117 & on)
Battery charging coil
Regulator/ rectifier

115 HP MODELS

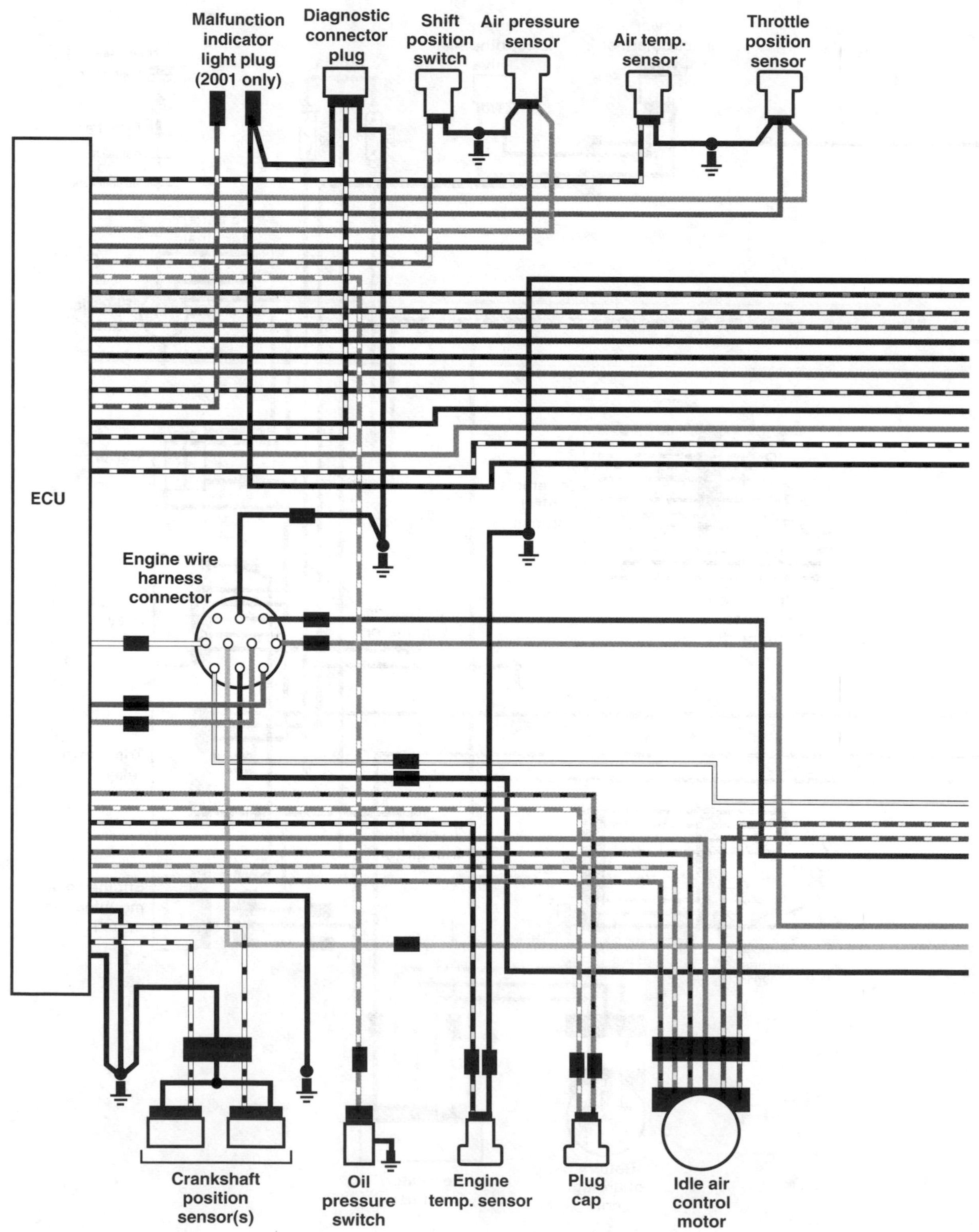

Malfunction indicator light plug (2001 only)
Diagnostic connector plug
Shift position switch
Air pressure sensor
Air temp. sensor
Throttle position sensor
ECU
Engine wire harness connector
Crankshaft position sensor(s)
Oil pressure switch
Engine temp. sensor
Plug cap
Idle air control motor

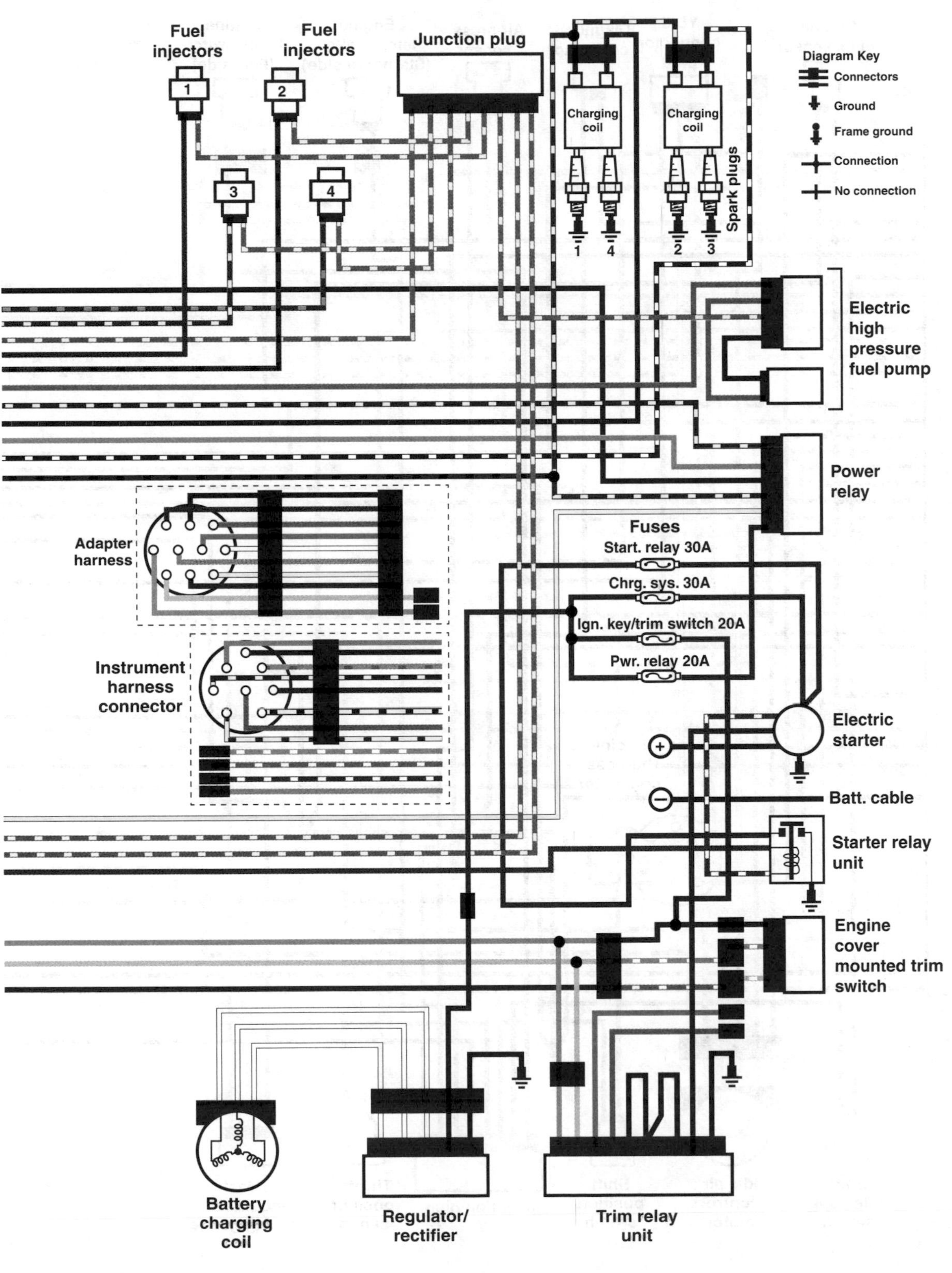
Fuel injectors
Fuel injectors
Junction plug
1
2
3
4
Charging coil
Charging coil
Spark plugs
1
4
2
3
Diagram Key
Connectors
Ground
Frame ground
Connection
No connection
Electric high pressure fuel pump
Power relay
Fuses
Start. relay 30A
Chrg. sys. 30A
Ign. key/trim switch 20A
Pwr. relay 20A
Adapter harness
Instrument harness connector
Electric starter
Batt. cable
Starter relay unit
Engine cover mounted trim switch
Battery charging coil
Regulator/ rectifier
Trim relay unit

13

225 HP MODELS

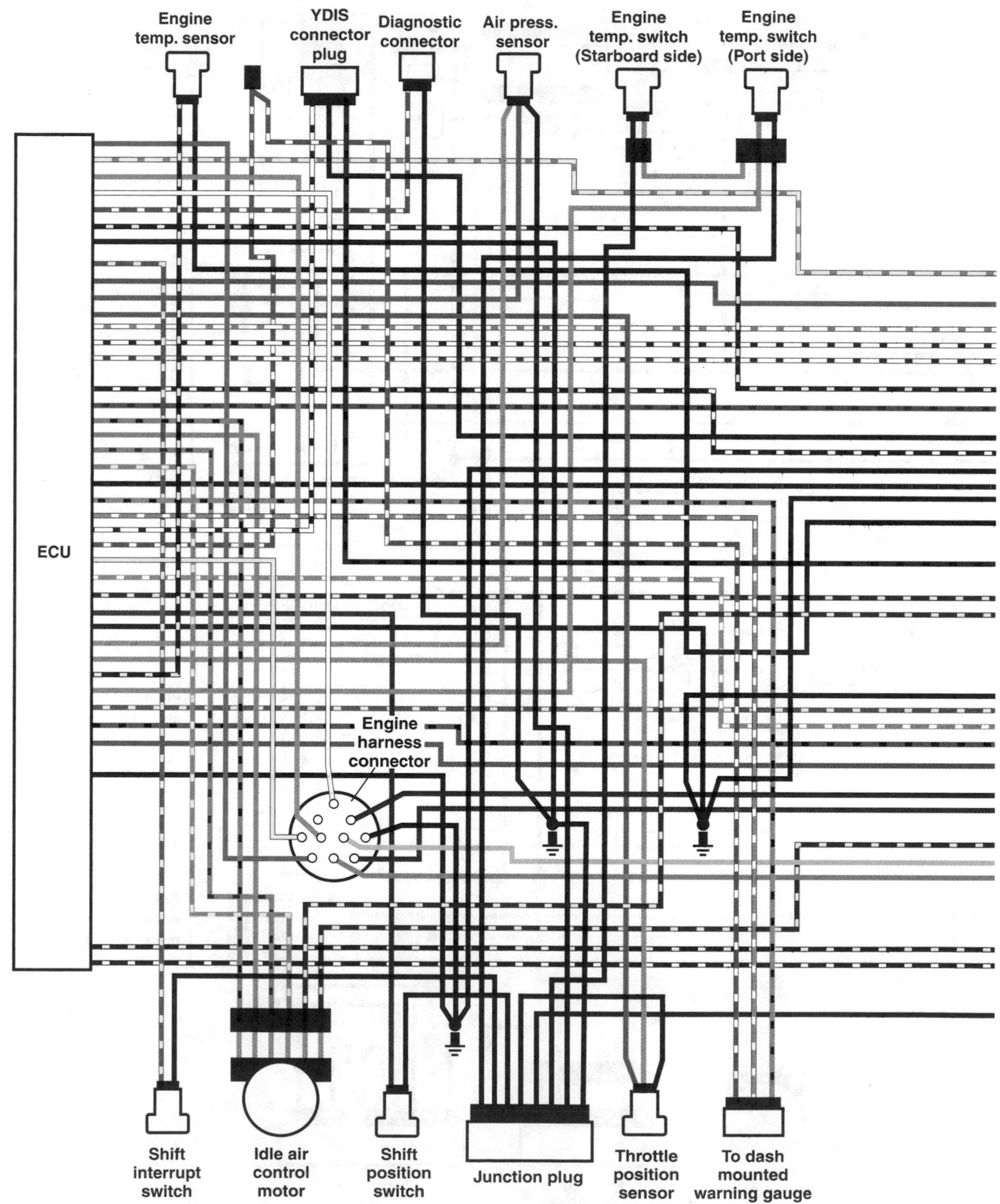

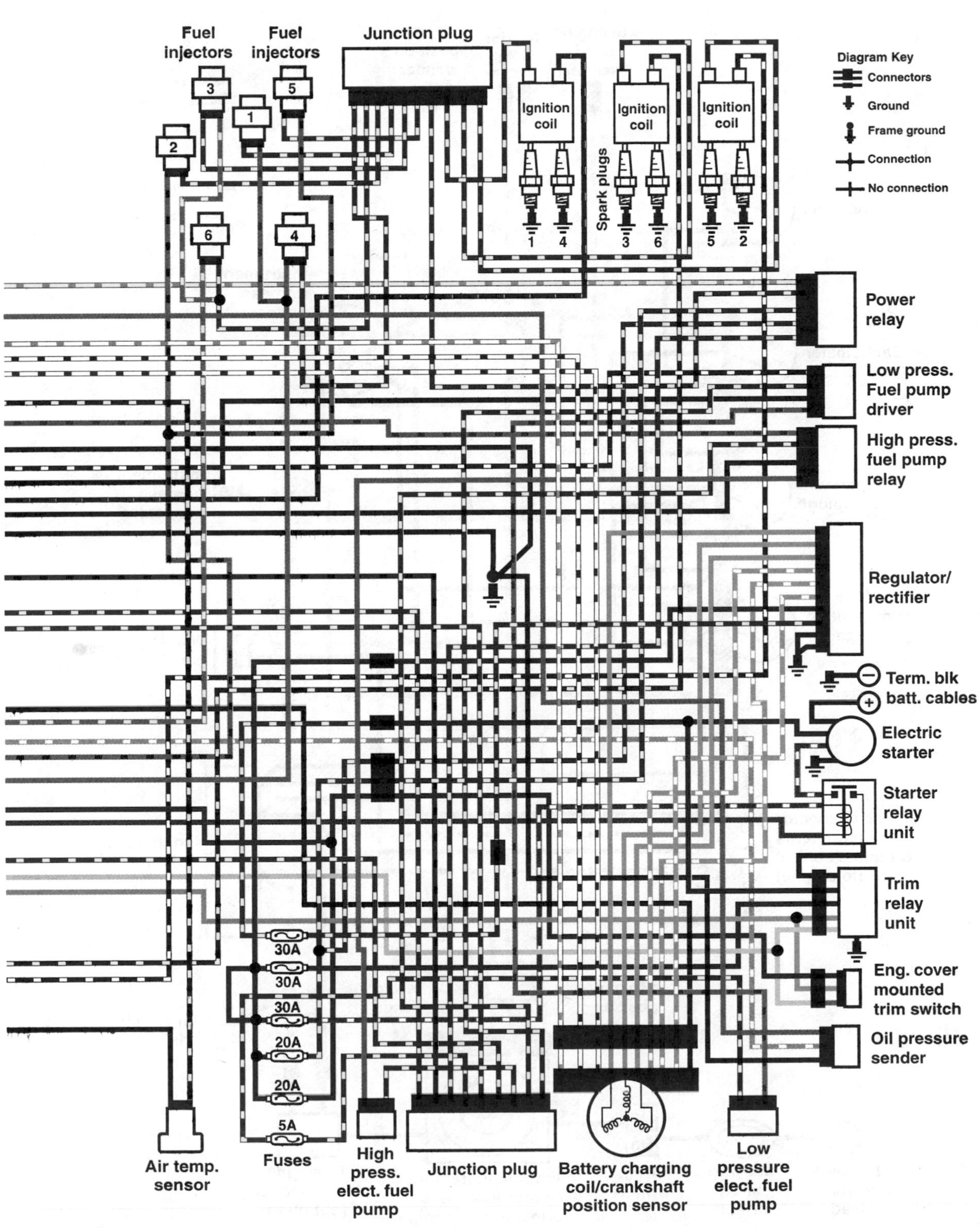
Fuel injectors
Fuel injectors
Junction plug
3
5
1
2
6
4
Ignition coil
Ignition coil
Ignition coil
Spark plugs
1
4
3
6
5
2
Diagram Key
Connectors
Ground
Frame ground
Connection
No connection
Power relay
Low press. Fuel pump driver
High press. fuel pump relay
Regulator/ rectifier
Term. blk batt. cables
Electric starter
Starter relay unit
Trim relay unit
Eng. cover mounted trim switch
Oil pressure sender
30A
30A
30A
20A
20A
5A
Air temp. sensor
Fuses
High press. elect. fuel pump
Junction plug
Battery charging coil/crankshaft position sensor
Low pressure elect. fuel pump

REMOTE CONTROL AND INSTRUMENT WIRING

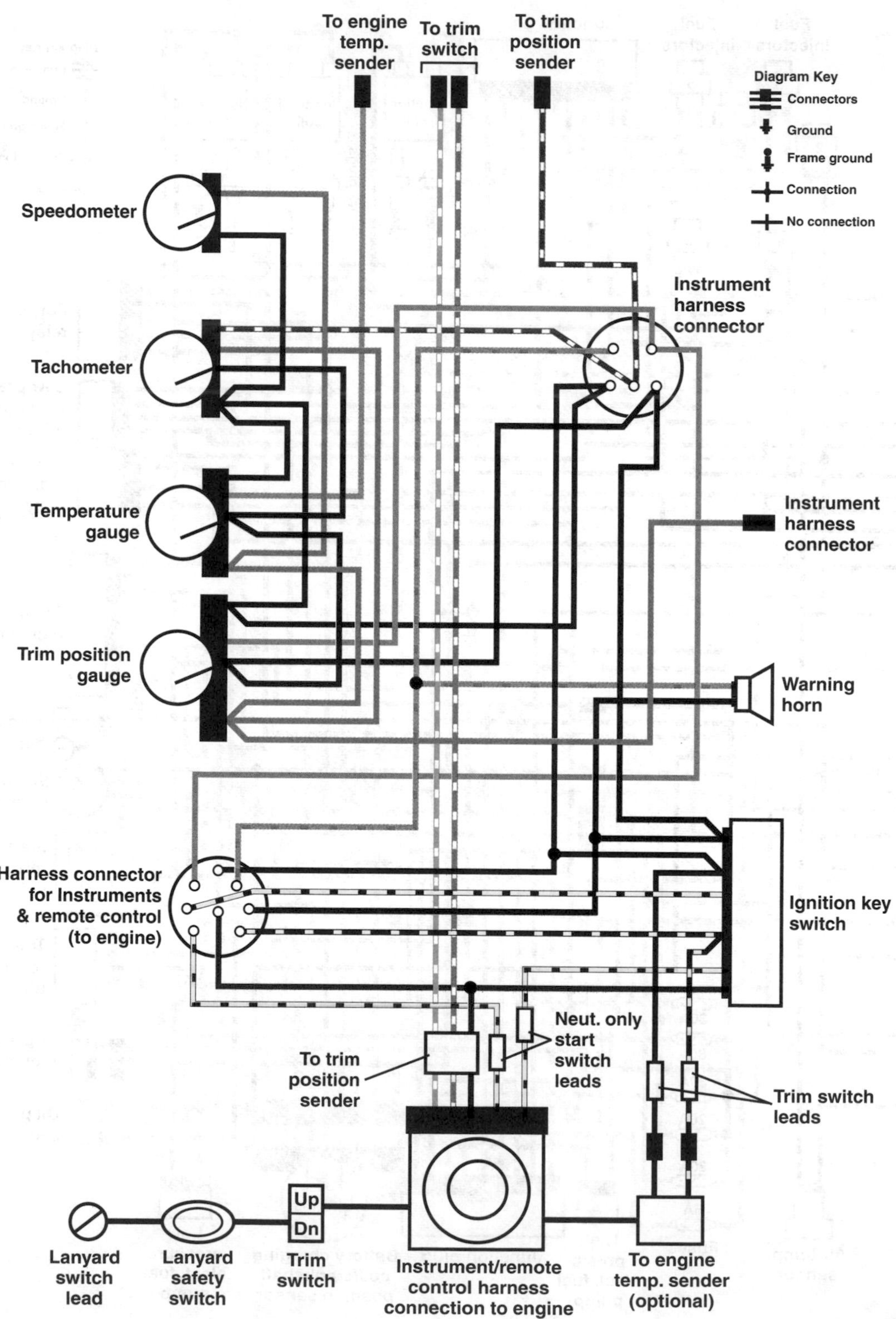

NOTES

NOTES

NOTES

NOTES

NOTES

MAINTENANCE LOG

Date	Engine Hours	Type of Service